Rick Steves'®

EASTERN EUROPE

DISCARDED

Rick Steves & Cameron Hewitt

D0967667
Baypo

Eastern Europe Overview
The maps on the following pages show more detail.
0 km 100 200 km
0 miles 50 100 m
Gdynia
Hel
Sopot
TRI-CITY
Gdańsk
Malbork
POMERANIA
Toruń
Warsaw
Wisła
Berlin
Poznań
WIELKOPOLSKA
MAZOVIA
GERMANY
Łódź
POLAND
Elbe
Leipzig
Wrocław
MAŁOPOLSKA
Dresden
Częstochowa
SILESIA
Wisła
Kraków
TEREZÍN
AUSCHWITZ
BOHEMIA
Labe
Prague
Kutná Hora
Ostrava
Olomouc
Zakopane
Levoča
Plzeň
Vltava
CZECH REPUBLIC
MORAVIA
HIGH TATRA MTNS.
Nürnberg
Brno
Poprad
Košice
Český Krumlov
SLOVAKIA
Danube
Bratislava
Eger
Melk
Vienna
Danube
DANUBE BEND
Munich
Salzburg
Győr
Sopron
Budapest
Szombathely
AUSTRIA
Innsbruck
TIROL
Graz
Lake Balaton
Klagenfurt
Maribor
HUNGARY
DOLOMITES
JULIAN ALPS
Bled
Pécs
Bolzano
Bled
Bohinj
Ljubljana
Kobarid
Zagreb
SERBIA
SLOVENIA
Osijek
Trieste
KARST
SLAVONIA
Danube
Piran
CROATIA
Venice
Motovun
Rijeka
ISTRIA
Plitvice Lakes National Park
Rovinj
Po
Pula
Bihać
Banja Luka
BOSNIA - HERZEGOVINA
ITALY
Adriatic Sea
Zadar
Sarajevo
Trogir
DALMATIAN COAST
Split
MEĐUGORJE
Florence
Ancona
Hvar
Mostar
MONTE-NEGRO
Siena
Korčula
Podgorica
Assisi
Dubrovnik
Kotor

LEGEND
A12 Freeway/Autobahn
Major Roads
Major Rail Line
Airport
Ruin, Museum, Other Point of Interest
Castle, Monument, Palace
Natural Wonder
0 km 50 100 km
0 miles 50 miles
Neubrandenburg
Pasewalk
Szczecin/ Stettin
Szczeciński/Stargard
Neustrelitz
Prenzlau
A1
Milmersdorf
Schwedt
Angermünde
Bad Freienwalde
SACHSENHAUSEN
Bernau
Gorzów Wielkopolski
Straussberg
Kostrzyń
Tegel
Berlin
Frankfurt an der Oder
Rzepin
A10
Potsdam
SANSSOUCI PALACE
Schönefeld
A12
Świebodzin
Brandenburg
A2
GERMANY
Zielona Góra
Magdeburg
Jüterbog
A9
Wittenberg
A13
Lubben
Guben
Gubin
Cottbus
Głogów
Dessau
Kothen
Aschersleben
Bitterfeld
Falkenburg
Doberlug
A15
Forst
Zary
Lauchhammer
Lubin
A4
Eisleben
Halle
Elbe
Howerswerda
Legnica
Wurzen
MORITZBURG
Görlitz
Bolesławiec
Leipzig
Meissen
A4
Bautzen
Zgorzelec
Jelenia Góra
Naumburg
Zeitz
SAXONY
Dresden
Bad Schandau
Zittau
Weimar
Gössnitz
Schmilka
Liberec
Erfurt
A4
Jena
Gera
Chemnitz
Freiberg
Hřensko
Děčín
Werdau
Glauchau
Altenberg
Zinnwald
Labe
Turnov
Nácho
A9
A72
Teplice
Ústí nad Labem
Saalfeld
Chomutov
Most
Litoměřice
Jičín
TEREZÍN
Mladá Boleslav
Hradec Králové
Plauen
Ruzyně
Mělník
Karlovy Vary
Kladno
Kolín
Pardubic
Coburg
Münchberg
Hof
KŘIVOKLÁT CASTLE
Prague
Cheb
Berouň
KARLŠTEJN CASTLE
Kutná Hora
Schirdning
A70
Bayreuth
Marktredwitz
Mariánské Lázni
E50
BOHEMIA
Plzeň
Příbram
Benešov
Havlíčkův Brod
A73
KONOPIŠTĚ CASTLE
E50
Pegnitz
Weiden
CZECH REPUBLIC
Jihla
A93
České Kubice
Tábor
Klatovy
Třeb
Nürnberg
Schwandorf
Furth
Strakonice
Písek
Vltava R.
Veselí nad Lužnicí
Telč
A6
Neumarkt
A3
Železná Ruda
Protovin
Třeboň
Slavon
Bayerisch Eisenstein
České Budějovice
A9
Regensburg
České Velenice
Gmund
Treuchtlingen
Straubing
Český Krumlov
Sigmundsherb
Ingolstadt
Danube
A93
Deggendorf
Plattling
A3
WACHA
Passau
Dingolfing
Summerau
Horní Dvoriště
Durnstein
Kre
BAVARIA
A92
Landshut
Danube
Spitz
St
Eggenfelden
MAUTHAUSEN
Pölten
Augsburg
Neumarkt
Linz
Melk
Strauss
Simbach
Ybbs
DACHAU
Mühldorf
Wels
St. Valentin
Amstetten
Inn R.
Braunau
Salzach
Attnang Puchheim
A1
Steyr
SCHNEEBER
Lands-berg
A96
Munich
Wasserburg
Herrsching
HERREN-CHIEMSEE
Gmunden
Kirchdorf
Mariazell
ANDECHS MONASTERY
Freilassing
AUSTRIA
A95
Rosenheim
A8
Prien
Salzburg
Bad Ischl

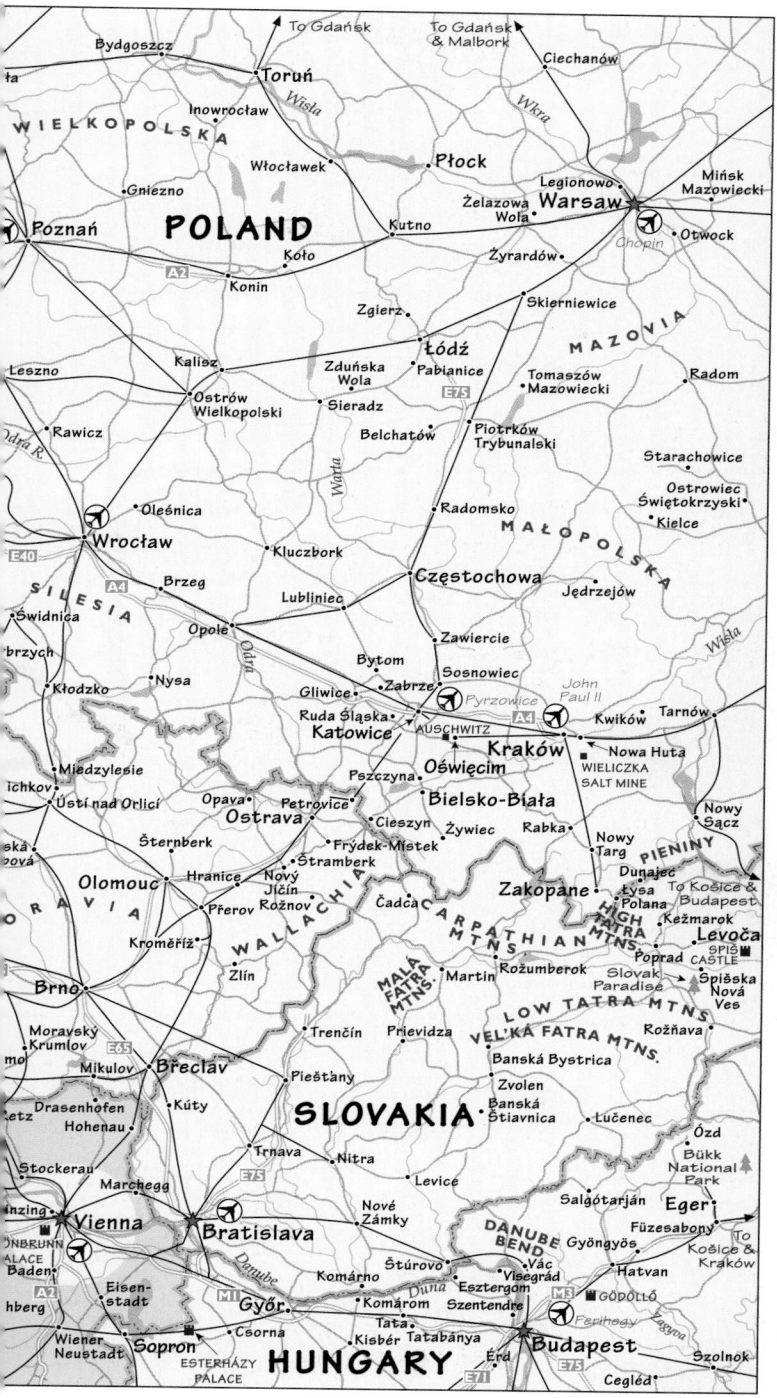
To Gdańsk
To Gdańsk & Malbork
Bydgoszcz
Toruń
Ciechanów
Wisła
Wkra
WIELKOPOLSKA
Inowrocław
Płock
Włocławek
Gniezno
Legionowo
Mińsk Mazowiecki
Żelazowa Wola
Warsaw
Chopin
Poznań
POLAND
Kutno
Otwock
Koło
Żyrardów
A2
Konin
Skierniewice
Zgierz
MAZOVIA
Łódź
Leszno
Kalisz
Zduńska Wola
Pabianice
Tomaszów Mazowiecki
Radom
Ostrów Wielkopolski
Sieradz
E75
Rawicz
Odra R.
Belchatów
Piotrków Trybunalski
Warta
Starachowice
Ostrowiec Świętokrzyski
Oleśnica
Radomsko
Kielce
MAŁOPOLSKA
Wrocław
E40
Kluczbork
Częstochowa
A4
Brzeg
SILESIA
Lubliniec
Jędrzejów
Świdnica
Opole
Zawiercie
Wisła
Odra
Bytom
Sosnowiec
Nysa
Kłodzko
Gliwice
Zabrze
John Paul II
Pyrzowice
Ruda Śląska
Katowice
AUSCHWITZ
Kraków
Kwików
Tarnów
Nowa Huta
WIELICZKA SALT MINE
Miedzylesie
Oświęcim
Pszczyna
Ústí nad Orlicí
Opava
Petrovice
Bielsko-Biała
Ostrava
Cieszyn
Żywiec
Rabka
Nowy Sącz
Nowy Targ
PIENINY
Šternberk
Frýdek-Místek
Štramberk
Olomouc
Hranice
Nový Jičín
Dunajec
Zakopane
Łysa Polana
To Košice & Budapest
Kežmarok
Přerov
Rožnov
Čadca
CARPATHIAN MTNS
HIGH TATRA MTNS
Kroměříž
WALLACHIA
Levoča
SPIŠ CASTLE
Poprad
Zlín
Martin
Rožumberok
Slovak Paradise
Spišská Nová Ves
Brno
MALA FATRA MTNS
LOW TATRA MTNS
Moravský Krumlov
Trenčín
Prievidza
VEĽKÁ FATRA MTNS.
Rožňava
E65
Mikulov
Břeclav
Banská Bystrica
Pieštany
Zvolen
Drasenhofen
Kúty
SLOVAKIA
Banská Štiavnica
Lučenec
Hohenau
Ózd
Bükk National Park
Stockerau
Trnava
Nitra
E75
Marchegg
Levice
Salgótarján
Eger
Vienna
Nové Zámky
Bratislava
DANUBE BEND
Gyöngyös
Füzesabony
To Košice & Kraków
Baden
Štúrovo
Vác
Hatvan
Danube
Komárno
Visegrád
Eisenstadt
Esztergom
Duna
M1
Győr
Komárom
Szentendre
M3
GÖDÖLLŐ
Ferihegy
Tata
Csorna
Kisbér
Tatabánya
Wiener Neustadt
Sopron
ESTERHÁZY PALACE
HUNGARY
Budapest
Erd
Szolnok
E71
Cegléd

BAVARIA
Augsburg
DACHAU
Munich
Landsberg
Herrsching
ANDECHS MONASTERY
Starnbergersee
WIESKIRCHE
Oberammergau
NEUSCHWANSTEIN
Garmisch-Partenkirchen
Mittenwald
ZUGSPITZE
Seefeld
Hall
HINTERHORNALM
ZILLERTALVALLEY
Innsbruck
EUROPABRÜCKE
TIROL
STUBAI GLACIER
BRENNER PASS
REIFENSTEIN CASTLE
Vipiteno
Brunico
Fortezza
Merano
Dobbiaco
Alpe Di Siusi
Castelrotto
ALPE DI SIUSI
Bolzano
Cortina
Calalzo
Cavalese
DOLOMITES
Belluno
Trento
Adige R.
Lago di Garda
Vicenza
Verona
Padova
Mestre
Venice
BRENTA CANAL VILLAS
Chioggia
Mantova
Po
POMPOSA ABBEY
Ferrara
Modena
Reggio Emilia
Bologna
Imola
Faenza
ITALY
Cesena
Rimini
SAN MARINO
Pesaro
Fano
San Leo
Urbino
Pistoia
Vespucci
Fiesole
Florence
Arno
Empoli
Poggibonsi
San Gimignano
Volterra
TUSCANY
Siena
Rubicon
Arezzo
UMBRIA
Gubbio
Macerata
Cortona
Terontola
Montepulciano
L. Trasimeno
Perugia
Assisi
Montalcino
Pienza
Chiusi
Deruta
Foligno
Ascoli Piceno
VIA AURELIA
Piombino
Grosseto
Orvieto
Todi
Baschi
Spoleto
Teramo
Pescara
Adriatic Sea
Eggenfelden
Simbach
Mühldorf
Braunau
Strauss
Inn R.
Wasserburg
Salzach
Attnang Puchheim
Danube
Neumarkt
Wels
Linz
MAUTHAUSEN
Spitz
St. Valentin
Ybbs
Melk
St. Pölten
Amstetten
Steyr
SCHNEEBERG
Mariazell
AUSTRIA
Kirchdorf
HERRENCHIEMSEE
Chiemsee
Freilassing
Salzburg
Gmunden
Attersee
Traunsee
Rosenheim
Prien
Bad Ischl
Berchtesgaden
Kufstein
Hallein
Hallstatt
Selzthal
Stainach Irdning
SALZKAMMERGUT
Leoben
St. Michael
Piber
Worgl
St. Johann
Kitzbühel
DACHSTEIN MTNS.
Bischofshofen
Schwarzach St. Veit
Zell am See
Bad Gastein
Unzmarkt
Mur R.
Koflach
Gra
Zell
Krimml
Mayrhofen
Tamsweg
KATSCHBERG TUNNEL
GROSSGLOCKNER PASS
TAUERN TUNNEL
Winklern
Spittal
Feldkirchen
St. Veit
HOCHOSTERWITZ CASTLE
Wolfsberg
Drau R.
Klagenfurt
Dravograd
Lienz
Arnbach
San Candido
PLÖCKENPASS
Tarvisio
Villach
Jesenice
LOGARSKA DOLINA
Velenje
VRŠIČ PASS
Bled
Lesce
Kadovljica
Bovec
TRIGLAV
Lake Bled
Bohinj
Kobarid
Kranj
Brnik
Celje
Ljubljana
Tolmin
JULIAN ALPS
Idrija
Soča R.
Udine
Gorizia
SLOVENIA
Nova Gorica
Novo Mesto
Pordenone
Palmanova
POSTOJNA CAVES
Postojna
Kočevje
Divača
Pivka
SKOCJAN CAVES
KARST
Grado
Trieste
Lipica
Črnomelj
Treviso
Marco Polo
Piran
Koper
Umag
Grožnjan
Motovun
Hum
Rijeka
Opatija
Pazin
Poreč
ISTRIA
Krk
KVARNER
Rovinj
Brijuni Islands
Pula
Cres
Rab
Jablanac
Pag
Lošinj
Dugi Otok

Vienna
Bratislava
SLOVAKIA
Nové Zámky
Štúrovo
DANUBE BEND
Gyöngyös
Füzesabony
To Eger
Hatvan
Vác
Visegrád
Esztergom
Szentendre
Budapest
GÖDÖLLŐ
Ferihegy
Szolnok
To Bucharest
Cegléd
Érd
Tatabánya
Tata
Komárom
Komárno
Győr
Sopron
ESTERHÁZY PALACE
Csorna
Kisbér
Wiener Neustadt
Eisenstadt
Neusiedler See
Mürzzuschlag
Köszeg
Szombathely
Pápa
Várpalota
Székesfehérvár
Veszprém
Ajka
Balatonfüred
Tihany
Siófok
Sárbogárd
Dunaújváros
Dunaföldvár
Kecskemét
Kiskőrös
Vasvár
Kőrmend
Rábafüzes
Szentgotthárd
Zalaegerszeg
Hévíz
Keszthely
BAKONY
Lake Balaton
HUNGARY
Kalocsa
Szeged
Murska Sobota
Maribor
Ptuj
Čakovec
Letenye
Nagykanizsa
Kaposvár
Szekszárd
Baja
Nagyatád
Csurgó
Gyékényes
Komló
MECSEK HILLS
Pécs
Mohács
Subotica
Varaždin
Koprivnica
Szigetvár
Barcs
Zabok
Sombor
SERBIA
Bjelovar
Vicovitica
Zagreb
CROATIA
Osijek
Vukovar
Đakovo
SLAVONIA
Požega
Kutina
Sisak
Karlovac
Novska
Slavonski Brod
Nova Gradiška
Županja
Šid
Brčko
To Belgrade
Prijedor
Banja Luka
Doboj
Bihać
BOSNIA - HERZEGOVINA
Tuzla
Gospić
Zenica
Travnik
Srebrenica
Gračac
Visoko
Sarajevo
Knin
Zadar
DINARIC MTNS.
Goražde
Perković
Konjic
Šibenik
Split
Trogir
Mostar
MEĐUGORJE
Buna
Makarska
Šolta
Brač
BOL
Drvenik
Vrgorac
Nevesinje
Počitelj
Gacko
Stari Grad
Hvar
Ploče
Metković
Ljubinje
Stolac
Bileća
MONTE-NEGRO
Vis
Komiža
Orebić
Pelješac Peninsula
Neum
Trebinje
Vela Luka
Korčula
Ston
Dubrovnik
Bay of Kotor
Polače
Elaphite Islands
Miljet
Lastovo
Lokrum
Podgorica
Kotor
Sobra
Cavtat
Četinje
Budva
Herceg Novi
Sveti Stefan
DALMATIAN COAST
To Bari, Italy

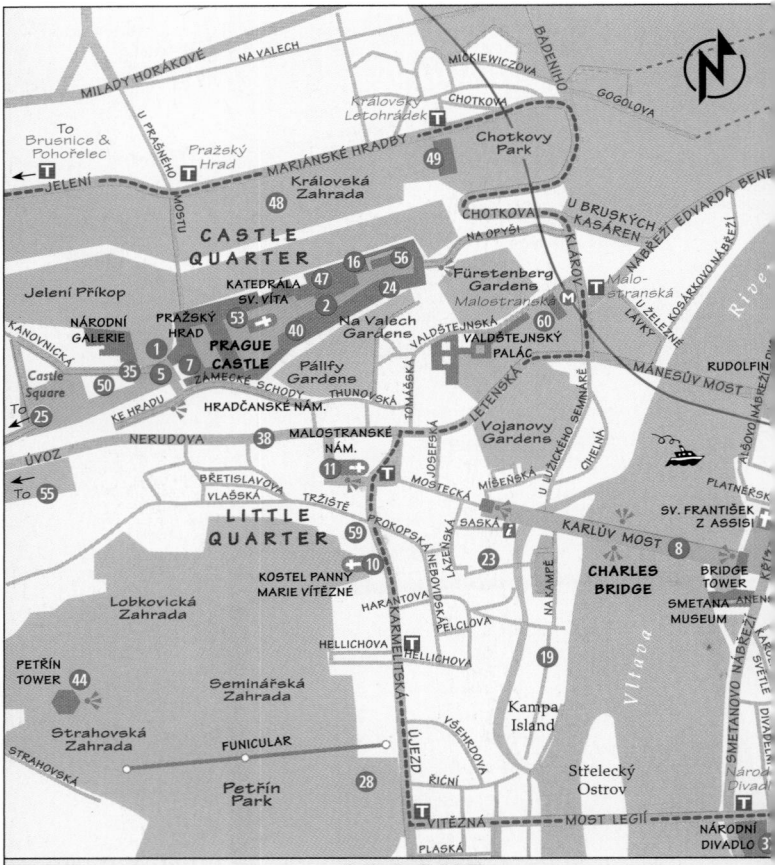

PRAGUE

1. Archbishop's Palace
2. Basilica & Convent of St. George
3. Bethlehem Chapel
4. Black Light Theaters (3)
5. Castle Square
6. Ceremonial Hall
7. Changing of the Guard
8. Charles Bridge
9. Charles University
10. Church of St. Mary the Victorious
11. Church of St. Nicholas (in Little Quarter)
12. Church of St. Nicholas (in Old Town)
13. To Dancing House
14. Dvořák Museum
15. Estates Theater
16. Golden Lane
17. Havelská Market
18. Jewish Quarter
19. Kampa Island
20. Karlova Street
21. Klaus Synagogue
22. Klementinum
23. Lennon Wall
24. Lobkowicz Palace
25. To Loreta Church
26. Lucerna Gallery
27. Maisel Synagogue
28. Monument to Victims of Communism Who Survived
29. Mucha Museum
30. Municipal House
31. Museum of Communism
32. Museum of Czech Cubism (in Black Madonna House)
33. Museum of Medieval Art at St. Agnes Convent
34. Na Příkopě Street
35. National Gallery in Sternberg Palace
36. National Museum
37. National Theater
38. Nerudova Street
39. Old Jewish Cemetery
40. Old Royal Palace
41. Old Town Hall, Astronomical Clock, Tower & Chapel
42. Old Town Square & Jan Hus Memorial
43. Old-New Synagogue
44. Petřín Tower & Mus. of Jára Cimrman
45. Pinkas Synagogue
46. Powder Tower
47. Prague Castle
48. Royal Gardens
49. Royal Summer Palace
50. Schwarzenberg Palace
51. Spanish Synagog
52. St. Martin in the Wall
53. St. Vitus Cathed
54. St. Wenceslas Statue
55. To Strahov Monastery & Library
56. Toy & Barbie Mus
57. Týn Church
58. Ungelt Courtyard & House at the Golden Ring Galle
59. Vrtba Garden
60. Wallenstein Palac Garden
61. Wenceslas Squar

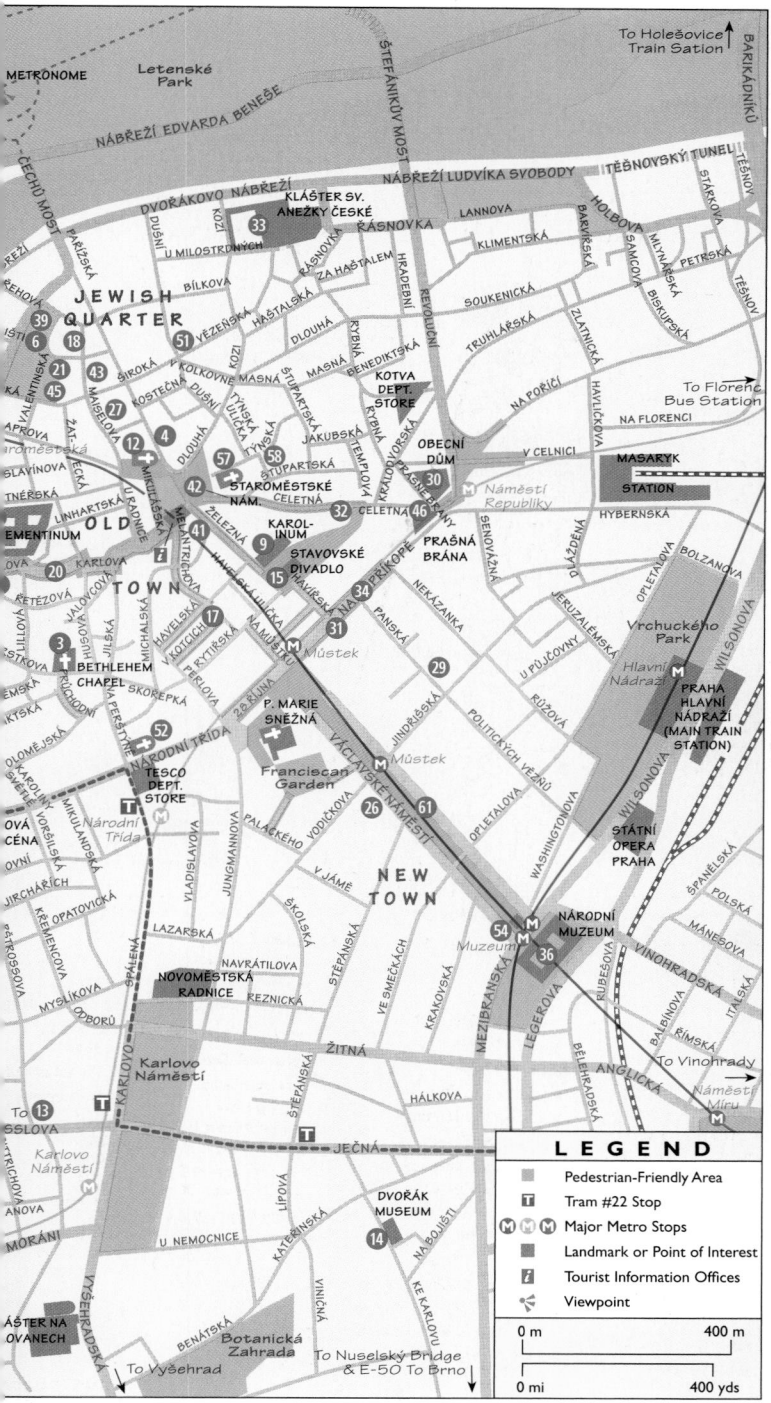
To Holešovice Train Station
METRONOME
Letenské Park
NÁBŘEŽÍ EDVARDA BENEŠE
ŠTEFÁNIKŮV MOST
BARIKÁDNÍKŮ
TĚŠNOVSKÝ TUNEL
NÁBŘEŽÍ LUDVÍKA SVOBODY
ČECHŮV MOST
DVOŘÁKOVO NÁBŘEŽÍ
KLÁŠTER SV. AŇEŽKY ČESKÉ
LANNOVA
HOLBOVA
STÁŘKOVA
TĚŠNOV
RÁSNOVKA
KLIMENTSKÁ
BARVÍŘSKÁ
MLÝNSKÁ
PETRSKÁ
PARÍŽSKÁ
DUŠNÍ
U MILOSTRDNÝCH
ZA HAŠTALEM
HRADEBNÍ
REVOLUČNÍ
SOUKENICKÁ
BÍLKOVA
JEWISH QUARTER
VÝŽEŇSKÁ
HAŠTALSKÁ
DLOUHÁ
RYBNÁ
TRUHLÁŘSKÁ
ZLATNICKÁ
BISKUPSKÁ
ŠIROKÁ
KOSTEČNÁ
MASNÁ
BENEDIKTSKÁ
KOTVA DEPT. STORE
NA POŘÍČÍ
HAVLÍČKOVA
To Florenc Bus Station
NA FLORENCI
MAISELOVA
ŠTUPARTSKÁ
JAKUBSKÁ
TEMPLOVÁ
KRÁLOVOVRŠSKÁ
OBECNÍ DŮM
V CELNICI
MASARYK STATION
Náměstí Republiky
STAROMĚSTSKÉ NÁM.
CELETNÁ
KAROLINUM
PŘÍKOPY
PRAŠNÁ BRÁNA
HYBERNSKÁ
OLD TOWN
KARLOVA
STAVOVSKÉ DIVADLO
NEKÁZANKA
PANSKÁ
SENOVÁŽNÉ
DLAŽDĚNÁ
OPLETALOVA
BOLZANOVA
Vrchuckého Park
JERUZALÉMSKÁ
U PŮJČOVNY
Hlavní Nádraží
PRAHA HLAVNÍ NÁDRAŽÍ (MAIN TRAIN STATION)
WILSONOVA
BETHLEHEM CHAPEL
SKOŘEPKA
P. MARIE SNĚŽNÁ
Franciscan Garden
Můstek
POLITICKÝCH VĚŽŇŮ
RŮŽOVÁ
NÁRODNÍ TŘÍDA
TESCO DEPT. STORE
Národní Třída
VÁCLAVSKÉ NÁMĚSTÍ
OPLETALOVA
WASHINGTONOVA
STÁTNÍ OPERA PRAHA
PALACKÉHO
VODIČKOVA
V JÁMĚ
NEW TOWN
ŠPANĚLSKÁ
POLSKÁ
MÁNESOVA
NÁRODNÍ MUZEUM
Muzeum
VINOHRADSKÁ
ITALSKÁ
LAZARSKÁ
NAVRÁTILOVA
NOVOMĚSTSKÁ RADNICE
KEŽNICKÁ
ŠKOLSKÁ
ŠTĚPÁNSKÁ
VE SMEČKÁCH
KRAKOVSKÁ
MEZIBRANSKÁ
LEGEROVA
RUBEŠOVA
BALBÍNOVA
RÍMSKÁ
To Vinohrady
ANGLICKÁ
Náměstí Míru
ŽITNÁ
HÁLKOVA
Karlovo Náměstí
KARLOVO
JEČNÁ
DVOŘÁK MUSEUM
LIPOVÁ
KATEŘINSKÁ
U NEMOCNICE
VINIČNÁ
KE KARLOVU
NA BOJIŠTI
MORÁNI
ÁSTER NA OVANECH
BENÁTSKÁ
Botanická Zahrada
To Vyšehrad
To Nuselský Bridge & E-50 To Brno
LEGEND
Pedestrian-Friendly Area
Tram #22 Stop
Major Metro Stops
Landmark or Point of Interest
Tourist Information Offices
Viewpoint
0 m
400 m
0 mi
400 yds

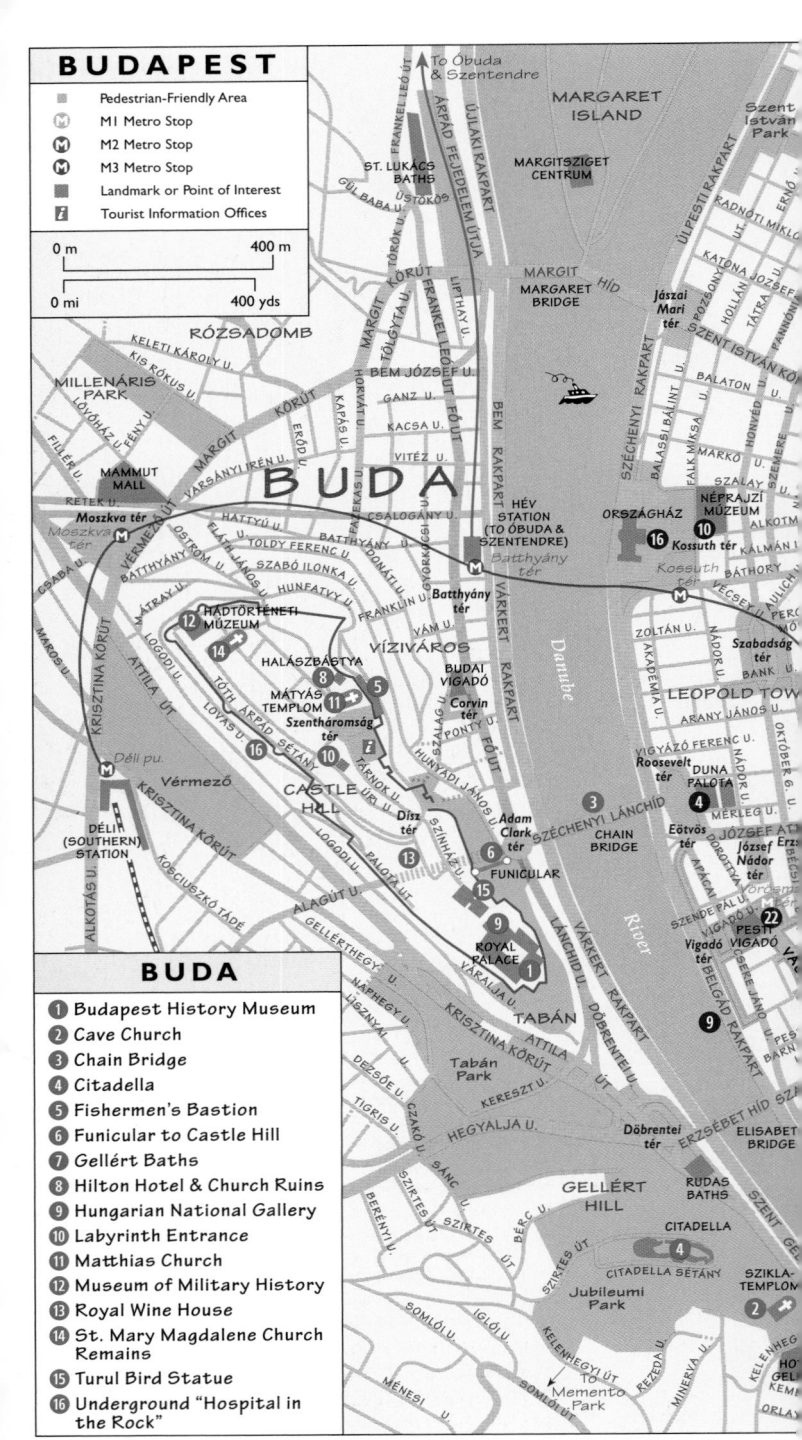
BUDAPEST
Pedestrian-Friendly Area
M1 Metro Stop
M2 Metro Stop
M3 Metro Stop
Landmark or Point of Interest
Tourist Information Offices
0 m
400 m
0 mi
400 yds
BUDA
1 Budapest History Museum
2 Cave Church
3 Chain Bridge
4 Citadella
5 Fishermen's Bastion
6 Funicular to Castle Hill
7 Gellért Baths
8 Hilton Hotel & Church Ruins
9 Hungarian National Gallery
10 Labyrinth Entrance
11 Matthias Church
12 Museum of Military History
13 Royal Wine House
14 St. Mary Magdalene Church Remains
15 Turul Bird Statue
16 Underground "Hospital in the Rock"
To Óbuda & Szentendre
MARGARET ISLAND
Szent István Park
ST. LUKÁCS BATHS
MARGITSZIGET CENTRUM
MARGIT HÍD
MARGARET BRIDGE
Jászai Mari tér
RÓZSADOMB
MILLENÁRIS PARK
BEM JÓZSEF U.
MAMMUT MALL
Moszkva tér
BUDA
HÉV STATION (TO ÓBUDA & SZENTENDRE)
Batthyány tér
ORSZÁGHÁZ
NÉPRAJZI MÚZEUM
Kossuth tér
HADTÖRTÉNETI MÚZEUM
HALÁSZBÁSTYA
MÁTYÁS TEMPLOM
Szentháromság tér
VÍZIVÁROS
BUDAI VIGADÓ
Corvin tér
Szabadság tér
LEOPOLD TOWN
Déli pu.
Vérmező
CASTLE HILL
Dísz tér
Adam Clark tér
FUNICULAR
Roosevelt tér
DUNA PALOTA
CHAIN BRIDGE
Eötvös tér
József Nádor tér
DÉLI (SOUTHERN) STATION
ROYAL PALACE
PEST VIGADÓ
Vigadó tér
TABÁN
Tabán Park
Döbrentei tér
ELISABET BRIDGE
GELLÉRT HILL
RUDAS BATHS
CITADELLA
Jubileumi Park
SZIKLA-TEMPLOM
Memento Park
Danube
River

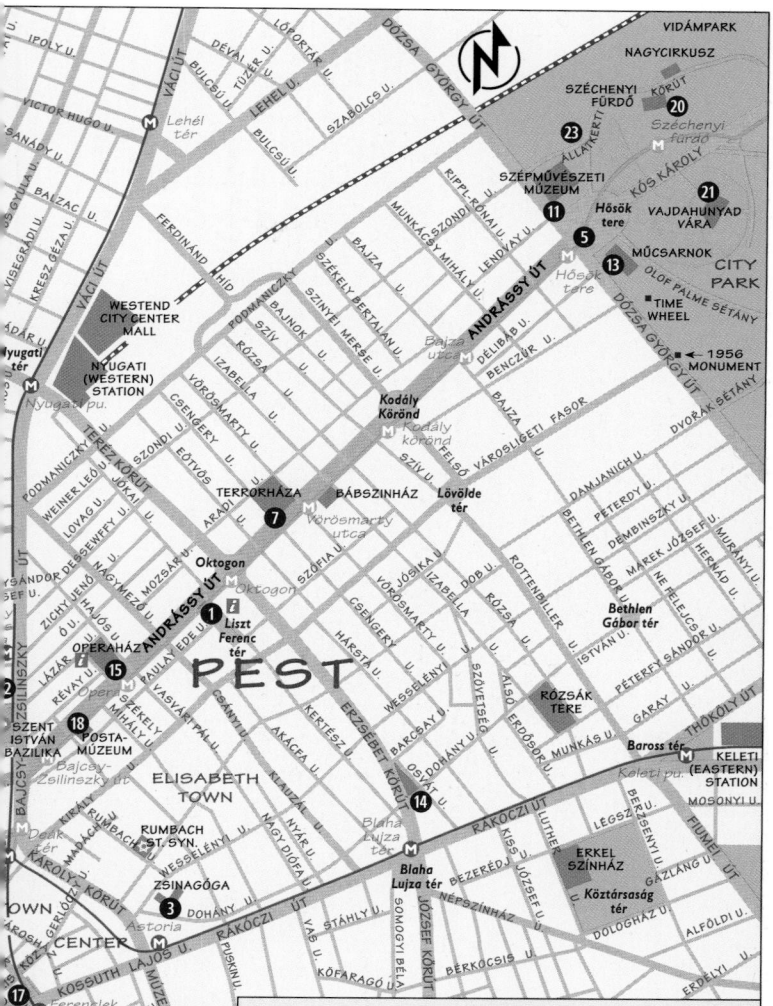
PEST
VIDÁMPARK
NAGYCIRKUSZ
SZÉCHENYI FÜRDŐ
Széchenyi fürdő
SZÉPMŰVÉSZETI MÚZEUM
Hősök tere
VAJDAHUNYAD VÁRA
MŰCSARNOK
CITY PARK
TIME WHEEL
1956 MONUMENT
WESTEND CITY CENTER MALL
NYUGATI (WESTERN) STATION
Nyugati pu.
Kodály Körönd
TERRORHÁZA
BÁBSZINHÁZ
Lövölde tér
Oktogon
Liszt Ferenc tér
OPERAHÁZ
SZENT ISTVÁN BAZILIKA
POSTA-MÚZEUM
ELISABETH TOWN
RUMBACH ST. SYN.
ZSINAGÓGA
Astoria
CENTER
KOSSUTH LAJOS U.
MAGYAR NEMZETI MÚZEUM
Kálvin tér
NAGYVÁSÁRCSARNOK
ROZSAK TERE
KELETI (EASTERN) STATION
Keleti pu.
Baross tér
ERKEL SZÍNHÁZ
Köztársaság tér
Blaha Lujza tér
Deák tér
Ferencek tere
VÁCI UTCA
ANDRÁSSY ÚT
KÁROLY KÖRÚT
KÖRÚT
RÁKÓCZI ÚT
DÓZSA GYÖRGY ÚT
VÁCI ÚT
KÓS KÁROLY
ÁLLATKERTI
OLOF PALME SÉTÁNY
DVORÁK SÉTÁNY
VÁROSLIGETI FASOR
ERZSÉBET KÖRÚT
JÓZSEF KÖRÚT
THÖKÖLY ÚT
FIUMEI ÚT
ALFÖLDI U.
GÁLLANG U.
DOLOGHÁZ U.
NÉPSZÍNHÁZ U.
PERKÓCSIS U.
ERDÉLYI U.
KŐFARAGÓ U.
MOSONYI U.
KÖZRAKTÁR U.
MÁTYÁS U.
VÁMHÁZ KÖRÚT
HÍD
RAKPART
VÁRADY U.
BÁSTYA U.
KIRÁLY U.
MAGYAR U.
FERECZY U.
VERŐS PÁLNÉ U.
SZERB U.
GERKEL U.
MÚZEUM KÖRÚT
KOSSUTH LAJOS U.
ÖRSÖD U.
ÖRSÖD U.
ÖRSÖD

DALMATIAN COAST
A1 Expressway
Major Road
Major Rail Line
Car Ferry
Passenger Boat
Airport
Ruin, Museum, Other Point of Interest
Castle, Monument, Palace
Natural Wonder
0 km 50 100 km
0 miles 50 miles
BOSNIA-HERZEGOVINA
MONTENEGRO
CROATIA
DINARIC MTNS.
To Sarajevo
Mostar
Neretva
Nevesinje
Gacko
Bileća
Bilećko
Podgorica
Livno
Buna
Blagaj
Stolac
Ljubinje
Njeguši
Cetinje
Kotor
Sveti Stefan
Bay of Kotor
Tivat
Herceg Novi
Budva
BUDVA RIVIERA
MEĐUGORJE
Počitelj
Čapljina
Trebinje
Mount Srđ
Dubrovnik
Cilipi
Cavtat
Lokrum
Knin
To Zadar & Zagreb
Sinj
A1
Veliki Prolog
Vrgorac
Metković
Neum
TRSTENO
Mali Ston
Ston
Koločep
Šipan
Lopud
MAKARSKA RIVIERA
NERETVA RIVER DELTA
Ploče
Perković
Makarska
Drvenik
Sućuraj
Solin
Split
Omiš
Šumartin
PELJEŠAC PENINSULA
ELAPHITE ISLANDS
Trpanj
Mljet
Sobra
To Zadar & Zagreb
Brač
Orebić
Polače
MLJET NATL. PARK
To Bari, Italy
Trogir
Supetar
BOL BEACH
Dominče
Pomena
Šibenik
Čiovo
Korčula
Stari Grad
Rogač
Šolta
Hvar
Korčula
To Zadar and Rijeka, Croatia
Vela Luka
Palmižana
Hvar
PAKLENI ISLANDS
Lastovo
Ubli
Vis
Vis
Komiža
To Ancona, Italy
Adriatic Sea
AUSTRIA
HUNGARY
SLOVENIA
CROATIA
BOSNIA-HERZEGOVINA
ITALY
Adriatic Sea

Rick Steves'®

EASTERN EUROPE

CONTENTS

Introduction **1**
Planning 4
Practicalities 12
Money 14
Sightseeing 21
Sleeping 23
Eating 29
Traveling as a Temporary Local 31
Back Door Travel Philosophy 32

Czech Republic **33**
▸ **Prague** 49
Sights 69
Sleeping 125
Eating 135
▸ **Near Prague** 150
Kutná Hora 150
Terezín Concentration Camp 158
Konopiště Castle 166
Karlštejn Castle 168
Křivoklát Castle 169
▸ **Český Krumlov** 171

Slovakia **191**
▸ **Bratislava** 200
Sights 211
Sleeping 216
Eating 217
▸ **The Spiš Region** 220
Levoča 221
The High Tatras 229

Poland **231**
▸ **Kraków** 248
Sights 274
Sleeping 302
Eating 310
▸ **Auschwitz-Birkenau** 317
▸ **Warsaw** 334
Sights 351
Sleeping 370
Eating 375
▸ **Gdańsk and the Tri-City** 379
Sights 396
Sleeping 415
Eating 418
Near Gdańsk: The Tri-City 423
▸ **Pomerania** 428
Malbork Castle 429
Toruń 442

Hungary **449**
▸ **Budapest** 472
Sights 497
Sleeping 561
Eating 574
▸ **Eger** 588
▸ **Pécs** 610

Slovenia **633**
▸ **Ljubljana** 645
Sights 659
Sleeping 676
Eating 680

▸ **Lake Bled** 687
Near Lake Bled 709
▸ **The Julian Alps** 716
Vršič Pass & Soča River Valley 719
Bovec 726
Kobarid 729

Croatia **735**
▸ **Dubrovnik** 758
Sights 778
Sleeping 797
Eating 806
▸ **Split** 812
Sights 828
Sleeping 837
Eating 842
▸ **Korčula** 851
▸ **Rovinj and Istria** 868
Pula 891
Motovun 905
▸ **Zagreb** 912
▸ **Plitvice Lakes National Park** 934

Gateway Cities
▸ **Mostar, Bosnia-Herzegovina** 948
Sights 956
Sleeping 969
Eating 971
▸ **Vienna, Austria** 978
Sights 1003
Sleeping 1048
Eating 1058

Understanding Yugoslavia **1069**

Appendix **1085**
Tourist Information 1085
Communicating 1086
Transportation 1096
Resources 1106
Holidays and Festivals 1111
Conversions and Climate 1114
Essential Packing Checklist 1117
Hotel Reservation Form 1118
Czech Survival Phrases 1119
Slovak Survival Phrases 1120
Polish Survival Phrases 1121
Hungarian Survival Phrases 1123
Slovenian Survival Phrases 1125
Croatian Survival Phrases 1127
German Survival Phrases 1129
Pronouncing Eastern European Place Names 1132

Index **1135**

Map Index **1157**

Top Destinations in Eastern Europe

INTRODUCTION

Until 1989, Eastern Europe was a foreboding place—a dark and gloomy corner of the "Evil Empire." But the dismal grays and preachy reds of communism live on only in history books, museums, and kitschy theme restaurants. Today's Eastern Europe is a traveler's delight, with friendly locals, lively squares, breathtaking sights, fascinating history, reasonable prices, and a sense of pioneer excitement.

This book breaks Eastern Europe into its top big-city, small-town, and back-to-nature destinations. It then gives you all the specifics and opinions necessary to wring the maximum value out of your limited time and money. If you're planning for a month or less in this region, this book is all you need.

Wander among Prague's dreamy, fairy-tale spires, bask in the energy of Kraków's Main Market Square, and soak with chess players in a Budapest bath. Ponder Europe's most moving Holocaust memorial at Auschwitz. Enjoy nature as you stroll on boardwalks through the Plitvice Lakes' waterfall wonderland, or glide across Lake Bled to a church-topped island in the shadow of the Julian Alps. Taste a proud Hungarian vintner's wine and say, *"Egészségedre!"* (or stick with "Cheers!").

Experiencing Europe's culture, people, and natural wonders economically and hassle-free has been my goal for three decades of traveling, tour guiding, and writing. With this book, I pass on to you all of the lessons I've learned.

I've been selective, including only the top destinations and sights. For example, Poland has dozens of medieval castles—but Malbork is a cut above the rest.

The best is, of course, only my opinion. But after spending a third of my adult life exploring and researching Europe, I've developed a sixth sense for what travelers enjoy. Just thinking about the places featured in this book makes me want to polka.

What Is "Eastern Europe"?

"Eastern Europe" means different things to different people. To most Americans, Eastern Europe includes any place that was once behind the Iron Curtain, from the former East Germany to Moscow. But people who actually live in many of these countries consider themselves "Central Europeans." (To them, "Eastern Europe" is *really* eastern: Russia, Ukraine, Belarus, and Romania.)

In this book, I use the term "Eastern Europe" the way most Americans do—to describe the **Czech Republic, Slovakia, Poland, Hungary, Slovenia,** and **Croatia.** I've also thrown in two cities worth a detour: **Vienna** (in Austria) and **Mostar** (in Bosnia-Herzegovina). Vienna is a "gateway city" that feels more Western than Eastern, but it has important historical ties to the region. And Mostar—a mostly Muslim city a short drive or bus trip from Croatia's Dalmatian Coast—provides an opportunity to splice in some diversity.

So what do my six core "Eastern European" countries have in common? All of these destinations fell under communist control during the last half of the 20th century. More importantly, for centuries leading up to World War I, they were all part of the Austrian Habsburg Empire. Before the Habsburgs, the kings and emperors of these countries also frequently governed their neighbors. And all of these countries (except Hungary) are populated by people of Slavic heritage.

I hope that natives, sticklers, and historians will understand the liberties I've taken with the title of this book. But, after all, would you buy a book called *Rick Steves' Former Habsburg Empire?*

About This Book

Rick Steves' Eastern Europe is a personal tour guide in your pocket. Better yet, it's actually two tour guides in your pocket: The co-author of this book is Cameron Hewitt. Cameron writes and edits guidebooks for my travel company, Rick Steves' Europe Through the Back Door. Inspired by his Polish roots and by the enduring charm of the Eastern European people, Cameron has spent the last decade closely tracking the exciting changes in this part of the world. Together, Cameron and I keep this book up-to-date and accurate (though for simplicity we've shed our respective egos to become "I" in this book).

This book is organized by destinations, each one a mini-vacation on its own, filled with exciting sights, strollable neighborhoods, affordable places to stay, and memorable places to eat. I update this book regularly, but things change. For the latest, visit www.ricksteves.com/update, and for reports and experiences—

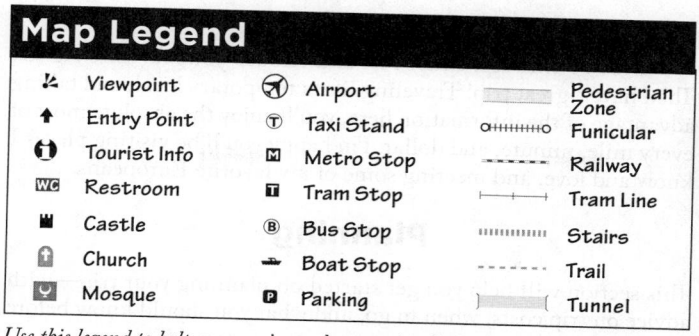

Use this legend to help you navigate the maps in this book.

good and bad—from fellow travelers, check www.ricksteves.com/feedback.

In the following chapters, you'll find these sections:

Planning Your Time suggests a schedule, with thoughts on how best to use your limited time.

Orientation includes specifics on public transportation, helpful hints, local tour options, easy-to-read maps, and tourist information (abbreviated **TI** in this book).

Self-Guided Walks take you through interesting neighborhoods, with a personal tour guide in hand.

Sights, described in detail, are rated:

▲▲▲—Don't miss
▲▲—Try hard to see
▲—Worthwhile if you can make it
No rating—Worth knowing about

Sleeping describes my favorite hotels, from good-value deals to cushy splurges.

Eating serves up a range of options, from inexpensive take-out joints to fancy restaurants.

Connections explains your options for reaching nearby destinations by train, bus, and boat. In car-friendly regions, I've included route tips for drivers, with recommended roadside attractions along the way.

Country Introductions give you an overview of each country's culture, customs, money, history, current events, cuisine, language, and other helpful hints.

The **Understanding Yugoslavia** chapter sorts out the various countries and conflicts, giving you a good picture of why Yugoslavia was formed, and why it broke apart.

The **appendix** is a traveler's tool kit, with telephone tips, useful phone numbers, transportation basics (on trains, buses, boats, car rentals, driving, and flying), recommended books and films, a festival list, a climate chart, a handy packing checklist, a hotel

reservation form, and useful survival phrases.

Browse through this book and choose your favorite sights. Then have a great trip! Traveling like a temporary local, and taking advantage of the information here, you'll enjoy the absolute most of every mile, minute, and dollar. I'm happy you'll be visiting places I know and love, and meeting some of my favorite Europeans.

Planning

This section will help you get started on planning your trip—with advice on trip costs, when to go, and what you should know before you take off.

Travel Smart

Your trip to Europe is like a complex play—easier to follow and really appreciate on a second viewing. While no one does the same trip twice to gain that advantage, studying this book before your trip accomplishes much the same thing. To avoid redundancy, many cultural or historical details are explained for one sight and not repeated for another; to get the full picture, read the entire chapter for each destination you'll visit.

Design an itinerary that enables you to visit the various sights at the best possible times. Note holidays, festivals, seasonal closures (especially in Croatia), and days when sights are closed. For example, most museums throughout Eastern Europe close on Mondays. Hotels are most crowded on Fridays and Saturdays, especially in resort towns.

Sundays have the same pros and cons as they do for travelers in the US (special events, limited hours, banks and many shops generally closed, limited public-transportation options, no rush hour). Rowdy evenings are rare on Sundays. Saturdays are virtually weekdays, with earlier closing hours and no rush hour (though transportation connections can be less frequent than on weekdays).

Be sure to mix intense and relaxed periods in your itinerary. To maximize rootedness, minimize one-night stands. Accommodations are more likely to give a good price to someone staying more than one night. Every trip (and every traveler) needs at least a few slack days (for picnics, laundry, people-watching, and so on). Pace yourself. Assume you will return.

Reread this book as you travel, and visit local TIs. Upon arrival in a new town, lay the groundwork for a smooth departure; write down (or print out from an online source) the schedule for the train, bus, or boat you'll take when you depart. Drivers can ask about the best route to their next destination.

While traveling, take advantage of the Internet and phones to

make your trip run smoothly. By going online (at Internet cafés or your accommodations) and using the phone (buy a phone card or carry a mobile phone), you can get tourist information, learn the latest on sights (special events, tour schedules, etc.), book tickets and tours, make reservations, reconfirm hotels, research transportation connections, and keep in touch with loved ones.

Connect with the culture. Set up your own quest for the best bit of communist kitsch, mug of Czech beer, bowl of borscht, scenic seafront perch, or whatever. Enjoy the hospitality of the local people. Slow down and be open to unexpected experiences. Ask questions—most locals are eager to point you toward their idea of the right direction. Keep a notepad in your pocket for organizing your thoughts. Wear your money belt, learn the local currency, and figure out how to estimate prices in dollars. Those who expect to travel smart, do.

Attitude Adjustment

Americans sometimes approach Eastern Europe expecting grouchy service, crumbling communist infrastructure, and grimy, depressing landscapes. But those who visit are pleasantly surprised at the beauty, friendliness, safety, and ease of travel here. Travel in Eastern Europe today is nearly as smooth as travel in the West. Most of the natives speak excellent English and are forever scrambling to impress their guests. Any remaining rough edges simply add to the charm and carbonate the experience.

The East-West stuff still fascinates us, but to locals, the Soviet regime is old news, Cold War espionage is the stuff of movies, and oppressive monuments to Stalin are a distant memory. More than two decades after the fall of the Iron Curtain, Eastern Europeans (or, as they prefer to be called, *Central* Europeans) think about communism only when tourists bring it up. Freedom is a generation old, and—for better or for worse—McDonald's, MTV, and mobile phones are every bit as entrenched here as anywhere else in Europe. Most of the countries in this book already belong to the European Union, the others are on track to join soon...and all of them are looking optimistically to the future.

Trip Costs

The Eastern European countries in this book—while just two decades removed from communism—are no longer Europe's bargain basement. Although local economies are struggling along with everyone else's due to the global financial crisis, the cost of living in most of Eastern Europe is nearly on par with the West. But it can still be a good value to travel here. Things that natives buy—such as food and transportation—remain fairly inexpensive. Hotels can be pricey, but if you use my listings to find the best

Eastern Europe at a Glance

Czech Republic

▲▲▲**Prague** Romantic Czech capital with a remarkably well-preserved Old Town, sprawling hilltop castle, informative Jewish Quarter, and rollicking pubs.

▲**Near Prague** Kutná Hora's offbeat bone church, Terezín's Nazi concentration camp memorial, and three countryside castles.

▲▲**Český Krumlov** Picturesque town hugging a river bend under a castle.

Slovakia

▲**Bratislava** The Slovak capital, with a rejuvenated Old Town and lots of new construction.

The Spiš Region Rugged northern corner of Slovakia, featuring sweeping mountain scenery, few tourists, and the diamond-in-the-rough town of Levoča.

Poland

▲▲▲**Kraków** Poland's cultural, intellectual, and historical capital, with a huge but cozy main square, easy-to-enjoy Old Town, thought-provoking Jewish quarter, and important castle.

▲▲▲**Auschwitz-Birkenau** The largest and most notorious Nazi concentration camp, now a compelling museum and memorial.

▲▲**Warsaw** Poland's modern capital, with an appealing urban tempo, a reconstructed Old Town, and good museums.

▲▲**Gdańsk and the Tri-City** Historic Hanseatic trading city, with a cancan of marvelous facades and the shipyard where the Solidarity trade union challenged the communists in 1980.

▲**Pomerania** The Teutonic Knights' gigantic, Gothic Malbork Castle; and the red-brick, gingerbread-scented city of Toruń.

Hungary

▲▲▲**Budapest** A grand Danube-spanning cityscape peppered with opulent late-19th-century buildings, excellent restaurants, layers of epic history, and uniquely exhilarating thermal baths.

▲▲**Eger** Strollable town with a gaggle of gorgeous Baroque buildings and locally produced wines.

▲▲**Pécs** Small city featuring a unique mosque-turned-church on its main square, good museums, and colorfully tiled facades.

Slovenia

▲▲**Ljubljana** Slovenia's vibrant, relaxing capital, with fine architecture and an inviting riverside promenade and market.

▲▲▲**Lake Bled** Photogenic lake resort huddled in mountain foothills, with a church-topped island and cliff-hanging castle.

▲▲**The Julian Alps** Cut-glass peaks easily conquered by a twisty mountain road over the Vršič Pass, ending in the tranquil Soča River Valley, with the fine WWI museum in Kobarid.

Croatia

▲▲▲**Dubrovnik** The "Pearl of the Adriatic" and Croatia's best destination: a giant walled Old Town with a scenic wall walk, tons of crowds, an epic past, and an inspiring recent history.

▲▲**Split** Dalmatian transit hub, with a people-filled seaside promenade next to the remains of a massive Roman palace.

▲**Korčula** Low-key island town with a fjord-like backdrop.

▲▲**Rovinj and Istria** Croatia's most enchanting small coastal town—with a romantic Venetian vibe—plus Roman ruins in the city of Pula and the hill town of Motovun.

▲**Zagreb** Croatia's underrated capital city, with interesting sightseeing and a lively urban bustle.

▲▲▲**Plitvice Lakes National Park** A forested canyon filled with crystal-clear lakes and stunning waterfalls, all laced together by boardwalks and trails.

Gateway Cities

▲▲▲**Mostar, Bosnia-Herzegovina** Fascinating town with a striking setting, vital Muslim culture, old Turkish architecture, evocative war damage, and an inspiring, rebuilt Old Bridge.

▲▲▲**Vienna, Austria** Glorious onetime Hapsburg capital boasting stately palaces and world-class museums, convivial wine gardens, a rich musical heritage, and a genteel elegance that has long outlived the emperor's reign.

accommodations deals, a trip to these countries can be substantially cheaper than visiting Italy, Germany, or France.

Five components make up your total trip cost: airfare, surface transportation, room and board, sightseeing and entertainment, and shopping and miscellany. The prices I've listed below are more or less average for all of the destinations in this book. Prices are generally lower in Poland, Slovakia, and Mostar, and higher in Slovenia, Croatia, and Vienna; the Czech Republic and Hungary are in between. Of course, big cities (such as Prague and Budapest) are much more expensive than smaller towns (like Český Krumlov and Eger).

Airfare: A basic round-trip flight from the US to Prague should cost $700 to $1,300 (cheaper in winter), depending on where you fly from and when. Always consider saving time and money in Europe by flying "open jaw"—into one city and out of another. The additional cost of flying into Prague and out of Dubrovnik is almost certainly cheaper than the added expense (and wasted time) of an overland return trip to Prague.

Surface Transportation: For the three-week whirlwind trip described in this chapter, allow $300 per person for public transportation (train, bus, and boat tickets). Train travelers will probably save money by simply buying tickets along the way, rather than purchasing a railpass (see "Transportation," page 1096). Depending on the country, renting a small car costs about $300–450 per week (including tolls, gas, and basic insurance). Long-term car rental is cheapest when arranged in advance from the US, but exorbitant fees for dropping off in a different country can make long-term car rental prohibitively expensive for a multi-country itinerary (see "Renting a Car," page 1100).

Room and Board: You can thrive in Eastern Europe on an average of $100 a day per person for room and board. A $100-a-day budget per person allows $15 for lunch, $25 for dinner, and $60 for lodging (based on two people splitting the cost of a $120 double room that includes breakfast). That's doable. Students and tightwads eat and sleep for $50 a day ($30 per hostel bed, $20 for groceries and snacks).

Sightseeing and Entertainment: Sightseeing is cheap here. Major sights generally cost $3–6, with some more expensive sights at around $10. Figure $10–25 for splurge experiences (e.g., going to concerts, taking an Adriatic cruise, or soaking in a Budapest bath). You can hire your own private guide for four hours for about $100–150—a great value when divided among two or more people. An overall average of $20 a day works for most people. Don't skimp here. After all, this category is the driving force behind your trip—you came to sightsee, enjoy, and experience Eastern Europe.

Shopping and Miscellany: Figure $2 per postcard, coffee,

beer, and ice-cream cone. Shopping can vary in cost from nearly nothing to a small fortune. Good budget travelers find that this category has little to do with assembling a trip full of lifelong and wonderful memories.

When to Go

The "tourist season" runs roughly from May through September. Summer has its advantages: the best weather, very long days (light until after 21:00), and the busiest schedule of tourist fun.

In spring and fall—May, June, September, and early October—travelers enjoy fewer crowds and milder weather. This is my favorite time to travel here. Cities are great at this time of year, but some small towns—especially resorts on the Croatian coast—get quieter and quieter the further off-season you get, and are downright deserted and disappointing in early May and late October.

Winter travelers find concert season in full swing, with absolutely no tourist crowds (except in always-packed Prague), but some accommodations and sights are either closed or run on a limited schedule. Croatian coastal towns are completely dead in winter. Confirm your sightseeing plans locally, especially when traveling off-season. The weather can be cold and dreary, and night will draw the shades on your sightseeing before dinnertime. You may find the climate chart in the appendix helpful.

Sightseeing Priorities

Depending on the length of your trip, here are my recommended priorities. Assuming you're traveling by public transportation, I've taken geographical proximity into account.

3 days:	Prague
5 days, add:	Budapest
7 days, add:	Kraków and Auschwitz
9 days, add:	Český Krumlov
12 days, add:	Ljubljana and Lake Bled
16 days, add:	Dubrovnik and Split
22 days, add:	Plitvice Lakes, Mostar, Eger, Rovinj

With more time or a special interest, choose among Vienna, Gdańsk, Pomerania, Toruń, Warsaw, Pécs, sights near Prague, Korčula, Zagreb, Slovakia's Spiš Region, and Bratislava.

The map on page 11 and the three-week itinerary on page 10 include most of the stops in the first 22 days.

Know Before You Go

Your trip is more likely to go smoothly if you plan ahead. Check this list of things to arrange while you're still at home.

You need a **passport**—but no visa or shots—to travel in the

Eastern Europe: Best Three-Week Trip by Public Transportation

Day	Plan	Sleep in
1	Arrive in Prague	Prague
2	Prague	Prague
3	Prague night train to Kraków	Night train
4	Kraków	Kraków
5	Kraków, day trip to Auschwitz	Kraków
6	Kraków, maybe side-trip to Wieliczka Salt Mine night train to Eger	Night train*
7	Eger	Eger
8	Early to Budapest	Budapest
9	Budapest	Budapest
10	Budapest	Budapest
11	To Ljubljana (catch direct 9-hr midday train; no night-train option)	Ljubljana
12	Ljubljana	Ljubljana
13	To Bled	Bled
14	Rent car for day trips around Julian Alps	Bled
15	To Zagreb, sightseeing, then early evening bus to Plitvice Lakes National Park	Plitvice
16	Plitvice hike in morning, then afternoon bus to Split	Split
17	Split	Split
18	Boat to Korčula (for beach fun) or bus to Mostar (for a taste of Bosnia)	Korčula or Mostar
19	Korčula or Mostar	Korčula or Mostar
20	Boat or bus to Dubrovnik	Dubrovnik
21	Dubrovnik	Dubrovnik
22	Side-trip to Mostar or fly home	

*The handy Kraków-Eger night train connection generally runs only in summer. At other times, you can take the Kraków-Budapest night train (which runs year-round). Once in Budapest, you can either side-trip to Eger, or skip the town entirely.

This ambitious, speedy, far-reaching itinerary works best by public transportation. Most of the time, you'll take the train. There are a few exceptions: Bled and Ljubljana are better connected by bus. To get from Bled to Plitvice, take the bus to Ljubljana, the train to Zagreb, and then the bus to Plitvice. To get from Plitvice to the coast, take the bus to Split. The Dalmatian Coast destinations are best connected to each other by boat or bus (no trains).

By **car,** this itinerary is exhausting, with lots of long road days. Instead, connect long-distance destinations by night train (e.g., Prague to Kraków, Kraków to Eger/Budapest), then strate-

gically rent cars for a day or two in areas that merit having wheels (e.g., the Czech or Slovenian countryside). Also consider adding a side-trip to Croatia's Rovinj (and skip Zagreb). But remember that international drop-off fees for rental cars can be astronomical, and plan accordingly (for example, you could drop off your rental car in Slovenia, take the train or bus into Croatia, and then pick up a different rental car for your Croatia visit). This can be a bit of a puzzle to figure out, but it can also save you plenty.

Vienna: The Austrian capital is a likely gateway between Western and Eastern Europe, but it's out of the way for the above itinerary. If you really want to see Vienna, give it two days between Budapest and Ljubljana (it also makes sense if you're going directly between Budapest and Prague).

Where Do I Find Information On...?

Credit Card Theft	See page 18.
Packing Light	See the packing list on page 1117.
Phoning	See "Telephones" on page 1088.
Language	See page 1086.
Making Hotel Reservations	See page 26.
Tipping	See page 18.
Tourist Information Offices	See page 1085.
Updates to This Book	See www.ricksteves.com/update

countries covered in this book. You may be denied entry into certain European countries if your passport is due to expire within three to six months of your ticketed date of return. Get it renewed if you'll be cutting it close. It can take up to six weeks to get or renew a passport (for more on passports, see www.travel.state.gov). Pack a photocopy of your passport in your luggage in case the original is lost or stolen.

Book rooms in advance if you'll be traveling during peak season (July and August), any major holidays and festivals (see page 1111 of appendix), and definitely for your first night.

Call your **debit and credit card companies** to let them know the countries you'll be visiting so that they won't deny your international charges. Confirm your daily withdrawal limit; consider asking to have it raised so you can take out more cash at each ATM stop.

If you plan to hire a **local guide,** reserve ahead by email. Popular guides can get booked up.

If you're planning on **renting a car** in Eastern Europe, bring your US driver's license. It's also recommended that you carry an International Driving Permit (IDP), available at your local AAA office ($15 plus two passport photos, www.aaa.com). Many countries require drivers to buy a toll sticker for driving on expressways; for details per country, see page 1104.

Since **airline carry-on restrictions** are always changing, visit the Transportation Security Administration's website (www.tsa.gov/travelers) for an up-to-date list of what you can bring on the plane with you...and what you have to check. Arrive early, leaving yourself plenty of time to get through security.

Practicalities

Emergency Telephone Numbers: In all of the countries in this book, dial 112 for medical or other emergencies (except Bosnia-Herzegovina, where it's 124). For police, dial 112 in Slovakia,

Major Holidays and Weekends

Popular places are even busier on weekends, and holidays can bring many businesses to a grinding halt. Plan ahead and reserve your accommodations and transportation well in advance, especially for the month of August. Mark these dates in red on your travel calendar: Easter (April 4 in 2010, April 24 in 2011), Ascension Day (May 13 in 2010, June 2 in 2011), Pentecost/Whitsunday and Whitmonday (May 23–24 in 2010, June 12–13 in 2011), Christmas, December 26, and New Year's Day. Also check the list of festivals and holidays in the appendix.

Hungary, Poland, or Austria; dial 158 in the Czech Republic; dial 113 in Slovenia; dial 92 in Croatia; and dial 122 in Bosnia-Herzegovina.

Borders: All of the countries in this book, except Croatia and Bosnia-Herzegovina, have officially joined the open-borders Schengen Agreement. That means that there are no border checks between any of these countries, or between them and Western European countries such as Germany, Austria, and Italy. You'll simply zip through the border without stopping.

Croatia and Bosnia-Herzegovina, however, have not yet entered the Schengen Agreement. Upon entering or exiting these countries, you'll still have to stop. But whether traveling by car, train, or bus, you'll find that border crossings are generally a non-event—flash your passport, maybe wait a few minutes, and move on. When you change countries, you must still change phone cards, postage stamps, and underpants.

Time: In Europe—and in this book—you'll use the 24-hour clock. It's the same through 12:00 noon, then keep going—13:00, 14:00, and so on. For anything after 12, subtract 12 and add p.m. (14:00 is 2:00 p.m.).

The countries listed in this book are generally six/nine hours ahead of the East/West Coasts of the US. The exceptions are the beginning and end of Daylight Saving Time: Europe "springs forward" the last Sunday in March (two weeks after most of North America), and "falls back" the last Sunday in October (one week before North America). For a handy online time converter, try www.timeanddate.com/worldclock.

Medical Help: If you get sick, do as the locals do and go to a pharmacist. They can help you with almost any ailment. If you need more in-depth attention, ask your hotel for the nearest hospital.

Watt's Up? Europe's electrical system is different from North America's in two ways: the shape of the plug (two round prongs)

and the voltage of the current (220 volts instead of 110 volts). For your North American plug to work in Europe, you'll need an adapter, sold inexpensively at travel stores in the US. As for the voltage, most newer electronics or travel appliances (such as hair dryers, laptops, and battery chargers) automatically convert the voltage—if you see a range of voltages printed on the item or its plug (such as "110–220"), it'll work in Europe. Otherwise, you can buy a converter separately in the US (about $20).

Discounts: Discounts are not listed in this book. However, youths (under 18) and students (with International Student Identity Cards, www.isic.org) often get discounts—but only by asking.

Smoking: While most Western European countries have banned smoking in public places, most Eastern European countries still lag behind—many restaurants and cafés here will give you a whiff of the old, nicotine-stained Europe. In Slovenia and Croatia, smoking is banned (to varying degrees) in indoor public spaces, such as restaurants. Some of the other countries have lesser measures, such as requiring a larger restaurant to have both smoking and non-smoking sections, but allowing the manager of smaller restaurants to choose between smoking and non-smoking. If you require a completely non-smoking section, you'll have to be very specific in your request, and understand that it may not be granted.

News: Americans keep in touch in Europe with the *International Herald Tribune,* published almost daily throughout Europe and online at www.iht.com. Other newsy sites are http://news.bbc.co.uk and www.europeantimes.com. Every Tuesday, the European editions of *Time* and *Newsweek* hit the stands with articles of particular interest to travelers in Europe. Sports addicts can get their fix from *USA Today*. News in English will be sold only where there's enough demand: in big cities and tourist centers (Prague and Budapest have weekly English-language newspapers). Many hotels have CNN or BBC television channels available.

Money

This section offers advice on exchange rates, getting cash, using credit and debit cards, dealing with lost or stolen cards, and tipping.

Exchange Rates

Most of the countries in this book still use their traditional currencies...for now. Through the end of 2011, only Slovenia, Slovakia, and Austria officially use the euro currency. But within a few years, the rest hope to also adopt it.

In countries that don't officially use the euro, many businesses

(especially hotels) quote prices in euros anyway. Even if places list prices in euros, they typically prefer payment in the local currency.

Here are the rough exchange rates for each country. Because of currency fluctuations, and to make things easier to convert in your head, these are very loose estimates (for the latest, see www.oanda.com):

1 euro (€) = about $1.40 (used in Slovakia, Slovenia, and Austria). To roughly convert prices in euros to dollars, add 40 percent: €20 is about $28, €50 is about $70, and so on.

18 Czech crowns (*koruna*, Kč) = about $1. To estimate prices in dollars, multiply by five and drop the last two digits (e.g., 1,000 Kč = about $50).

3 Polish złoty (zł, or PLN) = about $1. To roughly convert prices into dollars, divide by three (e.g., 85 zł = about $30).

200 Hungarian forints (Ft, or HUF) = about $1. To figure dollars, divide by two and drop the last two digits (e.g., 10,000 Ft = about $50).

5 Croatian kunas (kn, or HRK) = about $1. To estimate dollars, multiply by two and drop the last digit (e.g., 70 kn = about $14).

1.3 Bosnian convertible marks (KM, or BAM) = about $1. To roughly convert prices into dollars, subtract 30 percent: 15 KM is about $10. Note that most Bosnian merchants will take euros or Croatian kunas.

So, that 20-zł Polish woodcarving is about $7, the 5,000-Ft Hungarian dinner is about $25, and the 2,000-Kč taxi ride through Prague is...uh-oh.

Cash from ATMs

Throughout Europe, cash machines (ATMs) are the standard way for travelers to get local currency. Bring plastic—credit and/or debit cards. It's smart to bring two cards, in case one gets demagnetized or eaten by a temperamental machine. As an emergency backup, bring several hundred dollars in hard cash (in $20 bills rather than hard-to-exchange $100 bills). Don't use traveler's checks—they're a waste of time (long waits at slow banks) and a waste of money in fees.

Because most of these countries still have different currencies, you'll likely wind up with leftover cash from the previous country. Coins can't be exchanged once you leave the country, so try to spend them before you cross the border. But bills are easy to convert to the "new" country's currency. Regular banks have

the best rates for changing currency or traveler's checks (except in Poland, where *kantors,* or money-changing kiosks, generally offer good rates—check several to find the best). Post offices and train stations usually change money if you can't get to a bank.

You'll find cash machines (called a *Bankomat* in all of these countries) all over, always open, and providing quick transactions. To withdraw money, you'll need a debit card—ideally with a Visa or MasterCard logo for maximum usability—plus a PIN (Personal Identification Number). Know your PIN code in numbers; there are only numbers—no letters—on European keypads.

Before you go, confirm with your bank or credit-card company that your card will work overseas, and alert them that you'll be making withdrawals in Europe; otherwise, they may not approve transactions if they perceive unusual spending patterns. Also ask about international transaction fees; see "Credit and Debit Cards," later.

When using a cash machine, try to take out large sums of money to reduce your per-transaction bank fees. If the machine refuses your request, try again and select a smaller amount (some cash machines limit the amount you can withdraw, especially in Poland and Croatia—don't take it personally). If that doesn't work, try a different machine.

Bank machines often dispense high-denomination bills, which can be difficult to break (especially at odd hours). My strategy: Request an odd amount of money from the ATM (such as 2,800 Kč instead of 3,000 Kč); or, go as soon as possible to a bank or a large store (such as a supermarket) to break the big bills.

To keep your cash safe, use a money belt—a pouch with a strap that you buckle around your waist like a belt, and wear under your clothes. Thieves target tourists. A money belt provides peace of mind, allowing you to carry lots of cash safely. Don't waste time every few days tracking down a cash machine—withdraw a week's worth of money, stuff it in your money belt, and travel!

Credit and Debit Cards

For purchases, Visa and MasterCard are more commonly accepted than American Express. Just like at home, credit or debit cards work easily at larger hotels, shops, and restaurants, but smaller businesses prefer payment in local currency (ideally in smaller bills; break large bills at a bank or big store). If receipts show your credit-card number, don't toss these thoughtlessly.

Fees: Credit- and debit-card transactions—whether used for purchases or ATM withdrawals—often charge additional, tacked-on "international transaction" fees of up to 3 percent plus $5 per transaction. Note that if you use a credit card for ATM transactions, it's technically a "cash advance" rather than a "withdrawal"—and

EU Enlargement and the "New Europe"

The Czech Republic, Slovakia, Poland, Hungary, Slovenia, and five other countries joined the European Union in 2004, with Bulgaria and Romania joining in 2007. Today Croatia, Turkey, and the Republic of Macedonia are also candidates for membership. Though EU membership—and investment—should ultimately benefit everybody, old members and new members have both had their doubts.

For example, new EU member Poland survived the communist era without having to collectivize its small family farms. But after it joined the EU, collectivization became mandatory. Traditional Czech cuisine was also in jeopardy. EU hygiene standards dictate that cooked food can't be served more than two hours old. My Czech friend complained, "This makes many of our best dishes illegal." Czech specialties, often simmered, taste better the next day.

A wise Czech grandmother put it best. In her lifetime, she had lived in a country ruled from Vienna (Habsburgs), Berlin (Nazis), and Moscow (communists). She said, "Now that we're finally ruled from Prague, why would we want to turn our power over to Brussels?"

For their part, longstanding EU members have been skeptical about taking on more countries. Wealthy nations have already spent vast fortunes to improve the floundering economies of poorer member countries (such as Portugal, Greece, and Ireland). Most of the new members joined the union expecting a similar financial-aid windfall, especially during these uncertain times. Also on the financial front, Westerners are fretting about an influx of cheap labor from the East (see "The Polish Plumber Syndrome," page 28).

Finally, Western Europeans worry about their political power being diluted. With 12 new nations joining the EU—and more to come—the geographical center of Europe is gradually shifting from Brussels to Prague. In this "New Europe," the old powers of the West have sometimes been startled to find their spunky new Eastern comrades wielding their influence with gusto. The East eagerly embraces the future, intent on distancing itself from its painful recent history, while the West tentatively clings to the past, when its power was at its peak (and French, not English, was the world's language).

As the "New Europe" takes shape, players on both sides will continue to define their new roles and seek compromise. So far, the general consensus in the East is that joining the EU was the right move. In a few years, the Hungarians, Poles, Czechs, and their neighbors will all be working harder than ever and enjoying more coins jangling in their pockets...and they expect that those coins will be euros.

subject to an additional cash-advance fee.

To avoid unpleasant surprises, call your bank or credit-card company before your trip to ask about these fees. Ask your bank if it has agreements with any European banks for lower withdrawal fees. If the fees are too high, consider getting a card just for your trip: Capital One (www.capitalone.com) and most credit unions have low-to-no international transaction fees.

If merchants offer to convert your purchase price into dollars (called dynamic currency conversion, or "DCC"), refuse this "service." You'll pay even more in fees for the expensive convenience of seeing your charge in dollars.

Damage Control for Lost Cards

If you lose your credit, debit, or ATM card, you can stop people from using it by reporting the loss immediately to the respective global customer-assistance centers. Call these 24-hour US numbers collect: Visa (410/581-9994), MasterCard (636/722-7111), and American Express (623/492-8427).

At a minimum, you'll need to know the name of the financial institution that issued you the card, along with the type of card (classic, platinum, or whatever). Providing the following information will allow for a quicker cancellation of your missing card: full card number, whether you are the primary or secondary cardholder, the cardholder's name exactly as printed on the card, billing address, home phone number, circumstances of the loss or theft, and identification verification (your birth date, your mother's maiden name, or your Social Security number—memorize this, don't carry a copy). If you are the secondary cardholder, you'll also need to provide the primary cardholder's identification-verification details. You can generally receive a temporary card within two or three business days in Europe.

If you promptly report your card lost or stolen, you typically won't be responsible for any unauthorized transactions on your account, although many banks charge a liability fee of $50.

Tipping

A decade ago, tipping was unheard of in Eastern Europe. But then came the tourists. Today, some waiters and taxi drivers are beginning to expect Yankee-sized tips when they spot an American—especially in big cities such as Prague and Budapest. Tipping the appropriate amount—not feeling stingy, but also not contributing to the overtipping epidemic—is nerve-racking to conscientious visitors.

Relax! Many locals still don't tip at all, so any tip is appreciated. As in the US, the proper amount depends on your resources, tipping philosophy, and the circumstances, but some general

guidelines apply.

Restaurants: Tipping is an issue only at restaurants that have table service. If you order your food at a counter, don't tip.

At restaurants that have a waitstaff, round up the bill 5–10 percent after a good meal. My rule of thumb is to estimate about 10 percent, then round down slightly to reach a convenient total (for a 370-Kč meal, I pay 400 Kč—a tip of 30 Kč, or about 8 percent). I'm a little more generous in Budapest, where a minimum 10 percent tip is expected (I'll hand over 4,000 Ft for a 3,600-Ft bill—that's a 400-Ft tip, or 11 percent). Anywhere in Eastern Europe, a 15 percent tip is overly generous, verging on extravagant. At some tourist-oriented restaurants, a 10 or 15 percent "service charge" may be added to your bill, in which case an additional tip is not necessary. (More commonly, menus or bills remind you that the tip is *not* included.) If you're not sure whether your bill includes the tip, just ask.

Taxis: To tip the cabbie, round up about five percent (for a 71-kn fare, pay 75 kn). If the cabbie hauls your bags and zips you to the airport to help you catch your flight, you might want to toss in a little more. But if you feel like you're being driven in circles or otherwise ripped off, skip the tip.

Special Services: Tour guides at public sites sometimes hold out their hands for tips after they give their spiels. If I've already paid for the tour, I don't tip extra unless they've really impressed me. At hotels, if you let the porter carry your luggage, it's polite to give them the local equivalent of 50 cents for each bag. I don't tip the maid, but if you do, you can leave a dollar's worth of local cash per overnight at the end of your stay. In general, if someone in the service industry does a super job for you, a small tip (the equivalent of a dollar or two) is appropriate...but not required.

When in doubt, ask: If you're not sure whether (or how much) to tip for a service, ask your hotelier or the TI; they'll fill you in on how it's done on their turf.

VAT Refunds for Shoppers

Wrapped into the purchase price of your souvenirs is a Value-Added Tax (VAT) that varies per country. You're entitled to get most of that tax back if you make a purchase of more than a certain amount at a store that participates in the VAT refund scheme (see chart for VAT rates and minimum amounts).

Getting your refund is usually straightforward and, if you buy a substantial number of souvenirs, well worth the hassle. If you're lucky, the merchant will subtract the tax when you make your purchase. (This is more likely to occur if the store ships the goods to your home.) Otherwise, you'll need to:

Get the paperwork. Have the merchant completely fill out

VAT Rates and Minimum Purchases Required to Qualify for Refunds

Country of Purchase	VAT Standard Rate*	Minimum in Local Currency	Approx. Min. in US Dollars
Austria	20%	€75.01	$105
Croatia	23%	501 kn	$100
Czech Republic	19%	2,001 Kč	$112
Hungary	20%	42,001 Ft	$210
Poland	22%	200 zł	$66
Slovakia	19%	€150	$210
Slovenia	20%	€50	$70

* The VAT Standard Rates listed above—while listed as exact amounts—are intended to give you an idea of the rates and minimums involved. But VAT rates fluctuate based on many factors, including what kind of item you are buying. Your refund will also likely be less than the above rate, especially if it's subject to processing fees.

the necessary refund document, called a "cheque." You'll have to present your passport at the store.

Get your stamp at the border or airport. Process your cheque(s) at your last stop in the country with the customs agent who deals with VAT refunds. It's best to keep your purchases in your carry-on for viewing, but if they're too large or dangerous (such as knives) to carry on, track down the proper customs agent to inspect them before you check your bag. To qualify, your purchased goods should be unused. If you show up at customs wearing your chic Czech shirt, officials might look the other way—or deny you a refund.

Collect your refund. You'll need to return your stamped document to the retailer or its representative. Many merchants work with a service that has offices at major airports, ports, and border crossings, such as Global Refund (www.globalrefund.com) or Premier Tax Free (www.premiertaxfree.com). These services, which extract a 4 percent fee, can usually refund your money immediately in your currency of choice or credit your card (within two billing cycles). If the retailer handles VAT refunds directly, it's up to you to contact the merchant for your refund. You can mail the documents from home, or quicker, from your point of departure (using a stamped, addressed envelope you've prepared or one that's been provided by the merchant). You'll then have to wait—it could take months.

Customs for American Shoppers

You are allowed to take home $800 worth of items per person duty-free, once every 30 days. The next $1,000 is taxed at a flat 3 percent. After that, you pay the individual item's duty rate. You can also bring in duty-free a liter of alcohol (slightly more than a standard-size bottle of wine; you must be at least 21), 200 cigarettes, and up to 100 non-Cuban cigars. You may take home vacuum-packed cheeses; dried herbs, mushrooms, or spices (such as Hungarian paprika); and canned fruits or vegetables, including jams and vegetable spreads. Baked goods, candy, chocolate, oil, vinegar, mustard, and honey are OK. Fresh fruits or vegetables are not. Meats, even if canned, are generally not allowed. Remember that you'll need to carefully pack any bottles of *vino, slivovice, wódka,* or other liquid-containing items in your checked luggage, due to the three-ounce limit on liquids in carry-on baggage. To check customs rules and duty rates before you go, visit www.cbp.gov, and click on "Travel," then "Know Before You Go."

Sightseeing

Eastern Europe's best attractions are new, modern museums that chronicle the communist regime and celebrate its demise (such as Budapest's House of Terror and Memento Park, and Gdańsk's "Roads to Freedom" exhibit). But the majority of museums here are dusty, old-fashioned collections of art or historical artifacts. While these don't quite rank with the Louvre or the Prado, many are surprisingly engaging if you give them a chance. Generally, you'll follow a confusing, one-way tour route through a maze of rooms with squeaky parquet floors, monitored by grumpy grannies who listlessly point you in the right direction. While some museums label exhibits in English, most don't post full explanations; you'll have to buy a book or borrow laminated translations. In some cases, neither option is available. Audioguides are just catching on, and tend to be expensive and dull.

Sightseeing can be hard work. Use these tips to make your visits to Eastern Europe's finest sights meaningful, fun, efficient, and painless.

Plan Ahead

Set up an itinerary that allows you to fit in all your must-see sights. Most sights keep stable hours, but in some areas (especially Poland and coastal Croatia), hours tend to fluctuate from year to year and season to season. If you have your heart set on visiting particular sights, it's always smart to confirm the latest hours by checking their websites or asking at the local TI.

When possible, visit key museums first thing (when your

energy is best) and save other activities for the afternoon. Hit the highlights first, then go back to other things if you have the stamina and time.

At Sights

Here's what you can typically expect:

At churches—which often offer interesting art (usually free) and a welcome seat—a modest dress code (no bare shoulders or shorts) is encouraged, but rarely enforced.

Some important sights have metal detectors or conduct bag searches that will slow your entry.

Major museums and sights require you to check daypacks and coats. They'll be kept safely. If you have something you can't bear to part with, stash it in a pocket or purse. To avoid checking a small backpack, carry it under your arm like a purse as you enter. From a guard's point of view, a backpack is generally a problem, while a purse is not.

Photography is sometimes banned at major sights. Look for signs or ask. Even if cameras are allowed, flashes or tripods usually are not. Flashes damage oil paintings and distract others in the room. Even without a flash, a handheld camera will take a decent picture (or you can buy postcards or posters at the museum bookstore). If photos are permitted, video cameras generally are, too.

Many museums have special exhibits in addition to their permanent collection. Some exhibits are included in the entry price, while others come at an extra cost (which you may have to pay even if you don't want to see the exhibit).

Expect changes—paintings can be on tour, on loan, out sick, or shifted at the whim of the curator. To adapt, pick up any available free floor plans as you enter, and ask museum staff if you can't find a particular item.

A few sights rent audioguides offering recorded descriptions in English, but they're rarely worth the cost (about $6-8). If you bring along your own pair of headphones and a Y-jack, you can sometimes share one audioguide with your travel partner and save money.

Some sights have videos about the attraction. These are generally worth your time. I make it standard operating procedure to ask when I arrive at a sight if there is a film in English.

The WCs at many sights are free and clean. Some sights have an on-site café or cafeteria (usually a good place to rest and have a snack or light meal).

Many places sell postcards that highlight their attractions. Before you leave, scan the postcards and thumb through the biggest guidebook (or skim its index) to be sure you haven't overlooked something that you'd like to see.

Most sights stop admitting people 30–60 minutes before closing time, and some rooms close early (generally about 30 minutes before the actual closing time). Guards usher people out, so don't save the best for last.

Every sight or museum offers more than what is covered in this book. Use the information in this book as an introduction—not the final word.

Sleeping

I look for places that are friendly, clean, comfortable, professional-feeling, centrally located, English-speaking, and family-run. I also like local character and simple facilities that don't cater to American "needs." Obviously, a place meeting every criterion is rare, and all of my recommendations fall short of perfection—sometimes miserably. But I've listed the best values for each price category.

My favorites are small, family-run hotels (which aren't as prevalent in Eastern Europe as in the West), and friendly local people who rent "hotelesque" private rooms without a reception desk. I've also thrown in a few hostels and other cheap options for budget travelers.

Accommodations in Eastern Europe cost about as much as comparable beds in the West. While most accommodations listed in this book cluster at about $80–120 per double, they range from $15 bunks to $500-plus splurges (maximum plumbing and more).

Remember that some accommodations quote their rates in euros, while others use the local currency. I generally list the prices they give me. However, occasionally I've converted a few prices to make it easier for you to compare hotel rates—so you might notice a little variation between the rates listed here and those quoted by hotels.

If asked whether they have non-smoking rooms, most hoteliers in Eastern Europe will say yes. When pressed, they'll sheepishly admit, "Well, *all* of our rooms are non-smoking"...meaning they air them out after a smoker has stayed there. I've described accommodations as "non-smoking" only if they have specially designated rooms for this purpose. Be specific and assertive if you need a strictly non-smoking room.

For environmental reasons, towels are often replaced in hotels only when you leave them on the floor. In private accommodations and some cheap hotels, they aren't replaced at all, so hang them up to dry and reuse. The cord that dangles over the tub or shower in big resort hotels is not a clothesline—you pull it if you've fallen and can't get up.

Before accepting a room, confirm your understanding of

the complete price (including, for example, surcharges for short stays). Pay your bill the evening before you leave to avoid the time-wasting crowd at the reception desk in the morning, especially if you need to rush off to catch your train. The only tip my recommended accommodations would like is a friendly, easygoing guest. And, as always, I appreciate feedback on your experiences.

Types of Accommodations

Hotels

In Eastern Europe, you can choose from a delightful variety of stylish and charming hotels and guest houses. Although some dreary old communist-era hotels remain, they're no longer the norm. Because so many Eastern European hotels are relatively new (built since the end of communism), hotel prices can be higher than you might expect. You can find a central, basic, comfortable double for $100 just about anywhere. Plan on spending $90–130 per double in big cities, and $60–90 in smaller towns. You can uncover some bargains, but I think it's worth paying a little more for comfort and a good location.

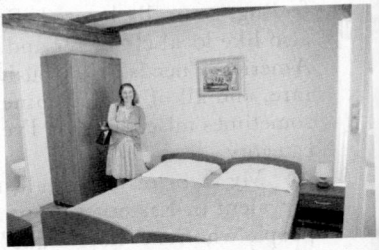

During these times of economic uncertainty, many larger hotels will likely be discounting deeply to snare what customers they can. Try to avoid paying the inflated, official "rack rates." If you email several big hotels and ask for their best prices, you'll find some eager to discount and others more passive. This can save you big bucks—with prices potentially far below those listed in this guidebook.

Three or four people can save money by requesting one big room. Traveling alone can be expensive: A single room is often only 20 percent cheaper than a double.

When you check in, the receptionist will normally ask for your passport and keep it for a couple of hours. Don't worry. Hotels are legally required to register each guest with the local police. Americans are notorious for making this chore more difficult than it needs to be.

You can assume that a buffet breakfast is included in the prices I've listed, unless otherwise noted. This usually includes rolls, cold cuts, cheese, cereal, yogurt, fruit, coffee, milk, and juice; some places also provide eggs.

Most hotel rooms have a TV and telephone, and Internet access (either wireless or with a cable) is increasingly common. Pricier hotels also have air-conditioning, a little safe, and a minibar. Rooms are secure. Still, keep cameras, laptops, and cash out of sight.

Sleep Code

To help you sort easily through the listings, I've divided the rooms into three categories based on the price for a standard double room with bath:

$$$ Higher Priced
$$ Moderately Priced
$ Lower Priced

Prices listed in this book are per room, not per person. Hotels usually accept credit cards and include a buffet breakfast (unless otherwise noted); private accommodations rarely do either. Virtually all of my recommended accommodations are run by people who speak English; if they don't, I mention it in the listing.

When there is a range of prices in one category, that means the price fluctuates with the season; the prices and seasons are posted at or near the hotel desk. To give maximum information in a minimum of space, I use the following code to describe the accommodations.

S = Single room (or price for one person in a double).
D = Double or twin. Double beds are usually big enough for non-romantic couples.
T = Triple (often a double bed with a single).
Q = Quad (usually two double beds).
b = Private bathroom with toilet and shower or tub.
s = Private shower or tub only (the toilet is down the hall).

According to this code, a couple staying at a "Db-2,700 Kč, cash only" place in Prague would pay a total of 2,700 Czech crowns (about $135) for a double room with a private bathroom. Credit cards are not accepted, but you can assume they speak English.

If I mention "Internet access" in a listing, there's a public terminal in the lobby for guests to use. If I specify "Wi-Fi" or "cable Internet," you can generally get online in your room (usually for free), but only if you have your own laptop.

Your hotelier, a good source of advice, can direct you to the nearest launderette and Internet café.

Private Rooms

Private accommodations—which are particularly prevalent in Croatia—offer travelers a characteristic and money-saving alternative for a fraction of the price of a hotel. A room in a private home is called a *sobe* in Slovenia and Croatia; the German word *Zimmer* works there, too, and throughout Eastern Europe. These places are

inexpensive, at least as comfortable as a cheap hotel, and a good way to get some local insight. The boss changes the sheets, so people staying several nights are most desirable—and those who stay less than three nights are often charged a lot more (typically 20–50 percent; this surcharge is often waived outside of peak season). For more on Croatian *sobe*, see page 737.

Hostels

For $20–30 a night, travelers of any age can stay at a youth hostel. While official IYHF hostels admit nonmembers for an extra fee, it can be easier to join the club and buy a youth hostel card before you go (call Hostelling International at US tel. 202/783-6161, or order online at www.hiayh.org). However, to increase your options, consider the many independent hostels that don't require a membership card.

If you're used to hosteling elsewhere in Europe, you may be unpleasantly surprised by some Eastern European hostels. In general, the official IYHF hostels are inconveniently located and particularly institutional, while independent hostels are more loosely run and grungier than the European norm. In each town, I've tried to list the best-established, most reputable hostel options, both independent and official—sometimes with lots of caveats. But this scene is evolving so fast that avid hostelers will do better getting tips from fellow travelers and searching on sites such as www.hostels.com, www.hostelworld.com, www.hostelz.com, and www.hostelseurope.com.

At hostels, cheap meals are sometimes available, and kitchen facilities are usually provided for do-it-yourselfers. While many hostels have a few doubles or family rooms available upon request for a little extra money, plan on dorms with 4- to 20-beds per room. At official hostels, dorms are generally gender-segregated; at independent hostels, it's more likely mixed. In summer, expect crowds, snoring, and lots of noisy backpacker bonding in the common room while you're trying to sleep. Hosteling is ideal for those traveling single: Prices are per bed, not per room, and you'll have an instant circle of friends. At most hostels, you can reserve online or by phoning ahead (usually with a credit card).

Phoning

To make international calls to line up hotel reservations, you'll need to know the country codes. For detailed instructions on telephoning, see page 1088 in the appendix.

Making Reservations

Given the erratic accommodations values in Eastern Europe—and the quality of the places I've found for this book—I'd recommend

that you reserve your rooms in advance, particularly if you'll be traveling during peak season. Book several weeks ahead, or as soon as you've pinned down your travel dates. Note that some holidays jam things up and merit your making reservations far in advance (see "Major Holidays and Weekends" sidebar on page 13). Just like at home, holidays that fall on a Monday, Thursday, or Friday can turn the weekend into a long holiday, so book the entire weekend well in advance. Finding accommodations as you travel is possible, but you're more likely to wind up in a poorly located and/or overpriced hotel than if you plan ahead.

Requesting a Reservation: To reserve, contact hotels directly by email, phone, or fax. Email is the clearest and most economical way to make a reservation. Or you can go straight to the hotel website; many hotels have secure online reservation forms and can instantly inform you of availability and any special deals. But be sure you use the hotel's official site and not a booking agency's site—otherwise you may pay higher rates than you should. If you're phoning from the US, be mindful of time zones (see page 13). Most recommended accommodations are accustomed to guests who speak only English.

Your hotelier or B&B host wants to know these key pieces of information (also included in the sample request form on page 1118):

- number and type of rooms
- number of nights
- date of arrival
- date of departure
- any special needs (e.g., bathroom in the room or down the hall, twin beds vs. double bed, air-conditioning, quiet, view, ground floor, etc.)

When you request a room in writing for a certain time period, use the European style for writing dates: day/month/year. Hoteliers need to know your arrival and departure dates. For example, for a two-night stay in July I would request: "1 double room for 2 nights, arrive 16/07/10, depart 18/07/10." (Consider in advance how long you'll stay; don't just assume you can tack on extra days once you arrive.)

If you don't get a reply to your email or fax, it usually means the place is already fully booked (but you can try sending the message again, or call to follow up).

Confirming a Reservation: If the hotel's response tells you its room availability and rates, it's not a confirmation. You must tell them that you want that room at the given rate. Many hoteliers will request your credit-card number for a one-night deposit to hold the room. While you can email your credit-card information (I do), it's safer to share that personal info via phone call, fax, two

The Polish Plumber Syndrome

You'll likely enjoy a taste of Eastern European culture on your next trip...to London or Dublin. When several Eastern European countries joined the European Union in 2004, three EU members immediately welcomed their new comrades to work without a visa: Great Britain, the Republic of Ireland, and Sweden. This sparked a wave of immigration into these wealthy counties, as Eastern Europeans flocked to the land of plenty to find work. Many ended up in the hospitality industry.

The result has been mixed in each region. The transplants enjoyed more money and an irreplaceable cross-cultural experience. But Eastern Europe went through a somewhat alarming "brain drain," as many of its youngest and most westward-thinking residents rushed away. In Britain and Ireland, tourists began to encounter desk clerks who didn't quite speak fluent English. More recently, the global financial crisis has tightened up the job market—making the arrangement less appealing both to the expat workers, and to the native job-seekers in the countries that are hosting them. Quite a few of these transplants have lost their jobs and returned home to the East.

Other Western European countries have contemplated opening their borders, but it's controversial. One popular symbol—invented by a right-wing French politician—was an invading "Polish plumber" who'd put French plumbers out of a job. The Polish tourist board countered by putting up clever ads in France featuring an alluring Polish hunk stroking a pipe wrench, saying, "I'm staying in Poland... come visit me!"

This is just one more step in the Europe-wide process of integration. Europeans in their twenties have been dubbed the "Erasmus Generation"—after the Erasmus Student Network, an EU organization that fosters study-abroad opportunities within Europe. As European twentysomethings have grown up accustomed to attending universities in other counties, it seems natural for them to identify as "Europeans" rather than as Spaniards, Slovenes, or Swedes. Multilingualism, international résumés, and cross-cultural marriages are the norm.

Ultimately, as with all aspects of EU enlargement, the resettlement of Poles, Czechs, and Hungarians to the bogs of Ireland will likely be good for everyone, despite a few growing pains. It's just one more step in the evolution of a truly united Europe.

successive emails, or secure online reservation form (if the hotel has one on its website).

Canceling a Reservation: If you must cancel your reservation, it's courteous to do so with as much advance notice as possible—at least three days. Simply make a quick phone call or send an email. Family-run hotels and B&Bs lose money if they turn away customers while holding a room for someone who doesn't show up. Understandably, many hoteliers bill no-shows for one night.

Hotels sometimes have strict cancellation policies: For example, you might lose a deposit if you cancel within two weeks of your reserved stay, or you might be billed for the entire visit if you leave early. Ask about cancellation policies before you book.

If canceling via email, request confirmation that your cancellation was received to avoid being accidentally billed.

Reconfirm Your Reservation: Always call to reconfirm your room reservation a few days in advance from the road. Smaller hotels and B&Bs appreciate knowing your estimated time of arrival. If you'll be arriving late (after 16:00), always alert your host or hotel. On the small chance that a hotel loses track of your reservation, bring along a hard copy of their emailed or faxed confirmation.

Reserving Rooms as You Travel: If you enjoy having a fluid itinerary, you can make reservations as you travel, calling hotels or B&Bs a few days to a week before your visit. If you prefer the flexibility of traveling without any reservations at all, you'll have greater success snaring rooms if you arrive at your destination early in the day. When you anticipate crowds (weekends are worst), call hotels at about 9:00 on the day you plan to arrive, when the hotel clerk knows who'll be checking out and just which rooms will be available. If you encounter a language barrier, ask the fluent receptionist at your current hotel to call for you.

Eating

Eastern Europe offers good food for relatively little money—especially if you steer clear of the easy-to-avoid tourist trap restaurants. This is affordable sightseeing for your palate.

Slavic cuisine has a reputation for being heavy and hearty, with lots of pork, potatoes and cabbage...which is true. But the food here is also delicious, and there's a lot more diversity from country to country than you might expect. Tune in to the regional and

How Was Your Trip?

Were your travels fun, smooth, and meaningful? If you'd like to share your tips, concerns, and discoveries, please fill out the survey at www.ricksteves.com/feedback. I value your feedback. Thanks in advance—it helps a lot.

national specialties and customs (see each country's introduction in this book for details).

Ethnic restaurants provide a welcome break from Slavic fare. Seek out vegetarian, Italian, Indian, Chinese, and other similar places. They're especially good in big cities such as Prague, Budapest, or Kraków (I've listed a few tasty options). Hungarian cuisine is rich and spicy (think paprika), while Slovenia and Croatia have good seafood and lots of Italian-style dishes (pastas and pizzas).

When restaurant-hunting, choose a spot filled with locals, not the place with the big neon signs boasting, "We Speak English and Accept Credit Cards." Venturing even a block or two off the main drag leads to local, higher-quality food for less than half the price of the tourist-oriented places. Most restaurants tack a menu onto their door for browsers and have an English menu inside. If the place isn't full, you can usually just seat yourself (get a waiter's attention to be sure your preferred table is OK)—the American-style "hostess," with a carefully managed waiting list, isn't common here. Once seated, feel free to take your time. In fact, it might be difficult to dine in a hurry. Only a rude waiter will rush you. Good service is relaxed (slow to an American).

When you're in the mood for something halfway between a restaurant and a picnic meal, look for take-out food stands, bakeries (with sandwiches and savory pastries to go), shops selling pizza by the slice, or simple little eateries offering fast and easy sit-down restaurant food. In Poland, don't miss the deliriously cheap "milk bar" cafeterias (see page 245). Many grocery stores sell pre-made sandwiches, and others might be willing to make one for you from what's in the deli case.

The Czech Republic is beer country, with Europe's best and cheapest brew. Poland also has fine beer, but the national drink is *wódka*. Hungary, Slovenia, and Croatia are known for their wines. Each country has its own distinctive liqueur, most of them a variation on *slivovice* (SLEE-voh-veet-seh)—a plum brandy so highly valued that it's the de facto currency of the Carpathian Mountains (often used for bartering with farmers and other mountain folk). Menus list drink size by the tenth of a liter, or deciliter (dl). Non-drinkers will find all the standard types of Coke and Pepsi, along

with some fun-to-sample local alternatives (such as Slovenia's Cockta, described on page 642).

Traveling as a Temporary Local

We travel all the way to Europe to enjoy differences—to become temporary locals. You'll experience frustrations. Certain truths that we find "God-given" or "self-evident," such as cold beer, ice in drinks, bottomless cups of coffee, hot showers, cigarette smoke being irritating, and bigger being better, are suddenly not so true. One of the benefits of travel is the eye-opening realization that there are logical, civil, and even better alternatives. A willingness to go local ensures that you'll enjoy a full dose of local hospitality.

Fortunately for you, hospitality is a local forte. The friendliness of the Eastern Europeans seems to have only been enhanced during the communist era: Tangible resources were in short supply, so an open door and a genial conversation were all that people had to offer. For many Eastern Europeans, the chance to chat with an American is still a delightful novelty. Even so, some people—hardened by decades of being spied on by neighbors and standing in long lines to buy food for their family—seem brusque at first. In my experience, all it takes is a smile and a little effort to befriend these residents of the former "Evil Empire."

Americans are enjoying a surge in popularity these days. But if there is a negative aspect to the image Europeans have of Americans, it's that we are big, loud, aggressive, impolite, rich, superficially friendly, and a bit naive.

Americans tend to be noisy in public places, such as restaurants and trains. My European friends place a high value on speaking quietly in these same places. Listen while on the bus or in a restaurant—the place can be packed, but the decibel level is low. Try to remember this nuance, and soften your speaking voice as a way of respecting their culture.

While Europeans look bemusedly at some of our Yankee excesses—and worriedly at others—they nearly always afford us individual travelers all the warmth we deserve.

Judging from all the happy feedback I receive from travelers who have used this book, it's safe to assume you'll enjoy a great, affordable vacation—with the finesse of an independent, experienced traveler.

Thanks, and happy travels!

Back Door Travel Philosophy

From *Rick Steves' Europe Through the Back Door*

Travel is intensified living—maximum thrills per minute and one of the last great sources of legal adventure. Travel is freedom. It's recess, and we need it.

Experiencing the real Europe requires catching it by surprise, going casual..."Through the Back Door."

Affording travel is a matter of priorities. (Make do with the old car.) You can eat and sleep—simply, safely, and enjoyably—anywhere in Europe for $120 a day plus transportation costs. In many ways, spending more money only builds a thicker wall between you and what you traveled so far to see. Europe is a cultural carnival, and time after time, you'll find that its best acts are free and the best seats are the cheap ones.

A tight budget forces you to travel close to the ground, meeting and communicating with the people. Never sacrifice sleep, nutrition, safety, or cleanliness to save money. Simply enjoy the local-style alternatives to expensive hotels and restaurants.

Connecting with people carbonates your experience. Extroverts have more fun. If your trip is low on magic moments, kick yourself and make things happen. If you don't enjoy a place, maybe you don't know enough about it. Seek the truth. Recognize tourist traps. Give a culture the benefit of your open mind. See things as different, but not better or worse. Any culture has plenty to share.

Of course, travel, like the world, is a series of hills and valleys. Be fanatically positive and militantly optimistic. If something's not to your liking, change your liking.

Travel can make you a happier American, as well as a citizen of the world. Our Earth is home to six and a half billion equally precious people. It's humbling to travel and find that other people don't have the "American Dream"—they have their own dreams. Europeans like us, but with all due respect, they wouldn't trade passports.

Thoughtful travel engages us with the world. In tough economic times, it reminds us what is truly important. By broadening perspectives, travel teaches new ways to measure quality of life.

Globetrotting destroys ethnocentricity, helping us understand and appreciate other cultures. Rather than fear the diversity on this planet, celebrate it. Among your most prized souvenirs will be the strands of different cultures you choose to knit into your own character. The world is a cultural yarn shop, and Back Door travelers are weaving the ultimate tapestry. Join in!

CZECH REPUBLIC

CZECH REPUBLIC

Česká Republika

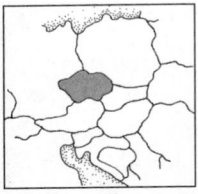

Despite their difficult 20th-century experience, the Czechs have managed to preserve their history. In Czech towns and villages, you'll find a simple joy of life—a holdover from the days of the Renaissance. The deep spirituality of the Baroque era still shapes the national character. The magic of Prague, the beauty of Český Krumlov, and the lyrical quality of the countryside relieve the heaviness caused by the turmoil that passed through here. Get beyond Prague and explore the country's medieval towns. These rugged woods and hilltop castles will make you feel as if you're walking through the garden of your childhood dreams.

Of the Czech Republic's three main regions—Bohemia, Moravia, and small Silesia—the best-known is Bohemia. It has nothing to do with beatnik bohemians, but with the Celtic tribe of Bohemia that inhabited the land before the coming of the Slavs. A longtime home of the Czechs, Bohemia is circled by a naturally fortifying ring of mountains and cut down the middle by the Vltava River, with Prague as its capital. The winegrowing region of Moravia (to the east) is more Slavic and colorful, and more about the land.

Tourists often conjure up images of Bohemia when they think of the Czech Republic. But the country consists of more than rollicking beer halls and gently rolling landscapes. It's also about dreamy wine cellars and fertile Moravian plains, with the rugged Carpathian Mountains on the horizon. Politically and geologically, Bohemia and Moravia are two distinct regions. The soils and climates in which the hops and wine grapes grow are very different...and so are the two regions' mentalities. The boisterousness of the Czech polka contrasts with the melancholy of the Moravian ballad; the political viewpoint of the Prague power broker is at odds with the spirituality of the Moravian bard.

Only a tiny bit of Silesia—around the town of Opava—is part of the Czech Republic today; the rest of the region is in Poland and Germany. (The Habsburgs lost traditionally Czech Silesia to Prussia in the 1740s, and 200 years later, Germany in turn ceded most of it to Poland.) People in Silesia speak a wide variety of

dialects that mix Czech, German, and Polish. Perhaps due to their diverse genes and cultural heritage, women from Silesia are famous for being intelligent and beautiful.

Since 1989, the year that Czechs won their independence from Soviet control, people have been working harder—but the average monthly wage is still only about $1,500. Roads have been patched up, facades have gotten facelifts, and supermarkets have been pushed out by hypermarkets.

In communist times, it was routine to be married and start a family by age 22. Once a Czech finished training school and (for men) the compulsory two-year military service, there was little else to aspire to. Everyone was assigned essentially the same mediocre job ("They pretended to pay us, we pretended to work"), with little hope of career progress—unless you were willing to cut ties with your friends by entering the Communist Party or working for the secret police. Children (and summer homes) were the only way for people to project their dreams. Parenting was subsidized. In the countryside, young families were guaranteed housing, and in cities, flats were allocated according to long waiting lists that gave priority to married couples with children.

But after the fall of communism in 1989, many more options became available to young people who, as children or teenagers, had not even dreamed of such possibilities. Young Czechs embraced the new freedoms: Everyone wanted to travel—to the West to study law, or to the East to meditate in a cave. And everyone wanted to work—for big bucks at a multinational investment bank, or for pennies at a nonprofit organization in Afghanistan. Marriage was no longer the expected "next step." And shacking up was no longer a problem; you needed money, rather than a marriage certificate, to get a place to live. More and more young adults

Czech Republic Almanac

Birth of Two Nations: The nation of Czechoslovakia—formed after World War I and dominated by the USSR after World War II—split on January 1, 1993, into two separate nations: the Czech Republic (Česká Republika) and Slovakia.

Population: 10.3 million people. About 90 percent are ethnic Czechs, who speak Czech. Unlike some of their neighbors (including the very Catholic Poles and Slovaks), Czechs are inclined to be agnostic: One in four is Roman Catholic, but the majority (60 percent) list their religion as unaffiliated.

Latitude and Longitude: 50°N and 15°E (similar latitude to Vancouver, British Columbia).

Area: 31,000 square miles (similar to South Carolina or Maine).

Geography: The Czech Republic is made up of three regions—Bohemia (Čechy), Moravia (Morava), and a small slice of Silesia (Slezsko). The climate is generally cool and partly cloudy.

Biggest Cities: Prague (the capital, 1.2 million), Brno (380,000), Ostrava (336,000), and Plzeň (165,000).

Economy: The gross domestic product equals about $220 billion (similar to that of Indiana). The GDP per capita is approximately $26,000 (about half that of the average American). Some major moneymakers for the country are machine parts, cars and trucks (VW subsidiary Škoda has become a highly respected automaker), and beer (including Pilsner Urquell and the original Budweiser—called "Czechvar" in the US). More than a third of trade is with next-door-neighbor Germany; Germany's economic

waited until after age 30 to get married, and those already married reconsidered their choices in the light of new circumstances. Fewer Czechs had children, and many got divorced.

By 2004, the falling birthrate and shrinking size of the Czech nation was a regular topic in newspaper columns. To stimulate production, the socialist government began paying new parents a baby bonus—one month's wages—in addition to the standard three years of paid maternity leave already promised to one parent.

Ironically—as if to prove that Czechs will never listen to what the government tells them to do—as soon as the newly elected conservatives revoked the monthly baby bonus in 2006, everyone between the ages of 25 and 35 suddenly decided to have children. The biggest baby boom in a generation is still on: Maternity wards are overflowing, signs regulating stroller traffic are popping up in public parks, and politicians are blaming each other for imprudently closing down many state-run nurseries.

Yet even faced with a bright and baby-filled future, some Czechs maintain a healthy dose of pessimism and seem reluctant

health one year will generally predict the Czech Republic's fortunes the next. Privatization of formerly government-run industries goes on. Next to be sold are the airlines and the energy company.

Currency: 18 Czech crowns (*koruna,* Kč) = about $1.

Government: From 1948 to 1989, Czechoslovakia was a communist state under Soviet control. Today, the Czech Republic is a member of the European Union (since 2004) and a vibrant democracy, with 68 percent of its eligible population voting in the 2006 election. Its parliament is made up of 200 representatives elected every four years and 81 senators elected for six years. No single political party dominates. The two big parties—the conservative Civic Democrats and the left-of-center Social Democrats—each won just a third of the vote in the 2006 election. The other three parties—the Communists, Christian Democrats, and the Greens—hold enough sway that the leader of the winning party typically heads a coalition government. The president (currently Václav Klaus, a conservative) is selected every five years by the legislators.

Flag: The Czech flag is red (bottom), white (top), and blue (a triangle along the hoist side).

The Average Czech: The average Czech has 1.2 kids (slowly rising after the sharp decline that followed the end of communism), will live 76 years, and has one television in the house.

to dive headlong into the Western rat race. Things still go a little slower here, and people find pleasure in simple things.

Czech children, adults, and grandparents delight in telling stories. In Czech fairy tales, there are no dwarfs and monsters. To experience the full absurdity and hilarity of Czech culture, you need a child's imagination and the understanding that the best fun comes from being able to laugh at yourself. Czech writers invented the robot, the pistol, and Black Light Theater (an absurd show of illusion, puppetry, mime, and modern dance—see page 122).

Literature and film are the most transparent window into the Czech soul. The most famous Czech literary figure is the title character of Jaroslav Hašek's *Good Soldier Švejk,* who frustrates the World War I Austro-Hungarian army he serves by cleverly playing dumb. Other well-known Czech writers include Václav Havel (playwright who went on to become Czechoslovakia's first post-communist president—he authored many essays and plays, including *The Garden Party*); Milan Kundera (author of *The Unbearable Lightness of Being,* set during the "Prague Spring" uprising); and

Karel Čapek (novelist and playwright who created the robot in the play *R.U.R.*). But the most famous Czech writer of all is the existentialist great, Franz Kafka, a Prague Jew who wrote in German about a person turning into a giant cockroach *(The Metamorphosis)* and an urbanite being pursued and persecuted for crimes he knows nothing about *(The Trial)*.

Ninety percent of the tourists who visit the Czech Republic see only Prague. But if you venture outside the capital, you'll enjoy traditional towns and villages, great prices, a friendly and gentle countryside dotted by nettles and wild poppies, and almost no Western tourists. Since the time of the Habsburgs, fruit trees have lined the country roads for everyone to share. Take your pick.

Helpful Hints

Telephone: Dial 112 for medical or other emergencies and 158 for police. If a number starting with 0800 doesn't work, replace the 0800 with 822. For more details on dialing, see page 1088.

Transportation: The Czech Republic is covered by its own railpass, a Germany-Czech railpass, the five-country European East pass, the Eurail Global pass, and the Eurail Selectpass. If your train travel will be limited to a handful of rides and/or short distances (e.g., within the Czech Republic), you're probably better off without a pass—Czech tickets are cheap to buy as you go. If you're combining Prague with international destinations, a railpass could save you money. For all the details, check out my free Railpass Guide at www.ricksteves.com/rail.

Czech History

The Czechs have always been at a crossroads of Europe—between the Slavic and Germanic worlds, between Catholicism and Protestantism, and between Cold War East and West. As if having foreseen all of this, the mythical founder of Prague—the beautiful princess Libuše—named her city "Praha" (meaning "threshold" in Czech). Despite these strong external influences, the Czechs have retained their distinct culture...and a dark, ironic sense of humor to keep them laughing through it all.

Charles IV and the Middle Ages

Prague's castle put Bohemia on the map in the ninth century. About a century later, the region was incorporated into the German Holy Roman Empire. Within a couple hundred years, Prague was one of Europe's largest and most highly cultured cities.

The 14th century was Prague's Golden Age, when Holy Roman Emperor Charles IV (1316–1378) ruled from here. Born to a Luxemburg nobleman and a Czech princess, Charles IV was a dynamic man on the cusp of the Renaissance. He spoke five languages, counted Petrarch as a friend, imported French architects to make Prague a grand capital, founded the first university north of the Alps, and invigorated the Czech national spirit. (He popularized the legend of the good king Wenceslas to give his people a near-mythical, King Arthur–type cultural standard-bearer.) Much of Prague's history and architecture (including the famous Charles Bridge, Charles University, and St. Vitus Cathedral) can be traced to this man's rule. Under Charles IV, the Czech people gained esteem among Europeans.

Jan Hus and Religious Wars

Jan Hus (c. 1370–1415) was a local preacher and professor who got in trouble with the Vatican a hundred years before Martin Luther. Like Luther, Hus preached in the people's language rather than in Latin. To add insult to injury, he complained about Church corruption. Tried for heresy and burned in 1415, Hus became both a religious and a national hero. While each age has defined Hus to its liking, the way he challenged authority while staying true to himself has long inspired and rallied the Czech people. (For more on Hus, see the sidebar on page 71.)

Inspired by the reformist ideas of Hus, the Czechs rebelled against both the Roman Catholic Church and German political control. This burst of independent thought led to a period of religious wars, and ultimately the loss of autonomy to Vienna. Ruled by the Habsburgs of Austria, Prague stagnated—except during the rule of King Rudolf II (1552–1612), a Holy Roman Emperor. With Rudolf living in Prague, the city again emerged as a cultural and intellectual center. Astronomers Johannes Kepler and Tycho Brahe and other scientists flourished, and much of the inspiration for Prague's great art can be attributed to the king's patronage.

Not long after this period, Prague entered one of its darker spells. The Thirty Years' War (1618–1648) began in Prague when Czech Protestant nobles, wanting religious and political autonomy, tossed two Catholic Habsburg officials out of the window of the castle. (This was one of Prague's many defenestrations—a uniquely Czech solution to political discord, in which offending politicians are thrown out the window.) The Czech Estates Uprising lasted for

two years, ending in a crushing defeat of the Czech army in the Battle of White Mountain (1620), which marked the end of Czech freedom. Twenty-seven leaders of the uprising were executed (today commemorated by crosses on Prague's Old Town Square), most of the old Czech nobility was dispossessed, and Protestants had to leave the country or convert to Catholicism. Often called "the first world war" because it engulfed so many nations, the Thirty Years' War was particularly tough on Prague. During this period, its population dropped from 60,000 to 25,000. The result of this war was 300 years of Habsburg rule from afar, as Prague became a German-speaking backwater of Vienna.

Czech National Revival

The end of Prague as a "German" city came gradually. As the Industrial Revolution attracted Czech farmers and peasants into the cities, the demographics of the Czech population centers began to shift. Between 1800 and 1900, though it remained part of the Habsburg Empire, Prague went from being an essentially German town to a predominantly Czech one. As in the rest of Europe, the 19th century was a time of great nationalism, when the age of divine kings and ruling families came to a fitful end. The Czech spirit was stirred by the completion of Prague's St. Vitus Cathedral, the symphonies of Antonín Dvořák, and the operas of Bedřich Smetana performed in the new National Theater.

After the Habsburgs' Austro-Hungarian Empire suffered defeat in World War I, their vast holdings broke apart and became independent countries. Among these was a union of Bohemia, Moravia, and Slovakia, the brainchild of a clever politician named Tomáš Garrigue Masaryk (described on page 156). The new nation, Czechoslovakia, was proclaimed in 1918, with Prague as its capital.

Troubled 20th Century

Independence lasted only 20 years. In the notorious Munich Agreement of September 1938—much to the dismay of the Czechs and Slovaks—Great Britain and France peacefully ceded to Hitler the so-called "Sudetenland" (a fringe around the edge of Bohemia, populated mainly by people of German descent). It wasn't long before Hitler seized the rest of Czechoslovakia...and the Holocaust began.

For centuries, Prague's cultural makeup had consisted of a rich mix of Czech, German, and Jewish people—historically, they were about evenly divided. But only 5 percent of the Jewish population survived the Holocaust. And after World War II ended, the three million people of Germanic descent who lived in Czechoslovakia were pushed into Germany. Their forced resettlement—which led

Notable Czechs

These prominent historical figures are listed in chronological order.

St. Wenceslas (907–935): Bohemian duke who allied the Czechs with the Holy Roman Empire. He went on to become the Czech Republic's patron saint, and it is he who is memorialized as a "good king" in the Christmas carol. For more on Wenceslas, see page 90.

Jan Hus (c. 1370–1415): Proto-Protestant Reformer who was burned at the stake (see page 39).

John Amos Comenius (Jan Amos Komenský in Czech, 1592–1670): "Teacher of Nations" and Protestant exile, whose ideas paved the way for modern education.

Antonín Dvořák (1841–1904): Inspired by a trip to America, he composed his *New World Symphony.*

Tomáš Garrigue Masaryk (1850–1937): Sociology professor, writer, politician, and spiritual reformer. He was idolized during his lifetime as the "dearest father" of the Czechoslovak democracy (see page 112).

Jára Cimrman (c. 1853–1914): Illustrious but fictional inventor, explorer, philosopher, and all-around genius. Despite being overwhelmingly voted the "Greatest Czech of All Time" in a recent nationwide poll, he was not awarded the title. For details on the controversy, see page 104.

Alfons Mucha (1860–1939): You might recognize his turn-of-the-century Art Nouveau posters of pretty girls entwined in vines. Visit his museum in Prague (page 94) and marvel at his stained-glass window in St. Vitus Cathedral (page 116).

Franz Kafka (1883–1924): While working for a Prague insurance firm, he wrote (in German) *The Metamorphosis* (man awakes as a cockroach), *The Trial, The Castle,* and other psychologically haunting stories and novels.

Milan Kundera (1929–): Wrote the novel *The Unbearable Lightness of Being* (which became a film).

Václav Havel (1936–): The country's first post-Soviet president, also known as a playwright and philosopher.

Martina Navrátilová (1956–): Tennis star of the 1980s.

to the deaths of untold numbers of Germans—was the idea, among others, of Czechoslovak President Edvard Beneš, who had been ruling from exile in London throughout the war (see page 178). As a result of both of these policies (the Holocaust and the expulsion of Germans), today's Czech Republic is largely homogenous—about 95 percent Czechs.

Although Prague escaped the bombs of World War II, it went directly from the Nazi frying pan into the communist fire. A local

uprising freed the city from the Nazis on May 8, 1945, but the Soviets "liberated" them on May 9.

The early communist chapter (1948–1968) was a mixture of misguided zeal, Stalinist repressions, and attempts to wed socialism with democracy. The "Prague Spring" period—initiated by a young generation of reform-minded communists in 1968—came to an abrupt halt under the treads of Soviet tanks.

The uprising's charismatic leader, Alexander Dubček, was exiled (and made a backwoods forest ranger), and the years following the unsuccessful revolt were particularly disheartening. In the late 1980s, the communists began constructing Prague's huge Žižkov TV tower (now the city's tallest structure)—not only to broadcast Czech TV transmissions, but also to jam Western signals. The Metro, built at about the same time, was intended for mass transit, but was also designed to be a giant fallout shelter for protection against capitalist bombs.

But the Soviet empire crumbled. Czechoslovakia regained its freedom in the student- and artist-powered 1989 "Velvet Revolution" (so called because there were no casualties...or even broken windows). Václav Havel, a writer who had been imprisoned by the communist regime, became Czechoslovakia's first post-communist president. In 1993, the Czech and Slovak Republics agreed on the "Velvet Divorce" and became two separate countries (see page 196). Two other major turning points were May 1, 2004, when the Czech Republic joined the European Union; and January 1, 2008, when the country entered the Schengen Agreement, effectively erasing its borders for the purposes of travel.

The Czech Republic Today

Havel ended his second (and, constitutionally, last) five-year term in 2003. While he's still admired by Czechs as a great thinker, writer, and fearless leader of the opposition movement during the communist days, many consider him to have been less successful as a president. Some believe that the split of Czechoslovakia was partly caused by Havel's initial insensitivity to Slovak demands.

The current president, Václav Klaus, was the pragmatic author of the economic reforms in the 1990s. Klaus' surprising election in 2003 symbolized a change from revolutionary times, when philosophers became kings, to modern humdrum politics, when offices are gained by bargaining with the opposition (Communist votes in the Parliament were the decisive factor in Klaus' election).

In 2008, Klaus was narrowly reelected by the Parliament for a second term, despite revelations that his economic reforms had resulted in widespread corruption in the privatizing business sector. In the first half of 2009, the Czech Republic held the rotating presidency of the EU, during which time they focused

Czech Sports

Prague's top sports are soccer (that's "football" here) and hockey. Surprisingly, the Czechs are a world power in both.

The Czech national **soccer** team reached the semifinals of Euro 2004, but were eliminated in the first round of the 2006 World Cup, and lost to Turkey in the final first-round game of Euro 2008 (Turkey scored 3 goals in the last 10 minutes of play). Within the Czech Republic, the two oldest and by far most successful soccer clubs are the bitter Prague rivals, Sparta and Slavia. Sparta's 1970s-era stadium is at Letná (behind the giant Metronome ticking above the river in Letenské Park). Slavia's brand-new stadium is in Vršovice (12 stops from the National Theater on tram #22).

Between 1996 and 2005, the Czech national **hockey** team won five of the annual world championships. In 1998, it won the gold medal at the Olympic Games in Nagano, Japan. However, the golden generation is retiring—though legendary goaltender Dominik Hašek, now in his 40s, still plays for his hometown team—and younger players have been slow to fill the gap. In each of the last three world championships, the Czech team lost in the quarterfinals. Currently, more than 50 Czech players take the ice in America's NHL. Think of Jaromír Jágr, one of the NHL's all-time leading scorers. Sparta and Slavia, the traditional Czech soccer powers, also have hockey teams, but the rivalry is less intense, as the teams from smaller towns are more than their equals. Slavia plays in the state-of-the-art Sazka Arena, built for the 2004 World Hockey Championships (right at the Českomoravská Metro stop).

Back in the old days, ice hockey was the only battleground on which Czechoslovaks could seek revenge on their Russian oppressors. The hockey rink is still where Czechs are proudest about their nationality. If you are in town in May during the hockey championships, join locals cheering their team in front of a giant screen on the Old Town Square, as well as on other main squares around the country.

Ice hockey is also the most popular sport in Slovakia. To understand the friendly relationship between Czechs and Slovaks after their Velvet Divorce in 1989, just walk into any Czech or Slovak pub during the hockey championships. Unless the two teams are playing each other, all Czechs passionately support the Slovak team, and vice versa.

on ending Europe's energy dependence on Russia and on more workforce mobility. Halfway through the presidency, Czech minority parties, along with two defectors from the conservatives, pushed a vote of non-confidence through the Parliament, leaving the country and the EU without a prime minister—and thereby effectively confirming the widespread European suspicion that the Czechs were unreliable. Ironically, one of the defectors' objections was the government's willingness to allow the US to build a part of its anti-missile defense system on Czech territory, a plan that was shelved by the Obama administration in September 2009.

Klaus has polarized the country like no other figure in modern history, bringing into visible confrontation the old attitude of suppressing past trauma, and the new attitude of learning from your history.

Today, while not without its problems, the Czech Republic is still enjoying a growing economy and a strong democracy, and Prague has emerged as one of the most popular tourist destinations in Europe.

Czech Food

The Czechs have one of Europe's most stick-to-your-ribs cuisines. Heavy on meat, potatoes, and cabbage, it's hearty and tasty—designed to keep peasants fueled through a day of hard work. Some people could eat this stuff forever, while others seek a break in the form of ethnic restaurants (fortunately, cosmopolitan Prague has plenty of options; I've recommended my favorites).

After a sip of beer, ask for the *jídelní lístek* (menu). *Polévka* (soup) is the most essential part of a meal. The saying goes: "The soup fills you up, and the dish plugs it up." Some of the thick soups for a cold day are *zelná* or *zelňačka* (cabbage), *čočková* (lentil), *fazolová* (bean), and *dršťková* (tripe—delicious if fresh, chewy as gum if not). The lighter soups are *hovězí* or *slepičí vývar s nudlemi* (beef or chicken broth with noodles), *pórková* (leek), and *květáková* (cauliflower). *Pečivo* (bread) is either delivered with the soup, or you need to ask for it; it's always charged separately depending on how many *rohlíky* (rolls) or slices of *chleba* (yeast bread) you eat.

Main dishes are divided into *hotová jídla* (quick, ready-to-serve standard dishes, in some places available only during lunch hours, 11:30–14:30) or the more specialized *jídla na objednávku* or *minutky* (plates prepared when you order). Even the supposedly quick *hotová jídla* will take longer than the fast food you're used to back home.

Hotová jídla come with set garnishes. The standard menu across the country includes *smažený řízek s bramborem* (fried pork fillet with potatoes), *svíčková na smetaně s knedlíkem* (beef tender-

loin in cream sauce with dumplings), *vepřová s knedlíkem a se zelím* (pork with dumplings and cabbage), *pečená kachna s knedlíkem a se zelím* (roasted duck with dumplings and cabbage), *mad'arský guláš s knedlíkem* (the Czech version of Hungarian goulash), and *pečené kuře s bramborem* (roasted chicken with potatoes).

In this landlocked country, fish options are typically limited to *kapr* (carp) and *pstruh* (trout), prepared in a variety of ways and served with potatoes or fries—although recently, Czech perch and Norwegian salmon have also cropped up on many local menus. Vegetarians can go for the delicious *smažený sýr s bramborem* (fried cheese with potatoes) or default to *čočka s vejci* (lentils with fried egg). If you are spending the night out with friends, have a beer and feast on the huge *vepřové koleno s hořčicí a křenem* (pork knuckle with mustard and horseradish sauce) with *chleba* (yeast bread).

The range of the *jídla na objednávku* (meals prepared to order) depends on the chef. You choose your starches and garnishes, which are charged separately.

Šopský salát, like a Greek salad, is usually the best salad option (a mix of tomatoes, cucumbers, peppers, onion, and feta cheese with vinegar and olive oil). The waiter will bring it with the main dish, unless you specify that you want it before.

For *moučník* (dessert), there are *palačinka* (crêpes served with fruit or jam), *lívance* (small pancakes with jam and curd), *zmrzlinový pohár* (ice-cream sundae), or fruit-filled dumplings. Many restaurants will offer different sorts of *koláče* (pastries) and *štrůdl* (apple strudel), but it's much better to get these directly from a bakery.

No Czech meal is complete without a cup of strong *turecká káva* (Turkish coffee—finely ground coffee that only partly dissolves, leaving "mud" on the bottom, drunk without milk). Although espressos and instant coffees have made headway in the past few years, some Czechs regard them as a threat to tradition.

Czech mineral waters (*minerálka)* have a high mineral content. They're naturally carbonated because they come from the springs in the many Czech spas (Mattoni, the most common brand, is from Carlsbad). If you want still water, ask for *voda bez bublinek* (water without bubbles). Tap water is generally not served. Water comes bottled and generally costs more than beer.

Bohemia is beer country, with Europe's best and cheapest brew (see sidebar on next page). Locals also like the herb liquor *becherovka*. Moravians prefer wine and the plum brandy called *slivovice* (SLEE-voh-veet-seh). *Medovina* ("honey wine") is mead.

In bars and restaurants, you can go wild with memorable liqueurs, most of which cost about a dollar a shot. Experiment. *Fernet,* a bitter drink made from many herbs, is the leading Czech

Czech Beer

Czechs are among the world's most enthusiastic beer *(pivo)* drinkers—adults drink an average of 80 gallons a year. The pub is a place to have fun, complain, discuss art and politics, talk hockey, and chat with locals and visitors alike. The *pivo* that was drunk in the country before the Industrial Revolution was much thicker, providing the main source of nourishment for the peasant folk. Even today, it doesn't matter whether you're in a *restaurace* (restaurant), a *hostinec* (pub), or a *hospoda* (bar)—a beer will land on your table upon the slightest hint to the waiter, and a new pint will automatically appear when the old glass is almost empty. (You must tell the waiter *not* to bring more.) Order beer from the tap (*točené* means "draft," *sudové pivo* means "keg beer"). A *pivo* is large (0.5 liter, or 17 oz); a *malé pivo* is small (0.3 liter, or 10 oz). Men invariably order the large size. *Pivo* for lunch has me sightseeing for the rest of the day on Czech knees.

The Czechs invented pilsner-style lager in nearby Plzeň ("Pilsen" in German), and the result, Pilsner Urquell, is on tap in many local pubs. But be sure to venture beyond this famous beer. The Czechs produce plenty of other good beers, including Krušovice, Gambrinus, Staropramen, and Kozel. Budvar, from the town of Budějovice ("Budweis" in German), is popular with Anheuser-Busch's attorneys. (The Czech and the American breweries for years disputed the "Budweiser" brand name. The solution: The Czech Budweiser is sold under its own name in Europe, China, and Africa, while in America it is marketed as Czechvar.)

The big degree symbol on bottles does not indicate the percentage of alcohol content. Instead, it is a measurement used by brewers to track the density of certain ingredients. As a rough guide, 10 degrees is about 3.5 percent alcohol, 12 degrees is about 4.2 percent alcohol, and 11 and 15 degrees are dark beers. The most popular Czech beers are about as potent as German beers and only slightly stronger than typical American beers.

Each establishment has only one kind of beer on tap; to try a particular brand, look for its sign outside. A typical pub serves only one brand of 10-degree beer, one brand of 12-degree beer, and one brand of dark beer. Czechs do not mix beer with anything, and do not hop from pub to pub (in one night, it is said, you must stay loyal to one woman and to one beer). *Na zdraví* means "to your health" in Czech.

aperitif. Absinthe, made from wormwood and herbs, is a watered-down version of the hallucinogenic drink that's illegal in much of Europe. It's famous as the muse of many artists (including Henri de Toulouse-Lautrec in Paris more than a century ago). *Becherovka,* made of 13 herbs and 38 percent alcohol, was used to settle upset aristocratic tummies and as an aphrodisiac. This velvety drink remains popular today. *Becherovka* and tonic mixed together is nicknamed *beton* ("concrete"). If you drink three, you'll find out why.

You can stay in a pub as long as you want—no one will bring you the *účet* (bill) until you ask for it: *"Pane vrchní, zaplatím!"* (PAH-neh VURCH-nee zah-plah-TEEM; "Mr. Waiter, now I pay!").

Czech Language

Czech is a Slavic language closely related to its Polish and Slovak neighbors. These days, English is commonly spoken, and you'll find the language barrier minimal. Among older people, German is a common second language.

Czech pronunciation can be tricky. The language has a dizzying array of diacritical marks (little doo-hickeys over some letters that affect pronunciation). Most notably, some letters can be topped with a *háček (č, š, ž, ň, ě).* Here are some clues for Czech pronunciation:

j sounds like "y" as in "yarn"
c sounds like "ts" as in "cats"
č sounds like "ch" as in "chicken"
š sounds like "sh" as in "shrimp"
ž sounds like "zh" as in "leisure"
ň sounds like "ny" as in "canyon"
ě sounds like "yeh" as in "yet"
d' sounds like the "dj" sound in "ledge"

Czech has one sound that occurs in no other language: ř (as in "Dvořák"), which sounds like a cross between a rolled "r" and "zh." It takes a lot of practice, but if you can master this sound, you'll impress the Czechs.

An acute accent *(á, é, í, ó, ú, ý)* means you linger on that vowel; it does not indicate stress, which invariably falls on the first syllable. For example, the word for "please" is *prosím,* with the emphasis on the first syllable but a long "i" sound at the end: PROH-zeeeem.

Prague is flooded with tourists, most of whom don't bother to learn a single word of the local language. To ingratiate yourself to your hosts—not to mention, be a sensitive traveler—take some time to learn the Czech essentials. You'll find a selection of Czech Survival Phrases on page 1119.

When navigating town, these words might be helpful: ***město*** (MYEHS-toh, town), ***náměstí*** (NAH-myehs-tee, square), ***ulica*** (OO-leet-sah, road), ***nábřeži*** (NAH-bzheh-zhee, embankment road), and ***most*** (mohst, bridge).

PRAGUE

For many travelers, Prague is their first stop in Eastern Europe. And for good reason. Few places in Eastern Europe can match Prague's over-the-top romance, evocative Old World charm, easy accessibility...and tourist crowds. Whether you use it as a tentative first foray into the East, or a springboard for a lengthy Slavic adventure, Prague (whose name means "threshold" in Czech) has always been a natural entry point to the East.

With its privileged position on a major river in the very center of bowl-shaped Bohemia, Prague has long been the beating heart and soul of the Czech people. From the Czechs' humble beginnings under a duke named Wenceslas, to the flourishing of culture under Holy Roman Emperor Charles IV, to the devastating Catholics-versus-Protestants warfare of the 17th century, Prague has seen more than its share of history rumble through its cobbled streets. In the 19th century—back when most of its residents were elite German-speakers proud to be subjects of the Habsburg monarchs—Prague was a low-rent mini-Vienna (and played host to the likes of Mozart). But by century's end, the city had become a hotbed for the Czech national revival, as people across Eastern Europe looked to Prague as the region's cultural capital and standard bearer for shunning imposed Germanic ways and embracing their deep Slavic roots.

While the 20th century (and its four decades of communism) was hard on Prague, at least the city escaped the bombs of the world wars—making it uniquely well-preserved among Central European capitals. Now that the shroud of communism has lifted, and the facades have been dutifully scrubbed, visitors can fully enjoy the streets and lanes of today's Prague—a veritable textbook

of architectural styles. I love bringing first-time visitors to Prague's Old Town Square at twilight. After gaping their way around the square, invariably they nudge me and whisper, "This is better than Disneyland!"

In addition to its glorious buildings, Prague intoxicates visitors with its almost mystically beautiful cityscape, entertains us with an endless array of cheap classical concerts, tickles our inner artist with slinky Art Nouveau works by Alfons Mucha, educates us with its historic sites and sobering Jewish Quarter, bends our minds with the uniquely Czech phenomenon of Black Light Theater, and keeps us lubricated with Europe's best beer. Hike up to the world's biggest castle for a lesson in Czech history and sweeping views across the city's spires and domes. Cross the famous Charles Bridge, communing with vendors, artists, tourists, and a stoic lineup of Czech saints in stone. Escape the crowds into the back lanes and pretend you're strolling through the 18th century. Join the local gang over a *pivo* at a rollicking beer hall and learn some Czech soccer songs. Delve into one of Europe's top stops.

Planning Your Time

Prague demands a minimum of two full days (with three nights, or two nights and a night train). You can easily fill more time, which also allows you to side-trip to nearby sights (such as Kutná Hora, Terezín Concentration Camp, or a variety of countryside castles—described in the next chapter). From Budapest, Warsaw, or Kraków, you can get here on a handy overnight train. From Vienna, Berlin, and Munich, Prague is a four- to six-hour train ride by day (you also have the option of a longer night train from Munich).

With two days in Prague, I'd spend one morning seeing the castle and another morning in the Jewish Quarter. Use your afternoons for loitering around the Old Town, Charles Bridge, and the Little Quarter, and split your nights between beer halls and live music. Keep in mind that Jewish Quarter sights close on Saturday. Some museums, mainly in the Old Town, are closed on Monday.

Orientation to Prague

Locals call their town "Praha" (PRAH-hah). It's big, with 1.2 million people, but during a quick visit, you'll focus on its relatively compact old center. As you wander, take advantage of brown street signs directing you to tourist landmarks. Self-deprecating Czechs note that while the signs are designed to help tourists (locals never use them), they're only printed in Czech. Still—thanks to the little icons—the signs can help smart visitors who are sightseeing on foot.

The Vltava River divides the west side (Castle Quarter and Little Quarter) from the east side (New Town, Old Town, Jewish Quarter, main train station, and most of the recommended hotels).

Prague addresses come with references to a general zone. Praha 1 is in the old center on either side of the river. Praha 2 is in the New Town, southeast of Wenceslas Square. Praha 3 and higher indicate a location farther from the center. Virtually everything I list is in Praha 1.

Tourist Information

TIs are at several key locations: **Old Town Square** (in the Old Town Hall, just to the left of the Astronomical Clock; Easter–Oct Mon–Fri 9:00–19:00, Sat–Sun 9:00–18:00; Nov–Easter Mon–Fri 9:00–18:00, Sat–Sun 9:00–17:00; tel. 224-482-018) and the castle side of **Charles Bridge** (Easter–Oct daily 10:00–18:00, closed Nov–Easter). For general tourist information in English, dial 12444 (Mon–Fri 8:00–19:00) or check the TIs' useful website: www.prague-info.cz.

The TIs offer maps, phone cards, a useful transit guide, information on guided walks and bus tours, and bookings for private guides, concerts, hotel rooms, and rooms in private homes.

Monthly event guides—all of them packed with ads—include the *Prague Guide* (29 Kč), *Prague This Month* (free), and *Heart of Europe* (free, summer only). The English-language weekly *Prague Post* newspaper is handy for entertainment listings and current events (60 Kč at newsstands).

Arrival in Prague

No matter how you arrive, your first priority is buying a city map, with trams and Metro lines marked and tiny sketches of the sights drawn in for ease in navigating (30–70 Kč, many different brands; sold at kiosks, exchange windows, and tobacco stands). It's a mistake to try doing Prague without a good map—you'll refer to it constantly. The *Kartografie Praha* city map, which shows all the tram lines and major landmarks, includes a castle diagram and a street index. It comes in two

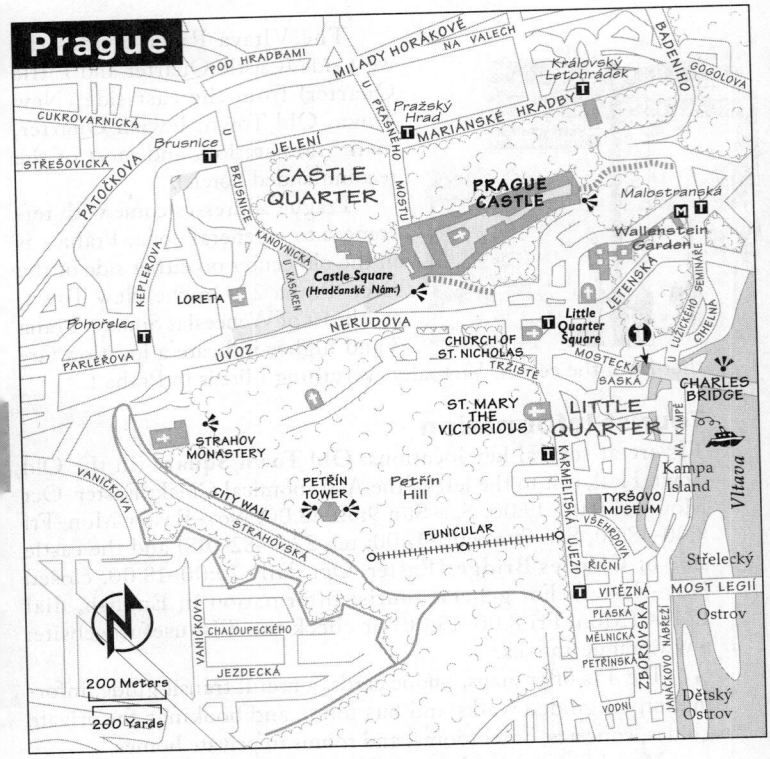

versions: 1:15,000 covers the city center, and 1:25,000 includes the whole city. The city center map is easier to navigate, and sufficient unless you're sleeping in the suburbs.

By Train

Prague has two international train stations. The Main Station (Hlavní Nádraží) serves trains from Kraków, Vienna, Frankfurt, Munich, and Salzburg; most trains within the Czech Republic, including the high-speed SC Pendolino trains; and the DB-ČD bus from Nürnberg. The secondary Holešovice Station (Nádraží Holešovice, located north of the river) handles all trains from Berlin and Budapest—though these may move to the Main Station as early as 2010.

Upon arrival, get money. Both stations have ATMs (best rates) and an exchange bureau (rates are generally bad; consider waiting until you can get to a bank in town to exchange money). Then buy a good map and confirm your departure plans.

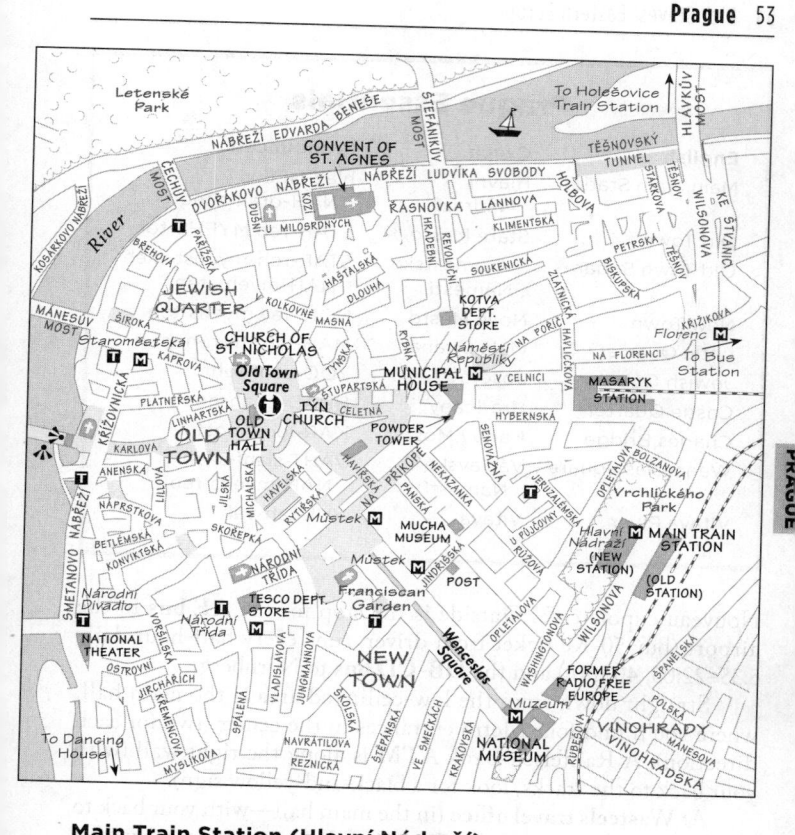

Main Train Station (Hlavní Nádraží)

The station's creepy, two-floor hall is the work of communist architects, who expanded a classy building to make it just big, then painted it the compulsory dreary gray with reddish trim. Originally named for Emperor Franz Josef, the station was later renamed for President Woodrow Wilson (see the commemorative plaque in the main exit hall leading away from the tracks), because his promotion of self-determination led to the creation of the free state of Czechoslovakia in 1918. Under the communists (who weren't big fans of Wilson), it was bluntly renamed Hlavní Nádraží—"Main Station." But a renovation is underway: Drunks and homeless people are being pushed out, and an Italian firm is refitting the station to Western European standards, filling every empty space with shiny clothing boutiques and convenience stores.

Three parallel tunnels connect the tracks to the arrival hall. The first area you reach (with low ceilings) has an exchange office and signs pointing to the "official" taxi stand to the right (avoid these rip-off cabbies—explained later). If you turn around and go up another floor, you'll find the **Fantova Kavárna,** a decrepit Art

Prague Essentials

English	Czech	Pronounced
Main Train Station	Hlavní Nádraží	hlav-NEE NAH-drah-zhee
Old Town	Staré Město	STAH-reh MYEHS-toh
Old Town Square	Staroměstské Náměstí	STAR-roh-myehst-skeh NAH-myehs-tee
New Town	Nové Město	NOH-vay myehs-toh
Little Quarter	Malá Strana	MAH-lah strah-nah
Jewish Quarter	Josefov	YOO-zehf-fohf
Castle Quarter	Hradčany	HRAD-chah-nee
Charles Bridge	Karlův Most	KAR-loov most
Wenceslas Square	Václavské Náměstí	VAHT-slahf-skeh NAH-myehs-tee
Vltava River	Vltava	VUL-tah-vah

Nouveau cupola café. Outside is the stop for the **AE bus** to the airport (buy 50-Kč ticket from driver, runs every half-hour daily 5:35–22:05, 40 min) and the **DB-ČD bus** to Nürnberg.

Straight down from the low-ceilinged area is the main hall, where you'll find four Metro entrances in the center (two for each direction). A Raiffeisen Bank **ATM** is along the right wall (with your back to the tracks, look for a black-and-yellow sign).

At **Wasteels travel office** (in the main hall—with your back to tracks, it's to the right under the stairs), Jaromír and Jaroslav offer reasonably friendly assistance. You can drop by here upon arrival to get a transit ticket without using the ATM (they take euro coins), and to confirm and buy your outbound train tickets. They can help you figure out international train connections, and they sell train tickets to anywhere in Europe—with domestic stopovers if you like—along with tickets for fast local trains and cheap international phone cards (no commission; Mon–Fri 9:00–17:00 or later, Sat 9:00–12:00 & 13:00–16:00, closed Sun, tel. 972-241-954, www.wasteels.cz). You can even leave your bags here for a short time.

The **Czech Railways ticket office** is in the middle of the main hall under the stairs. Its tiny ČD Travel center, on the left as you enter the main office, sells both domestic and international tickets, and is your best bet for information in English (Mon–Fri 9:00–17:00, closed Sat–Sun, tel. 972-241-861, www.cdtravel.cz). The regular ticket desks are faster if you already know your schedule and destination, but attendants are unlikely to speak English. You can also wait and get your tickets later at their more centrally located downtown branch (at Na Příkopě 31; see page 148).

Touristpoint (with your back to the tracks, it's on your right under the stairs) arranges last-minute rooms in hotels and pensions, as well as car rentals, sightseeing tours, and adrenaline experiences. They accept any currency and credit cards, and also sell maps and international phone cards. A phone is available for calling a cab—the driver will come to the desk to get you (daily 8:00–22:00, tel. 224-946-010, www.touristpoint.cz, info@touristpoint.cz).

Even though the Main Station is basically downtown, it can be a little tricky to get to your hotel. The biggest challenge is that the **taxi** drivers at the train station's run-down "official" stand are a gang of no-neck mafia thugs who wait around to charge an arriving tourist five times the regular rate. (This is likely to change as station reconstruction progresses.) To get an honest cabbie, exit the station's main hall through the big glass doors, then cross 50 yards through a park to Opletalova street (a few taxis are usually waiting in front of the Hotel Chopin, on the corner of Jeruzalémská street). You can also call a taxi from the Touristpoint office, described earlier (AAA Taxi—tel. 14-014; City Taxi—tel. 257-257-257). Before getting into a taxi, always confirm the maximum price to your destination, and make sure the driver turns on the meter—it should cost no more than 300 Kč to get to your hotel.

A better option may be to take the **Metro.** It's dirt-cheap and easy, with very frequent departures. Once you're on the Metro, you'll wonder why you would ever bother with a taxi (inside the station's main hall, look for the red M with two directions: Háje or Letňany). To purchase tickets from the automated machine by the Metro entrance, you'll need Czech coins (get change at a newsstand or grocery). Validate your ticket in the yellow machines *before* you go down the stairs to the tracks. To get to hotels in the Old Town, catch a Háje-bound train to the Muzeum stop, then transfer to the green line (direction: Dejvická) and get off at either Můstek or Staroměstská; these stops straddle the Old Town. For information on Prague's public transit, see "Getting Around Prague," later.

Most hotels I list in the Old Town are within a 20-minute **walk**. Exit the station into a small park. Walk across the park, and cross the street on the other side of it. Head down Jeruzalémská street to Jindřišská Tower and tram stop, walk under a small arch, then continue slightly to the right down Senovážná street. To the left at the end of the street, you'll see the Powder Gate, the grand entry into the Old Town. Alternatively, Wenceslas Square in the New Town is a 10-minute walk—exit the station, cross the park, and walk to the left along Opletalova street.

The nearest **tram** stop is to the right as you exit the station (about 200 yards). Tram #9 to takes you to the neighborhood near the National Theater and the Little Quarter, but is not useful for most hotels in the Old Town.

Rip-Offs in Prague

With its unprecedented recent influx of tourists, Prague has also become notorious for its scams. There's no particular risk of violent crime, but green, rich tourists do get taken by con artists. Simply be on guard, particularly when traveling on trains (thieves thrive on overnight trains), changing money (tellers with bad arithmetic and inexplicable pauses while counting back your change), dealing with taxis (see "Getting Around Prague—By Taxi," page 62), paying in restaurants (see "Eating in Prague," page 135), and wandering through seedy neighborhoods.

Anytime you pay for something, make a careful note of how much it costs, how much you're handing over, and how much you expect back. Count your change. Someone selling you a phone card marked 190 Kč might first tell you it's 790 Kč, hoping to pocket the difference. If you call his bluff, he'll pretend that it never happened.

Plainclothes policemen "looking for counterfeit money" are con artists. Don't show them any cash or your wallet. If you're threatened with an inexplicable fine by a "policeman," conductor, or other official, you can walk away, scare him away by saying you'll need a receipt (which real officials are legally required to provide), or ask a passerby if the fine is legit. On the other hand, do not ignore the plainclothes inspectors on the Metro and trams who have shown you their badges.

Pickpockets can be little children or adults dressed as professionals—or even as tourists. They target Western visitors.

Holešovice Train Station (Nádraží Holešovice)

This station, slightly farther from the center, is suburban mellow. The main hall has all the services of the Main Station in a more compact area. On the left are international and local ticket windows (open 24 hours), an information office, and an AVE (AEX) office with last-minute accommodations (daily 12:00–20:00, tel. 972-224-660). On the right is a little-frequented café with Internet access (1 Kč/min, daily 8:00–19:30). Two ATMs are immediately outside the first glass doors, and the Metro is 50 yards to the right (follow signs toward *Vstup*, which means "entrance"; it's three stops to Hlavní Nádraží—the Main Station—or four stops to the city-center Muzeum stop). Taxis and trams are outside to the right (allow 300 Kč for a cab to the center).

By Bus

Prague's main bus station is at Florenc, east of the Old Town (Metro: Florenc). But some connections use other stations, including Roztyly (Metro: Roztyly), Na Knížecí (Metro: Anděl), the

Many thieves drape jackets over their arms to disguise busy fingers. Thieves work the crowded and touristy places in teams. They use mobile phones to coordinate their bumps and grinds. Be careful if anyone creates a commotion at the door of a Metro or tram car (especially around the Národní Třída and Vodičkova tram stops, or on the made-for-tourists tram #22)—it's a smokescreen for theft.

Car theft is also a big problem in Prague (many Western European car-rental companies don't allow their rentals to cross the Czech border). Never leave anything valuable in your car—not even in broad daylight on a busy street.

The sex clubs on Skořepka and Melantrichova streets, just south and north of Havelská Market, routinely rip off naive tourists and can be dangerous. They're filled mostly with young Russian women and German and Asian men. Lately this district has become the rage for British "stag" parties, for guys who are happy to fly cheaply to get to cheap beer and cheap thrills.

This all sounds intimidating. But Prague is safe. It has its share of petty thieves and con artists, but very little violent crime. Don't be scared—just be alert.

Nádraží Holešovice train station (Metro: Nádraží Holešovice), or the main train station (Metro: Hlavní Nádraží).

By Plane

Prague's modern, tidy, low-key **Ruzyně Airport,** located 12 miles (about 30 min) west of the city center, is as user-friendly as any airport in Western Europe or the US. The new Terminal 2 serves destinations within the EU except for Great Britain (no passport controls); Terminal 1 serves Great Britain and everywhere else. The airport has ATMs (avoid the change desks); desks promoting their transportation services (such as city transit and shuttle buses); kiosks selling city maps and phone cards; and a tourist service with few printed materials. Airport info: tel. 220-113-314, operator tel. 220-111-111.

Getting to and from the airport is easy. Leaving either airport terminal, you have four options, listed below from cheapest to priciest:

Dirt Cheap: Take bus #119 to the Dejvická Metro station, or

#100 to the Zličín Metro station (20 min), then take the Metro into the center (26 Kč, info desk in airport arrival hall).

Budget: Take the airport express (AE) bus to the main train station (50 Kč, runs every half-hour daily 5:35–22:05, 40 min, look for the *AE* sign in front of the terminal and pay the driver, www.czech-transport.com). From the main train station, you can take the Metro, hire a taxi, or walk to your hotel, following the arrival instructions explained earlier (under "By Train"). However, note that Náměstí Republiky—served by the minibus shuttle described next—is a much handier place to arrive than the main train station, and well worth the negligible extra cost.

Moderate: Take the Čedaz minibus shuttle to Náměstí Republiky, at the entrance to the Old Town. The shuttle drops you off in front of the Czech Airlines office next to Hotel Marriott on V Celnici street (pay 120 Kč directly to driver, daily 7:30–19:00, 2/hr, info desk in arrival hall).

Expensive: Take a Čedaz minibus directly to your hotel, with a couple of stops likely en route (480 Kč for a group of up to four, tel. 221-111-111). Look for a dispatcher on the curb in front of the arrival hall.

Splurge: Catch a taxi. Cabbies wait at the curb directly in front of the arrival hall. Airport taxi cabbies are honest but more expensive. Carefully confirm the total price before getting in. It should be a fixed rate of 600–700 Kč, with no meter.

Helpful Hints

Medical Help: A 24-hour **pharmacy** is at Palackého 5 (a block from Wenceslas Square, tel. 224-946-982). For standard assistance, there are two state hospitals in the center: the **General Hospital** (open daily 24 hours, moderate wait time, right above Karlovo Náměstí at U Nemocnice 2, Praha 2, use entry G, tel. 224-962-564) and the **Na Františku Hospital** (on the embankment next to Hotel InterContinental, Na Františku 1, go to the main entrance, for English assistance call Mr. Hacker between 8:00–14:00, tel. 222-801-278 or tel. 222-801-371—serious problems only). The reception staff may not speak English, but doctors do.

For better-than-standard assistance in English (including dental service), consider the top-quality **Hospital Na Homolce** (less than 1,000 Kč for an appointment, from 8:00–16:00 call 252-922-146, for after-hours emergencies call 257-211-111; bus #167 from Anděl Metro station, Roentgenova 2, Praha 5). The **Canadian Medical Care Center** is a small, private clinic with an English-speaking Czech staff at Veleslavínská 1 in Praha 6 (3,000 Kč for an appointment, 4,500 Kč for a house call, halfway between the city and the airport, tel. 235-360-133,

after-hours emergency tel. 724-300-301).

Internet Access: Internet cafés are well-advertised and scattered through the Old and New Towns. Consider **Bohemia Bagel** near the Jewish Quarter (see page 142). **Káva Káva Káva Coffee,** on the boundary between the Old and New Towns, is in the Platýz courtyard off Národní 37.

Laundry: A full-service laundry near most of the recommended hotels is at Karolíny Světlé 11 (200 Kč/8-pound load, wash and dry in 3 hours, Mon–Fri 7:30–19:00, closed Sat–Sun, 200 yards from Charles Bridge on Old Town side, mobile 721-030-446); another is at Rybná 27 (290 Kč/8-pound load, same-day pick-up, Mon–Fri 8:00–18:00, Mon and Wed from 7:00, closed Sat–Sun, tel. 224-812-641). Or surf the Internet while your undies tumble-dry at the self-service launderette at Korunní 14 (160 Kč/load wash and dry, Internet access-2 Kč/min, daily 8:00–20:00, near Náměstí Míru Metro stop, Praha 2).

Local Help: Magic Praha is a tiny travel service run by Lída Jánská. A Jill-of-all-trades, she can help with accommodations and transfers throughout the Czech Republic, as well as private tours and side-trips to historic towns (mobile 604-207-225, www.magicpraha.cz, magicpraha@magicpraha.cz). Lída also speaks Spanish and Portuguese.

Bike Rental: Prague has recently improved its network of bike paths, making bicycles a feasible option for exploring the center of the town and beyond (see www.prahounakole.cz/mapa for an updated map). Two bike-rental shops located near the Old Town Square are **Praha Bike** (daily 9:00–22:00, Dlouhá 24, mobile 732-388-880, www.prahabike.cz) and **City Bike** (daily 9:00–19:00, Králodvorská 5, mobile 776-180-284, www.citybike-prague.com). They rent bikes for about 400 Kč for four hours or 500 Kč per day (with a 1,500-Kč deposit) and also organize guided bike tours.

Car Rental: All of the biggies have offices in Prague (check each company's website, or ask at the TI). For a locally operated alternative, consider **Alimex Thrifty** (toll-free tel. 800-150-170, www.alimex.eu). The cheaper models are a great value (584 Kč/day with basic insurance and limited mileage, plus 238 Kč/day for full theft and damage insurance; additional fees: 500-Kč tax for airport pickup, 357 Kč for delivery to your hotel; discounts if you book online, smart to reserve up to a week ahead in peak season). Note that the "super offer" cars have giant ads pasted on the side. Alimex has branches at the airport (daily 8:00–21:00, tel. 220-114-860) and near Holešovice Station (Mon–Fri 8:00–18:00, Sat 8:00–14:00, Sun 10:00–16:00, tel. 233-350-001).

Best Views: Enjoy the "Golden City of a Hundred Spires" during the early evening, when the light is warm and the colors are rich. Good viewpoints include the terrace at the Strahov Monastery (above the castle), the top of St. Vitus Cathedral (at the castle), the top of either tower on Charles Bridge, the Old Town Square clock tower (has an elevator), the recommended Restaurant u Prince Terrace overlooking the Old Town Square (also with an elevator), and the steps of the National Museum overlooking Wenceslas Square.

Getting Around Prague

You can walk nearly everywhere. But after you figure out the public transportation system, the Metro is slick, the trams fun, and the taxis quick and easy. For details, pick up the handy transit guide at the TI. City maps show the Metro, tram, and bus lines.

By Metro, Tram, and Bus

Affordable and excellent public transit is perhaps the best legacy of the communist era (locals ride all month for 550 Kč). The three-line Metro system is handy and simple, but doesn't always get you right to the tourist sights (landmarks such as the Old Town Square and Prague Castle are several blocks from the nearest Metro stops). Trams rumble by every 5–10 minutes and take you just about anywhere.

Tickets: The Metro, trams, and buses all use the same tickets:

- 20-minute basic ticket with limited transfer options (*základní s omezenou přestupností)*—18 Kč. With this ticket, no transfers are allowed on trams and buses, but on the Metro, you can go up to five stops with one transfer (not valid for night trams or night buses).
- 1.25-hour transfer ticket with unlimited transfers *(základní přestupní)*—26 Kč.
- 24-hour pass *(jízdenka na 24 hodin)*—100 Kč.
- 3-day pass *(jízdenka na 3 dny)*—330 Kč.
- 5-day pass *(jízdenka na 5 dní)*—500 Kč.

Buy tickets from your hotel, at newsstand kiosks, or from automated machines (select ticket price, then insert coins). For convenience, buy all the tickets that you think you'll need—but estimate conservatively. Remember, Prague is a great walking town, so unless you're commuting from a hotel far outside the center, you'll likely find that individual tickets work best. Be sure

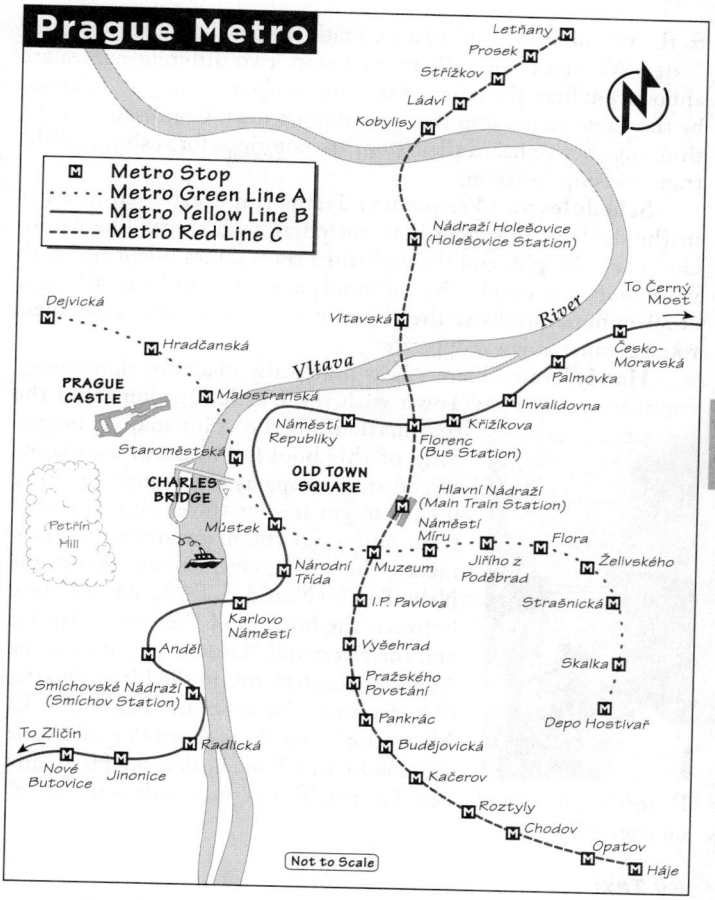

to validate your ticket as you board the tram or bus, or in the Metro station, by sticking it in the machine (which stamps a time on it; watch locals and imitate). Inspectors routinely ambush ticketless riders (including tourists) and fine them 700 Kč on the spot.

Tips: Navigate by signs that list the end stations. When you come to your stop, push the yellow button if the doors don't automatically open. Although it seems that all Metro doors lead

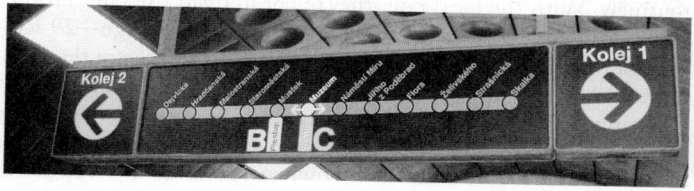

to the neighborhood of Výstup, that's simply the Czech word for "exit." When a tram pulls up to a stop, two different names are announced: first, the name of the stop you're currently at, followed by the name of the stop that's coming up next. Confused tourists, thinking they've heard their stop, are notorious for rushing off the tram one stop too soon.

Schedules and Frequency: Trams run every 5–10 minutes in the daytime (a schedule is posted at each stop). The Metro closes at midnight, and the nighttime tram routes (identified with white numbers on blue backgrounds at tram stops) run all night at 30-minute intervals. There's more information and a complete route planner at www.dpp.cz/en.

Handy Tram: Tram #22 is practically made for sightseeing, connecting the New Town with the Castle Quarter (find the line marked on the color map at beginning of this book). The tram uses some of the same stops as the Metro (making it easy to get to—or travel on from—the tram route). Of the many stops this tram makes, the most convenient are two in the New Town (Národní Třída Metro stop, between the bottom of Wenceslas Square and the river; and Národní Divadlo, at the National Theater), two in the Little Quarter (Malostranské Náměstí and Malostranská Metro stop), and three above Prague Castle (Královský Letohrádek, Pražský Hrad, and Pohořelec; for details, see "Getting to Prague Castle—By Tram" on page 107).

PRAGUE

By Taxi

Prague's taxis—notorious for hyperactive meters—are being tamed. New legislation is in place to curb crooked cabbies, and police will always take your side in an argument. Still, many cabbies are crooks who consider it a good day's work to take one sucker for a ride. You'll make things difficult for a dishonest cabbie by challenging an unfair fare.

While most hotel receptionists and guidebooks advise that you avoid taxis, I find Prague to be a great taxi town and use them routinely. With the local rate, they're cheap (read the rates on the door: drop charge starts at 36 Kč; per-kilometer charge—29 Kč; and waiting time per minute—5 Kč). The key is to be sure the cabbie turns on the meter at the #1 tariff (look for the word *sazba*, meaning "tariff," on the meter). Avoid cabs waiting at tourist attractions and train stations. To improve your odds of getting a fair meter rate—which starts only when you take off—call for a

cab (or have your hotel or restaurant call one for you). AAA Taxi (tel. 14-014) and City Taxi (tel. 257-257-257) are the most likely to have English-speaking staff—and honest cabbies. I also find that hailing a passing taxi usually gets me a decent price, although at a slightly higher rate than when reserving by phone. If a cabbie surprises you at the end with an astronomical fare, simply pay 300 Kč, which should cover you for a long ride anywhere in the center. Then go into your hotel. On the miniscule chance that he follows you, the receptionist will back you up.

Tours in Prague

Walking Tours—Many small companies offer walking tours of the Old Town, the castle, and more. For the latest, pick up the walking tour fliers at the TI. Since guiding is a routine side-job for local university students, you'll generally get hardworking young guides at good prices. While I'd rather go with my own private guide (described next), public walking tours are cheaper (about 450 Kč for a 4-hour tour), cover themes you might not otherwise consider, connect you with other English-speaking travelers, and allow for spontaneity. The quality depends on the guide rather than the company. Your best bet is to show up at the Astronomical Clock a couple of minutes before 8:00, 10:00, or 11:00, then chat with a few of the umbrella-holding guides there. Choose the one you click with. Guides also have fliers advertising additional walks.

▲▲Private Guides—In Prague, hiring a local guide is particularly smart—they're twice as helpful for half the price compared to guides in Western Europe. Because prices are usually per hour (not per person), small groups can inexpensively hire a guide for several days. Guides meet you wherever you like, and tailor the tour to your interests. Visit their websites in advance for details on various walks, airport transfers, countryside excursions, and other services offered, and then make arrangements by email.

Katka Svobodová, a hardworking anthropologist-historian-guide who knows her stuff, runs **Praguewalker,** which offers enthusiastic and friendly guides (600 Kč/hr for 1–4 people, 800 Kč/hr for 5–8 people, mobile 603-181-300, www.praguewalker.com, katerina@praguewalker.com).

Šárka Kačabová, who uses her teaching background to help you comprehend Czech culture, has hand-picked a team of personable and knowledgeable guides for her company **Personal Prague Guide** (600 Kč/hr for 2–3 people, 800 Kč/hr for 4–8 people, mobile 777-225-205, www.prague-guide.info, saraguide@volny.cz).

Jana Hronková has a natural style—a welcome change from the more strict professionalism of some of the busier guides

Prague's Four Towns

Until about 1800, Prague was actually four distinct towns with four town squares, all separated by fortified walls. Each town had a unique character, which came from the personality of the people who initially settled it. Today, much of Prague's charm survives in the distinct spirit of each of its towns.

Castle Quarter (Hradčany): Since the ninth century, when the first castle was built on the promontory overlooking a ford across the Vltava River, Castle Hill has been occupied by the ruling class. When Christianity arrived in the Czech lands, this hilltop—oriented along an east-west axis—proved a perfect spot for a church and, later, the cathedral (which, according to custom, must be built with the altar pointing east). Finally, the nobles built their representative palaces in proximity to the castle to compete with the Church for influence on the king. Even today, you feel like clip-clopping through this neighborhood in a fancy carriage. The Castle Quarter—which hosts the offices of the president and the foreign minister—has high art and grand buildings, little commerce, and few pubs.

Little Quarter (Malá Strana): This Baroque town of fine palaces and gardens rose from the ashes of a merchant settlement that burned down in the 1540s. The Czech and European nobility who settled here took pride in the grand design of their gardens. In the 1990s, after decades of decay, the gardens were carefully restored. While some are open only to the successors of the former nobility—including the Czech Parliament and the American, German, and Polish Embassies—many are open to visitors.

Old Town (Staré Město): Charles Bridge connects the Little Quarter with the Old Town. A boomtown since the 10th century, this area has long been the busy commercial quarter—filled with merchants, guilds, and supporters of Jan Hus (who wanted a Czech-style Catholicism). Trace the walls of this town in the modern road plan (the Powder Tower is a remnant of a wall system that completed a fortified ring, the other half of which was formed by the river). The marshy area closest to the bend—least inhabitable and therefore allotted to the Jewish community—became the ghetto (today's Josefov, or Jewish Quarter).

New Town (Nové Město): The New Town rings the Old Town—cutting a swath from riverbank to riverbank—and is fortified with Prague's outer wall. In the 14th century, the king cre-

(mobile 732-185-180, www.experience-prague.info, janahronkova@hotmail.com).

My readers also recommend **Renata Blažková,** who has a special interest in the history of Prague's Jewish Quarter (tel. 222-716-870, mobile 602-353-186, blazer@volny.cz); **Martin Bělohradský,** whose main area of expertise lies in fine arts and architecture (martinb@uochb.cas.cz, mobile 723-414-565); and **Václav**

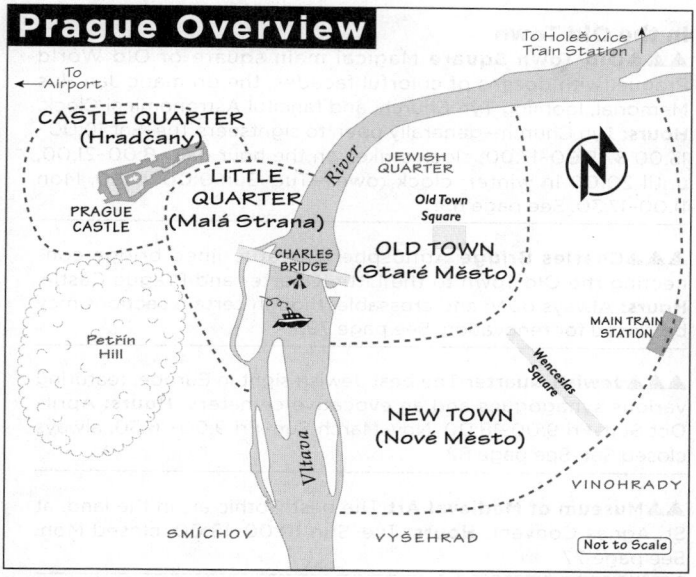

ated this town, tripling the size of what would become Prague. Wenceslas Square was once the horse market of this busy working-class district. Even today, the New Town is separated from the Old Town by a "moat" (the literal meaning of the street called Na Příkopě). As you cross bustling Na Příkopě, you leave the glass and souvenir shops behind, and you enter a town of malls and fancy shops that cater to locals and visitors alike.

The Royal Way: Slicing through the four towns—from St. Vitus Cathedral down to the Charles Bridge, and then from the bridge to the Powder Tower—is the Royal Way (Královská Cesta), the ancient path of coronation processions. Today, this city spine is marred by tacky trinket shops and jammed by tour groups. Use it for orientation only—try to avoid it if you want to see the real Prague.

Štorek, who specializes in history (vaclavstorek@post.cz). These guides typically charge about 2,000–2,500 Kč for a half-day tour. For a listing of more private guides, see www.guide-prague.cz.

Jewish-Themed Tours: Sylvie Wittmann, a native Czech Jew, has developed a diverse array of guides (some better than others) who aspire to bring Jewish traditions back to life in Prague. Consider her three-hour walking tour of the Jewish Quarter

Prague at a Glance

In the Old Town

▲▲▲Old Town Square Magical main square of Old World Prague, with dozens of colorful facades, the dramatic Jan Hus Memorial, looming Týn Church, and fanciful Astronomical Clock. **Hours:** Týn Church—generally open to sightseers Tue–Sat 10:00–13:00 & 15:00–17:00; clock strikes on the hour daily 8:00–21:00, until 20:00 in winter; clock tower—Tue–Sun 9:00–17:30, Mon 11:00–17:30. See page 69.

▲▲▲Charles Bridge Atmospheric, statue-lined bridge connecting the Old Town to the Little Quarter and Prague Castle. **Hours:** Always open and crossable, though certain sections may be closed for renovation. See page 79.

▲▲▲Jewish Quarter The best Jewish sight in Europe, featuring various synagogues and an evocative cemetery. **Hours:** April–Oct Sun–Fri 9:00–18:00, Nov–March Sun–Fri 9:00–16:30, always closed Sat. See page 82.

▲▲Museum of Medieval Art The best Gothic art in the land, at St. Agnes Convent. **Hours:** Tue–Sun 10:00–18:00, closed Mon. See page 77.

▲Havelská Market Colorful open-air market that sells crafts and produce. **Hours:** Daily 9:00–18:00. See page 78.

▲Klementinum National Library's lavish Baroque Hall and Observatory Tower (with views), open by 45-minute tour only. **Hours:** Mon–Fri 14:00–19:00, Sat–Sun 10:00–19:00, shorter hours off-season. See page 79.

In the New Town

▲▲Wenceslas Square Lively boulevard at the heart of modern Prague. **Hours:** Always open. See page 88.

▲▲Mucha Museum Easy-to-appreciate collection of Art Nouveau works by Czech artist Alfons Mucha. **Hours:** Daily 10:00–18:00. See page 94.

▲▲Municipal House Pure Art Nouveau architecture, including Prague's largest concert hall and several eateries. **Hours:** Daily 10:00–18:00. See page 95.

▲▲Museum of Communism The rise and fall of the regime, from start to Velvet finish. **Hours:** Daily 9:00–21:00. See page 96.

In the Little Quarter

Church of St. Nicholas Jesuit centerpiece of Little Quarter Square, with ultimate High Baroque decor and a climbable bell tower. **Hours:** Church—daily 9:00–17:00; tower—April–Oct daily 10:00–18:00, closed Nov–March. See page 102.

Petřín Hill Little Quarter hill with public art, a funicular, a replica of the Eiffel Tower, and the quirky museum of a nonexistent Czech hero. **Hours:** Funicular—daily 8:00–22:00; tower and museum—daily 10:00–22:00. See page 106.

In the Castle Quarter

▲▲▲St. Vitus Cathedral The Czech Republic's most important church, featuring a climbable tower and a striking stained-glass window by Art Nouveau artist Alfons Mucha. **Hours:** Daily April–Oct 9:00–17:00, Nov–March 9:00–16:00, closed Sunday mornings year-round for Mass. See page 115.

▲▲Prague Castle Traditional seat of Czech rulers, with St. Vitus Cathedral (see above), Old Royal Palace, Basilica of St. George, shop-lined Golden Lane, and lots of crowds. **Hours:** Castle sights—daily April–Oct 9:00–17:00, Nov–March 9:00–16:00; castle grounds—daily 5:00–23:00. See page 114.

▲Strahov Monastery and Library Baroque center of learning, with ornate reading rooms and old-fashioned science exhibits. **Hours:** Daily 9:00–11:45 & 13:00–17:00. See page 108.

Toy and Barbie Museum Several centuries of toys, starring an army of Barbies. **Hours:** Daily 9:30–17:30. See page 120.

Activities

▲▲Tourist Concerts Good yet affordable concerts in sumptuous venues. **Hours:** Daily between about 13:00 and 21:00. See page 122.

▲▲Private Guides A worthwhile two- to three-hour tour of this complex city by a hired, hardworking young guide. See page 63.

▲ Rowboat or Paddleboat Cruises An hour's paddle on the river on a hot, sunny day: peaceful, scenic, memorable...and good exercise. See page 69.

(880 Kč includes entry to the Jewish Museum and the Old-New Synagogue, May–Oct Sun–Fri at 10:30 and 14:00, Nov–Dec and mid-March–April Sun–Fri at 10:30 only, no tours Sat and Jan–mid-March) or her six-hour trip to Terezín Concentration Camp (1,150 Kč includes transportation and all entries, departs May–Oct daily at 10:00; mid-March–April and Nov–Dec no Mon, Wed, or Fri tours; Jan–mid-March by appointment only). All tours require prior reservation and meet in front of Hotel InterContinental at the end of Pařížská street (tel. & fax 222-252-472, mobile 603-168-427, www.wittmann-tours.com).

Outside Prague: To get beyond sights listed in most guidebooks, call **Tom and Marie Zahn** from **P.A.T.H. Finders International**. Tom is an American who married into the Czech Republic (Marie), and together they organize and lead family-friendly day excursions (in Prague or throughout the country). Their tours are creative and affordable, and they teach travelers how to find off-the-beaten-track destinations on their own. Their specialty is Personal Ancestral Tours & History (P.A.T.H.), and with sufficient notice, they can help people with Czech heritage find their ancestral homes, and perhaps even a long-lost relative. Tom and Marie can also help you with other parts of your Eastern European travel by hooking you up with associates in other countries, especially Germany, Hungary, Poland, Romania, Slovakia, and Ukraine (US tel. 360-450-5959, Czech tel. 257-940-113, www.pathfinders.cz, info@pathfinders.cz).

Reverend Jan Dus is another option. This enthusiastic pastor lived in the US for several years and now serves a small congregation about 100 miles east of Prague. Jan likes to help travelers connect with locals in little towns, particularly in northeastern Bohemia and in Moravia. He has an outstanding track record in providing genealogical services (toll-free US tel. 800-807-1562, www.revjan.com, rev.jan.services@gmail.com).

Bus Tours—While I generally recommend cheap big-bus orientation tours for an efficient, once-over-lightly look at great cities, Prague just isn't built for bus tours. In fact, most bus tours of the city are walking tours that use buses for pick-ups and transfers. The sightseeing core (Castle Quarter, Charles Bridge, and the Old Town) is not accessible by bus. So if you insist on a bus, you're playing basketball with a catcher's mitt.

Bus tours make more sense for day trips out of Prague. Several companies have kiosks on Na Příkopě where you can comparison-shop. **Premiant City Tours** offers 20 different tours, including Terezín Concentration Camp, Karlštejn Castle, and Český Krumlov (1,750 Kč, 10 hrs), and a river cruise. The tours feature live guides and depart from near the bottom of Wenceslas Square at Na Příkopě 23. Get tickets at an AVE travel agency, your hotel,

on the bus, or at Na Příkopě 23 (tel. 224-946-922, mobile 606-600-123, www.premiant.cz). Tour salespeople are notorious for telling you anything to sell a ticket. Some tours, especially those heading into the countryside, can be in as many as four different languages. Hiring a private guide, many of whom can drive you around in their car, can be a much better value (described earlier, under "Private Guides").

Cruises—Prague isn't ideal for a boat tour because you might spend half the time waiting to go through the locks. Still, the hour-long Vltava River cruises, which leave from near the castle end of Charles Bridge about hourly, are scenic and relaxing, though not informative (150–200 Kč).

▲Rowboat or Paddleboat Cruises—Renting a rowboat or paddleboat on the island by the National Theater is a better way to enjoy the river. You'll float at your own pace among the swans and watch local lovers cruise by in their own boats (40 Kč/hr for rowboats, 60 Kč/hr for paddleboats, bring photo ID for deposit).

Sights in Prague

I've arranged these sights according to which of Prague's four towns you'll find them in (see "Prague's Four Towns" sidebar): Old Town, New Town, Little Quarter, or Castle Quarter.

The Old Town (Staré Město)

From Prague's dramatic centerpiece, the Old Town Square, sightseeing options fan out in all directions. Get oriented on the square before venturing onward. You can learn about Jewish heritage in the Jewish Quarter (Josefov), a few blocks from the Old Town Square. Closer to the square, you'll find the quaint and historic Ungelt courtyard and Celetná street, which leads to the Museum of Czech Cubism and the landmark Estates Theater. If you're intrigued by Jan Hus, the preacher and martyr, look for his pulpit in the chapel on Bethlehem Square. Nearby, Karlova street funnels all the tourists to the famous Charles Bridge. All of the sights described here are within a five-minute walk of the magnificent Old Town Square.

▲▲▲Old Town Square (Staroměstské Náměstí)

The focal point for most visits, Prague's Old Town Square is one of the city's top sights. This has been a market square since the

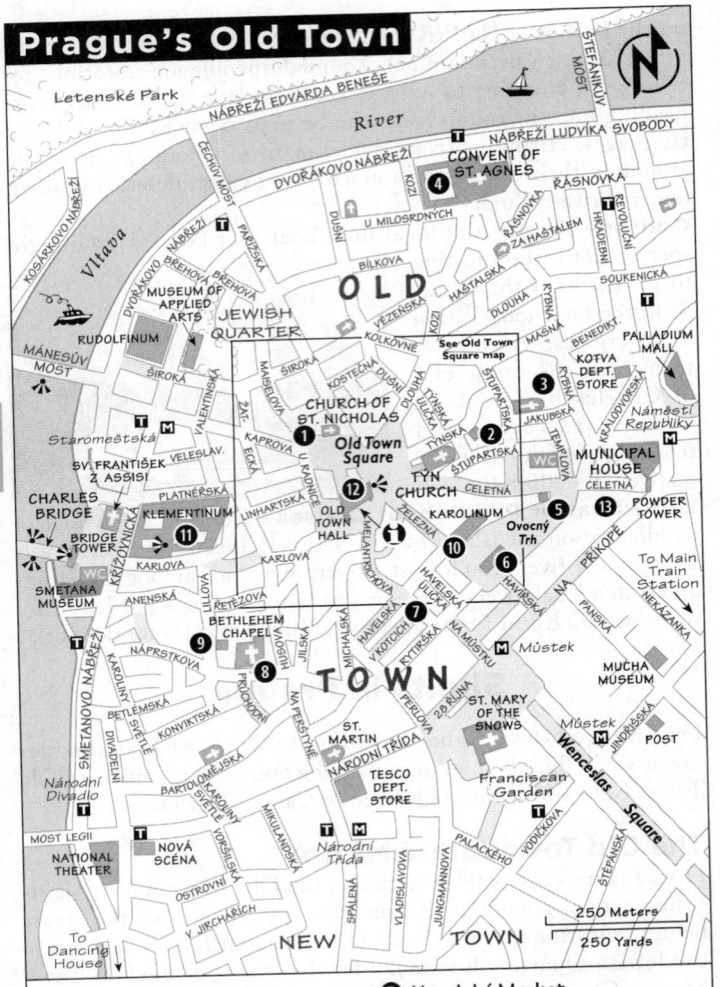
Prague's Old Town
Letenské Park
NÁBŘEŽÍ EDVARDA BENEŠE
River
NÁBŘEŽÍ LUDVÍKA SVOBODY
STEFÁNIKŮV MOST
CONVENT OF ST. AGNES
DVOŘÁKOVO NÁBŘEŽÍ
ČECHŮV MOST
PAŘÍZSKÁ
KOZÍ
DUŠNÍ
U MILOSRDNÝCH
ŘÁSNOVKA
ZA HAŠTALEM
REVOLUČNÍ
HRADEBNÍ
Vltava
KOSÁŘKOVO NÁBŘEŽÍ
BŘEHOVÁ
BÍLKOVÁ
OLD
HAŠTALSKÁ
SOUKENICKÁ
MUSEUM OF APPLIED ARTS
JEWISH QUARTER
VEZENSKÁ
DLOUHÁ
RUDOLFINUM
KOLKOVNĚ
See Old Town Square map
MÁNESŮV MOST
ŠIROKÁ
VALENTINSKÁ
MASNÁ
BENEDIKT
PALLADIUM MALL
KOTVA DEPT. STORE
KOSTEČNÁ
DUŠNÍ
DLOUHÁ
TÝNSKÁ
ŠTÚPARTSKÁ
MAISELOVA
ŽAT.
CHURCH OF ST. NICHOLAS
Staroměstská
KAPROVA
ECKA
U RADNICE
Old Town Square
TÝNSKÁ
ŠTÚPARTSKÁ
JAKUBSKÁ
KRÁLOVDVORSKÁ
Náměstí Republiky
MUNICIPAL HOUSE
CELETNÁ
TEMPLOVA
SV. FRANTIŠEK Z ASSISI
VELESLAV.
PLATNÉŘSKÁ
TYN CHURCH
CHARLES BRIDGE
KLEMENTINUM
LINHARTSKÁ
OLD TOWN HALL
ŽELEZNÁ
KAROLINUM
Ovocný Trh
POWDER TOWER
BRIDGE TOWER
KARLOVA
MELANTRICHOVA
HAVELSKÁ ULIČKA
HAVÍŘSKÁ
NA PŘÍKOPĚ
To Main Train Station
SMETANA MUSEUM
ANENSKÁ
ŘETĚZOVÁ
BETHLEHEM CHAPEL
HAVELSKÁ
V KOTCÍCH
NA MŮSTKU
PANSKÁ
NEKÁZANKA
NÁPRSTKOVA
JILSKÁ
MICHALSKÁ
Můstek
MUCHA MUSEUM
SMETANOVO NÁBŘEŽÍ
KAROLINY SVĚTLÉ
PRŮCHODNÍ
TOWN
BETLÉMSKÁ
KONVIKTSKÁ
NA PŘÍKOPĚ
RYTÍŘSKÁ
PERLOVÁ
28. ŘÍJNA
ST. MARY OF THE SNOWS
Můstek
JINDŘIŠSKÁ
POST
DIVADELNÍ
ST. MARTIN
NÁRODNÍ TŘÍDA
Wenceslas Square
Národní Divadlo
BARTOLOMĚJSKÁ
KAROLINY SVĚTLÉ
TESCO DEPT. STORE
Franciscan Garden
MOST LEGII
NOVÁ SCÉNA
MIKULANDSKÁ
Národní Třída
PALACKÉHO
VODIČKOVA
ŠTĚPÁNSKÁ
NATIONAL THEATER
OSTROVNÍ
V JIRCHÁŘICH
SPÁLENÁ
VLADISLAVOVA
JUNGMANNOVA
250 Meters
250 Yards
To Dancing House
NEW
TOWN
PRAGUE
1 Church of St. Nicholas
2 Ungelt Courtyard & House at the Golden Ring
3 Church of St. James
4 St. Agnes Convent & Museum of Medieval Art
5 Museum of Czech Cubism
6 Estates Theater
7 Havelská Market
8 Bethlehem Chapel
9 Family Museum of Postcards
10 Charles University
11 Klementinum (National Library)
12 Old Town Hall & Astronomical Clock
13 Czech Railways Ticket Office

Jan Hus and Martin Luther

The word *catholic* means "universal." The Roman Catholic Church—in many ways the administrative ghost of the Roman Empire—is the only organization to survive from ancient times. For more than a thousand years, it enforced its notion that the Vatican was the sole interpreter of God's word on earth, and the only legitimate way to be a Christian was as a Roman Catholic.

Jan Hus (c. 1369–1415) lived and preached a century before Martin Luther. Both were college professors, as well as priests. Both drew huge public crowds as they preached in their university chapels. Both condemned Church corruption and promoted a local religious autonomy. Both helped establish their national languages. (Hus gave the Czech alphabet its unique accent marks so that the letters could fit the sounds.) And both got in big trouble.

While Hus was burned, Luther survived. Thanks to the new printing press, invented by Gutenberg, Luther was able to spread his message cheaply and effectively. Since Luther was high-profile and German, killing him would have caused major political complications. While Hus may have loosened Rome's grip on Christianity, Luther orchestrated the Reformation that finally broke it. Today, both are honored as national heroes as well as religious reformers.

11th century. It became the nucleus of the Old Town (Staré Město) in the 13th century, when its Town Hall was built. Today, the old-time market stalls have been replaced by outdoor cafés and touristy horse buggies. But under this shallow surface, the square hides a magic power to evoke the history that has passed through here. The square's centerpiece is a memorial to Jan Hus.

Jan Hus Memorial—This monument, erected in 1915 (500 years after the Czech reformer's martyrdom by fire), symbolizes the long struggle for Czech freedom. Walk around the memorial. Jan Hus stands tall between two groups of people: victorious Hussite patriots and Protestants defeated by the Habsburgs in 1620. One of the patriots holds a chalice (cup); in the medieval Church, only priests could drink the wine at Communion. Since the Hussites fought for their right to take both the wine and the bread, the cup is their symbol. Hus looks proudly at the Týn Church (described later), which became the headquarters and leading church of his

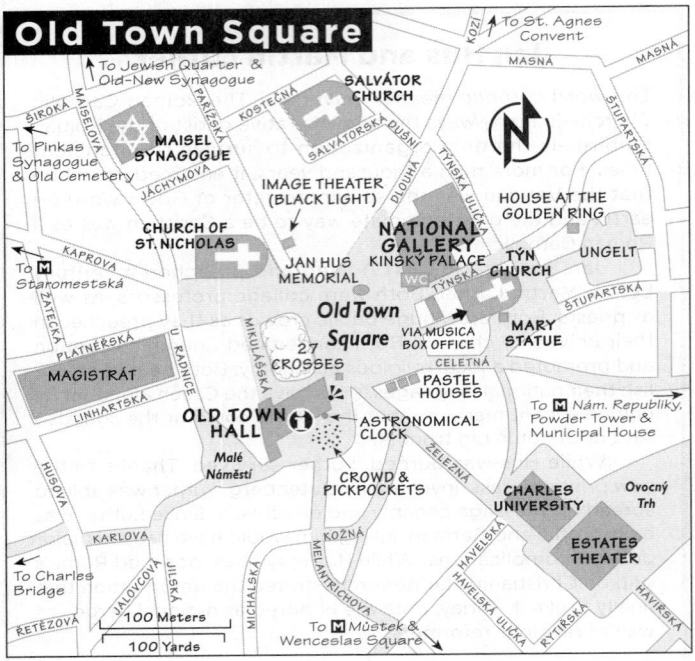

followers. A golden chalice once filled the now-empty niche under the gold bas-relief of the Virgin Mary on the church's facade. After the Habsburg (and, therefore, Catholic) victory over the Czechs in 1620, the Hussite chalice was melted down and made into the image of Mary that shines from that spot high over the square today.

Behind the statue of Jan Hus, the bronze statue of a mother with her children represents the ultimate rebirth of the Czech nation. Because of his bold stance for independence in the way common people worship God, Hus was excommunicated and burned in Germany, a century before the age of Martin Luther.

Old Town Square Orientation Spin-Tour—As this tour is designed to give you your bearings, most of the important sights are described in greater detail later. Whirl clockwise to get a look at Prague's diverse architectural styles: Gothic, Renaissance, Baroque, Rococo, and Art Nouveau. Start with the green domes of the Baroque **Church of St. Nicholas.** Originally Catholic,

now Hussite, this church is a popular venue for concerts. (There's another green-domed Church of St. Nicholas—also popular for concerts—by the same architect, across the Charles Bridge in the Little Quarter.) The **Jewish Quarter** (Josefov) is a few blocks behind the church, down the uniquely tree-lined Pařížská—"Paris street."

Pařížská, an eclectic cancan of mostly Art Nouveau facades, leads to a bluff that once sported a 100-foot-tall stone statue of Stalin. Demolished in 1962 after Khrushchev exposed Stalin's crimes, it was replaced in 1991 by a giant ticking **metronome**—partly to commemorate Prague's centennial exhibition (the 1891 exhibition is remembered by the Little Quarter's Eiffel-esque Petřín Tower), and partly to send the message that for every power, there's a time to go.

Spin to the right, past the Hus Memorial and the fine yellow Art Nouveau building. The large Rococo palace on the right (with a public WC in the courtyard) is part of the **National Gallery.** As of its May 2010 re-opening, the collection's focus is on Asian art—particularly Chinese and Japanese works (Tue–Sun 10:00–18:00, closed Mon).

To the right, you can't miss the towering, Gothic **Týn Church** (pronounced "teen"), with its fanciful spires flanking the gold bas-relief of Mary. For 200 years after Hus' death, this was Prague's leading Hussite church. A narrow lane leading to the church's entrance passes the **Via Musica,** the most convenient ticket office in town. Behind the Týn Church is a gorgeously restored medieval courtyard called **Ungelt.** The row of pastel houses in front of Týn Church has a mixture of Gothic, Renaissance, and Baroque facades. To the right of these buildings, shop-lined **Celetná street** leads to a square called Ovocný Trh (with the Estates Theater and Museum of Czech Cubism), and beyond that, to the Municipal House and Powder Tower in the New Town.

Continue spinning right, taking in more gloriously colorful architecture, until you reach the pointed 250-foot-tall spire marking the 14th-century **Old Town Hall** (which has the only elevator-accessible tower in town). The chunk of pink building attached to the tower of the Neo-Gothic City Hall is the town's "memorial" to bad losers. The building once stretched all the way to the Church of St. Nicholas. Then, in the last days of World War II (May 1945), German tanks knocked off this landmark—to the joy of many Prague citizens who considered it an ugly, oversized 19th-century stain on the medieval square. Across the square from the Old Town

Hall (opposite the Astronomical Clock), touristy **Melantrichova street** leads directly to the New Town's Wenceslas Square, passing the craft-packed Havelská Market along the way.

Twenty-Seven Crosses—Embedded in the pavement at the base of the Old Town Hall tower (near the snack stand), you'll see white inlaid crosses marking the spot where 27 Protestant nobles, merchants, and intellectuals were beheaded in 1621 after rebelling against the Catholic Habsburgs. The execution ended Czech independence for 300 years—and it's still one of the grimmest chapters in the country's history.

▲▲Astronomical Clock—Join the gang for the striking of the hour on the Town Hall clock (daily 8:00–21:00, until 20:00 in winter). As you wait, see if you can figure out how the clock works.

With revolving discs, celestial symbols, and sweeping hands, this clock keeps several versions of time. Two outer rings show the hour: Bohemian time (gold Gothic numbers on black background, counts from sunset—find the zero, between 23 and 1...supposedly the time of tonight's sunset) and modern time (24 Roman numerals, XII at the top being noon, XII at the bottom being midnight). Five hundred years ago, everything revolved around the earth (the fixed middle background—with Prague marking the center, of course).

To indicate the times of sunrise and sunset, arcing lines and moving spheres combine with the big hand (a sweeping golden sun) and the little hand (a moon that spins to show various stages). Look for the orbits of the sun and moon as they rise through day (the blue zone) and night (the black zone).

If this seems complex to us, it must have been a marvel 500 years ago. Because the clock was heavily damaged during World War II, much of what you see today is a reconstruction. The circle below (added in the 19th century) shows the signs of the zodiac, scenes from the seasons of a rural peasant's life, and a ring of saints' names—one for each day of the year, with a marker showing today's special saint (at top).

Four statues flanking the clock represent the 15th-century outlook on time and prejudices. A Turk with a mandolin symbolizes hedonism, a Jewish moneylender is greed, and the figure staring into a mirror stands for vanity. All these worldly goals are vain in the face of Death, whose hourglass reminds us that our time is unavoidably running out.

At the top of the hour (don't blink—the show is pretty quick): First, Death tips his hourglass and pulls the cord, ringing the bell; then the windows open and the 12 apostles parade by, acknowledging the gang of onlookers; then the rooster crows; and then the hour is rung. The hour is often off because of Daylight Saving Time (completely senseless to 15th-century clockmakers). At the top of the next hour, stand under the tower—protected by a line of banner-wielding concert salespeople in powdered wigs—and watch the tourists.

Clock Tour and Tower Climb: The main TI, to the left of the Astronomical Clock, contains an information desk and sells tickets for these two options: zipping up the Old Town Hall tower via elevator (60 Kč, Tue–Sun 9:00–17:30, Mon 11:00–17:30, fine views); or taking a 45-minute tour of the Old Town Hall, which includes a Gothic chapel and a close-up look at the inner guts of the Astronomical Clock (plus its statues of the 12 apostles; 50 Kč, 2/hr).

▲Týn Church—Though this church has a long history, it's most notable for its 200-year-stint as the leading church of the Hussite movement (generally open to sightseers Tue–Sat 10:00–13:00 & 15:00–17:00). It was Catholic before the Hussites, and returned to Catholicism after the Hussites were defeated. As if to insult Hus and his doctrine of simplicity, the church's once elegant and pure Gothic columns are now encrusted with noisy Baroque altars. While Gothic, the church interior is uncharacteristically bright because of its clear Baroque windowpanes and whitewash. Read the church's story (posted in English, rear-left side) for a Catholic spin on the church's events—told with barely a mention of Hus. The fine 16th-century, carved John the Baptist altar (right aisle) is worth a look. As you enjoy this church, try to ignore its unwelcoming signs—other than the Catholic-slanted history, the only English words you'll see here are commands that tell you what not to do.

Outside, on the side of the church facing Celetná street, find a statue of the Virgin Mary resting on a temporary column against the wall. The Catholics are still waiting for a chance to reinstall Mary in the middle of the Old Town Square, where she stood for

about 250 years until being torn down in 1918 by a mob of anti-Habsburg (and therefore anti-Catholic) demonstrators.

Behind Týn Church

▲Ungelt Courtyard (Týnský Dvůr)—Ever since the Old Town was established, the Ungelt courtyard—located directly behind the Týn Church—served as a hostel for foreign merchants, much like a Turkish caravanserai. Here the merchants (usually German) would store their goods and pay taxes before setting up stalls on the Old Town Square. Notice that there are only two entrances into the complex, for the purpose of guaranteeing the safety of goods and merchants. After decades of disuse, the courtyard had fallen into such disrepair by the 1980s that authorities considered demolishing it. Marvelously restored a few years ago, the Ungelt courtyard is now the most pleasant area in the Old Town for dining outdoors (such as at the recommended Indian Jewel), sorting through wooden crafts, and paging through English books (at Anagram Bookshop). Although Prague has undoubtedly lost some of its dreamy character to the booming tourist industry, places such as Ungelt stand as testimony to the miracles that money can work. Had the communists stayed in power for a few more years, Ungelt would have been a black hole by now. Ungelt also reminds us that Prague, for most of its history, has been a cosmopolitan center quite different from the rest of the country.

Church of St. James (Kostel Sv. Jakuba)—Perhaps the most beautiful church in the Old Town, the Church of St. James is just behind the Ungelt courtyard. The Minorite Order has occupied this church and the adjacent monastery almost as long as merchants have occupied Ungelt. A medieval city was a complex phenomenon: Side-by-side, there existed commerce, brothels, and a life of contemplation. (I guess it's not that much different from today.) Artistically, St. James (along with the Church of the Ascension of St. Mary at Strahov Monastery) is a stunning example of how simple Gothic spaces could be transformed into sumptuous feasts of Baroque decoration. The blue light in the altar highlights one of Prague's most venerated treasures—the bejeweled Madonna Pietatis. Above the *pietà,* as if held aloft by hummingbird-like angels, is a painting of the martyrdom of St. James (free, daily 9:30–12:00 & 14:00–16:00).

As you leave, find the black and shriveled-up arm with clenched fingers (15 feet above and to the left of the door). According to legend, a thief attempted to rob the Madonna Pietatis from the altar, but his hand was frozen the moment he touched the statue. The monks had to cut off the arm in order for it to let go. The desiccated arm now hangs here as a warning—and the entire delightful story is posted nearby in English.

North of the Old Town Square, near the River

▲▲Museum of Medieval Art—The St. Agnes Convent houses the Museum of Medieval Art in Bohemia and Central Europe (1200–1550). The 14th century was Prague's Golden Age, and the religious art displayed in this Gothic space is a testament to the rich cultural life of the period. Each exquisite piece is well-lit and thoughtfully described in English. Follow the arrows on a chronological sweep through Gothic art history. The various Madonnas and saints were gathered here from churches all over Central Europe (100 Kč, Tue–Sun 10:00–18:00, closed Mon, two blocks northeast of the Spanish Synagogue, along the river at Anežská 12).

Princess Agnes founded this Clarist convent in the 13th century as the first hospital in Prague. Agnes was canonized by Pope John Paul II (who loved to promote the Slavic faithful) in 1989. Since local celebrations of her sainthood on November 26 coincided with the Velvet Revolution (the peaceful overthrow of the Communist government in 1989), Agnes has since been regarded as the patron of the renascent Czech democracy (you'll see her on the rare 50-Kč bill).

On Celetná Street, Toward the New Town

Celetná, a pedestrian-only street, is a convenient and relatively untouristy way to get from the Old Town Square to the New Town (specifically the Municipal House and Powder Tower). Along the way, at the square called Ovocný Trh, you'll find these sights.

Museum of Czech Cubism—Cubism was a potent force in Prague in the early 20th century. The fascinating Museum of Czech Cubism in the Black Madonna House (Dům u Černé Matky Boží) offers the complete Cubist experience: Cubist architecture (stand back and see how masterfully it makes its statement while mixing with its neighbors... then get up close and study the details), a great café (one flight up), a ground-floor shop, and, of course, a museum.

Take the elevator to the top floor and work your way down. On three floors, you'll see paintings, furniture, graphics, and architectural drafts by Czech Cubists. This building is an example of what has long been considered the greatest virtue of Prague's architects: the ability to adapt their grandiose plans to the existing cityscape (100 Kč, Tue–Sun 10:00–18:00, closed Mon, corner of Celetná and

Ovocný Trh at Ovocný Trh 19, tel. 224-301-003, www.ngprague.cz). If you're not interested in touring the museum itself, consider a drink in the similarly decorated upstairs Grand Café Orient (described on page 144).

Estates Theater (Stavovské Divadlo)—Built by a nobleman in the 1770s, this Classicist building—gently opening its greenish walls onto Ovocný Trh—was the prime opera venue in Prague at a time when an Austrian prodigy was changing the course of music. Wolfgang Amadeus Mozart premiered *Don Giovanni* in this building, and personally directed many of his works here. Prague's theatergoers would whistle arias from Mozart's works on the streets the morning after they premiered. Today, the Estates Theater (part of the National Theater group) continues to produce *The Marriage of Figaro, Don Giovanni,* and occasionally *The Magic Flute.* For a more intimate encounter with Mozart, go to Villa Bertramka (see "Entertainment in Prague," later).

On Melantrichova Street

Skinny, tourist-clogged Melantrichova street leads directly from the Old Town Square's Astronomical Clock to the bottom of Wenceslas Square. But even along this most crowded of streets, a genuine bit of Prague remains...

▲Havelská Market—This open-air market, offering crafts and produce, was set up in the 13th century for the German trading community. Though heavy on souvenirs these days, the market still keeps hungry locals and vagabonds fed cheaply. It's ideal for a healthy snack; merchants are happy to sell a single vegetable or piece of fruit; and you'll find a washing fountain and plenty of inviting benches midway down the street. The market is also a fun place to browse for crafts. It's a homegrown, homemade kind of place; you'll often be dealing with the actual artist or farmer (market open daily 9:00–18:00, produce best on weekdays; more souvenirs, puppets, and toys on weekends). The many cafés and little eateries circling the market offer a fine and relaxing vantage point from which to view the action.

From Old Town Square to Charles Bridge

Karlova Street—Karlova street winds through medieval Prague from the Old Town Square to the Charles Bridge (it zigzags... just follow the crowds). This is a commercial gauntlet, and it's

here that the touristy feeding frenzy of Prague is most ugly. Street signs keep you on track, and *Karlův most* signs point to the bridge. Obviously, you'll find few good values on this drag. Two favorite places providing a quick break from the crowds are just a few steps off Karlova on Husova street: **Cream and Dream Ice Cream** (Husova 12) and the recommended **U Zlatého Tygra,** a colorful pub that serves great, cheap beer in a classic and untouristy setting (Husova 17).

▲Klementinum—The Czech Republic's massive National Library borders touristy Karlova street. The contrast could not be starker: Step out of the most souvenir-packed stretch of Eastern Europe, and enter into the meditative silence of Eastern Europe's biggest library. Jesuits built the Klementinum in the 1600s to house a new college; they had been invited to Prague by the Catholic Habsburgs to offset the influence of the predominantly Protestant Charles University nearby. The building was transformed into a library in the early 1700s, when the Jesuits took firm control of the university. Their books, together with the collections of several noble families (written in all possible languages...except Czech), form the nucleus of the National and University Library, which is now six million volumes strong. (Note that the Klementinum's Chapel of Mirrors is a popular venue for evening concerts.)

▲▲▲Charles Bridge (Karlův Most)

Among Prague's defining landmarks, this much-loved bridge offers one of the most pleasant and entertaining 500-yard strolls in Europe. Enjoy the bridge at different times of day. The bridge is most memorable early—before the crowds—and late, during photographers' "magic hour," when the sun is low in the sky.

At the Old Town end of the bridge, in a little square, is a statue of the bridge's namesake, **Charles IV** (Karlo Quatro—the guy on the 100-Kč bill), the Holy Roman Emperor who ruled his vast empire from Prague in the 14th century. This statue was erected in 1848 to celebrate the 500th birthday of Prague's university. Charles is holding a contract establishing the university, the first in Northern Europe. The women around the pedestal symbolize the school's four

Charles Bridge Reconstruction

Talked about for many years, financed by the city of Prague, and scheduled to last for more than a decade, the long-overdue reconstruction of the Charles Bridge finally began in the summer of 2007, days after the city celebrated the bridge's 650-year anniversary.

Aware of the blow that closing the entire bridge would deal to the tourist industry, the city chose a more costly and technologically challenging "chessboard" strategy. With this plan, only a small section is closed at any time, allowing people to continue using the bridge, but leading to midday crowds in the resulting bottleneck. To give everyone the opportunity to peek inside the centuries-old structure, and thus turn the bridge renovation into Prague's newest attraction, the mayor requested (to the dismay of many archaeologists) that the construction site be at all times surrounded only by light, transparent fences.

The reconstruction is being carried out in two stages. In the first major stage—preceded by archaeological excavations and scheduled to be completed sometime in 2010—gas lighting will return to the bridge, and the sewage system, insulation, and pavement will be installed. In the next stage, many of the deteriorated sandstone pieces will be replaced by new ones. In the past, builders often chose poor-quality sandstone, and this is precisely the mistake current workers want to avoid. To minimize impact on the nearby areas, most of the building materials will be transported by river.

subjects: the arts, medicine, law, and theology. (From the corner by the busy street, many think the emperor's silhouette makes it appear as if he's peeing on the tourists. Which reminds me, public WCs are in the passageway opposite the statue.)

Bridges had been built on this spot before, as the remnant tower from Judith Bridge testifies (see the smaller of the two bridge towers at the far end). All were washed away by floods. After a major flood in 1342, Emperor Charles IV decided to commission an entirely new structure rather than repair the old one. Until the 19th century, this was the only bridge in Prague that crossed the river.

Charles Bridge has long fueled a local love of legends—including one tied to numbers. According to medieval record, the

bridge's foundation was laid in 1357. In the late 1800s, an amateur astronomer noticed a curious combination of numbers, leading to a popular theory about Charles IV. Charles is known to have been interested in numerology and astrology, and was likely aware of the significance of this date: the ninth of July at 5:31 in the morning. Written out in digits—as the year, month, day, hour, and minute—it's a numerical palindrome: 135797531. It's speculated that Charles must have chosen that precise moment (which also coincides with a favorable positioning of the earth and Saturn) to lay the foundation stone of the bridge. Further "corroboration" of this remarkable hypothesis was provided by the discovery that the end of the bridge on the Old Town side aligns perfectly with the tomb of St. Vitus (in the cathedral across the river) and the setting sun at summer solstice. In the absence of accurate 14th-century records, this intriguing proposition has delighted the modern Czech imagination. The number "135797531" is bound to remain celebrated as the adopted birthday of Prague's most beloved structure.

The magically aligned spot on the Old Town side is now occupied by the **bridge tower,** considered one of the finest Gothic gates anywhere. Contemplate the fine sculpture on the Old Town side of the tower, showing the 14th-century hierarchy of kings, bishops, and angels. Climbing the tower rewards you with wonderful views over the bridge (40 Kč, daily 10:00–19:00, as late as 22:00 in summer).

In the 17th century, there were no statues on the bridge—only a **cross,** which you can still see as part of the third sculpture on the right. The gilded Hebrew inscription from the Book of Isaiah celebrates Christ ("Holy, holy, holy is the Lord of hosts"). The inscription was paid for by a fine imposed on a Prague Jew—the result of a rivalry within the Jewish community (fellow Jews turned him in for mocking the cross).

The bronze Baroque statue depicting **John of Nepomuk**—a saint of the Czech people—draws a crowd (look for the guy with the five golden stars around his head, near the Little Quarter end of the bridge on the right). John of Nepomuk was a 14th-century priest to whom the queen confessed all her sins. According to

a 17th-century legend, the king wanted to know his wife's secrets, but Father John dutifully refused to tell. He was tortured and eventually killed by being tossed off the bridge. When he hit the water, five stars appeared. The shiny plaque at the base of the statue depicts the heave-ho. Notice the date on the inscription: This oldest statue on the bridge was unveiled in 1683, on the supposed 300th anniversary of the martyr's death.

The reason for John of Nepomuk's immense Baroque popularity and 1729 canonization remains contested. Some historians claim that at a time when the Czechs were being forcibly converted to Catholicism, Nepomuk became the rallying national symbol ("We will convert, but our patron must be Czech"). Others argue that Nepomuk was a propaganda figure used by Catholic leaders to give locals an alternative to Jan Hus. You'll find statues like this one on squares and bridges throughout the country.

The actual spot of the much-talked-about river-toss is a few steps farther away from the castle—find a small **brass relief** depicting a floating figure with a semicircle of stars above him. This is a replica of a Baroque original that was badly damaged by a flood in 1890, later marred by protesters in the 1920s, and finally removed by the communists. In May of 2009, this replacement was installed by the Prague archbishop as part of an attempt to revive Baroque celebrations of the saint. Devout pilgrims believe that touching the relief here on the "magic" spot will make a wish come true. According to tradition, you get only one chance in life to make this wish, so think carefully before you touch the saint.

Most of the other Charles Bridge statues date from the late 1600s and early 1700s. Today, half of them are replicas—the originals are in city museums, out of the polluted air. At the far end of Charles Bridge, you reach the **Little Quarter,** described later.

▲▲▲Jewish Quarter (Josefov)

Prague's Jewish Quarter neighborhood and its well-presented, profoundly moving museum tell the story of this region's Jews. For me, this is the most interesting collection of Jewish sights in Europe, and well worth seeing. The Jewish Quarter is an easy walk from Old Town Square, up delightful Pařížská street (next to the green-domed Church of St. Nicholas).

As the Nazis decimated Jewish communities in the region, Prague's Jews were allowed to collect and archive their treasures here. While the archivists were ultimately killed in concentration camps, their work survives. Seven sights scattered over a three-block area make up the tourists' Jewish Quarter. Six of the sights—all except the Old-New Synagogue—are called "The Museum" and are covered by one admission ticket. Your ticket comes with a map that locates the sights and lists admission appointments—the

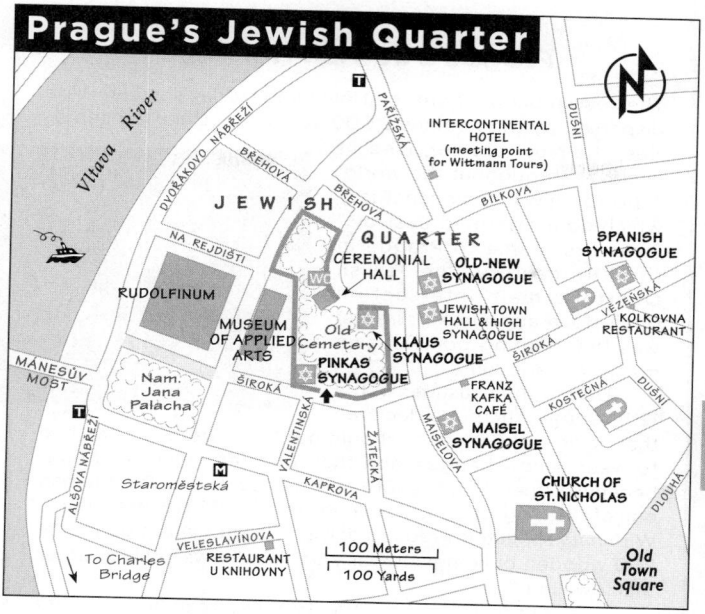

times you'll be let in if it's very busy. (Ignore the times unless it's really crowded.) You'll notice plenty of security.

Cost, Hours, Tours: To visit all seven sights, you'll pay 500 Kč (300 Kč for the six sights that make up the Museum, plus 200 Kč for the Old-New Synagogue). The Museum sights are open April–Oct Sun–Fri 9:00–18:00; Nov–March Sun–Fri 9:00–16:30; closed year-round on Sat—the Jewish Sabbath—and on Jewish holidays (Old-New Synagogue hours listed on page 86). Tel. 222-317-191, www.jewishmuseum.cz. Each sight is thoroughly and thoughtfully described in English, making a guided tour unnecessary for most visitors. Occasional guided walks in English start at the Maisel Synagogue (50 Kč, 3 hours).

Cemetery: The Old Jewish Cemetery—with its tightly packed, topsy-turvy tombstones—is, for many, the most evocative part of the experience. Unfortunately, there's no ticket just to see the cemetery, and they've closed off most free viewpoints. If the 300-Kč Museum ticket is too steep and you just want a free peek at the famous cemetery, climb the steps to the covered porch of the Ceremonial Hall (but don't rest your chin on the treacherous railing).

Planning Your Time: The most logical start (if you'll be seeing everything) is to buy your ticket at Pinkas Synagogue and visit this most powerful memorial of the museum complex first. From there, walk through the Old Jewish Cemetery, which leads to the

Prague's Jewish Heritage

The Jewish people from the Holy Land (today's Israel) were dispersed by the Romans 2,000 years ago. Over the centuries, their culture survived in enclaves throughout the world: "The Torah was their sanctuary which no army could destroy." Jews first came to Prague in the 10th century. The Jewish Quarter's main intersection (Maiselova and Široká streets) was the meeting point of two medieval trade routes.

During the Crusades in the 12th century, the pope declared that Jews and Christians should not live together. Jews had to wear yellow badges, and their quarter was walled in. It became a ghetto. In the 16th and 17th centuries, Prague had one of the biggest ghettos in Europe, with 11,000 inhabitants. Within its six gates, Prague's Jewish Quarter was a gaggle of 200 wooden buildings. It was said that "Jews nested rather than dwelled."

The "outcasts" of Christianity relied mainly on profits from money-lending (forbidden to Christians) and community solidarity to survive. While their money bought them protection (the kings highly taxed Jewish communities), it was often also a curse. Throughout Europe, when times got tough and Christian debts to the Jewish community mounted, entire Jewish communities were evicted or killed.

In the 1780s, Emperor Josef II, motivated more by economic concerns than by religious freedom, eased much of the discrimination against Jews. In 1848, the Jewish Quarter's walls were torn down, and the neighborhood—named Josefov in honor of the emperor who provided this small measure of tolerance—was incorporated as a district of the Old Town.

In 1897, ramshackle Josefov was razed and replaced by a new modern town—the original 31 streets and 220 buildings became 10 streets and 83 buildings. This is what you'll see today: an attractive neighborhood of pretty, mostly Art Nouveau buildings, with a few surviving historic Jewish structures. By the 1930s, Prague's Jewish community was hugely successful, thanks largely to their ability to appreciate talent—a rare quality in small Central European countries whose citizens, as the great Austrian novelist Robert Musil put it, "were equal in their unwillingness to let one another get ahead."

Of the 120,000 Jews living in the area in 1939, just 10,000 survived the Holocaust to see liberation in 1945. Today, only a few thousand Jews remain in Prague...but the legacy of their ancestors lives on.

Ceremonial Hall and Klaus Synagogue. After visiting those, head over to the Old-New Synagogue, have a coffee break (the recommended Franz Kafka Café is nearby). Next, visit the museum-like Maisel Synagogue, and finally the Spanish Synagogue. (Note that Prague's fine Museum of Medieval Art, described earlier, is only a few blocks from the Spanish Synagogue.)

Art Nouveau and the New Josefov: Going from sight to sight in the Jewish Quarter, you'll walk through perhaps Europe's finest Art Nouveau neighborhood. Make a point to enjoy the circa-1900 buildings with their marvelous trimmings and oh-wow entryways. While today's modern grid plan has replaced the higgledy-piggledy medieval streets of old, Široká ("Wide Street") was and remains the main street of the ghetto.

Pinkas Synagogue (Pinkasova Synagóga)—A site of Jewish worship for 400 years, this synagogue is a poignant memorial to the victims of the Nazis. The walls are covered with the handwritten names of 77,297 Czech Jews who were sent from here to the gas chambers at Auschwitz and other camps. (As you ponder this sad sight, you'll hear the somber reading of the names alternating with a cantor singing the Psalms.) Hometowns are in gold and family names are in red, followed in black by the individual's first name, birthday, and last date known to be alive. Notice that families generally perished together. Extermination camps are listed on the east wall. Climb eight steps into the women's gallery. When the communists moved in, they closed the synagogue and erased virtually everything. With freedom, in 1989, the Pinkas Synagogue was reopened and the names were rewritten. (The names in poor condition near the ceiling are original.) Note that large tour groups may disturb this small memorial's compelling atmosphere between 10:00 and 12:00.

Upstairs is the **Terezín Children's Art Exhibit** (very well-described in English), displaying art drawn by Jewish children who were imprisoned at Terezín Concentration Camp and later perished. Terezín makes an emotionally moving day trip from Prague (see next chapter).

Old Jewish Cemetery (Starý Židovský Hřbitov)—From the Pinkas Synagogue, you enter one of the most wistful scenes in Europe—Prague's Old Jewish Cemetery. As you wander among 12,000 evocative tombstones, remember that from 1439 until 1787, this was the only burial ground allowed for the Jews of Prague. Tombs were piled atop each other because of limited

space, the sheer number of graves, and the Jewish belief that the body should not be moved once buried. With its many layers, the cemetery became a small plateau. And as things settled over time, the tombstones got crooked. The Hebrew word for cemetery means "House of Life." Many Jews believe that death is the gateway into the next world. Pebbles on the tombstones are "flowers of the desert," reminiscent of the old days when rocks were placed upon the sand gravesite to keep the body covered. Wedged under some of the pebbles are scraps of paper that contain prayers.

Ceremonial Hall (Obřadní Síň)—Leaving the cemetery, you'll find a Neo-Romanesque mortuary house built in 1911 for the purification of the dead (on the left). It's filled with a worthwhile exhibition, described in English, on Jewish medicine, death, and burial traditions. A series of crude but instructive paintings (hanging on walls throughout the house) show how the "burial brotherhood" took care of the ill and buried the dead. As all are equal before God, the rich and poor alike were buried in embroidered linen shrouds similar to the one you'll see on display.

Klaus Synagogue (Klauzová Synagóga)—This 17th-century synagogue (also near the cemetery exit) is the final wing of a museum devoted to Jewish religious practices. Exhibits on the ground floor explain the Jewish calendar of festivals. The central case displays a Torah (the first five books of the Bible) and solid silver pointers used when reading—necessary since the Torah is not to be touched. Upstairs is an exhibit on the rituals of Jewish life (circumcisions, bar and bat mitzvahs, weddings, kosher eating, and so on).

Old-New Synagogue (Staronová Synagóga)—For more than 700 years, this has been the most important synagogue and the central building in Josefov. Standing like a bomb-hardened bunker, it feels as though it has survived plenty of hard times. Stairs take you down to the street level of the 13th century and into the Gothic interior. Built in 1270, it's the oldest synagogue in Eastern Europe. Snare an attendant, who is likely to love showing visitors around. The separate, steep 200-Kč admission keeps many away,

but even if you decide not to pay, you can see the exterior and a bit of the interior. (Go ahead...pop in and crane your cheapskate neck.)

The lobby (down the stairs, where you show your ticket) has two fortified old lockers—in which the most heavily taxed community in medieval Prague stored its money in anticipation of the taxman's arrival. As 13th-century Jews were not allowed to build, the synagogue was erected by Christians (who also built the St. Agnes Convent nearby). The builders were good at four-ribbed vaulting, but since that resulted in a cross, it wouldn't work for a synagogue. Instead, they made the ceiling using clumsy five-ribbed vaulting.

The interior is pure 1300s. The Shrine of the Ark in front is the focus of worship. The holiest place in the synagogue, it holds the sacred scrolls of the Torah. The old rabbi's chair to the right remains empty (notice the thin black chain) out of respect. The red banner is a copy of the one that the Jewish community carried through town during medieval parades. Notice the yellow-pointed hat within the Star of David (on the banner), which the pope ordered all Jewish men to wear in 1215. Twelve is a popular number (e.g., windows), because it symbolizes the 12 tribes of Israel. The horizontal slit-like windows are an 18th-century addition, allowing women to view the male-only services.

Cost and Hours: The Old-New Synagogue requires a separate 200-Kč admission that includes a worthwhile 10-minute tour—ask about it. It's open Sun–Thu 9:30–18:00, Fri 9:30–17:00 or until sunset, closed Sat. Tel. 222-317-191, www.synagogue.cz. Admission also includes entry to the Art Nouveau **Jerusalem Synagogue** in the New Town (described later).

Maisel Synagogue (Maiselova Synagóga)—This synagogue was built as a private place of worship for the Maisel family during the 16th-century Golden Age of Prague's Jews. Maisel, the wealthy financier of the Habsburg king, lavished his riches on the synagogue's Neo-Gothic interior. In World War II, it served as a warehouse for the accumulated treasures of decimated Jewish communities, a collection that Hitler planned to use for his "Museum of the Extinct Jewish Race." The one-room exhibit shows a thousand years of Jewish history in Bohemia and Moravia. Well-explained in English, topics include the origin of the Star of David, Jewish mysticism, the history of discrimination, and the creation of Prague's ghetto. Notice the eastern wall, with the Holy

Ark containing the scroll of the Torah. The central case shows the silver ornamental Torah crowns that capped the scroll.

Spanish Synagogue (Španělská Synagóga)—Displays of Jewish history through the 18th, 19th, and tumultuous 20th centuries continue in this ornate, Moorish-style synagogue built in the 1800s. The upstairs is particularly intriguing, with circa-1900 photos of Josefov, an exhibit on the fascinating story of this museum and its relationship with the Nazi regime, and life in Terezín. The Winter Synagogue (also upstairs) shows a trove of silver worshipping aids gathered from countryside Jewish neighborhoods that were depopulated in the early 1940s, thus giving a sense of what the Nazis stockpiled.

The New Town (Nové Město)

Enough of medieval Prague—let's leap into the modern era. The New Town, with Wenceslas Square as its focal point, is today's urban Prague. This part of the city offers bustling boulevards and interesting neighborhoods. The New Town is one of the best places to view Prague's remarkable Art Nouveau art and architecture, and to learn more about its recent communist past.

▲▲Wenceslas Square

More a broad boulevard than a square (until recently, trams rattled up and down its park-like median strip), this city landmark is named for King Wenceslas—featured both on the 20-Kč coin and the equestrian statue that stands at the top of the boulevard. Wenceslas Square (Václavské Náměstí) functions as a stage for modern Czech history: The creation of the Czechoslovak state was celebrated here in 1918; in 1968, the Soviets suppressed huge popular demonstrations at the square; and, in 1989, more than 300,000 Czechs and Slovaks converged here to claim their freedom.

➲Self-Guided Walk: Let's take a stroll down Prague's urban centerpiece. Start near the Wenceslas statue at the top (Metro: Muzeum), and look to the building crowning the top of the square.

National Museum (Národní Muzeum): This museum—likely to be closed for renovation in 2011–2012—stands grandly at the top. While its collection is dull, the building offers a powerful view, and the interior is richly decorated in the Czech Revival Neo-Renaissance style that heralded the 19th-century rebirth of the Czech nation. The light-colored patches in the museum's columns fill holes where Soviet bullets hit during the crackdown against the 1968 Prague

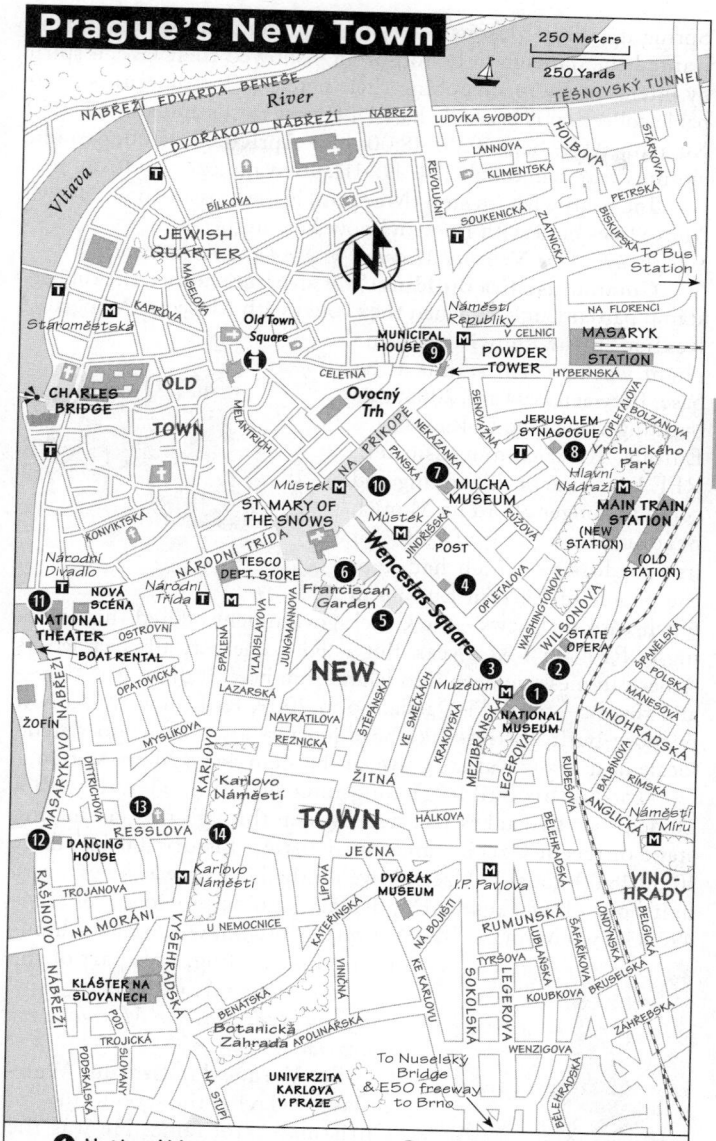

1. National Museum
2. Communist-Era Building
3. Memorial
4. Grand Hotel Evropa
5. Lucerna Gallery
6. Franciscan Garden
7. Mucha Museum
8. Jerusalem Synagogue
9. Municipal House
10. Museum of Communism
11. National Theater
12. Dancing House
13. Greek Orthodox Church
14. Charles Square

Spring uprising. Masons—defying their communist bosses, who wanted the damage to be forgotten—showed their Czech spirit by intentionally mismatching their patches. The museum's skippable collection is basically halls of Czech fossils and animals (150 Kč, daily May–Sept 10:00–18:00, Oct–April 9:00–17:00, periodic closures year-round, tel. 224-497-111, www.nm.cz).

The nearby Metro stop (Muzeum) is the crossing point of two Metro lines built with Russian know-how in the 1970s.

• *To the left of the National Museum (as you face it) is an ugly...*

Communist-Era Building: This structure housed the rubber-stamp parliament back when they voted with Moscow. A Socialist Realist statue showing triumphant workers still stands at its base. Between 1994 and 2008, this building was home to Radio Free Europe. After communism fell, RFE lost some of its funding and could no longer afford its Munich headquarters. In gratitude for its broadcasts—which had kept the people of Eastern Europe in touch with real news—the Czech government offered this building to RFE for 1 Kč a year. But as RFE energetically beamed its American message deep into Islam from here, it drew attention—and threats—from Al-Qaeda. So in 2009, RFE moved to a new purpose-built, fortress-like headquarters at an easier-to-defend locale near Franz Kafka's grave, at the Želivského Metro station.

Today, this building's long interior can be viewed with a guided tour that takes you step-by-step through this fascinating stage of recent Czech—and journalistic—history (80 Kč, daily 10:00-18:00, tours in Czech leave on the hour on weekdays, every half-hour on weekends, English audioguide provided, tel. 224-497-430, www.nm.cz). The National Museum, which now administers this building, uses part of the space for temporary exhibits.

• *In front of the National Museum is the equestrian...*

St. Wenceslas Statue: Wenceslas (Václav) is the "good king" of Christmas-carol fame. He was the wise and benevolent 10th-century Duke of Bohemia. A rare example of a well-educated and literate ruler, King Wenceslas I was credited by his people for Christianizing his nation and lifting up the culture. He

astutely allied the Czechs with Saxony, rather than Bavaria, giving the Czechs a vote when the Holy Roman Emperor was selected (and therefore more political clout).

After his murder in 929, Wenceslas was canonized as a saint. He became a symbol of Czech nationalism and statehood—and remains an icon of Czech unity whenever the nation has to rally. Supposedly, when the Czechs face their darkest hour, Wenceslas will come riding out of Blaník Mountain (east of Prague) with an army of knights to rescue the nation. In 1620, when Austria stripped the Czechs of their independence, many people went to Blaník Mountain to see whether it had opened up. They did the same at other critical points in their history (in 1938, 1948, and 1968)—but Wenceslas never emerged. Although the Czech Republic is now safely part of NATO and the EU, Czechs remain realistic: If Wenceslas hasn't come out yet, the worst times must still lie ahead...

Study the statue. Wenceslas, on the horse, is surrounded by the four other Czech patron saints. Notice the focus on books. A small nation without great military power, the Czech Republic chose national heroes who enriched the culture by thinking, rather than fighting. This statue is a popular meeting point. Locals say, "I'll see you under the tail."

• *Now begin walking down the square. Thirty yards below the big horse is a small garden with a low-key...*

Memorial: This commemorates victims of communism, such as Jan Palach. In 1969, a group of patriots decided that an act of self-immolation would stoke the fires of independence. Palach, a philosophy student who loved life—but wanted to live in freedom—set himself on fire on the steps of the National Museum for the cause of Czech independence. He died a few days later in a hospital ward. Czechs are keen on anniversaries, and huge demonstrations swept the city on the 20th anniversary of Palach's death. These protests led, 10 months later, to the overthrow of the Czech communist government in 1989.

This grand square is a gallery of modern architectural styles. As you wander downhill, notice the fun mix, all post-1850: Romantic Neo-Gothic, Neo-Renaissance, and Neo-Baroque from the 19th century; Art Nouveau from about 1900; ugly Functionalism from the mid-20th century (the "form follows function" and "ornamentation is a crime" answer to Art Nouveau); Stalin Gothic from the 1950s "communist epoch" (a good example is the Jalta building, halfway downhill on the right);

and the glass-and-steel buildings of the 1970s.

• *Walk a couple of blocks downhill through the real people of Prague (not tourists) to* ***Grand Hotel Evropa,*** *with its hard-to-miss, dazzling Art Nouveau exterior and plush café interior full of tourists. Stop for a moment to consider the events of...*

November of 1989: This huge square was filled every evening with more than 300,000 ecstatic Czechs and Slovaks who believed freedom was at hand. Assembled on the balcony of the building opposite Grand Hotel Evropa (look for the *Marks & Spencer* sign) were a priest, a rock star (famous for his unconventional style, which constantly unnerved the regime), Alexander Dubček (hero of the 1968 revolt), and Václav Havel (the charismatic playwright, newly released from prison, who was every freedom-loving Czech's Nelson Mandela). Through a sound system provided by the rock star, Havel's voice boomed over the gathered masses, announcing the resignation of the Politburo and saying that the Republic of Czechoslovakia's freedom was imminent. Picture that cold November evening, with thousands of Czechs jingling their key chains in solidarity, chanting at the government, "It's time to go now!" (To quell this revolt, government tanks could have given it the Tiananmen Square treatment—which had spilled patriotic blood in China just six months earlier. Locals believe that the Soviet head of state, Mikhail Gorbachev, must have made a phone call recommending a nonviolent response.) For more on the events leading up to this climactic rally, see "The Velvet Revolution of 1989" sidebar, later.

• *Immediately opposite Grand Hotel Evropa is the Lucerna Gallery (use entry marked* Pasáz Rokoko *and walk straight in).*

Lucerna Gallery: This grand mall retains some of its Art Deco glamour from the 1930s, with shops, theaters, a ballroom in the basement, and the fine Lucerna Café upstairs. You'll see a sculpture—called *Wenceslas Riding an Upside-Down Horse*—hanging like a swing from a glass dome. David Černý, who created the statue in 1999, is one of the Czech Republic's most original contemporary artists. Always aspiring to provoke controversy, Černý has painted a menacing Russian tank pink, attached crawling babies to the rocket-like Žižkov TV tower, defecated inside the National Gallery to protest the policies of its director, and sunk a shark-like Saddam Hussein inside an aquarium. His art hoax *Entropa* was created to commemorate the Czech presidency of the European Union in 2009. But when it was unveiled in Brussels, it insulted many EU nations with its satirical symbolism (Bulgaria was represented by squat toilets, Germany consisted of twisted autobahns hinting at a swastika, and so on).

Inside the gallery, you'll also find a **Ticketpro box office** (with all available tickets, daily 9:30–18:00), a lavish 1930s Prague cinema

(under the upside-down horse, shows artsy films in Czech with English subtitles or vice versa, 110 Kč), and the popular **Lucerna Music Bar** in the basement (disco themes from the '70s, '80s, and '90s, 100 Kč, nightly from 21:00).

Directly across busy Vodičkova street (with a handy tram stop) is the Světozor mall. Inside, you'll find the **World of Fruit Bar Světozor,** every local's favorite ice-cream joint. True to its name, the bar tops its ice cream with every variety of fruit. They sell cakes and milkshakes, too. Ask at the counter for an English menu.

• *Farther down the mall on the left is the entrance to the peaceful...*

Franciscan Garden (Františkánská Zahrada): Its white benches and spreading rosebushes are a universe away from the fast beat of the city, which throbs behind the buildings that surround the garden.

Back on Wenceslas Square, if you're in the mood for a mellow hippie teahouse, consider a break at the recommended **Dobrá Čajovna** ("Good Teahouse") near the bottom of the square (#14). Or, if you'd like an old-time wine bar, pop into the plain **Šenk Vrbovec** (nearby at #10); it comes with a whiff of the communist days, embracing the faintest bits of genteel culture from an age when refinement was sacrificed for the good of the working class. They serve traditional drinks, Czech keg wine, Moravian wines (listed on blackboard outside), *becherovka* (the 13-herb liqueur), and—only in autumn—*burčák* (this young wine tastes like grape juice turned halfway into wine).

The bottom of Wenceslas Square is called **Můstek,** which means "Bridge"; a bridge used to cross a moat here, allowing entrance into the Old Town (you can still see the original Old Town entrance down in the Metro station).

• *Running to the right from the bottom of Wenceslas Square is the street called...*

Na Příkopě: Meaning "On the Moat," this busy boulevard follows the line of the Old Town wall, leading to one of the wall's former gates, the Powder Tower. Along the way, it passes the Museum of Communism and a couple of Art Nouveau sights (described in the next section). City tour buses (see "Tours in Prague—Bus Tours," earlier) leave from along this street, which offers plenty of shopping temptations (such as these malls: Slovanský Dům at Na Příkopě 22, and Černá Růže at Na Příkopě 12, next door to Mosers, which has a crystal showroom upstairs).

Na Příkopě: Art Nouveau Prague

Stroll up Na Příkopě to take in two of Prague's best Art Nouveau sights: the Mucha Museum and the Municipal House. The first is on the street called Panská (turn right up the first street you reach as you walk up Na Příkopě from Wenceslas Square); the second is

Art Nouveau

Prague is the best Art Nouveau town in Europe, with fun-loving facades gracing streets all over town. Art Nouveau, born in Paris, is "nouveau" because it wasn't inspired by Rome. It's neo-nothing...a fresh answer to all the revival styles of the later 19th century and an organic response to the Eiffel Tower art of the Industrial Age. The style liberated the artist in each architect. Notice the unique curves and motifs expressing originality on each Art Nouveau facade. Artists such as Alfons Mucha believed that the style should include all facets of daily life. They designed everything from buildings and furniture to typefaces and cigarette packs.

Prague's three top Art Nouveau architects are Jan Koula, Josef Fanta, and Osvald Polivka (whose last name sounds like the Czech word for "soup"). Think "Cola, Fanta, and Soup"—easy to remember and a good way to impress your local friends.

Prague's Art Nouveau highlights include the facades lining the streets of the Jewish Quarter, the Jerusalem Synagogue, the Mucha window in St. Vitus Cathedral, and the Grand Hotel Evropa on Wenceslas Square. The top two sights for Art Nouveau fans are the Mucha Museum and the Municipal House.

two blocks farther up Na Příkopě, next to the big, Gothic Powder Tower.

▲▲Mucha Museum—This is one of Europe's most enjoyable little museums. I find the art of Alfons Mucha (MOO-kah, 1860–1939) insistently likeable. See the crucifixion scene he painted as an eight-year-old boy. Read how this popular Czech artist's posters, filled with Czech symbols and expressing his people's ideals and aspirations, were patriotic banners that aroused the national spirit. And check out the photographs of his models. With the help of an abundant supply of slinky models, Mucha was a founding father of the Art Nouveau movement. Partly overseen by Mucha's grandson, the museum is two blocks off Wenceslas Square and wonderfully displayed on one comfortable floor (120 Kč, daily 10:00–18:00, well-described in English, Panská 7, tel. 224-233-355, www.mucha.cz). The included 30-minute video is definitely worthwhile (in English, generally at :15 and :45 past the hour—ask for the starting time); it describes the main project of Mucha's life—the *Slav Epic,* currently on display in the town of Moravský

Krumlov, though there is talk of moving it to Prague.

• *Coming back to Na Příkopě and continuing toward the Powder Tower, notice the Neo-Renaissance* ***UniCredit Bank*** *building (formerly Živnostenská Banka, Prague's oldest banking institution) on the corner of Nekázanka. It houses a modern bank with classy circa-1900 ambience (enter and peek into the main hall upstairs).*

Consider a several-block detour down Nekázanka to visit another of Prague's Art Nouveau buildings—the Jerusalem Synagogue. (To skip this detour, just continue along Na Příkopě until you reach the big, yellow Municipal House, and skip down to that listing.) To find the synagogue, follow Nekázanka to Jindřišská street, turn left, then turn right onto Jeruzalémská street. About halfway down on your left is the...

Jerusalem Synagogue (Jeruzalémské Synagóga)—This colorful synagogue, also known as the Jubilee Synagogue, is a fascinating combination of Moorish Renaissance and Viennese Art Nouveau styles. It was built from 1905 to 1906 in commemoration of the first 50 years of Franz Josef's liberal rule. Recently restored, still serving the Prague Jewish community, and sparsely visited, this is the most contemplative and visually stunning of Prague's synagogues (200-Kč admission includes entry to Old-New Synagogue in the Jewish Quarter—described earlier, April–Oct Sun–Fri 13:00–17:00, closed Sat, closed in winter and on Jewish holidays, between Powder Tower and main train station at Jeruzalémská 7, tel. 222-319-002, www.synagogue.cz/Jerusalem).

• *Return to Jindřišská street and go left, passing the Jindřišská gate, then take a right on Senovážná street, which leads you to the...*

▲▲Municipal House (Obecní Dům)—The Municipal House is the "pearl of Czech Art Nouveau." Financed by cultural and artistic leaders, it was built (1905–1911) as a ceremonial palace to reinforce the self-awareness of the Czech nation. It features Prague's largest concert hall, a recommended Art Nouveau café (Kavárna Obecní Dům), and two other restaurants. Pop in and wander around the lobby of the concert hall. Walk through to the ticket office on the ground floor. For the best look, including impressive halls and murals you won't see otherwise, take one of the regular hour-long **tours** (open daily 10:00–18:00; tours—150 Kč; generally at 10:15, 12:00, 14:00, and 16:00; 2/day in English, buy ticket from ground-floor shop where tour departs; tel. 222-002-101, www.obecnidum.cz).

Standing in front of the Municipal House, you can survey

four different styles of architecture. First, enjoy the colorful facade of the Municipal House itself—a mixture of Neo-Baroque and Art Nouveau. Featuring a goddess-like Praha presiding over a land of peace and high culture, the *Homage to Prague* mosaic on the building's striking facade stoked cultural pride and nationalist sentiment. Across the street, the classical fixer-upper from 1815 was the customs house, which has recently been turned into a giant stage for Broadway-style musicals. The stark national bank building (Česká Národní Banka) is textbook Functionalism from the 1930s. Farther away, across the square, former Neo-Romanesque barracks have been transformed into central Prague's biggest shopping mall and underground parking lot.

Powder Tower—The big, black Powder Tower (not worth touring inside) was the Gothic gate of the town wall, built to house the city's gunpowder. The decoration on the tower, portraying Czech kings, is the best 15th-century sculpture in town. If you go through the tower, you'll reach Celetná street, which leads past a few sights (including the Estates Theater and Museum of Czech Cubism, both described earlier) to the Old Town Square.

Národní Třída: Communist Prague

From Můstek at the bottom of Wenceslas Square, you can head west on Národní Třída (in the opposite direction from Na Příkopě and the Art Nouveau sights) for an interesting stroll through urban Prague to the National Theater and the Vltava River. But first, consider dropping into the Museum of Communism, a few steps down Na Příkopě (on the right).

▲▲Museum of Communism—This museum traces the story of communism in Prague: the origins, dream, reality, and nightmare; the cult of personality; and finally, the Velvet Revolution. Along the way, it gives a fascinating review of the Czech Republic's 40-year stint with Soviet economics, "in all its dreariness and puffed-up glory." You'll find propaganda posters, busts of communist All-Stars (Marx, Lenin, Stalin), and a photograph of the massive stone Stalin that overlooked Prague until 1962. Slices of communist life are re-created here, from a bland store counter to a typical classroom (with textbooks using Russia's Cyrillic alphabet—no longer studied—and a poem on the chalkboard that extols the virtues of the tractor). Don't miss the Jan Palach exhibit and the 20-minute video (plays continuously, English subtitles) that shows how the Czech people chafed under the big Red yoke from the 1950s through 1989 (180 Kč, daily 9:00–21:00, Na Příkopě 10, above a

McDonald's and next to a casino—Lenin is turning over in his grave, tel. 224-212-966, www.muzeumkomunismu.cz).

• *Now head for the river (with your back to Wenceslas Square, go left down 28 Října to Národní Třída). Along the way, Národní Třída has a story to tell.*

Národní Třída and the Velvet Revolution—Národní Třída (National Street) is where you feel the pulse of the modern city. The street, which connects Wenceslas Square with the National Theater and the river, is a busy thoroughfare running through the heart of urban Prague. In 1989, this unassuming boulevard played host to the first salvo of a Velvet Revolution that would topple the communist regime.

Make your way down Národní Třída until you hit the tram tracks (just beyond the Tesco department store). On the left, look for the photo of Bill Clinton playing saxophone, with Václav Havel on the side (this is the entrance to **Reduta**, Prague's best jazz club; next door are two recommended eateries, Café Louvre and Le Patio). Just beyond that, you'll come to a short corridor with white arches. Inside this arcade is a simple memorial to the hundreds of students injured here by the police on November 17, 1989. For the fascinating story, see "The Velvet Revolution of 1989" sidebar on next page.

Along the Vltava River

I've listed these sights from north to south, beginning at the grand, Neo-Renaissance National Theater, which is five blocks south of Charles Bridge and stands along the riverbank at the end of Národní Třída.

National Theater (Národní Divadlo)—Opened in 1883 with Smetana's opera *Libuše*, t[illegible] theater was the first truly Czech ver[illegible] Prague. From the very start, it w[illegible] named the "Cradle of Czech[illegible] The building is a key symbo[illegible] national revival that bega[illegible] century. In 1800, "Pr[illegible] nantly German. The [illegible] brought Czechs from [illegible] the city, their new urban[illegible]

The Velvet Revolution of 1989

On the afternoon of November 17, 1989, 30,000 students gathered in Prague's New Town to commemorate the 50th anniversary of the suppression of student protests by the Nazis, which had led to the closing of Czech universities through the end of World War II. The 1989 demonstration—initially planned by the Communist Youth as a celebration of the communist victory over fascism—spontaneously turned into a protest *against* the communist regime. "You are just like the Nazis!" shouted the students. The demonstration was supposed to end in the National Cemetery at Vyšehrad (the hill just south of the New Town). But when the planned events concluded in Vyšehrad, the students decided to march on toward Wenceslas Square, making history.

As they worked their way north along the Vltava River toward the New Town's main square, the students were careful to keep their demonstration peaceful. Any hint of violence, the demonstrators knew, would incite brutal police retaliation. Instead, as the evening went on, the absence of police became conspicuous. (In the 1980s, the police never missed a chance to participate in any demonstration...preferably outnumbering the demonstrators). At about 20:00, as the students marched down this very stretch of street toward Wenceslas Square, three rows of policemen suddenly blocked the demonstration at the corner of Národní and Spálená streets. A few minutes later, military vehicles with fences on their bumpers (having crossed the bridge by the National Theater) appeared behind the marching students. This new set of cops compressed the demonstrators into the stretch of Národní Třída between Voršilská and Spálená. The end of Mikulandská street was also blocked, and policemen were hiding inside every house entry. The students were trapped.

At 21:30, the "Red Hats" (a special anti-riot commando force known for its brutality) arrived. The Red Hats lined up on both sides of this corridor. To get out, the trapped students had to run through the passageway as they were beaten from the left and right. Police trucks ferried captured students around the corner to the police headquarters (on Bartolomějská) for interrogation.

The next day, university students throughout Czechoslovakia decided to strike. Actors from theaters in Prague and Bratislava joined the student protest. Two days later, the students' parents—shocked by the attacks on their children—marched into Wenceslas Square. Sparked by the events of November 17, 1989, the wave of peaceful demonstrations ended later that year on December 29, with the election of Václav Havel as the president of a free Czechoslovakia.

by patriotic teachers and priests. By 1883, most of the city spoke Czech, and the opening of this theater represented the birth of the modern Czech nation. It remains an important national icon: The state annually pours more subsidies into this theater than into all of Czech film production. It's the most beautiful venue in town for opera and ballet, often with world-class singers (for more details on performances, see "Entertainment in Prague," later).

Next door (just inland, on Národní Třída) is the boxy, glassy facade of the **Nová Scéna.** This "New National Theater" building, dating from 1983 (the 100th anniversary of the original National Theater building), reflects the bold and stark communist aesthetic.

Across the street from the National Theater is the former haunt of Prague's intelligentsia, the recommended **Grand Café Slavia,** a Viennese-style coffeehouse that is fine for a meal or drink with a view of the river.

• *Just south of the National Theater in the Vltava, you'll find...*

Prague's Islands—From the National Theater, the Legions' Bridge (Most Legií) leads across the island called **Střelecký Ostrov.** Covered with chestnut trees, this island boasts Prague's best beach (on the sandy tip that points north to Charles Bridge). You might see a fisherman pulling out trout from a river that's now much cleaner than it used to be. Bring a swimsuit and take a dip just a stone's throw from Europe's most beloved bridge. In summer, the island hosts open-air movies (most in English or with English subtitles, nightly mid-July–early Sept at about 21:00, www.strelak.cz).

In the mood for boating instead of swimming? On the next island up, **Slovanský Ostrov,** you can rent a boat (40 Kč/hr for rowboats, 60 Kč/hr for paddleboats, bring a picture ID as deposit). A lazy hour paddling around Střelecký Ostrov—or just floating sleepily in the middle of the river surrounded by this great city's architectural splendor—is a delightful experience on a sunny day. It's cheap, easy fun (and it's good for you).

• *A 10-minute walk (or one stop on tram #17) south from the National Theater, beyond the islands, is Jirásek Bridge (Jiráskův Most), where you'll find the...*

Dancing House (Tančící Dům)—If ever a building could get your toes tapping, it would be this one, nicknamed "Fred and Ginger" by American architecture buffs. This metallic samba is the work of Frank Gehry (who designed the equally striking Guggenheim Museum in Bilbao, Spain, and Seattle's

Experience Music Project). Eight-legged Ginger's wispy dress and Fred's metal mesh head are easy to spot. The building's top-floor restaurant, La Perle de Prague, is a fine place for a fancy French meal (VIPs often eat and drink here, reservation needed even to get into the elevator, tel. 221-984-160).

• *Three blocks up Resslova street is...*

Charles Square (Karlovo Náměstí)—Prague's largest square is covered by lawns, trees, and statues of Czech writers. It's a quiet antidote to the bustling Wenceslas and Old Town squares. The Gothic New Town Hall at the top-left corner of the square has excellent views and labeled panoramic photographs that help you orient yourself to what you see. The little parlor across the street has some of the best gelato in town.

The Little Quarter (Malá Strana)

This charming neighborhood, huddled under the castle on the west bank of the river, is low on blockbuster sights but high on ambience. The most enjoyable approach from the Old Town is across Charles Bridge. From the end of the bridge (TI in tower), Mostecká street leads two blocks up to the Little Quarter Square (Malostranské Náměstí) and the huge Church of St. Nicholas. But before you head up there, consider a detour to Kampa Island.

Between Charles Bridge and Little Quarter Square

Kampa Island—One hundred yards before the castle end of the Charles Bridge, stairs on the left lead down to the main square of Kampa Island (mostly created from the rubble of the Little Quarter, which was destroyed in a 1540 fire). The island features relaxing pubs, a breezy park, hippies, lovers, a fine contemporary art gallery, and river access. From the main square, Hroznová lane (on the right) leads to a bridge. Behind the **old mill wheel,** notice the high-water marks from the flood of 2002. The water wheel is the last survivor of many that once lined the canal here. Each mill had its own protective water spirit *(vodník)*. Today, only one wheel—and one spirit (Mr. Kabourek)—remains.

• *Fifty yards beyond the bridge (on the right, under the trees) is the...*

Lennon Wall (Lennonova Zeď)—While Lenin's ideas hung like a water-soaked trench coat upon the Czech people, rock singer John Lennon's ideas gave many locals hope and a vision. When Lennon was killed in 1980, a large wall was spontaneously covered with memorial graffiti. Night after night, the police would

Prague's Little Quarter

Letenské Park
BADENIHO
GOGOLOVA
CHOTKOVA
MILADY HORÁKOVÉ
U PRÁŠNÉHO
Pražský Hrad
MARIÁNSKÉ HRADBY
Královský Letohrádek
Brusice
JELENÍ
STARÉ ZÁMECKÉ SCHODY (STAIRS)
CHOTKOVA
U BRUSKÝCH KASÁREN
CASTLE QUARTER
PRAGUE CASTLE
Malostranská
U BRUSNICE
U TŘÍSTUDNÉ
KANOVNICKÁ
Wallenstein Garden
U ŽELEZNÉ LÁVKY
ZÁMECKÉ SCHODY (Stairs)
LORETA CHURCH
Castle Square (Hradčanské Nám.)
THUNOVSKÁ
LETENSKÁ
MÁNESŮV MOST
Pohořelec
NERUDOVA
CHURCH OF ST. NICHOLAS
Little Quarter Square
U LUŽICKÉHO SEMINÁŘE
ÚVOZ
MOSTECKÁ
MISEŇSKÁ
CHARLES BRIDGE
PROKOPSKÁ
VLAŠSKÁ
LITTLE QUARTER
KARLŮV MOST
STRAHOV MONASTERY
NEBOVIDSKÁ
NA KAMPĚ
RIVER CRUISES
HARANTOVA
PETŘÍN TOWER
Petřín Hill
HELLICHOVA
PELCLOVA
Kampa Island
Vltava
STRAHOVSKÁ
FUNICULAR
KARMELITSKÁ
VŠEHRDOVA
ŘÍČNÍ
HUNGRY WALL
VÍTĚZNÁ
LEGIONS' BRIDGE (MOST LEGIÍ)
PLASKÁ
MĚLNICKÁ
ZBOROVSKÁ
JANÁČKOVO NÁBŘEŽÍ
Střelecký Ostrov
PETŘÍNSKÁ
HOLEČKOVA
KROFTOVA
VODNÍ
ELIŠKY PEŠKOVÉ
Dětský Ostrov
River
ŠTEFÁNIKOVA
MALÁTOVA
ZUBATÉHO
PAVLA ŠVANDY ZE SEMČIC
To Dancing House
DRTINOVA
KOŘENSKÉHO
VIKTORA HUGA
JIRÁSKŮV MOST
200 Meters
200 Yards
V BOTANICE
Dienzenhoferovy Park
MATOUŠOVA
KARTOUZSKÁ
LISNICKÁ
ŠÁRKOPKAMENNÁ
SVORNOSTI
HOŘEJŠÍ NÁBŘEŽÍ
PECHÁČKOVA
PALACKÉHO MOST
RADLICKÁ
PIZEŇSKÁ
LIDICKÁ
NA BĚLIDLE
Anděl

1. Kampa Island & Old Mill Water Wheel
2. Lennon Wall
3. Church of St. Nicholas
4. Wallenstein Palace Garden (Entrance)
5. Vrtba Garden
6. Church of St. Mary the Victorious
7. Monument to Victims of Communism Who Survived
8. Hungry Wall
9. Petřín Tower & Museum of Jára Cimrman
10. Mirror Maze
11. US Embassy

paint over the "All You Need Is Love" and "Imagine" graffiti. And day after day, it would reappear. Until independence came in 1989, travelers, freedom-lovers, and local hippies gathered here. Silly as it might seem, this wall is remembered as a place that gave hope to locals craving freedom. Even today, while the tension

and danger associated with this wall are gone, people come here to imagine. *"John žije"* is Czech for "John lives." In the left-hand corner of the wall, a small gate leads to a quiet courtyard with the recommended John & George Café.

• *From here, you can continue up to the Little Quarter Square.*

On or near Little Quarter Square

The focal point of this neighborhood, the Little Quarter Square (Malostranské Náměstí) is dominated by the huge Church of St. Nicholas. Note that there's a handy Via Musica ticket office across from the church.

Church of St. Nicholas (Kostel Sv. Mikuláše)—When the Jesuits came to Prague, they found the perfect piece of real estate for their church and its associated school—right on Little Quarter Square. The church (built 1703–1760) is the best example of High Baroque in town. It's giddy with curves and illusions. The altar features a lavish gold-plated Nicholas, flanked by the two top Jesuits: the founder, St. Ignatius Loyola, and his missionary follower, St. Francis Xavier. Climb up the **gallery** through the staircase in the left transept for a close-up look at a collection of large canvases and illusionary frescoes by Karel Škréta, the greatest Czech Baroque painter. Notice that at first glance, the canvases are utterly dark. But as sunbeams shine through the window, various parts of the painting brighten up. Like a looking-glass, the image reflects the light, creating a play of light and darkness. This painting technique represents a central Baroque belief: The world is full of darkness, and the only hope that makes it come alive comes from God. The church walls seem to nearly fuse with the sky, suggesting that happenings on earth are closely connected to heaven. Find St. Nick with his bishop's miter in the center of the ceiling, on his way to heaven (60 Kč, church open daily 9:00–17:00, opens at 8:30 for prayer).

Tower Climb: For a good look at the city and the church's 250-foot dome, climb 215 steps up the bell tower (50 Kč, April–Oct daily 10:00–18:00, closed Nov–March, tower entrance is outside the right transept).

Concerts: The church is also an evening concert venue; tickets are usually on sale at the door (450 Kč, generally nightly except Tue at 18:00, www.psalterium.cz).

• *From here, you can hike 10 minutes uphill to the castle (and five more minutes to the Strahov Monastery). For information on these sights, see "The Castle Quarter," later. If you're walking up to the castle, consider going via...*

Nerudova Street—This steep, cobbled street, leading from Little Quarter Square to the castle, is named for Jan Neruda, a gifted 19th-century journalist (and somewhat less talented fiction

writer). It's lined with old buildings still sporting the characteristic doorway signs (e.g., the lion, three violinists, house of the golden suns) that once served as street addresses. The surviving signs are carefully restored and protected by law. They represent the family name, the occupation, or the various passions of the people who once inhabited the houses. (If you were to replace your house number with a symbol, what would it be?) In 1777, in order to collect taxes more effectively, Habsburg empress Maria Theresa decreed that numbers be used instead of these quaint house names. This neighborhood is filled with old noble palaces, now generally used as foreign embassies and offices of the Czech Parliament.

North of Little Quarter Square, near Malostranská Metro Station

Twenty yards from the Malostranská Metro station (go left from the top of the escalator and turn right when you get outside), a few blocks north of Little Quarter Square, is a fine palace and garden. If you want to reach Little Quarter Square from here, follow Valdštejnská street.

Wallenstein Palace Garden (Valdštejnská Palac Zahrada)—Of the neighborhood's many impressive palace gardens, this is by far the largest and most beautiful. The complex—consisting of a palace (generally closed) and the surrounding garden (generally open and free to enter April–Oct daily 10:00–18:00, closed Nov–March)—was commissioned during the Thirty Years' War by the Habsburg general and Czech nobleman Albrecht z Valdštejna (or, in German, Albrecht von Wallenstein). The inconspicuous entry to the palace's Wallenstein Garden is by the Malostranská Metro station. The garden, renovated in the late 1990s, features a large pool surrounded by peacocks. The statues that line the central walkway, inspired by Greek mythology, were done by the Danish artist Adrian de Vries—arguably the best Renaissance sculptor outside of Italy. Notice the elegant classical shapes, a sharp contrast to the chubbiness of the Baroque figures on the Charles Bridge and elsewhere in the city. The original statues were stolen by invading Swedish armies in 1648, and are still in Sweden; the present replicas were cast in the early 1900s.

Near the Garden: For a terraced Baroque garden to compare to this Renaissance one, visit the **Vrtba Garden** (Vrtbovská Zahrada, 100 Kč, daily 10:00–18:00; just south of Little Quarter Square, on Karmelitská before the Church of St. Mary the Victorious—described next).

South of Little Quarter Square, to Petřín Hill

Karmelitská street, leading south (along the tram tracks) from Little Quarter Square, is home to these sights.

Jára Cimrman: When Optimists Should Be Shot

"I am such a complete atheist that I am afraid God will punish me." Such is the pithy wisdom of Jára Cimrman, the man overwhelmingly voted the "Greatest Czech of All Time" in a 2005 national poll. Who is Jára Cimrman? A philosopher? An explorer? An inventor? He is all of these things, yes, and much more. Today, a museum celebrates his life (see the Museum of Jára Cimrman on page 106).

Born in the mid-19th century to a Czech tailor of Jewish descent and an Austrian actress, Cimrman studied in Vienna before starting off on his journeys around the world. He traversed the Atlantic in a steamboat he designed himself, taught drama to peasants in Peru, and drifted across the Arctic Sea on an iceberg. Other astounding feats soon followed. Cimrman was the first to come within 20 feet of the North Pole. He was the first to invent the light bulb (unfortunately, Edison beat him to the patent office by five minutes). It was he who suggested to the Americans the idea for a Panama Canal, though, as usual, he was never credited. Indeed, Cimrman surreptitiously advised many of the world's greats: Eiffel on his tower, Einstein on his theories of relativity, Chekhov on his plays. ("You can't just have *two* sisters," Cimrman told the playwright. "How about three?") In 1886, long before the world knew of Sartre or Camus, Cimrman was writing tracts such as *The Essence of the Existence,* which would become the foundation for his philosophy of "Cimrmanism," also known as "non-existentialism." (Its central premise: "Existence cannot not exist.")

This man of unmatched genius would have won the honor of "Greatest Czech of All Time" if not for the bureaucratic narrow-mindedness of the poll's sponsors, who had a single objection to Cimrman's candidacy: He's not real. Jára Cimrman is the brainchild of two Czech humorists—Zdeněk Svěrák and Jiří Šebánek—who brought their patriotic Renaissance Man to life in 1967 in a satirical radio play. So, even though Cimrman handily won the initial balloting in January of 2005, Czech TV officials—blatantly biased against his non-existentialism—refused to let him into the final rounds of the competition.

How should we interpret the fact that the Czechs would

Church of St. Mary the Victorious (Kostel Panny Marie Vítězné)—This otherwise ordinary Carmelite church displays Prague's most worshipped treasure, the Infant of Prague (Pražské Jezulátko). Kneel at the banister in front of the tiny lost-in-gilded-Baroque altar, and find the prayer in your language (of the 13 in the folder). Brought to Czech lands during the Habsburg era by a Spanish noblewoman who came to marry a Czech nobleman, the Infant has become a focus of worship and miracle tales in Prague and Spanish-speaking countries. South Americans come

rather choose a fictional character as their greatest countryman over any of their flesh-and-blood national heroes—say, Charles IV (the 14th-century Holy Roman Emperor who established Prague as the cultural and intellectual capital of Europe), Jan Hus (the 15th-century religious reformer who challenged the legitimacy of the Catholic Church), Comenius (a 17th-century educator and writer, considered one of the fathers of modern education), or Martina Navrátilová (someone who plays a sport with bright green balls)? The more cynically inclined—many Czechs among them—might point out that the Czech people have largely stayed behind their mountains for the past millennia, with little interest in, or influence on, happenings elsewhere in the world. Perhaps Cimrman is so beloved because he embodies that most prickly of ironies: a Czech who was greater than all the world's greats, but who for some hiccup of chance has never been recognized for his achievements.

Personally, I like to think that the vote for Cimrman says something about the country's rousing enthusiasm for blowing raspberries in the face of authority. Throughout its history—from the times of the Czech kings who used crafty diplomacy to keep the German menace at bay, to the days of Jan Hus and his questioning of the very legitimacy of any ruler's power, to the flashes of anti-communist revolt that at last sparked the Velvet Revolution in 1989—the Czechs have maintained a healthy disrespect for those who would tell them what is best or how to live their lives. Other countries soberly choose their "Greatest" from musty tomes of history, but the Czechs won't play this silly game. Their vote for a fictional personage, says Cimrman's co-creator Svěrák, shows two things about the Czech nation: "That it is skeptical about those who are major figures and those who are supposedly the 'Greatest.' And that the only certainty that has saved the nation many times throughout history is its humor."

Cimrman would agree. A man of greatness, he was always a bit skeptical of those who saw themselves as great, or who marched forward under the banner of greatness. As Cimrman liked to say, "There are moments when optimists should be shot."

on pilgrimage to Prague just to see this one statue. An exhibit upstairs shows tiny embroidered robes given to the Infant, including ones from Habsburg Empress Maria Theresa of Austria (1754) and Vietnam (1958), as well as a video showing a nun lovingly dressing the doll-like sculpture (free, Mon–Sat 9:30–17:30, Sun 13:00–17:00, English-language Mass Sun at 12:00, Karmelitská 9, www.pragjesu.com).

• *Continue a few more blocks down Karmelitská to the south end of the Little Quarter (where the street is called Újezd, roughly across the*

Legions' Bridge from the National Theatre). Here you find yourself at the base of...

Petřín Hill—This hill, topped by a replica of the Eiffel Tower, features several unusual sights.

The figures walking down the steps in the hillside make up the **Monument to Victims of Communism Who Survived.** The monument's figures are gradually atrophied by the totalitarian regime. They do not die, but slowly disappear, one limb at a time. The statistics say it all: In Czechoslovakia alone, 205,486 people were imprisoned, 248 were executed, 4,500 died in prison, 327 were shot attempting to cross the border, and 170,938 left the country. To the left of the monument is the **Hungry Wall,** Charles IV's 14th-century equivalent of FDR's work-for-food projects. On the right (50 yards away) is the base of a handy **funicular**—hop on to reach Petřín Tower (uses tram/Metro ticket, runs daily, every 10–15 min from 8:00–22:00).

The summit of Petřín Hill is considered the best place in Prague to take your date for a romantic city view. Built for an exhibition in 1891, the 200-foot-tall **Petřín Tower** is one-fifth the height of its Parisian big brother, which was built two years earlier. But, thanks to this hill, the top of the tower sits at the same elevation as the real Eiffel Tower. Climbing the 400 steps rewards you with amazing views over the city. Local wives drag their men to Petřín Hill each May Day to reaffirm their love with a kiss under a blooming sour-cherry tree.

In the tower's basement is the funniest sight in Prague, the **Museum of Jára Cimrman, Genius Who Did Not Become Famous.** The museum traces Cimrman's (fictional) life, including pictures and English descriptions of the thinker's overlooked inventions (50 Kč includes tower and Cimrman museum, daily 10:00–22:00). For more on the mysterious Cimrman, see the sidebar.

The **mirror maze** next door is nothing special, but fun to quickly wander through since you're already here (50 Kč, daily 10:00–22:00).

The Castle Quarter (Hradčany)

Looming above Prague, dominating its skyline, is the Castle Quarter. Prague Castle and its surrounding sights are packed with Czech history, as well as with tourists. In addition to the castle itself, I enjoy visiting the nearby Strahov Monastery—which has a fascinating old library and beautiful views over all of Prague.

Castle Square (Hradčanské Náměstí)—right in front of the castle gates—is at the

center of this neighborhood. Stretching along the promontory away from the castle is a regal neighborhood that ends at the Strahov Monastery. Above the castle are the Royal Gardens, and below the castle are more gardens and lanes leading down to the Little Quarter.

Getting to Prague Castle

If you're not up for a hike, the tram offers a sweat-free ride up to the castle. Taxis are expensive, as they have to go the long way around (200 Kč).

By Foot: Begin in the Little Quarter, just across Charles Bridge from the Old Town. Hikers can follow the main cobbled road (Mostecká) from Charles Bridge to Little Quarter Square, marked by the huge, green-domed Church of St. Nicholas. (The nearest Metro stop is Malostranská, from which Valdštejnská street leads down to Little Quarter Square.) From Little Quarter Square, hike uphill along Nerudova street (described earlier). After about 10 minutes, a steep lane on the right leads to the castle. (If you continue straight, Nerudova becomes Úvoz and climbs to the Strahov Monastery.)

By Tram: Tram #22 takes you up to the castle. While you can catch the tram in various places, these three stops are particularly convenient: at the Národní Třída Metro stop (between Wenceslas Square and the National Theater in the New Town); in front of the National Theater (Národní Divadlo, on the riverbank in the New Town); and at Malostranská (the Metro stop in the Little Quarter). After rattling up the hill, the tram makes three stops near the castle: Get off at **Královský Letohrádek** for the scenic approach to the castle (through the Royal Gardens); stay on one more stop to get off at **Pražský Hrad** (most direct but least interesting—simply walk along U Prašného Mostu over the bridge into the castle); or go yet two more stops—passing the Brusnice stop—to **Pohořelec** to visit the Strahov Monastery before hiking down to the castle (explained above).

Tram Tips: When you're choosing which of the castle's three tram stops to get off at, consider the time of day. The castle is plagued with crowds. If you're visiting in the morning, use the Pražský Hrad tram stop for the quickest commute to the castle. Be at the door of St. Vitus Cathedral when it opens at 9:00 (except on Sunday mornings, when it's closed for Mass). If you arrive just 10–15 minutes later, it'll be swamped with tour groups. See the castle sights quickly, then move on to the Strahov Monastery. I'd avoid the castle entirely mid-morning, but by mid-afternoon, the tour groups are napping and the grounds are (relatively) uncrowded. If you're going in the afternoon, take the tram to the Pohořelec stop, see the Strahov Monastery, then wander down to the castle.

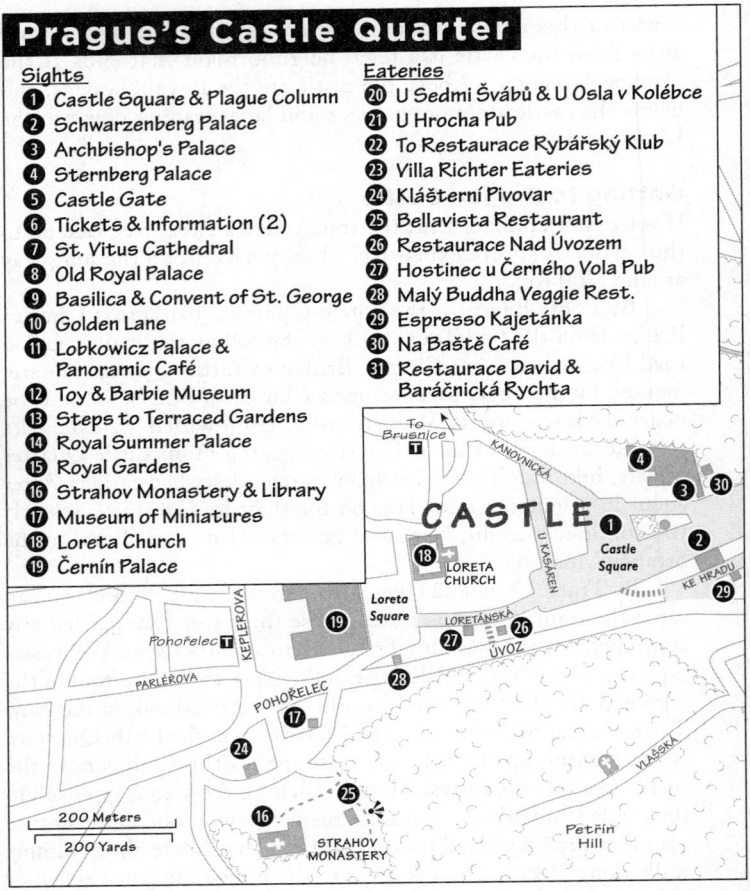

▲Strahov Monastery and Library, near the Pohořelec Tram Stop

Twin Baroque domes high above the castle mark the Strahov Monastery. This complex is best reached from the Pohořelec stop on tram #22 (from the stop, follow the tram tracks uphill for 50 yards, enter the fancy gate on the left near the tall red-brick wall, and you'll see the twin spires of the monastery; the library entrance is in front of the church on the right). If you're coming on foot from the Little Quarter, allow 15 minutes for the uphill hike. After seeing the monastery, hike down to the castle (a 5-min walk).

Monastery: The monastery (Strahovský Klášter Premonstrátů) had a booming economy of its own in its heyday, with vineyards, a brewery, and a sizeable beer hall—all still open. Its main church, dedicated to the Assumption of St. Mary, is an origi-

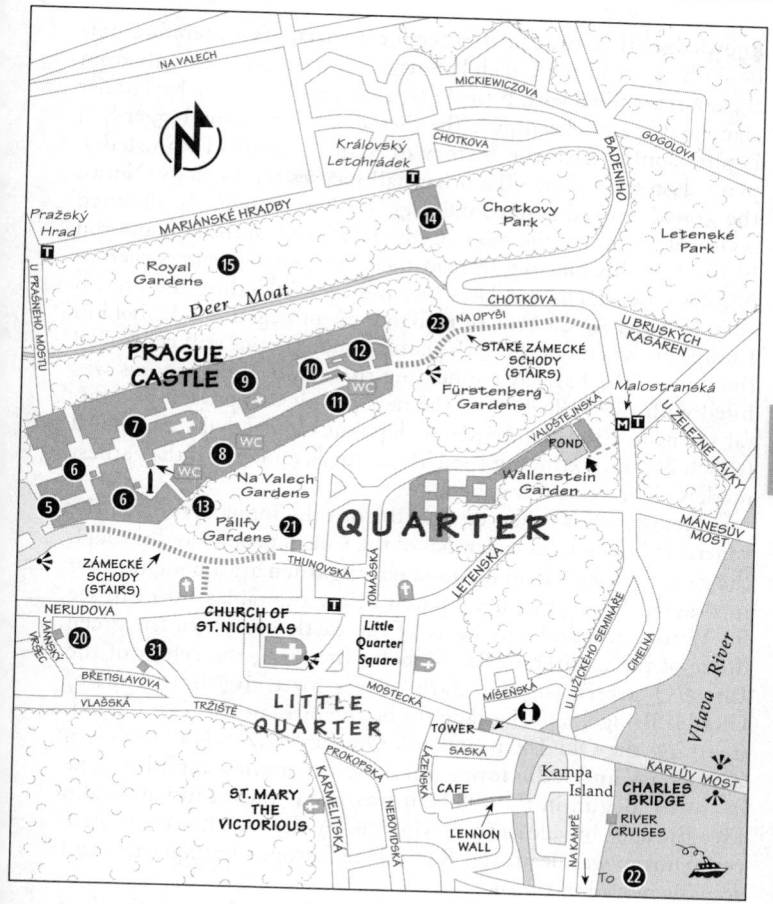

nally Romanesque structure decorated by the monks in textbook Baroque (usually closed, but look through the window inside the front door to see its interior).

Library: The adjacent library (Strahovská Knihovna) offers a peek at how enlightened thinkers in the 18th century influenced learning (80 Kč, daily 9:00–11:45 & 13:00–17:00). Cases in the library gift shop show off illuminated manuscripts (described in English). Some are in old Czech, but these are rare. Because the Enlightenment promoted the universality of

knowledge, there was little place for vernaculars—therefore, few books here are in the Czech language. Two rooms (seen only from the door) are filled with 10th- to 17th-century books, shelved under elaborately painted ceilings. The theme of the first and bigger hall is philosophy, with the history of man's pursuit of knowledge painted on the ceiling. The other hall focuses on theology. Notice the gilded, locked case containing the *libri prohibiti* (prohibited books) at the end of the room. Only the abbot had the key, and you had to have his blessing to read these books—by writers such as Nicolas Copernicus and Jan Hus, and even including the French encyclopedia. As the Age of Enlightenment began to take hold in Europe at the end of the 18th century, monasteries still controlled the books. The hallway connecting these two library rooms was filled with cases illustrating the new practical approach to natural sciences. Find the dried-up elephant trunks, baby dodo bird (which became extinct in the 17th century), and one of the earliest models of an electricity generator.

Nearby Views: Just downhill from the monastery, past the venerable linden trees (a symbol of the Czech people) and through the gate, the views from the **monastery garden** are among the best in Prague. From the public perch below the tables, you can see St. Vitus Cathedral (the heart of the castle complex), the green dome of the Church of St. Nicholas (marking the center of the Little Quarter), the two dark towers fortifying both ends of Charles Bridge, and the fanciful black spires of the Týn Church (marking the Old Town Square). On the horizon is the modern **Žižkov TV and radio tower** (marking the liveliest nightlife zone in town). Begun in the 1980s, it was partly meant to jam Radio Free Europe's broadcast from Munich. By the time it was finished, communism was dead, and Radio Free Europe's headquarters had actually moved to Prague.

Getting to the Castle: To reach the castle from Strahov Monastery, take Loretánská (the upper road, passing Loreta Square—described later); this is a more interesting route than the lower road, Úvoz, which takes you steeply downhill, below Castle Square.

Or, for one more little sight, consider visiting the Museum of Miniatures. From the monastery garden viewpoint, backtrack through the gate to the big linden trees, and leave through a passage on your right. At the door is the miniscule...

Museum of Miniatures: You'll see 40 teeny exhibits, each under a microscope, crafted by an artist from St. Petersburg. Yes, you could fit the entire museum in a carry-on-size suitcase, but good things sometimes come in very, very small packages—it's fascinating to see minutiae such as a padlock on the leg of an ant. An English flier explains it all (50 Kč, kids-20 Kč, daily 9:00–17:00).

On Loreta Square, between Strahov Monastery and Castle Square

From the monastery, take Loretánská street to Loreta Square (Loretánské Náměstí). As you wander this road, you'll pass several mansions and palaces, and an important pilgrimage church.

Loreta Church—This church has been a hit with pilgrims for centuries, thanks to its dazzling bell tower, peaceful yet plush cloister, sparkling treasury, and much-venerated Holy House (110 Kč, Tue–Sun 9:00–12:15 & 13:00–16:30, closed Mon).

Once inside, follow the one-way clockwise route. Strolling along the cloister, notice that the ceiling is painted with the many places Mary has miraculously appeared to the faithful in Europe.

In the garden-like center of the cloister stands the ornate **Santa Casa (Holy House),** considered by some pilgrims to be part of Mary's home in Nazareth. Because many pilgrims returning from the Holy Land docked at the Italian port of Loreto, it's called the Loreta Shrine. The Santa Casa is the "little Bethlehem" of Prague. It is the traditional departure point for Czech pilgrims setting out on the long, arduous journey to Europe's most important pilgrimage site, Santiago de Compostela, in northwest Spain. Inside, on the left wall, hangs what some consider to be an original beam from the house of Mary. It's overseen by a much-venerated statue of the Black Virgin. The Santa Casa itself might seem like a bit of a letdown, but consider that you're entering the holiest spot in the country for generations of believers.

The small Baroque church behind the Santa Casa is one of the most beautiful in Prague. The decor looks rich—but the marble and gold is all fake (tap the columns). From the window in the back, you can see a stucco relief on the Santa Casa that shows angels rescuing the house from a pagan attack in Nazareth and making a special delivery to Loreto in Italy.

Continue around the cloister. In the last corner is "St. Bearded Woman" (Svatá Starosta). This patron saint of unhappy marriages is a woman whose family arranged for her to marry a pagan man. She prayed for an escape, sprouted a beard...and the guy said, "No way." While she managed to avoid the marriage, it angered her father, who crucified her. The many candles here are from people suffering through unhappy marriages.

Take a left just before the exit and head upstairs, following signs to the treasury—a room full of jeweled worship aids (well-described in English). The highlight here is a monstrance

Tomáš Garrigue Masaryk
(1850–1937)

Tomáš Masaryk was the George Washington of Czechoslovakia. He founded the first democracy in Eastern Europe at the end of World War I, uniting the Czechs and the Slovaks to create Czechoslovakia. Like Václav Havel 70 years later, Masaryk was a politician whose vision extended far beyond the mountains enclosing the Bohemian basin.

Masaryk was born into a poor servant family in southern Moravia. After finishing high school, the village boy set off to attend university in Vienna. Masaryk earned his Ph.D. in sociology just in time for the opening of the Czech-language university in Prague. By then, he was married to an American music student named Charlotta Garrigue, who came from a prominent New York family. (The progressive Tomáš actually took her family name as part of his own.) Charlotta opened the doors of America's high society to Masaryk. Among the American friends he made was a young Princeton professor named Woodrow Wilson.

Masaryk was greatly impressed with America, and his admiration for its democratic system became the core of his gradually evolving political creed. He traveled the world and went to Vienna to serve in the parliament. By the time World War I broke

(Communion wafer holder) from 1699, with more than 6,000 diamonds.

Enjoy the short carillon concert at the top of the hour; from the lawn in front of the main entrance, you can see the racks of bells being clanged. (At the exit, you'll see a schedule of English-language Masses and upcoming *pouť*—pilgrimages—departing from here.)

Castle Square (Hradčanské Náměstí)

This is the central square of the Castle Quarter. Enjoy the awesome city view and the two entertaining bands that play regularly at the gate. (If the Prague Castle Orchestra is playing, say hello to friendly, mustachioed Josef, and consider getting the group's

out in 1914, Masaryk was 64 years old and—his friends thought—ready for retirement. But while most other Czech politicians stayed in Prague and supported the Habsburg Empire, Masaryk went abroad in protest and formed a highly original plan: to create an independent, democratic republic of Czechs and Slovaks. Masaryk and his supporters recruited an army of 100,000 Czech and Slovak soldiers who were willing to fight with the Allies against the Habsburgs...establishing a strong case to put on his friend Woodrow Wilson's Oval Office desk.

On the morning of October 28, 1918, news of the unofficial capitulation of the Habsburgs reached Prague. Local supporters of Masaryk's idea quickly took control of the city and proclaimed the free republic. As the people of Prague tore down double-headed eagles (a symbol of the Habsburgs), Czechoslovakia was born.

On November 11, 1918, four years after he had left the country as a political nobody, Masaryk arrived in Prague as the greatest Czech hero since the revolutionary priest Jan Hus. The dignified old man rode through the masses of cheering Czechs on a white horse. He told the jubilant crowd, "Now go home—the work has only started." Throughout the 1920s and 1930s, Masaryk was Europe's most vocal defender of democratic ideals against the rising tide of totalitarian ideologies.

In 2001, the US government honored Masaryk's dedication to democracy by erecting a monument to him in Washington, DC. He is one of only three foreign leaders (along with Gandhi and Churchill) to have a statue in the American capital.

terrific CD.) The recommended **Espresso Kajetánka** café, with dramatic city views, hides a few steps down (immediately to the right as you face the castle). From the café, stairs lead down to the Little Quarter.

Castle Square was a kind of medieval Pennsylvania Avenue—the king, the most powerful noblemen, and the archbishop lived here. Look uphill from the gate. The Renaissance **Schwarzenberg Palace** (on the left, with the big rectangles scratched on the wall) was where the Rožmberks "humbly" stayed when they were in town from their Český Krumlov estates. The Schwarzenberg family inherited the Krumlov estates and aristocratic prominence in Bohemia, and stayed in the palace until the 20th century. The palace now houses the National Gallery's collection of Czech Baroque paintings, displayed in recently restored rooms that also have great views of the city (150 Kč, Tue–Sun 10:00–18:00, cheaper after 16:00, closed Mon).

The archbishop still lives in the yellow Rococo **palace** across

the square (with the three white goose necks in the red field—the coat of arms of Prague's archbishops).

Through the portal on the left-hand side of the palace, a lane leads to the **Sternberg Palace** (Šternberský Palác), filled with the National Gallery's skippable collection of European paintings—including minor works by Albrecht Dürer, Peter Paul Rubens, Rembrandt, and El Greco (150 Kč, Tue–Sun 10:00–18:00, closed Mon).

The black Baroque sculpture in the middle of the square is a **plague column,** erected as a token of gratitude to the saints who saved the population from the epidemic, and an integral part of the main square of many Habsburg towns.

The statue marked *TGM* honors **Tomáš Garrigue Masaryk** (1850–1937), a university prof and a pal of Woodrow Wilson. At the end of World War I, Masaryk united the Czechs and the Slovaks into one nation and became its first president (see sidebar on previous page).

▲▲ Prague Castle (Pražský Hrad)

For more than a thousand years, Czech leaders have ruled from Prague Castle. Today, Prague's Castle is, by some measures, the biggest on earth. Four stops matter, and all are explained here: St. Vitus Cathedral, Old Royal Palace, Basilica of St. George, and the Golden Lane.

Hours: Castle sights are open daily April–Oct 9:00–17:00, Nov–March 9:00–16:00, last entry 15 minutes before closing; grounds are open daily 5:00–23:00. St. Vitus Cathedral is closed Sunday mornings for Mass. Be warned that the cathedral can be unexpectedly closed due to special services—consider calling ahead to confirm (tel. 224-373-368 or 224-372-434). If you're not interested in entering the museums, you could try a nighttime visit—the castle grounds are safe, peaceful, floodlit, and open late.

Tickets: The cathedral is free. For the other castle sights, rather than buying the comprehensive long-tour ticket (350 Kč), I recommend getting the short-tour ticket (250 Kč, covers the Old Royal Palace, Basilica of St. George, and the Golden Lane; buy in palace, Basilica, or the ticket offices on the two castle courtyards). To save time, skip the packed Golden Lane during the day, and

return at night for a romantic, crowd-free visit (free before 9:00 and after 18:00, or after 17:00 in winter).

Tours: Hour-long tours in English depart from the main ticket office across from the cathedral entrance about three times a day, but cover only the cathedral and Old Royal Palace (100 Kč plus entry ticket, tel. 224-373-368). You can rent an **audioguide** for 200 Kč (good all day)—pick it up at the main desk, and show this book for this rate (promised through 2011 by the manager Tomáš Kuha). The audioguide also entitles you to priority entrance at the cathedral—when the line in front of the entrance is long, walk to the exit door on the right and show the audioguide to the guard to be let in.

Crowd-Beating Tips: Huge throngs of tourists turn the castle grounds into a sea of people during peak times (9:30–12:30). St. Vitus Cathedral is the most crowded part of the castle complex. If you're visiting in the morning, be at the cathedral entrance promptly at 9:00, when the doors open. For 10 minutes, you'll have the sacred space to yourself (after about 9:15, tour guides jockeying unwieldy groups from tomb to tomb turn the church into a noisy human traffic jam). Late afternoon is least crowded.

Castle Gate and Courtyards—Begin at Castle Square. From here, survey the castle—the tip of a 1,500-foot-long series of courtyards, churches, and palaces. The guard changes on the hour (5:00–23:00), with the most ceremony and music at noon.

Walk under the fighting giants, under an arch, through the passageway, and into the courtyard. The modern green awning with the golden-winged cat (just past the ticket office) marks the offices of the Czech president, who is elected by the parliament rather than by popular vote and serves as more of a figurehead than a power broker. The current president is Václav Klaus. His consistent politics have brought him popularity from like-minded Czechs, but bitter resentment from those who see him as incapable of considering points of view other than his own. Outside the Czech Republic, Klaus is known for his unconstructive criticism of the European Union and denunciation of the campaign against global warming (the reality of which he denies).

• *As you walk through another passageway, you'll find yourself facing...*

▲▲▲St. Vitus Cathedral (Katedrála Sv. Víta)—The Roman Catholic cathedral symbolizes the Czech spirit—it contains the tombs and relics of the most important local saints and kings, including the first three Habsburg kings.

➲Self-Guided Tour: The following commentary will bring meaning to your cathedral visit.

Cathedral Facade: Before entering, check out the facade. What's up with the guys in suits carved into the facade below the big, round window? They're the architects and builders who finished the church. Started in 1344, construction was stalled by wars and plagues. But, fueled by the 19th-century rise of Czech nationalism, Prague's top church was finished in 1929 for the 1,000th anniversary of the death of St. Wenceslas. While it looks wholly Gothic, it's actually two distinct halves: the original 14th-century Gothic around the high altar, and the modern Neo-Gothic nave. For 400 years, a temporary wall sealed off the functional, yet unfinished, cathedral.

Mucha Stained-Glass Window: Enter through the gate on the left with the fenced-off queuing area, and find the third window on the left. This masterful 1931 Art Nouveau window is by Czech artist Alfons Mucha (if you like this, you'll love the Mucha Museum in the New Town, described on page 94).

Notice Mucha's stirring nationalism: Methodius and Cyril, widely considered the fathers of Slavic-style Christianity, are top and center. Cyril—the monk in black holding the Bible—brought the word of God to the Slavs. They had no written language in the ninth century—so he designed the necessary alphabet (Glagolitic, which later developed into Cyrillic). Methodius, the bishop, is shown baptizing a mythic, lanky, long-haired Czech man—a reminder of how he brought Christianity to the Czech people. Scenes from the life of Cyril, on the left, and scenes from the life of Methodius, on the right, bookend the stirring and epic Slavic scene. In the center are a kneeling boy and a prophesying elder—that's young St. Wenceslas and his grandmother, St. Ludmila. In addition to being specific historical figures, these characters are also symbolic: The old woman, with closed eyes, stands for the past and memory, while the young boy, with a penetrating stare, represents the hope and future of a nation. Notice how master designer Mucha draws your attention to these two figures through the use of colors—the dark blue on the outside gradually turns into green,

then yellow, and finally the gold of the woman and the crimson of the boy in the center. In Mucha's color language, blue stands for the past, gold for the mythic, and red for the future. Besides all the meaning, Mucha's art is simply a joy to behold. (And on the bottom, the tasteful little ad for *Banka Slavie,* which paid for the work, is hardly noticeable.)

Habsburg Emperor's Tomb: Continue circulating around the apse. The big royal tomb (within the black iron fence) is of the first Habsburg emperor. It dates from 1590, when Prague was a major Habsburg city.

Relief of Prague: As you walk around the high altar, study the fascinating carved-wood relief of Prague. It depicts the victorious Habsburg armies entering the castle after the Battle of White Mountain, while the Protestant King Frederic escapes over the Charles Bridge (before it had any statues). Carved in 1630, 10 years after the famous event occurred, the relief also gives you a peek at Prague in 1620, stretching from the Týn Church to the cathedral (half-built at that time, up to where you are now). Notice that back then, the Týn Church was Hussite, so the centerpiece of its facade is not the Virgin Mary—but a chalice, symbol of Jan Hus' ideals. The old city walls—now replaced by the main streets of the city—stand strong. The Jewish Quarter (the slummy, muddy zone along the riverside below the bridge on the left) fills land no one else wanted.

Apse: Circling around the high altar, you pass graves of bishops, including the tomb of St. Vitus (behind the chair of the bishop). The stone sarcophagi contain kings from the Přemysl dynasty (12th–14th centuries). Locals claim the gigantic, shiny tomb of St. John of Nepomuk has more than a ton of silver (for more on St. John of Nepomuk, see page 1021). After the silver tomb, look up at the royal box from where the king would attend Mass in his jammies (an elevated corridor connected his private apartment with his own altar-side box pew).

Look for the finely carved wood panel that gives a Counter-Reformation spin on the Wars of Religion. It shows the "barbaric" Protestant nobles destroying the Catholic icons in the cathedral after their short-lived victory.

Wenceslas Chapel: A fancy roped-off chapel (right transept) houses the tomb of St. Wenceslas, surrounded by precious 14th-century murals showing scenes of his life (see description on page 90), and a locked door leading to the crown jewels. The Czech kings used to be crowned right here in front of the coffin, draped in red. The chapel is roped off because the wallpaper is encrusted with precious and semiprecious stones. (Lead us not into temptation.) You can view the chapel from either door (if the door facing the nave is crowded, duck around to the left to find a door that is most likely open).

Spire: You can climb 287 steps up the spire for one of the best views of the whole city (may be closed for reconstruction, otherwise April–Oct daily 9:00–17:00 except Sun morning, Nov–March until 16:00, last entry 45 min before closing).

Back Outside the Cathedral: Leaving the cathedral, turn left (past the public WC). The **obelisk** was erected in 1928—a single piece of granite celebrating the 10th anniversary of the establishment of Czechoslovakia and commemorating the soldiers who fought for its independence. It was originally much taller, but broke in transit—an inauspicious start for a nation destined to last only 70 years. Up in the fat, green tower of the cathedral is the Czech Republic's biggest bell, nicknamed "Zikmund." In June of 2002, it cracked, and two months later, the worst flood in recorded history hit the city—which the locals saw as a sign. As a nation sandwiched between great powers, Czechs are deeply superstitious when it comes to the tides of history. Often feeling unable to influence the course of their own destiny, they helplessly look at events as we might look at the weather and other natural phenomena—trying to figure out what fate has in store for them next.

Find the 14th-century **mosaic** of the Last Judgment outside on the right transept. It was commissioned in the Italian style by King Charles IV, who was modern, cosmopolitan, and ahead of his time. Jesus oversees the action, as some go to heaven and some go to hell. The Czech king and queen kneel directly below Jesus and the six patron saints. On coronation day, they would walk under this arch, which would remind them (and their subjects) that even those holding great power are not above God's judgment. The royal crown and national jewels are kept in a chamber (see the grilled windows) above this entryway, which was the cathedral's main entry for centuries while the church remained uncompleted.

Across the square and 20 yards to the right, a door leads into the Old Royal Palace (in the lobby, there's a WC with a window shared by the men's and women's sections—meet your partner to enjoy the view).

Old Royal Palace (Starý Královský Palác)—Starting in the 12th century, this was the seat of the Bohemian princes. While extensively rebuilt, the **large hall** is late Gothic, designed as a multipurpose hall for the old nobility. It's big enough for jousts—even the staircase was designed to let a mounted soldier gallop in. It was filled with market stalls, giving nobles a chance to shop

without actually going into town. In the 1400s, the nobility met here to elect their king. The tradition survived until modern times, as the parliament crowded into this room until the late 1990s to elect the Czechoslovak (and later Czech Republic) president. (The last three elections happened in another, far more lavish hall in the castle.) Look up at the flower-shaped, vaulted ceiling.

On your immediate right, enter the two small Renaissance rooms known as the **"Czech Office."** From these rooms (empty today except for their 17th-century porcelain heaters), two governors used to oversee the Czech lands for the Habsburgs in Vienna. In 1618, angry Czech Protestant nobles poured into these rooms and threw the two Catholic governors out of the window. An old law actually permits defenestration—throwing people (usually bad politicians) out of windows when necessary. Old prints on the wall show the second of Prague's many defenestrations. The two governors landed—fittingly—in a pile of horse manure. Even though they suffered only broken arms and bruised egos, this event kicked off the huge and lengthy Thirty Years' War.

Look down on the chapel from the end, and go out on the balcony for a fine Prague view. Is that Paris' Eiffel Tower in the distance? No, it's Petřín Tower (described earlier)—a fine place for a relaxing day at the park, offering sweeping views over Prague.

As you exit through the side door, pause at the door to consider the subtle yet racy little Renaissance knocker. Go ahead—play with it for a little sex in the palace (be gentle).

• *Across from the palace exit is the...*

Basilica and Convent of St. George (Bazilika Sv. Jiří)—Step into the beautiful-in-its-simplicity Basilica of St. George to see Prague's best-preserved Romanesque church. Notice the characteristic double windows on the gallery, as well as the walls made of limestone (the rock that Prague rests on). In those early years, the building techniques were not yet advanced, and the ceiling is made of wood, rather than arched with stone. St. Wenceslas' grandmother, St. Ludmila, who established this first Bohemian convent, was reburied here in 973. Look for Gothic frescoes depicting this cultured

woman (to the right of the altar space). The Baroque front—which dates from much later—was added on the exterior at the same time as the St. John of Nepomuk chapel (through which you exit the church). The scary-looking bones under the chapel altar are replicas—neither St. John's nor real.

Today, the **convent** next door houses the National Gallery's collection of 19th-century Czech paintings (150 Kč, Tue–Sun 10:00–18:00, closed Mon).

• *Continue walking downhill through the castle grounds. Turn left on the first street, which leads into the...*

Golden Lane (Zlatá Ulička)—This street of old buildings, which originally housed goldsmiths, is jammed with tourists during the day and lined with overpriced gift shops. Franz Kafka lived briefly at #22. There's a deli/bistro at the top. In the morning (before 9:00) and at night (after 18:00 in summer, after 17:00 in winter), the tiny street is empty and romantic. Exit the lane through a corridor at the last house (#12).

Lobkowicz Palace (Lobkowiczký Palác)—At the bottom of the castle complex just after you leave the Golden Lane, this palace displays the private collection of a prominent Czech noble family, including paintings, ceramics, and musical scores (275 Kč, includes audioguide, not included in any castle tickets, Tue–Sun 10:30–18:00, last entry one hour before closing, closed Mon, tel. 233-312-925, www.lobkowiczevents.cz). The **Panoramic Café** by the exit has a creative cosmopolitan menu and stunning views of the city (daily 10:00–18:00).

Toy and Barbie Museum (Muzeum Hraček)—Across the street from Lobkowicz Palace, a courtyard and a long wooden staircase lead to two entertaining floors of old toys and dolls, thoughtfully described in English. You'll see a century of teddy bears, 19th-century model train sets, and an incredible Barbie collection (the entire top floor). Find the buxom 1959 first edition, and you'll understand why these capitalistic sirens of material discontent weren't allowed here until 1989 (70 Kč, 120 Kč family ticket, not included in any castle tickets, daily 9:30–17:30, WC next to entrance).

After Your Castle Visit: Tourists squirt slowly through a fortified door at the bottom end of the castle. From there, you can follow the steep lane directly back to the riverbank...or turn right about halfway down the steps to visit the recently reopened **Fürstenberg Gardens,** with 3,500 flowering plants and 2,200 rose bushes (80

Kč, April–Oct daily from 10:00 until one hour before sunset). Either way, you'll end up at the Malostranská Metro station.

Or, as you walk out of the castle gate, you can take a hard right and stroll through the long, delightful park. Along the way, notice the Modernist design of the **Na Valech Garden,** which was carried out by the court architect of the 1920s, Jože Plečnik of Slovenia (see page 672).

Halfway through the long park is a viewpoint overlooking the terraced **Pálffy Gardens;** you can zigzag down through these gardens into the Little Quarter (80 Kč, April–Oct daily 10:00–18:00, closed Nov–March).

If you continue through the park all the way to Castle Square, you'll find two more options: a staircase leading down into the Little Quarter, or a cobbled street taking you to historic Nerudova street (described earlier).

Congratulations. You've conquered the castle.

Entertainment in Prague

Prague booms with live and inexpensive theater, classical music, jazz, and pop entertainment. Everything is listed in several monthly cultural events programs (free at TIs) and in the *Prague Post* newspaper (60 Kč at newsstands).

You'll be tempted to gather fliers as you wander through the town. Don't bother. To really understand all your options (the street Mozarts are pushing only their concerts), drop by a **Via Musica** box office. There are two: One is next to Týn Church on the Old Town Square (daily 10:30–19:30, tel. 224-826-969), and the other is in the Little Quarter across from the Church of St. Nicholas (daily 10:30–18:00, tel. 257-535-568). The event schedule posted on the wall clearly shows everything that's playing today and tomorrow, including tourist concerts, Black Light Theater, and marionette shows, with photos of each venue and a map locating everything (www.viamusica.cz).

Ticketpro sells tickets for the serious concert venues and most music clubs (daily 8:00–12:00 & 12:30–16:30, Rytířská 31, between Havelská Market and Estates Theater; also has a booth in Tourist Center at Rytířská 12, daily 9:00–20:00; English-language reservations tel. 296-329-999).

Consider buying concert tickets directly from the actual venues. You won't save money, but more of your money will go to the musicians.

Locals dress up for the more "serious" concerts, opera, and ballet, but many tourists wear casual clothes—as long as you don't show up in shorts, sneakers, or flip-flops, you'll be fine.

Black Light Theater

A kind of mime/modern dance variety show, Black Light Theater has no language barrier and is, for many, more entertaining than a classical concert. Unique to Prague, Black Light Theater originated in the 1960s as a playful and mystifying theater of the absurd. These days, aficionados and critical visitors lament that it's becoming a cheesy variety show, while others are uncomfortable with the sexual flavor of some acts. Still, it's an unusual theater experience that most enjoy. Shows last about an hour and a half. Avoid the first four rows, which get you so close that it ruins the illusion. Each theater has its own spin on what Black Light is supposed to be:

Ta Fantastika is traditional and poetic, with puppets and a little artistic nudity (*Aspects of Alice* nightly at 21:30, 650 Kč, reserved seating, near east end of Charles Bridge at Karlova 8, tel. 222-221-366, www.tafantastika.cz).

Image Theater has more mime and elements of the absurd, with shows including *Clonarium, Fiction,* and *The Best of Image:* "It's precisely the fact that we are all so different that unites us" (shows nightly at 18:00 and 20:00, 480 Kč, open seating—arrive early to grab a good spot, just off Old Town Square at Pařížská 4, tel. 222-314-448, www.imagetheatre.cz).

Laterna Magica, in the big, glassy building next to the National Theater, mixes Black Light techniques with film projection into a multimedia performance that draws Czech audiences (*Wonderful Circus, Rendezvous, Graffiti,* shows Mon–Sat at 20:00, no shows on Sun, 680 Kč, tel. 224-931-482, www.laterna.cz).

The other Black Light theaters advertised around town aren't as good.

Concerts

Each day, six to eight classical concerts designed for tourists fill delightful Old World halls and churches with music of the crowd-pleasing sort: Vivaldi, Best of Mozart, Most Famous Arias, and works by the famous Czech composer Antonín Dvořák. Concerts typically cost 400–1,000 Kč, start anywhere from 13:00 to 21:00, and last about an hour. Typical venues include two buildings on the Little Quarter Square (the Church of St. Nicholas and the Prague Academy of Music in Liechtenstein Palace); the Klementinum's Chapel of Mirrors; the Old Town Square (in a different Church of St. Nicholas); and the stunning Smetana Hall in the Municipal House (see page 95). The artists vary from excellent to amateurish.

A sure bet is the jam session held every Monday at 17:00 at **St. Martin in the Wall,** where some of Prague's best musicians gather to tune in and chat with each other (400 Kč, Martinská street, just north of the Tesco department store in the Old Town).

The **Prague Castle Orchestra,** one of Prague's most entertaining acts, performs regularly on Castle Square. This trio—Josef on flute, Radek on accordion, and Zdeněk on bass—plays a lively Czech mélange of Smetana, swing, old folk tunes, and 1920s cabaret songs. Look for them if you're visiting the castle, and consider picking up their fun CD. They're also available for private functions (mobile 603-552-448, josekocurek@volny.cz).

Serious music-lovers should consider Prague's two top ensembles: The **Czech Philharmonic,** which performs in the classical Neo-Renaissance Rudolfinum (on Palachovo Náměstí, in the Jewish Quarter on the Old Town side of Mánes Bridge—ticket office on right side, under the stairs; 250–1,000 Kč, open Mon–Fri 10:00–18:00, and until just before the show starts on concert days, tel. 227-059-352, www.ceskafilharmonie.cz, info@cfmail.cz), and the **Prague Symphony Orchestra,** based in the gorgeous Art Nouveau Municipal House (ticket office on the right side, on U Obecního Domu street opposite Hotel Paris; Mon–Fri 10:00–18:00, tel. 222-002-336, www.fok.cz, pokladna@fok.cz). Both orchestras perform in their home venues about five nights a month from September through June. Most other nights these spaces are rented to agencies that organize tourist concerts of varying quality for double the price (as described earlier). Check first whether your visit coincides with either ensemble's performance.

During his frequent visits to Prague, Austrian Wolfgang Amadeus Mozart (1756–1791) stayed with his friends in the beautiful, small, Neoclassical **Villa Bertramka,** now the Mozart Museum. Surrounded by a peaceful garden, the villa preserves the time when the Salzburg prodigy felt more appreciated in Prague than in Austria. Intimate concerts are held some afternoons and evenings, either in the garden or in the small concert hall (110 Kč, daily April–Oct 9:30–18:00, Nov–March 9:30–17:00, Mozartova 169, Praha 5; from Metro: Anděl, it's a 10-min walk—head to Hotel Mövenpick and then go up alley behind hotel; tel. 257-317-465, www.bertramka.cz).

Opera and Ballet

The **National Theater** (Národní Divadlo, on the New Town side of Legií Bridge)—with a must-see Neo-Renaissance interior (see page 97)—is best for opera and ballet (shows from 19:00, 300–1,000 Kč, tel. 224-912-673, www.nationaltheatre.cz). The **Estates Theater** (Stavovské Divadlo) is where Mozart premiered and personally directed many of his most beloved works (see page

78). *Don Giovanni, The Marriage of Figaro,* and *The Magic Flute* are on the program a couple of times each month (shows from 20:00, 800–1,400 Kč, between the Old Town Square and the New Town on a square called Ovocný Trh, tel. 224-214-339, www.estatestheatre.cz). A handy ticket office for both of these theaters is in the little square (Ovocný Trh) behind the Estates Theater, next to a pizzeria.

The **State Opera** (Státní Opera) operates on a smaller budget and is also not as architecturally rewarding as the National Theater (shows at 19:00 or 20:00, 400–1,200 Kč, buy tickets at the theater, on the busy street between the main train station and Wenceslas Square at Wilsonova 101—see map on page 89, tel. 224-227-693, www.opera.cz).

Festivals

World-class musicians are in town during these musical festivals: **Prague Spring** (last three weeks of May, www.festival.cz), **Prague Proms** (July–Aug, www.pragueproms.cz), and the newer **Dvořák's Prague** (Aug–Sept, www.dvorakovapraha.cz).

Shopping in Prague

Prague's entire Old Town seems designed to bring out the shopper in visitors. Puppets, glass, and ceramics are traditional. Shop your way from the Old Town Square up Celetná street to the Powder Tower, then along Na Příkopě to the bottom of Wenceslas Square (Václavské Náměstí). The city center is tourist-oriented—most locals do their serious shopping in the suburbs.

Celetná is lined with big stores selling all the traditional Czech goodies. Tourists wander endlessly here, mesmerized by the window displays. Celetná Crystal, about midway down the street, offers the largest selection of affordable crystal. You can have the glass safely shipped home directly from the shop.

Náměstí Republiky (Republic Square) boasts Prague's newest and biggest mall, Palladium (Sun–Wed 9:00–21:00, Thu–Sat 9:00–22:00). It's hidden behind a pink Neo-Romanesque facade and the brown steel-and-glass 1980s department store Kotva (Anchor)—an obsolete beast on the verge of extinction (Mon–Fri 9:00–20:00, Sat–Sun 10:00–18:00).

Na Příkopě has a couple of good modern malls. The best is

Slovanský Dům (daily 10:00–20:00, Na Příkopě 22), where you'll wander deep past a 10-screen multiplex into a world of classy restaurants and designer shops surrounding a peaceful, park-like inner courtyard. Another modern mall is Černá Růže (daily 10:00–20:00, Na Příkopě 12), with a great Japanese restaurant around a small garden. Next door is Moser, which has a museum-like crystal showroom upstairs. The Galerie Myslbek, directly across the street, has fancy stores in a space built to Prague's scale.

Národní Třída (National Street) is less touristy and lined with some inviting stores. The big Tesco department store in the middle sells anything you might need, from a pin for a broken watchband to a swimsuit (generally daily 9:00–21:00, Národní Třída 26).

Crystal: Along with shops on Celetná and Na Příkopě, a small square just off the Old Town Square, Malé Náměstí, is ringed by three major crystal retailers (generally open daily 10:00–20:00): Moser, Rott Crystal, and Crystalex (which claims to have "factory-direct" prices, at #6 on the square).

Garnets: This extraordinary stone of fiery red color, with unique refractive—some claim even curative—properties, is found only in Bohemia. The characteristic design of garnet jewelry, with the gems overwhelming the metal setting, became popular in the 1890s and remains so today. Although garnet jewelry is sold in most crystal shops, the Turnov Granát Co-op has the largest selection (with shops at Dlouhá 30 and Panská 1, www.granat.eu). It oversees its own mining and represents more than 300 traditional goldsmiths and jewelers. If you buy garnet jewelry, make sure to ask your vendor for a certificate of authenticity—many shops sell glass imitations.

Sleeping in Prague

Peak season for hotels in Prague is May, June, and September. Easter and New Year's are the most crowded times, when prices are jacked up a bit. I've listed peak-time prices—if you're traveling in July or August, you'll find rates generally 15 percent lower, and from November through March, about 30 percent lower.

Room-Booking Services

Prague is awash with fancy rooms on the push list; private, small-time operators with rooms to rent in their apartments; and roving agents eager to book you a bed and earn a commission. You

Sleep Code

(18 Kč = about $1, country code: 420)
S = Single, **D** = Double/Twin, **T** = Triple, **Q** = Quad, **b** = bathroom, **s** = shower only. Unless otherwise noted, credit cards are accepted, and breakfast and tax are included. Everyone listed here speaks English.

To help you sort easily through these listings, I've divided the rooms into three categories based on the price for a standard double room with bath:

$$$ Higher Priced—Most rooms 3,500 Kč or more.
$$ Moderately Priced—Most rooms between 2,500-3,500 Kč.
$ Lower Priced—Most rooms 2,500 Kč or less.

can save about 30 percent by showing up in Prague without a reservation and finding accommodations upon arrival. However, it can be a hassle, and you won't necessarily get your ideal choice. If you're coming in by train or car, you'll encounter booking agencies. They can almost always find you a reasonable room, and, if it's in a private guest house, your host can even come and lead you to the place.

Athos Travel has a line on 200 properties (ranging from hostels to five-star hotels), 90 percent of which are in the historical center. To book a room, call them or use their handy website, which allows you to search for a room, based on various criteria (best to arrange in advance during peak season, can also help with last-minute booking off-season, tel. 241-440-571, fax 241-441-697, www.a-prague.com, info@a-prague.com). Readers report that Athos is aggressive with its business policies—while there's no fee to cancel well in advance, they strictly enforce penalties on cancellations within 48 hours.

Touristpoint, at the main train station (Hlavní Nádraží), is another booking service (daily 8:00–22:00). They have a slew of hotels and small pensions available (2,000-Kč pension doubles in old center, 1,500-Kč doubles a Metro ride away). You can reserve by email, using your credit card as a deposit (tel. 224-946-010, www.touristpoint.cz, info@touristpoint.cz), or just show up at the office and request a room. Be clear on the location before you make your choice.

Lída Jánská's **Magic Praha** can help with accommodations (mobile 604-207-225, www.magicpraha.cz, magicpraha@magicpraha.cz; see "Helpful Hints," earlier). Lída rents a well-located apartment with a river view near the Jewish Quarter.

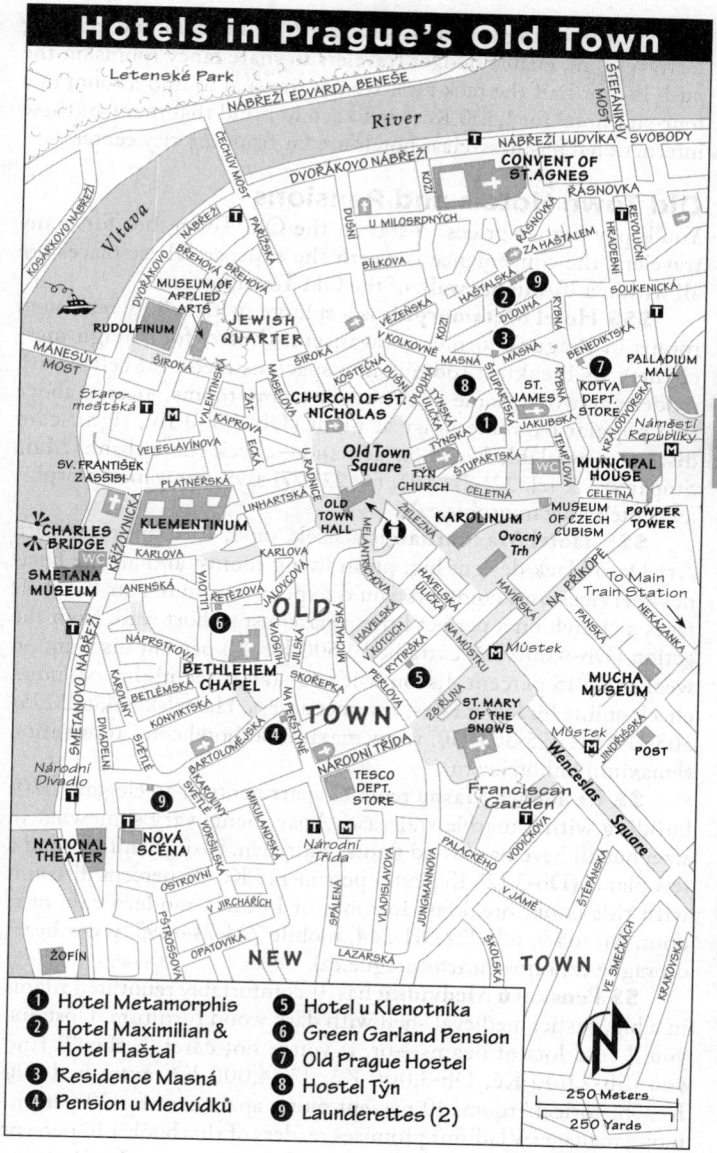
Hotels in Prague's Old Town
Letenské Park
NÁBŘEŽÍ EDVARDA BENEŠE
River
ŠTEFÁNIKŮV MOST
NÁBŘEŽÍ LUDVÍKA SVOBODY
CONVENT OF ST. AGNES
ČECHŮV MOST
DVOŘÁKOVO NÁBŘEŽÍ
RÁSNOVKA
Vltava
KOZÁKOVO NÁBŘEŽÍ
NÁBŘEŽÍ
PAŘÍZSKÁ
DUŠNÍ
U MILOSRDNÝCH
RÁSNOVKA
ZA HAŠTALEM
HRADEBNÍ
REVOLUČNÍ
DVOŘÁKOVO
BŘEHOVÁ
BŘEHOVÁ
BÍLKOVÁ
MUSEUM OF APPLIED ARTS
HAŠTALSKÁ
SOUKENICKÁ
RUDOLFINUM
JEWISH QUARTER
VĚŽENSKÁ
DLOUHÁ
RYBNÁ
V KOLKOVNĚ
KOZÍ
BENEDIKTSKÁ
MÁNESŮV MOST
ŠIROKÁ
ŠIROKÁ
MASNÁ
MASNÁ
PALLADIUM MALL
Staroměstská
VALENTINSKÁ
MASELNÁ
KOSTELNÁ
DUŠNÍ
DLOUHÁ
STŮPARTSKÁ
ST. JAMES
RYBNÁ
KOTVA DEPT. STORE
ŽAT.
CHURCH OF ST. NICHOLAS
TÝNSKÁ
ULIČKA
KAPROVA
ECKÁ
JAKUBSKÁ
KRÁLOVSKÁ
Náměstí Republiky
VELESLAVÍNOVA
U RADNICE
Old Town Square
TÝNSKÁ
STŮPARTSKÁ
TEMPLOVÁ
MUNICIPAL HOUSE
SV. FRANTIŠEK ZASSISI
PLATNÉRSKÁ
TÝN CHURCH
CELETNÁ
CELETNÁ
LINHARTSKÁ
OLD TOWN HALL
ŽELEZNÁ
KAROLINUM
MUSEUM OF CZECH CUBISM
POWDER TOWER
CHARLES BRIDGE
KLEMENTINUM
KŘIŽOVNICKÁ
MELANTRICHOVA
Ovocný Trh
KARLOVA
KARLOVA
SMETANA MUSEUM
ANENSKÁ
LILLOVA
ŘETĚZOVÁ
JÁLOVCOVÁ
HAVELSKÁ ULICKA
HAVÍŘSKÁ
NA PŘÍKOPĚ
To Main Train Station
OLD
HAVELSKÁ
V KOTCÍCH
MICHALSKÁ
NÁPRSTKOVÁ
VÁCLAVSKÁ
JILSKÁ
RYTÍŘSKÁ
NA MŮSTKU
Můstek
PANSKÁ
NEKÁZANKA
SMETANOVO NÁBŘEŽÍ
BETHLEHEM CHAPEL
KAROLINY
BETLÉMSKÁ
SKOŘEPKA
PERLOVÁ
MUCHA MUSEUM
KONVIKTSKÁ
NA PERŠÝNĚ
TOWN
28 ŘÍJNA
ST. MARY OF THE SNOWS
DIVADELNÍ
SVĚTLE
BARTOLOMĚJSKÁ
NÁRODNÍ TŘÍDA
Můstek
JINDŘIŠSKÁ
POST
Wenceslas Square
Národní Divadlo
SVĚTLE
KAROLINY
TESCO DEPT. STORE
Franciscan Garden
MIKULANDSKÁ
NATIONAL THEATER
NOVÁ SCÉNA
VOKŠÍLSKÁ
Národní Třída
PALACKÉHO
VODIČKOVA
OSTROVNÍ
V JIRCHÁŘICH
SPÁLENÁ
VLADISLAVOVA
JUNGMANNOVA
V JÁMĚ
ŠTEFÁNIKOVA
PŠTROSOVA
OPATOVICKÁ
ŽOFÍN
NEW
LAZARSKÁ
ŠKOLSKÁ
TOWN
VE SMEČKÁCH
NRAKOVSKÁ
1 Hotel Metamorphis
2 Hotel Maximilian & Hotel Haštal
3 Residence Masná
4 Pension u Medvídků
5 Hotel u Klenotníka
6 Green Garland Pension
7 Old Prague Hostel
8 Hostel Týn
9 Launderettes (2)
250 Meters
250 Yards

Web-booking services, such as Priceline.com and Bidding fortravel.com, enable budget travelers to snare fancy rooms on the push list for half the rack rate. It's not unusual to find a room in a four-star hotel for 1,300 Kč—but keep in mind that many of these international business-class hotels are far from the city center.

Old Town Hotels and Pensions

You'll pay higher prices to stay in the Old Town, but for many travelers, the convenience is worth the expense. These places are all within a 10-minute walk of the Old Town Square.

$$$ Hotel Metamorphis is a splurge, with solidly renovated rooms in Prague's former caravanserai (hostel for foreign merchants). Its breakfast room is in a spacious medieval cellar with modern artwork. Some of the street-facing rooms, located above two popular bars, are noisy at night (Db-4,800 Kč, significant discounts available based on demand—check the website, Malá Štupartská 5, tel. 221-771-011, fax 221-771-099, www.metamorphis.cz, hotel@metamorphis.cz).

$$$ Hotel Maximilian is a sleek, mod, 70-room place with Art Deco black design; big, plush living rooms; and all the business services and comforts you'd expect in a four-star hotel. It faces a church on a perfect little square just a short walk from the action (Db-4,000 Kč, extra bed-1,500 Kč, 20 percent discount on weekends, 15 percent discount if you stay three nights or more, check online for lower rates, Internet access, Haštalská 14, tel. 225-303-111, fax 225-303-110, www.maximilianhotel.com, reservation@maximilianhotel.com).

$$ Residence Masná rents 12 apartments in an elegant 1930s building with a marble staircase. Apartments vary somewhat in size, but all have hardwood floors, a kitchen, basic furniture, and a few plants (Db-3,125 Kč, extra person-125 Kč, 25 percent discount with this book, breakfast in room or in ultra-modern café next door, Masná 9, tel. 222-311-244, mobile 724-744-395, www.heartofprague.cz, info@heartofprague.cz).

$$ Pension u Medvídků has 31 comfortably renovated rooms in a big, rustic, medieval shell with dark wood furniture. Upstairs, you'll find lots of beams—or, if you're not careful, they'll find you (Sb-2,000 Kč, Db-3,000 Kč, Tb-4,000 Kč, extra bed-500 Kč, "historical" rooms 10 percent more, apartment for 20 percent more, manager Vladimír promises readers of this book a 10 percent discount with cash if you book direct, Internet access, Na Perštýně 7, tel. 224-211-916, fax 224-220-930, www.umedvidku.cz, info@umedvidku.cz). The pension runs a popular beer-hall restaurant with live music most Fridays and Saturdays until 23:00—request an inside room for maximum peace.

$$ Hotel u Klenotníka ("At the Jeweler"), with 11 modern, comfortable rooms in a plain building, is three blocks off the Old Town Square (Sb-2,000 Kč, small double-bed Db-2,750 Kč, bigger twin-bed Db-3,300 Kč, Tb-3,750 Kč, 10 percent off with this book, Wi-Fi, Rytířská 3, tel. 224-211-699, fax 224-221-025, www.uklenotnika.cz, info@uklenotnika.cz, Marie and Helena).

$ Green Garland Pension (U Zeleného Věnce), on a central but delightfully quiet cobbled lane, has a warm and personal feel rare for the Old Town. Located in a thick 14th-century building with open beams, it has a blond-hardwood charm decorated with a woman's touch. Its nine rooms are clean and simply furnished (big Sb-1,700 Kč, Db-2,200 Kč, bigger Db-2,500 Kč, Tb-2,800 Kč, family suite, Wi-Fi, Řetězová 10, tel. 222-220-178, fax 224-248-791, www.uzv.cz, pension@uzv.cz).

$ Hotel Haštal is next to Hotel Maximilian (listed earlier) on the same quiet, hidden square in the Old Town. A popular hotel back in the 1920s, it has been tactfully renovated to complement the neighborhood's vibrant circa-1900 architecture. Its 24 rooms are comfortable, but the walls are a bit thin (Sb-1,500 Kč, Db-2,000 Kč, extra bed-550 Kč, book by email to avoid online booking fee, air-con, Wi-Fi, Haštalská 16, tel. 222-314-335, www.hastal.com, info@hastal.com). The hotel's small restaurant is understandably popular with locals for its reasonably priced lunch specials and draft beer.

Under the Castle, in the Little Quarter

The first and third listings below are buried on quiet lanes deep in the Little Quarter, among cobbles, quaint restaurants, rummaging tourists, and embassy flags. Hotel Julián is a 10-minute walk up the river on a quiet and stately street, with none of the intense medieval cityscape of the others.

$$$ Vintage Design Hotel Sax recently remodeled its 22 rooms in a retro, meet-the-Jetsons fashion. With a fruity atrium and a distinctly modern, stark feel, this is a stylish, no-nonsense place (Sb-3,800–4,300 Kč, Db-3,800–4,500 Kč, Db suite-5,000 Kč, extra bed-750 Kč, 10 percent off with this book, elevator, Internet access, Jánský Vršek 3, tel. 257-531-268, fax 257-534-101, www.sax.cz, hotel@sax.cz).

$$$ Hotel Julián is an oasis of professional, predictable decency in an untouristy neighborhood. Its 32 spacious, fresh, well-furnished rooms and big, homey public spaces hide behind a noble Neoclassical facade. The staff is friendly and helpful (Sb-3,680 Kč, Db-3,980 Kč, Db suite-4,800 Kč, extra bed-900 Kč, check website for lower rates, 15 percent discount off rack rate with this book, free tea and coffee in room, air-con, Wi-Fi, elevator, plush and inviting lobby, summer roof terrace has view of Prague Castle, parking

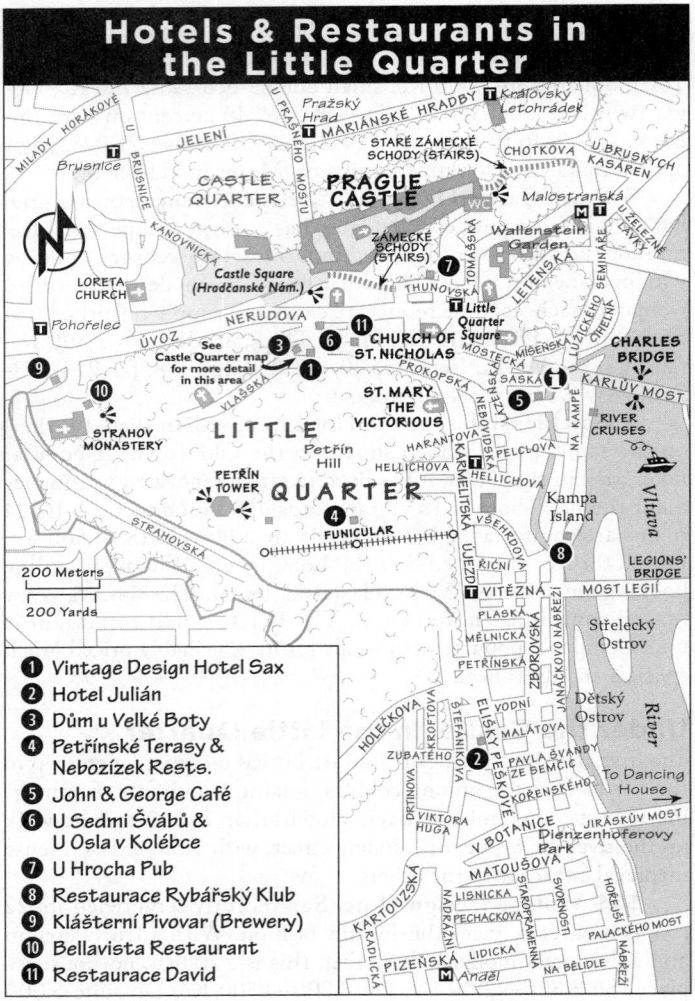

lot; Metro: Anděl, then an 8-min walk, or take tram #6, #9, #12, #20, or #58 for two stops; Elišky Peškové 11, Praha 5, reservation tel. 257-311-150, reception tel. 257-311-145, fax 257-311-149, www.julian.cz, info@julian.cz). Free lockers and a shower are available for those needing a place to stay after check-out (for example, while waiting for an overnight train). Mike's Chauffeur Service, based here, is reliable and affordable (see page 149).

$$ Dům u Velké Boty ("House at the Big Boot"), on a quiet square in front of the German Embassy, is the rare quintessential family hotel in Prague: homey, comfy, and extremely friendly.

Charlotta, Jan, and their two sons treat every guest as a (thirsty) friend, and the wellspring of their stories never runs dry. Each of their 12 rooms is uniquely decorated, most in tasteful 19th-century Biedermeier style (tiny S-2,100 Kč, two D rooms that share a bathroom-2,250 Kč each, Db-2,900–3,600 Kč, extra bed-725 Kč, 10 percent off with advance reservation and this book, prices can be soft when slow, cash only, children up to 10 free—toys provided, free Internet access and Wi-Fi, Vlašská 30, tel. 257-532-088, www.bigboot.cz, info@bigboot.cz). There's no hotel sign on the house—look for the splendid geraniums that Jan nurtures in the windows.

Away from the Center

Moving just outside central Prague saves you money—and gets you away from the tourists and into some more workaday residential neighborhoods. The following listings (great values compared to the downtown hotels listed previously) are all within a 5- to 15-minute tram or Metro ride from the center.

Beyond Wenceslas Square

These hotels are in urban neighborhoods on the outer fringe of the New Town, beyond Wenceslas Square. But they're still within several minutes' walk of the sightseeing zone, and are well-served by trams.

$$$ Sieber Hotel, with 20 rooms, is a quality, four-star, business-class hotel in an upscale circa-1900 residential neighborhood (Vinohrady) that has recently become popular with Prague's expat community. They do a good job of being homey and welcoming (Sb-4,480 Kč, Db-4,780 Kč, extra bed-990 Kč, fourth night free, 20 percent discount with this book, 30 percent discount for last-minute reservations, air-con, elevator, Internet access, 3-min walk to Metro: Jiřího z Poděbrad, or tram #11, Slezská 55, Praha 3, tel. 224-250-025, fax 224-250-027, www.sieber.cz, reservations@sieber.cz).

$$ Hotel 16 is a sleek and modern business-class place with an intriguing Art Nouveau facade, polished cherry-wood elegance, high ceilings, and 14 fine rooms (Sb-2,800 Kč, Db-3,500 Kč, bigger Db-3,700 Kč, Tb-4,400 Kč, 10 percent discount with this book, check website for last-minute rates, triple-paned windows, back rooms facing the garden are quieter, air-con, elevator, Internet access, 10-min walk south of Wenceslas Square, Metro: I.P. Pavlova, Kateřinská 16, Praha 2, tel. 224-920-636, fax 224-920-626, www.hotel16.cz, hotel16@hotel16.cz).

$ Hotel Anna offers 24 bright, simple, pastel rooms and basic service. It's a bit closer in—just 10 minutes by foot east of Wenceslas Square (Sb-1,600 Kč, Db-1,900 Kč, Tb-2,100 Kč, special online offers, elevator, Budečská 17, Praha 2, Metro: Náměstí

Hotels & Restaurants in the New Town & Beyond

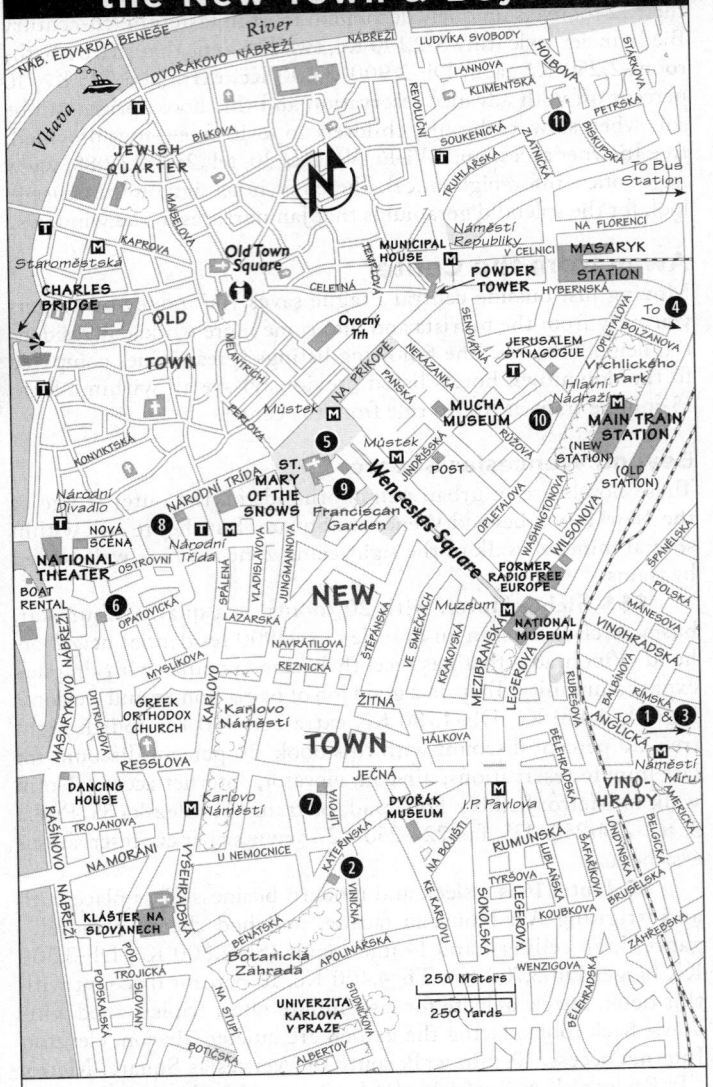

1. To Sieber Hotel
2. Hotel 16
3. To Hotel Anna
4. To Hostel Elf
5. Restaurace u Pinkasů
6. Hospoda u Nováka
7. Pivovarský Dům
8. Le Patio & Café Louvre
9. Dobrá Čajovna Teahouse
10. Čajový Klub Cha Dao
11. Restaurant Červená Tabulka

Míru, tel. 222-513-111, fax 222-515-158, www.hotelanna.cz, sales @hotelanna.cz). They run a similar hotel (same standards and prices) nearby.

The Best Values, Farther from the Center

These accommodations are a 10- to 20-minute tram ride from the center, but once you make the trip, you'll see it's no problem—and you'll feel pretty smug saving $50 to $100 a night per double by not sleeping in the Old Town. Hotel u Šemíka and Guest House Lída are within a stone's throw of peaceful Vyšehrad Park, with a legendary castle on a cliff overlooking the Vltava River. Hotel Adalbert is on the grounds of an ancient monastery, and Pension Větrník is adjacent, with two of Prague's best-preserved natural areas (Star Park and Šárka) just a short walk away.

$$ Hotel Adalbert occupies an 18th-century building in the Břevnov Monastery (one of the Czech Republic's oldest monastic institutions, founded in 993). Meticulously restored after the return of the Benedictine monks in the 1990s, the monastery complex is the ultimate retreat for those who come to Prague for soul-searching or just wanting a quiet place away from the bustle. Join the monks for morning (7:00) and evening (18:00) Mass in the St. Margaret Basilica, a large and elegant Baroque church decorated with unusual simplicity. You can help yourself in the monastery fruit orchard, and eat in the atmospheric monastery pub (Klášterní Šenk). The hotel itself caters primarily to business clientele and takes ecology seriously: recycling, water conservation, and free tram tickets for guests. I prefer the first-floor rooms, as some of the attic rooms—room numbers in the 200s—feel a bit cramped (Sb-2,300 Kč, Db-3,200 Kč, extra bed-1,050 Kč, less on weekends, ask for 15 percent Rick Steves discount when you reserve, Wi-Fi, free parking, halfway between city and airport at Markétská 1, Praha 6, tram #22 to Břevnovský Klášter; 5 min by tram beyond the castle, 20 min from Old and New Towns; tel. 220-406-170, fax 220-406-190, www.hoteladalbert.cz, info@hoteladalbert.cz).

$$ Hotel u Šemíka, named for a heroic mythical horse, offers 25 rooms in a quiet residential neighborhood just below Vyšehrad Castle and the Slavín cemetery where Dvořák, Mucha, and Čapek are buried. It's a 10-minute tram ride south of the Old Town (Sb-2,000 Kč, Db-2,650 Kč, apartment-3,350–3,700 Kč for 2–4 people, extra bed-600 Kč, ask for the "direct booking" Rick Steves 10 percent discount, Internet access; from the center, take tram #3, #17, or #21 to Výtoň, go under rail bridge, and walk 3 blocks uphill to Vratislavova 36; Praha 2, tel. 224-920-736, fax 224-911-602, www.usemika.cz, usemika@usemika.cz).

$ Pension Větrník fills an attractive white-and-orange former 18th-century windmill in one of Prague's most popular

residential areas, right next to the Břevnov Monastery and midway between the airport and the city. The talkative owner, Miloš Opatrný, is a retired, prizewinning Czech chef whose culinary work took him as far as Japan. On request, he will gladly prepare a meal you won't forget. The six rooms here are the pride of the Opatrný family, who live on the upper floors. The garden has a red-clay tennis court—rackets and balls are provided (Db-2,200 Kč, suite-3,300 Kč, extra bed-550 Kč, Internet access, U Větrníku 1, Praha 6; airport bus #179 stops near the house, tram #18 goes straight to Charles Bridge, both take 20 min; tel. 220-612-404, fax 220-513-390, www.vetrnik1722.cz, pension@vetrnik1722.cz).

$ Guest House Lída, with 12 homey and spacious rooms, fills a big house in a quiet residential area farther inland, a 15-minute tram ride from the center. Jan, Jiří, and Jitka Prouza, who run the place, are a wealth of information and know how to make people feel at home (Sb-1,380 Kč, small Db-1,440 Kč, Db-1,760 Kč, Tb-2,110 Kč, Qb-2,530 Kč, cash only, family rooms, top-floor family suite with kitchenette, Internet access, parking garage-200 Kč/day, Metro: Pražského Povstání; exit Metro and turn left on Lomnického between the Metro station and big blue-glass ČSOB building, follow Lomnického for 500 yards, then turn left on Lopatecká, go uphill and ring bell at Lopatecká #26, no sign outside; Praha 4, tel. & fax 261-214-766, www.lidabb.eu, lidabb@seznam.cz). The Prouza brothers also rent four **apartments** across the river, an equal distance from the center (Db-1,600 Kč, Tb-1,900 Kč, Qb-2,100 Kč).

Hostels in the Center

It's tough to find a double for less than 2,500 Kč in the old center. But Prague has an abundance of fine hostels—each with a distinct personality, and each excellent in its own way for anyone wanting a 300-500-Kč dorm bed or an extremely simple, twin-bedded room for about 1,300 Kč. With travelers seeking cheaper options these days, it's good to keep in mind that hostels are no longer the exclusive domain of backpackers. The first two hostels are centrally located; the last two are found in workaday neighborhoods and have atmospheric interiors.

$ Old Prague Hostel is a small and friendly place with 70 beds on the second and third floors of an apartment building on a back alley near the Powder Tower. The spacious rooms were once apartment bedrooms, so it feels less institutional than most hostels. You can hang out in the comfy TV lounge/breakfast room. Older travelers would feel comfortable in this mellow place (D-1,400 Kč, bunk in 4- to 8-person room-400–500 Kč; includes breakfast, sheets, towels, lockers, and free Internet access; in summer reserve 2 weeks ahead for doubles, a few days ahead for bunks; Benediktská

2, see map on page 127 for location, tel. 224-829-058, fax 224-829-060, www.oldpraguehostel.com, oldpraguehostel@seznam.cz).

$ Hostel Týn is hidden in a silent courtyard two blocks from the Old Town Square. Because the management is aware of its value, they don't bother being too friendly (D-1,240 Kč, T-1,410 Kč, bunk in 4- to 5-bed co-ed room-420 Kč, lockers, Internet access, kitchen, no breakfast, reserve one week ahead, Týnská 19, see map on page 127, tel. 224-828-519, mobile 776-122-057, www.hosteltyn.com, roomservice@seznam.cz).

$ Sir Toby's is in a 1930s working-class neighborhood—a newly popular residential and dining-out area that's a 12-minute tram ride from the center. Sir Toby's owners have taken great pains to stamp the place with character: restored hardwood floors, a back garden with tables made out of sewing machines, and rooms filled with vintage 1930s furniture and photographs. Amenities include self- and full-service laundry, an on-site pub, and a friendly staff (120 beds, S-1,200 Kč, Db-1,640 Kč, Tb-1,840 Kč, bunk in 4- to 6-bed co-ed room-480 Kč, bunk in 8- to 10-bed co-ed room-340 Kč, take tram #5 from the main train station or tram #3 from the middle of Wenceslas Square to Dělnická, at Dělnická 24, Praha 7, tel. 246-032-610, www.sirtobys.com). They also run two contemporary-design hostels in Vinohrady.

$ Hostel Elf, a 10-minute walk from the main train station or one bus stop from the Florenc Metro station, is fun-loving, ramshackle, covered with noisy, self-inflicted graffiti, and the wildest of these hostels. They offer cheap, basic beds, a helpful staff, and lots of creative services—kitchen, free luggage room, free Internet access, laundry, no lockout, free tea, cheap beer, a terrace, and lockers (120 beds, D-1,100 Kč, bunk in 6- to 11-person room-320 Kč, includes sheets and breakfast, cash only, reserve four days ahead, Husitská 11, Praha 3, take bus #133 or #207 from Florenc Metro station for one stop to U Památníku, tel. 222-540-963, www.hostelelf.com, info@hostelelf.com).

Eating in Prague

A big part of Prague's charm is found in wandering aimlessly through the city's winding old quarters, marveling at the architecture, watching the people, and sniffing out fun restaurants. You can eat well here for very little money. What you'd pay for a basic meal in Vienna or Munich will get you a feast in Prague. In addition to meat-and-potatoes Czech cuisine (see "Czech Food" on page 44), you'll find trendy, student-oriented bars and lots of fine ethnic eateries. For ambience, the options include traditional, dark Czech beer halls; elegant Art Nouveau dining rooms; and hip, modern cafés.

Watch out for scams. Many restaurants put more care into ripping off green tourists (and even locals) than into their cooking. Tourists are routinely served cheaper meals than what they ordered, given a menu with a "personalized" price list, charged extra for things they didn't get, or shortchanged. Speak Czech. Even saying "Hello" in Czech (see the Czech Survival Phrases on page 1119) will get you better service. Avoid any menu without clear and explicit prices. Be careful of waiters padding the tab. Closely examine your itemized bill and understand each line (a 10 percent service charge is sometimes added—in that case, there's no need to tip extra). Tax is always included in the price, so it shouldn't be tacked on later. Part with very large bills only if necessary, and deliberately count your change. Never let your credit card out of your sight. Make it a habit to get cash from an ATM to pay for your meals. (Credit cards can cost merchants as much as 10 percent.) Remember, there are two parallel worlds in Prague: the tourist town and the real city. Generally, if you walk two minutes away from the tourist flow, you'll find better value, atmosphere, and service. (For more on scams, see "Rip-Offs in Prague," page 56.)

I've listed these eating and drinking establishments by neighborhood. The most options—and highest prices—are in the Old Town. If you want a memorable splurge, see the "Dining with Style" section. For a light meal, consider one of Prague's many cafés (see the "Cafés" section). Many of the places listed here are handy for an efficient lunch, but may not offer fine evening dining. Others make less sense for lunch, but are great for a slow, drawn-out dinner. Read the descriptions to judge which is which.

Fun, Touristy Neighborhoods: Several areas are pretty and well-situated for sightseeing, but lined only with touristy restaurants. While these places are not necessarily bad values, I've listed only a few of your many options—just survey the scene in these spots and choose whatever looks best. Kampa Square, just off the Charles Bridge, feels like a small-town square. Havelská Market is surrounded by colorful little eateries, any of which give a fine perch for viewing the market scene while you munch. The massive Old Town Square is *the* place to nurse a drink or enjoy a meal while watching the tide of people, both tourists and locals, sweep back and forth. There's often some event on this main square, and its many restaurants provide tasty and relaxing vantage points.

Dining with a View: For great views, consider these options: **Restaurant u Prince Terrace** (rooftop dining above a fancy hotel, completely touristy but awesome views, described on page 60); **Villa Richter** (next to Prague Castle, above Malostranská Metro stop, described on page 146); the **Bellavista Restaurant** at Strahov Monastery; **Petřínské Terasy** and **Nebozízek** next to the funicular stop halfway up Petřín Hill; and the many overpriced but elegant places serving scenic meals along the riverbanks. For the best cheap riverside dinner, have a picnic on a paddleboat (see page 69). There's nothing like drifting down the middle of the Vltava River as the sun sets, while munching on a picnic meal and sipping a beer with your favorite travel partner.

In or near the Old Town

Characteristically Czech Places

With the inevitable closing of cheap student pubs (replaced by shops and hotels that make more money), it's getting difficult to find a truly Czech pub in the historic city center. Most Czechs no longer go to "traditional" eateries, preferring the cosmopolitan taste of the world to the mundane taste of sauerkraut. As a result, ancient institutions with "authentic" Czech ambience have become touristy—but they're still great fun, a good value, and respected by locals. Expect wonderfully rustic spaces, smoke, surly service, and reasonably good, inexpensive food. Understand every line on your bill.

Restaurace u Pinkasů, with a menu that reads like a 19th-century newspaper, is a Prague institution, founded in 1843. It's best in summer, when you sit in the garden behind the building, in the shade of the Gothic buttresses of the St. Mary of the Snows Church. But its waiters could win the award for the rudest service in town (daily 9:00–24:00, tucked in a courtyard near the bottom of Wenceslas Square, on the border between Old and New towns—for location see map on page 132, Jungmannovo Náměstí 16, tel. 221-111-150).

Restaurace u Provaznice ("By the Ropemaker's Wife") has all the Czech classics, peppered with the story of a once-upon-a-time-faithful wife. (Check the menu for details of the gory story.) It's less touristy and less expensive than the other restaurants in this area. Natives congregate here for their famously good "pig leg" with horseradish and Czech mustard (daily 11:00–24:00, a block into the Old Town from the bottom of Wenceslas Square at Provaznická 3, tel. 224-232-528).

U Medvídků ("By the Bear Cubs"), which started out as a brewery in 1466, is now a flagship beer hall of the Czech Budweiser. The one large room is bright, noisy, touristy, and a bit smoky (daily 11:30–23:00, a block toward Wenceslas Square from Bethlehem

Restaurants in the Old Town

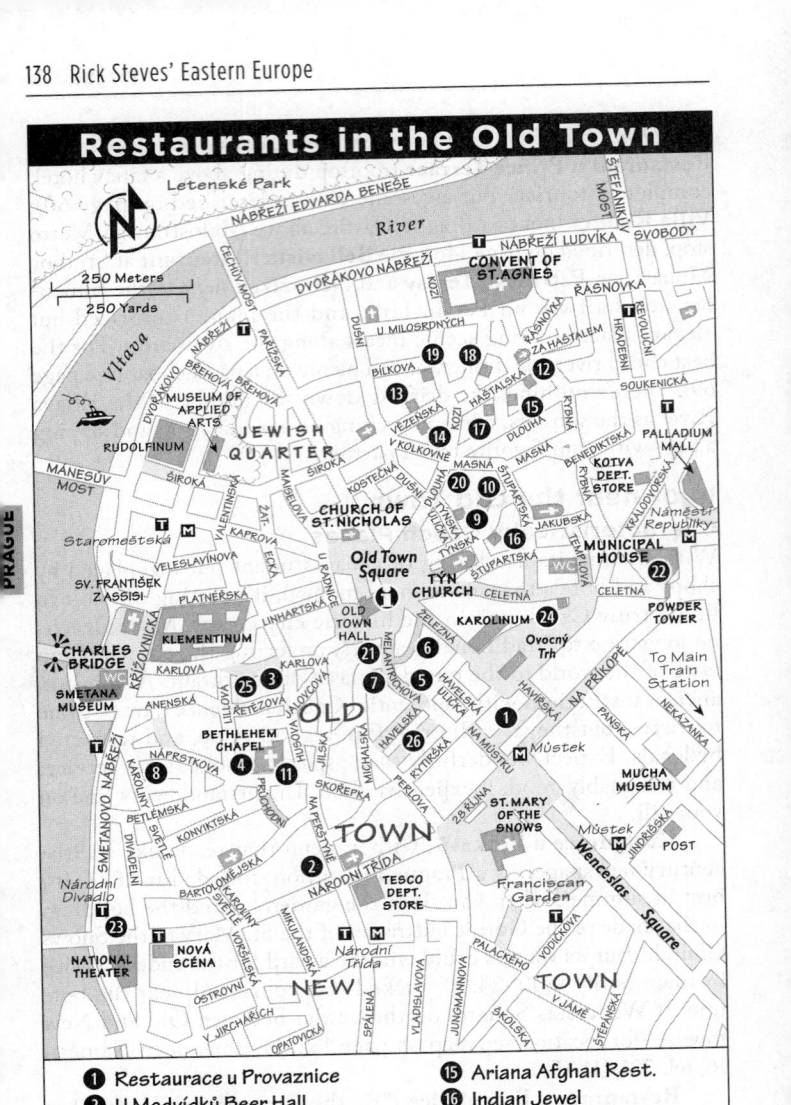

1. Restaurace u Provaznice
2. U Medvídků Beer Hall
3. U Zlatého Tygra Pub
4. Restaurace u Betlémské Kaple
5. Česká Kuchyně
6. Restaurace Mlejnice
7. Country Life Vegetarian Rest.
8. Lehká Hlava Vegetarian Rest.
9. Restaurace Maitrea
10. Beas Vegetarian Restaurant
11. Klub Architektů
12. Chez Marcel
13. Amici Miei Restaurant
14. Aldente Trattoria
15. Ariana Afghan Rest.
16. Indian Jewel
17. Orange Moon
18. Molly Malone's Irish Pub
19. La Casa Blů
20. Bohemia Bagel
21. Restaurant u Prince Terrace
22. Municipal House Eateries
23. Grand Café Slavia
24. Grand Café Orient
25. Café Montmartre & Ebel Coffee House
26. Havelská Market

Square at Na Perštýnì 7, tel. 224-211-916). The small beer bar next to the restaurant (daily 16:00–3:00 in the morning) is used by university students during emergencies—such as after most other pubs have closed.

U Zlatého Tygra ("By the Golden Tiger") has long embodied the proverbial Czech pub, where beer turns strangers into kindred spirits, who cross the fuzzy line between memory and imagination as they tell their hilarious life stories to each other. Today, "The Tiger" is a buzzing shrine to one of its longtime regulars, the writer Bohumil Hrabal, whose fictions immortalize many of the colorful characters that once warmed the wooden benches here. Only regulars have reserved tables. If you find a rare empty spot, you'll be treated as a surprise guest rather than a customer (daily 15:00–23:00, just south of Karlova at Husova 17, tel. 222-221-111).

Hospoda u Nováka, behind the National Theater (i.e., not so central), is emphatically Czech, with few tourists. It takes good care of its regulars (you'll see the old monthly beer tabs in a rack just inside the door). Nostalgic communist-era signs are everywhere. During that time, pubs like this were close-knit communities where regulars escaped from the depression of daily life. Today, the U Nováka is a bright and smoky hangout where you can still happily curse whatever regime you happen to live under. While the English menu lists the well-executed Czech classics, it doesn't list the cheap daily specials (daily 10:00–23:00, V Jirchářích 2—see map on page 132, tel. 224-930-639).

Pivovarský Dům ("The Brewhouse"), on the corner of Ječná and Lípová in the New Town, is popular with locals for its rare variety of fresh beers (yeast, wheat, and fruit-flavored), fine classic Czech dishes, and an inviting interior that mixes traditonal and modern (daily 11:00–23:00, reservations recommended in the evenings; walk up Štěpánská street from Wenceslas Square for 10 minutes, or take tram #22 for two stops from Národní to Štěpánská; Lípová 15—see map on page 132, tel. 296-216-666, variety of beer mugs sold).

Restaurace u Betlémské Kaple, behind Bethlehem Chapel, is not "ye olde" Czech. It has light wooden decor, cheap lunch deals, and fish specialties that attract natives and visitors in search of a good Czech bite for Czech prices (daily 11:00–23:00, Betlémské Náměstí 2, tel. 222-221-639).

Česká Kuchyně ("Czech Kitchen") is a blue-collar cafeteria serving steamy old Czech cuisine to a local clientele. It's fast, practical, cheap, and traditional as can be. There's no English inside, so—if you want apple charlotte, but not tripe soup—be sure to review the small English menu in the window outside before entering. Note the numbers of your preferred dishes (they correspond to the Czech menu inside), pick up your tally sheet as you enter, grab

a tray, point liberally to whatever you'd like, and keep the paper to pay as you exit. It's extremely cheap...unless you lose your paper (daily 9:00–20:00, very central, across from Havelská Market at Havelská 23, tel. 224-235-574).

Restaurace Mlejnice ("The Mill") is a fun little pub strewn with farm implements and happy eaters, located just out of the tourist crush two blocks from the Old Town Square. They serve hearty traditional and modern Czech plates for 150–180 Kč. Reservations are smart in the evening (daily 11:00–24:00, between Melantrichova and Železná at Kožná 14, tel. 224-228-635).

Hip Restaurants

Country Life Vegetarian Restaurant is a bright, easy, non-smoking cafeteria with a well-displayed buffet of salads and hot veggie dishes. It's midway between the Old Town Square and the bottom of Wenceslas Square. They're serious about their vegetarianism, serving only plant-based, unprocessed, and unrefined food. Its dining area is quiet and elegantly woody for a cafeteria, with three tables and wicker chairs outside in the courtyard (Sun–Thu 9:00–20:30, Fri 9:00–17:00, closed Sat, through courtyard at Melantrichova 15/Michalská 18, tel. 224-213-366).

Lehká Hlava Vegetarian Restaurant ("Clear Head"), tucked away on a cul-de-sac, has a mission to provide a "clear atmosphere for enjoying food." Sitting in an enchanted-forest setting, diners enjoy dishes from around the world. Reserve in advance for evenings (100–150-Kč plates, two-course 90-Kč daily special, no eggs, no smoke, lots of vegan dishes, daily 11:30–23:30, between Bethlehem Chapel and the river at Boršov 2, tel. 222-220-665).

Restaurace Maitrea, just off the Old Town Square alongside the Týn Church, builds on the success of its older sibling, Lehká Hlava (listed above). Every inch of the modern interior is curved to ensure the "unobstructed flow of energy." None of the imaginative vegetarian dishes duplicates those served at Lehká Hlava. The 105-Kč lunch special is a great value (Mon–Fri 11:30–23:30, Sat–Sun 12:00–23:30, Týnská ulička 6, tel. 221-711-631).

Beas is a cheap vegetarian restaurant ruled by a Punjabi chef who concocts mild *thalis* (mixed platters in the style of the north Indian plains) and *dosas* (south Indian crêpes). Tucked away in a courtyard behind the Týn Church, this place is popular with university students (Mon–Sat 9:30–20:00, Sun 10:00–18:00, Týnská 19, mobile 608-035-727).

Klub Architektů, next to Bethlehem Chapel, is a modern hangout in a medieval cellar that serves excellent original dishes, hearty salads, Moravian wines, and Slovak beer (daily, Betlémské Náměstí 169, tel. 224-401-214).

At **Le Patio,** on the big and busy Národní Třída, the first

thing you'll notice are the many lanterns suspended from the ceiling—and the big ship moored out back (OK, just its hulking bow). Le Patio has a hip, continental feel, but for a place that also sells furniture (head straight back and down the stairs), it definitely needs comfier dining chairs. The atmosphere is as pleasant and carefully designed as the dishes, with international fare from India, France, and points in between. There's always a serious vegetarian option available (200–350-Kč plates, daily 8:00–23:00, Národní 22—see map on page 132, tel. 224-934-375). Diners enjoy live music on Friday and Saturday nights (19:30–22:30).

Ethnic Eateries and Bars near Dlouhá Street

Dlouhá, the wide street leading away from the Old Town Square behind the Jan Hus Memorial (left of Týn Church), is lined with ethnic restaurants catering mostly to cosmopolitan locals. Within a couple of blocks, you can eat your way around the world. From Dlouhá, wander the Rámová/Haštalská/Vězeňská area to survey a United Nations of eateries: You'll find French (**Chez Marcel** at Haštalská 12 is understandably popular—with a fun-loving wait-staff, cash only); Italian (**Amici Miei** at Vězeňská 5 prides itself on fresh *pesci* and *frutti di mare*, while the **Aldente Trattoria,** directly across the street, has a genuinely rustic Italian feel); and Afghan (**Ariana** at Rámová 6 serves up a taste of Central Asia at Czech prices). These five deserve special consideration:

Indian: **Indian Jewel**, in the Ungelt courtyard behind the Týn Church, is the best place in Prague to find a full Indian menu that actually tastes Indian. Located in a pleasant, artfully restored courtyard, this is my choice for outdoor dining, with seriously executed subcontinental classics and good-value lunch specials (daily 11:00–23:00, Týn 6, tel. 222-310-156).

Thai: **Orange Moon** specializes in Thai curries, but you'll also find dishes from Myanmar (Burma) and India, served in a space delightfully decorated with artwork from Southeast Asia. This restaurant attracts a mixture of locals, expats, and tourists—as well as a mixture of wait-staff attitudes (daily 11:30–23:30, reservations recommended, Rámová 5, tel. 222-325-119).

Irish: **Molly Malone's Irish Pub,** hidden in a forgotten corner of the Jewish Quarter, may seem like a strange recommendation in Prague—home of some of the world's best beer—but it has the kind of ambience that locals (and few tourists) seek out. Molly Malone's has been the expat and local favorite for Guinness ever since the Velvet Revolution enabled the Celts to return to one of their homelands. Worn wooden floors, dingy walls, and the Irish manager transport you right into the heart of blue-collar Dublin—which is, after all, a popular place for young Czechs to find jobs in the high-tech industry (Sun–Thu 11:00–1:00 in the morning,

Fri–Sat 11:00–2:00 in the morning, U Obecního Dvora 4, tel. 224-818-851).

Latin American: **La Casa Blů,** with cheap lunch specials, Mexican plates, Staropramen beer, and greenish *mojitos,* is your own little pueblo in Prague. It's one of the last student bastions in the Old Town—and one of the first bars in the city to go non-smoking. Painted in warm orange-and-red and guarded by creatures from Mayan mythology, La Casa Blů is packed nightly with guitar music and a fusion of Czechs and Chileans (Mon–Sat 11:00–23:00, Sun 14:00–23:00, on the corner of Kozí and Bílkova, tel. 224-818-270).

North American: **Bohemia Bagel** is hardly authentic—exasperated Czechs insist that bagels have nothing to do with Bohemia. Owned by an American, this practical café caters mostly to youthful tourists, with good sandwiches (100–125 Kč), a little garden out back, and Internet access (1.50 Kč/min). If homesick, you'll love the menu, with everything from Philly cheesesteaks to bacon and eggs (daily 7:00–24:00, Masná 2, tel. 224-812-560).

In the Jewish Quarter

These three eateries are well-located to break up a demanding tour of the Jewish Quarter—all within two blocks of each other on or near Široká (see map on page 83). Also consider the nearby ethnic eateries listed above.

Kolkovna, the flagship of a franchise owned by Pilsner Urquell, is big and woody, yet modern, serving a fun mix of Czech and international cuisine—ribs, salads, cheese plates, and good beer (a bit overpriced but good energy, daily 11:00–24:00, across from Spanish Synagogue at V Kolkovně 8, tel. 224-819-701).

Franz Kafka Café, with a cool, dark, and woody interior strewn with historic photos of the ghetto and a few good sidewalk tables, is great for a relaxing salad, sandwich, snack, or drink (150-Kč salads, daily 10:00–21:00, one block from the cemetery at Široká 12).

Restaurace U Knihovny ("By the Library"), situated steps away from the City and National Libraries as well as the Pinkas Synagogue, is a favorite lunch spot for locals who work nearby. Their cheap daily lunch specials consist of seven imaginative variations on traditional Czech themes. The service is friendly, and the stylish red-brick interior is warm. Smoking is not permitted during lunch (daily 11:00–23:00, on the corner of Veleslavínova and Valentinská, mobile 732-835-876).

Dining with an Old Town Square View

Restaurant u Prince Terrace, in the five-star U Prince Hotel facing the Astronomical Clock, is designed for foreign tourists.

A sleek elevator takes you to its rooftop, where every possible inch is used to serve good food (international with plenty of fish) from their open-air grill. The view is arguably the best in town—especially at sunset. The menu is a fun but overpriced mix, with photos that make ordering easy. Being in such a touristy spot, waiters are experts at nicking you with confusing menu charges; don't be afraid to confirm exact prices before ordering. This place is also great for just a drink at sunset or late at night (fine salads, 240–300-Kč plates, daily until 24:00, brusque staff, outdoor heaters when necessary, Staroměstské Náměstí 29, tel. 224-213-807—but no reservations possible).

Art Nouveau Splendor in the Municipal House

The Municipal House (Obecní Dům), the sumptuous Art Nouveau concert hall, has three restaurants: a café, a French restaurant, and a beer cellar (all at Náměstí Republiky 5). The dressy café, **Kavárna Obecní Dům,** is drenched in chandeliered, Art Nouveau elegance and offers the best value and experience here. Light, pricey meals and drinks come with great atmosphere and bad service (250-Kč three-course special daily for lunch or dinner, open daily 7:30–23:00, live piano or jazz trio 16:00–20:00, tel. 222-002-763). The fine and formal French restaurant in the next wing oozes Mucha elegance (700–1,000-Kč meals, daily 12:00–16:00 & 18:00–23:00, tel. 222-002-777). The beer cellar is overpriced and touristy (daily 11:30–23:00).

Cafés

Dripping with history, these places are as much about the ambience as they are about the coffee. Most cafés also serve sweets and light meals.

Grand Café Slavia, across from the National Theater (facing the Legií Bridge on Národní street), is a fixture in Prague, famous as a hangout for its literary elite. Today, it's tired and clearly past its prime, with an Art Deco interior, lousy piano entertainment, and celebrity photos on the wall. But its iconic status makes it a fun stop for a coffee—skip the food (daily 8:00–23:00, sit as near the river as possible, tel. 224-218-493). Notice the *Drinker of Absinthe* painting on the wall (and on the menu for 55 Kč)—with the iconic Czech writer struggling with reality.

Café Louvre is a longtime elegant favorite (opened in 1902) that still draws an energetic young crowd. From the big and busy Národní street, you walk upstairs into a venerable world of

newspapers on sticks (including English) and waiters in vests and aprons. The back room has long been the place for billiard tables (100 Kč/hr). An English flier tells its history (200-Kč plates, 120-Kč two-course lunch offered 11:00–15:00, open daily 8:00–23:30, Národní 22—see map on page 132, tel. 224-930-949).

Grand Café Orient is just one flight up off busy Celetná street, yet a world away from the crush of tourism below. Located in the Black Madonna House, the café is upstairs from the entrance to the Museum of Czech Cubism and fittingly decorated with a Cubist flair. With its stylish, circa-1910 decor toned to dark green, this space is full of air and light—and a good value as well (salads, sandwiches, great balcony seating, Mon–Fri 9:00–22:00, Sat–Sun 10:00–22:00, Ovocný Trh 19, at the corner of Celetná near the Powder Tower, tel. 224-224-240).

Café Montmartre, on a small street parallel to Karlova, combines Parisian ambience with unbeatable Czech prices for coffee (no food served). Dreamy Czech minds found their quiet asylum here after Grand Café Slavia (listed earlier) and other longtime favorites either closed down or became stuck in their past. The main room is perfect for discussing art and politics, while the intimate room behind the courtyard is where you recite poetry to your date (Mon–Fri 9:00–23:00, Sat–Sun 12:00–23:00, Řetězová 7, tel. 222-221-244).

Ebel Coffee House, next door to Café Montmartre, prides itself on its wide assortment of fresh brews from every coffee-bean-growing country in the world, inviting cakes, and a colorful setting that delights the mind as much as the caffeine does (daily 9:00–22:00, Řetězová 3, tel. 224-895-788).

John & George Café, in the courtyard on the other side of the Lennon Wall, is a secluded spot serving raspberry drinks, fresh sandwiches, and Italian coffee next to a flower garden, an English lawn, and one of the oldest trees in Prague (daily 11:00–22:00, Velkopřevorské Náměstí 4, look for small gate at left end of Lennon Wall, entrance to indoor seating area is another 20 yards to the left, see map on page 130, tel. 257-217-736).

Teahouses

Many Czech people are bohemian philosophers at heart and prefer the mellow, smoke-free environs of a teahouse to the smoky, traditional beer hall. Young Czechs are much more interested in traveling to exotic destinations like Southeast Asia, Africa, or Peru than to Western Europe, so the Oriental teahouses set their minds in vacation mode.

While there are teahouses all over town, a fine example in a handy locale is Prague's original one, established in 1991. **Dobrá Čajovna** ("Good Teahouse"), just a few steps off the

bustle of Wenceslas Square, takes you into a very peaceful world that elevates tea to an almost religious ritual. At the desk, you'll be given an English menu and a bell. Grab a seat and study the menu, which lovingly describes each tea. The menu lists a world of tea (very fresh, prices by the small pot), "accompaniments" (such as Exotic Miscellany), and light meals "for hungry tea drinkers." When you're ready to order, ring your bell to beckon a tea monk—likely a member of the Lovers of Tea Society (Mon–Sat 10:00–21:30, Sun 14:00–21:30, near the base of Wenceslas Square, opposite McDonald's at Václavské Náměstí 14, tel. 224-231-480).

For actual taste of tea from Prague's newly emerging Chinese middle class (rather than from some Czech's dreams of the Orient), head to **Čajový Klub** ("Tea Club") **Cha Dao**, just opposite the Jerusalem Synagogue. Creatively run by a cultured man from Beijing, here you'll find red cherry-wood decor, expertly served tea, and the freshest green leaves in town (Mon–Fri 10:00–21:00, Sat 11:00–21:00, closed Sun, Jeruzalémská 10, tel. 222-721-072).

In the Little Quarter

These characteristic eateries are handy for a bite before or after your Prague Castle visit. For locations, see the map on page 130.

U Sedmi Švábů ("By the Seven Roaches") is an ever-more-touristy den where even the cuisine is medieval. Since America had not yet been discovered in the Middle Ages, you won't find any corn, potatoes, or tomatoes on the menu. The salty yellow things that come with the Krušovice beer are chickpeas. Carnivores thrive here: Try the skewered meats *(špíz u Sedmi Švábů)*, flaming beef *(flambák)*, or pork knuckle (daily 11:00–23:00, Janský Vršek 14, tel. 257-531-455).

U Osla v Kolébce ("By the Donkey in the Cradle") fills a peaceful courtyard just a minute off the touristy hubbub of Nerudova. The laid-back scene consists of two restaurants with nearly identical simple menus, dominated by tasty sausages and salads (daily 10:00–22:00, Jánský Vršek 8, below Nerudova, next door to U Sedmi Švábů, mobile 731-407-036).

U Hrocha ("By the Hippo"), a very authentic little pub packed with beer-drinkers and smoke, serves simple, traditional meals—basically meat starters with bread. Just below the castle near Little Quarter Square (Malostranské Náměstí), it's actually the haunt of many members of parliament, which is located just around the corner (daily 12:00–23:00, chalkboard lists daily meals in English, Thunovská 10, tel. 257-533-389).

Restaurace Rybářský Klub, on Kampa Island overlooking the river, is run by the Society of Czech Fishermen and serves one of the widest selections of freshwater fish in Prague. Dine on fish-cream soup, pike, trout, carp, or catfish under the imaginative

artwork of Little Quarter painter Mr. Kuba. On warm evenings, late May through October, the Society fills its dock with tables—my choice for the best riverside dining in town (three-course meal for around 500 Kč, riverside menu not as extensive as indoor restaurant menu, daily 12:00–23:00, U Sovových Mlýnů 1, tel. 257-534-200).

In the Castle Quarter

To locate the following restaurants, see the map on page 108.

Villa Richter, at the end of the castle promontory and surrounded by newly replanted vineyards, consists of three classy restaurants: the ground-floor Piano Terra, with a menu built on Czech cooking (200–300-Kč entrées); the first-floor Piano Nobile, inspired by French and Italian cuisine (700-Kč entrées); and the outdoor Panorama Pergola, with superb views and ideal for an after-castle Caesar salad and glass of wine (all three open daily 10:00–23:00, Staré Zámecké Schody 6, tel. 257-219-079). Walk out of the castle gate near the Golden Lane, then turn left onto the path between the vines.

Klášterní Pivovar ("Monastery Brewery"), founded by an abbot in 1628 and reopened in 2004, has two large rooms, a pleasant courtyard, and typically unpleasant staff. This is the place to taste rare, unpasteurized yeast beer, brewed on the premises. The wooden decor and circa-1900 newspaper clippings (including Habsburg Emperor Franz Josef's "Proclamation to My Nations," announcing the beginning of the First World War) evoke the era when Vienna was Europe's artistic capital, Prague was building its faux Eiffel Tower, and life moved much slower than today. To accompany the beer, try the beer-flavored cheese served on toasted black-yeast bread (daily 10:00–22:00, Strahovské Nádvoří 301, tel. 233-353-155). It's directly across from the entrance to the Strahov Library (not to be confused with the enormous, group-oriented Klášterní Restaurace next door, to the right).

Restaurace Nad Úvozem is hidden in the middle of a staircase that connects Loretánská and Úvoz streets. This secret spot, which boasts super views of the Little Quarter and Petřín Hill, is one of the few places in the area for decent—but by no means exceptional—food in a secluded space. Try the roast beef in plum sauce (170 Kč). The service is slower when the restaurant is full, as the kitchen has limited space. Check your bill for "special charges" before you pay (daily 12:00–21:00; as you go down Loretánská watch for pans, scoops, and spoons hanging on chains on your right at #15; tel. 220-511-532). To discourage pub-goers from mingling with diners, the beer here is terribly overpriced (69 Kč).

Hostinec u Černého Vola ("By the Black Ox") is a smoky, dingy old-time pub—its survival in the midst of all the castle

splendor and tourism is a marvel. It feels like a kegger on the banks of the river Styx, with classic bartenders serving up Kozel beer (traditional "Goat" brand with excellent darks) and beer-friendly light meals. The pub is located on Loretánská (no sign outside, sniff for cigarette smoke and look for the only house on the block without an arcade, daily 10:00–22:00, English menu on request, tel. 220-513-481).

Malý Buddha ("Little Buddha") serves delightful food—especially vegetarian—and takes its theme seriously. You'll step into a mellow, low-lit escape of bamboo and peace, where you'll be served by people with perfect complexions and almost no pulse (Tue–Sun 13:00–22:30, closed Mon, non-smoking, between the castle and Strahov Monastery at Úvoz 46, tel. 220-513-894).

Espresso Kajetánka, just off Castle Square, has magnificent city views. It's a good-if-overpriced place for a drink or snack as you start or end your castle visit (daily 10:00–20:00, Ke Hradu, tel. 257-533-735).

Na Baště, more convenient but not as scenic, is in a garden through the gate to the left of the main castle entry. The outdoor seating, among Jože Plečnik's ramparts and obelisks, is the castle at its most peaceful (Sun–Thu 11:00–23:00, Fri–Sat 11:00–24:00, tel. 281-933-010).

Dining with Style

In Prague, a fancy candlelit dinner with fine wines and connoisseur-approved dishes costs more than most locals can afford—but it's still a bargain in comparison to similar restaurants in Paris or Dallas. I list only two such splurges: one aristocratic, Old World, and under the castle; one more modern, untouristy, and near the Old Town Square.

Restaurace David, with two little 18th-century rooms hiding on a small cobblestone street opposite the American Embassy in the Little Quarter, is my choice for a romantic splurge. The exquisite cuisine—a modern incarnation of traditional Czech dishes with French and European influences—ranges from game to roasted duck and liver. Your meal comes with the gourmet quotient of knives and fancy glasses, and measured, no-nonsense service (most meals 600–1,000 Kč, open daily, Tržiště 21—see map on page 130, tel. 257-533-109).

Restaurant Červená Tabulka ("Red Chalkboard") is in a low, nondescript townhouse in a quiet neighborhood outside of the tourist circus. Sit in the dressy candlelit interior or on the quiet and breezy cobbled courtyard. Either way, there's not a dumpling in sight. The menu features modern international dishes with a focus on fish (fine 300-Kč plates and gourmet presentation). The wines are excellent and a great value (daily 11:30–23:00, Lodecká 4, tel.

224-810-401). To get to the restaurant from the Municipal House, cross Náměstí Republiky and turn right onto Truhlářská; it's 200 yards down the street on the corner of quiet Petrské Náměstí Square (see map on page 132).

Prague Connections

Centrally located Prague is a logical gateway between Western and Eastern Europe. Prague is connected by convenient night trains to Budapest, Kraków, and Warsaw. Direct overnight trains also connect Prague to Amsterdam, Frankfurt, and Zürich; and several daily trains leave from Munich, Berlin, and Vienna. For information on Prague's airport, see "Arrival in Prague—By Plane," page 57.

You'll find handy Czech train and bus schedules at www.idos.cz; for trains, you can also check out Germany's all-Europe timetable at http://bahn.hafas.de/bin/query.exe/en. Remember that for all train connections, it's important to confirm which of Prague's stations to use.

Tickets: You can make express or international reservations and buy tickets at the conveniently located **Czech Railways' travel center** in the Broadway Mall between Na Příkopě and Celetná streets, near the Powder Tower (see map on page 89). Ask whether discounts are available for your journey, as the rail company has a complex scheme of special offers (Mon–Fri 9:00–17:00, closed Sat–Sun; quick, helpful, English-speaking staff; inside the mall passageway by T.G.I. Friday's, look for blue neon *ČD* sign on your right, Na Příkopě 31; tel. 972-243-071, www.cdtravel.cz, prodej@cdtravel.cz).

From Prague by Train to: Konopiště Castle (train to **Benešov**, hourly, 1 hr, then 30-min walk to castle), **Karlštejn** (2/hr, 40 min, then a 20-min walk to castle), **Křivoklát** (hourly, 1.5 hrs, transfer in Beroun), **Kutná Hora** (11/day, 1 hr, more with change in Kolín), **Terezín** (train to Bohušovice station, nearly hourly, 1–1.5 hrs; then 5-min taxi or bus ride), **Český Krumlov** (8/day, 1/day direct, 4 hrs—bus is faster, cheaper, and easier), **Budapest** (3/day, 7 hrs; more with 2–3 changes, 8.5 hrs; 1 night train, 7.5 hrs), **Kraków** (1/night direct, 10 hrs; 3/day including 1 direct, 8.5 hrs), **Warsaw** (2/day direct including 1 night train, more with changes, 8.5–10 hrs), **Vienna** (5/day direct, 4–4.5 hrs, more with 1 change, 5–6 hrs), **Berlin** (6/day, 4.5–5 hrs), **Munich** (2/day direct, 6.25 hrs; 6 more/day with express bus to Nürnberg then train to Munich, 5.25 hrs total; no night train), **Frankfurt** (almost hourly, 7–8.25 hrs).

From Prague by Bus to: Terezín (hourly, 50 min, departs from Nádraží Holešovice train station), **Český Krumlov** (7/day, 3.5

hrs, some leave from Florenc station, others leave from Na Knížecí station or Roztyly station.

By Car with a Driver: Mike's Chauffeur Service is a reliable, family-run company with fair and fixed rates around town and beyond. Friendly Mike's motto is, "We go the extra mile for you" (round-trip fares, with waiting time included, guaranteed through 2010 with this book: Český Krumlov-3,800 Kč, Terezín-1,900 Kč, Karlštejn-1,800 Kč, plus 5 percent gas surcharge, 4 percent surcharge for credit-card payment, these prices for up to 4 people, minivan for up to 6 and brand-new minibus for 7 also available, tel. 241-768-231, mobile 602-224-893, www.mike-chauffeur.cz, mike .chauffeur@cmail.cz). On the way to Krumlov, Mike will stop at no extra charge at Hluboká Castle or České Budějovice, where the original Bud beer is made.

Mike also offers "Panoramic Transfers" to **Vienna** (7,000 Kč, depart Prague at 8:00, arrive Český Krumlov at 10:00, stay up to 6 hrs, 1-hr scenic Czech riverside-and-village drive, then a 2-hr autobahn ride to your Vienna hotel, maximum 4 people), **Budapest** (8,900 Kč, 2 hrs to Český Krumlov, then 1-hr scenic drive to Linz, followed by 5–6 hrs on expressway to Budapest), and **Kraków** (8,900 Kč, with a stop at Auschwitz). Check Mike's website for special deals on last-minute transfers.

NEAR PRAGUE

Kutná Hora • Terezín Concentration Camp • Konopiště Castle • Karlštejn Castle • Křivoklát Castle

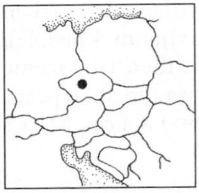

Prague has plenty to keep a traveler busy, but don't overlook the enjoyable day trips in the nearby Bohemian countryside. Within an hour of Prague (in different directions), you'll find a rich medieval town, a sobering concentration camp, and three grand castles.

Down-to-earth Kutná Hora was once home to the world's largest silver mine; it's now known for its opulent cathedral, built with riches from the mining bonanza. Terezín, a walled town, served as an internment camp for Jews during World War II. Two of the country's most popular castles—Konopiště (better interior) and Karlštejn (better exterior)—give you a good look at the Czech version of this European medieval architectural form. And Křivoklát Castle is one of the purest Gothic structures in the country, and a less touristy alternative to the other two castles.

Kutná Hora

Kutná Hora (KOOT-nah HO-rah) is a refreshingly authentic town of 20,000, on top of what was once Europe's largest silver mine. In its heyday, the mine was so productive that Kutná Hora was Bohemia's "second city" after Prague. The standard coinage of much of Europe was minted here. By about 1700, the mining and minting petered out, and the city slumbered. Once rich, then ignored, Kutná Hora is now newly appreciated by tourists looking for a handy side-trip from Prague. Visitors are charmed by the wonderfully preserved town and its interesting sights: the

fine St. Barbara's Cathedral, the fascinating silver mine, and the eerie Sedlec Bone Church.

Kutná Hora, unlike dolled-up Český Krumlov, is a typical Czech town. The shops on the main square cater to locals, and the factory between the Sedlec Bone Church and the train station has been the biggest tobacco processor in the country since the 1930s; it's now Philip Morris' headquarters for Central Europe. After touristy Prague, Kutná Hora is about as close to quintessential Czech life as you can get.

Getting to Kutná Hora

The town is 40 miles east of Prague. Direct trains from Prague's Main Station stop at Kutná Hora's Main Station, two miles from the town center (11/day, 1 hr; other trains are slower and require transfer in Kolín). From there, a local train shuttles visitors to Sedlec Station (near the Sedlec Bone Church), then to the central Město Station (near the rest of the sights).

In Prague, make sure to buy a ticket to the Kutná Hora Město Station rather than its Main Station—the price is nearly the same, and this gives you the flexibility to get off and on at any of the three Kutná Hora stations.

Planning Your Time

For the most efficient visit, visit the Sedlec Bone Church first. At Kutná Hora's Main Station, transfer to the local train or walk 10 minutes to the church. After your visit, ride the Bone Church's tourist minivan to St. Barbara's Cathedral in the town center. From the cathedral, walk to the silver museum and reserve your spot on the next English-language tour (or call the museum ahead to find out the schedule and reserve).

Orientation to Kutná Hora

Tourist Information

The main TI is on **Palackého Náměstí**, housed in the same building as the Alchemy Museum (April–Sept daily 9:00–18:00; Oct–March Mon–Fri 9:00–17:00, Sat–Sun 9:00–16:00; tel. 327-512-378, www.kutnahora.cz). It offers Internet access and also rents bicycles (220 Kč/day, mobile 605-802-874).

A small TI kiosk, with handy WCs, is in front of the **cathedral**; you can hire a local guide here. Ideally, reserve ahead (500 Kč/hr Tue–Sun, no tours Mon, tel. 327-516-710, mobile 736-485-408, infocentrum@kh.cz).

Sights in Kutná Hora

St. Barbara's Cathedral (Chrám Sv. Barbory)—The cathedral was founded in 1388 by miners, who dedicated it to their patron. The dazzling interior celebrates the town's sources of wealth, with frescoes featuring mining and minting. Even the Renaissance vault—a stunning feat of the two Gothic geniuses of Prague, Matyáš Rejsek and Benedict Ried—is decorated with miners' coats of arms. The artistic highlight is the Smíšek Chapel to the right of the altar. The late-Gothic frescoes—*The Arrival of the Queen of Sheba, The Trial of Trajan,* and especially the fresco under the chapel's window depicting two men with candles—are the only

works of a Dutch-trained master in Gothic Bohemia (50 Kč, daily 9:00–18:00 in summer, shorter hours off-season).

As you exit the cathedral, you'll see the Baroque Jesuit college on your left (currently being converted into an art gallery). Jesuits arrived here in 1626 with a mission: to make the Protestant population Catholic again. The statues of saints on the artificial terrace in front of the college were inspired by the statues on Charles Bridge in Prague.

Hrádek and the Czech Museum of Silver—At this museum, located in Kutná Hora's 15th-century castle, you'll see an exhibit on mining and an intriguing horse-powered winch that hoisted 2,000 pounds of rock at a time out of the mine. Then you'll don a miner's coat and helmet and climb deep into the mine for a wet, dark, and claustrophobic 45-minute tour of the medieval shafts that honeycomb the rock beneath the town (110 Kč, April–Oct Tue–Sun 10:00–18:00, closed Mon and Nov–March, tours generally every half-hour, tel. 327-512-159, www.cms-kh.cz). Try to time your visit to join an English-language tour (ask for Mr. Matuška, a charming retired miner). You can try calling ahead (the day before or the morning of your visit) to ask when English tours are scheduled—wait through the Czech recording, ask to speak with an English-speaker, and reserve a slot. Otherwise, drop by the museum soon after you arrive in Kutná Hora to find out the schedule and reserve.

Stone Fountain (Kamenná Kašna)—Because of intensive mining under the town, Kutná Hora has always struggled with the problem of obtaining clean drinking water. Water was brought to town by a sophisticated system of water pipes and stored in large tanks. At the end of the 15th century, the architect Rejsek built a 12-sided, richly decorated Gothic structure over one of these tanks. While no longer functioning, the fountain survives unchanged—the only structure like it in Bohemia (on the square called Rejskovo Náměstí).

Stone House (Kamenný Dům)—Notice the meticulous detail in the grape leaves, branches, and animals on this house's facade and up in its gable. Talented Polish craftsmen delicately carved the brittle stone into what was considered a marvel of its time. Skip the boring museum of local arts and crafts inside (40 Kč, daily 10:00–17:00, Radnická 183).

Alchemy Museum—The only one of its kind in the Czech Republic, this place is run by a gracious, eccentric Englishman who (upon request) will personally guide you into the surprisingly deep medieval cellars of this otherwise unassuming house. There you'll find a laboratory dedicated to the pursuit of *prima materia* (primal matter). The English descriptions do a good job explaining the goals and methods of alchemy, and the fate of its failed

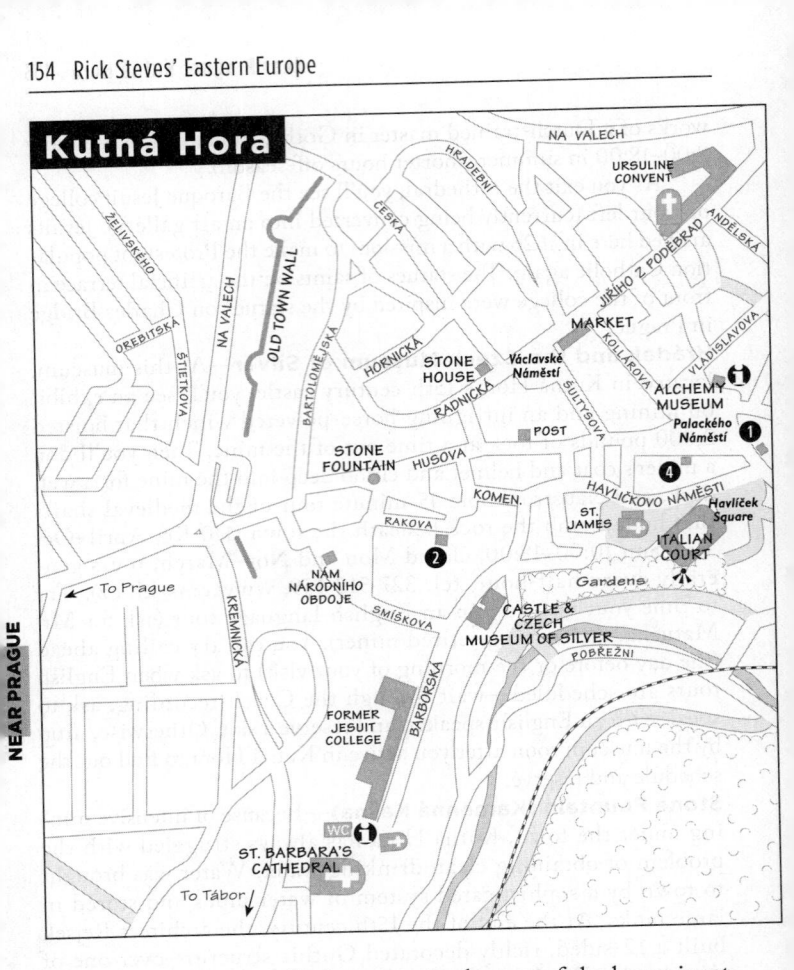

practitioners. The rare Gothic tower in the rear of the house is set up as an alchemist's study (complete with ancient books), looking much as it did when a prince used this vaulted space in his quest to purify matter and spirit (50 Kč, daily April–Oct 10:00–17:00, Nov–March 10:00–16:00, on the main square in the same building as the TI, tel. 327-511-259, mobile 603-308-024, www.alchemy.cz).

Upstairs from the TI is another quirky museum, featuring a collection of baby strollers from the Victorian era to the present.

Italian Court (Vlašský Dvůr)—This palace, located on the site where Czech currency was once made, became Europe's most important mint and the main residence of Czech kings in the 1400s. Today, it hosts a museum on minting and local history. The entry fee gets you into the main Gothic hall (now a wedding chamber) and the Art Nouveau–decorated St. Wenceslas Chapel (70 Kč, April–Sept daily 9:00–18:00, shorter hours Oct–March, Havlíčkovo Náměstí). Neither the museum nor the building

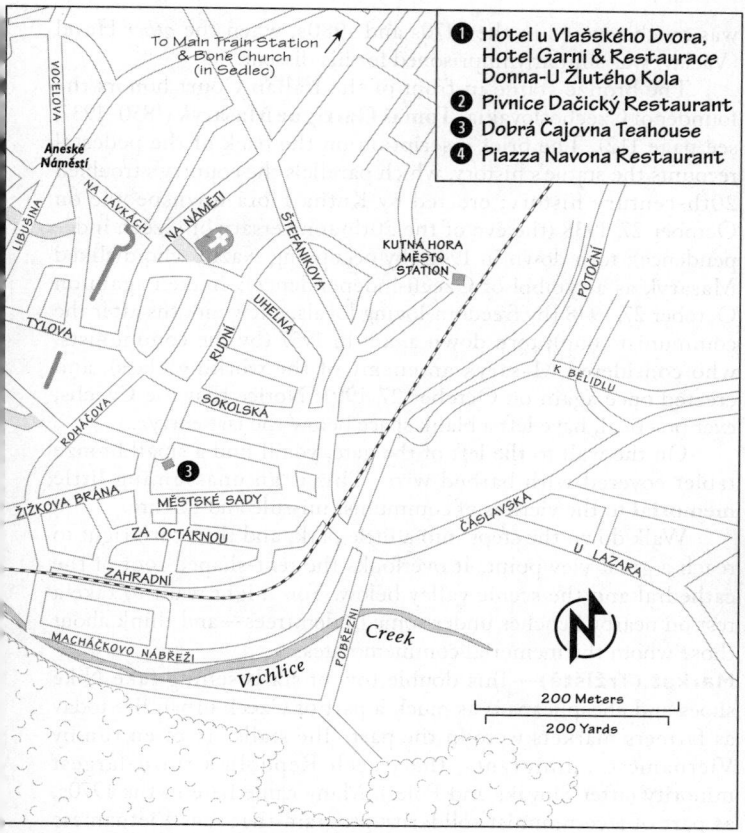

itself—largely a 19th-century imitation of the former palace—is particularly interesting. The flower-filled square in front, on the other hand, is worth a look...

Havlíček Square (Havlíčkovo Náměstí)—The monuments on this square are a *Who's Who* of important Czech patriots.

The statue in the middle of the square (and the square's namesake) is **Karel Havlíček** (1821–1856), the founder of Czech political journalism. From Kutná Hora, Havlíček ran an influential magazine highly critical of the Habsburg government. In 1851, he was forced into exile and detained for five years in the Tirolean Alps under police surveillance. His integrity is reflected by the quote inscribed on the statue: "You can try to bribe me with favors, you can threaten me, you can torture me, yet I will never turn a traitor." His motto became an inspiration for generations of Czech intellectuals, most of whom faced a similar combination of threats and temptations. Havlíček (whose name means "little Havel")

was much revered in the 1970s and 1980s, when the *other* Havel (Václav) was similarly imprisoned for his dissent.

The bronze statue in front of the Italian Court honors the founder of Czechoslovakia, **Tomáš Garrigue Masaryk** (1850–1937; see page 112). The brief inscription on the back of the pedestal recounts the statue's history, which parallels the country's troubled 20th-century history: erected by Kutná Hora townspeople on October 27, 1938 (the eve of the 20th anniversary of Czech independence); torn down in 1942 (by occupying Nazis, who disliked Masaryk as a symbol of Czech independence); erected again on October 27, 1948 (by freedom-loving locals, a few months after the communist coup); torn down again in 1957 (by the communists, who considered Masaryk an enemy of the working class); and erected once again on October 27, 1991. Notice that the Czechs, ever practical, have left a blank space below the last entry....

On the wall to the left of the gate, you'll find a small bronze tablet covered with barbed wire. This is an unassuming little **memorial** to the victims of communist misrule and torture.

Walk down the steps into a little park, and then turn right to reach a great viewpoint. It overlooks the tent-shaped roof of the cathedral and the scenic valley below. You might want to take a rest on nearby benches under some linden trees—and think about those whom the memorial commemorates.

Market (Tržiště)—This double row of stalls selling fake Nike shoes and cheap jeans is as much a part of Czech urban life today as farmers markets were in the past. The stalls are often run by Vietnamese immigrants, the Czech Republic's third-largest minority (after Slovaks and Poles). Many came here in the 1970s, as part of a communist solidarity program that sent Vietnamese workers to Czech textile factories. They learned the language, adapted to the environment, and, after 1989, set off on a road to entrepreneurial success that allowed them to bring over friends and relatives (Mon–Fri 7:30–16:45, shorter hours Sat, closed Sun, near Stone House).

Near Kutná Hora

Sedlec Bone Church (Kostnice u Sedlci)—Located a mile away from the center of town, in Sedlec, this little church looks normal on the outside. But inside, the bones of 40,000 people decorate the walls and ceilings. The 14th-century plagues and 15th-century wars provided all the raw material necessary for the creepily creative monks who made these designs. Those who first placed these bones 400 years ago

Sleep Code

(18 Kč = about $1, country code: 420)
S = Single, **D** = Double/Twin, **T** = Triple, **Q** = Quad, **b** = bathroom, **s** = shower only. Unless otherwise noted, prices include breakfast.

To help you sort easily through these listings, I've divided the rooms into three categories based on the price for a standard double room with bath:

$$$ Higher Priced—Most rooms 1,500 Kč or more.
$$ Moderately Priced—Most rooms between 1,000–1,500 Kč.
$ Lower Priced—Most rooms 1,000 Kč or less.

wanted viewers to remember that the earthly church is a community of both the living and the dead, a countless multitude that will one day stand before God. Later bone-stackers were more interested in design than theology...as evidenced by the chandelier that includes every bone in the human body (50 Kč, daily April–Sept 8:00–18:00, March and Oct 9:00–17:00, Nov–Feb 9:00–16:00, tel. 327-561-143, www.kostnice.cz).

The Bone Church runs a **tourist minivan** that can shuttle you around town (35 Kč/person, requires three passengers or else pay the 105-Kč minimum fee, April–Sept 9:00–18:00, Oct–March 9:00–17:00, inquire at the desk, mobile 733-551-011).

Sleeping in Kutná Hora

Although one day is enough for Kutná Hora, staying overnight saves you money (hotels are much cheaper here than in Prague) and allows you to better savor the atmosphere of a small Czech town.

$$ Hotel u Vlašského Dvora and **Hotel Garni** are two newly renovated townhouses run by the same management. Furnished in a mix of 1930s and modern style, the hotels come with access to a fitness center and sauna. Hotel Garni is slightly nicer (Db-1,200 Kč, a few steps off main square at Havlíčkovo Náměstí 513, tel. 327-515-773, www.vlasskydvur.cz).

Eating in Kutná Hora

Pivnice Dačický has made a theme of its namesake, a popular 17th-century author who once lived in the house. Solid wooden tables rest under perky illustrations of medieval town life, and a once-local brew, also named after Dačický, flows from the tap.

They serve standard Czech fare, as well as excellent game and fish. While its regulars still come here for the cheap lunch specials, during tourist season the crowd is mostly international. Service can be slow when a group arrives (daily 11:00–23:00, Rakova 8, tel. 327-512-248, mobile 603-434-367).

Dobrá Čajovna Teahouse also offers the chance to escape—not to medieval times, but to a Thai paradise. Filled with tea cases, water pipes, and character, this place is an ideal spot to dawdle away the time that this ageless town has reclaimed for you (daily 14:00–22:00, Jungmannovo Náměstí 16, mobile 777-028-481).

Restaurace Donna-U Žlutého Kola serves the fastest and tastiest Czech dishes in town, attracting a local crowd. There's a long menu in English, but the lunch specials are only listed on a separate sheet in Czech. When the weather's nice, sit in the shady courtyard behind the restaurant (open daily, lunch specials until 15:00, on Havlíčkovo Náměstí, right above Hotel Garni).

Piazza Navona features irritating English-language advertising ("the only true Italian restaurant in town"), but it still draws loyal customers thanks to its decent food and superb location on the main square (open daily).

Terezín Concentration Camp

Terezín (TEH-reh-zeen), an hour by bus from Prague, was originally a fortified town named after Habsburg Empress Maria Theresa (it's called "Theresienstadt" in German). It was built in the 1780s with state-of-the-art, star-shaped walls designed to keep out the Prussians. In 1941, the Nazis removed its 7,000 inhabitants and brought in 60,000 Jews, creating Terezín Concentration Camp. Ironically, the town's medieval walls, originally meant to keep Germans out, were later used by Germans to keep the Jews in.

This was the Nazis' model "Jewish town," a concentration camp dolled up for propaganda purposes. Here, in this "self-governed Jewish resettlement area," Jewish culture seemed to thrive, as "citizens" put on plays and concerts, published a magazine, and raised their families. But it was all a carefully planned deception, intended to convince Red Cross inspectors that the Jews were being treated well. Virtually all of Terezín's Jews (155,000 over the course of the war) ultimately ended up dying either here

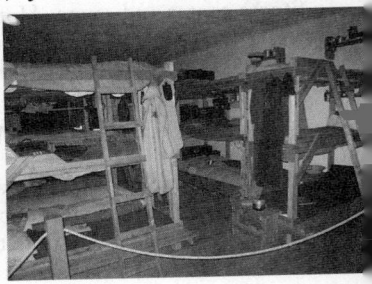

Petr Ginz, Young Artist and Writer

Born in 1928 to a Jewish father and non-Jewish mother, Prague teenager Petr Ginz excelled at art and was a talented writer who penned numerous articles, short stories, and even a science-fiction novel. Petr was sent to the concentration camp at Terezín in 1942, where he edited the secret boys' publication *Vedem (We Are Ahead)*, writing poetry and drawing illustrations, and paying contributors with food rations he received from home.

Some of Petr's artwork and writings were preserved by Terezín survivors and archived by the Jewish Museum in Prague. In 2003, Ilan Ramon, the first Israeli astronaut and the son of a Holocaust survivor, took one of Petr's drawings—titled *Moon Country*—into space aboard the final, doomed mission of the space shuttle Columbia.

The publicity over the Columbia's explosion and Petr's drawing spurred a Prague resident to come forward with a diary he'd found in his attic. It was Petr's diary from 1941 to 1942, hidden decades earlier by Petr's parents, and chronicling the year before the teen's deportation to Terezín. *The Diary of Petr Ginz* has since been published in more than 10 languages.

In the diary, Petr matter-of-factly documented the increasing restrictions on Jewish life in occupied Prague, interspersing the terse account with dry humor. In the entry for September 19, 1941, Petr wrote, "They just introduced a special sign for Jews" and drew the Star of David. He continued, "On the way to school I counted 69 'sheriffs,'" referring to people wearing the star.

Petr spent two years at Terezín before being sent to Auschwitz, where he died in a gas chamber. He was 16.

(35,000) or in extermination camps farther east.

One of the notable individuals held at Terezín was the Viennese artist Friedl Dicker-Brandeis. This daring woman, a leader in the Bauhaus art movement, found her life's calling in teaching children freedom of expression. She taught the kids in the camp to distinguish between the central things—trees, flowers, lines—and peripheral things, such as the conditions of the camp. In 1944, Dicker-Brandeis volunteered to be sent to Auschwitz after her husband was transported there; she was killed a month later.

Of the 15,000 children who passed through Terezín from 1942–1944, fewer than 100 survived. The artwork they created at Terezín is a striking testimony to the cruel horror of the Holocaust. In 1994, Hana Volavková, a Terezín survivor and the director of the Jewish Museum in Prague, collected the children's artwork and poems in the book *I Never Saw Another Butterfly*. Selections

of the Terezín drawings are also displayed and well-described in English in Prague's Pinkas Synagogue (see page 85).

The most well-known of the cultural activities that took place at Terezín was the children's opera *Brundibár*. Written just before the war, the anti-Fascist opera premiered secretly in Prague at a time when Jewish activities were no longer permitted. From 1943 to 1944, the play, performed in Czech, ran 55 times in the camp. After the war it was staged internationally (including a successful run on Broadway) and was recently rewritten in the US as a successful children's book.

Today, Terezín is an unforgettable day trip from Prague for those interested in touring a concentration camp memorial and museum. Allow three to six hours to see the entire camp.

Getting to Terezín

The camp is about 40 miles northwest of Prague. It's most convenient to visit Terezín by bus (described next) or tour bus (see page 68).

Buses to Terezín leave hourly from Prague's Holešovice train station (Nádraží Holešovice, on Metro line C). When you get off the Metro (coming from the city center), head toward the front of the train, go upstairs, turn right, and walk to the end of the corridor. You'll see bus stands directly ahead, outside the station. The Terezín bus departs from platform 7 (direction: Litoměřice, buy ticket from driver).

You'll arrive in Terezín 50 minutes later at the public bus stop on the main square, around the corner from the Museum of the Ghetto. Some buses also stop earlier, by the Small Fortress. The driver and fellow passengers may tell you to get off there, but my self-guided tour works best if you begin at the stop in town (after the bus passes a field of crosses on your right and travels across the river).

For schedules, see www.idos.cz—you want "Terezín LT" (be sure to check the return schedule, too; for details on getting back to Prague, see "Terezín Connections," later).

Orientation to Terezín

Cost, Hours, Information: The 200-Kč combo-ticket includes all parts of the camp. Most sights, including the Museum of the Ghetto, Magdeburg Barracks, and Hidden Synagogue, are open daily April–Oct 9:00–18:00, Nov–March 9:00–17:30. The Columbarium and Crematorium are closed Sat. The Crematorium opens at 10:00 year-round and closes at 16:00 Nov–March, and the Small Fortress opens at 8:00 year-round and closes at 16:30 Nov–March. Tel. 416-782-225, mobile 606-632-914, www.pamatnik-terezin.cz.

Self-Guided Tour

Terezín Concentration Camp

On this visit, you'll see Terezín town and the Small Fortress, which is a long half-mile to the east across the river.

The bus from Prague drops you off at Terezín town's spacious ❶ **main square** (Náměstí Československé Armády). Picture the giant circus tent and barbed-wire fence that stood on this square for two years during the war. Inside, Jewish workers boxed special motors for German vehicles being used on the frigid Soviet front. As part of year-long preparations for the famous Red Cross visit (which lasted all of six hours on June 23, 1944), the tent and fence were replaced by flower beds (which you still see on the square today) and a pavilion for outdoor music performances.

Walk around the corner to the ❷ **Museum of the Ghetto,** where you can buy the Terezín combo-ticket (note show times for movies). You'll find two floors of exhibits about the development of the Nazis' "Final Solution" and a theater showing four excellent films. One film documents the history of the ghetto, and two focus on children's art in the camp. The fourth is made up of clips from *Der Führer schenkt den Juden eine Stadt (The Führer Gives a City to the Jews)* by Kurt Gerron. Gerron, a Berlin Jew, was a 1920s movie star who appeared with Marlene Dietrich in *Blue Angel.* Deported to Terezín, Gerron in 1944 was asked by the Nazis to produce a propaganda film. The resulting film depicts healthy (i.e., recently arrived) "Jewish settlers" in Terezín happily viewing concerts, playing soccer, and sewing in their rooms—yet an unmistakable, deadly desperation radiates from their pallid faces. The only moment of genuine emotion comes toward the end, when a packed room of children applauds the final lines of the popular anti-Nazi opera *Brundibár*: "We did not let ourselves down, we chased the nasty Brundibár away. With a happy song, we won it all." Even the Nazis were not fooled: Gerron and his wife were shipped to Auschwitz and the film was never shown in public.

To learn more about living conditions in the camp, walk over to the ❸ **Magdeburg Barracks.** Peek inside the large courtyard (you'll recognize it as the "soccer stadium" in Gerron's film), then continue upstairs. On the right are rooms reproducing the camp cabaret stage and exhibits documenting the prisoners' literary, musical, and theatrical activities. On the left is a meticulously restored camp dormitory, complete with three-tiered beds, eyeglasses, dolls, chessboards, and sewing kits.

As you exit from the barracks (notice the high-water marks from the 2002 flood on the house opposite), turn right around the corner and walk 100 yards to a brick gate. As you cross a bridge over a ❹ **dry moat,** imagine the moat filled with plots of vegetables

To Litoměřice
FORMER DEUTSCHES REICH
FORMER PROTECTORATE BOHEMIA AND MORAVIA
TEREZÍN TOWN
To Ústí nad Labem
FORMER BORDER SUDETENLAND
PRAŽSKÁ
MICHOVA
HUSOVA
FUČÍKOVA
5 KVĚTNA
Nám. Česko. Armády
WATER GATE
28 ŘÍJNA
DLOUHÁ
PALACKÉHO
VODÁRENSKÁ
TYŠOVA
FORTRESS WALLS
400 Meters
400 Yards
Vegetable Plots
To Bohušovice

grown by starving Jews for well-fed SS officers.

Turn left and walk along the moat. The top of the fortification walls on the other side were once equipped with benches and pathways. When you reach the main road, turn right across the New Ohře River (the original course of the river was diverted here when Terezín was built) and walk past the vast cemetery to the ❺ **Small Fortress**—you'll see its black-and-white-striped gate. From 1940 to 1945, this fortress functioned as a Gestapo prison, through which 32,000 inmates passed (of whom nearly 10 percent

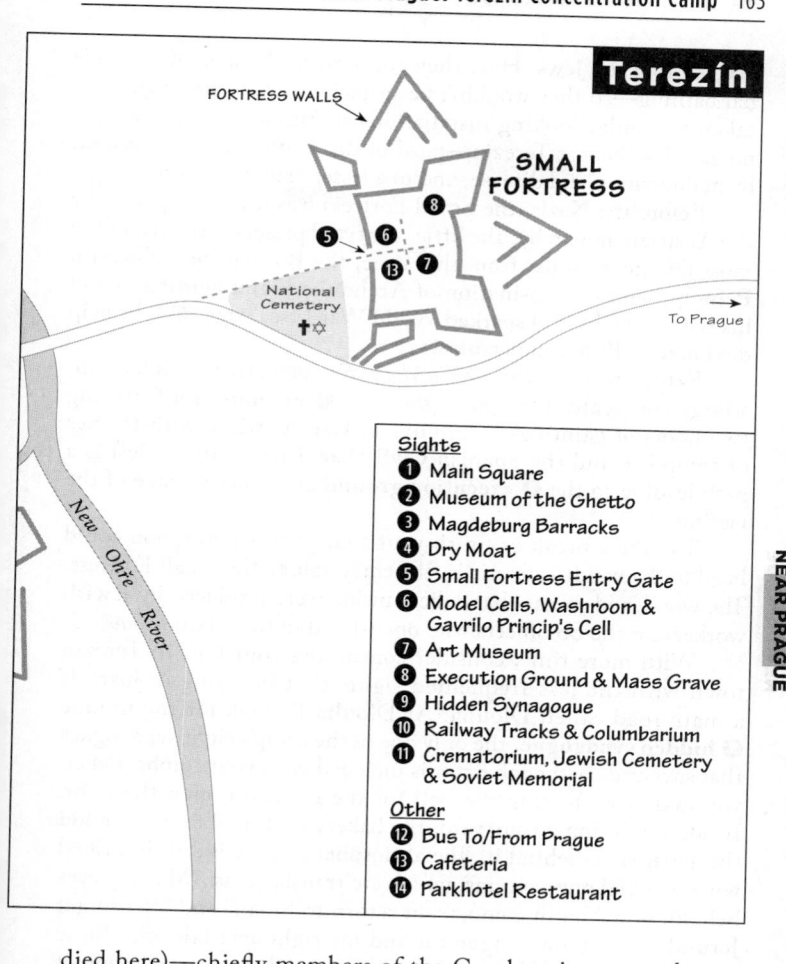

died here)—chiefly members of the Czech resistance and communists. The 1,500 Jews interned here were treated with particular severity.

Inside the gate, turn left toward the notorious *Arbeit Macht Frei* sign (a postwar replica), painted above an arched gate. In the courtyard behind, you will first find ❻ **model prison cells.** The **washroom** in the left corner was built solely for the purpose of fooling Red Cross inspectors. Turn the faucets: No pipes were ever installed to bring in water. The **shower room** farther to the left, on the other hand, was

used to fool the Jews. Here they got used to the idea of communal bathing—so they wouldn't be suspicious when they were later taken to similar-looking installations at Auschwitz. (There were no gas chambers at Terezín—most of the deaths here were caused by malnutrition and disease, and to a lesser extent, executions.)

Before the Nazis, the Small Fortress was used as a prison by the Austrian monarchy. The little courtyard preserves the cell of the most famous prisoner from that time, the Bosnian Serb **Gavrilo Princip,** whose assassination of Archduke Franz Ferdinand and his wife Žofie in 1914 sparked World War I (see page 167). Princip died here in 1918 of tuberculosis.

Return through the *Arbeit Macht Frei* gate, then turn left into a large courtyard. On your right is an ❼ **art museum** featuring two floors of paintings by prominent Czech artists, with themes of camp life and the Spanish Civil War. Farther to the left is a path leading to the ❽ **execution ground** and a **mass grave** of the victims.

To take a break or finish your tour at this point, you could head to the handy cafeteria by the entry gate to the Small Fortress. The wood-and-metal chandeliers inside were produced by Jewish workers for the SS officers who once dined in these two rooms.

With more time, consider continuing your tour in Terezín town with the less-frequented sights that lie along or just off a main road called Dlouhá. At Dlouhá 17, look for the unique ❾ **hidden synagogue,** the only one of the camp's eight synagogues that survived. Although entry is included with your combo-ticket, you may need to ring the bell for the guard to open the door. Inside you'll find a courtyard; the bakery that used to be here hid the synagogue behind it. The atmospheric space is still inscribed with two Hebrew captions, which are translated as: "May my eyes behold, how You in compassion return to Sinai," and "If I forget Jerusalem, may my tongue rot and my right arm fall off." These words indicate that the prayer room belonged to a congregation of Zionists (advocates of a Jewish state), who, one would expect, were specifically targeted by the Nazis.

Continue down Dlouhá to the Bohušovice gate. On the ground, look for the remnants of ❿ **railway tracks.** In the early years of the camp, Jews arrived at the train station in the nearby town of Bohušovice and then had to walk the remaining two miles to Terezín. This was too public a display for the Nazis, who didn't want locals to observe the transports and become suspicious. So

the Jewish prisoners at Terezín were forced to construct a railway line that led right to Terezín...and back out again to Auschwitz.

As you exit the walled-in area, on the right you will find Jewish and Christian ceremonial halls and the main morgue, while on the left is a **Columbarium,** or storage space for funerary urns. The Germans originally promised that the urns would be properly reburied after the war, but in 1945, to erase evidence, the ashes of Terezín victims (stored mainly in cardboard boxes) were dumped into the New Ohře River.

Continue along the road, then turn left past bucolic vegetable plots and fruit gardens to reach the ⓫ **Crematorium, Jewish Cemetery,** and a **Memorial to Soviet Soldiers.** Days before Terezín was liberated (on May 8, 1945), an epidemic of typhus spread through the camp. In the weeks after the war ended, scores of Soviet soldiers and medical workers who tried to contain the epidemic died, along with hundreds of former prisoners.

Our tour ends here. As you ponder Terezín, remember the message of all such memorials: Never again.

Eating in Terezín

In Terezín town, the **Parkhotel Restaurant** is the most elegant place for lunch (daily 10:00–22:00, around the block from the Museum of the Ghetto at Máchova 163, tel. 416-782-260).

The Small Fortress has a **cafeteria**. But avoid the stale sandwiches in the Museum of the Ghetto's dingy basement cafeteria, where most tour guides inexplicably shove their clients.

Terezín Connections

The bus for **Prague** leaves from Terezín's main square. If the return bus doesn't fit your schedule, consider taking a taxi from Terezín to the Bohušovice station (5 min from Terezín, trains to Prague depart nearly hourly, 1–1.5 hrs). There is no taxi service from Bohušovice *to* Terezín, making the train a good option only for the return journey. If you're continuing from Terezín to **Dresden,** Germany, take the train from Bohušovice to Ústí, then switch to the international express train.

Konopiště Castle

Konopiště (KOH-noh-peesh-tyeh), the huge, Neo-Gothic residence of the Archduke Franz Ferdinand d'Este, is 30 miles south of Prague.

Construction of the castle began in the 14th century, but today's exterior and furnishings date from about 1900, when the heir to the Habsburg throne, Archduke Franz Ferdinand, renovated his new home. As one of the first castles in Europe to have an elevator, a WC, and running water, Konopiště shows "modern" living at the turn of the 20th century. Touring the castle gives you a good sense of who this powerful Habsburg was, as well as a glimpse at one of the best medieval arms collections in the world (and lots of hunting trophies).

While the stretch between the parking lot and the castle entrance is overrun by tour groups, the **gardens** and the **park** are surprisingly empty. In the summer, the flowers and goldfish in the rose garden are a big hit with visitors. The peaceful 30-minute walk through the woods around the lake (wooden bridge at the far end) offers gorgeous castle views.

Tucked away in the bushes behind the pond is a pavilion coated with tree bark, a perfect picnic spot. This simple structure, nicknamed the **Kaiser's Pavilion,** was the site of a fateful meeting between the German Kaiser Wilhelm and the Archduke Franz Ferdinand (explained in the sidebar).

Cost and Tours: Entrance to the castle is by one-hour guided tour only. Choose from three different routes: Route I (190 Kč, includes public and guest rooms, hunting hall, and shooting range), Route II (190 Kč, includes the oldest part of the castle, armory, elevator, and chapel), and Route III (300 Kč, includes private top-floor rooms of Franz Ferdinand and his family). All tickets are 30 percent cheaper if you join a Czech-speaking tour. While Route II gives you the most comprehensive look into the castle, its history, and celebrated collections, Route III—reopened after the rooms were meticulously restored to match 1907 photographs—launches you right into a turn-of-the-20th-century time capsule.

Hours and Information: Castle open May–Aug Tue–Sun 9:00–12:30 & 13:00–17:00; April and Oct Tue–Fri 9:00–15:00, Sat–Sun 9:00–16:00; Sept Tue–Fri 9:00–16:00, Sat–Sun 9:00–17:00; closed Nov–March and Mon year-round. Tel. 317-721-366, www.zamek-konopiste.cz.

Archduke Franz Ferdinand
(1863–1914)

Archduke Franz Ferdinand was the nephew of the Habsburg Emperor Franz Josef, who ruled from 1848–1916 (longer than Queen Victoria). Ferdinand was the impatient successor to the Austro-Hungarian throne. Local legends (whose veracity historians categorically deny) say that Franz Ferdinand even built a chapel at Konopiště for the sole purpose of praying that his old, hated uncle might soon die...but the emperor went on to outlive the young archduke.

Franz Ferdinand fell out of his uncle's favor when he married a beautiful but low-ranking Czech countess, Žofie Chotková (often known by her German name, Sophie). Žofie was "only" aristocratic, not royal. To get out of sight of his relatives, Franz Ferdinand bought Konopiště and moved here.

Obsessed with hunting, Franz Ferdinand traveled around the world twice, shooting at anything in sight: deer, bears, tigers, elephants, and crocodiles. He eventually killed 300,000 animals, many of whom stare morbidly at you as hunting trophies covering the walls at Konopiště.

In the Kaiser's Pavilion on the grounds of Konopiště, Franz Ferdinand met with German Kaiser Wilhelm and tried to talk him out of plotting a war against Russia. Wilhelm argued that a war would work to the mutual benefit of Germany and Austria: Germans wanted colonies, and Austria—crippled by the aspirations of its many nationalities—could use a war to divert attention from its domestic problems. But Franz Ferdinand foresaw that war would be suicidal for Austria's overstretched monarchy.

Soon after, Franz Ferdinand and his wife went to Sarajevo, in the Habsburg-annexed territories of Bosnia and Herzegovina. On that trip, young Gavrilo Princip, a Bosnian Serb, shot the Habsburg archduke who so loved shooting. (Princip also shot and killed Žofie.) Franz Ferdinand's assassination ironically gave the Germans (and their pro-war allies in the Austro-Hungarian administration) the pretext for starting the war against Serbia and its ally, Russia. World War I soon broke out. The event Franz Ferdinand had tried to prevent was, in fact, sparked by his death.

Getting to Konopiště Castle: Trains from Prague's Main Station drop you in Benešov (hourly, 1 hr); a well-marked trail goes from the station to the castle (1.5 miles). As you exit the Benešov train station, turn left and walk along the street parallel to the railroad tracks. Turn left at the first bridge you see crossing over the tracks. Along the way you'll see trail markers on trees, walls, and lampposts—one yellow stripe between two white stripes. Follow these markers. As you leave town, watch for a marker with

an arrow pointing to a path in the woods. Take this path to bypass the castle's enormous parking lot, which is clogged with souvenir shops and bus fumes.

Eating at Konopiště Castle

Three touristy restaurants sit under the castle, but I'd bring picnic supplies from Prague (or buy them at the grocery store by the Benešov train station). While the crowds wait to pay too much for lousy food in the restaurants, you'll enjoy the peace and thought-provoking ambience of a **picnic** in the shaded Kaiser's Pavilion. Or eat cheaply with locals on Benešov's main square (try **U Zlaté Hvězdy**—"The Golden Star").

Karlštejn Castle

One of the Czech Republic's top attractions, Karlštejn Castle (KARL-shtayn) was built by Charles IV in about 1350 to house the crown jewels of the Holy Roman Empire. While a striking, fairy-tale castle from a distance, it's not much inside. The highlight of the castle's interior—the much venerated and sumptuous Chapel of the Holy Cross (built to house the crown jewels)—can be seen only with an advance reservation.

Cost and Tours: The Chapel of the Holy Cross—basically the only thing inside Karlštejn worth seeing—is part of tour Route II (300 Kč). You can only visit this route with a group (15 people maximum per group, 1 group per hour), and reservations are required (30-Kč reservation fee per person, tel. 274-008-154 or 274-008-155, rezervace@stc.npu.cz). Route I is nowhere near as interesting (220 Kč, no reservation required, bigger groups, shorter tour).

Hours and Information: May–Sept Tue–Sun 9:00–12:00 & 13:00–18:00; April and Oct Tue–Sun 9:00–12:00 & 13:00–15:00; closed Nov–March and Mon year-round; tel. 274-008-154, www.hradkarlstejn.cz.

Getting to Karlštejn Castle: The castle, 20 miles southwest of Prague, is accessible by train (2/hr, 40 min, then a 20-min walk; depart from Prague's Main Station in the direction of Beroun). When you leave the Karlštejn station, turn right, walk to the next road, turn left, and cross the bridge over the river. From here,

follow the pedestrian-only street up to the castle. Warning: This half-mile stretch has a concentration of crystal and souvenir shops as intense as Karlova street in Prague.

Hike to Srbsko: From Karlštejn Castle, an easy one-hour hike along a well-marked trail (look for markers with one red stripe between two white stripes) leads away from the tourists through a quiet forest to Srbsko. There, you'll find two good Czech restaurants and a train station (the Karlštejn–Prague train stops in Srbsko).

Křivoklát Castle

Křivoklát (KREE-vohk-laht), an original 14th-century castle, is beautiful for its simplicity and setting, amid hills and deep woods near the lovely Berounka River valley. Originally a hunting residence of Czech kings, it was later transformed into a royal prison that "entertained" a number of distinguished guests, among them the most notorious alchemist of the 1500s, the Englishman Edward Kelly.

In summer, Křivoklát comes alive with craftspeople—woodcarvers, blacksmiths, and basket-weavers—who work as if it were the 15th century. The absence of tacky souvenir shops, the plain Gothic appearance, and the background noise of hammers and wood chisels give Křivoklát an engaging character.

The tour of the interior lasts a sensible half-hour. The highlight is the king's audience hall, with its delicately arched ceiling.

Cost, Hours, Information: 150 Kč with an English-speaking guide; 100 Kč if you go with a Czech group (pick up an explanation sheet in English, and you'll be fine with the Czechs). Open June–Aug Tue–Sun 9:00–12:00 & 13:00–17:00, closed Mon; May and Sept Tue–Sun 9:00–16:00, closed Mon; April and Oct Tue–Sun 9:00–15:00, closed Mon; Nov–Dec Sat–Sun 9:00–15:00, closed Mon–Fri; closed Jan–March, tel. 313-558-440, www.krivoklat.cz.

Getting to Křivoklát Castle: Trains leave Prague's Main Station for Beroun (hourly, 40 min), running through the delightful valley of the dreamy Berounka River. In Beroun, transfer to the cute little motor train to Křivoklát (dubbed by Czech hikers the "Berounka Pacific"; allow 1.5 hrs total for trip from Prague). From Křivoklát's train station, it's a 10-minute walk uphill to the castle. At the train station, confirm the return schedule—one train leaves just before noon, and three others depart during the afternoon.

Sleeping and Eating near Křivoklát

$ Hotel and Restaurant Sýkora, below the castle near the train station, has been a favorite among Czech hikers since the 1930s. If you want to stay for an evening concert in the castle courtyard or for a hike in the nearby woods, sleep in one of the hotel's 11 renovated rooms (Db-600 Kč, tel. 313-558-114, www.hotel-sykora.krivoklatsko.com, hotel.sykora@krivoklatsko.com, only Czech and German spoken). Insist on this promised price or cross the street to the nearby, much classier **$$ Hotel and Restaurant U Jelena** (Db-1,200 Kč, tel. 313-558-529, www.ujelena.eu, krivoklat@ujelena.eu).

ČESKÝ KRUMLOV

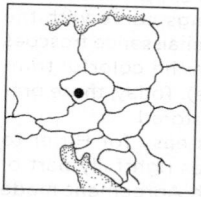

Lassoed by its river and dominated by its castle, this enchanting town feels lost in a time warp. While Český Krumlov is the Czech Republic's answer to Germany's Rothenburg, it has yet to be turned into a medieval theme park. When you see its awe-inspiring castle, delightful Old Town of shops and cobbled lanes, characteristic little restaurants, and easy canoeing options, you'll understand why having fun is a slam-dunk here.

Český Krumlov (CHESS-key KROOM-loff) means, roughly, "Czech Bend in the River." Calling it "Český" for short sounds silly to Czech-speakers (since dozens of Czech town names begin with "Český"). "Krumlov" for short is okay.

Since Krumlov is the Czech Republic's second-most-visited town (1.5 million visits annually), there's enough tourism to make things colorful and easy—but not so much that it tramples the place's charm. This town of 15,000 attracts a young, bohemian crowd, drawn here for its simple beauty, cheap living, and fanciful bars.

Planning Your Time

Because the castle and theater can be visited only with a guide (and English-language tours are offered just a few times a day), serious sightseers should reserve both tours first thing in the morning in person at the castle and theater (or call the castle), and then build their day around the tour times. Those who hate planning ahead on vacation can join a Czech tour anytime with an English information sheet.

A paddle down the river to Zlatá Koruna Abbey is a highlight (three hours), and a 20-minute walk up to the Křížový Vrch

Český Krumlov's History

With the natural moat provided by the sharp bend in the Vltava, it's no wonder this has been a choice spot for eons. Celtic tribes first settled here a century before Christ. Then came German tribes. The Slavic tribes arrived in the ninth century. The Rožmberks—Bohemia's top noble family—ran the city from 1302 to 1602. You'll see their rose symbol all over town. In many ways, the 16th century was the town's Golden Age, when Český Krumlov hosted artists, scientists, and alchemists from all over Europe. In 1588, the town became home to an important Jesuit college. The Habsburgs bought the region in 1602, ushering in a more Germanic period. (After that, as many as 75 percent of the town's people were German—until 1945, when most Germans were expelled.)

The rich mix of Gothic, Renaissance, and Baroque buildings is easy to under-appreciate. As you wander, look up...notice the surviving details in the stonework. Step into shops. Snoop into back lanes and tiny squares. Gothic buildings curve with the winding streets. Many precious Gothic and Renaissance frescoes were whitewashed in Baroque times (when the colorful trimmings of earlier periods were way out of style). Today, these precious frescoes are being rediscovered and restored.

With its rich German heritage, it was easy for Hitler to claim that this region—the Sudetenland—was rightfully part of Germany, and in 1938, the infamous Munich Agreement made it his. Americans liberated the town in 1945. Due to Potsdam

(Hill of the Cross) rewards you with a fine view of the town and its unforgettable riverside setting. Other sights are quick visits and worthwhile only if you have a particular interest (Viennese artist Egon Schiele, puppets, torture, and so on).

The town itself is the major attraction. Evenings are for atmospheric dining and drinking. Sights are generally open 10:00–17:00 and closed on Monday.

Orientation to Český Krumlov

Český Krumlov is extremely easy to navigate. The twisty Vltava River, which makes a perfect S through the town, ropes the Old Town into a tight peninsula. Above the Old Town is the Castle Town. Český Krumlov's one main street starts at the isthmus and heads through the peninsula. It winds through town and continues across a bridge before snaking through the Castle Town, the castle complex (a long series of courtyards), and the castle gardens high above. The main square, Náměstí Svornosti—with the TI, ATMs, and taxis—dominates the Old Town and marks the center of the

Treaty-approved ethnic cleansing, three million Germans in Czech lands were sent west to Germany. Emptied of its German citizenry, Český Krumlov turned into a ghost town, partially inhabited by Roma (Gypsies).

In the post-WWII world drawn up by Stalin, Churchill, and FDR at Yalta, the border of the Soviet and American spheres of influence fell about here. While the communist government established order, the period from 1945 to 1989 was a smelly interlude, as the town was infamously polluted. Its now-pristine river was foamy with effluent from the paper mill just upstream, while the hills around the town were marred with apartment blocks of prefabricated concrete. The people who moved in never fully identified with the town—in Europe, a place without ancestors is without life. But the bleak years of communism paradoxically provided a cocoon to preserve the town. There was no money, so little changed, apart from a build-up of grime.

In the early 1990s, tourists discovered Český Krumlov, and the influx of money saved the buildings from ruin. Color returned to the facades, waiters again dressed in coarse linen shirts, and the main drag was flooded with souvenir shops.

With its new prosperity, the center of today's Český Krumlov looks like a fairy-tale town. In fact, movie producers consider it ideal for films. *The Adventures of Pinocchio* was filmed here in 1995, as was the opening sequence for the 2006 film *The Illusionist*.

peninsula. All recommended restaurants and hotels are within a few minutes' walk of this square. No sight in town is more than a five-minute stroll away.

Tourist Information

The helpful TI is on the **main square** (daily 9:00–19:00, July–Aug until 20:00, shorter hours in winter, tel. 380-704-622, www.ckrumlov.cz). Pick up the free city map. The 129-Kč *City Guide* book explains everything in town and includes a fine town and castle map in the back. The TI can check train, bus, and flight schedules. Ask about concerts, city walking tours in English, and canoe trips on the river.

A second, less-crowded TI—actually a private business—is just below the **castle** (daily 9:00–19:00, tel. 380-725-110).

Arrival in Český Krumlov

By Train: The train station is a 20-minute walk from town (turn right out of the station, then walk downhill onto a steep cobbled path leading to an overpass into the town center). Taxis are

standing by to zip you to your hotel (about 100 Kč), or call 602-113-113 to summon one.

By Bus: The bus station is just three blocks away from the Old Town (from the bus station lot, drop down to main road and turn left, then turn right at Potraviny grocery store to reach the center). Figure on 60 Kč for a taxi from the station to your hotel.

Helpful Hints

Internet Access: Fine Internet cafés are all over town, and many of my recommended accommodations offer Wi-Fi or Internet access. The TI on the main square has several fast, cheap, stand-up stations. Perhaps the best cybercafé is behind the TI by the castle (tel. 380-725-117).

Bookstore: Shakespeare and Sons is a good little English-language bookstore (daily 11:00–20:00, a block below the main square at Soukenická 44, tel. 380-711-203).

Laundry: The recommended **Pension Lobo** runs a self-service launderette near the castle. Since there are only a few machines, you may have to wait (200 Kč to wash and dry, includes soap, daily 9:00–20:00, Latrán 73).

Festivals: Locals drink oceans of beer and celebrate their medieval roots at big events such as the Celebration of the Rose (Slavnosti Růže), where blacksmiths mint ancient coins, jugglers swallow fire, mead flows generously, and pigs are roasted on open fires (June 18–20 in 2010). The summer also brings a top-notch international jazz and alternative music festival to town, performed in pubs, cafés, and the castle gardens (July 18–Aug 23 in 2010). During the St. Wenceslas celebrations, the square becomes a medieval market and the streets come alive with theater and music (Sept 24–28 in 2010). Reserve a hotel well in advance if you'll be in town for these events (for more details, see www.ckrumlov.cz).

Tours in Český Krumlov

Walking Tours—Since the town itself, rather than its sights, is what it's all about here, taking a guided walk is the key to a meaningful visit. The TI sells tickets for two different guided walks. They are affordable, in English, and well worth your time. Both meet in front of the TI on the main square. No reservations are necessary—just drop in and pay the guide. The **Old Town Tour** offers the best general town introduction and is most likely to run (250 Kč, daily May–Oct at 10:30 and 15:00, Nov–April at 11:00, weekends only in Feb, 1.5 hours). The **Brewing History Tour,** the most intimate of the many brewery tours in this land that so loves its beer, takes you through the Eggenberg Brewery (200 Kč, daily

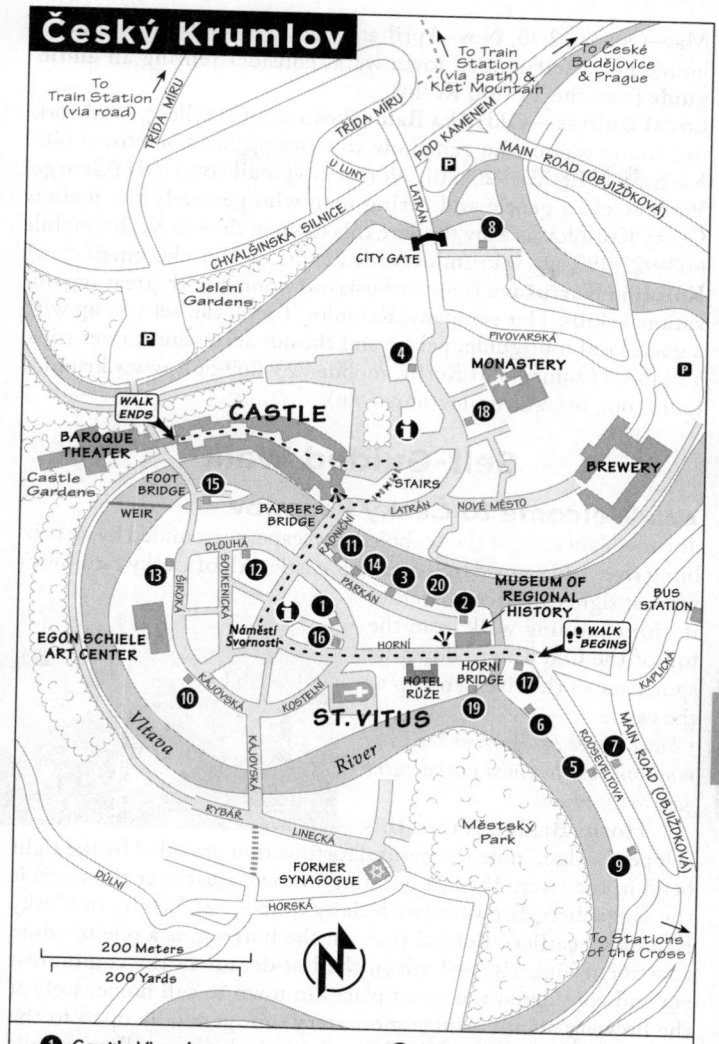

1. Castle View Apts.
2. Hotel Mlýn
3. Pension Olšakovský
4. Pension Lobo & Pension Danny
5. Pension Teddy
6. Pension Myší Díra & Maleček Boat Rental
7. Pension Anna
8. Hostel 99 & Hospoda 99 Rest.
9. Krumlov House Hostel
10. Na Louži Restaurant
11. Krčma u Dwau Maryí
12. Cikánská Jizba
13. Rest. u Dobráka
14. Laibon Restaurant
15. Rybářská Restaurace
16. Krčma v Šatlavské
17. Restaurace Barbakán
18. Dobrá Čajovna Teahouse
19. Start Short River Float
20. End Short River Float & Start Zlatá Koruna Float

May–Oct at 12:30, Nov–April at 13:00, weekends only in Feb, 1 hour). For a self-guided town walk, consider renting an **audio-guide** from the TI (100 Kč/hr).

Local Guides—Oldřiška Baloušková is an excellent, hardworking young guide who can show you around her hometown (400 Kč/hr, mobile 737-920-901, oldriskab@gmail.com). **Jiří (George) Václavíček,** a gentle and caring man who perfectly fits mellow Český Krumlov, is a joy to share this town with (450 Kč/hr, mobile 603-927-995, www.krumlovguide.cz, jiri.vaclavicek@gmail.com). **Karolína Kortušová** is an enthusiastic woman with great organizational skills. Her company, Krumlov Tours, can set you up with a good local tour guide, palace and theater admissions, river trips, and more (guides-400 Kč/hr, mobile 723-069-561, www.krumlovtours.com, info@krumlovtours.com).

Self-Guided Walk

▲▲▲Welcome to Český Krumlov

The town's best sight is its cobbled cityscape, surrounded by its babbling river and capped by a dramatic castle. All of Český Krumlov's modest sights are laced together in this charming walk from the top of the Old Town, down its spine, across the river, and up to the castle.

• *Start at the bridge over the isthmus, once the fortified grand entry gate to the town.*

Horní Bridge: From this "Upper Bridge," note the natural fortification provided by the tight bend in the river. The last building in town (just over the river) is the Eggenberg Brewery (with daily tours—see "Tours in Český Krumlov," earlier). Behind that, on the horizon, is a pile of white apartment high-rises—built in the last decade of the communist era and considered the worst places in town to call home. Left of the brewery stands a huge monastery (not generally open to the public). Behind that on Kleť Mountain, the highest hilltop, stands a TV tower that locals say was built to jam Voice of America broadcasts. Facing the town, on your left, rafters take to the river for the sloppy half-hour float around town to the take-out spot just on your right.

• *A block downhill on Horní (Upper) street is the...*

Museum of Regional History: This small museum gives you a quick look at regional costumes, tools, and traditions. When you pay, pick up the English translation of the displays (it also includes a lengthy history of Krumlov). Start on the top floor, where you'll

see a Bronze Age exhibit, old paintings, a glimpse of noble life, and a look at how the locals rafted lumber from Krumlov all the way to Vienna (partly via canal). Don't miss the fun-to-study ceramic model of Český Krumlov in 1800 (note the extravagant gardens high above the town). The lower floor comes with fine folk costumes and domestic art (50 Kč, daily 10:00–17:00, July–Aug until 18:00, Horní 152, tel. 380-711-674).

• *Below the museum, a little garden overlook affords a fine castle view. Immediately across the street, notice the Renaissance facade of...*

Hotel Růže: This former Jesuit college hides a beautiful courtyard. Pop inside to see a couple of bronze busts that stand like a shrine to the founders of Czechoslovakia. The one on the right, dedicated by the Czech freedom fighters, commemorates the first Czechoslovak president, Tomáš Garrigue Masaryk (in office 1918–1934; see sidebar on page 112). The bust on the left recalls Masaryk's successor, Edvard Beneš (in office 1934–1948; see sidebar on next page).

• *Walk another block down the main drag, until you reach steps on the left leading to the...*

Church of St. Vitus: Český Krumlov's main church was built as a bastion of Catholicism in the 15th century, when the Roman Catholic Church was fighting the Hussites. The 17th-century Baroque high altar shows a totem of religious figures: the Virgin Mary (crowned in heaven), St. Vitus (above Mary), and way up on top, St. Wenceslas, the patron saint of the Czech people—long considered their ambassador in heaven. The canopy in the back, while empty today, once supported a grand statue of a Rožmberk atop a horse. The statue originally stood at the high altar. Too egotistical for Jesuits, it was later moved to the rear of the nave, and then lost for good. As you listen to the river, notice the empty organ case. While the main organ is out for restoration, the cute little circa-1716 Baroque beauty is getting plenty of use (see photos of the restoration work on the far wall, church open daily 10:00–19:00, Sunday Mass at 9:30, tel. 380-711-336).

• *Continuing on Horní street, you'll come to the...*

Main Square (Náměstí Svornosti): Lined by a mix of Renaissance and Baroque homes of burghers (all built upon 12th-century Gothic foundations), the main square has a grand charm. There's continuity here. Lékárna, with the fine red Baroque facade on the lower corner of the square, is still a pharmacy, as it has been since 1620. McDonald's tried three times to get a spot here but was turned away. The Town Hall flies the Czech flag and the town flag, which shows the rose symbol of the Rožmberk family, who ruled the town for 300 years.

Imagine the history that this square has seen: In the 1620s, the rising tide of Lutheran Protestantism threatened Catholic Europe.

Edvard Beneš and the German Question

Czechoslovakia was created in 1918, when the vast, multi-ethnic Habsburg Empire broke into smaller nations after losing World War I. The principle that gave countries such as Poland, Czechoslovakia, and Romania independence was called "self-determination": Each nation had the right to its own state within the area where its people were in the majority. But the peoples of Eastern Europe had mixed over the centuries, making it impossible to create functioning states based purely on ethnicity. In the case of Czechoslovakia, the borders were drawn along historical rather than ethnic boundaries. While the country was predominantly Slavic, there were also areas with overwhelmingly German and Hungarian majorities. One of these areas—a fringe around the western part of the country, mostly populated by Germans—was known as the Sudetenland.

At first, the coexistence of Slavs and Germans in the new republic worked fine. German parties were important power brokers and participated in almost every coalition government. Hitler's rise to power, however, led to the growth of German nationalism, even outside Germany. Soon 70 percent of Germans in Czechoslovakia voted for the Nazis. In September 1938, the Munich Agreement ceded the Sudetenland to Germany—and the Czech minority had to leave.

Edvard Beneš was the first Czechoslovak secretary of state (1918–1934) and later became the country's second president (1934–1948). Beneš led the Czechoslovak exile government in London during World War II. Like most Czechs and Slovaks, Beneš believed that after the hard feelings produced by the Munich Agreement, peaceful coexistence of Slavs and Germans in a single state was impossible. His postwar solution: move the Sudeten Germans to Germany, much as the Czechs had been forced out of the Sudetenland before. Through skillful diplomacy,

Krumlov was a seat of Jesuit power and learning, and the intellectuals of the Roman church allegedly burned books on this square. Later, when there was a bad harvest, locals blamed witches—and burned them, too. Every so often, terrible plagues rolled through the countryside. In a nearby village, all but two residents were killed by a plague.

But the plague stopped before devastating the people of Český Krumlov, and in 1715—as thanks to God—they built the plague monument that stands on the square today. Much later, in 1938, Hitler stood right here

Beneš got the Allies to sign on to this idea.

Shortly after the end of World War II, three million people of German ancestry were forced to leave their homes in Czechoslovakia. Millions of Germanic people in Poland, Romania, Ukraine, and elsewhere met with a similar fate. Many of these families had been living in these areas for centuries. The methods employed to expel them included murder, rape, and plunder. (Today, we'd call it "ethnic cleansing.")

In 1945, Český Krumlov lost 75 percent of its population, and Czechs moved into vacated German homes. Having easily acquired the property, the new residents didn't take much care of the houses. Within a few years, the once-prosperous Sudetenland was reduced to shabby towns and uncultivated fields—a decaying, godforsaken region. After 1989, displaced Sudeten Germans—the majority of whom now live in Bavaria—demanded that the Czechoslovak government apologize for the violent way in which the expulsion was carried out. Some challenged the legality of the decrees, and for a time the issue threatened otherwise good Czech-German relations.

Although no longer such a hot-button diplomatic issue, the so-called Beneš Decrees remain divisive in Czech politics. While liberals consider the laws unjust, many others—especially the older generations—see them as fair revenge for the behavior of the Sudeten Germans prior to and during the war. In the former Sudetenland, where Czech landowners worry that the Germans will try to claim back their property, Beneš is a hugely popular figure. His bust in Český Krumlov's Hotel Růže is one of the first memorials to Beneš in the country. The bridge behind the Old Town has been named for Beneš since the 1990s. The main square—the center of a thriving German community 70 years ago—is now ironically called "Square of Concord."

before a backdrop of long Nazi banners to celebrate the annexation of the Sudetenland. And in 1968, Russian tanks spun their angry treads on these same cobblestones to intimidate locals who were demanding freedom. Today, thankfully, this square is part of an unprecedented time of peace and prosperity for the Czech people.

• *The following three museums are grouped around the main square.*

Puppet Museum: You'll see fascinating displays in three small rooms of more than 300 movable creations (overwhelmingly of Czech origin, but also some from Burma and Rajasthan). At the model stage, children of any age can try their hand at pulling the strings on their favorite fairy tale (80 Kč, daily 10:00–18:00, longer hours in July-Aug, Radniční 29, tel. 380-713-422, www.inspirace.krumlov.cz).

Torture Museum: This is just a lame haunted house: dark, with sound effects, cheap modern models, and prints showing off the cruel and unusual punishments of medieval times (80 Kč, daily 9:00–20:00, English descriptions, Náměstí Svornosti 1, tel. 380-766-343).

Egon Schiele Art Center: This classy contemporary art gallery has temporary exhibits, generally featuring 20th-century Czech artists. The top-floor permanent collection celebrates the Viennese artist Egon Schiele (pronounced "Sheila"), who once spent a few weeks here during a secret love affair. A friend of Gustav Klimt and an important figure in the Secession movement in Vienna, Schiele lived a short life, from 1890–1918. His cutting-edge lifestyle and harsh art of graphic nudes didn't always fit the conservative, small-town style of Český Krumlov, but townsfolk are happy enough today to charge you to see this relatively paltry collection (180 Kč, daily 10:00–18:00, Široká 70, tel. 380-704-011, www.schieleartcentrum.cz). The Schiele collection in Vienna's Belvedere Palace is far better (see page 1032).

• *From the main square, walk up Radničí street and cross the...*

Barber's Bridge (Lazebnicky Most): This wooden bridge, decorated with two 19th-century statues, connects the Old Town and the Castle Town. In the center stands a statue of St. John of Nepomuk, who's also depicted by a prominent statue on Prague's Charles Bridge (see page 81). Among other responsibilities, he's the protector against floods. In the great floods of August 2002, the angry river submerged the bridge (but removable banisters minimized the damage). Stains just above the windows of the adjacent building show how high the water rose.

• *After crossing the bridge, hike on up the hill. Your next stop is Krumlov Castle.*

Sights in Český Krumlov

▲▲Krumlov Castle (Krumlovský Zámek)

No Czech town is complete without a castle—and now that the nobles are gone, their mansions are open to us common folk. The Krumlov Castle complex includes bear pits, the castle itself, a rare Baroque theater, and groomed gardens (www.castle.ckrumlov.cz).

Round Tower (Zâmecká Věž)—The strikingly colorful round tower marks the location of the first castle, built here to guard the medieval river crossing. With its

16th-century Renaissance paint job colorfully restored, it looks exotic, featuring fancy astrological decor, terra-cotta symbols of the zodiac, and a fine arcade. Climb its 162 steps for a great view (30 Kč, daily 9:00–18:00, last entry 17:30).

Bear Pits—At the site of the castle drawbridge, the bear pits hold a family of European brown bears, as they have since the Rožmberks added bears to their coat of arms in the 16th century to demonstrate their (fake) blood relation to the distinguished Italian family of Orsini (the name means "bear-like"). Featured on countless coats of arms, bears have long been totemic animals for Europeans. Pronouncing the animal's real name was taboo in many cultures, and Czechs still refer to bears only indirectly. For example, in most Germanic languages the word "bear" is derived from "brown," while the Slavic *medvěd* literally means "honey-eater."

Castle—The immense castle is a series of courtyards with shops, contemporary art galleries, and tourist services. The interior is accessible only by tour, which gives you a glimpse of the places where the Rožmberks, Eggenbergs, and Schwarzenbergs dined, studied, worked, prayed, entertained, and slept. (By European standards, the castle's not much, and the tours move slowly.) Imagine being an aristocratic guest here, riding the dukes' assembly line of fine living: You'd promenade through a long series of elegant spaces and dine in the sumptuous dining hall before enjoying a concert in the Hall of Mirrors, which leads directly to the Baroque Theater (described next). After the play, you'd go out into the château garden for a fireworks finale.

Cost, Hours, Tours: To see the interior, you must take a one-hour escorted tour: Tour I (Gothic and Renaissance rooms, of the most general interest) or Tour II (19th-century castle life). Tours run June–Aug Tue–Sun 9:00–12:00 & 13:00–18:00, spring and fall until 17:00, closed Mon and Nov–March. Tours in Czech cost 130 Kč plus a 10-Kč reservation fee, leave regularly, and include an adequate flier in English that contains about half the information imparted by the guide (generally a student who's just memorized the basic script). English tours are preferable, but cost more (240 Kč plus a 10-Kč reservation fee), run less frequently, and are often booked solid. Make your reservation when you arrive in town—just walk up to the castle office—or you can call 380-704-721, though the number is often busy. You'll be issued a ticket with your tour time printed on it. Be in the correct courtyard at that time, or you'll be locked out.

▲▲Baroque Theater (Zámecké Divadlo)—Europe once had several hundred fine Baroque theaters. Using candles for light and fireworks for special effects, most burned down. Today, only two survive in good shape and are open to tourists: one at Stockholm's Drottningholm Palace, and one here, at Krumlov Castle. During the 45-minute tour, you'll sit on benches in the theater and then go under the stage to see the wood-and-rope contraptions that enabled scenes to be scooted in and out within seconds (while fireworks and smoke blinded the audience). Due to the theater's fragility, the number of visitors is strictly regulated. There are only five English tours a day, limited to 25 people per group and generally sold out in advance. While it's a lovely little theater with an impressive 3-D effect that makes the stage look deeper than it really is, I wouldn't bother with the tour unless you can snare a spot on an English one. The theater is used only once a year for an actual performance, with attendance limited to Baroque theater enthusiasts. You can call 380-704-721 to get English-language tour times and reserve a space; but as with the castle tour, you will likely do best by visiting the ticket office in person (380 Kč plus a 10-Kč reservation fee for English tour, 250 Kč plus a 10-Kč reservation fee for Czech tour, tours daily May–Oct only; English departures at 10:00, 11:00, 13:00, 14:00, and 15:00; buy theater tour tickets at castle ticket office).

Castle Gardens—This 2,300-foot-long garden crowns the castle complex. It was laid out in the 17th century, when the noble family would light it with 22,000 oil lamps, torches, and candles for special occasions. The lower part is geometrical and symmetrical—French-style. The upper is rougher—English-style (free, May–Sept daily 8:00–19:00, April and Oct daily 8:00–17:00, closed Nov–March).

Near Český Krumlov

Zlatá Koruna Abbey—Directly above the river at the end of a three-hour float by raft or canoe (see "Activities in Český Krumlov," next), this abbey was founded in the 13th century by the king to counter the growing influence of the Vítek family, the ancestors of the mighty Rožmberks. As you enter the grounds, notice the central linden tree, with its strange, cape-like leaves; it's said to have been used by the anti-Catholic Hussites when they hanged the monks. The short guided abbey tour takes you through the rare two-storied Gothic Chapel of the Guardian Angel, the main church, and the cloister. After the order was dissolved in 1785, the abbey functioned shortly as a village school, before being turned into a factory during the Industrial Revolution. Damage from this period is visible on the cloister's crumbling arches. The abbey was restored in the 1990s and opened to the public only a few years ago

(95 Kč for a tour in Czech—generally runs hourly, 180 Kč for an English tour, Tue–Sun 9:00–15:30, until 16:30 June–Aug, closed Mon and Oct–March, call 380-743-126 to pre-arrange an English tour, access via river float, www.klaster-zlatakoruna.eu).

Activities in Český Krumlov

Český Krumlov lies in the middle of a valley popular for canoeing, rafting, hiking, and horseback riding. Boat-rental places are convenient to the Old Town, and several hiking paths start right in town.

▲▲▲Canoeing and Rafting the Vltava

Splash a little river fun into your visit by renting a rubber raft or fiberglass canoe for a quick 30-minute spin around Český Krumlov. Or go for a three-hour float and paddle through the Bohemian forests and villages of the nearby countryside. You'll end up at Zlatá Koruna Abbey (described earlier), where the rafting company will shuttle you back to town—or provide you with a bicycle to pedal back on your own along a bike path. This is a great hot-weather activity. Though the river is far from treacherous, be prepared to get wet.

On any trip, you'll encounter plenty of inviting pubs and cafés for breaks along the way. There's a little whitewater, but the river is so shallow that if you tip, you simply stand up and climb back in. (When that happens, pull the canoe up onto the bank to empty it, since you'll never manage to pour the water out while still in the river.)

Choose from a kayak, a canoe (fastest, less work, more likely to tip), or an inflatable raft (harder rowing, slower, but very stable). Prices are per boat (2–6 people) and include a map, a waterproof container, and transportation to or from the start and end points. Here are your options:

Quickie Circle-the-Town Float: The easiest half-hour experience is to float around the city's peninsula, starting and ending at opposite sides of the tiny isthmus. Heck, you can do it twice (350 Kč for 1–2 people in a canoe or raft).

Three-Hour Float to Zlatá Koruna Abbey: This is your best basic trip, with pastoral scenery, a riverside pub on the left after two hours, and a beautiful abbey as your destination (about 9 miles, 700 Kč for 1–2 people). From there you can bike back or

catch a shuttle bus home—simply arrange a return plan with the rental company.

Longer and Faster Trips: If you start upriver from Krumlov (direction: Rožmberk), you'll go faster with more whitewater, but the river parallels a road so it's a little less idyllic. Longer trips in either direction involve lots of paddling, even though you're going downstream. Rafting companies can review the many day-trip options with you.

Rental Companies: Several companies offer this lively activity. Perhaps the handiest are **Půjčovna Lodí Maleček Boat Rental** (open long hours daily April–Oct, closed Nov–March, at recommended Pension Myší Díra, Rooseveltova 28, tel. 380-712-508, www.malecek.cz, lode@malecek.cz) and **Cestovní Agentura Vltava** (April–Oct daily 9:00–18:00, closed Nov–March, in Pension Vltava at Kájovská 62, tel. 380-711-988, www.ckvltava.cz). Vltava also rents mountain bikes (320 Kč/day) and can bring a bike to the abbey for you to ride back.

Hiking

For an easy 20-minute hike to Křížový Vrch (Hill of the Cross), walk to the end of Rooseveltova street, cross at the traffic light, then head straight for the first (empty) chapel-like Station of the Cross. Turning right, it's easy to navigate along successive Stations of the Cross until you reach the white church on the hill (closed), set in the middle of wild meadows. Looking down into the valley at the medieval city nestled within the S-shaped river, framed by the rising hills, it's hard to imagine any town with a more powerful *genius loci* (spirit of the place). The view is best at sunset.

For longer hikes, start at the trailhead by the bear pits below the castle. Red-and-white trail markers will take you on an easy six-mile hike around the neighboring slopes and villages. The green-and-yellow stripes mark a five-mile hiking trail up Kleť Mountain—with an altitude gain of 1,800 feet. At the top, you'll find the Kleť Observatory, the oldest observatory in the country (now a leading center for discovering new planets). On clear days, you can see the Alps (observatory tours-30 Kč, hourly July–Aug Tue–Sun 10:30–15:30, closed Mon, www.hvezdarna.klet.cz).

Sleeping in Český Krumlov

Krumlov is filled with small, good, family-run pensions offering doubles with baths from 1,000–1,500 Kč and hostel beds for 300 Kč. Summer weekends and festivals (see page 174) are busiest and most expensive; reserve ahead when possible. Hotels (not a Krumlov forte) have staff that speak some English and accept credit cards; pensions rarely have or do either. While you can find

Sleep Code

(18 Kč = about $1, country code: 420)
S = Single, **D** = Double/Twin, **T** = Triple, **Q** = Quad, **b** = bathroom, **s** = shower only. Unless otherwise noted, prices include breakfast.

To help you sort easily through these listings, I've divided the rooms into three categories based on the price for a standard double room with bath:

$$$ Higher Priced—Most rooms 1,500 Kč or more.
$$ Moderately Priced—Most rooms between 1,000–1,500 Kč.
$ Lower Priced—Most rooms 1,000 Kč or less.

a room upon arrival here, it's better to book at least a few days ahead if you want to stay in the heart of town. Cars are not very safe overnight—locals advise paying for a garage.

In the Old Town

$$$ Castle View Apartments, run by local guide Jiří Václavíček, rents seven apartments. These are the plushest and best-equipped rooms I found in town—the bathroom floors are heated, all come with kitchenettes, and everything's done just right. Their website describes each of the stylish apartments (1,800–4,500 Kč depending on size, view, and season; the big 4,500-Kč apartment sleeps up to six, complex pricing scheme, reserve direct with this book to claim a 10 percent discount off their online prices, fourth night free, non-smoking, breakfast in a nearby hotel, Šatlavská 140, tel. 380-727-015, mobile 731-108-677, www.castleview.cz, info@castleview.cz).

On Parkán Street, Below the Square

Secluded Parkán street, which runs along the river below the square, has a row of pensions with three to five rooms each. These places have a family feel and views of the looming castle above.

$$$ Hotel Mlýn, at the end of Parkán, is a newly opened and tastefully furnished hotel with more than 30 rooms and all the amenities (Sb-2,400 Kč, Db-3,000 Kč, elevator, parking extra, Parkán 120, tel. 380-731-133, fax 380-747-054, www.hotelmlyn.eu, info@hotelmlyn.eu).

$$ Pension Olšakovský, which has a delightful breakfast area on a terrace next to the river, treats visitors as family guests (Db-1,000–1,250 Kč, includes parking, Parkán 114, tel. & fax 380-714-333, mobile 604-430-181, www.olsakovsky.cz, J.Olsakovsky@post.cz).

On Latrán Street, at the Base of the Castle

A quiet, cobbled pedestrian street (Latrán) runs below the castle just over the bridge from the Old Town. It's a 10-minute walk downhill from the train station. Lined with characteristic shops, the street has a couple of fine little family-run, eight-room pensions.

$$ Pension Lobo fills a modern, efficient, concrete building with eight rooms. The pension operates a shuttle bus to Linz, Salzburg, and Vienna—see details later under "Český Krumlov Connections" (Db-1,200 Kč, Tb-1,600 Kč, includes parking, Latrán 73, tel. & fax 380-713-153, www.pensionlobo.cz, lobo@ckrumlov.cz).

$ Pension Danny is a little funkier, with homier rooms and a tangled floor plan above a restaurant (Db-990 Kč, apartment Db-1,190 Kč, breakfast in room, Latrán 72, tel. 380-712-710, www.pensiondanny.cz, recepce@pensiondanny.cz).

On Rooseveltova Street, Between the Bus Station and the Old Town

Rooseveltova street, midway between the bus station and the Old Town (a four-minute walk from either), is lined with several fine little places, each with easy free parking. The key here is tranquility—the noisy bars of the town center are out of earshot.

Little **$$ Pension Teddy** offers three deluxe rooms that share a balcony overlooking the river and have original 18th-century furniture. Or stay in one of four modern-style rooms, some which also face the river (Db-1,250 Kč, deluxe Db-1,400 Kč, cash only, staff may be unhelpful, free Wi-Fi and Internet access, parking-200 Kč, Rooseveltova 38, tel. 380-711-595, mobile 724-003-981, www.pensionteddy.cz, info@pensionteddy.cz).

$$ Pension Myší Díra ("Mouse Hole") hides eight sleek, spacious, bright, and woody Bohemian contemporary rooms overlooking the Vltava River just outside the Old Town (Db-900–1,400 Kč, bigger deluxe riverview Db-1,900 Kč, prices include transfer to/from bus or train station, Rooseveltova 28, tel. 380-712-853, fax 380-711-900, www.malecek.cz). The no-nonsense reception, which closes at 20:00, runs the recommended boat rental company (Půjčovna Lodí Maleček, at the same address), along with three similar pensions with comparable prices: **Pension Wok** down by the river, **Pension Margarita** farther along Rooseveltova, and **Pension u Hada.**

$$ Pension Anna is well-run, with two doubles, five apartments, and a restful little garden. Its apartments are spacious suites, with a living room and stairs leading to the double-bedded loft. The upstairs rooms can get stuffy during the summer (Db-1,250 Kč, Db apartment-1,550 Kč, extra bed-350 Kč, Rooseveltova

41, tel. & fax 380-711-692, www.pensionanna.euweb.cz, pension .anna@quick.cz). If you book a standard Db and they bump you up to an apartment, don't pay more than the Db rate.

Hostels

There are several hostels in town. Hostel 99 (closest to the train station) is clearly the high-energy, youthful party hostel. Krumlov House (closer to the bus station) is more mellow. Both are well-managed, and each is a five-minute walk from the main square.

$ Hostel 99's picnic-table terrace looks out on the Old Town. While the gentle sound of the river gurgles outside your window late at night, you're more likely to hear a youthful international crowd having a great time. The hostel caters to its fun-loving young guests, offering free inner tubes for river floats, rental bikes, and a free keg of beer each Wednesday. The adjacent and recommended Hospoda 99 restaurant serves good, cheap soups, salads, and meals (65 beds in 4- to 10-bed coed rooms-300 Kč, D-700 Kč, T-990 Kč, Internet access-1 Kč/min, laundry-200 Kč/load, use the lockers, no curfew or lockout, 10-min downhill walk from train station or two bus stops to Spicak, Vezni 99, tel. & fax 380-712-812, www .hostel99.com, hostel99@hotmail.com).

$ Krumlov House Hostel is take-your-shoes-off-at-the-door, shiny, hardwood-with-throw-rugs mellow. Efficiently run by a Canadian, it has a hip and trusting vibe and feels welcoming to travelers of any age (24 beds, 6 beds in two dorms-300 Kč per bed, Db-800 Kč, 2-person apartment-900 Kč, family room, no breakfast but there is a guests' kitchen, DVD library, laundry facilities, Rooseveltova 68, tel. 380-711-935, www.krumlovhostel.com, info @krumlovhostel.com).

Eating in Český Krumlov

Krumlov, with a huge variety of creative little restaurants, is a fun place to eat. In peak times, the good places fill fast, so make reservations or eat early.

Na Louži seems to be everyone's favorite little Czech bistro, with 40 seats in one 1930s-style room decorated with funky old advertisements. They serve inexpensive, tasty local cuisine and hometown Eggenberg beer on tap. If you've always wanted to play the piano for an appreciative Czech crowd in a colorful little tavern...do it here (daily 10:00–23:00, Kájovská 66, tel. 380-711-280).

Krčma u Dwau Maryí ("Tavern of the Two Marys") is a characteristic old place with idyllic riverside picnic tables, serving ye olde Czech cuisine and drinks. The fascinating menu explains the history of the house and makes a good case that the food of the poor medieval Bohemians was tasty and varied. Buck up for

buckwheat, millet, greasy meat, or the poor-man's porridge (daily 11:00–23:00, Parkán 104, tel. 380-717-228).

Cikánská Jizba ("Gypsy Pub") is a Roma tavern filling one den-like, barrel-vaulted room. The Roma staff serves Slovak-style food (Slovakia is where most of the Czech Republic's Roma population came from). Krumlov has a long Roma history, and even today 1,000 Roma people live in the town. While this rustic little restaurant—which packs its 10 tables under a mystic-feeling Gothic vault—won't win any cuisine awards, you never know what festive and musical activities will erupt, particularly on Friday nights when the owner's son's band Cindži Renta (Wet Rag) performs here (Mon–Sat 15:00–24:00, closed Sun, 2 blocks toward castle from main square at Dlouhá 31, tel. 380-717-585). For more on the Roma of Eastern Europe, see page 224.

Restaurace u Dobráka ("Good Man") is like eating in a medieval garage, with a giant poster of Karl Marx overseeing the action. Lojza, who's been tossing steaks on his open fire for years, makes sure you'll eat well. Locals know it as the best place for grilled steak and fish—expect to pay 350 Kč for a full meal. He charges too much for his beer in order to keep the noisy beer-drinkers away (open daily 17:30–24:00 from Easter until Lojza "has a shoebox full of money," Široká 74, tel. 380-717-776).

Laibon is the modern vegetarian answer to the carnivorous Middle Ages. Settle down inside or head out onto the idyllic river terrace, and lighten up your pork-loaded diet with soy goulash or Mútábúr soup (daily 11:00–23:00, Parkán 105).

Rybářská Restaurace ("Fisherman's Restaurant") doesn't look particularly inviting from outside, but don't get discouraged. This is *the* place in town to taste freshwater fish you've never heard of (and never will again). Try eel, perch, shad, carp, trout, and more. Choose between indoor tables under fishnets or riverside picnic benches outside (daily 11:00–22:00, on the island by the millwheel).

Krčma v Šatlavské is an old prison gone cozy, with an open fire, big wooden tables under a rustic old medieval vault, and tables outdoors on the pedestrian lane. It's great for a late drink or game cooked on an open spit. *Medovina* is the hot honey wine (daily 12:00–24:00, on Šatlavská, follow lane leading to the side from TI on main square, mobile 608-973-797).

Restaurace Barbakán is built into the town fortifications,

with a terrace hanging high over the river. It's a good spot for old-fashioned Czech cooking and beer, at the top of town and near the recommended Rooseveltova street accommodations (open long hours daily, reasonable prices, Horní 26, tel. 380-712-679).

Hospoda 99 Restaurace serves good and cheap soups, salads, and meals. It's the choice of hostelers and locals alike for its hamburgers, vegetarian food, Czech dishes, and cheap booze (meals served 10:00–22:00, bar open until 24:00, at Hostel 99, Vezni 99, tel. 380-712-812). This place is booming until late, when everything else is hibernating.

Dobrá Čajovna is a typical example of the quiet, exotic-feeling teahouses that flooded Czech towns in the 1990s as alternatives to smoky, raucous pubs. While directly across from the castle entrance, it's a world away from the touristic hubbub. As is so often the case, if you want to surround yourself with locals, don't go to a traditional place...go ethnic. With its meditative karma inside and a peaceful terrace facing the monastery out back, it provides a relaxing break (daily 13:00–22:00, Latrán 54, mobile 777-654-744).

Český Krumlov Connections

Almost all trains to and from Český Krumlov require a transfer in the city of České Budějovice, a transit hub just to the north. České Budějovice's bus and train stations are next to each other. All bus and train timetables are online at www.idos.cz.

From Český Krumlov by Train to: České Budějovice (6/day, 1 hr), **Prague** (8/day, 1/day direct, 4 hrs; bus is faster, cheaper, and easier—see below), **Vienna** (5–6/day, 5–6 hrs, 1–2 changes), **Budapest** (6/day with at least one change, 10–15 hrs).

From Český Krumlov by Bus to: Prague (7/day, 3.5 hrs, 180 Kč; 2 of the daily departures—12:00 and 16:45—can be reserved and paid for at TI, tickets can be bought from driver if seats are available), **České Budějovice** (transit hub for other destinations; about 2/hr, 30–50 min, 30 Kč). The Český Krumlov bus station, a five-minute walk out of town, is just a big parking lot with numbered stalls for various buses (bus info tel. 380-711-190). A good place to buy bus tickets online is www.studentagency.cz.

By Shuttle Bus or Private Car to Linz and Beyond: If you get to Linz, Austria, by shuttle bus or car, you'll have your choice

of fast trains that run hourly from Linz to Munich, Salzburg, and Vienna. **Pension Lobo** in Český Krumlov runs a shuttle bus service to and from **Linz** (3/day, 75 min, 380 Kč), **Vienna** (1/day, 3 hrs, 950 Kč), and **Salzburg** (1/day, 3 hrs, 950 Kč). Reservations are required—call 380-713-153 or 777-637-374, send an email to lobo @ckrumlov.cz, or reserve in person at Pension Lobo or at the shuttle office on the main square (www.shuttlelobo.cz).

SLOVAKIA

SLOVAKIA

Slovensko

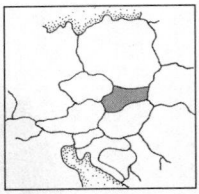

In many ways, Slovakia is the West Virginia of Europe—poor and relatively undeveloped, but stunningly beautiful in its own rustic way. Sitting quietly in the very center of Central Europe, wedged between bigger and stronger nations (Hungary, Austria, the Czech Republic, and Poland), Slovakia was brutally disfigured by the communists, then overshadowed by the Czechs. In recent years, however, this fledgling republic has begun to find its wings.

Recent economic reforms are causing two very different Slovakias to emerge: the west is modern, industrialized, flat, affluent, and centered in the capital of Bratislava; the east is traditional, remote, mountainous, poor, and has high unemployment.

Slovakia is fairly ethnically diverse: In addition to the Slavic Slovaks, it's home to many ethnic Hungarians (about 10 percent of the population, "stranded" here when Hungary lost this land after World War I) and Roma (Gypsies, also about 10 percent). Slovakia has struggled to incorporate both of these large and often-mistreated minority groups. Rounding out the cultural cocktail are Czechs, Ruthenians (Carpathian Mountain peasants of Ukrainian origin), and a smattering of Germans.

Though the Slovaks are more closely associated with their former countrymen, the Czechs, they actually have more in common culturally with their neighbors to the north, the Poles. While the Czechs take pride in a marked agnosticism, the Slovaks tend to be devout Catholics. Also like the Poles, the Slovaks have a strong agricultural (rather than industrial) heritage.

The Slovak capital city, Bratislava—between Vienna and Budapest on the Danube—is sprucing itself up and racing into the future. It becomes a more enticing destination with each passing year. Yet in many ways, it seems to be leaving the rest of the

country in its dust. To the north and east, near the Polish border, are the poorest and most beautiful parts of this mountainous nation: the rolling hills of the Spiš Region and the jagged peaks of the High Tatras.

Among travelers, there seem to be two schools of thought about the rural, rough-around-the-edges eastern part of the country. Some people adore the region for its stark natural beauty and cultural authenticity, which provides an exciting detour off the prettified tourist mainstream. Rural Slovakia gives more adventurous travelers the opportunity to feel the pulse of a place that's still struggling to transition into democracy—and yet is stable and safe enough for a comfortable visit. These people enjoy hiking along Slovakia's glorious mountain trails, driving through its humble villages, interacting with its kind people, and pondering the blemishes that communism left on its pastoral landscape.

Other people can't wait to leave rural Slovakia, turned off by its drab industrial skeletons, relative poverty, and dearth of must-see sights compared to the rest of Eastern Europe. Tourists focusing on pretty-as-a-postcard Eastern Europe will want to spend more time elsewhere...and should.

What is clear is that Slovakia is not your standard European country. With lots of pleasant surprises, Slovakia is worth a peek for more adventurous travelers.

For more in-depth information about Slovakia, pick up a copy of *Spectacular Slovakia,* an excellent annual magazine produced by the English-language newspaper in Bratislava (www.spectacularslovakia.sk).

Slovak History

Slovakia has spent most of its history as someone else's backyard. For centuries, Slovakia was ruled from Budapest and known as "Upper Hungary." In fact, in the 16th and 17th centuries, when the

Slovakia Almanac

Official Name: Slovenská Republika, though locals call it Slovensko. The nation is the eastern half of the former Czechoslovakia (split peaceably in 1993).

Population: 5.4 million people. The majority are native Slovaks who are Roman Catholic and speak Slovak. But one in ten has Hungarian roots, and an estimated one in ten is Roma (Gypsy).

Latitude and Longitude: 48°N and 20°E (similar latitude to Paris or Vancouver, BC).

Area: 19,000 square miles (the size of Massachusetts and New Hampshire put together).

Geography: The northeastern half of Slovakia features the beautiful rolling hills and spiky, jagged peaks of the Carpathian Mountains. The southwestern half is quite flat—a continuation of the Hungarian Plain. The climate is generally cool and cloudy.

Biggest Cities: Only two cities have more than 100,000 inhabitants: Bratislava in the west (the capital, 450,000) and Košice in the east (235,000).

Economy: The Gross Domestic Product is about $120 billion, and the GDP per capita is $22,000 (roughly two-thirds that of the average German). Since the initial changeover to capitalism, the unemployment rate has steadily declined, and is currently sitting at about 8 percent.

Currency: Slovakia uses the euro currency (€1 = about $1.40). You might still see references to the old currency, the Slovak koruna (30 Sk = about €1).

Government: President Ivan Gašparovič heads a government that isn't dominated by any single political party. Slovakia also has a 150-seat National Council (like a parliament).

Flag: Horizontal bands of white, blue, and red with a shield bearing a "patriarchal cross" (with two crossbars instead of one) atop three humps. The three humps represent three historic mountain ranges of Slovakia: Mátra (now in northern Hungary, near Eger), Fatra, and Tatra. The double-barred cross represents St. Stephen (István) of Hungary, commemorating the many centuries that Slovakia was part of Hungary.

Slovaks You May Recognize: Andy Warhol (American Pop artist who gained more than his 15 minutes of fame, born to Slovak immigrants), Martina Hingis (Swiss tennis player born in Slovakia), and Štefan Bani (emigrated to America and invented the parachute).

Ottomans occupied most of Hungary, the Hungarians moved their capital to Bratislava. At other times, Slovakia was an important chunk of the Habsburg Empire, ruled from neighboring Vienna. More recently was the 75-year era—still fresh in the collective memory—in which Slovakia was joined with the Czech Republic as the country of "Czechoslovakia."

Czechoslovakia

Czechoslovakia was formed at the end of World War I, when the Austro-Hungarian Empire was splitting into pieces. During this flurry of new nation-building, a small country of 10 million Czechs or five million Slovaks was unlikely to survive. The Czechs were concerned about the huge number of Germans in their territory (in an area called the Sudetenland), while the Slovaks—who had endured relatively oppressive conditions under the Hungarian half of the empire—were unsure of their ability to steer their own nation.

These two Slavic peoples decided there was safety in numbers. (It was a delicate balance—there were more Sudeten Germans in Czechoslovakia than there were Slovaks.) The union was logical enough—especially in the eyes of Tomáš Masaryk, Czechoslovakia's first president (and a buddy of Woodrow Wilson's from Princeton). Masaryk was from the border of the two regions and spoke a dialect that mixed elements of Czech and Slovak (for more on Masaryk, see page 112). Czechoslovakia was born.

The Czechs and the Slovaks were constantly reminded that they were countrymen in name only. In a prelude to World War II, these two peoples were again split along the cultural fault that always divided them: Today's Czech Republic was absorbed into Germany, while much of the Slovak land went to Nazi-allied Hungary.

During the post-war communist era, the regime decided to convert the Slovak economy from a low-key agricultural model to a base of heavy industry. Since the industry was centrally planned for communist purposes (relying on raw materials imported from elsewhere within the Eastern Bloc), it made sense only as a cog in the communist machine. Many of Slovakia's factories built heavy arms, making the country the biggest producer of tanks in the world. Slovakia became one of the ugliest and most polluted corners of Eastern Europe. The Slovak environment—and economy—are still recovering.

When the wave of uprisings spread across Eastern Europe in 1989, Czechoslovakia peacefully achieved its own freedom with the Velvet Revolution. Then, on January 1, 1993, with the so-called Velvet Divorce, Czechoslovakia amicably split into two nations: the Czech and Slovak Republics (see sidebar). At first, many

It's Not You, It's Me: The Velvet Divorce

In the autumn of 1989, hundreds of thousands of Czechs and Slovaks streamed into Prague to demonstrate on Wenceslas Square. Their "Velvet Revolution" succeeded, and Czechoslovakia's communist regime peacefully excused itself. But that was only the first step. In that age of new possibility, the two peoples of Czechoslovakia began to wonder if they belonged together, after all.

Ever since they joined with the Czechs in 1918, the Slovaks felt they were ruled from Prague (unmistakably the political, economic, and cultural center of the country), rather than from their own capital. And the Czechs, for their part, resented the financial burden of carrying their poorer neighbors to the east. In the post-communist world, the Czechs found themselves with a 10 percent unemployment rate...compared to 20 or 30 percent unemployment in the Slovak lands. In this new world of flux and freedom, long-standing tensions came to a head.

The dissolution of Czechoslovakia began over a hyphen, as the Slovaks wanted to rename the country Czecho-Slovakia. Ideally, this symbolic move would come with a redistribution of powers: two capitals and two UN reps, but one national bank and a single currency. The Slovaks were also less enthusiastic about abandoning the communist society altogether, since the Soviet regime had left them with a heavily industrialized economy that depended on a socialist system for survival.

Initially, many Czechs couldn't understand the Slovaks' Slovaks weren't sure this was so wise. More recently, however, it seems that the Czechs and Slovaks are getting along better than ever—by choice, not because they're compelled to. Czechs root for the Slovak hockey team, and Slovaks cheer on the Czech soccer powerhouse...unless, of course, their teams are playing against each other.

After the Divorce: Slovakia Today

Finally on their own after the Velvet Divorce, the Slovaks were initially faced with some challenging times. Communist rule had been particularly unkind to them, and their economy was in a shambles. The first president of Slovakia was a former boxer named Vladimír Mečiar, whose authoritarian rule was not much better than the communists'. Mečiar was frequently accused of corruption (including pulling issues off the ballot when the polls seemed to be going against him), and it was alleged that he was involved in the kidnapping, torture, and humiliation of one of his political opponent's sons in 1995. He was also notorious for making offensive statements about his country's substantial Hungarian

demands. The first post-communist president of Czechoslovakia, the Czech Václav Havel, inadvertently widened the gap when he took a rare trip to the Slovak half of his country in 1990. In a fit of terrible judgment, Havel boldly promised he'd close the ugly, polluting Soviet factories in Slovakia...seemingly oblivious to the fact that many Slovaks still depended on these factories for survival. Havel left in disgrace and visited the Slovak lands only twice more in the following two and a half years.

In June 1992, the Slovak nationalist candidate Vladimír Mečiar fared surprisingly well in the elections—suggesting that the Slovaks were serious about secession. The politicians plowed ahead, getting serious about the split in September 1992. The transition took only three months from start to finish.

The people of Czechoslovakia never actually voted on the separation; in fact, public opinion polls in both regions were two-thirds *against* the split. This makes Slovakia quite possibly the only country ever to gain independence against the will of its citizens.

The Velvet Divorce became official on January 1, 1993, and each country ended up with its own capital, currency, and head of state. The Slovaks let loose a yelp of excitement, and the Czechs emitted a sigh of relief. For most, the divorce dissolved tensions, and nearly two decades later, Czechs and Slovaks still feel closer to each other than to any other nationality.

and Roma minorities. Mečiar drew criticism from neighboring Eastern and Western European nations, as well as the US. He was finally defeated at the polls in 2000, but—like a bad penny—he kept turning up, nearly winning elections in 2002 and 2004.

As Mečiar (and his voting base) gets along in years, Slovakia appears to be turning to more mainstream politics. Over the last decade, visionary leaders have set forth bold solutions—including the 2003 implementation of a Steve Forbes–style flat tax (19 percent), followed by EU membership in 2004. Before long, a funny thing started happening—major international corporations began to notice the same thing the communists had: This is a great place to build stuff, thanks to an extremely handy location, low labor costs, and a well-trained workforce. Multiple foreign automakers have built plants here, making Slovakia the world's biggest car producer (per capita) and leading *The New York Times* to dub Slovakia "the European Detroit." Ireland's "Celtic Tiger" economic boom has led people to make comparisons with Slovakia, even predicting the coming of a "Tatra Tiger" (named for the Slovak mountain range).

While the flat tax is not without its critics—especially in the very impoverished eastern half of the country, where poor people feel they're becoming even poorer—there's no doubt it has been a boon for middle-class areas in the west. In 2007, Slovakia had Europe's fastest-growing economy (10.4 percent). And in 2009, Slovakia became the first former Warsaw Pact country to adopt the euro currency.

Slovak Food

Slovak cuisine shows some Hungarian influence, but in most ways it's closer to Czech cuisine—with lots of starches and gravy, and plenty of pork, cabbage, and potatoes (see "Czech Food," page 44). Slovakia also has a strong tradition of grilling pickled meats. Keep an eye out for Slovakia's national dish, *bryndzové halušky* (small potato dumplings with sheep's cheese and bits of bacon). Like the Czechs, the Slovaks produce excellent beer (*pivo*, PEE-voh). One of the top brands is Zlatý Bažant ("Golden Pheasant").

Slovak Language

Many people assume Slovak is virtually the same as Czech. To be sure, there are similarities—but they're hardly identical.

Slovak is handy as a sort of a lingua franca of Slavic tongues. Czechs can understand Poles, but not Slovenes; Poles can understand Croatians, but not Czechs. But Slovak speakers generally find they can understand—and be understood in—any of these languages.

Slovak's similarity to Czech was exaggerated during the 75 years that these languages shared a country. Soccer games would be broadcast with two commentators—one spoke Czech, and the other spoke Slovak. Anyone growing up in this era grew comfortable using the languages interchangeably. But today's teenagers—who have only spoken exclusively Czech or Slovak—find they have trouble understanding each other across the border.

Slovak uses many of the same diacritical markings as Czech. Many letters are topped with a *mäkčeň* ("softener"), including *č, š, ž,* and *ň).* Here are some guidelines for pronouncing Slovak:

j sounds like "y" as in "yarn"
c sounds like "ts" as in "cats"
č sounds like "ch" as in "chicken"
š sounds like "sh" as in "shrimp"
ž sounds like "zh" as in "leisure"
ň sounds like "ny" as in "canyon"
ä sounds like "eh" as in "get"

An acute accent *(á, é, í, ó, ú, ý)* means you linger on that vowel. What looks like an apostrophe after a consonant—such as ***d'***, ***t'***, and ***l'***—indicates that the sound has a palatal pronunciation; this

means that you make the sound by tapping the flat part of your tongue to the roof of your mouth (so *ď* sounds not quite like "d," but closer to the "dj" sound in "ledge").

The local "ciao"—used informally for both "hi" and "bye"—is easy to remember: *ahoj* (pronounced "AH-hoy," like a pirate). For more, see the Slovak Survival Phrases on page 1120.

When navigating town, these words might be helpful: ***mesto*** (MEHS-toh, town), ***námestie*** (NAH-mehs-tee, square), ***ulica*** (OO-leet-sah, road), ***nábrežie*** (NAH-breh-zhee, embankment road), and ***most*** (mohst, bridge).

BRATISLAVA

Pozsony/Pressburg

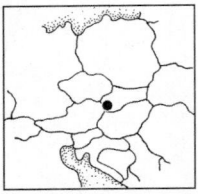

Bratislava (brah-tee-SLAH-vah), long a drab lesson in the failings of the communist system, is turning things around...fast. A decade ago, the city center was grim, deserted, and dangerous—a place where only thieves and fools dared to tread. Today it's downright charming, bursting with colorfully restored facades, lively outdoor cafés, swanky boutiques, in-love-with-life locals, and (on sunny days) an almost Mediterranean ambience.

The rejuvenation doesn't end in the Old Town. The ramshackle quarter to the east is gradually being flattened and redeveloped into a new forest of skyscrapers. Bratislava is working together with its neighbor Vienna to forge a new super-capital for trade and commerce, bridging the former Western Europe and the former Eastern Europe. The hilltop castle is getting a facelift. And even the glum commie suburb of Petržalka is getting a Technicolor makeover. Before our eyes, Bratislava is becoming the quintessential post-communist Central European city...an example of what can happen when government and business leaders make a concerted effort to jump-start a failing city.

You get the feeling that workaday Bratislavans—who strike some visitors as gruff—are being pulled to the cutting edge of the 21st century kicking and screaming. But many Slovaks embrace the changes, and fancy themselves as the yang to Vienna's yin: If Vienna is a staid, elderly aristocrat sipping coffee, then Bratislava is a vivacious young professional jet-setting around Europe.

Bratislava is not worth going far out of your way for. But its priceless location—on the Danube (and the tourist circuit) smack-dab between Budapest and Vienna—makes it worth considering as an illuminating "on the way" destination. Frankly, the city used to

leave me cold. But all the new changes are positively inspiring. See Bratislava now...in a few years, it'll be a different city.

Planning Your Time

A few hours is enough to get the gist of Bratislava. Head straight for the Old Town and follow my self-guided walk, dropping into your choice of museums. With more time, ascend to the "UFO" observation deck atop the funky suspension bridge. Or hike up to the castle, which offers great views over town (even though its interior is closed for renovation). Spend the night if you like, but I find hotel values and evening fun better in Budapest and Vienna.

Orientation to Bratislava

(area code: 02)

Bratislava, with nearly half a million residents, is Slovakia's capital and biggest city. It has a small, colorful Old Town (Staré Mesto), with the castle on the hill above it. This small area is surrounded by a vast construction zone of new buildings and a few colorized communist suburbs (including Petržalka, across the river). The north and west of the city is hilly and cool (these "Little Carpathians" are draped with vineyards), while the south and east is flat and warmer.

Tourist Information

The TI has two branches in the heart of the city. There's a small window in the **train station** (June–Oct Mon–Fri 8:00–19:00, Sat–Sun 9:00–17:00; Nov–May Mon–Fri 9:00–17:00, Sat–Sun 9:00–14:00; tel. 02/5249-5906), and a main branch on **Primate's Square** behind the Old Town Hall (June–Sept Mon–Fri 8:30–19:00, Sat 9:00–17:00, Sun 10:00–17:00; Oct–May Mon–Fri 8:30–18:00, Sat 9:00–16:00, Sun 10:00–15:00; Klobučnícka 2, tel. 02/5443-3715, www.bkis.sk and www.bratislava.sk). There are also TI windows at the airport and passenger boat terminals.

At any TI, pick up the free *Bratislava Guide* (with map) and browse their brochures. They can help you find a room for a modest fee. The **Bratislava City Card,** which includes free transit and sightseeing discounts, is worthwhile only if you're doing the Old Town walking tour (see "Tours in Bratislava," later; €10/day, includes walking tour April–Oct, 50 percent discount on tour Nov–March, sold at TI).

Arrival in Bratislava

By Train: Bratislava's main train station, called Bratislava Hlavná Stanica, is about a half-mile north of the Old Town. The city plans to tear down most of the station and start from scratch in the next

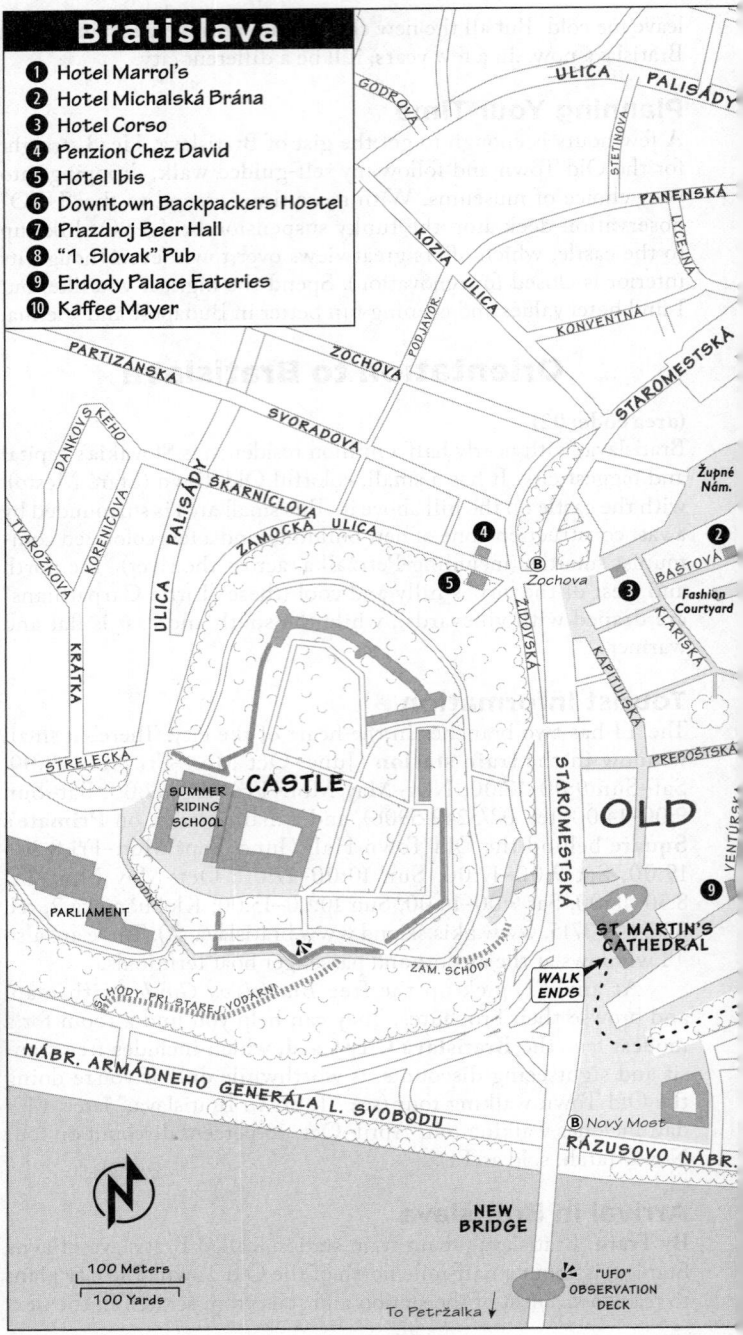
Bratislava
1 Hotel Marrol's
2 Hotel Michalská Brána
3 Hotel Corso
4 Penzion Chez David
5 Hotel Ibis
6 Downtown Backpackers Hostel
7 Prazdroj Beer Hall
8 "1. Slovak" Pub
9 Erdody Palace Eateries
10 Kaffee Mayer
GODROVÁ
ULICA PALISÁDY
ŠTEFÁNIKOVA
PANENSKÁ
LÝCEJNÁ
KOZIA ULICA
KONVENTNÁ
PODJAVOR
ZOCHOVA
PARTIZÁNSKA
STAROMESTSKÁ
SVORADOVA
DANKOVSKÉHO
ŠKARNÍCLOVA
Župné Nám.
TVAROŽKOVÁ
KORENICOVA
ZÁMOCKÁ ULICA
ULICA PALISÁDY
Zochova
BAŠTOVÁ
Fashion Courtyard
KLARISKÁ
ŽIDOVSKÁ
KAPITULSKÁ
KRÁTKA
STRELECKÁ
PREPOŠTSKÁ
SUMMER RIDING SCHOOL
CASTLE
OLD
STAROMESTSKÁ
VENTÚRSKA
VODNÝ
PARLIAMENT
ST. MARTIN'S CATHEDRAL
ZÁM. SCHODY
WALK ENDS
CHODY PRI STAREJ VODÁRNI
NÁBR. ARMÁDNEHO GENERÁLA L. SVOBODU
Nový Most
RÁZUSOVO NÁBR.
NEW BRIDGE
100 Meters
100 Yards
"UFO" OBSERVATION DECK
To Petržalka

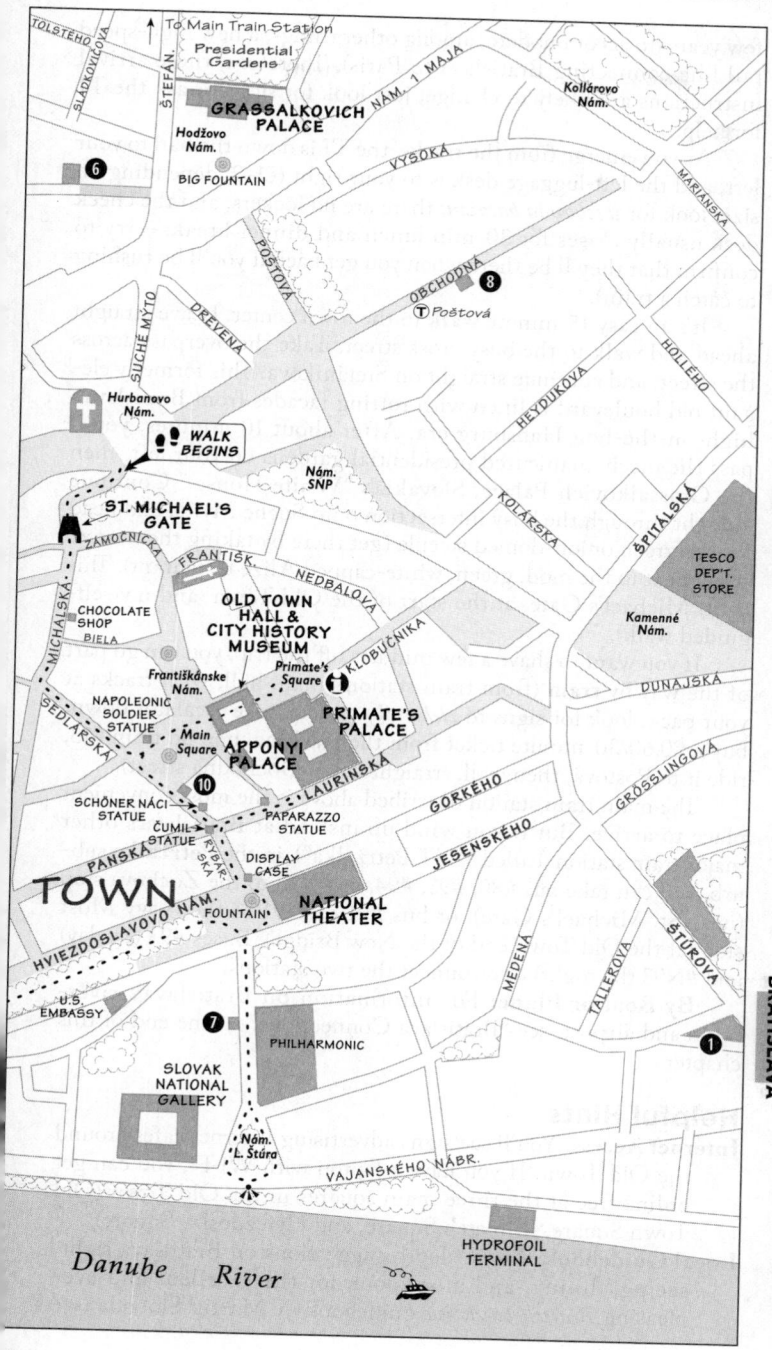
To Main Train Station
Presidential Gardens
TOLSTÉHO
SLÁDKOVIČOVA
ŠTEFÁNIKOVA
GRASSALKOVICH PALACE
NÁM. 1 MAJA
Kollárovo Nám.
Hodžovo Nám.
BIG FOUNTAIN
VYSOKÁ
MARIÁNSKA
POŠTOVÁ
OBCHODNÁ
Poštová
DREVENÁ
SÚCHE MÝTO
HEYDUKOVA
HOLLÉHO
Hurbanovo Nám.
WALK BEGINS
Nám. SNP
ST. MICHAEL'S GATE
ZÁMOČNÍCKA
FRANTIŠK.
NEDBALOVA
KOLÁRSKA
ŠPITÁLSKÁ
TESCO DEP'T. STORE
MICHALSKÁ
CHOCOLATE SHOP
BIELA
OLD TOWN HALL & CITY HISTORY MUSEUM
KLOBUČNÍKA
Kamenné Nám.
Františkánske Nám.
Primate's Square
DUNAJSKÁ
NAPOLEONIC SOLDIER STATUE
PRIMATE'S PALACE
ŠEDLÁRSKÁ
Main Square
APPONYI PALACE
LAURINSKÁ
GORKÉHO
GRÖSSLINGOVÁ
SCHÖNER NÁCI STATUE
PAPARAZZO STATUE
ČUMIL STATUE
JESENSKÉHO
PANSKÁ
RYBÁRSKA
DISPLAY CASE
TOWN
NATIONAL THEATER
FOUNTAIN
HVIEZDOSLAVOVO NÁM.
ŠTÚROVA
MEDENÁ
TALLEROVA
U.S. EMBASSY
PHILHARMONIC
SLOVAK NATIONAL GALLERY
Nám. L. Štúra
VAJANSKÉHO NÁBR.
HYDROFOIL TERMINAL
Danube River

few years (to accommodate, among other things, a new high-speed rail line connecting Bratislava to Paris). Therefore, these arrival instructions are likely to change; just look for signs or ask the TI for help.

As you emerge from the tracks, the TI is down the hall to your left, and the left-luggage desk is to your right (€1–2, depending on size; look for *ú schovňa batožín;* there are no lockers, and the check desk usually closes for 30-min lunch and dinner breaks—try to confirm that they'll be there when you get back if you'll be rushing to catch a train).

It's an easy 15-minute **walk** to the town center. Leave straight ahead and walk to the busy cross street. Take the overpass across the street, and continue straight on Štefánikova. This formerly elegant old boulevard is lined with rotting facades from Bratislava's high-on-the-hog Habsburg era. After about 10 minutes, you'll pass the nicely manicured presidential gardens on your left, then the Grassalkovich Palace, Slovakia's "White House." Continue straight through the busy intersection onto Súche Mýho, and head for the green onion-domed steeple (get there by taking the narrow street next to the mod, green, white-capped Alizé restaurant). This is St. Michael's Gate, at the start of the Old Town (and my self-guided walk).

If you want to shave a few minutes off the trip, you can go part of the way by **tram** (from train station's main hall, with tracks at your back, look for signs to *električky* on left; take escalator down, buy a €0.60/30-minute ticket from the machine, hop on tram #13, ride it to Poštová, then walk straight down Obchodná street).

The main train station described above is the most convenient place to arrive. But if you wind up instead at Bratislava's other major train station (called "ŽST Petržalka"), in the **Petržalka** suburb, you can take bus #80, #93, #94, or #N93 to the Zochova stop (near St. Michael's Gate), or bus #91 or #191 to the Nový Most stop (at the Old Town end of the New Bridge). Buses #93 (by day) and #N93 (by night) also connect the two stations.

By Boat or Plane: For information on Bratislava's riverboats and airport, see "Bratislava Connections," at the end of this chapter.

Helpful Hints

Internet Access: You'll see signs advertising Internet cafés around the Old Town. If you have a laptop with Wi-Fi, you can get online free at the three main squares in the Old Town (Old Town Square, Primate's Square, and Hviezdoslav Square).

Local Guidebook: For in-depth suggestions on Bratislava sightseeing, dining, and more, look for the excellent and eye-pleasing *Bratislava Active* guidebook by Martin Sloboda (see

"Tours in Bratislava," next; around €10, sold at every postcard rack).

Tours in Bratislava

Walking Tour—The TI offers a one-hour Old Town walking tour in English every day in the summer at 14:00 (€12.50, free or discounted with Bratislava City Card; runs sporadically based on demand Nov–March—call ahead to confirm, tel. 02/5443-4059, guides@bkis.sk).

Local Guide—MS Agency, run by **Martin Sloboda** (a can-do entrepreneur and tireless Bratislava booster, and author of the great local guidebook described above), will set you up with a good local guide (€120/3 hrs, €150/4 hrs), and can help you track down your Slovak roots (tel. 02/5464-1467, www.msagency.sk, info @msagency.sk).

Self-Guided Walk

Bratislava's Old Town

This orientation walk through the heart of delightfully traffic-free old Bratislava takes about an hour (not including stops). If you're coming from the station, make your way toward the green onion-domed steeple of St. Michael's Gate (explained in "Arrival in Bratislava," earlier). Before going through the passage into the Old Town, peek over the railing on your left to the inviting garden below—once part of the city moat.

• *Step through the first gate, walk along the passageway, and pause as you come through the onion-domed...*

St. Michael's Gate (Michalská Brána)

This is the last surviving tower of the city wall. Just below the gate, notice the "kilometer zero" plaque in the ground, marking the point from which distances in Slovakia are measured.

• *You're at the head of...*

Michalská Street

Pretty as it is now, the Old Town was a decrepit ghost town during the communist era. Locals avoided this desolate corner of the city, preferring to spend time in the Petržalka suburb across the river. But after the fall of communism, city leaders decided to

revitalize this zone. They replaced all of the cobbles, spruced up the public buildings, and encouraged the new private owners of other buildings to invest in careful restoration. It worked: Today the Old Town is gleaming, and packed with locals and tourists alike.

The cafés and restaurants that line this street are inviting, especially in summer. But if you don't look beyond the facades and outdoor tables, you'll miss much of Bratislava's charm. Courtyards and galleries—most of them open to the public—burrow through the city's buildings. For example, a half-block down on the right, the gallery at #7 is home to several fashion designers.

Speaking of fashion...are you noticing a lot of skin? Tight jeans? Low-cut tops? Slovak women are known for their provocative dress. When pressed for a reason for this, local men smirk and say, "That's just the way it is."

On the left (at #6), the **Čokoládovňa pod Michalom** chocolate shop is highly regarded among locals for its delicious, creamy truffles (Mon–Fri 9:00–21:00, Sat–Sun 10:00–21:00, tel. 02/5443-3945).

Look over the shop's entrance and find the **cannonball** embedded in the wall above the seal. This commemorates Napoleon's two sieges of Bratislava, which together caused massive devastation—even worse than the city suffered during World War II. Keep an eye out for these cannonballs all over town...somber reminders of one of Bratislava's darkest times.

• *Two blocks down from St. Michael's Gate, the name of this main drag changes to Ventúrska, the street jogs to the right, and the café scene continues. At the jog, detour left (along Sedlárska) and head for the...*

Main Square (Hlavné Námestie)

This is the bustling centerpiece of Old World Bratislava. Virtually every building around this square dates from a different architectural period, from Gothic (the yellow tower) to Art Nouveau (the fancy facade facing it from across the square). When these buildings were restored a few years ago, great pains were taken to achieve authenticity—each one matches the color most likely used when it was originally built. Extremely atmospheric cafés line the bottom of the square. **Kaffee Mayer** is the classic choice (described later, under "Eating in Bratislava"), but you can't go wrong along here. Choose the ambience you like best (indoors or out) and nurse a drink with arguably Slovakia's best urban view.

Peering over one of the benches is a cartoonish statue of a

Napoleonic officer (notice the French flag marking the embassy right behind him). With bare feet and a hat pulled over his eyes, it's hardly a flattering portrait—you could call it the Slovaks' revenge for the difficulties they faced at Napoleon's hands.

At the top of the Main Square is the impressive **Old Town Hall** (Stará Radnica), marked by a bold yellow tower. Near the bottom of the tower (to the left of the window), notice the cannonball embedded in the facade—yet another reminder of Napoleon's impact on Bratislava. Over time, the Old Town Hall gradually grew, annexing the buildings next to it—creating a mishmash of architectural styles along this side of the square. (A few steps down the street to the right are the historic apartments and wine museum at the Apponyi House—see "Sights in Bratislava," later.)

Step through the passageway into the Old Town Hall's gorgeously restored **courtyard,** with its Renaissance arcades. (If the City History Museum is open, its entrance is here—see "Sights in Bratislava," later.)

Then, to see another fine old square, continue through the other end of the courtyard into **Primate's Square** (Primaciálne Námestie). The pink mansion on the right is the Primate's Palace, with a fine interior decorated with six English tapestries (see "Sights in Bratislava," later). Do you see a lot of people using laptops? In a progressive move befitting its status as an emerging business center of Europe, Bratislava provides free Wi-Fi on three squares in the Old Town. The huge student population (not to mention tourists) happily surfs in this beautiful setting. At the far end of this square is the main branch of the TI.

• *Backtrack to the Main Square. With your back to the Old Town Hall, go to the end of the square and follow the street to the left (Rybárska Brána). Soon you'll pass a series of...*

Whimsical Statues

Several playful statues (such as the Napoleonic officer we met earlier) dot Bratislava's Old Town. Most of these date from the late 1990s, when city leaders wanted to entice locals back into the newly prettied-up Old Town.

A half-block down this street (on the left), you'll come to a jovial chap doffing his top hat. This is a statue of **Schöner Náci,** who lived in Bratislava until the 1960s. This eccentric old man, a poor carpet cleaner, would dress up in his one black suit and top

City of Three Cultures: Pressburg, Pozsony, Bratislava

Historically a Hungarian and Austrian city as much as a Slovak one, Bratislava has always been an Eastern European melting pot. The Hungarians used Pozsony (as they called it) as their capital during the century and a half that Buda and Pest were occupied by Ottoman invaders. Later, the city was a favorite retreat of Habsburg Empress Maria Theresa (who used its German name, Pressburg). Everyone from Hans Christian Andersen to Casanova sang the wonders of this bustling burg on the Danube.

By its late-19th-century glory days, the city was a rich intersection of cultures. Shop clerks had to be able to greet customers in German, Hungarian, and Slovak. It was said that the mornings belonged to the Slovaks (farmers who came into the city to sell their wares at market), the afternoons to the Hungarians (diplomats and office-workers filling the cafés), and the evenings to the Austrians (wine-producers who ran convivial neighborhood wine pubs where all three groups would gather). In those wine pubs, the vintner would listen to which language his customers used, then automatically bring them the correct size glass: 0.3 liters for Hungarians, 0.25 liters for Austrians, and 0.2 liters for Slovaks (a distinction that still exists today). Jews (one-tenth of the population), Romanians, and Roma (Gypsies) rounded out the city's ethnic brew.

When the new nation of Czechoslovakia was formed from the rubble of World War I, the city shed its German and Hungarian names, proudly taking the new Slavic name Bratislava. The Slovak population—which had been at only about 10 percent—was on the rise, but the city remained tri-cultural.

World War II changed all of that. With the dissolution of Czechoslovakia, Slovakia became an "independent" country

hat, and go strolling through the city, offering gifts to the women he fancied. (He'd often whisper *"schön"*—German for "pretty"—to the women, which is how he got his nickname.) After spending his life cheering up the gloomy streets of communist Bratislava, Schöner Náci now gets to spend eternity greeting visitors in front of his favorite café, Kaffee Mayer.

As a sad epilogue, Schöner Náci's arm was broken off recently by a bunch of drunks. As Prague gets more expensive, Bratislava is becoming the cheaper alternative for weekend "stag parties,"

under the thumb of the Nazis—who decimated the Jewish population. Then, at the end of the war, in retribution for Hitler's misdeeds, a reunited Czechoslovakia expelled people of Germanic descent (including all of those Austrians). And finally, a "mutual exchange of populations" sent the city's Hungarians back to Hungary.

Bratislava suffered terribly under the communists. It became the textbook example of a historic city whose multilayered charm and delicate cultural fabric were ripped apart, then shrouded in gray by the communist regime. For example, the communists were more proud of their ultramodern New Bridge than of the historic Jewish quarter they razed to make way for it. Now the bridge and its highway slice through the center of the Old Town, and the heavy traffic rattles the stained-glass windows of St. Martin's Cathedral.

But Bratislava's most recent chapter is one of great success. Over the last decade, the city has gone from gloomy victim of communism to thriving economic center and social hub. Its population of 450,000 includes some 70,000 students (at the city's six universities), creating an atmosphere of youthful energy and optimism. Its remarkable position on the Danube, a short commute from Vienna, is prompting its redevelopment as one of Europe's most up-and-coming cities.

Bratislava and Vienna have realized it's in both cities' interest to work together to bring the Slovak capital up to snuff. They're cooperating as a new "twin city" commercial super-zone...and things are happening at an astonishing pace. In the coming years, foreign investors plan to erect a skyline of 600-foot-tall skyscrapers and a clutch of glittering new mega-malls. You'd never have guessed it a few years ago, but today calling Bratislava "the next Berlin, on a smaller scale" is only a bit of a stretch.

popular with Brits lured here by cheap flights and cheap beer. Locals hope this is a short-lived trend, and that those rowdy louts will move farther east before long.

• *Continue down Rybárska.*

At the end of this block, at the intersection with Panská, watch out on the right for **Čumil** ("the Peeper"), grinning at passersby from a manhole. This was the first and is still the favorite Bratislava statue. There's no story behind this one—the artist simply wanted to create a fun icon and let the townspeople make up their own

tales. Čumil has survived being driven over by a truck—twice—and he's still grinning.

For a peek at a third statue—a nosy **Paparazzo**—you can turn left up Panská and go one block, watching the corner on the left.

• *Continuing straight past Čumil, you'll reach the long, skinny square called...*

Hviezdoslav Square (Hviezdoslavovo Námestie)

This square, named for a beloved Slovak poet, is yet another part of Bratislava that has undergone a much-needed sprucing-up. The landscaped park in the center is particularly inviting. At this end of the square is the impressive, silver-topped Slovak National Theater (Slovenské Národné Divadlo). Beyond that, the opulent yellow building that seems to be melting is the Philharmonic. The prominence of these two venues is evidence of Bratislava's strong performing arts tradition.

Right in front of the theater (by the McDonald's), look down into the glass **display case** to see the foundation of the one-time Fishermen's Gate into the city. Surrounding the base of the gate is water. This entire square was once a tributary of the Danube, and the Carlton Hotel across the way was a series of inns on different islands. The buildings along the Old Town side of the square mark where the city wall once stood.

• *From here, it's just a block to the Danube—passing the Slovak National Gallery, for those curious about local art (lime-green building on the corner with a modern annex). Once at the Danube, cross the street and belly up to the railing.*

The Danube (Dunaj)

Here you get a good look at the communists' pride and joy, the **New Bridge** (Nový Most, a.k.a. Most SNP). As with most Soviet-era landmarks in former communist countries, locals aren't crazy about this structure—not only for the questionable starship *Enterprise* design, but also because

of the oppressive regime it represents. However, the restaurant and observation deck up top—long a stale holdover from communist times—was recently renovated into a posh eatery called (appropriately enough) "UFO." You can visit for the views, a drink, or a full meal (described later, under "Sights in Bratislava").

• *Backtrack to the silver-topped National Theater at Hviezdoslav Square. Follow this square to the left, passing some fun public art: a statue of the square's namesake; the heavily fortified US Embassy (on the left); a glass pavilion (popular venue for summer concerts); and, on the right near the end, a statue of Hans Christian Andersen (the Danish storyteller, who enjoyed his visit to Bratislava).*

Reaching the end of the square (at the column with the big highway behind it), jog right and head for the big...

St. Martin's Cathedral (Dóm Sv. Martina)

This historic church isn't looking too sharp these days—and the highway thundering a few feet in front of its door (courtesy of the Soviets) doesn't help matters. If it were any closer, the off-ramp would go through the nave. Sad as it is now, the cathedral has been party to some pretty important history. While Buda and Pest were occupied by Ottomans for a century and a half, Bratislava was the capital of Hungary. A total of 19 Hungarian kings and queens were crowned in this church—more than have been crowned anywhere in Hungary. A replica of the Hungarian crown still tops the steeple.

• *Our walk is finished. From here, you have some sightseeing options (described in detail under "Sights in Bratislava," next). To reach the* ***castle****, take the underpass beneath the highway, go up the stairs on the right (marked by Hrad/Castle sign), then turn left up the stepped lane marked Zámocké Schody. Or, to get to the* ***New Bridge's "UFO" view*** *platform, turn left, walk toward the Danube, then walk the length of the bridge (pedestrian walkway on lower level) to reach the tower's entrance at the far end.*

Sights in Bratislava

It seems that all of Bratislava's sights have just reopened after a renovation...or are about to undergo one. In any event, most of Bratislava's charm is in its streets, not its museums. But these sights are fine for a rainy day or for "extra credit."

On or near the Old Town's Main Square

These three museums cluster within a few steps of the Main Square.

City History Museum (Mestské Múzeum)—This museum, in the Old Town Hall, will likely be closed through 2010 for a long-overdue renovation. When open, it offers an exhibit on town history (including torture equipment, or "instruments of feudal justice") and a chance to climb the Old Town Hall tower for a view of the square (if open, likely €3, Tue–Fri 10:00–17:00, Sat–Sun 11:00–18:00, closed Mon, enter through courtyard of Old Town Hall, tel. 02/5920-5130, www.muzeum.bratislava.sk).

▲Apponyi House (Apponyiho Palác)—This brand-new museum, which reopened in 2008 in the gorgeously restored mansion of a Hungarian aristocrat, comes in two parts. The cellar holds an interesting exhibit on the vineyards of the nearby "Little Carpathian" hills, with historic presses and barrels, and a replica of an old-time wine-pub table. Upstairs are two floors of urban apartments from old Bratislava: The first floor up shows off the 18th-century Rococo-style rooms of the nobility, while the second floor up (with lower ceilings and simpler wall decorations) illustrates 19th-century bourgeois/middle-class lifestyles, including some fine Empire-style furniture (€7, Tue–Fri 10:00–17:00, Sat–Sun 11:00–18:00, closed Mon, Radničná ulica 1, tel. 02/5920-5135).

▲Primate's Palace (Primaciálny Palác)—Probably Bratislava's most interesting museum, this tastefully restored French-Neoclassical mansion (formerly the residence of the archbishop, or "primate") dates from 1781. The smaller rooms were the archbishop's private quarters, now decorated with Dutch, Flemish, German, and Italian paintings. You'll peer from a bay window down into the archbishop's own, private marble chapel. When the archbishop became too ill to walk down to Mass, this window was built for him to take part in the service. The larger rooms were public...designed to impress. Among these is the Mirror Hall, used for concerts, city council meetings, and other important events.

But the museum's highlight is its series of six English tapestries, illustrating the ancient Greek myth of the tragic love between Hero and Leander. The tapestries—the only complete cycle of their kind in existence—were woven in England by Flemish weavers for the court of King Charles I (in the 1630s). After the king was deposed and beheaded, the tapestries disappeared. Centuries later, in 1903, restorers broke through a false wall in this mansion and

discovered the six tapestries, neatly folded and perfectly preserved. Nobody knows how they got there (perhaps they were squirreled away during the Napoleonic invasion, and whoever hid them didn't survive). The archbishop—who had just sold the palace to the city, but emptied it of furniture before he left—cried foul and tried to get the tapestries back...but the city said, "a deal's a deal" (€2, Tue–Fri 10:00–17:00, Sat–Sun 11:00–18:00, closed Mon, Primaciálne Námestie 3, tel. 02/5935-6394).

Bratislava Castle (Bratislavský Hrad)

This imposing fortress, nicknamed the "upside-down table," is the city's most prominent landmark. There surely has been a castle on this spot for centuries, but the oldest surviving chunk is the 13th-century Romanesque watchtower (the one slightly taller than the other three). When Habsburg Empress Maria Theresa took a liking to Bratislava in the 18th century, she transformed the castle from a military fortress to a royal residence suitable for holding court. She added a summer riding school (the U-shaped complex next to the castle), an enclosed winter riding school out back, and lots more...and then she painted the whole thing yellow. Maria Theresa's favorite daughter, Maria Christina, lived here with her husband, Albert, when they were newlyweds. Locals nicknamed the place "little Schönbrunn," in reference to the Habsburgs' summer palace on the outskirts of Vienna.

But M.T.'s castle burned to the ground in an 1811 fire, and it was left as a ruin for a century and a half—not reconstructed until 1953. Unfortunately, the communist rebuild was drab and uninviting; the inner courtyard felt like a prison exercise yard.

The good news is that the city is in the midst of a five-year renovation project to rehabilitate the castle from top to bottom. They've already reconstructed the summer riding school, and plan to rebuild the winter riding school and terraced French gardens out back...as well as paint the whole thing that pretty "Habsburg yellow" once again. The bad news is that during the restoration, the castle interior is closed to visitors. But more good news: The interior

was never appealing anyway, so the main reason to visit—for up-close views of the castle, over the rooftops of the Old Town, and across the Danube to Petržalka—remains the same (and free).

For details on the best way to hike up to the castle, see page 211.

The "UFO" at New Bridge (Nový Most)

The bizarre, flying-saucer-capped bridge near the Old Town—completed in 1972 in heavy-handed communist style—has been reclaimed by capitalists. It's been spruced up and turned into an overpriced café/restaurant, with an observation deck that allows visitors sweeping 360-degree views of Bratislava from about 300 feet above the Danube. Think of it as the "Slovak Space Needle."

Cost and Hours: €7, daily 10:00–23:00, elevator free if you have a meal reservation—main courses steeply priced at €25–30, tel. 02/6252-0300, www.u-f-o.sk/en.

Getting There: Just walk across the New Bridge from the Old Town—the elevator entrance is underneath the tower on the Petržalka side.

➲ **Self-Guided Tour:** The **"elevator"** that takes you up is actually a funicular—you'll notice you're moving at an angle. At the top, walk up the stairs to the observation deck.

Begin by viewing the **castle** and **Old Town.** Notice the massive construction zone to the right of the Old Town. If you set up a time-lapse camera here over the next few years, you'd watch skyscrapers pop up like dandelions. International investors are throwing many billions of euros at Bratislava, before rents skyrocket. (Imagine having so much prime, undeveloped real estate available downtown in the capital of an emerging European economic power...just an hour down the road from Vienna, no less.) Most of the development is taking place along the banks of the Danube. In a decade, this will be a futuristic city.

The huge, pointy monument back toward the train station (behind the Old Town) is **Slavín,** where more than 6,800 Soviet

soldiers who fought to liberate Bratislava from the Nazis are buried. A nearby church had to take down its steeple so as not to draw attention away from the huge Soviet soldier on top of the monument.

Now turn 180 degrees to face **Petržalka,** a planned communist suburb that sprouted here in the 1970s. The site was once occupied by a village, and the various districts of modern Petržalka still carry their original names (which now seem ironic): "Meadows" *(Háje),* "Woods" *(Lúky),* and "Courtyards" *(Dvory).* The ambitious Soviet planners envisioned a city laced with Venetian-style canals to help drain the marshy land, but the plans were abandoned after the harsh crackdown on the 1968 Prague Spring uprising. Today, one in four Bratislavans lives in Petržalka. A few years ago, this was a grim and decaying sea of miserable communist apartment *panelák* ("panel buildings," so called because they're made of huge prefab concrete panels that were built elsewhere, then brought here to assemble on-site). But things are changing fast. Many of the *panelák* are being retrofitted with new layers of insulation, and the apartments inside are being updated. And, like Dorothy opening the door to Oz, the formerly drab buildings are being splashed with bright new colors. Far from being a slum, Petržalka is a popular neighborhood for Bratislavan yuppies who can't yet afford to build their dream house. Locals read the Czech-language home-improvement magazine *Panel Plus* for ideas on how to give their *panelák* apartments some style (www.panelplus.cz).

Still facing Petržalka, notice that new construction is also happening along this riverbank (such as the supermall down below). But there's still history here. The **park** called Sad Janka Kráľa, a.k.a. "Aupark"—just downriver from the bridge—was technically the first public park in Europe, and is still a popular place for locals to relax and court.

Scanning the **horizon** beyond Petržalka, two things stick out: on the left, the old communist refinery (which has been fully updated); and on the right, a sea of modern windmills. These are just over the border, in Austria...and Bratislava is sure to grow in that direction quickly.

Before you leave, consider nursing a drink at the café (€3 coffee or beer, €5–15 cocktails). If nothing else, be sure to use the memorable WCs.

Sleeping in Bratislava

A few years ago, there were no sleepable hotels near Bratislava's Old Town. But new accommodations open every year, so the scene is rapidly improving. Hotel values here still aren't great; I'd rather sleep in Budapest or Vienna. But if the city entices you to stay longer than a day trip, these options are all inside or within a short walk of the Old Town. Business-oriented places charge more on weekdays (Mon–Thu) than on weekends (Fri–Sun).

$$$ Hotel Marrol's is the town's most enticing splurge. Although it's in a drab urban neighborhood, it's a five-minute walk from the Old Town, and the 54 rooms are luxurious and tastefully appointed Old World country-style. While pricey, the rates drop to tempting lows on weekends (Mon–Thu: Sb-€227, Db-€255; Fri–Sun: Sb-€134, Db-€153; air-con, non-smoking, free cable Internet, gorgeous lounge, Tobrucká ulica 4, tel. 02/5778-4600, www.hotelmarrols.sk, rec@hotelmarrols.sk).

$$$ Hotel Michalská Brána is a charming boutique hotel hiding down a tight, atmospheric little lane just inside St. Michael's Gate in the Old Town. The 14 rooms are sleek, mod, and classy (Mon–Thu: Sb-€150, Db-€160; Fri–Sun: Sb-€125, Db-€135; pricier suites also available, air-con, non-smoking, free cable Internet, elevator, Baštová 4, tel. 02/5930-7200, www.michalskabrana.com, michalskabrana@gmail.com).

$$ Hotel Corso has four rooms at the top floor of an office building right on the edge of the Old Town (Sb-€69, Db-€81, Tb-€104, cash only, elevator and some stairs, free Wi-Fi, some tram noise, Kapucínska 7, tel. 02/5441-6450, www.bratislavahotel.sk).

$$ Penzion Chez David is a simple, Jewish-themed hotel with 10 budget rooms just outside the Old Town (Mon–Thu: Sb-€64,

Sleep Code

(€1 = about $1.40, country code: 421, area code: 02)
S = Single, **D** = Double/Twin, **T** = Triple, **Q** = Quad, **b** = bathroom. English is spoken at each place. Unless otherwise noted, breakfast is included and you can pay by credit card.

To help you sort easily through these listings, I've divided the rooms into three categories, based on the price for a standard double room with bath:

$$$ Higher Priced—Most rooms €100 or more.
$$ Moderately Priced—Most rooms between €50–100.
$ Lower Priced—Most rooms €50 or less.

Db-€88; Fri–Sun: Sb-€54, Db-€78; pay Wi-Fi, some street noise from busy road and tram—request quieter room, Zámocká 13, tel. 02/5441-3824, www.chezdavid.sk, recepcia@chezdavid.sk).

$$ Hotel Ibis, part of the cookie-cutter chain, offers 120 rooms overlooking a busy tram junction across the street from Penzion Chez David (Mon–Thu: Sb/Db-€94; Fri–Sun: Sb/Db-€79; rates flex with demand, optional breakfast-€10 per person, Zámocká 38, tel. 02/5929-2000, fax 02/5929-2111, www.ibishotel.com, h3566@accor.com).

$ Downtown Backpackers Hostel is Bratislava's best hostel option. Funky but well-run, it's near the Grassalkovich (presidential) Palace about a five-minute walk from the Old Town (61 beds in 12 rooms, Db-€70, D-€55, bunk in Qb-€25, bunk in 7–8-bed dorm-€20, bunk in 10-bed dorm-€18, Panenská 31, tel. 02/5464-1191, www.backpackers.sk, info@backpackers.sk).

Eating in Bratislava

Bratislava is packed with inviting new eateries. In addition to the heavy Slovak staples, you'll find trendy new bars and bistros, and a wide range of ethnic offerings. The best plan may be to stroll the Old Town and keep your eyes open for the setting and cuisine that appeals to you most. Or consider one of these options.

Prazdroj ("Urquell") is a Czech-style beer hall with lively ambience and good traditional food. It sprawls through several rooms of a building just off Hviezdoslav Square at the edge of the Old Town (€7–10 main dishes, Mon–Fri 10:00–24:00, Sat–Sun 11:00–24:00, Mostová 8, tel. 02/5441-1108).

"1. Slovak" Pub (as in "the first") is the Slovak equivalent of Prazdroj, attracting a younger crowd. Enter from a bustling modern shopping street just outside the Old Town, and climb the stairs into a vast warren of rustic old countryside-style pub rooms. While enjoying the lively, loud, almost chaotic ambience, you'll dine on affordable and truly authentic Slovak fare, made with products from the pub's own farm. This is a good place to try the Slovak specialty, *bryndzové halušky* (€6–9 main dishes, Mon–Sat 10:00–24:00, Sun 12:00–24:00, Obchodná 62, tel. 02/5292-6367).

Erdody Palace, a newly renovated mansion in the center of the Old Town at Ventúrska 1, is a great place to splurge at one of two eateries with an Andy Warhol theme (after all, he was Slovak). As the owner is a huge Warhol fan, original Warhols hang in each

restaurant, named for the theme of the works: **Flowers** dishes up Mediterranean fare in a bright, covered courtyard (€7–14 pastas, €15–25 main dishes, daily 11:30–1:00 in the morning, tel. 02/2092-2733); the stuffier **Camouflage** features nouvelle cuisine in a somewhat snooty white-minimalist setting (€15–30 main dishes, Mon–Sat 11:30–1:00 in the morning, closed Sun, reservations smart, tel. 02/2092-2711). Even if you're not eating here, peek in the window at Camouflage to see Warhol enjoying the place.

Fast and Cheap: A local chain called **Coffee & Co,** with branches throughout the Old Town and beyond, serves up good €3–4 sandwiches—ideal for a bite on the run (various locations, all open long hours daily).

Classic Coffee House: The venerable **Kaffee Mayer,** at the corner of the main square, is an institution—they've been selling coffee and cakes to a genteel clientele since 1873. You can enjoy your pick-me-up in the swanky old interior, or out on the square (€2–3 cakes, Mon–Fri 9:30–22:00, Sat–Sun 9:30–23:00, Hlavné Námestie 4, tel. 02/5441-1741).

Bratislava Connections

By Train

Bratislava has two major train stations. The main train station (Hlavná Stanica, abbreviated "Bratislava hl. st." on schedules) is closer to the Old Town, while the Petržalka station (ŽST Petržalka), in the suburb across the river, can be more convenient for some connections. When checking schedules (http://bahn.hafas.de/bin/query.exe/en is helpful), pay attention to which station your train uses. Bus #93 connects these two Bratislava stations (5–12/hr, 10 min; or use bus #N93 at night).

From Bratislava by Train to: Budapest (5/day direct, 2.5 hrs; more with transfers), **Sopron** (at least hourly, 2.5 hrs, transfer at Vienna's Südbahnhof), **Vienna** (2/hr, 1–1.5 hrs), **Prague** (3/day direct, 4.25–5.5 hrs). For more Hungarian destinations (such as **Eger** or **Pécs**), you'll connect through Budapest.

By Boat

Riverboats connect Bratislava to the nearby capitals of Budapest and Vienna. Conveniently, these boats dock right along the Danube in front of Bratislava's Old Town. While they are more expensive, less frequent, and slower than the train, some travelers enjoy getting out on the Danube.

To Budapest: For details on the Mahart boats to and from Budapest, see page 586 in "Budapest Connections."

To Vienna: The Vienna-based DDSG line offers several daily boat trips between Bratislava and Vienna's Schwedenplatz

(where Vienna's town center hits the canal; €28 each way, €17 at less convenient times, €2 more on weekends, 1.25-hr trip; daily April–Oct only, Austrian tel. 01/58880, www.ddsg-blue-danube.at). The Budapest-based Mahart boat connects Bratislava to Vienna's Reichsbrücke dock once daily (€29 one-way, €39 round-trip, 1.5–2 hrs, daily late April–early Oct only; for more details, see page 586).

Bratislava Airport (Letisko Bratislava)

Bratislava Airport (airport code: BTS, www.letiskobratislava.sk) is six miles northeast of downtown Bratislava. The low-cost carriers who fly here sometimes market it as "Vienna–Bratislava," thanks to its proximity to both capitals. The airport is officially named for Milan Rastislav Štefánik, who worked toward the creation of Czechoslovakia at the end of World War I. It's compact and manageable, with all the usual amenities (including ATMs).

To Downtown Bratislava: The airport has easy **public bus** connections to Bratislava's main train station (€0.60, plus €0.30 ticket for each big bag, bus #61, 6/hr in peak times, 3/hr in slow times, trip takes 30 min). To reach the bus stop, exit straight out of the arrivals hall, cross the street, buy a ticket at the kiosk, and look for the bus stop on your right. For directions from the train station into the Old Town, see "Arrival in Bratislava," earlier. A **taxi** from the airport into central Bratislava should cost less than €20.

To Budapest: Take the bus or taxi to Bratislava's train station (described above), then hop a train to Budapest.

To Vienna: A slow option is to connect through Bratislava's train station (described above). More direct and still affordable, you can take a Eurolines bus from Bratislava Airport to the Erdberg stop of Vienna's U-3 subway line (9/day, €10, trip takes about an hour, book in advance, www.gratislava.at). A taxi from Bratislava Airport directly to Vienna costs €60–90 (depending on whether you use a cheaper Slovak or more expensive Austrian cab).

THE SPIŠ REGION

Levoča • The High Tatras

The most beautiful part of Slovakia is the mountainous north-central region, comprising the jagged High Tatras and the Spiš Region. The dramatic Carpathian Mountains slice through Eastern Europe here, dividing the Poles and Czechs in the north from the Hungarians and Yugoslavs in the south. With these Carpathian peaks as a backdrop, this region offers fine high-mountain scenery; easy river-rafting trips with fun-loving guides through a breathtaking gorge; a classic Old World walled town with one of Europe's finest Gothic altarpieces; a glimpse at Slovakia's complicated ethnic mix; and treacherous but legendary hiking trails in a place so pretty, they call it "paradise."

Planning Your Time

The Spiš Region is a handy place for drivers to break up the long journey between Kraków and Hungary—on this route, Levoča is worth an overnight to recharge and get a taste of rural Slovakia. But unless you have a special interest, don't go out of your way to reach this area. Train travelers or those on a speedy itinerary should skip it (sleep through Slovakia on the night train).

Getting to the Spiš Region

Seeing the Spiš Region is a real headache without a car. If you're going between Kraków and Hungary (Eger or Budapest), the train line veers around Levoča far to the east, through Košice. From Košice, trains will get you to Prešov or Spišská Nová Ves, and the bus will take you the rest of the way to Levoča. From the west, buses run between Bratislava and Levoča (though it's often

faster to take the train to Poprad, then bus to Levoča). For specific schedules, see www.cp.sk.

Levoča

Levoča (LEH-voh-chah) is a diamond in the rough. If you can look past the crumbling facades and potholed roads, you'll see Slovakia's finest small town—with a mostly intact medieval wall, a main square ringed by striking Renaissance facades, and one of the greatest Gothic altarpieces in all of Europe.

Levoča boomed in the Middle Ages, when trade between Hungary and Poland brought abundant merchant traffic through its gates. In the 15th century, the town's centerpiece was built: St. James Church. A local woodcarver named Master Pavol packed the church with one of the most impressive collections of altarpieces in the world—including the pièce de résistance, an exquisite 60-foot-high main altar.

History of the Spiš Region

The Spiš (pronounced "speesh") region is one of the most historic and scenic corners of Slovakia. The area was named Szepes ("beautiful") by the Hungarians, who controlled this area in the Middle Ages. After the Tatars swept through in the 13th century, decimating the local population, the Hungarians invited Saxons (from the region around Dresden in today's Germany) to come and resettle the land. Silver, copper, and iron ore were discovered, and the Spiš became a prosperous mining region, with 24 bustling, richly decorated Saxon towns (including Levoča). The region became a showcase of Gothic and, later, Renaissance architecture.

For centuries, the Spiš was populated by a colorful mix of Saxons, Jews, and Slovaks. But after World War II, Czechoslovakia forced out people of German heritage—including descendents of those Saxon settlers who had arrived here centuries before. The Spiš was abandoned, and many towns were repopulated by Slovaks, while others were settled by Roma (see sidebar on page 224).

Today's Spiš, while still suffering from economic ills, is emerging as a popular tourist destination.

In the 19th century, Levoča vied with Spišská Nová Ves, a town eight miles south, to host a station on an important rail line that was being built. S.N.V. won, and became a transportation hub for the region. While unfortunate for Levoča's economy at the time, this lack of train access has allowed Levoča to remain a wonderfully well-preserved Old World village of 10,000. If all of this makes Levoča feel off the beaten track, so much the better.

Orientation to Levoča

(area code: 053)

Levoča is small—you can walk from one end of the walled burg to the other in 15 minutes—and all roads lead to the town's main square, which is named for the important woodcarver Master Pavol (Námestie Majstra Pavla). The **TI** can answer your questions about the town, and put you in touch with a local guide (May–Sept daily 9:00–16:00; Oct–April Mon–Fri 9:00–16:00, closed Sat–Sun; on the main square at #58, tel. 053/451-3763, www.levoca.sk).

Sights in Levoča

▲Church of St. James (Chrám Sv. Jakuba)—This huge Gothic church, dominating Levoča's main square, contains 11 ornately decorated altars—including the tallest wooden altarpiece in the world.

Cost, Hours, Tours: The cost is €2, and you can visit only at the times posted on the door of the church office, across the street from the church entrance (on the north side of the church, facing the top of the square). You'll be accompanied by a guide, but you don't have to listen to her spiel (usually Slovak only—but try asking for English). Use my self-guided tour (below) to appreciate the church, or find the talking box in the back of the nave and insert a coin for English. The church is open July–Aug Tue–Sat 9:00–17:00, Sun 13:00–17:00, Mon 11:00–17:00, tours every 30 min; Easter–June and Sept–Oct Tue–Sat 8:30–16:00, Sun 13:00–16:00, Mon 11:30–16:00, tours roughly hourly, though not always at the top of the hour; Nov–Easter Tue–Sat 8:30–16:00, closed Sun–Mon, tours roughly hourly. Tel. 053/451-2347, mobile 0907-521-673, www.chramsvjakuba.sk.

➲ **Self-Guided Tour:** The church dates from the 14th century. In the late 15th century, neighboring VIPs visited here. The greatest Hungarian king, Mátyás Corvinus, came in 1474 (for more on Corvinus, see sidebar on page 502). Two decades later, representatives of Poland's powerful Jagiellonian dynasty paid a visit. These important guests—both commemorated inside the church—are a reminder that Slovakia sits at the center of Eastern Europe.

In the early 16th century, the great sculptor Master Pavol left his mark on the church. Master Pavol's unique, almost cartoonish style features figures with too-big heads, strangely weepy eyes, and honest-to-goodness personalities. Pavol's masterpiece is the church's single most impressive sight: the 60-foot-tall **main altar,** carved out of linden wood and bathed in gold paint. The large central figures represent Mary and the Baby Jesus, flanked by St. James (the church's namesake, on left) and St. John the Evangelist (on right). The four panels surrounding these figures depict scenes from James' and John's lives and deaths. Beneath them is a depiction of the Last Supper. Unusual in Gothic art, each apostle has his own individual features (based on the local merchants who financed the work). With this and his other carvings, Master Pavol was knocking on the door of the Renaissance.

The nave is lined with several other altarpieces—some by Master Pavol, some by others. At the front of the right nave (right-hand corner), look for the altar depicting the **Passion of Christ,** carved for the 1474 visit of Hungarian King Mátyás Corvinus. Jesus looks like Mátyás, Mary resembles his Italian wife, and the altar was supposed to bring the couple good luck in having a child.

To the left as you view the main altar, notice the interesting medieval **frescoes** on the wall (splotchy from a bad 19th-century renovation). The frescoes on the left depict the life of St. Dorothy. On the right are two strips. The upper strip shows a couple performing good deeds (feeding the hungry, visiting prisoners,

The "Gypsy Question"

Eastern Europe is home to a silent population—mostly in Romania, Bulgaria, Hungary, and Slovakia—of millions of dark-skinned people who speak a unique language and follow their own culture. The once-common term "Gypsy" is now considered both derogatory and inaccurate. It was derived from "Egypt"—the place where these people were once mistakenly thought to have originated. While "Gypsy" is not overtly offensive to most, today's preferred term for these people is "Roma."

The Roma are descended from several low north-Indian castes. (In fact, the language still spoken by about two-thirds of today's European Roma—called Romany—is related to contemporary Indian languages.) A thousand years ago, the Roma began to migrate through Persia and Armenia into the Ottoman Empire, which later stretched across much of southeastern Europe. Known for their itinerant lifestyles, expertise in horse trading, skilled artisanship, and flexibility regarding private property, the Roma were both sought out and suspected in medieval Europe. Similarly, the *gadjos* (non-Roma) and their customs came to be distrusted by the Roma.

The Industrial Revolution removed the Roma's few traditional means of earning a livelihood, making their wandering lifestyle difficult to sustain. Roma became entertainers (fortune telling, music and dancing, horse shows, dancing bears), outlaws, and metalworkers.

Roma were initially not allowed to enter Austrian territory, but as the Habsburgs recaptured lands once controlled by the Ottomans (including Slovakia and Hungary), they permitted the Roma already living there to stay. In the 18th and 19th centuries, as "Gypsy music" funneled into the theaters of Vienna and Budapest, a romantic image of the Roma emerged: a happy-go-lucky nomadic lifestyle; intoxicating music, with dancers swirling around a campfire; and mystical powers over white Europeans.

But white Europe's image of the Roma also had a sinister side. Even today, people might warn their children, "If you don't behave, I'll sell you to the Gypsies!" And when someone is cheated, we say they've been "gypped"—an ethnic slur so deeply ingrained, most don't even realize its origin. This widespread bigotry culminated in the Holocaust—when at least a quarter of a million Roma people were murdered in Nazi death camps.

After World War II, communist governments in the Soviet Bloc implemented a policy of forced assimilation: Roma were required to speak the country's major language, settle in *gadjo* towns, and work in new industrial jobs. But rather than producing well-adjusted citizens, the policy eroded time-honored Roma values and shattered the cohesiveness of their traditional communities. It left the new Roma generation prone to sexual, alcohol, and drug abuse, and filled state-run orphanages with deprived Roma toddlers. When the "obligation and right to work" disappeared with the communist regimes in 1989, rampant unemployment

and dependence on welfare joined the list of Roma afflictions.

Today's Roma are Europe's forgotten population—estimates range from 6 to 12 million throughout the continent. As people all over Eastern Europe have found it difficult to adjust to the new economic realities, they've again turned on the Roma as scapegoats, fueling the latent racism that is so characteristic of European history. For example, a small Czech town tried to build a wall between its wealthy neighborhood and the Roma ghetto. And obstetricians in the Czech Republic were accused of sterilizing their female Roma patients without their informed consent.

Those Roma who do their best to integrate with their white neighbors often find themselves shunned both by their fellow Roma, and by the white Europeans they're emulating. Those who make it against the odds and succeed in mainstream society typically do so by turning their backs on their Roma heritage.

Many Roma resist assimilation and live in segregated ghettos, where even the most talented of their children are forced to attend schools for the mentally disabled. For example, in the Spiš Region, some Roma live in small, remote, self-contained villages—a long walk up a dirt road away from the mainstream "civilization." Polygamy is not uncommon, and some girls marry and begin having children at a very early age. Most children start attending school, but a high percentage drop out.

The large Roma population also puts an enormous strain on the already overtaxed social-welfare networks. Unemployment in the Spiš Region among Roma is about 50 percent in the summer (when some seasonal work is available) to 80 percent in the winter. To a white Slovak struggling to succeed, Roma people are often seen as freeloaders. After Romania (with Europe's highest concentration of Roma) joined the EU, various other member nations implemented strict entry requirements for "Romanians"—a thinly veiled measure designed to keep out Roma.

It's easy to criticize these seemingly closed-minded attitudes. But, in the eyes of many white Europeans, the Roma's poor reputation is at least partly deserved. While many Roma are upstanding citizens, others do turn to thievery for survival. The tour-guide refrain, "Watch out for Gypsy thieves!" might seem racist—but it's not necessarily bad advice.

What emerges is a seemingly unsolvable problem—a fundamental cultural misunderstanding, tinged with racist undertones, that separates the people of this region. But the white European community is beginning to take note. The Decade of Roma Inclusion—launched in 2005 by Hungarian-American businessman George Soros—is an initiative being undertaken by nine Eastern European countries to better address the human rights of their Roma citizens (www.romadecade.org). Many are hopeful that with the EU's increased focus on cooperation and human rights, the Roma will find a place in the new, united Europe.

burying the dead, and so on). In the lower strip, they sit on animals representing the mortal sins.

As you leave, at the back of the left nave, look for another Master Pavol altar with an iconic statue of **Mary.** When the Reformation swept Europe in the 16th century, locals hid statues like Mary (who was tucked away in the Town Hall) to protect them from iconoclasts, Protestants who destroyed religious symbols to simplify their communion with God. Two centuries later, the long-forgotten statues were miraculously discovered and brought back to the church...for you to enjoy.

House of Master Pavol—The downside of the Church of St. James is that you can see the breathtaking altarpieces only from a distance, so you can't get a sense of what made Pavol the Master. At this museum, replicas of the statues allow you to look Pavol's creations right in their big, weepy eyes (€2, daily 9:00–17:00, tel. 053/451-3496).

Levoča Town Hall (Radnica v Levoči)—The huge, Renaissance-style building behind the Church of St. James used to be the Town Hall; now it's a museum devoted to the town and region's history and colorful folk cultures. You'll watch a movie in English before wandering though a grand, wood-carved meeting hall (with a beautifully painted ceiling) and rooms of maps of historic Levoča and the Spiš Region (€2, skimpy English information, daily 9:00–17:00, tel. 053/451-2786).

Mariánska Hora—This humble church, overlooking Levoča from a perch on a nearby hill, has been an important site for pilgrimages for centuries. Every year, on the first weekend of July, hundreds of thousands of Slovaks flock to the hill from the surrounding countryside—many walking as far as 30 miles. In 1995, Pope John Paul II made a pilgrimage here, saying Mass in front of some 650,000 people.

Near Levoča

Spiš Castle (Spišský Hrad)—Just a few miles from Levoča lies one of Europe's largest castles. Spiš Castle watches over the region from high on a bluff, overlooking a desolate terrain. Though there have been castles on this strategic spot for as long as people have lived here, the current version was built during the 15th century. Since its destruction in 1781, only evocative, photogenic ruins remain.

The interior is tourable, though it pales in comparison to the

dramatic hilltop setting (€5, daily May–Sept 9:00–19:00, March–April 9:00–17:00, Oct 10:00–16:30, Nov 10:00–16:00, closed Dec–Feb, last entry one hour before closing, tel. 053/454-1336, www.spisskyhrad.sk). However, views of the castle from the surrounding countryside are majestic.

Spiš Castle is the centerpiece of a cluster of interesting sights. The town just below the castle is **Spišské Podhradie** ("Under the Spiš Castle"). On a ridge opposite Spiš Castle is **Spišská Kapitula,** the site of the Spiš Region's cathedral, surrounded by a modest village and an imposing 14th-century wall. And tucked behind Spiš Castle is **Žehra,** a village with a simple, onion-domed church that contains some 13th- to 15th-century wall paintings.

Getting There: From Levoča, take the main road (E-50) east. After 7.5 miles, you'll see the first turnoff, which takes you scenically past Spišská Kapitula and through Spišské Podhradie (park near town and hike all the way up, or cut through town back to the main road and wind around to the second exit). To get to the castle more directly, stay on E-50 past the first exit, and go another two miles, where you'll reach another turnoff to the right leading up to the parking lot behind the castle.

Slovak Paradise (Slovenský Raj)—Outdoors enthusiasts from all over Eastern Europe flock to this national park, and for good reason—it features steep river gorges lined with waterfalls, and plateaus pocked by caves, offering some of the most enjoyable hikes this side of the Plitvice Lakes (see page 934). The Slovak Paradise is known for its seemingly treacherous trails—one often-photographed stretch features ladders laid at sharp uphill angles, spanning a gaping gorge. The faint of heart should steer clear of these more challenging hikes, but in other parts of the park, you'll find trails suitable for any hiker (www.slovenskyraj.sk). Spišská Nová Ves is the handiest gateway, on the northeastern fringe of the park (and with a convenient train station).

River Rafting in the Pieniny—A few miles north of Levoča, at the border with Poland, is the Pieniny region (www.pieniny.sk). Here, the Dunajec (DOO-nah-yets) River flows through a dramatic gorge in the shadow of sheer limestone cliffs, with Poland on one bank and Slovakia on the other. Floating through this scenery feels like

living a scene from *The Lord of the Rings*.

The best way to experience the Pieniny is on a boat cruise. You'll board a *plť*—a strange, pontoon-type raft made up of five canoe-like skiffs lashed together and bridged with long benches—and ply the waters of the Dunajec River. Your lively conductor is dressed in the traditional costume of the Góral folk who populate this region. The trip is generally smooth—no whitewater to speak of—and offers a lazy chance to enjoy the scenery.

Rafting trips go roughly from early May through late October, weather permitting (daily 8:30–17:00, until 15:00 Sept–Oct, about €10 per person, float lasts about one hour). The best stretch of river is 5.5-mile-long, U-shaped **Dunajec Canyon,** which begins near the town of **Červený Kláštor** ("Red Cloister"—this old building is near the town itself) and ends at the town of **Lesnica.** Hop on at a raft landing—marked as *prístav plťí* on signs and maps. When you reach Lesnica, catch the bus back to your starting point...or hike the three miles back to Červený Kláštor.

Sleeping in Levoča

The presidents of all of Central Europe's countries converged on Levoča for a conference in 1998, and you'll see photos of many of them decorating the few proud hotels in town. All of these hotels are right on the main square, Námestie Majstra Pavla.

$$ Hotel u Leva is the town splurge, with 23 nicely decorated rooms (Sb-€50, Db-€73, apartment-€99, breakfast-€5, elevator, cable Internet, Námestie Majstra Pavla 25, tel. 053/450-2311, fax 053/450-2340, www.uleva.sk, hotel@uleva.sk).

$ Hotel Arkada, popular with tours, has 32 nondescript rooms (Sb-€35, Db-€50, suite-€62, 20 percent cheaper mid-Oct–April, extra bed-€12, breakfast-€4, Námestie Majstra Pavla 26, tel. 053/451-2372, fax 053/451-2255, www.arkada.sk, hotelarkada@arkada.sk).

Sleep Code

(€1 = about $1.40, country code: 421, area code: 053)
S = Single, **D** = Double/Twin, **T** = Triple, **Q** = Quad, **b** = bathroom, **s** = shower only. Credit cards are accepted and English is spoken at each place. These rates do not include breakfast.

To help you sort easily through these listings, I've divided the rooms into two categories, based on the price for a standard double room with bath:

$$ Higher Priced—Most rooms €60 or more.
$ Lower Priced—Most rooms less than €60.

$ Hotel Barbakan, near the top of the main square, feels traditional. Though its 15 rooms are darkly furnished, it's a decent option for the price (Sb-€35, Db-€46, suite-€52, 15 percent cheaper Oct–April, extra bed-€12, breakfast-€5, lots of stairs with no elevator, Košická 15, tel. 053/451-4310, fax 053/451-3609, www.barbakan.sk, recepcia@barbakan.sk).

Eating in Levoča

Hotel Barbakan, listed earlier, has a restaurant. But **Reštaurácia u 3 Apoštolov** ("Three Apostles"), also right on the square, is a cut above, serving tasty Slovak cuisine. The decor is nothing special, but the food is delicious and cheap: pungent garlic soup, excellent trout, and the tasty "Apostle Specialty"—sautéed beef and vegetables in a spicy sauce, wrapped in a potato pancake (€6–8 main dishes, long hours daily, Námestie Majstra Pavla 11, tel. 053/451-2302).

The High Tatras (Vysoké Tatry)

While not technically in the Spiš Region, Slovakia's most breathtaking mountain range is nearby. The High Tatras mountain range is small but mighty—dramatic, nearly 9,000-foot-tall granite peaks spike up from the plains, covering an area of about 100 square miles. The High Tatras are the northernmost and highest part of the Carpathian Mountains, which stretch across the heart of Eastern Europe all the way to Romania. These cut-glass peaks have quickly become legendary among hardy, in-the-know travelers for their inexpensive, off-the-beaten-track hiking and skiing opportunities.

The High Tatras make up the Polish–Slovak border. Without a car, the most accessible approach is from the Polish resort town of **Zakopane** (an easy 1.5-hour bus or train connection from Kraków). But for more rugged beauty, head to the southern part of the range, in Slovakia.

The mid-sized city of **Poprad**—located on a plain about 10 miles from the mountains—is the most convenient launchpad for venturing into Slovakia's High Tatras. Along the base of the High Tatras are various modest resort towns (including the biggest, Starý Smokovec). There's no shortage of scenic hikes all over the

region (good maps and guidebooks available locally). The best no-sweat high-altitude option is to take the **cable car** from the resort village of Tatranská Lomnica up to the viewpoint at Lomnický Štít (8,640 feet; popular and crowded, so visit early).

By car, take road 537 along the base of the High Tatras to connect the various towns. By public transportation, you'll commute by electric trains *(električky)* from Poprad into Starý Smokovec. (There are also direct, one-hour buses from Levoča to Starý Smokovec.) From Starý Smokovec, you can continue by electric train on to Tatranská Lomnica and other villages. Each town has its share of simple resort-type hotels, but serious hikers enjoy staying in the High Tatras' many *chaty* (mountain huts). For more details on the High Tatras, visit www.tanap.sk or www.tatry.net. *Spectacular Slovakia* magazine, mentioned on page 193, also has good coverage of the region (www.spectacularslovakia.sk).

POLAND

POLAND

Polska

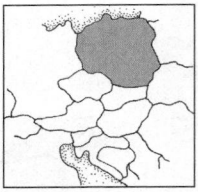

Americans who think of Poland as rundown—full of rusting factories, smoggy cities, and gloomy natives—are speechless when they step into Kraków's vibrant main square, Gdańsk's colorful pedestrian drag, or Warsaw's lively Old Town. While parts of the country are still cleaning up the industrial mess left by the Soviets, Poland also has some breathtaking medieval cities that show off its warm and welcoming people, dynamic history, and unique cultural fabric.

The Poles are a proud people—as moved by their spectacular failures as by their successes. Their quiet elegance has been tempered by generations of abuse by foreign powers. The Poles place a lot of importance on honor, and you'll find fewer scams and con artists here than in other Eastern European countries.

In a way, there are two Polands: lively, cosmopolitan urban centers, and countless tiny farm villages in the countryside. City-dwellers often talk about the "simple people" of Poland—those descended from generations of farmers, working the same plots for centuries and living an uncomplicated, traditional lifestyle. This large contingent of old-fashioned, salt-of-the-earth folks—who like things the way they are—is a major reason why Poland was so hesitant to join the European Union (see page 242).

Poland is one of Europe's most devoutly Catholic countries. Catholicism has long defined these people, holding them together through times when they had little else. Squeezed between Protestant Germany (originally Prussia) and Orthodox Russia, Poland wasn't even a country for generations (1795–1918). Its Catholicism helped keep its spirit alive. In the last century, while "under communism" (as that age is referred to), Poles found their religion a

source of strength as well as rebellion—they could express dissent against the atheistic regime by going to church. Some of Poland's best sights are churches, usually filled with locals praying silently. While these church interiors are worth a visit, be especially careful to show the proper respect (maintain silence, keep a low profile, and if you want to snap pictures, do so discreetly).

Visitors are sometimes surprised at how much of Poland's story is a Jewish story. Before World War II, 80 percent of the world's Jews lived in Poland. Warsaw was the world's second-largest Jewish city (after New York) with 380,000 Jews (out of a total population of 1.2 million). Poland was a magnet for Jews because of its relatively welcoming policies. Still, Jews were forbidden from owning land; that's why they settled mostly in the cities. But the Holocaust (and a later Soviet policy of sending "troublemaking" Jews to Israel) decimated the Jewish population. This tragic chapter, combined with postwar border shifts and population movements, made Poland one of Europe's most ethnically homogenous countries. Today, virtually everyone in the country speaks Polish, and only a few thousand Polish Jews remain.

Poland is historically extremely pro-American. Of course, their big neighbors (Russia and Germany) have been their historic enemies. And when Hitler invaded in 1939, the Poles felt let down by their supposed European friends (France and Britain), who declared war on Germany but provided virtually no military support to the Polish resistance. America has always been regarded as the big ally from across the ocean. In 1989, when Poland finally won its freedom, many Poles only half-joked that they should apply to become the 51st state of the United States.

Poland Almanac

Official Name: Rzeczpospolita Polska (Republic of Poland), or Polska for short.

Snapshot History: This thousand-year-old country has been dominated by foreigners for much of the last two centuries, finally achieving true independence (from the Soviet Union) in 1989.

Population: Nearly 38.5 million people, slightly more than California. About 97 percent are ethnically Polish and speak Polish (though English is also widely spoken). Three out of every four Poles are practicing Catholics. The population is younger than most European countries, with an average age of 37 (Germany's is 42).

Latitude and Longitude: 52°N and 20°E (similar latitude to Berlin, London, and Edmonton, Alberta).

Area: 122,000 square miles, the same as New Mexico (or Illinois and Iowa put together).

Geography: Because of its overall flatness, Poland has been a corridor for invading armies since its infancy. The Vistula River (680 miles) runs south-to-north up the middle of the country, passing through Kraków and Warsaw, and emptying into the Baltic Sea at Gdańsk. Poland's climate is generally cool and rainy—40,000 storks love it.

Biggest Cities: Warsaw (the capital, 1.7 million), Łódź (790,000), and Kraków (757,000).

Economy: The Gross Domestic Product is $670 billion, with a GDP per capita of $17,400. The 1990s saw an aggressive and successful transition from state-run socialism to privately owned capitalism. Still, Poland's traditional potato-and-pig-farming society is behind the times, with 16 percent of the country's workers producing less than 3 percent of its GDP. About one in ten Poles is unemployed, and nearly one in five lives in poverty. Poland's entry into the European Union in 2004 brought substantial financial aid that is improving things.

In 2012, Poland—jointly with Ukraine—will host the Euro Cup soccer championship. (For Europeans, this is just one step down from hosting the Olympics.) Cities hosting matches include Warsaw, Gdańsk, Poznań, and Wrocław. Throughout the country—but especially in these four cities—a wave of new construction and refurbishment is sweeping dingy old quarters, leaving them refreshed and reenergized. Poland is also using the Euro Cup as an excuse to beef up its rail system, as it creates a network of high-speed trains to more quickly and smoothly link together its major cities. (Unfortunately, in the short term this means that

Currency: 1 złoty (zł, or PLN) = 100 groszy (gr) = about 30 cents; 3 zł = about $1.

Real Estate: A typical one-bedroom apartment in Warsaw (250 square feet) rents for roughly $600 a month.

Government: Poland's mostly figurehead president selects the prime minister and Cabinet, with legislators' approval. They govern along with a two-house legislature (Sejm and Senat) of 560 seats. Donald Tusk, leader of the centrist Civic Platform, became prime minister in 2007. Current president Leck Kaczyński's five-year term expires in 2010. (For more on Polish politics, see page 243.)

Flag: The upper half is white, and the lower half is red—the traditional colors of Poland. Poetic Poles claim the white represents honor, and the red represents the enormous amounts of blood spilled by the Poles to honor their nation. The flag sometimes includes a coat of arms with a crowned eagle (representing Polish sovereignty). Under Poland's many oppressors (including the Soviets), the crown was removed from the emblem, and its talons were trimmed. On regaining its independence, Poland coronated its eagle once more.

The Average Pole: New prosperity aside, the average Pole spends just 4 percent of what a German spends on personal consumption. Half of all Poles use the Internet, and the average Pole will live to about age 75. The average woman gets married at 24 and will have 1.25 children.

Not-so-Average Poles: Despite the many "Polack jokes" you've heard (and maybe repeated), you actually know of many famous Polish intellectuals—you just don't realize they're Polish. The "Dumb Polack" Hall of Fame includes Karol Wojtyła (Pope John Paul II), Mikołaj Kopernik (Nicolas Copernicus), composer Fryderyk Chopin, scientist Marie Curie (née Skłodowska), writer Teodor Józef Korzeniowski (better known as Joseph Conrad, author of *Heart of Darkness*), filmmaker Roman Polański *(Chinatown, The Pianist)*, politician Lech Wałęsa...and one of this book's co-authors.

many rail journeys are taking much longer than normal, because of construction-related delays.)

On my first visit to Poland, I had a poor impression of Poles, who seemed brusque and often elbowed ahead of me in line. I've since learned that all it takes is a smile and a cheerful greeting—preferably in Polish—to break through the thick skin that helped these kind people survive the difficult communist times. With a friendly hello *(Dzień dobry!)*, you'll turn any grouch into a new friend.

Helpful Hints

Restroom Signage: To confuse tourists, the Poles have devised a secret way of marking their WCs. You'll see doors marked with *męska* (men) and *damska* (women)—but even more often, you'll simply see a triangle (for men) or a circle (for women). A sign with a triangle, a circle, and an arrow is directing you to the closest WCs.

Pay to Pee: Many Polish bathrooms charge a small fee. You may even be charged at a restaurant where you're paying to dine. Don't let this minor inconvenience interfere with your enjoyment of your trip. Yes, it's an annoying hassle—but at least it's cheap (usually around 1 zł).

Train Station Lingo: "PKP" is the abbreviation for Polish National Railways ("PKS" is for buses). In larger towns with several train stations, you'll normally use the one called Główny (meaning "Main"—except in Warsaw, where it's Centralna). Underneath most larger stations are mazes of walkways—lined with market stalls—that lead to platforms *(peron)* and exits *(wyjście)*. Most stations have several platforms, each of which has two tracks *(tor)*. Departures are generally listed by the *peron*, so keep your eye on both tracks for your train. Arrivals are *przyjazdy*, and departures are *odjazdy*. Left-luggage counters or lockers are marked *przechowalnia bagażu*. *Kasy* are ticket windows. These can be marked (sometimes only in Polish) for specific needs—domestic tickets, international tickets, and so on; ask fellow travelers to be sure you select the right line. Ticket and "information" windows are more often than not staffed by monolingual grouches. Smile sweetly, write down your destination and time, and hang onto your patience. The line you choose will invariably be the slowest one—leave plenty of time to buy your ticket before your train departs (or, if you're running out of time, buy it on board for a few dollars extra). For longer and/or express journeys, you'll likely be given two separate tickets: one for the trip itself, and the other for your seat assignment. On arriving at a station, to get into town, follow signs for *wyjście do centrum* or *wyjście do miasta*. Ongoing construction to improve Poland's rail lines (mostly in anticipation of Euro 2012) may make some of your train journeys take much longer than normal, and delays are common.

Museum Tips: Virtually every museum in Poland is closed on Monday. The ticket window for any museum typically closes a half-hour before the museum's closing time, and this last-entry deadline is strictly enforced. Poland's museums are notorious for constantly tweaking their opening times. I've tried to list the correct hours, but be aware that they're almost impossible to predict from year to year—try to confirm locally if you have your heart set on a particular place.

Polish Artists: Though Poland has produced world-renowned

Top 10 Dates That Changed Poland

A.D. 966—The Polish king, Mieszko I, is baptized a Christian, symbolically uniting the Polish people and founding the nation.

1385—The Polish queen (called a "king" by sexist aristocrats of the time) marries a Lithuanian duke, starting the two-century reign of the Jagiełło family.

1410—Poland defeats the Teutonic Knights at the Battle of Grunwald, part of a Golden Age of territorial expansion and cultural achievement.

1572—The last Jagiellonian king dies, soon replaced by bickering nobles and foreign kings. Poland declines.

1795—In the last of three Partitions, the country is divvied up by its more-powerful neighbors: Russia, Prussia, and Austria.

1918—Following World War I, Poland gets back its land and sovereignty.

1939—The Free City of Gdańsk (then called Danzig) is invaded by Nazi Germany, starting World War II. At war's end, the country is "liberated" (i.e., occupied) by the Soviet Union.

1980—Lech Wałęsa leads a successful strike, demanding more freedom from the communist regime.

1989—The Berlin Wall falls, and Poland soon gains independence under its first president—Lech Wałęsa.

2004—Poland joins the European Union, pedaling fast to catch up to its more-prosperous neighbors.

scientists, musicians, and writers, the country isn't known for its artists. Polish museums greet foreign visitors with fine artwork by unfamiliar names. If you're planning to visit any museums in Poland, two artists in particular are worth remembering: **Jan Matejko,** a 19th-century positivist who painted grand historical epics (see page 360); and one of his students, **Stanisław Wyspiański,** a painter and playwright who led the charge of the Młoda Polska movement—the Polish answer to Art Nouveau—in the early 1900s (see page 266).

Telephones: Remember these Polish prefixes: 0800 is toll-free, and 0700 is expensive (like phone sex). Many Poles use mobile phones (which come with 060 and 050 prefixes). If you are dialing from a Polish mobile phone, leave off the initial 0 of the phone numbers listed in this book. For more details on how to dial, see page 1088.

Polish History

Poland is flat. Take a look at a topographical map of Europe, and you can see the Poles' historical dilemma: The path of least

resistance from northern Europe to Russia leads right through Poland. Over the years, many invaders—including Napoleon and Hitler—have taken advantage of Poland's strategic location. The country is nicknamed "God's playground" for the many wars that have rumbled through its territory. Poland has been invaded by Soviets, Nazis, French, Austrians, Russians, Prussians, Swedes, Teutonic Knights, Tatars, Bohemians, Magyars—and, about 1,300 years ago, Poles.

Medieval Greatness

The first Poles were a tribe called the Polonians ("people of the plains"), a Slavic band that showed up in these parts in the eighth century. In 966, Mieszko I, Duke of the Polonian tribe, adopted Christianity and founded the Piast dynasty (which would last for more than 400 years). Poland was born.

Poland struggled with two different invaders in the 13th century: the Tatars (Mongols who ravaged the south) and the Teutonic Knights (Germans who conquered the north—see page 434). But despite these challenges, Poland persevered. The last king of the Piast dynasty was also the greatest: Kazimierz the Great, who famously "found a Poland made of wood and left one made of brick and stone"—bringing Poland (and its capital, Kraków) to international prominence (see page 265). The progressive Kazimierz also invited Europe's much-persecuted Jews to settle here, establishing Poland as a haven for the Jewish people—which it would remain until the Nazis arrived.

Kazimierz the Great died at the end of the 14th century without a male heir. His grand-niece, Princess Jadwiga, became "king" (the Poles weren't ready for a "queen") and married Lithuanian Prince Władysław Jagiełło, uniting their countries against a common enemy, the Teutonic Knights. Their marriage marked the beginning of the Jagiellonian dynasty and set the stage for Poland's Golden Age. With territory spanning from the Baltic Sea to the Black Sea, Poland flourished.

Foreign Kings and Partitions

When the Jagiellonians died out in 1572, political power shifted to the nobility. Poland became a Republic of Nobles governed by its wealthiest 10 percent—the *szlachta*, who elected a series of foreign kings. Many of these kings made bad diplomatic decisions and squandered the country's resources. To make matters worse,

the nobles' parliament (Sejm) introduced the concept of *liberum veto,* whereby any measure could be vetoed by a single member of parliament. This policy—which effectively demanded unanimous approval for any law to be passed—paralyzed the Sejm's waning power.

By the late 18th century, Poland was floundering—and surrounded by three land-hungry empires (Russia, Prussia, and Austria). Over the course of less than 25 years, these countries divided Poland's territory among themselves in a series of three Partitions. In 1795, "Poland" (nicknamed "the cake of kings"—to be sliced and eaten at will) disappeared from Europe's maps, not to return until 1918.

Even though Poland was gone, the Poles wouldn't go quietly. As the Partitions were taking place, Polish soldier Tadeusz Kościuszko (a hero of the American Revolution) returned home to lead an unsuccessful military resistance against the Russians. After another failed uprising against Russia in 1830, many of Poland's top artists and writers fled to Paris—including pianist Fryderyk Chopin and Romantic poet Adam Mickiewicz (whose statue adorns Kraków's main square and Warsaw's Royal Way). These Polish artists tried to preserve the nation's spirit with music and words; those who remained in Poland continued to fight with swords and fists. By the end of the 19th century, the image of the Pole as a tireless, idealistic insurgent emerged. During this time, some Romantics—with typically melodramatic flair—dubbed Poland "the Christ of nations" for the way it was misunderstood and persecuted by the world.

At the end of World War I, Poland finally regained its independence...but the peace didn't last long.

Saddle on a Cow: World War II and Communism

In the early 20th century, Poland enjoyed a diverse ethnic mix—including Germans, Russians, Ukrainians, Lithuanians, and an enormous Jewish minority. A third of Poland spoke no Polish. In fact, the historic Baltic port city of Gdańsk—which was bicultural (German and Polish)—had been given a special "free city" status following World War I to avoid dealing with the prickly issue of whether to assign it to Germany or Poland.

But then, on September 1, 1939, Hitler began World War II by attacking Gdańsk to bring it into the German fold. With six million deaths in the next six years, Poland suffered the worst per-capita WWII losses of any nation.

At the war's end, as the victorious Allies shifted Poland's borders significantly westward, a massive movement of populations took place: Germans from western Poland were forced into Germany, and Poles from what would become Ukraine were

The Heritage of Communism

While Poland has been free, democratic, and capitalist since 1989, even young adults carry lots of psychological baggage from living under communism. Although the young generally embrace the fast new affluence with enthusiasm, many older people tend to be nostalgic about that slower-paced time that came with more security. And even young professionals, with so much energy and hope now, don't condemn everything about that stretch of history. A friend who was 13 in 1989 recalled those days this way:

"My childhood is filled with happy memories. Under communism, life was family-oriented. Careers didn't matter. There was no way to get rich, no reason to rush, so we had time. People always had time.

"But there were also shortages—many things were 'in deficit.' Sometimes my uncle would bring us several toilet paper rolls, held together with a string—absolutely the best gift anyone could give. I remember my mother and father had to 'organize' for special events...somehow find a good sausage and some Coca-Cola.

"Boys in my neighborhood collected pop cans. Since drinks were very limited in Poland, cans from other countries represented a world of opportunities beyond our borders. Parents could buy their children these cans on the black market, and the few families who were allowed to travel returned home with a treasure trove of cans. One boy up the street from me went to Italy, and proudly brought home a Pepsi can. All of the boys in the neighborhood wanted to see it—it was a huge status symbol. But a month later, communism ended, you could buy whatever you wanted, and everyone's can collections were worthless.

"We had real chocolate only for Christmas. The rest of the year, for treats we got something called 'chocolate-like product', which was sweet, dark, and smelled vaguely of chocolate. And we had oranges from Cuba for Christmas, too. Everybody was excited when the newspapers announced, 'The boat with the oranges from Cuba is just five days from Poland.' We waited with excitement all year for chocolate and those oranges. The smell of Christmas was so special. Now we have that smell every day. Still, my happiest Christmases were under communism."

transplanted to Poland proper. After millions died in the war, millions more were displaced from their ancestral homes. When the dust settled, Poland was in rubble...and almost exclusively Polish.

Poland was arguably hit harder by the Soviet regime than the other countries in this book. As conditions worsened in the 1970s, food shortages were the norm. Stores were marked by long lines stretching around the block. Poles were issued ration coupons for food staples, and cashiers clipped off a corner when a purchase was made...assuming, of course, the item was in stock. It often wasn't.

The little absurdities of communist life—which today seem almost comical—made every day a struggle. For years, every elderly woman in Poland had hair the same strange magenta color. There was only one color of dye available, so if you had dyed hair, the choice was simple: Let your hair grow out (and look clownishly half red and half white), or line up and go red.

During these difficult times, the Poles often rose up—staging major protests in 1956, 1968, 1970, and 1976. Stalin famously noted that introducing communism to the Poles was like putting a saddle on a cow.

When an anti-communist Polish cardinal named Karol Wojtyła was elected Pope in 1978, then visited his homeland in 1979, it was a sign to his countrymen that change was in the air. (For more on Pope John Paul II, see page 270.) In 1980, Lech Wałęsa, an electrician at the shipyards in Gdańsk, became the leader of the Solidarity movement, the first workers' union in communist Eastern Europe. After an initial 18-day strike at the Gdańsk shipyards, the communist regime gave in, legalizing Solidarity (for more on Solidarity, see page 404).

But the union grew too powerful, and the communists felt their control slipping away. On Sunday, December 13, 1981, Poland's head of state, General Wojciech Jaruzelski, declared martial law in order to "forestall Soviet intervention." (Whether the Soviets actually would have intervened remains a hotly debated issue.) Tanks ominously rolled through the streets of Poland on that snowy December morning, and the Poles were terrified.

Martial law lasted until 1983. Each Pole has his or her own chilling memories of this frightening time. During riots, the people would flock into churches—the only place they could be safe from the ZOMO (riot police). But Solidarity struggled on, going underground and becoming a united movement of all demographics, 10 million members strong (more than a quarter of the population).

In July 1989, the ruling Communist Party agreed to hold open elections (reserving 65 percent of representatives for themselves). Their goal was to appease Solidarity, but the plan backfired: Communists didn't win a single contested seat. These elections

Polish Jokes

Through the dreary communist times, the Poles managed to keep their sense of humor. A popular target of jokes was the riot police, called the ZOMO. Here are just a few of the things Poles said about these unpopular cops:

- It's better to have a sister who's a whore than a brother in the ZOMO.
- ZOMO police are hired based on the 90-90 principle: They have to weigh at least 90 kilograms (200 pounds), and their I.Q. must be less than 90.
- ZOMO are dispatched in teams of three: one who can read, one who can write, and a third to protect those other two smart guys.
- A ZOMO policeman was sitting on the curb, crying. Someone came up to him and asked what was wrong. "I lost my dog!" he said. "No matter," the person replied. "He's a smart police dog. I'm sure he can find his way back to the station." "Yes," the ZOMO said. "But without him, *I* can't!"

The communists gave their people no options at elections: If you voted, you voted for the regime. Poles liked to joke that in some ways, this made communists like God—who created Eve, then said to Adam, "Now choose a wife." It was said that communists could run a pig as a candidate, and it would still win; a popular symbol of dissent became a pig painted with the words, "Vote Red."

There were even jokes about jokes. Under communism, Poles noted that there was a government-sponsored prize for the funniest political joke: 15 years in prison.

helped spark the chain reaction across Eastern Europe that eventually tore down the Iron Curtain. Lech Wałęsa became Poland's first post-communist president. (For more on Lech Wałęsa, see page 406.)

Poland in the 21st Century: The European Union

When 10 new countries joined the European Union in May 2004, Poland was the most ambivalent of the bunch. After centuries of being under other empires' authority, the Poles were hardly eager to relinquish some of their hard-fought autonomy to Brussels. Many Poles thought that EU membership would make things worse (higher prices, a loss of traditional lifestyles) before they got better. But most people agreed that their country had to join to survive in today's Europe. Today most Poles begrudgingly acknowledge that the benefits of EU membership have outweighed the drawbacks.

While other countries were planning their fireworks displays to celebrate EU enlargement on May 1, 2004, Poland was seized

by a strange sort of mass hysteria. The country buzzed with rumors of increased prices. When the news reported that sugar would be subject to a higher tax rate, there was a run on the stores, as the Poles bought up as much sugar as they could stockpile. The result? A shortage of sugar...and higher prices, even before May 1.

The most obvious initial impact of EU membership was the tremendous migration of young Poles seeking work in other EU countries (mostly Britain, Ireland, and Sweden, which waive visa requirements for Eastern European workers). Many of them found employment at hotels and restaurants. Visitors to London and Dublin are still likely to notice a surprising language barrier at the front desks of hotels, and Polish-language expat newspapers have joined British gossip rags on newsstands. Those who remained in Poland were concerned about the "brain drain" of bright young people flocking out of their country. But with the recent global economic crisis, quite a few Polish expats have returned home. For more on this phenomenon, see "The Polish Plumber Syndrome" on page 28.

Poland is by far the most populous of the recent EU members, with nearly 39 million people (about the same as Spain, or about half the size of Germany). This makes Poland the sixth-largest of the 27 EU member states—giving it serious political clout, which it has already asserted...sometimes to the dismay of the EU's more established powers. Poland seems poised to take a leading role in the "New Europe."

The Kaczyński Brothers: Those Two Who Would Lead Poland

Poland's political process took a surprising turn in the 2005 presidential election, won by Lech Kaczyński and his conservative Law and Justice party. The party's platform is pro-tax cuts, fiercely Euroskeptic (anti-EU), and very Catholic. This suits the Poles fine. Like a nation of Newt Gingriches, Poles are phobic when it comes to "big government," since they've been subjugated and manipulated so much by foreign oppressors over the centuries. This is partly why the infrastructure here still lags somewhat behind other Eastern European countries (lower taxes = less investment in roads). On the American spectrum, Poland may be the most politically "conservative" country in Europe.

In a queasy twist, several months after his election, President Lech Kaczyński took the controversial step of appointing his identical twin brother (and Law and Justice party co-founder) Jarosław as Poland's prime minister. The Kaczyński brothers were child actors who appeared in several popular movies together—their biggest hit was titled *Those Two Who Would Steal the Moon.* As teenagers, they would switch identities and take tests for each

other. Today the 45-minute-older, unmarried, and slightly more handsome Jarosław, who still lives with the twins' mother, is considered one of Poland's most eligible bachelors. (You can't make this stuff up.)

The political pendulum took a hard swing back to the center in October of 2007, when the Kaczyński brothers' main political rival, the pro-EU Donald Tusk, led his Civic Platform party to victory in the parliamentary elections. Tusk was named prime minister, though Lech Kaczyński remains president through at least 2010. As Poland marches into the 21st century, its future will be guided by Donald Tusk and the Kaczyńskis—the yin and yangs of Polish politics. The name Kaczyński loosely means "duck"—so the Poles quip that they're led by "Donald and the Ducks."

Polish Food

Polish food is hearty and tasty. Since Poland is north of the Carpathian Mountains, its weather tends to be chilly, which limits the kinds of fruits and vegetables that flourish here. Like other northern European countries (such as Russia or Scandinavia), dominant staples include potatoes, dill, berries, beets, and bread. Much of what you might think of as "Jewish food" turns up on Polish menus (gefilte fish, potato pancakes, chicken soup, and so forth)—which makes sense, given that Poles and Jews lived in the same area for centuries under the same climatic and culinary influences.

Polish soups are a highlight. The most typical are *żurek* and *barszcz*. *Żurek* (often translated as "sour soup" on menus) is a light-colored soup made from a sourdough base, usually containing a hard-boiled egg and pieces of *kiełbasa* (sausage). *Barszcz,* better known to Americans as borscht, is a savory beet soup that you'll see in several varieties: *Barszcz czerwony* (red borscht) is a broth with a deep red color, sometimes containing dumplings or a hard-boiled egg. *Barszcz ukraiński* (Ukrainian borscht) is similar, but has vegetables mixed in (usually cabbage, beans, and carrots). In summer, try the "Polish gazpacho"—*chłodnik,* a cream soup with beets, onions, and radishes that's served cold.

Another familiar Polish dish is pierogi. These ravioli-like dumplings come with various fillings. The most traditional are minced meat, sauerkraut, mushroom, cheese, and blueberry; many restaurants also experiment with more exotic fillings. Pierogi are often served with specks of fatty bacon to add flavor. Pierogi are a

Bar Mleczny (Milk Bar)

When you see a "bar" in Poland, it doesn't mean alcohol—it means cheap grub. Eating at a *bar mleczny* (bar MLECH-neh) is an essential Polish sightseeing experience. These cafeterias, which you'll see all over the country, are an incredibly cheap way to get a good meal...and, with the right attitude, a fun cultural experience.

In the communist era, the government subsidized the food at milk bars, allowing lowly workers to enjoy a meal out. The tradition continues, and today, Poland still foots the bill for most of your milk-bar meal. Prices are astoundingly low—my bill for a big meal usually comes to about $4–5—and, while communist-era fare was gross, today's milk-bar cuisine is usually quite tasty.

Milk bars usually offer many of the traditional tastes listed in the "Polish Food" section. Common items are soups (like *żurek* and *barszcz*), a variety of cabbage-based salads, *kotlet* (fried pork chops), pierogi (like ravioli, with various fillings), and *naleśniki* (pancakes). You'll see glasses of juice and (of course) milk, but most milk bars also stock bottles of water and Coke.

There are two types of milk bars: updated, modern cafeterias that cater to tourists (English menus), add some modern twists to their traditional fare, and charge about 50 percent more; and time-machine dives that haven't changed for decades. At truly traditional milk bars, the service is aimed at locals—which means no English menu and a confusing ordering system.

Every milk bar is a little different, but here's the general procedure: Head to the counter, wait to be acknowledged, and point to what you want. Handy vocabulary: *to* (sounds like "toe") means "this"; *i* (pronounced "ee") means "and."

If the milk-bar lady asks you any questions, you have three options: nod stupidly until she just gives you something; repeat one of the things she just said (assuming she's asked you to choose between two options, like meat or cheese in your pierogi); or hope that a kindly English-speaking Pole in line will leap to your rescue. If nothing else, ordering at a milk bar is an adventure in gestures. Smiling seems to slightly extend the patience of milk-bar staffers.

Once your tray is all loaded up, pay the cashier, do a double-take when you realize how cheap your bill is, then find a table. After the meal, it's generally polite, if not expected, to bus your own dishes to the little window (watch locals and imitate).

budget traveler's dream: Restaurants serving them are everywhere, and they're generally cheap, filling, and tasty.

Bigos is a rich and delicious sauerkraut stew cooked with meat, mushrooms, and whatever's in the pantry. *Gołąbki* is a dish of cabbage leaves stuffed with minced meat and rice in a tomato or mushroom sauce. *Kotlet schabowy* (fried pork chop)—once painfully scarce in communist Poland—remains a local favorite to this day. *Kaczka* (duck) is popular, as is fish: Look for *pstrąg* (trout), *karp* (carp, beware of bones), and *węgorz* (eel). Poles eat lots of potatoes, which are served with nearly every meal.

For a snack on the go, Poles love *zapiekanki* (singular *zapiekanek*): a toasted baguette with cheese, ketchup, rubbery mushrooms from a can, and sometimes onions or other toppings. It's like the poor cousin of a French-bread pizza. *Zapiekanki* are an acquired taste, but at least they're very cheap. The bagel-like rings you'll see sold on the street, *obwarzanki* (singular *obwarzanek*), are also cheap, and usually fresh and tasty.

Poland has good pastries. A *piekarnia* is a bakery specializing in breads. But if you really want something special, look for a *cukiernia* (pastry shop). The classic Polish treat is *pączki*, glazed jelly doughnuts. They can have different fillings, but most typical is a wild-rose jam. *Szarlotka* is apple cake—sometimes made with chunks of apples (especially in season), sometimes with apple filling. *Sernik* is cheesecake, and *makowiec* is poppy-seed cake. *Winebreda* is an especially gooey Danish. *Babeczka* is like a cupcake filled with pudding. You may see *jabłko w cieście*—slices of apple cooked in dough, then glazed. *Napoleonka* is a French-style treat with layers of crispy wafers and custard.

Lody (ice cream) is popular. The tall, skinny cones of soft-serve ice cream are called *świderki*, sometimes translated as "American ice cream." The most beloved traditional candy is *ptasie mleczko* (birds' milk), which is like a semi-sour marshmallow covered with chocolate. E. Wedel is the country's top brand of chocolate, with outlets in all the big cities (see page 377).

Thirsty? *Woda* is water, *woda mineralna* is bottled water (*gazowana* is with gas/carbonation, *niegazowana* is without), *kawa* is coffee, *herbata* is tea, *sok* is juice, and *mleko* is milk. Żywiec and Okocim are the best-known brands of *piwo* (beer).

Wódka (vodka) is a Polish staple—the name means, roughly, "precious little water." Żubrówka, the most famous brand of vodka, comes with a blade of grass from the bison reserves in eastern Poland (look for the bottle with the bison). The bison "flavor" the grass...then the grass flavors the vodka. Poles often mix Żubrówka with apple juice, and call this cocktail *szarlotka* ("apple cake"); it also goes by the name *tatanka* (a Native American word for "bison"). For "Cheers!" say, "*Na zdrowie!*" (nah ZDROH-vyeh).

Unusual drinks to try if you have the chance are *kwas* (a cold, fizzy, Ukrainian-style non-alcoholic beverage made from day-old rye bread) and *kompot* (a hot drink made from stewed berries). Poles are unusually fond of carrot juice (often cut with fruit juice); Kubuś is the most popular brand.

"Bon appétit" *is "Smacznego"* (smatch-NEH-goh). To pay, ask for the *rachunek* (rah-KHOO-nehk).

Polish Language

Polish is closely related to its neighboring Slavic languages (Slovak and Czech), with the biggest difference being that Polish has lots of fricatives (hissing sounds—"sh" and "ch"—often in close proximity). Consider the opening line of Poland's most famous tongue-twisting nursery rhyme: *W Szczebrzeszynie chrzaszcz brzmi w trzcinie* ("In Szczebrzeszyn, a beetle is heard in the reeds"—pronounced vuh shih-chehb-zheh-shee-nyeh khzhahshch bzh-mee vuh tzhuh-cheen-yeh...or something like that).

Polish intimidates Americans with long, difficult-to-pronounce words. But if you take your time and sound things out, you'll quickly develop an ear for it. One rule of thumb to help you out: The stress is always on the next-to-last syllable.

Polish has some letters that don't appear in English, and some letters and combinations are pronounced differently than in English:

ć, ci, and **cz** all sound like "ch" as in "church"
ś, si, and **sz** all sound like "sh" as in "short"
ż, zi, and **rz** all sound like "zh" as in "leisure"
ń and **ni** sound like "ny" as in "canyon"
ę and **ą** are pronounced nasally, as in French: "en" and "an"
c sounds like "ts" as in "cats"
j sounds like "y" as in "yellow"
w sounds like "v" as in "Victor"
ł sounds like "w" as in "with"

So to Poles, "Lech Wałęsa" isn't pronounced "lehk wah-LEH-sah," as Americans tend to say—but "lehkh vah-WEHN-sah."

The Polish people you meet will be impressed and flattered if you take the time to learn a little of their language. To get started, check out the selection of Polish Survival Phrases on page 1121.

As you're tracking down addresses, these words will help: ***miasto*** (mee-AH-stoh, town), ***plac*** (plahts, square), ***rynek*** (REE-nehk, big market square), ***ulica*** (OO-leet-sah, road), ***aleja*** (ah-LAY-yah, avenue), and ***most*** (mohst, bridge).

KRAKÓW

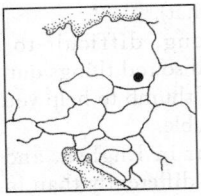

Kraków is easily Poland's best destination: a beautiful, old-fashioned city buzzing with history, enjoyable sights, tourists, and college students. Even though the country's capital moved from here to Warsaw 400 years ago, Kraków remains Poland's cultural and intellectual center. Of all of the Eastern European cities laying claim to the boast "the next Prague," Kraków is for real.

Kraków grew wealthy from trade in the late 10th and early 11th centuries. Traders who passed through were required to stop here for a few days and sell their wares at a reduced cost. Local merchants turned around and sold those goods with big price hikes...and Kraków thrived. In 1038, it became Poland's capital.

Tatars invaded in 1241, leaving the city in ruins. Krakovians took this opportunity to rebuild their streets in a near-perfect grid, a striking contrast to the narrow, mazelike lanes of most medieval towns. The destruction also paved the way for the spectacular Main Market Square—still Kraków's best attraction.

King Kazimierz the Great sparked Kraków's Golden Age in the 14th century (see page 265). In 1364, he established the university that still defines the city (and counts Copernicus and Pope John Paul II among its alumni).

But Kraków's power waned as Poland's political center shifted to Warsaw. In 1596, the capital officially moved north. At the end of the 18th century, three neighboring powers—Russia, Prussia, and Austria—partitioned Poland, annexing all of its territory and dividing it among themselves. Warsaw ended up as a satellite of oppressive Moscow, and Kraków became a poor provincial backwater of Vienna. But despite Kraków's reduced prominence,

Kraków Essentials

English	Polish	Pronounced
Main Train Station	Kraków Główny	KROCK-oof GWOHV-nee
Old Town	Stare Miasto	STAH-reh mee-AH-stoh
Main Market Square	Rynek Główny	REE-nehk GWOHV-nee
Cloth Hall	Sukiennice	soo-kyeh-NEET-seh
Floriańska Street	Ulica Floriańska	OOH-leet-suh floh-ree-AHN-skah
Park around the Old Town	Planty	PLAHN-tee
Castle Hill	Wawel	VAH-vehl
Jewish Quarter	Kazimierz	kah-ZHEE-mehzh
Vistula River	Wisła	VEES-wah
Salt Mine	Wieliczka	vee-LEECH-kah
Planned Communist Suburb	Nowa Huta	NOH-vah HOO-tah

Austria's comparatively liberal climate helped turn the city into a haven for intellectuals and progressives (including a young revolutionary thinker from Russia named Vladimir Lenin).

Kraków's cityscape emerged from World War II virtually unscathed. But when the communists took over, they decided to give intellectual (and potentially dissident) Kraków an injection of good Soviet values—in the form of heavy industry. They built Nowa Huta, an enormous steelworks and planned town for workers, on Kraków's outskirts—dooming the city to decades of smog. Thankfully, Kraków is now much cleaner than it was 20 years ago.

Pope John Paul II was born (as Karol Wojtyła) in nearby Wadowice, and served as archbishop of Kraków before being called to Rome. Kraków might be the most Catholic town in Europe's most Catholic country—so be sure to visit a few of its many churches. University life, small but thought-provoking museums, great restaurants, sprawling parks, and Jewish history round out the city's appeal.

Over the last few years, Kraków has gone through a boom and bust. The early 2000s were kind to the city, but tourist interest peaked in 2006. These days, it seems that many tourists have moved on—leaving local hoteliers scratching their heads and lowering their rates. Where all those travelers have gone, I'll never know. But their loss is your gain. Kraków is a gem. Enjoy it.

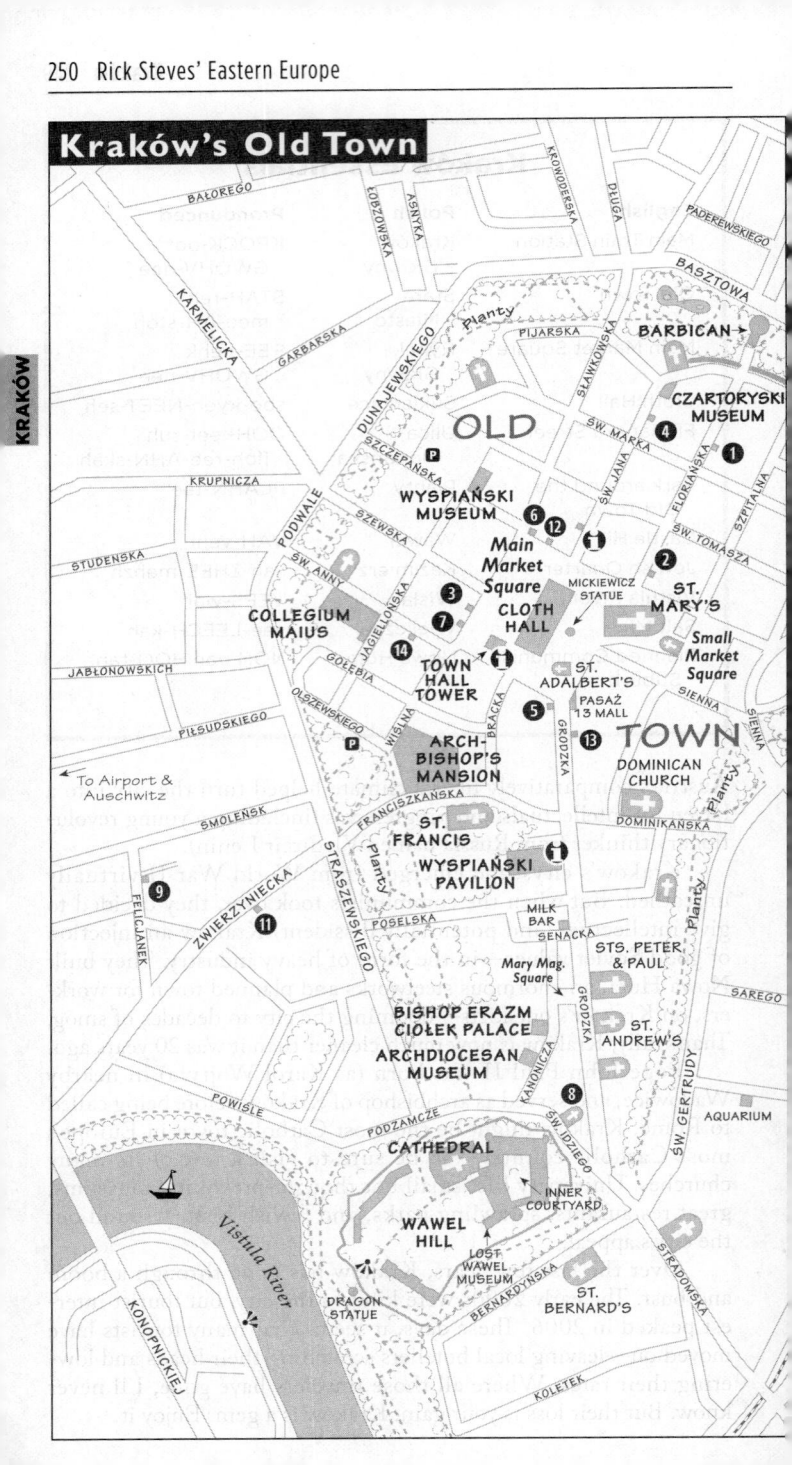
Kraków's Old Town
BAŁOREGO
ŁOBZOWSKA
ASNYKA
KROWODERSKA
DŁUGA
PADEREWSKIEGO
BASZTOWA
KARMELICKA
GARBARSKA
Planty
PIJARSKA
SŁAWKOWSKA
BARBICAN
DUNAJEWSKIEGO
OLD
TOWN
CZARTORYSKI MUSEUM
ŚW. MARKA
ŚW. JANA
FLORIAŃSKA
SZPITALNA
SZCZEPAŃSKA
KRUPNICZA
WYSPIAŃSKI MUSEUM
PODWALE
SZEWSKA
Main Market Square
ŚW. TOMASZA
STUDENSKA
ŚW. ANNA
MICKIEWICZ STATUE
ST. MARY'S
COLLEGIUM MAIUS
JAGIELLOŃSKA
CLOTH HALL
Small Market Square
JABŁONOWSKICH
GOŁĘBIA
TOWN HALL TOWER
ST. ADALBERT'S
OLSZEWSKIEGO
BRACKA
PASAŻ 13 MALL
SIENNA
PIŁSUDSKIEGO
WIŚLNA
GRODZKA
ARCH-BISHOP'S MANSION
DOMINICAN CHURCH
To Airport & Auschwitz
FRANCISZKAŃSKA
SMOLEŃSK
ST. FRANCIS
DOMINIKAŃSKA
WYSPIAŃSKI PAVILION
STRASZEWSKIEGO
ZWIERZYNIECKA
FELICJANEK
POSELSKA
MILK BAR
SENACKA
STS. PETER & PAUL
Mary Mag. Square
SAREGO
BISHOP ERAZM CIOŁEK PALACE
ST. ANDREW'S
ARCHDIOCESAN MUSEUM
KANONICZA
POWIŚLE
PODZAMCZE
ŚW. IDZIEGO
ŚW. GERTRUDY
AQUARIUM
CATHEDRAL
INNER COURTYARD
Vistula River
WAWEL HILL
LOST WAWEL MUSEUM
DRAGON STATUE
BERNARDYŃSKA
ST. BERNARD'S
STRADOWSKA
KONOPNICKIEJ
KOLETEK

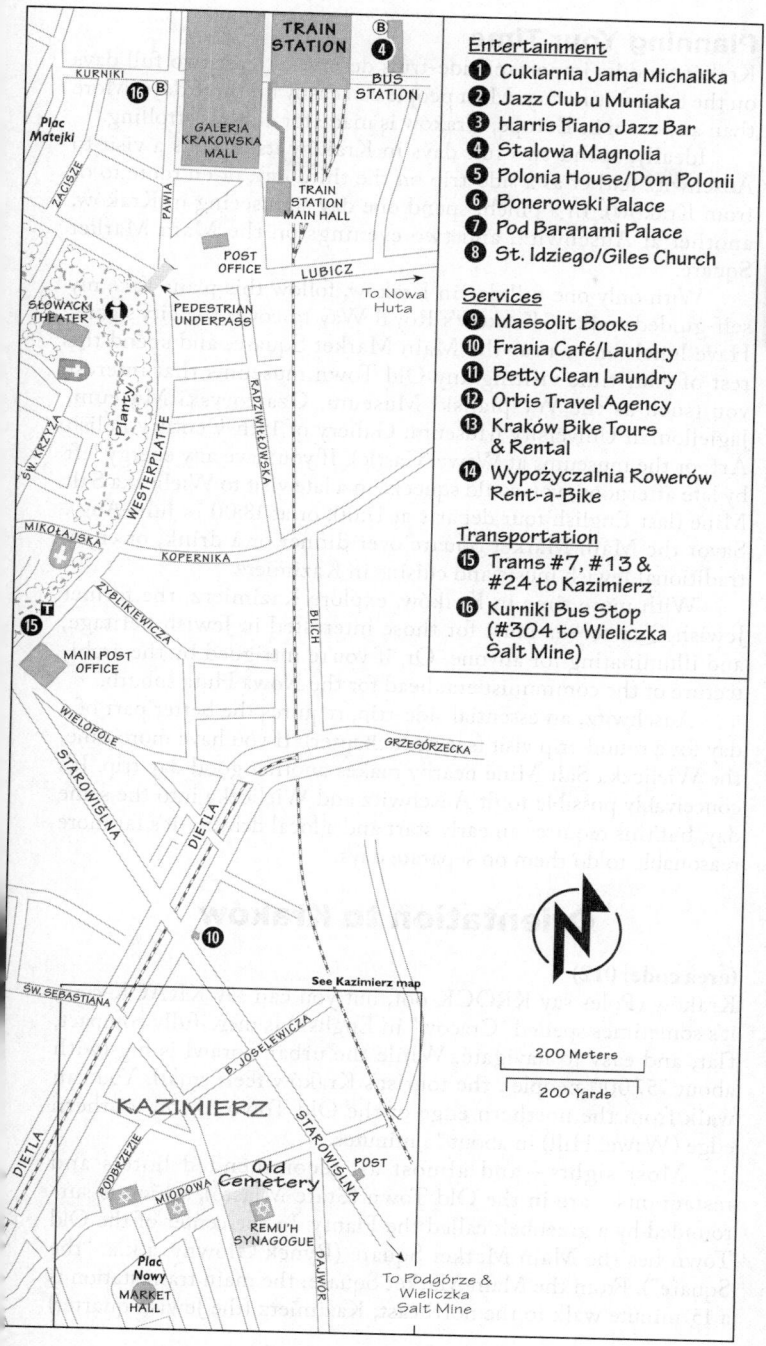
TRAIN STATION
BUS STATION
KURNIKI
Plac Matejki
GALERIA KRAKOWSKA MALL
ZACISZE
PAWIA
TRAIN STATION MAIN HALL
POST OFFICE
LUBICZ
To Nowa Huta
SŁOWACKI THEATER
PEDESTRIAN UNDERPASS
Planty
ŚW. KRZYŻA
WESTERPLATTE
RADZIWIŁŁOWSKA
MIKOŁAJSKA
KOPERNIKA
ZYBLIKIEWICZA
BLICH
MAIN POST OFFICE
WIELOPOLE
GRZEGÓRZECKA
STAROWIŚLNA
DIETLA
ŚW. SEBASTIANA
See Kazimierz map
B. JOSELEWICZA
KAZIMIERZ
STAROWIŚLNA
POST
PODBRZEZIE
MIODOWA
Old Cemetery
REMU'H SYNAGOGUE
DAJWOR
Plac Nowy
MARKET HALL
To Podgórze & Wieliczka Salt Mine
200 Meters
200 Yards
Entertainment
1 Cukiernia Jama Michalika
2 Jazz Club u Muniaka
3 Harris Piano Jazz Bar
4 Stalowa Magnolia
5 Polonia House/Dom Polonii
6 Bonerowski Palace
7 Pod Baranami Palace
8 St. Idziego/Giles Church
Services
9 Massolit Books
10 Frania Café/Laundry
11 Betty Clean Laundry
12 Orbis Travel Agency
13 Kraków Bike Tours & Rental
14 Wypożyczalnia Rowerów Rent-a-Bike
Transportation
15 Trams #7, #13 & #24 to Kazimierz
16 Kurniki Bus Stop (#304 to Wieliczka Salt Mine)

Planning Your Time

Kraków and its important side-trips deserve at least two full days on the busiest itinerary. Most people can easily fill three days. More than any town in Europe, Kraków is made for aimless strolling.

Ideally, spend two full days in Kraków itself, plus a visit to Auschwitz (either as a side-trip on the third day, or en route to or from Kraków). In a pinch, spend one day sightseeing in Kraków, another at Auschwitz, and two evenings on the Main Market Square.

With only one full day in Kraków, follow this plan: Take my self-guided walk of Kraków's Royal Way to cover the city's core. Have lunch on or near the Main Market Square, and spend the rest of your time visiting any Old Town museums that interest you (such as the Wyspiański Museum, Czartoryski Museum, Jagiellonian University Museum, Gallery of 19th-Century Polish Art, or the museums at Wawel Castle). If you have any energy left by late afternoon, you could squeeze in a late visit to Wieliczka Salt Mine (last English tour departs at 17:00, or at 18:00 in July–Aug). Savor the Main Market Square over dinner or a drink, or enjoy traditional Jewish music and cuisine in Kazimierz.

With more time in Kraków, explore Kazimierz, the former Jewish Quarter—a must for those interested in Jewish heritage, and illuminating for anyone. Or, if you're intrigued by the architecture of the communist era, head for the Nowa Huta suburb.

Auschwitz, an essential side-trip, requires the better part of a day for a round-trip visit (see next chapter). If you have more time, the Wieliczka Salt Mine nearby makes another good day trip. It's conceivably possible to fit Auschwitz and Wieliczka into the same day, but this requires an early start and a local driver—it's far more reasonable to do them on separate days.

Orientation to Kraków

(area code: 012)

Kraków (Poles say KROCK-oof, but you can say KRACK-cow; it's sometimes spelled "Cracow" in English) is mercifully compact, flat, and easy to navigate. While the urban sprawl is big (with about 757,000 people), the tourist's Kraków feels small. You can walk from the northern edge of the Old Town to the southern edge (Wawel Hill) in about 15 minutes.

Most sights—and almost all recommended hotels and restaurants—are in the Old Town (Stare Miasto), which is surrounded by a greenbelt called the Planty. In the center of the Old Town lies the Main Market Square (Rynek Główny, a.k.a. "the Square"). From the Main Market Square, the main train station is a 15-minute walk to the northeast; Kazimierz (the Jewish quarter)

is a 20-minute walk to the southeast; and Wawel Hill (with a historic castle, museums, and Poland's national church) is a 10-minute walk south. Just beyond Wawel is the Vistula River.

Tourist Information

Kraków has several helpful TIs. Four are in the Old Town (open daily May–Sept 9:00–19:00, Oct–April 9:00–17:00, unless otherwise noted): in the **Planty** park, between the main train station and Main Market Square (in round kiosk at ulica Szpitalna 25, tel. 012-432-0110); just north of the Main Market Square on **ulica Św. Jana** (specializes in concert tickets, daily 10:00–18:00, at #2, tel. 012-421-7787); in the **Old Town Hall Tower** right on the Main Market Square (sometimes 10:00–18:00 in winter, tel. 012-433-7310); and in the **Wyspiański Pavilion** just south of the Square on ulica Grodzka (plac Wszystkich Świętych 3, not at the window but inside the building, tel. 012-616-1886). Other branches are in **Kazimierz** (daily 9:00–17:00, ulica Józefa 7, tel. 012-422-0471), **Nowa Huta** (Tue–Fri 10:00–14:00, Sat 10:30-14:30, closed Sun–Mon, os. Słoneczne 16, tel. 012-643-0303), and the **airport** (Mon–Fri 8:00–19:00, Sat 9:30–21:30, Sun 9:30–17:30, tel. 012-285-5341). The website for all TIs is www.krakow.travel. Be warned that many private travel agencies, room-booking services, and tour operators masquerade as TIs, with deceptive blue-and-white "i" signs. If they're not listed above, they're not a real TI.

At any TI, ask what's new in fast-changing Kraków, browse the brochures, and pick up the free one-page map and the *Kraków Tourist Information Compendium* booklet. The TIs also offer a free room-finding service, and sell tickets for walking and bus tours (see "Tours in Kraków," later).

I'd skip the TI's **Kraków Tourist Card,** which covers public transportation in Kraków, admission to several city museums, and moderate discounts to outlying sights and tours (50 zł/2 days, 65 zł/3 days). Since public transportation is mostly unnecessary and museums are cheap, this card doesn't make sense for most visitors.

Arrival in Kraków

By Train: Kraków's main train station (called "Kraków Główny") is just northeast of the Old Town. It shares a broad plaza (plac Dworcowy) with the giant, modern Galeria Krakowska shopping mall.

Taxis from the station are cheap and easy: From the tracks, take the elevator or stairs to the rooftop above you, where you'll find a giant parking lot where taxis wait. Be sure to use a taxi clearly marked with a company name and telephone number. The usual metered rate to downtown is a reasonable 10–15 zł.

Most hotels are within easy **walking** distance. It's about a

15-minute stroll to the Main Market Square—just follow signs to the center (*wyjście do centrum* or *wyjście do miasta*). From the tracks, you'll first walk down some stairs and pass through an underground passage. When you emerge, turn left up the stairs and walk under the long green canopy to the yellow main terminal building. Exiting on the other side of the main terminal, you'll emerge into the wide-open plaza called plac Dworcowy, fronted by the Galeria Krakowska mall and an old-fashioned yellow post office. Beyond the post office, a broad ramp leads down into a pedestrian underpass beneath the busy ring road; as you emerge from this underpass, bear right (following signs for *Rynek Główny/ Main Market*) and head into the Planty park. You'll see the round TI kiosk on your left, and the Main Market Square is a few blocks straight ahead.

By Bus: The new, slick bus station is right behind the main train station. To get into town, use the passage that takes you under the train tracks (following signs for *PKP*—the train station—and *centrum*). Once at the train station, follow the directions above.

To get *to* the bus station from the Old Town (such as to catch a bus to Auschwitz), first head to the main train station (go through the Planty park and use the underpass). From the train station's main terminal, walk under the long green canopy to the train platforms. Use the pedestrian underpass to go under the tracks (following signs for *dojście do dworca autobusowego*); when you emerge on the other side, the bus station is the blocky, modern building on your left (marked *RDA Dworzec Autobusowy*). Inside are the standard amenities (lockers and toilets), domestic and international ticket windows, and an electronic board showing the next several departures. Some bus departures, marked on the board with a *G*, leave from the upper *(gorna)* stalls, which you can see out the window. Other bus departures, marked with a *D*, leave from the lower *(dolna)* stalls; to find these, go down the easy-to-miss stairs (marked *zejście na dolna płytę*) on the left just beyond the ticket windows. Note that some minibuses, such as those to Auschwitz, also leave from at or near this station.

By Car: *Centrum* signs lead you into the Old Town—you'll know you're there when you hit the ring road that surrounds the Planty park. Parking garages surround the Old Town. Your hotelier can advise you on directions and parking.

By Plane: The small, modern **John Paul II Kraków-Balice Airport** is about 10 miles west of the center, with separate international and domestic terminals. A train station near the airport allows you to zip quickly downtown (as you exit the main/international terminal, turn right and look for the *PKP* sign to catch the blue shuttle bus, which will take you to the station nearby; then buy the 8-zł ticket on the train for the 15-min trip to

Kraków's main train station—see train arrival instructions earlier; you can also catch this shuttle bus from in front of the domestic terminal). You can also catch public bus #208, #292, or (at night) #902 from in front of the airport to Kraków's main bus station (3 zł, 50-min trip depending on traffic, see bus station arrival instructions earlier). Or, for door-to-door service, catch a cab from the taxi stand in front of the terminal (ask about the fare up front—should be around 70–80 zł, more expensive at night, about 30 min). You can also arrange a taxi transfer in advance (such as with recommended driver Adrzej Durman, listed later, under "Tours in Kraków"). Airport info: tel. 012-295-5800, www.krakowairport.pl.

Note that many budget flights—including those on Wizz Air and Ryanair—use the **International Airport Katowice in Pyrzowice** (Międzynarodowy Port Lotniczy Katowice w Pyrzowicach, www.katowice-airport.com). This airport is about 18 miles from the city of Katowice, which is about 50 miles west of Kraków. Direct buses run sporadically between Katowice Airport and Kraków's main train station (50 zł, trip takes 1.75 hrs, generally scheduled to meet incoming flights). You can also take the bus from Katowice Airport to Katowice's train station (hourly, 50 min), then take the train to Kraków (hourly, 1.5 hrs). Wizz Air's website is useful for figuring out your connection: www.wizzair.com.

Helpful Hints

Sightseeing Schedules: Most Old Town museums are closed Monday. The TI hands out a thoughtful little flier listing attractions that are open on Monday, including the Jagiellonian University Museum and—in summer—a few of the Wawel attractions. In Kazimierz, most of the Jewish-themed sights are open on Monday (however, the Ethnographic Museum and—likely—Schindler's Factory are closed). Conversely, Kazimierz is very quiet on Saturday. Hours at museums tend to change frequently; it's important to carefully confirm the opening times of sights at the TI.

Internet Access: Virtually every hotel in Kraków has an Internet terminal in its lobby and/or Wi-Fi or cable Internet in its rooms. Otherwise, take your pick of the city's many Internet cafés—it seems there's one on every corner.

Post Office: The main post office (Poczta Główna) is at the intersection of Starowiślna and the Westerplatte ring road, a few blocks east of the Main Market Square (Mon–Fri 7:30–20:30, Sat 8:00–14:00, closed Sun).

Bookstore: For an impressive selection of new and used English books, try **Massolit Books,** just west of the Old Town. They also have a café with drinks and light snacks, and a good

children's section (Sun–Thu 10:00–20:00, Fri–Sat 10:00–21:00, ulica Felicjanek 4, tel. 012-432-4150).

Laundry: Frania Café is a dream come true for a traveler with dirty laundry. Halfway between the Old Town and Kazimierz, this inviting café/pub has ample washers and driers, relaxing ambience, free Wi-Fi and a loaner laptop, a full bar serving up espresso drinks and laundry-themed hard drinks, very long hours, and a friendly staff. Those in search of a mellow hangout might want to come here even if they don't need to wash clothes (16 zł/load self-service, 21 zł for them to do it for you in two hours—consider dropping it off on your way to Kazimierz and picking it up on the way back, likely open daily 10:30-24:00, ulica Starowiślna 26, tel. 012-395-3633, www.laundromat.pl).

If you must have something laundered closer to the Old Town, **Betty Clean** is relatively central, but pricey (about 12 zł/shirt, 17 zł/pants, 1 zł/pair of socks or underwear, takes 24 hours, pay 50 percent more for express 3-hour service, Mon–Fri 7:30–19:30, Sat 8:00–15:30, closed Sun, just outside the Planty park at ulica Zwierzyniecka 6, tel. 012-423-0848).

Travel Agencies: Orbis, at the top of the Main Market Square, has an English-speaking staff that books bus tours, changes money, and sells train, plane, and international bus tickets (May–Sept Mon–Fri 9:00–18:00, Sat 10:00–14:00, closed Sun, Rynek Główny 41, www.orbis.krakow.pl, tel. 012-619-2449). The agency posts a handy complete train schedule in their window. Buy your train tickets in this central location (no fee, English spoken) to avoid the trip to (and often long lines at) the station.

Getting Around Kraków

Kraków's top sights and best hotels are easily accessible by foot. You'll only need wheels if you're going to the Kazimierz Jewish quarter or the Nowa Huta suburb.

By Public Transit: Trams and buses zip around Kraków's urban sprawl. While most trams are new and modern, a few rickety old trams with big windows (dubbed "aquariums" by locals) also rattle around the city. The same tickets are used for both trams and buses, and can be purchased at most kiosks or at the new automated machines you'll find at most stops. You can buy a ticket from the driver for 0.50 zł extra, but they sometimes run out, so it's safer to get one before you board. A *bilet jednoprzejazdowy* (basic single ticket, no transfers) costs 2.50 zł; a *bilet godzinny* (one-hour ticket) allows transfers and costs 3.10 zł. Almost everything in Kraków is covered by the basic "one-zone" ticket, unless you're headed for the airport or Wieliczka Salt Mine, which are beyond the city limits

and require a slightly more expensive *aglomeracyjny* ticket. Always validate your ticket when you board the bus or tram. You can also get longer-term tickets for 24 hours (15 zł), 48 hours (18.80 zł), and 72 hours (25 zł). These must be validated the first time you use them; the 24-hour tickets can only be purchased at the new automated machines, and the other two must be bought at special MPK ticket booths (the handiest is in the Planty park near the TI).

By Taxi: Just as in other Eastern European cities, only take cabs that are clearly marked with a company logo and telephone number. Kraków taxis start at 7 zł and charge about 3 zł per kilometer. Rides are very short and generally run less than 15 zł. You're more likely to get the fair metered rate by calling or hailing a cab, rather than taking one waiting at tourist spots. To call a cab, try **Radio Taxi** (tel. 19191).

By Bike: Biking the Planty park and along the riverside promenades gets you out of the prettied-up Old Town to see a slice of untouristy Kraków. **Kraków Bike Tours** rents a wide variety of new, good-quality bikes (10 zł/first hour, cheaper per hour for longer rentals, 45 zł/day, 55 zł/24 hours, daily 10:00–19:00, just off the Square at Grodzka 2; see listing later, under "Tours in Kraków"). Nearby at **Wypożyczalnia Rowerów Rent-a-Bike,** easygoing Michał Bisping rents cheaper bikes (5 zł/hr, 35 zł/day, April–Oct daily 9:00–dusk, less in bad weather, closed Nov–March, ulica Św. Anny 4, mobile 0501-745-986).

Tours in Kraków

You can buy tickets for the walking tours and bus tours at any TI.

Local Guides—Kraków has several affordable guides. I've enjoyed working with two in particular, both of whom can show you the sights in Kraków and also have cars for day-tripping into the countryside: **Marta Chmielowska** (250 zł/half-day, 300 zł with her car, full day just a little more, mobile 0603-668-008, martachm@op.pl; for road trips she might send you with her driver/husband Czesław, a.k.a. Chester) and **Anna Gega** (by foot: 250 zł/4 hours, 350 zł/day; by car: 300 zł/4 hours, 500 zł/day—maybe more for long-distance trips; mobile 0604-151-293, leadertour@wp.pl).

Either of these guides can also take you to **Auschwitz** for the day for around 600-700 zł. However, only official Auschwitz guides can legally give tours at the concentration camp museum. Therefore, your local guide will probably either do the tour herself (and pay to hire a Polish-speaking guide to tag along and act "official"), or send you with one of the regularly departing English tours. Because of the added expense of hiring the local guide, it's pricey to visit Auschwitz with Marta or Anna—Andrew, below, is a better value.

Kraków at a Glance

Be Warned: Kraków's museum hours tend to fluctuate. To be sure you can get into a certain sight, confirm the hours in advance.

▲▲▲**Main Market Square** Stunning heart of Kraków and a people magnet any time of day. **Hours:** Always open. See page 264.

▲▲**Planty** Once a moat, now a scenic park encircling the city. **Hours:** Always open. See page 261.

▲▲**St. Mary's Church** Landmark church with extraordinary wood-carved Gothic altarpiece. **Hours:** Mon–Sat 11:30–18:00, Sun 14:00–18:00. See page 263.

▲▲**Cloth Hall** Fourteenth-century market hall with 21st-century souvenirs. **Hours:** Summer Mon–Fri 9:00–18:00, Sat–Sun 9:00–15:00, sometimes later; winter Mon–Fri 9:00–16:00, Sat–Sun 9:00–15:00. See page 267.

▲▲**St. Francis' Basilica** Lovely Gothic church with some of Poland's best Art Nouveau. **Hours:** Open long hours daily. See page 269.

▲▲**Wawel Cathedral** Poland's splendid national church, with tons of tombs, a crypt, and a climbable tower. **Hours:** May–Sept Mon–Sat 9:00–17:00, Sun 12:30–17:00; Oct–April Mon–Sat 9:00–16:00, Sun 12:30–17:00. See page 275.

▲▲**Wawel Castle Grounds** Historic hilltop with views, castle, cathedral, courtyard with chakras, and a passel of museums. **Hours:** Grounds open daily 6:00 until dusk. See page 277.

▲▲**Jewish Cemeteries** Two touching burial sites—the Old (1552–1800) and New (post-1800)—in Kazimierz. **Hours:** Old Cemetery—Sun–Fri 9:00–16:00, sometimes until 18:00 May–Aug, closes earlier in winter and at sundown on Fri, always closed Sat; New Cemetery—Sun–Fri 8:00–18:00, until 16:00 in winter, closed Sat. See page 291.

Driver—Since Kraków is such a useful home base for day trips, it can be handy to splurge on a private driver for door-to-door service. **Andrew (Andrzej) Durman,** a Pole who lived in Chicago and speaks great English, is a gregarious driver, translator, miracle worker, and all-around great guy. While not an officially trained or licensed tour guide, Andrew is an eager conversationalist and loves to provide lively commentary while you roll. Although you can hire Andrew for a simple airport transfer or Auschwitz

▲▲**Gallery of 19th-Century Polish Art** Worthwhile collection of paintings by should-be-famous artists (due to re-open the Cloth Hall in mid-2010). **Hours:** If open, it's Tue–Sat 10:00–18:00, Sun 10:00–16:00, closed Mon. See page 284.

▲**Czartoryski Museum** Varied collection, with European paintings (da Vinci and Rembrandt) and Polish armor, handicrafts, and decorative arts. **Hours:** Likely closed for restoration, otherwise Tue–Sat 10:00–18:00, Sun 10:00–16:00, closed Mon. See page 281.

▲**Wyspiański Museum** Art by the talented leader of the Młoda Polska Art Nouveau movement. **Hours:** Wed–Sat 10:00–18:00, Sun 10:00–16:00, closed Mon–Tue. See page 283.

▲**Jagiellonian University Museum: Collegium Maius** Proud collection of historic university, surrounding a tranquil courtyard where medieval professors lived. **Hours:** Two different tours; 30-min version—departs every 20 min Mon, Wed, and Fri 10:00–14:20; Tue and Thu 10:00–17:20; Sat 10:00–13:20; none Sun; 60-min version Mon–Fri at 13:00, none Sat–Sun. See page 286.

▲**Ethnographic Museum** Traditional rural Polish life on display. **Hours:** Tue–Sat 11:00–19:00, Thu until 21:00, Sun 11:00–15:00, closed Mon. See page 293.

▲**Pharmacy Under the Eagle** Small Podgórze exhibit about the Holocaust in Kraków, including three evocative historic films. **Hours:** May–Oct Mon 10:00–14:00, Tue–Sat 9:30–17:00, closed Sun; Nov–April Mon 10:00–14:00, Tue–Thu and Sat 9:00–16:00, Fri 10:00–17:00, closed Sun and the first Tue of each month. See page 294.

▲**Schindler's Factory** Brand-new museum covering Kraków's WWII experience—and how Oskar Schindler saved the lives of his Jewish workers. **Hours:** Opens sometime in 2010, likely Tue–Sun 10:00–17:30, closed Mon. See page 295.

day-trip, he also loves to tackle more ambitious itineraries, from helping you track down your Polish roots to multiple-day journeys around Poland and beyond (prices are for up to four people if you book direct: 380 zł to Auschwitz—he'll help you meet up with an English tour group there at your own expense, 180 zł to Wieliczka Salt Mine, 50 zł for transfer from Kraków airport, 400 zł for transfer from Katowice airport, 600 zł for an all-day trip into the countryside—such as into the High Tatras or to track down your

Polish roots near Kraków, more to cover gas costs for long-distance trips, mobile 0602-243-306, tel. 012-411-5630, www.tour-service.pl, andrew@tour-service.pl). The local guides listed above can also drive you on day trips.

Walking Tours—Various companies run city walking tours in English daily in summer. Most do a 2.5-hour tour of the Old Town as well as a 2.5-hour tour of Kazimierz, the Jewish district (40–60 zł per tour, depending on company). Because the scene is continually evolving, it's best to pick up fliers locally (at the TI or your hotel) and choose the one that fits your interests and schedule. Four people can hire their own great local guide for about the same amount of money.

Crazy Guides—This irreverent company offers tours to the communist suburb of Nowa Huta and other outlying sights. For details, see page 298.

Bike Tours—**Kraków Bike Tours** is a well-established operation that runs four-hour bike tours in English daily in summer. The tours make 25 stops in the Old Town, Kazimierz, and Podgórze (70 zł, includes loaner bike, April-Oct daily at 13:00, reservations recommended but not required, meet tour at their office down the passage at Grodzka 2—right at the bottom of the Square, mobile 0788-800-231, tel. 012-430-2034, www.krakowbiketour.com, krakowbiketour@gmail.com).

Bus Tours—As Kraków is so easily seen on foot, taking a bus tour doesn't make much sense to me here. But they can be handy for reaching outlying sights. Various tour companies run bus-plus-walking itineraries (each of them around 100–130 zł), including a general city overview of Kraków (3 hrs), Auschwitz (6 hrs), Wieliczka Salt Mine (4 hrs), and other regional side-trips. I'd skip the double-decker, hop-on, hop-off bus tour, which has a meager frequency (8 stops in the Old Town and Kazimierz, 39 zł/24 hours, buy tickets on bus). Get information on all tour companies at the TI.

Buggy Tours—Romantic, horse-drawn buggies trot around Kraków from the Square. The going rate is a hefty 100 zł for a 30-minute tour.

Golf-Cart Tours—Several outfits around town (including on the Square) offer tours on a golf cart with recorded commentary (prices are for up to 4 people: 120 zł for half-hour tour of Old Town or Kazimierz, 200 zł for hour-long tour of both the Old Town and Kazimierz).

Self-Guided Walk

Kraków's Royal Way

Most of Kraków's major sights are conveniently connected by this self-guided walking tour. This route is known as the "Royal Way"

because the king used to follow this same path when he returned to Kraków after a journey. After the capital moved to Warsaw, most kings were still crowned and buried in Wawel Cathedral at the far end of town—and they followed this same route for both occasions. You could sprint through this walk in under an hour (less than a mile altogether), but it's much more fun if you take it slow.

• *Begin just outside the main gate at the north end of the Old Town.*

▲Barbican (Barbakan), Florian Gate (Brama Floriańska), and City Walls

Tatars invaded Kraków three times in the 13th century. After the first attack destroyed the city in 1241, Krakovians built this wall. The original rampart had 47 watchtowers and eight gates. The big, round defensive fort standing outside the wall is a barbican. Structures like this provided extra fortification to weak sections. Imagine how it looked in 1500, when this barbican stood outside the town moat with a long bridge leading to the Florian Gate—the city's main entryway. Today you can pay 6 zł to scramble along the passages and fortifications of the barbican (May–Oct daily 10:30–18:00, last entry 30 min before closing, closed Nov–April). There's little to see inside...except for once a month in the summer, when a battle of knights is staged here (generally some Saturdays 12:00–14:30, get details at TI). The same ticket also lets you climb up onto the surviving stretch of Old Town walls flanking the Florian Gate (entry from inside walls).

• *Before entering the Old Town, look to the left and right of the barbican to see the...*

▲▲Planty

By the 19th century, Kraków's no-longer-necessary city wall had fallen into disrepair. Krakovians decided to tear down what remained, fill in the moat, and plant trees. (The name comes not from the English "plant," but from the Polish *plantovac,* or "flat"—since they flattened out this area to create it.) Today, the Planty is a beautiful park that stretches 2.5 miles around the entire perimeter of Kraków's Old Town.

• *Go through the Florian Gate into the Old Town. Inside the gate, notice the little chapel with a replica of the famous Black Madonna of Częstochowa, a very important religious symbol among all Poles. Once through the gate, you're standing at the head of Kraków's historic (and now touristic) gamut...*

▲Floriańska Street (Ulica Floriańska)

On the inside of the city wall, you'll see a makeshift **art gallery,** where starving students hawk the works they've painted at the Academy of Fine Arts (across the busy street from the barbican). Portraits, still lifes, landscapes, local scenes, nudes... this might just be Kraków's best collection of art. If you were to detour along the gallery (to the right with your back to the gate), in a block you'd arrive at another fine collection—the eclectic Czartoryski Museum, home to a rare Leonardo da Vinci oil painting (see "National Museum Branches," later, under "Sights in Kraków").

Walking down Floriańska street, you can't miss the **McDonald's** on the left. When renovating this building, they discovered a Gothic cellar—so they excavated it and added seating. Today, you can super-size your ambience by dining on a Big Mac and fries under a medieval McVault.

About halfway down the long block, on the left (at #45, round green sign), look for **Cukiarnia Jama Michalika** ("Michael's Cave"). This dark, atmospheric café, popular with locals for its coffee and pastries, began in 1895 as a simple bakery in a claustrophobic back room. A brothel upstairs scared off respectable patrons, so the owner attracted students by creating a cabaret act called "The Green Balloon." To this day, the cabaret—political satire set to music—still runs (in Polish only, Sun at 12:00). Around the turn of the 20th century, this was a hangout of the Młoda Polska (Young Poland) movement—the Polish answer to Art Nouveau (explained on page 266). The walls are papered with sketches from poor artists who couldn't pay their tabs. Poke around inside, appreciating this unique art gallery. Consider having coffee and dessert here (Sun–Thu 9:00–22:00, Fri–Sat 9:00–23:00), but expect a grouchy greeting and a fee for the obligatory coat-check.

Continue strolling down Floriańska street. Two blocks ahead on the left (at #3, 50 yards before the big church), you'll see **Jazz Club u Muniaka.** In the 1950s, Janusz Muniak was one of the first Polish jazzmen. Now he owns this place, and jams regularly here in a cool cellar surrounded by jazzy art. If you hang around the

bar before the show, you might find yourself sitting next to Janusz himself, smoking his pipe...and getting ready to smoke on the saxophone (for details, see "Entertainment in Kraków," later).

• *Continue into the Main Market Square, where you'll run into...*

▲▲St. Mary's Church (Kościół Mariacki)

A church has stood on this spot for 800 years. The original church was destroyed by the first Tatar invasion in 1241, but all subsequent versions—including the current one—have been built on the same foundation. You can look down the sides to see how the Main Market Square has risen about seven feet over the centuries.

How many church towers does St. Mary's have? Technically, the answer is one. The shorter tower belongs to the church; the taller one is a municipal watchtower, from which you'll hear a bugler playing the hourly ***hejnał*** song. According to Kraków's favorite legend, during that first Tatar invasion, a town watchman saw the enemy approaching and sounded the alarm. Before he could finish the tune, an arrow pierced his throat—which is why, even today, the *hejnał* stops *subito* partway through. Today's buglers—12 in all—are firemen first, musicians second. Each one works a 24-hour shift up there, playing the *hejnał* on the hour, every hour (broadcast on national Polish radio at noon).

In the summer, you can actually climb up the 239 stairs to the top of the taller **tower** to visit the *hejnał* fireman. While it's a huff—with some claustrophobic stone stairs, followed by some steep, acrophobic wooden ones—the view up top is the best you'll find of the Square (5 zł, buy ticket at little kiosk next to front door, May–Sept Tue, Thu, and Sat 9:00–11:30 & 13:00–17:30, closed Oct–April).

To get inside, the church's front door is open 14 hours a day and is free to those who come to pray. Tourists use the door around the right side (6 zł, buy ticket across the little square, Mon–Sat 11:30–18:00, Sun 14:00–18:00). The church's highlight, its wooden altarpiece, is open daily between noon and 18:00. Try to be here by 11:50 for the ceremonial opening or at 18:00 for the closing (except on Saturday, when they leave it open for the next day's service). The rusty neck-stock (behind the tourists' left door) was used for public humiliation until the 1700s.

Inside, you're drawn to one of the best medieval wood-carvings in existence—the exquisite, three-part Gothic **altarpiece**

by German Veit Stoss (Wit Stwosz in Polish). Carved in 12 years and completed in 1489, it's packed with emotion rare in Gothic art. Stoss used oak for the structural parts and linden trunks for the figures. When the altar doors are closed, you see scenes from the lives of Mary and Jesus. The open altar depicts the Dormition (death) of the Virgin. The artist catches the apostles (11, without Judas) around Mary, reacting in the seconds after she collapses. Mary is depicted in three stages: dying, being escorted to heaven by Jesus, and (at the very top) being crowned in heaven (flanked by two Polish saints—Adalbert and Stanisław). The six scenes on the sides are the Annunciation, birth of Jesus, visit by the Three Magi, Jesus' Resurrection, his Ascension, and Mary becoming the mother of the apostles at Pentecost.

There's more to St. Mary's than the altar. While you're admiring this church's art, notice the flowery Neo-Gothic painting covering the choir walls. Stare up into the starry, starry blue ceiling. As you wander around, consider that the church was renovated a century ago by three Polish geniuses from two very different artistic generations: the venerable positivist Jan Matejko and his Art Nouveau students, Stanisław Wyspiański and Józef Mehoffer (we'll learn more about these two later on our walk). The huge silver bird under the organ loft in back is a crowned eagle, the symbol of Poland.

• *Leaving the church, enjoy the...*

▲▲▲Main Market Square (Rynek Główny), a.k.a. "The Square"

Kraków's marvelous Square, one of Europe's most gasp-worthy public spaces, bustles with street musicians, colorful flower stalls, cotton-candy vendors, loitering teenagers, businesspeople commuting by foot, gawking tourists, and the lusty coos of pigeons. This Square is where Kraków lives. On my last visit, local teens practiced break-dancing moves at one end of the Square while farmers protested Poland's EU membership at the other. The Square is often filled with various special

Kazimierz the Great
(1333–1370)

Out of the many centuries of Polish kings, only one earned the nickname "great," and he's the only one worth remembering: Kazimierz the Great.

K. the G., who ruled Poland from Kraków in the 14th century, was one of those larger-than-life medieval kings who left his mark on all fronts—from war to diplomacy, art patronage to womanizing. His scribes bragged that Kazimierz "found a Poland made of wood, and left one made of brick and stone." He put Kraków on the map as a major European capital. He founded many villages (some of which still bear his name) and replaced wooden structures with stone ones (such as Kraków's Cloth Hall). Kazimierz also established the Kraków Academy (today's Jagiellonian University), the second-oldest university in Central Europe. And to protect all these new building projects, he heavily fortified Poland by building a series of imposing forts and walls around its perimeter.

Most of all, Kazimierz is remembered as a progressive, tolerant king. In the 14th century, other nations were deporting—or even interning—their Jewish subjects, who were commonly scapegoated for anything that went wrong. But the enlightened and kindly Kazimierz actively encouraged Jews to come to Poland by granting them special privileges, often related to banking and trade—establishing the country as a safe haven for Jews in Europe.

Kazimierz the Great was the last of Poland's long-lived Piast dynasty. Although he left no male heir—at least, no legitimate one—Kazimierz's advances set the stage for Poland's Golden Age (14th–16th centuries). After his death, Poland united with Lithuania (against the common threat of the Teutonic Knights), the Jagiellonian dynasty was born, and Poland became one of Europe's mightiest medieval powers.

events, markets, and festivals. The biggest are the seasonal markets before Easter and Christmas, but you're also likely to stumble on something special going on here anytime between June and August.

The Square was established in the 13th century, when the city had to be rebuilt after being flattened by the Tatars. At the time, it was the biggest square in medieval Europe. It was illegal to sell anything on the street, so everything had to be sold here on the Main Market Square. It was divided into smaller markets, such as the butcher stalls, the ironworkers' tents, and the still-standing Cloth Hall (described later). Recent work to renovate the Square's pavement has revealed a wealth of remains from previous structures.

Młoda Polska (Young Poland)

Polish art in the late 19th century was ruled by positivism, a school with a very literal, straightforward focus on Polish history (Jan Matejko led the charge; see page 360). But when the new generation of Kraków's artists came into their own in the early 1900s, they decided that the old school was exactly that. Though moved by the same spirit and goals as the previous generation—evoking Polish patriotism at a time when their country was being occupied—these new artists used very different methods. They were inspired by a renewed appreciation of folklore and peasant life. Rather than being earnest and literal (an 18th-century Polish war hero on horseback), the new art was playful and highly symbolic (the artist frolicking in a magical garden in the idyllic Polish countryside). This movement became known as Młoda Polska (Young Poland)—Art Nouveau with a Polish accent.

Stanisław Wyspiański (vees-PAYN-skee, 1869–1907) was the leader of Młoda Polska. He produced beautiful artwork, from simple drawings to the stirring stained-glass images in Kraków's St. Francis' Basilica. Wyspiański was an expert at capturing human faces with realistic detail, emotion, and personality. The versatile Wyspiański was also an accomplished stage designer and writer. His patriotic play *The Wedding*—about the nuptials of a big-city artist and a peasant girl—is regarded as one of Poland's finest dramas. The largest collection of Wyspiański's art is in Kraków's Wyspiański Museum, but you'll also see examples in Kraków's St. Francis' Basilica and Warsaw's National Museum.

Józef Mehoffer (may-HOH-fehr), Wyspiański's good friend and rival, was another great Młoda Polska artist. Mehoffer's style is more expressionistic and abstract than Wyspiański's, often creating an otherworldly effect. See Mehoffer's work in Kraków's St. Francis' Basilica and at the artist's former residence; and in Warsaw, at the National Museum.

Other names to look for include **Jacek Malczewski** (mahl-CHEHV-skee), who specialized in self-portraits, and **Olga Boznańska** (bohz-NAHN-skah), the movement's only prominent female artist. Both are featured in Warsaw's National Museum.

The statue in the middle of the Square is of Romantic poet **Adam Mickiewicz** (1789–1855). His epic masterpiece, *Pan Tadeusz*, is still regarded as one of the greatest works in Polish, and Mickiewicz is considered the "Polish Shakespeare." A wistful, nostalgic tale of Polish-Lithuanian nobility, *Pan Tadeusz* stirred patriotism in a Poland that had been dismantled by surrounding empires.

Near the end of the Square, you'll see the tiny, copper-domed **Church of St. Adalbert,** the oldest church in Kraków (10th century). This Romanesque structure predates the Square. Like St. Mary's (described above), it seems to be at an angle because it's aligned east–west, as was the custom when it was built. (In other words, the churches aren't crooked—the Square is.)

Drinks are reasonably priced at cafés on the Square (most around 10 zł). Find a spot where you like the view and the chairs, then sit and sip. Enjoy the folk band. Tip them, and you can photograph their traditional Kraków garb up close. (A big tip gets you *The Star-Spangled Banner.*)

As the Square buzzes around you, imagine this place before 1989. There were no outdoor cafés, no touristy souvenir stands, and no salesmen hawking cotton candy and quacking mouthpieces. The communist government shut down all but a handful of the businesses. They didn't want people to congregate here—they should be at home, resting, because "a rested worker is a productive worker." The buildings were covered with soot from the nearby Lenin Steelworks in Nowa Huta. The communists denied the pollution, and when the student "Green Brigades" staged a demonstration in this Square to raise awareness in the 1970s, they were immediately arrested. How things have changed.

• *The huge, yellow building right in the middle of the Square is the...*

▲▲Cloth Hall (Sukiennice)

In the Middle Ages, this was the place where cloth-sellers had their market stalls. Kazimierz the Great turned the Cloth Hall into a permanent structure in the 14th century. In 1555, it burned down, and was replaced by the current building. The letter *S* (at the top of the gable above the entryway) stands for King Sigismund the Old, who commissioned this version of the hall. As Sigismund fancied all things Italian (including women—he married an Italian princess), this structure is in the Italianate Renaissance style. Sigismund kicked off a nationwide trend, and you'll still see Renaissance buildings like this one all over the country—making the style as typically Polish as it is typically Italian. We'll see more works by Sigismund's imported Italian architects at Wawel Castle.

The Cloth Hall is still a functioning market—mostly souvenirs, including wood carvings, chess sets, jewelry (especially amber), painted boxes, and trinkets (summer Mon–Fri 9:00–18:00,

Sat–Sun 9:00–15:00, sometimes later; winter Mon–Fri 9:00–16:00, Sat–Sun 9:00–15:00). Cloth Hall prices are slightly inflated, but still cheap by American standards. You're paying a little extra for the convenience and the atmosphere, but you'll see locals buying gifts here, too.

WCs and telephones are at each end of the Cloth Hall. The upstairs of the Cloth Hall is home to the very good **Gallery of 19th-Century Polish Art.** The collection was moved to a castle outside of town during a recent renovation, but should re-open here in mid-2010 (described later, under "Sights in Kraków").

• *Browse through the Cloth Hall passageway. As you emerge into the other half of the Square, the big tower on your left is the...*

Town Hall Tower

This is all that remains of a Town Hall building from the 14th century—when Kraków was the powerful capital of Poland. After the 18th-century partitions of Poland, Kraków's prominence took a nosedive. By the 19th century, Kraków was Nowheresville. As the town's importance crumbled, so did its Town Hall. It was cheaper to tear down the building than to repair it, and all that was left standing was this nearly 200-foot-tall tower. In summer, you can climb the tower, stopping along the way to poke around an exhibit on Kraków history—but the views from up top are disappointing (6 zł, May–Oct daily 10:30–14:00 & 14:30–18:00, last entry 30 min before closing, closed Nov–April). In the bottom of the tower is a TI, where you buy your ticket for the tower.

The **gigantic head** at the base of the Town Hall Tower (the opposite end from the Cloth Hall) is a sculpture by contemporary artist Igor Mitoraj, who studied here in Kraków. Typical of Mitoraj's works, the head is an empty shell that appears to be wrapped in cloth. It was originally intended to be placed near the train station. But because of construction delays at the station, it found a home here on the Square. While some locals enjoy having a work by their fellow Krakovian in such a prominent place, others disapprove of its sharp contrast with the Square's genteel Old World ambience. Tourists enjoy playing peek-a-boo with the head's eyes.

• *When you're finished on the Square, we'll head toward Wawel Hill. But we'll take a one-block detour from the Royal Way to introduce you to one of Kraków's best churches. Leave on the street called ulica Bracka, in the middle of the bottom of the Square (next to the Deutsche Bank,*

at the end of the Cloth Hall). Follow this one long block (and across the busy Franciszkańska street) directly to the side door of a big red-brick church. Go ye.

▲▲St. Francis' Basilica (Bazylika Św. Franciszka)

This beautiful Gothic church, which was Pope John Paul II's home church while he was archbishop of Kraków, features some of Poland's best Art Nouveau *in situ* (in the setting for which it was intended) and is open long hours daily. After an 1850 fire, it was redecorated by the two leading members of the Młoda Polska (Young Poland) movement: Stanisław Wyspiański and Józef Mehoffer. These two talented and fiercely competitive Krakovians were friends who apprenticed together under Poland's greatest painter, Jan Matejko. The glorious decorations of this church are the result of their great rivalry run amok. (For more Wyspiański or Mehoffer, visit their museums—described later, under "Sights in Kraków.")

➲ **Self-Guided Tour:** Entering through the side door, turn left into the altar area to enjoy the paintings and stained-glass windows by **Stanisław Wyspiański.** The windows flanking the high altar represent the Blessed Salomea (left, the church's founder, buried in a side chapel) and St. Francis (right, the church's namesake). Salomea was a medieval Polish woman who became queen of Hungary, but later returned to Poland and entered a convent after her husband's death. Notice she's dropping a crown—repudiating the earthly world and giving herself over to the simple, stop-and-smell-God's-roses lifestyle of St. Francis. As you face the back of the church, look at the window in the rear of the nave: *God the Father Let It Be*, Wyspiański's finest masterpiece. The colors beneath the Creator change from yellows and oranges (fire) to soothing blues (water), depending on the light. Wyspiański was supposedly inspired by Michelangelo's vision of God in the Sistine Chapel, though he used a street beggar to model the specific features of God. Wyspiański also painted the delightful floral designs decorating the walls of the nave—fitting for a church dedicated to a saint so famous for his spiritual connection to nature. (For more on Wyspiański, see page 266.)

The chapel on the right side of the nave (as you face the back of the church) contains some evocative Stations of the Cross. This is **Józef Mehoffer**'s response to Wyspiański's work. The centerpiece of the room is a replica of the Shroud of Turin—which, since it touched the original shroud, is also considered a holy relic.

Karol Wojtyła (1920–2005): The Life and Death of the Greatest Pole

Karol Wojtyła was born to a humble family in the town of Wadowice near Kraków on May 18, 1920. Karol's mother died when he was a young boy. When he was older, he moved with his father to Kraków to study philosophy and drama at Jagiellonian University. Young Karol was gregarious and athletic—an avid skier, hiker, swimmer, and soccer goalie. During the Nazi occupation in World War II, he was forced to work in a quarry. In defiance of the oppressive Nazis, he secretly studied theology and appeared in illegal underground theatrical productions. When the war ended, he resumed his studies, this time at the theology faculty.

After graduating in 1947, Wojtyła swiftly rose through the ranks of the Catholic Church hierarchy. By 1964, he was archbishop of Kraków, and just three years later, he became the youngest cardinal ever in the Roman Catholic Church. Throughout the 1960s, he fought an ongoing battle with the regime when they refused to allow the construction of a church in the Kraków suburb of Nowa Huta. After years of saying Mass for huge crowds in open fields, Wojtyła finally convinced the communists to allow the construction of the Lord's Ark Church in 1977. A year later, just as Poland was facing its darkest hour, Karol Wojtyła was called to the papacy—the first non-Italian pope in more than four centuries. In 1979, he paid a visit to his native Poland. In a series of cautiously provocative speeches, he demonstrated to his countrymen the potential for mass opposition to communism.

Imagine you're Polish in the 1970s. Your country was devastated by World War II, and has struggled under an oppressive regime ever since. Food shortages are epidemic. Lines stretch around the block even to buy a measly scrap of bread. Life is bleak, oppressive, and hopeless. Then someone who speaks your language—someone you've admired your entire life, and one of the only people you've seen successfully stand up to the regime—becomes one of the world's most influential people. A Pole like you is the leader of a billion Catholics. He makes you believe that the impossible can happen. He says to you again

Back out in the nave, the modern painting (with an orange-and-blue background, midway up the nave on the left as you face the back of the church) depicts **St. Maksymilian Kolbe,** the Catholic priest who traded his own life to save a fellow inmate at Auschwitz (see his story on page 326). Kolbe is particularly beloved here, as he actually served at this church.

Just before going out the back door (below Wyspiański's stained-glass window), find the **silver plate** labeled "Jan Paweł II" on the second pew from the last (on right); this was Pope John Paul II's favorite place to pray when he lived in the Archbishop's

and again: *"Nie lękajcie się"*—"Have no fear." And you begin to believe it.

In addition to encouraging his countrymen, the Pope had a knack for challenging the communists. He'd push at them strongly enough to get his point across, but never went so far as to jeopardize the stature of the Church in Poland. Gentle but pointed wordplay was his specialty. The inspirational role he played in the lives of Lech Wałęsa and the other leaders of Solidarity gave them the courage to stand up to the communists (for more on Solidarity, see page 404). Many people (including Mikhail Gorbachev) credit Pope John Paul II for the collapse of Eastern European communism.

Even as John Paul II's easy charisma attracted new worshippers to the Church (especially young people), his conservatism on issues such as birth control, homosexuality, and female priests pushed away many Catholics. Under his watch, the Church struggled with embarrassing pedophilia scandals in the US, Ireland, and elsewhere. By the end of his papacy, John Paul II's failing health and old-fashioned politics had caused him to lose stature in worldwide public opinion. And yet, approval of the Pope never waned in Poland. His countrymen—even the relatively few atheists and agnostics—saw John Paul II both as the greatest hero of their people...and as a member of the family, like a kindly grandfather.

When Pope John Paul II died on April 2, 2005, the mourning in Poland was deep and sustained. Though the Pope's passing was hardly unexpected, it created an overwhelming wave of grief that flooded the country for weeks. Musical performances of all kinds were canceled for a week after his death, and the irreverent MTV-style music channel simply went off the air out of respect.

Karol Wojtyła has already been fast-tracked for sainthood. Out of 265 popes, only two have been given the title "great." There's already talk in Rome of increasing that number to three. Someday soon we may speak of this man as "John Paul the Great." His countrymen already do.

Palace across the street.

• *Stepping outside (through the back door), look to the right. The light-yellow building across the street is the...*

Archbishop's Palace

This building (specifically, the window over the stone entryway) was Pope John Paul II's residence when he was the archbishop of Kraków. When he became Pope, it remained his home-away-from-Rome for visits to his hometown. After a long day of saying formal Mass during his visits to Kraków, he'd wind up here. Weary as he

was, before going to bed he'd stand in the window for hours, chatting casually with the people assembled below—about religion, but also about sports, current events, and whatever was on their minds. In 2005, when the Pope's health deteriorated, this street filled with his supporters, even though the Pope was in Rome. For days, somber locals focused their vigil on this same window, their eyes fixed on a black crucifix that had been placed here. At 21:37 on the night of April 2, 2005, the Pope passed away in Rome. Ten thousand Krakovians were in this street, under this window, listening to a Mass broadcast on loudspeakers from the church. When the priest announced the Pope's death, every single person simultaneously fell to their knees in silence. For the next several days, thousands of the faithful continued to stand in this street, staring intently at the window where they last saw the man they considered to be the greatest Pole.

• *Now turn right, walk along the side of the church, pass a few monuments and a tram stop, and turn right again down busy...*

Grodzka Street

Now you're back on the Royal Way proper. At the corner of Grodzka street stands the modern, copper-colored **Wyspiański Pavilion.** In addition to housing a handy TI (inside—not the ticket window out front) and a conference center, this building features three new stained-glass windows based on designs Wyspiański once submitted for a contest to redecorate Wawel Cathedral. While these designs were rejected back then, they were finally realized on the hundredth anniversary of his death (in 2007). Visible from inside the building during the day (step inside to see them), and gloriously illuminated to be seen outside the building at night, they represent three Polish historical figures: The gaunt St. Stanisław (Poland's first saint), the skeletal Kazimierz the Great (in the middle), and the swooning King Henry the Pious.

Now continue down Grodzka street. This lively thoroughfare, connecting the Square with Wawel, is teeming with shops—and some of Kraków's best restaurants (see "Eating in Kraków," later). Survey your options now, and choose (and maybe reserve) your favorite for dinner tonight.

This is also a good street to find some of Kraków's **milk bars** (three are listed on page 313). The most traditional one is about two blocks down, on the right (at #45), with a simple *Bar Mleczny* sign.

These government-subsidized cafeterias are the locals' choice for a quick, cheap, filling, lowbrow lunch. Prices are deliriously cheap (soup costs less than a dollar), and the food isn't bad. For more on milk bars, see page 245. Or, for an even quicker bite, buy an *obwarzanek* (ring-shaped roll, typically fresh) from a street vendor.

• *One more block ahead, the small square on your right is...*

Mary Magdalene Square (Plac Św. Marii Magdaleny)

Back when Kraków was just a village, this was its main square. Today it offers a great visual example of Kraków's deeply religious character. In the Middle Ages, Kraków was known as "Small Rome" for its many churches. Today, there are 142 churches and monasteries within the city limits (32 in the Old Town alone)—more per square mile than anywhere outside Rome. You can see several of them from this spot: The nearest, with the picturesque white facade and red dome, is the **Church of Saints Peter and Paul** (Kraków's first Baroque church, and a popular tourist concert venue). The statues lining this church's facade are the 11 apostles (minus Judas), plus Mary Magdalene, the square's namesake. The next church to the right, with the twin towers, is the Romanesque **St. Andrew's** (now with a Baroque interior). According to legend, a spring inside this church provided water to citizens who holed up here during Tatar invasions in the 13th century. If you look farther down the street, you can see three more churches. And the square next to you used to be a church, too—it burned in 1855, and only its footprint survives.

• *Go through the square (admiring the sculpture on the column that won Kraków's distinguished "ugliest statue" award in 2002), and turn left down...*

Kanonicza Street (Ulica Kanonicza)

With so many churches around here, the clergy had to live somewhere. Many lived on this well-preserved street—supposedly the oldest street in Kraków. As you walk, look for the cardinal hats over three different doorways. The Hotel Copernicus, on the left, has hosted visitors both famous (Copernicus himself) and infamous (George W. Bush). On the right at #17, the **Bishop Erazm Ciołek Palace** hosts a good exhibit of medieval art and Orthodox icons. Next door, the yellow house on the right (#19) is where Karol Wojtyła lived for 10 years after World War II—long before he became Pope John Paul II. Today this building houses the **Archdiocesan Museum,** which features a few sparse exhibits about Kraków's favorite son; in lieu of a true "John Paul II Museum," this place is worth visiting if you're a fan of the late pontiff. Both sights are described later, under "Sights in Kraków."

• *At the end of Kanonicza street, our self-guided walk is finished. But*

there's still more to see. Across the busy street, a ramp leads up to the most important piece of ground in all of Poland: Wawel.

Sights in Kraków

Wawel Hill

Wawel (VAH-vehl), a symbol of Polish royalty and independence, is sacred territory to every Polish person. A castle has stood here since the beginning of Poland's recorded history. Today, Wawel—awash in tourists—is the most visited sight in the country. Crowds and an overly complex admissions system for the hill's many historic sights can be exasperating. Thankfully, a stroll through the cathedral and around the castle grounds requires no tickets, and—with the help of the following commentary—is enough. I've described these sights in the order of a handy self-guided walk. The many museums on Wawel (all described in this section) are mildly interesting, but can be skipped (grounds open daily from 6:00 until dusk, inner courtyard closes 30 min earlier).

• *From Kanonicza street—where my self-guided walk ends—head up the long ramp to the castle entry.*

Entry Ramp

When Kraków was part of the Habsburg Empire in the 19th century, the Austrians turned this castle complex into a fortress—destroying much of its delicate beauty. When Poland regained its independence after World War I, the castle was returned to its former glory. The bricks you see on your left as you climb the ramp bear the names of Poles from around the world who donated to the cause.

The jaunty equestrian statue ahead is **Tadeusz Kościuszko** (1746–1817)—a familiar name to American history buffs. Kościuszko was a hero of the American Revolution and helped design West Point. When he returned to Poland, he fought bravely but unsuccessfully against the Russians (during the Partitions that would divide Poland's territory among three neighboring powers).

• *Hiking through the Heraldic Gate next to Kościuszko, you pass the ticket office (if you'll be going into the museums, use the other ticket office, with shorter lines, on top of the hill—see "Tickets and Reservations," later). As you crest the hill, on your left is...*

▲▲Wawel Cathedral

Poland's national church is its Westminster Abbey. While the history buried here is pretty murky to most Americans, to Poles, this church is *the* national mausoleum. It holds the tombs of nearly all of Poland's most important rulers and greatest historical figures.

Cathedral Exterior—Go around to the far side of the cathedral to take in its profile. This uniquely eclectic church is the product of centuries of haphazard additions...yet somehow, it works. It began as a simple, stripped-down Romanesque church in the 12th century. (The white base of the nearest tower is original. In fact, anything at Wawel that's made of white limestone like this was probably part of the earliest Romanesque structures.)

Kazimierz the Great and his predecessors gradually surrounded the cathedral with some 20 chapels, which were further modified over the centuries—making this beautiful church a happy hodgepodge of styles. To give you a sense of the historical sweep, scan the chapels from left to right: 14th-century Gothic, 12th-century Romanesque (the base of the tower), 17th-century Baroque (the inside is Baroque, though the exterior is a copy of its Renaissance neighbor), 16th-century Renaissance, and 18th- and 19th-century Neoclassical. (This variety in styles is even more evident in the chapels' interiors, which we'll see soon.)

Pay attention to the two particularly interesting domed chapels to the right of the tall tower. The gold one is the Sigismund's Chapel, housing memorials to the Jagiellonian kings—including Sigismund the Old, who was responsible for Kraków's Renaissance renovation in the 16th century. Poles consider this chapel, made with 80 pounds of gold, to be the finest Renaissance chapel north of the Alps. The green chapel next to it, home to the Swedish Waza dynasty, resembles its neighbor (but it's a copy built 150 years later, and without all that gold). The tallest tower, called the Sigismund Tower, has a clock with only an hour hand.

Go back around and face the front entry for more architectonic silliness. You see Gothic chapels flanking the door, a Renaissance ceiling, lavish Baroque decoration over the door, and some big bones (thought to have come from extinct animals). Years ago, these were taken for the bones of giants and put here as an oddity to be viewed by the public. (Back then, there were no museums, so notable items like these were used to lure people to the church.) It's said that as long as the bones hang here, the cathedral will stand. The door is the original from the 14th century, with fine

wrought-iron work. The *K* with the crown stands for Kazimierz the Great. The black marble frame is made of Kraków stone from nearby quarries.

Cathedral Interior—The cathedral interior is slathered in Baroque memorials and tombs, decorated with tapestries, and soaked in Polish history.

Cost and Hours: Visitors can usually walk around the main part of the church for free. You must buy a 10-zł ticket to climb up the tallest tower or visit the crypt and the royal tombs. Buy the ticket at the house across from the cathedral entry, where you can also rent a 5-zł audioguide. The cathedral is open May–Sept Mon–Sat 9:00–17:00, Sun 12:30–17:00; Oct–April Mon–Sat 9:00–16:00, Sun 12:30–16:00; last entry always 15 min before closing.

➲ **Self-Guided Tour:** After you step inside, you'll follow the one-way, clockwise route that leads you through the choir, then around the back of the apse, then back to the entry.

At the entry, look straight ahead to see the silver tomb under a **canopy,** inspired by the one in St. Peter's at the Vatican. It contains the remains of the first Polish saint, Stanisław (from the 11th century).

Go behind this canopy into the ornately carved **choir** area. For 200 years, the colorful chair to the right of the high altar has been the seat of Kraków's archbishops, including Karol Wojtyła, who served here for 14 years before becoming pope.

Now you'll continue into the left nave. From here, if you have a ticket, you can enter two of the optional attractions: Claustrophobic wooden stairs lead up to the 11-ton **Sigismund Bell** and pleasant views of the steeples and spires of Kraków. Then, closer to the front of the church, descend into the little **crypt** (with a rare, purely Romanesque interior), which houses the remains of Adam Mickiewicz—the Romantic poet whose statue dominates the Main Market Square.

Now continue around the apse (behind the main altar). After curving around to the right, look for the red-marble tomb (on the right) of The Great One—**Kazimierz,** of course. (Look for *Kazimierz Wielki*—at his feet is what appears to be a beaver.) A few more steps toward the entrance, on the right, is the white sarcophagus of **St. Jadwiga** (with a dog at her feet). This 14th-century "King of Poland" helped Christianize Lithuania, fought the Teutonic Knights, kicked off the grand Jagiellonian dynasty, and was sainted by Pope John Paul II in 1997. (The sexist bigwigs of the time begrudgingly allowed her to take the throne, but refused to call her "Queen.") All the flowers here prove she remains popular with Poles today. Across from Jadwiga, peek into the gorgeous 16th-century **Sigismund Chapel,** with its silver altar (this is the gold-roofed chapel you just saw from outside).

Just beyond the Sigismund Chapel is a door leading back outside. If you don't have a ticket, your tour is finished—head out here. But those with a ticket can keep circling around.

To the left of the main door, take a look at the **Gothic chapel,** with its Orthodox–style 14th-century frescoes.

In the back corner of the church is the entrance to the **royal tombs** (you'll exit outside the church, so be sure you're done in here first). The first big room houses Poland's greatest war heroes: Kościuszko (of American Revolution fame), Jan III Sobieski (who successfully defended Vienna from the Ottomans; in the simple black coffin with the gold inscription *J III S*), Sikorski, Poniatowski, and so on. Then you'll wander through several rooms of second-tier Polish kings, queens, and their kids. Marshal Józef Piłsudski, the WWI hero who seized power and ruled Poland from 1926 to 1935, has the last grave (in the room on the right, just before you exit). His tomb was moved here so the rowdy soldiers who came to pay their respects wouldn't disturb the others. You may notice that there's one VIP (Very Important Pole) who's missing...Karol Wojtyła, a.k.a. John Paul II, once the bishop of this cathedral. John Paul II left no specific requests for his body, and the Vatican controversially (to Poles, at least) chose to entomb him under St. Peter's Basilica, instead of sending him back home to Wawel.

• *Up the little staircase across from the cathedral entry is the...*

Cathedral Museum—This small museum features various holy robes and replicas of what's buried with the kings, plus the Sigismund Bell's original clapper (covered by 10-zł cathedral ticket, Mon–Sat 9:00–17:00, closed Sun).

• *When you're finished in the cathedral, stroll around the...*

▲▲Wawel Castle Grounds

In the rest of the castle, you'll uncover more fragments of Kraków's history, and have the opportunity to visit several museums. While I consider the museums skippable, if you want to visit them, buy tickets before you enter the inner courtyard. Read the descriptions on page 280 to decide which museums appeal to you.

➲ **Self-Guided Walk:** This tour, which doesn't enter any of the attractions, is plenty for most visitors.

• *Behind the cathedral, a grand green-and-pink entryway leads into the palace's dramatically Renaissance-style...*

Inner Courtyard: If this space seems to have echoes of Florence, that's because it was designed and built by young Florentines after Kazimierz's original castle burned down. Notice the three distinct levels: The ground floor housed the private apartments of the higher nobility (governors and castle administrators); the middle level held the private apartments of the king; and the

top floor—much taller, to allow more light to fill its large spaces—were the public state rooms of the king. The ivy-covered wing to the right of where you entered served as the headquarters of the notorious Nazi governor of German-occupied Poland, Hans Frank. (He was tried and executed in Nürnberg after the war.) At the far end of the courtyard is a false wall, designed to create a pleasant Renaissance symmetry, and also to give the illusion that the castle is bigger than it is. Looking through the windows, notice that there's nothing but air on the other side. When foreign dignitaries visited, these windows could be covered to complete the illusion. The entrances to most Wawel museums are around this courtyard, and some believe that you'll find something even more special: chakra.

Adherents to the Hindu concept of **chakra** believe that a powerful energy field connects all living things. Some believe that, mirroring the seven chakra points on the body (from head to groin), there are seven points on the surface of the earth where this energy is most concentrated: Delhi, Delphi, Jerusalem, Mecca, Rome, Velehrad...and Wawel Hill—specifically over there in the corner (immediately to your left as you enter the courtyard). Look for peaceful people (here or elsewhere on the castle grounds) with their eyes closed. One thing's for sure: They're not thinking of Kazimierz the Great. The smudge marks on the wall are from people pressing up against this corner, trying to absorb some good vibes from this chakra spot.

The Wawel administration seems creeped out by all this. They've done what they can to discourage this ritual (such as putting up information boards right where the power is supposedly most focused), but believers still gravitate from far and wide to hug the wall. Give it a try...and let the Force be with you. (Just for fun, ask a Wawel tour guide about the chakra, and watch her squirm—they're forbidden to talk about it.)

• *If you want to visit some of the castle museums (you can enter four of the five from this courtyard), you'll first need to buy tickets elsewhere. Stick with me for a little longer to finish up our tour of the grounds, and we'll wind up near a ticket office.*

Head back out to the side of the cathedral to survey the...

Field of History: This hilltop has seen lots of changes over the years. Kazimierz the Great turned a small fortress into a mighty Gothic castle in the 14th century. Today, you'll see the

cathedral and a castle complex, but little remains of Kazimierz's grand fortress, which burned to the ground in 1499. In the grassy field across from the cathedral, you'll see the **foundations** of two Gothic churches that were destroyed when the Austrians took over Wawel in the 19th century and needed a parade ground for their troops. (They built the red-brick hospital building beyond the field, now used by the Wawel administration.)

• *Head across to the gap in the buildings beyond the field, to the...*

Viewpoint over the Vistula: Belly up to the wall and enjoy the panorama over the Vistula River and Kraków's outskirts. From here, you can see some unusual landmarks, including the odd wavy-roofed building just across the river (which houses the Manggha Japanese art gallery). The symmetrical little bulge that tops the highest hill on the horizon is the **Kościuszko Mound,** erected in 1823 to honor the Polish and American military hero. The mound—which was recently reinforced with steel and cement to prevent it from eroding away—is actually made of soil that was brought here from battlefields where the famous general fought... both in Poland, and in the American Revolution.

Now look directly below you, along the riverbank, to find a fire-belching monument to the **dragon** that was instrumental in the founding of Kraków. Once upon a time, a prince named Krak founded a town on Wawel Hill. It was the perfect location—except for the fire-breathing dragon who lived in the caves under the hill and terrorized the town. Prince Krak had to feed the dragon all of the town's livestock to keep the monster from going after the townspeople. But Krak, with the help of a clever shoemaker, came up with a plan. They stuffed a sheep's skin with sulfur and left it outside the dragon's cave. The dragon swallowed it, and before long, developed a terrible case of heartburn. To put the fire out, the dragon started drinking water from the Vistula. He kept drinking and drinking until he finally exploded. The town was saved, and Kraków thrived.

If you want to head down to see the Vistula and the dragon close up, take a shortcut through the nearby **Dragon's Den** (Smocza Jama, enter at the little copper-roofed brick building). It's just a 135-step spiral staircase and a few underground caverns—worthwhile only as a quick way to get from the top of Wawel down to the banks of the Vistula (3 zł, pay at machine—coins only, April–Oct daily 10:00–17:00, July–Aug until 18:00, closed Nov–March).

• *Our Wawel tour is finished. If you'd like to visit some of the museums, you can buy your tickets in the nearby Tourist Center (head back into the main Wawel complex—with the empty field—and turn right); here you'll also find WCs, a café, a gift shop, and other amenities.*

Wawel Castle Museums

There are five museums and exhibits in Wawel Castle (not including the cathedral and Cathedral Museum). Each has its own admission and slightly different hours (tel. 012-422-5155, ext. 219, www.wawel.krakow.pl).

Tickets and Reservations: Wawel has two ticket windows. Most people line up at the top of the entry ramp, but it's faster to buy tickets at the Tourist Center at the far corner of the castle grounds (across the field from the cathedral, near the café). A limited number of tickets are sold for the Royal State Rooms, Crown Treasury and Armory, and Royal Private Apartments (which can be visited only with an included tour). Boards show how many tickets for each of these are still available on the day you're there. Tickets come with an assigned entry time (though you can usually sneak in before your scheduled appointment). In the summer, ticket lines can be long, and sights can sell out by midday. You can reserve tickets ahead for the tour of the Royal Private Apartments (no fee) and the Royal State Rooms and the Crown Armory and Treasury (16-zł reservation fee for up to 9 people; tel. 012-422-1697). Frankly, the sights aren't worth all the fuss—if they're sold out, you're not missing much.

Hours: Unless otherwise noted, the museums are open April–Oct Tue-Fri 9:30–17:00, Sat–Sun 11:00–18:00, closed Mon; Nov–March Tue–Sat 9:30–16:00, closed Sun-Mon; last entry one hour before closing. In summer (April–Oct), visiting on Mondays has its advantages (Lost Wawel and Crown Treasury and Armory are free and open 9:30–13:00) and its disadvantages (the other three museums are closed). Off-season (Nov–March), similar caveats apply to Sundays, while everything is closed on Monday.

▲Royal State Rooms (Komnaty Królewskie)—While precious to Poles, these rooms are mediocre by European standards. Still, this is the best of the Wawel museums (17 zł, Nov–March also open—and free—Sun 10:00–16:00; enter through courtyard). First you'll wander through some ho-hum halls to get to the Throne Room, with 30 carved heads in the ceiling. According to legend, one of these heads got mouthy when the king was trying to pass judgment—so its mouth has been covered to keep it quiet. Then you'll walk along the outdoor gallery (enjoying views down into the courtyard) before heading upstairs. These top-floor rooms are best, with remarkably decorated wooden ceilings, gorgeous leather-tooled walls, and 16th-century Brussels tapestries (140 of the original series of 300 survive). Wandering these halls (with their period furnishings), you get a feeling for the 16th- and 17th-century glory days of Poland, when it was a leading power in Eastern Europe. The Senate Room, with its throne and fine tapestries, is the climax.

Royal Private Apartments (Prywatne Apartamenty Królewskie)—These are more of the same, and the only part of the complex that must be visited with a guided tour (24 zł, request English tour when buying your ticket—they depart 3/hr, enter through courtyard).

Crown Treasury and Armory (Skarbiec i Zbrojownia)—This is a decent collection of swords, saddles, and shields; ornately decorated muskets and crossbows; and cannons in the basement (17 zł, April–Oct also open—and free—Mon 9:30–13:00; enter through courtyard).

Oriental Art (Sztuka Wschodu)—While small, this exhibit displays swords, carpets, vases, and remarkable Turkish tents (upstairs, next to the Senate Room) used by the Ottomans during the 1683 Battle of Vienna. These are trophies of Jan III Sobieski, the Polish king who led a pan-European army to victory in that battle (8 zł, tickets sold at the door, enter through courtyard, don't miss entry on your way back downstairs from Royal State Rooms).

▲Lost Wawel (Wawel Zaginiony)—This exhibit traces the history of the hill and its various churches and castles. The one-way route leads through excavations of a 10th-century church. The collection includes a model of the cathedral in its original Romanesque form (much simpler, before all the colorful, bulbous domes, chapels, and towers were added). There's also a replica of the entire castle complex in the 18th century (pre-Austrian razing). A display shows fascinating decorative tiles from 16th-century stoves that once heated the place, plus some medieval artifacts (8 zł, tickets sold at the door, April–Oct also open—and free—Mon 9:30–13:00; Nov–March also open—and free—Sun 10:00–16:00; enter near snack bar across from side of cathedral).

National Museum Branches

Kraków's National Museum (Muzeum Narodowe) is made up of a series of small but interesting collections scattered throughout the city (www.muzeum.krakow.pl). I've listed the best of the National Museum's branches below. All of these are free to enter on Sunday.

Be warned: The hours of these museums can be maddeningly sporadic. If you have your heart set on a particular museum, confirm the opening times carefully before you visit.

▲Czartoryski Museum (Muzeum Czartoryskich)—This eclectic collection, displaying armor, handicrafts, decorative arts, and paintings, is one of Kraków's best-known (and most overrated) museums. It recently closed for a major restoration, during which most of its collection is scheduled to be temporarily exhibited at a castle outside of town (not worth the trip). However, its two best works—oil paintings by Leonardo da Vinci *(Lady with an Ermine)*

Kraków's Art Treasures

This city's two greatest artistic treasures originate not from Poland, but from Italy and the Netherlands: One is a work by a Renaissance genius, and the other by a Dutch Master. Usually these two paintings are displayed in the Czartoryski Museum. However, during that museum's renovation, they might be on loan in other cities, or displayed elsewhere in Kraków (likely in the Gallery of 19th-Century Polish Art above the Cloth Hall). Art-lovers should ask around to track down these wonderful works.

***Lady with an Ermine* (1489 or 1490) by Leonardo da Vinci:** This small (21" x 16"), simple portrait of a teenage girl is one of the most influential paintings in art history and a rare surviving work by one of history's greatest minds. The girl is likely Cecilia Gallerani, the young mistress of the Duke of Milan, Leonardo's employer. The ermine (white during winter) suggests several overlapping meanings, including a symbol of chastity (thus praising Cecilia's questioned virtue) and a naughty reference to the Duke's nickname, "Ermellino"—notice that his mistress is sensually, um, "stroking the ermine."

Painted before the *Mona Lisa,* the portrait was immediately recognized as revolutionary. Cecilia turns to look off-camera at someone. Leonardo catches her in an unguarded moment, giving the viewer a behind-the-scenes look unheard-of in the days of the posed, front-facing formal portrait. Her simple gestures and faraway gaze speak volumes about her inner thoughts and personality. Leonardo tweaks the generic Renaissance "pyramid"

and Rembrandt *(Landscape with the Good Samaritan)*—are worth seeking out (see sidebar). If the museum is still closed during your visit, ask around to see if the paintings are being displayed elsewhere in town.

Inspired by Poland's 1791 constitution (Europe's first), Princess Izabela Czartoryska began collecting bits of Polish history and culture. She fled with the collection to Paris after the 1830 insurrection, and 45 years later, her grandson returned it to its present Kraków location. When he ran out of space, he bought part of the monastery across the street, joining the buildings with a fancy passageway. The Nazis took the collection to Germany, and although most of it has been returned, some pieces are still missing.

If the museum is open, in addition to seeing the two great paintings, you'll wander through rooms of ornate armor (includ-

composition by turning it to three-quarters angle and softening it with curved lines—from her eyes, down her cheek and sloping shoulders, then doubling back across her folded arms. The background—once gray and blue—was painted black in the 19th century.

Lady with an Ermine is one of only three surviving oil paintings by Leonardo. It's better preserved than her famous cousin in Paris *(Mona Lisa)*, and—many think—simply more beautiful. Can we be sure it's really by the enigmatic Leonardo? Well, recently they found the master's fingerprint—literally—pressed into the paint.

***Landscape with the Good Samaritan* (1638) by Rembrandt van Rijn:** This small, remarkably detailed painting depicts the popular parable. On the right, the barely visible Samaritan helps the wounded, half-naked man onto his horse (as a little boy and girl look on). To the left, much farther down the road (just beyond the waterfall and bridge), find the two tiny figures walking: the priest and the Levite who had passed the injured man by. The churning sky—with bright sunlight clashing against black clouds—seems to reflect the inner conflict that comes with doing the right thing...or not. Instead of using a strict interpretation of the parable's Holy Land setting, Rembrandt chooses to combine disparate elements—such as the juxtaposition of classic Dutch windmills with the domed city of Jericho in the distance—to make the parable feel even more universal and immediate.

ing a ceremonial Turkish tent from the 1683 siege of Vienna, plus feathered Hussar armor), tapestries, treasury items, majolica, and Meissen porcelain figures. Rounding out the exhibits are painting galleries (including Italian, French, and Dutch High Renaissance and Baroque, as well as Czartoryski family portraits) and ancient art (mostly sculptures and vases).

Cost, Hours, Location: If the museum is open, it's likely 12 zł, free on Sun, open Tue–Sat 10:00–18:00, Sun 10:00–16:00, closed Mon, last entry 30 min before closing, 2 blocks north of the Main Market Square at ulica Św. Jana 19, tel. 012-422-5566.

Audioguide: The exhibits are poorly described in English. The dense, dry, but informative 15-zł audioguide helps make things meaningful.

▲Wyspiański Museum (Muzeum Wyspiańskiego)—If you enjoyed Stanisław Wyspiański's stained glass and wall paintings in St. Francis' Basilica, visit the museum that collects his work. Housed in a renovated mansion, this museum traces the personal history and artistic development of the Młoda Polska poster boy. For more on Wyspiański, see page 266.

Cost, Hours, Location: 8 zł, free on Sun, good English descriptions posted in most rooms, Wed–Sat 10:00–18:00, Sun 10:00–16:00, closed Mon–Tue, last entry 30 min before closing, 1 block northwest of the Main Market Square at ulica Szczepańska 11, tel. 012-292-8183.

➲ **Self-Guided Tour:** The museum layout is frequently rearranged, so keep your eyes open for the following highlights.

Buy your ticket and climb the stairs. Turn left at the top of the first flight of stairs, and begin circling this floor clockwise. Find the room devoted to Wyspiański's youth, including some of his precocious childhood sketchbooks. In the next room are works (including designs for beautiful stained-glass windows) from Wyspiański's youthful collaboration with his teacher Jan Matejko and his friend Józef Mehoffer; together they renovated St. Mary's Church. The "applied art" section shows off furniture Wyspiański designed, and a fine pastel drawing of St. Mary's spires. Hiding behind a curtain (to protect it from damaging sunlight—ask an attendant to raise it for you) is his design for the dramatic stained-glass *Apollo,* which hangs in the House of the Medical Society (which, unfortunately, is closed to the public). A room of portraits by various artists includes a self-portrait by Wyspiański himself. The next section demonstrates that Wyspiański was also a playwright—you'll see costumes and sets he designed for his own plays, and copies of his printed works (which he also designed himself). Finally are more portraits, including some by other artists (such as Wyspiański's talented Młoda Polska compatriot, Jacek Malczewski).

In the stairwell up to the third floor are more stained-glass designs, this time for Wyspiański's masterpiece, *God the Father Let It Be,* from St. Francis' Basilica. On the top floor, go left and circle the collection clockwise. After seeing various furniture and lesser works by other artists, you'll reach the model of the elaborate acropolis Wyspiański planned for the top of Wawel Hill, with a domed palace, an amphitheater, and a circus maximus. Nearby is a haunting painting of the Planty in winter, with Wawel Castle hovering in the background. The next few rooms contain more stained-glass designs, and designs for the painted floral decorations of St. Francis' Basilica. Then, filling another room, are portraits of Wyspiański's family—including his daughter Helenka just waking up, and his wife breast-feeding their son Staś. Helenka circles around to get good views of both of them, appearing twice in the painting. Yet another Helenka portrait shows her curiously fingering a vase of flowers. Rounding out the collection is a room filled with countryside scenes.

▲▲Gallery of 19th-Century Polish Art (Galeria Sztuki Polskiej XIX Wieku)—This surprisingly enjoyable collection of works by obscure Polish artists is usually displayed on the upper

level of the Cloth Hall. For years, it was relocated to a faraway countryside castle while the Cloth Hall was being renovated, but it's due to return to Kraków in mid-2010. Better yet, it will likely be hosting two other great works—da Vinci's *Lady with an Ermine* and Rembrandt's *Landscape with the Good Samaritan* (both described in the sidebar on page 282)—while the Czartoryski Museum is closed (likely 12 zł, free on Sun, open Tue–Sat 10:00–18:00, Sun 10:00–16:00, closed Mon, entrance on side of Cloth Hall facing Adam Mickiewicz statue, tel. 012-422-1166).

While you probably won't recognize any of the Polish names in here, some of these paintings are just plain good. The biggest works are by the historical painter Jan Matejko (for more on Matejko, see page 360). One of Matejko's paintings depicts Tadeusz Kościuszko—a hero of the American Revolution, now back in his native Poland fighting the Russians—doffing his hat after his unlikely victory at the battle at Racławice. Another Matejko painting shows the last Grand Master of the fearsome Teutonic Knights swearing allegiance to the Polish king in 1525. This historic ceremony took place in the Main Market Square of the capital at the time, Kraków. Notice the Cloth Hall and the spires of St. Mary's Church in the background. Matejko has painted his own face on one of his favorite historical figures, the jester Stańczyk (at the foot of the throne; for more on Stańczyk, see page 361).

Other excellent, but more obscure, painters are also represented. Find Józef Chełmoński's energy-charged *Four-in-Hand* (depicting a Ukrainian horseman giving a lift to a pipe-smoking nobleman) and misty *Cranes*. And my favorite: Władysław Podkowiński's gripping *Frenzy,* with a pale, sensuous woman clutching an all-fired-up black stallion. The painting caused a frenzy indeed at its 1894 unveiling—leading the unbalanced artist to attack his creation with a knife.

Bishop Erazm Ciołek Palace (Pałac Biskupa Erazma Ciołka)—This new branch of the National Museum features two separate art collections. Upstairs, the extensive "Art of Old Poland" section shows off works from the 12th through the 18th centuries, with room after room of altarpieces, sculptures, paintings, and more. The "Orthodox Art of the Old Polish Republic" section on the ground floor offers a taste of the remote Eastern reaches of Poland, with icons and other ecclesiastical art from the Orthodox faith. You'll see a sizeable section of the iconostasis (wall of icons) from the town of Lipovec. Both collections are covered by the same ticket and are very well-presented in a modern facility; while items are labeled in English, there's not much description (12 zł, free on Sun, 10-zł audioguide, Tue–Sat 10:00–18:00, Sun 10:00–16:00, closed Mon, Kanonicza 17, tel. 012-424-9371).

More National Museum Branches—While less interesting than the branches listed above, the National Museum's **Main Branch** (Gmach Główny) is worth a visit for museum completists. It features 20th-century Polish art and temporary exhibits (8 zł, west of the Main Market Square at aleja 3 Maja 1). You can also check out the museum of Wyspiański's friend and rival, the **Józef Mehoffer House** (Dom Józefa Mehoffera, 6 zł, ulica Krupnicza 26, tel. 012-421-1143), and the former residence of their mentor, the **Jan Matejko House** (Dom Jana Matejki, 6 zł, ulica Floriańska 41, tel. 012-422-5926).

Other Attractions

The following sights are worth considering if you're looking to fill out your Kraków sightseeing experience.

▲Jagiellonian University Museum: Collegium Maius—Kraków had the second university in Central Europe (after Prague's), boasting over the centuries such illustrious grads as Copernicus and Pope John Paul II. With around 150,000 students, this city is still very much a university town, and Jagiellonian University proudly offers tours of its historic oldest building, the 15th-century Collegium Maius (one block west of the Main Market Square at ulica Jagiellońska 15). In the Middle Ages, professors were completely devoted to their scholarly pursuits. They were unmarried, and lived, ate, and slept here in an almost monastic environment. They taught downstairs and lived upstairs. In many ways, this building feels more like a monastery than a university.

Student guides lead visitors through the musty and mildly interesting interior of the complex. You'll choose between two different guided tours. The shorter 30-minute "main exhibition" route includes the library, refectory (with a gorgeously carved Baroque staircase), treasury (including Polish filmmaker Andrzej Wajda's honorary Oscar), assembly hall, and some old scientific instruments (12 zł, a few tours per day in English; leaves every 20 min Mon, Wed, and Fri 10:00–14:20; Tue and Thu 10:00–17:20; Sat 10:00–13:20; none Sun). The one-hour deluxe version adds some more interiors, room after room of more old scientific instruments, medieval art (mostly church sculptures), a Rubens, a small landscape from the shop of Rembrandt, and Chopin's piano (16 zł, usually in English, Mon–Fri at 13:00, none Sat–Sun). It's smart to call ahead to find out when the shorter tour is scheduled in English, and to reserve for either tour (tel. 012-663-1307). The shorter tour is especially popular and books up long in advance (20 people maximum).

Aside from the courtyard, the only part of the Colleguim Maius you can see without a tour is an interactive exhibit that allows you to tinker with replicas of old scientific tools (7 zł, open Mon–Sat 9:00–13:30, closed Sun).

Before you leave, enjoy a cup of hot chocolate at the chocolate shop (down the stairs near the entrance)—widely regarded as the best in town.

Archdiocesan Museum (Muzeum Archidiecezjalne)—Kraków does not yet have a comprehensive museum devoted to its most famous resident, Pope John Paul II. But this museum, in a building where JPII lived both as a priest and as a bishop, does its best to capture some of his story. The museum consists of several parts: the underwhelming ground-floor collection of sacral art (with altars, paintings, and vestments); various temporary exhibits; and the top-floor museum devoted to John Paul II. Wandering past the scores of paintings and photographs, JPII's cult of personality is almost palpable. Unfortunately, since the collection mostly consists of elaborate gifts received by the Holy Father from around the world, it offers little intimacy or insight into the man himself. Still, JPII admirers will appreciate it (5 zł, Tue–Fri 10:00–16:00, Sat–Sun 10:00–15:00, closed Mon, Kanonicza 19–21, tel. 012-421-8963).

Kraków Aquarium—Landlocked Kraków and marine life don't quite seem to go together. But this facility—the brainchild of an armchair ichthyologist and expat American—is surprisingly modern and engaging, and one of the only truly kid-friendly attractions in town. With 130 different species of fish, reptiles, snakes, and even tamarinds (cute little monkeys) thoughtfully displayed on two floors, it offers a refreshing break from historic old Kraków. High-tech touchscreen displays give you more detail on each of the animals, and everything's kid-oriented and well-described in English. Rounding out the collection are items from the former Natural History Museum that once filled this building, including the skeleton of a 30,000-year-old wooly rhinoceros and two mammoth skulls (adults-18 zł, kids under 16–12 zł, Mon–Fri 9:00–20:00, Sat–Sun 9:00–21:00, near Wawel Hill just outside the Planty at ulica Św. Sebastiana 9, tel. 012-429-1049, www.aquariumkrakow.com).

Kazimierz (Jewish Quarter)

The neighborhood of Kazimierz (kah-ZHEE-mezh), 20 minutes by foot southeast of Kraków's Old Town, is the historic heart of Kraków's once-thriving Jewish community. After years of neglect, the district has been rediscovered by Krakovians and tourists alike. Visitors expecting a polished, touristy scene like Prague's Jewish Quarter will be surprised...and maybe disappointed. This is basically a local-feeling, slightly run-down neighborhood with

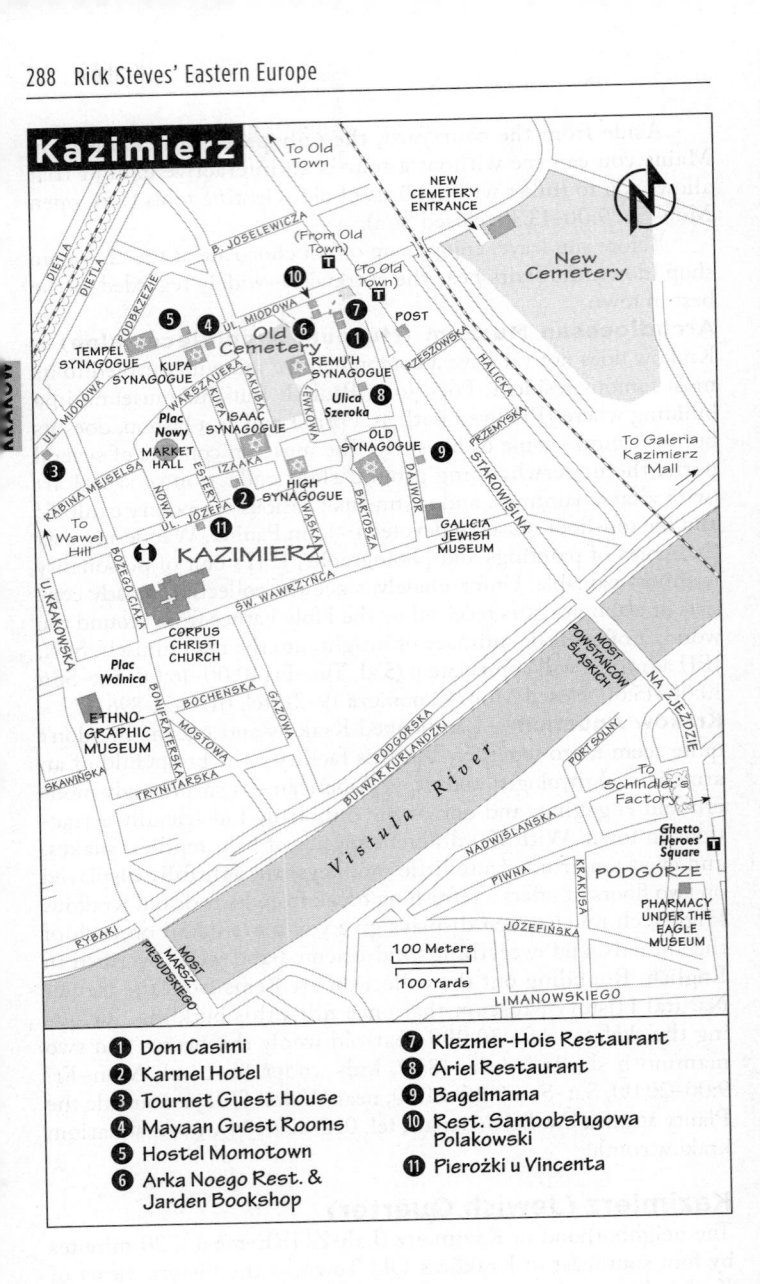

1. Dom Casimi
2. Karmel Hotel
3. Tournet Guest House
4. Mayaan Guest Rooms
5. Hostel Momotown
6. Arka Noego Rest. & Jarden Bookshop
7. Klezmer-Hois Restaurant
8. Ariel Restaurant
9. Bagelmama
10. Rest. Samoobsługowa Polakowski
11. Pierożki u Vincenta

a handful of Jewish cemeteries, synagogues, and restaurants, and often a few pensive Israeli tour groups wandering the streets. But for many, this is where you'll find the true soul of the European Jewish experience.

Try to visit any day except Saturday, when only the Old Synagogue and Galicia Jewish Museum are open. (While most Jewish-themed sights are open on Monday, the Ethnographic Museum and—most likely—Schindler's Factory are closed.) Note that it's respectful for men to cover their heads while visiting a Jewish cemetery or synagogue. While some of these sights offer loaner yarmulkes, it's easiest to just bring your own hat.

Getting to Kazimierz: From the Old Town, it's about a 20-minute **walk,** which gets you out of the fairy-tale tourist zone, and into the real, soot-stained, workaday Kraków (that's a good thing). From the Main Market Square, walk down ulica Sienna (near St. Mary's Church). At the fork, bear right through the Planty park. At the intersection with the busy Westerplatte ring road, you'll continue straight ahead (bear right at fork, then continue straight across the busy ring road) down Starowiślna for 15 more minutes. To hop the **tram,** go to the stop on the left-hand side of ulica Sienna (at the intersection with Westerplatte, across the street from the Poczta Główna, or main post office). Catch tram #7, #13, or #24 and go two stops to Miodowa. Walking or by tram, at the intersection of Starowiślna and Miodowa, you'll see a small park across the street and to the right. To reach the heart of Kazimierz—ulica Szeroka—cut through this park. To return to the Old Town, catch tram #7, #13, or #24 from the intersection of Starowiślna and Miodowa (kitty-corner from where you got off the tram) and go two stops back to the Poczta Główna stop.

Orientation: Start your visit to Kazimierz on **ulica Szeroka,** which is more of a long, parking-lot square than a street, surrounded by Jewish-themed restaurants, hotels, and synagogues.

Check in at the **Jarden Bookshop** at the top of the square (Mon–Fri 9:00–18:00, Sat–Sun 10:00–18:00, ulica Szeroka 2, tel. 012-429-1374, www.jarden.pl, jarden@jarden.pl). While there are many new bookstores in Kazimierz (mostly inside the various museums and synagogues), this is the original. It serves as a sort of TI for the neighborhood, and sells a wide variety of fairly priced books on Kazimierz and Jewish culture in the region (including a good 4-zł Kazimierz map and well-illustrated 18-zł *Jewish Kraków* guidebook). They also run several tours (prices based on the number of people; I've listed the price per person for 2 people): Jewish Kazimierz overview (55 zł, 2 hrs, walking tour), Kazimierz and the WWII ghetto (70 zł, 3 hrs, walking, the best overview), *Schindler's List* sights (100 zł, 2 hrs, by car), and Auschwitz-Birkenau (180 zł, 6–7 hrs, by car). Call to reserve ahead, as tours are by appointment

Jewish Kraków

After King Kazimierz the Great encouraged Jews to come to Poland in the 14th century, a large Jewish community settled in and around Kraków. According to legend, Kazimierz (the king) established Kazimierz (the village) for his favorite girlfriend—a Jewish woman named Ester—just southeast of the city walls. (If you have a 50-zł note, take a look at it: that's Kazimierz the Great on the front, and on the back are his capital, Cracovia, and the most important town he founded, Casmirus.)

It's a cute legend, but the village of Kazimierz didn't really become a Jewish enclave until much later. By the end of the 15th century, there were large Jewish populations in both Kazimierz and in Kraków. Kraków's Jewish community and the university students clashed, and when a destructive fire broke out in 1495, the Jews were blamed. The king at the time forced all of Kraków's Jews to move to Kazimierz.

Kazimierz was an autonomous community, with its own Town Hall, market square, and city walls (though many Jews still commuted into Kraków's Main Market Square to do business). Within Kazimierz, the Christian (west) and Jewish (east) neighborhoods were also separated by a wall. But by 1800, the walls came down, Kazimierz became part of Kraków, and the Jewish community flourished.

By the start of World War II, 65,000 Jews lived in Kraków (mostly in Kazimierz)—making up more than a quarter of the city's population. When the Nazis arrived, they immediately sent most of Kraków's Jews to the ghetto in the eastern Polish city of Lublin. Soon after, they forced Kraków's remaining 15,000 Jews into a walled ghetto at Podgórze, across the river. The Jews' cemeteries were defiled, and their buildings ransacked and destroyed. In 1942, the Nazis began transporting Kraków's Jews to death camps (including Płaszów—just on Kraków's outskirts—and Auschwitz). Many others were worked to death in the Podgórze ghetto. Only a few thousand Kraków Jews survived the war.

Today's Kraków has only about 200 Jewish residents. During the communist era, this waning population was ignored or mistreated. But in recent years, Kazimierz has enjoyed a renaissance of Jewish culture—thanks largely to the popularity of *Schindler's List* (which was partly filmed here). Look for handwritten letters from Steven Spielberg and the cast in local restaurants (such as Ariel) and hotels. While few Jews live here now, the spirit of the Jewish tradition lives on in the many synagogues, as well as in the soulful cemeteries.

only. Tours will run if a minimum of three people sign up, but pairs or singles can join an already scheduled tour.

Note that an official **TI** is just a few blocks off the bottom of ulica Szeroka, at ulica Józefa 7 (daily 9:00–17:00, tel. 012-422-0471). For hotel and restaurant suggestions, see page 302 of "Sleeping in Kraków" and page 310 of "Eating in Kraków." Several restaurants offer live traditional Jewish klezmer music nightly in summer.

▲▲Jewish Cemeteries—Kazimierz has two very different Jewish cemeteries that are worth a visit.

The small **Old Cemetery** (Stary Cmentarz) was used to bury members of the Jewish community from 1552 to 1800. It has been renovated—so in a way, it actually feels "newer" than the New Cemetery. After the New Cemetery (described next) was opened in 1800, this cemetery gradually fell into disrepair. What remained was further desecrated by the Nazis during World War II. In the 1950s, it was discovered, excavated, and put back together as you see here. Shattered gravestones form a mosaic wall around the perimeter. As in all Jewish cemeteries, you may see small stones stacked on the graves (originally placed over desert graves to cover the body and prevent animals from disturbing it). Behind the little synagogue to the left, the tallest tombstone next to the tree belonged to Moses Isserle (a.k.a. Remu'h), an important 16th-century rabbi. He is believed to have been a miracle worker, and his grave was one of the only ones that remained standing after World War II. The knee-high metal receptacle nearby is for written prayers (5 zł, very sporadic hours according to demand—especially outside of peak season—but generally open Sun–Fri 9:00–16:00, can be open until 18:00 May–Aug, closes earlier off-season and by sundown on Fri, always closed Sat, enter through Remu'h Synagogue at ulica Szeroka 40).

The much larger **New Cemetery** (Nowy Cmentarz) has graves of those who died after 1800. Nazis vandalized this cemetery, selling many of its gravestones to stonecutters, and using others as pavement in their concentration camps. Many of the gravestones have since been returned to their original positions. Other headstones could not be replaced, and were used to create the moving mosaic wall and Holocaust monument (on the right as you enter). Most gravestones are in one of four languages: Hebrew (generally the oldest, especially if there's no other language); Yiddish (sounds like a mix of German and Hebrew, and uses the Hebrew

alphabet); Polish (Jews who assimilated into the Polish community); and German (Jews who assimilated into the German community). The earliest graves are simple stones, while later ones imitate graves in Polish Catholic cemeteries—larger, more elaborate, and with a long stone jutting out to cover the body. Notice that some new-looking graves have old dates. These were most likely put here well after the Holocaust (or even after communism) by relatives of the dead (free, Sun–Fri 8:00–18:00, until 16:00 in winter, closed Sat, tricky to find—go under railway bridge at east end of ulica Miodowa, jog left as you emerge, cemetery is to your right, enter through gate with small *cmentarz żydowski* sign).

Synagogues—Six different synagogues in Kazimierz welcome visitors. Each of the interiors is a variation on the same theme: A large central prayer hall, often with an altar (facing east, toward Jerusalem) where the Torah is kept. The elevated platform in the center, sometimes surrounded by a cage-like structure, is the equivalent of a pulpit in a Christian church. You may see separate areas (often a balcony or an arcade) where women would worship, separately from men. Some synagogues have been converted into museums, while others are still used for services. The first two synagogues listed below are on Kazimierz's main square, ulica Szeroka; the next four are all within three blocks to the west (all are shown on the map on page 288).

Remu'h Synagogue, from 1553, has been carefully renovated and is fully active (included in 5-zł entry fee for Old Cemetery, same unpredictable hours as Old Cemetery, ulica Szeroka 40).

The **Old Synagogue** (Stara Synagoga), the oldest surviving Jewish building in Poland, is now a good three-room museum on local Jewish culture, with informative English descriptions. Most of the exhibits are displayed in the impressive main prayer hall (8 zł, free on Mon; April–Oct Mon 10:00–14:00, Tue–Sun 10:00–17:00; Nov–March Mon 10:00–14:00, Wed–Thu and Sat–Sun 9:00–16:00, Fri 10:00–17:00, closed Tue; ulica Szeroka 24).

The recently renovated **High Synagogue**—so called because its prayer room is upstairs—displays changing exhibits, most of which focus on the people who lived here before and after the Holocaust (9 zł, daily 9:00–19:00, shorter hours in winter, just around the corner from the Old Synagogue at ulica Józefa 38).

Isaac Synagogue (Synagoga Izaaka), one of Kraków's biggest, was built in the 17th century. On the walls in the prayer hall are

giant wall paintings of prayers for worshippers who couldn't afford to buy books (with translations posted below). It also serves as the local center for the Hasidic Jewish group Chabad, with a kosher restaurant and a library (5 zł; Sun–Thu 9:00–18:00, Fri 9:00–13:00; closes one hour later April–Sept; closed Sat, a block west of ulica Szeroka at ulica Kupa 18, tel. 012-430-2222).

Tempel Synagogue (Synagoga Templu) has the grandest interior—big and dark, with elaborately decorated, gilded ceilings and balconies—and the most lived-in feel of the bunch (5 zł, Sun–Fri 10:00–16:00, sometimes until 18:00, closed Sat, corner of ulica Miodowa and ulica Podbrzezie).

The smaller **Kupa Synagogue** (Synagoga Kupa), clean and brightly decorated, sometimes hosts temporary exhibits (Miodowa 27).

Galicia Jewish Museum (Galicja Muzeum)—This museum focuses on the present rather than the past. With a series of photographs displayed around a restored Jewish furniture factory, the permanent "Traces of Memory" exhibit shows today's remnants of yesterday's Judaism in the area around Kraków (a region known as "Galicia"). From forgotten synagogues to old Jewish gravestones flipped over and used as doorsteps, these giant postcards of Jewish artifacts (with good English descriptions) ensure that an important part of this region's heritage won't be forgotten. Complementing this permanent collection are good temporary exhibits (14 zł, daily 10:00–18:00, 1 block east of ulica Szeroka at ulica Dajwór 18, tel. 012-421-6842, www.galiciajewishmuseum.org). The museum also serves as a sort of cultural center, with a good bookstore, café, and programming that caters to both locals and visitors (such as Jewish dancing lessons on some Saturday mornings; pick up the monthly program).

Kazimierz Market Square (Plac Nowy)—The natives shop at plac Nowy's market stalls. This is a gritty, factory-workers-on-lunch-break contrast to Kraków's touristy Main Market Square (stalls open Tue–Sun 6:00–14:00, a few also open later, closed Mon). Consider dropping by here for some shopping, people-watching, or a quick, cheap, and local lunch (see page 314). More recently, several trendy bars and nightclubs have popped up around this square.

▲Ethnographic Museum (Muzeum Etnograficzne)—This clever and refreshingly good museum hides a few blocks west of the Jewish area of Kazimierz, in the former town hall. It sits on plac Wolnica, which was Kazimierz's primary market square and was once almost as big as Kraków's. On the ground floor, you'll find models of traditional rural Polish homes, as well as musty replicas of the interiors (like an open-air folk museum moved inside). The exhibit continues upstairs, where each in a long lineup

of traditional Polish folk costumes is identified by specific region. You'll see exhibits on village lifestyles, rustic tools, and musical instruments (including a Polish bagpipe). A highlight is the explanation of traditional holiday celebrations—from elaborate crèche scenes at Christmas, to a wall of remarkably painted Easter eggs. Some items are labeled in English, and you can borrow English descriptions in a few of the rooms. The top floor features temporary exhibits (8 zł, free on Sun, open Tue–Sat 11:00–19:00, Thu until 21:00, Sun 11:00–15:00, closed Mon, ulica Krakowska 46, tel. 012-430-6023, www.etnomuzeum.eu).

Near Kazimierz: Podgórze

The neighborhood called Podgórze (POD-goo-zheh), directly across the Vistula from Kazimierz, is where the Nazis forced Kraków's Jews into a ghetto in early 1941. (*Schindler's List* and the films in the Pharmacy Under the Eagle museum depict the sad scene of the Jews loading their belongings onto carts and trudging over the bridge into Podgórze.) The ghetto was surrounded by a wall with a fringe along the top that resembled Jewish gravestones—a chilling premonition of what was to come. A short section of this wall still stands along Lwowska street.

Getting There: To get to Ghetto Heroes' Square, continue through Kazimierz on tram #7, #13, or #24 (described earlier, under "Getting to Kazimierz") to the stop called plac Bohaterow Getta. You can also simply continue walking along Starowiślna, about 10 minutes past the other Kazimierz sights—it's just across the bridge.

Ghetto Heroes' Square (plac Bohaterow Getta)—This unassuming square is the focal point of the visitor's Podgórze. Today the square is filled with a recent monument consisting of several empty metal chairs. This is intended to remind viewers that the Jews of Kazimierz were forced to carry all of their belongings—including furniture—to the ghetto on this side of the river. It was also here that many Jews waited to be sent to extermination camps. The small, grey building across Ghetto Heroes Square feels like a train car inside, evocative of the wagons that carried people from here to certain death.

▲Pharmacy Under the Eagle (Apteka pod Orłem)—This modest museum, on Ghetto Heroes' Square, tells the story of Tadeusz Pankiewicz, a Polish Catholic pharmacist who chose to remain in Podgórze when it became a Jewish ghetto. During this time, the pharmacy was an important meeting point for the ghetto residents, and Pankiewicz and his staff heroically aided and hid Jewish victims of the Nazis. (Pankiewicz survived the war and was later acknowledged by Israel as one of the "Righteous Among the Nations"—non-Jews who risked their lives to help the Nazis'

victims during World War II.) Today the pharmacy hosts a small exhibit about the Jewish ghetto. Three video screens display footage from that era: One shows Kazimierz before the Nazis arrived; another documents the forced transition to the Podgórze ghetto; and a third is secret surveillance footage of Płaszów Concentration Camp, on Kraków's outskirts (5 zł, free on Mon, some English descriptions, good 10-zł audioguide gives 45 min of commentary; May–Oct Mon 10:00–14:00, Tue–Sat 9:30–17:00, closed Sun; Nov–April Mon 10:00–14:00, Tue–Thu and Sat 9:00–16:00, Fri 10:00–17:00, closed Sun and the first Tue of each month; plac Bohaterow Getta 18, tel. 012-656-5625).

Most people coming to Podgórze are actually looking for...

▲Schindler's Factory—Fans of the movie and book—and of the compassionate Kraków businessman who did his creative best to save the lives of his Jewish workers—can make a pilgrimage to Oskar Schindler's actual factory, named "Emalia." This is where Schindler worked, and where Spielberg filmed much of *Schindler's List*. The factory went bust a few years back, but curious tourists kept seeking it out. Now the Kraków Historical Museum has completely refurbished the complex, and turned it into a brand-new museum that's due to open in mid-2010. In addition to telling the history of the factory and of Schindler himself, the exhibit traces Kraków's World War II experience. You'll learn about the initial Nazi occupation in September 1939, see a replica of the wall that enclosed the Podgórze ghetto, watch testimonial footage of Schindler's grateful employees, and find out more about the nearby Płaszów Concentration Camp (also featured in *Schindler's List*). The "room of choices" leads visitors to reflect on the unthinkably difficult decisions that faced everyday people during those horrific times. Just inside the gate (on the left) is the long staircase—immortalized in a scene from *Schindler's List*—that leads to a replica of Oskar Schindler's office, with a giant pile of enamel pots and pans (like those that were made in this factory). Just behind the main building are several factory buildings, which might be converted into a gallery for modern art.

Because this project has been perpetually delayed, check with the TI or ask around Kazimierz to see what's open before making the long trek out here; even if the museum's not fully open, you might be able to tour the interior and see part of the exhibit (possibly 15 zł; hours uncertain but likely Tue–Sun 10:00–17:30, closed Mon; tel. 012-257-1017, www.mhk.pl).

Getting There: It's in a depressed industrial area a five-minute walk from Ghetto Heroes' Square (plac Bohaterow Getta): Head up Kącik street (to the left of the big, glass skyscraper), go under the railroad underpass marked *Kraków-Zabłocie,* and continue two blocks to the second big building on the left (ulica Lipowa 4).

Closer to the center, **Schindler's apartment** is a block from Wawel Castle at ulica Straszewskiego 7 (unmarked and not available for tours).

▲▲Wieliczka Salt Mine (Kopalnia Soli Wieliczka)

Wieliczka (veel-EECH-kah), a salt mine 10 miles southeast of Kraków, is beloved by Poles. Deep beneath the ground, the mine is filled with sculptures that miners have lovingly carved out of the salt. You'll explore this unique gallery—learning both about the art, and about medieval mining techniques—on a required tour. Though the sight is a bit overrated, it's unique and practically obligatory if you're in Kraków for at least two days.

Cost, Hours, Information: Visits are by tour only (65 zł to join a guided tour). English tours are offered daily year-round—with the exception of a few holidays when the mine is closed—but the schedule depends on the time of year (July–Aug every half-hour 8:30–18:00; June at 9:00, 10:00, 11:30, 12:30, 13:45, 15:00, 16:00, 17:00; Sept every 30 min 9:00–15:00, plus 16:00 and 17:00; Oct–May at 10:00, 11:00, 11:30, 12:30, 13:45, 15:00, 16:00, and 17:00). If you miss the English-language tour (or decide to just show up and take whatever's going next), buy the informative guidebook, which narrates the exact route the tours follow (mine open and tours run daily April–Oct 7:30–19:30, Nov–March 8:00–17:00, ulica Daniłowicza 10, tel. 012-278-7302, www.kopalnia.pl).

You'll pay an extra 10 zł for permission to use your camera—but be warned that flash photos often don't turn out, thanks to the irregular reflection of the salt crystals. Dress warmly—the mine is a constant 57 degrees Fahrenheit.

Your ticket includes a dull **mine museum** at the end of the tour. It adds an hour to the mine tour and is discouraged by locals ("1.5 miles more walking, colder, more of the same"). Make it clear when you buy your ticket that you're not interested in the museum.

Background: Wieliczka Salt Mine has been producing salt since at least the 11th century. Under Kazimierz the Great, one-third of Poland's income came from these precious deposits. Wieliczka miners spent much of their lives underground, leaving for work before daybreak and returning after sundown, rarely emerging into daylight. To pass the time, and to immortalize their national pride and religiosity in art, 19th-century miners began to

carve figures, chandeliers, and eventually even an elaborate chapel out of the salt. Until a few years ago, the mine still produced salt. Today's miners—about 400 of them—primarily work on maintaining the 200 miles of chambers. This entire network is supported by wooden beams (because metal would rust).

Highlights: From the lobby, your guide leads you 380 steps down a winding staircase. From this spot you begin a 1.5-mile stroll, generally downhill (more than 800 steps down all together), past 20 of the mine's 2,000 chambers (with signs explaining when they were dug), finishing 443 feet below the surface. When you're done, an elevator beams you back up.

The tour shows how the miners lived and worked, using horses who spent their whole lives without ever seeing the light of day. It takes you through some vast underground caverns, past subterranean lakes, and introduces you to some of the mine's many sculptures (including one of Copernicus—who actually visited here in the 15th century—as well as an army of salt elves, and this region's favorite son, Pope John Paul II). Your jaw will drop as you enter the enormous **Chapel of St. Kinga,** carved over three decades in the early 20th century. Look for the salt-relief carving of the Last Supper (its 3-D details are astonishing, considering it's just six inches deep).

While advertised as two hours, your tour finishes in a deep-down shopping zone 1.5 hours after you started (they hope you'll hang out and shop). Note when the next elevator departs (just 3/hr), and you can be outta there on the next lift. Zip through the shopping zone in two minutes, or step over the rope and be immediately in line for the great escape (you'll be escorted 300 yards to the skinny industrial elevator, into which you'll be packed like mine workers).

▲Nowa Huta

Nowa Huta (NOH-vah HOO-tah, "New Steel Works"), an enormous planned workers' town, offers a glimpse into the stark, grand-scale aesthetics of the communists. Since it's five miles east of central Kraków and a little tricky to see on your own, skip it unless you're determined. But architects and communist sympathizers may want to make a pilgrimage here.

Getting There: Trams #4 and #15 go from near Kraków's Old Town (catch the tram on the ring road near Kraków's main train station, at the Basztowa stop) along Pope John Paul II Avenue (aleja Jana Pawła II) to Nowa Huta's main square, plac Centralny

(about 30 min total). From there, tram #4 (but not #15) continues a few minutes farther to the main gate of the Tadeusz Sendzimir Steelworks, and then it returns to Kraków.

Tours: True to its name, Mike Ostrowski's **Crazy Guides** is a loosely run operation that takes tourists to Nowa Huta in genuine communist-era vehicles (mostly Trabants and Polski Fiats). While the content is good, Mike and his comrades are laid-back, very informal, and sometimes crude. If you're offended by a foul-mouthed guide who reminds you of a scruffy college student, or if you don't like the idea of careening down the streets of Kraków in a car that feels like a cardboard box with a lawnmower engine, skip this tour. For the rest of us, it's a fun and convenient way to experience Nowa Huta (129 zł/person for 2.5-hr Nowa Huta tour; 169 zł/person for 4-hr Communism Deluxe tour that also includes their makeshift "museum"—a communist-era apartment that's decorated to give you a taste of the way things were; 159 zł/person for 4-hr Real Kraków tour that covers the basic Nowa Huta trip plus other outlying sights; other crazy experiences also available, cash only, reserve ahead and they'll pick you up at your hotel, mobile 0500-091-200, www.crazyguides.com, info@crazyguides.com).

History: Nowa Huta was the communists' idea of paradise. It's one of only three towns outside the Soviet Union that were custom-built to showcase socialist ideals. (The others are Dunáujváros—once called Sztálinváros—south of Budapest, Hungary; and Eisenhüttenstadt—once called Stalinstadt—near Brandenburg, Germany.) Completed in just 10 years (1949–1959), Nowa Huta was primarily built because the Soviets felt that smart and sassy Kraków needed a taste of heavy industry. Farmers and villagers were imported to live and work in Nowa Huta. Many of the new residents weren't accustomed to city living, and brought along their livestock (who grazed in the fields around unfinished buildings). For commies, it was downright idyllic: Dad would cheerily ride the tram into the steel factory, mom would dutifully keep house, and the kids could splash around at the man-made beach and learn how to cut perfect red stars out of construction paper. But Krakovians had the last laugh: Nowa Huta, along with Lech Wałęsa's shipyard in Gdańsk, was one of the home bases of the Solidarity strikes that eventually brought down the regime. Now, with the communists long gone, Nowa Huta remains a sooty suburb of Poland's cultural capital, with a whopping 200,000 residents.

Sights: Nowa Huta's focal point used to be known simply as **Central Square** (plac Centralny), but in a fit of poetic justice,

it was recently renamed for the anti-communist Ronald Reagan. This square is the heart of the planned town. A map of Nowa Huta looks like a clamshell: a semi-circular design radiating out from Central/Reagan Square. Numbered streets fan out like spokes on a wheel, and trolleys zip workers directly to the immense factory.

Believe it or not, the inspiration for Nowa Huta was the Renaissance (which, thanks to the textbook Renaissance design of the Cloth Hall and other landmarks, Soviet architects considered typically Polish). Notice the elegantly predictable arches and galleries that would make Michelangelo proud. When first built (before it was layered with grime), Nowa Huta was delightfully orderly, primly painted, impeccably maintained, and downright beautiful...if a little boring. It was practical, too: Each of the huge apartment blocks is a self-contained unit, with its own grassy inner courtyard, school, and shops. Driveways (which appear to dead-end at underground garage doors) lead to vast fallout shelters.

Today's Nowa Huta is a far cry from its glory days. Wander around. Poke into the courtyards. Reflect on what it would be like to live here. It may not be as bad as you imagine. Ugly as they seem from the outside, these buildings are packed with happy little apartments filled with color, light, and warmth.

The wide boulevard running northeast of Central/Reagan Square, now called Solidarity Avenue (aleja Solidarności, lined with tracks for tram #4), leads to the **Tadeusz Sendzimir Steelworks.** Originally named for Lenin, this factory was supposedly built using plans stolen from a Pittsburgh plant. It was designed to be a cog in the communist machine—reliant on iron ore from Ukraine, and therefore worthless unless Poland remained in the Soviet Bloc. Down from as many as 40,000 workers at its peak, the steelworks now employs only about 10,000. Today there's little to see other than the big sign, stern administration buildings, and smokestacks in the distance. Examine the twin offices flanking the sign—topped with turrets and a decorative frieze inspired by Italian palazzos, these continue the Renaissance theme of the housing districts.

Another worthwhile sight in Nowa Huta is the **Lord's Ark Church** (Arka Pana, several blocks northwest of Central/Reagan Square on ulica Obrońców Krzyża). Back when he was archbishop of Kraków, Karol Wojtyła fought for years to build a church in this most communist of communist towns. When the regime refused, he insisted on conducting open-air Masses before crowds in fields—until the communists finally

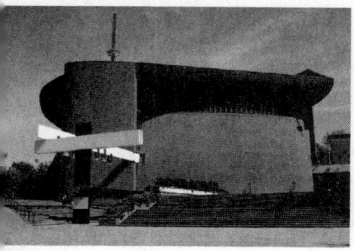

capitulated. Consecrated on May 15, 1977, the Lord's Ark Church has a Le Corbusier–esque design that looks like a fat, exhausted Noah's Ark resting on Mount Ararat—encouraging Poles to persevere through the floods of communism. While architecturally interesting, the church is mostly significant as a symbol of an early victory of Catholicism over communism.

Shopping in Kraków

Two of the most popular Polish souvenirs—amber and pottery—come from areas far from Kraków. Amber *(bursztyn)* is found on northern Baltic shores (see page 397). "Polish pottery," the distinctive blue-and-white pieces, is made in the region of Silesia, west of Kraków (mostly in the town of Bolesławiec). Because neither of these items actually comes from Kraków, you won't find any great bargains. Somewhat more local are the many wood carvings you'll see.

The **Cloth Hall,** smack-dab in the center of the Main Market Square, is the most convenient place to pick up any Polish souvenirs. It has a great selection, respectable prices, and the city's highest concentration of pickpockets (summer Mon–Fri 9:00–18:00, Sat–Sun 9:00–15:00, sometimes later; winter Mon–Fri 9:00–16:00, Sat–Sun 9:00–15:00).

A small but swanky mall called **Pasaż 13** is a few steps off the southeast corner of the Main Market Square, where Grodzka street enters the Square. Enter the mall under the balcony marked *Pasaż 13* (Mon–Sat 9:00–21:00, Sun 11:00–17:00).

Two new, enormous shopping malls lie just beyond the tourist zone. The gigantic **Galeria Krakowska,** with 270 shops, shares a square with the train station (Mon–Sat 9:00–22:00, Sun 10:00–21:00, can't miss it right next to the main train station). Note that nearby landmarks are signposted inside this massive, labyrinthine mall (*PKP/PKS* leads to the train and bus stations; *Stare Miasto* goes to the Old Town). Only slightly smaller is the **Galeria Kazimierz** (Mon–Sat 10:00–22:00, Sun 10:00–20:00, just a few blocks east of the Kazimierz sights, along the river at Podgórska 24).

Entertainment in Kraków

As a town full of both students and tourists, Kraków has plenty of entertainment options.

Concerts—You'll find a wide range of musical events, from tourist-oriented "Chopin's greatest hits" in quaint old ballrooms, to folk-dancing shows, to serious philharmonic performances. Popular venues include churches (such as the churches of Sts. Peter

and Paul on ulica Grodzka, St. Adalbert on the Main Market Square, or St. Idziego/Giles at the foot of Wawel Hill), various gardens around town (July–Aug only), and fancy mansions on the Main Market Square (including the Polonia House/Dom Polonii at #14, near ulica Grodzka; the Bonerowski Palace near the top of the Square at ulica Św. Jana 1; and the Pod Baranami Palace, at #27). Because Kraków's live-music scene is continually evolving, it's best to inquire locally about what's on during your visit. Hotel lobbies are stocked with fliers for upcoming concerts. But to get all of your options, visit any TI. The TI on ulica Św. Jana, which specializes in cultural events, can book tickets for most concerts (no extra fee), and tell you how to get tickets for the others. The monthly *Karnet* cultural events book lists everything (4 zł, half in Polish and half in English, also online at www.karnet.krakow.pl).

Jazz—For something a little more edgy, delve into Kraków's thriving jazz scene. Several popular clubs hide on the streets surrounding the Main Market Square (open nightly, most shows start around 21:30). The most famous and best for all-around jazz in a sophisticated cellar environment is **Jazz Club u Muniaka** (10–20-zł cover, open nightly 19:00–1:00 in the morning, live music nightly from 21:30, best music when the owner Janusz plays on Thu–Sat, ulica Floriańska 3, tel. 012-423-1205; described earlier on my self-guided walk). **Harris Piano Jazz Bar,** right on the Square (at #28), is more casual and offers a mix of traditional and updated "fusion" jazz, plus blues (free or 5-zł cover most nights, 15–35-zł cover for more serious shows on Sat, music nightly from 21:30, tel. 012-421-5741, www.harris.krakow.pl). **Stalowa Magnolia** is a bit more youthful, clubby-feeling, and snooty, with jazz about two nights a week and rock or pop the other nights (no cover on weeknights, on weekends 15-zł cover for men and free for women, music nightly from 22:00, ulica Św. Jana 15, www.stalowemagnolie.com).

Nightlife in the Old Town—The entire Old Town is crammed with nightclubs and discos pumping loud music on weekends. On a Saturday, the pedestrian streets can be more crowded at midnight than at noon. The scene is too fast-changing to list specifics here; if this is your idea of fun, ask around for tips, or just follow the beat.

Nightlife in Kazimierz—Young people willing to venture farther afield enjoy the lively nightlife in Kazimierz. Because the neighborhood has more affordable rents than the Old Town and it's not too far away (a 20-min walk or a 5-min tram ride), it has emerged as a cutting-edge after-hours mecca. Especially around plac Nowy, the streets teem with innovative, trendy pubs and nightclubs. Ask locals for tips on this always-evolving scene.

Klezmer Music in Kazimierz—For something a bit more sedate and cultured, consider the nightly klezmer music concerts of traditional Jewish music, also in Kazimierz (page 314).

Sleeping in Kraków

Healthy competition—with new, cleverly run places cropping up all the time—keeps Kraków's accommodation prices reasonable and makes choosing a hotel fun rather than frustrating. Rates are soft. Hoteliers don't need much of an excuse to offer you 10 to 20 percent off, especially on weekends or in the off-season. I've focused my accommodations on two areas: in and near the Old Town; and in Kazimierz, a local-style, more affordable neighborhood that is home to both the old Jewish quarter and a thriving dining and nightlife zone.

While the Old Town used to be sleepy, it's now jam-packed with discos that thump loud music on weekend nights to attract roving gangs of rowdy students, backpackers, and obnoxious "stag parties" of drunken louts from the UK in town for a weekend of carousing. The "quiet after 22:00" law is flagrantly ignored. Kazimierz is also home to various hip dance clubs. Virtually all of my accommodations come with some risk of noise; to help your odds, ask for a quiet room when you reserve, and bring earplugs.

In the Old Town

While you could stay away from the center, accommodations values here are so good that there's little sense in sleeping beyond the Planty park. Most of my listings are inside (or within a block or two of) the former city walls.

The Old Town has four basic types of accommodations: small, well-run guest houses (my favorite); big hotels (comfortable but overpriced); apartments (cheap, but you're on your own); and funky youth hostels. I've listed the best of each type.

Guest Houses

These good-value pensions almost invariably come with lots of stairs (no elevators), and are run by smart, can-do, entrepreneurial owners. They're all located in the heart of the Old Town along busy pedestrian streets, and most don't have air-conditioning—so they can be noisy with the windows open in the summer, especially on weekends. (Light sleepers should request quiet rooms.) These places book up fast, especially in summer—reserve as far ahead as possible. Don't expect a 24-hour reception desk; it's always smart to tell them your arrival time, especially if it's late in the day.

$$ Tango House, run by tango dance instructor Marcin Miszczak, is in a well-located building with an ancient-feeling stairwell decorated with faded Art Nouveau paintings. Its eight long, skinny, stylish rooms have parquet floors (tiny Sb-220 zł, standard Sb-300 zł, Db-340 zł, big Db-380 zł, prices can be soft in slow times, about 100 zł cheaper Nov-March, free Wi-Fi, ask for

Sleep Code

(3 zł = about $1, country code: 48)
S = Single, **D** = Double/Twin, **T** = Triple, **Q** = Quad, **b** = bathroom, **s** = shower only. Breakfast is included, credit cards are accepted, and English is spoken (unless otherwise noted).

To help you sort easily through these listings, I've divided the rooms into three categories, based on the price for a standard double room with bath:

$$$ Higher Priced—Most rooms 400 zł or more.
$$ Moderately Priced—Most rooms between 300–400 zł.
$ Lower Priced—Most rooms 300 zł or less.

quieter courtyard room to avoid rowdy street noise on weekends, ulica Szpitalna 4, tel. 012-429-3114, www.tangohouse.pl, info @tangohouse.pl).

$ Golden Lion Guest House has 12 smallish rooms with modern flair on a bustling pedestrian street a block off the Main Market Square (S-180 zł, Sb-200 zł, Db-300 zł, 10 percent cheaper Nov–Feb, free Internet access and Wi-Fi, guest kitchen, ask for quieter room in back, no parking, ulica Szewska 19, tel. 012-422-9323, fax 012-421-9775, www.goldenlion.pl, reservation@golden lion.pl, Anna and the Łodziński family).

$ At **Pensjonat Trecius,** Michał Palarczyk offers surprising class for low prices. Hiding upstairs in a nondescript building overlooking the bustling (and sometimes noisy) Floriańska pedestrian street, its eight rooms are nicely decorated, except for the two cheaper, unrenovated rooms on the top floor (S-120 zł, Sb-150–220 zł depending on size, D-150 zł, Db-200–300 zł depending on size, extra bed-50 zł, 5 percent cheaper if you pay cash, continental breakfast-8 zł, full breakfast-16 zł, non-smoking, reception open Mon–Fri 8:00–20:00, Sat–Sun 8:00–15:00, free Internet access, free cable Internet, 2 blocks from the Main Market Square at ulica Św. Tomasza 18, tel. 012-421-2521, fax 012-426-8730, www .trecius.krakow.pl, hotel@trecius.krakow.pl).

$ Globtroter Guest House offers 15 rustic-feeling rooms with high ceilings and big beams around a serene garden courtyard. Jacek (Jack), who really understands and respects travelers, conscientiously focuses on value—keeping prices as low as possible by not offering needless extras (June–Aug: Sb-170 zł, Db-280 zł; April–May and Sept–Oct: Sb-155 zł, Db-260 zł; Nov–March: Sb-150 zł, Db-210 zł; ask for 10 percent discount with this book, 2 people can cram into a single to save money—a little more than the Sb price, larger suites for up to five also available, no breakfast at

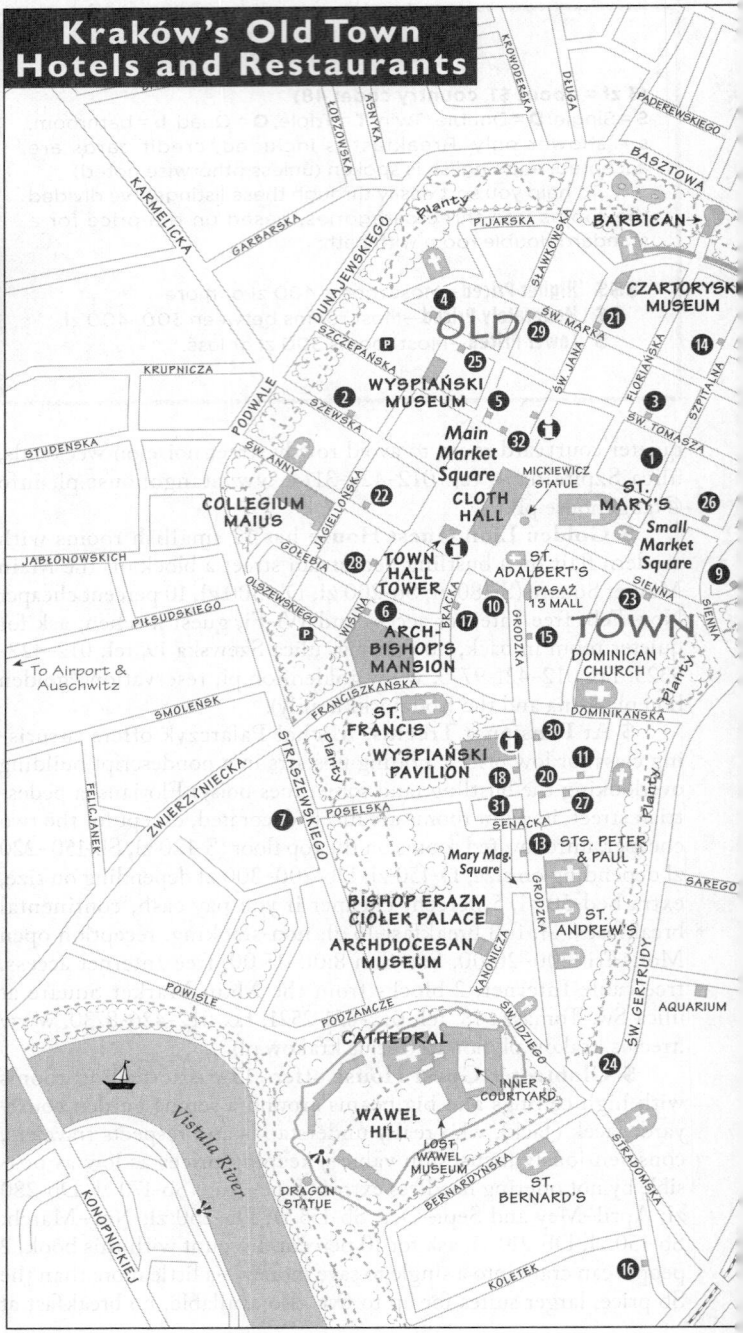
Kraków's Old Town
Hotels and Restaurants
KRONODEKSKA
DŁUGA
PADEREWSKIEGO
BASZTOWA
BARBICAN
LOBZOWSKA
ASNYKA
KARMELICKA
GARBARSKA
Planty
PIJARSKA
SŁAWKOWSKA
CZARTORYSKI MUSEUM
DUNAJEWSKIEGO
OLD
ŚW. MARKA
ŚW. JANA
FLORIAŃSKA
SZPITALNA
SZCZEPAŃSKA
KRUPNICZA
WYSPIAŃSKI MUSEUM
SZEWSKA
ŚW. TOMASZA
PODWALE
STUDENSKA
Main Market Square
MICKIEWICZ STATUE
ŚW. ANNY
COLLEGIUM MAIUS
JAGIELLOŃSKA
CLOTH HALL
ST. MARY'S
Small Market Square
JABŁONOWSKICH
GOŁĘBIA
TOWN HALL TOWER
ST. ADALBERT'S
PASAŻ 13 MALL
SIENNA
OLSZEWSKIEGO
BRACKA
PIŁSUDSKIEGO
WIŚLNA
ARCH-BISHOP'S MANSION
GRODZKA
TOWN
To Airport & Auschwitz
DOMINICAN CHURCH
FRANCISZKAŃSKA
SMOLENSK
ST. FRANCIS
DOMINIKAŃSKA
WYSPIAŃSKI PAVILION
STRASZEWSKIEGO
ZWIERZYNIECKA
FELICJANEK
POSELSKA
SENACKA
STS. PETER & PAUL
Mary Mag. Square
SAREGO
BISHOP ERAZM CIOŁEK PALACE
ST. ANDREW'S
ARCHDIOCESAN MUSEUM
KANONICZA
ŚW. GERTRUDY
POWIŚLE
PODZAMCZE
ŚW. IDZIEGO
AQUARIUM
CATHEDRAL
INNER COURTYARD
Vistula River
WAWEL HILL
LOST WAWEL MUSEUM
DRAGON STATUE
BERNARDYŃSKA
ST. BERNARD'S
STRADOWSKA
KONOPNICKIEJ
KOŁETEK

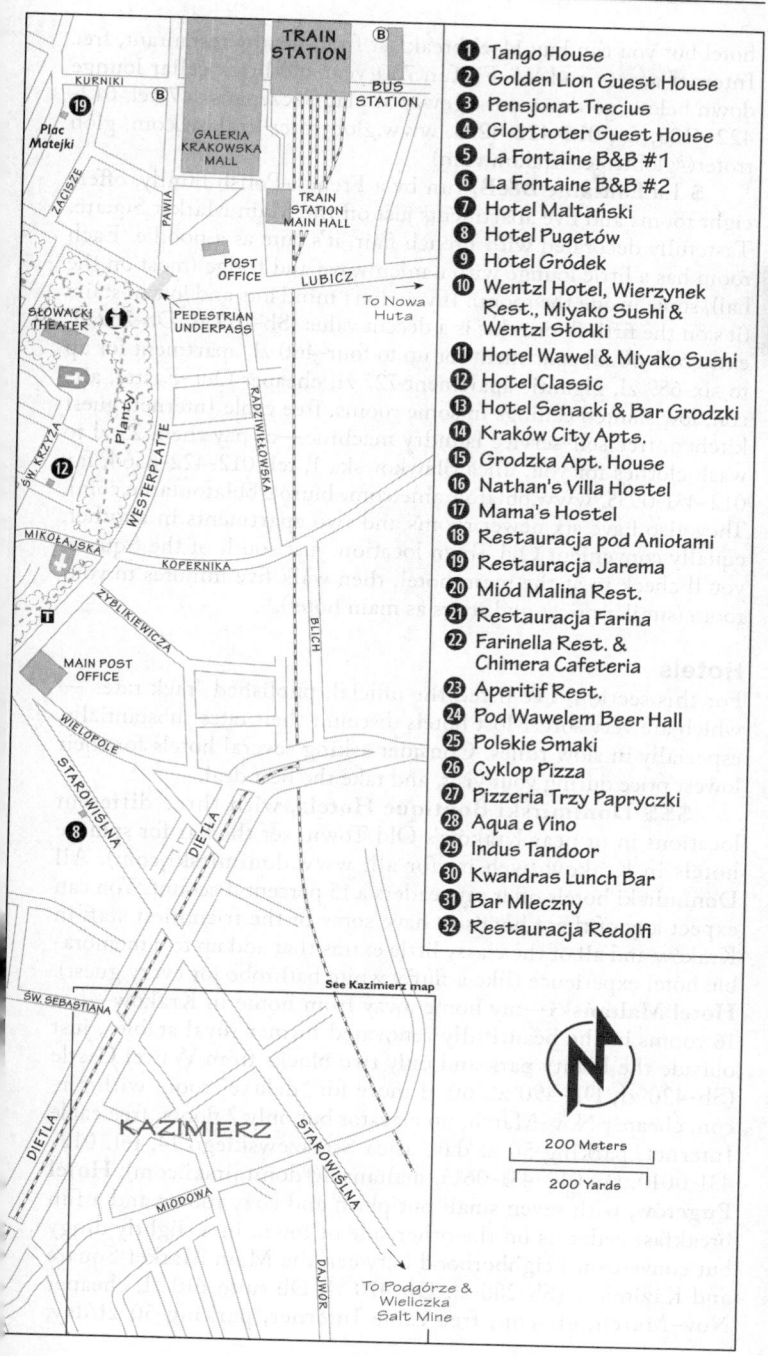
TRAIN STATION
BUS STATION
KUKNIKI
Plac Matejki
GALERIA KRAKOWSKA MALL
ZACISZE
PAWIA
TRAIN STATION MAIN HALL
POST OFFICE
LUBICZ
To Nowa Huta
SŁOWACKI THEATER
PEDESTRIAN UNDERPASS
Planty
ŚW. KRZYŻA
WESTERPLATTE
RADZIWIŁŁOWSKA
MIKOŁAJSKA
KOPERNIKA
ZYBLIKIEWICZA
BLICH
MAIN POST OFFICE
WIELOPOLE
STAROWIŚLNA
DIETLA
ŚW. SEBASTIANA
See Kazimierz map
KAZIMIERZ
MIODOWA
DAJWÓR
To Podgórze & Wieliczka Salt Mine
200 Meters
200 Yards
1 Tango House
2 Golden Lion Guest House
3 Pensjonat Trecius
4 Globtroter Guest House
5 La Fontaine B&B #1
6 La Fontaine B&B #2
7 Hotel Maltański
8 Hotel Pugetów
9 Hotel Gródek
10 Wentzl Hotel, Wierzynek Rest., Miyako Sushi & Wentzl Słodki
11 Hotel Wawel & Miyako Sushi
12 Hotel Classic
13 Hotel Senacki & Bar Grodzki
14 Kraków City Apts.
15 Grodzka Apt. House
16 Nathan's Villa Hostel
17 Mama's Hostel
18 Restauracja pod Aniołami
19 Restauracja Jarema
20 Miód Malina Rest.
21 Restauracja Farina
22 Farinella Rest. & Chimera Cafeteria
23 Aperitif Rest.
24 Pod Wawelem Beer Hall
25 Polskie Smaki
26 Cyklop Pizza
27 Pizzeria Trzy Papryczki
28 Aqua e Vino
29 Indus Tandoor
30 Kwandras Lunch Bar
31 Bar Mleczny
32 Restauracja Redolfi

hotel but you can buy 14-zł breakfast from nearby restaurant, free Internet access and Wi-Fi, fun 700-year-old brick cellar lounge down below, go down passageway at plac Szczepańska 7, tel. 012-422-4123, fax 012-422-4233, www.globtroter-krakow.com, globtroter@globtroter-krakow.com).

$ La Fontaine B&B, run by a French-Polish family, offers eight rooms and five apartments just off the Main Market Square. Tastefully decorated with French flair, it's cute as a poodle. Each room has a little lounge with a microwave and fridge (most on the hall, some inside the room). If you don't mind lots and lots of stairs (it's on the fifth floor), this is a decent value (Sb-209 zł, Db-269 zł, extra bed-60 zł, apartment for up to four-460 zł, apartment for up to six-659 zł, gigantic apartment-727 zł, cheaper Oct–Easter, air-con, low slanted ceilings in some rooms, free cable Internet, guest kitchen, free self-service laundry machine—or pay them 25 zł to wash clothes for you, ulica Sławkowska 1, tel. 012-422-6564, fax 012-431-0955, www.bblafontaine.com, biuro@bblafontaine.com). They also have six newer rooms and two apartments in another, equally convenient Old Town location, just south of the Square; you'll check in at the main hotel, then walk five minutes to your room (similar prices and stairs as main hotel).

Hotels

For this section, I've listed the official, published "rack rates"—which are very soft. Most hotels discount their rates substantially, especially in slow times. Consider asking several hotels for their lowest price during your visit, and take the best deal.

$$$ Donimirski Boutique Hotels, with three different locations in or near Kraków's Old Town, set the bar for splurge hotels in Kraków (website for all: www.donimirski.com). All Donimirski hotels offer my readers a 15 percent discount. You can expect any of these hotels to have some of the friendliest staff in Kraków and all of the classy little extras that add up to a memorable hotel experience (like a fluffy white bathrobe for every guest). **Hotel Maltański**—my home away from home in Kraków—has 16 rooms in the beautifully renovated former royal stables, just outside the Planty park and only two blocks from Wawel Castle (Sb-420 zł, Db-490 zł, 60 zł more for "deluxe" room with air-con, cheaper Nov–March, no elevator but only 2 floors, free cable Internet, parking-50 zł/day, ulica Straszewskiego 14, tel. 012-431-0010, fax 012-431-0615, maltanski@donimirski.com). **Hotel Pugetów,** with seven small but plush and cozy rooms and a fun breakfast cellar, is on the other side of town, in a slightly dingy but convenient neighborhood between the Main Market Square and Kazimierz (Sb-280 zł, Db-470 zł, Db suite-610 zł, cheaper Nov–March, air-con, free cable Internet, parking-50 zł/day,

ulica Starowiślna 13–15, tel. 012-432-4950, pugetow@donimirski.com). **Hotel Gródek**—by far the fanciest and most central of the bunch—offers 23 rooms a three-minute walk behind St. Mary's Church on a quiet dead-end street overlooking the Planty park. This place is easily the best splurge in town, with a handy location, gorgeously decorated rooms, and a top-notch breakfast served in a room surrounded by a mini-museum of artifacts discovered during the recent renovation (Sb-450 zł, bigger "deluxe" Sb-610 zł, Db-590 zł, bigger "deluxe" Db-670 zł, suite-840 zł, cheaper Nov–March, free Internet access, free cable Internet, good cellar restaurant serves Polish cuisine, parking-50 zł/day, Na Gródku, tel. 012-431-9030, grodek@donimirski.com). If you have a car, ask about rooms at their countryside castle, Zamek Korzkiew. Their fifth property, Hotel Kościuszko, has five stars and reasonable prices, but is located far from the center.

$$$ Wentzl Hotel is your splurge-right-on-the-Square option, with 18 rooms. The decor is classy Old World with modern touches, like state-of-the-art TVs and bathrooms. When reserving, request a room with a view on the Square—which can be noisy, especially on weekends—or a quieter back room (Sb-665 zł, Db-700 zł, bigger "deluxe" rooms cost 50 zł more, elevator, air-con, free Wi-Fi, Rynek Główny 19, tel. 012-430-2664, fax 012-430-2665, www.wentzl.pl, hotel@wentzl.pl).

$$$ Hotel Wawel has 39 beautifully renovated rooms on a well-located street that's quieter than the Old Town norm. It feels elegant for the price; above the swanky marble lobby are hallways creatively painted with the history of the building and images from around Kraków (Sb-330 zł, Db-460 zł, extra bed-100 zł/adult or 50 zł/child, non-smoking, air-con, free Internet access and Wi-Fi, elevator—but doesn't go to top floor, ulica Poselska 22, tel. 012-424-1300, fax 012-424-1333, www.hotelwawel.pl, hotel@hotelwawel.pl).

$$$ Hotel Classic, a modern home in old Kraków (on a non-descript street just inside the Planty park), has 30 rooms, a sleek marble lobby, professional staff, decent prices, and little character (April–Oct: Sb-440 zł, Db-480 zł, suite-640 zł; Nov–March: Sb-300 zł, Db-340 zł, suite-540 zł; Rick Steves readers get a 20 percent discount on weekdays and 25 percent discount Fri–Sun with a 2-night minimum stay, non-smoking floor, air-con, elevator, free cable Internet, request quiet back room to avoid disco noise from across the street, ulica Św. Tomasza 32, tel. 012-424-0303, fax 012-429-3680, www.hotel-classic.pl, hotel@hotel-classic.pl).

$$$ Hotel Senacki is a business-class place renting 20 aging rooms with parquet floors between Wawel Castle and the Main Market Square. Nine of the rooms have air-conditioning for no extra charge—if you'll be here in summer, request this when

you reserve (Sb-400 zł, Db-460–540 zł, lower price is for "attic" rooms with skylight windows and a flight of stairs after the elevator, deluxe Db-615 zł, all rates 40 zł cheaper Fri–Sun and very soft in general, extra bed-90 zł, 15 percent cheaper Nov–March, parking-50 zł/day, non-smoking rooms, elevator—but doesn't go to "attic" rooms, free cable Internet, ulica Grodzka 51, tel. 012-422-7686, fax 012-422-7934, www.osti-hotele.pl, senacki@osti-hotele.pl).

Apartments

You can save money by staying in your own apartment rather than a hotel. Apartments come with great locations, simple kitchens, and relatively low prices, but no reception desk or big-hotel services (such as having your room cleaned daily)...you're on your own. Apartments aren't just for long stays—these places welcome even one-nighters. While the apartments themselves are neat and modern, most are in old buildings with dreary entryways and stairways. Be sure to clearly communicate your arrival time.

$ Kraków City Apartments, conscientiously run by Andzej and Katarzyna, is 10 clean, modern apartments tucked away in a quiet courtyard at the corner of the Old Town (small Db-200 zł, standard Db-260 zł, bigger apartment-400 zł, 15 percent cheaper Oct–mid-April, non-smoking, elevator, free cable Internet, ulica Szpitalna 34, tel. 012-431-0041, mobile 0504-235-925, www.krakowapartments.info, info@krakowapartments.info).

$ Grodzka Apartment House offers 11 new-feeling, stylishly decorated apartments around a courtyard along one of Kraków's most happening streets, just a few steps off the Main Market Square. The studio apartments are as nice as a hotel room and a good value (studio-240 zł, 1-bedroom-280–300 zł, 2-bedroom-450 zł, prices soft, cheaper Nov–March, no breakfast but can buy 18-zł breakfast at nearby café, reception open daily 11:00–21:00, some apartments have street noise—light sleepers ask for quiet room, lots of stairs with no elevator, free cable Internet, go down the passage at Grodzka 4, tel. 012-421-4835, mobile 0660-541-085, www.grodzka.net.pl, info@grodzka.net.pl, Mikołaj). They also have more apartments (though not quite as nice) in two other Old Town buildings.

Hostels

New hostels are born—and go extinct—every other day in Kraków. But these three are well-established.

$ Nathan's Villa Hostel, in an up-and-coming neighborhood between Wawel Hill and Kazimierz, is well-run by an energetic young Bostonian and his wife. It's loose, easygoing, and fun, with 120 beds in 21 cleverly painted rooms, a bar, a beer garden,

an art gallery, a cheap BBQ every night in summer, and plenty of backpacker bonding. Their advertising promises advice on how to "get hammered," and the bar has regular drinking contests... if that's not your scene, sleep elsewhere (bunk in 4-bed room-65 zł, in 6-bed room-60 zł, in 8-bed room-55 zł, in 10-bed room-45 zł, D-160 zł, Db-180 zł, apartment with kitchenette for up to four-280 zł, rates are 5 zł/person less Nov–Feb; includes breakfast, sheets, laundry facilities, and lockers; free Internet access and Wi-Fi, non-smoking, no curfew or lockout time, ulica Św. Agnieszki 1, tel. 012-422-3545, www.nathansvilla.com, krakow@nathansvilla.com).

$ Mama's Hostel is ideally located (just steps off the Main Market Square) and more dignified than most hostels—like an old apartment taken over by vagabonds with good manners, but who still know how to have a good time. With 50 beds in seven rooms and mellow public spaces, it's a winner (60 zł/person in a 6-bed room, 55 zł in a 10-bed room, 50 zł in a 12-bed room, D-180 zł; includes sheets, breakfast, laundry, and lockers; non-smoking, no curfew, free Internet access and Wi-Fi, kitchen, lots of stairs with no elevator, ulica Bracka 4, tel. & fax 012-429-5940, www.mamashostel.com.pl, hostel@mamashostel.com.pl).

$ Hostel Momotown, in Kazimierz (described next), is a smidge more institutional and less party-oriented than the above options, but still loose and friendly. Run by Paweł Momot, it has 52 dorm beds and a fun garden for hanging out (bunk in 4-bed dorm-60 zł, in 6-bed dorm-55 zł, in 8-bed dorm-50 zł, in 10-bed dorm-45 zł, includes breakfast and sheets but not towels, kitchen, laundry, pay Internet access, free Wi-Fi, ulica Miodowa 28, tel. 012-429-6929, www.momotownhostel.com, info@momotownhostel.com). Two blocks away, they also rent 14 basic but cheap private rooms that share a kitchenette, overlooking Kazimierz's main square, ulica Szeroka (Sb-140 zł, Db-180 zł).

In Kazimierz

Sleep in Kazimierz to be close to Kraków's Jewish heart—or simply to experience a cheaper, less touristy, more local-feeling neighborhood outside the Old Town. With the highest concentration of pubs and nightclubs in town, Kazimierz is *the* spot for nightlife—which means that all of these places can be subject to some noise, especially on weekends. Keep in mind that these accommodations put you a 20-minute walk or a five-minute tram ride from the medieval ambience of Kraków's old center (for details on getting to Kazimierz from the Old Town, see page 287). Some of the klezmer music restaurants listed under "Eating in Kraków" also rent rooms, but they're generally an afterthought to the food and music, and not a good value. Note that Hostel

Momotown—listed above—is also in Kazimierz. For locations, see the map on page 288.

$$ Dom Casimi is nicely located, with 12 rooms at the top of ulica Szeroka in the heart of Jewish Kazimierz (Sb-199–260 zł, Db-290–370 zł, Tb-330–430 zł, price depends on size and style of room—pricier rooms have antique furniture, 15 percent cheaper Oct–March, stairs with no elevator, free cable Internet, free loaner bikes for guests, ulica Szeroka 7/8, tel. 012-426-1193, fax 012-426-1194, www.casimi.pl, casimi@casimi.pl).

$$ Karmel Hotel, with 11 rooms on a pleasant side street near the heart of Kazimierz, feels elegant for the price (Sb-250 zł, tight twin Db-298 zł, more spacious "komfort plus" Db with one big bed and air-con-398 zł, pricier suites also available, extra bed-70 zł, about 15–20 percent less Nov–March, upstairs with no elevator, free Internet access and Wi-Fi, some night noise on weekends, ulica Kupa 15, tel. 012-430-6697, fax 012-430-6726, www.karmel.com.pl, hotel@karmel.com.pl).

$ Tournet Guest House, well-run by friendly Piotr and Sylwia Działowy, is a great budget option offering 17 clean, colorful rooms near the edge of Kazimierz toward Wawel Hill. The "basic" rooms don't include breakfast (7.50 zł extra) or TV sets (basic Sb-110 zł, standard Sb-150 zł, basic Db-140 zł, standard Db-200 zł, Tb-250 zł, extra bed-50 zł, 20 zł less Nov–March, continental breakfast served in room, lots of stairs with no elevator, free Wi-Fi, reception open 7:00–22:00, ulica Miodowa 7, tel. 012-292-0088, fax 012-292-0089, www.accommodation.krakow.pl, tournet@accommodation.krakow.pl).

$ Maayan Guest Rooms offers 11 simple but comfortable rooms surrounding the 17th-century Kupa Synagogue. You can walk through the balconies overlooking the synagogue's prayer hall (S-70 zł, Sb-110 zł, D-100 zł, Db-180 zł, cash only, no breakfast, non-smoking, free Wi-Fi, some nightclub noise on weekends—ask for quiet room, ulica Miodowa 27, tel. 012-431-0170, maayanhotel@gmail.com, Wasilewski family).

Eating in Kraków

Kraków has a wide array of excellent restaurants—for every one I've listed, there are two or three nearly as good. The Old Town is very strong on traditional Polish and Italian, but less successful with other cuisines. Kazimierz has a more diverse selection, including Jewish restaurants with live klezmer music.

In the Old Town

Kraków's Old Town is littered with great restaurants. Prices are reasonable even on the Main Market Square. And a half-block

away, they get even better. All of these eateries (except the milk bars) are likely to be booked up on weekends—always reserve ahead.

Restauracja pod Aniołami ("Under Angels") offers a dressy, candlelit atmosphere on a covered patio, or in a deep, steep, romantic cellar with rough wood and medieval vaults. The cuisine is traditional Polish, with an emphasis on grilled meats and trout (on a wood-fired grill). Don't go here if you're in a hurry—only if you want to really slow down and enjoy your dinner (40–65-zł main dishes, daily 13:00–24:00, reservations smart, ulica Grodzka 35, tel. 012-421-3999).

Restauracja Jarema (yah-RAY-mah) offers a tasty reminder that Kraków used to rule a large swath of Ukraine and Lithuania. They serve eastern Polish/Ukrainian cuisine (with well-described specialties) amid 19th-century aristocratic elegance—you'll feel like you're dining in an old mansion (30–70-zł main dishes, several good vegetarian options, daily 12:00–22:00, usually live music from 19:00, reservations wise, across the street from barbican at plac Matejki 5, tel. 012-429-3669).

Miód Malina ("Honey Raspberry") is a delightful Polish-Italian fusion restaurant filled with the comforting aroma of its wood-fired oven. The menu is half Polish and half Italian—yet, remarkably, they do both cuisines equally well. For example, you can start with borscht and follow it with lasagna Bolognese. Sit in the cozy, warmly painted interior, or out in the courtyard (18-zł pierogi, 25-zł pastas, 30–60-zł main dishes, reservations smart, daily 12:00–23:00, ulica Grodzka 40, tel. 012-430-0411).

Restauracja Farina, with a fish-and-bottles theme, features a welcoming atmosphere and Polish and Mediterranean cuisine with an emphasis on fresh fish (30–35-zł pastas, 30–60-zł main dishes). They serve some special seafood dishes (60–100 zł) only on the days that they get their fresh delivery (open daily 12:00–23:00, 2 blocks north of the Square at ulica Św. Marka 16, at intersection with ulica Św. Jana, tel. 012-422-1680). They have a smaller branch, called **Farinella,** with more traditional Polish food (20–45-zł main dishes, daily 9:00–22:00, ulica Św. Anny 5, tel. 012-422-2121).

Chimera, just off the Main Market Square, is a cafeteria that serves fast traditional meals to a steady stream of students. You'll eat either outside on their quiet courtyard, or inside in what seems like a fake Old World stage set. In most of the restaurant, you'll order at the counter (good salad buffet: small plate-12 zł, big plate-16 zł, 12–19-zł main dishes), but part of the downstairs area has table service (25–30-zł main dishes; both parts good for vegetarians, daily 10:00–22:00, near university at ulica Św. Anny 3). I'd skip their expensive full-service restaurant,

U Artura, one door closer to the Square (40–60-zł main dishes, daily 12:00–24:00).

Aperitif is a stylish bistro serving tasty international cuisine with Mediterranean flair on the appealing Small Market Square (Mały Rynek) behind St. Mary's Church. It's classy but casual, with a cozy interior and a pleasant garden in back. Their 19-zł lunch specials, served on weekdays, are a great deal (21–29-zł pastas, 35–55-zł main dishes, daily 10:00–23:00, ulica Sienna 9, tel. 012-432-3333).

Beer Hall: **Pod Wawelem** ("Under Wawel") is a rollicking Austrian-style beer hall right on the Planty park near Wawel Castle. It's packed with locals seeking out big, sloppy, greasy portions of meaty fare, with giant mugs of various beers on tap (including Polish and Bavarian). Choose between the bustling interior, or the outdoor terrace right on the Planty (20–30-zł main dishes, different specials every day—such as giant schnitzel, pork ribs, or roasted chicken; daily 12:00–24:00, ulica Św. Gertrudy 26–29, tel. 012-421-2336).

Fast and Cheap: For a step up from the milk bars described below, **Polskie Smaki** ("Polish Flavors") is a homey little self-service cafeteria with a surprisingly elegant interior. They serve fast, inexpensive, and tasty traditional meals a block off the Main Market Square, with good borscht and *gołąbki* (stuffed cabbage rolls) at a fraction of what you'd pay elsewhere (7–13-zł main dishes, daily 10:00–22:00, ulica Św. Tomasza 5, tel. 012-422-4822).

Pizza: **Cyklop,** with 10 tables wrapped around the cook and his busy oven, has excellent wood-fired pizzas (14–22-zł one-person pizzas, 15-25-zł two-person pizzas, daily 11:30–22:00, near St. Mary's Church at Mikołajska 16, tel. 012-421-6603). **Pizzeria Trzy Papryczki** ("Three Peppers")—also dishing out wood-fired pizzas (though not quite as good as Cyklop's)—has better ambience, either inside or out in the welcoming garden (18–24-zł one-person pizzas, 20–28-zł two-person pizzas, daily 11:00–23:00, ulica Poselska 17, tel. 012-292-5532).

Serious Italian: The Italian-owned **Aqua e Vino** offers good food in a mellow, mod, black-and-white cellar decorated with giant stills from old movies. Probably the most authentic Italian eatery in town, it has a loyal following among the Italian expat community (25–35-zł pastas, 40–55-zł main dishes, daily 12:00–24:00, ulica Wiślna 5/10, tel. 012-421-2567).

Indian: **Indus Tandoor** is Kraków's oldest Indian restaurant, and the best I've tried in town. If you're ready for a break from Polish fare, this is the place (20–35-zł dishes, daily 12:00–22:00, Fri–Sat until 24:00, Sławkowska 13–15, tel. 012-423-2282). They also have a garden out back, where you can sip a drink and smoke a hookah (water pipe with flavored tobacco, 25 zł).

Milk Bars on Grodzka Street

Ulica Grodzka, the busy street that cuts south from the Main Market Square, has a convenient little pocket of three milk bars within a few steps of each other (all are open daily for lunch and dinner, but only until 19:00 or 20:00, sometimes later in summer). Survey all three options before you dive in. If they look full, just wait—there's a lot of turnover, so a table should free up soon. For pointers on eating at a milk bar, review the sidebar on page 245.

Approaching from the Square, the first one you'll come to (just after the modern copper-colored Wyspiański Pavilion, on the left) is the most modern and trendy of the three, more popular with students than with their grandparents: **Kwandras Lunch Bar** ("Quarter"—as in, you can eat here in a quarter-hour; pierogi and other dishes for 9–12 zł, full dinner for 13 zł, ulica Grodzka 32, tel. 012-294-2222).

Two blocks down the street and on the right (at the corner with Senacka) is the most basic and traditional milk bar, with a sign reading simply **Bar Mleczny** ("Milk Bar"; low-profile sign over the door reads *Restauracja "pod Temidą"*). The next best thing to a time machine to the communist era, this place has grumpy monolingual service, a mostly local clientele, and cheap but good food (6–12-zł main dishes).

A few more steps down, also on the right (just before the two churches), is **Bar Grodzki,** a single tight little room with shared tables. In addition to the standard milk-bar fare, Bar Grodzki specializes in tasty potato pancake dishes *(placki ziemniaczane).* Order high on the menu and try the rich and hearty "Hunter's Delight"—potato pancake with sausage, beef, melted cheese, and spicy sauce for 17 zł. The English menu posted by the counter makes ordering easy. Order, sit, and wait to be called to fetch your food (most main dishes 9–17 zł).

Splurging on the Main Market Square

You'll find plenty of relatively expensive, tourist-oriented restaurants on the Square. While all of these places have rich interiors, there's not much point in paying a premium to dine here unless you're sitting outside on the Square (one exception is Pod Krzyżkiem at #39, with a surrealistic interior that boldly attempts to one-up Eastern Europe's top square). While tourists go for the ye olde places, natives hang out at pizza joints (like Sphinx, part of a wildly popular Poland-wide chain). Poles generally afford this zone on their meager incomes by just having a drink on the Square after eating at home.

Wierzynek is the most famous restaurant on the Square (and maybe in all of Poland), with a heritage dating back to 1364 and a guest list of notables ranging from heads of state to movie stars. It

lives up to its big reputation with good food at not-too-outrageous prices in two dining zones (both with seating either indoors, or out on the Square—if dining outside, be clear on which area you want). The fancier restaurant serves sophisticated Polish fare (15–50-zł starters, 60–100-zł main dishes, daily 13:00–23:00), while the simpler café is a good budget alternative, with salads for under 30 zł and 15–40-zł Polish traditional classics (daily 10:00–23:00; both at #15, tel. 012-424-9600).

Restauracja Redolfi comes with my favorite Square view, great salads, international cuisine, and a wide selection of desserts (30-zł salads and pastas, 50–60-zł main dishes, daily 9:00–24:00, Rynek Główny 38, tel. 012-423-0579).

Miyako Sushi is the place to mix your Square views with raw fish. Offering a wide range of Japanese cuisine—from fresh sushi (10–20-zł rolls and nigiri) to cooked dishes (30–40 zł)—it's a favorite of local sushi fans (daily 12:00–23:00, at #19, tel. 012-429-5299). There's another location with the same menu a couple of blocks away, just off Grodzka (same hours, ulica Poselska 22, tel. 012-430-2090), and yet another at the Galeria Krakowska mall near the train station (daily 10:00–22:00, tel. 012-628-7252).

And for Dessert: **Wentzl Słodki** ("Sweets") is a local favorite for enjoying dessert on the Square. Consider dining more cheaply elsewhere, then finishing up with coffee, ice cream, or cake here (12–25-zł desserts, daily 11:00–23:00, at #19).

In Kazimierz

The entire district is bursting with lively cafés and bars—it's a happening night scene. Jewish food is the specialty here, but in general the neighborhood offers more diversity than the Old Town. The non-Jewish places I've listed are fast, cheap, and convenient. For locations, see the map on page 288.

Klezmer Concerts and Jewish Food

Kazimierz is a hub of Jewish restaurants, featuring cuisine and music that honors the neighborhood's Jewish heritage (and caters to its Jewish visitors). On a balmy summer night, the air is filled with the sound of klezmer music—traditional Jewish music from 19th-century Poland, generally with violin, string bass, clarinet, and accordion. Skilled klezmer musicians can make their instruments weep or laugh like human voices. Several places on ulica Szeroka (Kazimierz's main square) offer klezmer concerts around 20:00. All of these have several rooms, which the musicians move between as the evening goes on. While most places claim to do concerts nightly year-round, in reality they can be canceled anytime it's slow (especially off-season). For this reason—and because

these places fill up—it's important to reserve ahead. (If you're in Kazimierz for some daytime sightseeing, visit several places, pick your favorite, and reserve dinner.) Each restaurant has a similar menu, with main dishes for 20–50 zł. Sometimes you'll need to order sides and starches separately. You'll pay an additional cover charge just for the music (about 20–22 zł/person). Don't expect great cuisine—you're here for the music.

Arka Noego ("Noah's Ark") has a good reputation for its music and its food (slightly cheaper food than the others, daily 10:00–2:00 in the morning, shares building with Jarden Bookshop at #2, tel. 012-429-1528).

At **Klezmer-Hois,** which fills a venerable former Jewish ritual bathhouse, you'll feel like you're dining in a rich grandparent's home (daily 8:00–22:00, at #6, tel. 012-411-1245).

Ariel is popular but has gone downhill in recent years, and receives mixed reviews for its food (daily 10:00–24:00, music in up to four different rooms, best upstairs in the larger dining hall, at #18, tel. 012-421-7920).

Fast and Cheap

Bagelmama, run by an American named Nava, is a casual bagel shop serving up a wide range of sandwiches, soups, salads, burritos, desserts, and good espresso drinks. The bagels come dressed with a wide variety of spreads, from simple cream cheese or peanut butter to lox, tuna, or curry chicken. You can eat in or get it to go (most items 7–16 zł, Mon–Sat 9:00–21:00, Sun 9:00–19:00, ulica Dajwór 10, tel. 012-346-1646).

Restauracja Samoobsługowa Polakowski is a glorified milk bar with country-kitchen decor and cheap and tasty Polish fare. Curt service...cute hats (8–14-zł main dishes, borrow the English menu and/or point to what you want, daily 8:00–22:00, just behind the top of ulica Szeroka at ulica Miodowa 39).

Pierożki u Vincenta is a tiny, Vincent van Gogh–inspired eatery serving great pierogi (Polish-style ravioli) with both traditional fillings and creative newfangled versions (most around 8–12 zł, Sun–Thu 12:00–21:00, Fri–Sat 12:00–22:00, closes one hour earlier in winter, Bożego Ciała 12, tel. 012-430-6834).

The **plac Nowy market** offers a fully authentic, very cheap, blue-collar Polish experience—join the workers on their lunch break at the little food windows on Kazimierz's market square. This area is particularly known for its *zapiekanki*—the uniquely Polish fast food of a toasted baguette with cheese, ketchup, and other toppings (Bar Endzior is well-regarded). More recently, a wide range of trendy restaurants and bars has sprung up around the square. Survey your options and pick your favorite.

Kraków Connections

For getting between Kraków and **Auschwitz,** see page 333 in the next chapter.

From Kraków by Train to: Warsaw (hourly, 2.75 hrs, requires seat reservation, see below), **Gdańsk** (4/day direct, 2 more with change in Warsaw, 7.75 hrs; plus 1 direct night train, 11 hrs), **Toruń** (1/day direct, 7.75 hrs; better to transfer at Warsaw's Zachodnia station: 4/day, 5.75–6.5 hrs), **Prague** (1 early-morning direct train/day, 7 hrs; 3 more/day with 1–2 changes, 7.5–8 hrs; 1 night train, 8.75 hrs), **Berlin** (2/day direct, including 1 night train, 9.5–10.5 hrs; otherwise transfer in Warsaw, 9–11 hrs), **Budapest** (2/day, 9.5–11.5 hrs, transfer in Katowice, Poland, and Břeclav, Czech Republic; plus 1 direct night train/day, 10.5 hrs), and **Vienna** (1/night direct, 7.5 hrs; 3 decent daytime options, 6.25 hrs direct or 7–8.5 hrs with 1–3 changes).

The express train to **Warsaw**—which requires a reservation, even if you have a railpass—is particularly pleasant: A speedy 2.75 hours without stopping, from city center to city center. You'll be offered a free drink and snack to nibble on as you enjoy the pastoral scenery.

Night Trains to Hungary: If your next stop is Hungary, it can be convenient to sleep your way there on a night train. A night train from Kraków to **Budapest** runs nightly year-round (10.5 hours). If you'd rather head for **Eger,** in the summer (late June–late Aug) it's generally possible to take a night train to Füzesabony, Hungary, where you can change to an Eger-bound train. However, this service has been in flux in recent years. If it's not running, ride the night train from Kraków to Budapest, then connect to Eger (either right away, or as a side-trip later). To research the latest schedules, see http://bahn.hafas.de/bin/query.exe/en.

AUSCHWITZ-BIRKENAU

The unassuming regional capital of Oświęcim (ohsh-VEENCH-im) was the site of one of humanity's most unspeakably horrifying tragedies: the systematic murder of at least 1.1 million innocent people. From 1941 until 1945, Oświęcim was the home of Auschwitz, the biggest, most notorious concentration camp in the Nazi system. Today, Auschwitz is the most poignant memorial anywhere to the victims of the Holocaust.

A visit here is obligatory for Polish 14-year-olds; students usually come again during their last year of school, as well. You'll often see Israeli high school groups walking through the grounds waving their Star of David flags. Many visitors, including Germans, leave flowers and messages. One of the messages reads, "Nations who forget their own history are sentenced to live it again."

Orientation to Auschwitz

"Auschwitz" (OWSH-vits) actually refers to a series of several camps in Poland—most importantly Auschwitz I, in the village of Oświęcim (50 miles, or a 1.25-hour drive, west of Kraków), and Auschwitz II, a.k.a. Birkenau (about 2 miles west of Oświęcim). Those visiting Auschwitz generally see both parts. **Auschwitz I,** where public transportation from Kraków arrives, has the main museum building, the *Arbeit Macht Frei* gate, and indoor museum exhibits in former prison buildings. Then a brief shuttle-bus ride takes visitors to **Birkenau** (BEER-keh-now)—on a much bigger scale and mostly outdoors, with the famous guard tower (and another bookshop and more WCs), a vast field with ruins of barracks, a few tourable rough barracks, the notorious "dividing

Why Visit Auschwitz?

Why visit a notorious concentration camp on your vacation? Auschwitz-Birkenau is one of the most moving sights in Europe, and certainly the most important of all the Holocaust memorials. Seeing the camp can be difficult: Many visitors are overwhelmed by a combination of sadness and anger over the tragedy, as well as inspiration at the remarkable stories of survival. Auschwitz survivors and victims' families want tourists to come here and experience the scale and the monstrosity of the place. In their minds, a steady flow of visitors will ensure that the Holocaust is always remembered—so nothing like it will ever happen again.

Auschwitz isn't for everyone. But I've never met anyone who toured Auschwitz and regretted it. For many, it's a profoundly life-altering experience—and at the very least, it will forever affect the way you think about the Holocaust.

platform," a giant monument flanked by remains of destroyed crematoria, and a prisoner processing facility called "the Sauna."

Begin at Auschwitz I. The museum's main building has ticket booths (to pay for a tour or to make a donation), bookshops (consider the good *Guide-Book* brochure or the bigger laminated map), exchange offices, WCs, and basic eateries. You'll also find maps of the camp (posted on the walls) and a theater that shows a powerful film. A helpful **information desk**—where you can ask questions, buy tickets for the tour (see "Tours at Auschwitz," later), and find out about bus schedules for the return trip to Kraków—is halfway down the main entrance hall on the right, in the back corner behind the little tables.

Cost, Hours, Information: Entrance to the camp is free, but donations are gladly accepted. During busy times (May–Sept 9:00–15:00), you'll pay 33 zł to join a required organized tour (private guides also available; see "Tours at Auschwitz," later). The museum opens every day at 8:00, and closes June–Aug at 19:00, May and Sept at 18:00, April and Oct at 17:00, March and Nov at 16:00, and Dec–Feb at 15:00. Information: tel. 033-844-8100, www.auschwitz.org.pl.

Getting There: For details on getting between Kraków and Auschwitz, see "Auschwitz Connections," at the end of this chapter.

Getting from Auschwitz I to Birkenau: Buses shuttle visitors two miles between the camps (free, about 4/hr in peak season, less off-season, times posted at the bus stop outside the main building of each site, timed to correspond with tours). Taxis are also standing by (about 15 zł). Many visitors, rather than wait for the next bus, decide to walk the 20 minutes between the camps—offering a much-needed chance for reflection. Along the way, you'll pass the Judenrampe, an old train car like the ones used to transport prisoners, explained by an informational sign.

Film: The 17-minute movie (too graphic for children) was shot by Ukrainian troops days after the Red Army liberated the camp (3.50 zł, buy ticket on arrival; always in English at 10:00, 11:00, 13:00, and 15:00, sometimes more—ask when you arrive).

Photography: Because the philosophy of the camp is to spread the story of Auschwitz, taking photographs of anything outside is encouraged. However, to ease the movement of visitors, photography is not allowed inside the museum buildings.

Eating: There's a café and decent cafeteria (Bar Smak) at the main Auschwitz building. More options are in the commercial complex across the street.

Etiquette: The camp encourages visitors to remember that Auschwitz is the place where more than a million people lost their lives; behave here as you would at a cemetery.

Tours at Auschwitz

Visiting Auschwitz on your own works well, given the abundance of English descriptions (and this chapter's self-guided tour). However, due to crowd-control issues, individual visitors are not allowed to enter the Auschwitz I part of the complex on their own in the summer (May–Sept) between the peak times of 9:00 and 15:00. Instead, you're required to either join one of the museum's organized tours, or reserve your own private museum guide (both options are explained below). Note that even during these busy times, individuals may enter the Auschwitz II/Birkenau part of the complex without a guide. As this is a new policy, consider calling ahead to confirm the details if you're planning to visit the camp on your own.

Organized Museum Tours—The Auschwitz Museum's network of excellent guides are serious and frank, and feel a strong sense of responsibility about sharing the story of the camp. Appropriately, these well-trained guides are more historians than entertainers. The regularly scheduled 3.5-hour English tour covers Auschwitz, Birkenau, and the film (33 zł, buy ticket halfway down the main entry hall, on the right, in the back corner behind the tables). Most of the year, there are generally at least four English tours scheduled

Auschwitz Renovation

The International Auschwitz Council is planning to renovate the site over the next several years. The museum at Auschwitz I, widely considered the oldest Holocaust exhibit in the world, has remained largely unchanged in the more than 50 years since it opened. Now the museum displays will be modernized and better organized to accommodate the growing number of visitors. The key elements described in this chapter (such as the displays of human hair, eyeglasses, and suitcases) will still be part of the exhibit, but will likely be spread into more buildings (mostly on the ground floor, to avoid congestion on stairways). At Birkenau, restorers will build retaining walls to prevent the remains of the huge crematoria—key evidence of Nazi crimes—from slowly sinking into the ground.

Because of the renovation, be aware that the information in this chapter (especially the locations of exhibits on the self-guided tour) is subject to change. Ask about recent developments when you arrive at the camp.

each day. You'll watch the film first, and the actual tour begins 30 minutes later (film at 10:00, 11:00, 13:00, and 15:00; possibly more with demand—as soon as 10 English-speakers gather, ask for a tour; in winter generally at 11:00 and 13:00, maybe also at 15:00). Try to arrive at least 20 minutes ahead, because if the tour's full, you might have to wait until the next one.

Private Official Museum Guides—If you have a special interest, a small group, or just want a more personalized visit, it's affordable and worthwhile to hire one of the museum's guides for a private tour. Choose between the basic 3.5-hour tour of the camp (247 zł), or a longer "study tour" (462 zł/6 hrs, 550 zł/8 hrs spread over 2 days). Because English-speaking guides are limited, it's essential to reserve as far ahead as possible—at least two weeks in advance (fill out the online form at www.auschwitz.org.pl, or call 033-844-8099 or 033-844-8100). At busy times, individuals might not be able to reserve a private guide between 10:00 and 14:00, when they're needed for bigger groups.

Tours from Kraków—Various Kraków-based companies sell round-trip tours from Kraków to Auschwitz (see "Tours in Kraków," page 257). While these take care of transportation for you and include a guided tour, you'll pay triple and have to adhere to a strict schedule.

Local Guides and Drivers From Kraków—For hassle-free transportation to the camp, you can hire a Kraków-based local guide or driver to bring you to Auschwitz; I've listed my favorites on page 257. However, since these people are not officially regis-

tered museum guides, they technically aren't allowed to show you around the site. Instead, they will most likely arrange a private museum guide to join you, or time your visit so you can join an organized English tour (both options described above). While it's pricey, some travelers consider hiring a driver/guide to be a worthwhile splurge, since you'll have door-to-door service to the camp and three hours in the car with a local expert.

Self-Guided Tour

Auschwitz I

Before World War II, this camp was a base for the Polish army. When Hitler occupied Poland, he took over these barracks and turned it into a concentration camp for his Polish political enemies. The location was ideal, with a nearby rail junction and rivers providing natural protective boundaries. In 1942, Auschwitz became a death camp for the extermination of European Jews and others whom Hitler considered "undesirable." By the time the camp was liberated in 1945, at least 1.1 million people had been murdered here—approximately 960,000 of them Jewish.

As you exit the entry building's back door and go toward the camp, you see the notorious **gate** with the cruel message, *Arbeit Macht Frei* ("Work Sets You Free"). Note that the B was welded on upside down by belligerent inmates. On their arrival, new prisoners were told the truth: The only way out of the camp was through the crematorium chimneys. This gate was in the news in December of 2009, when the original sign that still hung here was stolen one night, then recovered cut into three pieces two days later. It was re-assembled and re-mounted atop this gate.

Just inside the gate and to the right, the camp orchestra (made up of prisoners) used to play marches; having the prisoners march made them easier to count.

The main road leads past the barracks. An average of 14,000 prisoners were kept at this camp at one time. (Birkenau could hold up to 100,000.)

The first row of barracks contains the **National Memorials,** created by the home countries of the camps' victims. As these memorials overlap with the general exhibits, and are designed for Europeans to learn more about the victims from their own home countries, most visitors skip this part of the site. But if you have

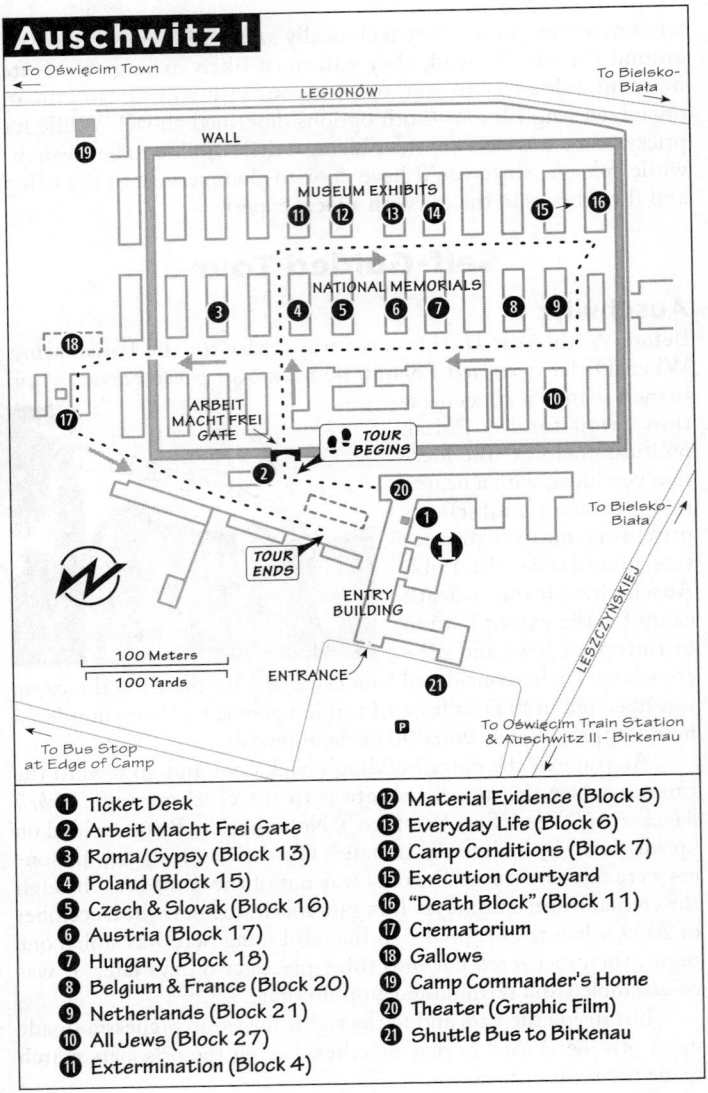

time later to take a look, consider circling back here to see those that interest you. Block 13 houses the **Roma (Gypsy)** exhibit. You'll learn that the Roma, along with the Jews, were considered no better than "rats, bedbugs, and fleas," and explore elements of the so-called *Zigeunerfrage*—the "Gypsy question" about what to do with this "troublesome" population. Block 15 honors victims from **Poland,** focusing on the 1939 Nazi invasion of the country,

which resulted in the immediate internment of Polish political prisoners. Exhibits explain the process of "Germanization"—such as renaming Polish streets with German names—and (upstairs) the underground resistance that fought to re-assert some control over Poland. Block 16 contains a new and well-presented exhibit about **Czech and Slovak** victims. Block 17 contains a new presentation about victims from **Austria** (but only in German and Polish). Block 18 holds a very modern, conceptual exhibit about **Hungary**'s victims, with an eerie heartbeat sound pervading the space. Block 20, a former hospital block, is shared by **Belgium** and **France.** A room near the entrance explains how prisoners were killed by lethal injection, with portraits and biographical sketches of victims. Upstairs is the powerful Belgium exhibit, with a room featuring portraits of victims. Block 21 honors **Dutch Jews;** like Hungary's, the exhibit is experiential, with a walk-through tunnel. Finally, Block 27 is devoted to a dark, somber memorial to **all Jews,** titled the "Suffering, Struggle, and Destruction of the Jews."

The most interesting part of the camp is the second row of barracks, which holds the museum exhibitions. Blocks 4 and 5 focus on how Auschwitz prisoners were killed. Blocks 6, 7, and 11 explore the conditions for prisoners who survived here a little longer than most.

Block 4 features exhibits on **extermination.** In the first room is a map showing all of the countries from which Auschwitz prisoners were brought—as far away as Norway and Greece. You'll also find an urn filled with ashes, a symbolic memorial to all of the camp's victims. In Room 2, a map shows that victims were transported here from all over Europe. To prevent a riot, the Nazis claimed at first that this was only a transition camp for resettlement in Eastern Europe. Room 3 displays some of the only photos that exist of victims inside the camp—taken by arrogant SS men.

Upstairs in Room 4 is a chilling model of a Birkenau crematorium. People entered on the left, then got undressed in the underground rooms (hanging their belongings on numbered hooks and encouraged to remember their numbers to retrieve their clothes later). They then moved into the "showers" and were killed by Zyklon-B gas. This efficient factory of murder took about 20 minutes to kill 20,000 people in four gas chambers. Elevators brought the bodies up to the crematorium. Members of the *Sonderkommand*—Jewish inmates who were kept isolated and forced by the Nazis to work here—removed the corpses' gold

Chilling Statistics: The Holocaust in Poland

The majority of people murdered by the Nazis during the Holocaust were killed right here in Poland. For centuries, Poland was known for its relative tolerance of Jews, and right up until the beginning of World War II, Poland had Europe's largest concentration of Jews: 3,500,000. Throughout the Holocaust, the Nazis murdered 4,500,000 Jews in Poland (many of them brought in from other countries) at camps, including Auschwitz, and in ghettos such as Warsaw's.

By the end of the war, only 300,000 Polish Jews had survived—less than 10 percent of the original population. Many of these survivors were granted "one-way passports" (read: deported) to Israel by the communist government in 1968 (following a big student demonstration with a strong Jewish presence). Today, only about 10,000 Jews live in all of Poland.

teeth and shaved off their hair (to be sold) before putting the bodies in the ovens. It wasn't unusual for a *Sonderkommand* worker to discover a wife, child, or parent among the dead. A few committed suicide by throwing themselves at electric fences; those who didn't were systematically executed by the Nazis after a two-month shift. Across from the model of the crematorium are canisters of Zyklon-B (hydrogen cyanide), the German-produced cleaning agent that is lethal in high doses. Across the hall in Room 5 is a wall of victims' hair—4,400 pounds of it. Also displayed is cloth made of the hair, used to make Nazi uniforms.

Back downstairs in Room 6 is an exhibit on the plunder of victims' personal belongings. People being transported here were encouraged to bring luggage—and some victims had even paid in advance for houses in their new homeland. After they were killed, everything of value was sorted and stored in warehouses that prisoners named "Canada" (after a country they associated with great wealth). Although the Canada warehouses were destroyed, you can see a few of these items in the next building.

Block 5 focuses on **material evidence** of the crimes that took place here. It consists mostly of piles of the victims' goods, a tiny fraction of everything the Nazis stole. As you wander through the rooms, you'll see eyeglasses; fine Jewish prayer shawls; crutches and prosthetic limbs (the first people the Nazis ever exterminated were mentally and physically ill German citizens); a seemingly endless mountain of shoes; and suitcases with names of victims—many marked *Kind,* or "child." Visitors often wonder if the suitcase with the name "Frank" belonged to Anne, one of the Holocaust's most famous victims. After being discovered in Amsterdam by the

Nazis, the Frank family was transported here to Auschwitz, where they were split up. Still, it's unlikely this suitcase was theirs. Anne Frank and her sister Margot were sent to the Bergen-Belsen camp in northern Germany, where they died of typhus shortly before the war ended. Their father, Otto Frank, survived Auschwitz and was found barely alive by the Russians, who liberated the camp in January of 1945.

Although the purpose of Auschwitz was to murder its inmates, not all of them were killed immediately. After an initial evaluation, some prisoners were registered and forced to work. (This did not mean they were chosen to live—but rather to die later.) In Block 6, you see elements of the **everyday life** of prisoners. The halls are lined with photographs of victims. Notice the dates of arrival *(przybył)* and death *(zmarł)*—those who were registered survived here an average of two to three months. (Flowers are poignant reminders that these victims are survived by loved ones.) Room 1 displays drawings of the arrival process—sketched by survivors of the camp. After the initial selection, those chosen to work were showered, shaved, and photographed. After a while, photographing each prisoner got to be too expensive, so prisoners were tattooed instead (see photographs): on the chest, on the arm, or—for children—on the leg. A display shows the symbols that prisoners had to wear to show their reason for internment—Jew, Roma (Gypsy), homosexual, political prisoner, and so on.

Room 4 shows the starvation that took place. The 7,500 survivors that the Red Army found here when the camp was liberated were living skeletons (the healthier ones had been forced to march to Germany). Of those liberated, 20 percent died soon after of disease and starvation. Look for the prisoners' daily ration (in the glass case): a pan of tea or coffee in the morning; thin vegetable soup in the afternoon; and a piece of bread (often made with sawdust or chestnuts) for dinner. This makes it clear that Auschwitz was never intended to be a "work camp," where people were kept alive, healthy, and efficient to do work. Rather, people were meant to die here—if not in the gas chambers, then through malnutrition and overwork.

You can see scenes from the prisoner's workday (sketched by survivors after liberation) in Room 5. Prisoners worked as long as the sun shone—eight hours in winter, up to twelve hours in summer—mostly on farms or in factories. Room 6 is about Auschwitz's child inmates, 20 percent of the camp's victims. Blond, blue-eyed

St. Maksymilian Kolbe
(1894–1941)

Among the many inspirational stories of Auschwitz is that of a Polish priest named Maksymilian Kolbe. Before the war, Kolbe traveled as a missionary to Japan, then worked in Poland for a Catholic newspaper. While he was highly regarded for his devotion to the Church, some of his writings had an unsettling anti-Semitic sentiment. But during the Nazi occupation, Kolbe briefly ran an institution that cared for refugees—including Jews.

In 1941, Kolbe was arrested and interned at Auschwitz. When a prisoner from Kolbe's block escaped in July of that year, the Nazis punished the remaining inmates by selecting 10 of them to put in the Starvation Cell until they died—based on the Nazi "doctrine of collective responsibility." After the selection had been made, Kolbe offered to replace a man who expressed concern about who would care for his family. The Nazis agreed. (The man Kolbe saved is said to have survived the Holocaust.)

All 10 of the men—including Kolbe—were put into Starvation Cell 18. Two weeks later, when the door was opened, only Kolbe had survived. The story spread throughout the camp, and Kolbe became an inspiration to the inmates. To squelch the hope he had given the others, Kolbe was executed by lethal injection.

In 1982, Kolbe was canonized by the Catholic Church. Some critics—mindful of his earlier anti-Semitic rhetoric—still consider Kolbe's sainthood controversial. But most Poles feel he redeemed himself for his earlier missteps through this noble act at the end of his life.

children—like the girl in the bottom row on the right—were either "Germanized" in special schools or, if younger, adopted by German families. Dr. Josef Mengele conducted experiments on children, especially twins and triplets, to try to figure out ways to increase fertility for German mothers.

Block 7 shows **living and sanitary conditions** at the camp—which you'll see in more detail later at Birkenau. Blocks 8–10 are vacant (medical experiments were carried out in Block 10).

Step into the **courtyard** between Blocks 10 and 11. The wall at the far end is where the Nazis shot several thousand political prisoners, leaders of camp resis-

tance, and religious leaders. Notice that the windows are covered, so that nobody could witness the executions. Also take a close look at the memorial—the back of it is made of a material designed by Nazis to catch the bullets without a ricochet. Inmates were shot at short range—about three feet. The pebbles represent prayers from Jewish visitors.

The most feared place among prisoners was the **"Death Block"** (#11), from which nobody ever left alive. In Room 5, you can see how prisoners lived in these barracks—three-level bunks, with three prisoners sleeping in each bed (they had to sleep on their sides so they could fit). Death here required a trial (the room in which sham trials were held—lasting about 2 minutes each—is on display). In Room 6, people undressed before they were executed. In the basement, you'll see several different types of cells. The Starvation Cell (#18) held prisoners selected to starve to death when a fellow prisoner escaped; Maksymilian Kolbe spent two weeks here to save a man's life (see sidebar). In the Dark Cell (#20), which held up to 30, people had only a small window for ventilation—and if it became covered with snow, the prisoners suffocated. At the end of the hall in Cell 21, you can see where a prisoner scratched a crucifix (left) and image of Jesus (right) on the wall. In the Standing Cells (#22), four people would be forced to stand together for hours at a time (of course, the bricks went all the way to the ceiling then). Upstairs is an exhibit on resistance within the camp.

Before you leave Auschwitz, visit the **crematorium** (from Block 11, exit straight ahead and go past the first row of barracks, then turn right and go straight on the road between the two rows of barracks; pass through the gap in the fence and look for the chimney on your left). People undressed outside, or just inside the door. Up to 700 people at a time could be gassed here. Inside the door, go into the big room on the right. Look for the vents in the ceiling—this is where the SS men dropped the Zyklon-B. Through the door is a replica of the furnace. This facility could burn 340 bodies a day—so it took two days to burn all of the bodies from one round of executions. The Nazis didn't like this inefficiency, so they built four more huge crematoria at Birkenau.

Shortly after the war, camp commander Rudolf Höss was tried, convicted, and sentenced to death. Survivors requested that he be executed at Auschwitz. In 1947, he was hanged. These **gallows** are preserved behind the crematorium (about a hundred yards from his home where his wife—who loved her years here—read stories to their children, very likely by the light of a human-skin lampshade).

Take your time with Auschwitz I. When you're ready, continue to the second stage of the camp—Birkenau (see "Getting from Auschwitz I to Birkenau," page 319).

Auschwitz II—Birkenau

In 1941, when the original Auschwitz camp got to be too small for the capacity the Nazis envisioned, they began a second camp in some nearby farm fields. The original plan was for a camp that could hold 200,000 people, but at its peak, Birkenau (Brzezinka) held only about 100,000. They were still adding onto it when the camp was liberated in 1945.

Train tracks lead past the main building and into the camp. The first sight that greeted prisoners was the **guard tower** (familiar to many visitors from the stirring scenes in *Schindler's List*). Climb to the top of the entry building (also houses WCs and bookstore) for an overview of the massive camp. As you look over the camp, you'll see a vast field of chimneys and a few intact wooden and brick barracks. The train tracks lead straight back to the dividing platform, and then dead-end at the ruins of the crematorium and camp monument at the far side.

Some of the barracks were destroyed by Germans. Most were dismantled to be used for fuel and building materials shortly after the war. But the first row has been reconstructed (using components from the original structures). Visit the barracks on the right.

The first of these barrack buildings was the **latrine:** The front half of the building contained washrooms, and the back was a row of toilets. There was no running water; prisoners were in charge of keeping these clean. Because of the unsanitary conditions and risk of disease, the Nazis were afraid to come in here—so it was the heart of the black market and the inmates' resistance movement.

The fourth **barrack** was a bunk building. Each inmate had a personal number, a barrack number, and a bed number. Inside, you can see the beds (angled so that more could fit). An average of 400 prisoners—but up to

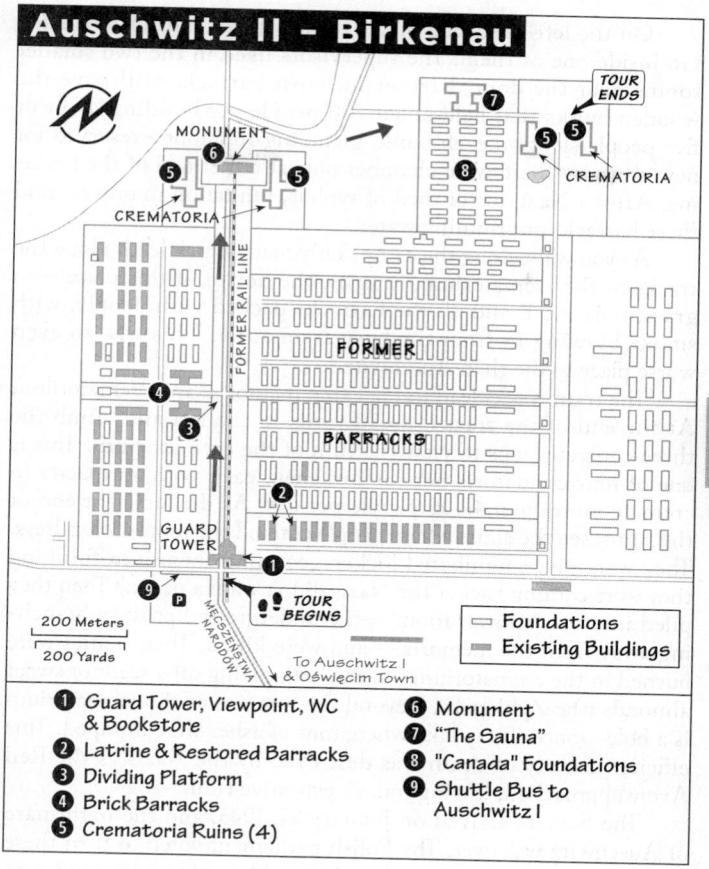

1,000—would be housed in each of these buildings. These wooden structures, designed as stables by a German company (look for the horse-tying rings on the wall), came in prefab pieces that made them cheap and convenient. Two chimneys connected by a brick duct provided a little heat. The bricks were smoothed by inmates who sat here to catch a bit of warmth.

Follow the train tracks toward the monument about a half-mile away, at the back end of Birkenau. At the intersection of these tracks and the perpendicular gravel road (halfway to the monument) was the gravel **dividing platform.** A Nazi doctor would stand facing the guard tower and evaluate each prisoner. If he pointed to the right, the prisoner was sentenced to death, and trudged—unknowingly—to the gas chamber. If he pointed to the left, the person would be registered and live a little longer. It was here that families from all over Europe were torn apart forever.

On the left-hand side of the tracks are some **brick barracks.** Go inside one of them. The supervisors lived in the two smaller rooms near the door. Farther in, most barracks still have the wooden bunks that held about 700 people per building. Four or five people slept on each bunk, including the floor—reserved for new arrivals. There were chamber pots at either end of the building. After a Nazi doctor died of typhus, sanitation improved, and these barracks got running water.

As you walk along the camp's only road, which leads along the tracks to the crematorium, imagine the horror of this place—no grass, only mud, and all the barracks packed with people, with smoke blowing in from the busy crematoria. This was an even worse place to die than Auschwitz I.

The train tracks lead to the camp memorial and crematorium. At the end of the tracks, go 50 yards to the left and climb the three concrete steps to view the ruin of the **crematorium.** This is one of four crematoria here at Birkenau, each with a capacity to cremate more than 4,400 people per day. At the far-right end of the ruins, see the stairs where people entered the rooms to undress. They were given numbered lockers, conning them into thinking they were coming back. (The Nazis didn't want a panic.) Then they piled into the "shower room"—the underground passage branching away from the memorial—and were killed. Their bodies were burned in the crematorium (on the left), giving off a scent of sweet almonds (the Zyklon-B). Beyond the remains of the crematorium is a hole—once a gray lake where tons of ashes were dumped. This efficient factory of death was destroyed by the Nazis as the Red Army approached, leaving today's evocative ruins.

The Soviets arrived on January 27, 1945, and the nightmare of Auschwitz was over. The Polish parliament voted to turn these grounds into a museum, so that the world would understand, and never forget, the horror of what happened here. The **monument** at the back of the camp, built in 1967 (by the communist government in its heavy "Social Realist" style), represents gravestones and the chimney of a crematorium. The plaques, written in each of the languages spoken by camp victims (including English, far right), explain that the memorial is "a cry of despair and a warning to humanity."

With more time, you could continue deeper into the camp—to the reception and disinfection building that prisoners called **"the Sauna"** (the long building with four chimneys). It was here that prisoners would be forced to strip and be de-loused; their belong-

On the Way to Auschwitz: The Polish Countryside

You'll spend about an hour gazing out the window as you drive or ride to Auschwitz. This may be your only real look at the Polish countryside. Ponder these thoughts about what you're passing...

The small houses you see are traditionally inhabited by three generations at the same time. Nineteenth-century houses (the few that survive) often sport blue stripes. Back then, parents announced that their daughters were now eligible by getting out the blue paint. Once they saw these blue lines, local boys were welcome to come a-courtin'.

Big churches mark small villages. Tiny roadside memorials and crosses indicate places where fatal accidents have occurred.

Polish farmers traditionally had small lots that were notorious for not being very productive. These farmers somewhat miraculously survived the communist era without having to merge their farms. For years, they were Poland's sacred cows: producing little, paying almost no tax, and draining government resources. But since Poland joined the European Union in 2004, they're being forced to get up to snuff...and, in many cases, collectivize their farms after all.

Since most people don't own cars, bikes are common and public transit is excellent. There are lots of bus stops, as well as minibuses that you can flag down anywhere for a 2-zł ride. The bad roads are a legacy of communist construction, exacerbated by heavy truck use and brutal winters.

Poland has more than 2,000 counties, or districts, each with its own coat of arms; you'll pass several along the way. The forests are state-owned, and locals enjoy the right to pick berries in the summer and mushrooms in the autumn (you may see people—often young kids—selling their day's harvest by the side of the road). The mushrooms are dried and then boiled to make tasty soups in the winter.

ings were seized and taken to the "Canada" warehouses to be sorted. Walking through here (on glass floors designed to protect the original structure below), you'll see artifacts of the queasy efficiency with which prisoners were "processed"—their heads were shaved, they were tattooed with a serial number, and they were assigned uniforms and wooden clogs to wear. Portraits at the end of the building humanize those who passed through here. Look for the cart, which was used to dispose of ashes. In front of the Sauna is a field of foundations of the **"Canada" warehouses.** Nearby are the other two destroyed **crematoria.**

Auschwitz Connections

Remember that the Auschwitz Museum is in the town of Oświęcim, about 50 miles west of Kraków.

From Kraków to Auschwitz

The easiest way to reach Auschwitz is with a package tour or private guide or driver (described on page 257). But if you're using public transportation, here are your options:

Frequent **buses** connect Kraków and Auschwitz, mostly run by PKS Oświęcim (11 zł, at least hourly, 1.75 hrs, get the most recent schedule at any Kraków TI, buses depart from Kraków's main bus station behind the train station). Buy a one-way ticket from the driver to leave your options open for getting home. Look for buses to "Oświęcim" (not necessarily "Auschwitz"). Note that these buses can be full, and since most come from other towns, there's no way to reserve a seat—so line up early (generally about 15 min ahead). If you don't get on a bus, you'll have to wait for the next one. Once in the town of Oświęcim, buses from Kraków stop first at the train station, then continue on to one of two stops near the museum: About half of the buses go directly into the parking lot at the museum itself, while the rest use a low-profile bus stop on the edge of the Auschwitz camp grounds (you'll see a small *Muzeum Auschwitz* sign on the right just before the stop, and a blue *Oświęcim Muzeum PKS* sign on the stop itself). From this bus stop, follow the sign down the road and into the parking lot; the main museum building is across the lot on your left. Note that since some buses don't actually go into the museum's parking lot, the Auschwitz stop can be easy to miss—don't be shy about letting your driver know where you want to go: *"Muzeum?"*

Several **minibuses** from Kraków head for Auschwitz (7.10 zł, sporadic departures—generally 1–2/hr, 1.75 hrs). Like the buses, some go right to the museum, while others use the bus stop at the edge of camp (see above). These generally depart from the lower platform of the main bus station (but confirm the departure point at the TI).

You could ride the **train** to Oświęcim, but it's less convenient than the bus because it leaves you at the train station, farther from the museum (8/day, less Sat–Sun, 1.5 hrs, 11 zł).

If you wind up at the **Oświęcim train station,** it's about a 20-minute walk to the camp (turn right out of station, go straight, then turn left at roundabout, camp is several blocks ahead on left). Or you can take a taxi (around 15 zł).

Returning from Auschwitz to Kraków

Upon arrival at Auschwitz I, visit the information window inside the main building (halfway down the main entry hall, on the right, in the back corner behind the tables). They can give you a schedule of departures and explain where the bus or minibus leaves from. (If you'll be staying late into the afternoon, make a point of figuring out the last possible bus or train back to Kraków, and plan accordingly.) Remember to allow enough time to make it from Birkenau back to Auschwitz I to catch your bus.

Some buses and minibuses back to Kraków do not leave from the camp parking lot itself (though some buses do). Instead, you'll most likely catch the bus from the stop on the edge of the Auschwitz I grounds. To reach this bus stop, leave the Auschwitz I building through the main entry and walk straight along the parking lot, then turn right on the road near the end of the lot. At the dead end, cross the street to the little bus stop with the blue *Oświęcim Muzeum PKS* sign. Don't be distracted by the ads for a nearby travel agency—you can buy tickets on board. Note that there's no public transportation back to Kraków from Birkenau, where most people end their tours; you'll have to take the shuttle bus back to Auschwitz I first.

WARSAW

Warszawa

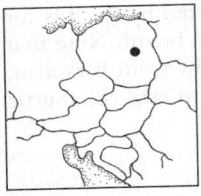

Warsaw (Warszawa, vah-SHAH-vah in Polish) is Poland's capital and biggest city. It's huge, famous, and important...but not particularly romantic. If you're looking for Old World quaintness, head for Kraków. If you're tickled by spires and domes, get to Prague. But if you want to experience a truly 21st-century city, Warsaw's your place.

Stroll down revitalized boulevards that evoke the city's glory days, pausing at an outdoor café to sip coffee and nibble at a *pączki* (the classic Polish jelly doughnut). Commune with the soul of Poland through its artists (at the National Museum), its favorite composer (at the Chopin Museum), its dramatic history (at the Warsaw Historical Museum and Warsaw Uprising Museum), and its Jewish story (in the former Jewish Ghetto). And ponder the wide range of Warsaw's postwar urban architecture, from dreary communist monstrosities to designer shopping malls.

Like Berlin, Warsaw is modernizing—fast. Mindful of its history, yet optimistic about its future, Warsaw has happily emerged from a long hibernation. Varsovians are embracing their role as the capital city of an influential nation in the "New Europe." The European Union has two universities aimed at educating future political leaders (or "Eurocrats"). One is in Bruges, Belgium, just down the road from the EU capital of Brussels. The other one is right here. You can almost feel Warsaw peeling back the layers of communist grime as it replaces potholed highways with pedestrian-friendly parks. Today's Warsaw also has gleaming new skyscrapers and street signs, stylishly dressed locals, cutting-edge shopping malls, swarms of international

businesspeople, and a gourmet coffee shop on every corner. And now the city is gaining a futuristic new stadium and an even more spiffed-up infrastructure as it prepares to host the Euro 2012 soccer championship.

Warsaw has good reason to be a city of the future: The past hasn't been very kind. Since becoming Poland's capital in 1596, Warsaw has seen wave after wave of foreign rulers and invasions—especially during the last hundred years. But in this horrific crucible, the enduring spirit of the Polish people was forged. As one proud Varsovian told me, "Warsaw is ugly because its history is so beautiful."

The city's darkest days came during the Nazi occupation of World War II. First, its Jewish residents were forced into a tiny ghetto. They rose up...and were slaughtered. Then, its Polish residents rose up...and were slaughtered. Hitler sent word to systematically demolish this troublesome city. At the war's end, Warsaw was devastated. An estimated 800,000 residents were dead—almost two out of every three Varsovians.

The Poles almost gave up on what was then a pile of rubble to build a brand-new capital city elsewhere. But ultimately they decided to rebuild, creating a city of contrasts: painstakingly restored medieval lanes, crumbling communist apartment blocks (*bloki* in Polish), and sleek, super-modern, glass-and-steel skyscrapers. Between the buildings, you'll find fragments of a complex, sometimes tragic, and often inspiring history.

A product of its complicated past, sprinkled with the big-city style and sophistication of its present, Warsaw remains quintessentially Polish. It is a place worth grappling with to understand the Poland of today...and the Europe of tomorrow.

Planning Your Time

Warsaw can easily fill two or three days, but if you're pressed for time, one full day is enough for most people. Get your bearings by taking a stroll through Polish history on the Royal Way, using my self-guided walk. Then enjoy the Old Town area. Visit other sights according to your interests: Polish artists, Holocaust history, the Warsaw Uprising, royalty, or Chopin. To slow down and take a break from the city, relax in Łazienki Park.

Orientation to Warsaw

(area code: 022)

Warsaw sprawls with 1.7 million residents. Everything is on a big scale—it seems to take forever to walk just a few "short" blocks. Get comfortable with public transportation and plan your sightseeing wisely to avoid backtracking.

Virtually everything of interest to travelers is on a mild hill on the west bank of the Vistula River. The city's central train station (Warszawa Centralna) is in the shadow of its biggest landmark: the can't-miss-it, skyscraping Palace of Culture and Science. From here, the avenue called aleja Jerozolimskie runs east toward the river, past the National Museum. It crosses the "Royal Way" boulevard, which connects the sights in the north (Old Town and New Town) with those in the south (Łazienki Park, and at the outskirts of town, Wilanów Palace). Most major sights and recommended hotels and restaurants are along this axis (Royal Way and aleja Jerozolimskie).

Another tip: You'll hear about two distinct uprisings against the Nazis during World War II. They're easy to confuse, but try to keep them straight: the **Ghetto Uprising** was staged by Warsaw's dwindling Jewish population in the spring of 1943 (see page 364); the **Warsaw Uprising,** a year later, was led by the (mostly non-Jewish) Polish Home Army (see page 368).

Tourist Information

Warsaw's helpful, youthful TI has three offices: on the **Royal Way** near Castle Square (daily May–Sept 9:00–20:00, Oct–April 9:00–18:00, Krakowskie Przedmieście 65), at the **central train station** (daily May–Sept 8:00–20:00, Oct–April 8:00–18:00), and at the **airport** (same hours as central train station TI). The general information number for all TIs is 19431 from inside Warsaw, or 022-19431 from outside Warsaw (www.warsawtour.pl). All of the branches offer several free, useful materials: a city map (with key phone numbers on the back), a well-produced booklet called *Warsaw: In Short,* and a series of brochures on sights and activities ("city breaks," Jewish heritage, Chopin, and so on, as well as info for kids, active types, and wheelchair-users). The TI also has a free room-booking service.

Warsaw has a thriving live-music scene. Ask the TI for a weekly performance schedule. For light, enjoyable music events in summer, consider the Chopin concerts in Łazienki Park (only on

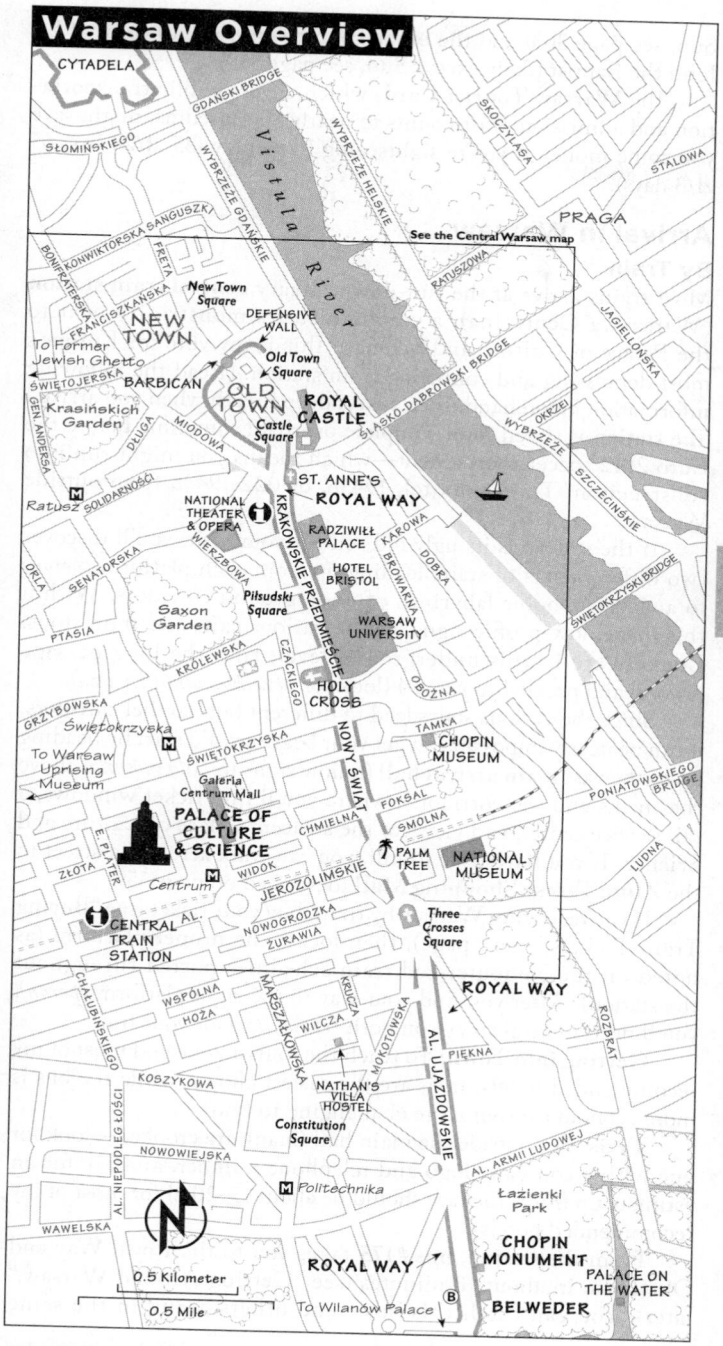
Warsaw Overview
CYTADELA
GDAŃSKI BRIDGE
SŁOMIŃSKIEGO
WYBRZEŻE GDAŃSKIE
Vistula River
WYBRZEŻE KIELSKIE
SKOCZYLASA
STALOWA
PRAGA
SANGUSZKI
KONWIKTORSKA
BONIFRATERSKA
FRETA
See the Central Warsaw map
RATUSZOWA
New Town Square
FRANCISZKAŃSKA
NEW TOWN
DEFENSIVE WALL
To Former Jewish Ghetto
ŚWIĘTOJERSKA
BARBICAN
Old Town Square
OLD TOWN
ROYAL CASTLE
Castle Square
JAGIELLOŃSKA
ŚLĄSKO-DĄBROWSKI BRIDGE
Krasińskich Garden
GEN. ANDERSA
DŁUGA
MIODOWA
OKRĘŻE
WYBRZEŻE SZCZECIŃSKIE
Ratusz
SOLIDARNOŚCI
ST. ANNE'S
ROYAL WAY
NATIONAL THEATER & OPERA
KRAKOWSKIE PRZEDMIEŚCIE
RADZIWIŁŁ PALACE
KARÓWA
WIERZBOWA
HOTEL BRISTOL
BROWARNA
DOBRA
ORLA
SENATORSKA
Pilsudski Square
Saxon Garden
WARSAW UNIVERSITY
ŚWIĘTOKRZYSKI BRIDGE
PTASIA
KRÓLEWSKA
CZACKIEGO
HOLY CROSS
OBOŹNA
GRZYBOWSKA
Świętokrzyska
ŚWIĘTOKRZYSKA
NOWY ŚWIAT
TAMKA
CHOPIN MUSEUM
To Warsaw Uprising Museum
Galeria Centrum Mall
PALACE OF CULTURE & SCIENCE
FOKSAL
PONIATOWSKIEGO BRIDGE
CHMIELNA
SMOLNA
E. PLATER
ZŁOTA
Centrum
WIDOK
PALM TREE
NATIONAL MUSEUM
LUDNA
JEROZOLIMSKIE
AL.
CENTRAL TRAIN STATION
NOWOGRODZKA
ŻURAWIA
Three Crosses Square
ROYAL WAY
CHAŁUBIŃSKIEGO
WSPÓLNA
HOŻA
MARSZAŁKOWSKA
KRUCZA
WILCZA
MOKOTOWSKA
AL. UJAZDOWSKIE
ROZBRAT
PIĘKNA
KOSZYKOWA
NATHAN'S VILLA HOSTEL
Constitution Square
AL. NIEPODLEGŁOŚCI
NOWOWIEJSKA
AL. ARMII LUDOWEJ
Politechnika
Łazienki Park
WAWELSKA
CHOPIN MONUMENT
0.5 Kilometer
ROYAL WAY
PALACE ON THE WATER
0.5 Mile
To Wilanów Palace
BELWEDER

Sun, see page 363) and the organ concerts in the Cathedral of St. John the Baptist (daily except Sun, see page 355).

The **Warsaw Tourist Card,** which covers public transportation and admission or discounts to nearly 30 museums, might save you some money if you're sightseeing like crazy (35 zł/24 hrs, 65 zł/3 days).

Arrival in Warsaw

By Train

Most trains arrive at the run-down, dreary **central train station** (Warszawa Centralna), a communist-era monstrosity next to the Palace of Culture and Science. This is my vote for Europe's most depressing and confusing train station. (Read the following information beforehand, then take a deep breath when you arrive.) The station is slated for a complete overhaul sometime before the Euro 2012 soccer tournament—which means you might run into construction. Train info: tel. 19436, or 022-19436 from outside Warsaw.

If the station is its ugly old self for your visit, you'll discover two different sets of stairs leading up from each platform *(peron)* to a claustrophobic labyrinth of underground corridors. Within this maze, low-profile signs lead to various exits and tram stops. **Lockers** are in this underground level; find the long passage beyond and parallel to *peron* 4 (look for *przechowalnia bagażu*).

Since the various stairs lead to different but parallel corridors, it can be nearly impossible to get your bearings. I'd start by heading up to the vast **main arrival hall** (follow signs to *hala główna,* above the tracks and the corridors), where you'll find ticket windows, a rail service center, and views of the adjacent Palace of Culture and Science. If you have time to kill, you can walk across the street to the **Złote Tarasy Shopping Mall** (described on page 359).

If you're leaving Warsaw by train, buy your ticket (see "Buying Train Tickets," next page), then locate the proper platform (as noted on the computerized train schedules posted throughout the station). After you find your way to the right platform *(peron),* you'll need to keep an eye on both tracks *(tor)* for your train.

Getting into Town: To reach the tourist zone and most of my recommended hotels, taxis are the easiest choice, while the bus is more economical (but more challenging to find).

Taxis wait outside the main hall (many are crooked—look for one with a company logo and telephone number, and ask for an estimate up front; the fare should be about 15–20 zł for most of my recommended hotels).

From the station, **bus #175** takes you to the Royal Way and Old Town in about 10 minutes (see "Getting Around Warsaw," later). You can catch this bus—and others going in the same

Warsaw Essentials

English	Polish	Pronounced
Warsaw	Warszawa	vah-SHAH-vah
Central Train Station	Warszawa Centralna	vah-SHAH-vah tsehn-TRAHL-nah
Palace of Culture and Science	Pałac Kultury i Nauki (or "simply Pałac")	PAH-wahts nah-OO-kee
New Town	Nowe Miasto	NOH-vay mee-AH-stoh
Old Town	Stare Miasto	STAH-reh mee-AH-stoh
Old Town Market Square	Rynek Starego Miasta	REE-nehk stah-RAY-goh mee-AH-stah
Royal Way	Szłak Królewski	shwock kroh-LEHV-skee
Popular restaurant street on Royal Way	Nowy Świat	NOH-vee SHVEE-aht
Attraction-lined street on Royal Way	Krakowskie Przedmieście	krah-KOHV-skyeh pzhehd-MYESH-cheh
Royal Castle	Zamek Królewski	ZAH-mehk kroh-LEHV-skee
Castle Square	Plac Zamkowy	plahts zahm-KOH-vee
Piłsudski Square	Plac Marszałka Józefa Piłsudskiego	plahts mar-SHAW-kah yoh-ZEH-fah pew-sood-SKYAY-goh
Łazienki Park	Park Łazienkowski	park wah-zhehn-KOV-skee
Vistula River	Wisła	VEES-wah

direction—in front of the skyscraper with the LOT airlines office and Hotel Marriott across busy aleja Jerozolimskie from the station. From the corridors under the main hall, carefully track *Al. Jerozolimskie* signs. Several different exits are marked this way, but if you hone in on *Hotel Marriott* signs, you'll reach a pedestrian underpass that pops you out just next to the bus stop. Note that it's easiest to buy your bus ticket in the underground zone (at any kiosk marked *RUCH*) before you surface.

Buying Train Tickets: Lining one wall of the main arrival hall (*hala główna*) are **ticket windows,** some of which are

designated for international tickets (*kasa międzynarodowa*). A much more user-friendly **customer service center** is in the corner (under the big, orange *Apteka Non Stop* sign). While it can be slower to buy tickets or make reservations here (take a number as you enter), staff members speak English and are generally more patient in helping explain your options. If you're in a hurry and the lines at the ticket windows in the main hall are way too long, you can find more ticket windows (marked *PKP*) in the maze of corridors under the station. Allow yourself plenty of time to wait in line to buy tickets. Some locals bypass these lines altogether and buy their tickets on the train for an extra charge (about 7 zł extra; find the conductor before he finds you).

Note that even if you have a railpass, a reservation is still required on certain trains (including the express trains to Kraków)—if you're not sure, it's worth asking at the rail service center.

By Plane

Warsaw's **Fryderyk Chopin International Airport** (Port Lotniczy im. Fryderyk Chopina) is about six miles southwest of the center. The two main terminals are next to each other: Terminal 1 and the newer Terminal 2 (which handles most arrivals for both terminals). A third terminal, called Etiuda, is used by discount airlines. At the airport, you'll find a TI, ATMs, and exchange offices *(kantor)*.

From any terminal, **bus** #175 runs into the center (central train station, Royal Way, and Old Town; 2.80 zł, buy ticket at kiosk or from driver—though sometimes drivers can't make change and require the exact amount, 4–6/hr, 30–45 min). Only three **taxi** companies (MPT, Sawa, and Merc) are authorized to pick up arriving travelers at the airport; use a cab marked with one of these company names, and avoid random hucksters offering you a ride out front (these creeps are notorious for overcharging). The 30-minute taxi ride to the center shouldn't cost you more than 40 zł. The trip into town can take much longer during rush hour. Airport info: tel. 022-650-4220, www.lotnisko-chopina.pl.

To increase capacity for the Euro 2012 festivities, a new airport is being planned.

By Car

Warsaw is a stressful city to drive and park in. Arrange parking with your hotel, and get around by foot or public transit.

Getting Around Warsaw

By Public Transit: In this big city, it's essential to get a handle on public transportation. The Metro is mostly useless to tourists, but the buses and trams are great. All three systems use the

same tickets. A single ticket costs 2.80 zł (called *bilet jednorazowy,* good for one trip, no transfers); a 24-hour ticket costs 9 zł *(bilet dobowy)*; and a three-day ticket is 16 zł *(bilet trzydniowy).* For shorter trips, you can also buy time-limited tickets, such as the 2-zł "20-minute city travelcard" (*bilet 20-minutowy;* also available in 40- and 60-minute versions). Buy your ticket at any kiosk with a *RUCH* sign (and some others), and be sure to validate it as you board by inserting it in the little yellow box (24-hour and three-day tickets need only be validated the first time you ride). While you can usually buy the basic one-ride tickets from your bus or tram driver, it's best to purchase them before boarding, as drivers expect exact change and often run out of tickets. Some (but not all) buses have automated machines for buying tickets on board. Transit info: www.ztm.waw.pl.

Most of the city's major attractions line up on a single axis, the Royal Way, which is served by several different buses (but no trams). The designed-for-tourists **bus #180** conveniently connects virtually all of the significant sights and neighborhoods: the former Jewish Ghetto, Castle Square/Old Town, the Royal Way, Łazienki Park, and Wilanów Palace (south of the center). This particularly user-friendly bus lists sights in English on the posted schedule inside (other buses don't). **Bus #175** links the airport, the central train station, the Royal Way, and Old Town. Those two buses, as well as buses #116 and #195, go along the most interesting stretch of the Royal Way (between aleja Jerozolimskie and Castle Square in the Old Town). Bus routes beginning with "E" are express, so they go long distances without stopping.

Note that on Saturdays and Sundays in summer (June–Sept), the Nowy Świat section of the Royal Way is closed to buses, so the above routes take a detour along a parallel street.

By Taxi: As in most big Eastern European cities, it's wise to use only cabs that are clearly marked with a company logo and telephone number (or call your own: Locals like MPT Radio Taxi, tel. 19191; or Elle taxi, tel. 022-811-1111). All official taxis have similar rates: 6 zł to start, then 3 zł per kilometer (more after 22:00 or in the suburbs). The drop fee may be higher if you catch the cab in front of a fancy hotel.

Tours in Warsaw

Each year, new companies crop up offering **walking tours** in Warsaw. As none is well-established yet, get the latest advice from the TI. Various companies offer **bus tours** (which include some walking; 140 zł, 3 hrs, get information at TI or your hotel). A **tourist train** does a 30-minute circuit, leaving from in front of the Royal Castle (22 zł, daily May–Oct, doesn't run Mon Nov–April).

Warsaw at a Glance

▲▲**Royal Castle** Warsaw's best palace, rebuilt after World War II, but still retaining its former opulence and many original furnishings. **Hours:** May–Sept Mon–Sat 10:00–18:00, Sun 11:00–18:00; Oct–April Tue–Sat 10:00–16:00, Sun 11:00–16:00, closed Mon; oriental carpet exhibition open daily 12:00–16:00. See page 353.

▲▲**Old Town Market Square** Re-creation of Warsaw's glory days, with lots of colorful architecture. **Hours:** Always open. See page 356.

▲▲**National Museum** Collection of mostly Polish art, with unknown but worth-discovering works by Jan Matejko and the Młoda Polska (Art Nouveau) crew. **Hours:** Tue 10:00–17:00, Wed–Thu 10:00–16:00, Fri 12:00–21:00, Sat–Sun 12:00–18:00, closed Mon. See page 360.

▲**Castle Square** Colorful spot with whiffs of old Warsaw—Royal Castle, monuments, and a chunk of the city wall—and cafés just off the square. **Hours:** Always open. See page 352.

▲**Chopin Museum** Elegant old mansion with Chopin bric-a-brac and occasional piano concerts. **Hours:** Tue–Sun 12:00–21:00, Oct–April until 20:00, closed Mon. See page 362.

Self-Guided Walk

Warsaw's Royal Way

The Royal Way (Szłak Królewski) is the six-mile route that the kings of Poland used to take from their main residence (at Castle Square in the Old Town) to their summer home (Wilanów Palace, south of the center and not worth visiting). In the heart of the city, the Royal Way is a busy boulevard with two different names: At the south end, hip and vibrant **Nowy Świat** offers lots of shops and restaurants, and a good glimpse of urban Warsaw; to the north, and ending at the Old Town, **Krakowskie Przedmieście** is lined with historic landmarks and better for sightseeing.

Since this spine connects most hotels, restaurants, and sights, you'll almost certainly use it—on foot or by bus—sometime during your trip (key buses are noted earlier, under "Getting Around Warsaw"). This self-guided walk should make your commute more interesting. Not counting sightseeing stops, figure about 10 minutes to walk along Nowy Świat ("Part 1"), then another 20 minutes along Krakowskie Przedmieście to the Old Town ("Part 2").

▲**Łazienki Park** Lovely, sprawling green space with Chopin statue, peacocks, and Neoclassical buildings. **Hours:** Always open. See page 363.

▲**Warsaw Uprising Museum** High-tech exhibit tracing the history of the Uprising and celebrating its heroes. **Hours:** Mon, Wed, and Fri 8:00–18:00; Thu 8:00–20:00; Sat–Sun 10:00–18:00; closed Tue. See page 367.

Warsaw Historical Museum Glimpse of the city before and after World War II, with excellent movie in English. **Hours:** Museum—Tue and Thu 11:00–18:00, Wed and Fri 10:00–15:30, until 18:00 mid-July–Sept, Sat–Sun 10:30–16:30, closed Mon; Movie—Tue–Sun at noon. See page 356.

Palace of Culture and Science Huge "Stalin Gothic" skyscraper with a more impressive exterior than interior, housing theaters, multiplex cinema, observation deck, and more. **Hours:** Observation deck—daily June–Sept 9:00–20:00, until 23:00 Fri–Sat; Oct–May 9:00–18:00. See page 359.

Jewish Ghetto: Path of Remembrance Pilgrimage from Ghetto Heroes Square to the infamous Nazi "transfer spot" where Jews were sent to death camps. **Hours:** Always open. See page 366.

Royal Way Walk Part 1: Nowy Świat

Begin at the head of the boulevard called Nowy Świat, at the intersection with busy **aleja Jerozolimskie** ("Jerusalem Avenue"). This street once led to a Jewish settlement called New Jerusalem. Like so much else in Warsaw, it's changed names many times. Between the World Wars, it became "May 3rd Avenue," celebrating Poland's 1791 constitution (Europe's first). But this was too nationalistic for the occupying Nazis, who called it simply Bahnhofstrasse ("Train Station Street"). Then the communists switched it back to "Jerusalem"—strangely disregarding the religious connotations of that name. (Come on, guys—what about a good, old-fashioned "Stalin Avenue"?)

You can't miss the giant, out-of-place **palm tree** in the middle of aleja Jerozolimskie. When a local artist went to the real Jerusalem, she was struck at how many palm trees she saw there. She decided it was only appropriate that one

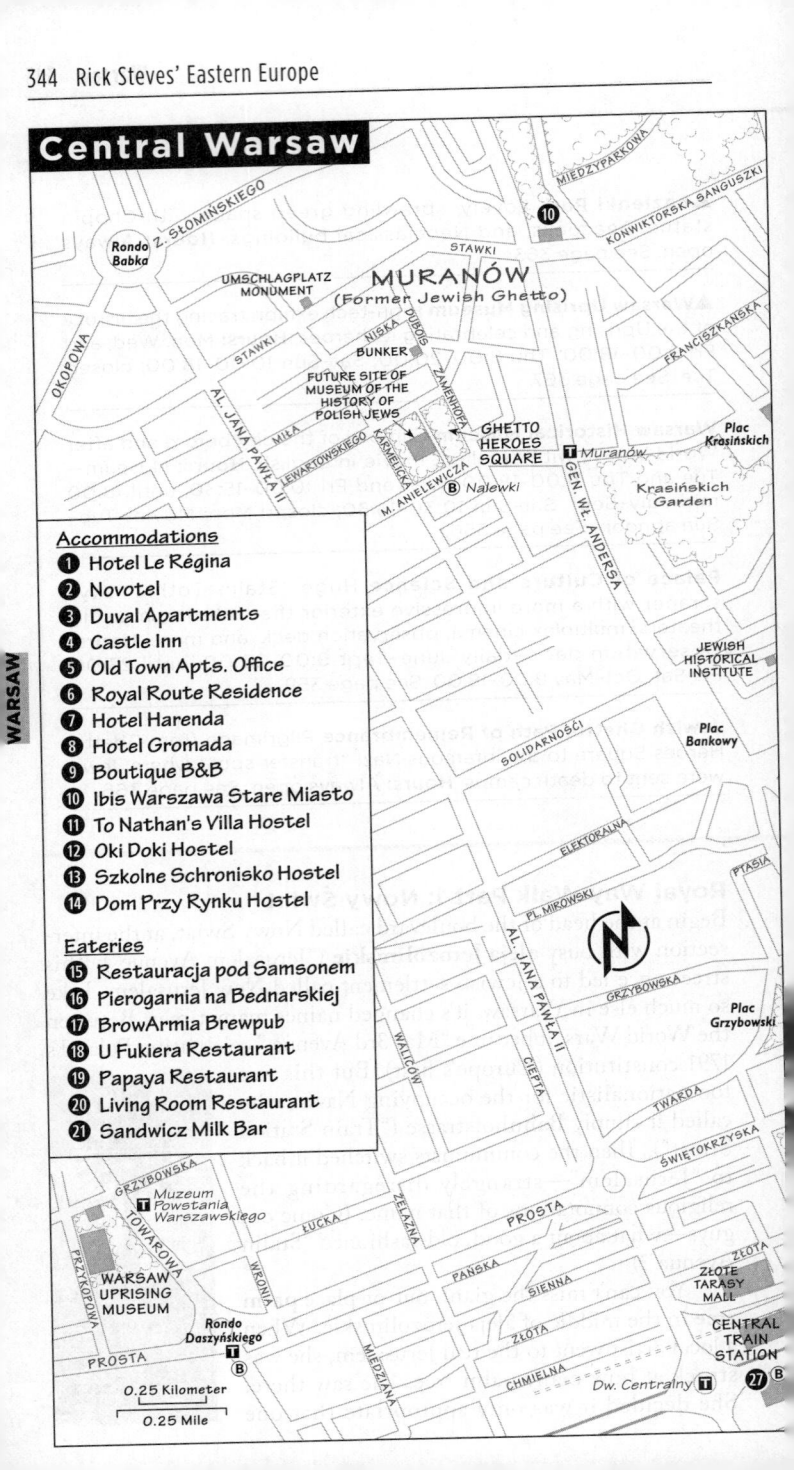
Central Warsaw
Rondo Babka
Z. SŁOMIŃSKIEGO
UMSCHLAGPLATZ MONUMENT
MURANÓW
(Former Jewish Ghetto)
STAWKI
MIĘDZYPARKOWA
KONWIKTORSKA
SANGUSZKI
FRANCISZKAŃSKA
OKOPOWA
NISKA
DUBOIS
BUNKER
ŻAMENHOFA
FUTURE SITE OF MUSEUM OF THE HISTORY OF POLISH JEWS
AL. JANA PAWŁA II
MIŁA
LEWARTOWSKIEGO
KARMELICKA
M. ANIELEWICZA
GHETTO HEROES SQUARE
Muranów
Nalewki
GEN. WŁ. ANDERSA
Plac Krasińskich
Krasińskich Garden
JEWISH HISTORICAL INSTITUTE
Plac Bankowy
SOLIDARNOŚCI
ELEKTORALNA
PTASIA
PL. MIROWSKI
AL. JANA PAWŁA II
GRZYBOWSKA
Plac Grzybowski
WALICÓW
CIEPŁA
TWARDA
ŚWIĘTOKRZYSKA
Accommodations
1 Hotel Le Régina
2 Novotel
3 Duval Apartments
4 Castle Inn
5 Old Town Apts. Office
6 Royal Route Residence
7 Hotel Harenda
8 Hotel Gromada
9 Boutique B&B
10 Ibis Warszawa Stare Miasto
11 To Nathan's Villa Hostel
12 Oki Doki Hostel
13 Szkolne Schronisko Hostel
14 Dom Przy Rynku Hostel
Eateries
15 Restauracja pod Samsonem
16 Pierogarnia na Bednarskiej
17 BrowArmia Brewpub
18 U Fukiera Restaurant
19 Papaya Restaurant
20 Living Room Restaurant
21 Sandwicz Milk Bar
WARSAW
GRZYBOWSKA
Muzeum Powstania Warszawskiego
ŁUCKA
ŻELAZNA
PROSTA
OWARNA
PRZYKOPOWA
WARSAW UPRISING MUSEUM
WRONIA
PAŃSKA
SIENNA
ZŁOTA
ZŁOTE TARASY MALL
Rondo Daszyńskiego
MIEDZIANA
CHMIELNA
CENTRAL TRAIN STATION
Dw. Centralny
0.25 Kilometer
0.25 Mile

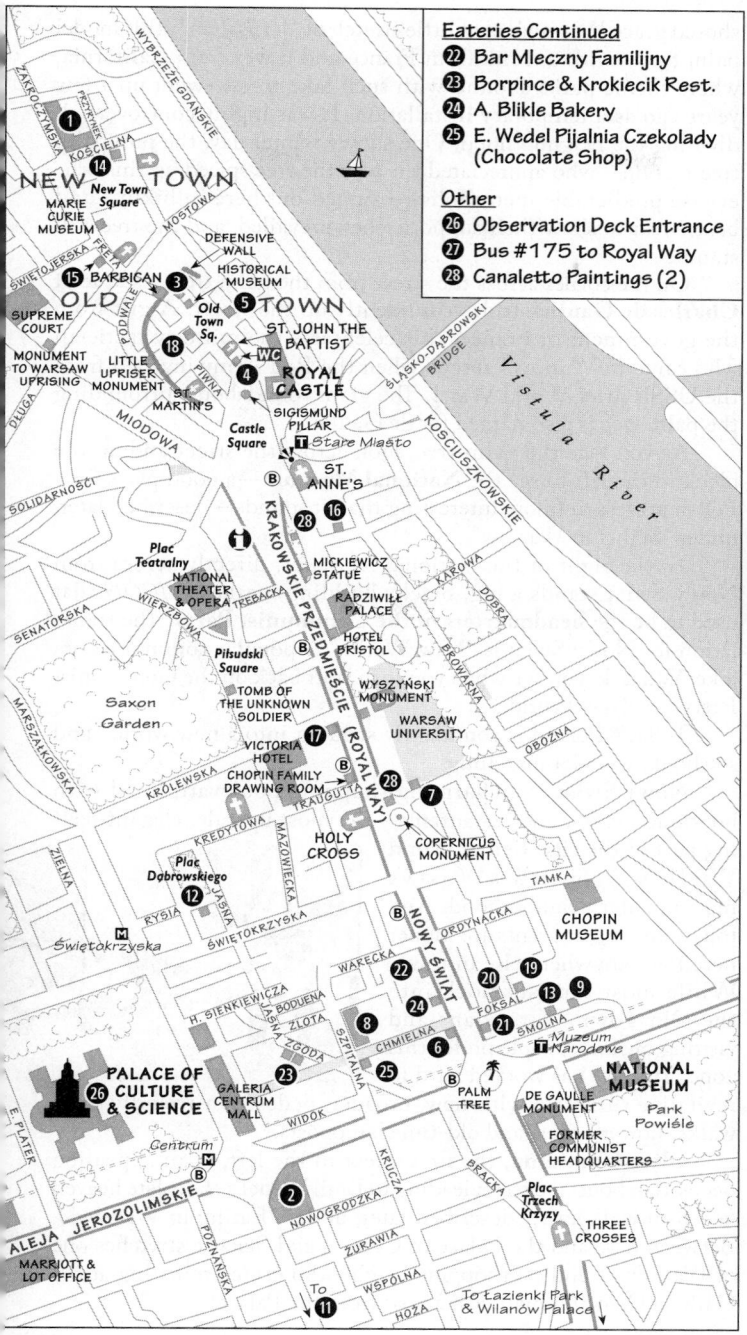
Eateries Continued
22 Bar Mleczny Familijny
23 Borpince & Krokiecik Rest.
24 A. Blikle Bakery
25 E. Wedel Pijalnia Czekolady (Chocolate Shop)
Other
26 Observation Deck Entrance
27 Bus #175 to Royal Way
28 Canaletto Paintings (2)
NEW TOWN
New Town Square
MARIE CURIE MUSEUM
DEFENSIVE WALL
HISTORICAL MUSEUM
BARBICAN
OLD TOWN
Old Town Sq.
SUPREME COURT
ST. JOHN THE BAPTIST
MONUMENT TO WARSAW UPRISING
LITTLE UPRISER MONUMENT
ST. MARTIN'S
ROYAL CASTLE
SIGISMUND PILLAR
Castle Square
Stare Miasto
ST. ANNE'S
Vistula River
Plac Teatralny
NATIONAL THEATER & OPERA
MICKIEWICZ STATUE
RADZIWIŁŁ PALACE
HOTEL BRISTOL
Piłsudski Square
Saxon Garden
TOMB OF THE UNKNOWN SOLDIER
WYSZYŃSKI MONUMENT
WARSAW UNIVERSITY
VICTORIA HOTEL
CHOPIN FAMILY DRAWING ROOM
KRAKOWSKIE PRZEDMIEŚCIE (ROYAL WAY)
HOLY CROSS
COPERNICUS MONUMENT
Plac Dąbrowskiego
Świętokrzyska
CHOPIN MUSEUM
NOWY ŚWIAT
Muzeum Narodowe
NATIONAL MUSEUM
PALACE OF CULTURE & SCIENCE
GALERIA CENTRUM MALL
PALM TREE
DE GAULLE MONUMENT
Park Powiśle
FORMER COMMUNIST HEADQUARTERS
Centrum
Plac Trzech Krzyży
THREE CROSSES
ALEJA JEROZOLIMSKIE
MARRIOTT & LOT OFFICE
To Łazienki Park & Wilanów Palace

should grace Warsaw's own little stretch of "Jerusalem." This model palm tree—with a trunk from France and leaves from California, where theme parks abound with such fake trees—went up a few years ago as a temporary installation. It was highly controversial, dividing the neighborhood. One snowy winter day, the pro–palm tree faction—who appreciated the way the tree spiced up this otherwise predictable metropolis—camped out here in bikinis and beachwear to show their support. They prevailed, and the tree still stands.

On the corner across the street from the palm tree, a statue of **Charles de Gaulle** strides confidently up the street. A gift from the government of France, this celebrates the military tactician who came to Warsaw's rescue when the Red Army invaded from the USSR after World War I. The giant roundabout surrounding the palm tree is also named for de Gaulle.

As you face the palm tree, look across the street and up the block to the left to see the **National Museum**—a good place for a Polish art lesson (more interesting than it sounds—described later, under "Sights in Warsaw").

To the right of the National Museum, directly across from Nowy Świat stands a big, blocky building marked *RICOH* that used to be the **headquarters of the Communist Party.** The translation for Nowy Świat is "New World." A popular communist-era joke: What do you see when you turn your back on the Communist Party? A "New World."

Today's Poland is confidently striding into a new world...and so should we. Get marching.

Nowy Świat is a charming shopping boulevard lined with boutiques, cafés, and restaurants—the most upscale, elegant-feeling part of the city. Before World War II, Nowy Świat was Warsaw's most popular neighborhood. And today, once again, rents are higher here than anywhere else in town. While most tourists flock into the Old Town, Varsovians and visiting businesspeople prefer this zone. The city has worked hard to revitalize this strip with new, broader, pedestrian-friendly sidewalks, flower boxes, and old-time lampposts.

Ulica Chmielna, the first street to the left, is an appealing pedestrian boutique street leading to Emil Wedel's chocolate heaven (a 5-min walk away; described later, under "Eating in Warsaw"). Between here and the Palace of Culture and Science stretches one of Warsaw's trendiest shopping neighborhoods (culminating at the Galleria Centrum mall, just across from the Palace).

Across the street from Chmielna (on the right) is the street called **Foksal,** which is emerging as one of Warsaw's most pleasant and trendy dining zones. On a balmy summer evening, this street is filled with chatty al fresco diners, sipping drinks and nibbling at plates of cutting-edge international cuisine (I've recommended some eateries here under "Eating in Warsaw," later).

A few steps down Nowy Świat, on the left, don't miss the recommended **A. Blikle** pastry shop and café—*the* place in Poland to buy sweets, especially *pączki* (rose-flavored jelly doughnuts; see page 377). If you're homesick for Starbucks, drop into one of the many gourmet coffee shops that line this stretch of Nowy Świat—with American-style lattes "to go."

A half-block down the street (on the left) is a rare surviving bit of pre-glitz Nowy Świat: Bar Mleczny Familijny, a classic **milk bar**—a government-subsidized cafeteria filled with locals seeking a cheap meal (described later, under "Eating in Warsaw"; for more about milk bars, see page 245). Don't be surprised if it's gone by the time you visit; in this high-rent district, it's unlikely that these few remaining holdovers from the old days will survive for much longer.

The next two blocks are more of the same. Eat and shop your way up Nowy Świat, until you reach the big Copernicus statue.

Royal Way Walk Part 2: Krakowskie Przedmieście

The street name changes to Krakowskie Przedmieście (roughly translated as "Suburb in the Direction of Kraków") at the big statue of **Copernicus,** in front of the Polish Academy of Science. Mikołaj Kopernik (1473–1543) was born in Toruń and went to college in Kraków. The Nazis stole this statue and took it to Germany (which, like Poland, claims Copernicus as its own). Now it's back where it belongs. Nearby, find the Canaletto painting of this same street scene in 1778, and compare it to today's reality. (Paintings like this were used to rebuild the city after World War II.)

We'll pass many churches along this route, but the **Church of the Holy Cross** is unique (Kościół Św. Krzyża, across from Copernicus, free entry). Composer Fryderyk Chopin's heart is inside one of the pillars of the nave (second big pillar on the left, look for the marker). After two decades of exile in France, Chopin's final wish was to have his heart brought back to his native Poland. During World War II, the heart was hidden away in the countryside for safety. Chopin's organs aside, this

church feels more alive than most. Locals often drop in. Check out the bright gold chapel, located on the left as you face the altar, near the front of the church. It's dedicated to a saint whom Polish Catholics believe helps them with "desperate and hopeless causes." People praying here are likely dealing with some tough issues. The beads draped from the altarpieces help power their prayers, and the many little brass plaques are messages of thanks for prayers answered. In the back-right corner (as you face the altar), behind the giant barbed wire, is a memorial to the 20,000 Polish POWs—mostly officers and prominent civilians—massacred by Soviet soldiers in 1940 near Katyń, a village in today's Russia.

Leave the church and cross the street (appreciating how pedestrian-friendly it's become in recent years). About a block up the street on the right, you'll see the gates (marked *Uniwersytet*) to the main campus of **Warsaw University,** founded in 1816. This area is a lively student district with plenty of bookstores and cafés.

The 18th century was a time of great political decline for Poland, as a series of incompetent foreign kings mishandled crises and squandered funds. But ironically, it was also Warsaw's biggest economic boom time. Along this boulevard, aristocratic families of the period built **mansions**—most of them destroyed during World War II and rebuilt since. Some have curious flourishes (just past the university on the right, look for the doorway supported by four bearded brutes admiring their overly defined abs.) Over time, many of these families donated their mansions to the university. (Across the street on the corner, look for the recommended BrowArmia brewpub, with some of the best people-watching al fresco tables on the Royal Way.)

The yellow church a block up from the university is the Church of the Nuns of the Visitation (Kościół Sióstr Wizytek). The monument in front commemorates **Cardinal Stefan Wyszyński,** who was the Polish primate (the head of the Polish Catholic Church) from 1948 to 1981. He took this post soon after the arrival of the communists, who opposed the Church, but also realized it would be risky for them to shut down the churches in such an ardently religious country. The Communist Party and the Catholic Church coexisted tensely in Poland, and when Wyszyński protested a Stalinist crackdown in 1953, he was arrested and imprisoned. Three years later, in a major victory for the Church, Wyszyński was released. He continued to fight the communists, becoming a great

hero of the Polish people in their struggle against the regime.

Farther up, you'll see the elegant, venerable **Hotel Bristol.** Leave the Royal Way briefly here to reach Piłsudski Square (a block away on the left, up the street opposite Hotel Bristol).

The vast, empty-feeling **Piłsudski Square** (Plac Marszałka Józefa Piłsudskiego) has been important Warsaw real estate for centuries, constantly changing with the times. In the 1890s, the Russians who controlled this part of Poland began construction of a huge and magnificent Orthodox cathedral on this spot. But soon after it was completed, Poland regained its independence, and anti-Russian sentiments ran hot. So in the 1920s, just over a decade after the cathedral went up, it was torn down again. During the Nazi occupation, this square took the name "Adolf-Hitler-Platz." Under the communists, it was Zwycięstwa, meaning "Victory" (of the Soviets over Hitler's fascism). When the regime imposed martial law in 1981, the people of Warsaw silently protested by filling the square with a giant cross made of flowers. The huge plaque in the ground near the road commemorates two monumental communist-era Catholic events on this square: John Paul II's first visit as pope to his homeland on June 2, 1979; and the May 31, 1981 funeral of Cardinal Stefan Wyszyński, whom we met across the street. The cross nearby also honors the 1979 papal visit, with one of his most famous and inspiring quotes to his countrymen: "Let thy spirit descend, let thy spirit descend, and renew the face of the earth—*this* earth" (meaning Poland, in a just-barely-subtle-enough dig against the communist regime that was tolerating his visit).

Stand near the giant plaque, with the Royal Way at your back, for this quick spin-tour orientation: Ahead are the Tomb of the Unknown Soldier and Saxon Garden (explained later); 90 degrees to the right is the old National Theater, eclipsed by a modern business center/parking garage; another 90 degrees to the right is a statue of Piłsudski (which you passed to get here—described later); and 90 more degrees to the right is the Victoria Hotel, the ultimate plush, top-of-the-top hotel where all communist-era VIPs stayed. To the right of the hotel, on the horizon, you can see Warsaw's newly emerging skyline. The imposing Palace of Culture and Science, which once stood alone over the city, is now joined by a cluster of brand-new skyscrapers, giving Warsaw a Berlin-esque vibe befitting its important role as a business center of the "New Europe."

Walk to the fragment of colonnade by the park that marks the **Tomb of the Unknown Soldier** (Grób Nieznanego Żołnierza). The colonnade was once part of a much larger palace built by the Saxon prince electors (Dresden's Augustus the Strong and his son), who became kings of Poland in the 18th century. After the palace

was destroyed in World War II, this fragment was kept to memorialize Polish soldiers. The names of key battles are etched into the columns, the urns contain dirt from major Polish battlefields, and the two soldiers are pretty stiff.

Just behind the Tomb is the stately **Saxon Garden** (Ogród Saski), inhabited by genteel statues and a spurting fountain. This park was also built by the Saxon kings of Poland. Like most foreign kings, Augustus the Strong and his son cared little for their Polish territory, building gardens like these for themselves instead of investing in more pressing needs. Poles say that foreign kings such as Augustus did nothing but "eat, drink, and loosen their belts" (it rhymes in Polish). According to Poles, these selfish absentee kings were the culprits for Poland's eventual decline.

Walk back out toward the Royal Way, stopping at the statue you passed earlier. In 1995, the square was again renamed—this time for **Józef Piłsudski** (1867–1935), the guy with the big walrus moustache. With the help of the French General de Gaulle (whom we met earlier), Piłsudski forced the Russian Bolsheviks out of Poland in 1920 in the so-called Miracle on the Vistula. Piłsudski is credited with creating a once-again-independent Poland after more than a century of foreign oppression, and he essentially ran Poland as a virtual dictator after World War I. Of course, under the communists, Piłsudski was swept under the rug. But since 1989, he has enjoyed a renaissance as many Poles' favorite prototype anti-communist hero (his name adorns streets, squares, and bushy-mustachioed monuments all over the country).

Return to Hotel Bristol, turn left, and continue your Royal Way walk. Next door to the hotel, you'll see the huge **Radziwiłł Palace.** The Warsaw Pact was signed here in 1955, officially uniting the Soviet satellite states in a military alliance against NATO. This building also serves as the Polish "White House," with the offices of Poland's figurehead

president, Lech Kaczyński. For more on Kaczyński—and his identical twin brother Jarosław—see page 243.

Beyond Radziwiłł Palace, you'll reach a statue (on a pillar) of **Adam Mickiewicz,** Poland's national poet. Polish high school students have a big formal ball (like a prom) 100 days before graduation. After the ball, if students come here and hop around the statue on one leg, it's supposed to bring them good luck on their finals. Mickiewicz, for his part, looks like he's suffering from a heart attack—perhaps in response to the impressively ugly National Theater and Opera a block in front of him.

At the end of the little park around the Mickiewicz statue, notice another before-and-after Canaletto painting of old Warsaw. The TI is across the street (on the left) and a few steps up. Continue to the end of the Royal Way, marked by the big pink palace. For a scenic finale to your Royal Way stroll, climb the 150 steps of the view tower by **St. Anne's Church** (4 zł, sporadic hours but generally open daily 10:00–18:00, in summer until 21:00 or 22:00 depending on weather, closed in bad winter weather, on the right just before Castle Square). You'll be rewarded with a great view of the Old Town, river, and Warsaw's skyline.

From St. Anne's Church, it's just another block—past inviting art galleries and restaurants—to the Castle Square, the TI, and the start of the Old Town.

Sights in Warsaw

The Old Town

In 1945, not a building remained standing in Warsaw's "Old" Town (Stare Miasto). Everything you see is rebuilt, mostly finished by 1956. Some think the Old Town feels artificial and phony, in a Disney World kind of way. For others, the painstaking postwar reconstruction feels just right, with Old World squares and lanes charming enough to give Kraków a run for its money. Before 1989, stifled by communist repression and choking on smog, the Old Town was an empty husk of its historic self. But now, the outdoor restaurants and market stalls have returned, and the locals and tourists are out strolling.

These sights are listed in order from south to north, beginning at the Castle Square and ending at the entrance to the New Town. For the best route from the central train station to the Old Town,

see the "Royal Way" self-guided walk, earlier.

▲Castle Square (Plac Zamkowy)—This lively square is dominated by the big, pink Royal Castle that is the historic heart of Warsaw's political power.

After the second great Polish dynasty—the Jagiellonians—died off in 1572, it was replaced by the Republic of Nobles (about 10 percent of the population), which elected various foreign kings to their throne. The guy on the 72-foot-tall **pillar** is Sigismund III, the first Polish king from the Swedish Waza family. In 1596, he relocated the capital from Kraków to Warsaw. This move made sense, since Warsaw was closer to the center of 16th-century Poland (which had expanded to the east), and because the city had gained political importance over the past 30 years as the meeting point of the Sejm, or parliament of nobles. Along the right side of the castle, notice the two previous versions of this pillar lying on a lawn. The first one, from 1644, was falling apart and had to be replaced in 1887 by a new one made of granite. In 1944, a Nazi tank broke this second pillar—a symbolic piece of Polish heritage—into the four pieces (still pockmarked with bullet holes) that you see here today. As Poland rebuilt, its citizens put Sigismund III back on his pillar.

Across the square from the castle, you'll see the partially reconstructed defensive wall. This rampart once enclosed the entire Old Town. Warsaw—like all of Poland—has seen invasion from all sides.

Explore the café-lined lanes that branch off Castle Square. Street signs indicate the year that each lane was originally built.

The first street leading off the square is **ulica Piwna** ("Beer Street"), where you'll find **St. Martin's Church** (Kościół Św. Martina, on the left). Run by Franciscan nuns, this church has a simple, modern interior. Notice the partly destroyed crucifix—all that survived World War II. Across the street and closer to Castle Square, admire the carefully carved doorway of Restauracja pod Gołębiami ("Under Doves")—dedicated to the memory of an old woman who fed birds amidst the Old Town rubble after World War II.

Back on the Castle Square, find the white **plaque** in the middle of the second block (by plac Zamkowy 15/19). It explains that 50 Poles were executed by Nazis on this spot on September 2, 1944. You'll see plaques like this all over the Old Town, each one commemorating victims or opponents of the Nazis. The brick

planter under the plaque is often filled with fresh flowers to honor the victims.

▲▲Royal Castle (Zamek Królewski)—A castle has stood here since the Mazovian dukes built a wooden version in the 14th century. It has shifted shape with the tenor of the times, being rebuilt and remodeled by many different kings. When Warsaw became the capital in 1596, this massive building served a dual purpose: It was both the king's residence and the meeting place of the parliament (Sejm). After it was destroyed in World War II, rebuilding began again in the 1950s and was not completed until the 1970s.

Warsaw's Royal Castle has a gorgeous interior—the most opulent I've seen in Poland. Many of the furnishings are original (hidden away when it became clear the city would be demolished in World War II). A visit to the castle is like perusing a great Polish history textbook. In fact, you'll likely see grade-school classes sitting cross-legged on the floors. Watching the teachers quizzing eager young history buffs, you can only imagine what it's like to be a young Pole, with such a tumultuous recent history.

The downside is that the castle can be more complicated to visit than it should be. The castle opening times, ticket options, and even layout are maddeningly unpredictable (though posted English descriptions help identify each room). Things frequently change, depending on special events, temporary exhibitions, the direction the wind is blowing, and the inexplicable whims of palace administrators. Don't be surprised if your experience doesn't match my self-guided tour.

Cost, Hours, Information: 22 zł, free on Sun; open May–Sept Mon–Sat 10:00–18:00, Sun 11:00–18:00; Oct–April Tue–Sat 10:00–16:00, Sun 11:00–16:00, closed Mon; last entry one hour before closing; Plac Zamkowy 4, tel. 022-355-5170, www.zamek-krolewski.com.pl. A public WC is on the courtyard just around the corner of the castle.

➲ Self-Guided Tour: You can use this commentary to follow the one-way route through the castle. But because the castle visit procedure is always changing, there's a good chance you won't see these rooms in this exact order; if that happens, match the labels in each room to the corresponding text below.

Head upstairs, where you'll begin wandering through two different types of royal apartments: public state rooms and private chambers. The **Great Assembly Hall** is heavy with marble and chandeliers. The **Knights' Hall** features the Polish Hall of

Fame, with paintings of great events and busts and portraits of VIPs—Very Important Poles. Just off of this room is the **Marble Room,** with more portraits of Polish greats.

Continuing back through the Knights' Hall, you'll wind up in the remarkable **Throne Room.** Notice the crowned eagle, the symbol of Poland, decorating the banner behind the throne. The Soviets didn't allow anything royal or aristocratic, so postwar restorations came with crown-less eagles. Only after 1989 were the crowns replaced (in the case of this banner, sewn on).

After four more grand rooms (including the King's Bedroom), you'll enter the **Canaletto Room,** filled with canvases of late-18th-century Warsaw painted in exquisite detail by this talented artist. These paintings came in handy when the city needed to be rebuilt. (This Canaletto, also known for his panoramas of Dresden, was the nephew of another artist with the same nickname, famous for painting Venice's canals.) Paintings like these helped post-WWII restorers resurrect the city from its rubble.

As you cross over to the other part of the castle, you'll pass some faded tapestries before entering a few rooms occupied by the **houses of parliament**—a reminder that this "castle" wasn't just the king's house, but also the meeting place of the legislature.

After several rooms, you'll reach the grand **Senators' Chamber,** with the king's throne, surrounded by different coats of arms. Each one represents a region that was part of Poland during its Golden Age, back when it was united with Lithuania and its territory stretched from the Baltic to the Black Sea (see the map on the wall). In this room, Poland adopted its 1791 constitution. It was the first in Europe, written soon after America's and just months before France's. And, like the Constitution of the United States, it was very progressive, based on the ideals of the Enlightenment. But when the final partitions followed in 1793 and 1795, Poland was divided between neighboring powers and disappeared from the map until 1918—so the constitution was never really put into action.

The next room features paintings by **Jan Matejko** that capture the excitement surrounding the adoption of this ill-fated constitution (for more on Matejko, see page 360). Finally, you'll wind through more rooms with paintings of great historical events and portraits of famous Poles.

Other Castle Sights: Consider a detour to the **Kubicki Arcades** (Arkady Kubiciego), the impressively excavated arcades deep beneath the castle. From the entrance lobby, head downstairs

to the area with the cloakroom, bathrooms, and bookshop, then find the long escalator that takes you down to the arcades. It's free to wander the long, cavernous, and newly clean and gleaming space, made elegant by grand drapes. To visit the exhibit branching off the arcade, which explains the excavation and refurbishment, you'll have to buy an 8-zł ticket (free on Sun, purchase from main ticket desk). I'd skip the exhibit and just enjoy the space.

The castle has a vast collection, which it organizes into various exhibitions—some permanent (well, as permanent as anything around here) and some temporary. The extensive **oriental carpet collection** in the "tin-roofed castle" (Pałac pod Blachą) is sparsely described and skippable for most (6 zł, free on Sun, open daily 12:00–16:00, last entry at 15:00, around the right side of the castle as you face it—past the two fallen columns, buy ticket at main ticket desk). When you're buying your castle ticket, keep an eye out for **temporary exhibits** of interest.

• *After you finish touring the castle and are ready to resume exploring the Old Town, turn left at the end of the square onto...*

St. John's Street (Świętojańska)—On the plaque under the street name sign, you can guess what the dates mean, even if you don't know Polish: This building was constructed from 1433 to 1478, destroyed in 1944, and rebuilt from 1950 to 1953.

• *Partway down the street on the right, you'll come to the big brick...*

Cathedral of St. John the Baptist (Katedra Św. Jana Chrzciciela)—This cathedral-basilica is the oldest (1339) and most important church in Warsaw. Poland's constitution was consecrated here on May 3, 1791. Much later, this church became the final battleground of the 1944 Warsaw Uprising—when a Nazi tank (appropriately named *Goliath*) drove into the church and intentionally exploded, massacring the rebels. You can still see part of that tank's tread hanging on the outside wall of the church (through the passage on the right side, near the end of the church).

Despite the church's historical significance, its interior is pretty dull (free, open to tourists daily 10:00–13:00 & 15:00–17:30, closed during services and

organ concerts). Typical of brick churches, it has a "hall church" design, with three naves of equal height. Look for the crucifix ornamented with real human hair (chapel left of high altar). The high altar holds a copy of the Black Madonna—proclaimed "everlasting queen of Poland" after a victory over the Swedes in the 17th century. The original Black Madonna is in Częstochowa (125 miles south of Warsaw)—a mecca for Slavic Catholics, who visit in droves in hopes of a miracle.

The cathedral also hosts organ **concerts** in summer (9 zł, May–late Sept Mon–Sat at 12:00, 25 min, no concerts Sun or late Sept–April).

• *Continue up the street and enter Warsaw's grand...*

▲▲Old Town Market Square (Rynek Starego Miasta)—Seventy-five years ago, this was one of the most happening spots in Central Europe. Sixty-five years ago, it was rubble. And today, like a phoenix from the ashes, it's risen to remind residents and tourists alike of the pre-war glory of the Polish capital.

Go to the **mermaid fountain** in the middle of the square. The mermaid is an important symbol in Warsaw—you'll see her everywhere. Legend has it that a mermaid *(syrenka)* lived in the Vistula River and protected the townspeople. While this siren supposedly serenaded the town, Varsovians like her more for her strength (hence the sword). In fact, the woman who modeled for this sculpture, Krystyna Krahelska (code name: "Danuta"), served as a paramedic for the Polish Home Army during the Warsaw Uprising. On the second day of the fighting, she was shot in the chest and died, becoming a martyr for the Polish people. But life goes on in Warsaw, as it always has. I've often seen children frolicking here, oblivious to the turmoil their forebears withstood. When the fountain gurgles, the kids giggle.

Each of the square's four sides is named for a prominent 18th-century Varsovian: Kołłątaj, Dekert, Barss, and Zakrzewski. These men served as "Presidents" of Warsaw (mayors, more or less), and Kołłątaj was also a framer of Poland's 1791 constitution. Take some time to explore the square. Enjoy the colorful architecture. Notice that many of the buildings were intentionally built to lean out into the square—to simulate the higgledy-piggledy wear and tear of the original buildings.

• *On the Dekert (north) side of the square is the...*

Warsaw Historical Museum (Muzeum Historyczne Warszawy)—This labyrinthine museum rambles through several

reconstructed buildings fronting the Old Town Market Square. Although parts of the exhibit were recently redone, the English descriptions are limited, making it all a bit difficult to appreciate. As you twist your way through room after room of historical bric-a-brac, keep an eye out for the model of 18th-century Warsaw, which is worth a close look. The final third of the collection, which focuses on the tumultuous 20th century, is the most updated—and the most interesting (8 zł, free on Sun, open Tue and Thu 11:00–18:00, Wed and Fri 10:00–15:30—until 18:00 mid-July–Sept, Sat–Sun 10:30–16:30, closed Mon, last entry 45 min before closing, Rynek Starego Miasta 28/42, tel. 022-635-1625).

Unless you're fascinated by Warsaw's history, I'd skip the museum collection and just buy the separate 6-zł ticket to watch the excellent 20-minute **film** in English, worth ▲▲; unfortunately, it runs only at 12:00 (Tue–Sun). With somber narration and black-and-white scenes from before, during, and after the wartime devastation, this film is best appreciated after you've had a chance to see some of today's Warsaw (especially along the Royal Way). The movie ends with, "They say that there are no miracles. Then what is this city on the Vistula?" Emotionally drained, you can only respond, "Amen."

• *Leave the square on Nowomiejska (at the mermaid's 2 o'clock, by the second-story niche sculpture of St. Anne). After a block, you'll reach the...*

Barbican (Barbakan)—This defensive gate of the Old Town, similar to Kraków's, protected the medieval city from invaders. Just outside the gate, you may be accosted by a pair of village idiots, dressed as **medieval executioners.** These unemployed (but undeniably creative) punks, in a sort of aggressive, costumed panhandling, will steer you to their "executioner's block" and playfully threaten to liberate your head from your body until you give them some pocket change. Actually, these guys speak English, and if you talk to them, they'll explain that at least two buildings within the Old Town really were used for executions once upon a time.

• *Once you've crossed through the barbican and have been granted a stay of execution, you're officially in Warsaw's...*

New Town (Nowe Miasto)—This 15th-century neighborhood is "new" in name only: It was the first part of Warsaw to spring up outside of the city walls (and therefore slightly newer than the Old Town). The New Town is a fun place to wander: Only a little less charming than the Old Town, but with a more real-life feel—like

people live and work here. It also has some good Polish restaurants that are cheaper than the Old Town options (described later, under "Eating in Warsaw"). Its centerpiece is the **New Town Square** (Rynek Nowego Miasta), watched over by the distinctive green dome of St. Kazimierz Church.

Scientists might want to pay homage at the museum (and birthplace) of Warsaw native **Marie Skłodowska-Curie** (1867–1934). This Nobel Prize winner was the world's first radiologist—discovering both radium and polonium (named for her native land) with her husband, Pierre Curie. Since she lived at a time when Warsaw was controlled by oppressive Russia, she conducted her studies in France. The museum—with photos, furniture, artifacts, and a paucity of English information—is a bit of a snoozer, best left to true fans (overpriced at 10 zł, Tue 8:30–16:00, Wed–Fri 9:30–16:00, Sat 10:00–16:00, Sun 10:00–15:00, closed Mon, ulica Freta 16).

From the New Town to Castle Square: You can backtrack the way you came, or, to get a look at Warsaw's back streets, consider this route from the big, round barbican gate (where the New Town meets the Old): Go back through the barbican and over the little bridge, turn right, and walk along the houses that line the inside of the wall. You'll pass a leafy garden courtyard on the left—a reminder that people actually live in the tourist zone within the Old Town walls. Just beyond the garden on the right, look for the carpet-beating rack, used to clean rugs (these are common fixtures in people's backyards). Go left into the square called Szeroki Dunaj ("Wide Danube") and look for another mermaid (over the Thai restaurant). Continue through the square and turn right at Wąski Dunaj ("Narrow Danube"). After about 100 yards, you'll pass the city wall. Just to the right (outside the wall), you'll see the monument to the **Little Upriser** of 1944, an imp wearing a grown-up's helmet and too-big boots, and carrying a machine gun. Children—and especially Scouts (Harcerze)—played a key role in the resistance against the Nazis. Their job was mainly carrying messages and propaganda.

Now continue around the wall (the upper, inner part is more pleasant). Admire more public art as you head back to Castle Square.

Near Nowy Świat and the Central Train Station

These sights are near Nowy Świat, within a few blocks of the central train station.

Palace of Culture and Science (Pałac Kultury i Nauki, or PKiN)—This massive skyscraper, dating from the early 1950s, is Poland's tallest building (760 feet). It was a "gift" from Stalin that the people of Warsaw couldn't refuse. Varsovians call it "Stalin's Penis"...using cruder terminology than that. (There were seven such "Stalin Gothic" erections in Moscow.) Because it was to be "Soviet in substance, Polish in style," Soviet architects toured Poland to absorb local culture before starting the project. Notice the frilly decorative friezes that top each level—evocative of Poland's many Renaissance buildings (such as Kraków's Cloth Hall). The clock was added in 1999 as part of the millennium celebrations. Since the end of communism, the younger generation doesn't mind the structure so much—and some even admit to liking it for the way it enlivens the new, predictable, glass-and-steel skyline springing up around it.

Everything about the Pałac is big. It's designed to show off the strong, grand-scale Soviet aesthetic and architectural skill. The Pałac contains various theaters (the Culture), museums of evolution and technology (the Science), a congress hall, a multiplex (showing current movies), an observation deck, and lots of office space. With all of this culture and science under one roof, it's a shame that none of it makes for worthwhile sightseeing. While the interior is highly skippable, viewing the building from the outside is a quintessential Warsaw experience, worth ▲▲.

If you're killing time between trains, you could zip up to the observation deck in 20 seconds on the retrofitted Soviet elevators. Better yet, snap a photo from down below and save your money—it's overpriced and the view's a letdown. While you'll get a nice overview of Warsaw's forest of new skyscrapers, you can hardly see the Old Town, and Warsaw's most prominent big building—the Pałac itself—is missing (20 zł, includes Polish-oriented special exhibitions; daily June–Sept 9:00–20:00, until 23:00 Fri–Sat for 5 zł less; Oct–May 9:00–18:00, enter through main door on east side of Pałac—opposite from train station, tel. 022-656-7600, www.pkin.pl).

Złote Tarasy Shopping Mall—Tucked behind the train station, "Golden Terraces" is a super-modern shopping mall with a funky, undulating glass-and-steel roof. Even though you didn't come all the way to Poland to visit a shopping mall, it's worth detouring here to get a taste of Poland's race into the future. In many ways, this—and not humble farmers munching pierogi—is the face of

Jan Matejko
(1838–1893)

Jan Matejko (yawn mah-TAY-koh) is Poland's most important painter, period. In the late 19th century, the nation of Poland had been dissolved by foreign powers, and Polish artists struggled to make sense of their people's place in the world. Rabble-rousing Romanticism seemed to have failed (inspiring many brutally suppressed uprisings), so Polish artists and writers turned their attention to educating the people about their history, with the goal of keeping their traditions alive.

Matejko was at the forefront of this so-called "positivist" movement. Matejko saw what the tides of history had done to Poland, and was determined to make sure his countrymen learned from it. He painted two types of works: huge, grand-scale epics depicting monumental events in Polish history; and small, intimate portraits of prominent Poles. Polish schoolchildren study history from books with paintings of virtually every single Polish king—all painted by the incredibly prolific Matejko.

Matejko is admired not for his technical mastery (he's an unexceptional painter), but for the emotion behind—and inspired by—his works. His paintings are utilitarian, straightforward, and dramatic enough to stir the patriot in any Pole. The intense focus on history by Matejko and other positivists is one big reason why today's Poles are still so in touch with their heritage.

You'll see Matejko's works in Warsaw's National Museum and Royal Castle, as well as in Kraków's Gallery of 19th-Century Polish Art (above the Cloth Hall). You can also visit his former residence in Kraków.

today's Poland (Mon–Sat 10:00–22:00, Sun 10:00–20:00, lots of designer shops, good food court on top level, www.zlotetarasy.pl).

▲▲National Museum (Muzeum Narodowe)—While short on big-name pieces, this museum interests art-lovers and offers a good, accessible introduction to some talented Polish artists who are largely unknown outside their home country.

Cost, Hours, Location: 12 zł, more for temporary exhibits, permanent collection free on Sat; open Tue 10:00–17:00, Wed–Thu 10:00–16:00, Fri 12:00–21:00, Sat–Sun 12:00–18:00, last entry 45 min before closing, closed Mon; 1 block east of Nowy Świat at aleja Jerozolimskie 3, tel. 022-629-3093, www.mnw.art.pl.

➲ Self-Guided Tour: On the ground floor are exhibits of ancient art (from Egyptian and Greek pieces to works by early Polish tribes), as well as room upon room of medieval altarpieces and crucifixes (including some of the most graphic ones I've seen). The upper floors have temporary exhibits and collections of Polish

and European decorative arts and European paintings. But the reason we're here is the Gallery of Polish Painting, one floor up. Focus on the two most important eras, at opposite ends of the building.

First, find the **Jan Matejko** room. From the lobby, take the left staircase up one level, then walk along the railing and go in the door on the left. Bear right through this door, then walk to the very back of this wing, where Matejko hides (if you can't find him, ask the guards, "mah-TAY-koh?"). On the way, you'll pass through a whole room of Napoleon portraits. The Poles loved Napoleon, who bravely marched on Russia in an era when this part of Poland was occupied and oppressed by the Russians...sadly, not for the last time.

The Matejko room is dominated by the enormous *Battle of Grunwald.* This epic painting commemorates one of Poland's high-water marks—the dramatic victory of a Polish-Lithuanian army over the Teutonic Knights, who had been terrorizing northern Poland for decades (for more on the Teutonic Knights, see page 434). On July 15, 1410, some 40,000 Poles and Lithuanians (led by the sword-waving Lithuanian in red, Grand Duke Vytautas) faced off against 27,000 Teutonic Knights (under their Grand Master, in white) in one of the medieval world's bloodiest battles. Matejko plops us right in the thick of the battle's chaos, painting life-size figures and framing off a 32-foot-long slice of the actual two-mile battle line.

In the center of the painting, the Teutonic Grand Master is about to become a shish kebab. Duke Vytautas, in red, leads the final charge. And waaaay up on a hill (in the upper right-hand corner, on horseback, wearing a silver knight's suit) is Władysław Jagiełło, the first king of the Jagiellonian dynasty...ensuring his bloodline will survive another 150 years.

Matejko spent three years covering this 450-square-foot canvas in paint. The canvas was specially made in a single seamless piece. This was such a popular work that almost as many fans turned out for its unveiling as there are figures in the painting.

From Poland's high point in the *Battle of Grunwald,* turn to the canvas immediately to the left, *Stańczyk after the Loss of Smolensk,* to see how Poland's fortunes shifted drastically a century later. This smaller, more intimate portrait by Matejko depicts a popular Polish figure: the court jester Stańczyk, who's smarter than the king, but not allowed to say so. This complex character, representing the national conscience, is a favorite symbol of Matejko's. Stańczyk slumps in gloom. He's just read the news (on the table beside him) that the city of Smolensk has fallen to the Russians after a three-year siege (1512–1514). The jester had tried to warn the king to send more troops, but the king was too busy partying

(behind the curtain). The painter Matejko—who may have used his own features for Stańczyk's face—also blamed the nobles of his own day for fiddling while Poland was partitioned.

Other Matejko paintings include one depicting the tragic couple of the last Jagiellonian king, Stanisław August Poniatowski (here identified as Sigismund Augustus), and his wife, Barbara—whom the king loved deeply, even though she couldn't bear him an heir. (In the next room, see the painful end to their sad tale: Barbara on her deathbed.)

Next, take a look at the **Młoda Polska** ("Young Poland") collection, featuring paintings from Poland's version of Art Nouveau (see page 266). It's in the same position as the Matejko room, only on the opposite side of the building: From the lobby, take the right staircase up, then go in the right-hand door, bear left, and work around all the way to the back. In addition to a room of works by movement headliner Stanisław Wyspiański, you'll see the hypnotic *Strange Garden* by Wyspiański's friend and rival, Józef Mehoffer. In the next room are several paintings by Jacek Malczewski, many of them depicting the goateed, close-cropped artist in a semi-surrealistic, Polish countryside context. There's also a room of canvases by the only prominent female Polish painter, Olga Boznańska (past the Wyspiański room)—with a softer and more impressionistic touch than her male Młoda Polska counterparts.

▲Chopin Museum (Muzeum Fryderyka Chopina)—The reconstructed Ostrogski Castle houses this museum honoring Poland's most famous composer. The museum recently enjoyed an extensive upgrade in preparation for the "Year of Chopin" in 2010, when all of Poland celebrates the composer's 200th birthday. The modern, well-presented exhibit tells the story of Chopin's life and music, and displays some of his manuscripts, letters, and original handwritten compositions. You'll also see a replica of Chopin's drawing room in Paris, and his last piano, which he used for composing during the final two years of his life (1848–1849). Chopin's bronze death mask features his distinctively Polish nose, shaped like an eagle's beak. Rounding out the museum are multimedia exhibits and a children's area. You might notice several Japanese visitors; Chopin's music is popular in Japan, and Japanese music-lovers flock here, almost as a pilgrimage (22 zł, free on Tue, open Tue–Sun 12:00–21:00, Oct–April until 20:00, closed Mon, 3 blocks east of Nowy Świat at ulica Okólnik 1, tel. 022-827-5473, www.chopin.museum).

In the cellar under the palace is a new **concert hall,** open for special concerts. If you're in town for one, go. There's nothing like hearing Chopin's music passionately played by a teary-eyed Pole who really feels the music (call museum to ask for concert schedule).

The **Ostrogski Castle** was destroyed down to the brick cellar

in World War II. A plaque by the staircase around back notes that it was "voluntarily reconstructed" by the communists in 1970 "to celebrate the 25th anniversary of the People's Republic of Poland." In the courtyard behind is a statue of a golden duck *(złota kaczka),* a mythical creature that supposedly lived in the castle's cellar. A strangely anticlimactic parable explains that this duck gave a cobbler's apprentice a huge amount of money, telling him that if he frittered it away by the end of the day, he'd win great riches. The boy gave some to a beggar, which didn't fit the duck's idea of "frittering"—but the boy found true happiness anyway.

Other Chopin Sights: Serious fans of the composer might enjoy two other Chopin sights. The **Chopin Family Drawing Room,** in the Royal Way apartment where Chopin lived with his family, is where he wrote and premiered many of his earliest compositions (3 zł, free on Wed, open Mon–Fri 10:00–18:00, closed Sat–Sun, upstairs in the Krasiński Palace—now the Academy of Fine Arts—at Krakowskie Przedmieście 5, tel. 022-320-0275). Chopin's tourable birth house is in **Żelazowa Wola,** 34 miles from Warsaw. While interesting to Chopin devotees, it's not worth the trek for most (7 zł, 39 zł also includes museum in Warsaw, Tue–Sun 9:00–16:00, closed Mon, tel. 046-863-3300). On summer weekends, the Chopin Museum sometimes runs a handy bus to visit the house (ask at the museum).

South of the Center

▲Łazienki Park (Park Łazienkowski)—This huge, idyllic park is where Varsovians go to play. The park is sprinkled with fun Neoclassical buildings, strutting peacocks, and young Poles in love. It was built by Poland's very last king (before the final partition), Stanisław August Poniatowski, to serve as his summer residence and provide a place for his citizens to relax.

On the edge of the park (along Belwederska) is a **monument to Fryderyk Chopin.** The monument, in a rose garden, is flanked by platforms, where free summer piano **concerts** are given weekly (mid-May–mid-Sept only, generally Sun at 12:00 and 16:00—confirm at TI). The statue shows Chopin sitting under a wind-blown willow tree. While he spent his last 20 years and wrote most of his best-known music in France, his inspiration came from wind blowing through the willow trees of his native land, Poland. The Nazis melted the original statue (from 1926) down for its metal. Today's copy was recast after World War II.

Warsaw's Jews and the Ghetto Uprising

From the Middle Ages until World War II, Poland was a safe haven for Europe's Jews. While other kings were imprisoning and deporting Jews in the 14th century, the progressive king Kazimierz the Great welcomed Jews into Poland, even granting them special privileges (see page 265).

By the 1930s, there were more than 380,000 Jews in Warsaw—nearly a third of the population (and the largest concentration of Jews in the world). The Nazis arrived in 1939. Within a year, they had pushed all of Warsaw's Jews into one neighborhood and surrounded it with a wall, creating a miserably overcrowded ghetto (crammed full of half a million people, including many from nearby towns). Over the next year, the Nazis brought in more Jews from throughout Poland, and the number grew by a million.

By the summer of 1942, more than a quarter of Warsaw's Jews had either died of disease, committed suicide, or been murdered. The Nazis started moving Warsaw's Jews (at the rate of 5,000 a day) into what they claimed were "resettlement camps." Most of these people were actually murdered at Treblinka or Auschwitz. After hundreds of thousands of Jews had been taken away, the waning population—now about 60,000—began to get word from concentration camp escapees about what was actually going on there. Spurred by this knowledge, Warsaw's surviving Jews staged a dramatic uprising.

On April 19, 1943, the Jews attacked Nazi strongholds and had some initial success—but within a month, the Nazis crushed the Ghetto Uprising. The ghetto's residents and structures were "liquidated." About 300 of Warsaw's Jews survived, thanks in part to a sort of "underground railroad" of courageous Varsovians.

Warsaw's Jewish sights are moving, but even more so if you know some of their stories. You may have heard of **Władysław Szpilman,** a Jewish concert pianist who survived the war with the help of Jews, Poles, and even a Nazi officer. Szpilman's life story was turned into the highly acclaimed, Oscar-winning 2002 film *The Pianist,* which powerfully depicts events in Warsaw during World War II.

Less familiar to non-Poles—but equally affecting—is the story of Henryk Goldszmit, better known by his pen name, **Janusz Korczak.** Korczak wrote imaginative children's books that are still enormously popular among Poles. He worked at an orphanage in the Warsaw ghetto. When his orphans were sent off to concentration camps, the Nazis offered the famous author a chance at freedom. Korczak turned them down, and chose to die at Treblinka with his children.

Savor this spot; it's great in summer, with roses wildly in bloom, and in autumn, when the trees provide a golden backdrop for the black, romantic statue.

Venture to the center of the park, where (after a 10-min hike) you'll find King Poniatowski's striking **Palace on the Water** (Pałac na Wodzie)—literally built in the middle of a river. Nearby, you'll spot a clever amphitheater with seating on the riverbank and the stage on an island. The king was a real man of the Enlightenment, hosting weekly dinners here for artists and intellectuals. But Poland's kings are long gone, and proud peacocks now rule this roost.

Getting There: The park is just south of the city center on the Royal Way. Buses #116, #180, and #195 run from Castle Square in the Old Town along the Royal Way directly to the park (get off at the stop called Łazienki Królewskie, by Belweder Palace—you'll see Chopin squinting through the trees on your left). Maps at park entrances locate the Chopin monument, Palace on the Water, and other park attractions.

Jewish Warsaw

After centuries of living peacefully in Poland, Warsaw's Jews suffered terribly at the hands of the Nazis. Several sights in Warsaw commemorate those who were murdered, and those who fought back. Because the Nazis leveled the ghetto, there is literally nothing left except the street plan, some monuments, and the heroic spirit of its former residents.

Ghetto Walking Tour—For a quick walking tour of the former ghetto site, begin at **Ghetto Heroes Square** (plac Bohaterow Getta). To get here from the Old Town you can hop a taxi (10 zł), take a bus (to Nalewki stop, bus #180 is particularly useful), or walk (go through barbican gate two blocks into New Town, turn left on Świętojerska, and walk straight 10 min—passing the new green-glass Supreme Court building—until you reach a grassy park on Zamenhofa Street). The square is in the heart of what was the Jewish ghetto—now surrounded by bland Soviet-style apartment blocks. After the uprising, the entire ghetto was reduced to dust by the Nazis—leaving the communists to rebuild to their own specifications. The district is called Muranów ("Rebuilt") today.

The **monument** in the middle of the square commemorates those who fought and died, "for the dignity and freedom of the Jewish Nation, for a free Poland, and for the liberation of humankind."

The big construction zone across the street is the future site of the **Museum of the History of Polish Jews,** slated to open in 2012. When finished, the cutting-edge museum will be one of Warsaw's best, and one of Europe's top Jewish museums (for the latest, see www.jewishmuseum.org.pl).

Facing the monument, head left (with the park on your left) up Zamenhofa—which, like many streets in this neighborhood, is named for a hero of the Ghetto Uprising. From the monument, you'll follow a series of three-foot-tall black stone monuments to uprising heroes—the **Path of Remembrance.** Like Stations of the Cross, each recounts an event of the uprising. Every April 19th (the day the uprising began), huge crowds follow this path. In a block, at the corner of Miła (partly obscured by some bushes), you'll find a **bunker** where organizers of the uprising hid (and where they committed suicide when the Nazis discovered them on May 8, 1943).

Continue following the black stone monuments up Zamenhofa (which becomes Dubois), then turn left at the corner and, later on that same block, cross busy Stawki street. A long block up Stawki and on the right, you'll see the **Umschlagplatz** monument—shaped like a cattle car. That's German for "transfer place," and it marks the spot where the Nazis brought Jewish families to prepare them to be loaded onto trains bound for Treblinka or Auschwitz (a harrowing scene vividly depicted in *The Pianist*). In the walls of the monument are inscribed the first names of some of the victims.

Jewish Historical Institute of Poland (Żydowski Instytut Historyczny)—For more in-depth information about Warsaw's Jewish community, including the Ghetto Uprising, visit this museum housed in the former Jewish Library building. The main floor displays well-described old photos. The 37-minute movie about life and death in the ghetto—played in English upon request—is graphic and powerful. Upstairs, you'll find more on Jewish art and culture, along with temporary exhibits (10 zł, Mon–Wed and Fri 9:00–16:00, Thu 11:00–18:00, closed Sat–Sun, last entry 30 min before closing, just north of Saxon Garden at ulica Tłomackie 3/5, tel. 022-827-9221, www.jhi.pl).

The Peugeot building next door—appropriately dubbed "the blue tower" by locals—was built on the former site of Warsaw's biggest synagogue, destroyed by the Nazis as a victorious final kick.

Warsaw Uprising Sights

While the 1944 Warsaw Uprising is a recurring theme in virtually all Warsaw sightseeing, two sights in particular—one a monument, the other a museum—are worth a visit for anyone with a special interest. Neither is right on the main tourist trail; the

monument is closer to the sightseeing action, while the museum is a tram or taxi ride away.

Warsaw Uprising Monument—The most central sight relating to the Warsaw Uprising is the monument at plac Krasińskich (intersection of ulica Długa and Miodowa, one long block and about a five-minute walk northwest of the New Town). Larger-than-life soldiers and civilians race for the sewers in a desperate attempt to flee the Nazis. Just behind the monument is the rusting copper facade of Poland's Supreme Court.

▲Warsaw Uprising Museum (Muzeum Powstania Warszawskiego)—This museum opened on August 1, 2004—the 60th anniversary of the Warsaw Uprising. Thorough, modern, and packed with Polish field-trip groups, the museum celebrates the heroes of the uprising. It's a bit cramped, and finding your way through the exhibits can be confusing, but it thoughtfully illuminates this complicated chapter of Warsaw's history. The location is inconvenient (a 10-min tram ride west of central train station), and probably not worth the trek for those with a casual interest. But for history buffs, it's Warsaw's single best museum.

Getting There: It's on the western edge of downtown at ulica Przyokopowa 28. While it looks close on the map, it's actually a long hike through Warsaw's dullest quarter. Instead, take tram #24 from near the central train station (from the underground passageways, follow signs for *Ochota* to find the tram tracks), or from across the street from the National Museum (near the start of Nowy Świat). Get off at the stop called Muzeum Powstania Warszawskiego, cross the tracks and the busy street, walk straight one short block up Grzybowska, and take a left on Przyokopowa. The museum is the big, red-brick building on the left. You can also get to the museum by taking bus #105 (meet it across the street from the central train station—in front of the Palace of Culture and Science; get off at the Rondo Daszyńskiego stop and look for the watchtower with the P-and-W symbol and Polish flag, hiding behind the Bank BPH). From the Old Town, tram #32 goes to the museum (to reach the tram stop, go down the stairs between St. Anne's Church and the Royal Castle; ride it to the Muzeum Powstania Warszawskiego stop).

Cost and Hours: 5 zł; Mon, Wed, and Fri 8:00–18:00; Thu 8:00–20:00; Sat–Sun 10:00–18:00; closed Tue; last entry 30 min before closing, tel. 022-539-7947, www.1944.pl.

Audioguide: The informative, two-hour audioguide is ideal if

The Warsaw Uprising

By the summer of 1944, it was becoming clear that the Nazis' days in Warsaw were numbered. The Red Army drew near, and by late July, Soviet tanks were within 25 miles of downtown Warsaw.

The Varsovians could have simply waited for the Soviets to cross the river and force the Nazis out. But they knew that Soviet "liberation" would also mean an end to Polish independence. The Polish Home Army numbered 400,000—30,000 of them in Warsaw alone—and was the biggest underground army in military history. The uprisers wanted Poland to control its own fate, and they took matters into their own hands. The resistance's symbol was an anchor made up of a P atop a W (which stands for *Polska Walcząca*, or "Poland Fighting"—you'll see this icon all around town). Over time, the Home Army had established an extensive network of underground tunnels and sewers, which allowed them to deliver messages and move around the city without drawing the Nazis' attention. These tunnels gave the Home Army the element of surprise.

On August 1, 30,000 Polish resistance fighters launched an attack on their Nazi oppressors. They poured out of the sewers and caught the Nazis off guard, initially having great success.

But the Nazis regrouped quickly, and within a few days, they had retaken several areas of the city—murdering tens of thousands of innocent civilians as they went. In one notorious incident, some 5,500 Polish soldiers and 6,000 civilians who were surrounded by Nazis in the Old Town were forced to flee through the sewers; many drowned or were shot. (This scene is depicted in the Warsaw Uprising Monument on plac Krasińskich.)

Just two months after it had started, the Warsaw Uprising was over. The Home Army called a cease-fire. About 18,000 Polish uprisers had been killed, along with nearly 200,000 innocent civilians. An infuriated Hitler ordered that the city be destroyed—which it was, systematically, block by block, until virtually nothing remained.

Through all of this, the Soviets stood still, watched, and waited. When the smoke cleared and the Nazis left, the Red Army marched in and claimed the wasteland that was once called Warsaw. After the war, General Dwight D. Eisenhower said that the scale of destruction here was the worst he'd ever seen.

Depending on whom you talk to, the desperate uprising of Warsaw was incredibly brave, stupid, or both. As for the Poles, they remain fiercely proud of their struggle for freedom. The city of Warsaw has recently commemorated this act of bravery with the new Warsaw Uprising Museum.

you really want to delve into the whole story (5 zł, rent it in the gift shop). A well-illustrated, 20-zł guidebook is also sold in the shop. For a quick overview, take my self-guided tour.

➲ **Self-Guided Tour:** The museum has several parts. The beautifully restored 1905 red-brick building, once an electrical plant, houses the permanent exhibition. The more recent gray addition behind it displays temporary exhibitions. And the park stretching around the back of the complex also has some moving sights. Buy your ticket at the little house on the left (marked *kasa*), then head into the main hall.

The high-tech **main exhibit** sprawls across three floors. It chronologically tells the story of the uprising, with a keen focus on military history. While it's easy to get turned around, look for directional signs and don't be afraid to explore. Everything is well-described in English; also look for the printed pages of English information.

The ground floor focuses on Germany's invasion and occupation of Poland. The children's area (to the right as you enter) reminds visitors that Varsovian kids played a role in the Warsaw Uprising, too. Then you'll take the elevator up to the top floor (signed *2*), which features exhibits on the uprising itself. You'll meet some of the uprising's heroes, and learn about their weapons and methods. Inside the big tent is an exhibit about the Wola Massacre, during which 40,000 people were killed after the Nazis issued a take-no-prisoners decree in retribution for the uprising. Another exhibit looks at its impact on civilians and hospitals. The "Kino Palladium" movie screen shows subtitled Home Army newsreel footage from the period. To the right of the screen, you'll walk through a simulated sewer, reminiscent of the one that many Home Army soldiers and civilians used to evade the Germans. Imagine terrified troops quietly traversing a more than mile-long sewer line like this one (but with lower ceilings)—and doing it while knee-deep in liquid sewage.

The exhibit continues downstairs. If you need a break, straight ahead from the stairs are WCs and a café (past the exhibit on the USSR's role in the Warsaw Uprising, and in "liberating" and terrorizing postwar Poland). The café is oddly pleasant, serving drinks and light snacks amidst genteel ambience from pre-war Warsaw.

Back in the main exhibit, one room honors the Field Postal Service, which, at great personal risk, continued mail delivery of both military communiqués and civilian correspondences. Many of these brave "mailmen" were actually Scouts who were too young to fight. The later days of the uprising are outlined, battle by battle. A chilling section describes how Warsaw became a "city of graves," with burial mounds and makeshift crosses scattered everywhere. As you learn about the uprising's aftermath, consider that the

Nazis destroyed Warsaw four separate times during World War II (at the outbreak of war, to put down the Ghetto Uprising, to put down the Warsaw Uprising, and finally just to be mean).

Occupying the center of the main hall are two large-scale exhibits: a replica of an RAF Liberator B-24 J, used for airborne surveillance of wartime Warsaw; and a giant movie screen showing more fascinating newsreels assembled by the Home Army's own propaganda unit during the uprising. Under the screen, behind the black curtains, is yet another exhibit, this one about life in Nazi-occupied Warsaw, along with another, more claustrophobic walk-through sewer.

The **park** features several thought-provoking sights. Around the right side are several monuments, with photographs along the side wall showing the history of the museum building. Along the back is the Wall of Memory, a Vietnam Wall–type monument to soldiers of the Polish Home Army who were killed in action. You'll see their rank and name, followed by their codename, in quotes. The Home Army observed a strict policy of anonymity, forbidding members from calling each other by anything but their codenames. The bell in the middle is dedicated to the commander of the uprising, Antoni Chruściel (codename "Monter").

Sleeping in Warsaw

Most accommodations in central Warsaw are either overpriced business-class hotels (whose rates can drop dramatically when demand is low—especially on weekends and in summer), or gloomy, impersonal communist-holdover hotels. Thankfully, there are a few happy exceptions—such as Boutique B&B and Duval Apartments, easily the best options in Warsaw. For locations, see the map on page 344.

$$$ Hotel Le Régina is a tempting splurge buried in the quiet and charming New Town (just beyond the Old Town). From its elegant public spaces to its 61 top-notch rooms, everything here is done with class. Choose between plenty nice "standard" and "classic" rooms, or pay an extra 200 zł for bigger "superior" rooms, with hand-painted frescoes over each bed. While the official rates are ridiculously high (standard Db-1,500 zł, superior Db-1,700 zł), you'll often find amazingly lower promotional prices on their website (for a standard room in summer figure Db-500–600 zł on weekdays, as low as 300 zł on weekends, prices change constantly—

Sleep Code

(3 zł = about $1, country code: 48)
S = Single, **D** = Double/Twin, **T** = Triple, **Q** = Quad, **b** = bathroom, **s** = shower only. Unless otherwise noted, English is spoken, breakfast is included, and credit cards are accepted.

To help you sort easily through these listings, I've divided the rooms into three categories, based on the price for a standard double room with bath:

$$$ Higher Priced—Most rooms 400 zł or more.
$$ Moderately Priced—Most rooms between 300–400 zł.
$ Lower Priced—Most rooms 300 zł or less.

check online for latest deals, more expensive during winter convention season, prices don't include 7 percent tax or 90 zł/person breakfast—skip this very overpriced option, pricier suites, elevator, non-smoking floor, free Wi-Fi, exercise room, pool, Kościelna 12, tel. 022-531-6000, www.leregina.com, info@leregina.com).

$$$ Novotel, with 733 uninspired cookie-cutter rooms across the street from the Palace of Culture and Science, overlooks Poland's busiest intersection. Recently renovated inside and out, this is a good option for a big, business-class, downtown hotel that's handy to the train station (official rate is Sb/Db-550 zł, but in slow times—especially weekends—you might pay 300–450 zł, best deals are online, optional breakfast-60 zł, non-smoking rooms, elevator, pay Internet access, free cable Internet, Marszałkowska 94/98, tel. 022-621-0271, fax 022-625-0476, www.orbis.pl, nov.warszawa@orbis.pl).

$$ Duval Apartments, named for a French woman who supposedly had an affair with the Polish king in this building, offers four beautifully appointed rooms above a restaurant (called Same Fusy) a few steps off the square in the Old Town. Each room has a different theme: traditional Polish, Japanese, glass, or retro (Sb-275 zł, Db-320 zł, Tb-400 zł, more for 1-night stays, includes breakfast, lots of stairs with no elevator, some restaurant noise—light sleepers should request a quiet room, free Wi-Fi, Nowomiejska 10, mobile 0608-679-346, tel. & fax 022-831-9104, www.duval.net.pl, duval@duval.net.pl). There's no reception, and the rooms aren't affiliated with the restaurant, so arrange a meeting time with Agnieszka when you reserve. On arrival, go up the stairs and ring doorbell #5.

$$ Castle Inn, sitting right on Castle Square at the entrance to the Old Town, is the next rung up the ladder for youth hostelers who've outgrown the grungy backpacker scene. Run by the owners

of Oki Doki Hostel (described later), it has 22 creative and colorful rooms, each with completely different but equally artsy decor. Youthful and funky, it provides a welcome jolt of new energy on Warsaw's hotel scene (very slushy rates depending on demand, generally Sb-255–303 zł, Db-270–327 zł, "delux" Db-350–440 zł, "delux" Tb-355–492 zł, 22 zł extra for continental breakfast—have it delivered to your room for the same price, free Wi-Fi, Świętojańska 2, tel. 022/425-0100, www.castleinn.pl, castleinn@castleinn.pl).

$$ Old Town Apartments offers 25 studio, one-bedroom, and two-bedroom apartments (all with kitchen) inside Warsaw's Old Town. The prices are good and the location is excellent, but you're pretty much on your own (no real reception, no breakfast). View the apartments on their website, pick the one that looks best, and set up a meeting to get the keys at their office (prices flex with demand, but figure studio-300 zł, 1-bedroom-350 zł, 2-bedroom-450 zł, some more expensive "featured" apartments on the square also available, slightly cheaper Oct–April and last-minute, tel. 022-887-9800, fax 022-831-4956, www.apartmentsapart.com, warsaw@bookaa.net). They have an office right on the Old Town Market Square that acts as a sort of reception desk (Mon–Fri 9:00–20:00, Sat–Sun 9:00–17:00, Rynek Starego Miasta 12/14 #2). They also rent 15 pricey apartments on Nowy Świat, called **Royal Route Residence** (studio-400 zł, 1-bedroom-500 zł, 2-bedroom-600 zł, breakfast-25 zł, corner of Nowy Świat and Chmielna, office open Mon–Fri 10:00–18:00—at other times arrange a meeting to get the keys, tel. 022-692-8495, same booking info as above).

$$ Hotel Harenda rents 43 rooms with leatherbound doors on the second and third floors of an office building right in the middle of the Royal Way, by the Copernicus monument. The tired, communist-era rooms are crying out for a renovation, but the location is convenient, and the ground-floor pub is a popular hangout spot (May–June and Sept–Oct: Sb-340 zł, Db-380 zł; July–Aug and Jan–Feb: Sb-295 zł, Db-340 zł; March–April and Nov–Dec: Sb-310 zł, Db-340 zł; breakfast-25 zł, second night is free Fri–Sun, some rowdy street noise—especially on weekends—so request a quiet room, lots of stairs with no elevator, free Internet access and Wi-Fi, Krakowskie Przedmieście 4/6, tel. & fax 022-826-0071, www.hotelharenda.com.pl, rezerwacja@hotelharenda.com.pl).

$$ Hotel Gromada, a 320-room conference hotel, has a dreary communist exterior, but the lobby and most rooms have been refurbished. There are three types of rooms, all of which are pretty similar: "tourist" (lightly renovated since the communist days); "standard" (a little nicer, with newer bathrooms,

but still scruffy); and "plus" (much better and in a newer building). While the place is dull, it has a fine location—between the Palace of Culture and Science and Nowy Świat (tourist rooms: Sb-250 zł, Db-300 zł; standard rooms: Sb-320 zł, Db-350 zł; plus rooms: Sb-420 zł, Db-450 zł; about 25 percent cheaper Fri–Sat, non-smoking rooms, elevator, free Wi-Fi or cable Internet, plac Powstańców Warszawy 2, tel. 022-582-9900, fax 022-582-9527, www.gromada.pl, warszawahotel.centrum@gromada.pl).

$ Boutique B&B offers more comfort and class than a hotel twice its price, in a beautifully renovated and well-located old building. Jarek Chołodecki, who lived near Chicago for many years, returned to Warsaw and converted apartments into this wonderful bed-and-breakfast with seven rooms. It's a friendly, casual, stylish place, creatively decorated and impeccably maintained. You'll feel like you're staying with your Warsaw sophisticate cousin—quirky, charismatic Jarek loves to chat with his guests, many of whom return and become his good friends. Each morning, lively conversation percolates at the big, family-style breakfast table over a morning meal made mostly from organic and locally sourced foods. A small drawing room plays host to occasional piano concerts and other convivial activities. When Jarek is out of town, his right-hand-man Paweł capably holds down the fort. Let them know what time you'll be arriving (Sb-250 zł, standard Db-280 zł, junior suite-320 zł, big suite-420 zł, elevator, free Internet access and Wi-Fi in some rooms, ulica Smolna 14, tel. 022-829-4801, fax 022-829-4802, www.bedandbreakfast.pl, office@bedandbreakfast.pl). To make things easier, Jarek can arrange for a no-stress ride in from the airport for the same price as a taxi (40 zł, more at night, request when you reserve your room).

$ Ibis Warszawa Stare Miasto, with 333 cookie-cutter rooms, is the place for predictable comfort with zero personality. This hotel, part of the popular European chain, overlooks a WWII memorial in a nondescript, businessy-feeling neighborhood a 10-minute walk north of the Old Town (Sb/Db-289 zł, or 219 zł Fri–Sun, sometimes better deals online, breakfast-33 zł, air-con, non-smoking rooms, elevator, Muranowska 2, tel. 022-310-1000, fax 022-310-1010, www.ibishotel.com, h3714@accor.com).

Hostels

$ Nathan's Villa Hostel is the most appealing hostel option in Warsaw. Run by a sharp Bostonian entrepreneur with hostels all

over Poland, Nathan's has 13 rooms (with 95 beds) overlooking a cozy courtyard, and plenty of opportunities for backpacker bonding. The catch: It's less conveniently located than my other listings, requiring a 15-minute walk or easy bus ride south of the train station area (dorm bed in 4-bed room-60 zł, in 5-bed room-55 zł, in 6-bed room-50 zł, in 8-bed room-45 zł, in 10-bed room-40 zł, in 12-bed room-36 zł, 5 zł more Fri–Sat; D-170 zł, Db-180–190 zł, 10 zł more Fri–Sat; includes breakfast and sheets, lockers, free Internet access and Wi-Fi, laundry service-15 zł, guest kitchen, hiding behind a modern glass office building at ulica Piękna 24/26—the nearby square called plac Konstytucji has easy bus connections, for location see map on page 344, tel. & fax 022-622-2946, www.nathansvilla.com).

$ Oki Doki Hostel, on a pleasant square a few blocks in front of the Palace of Culture and Science, is colorful, creative, and easygoing. Each of its 37 rooms was designed by a different artist with a special theme—such as Van Gogh, Celtic spirals, heads of state, or Lenin. It's run by Ernest—a Pole whose parents loved Hemingway—and his wife Łucja, with help from their sometimes-jaded staff (complicated pricing structure flexes with demand: dorm bed in 4-bed room-50–67 zł, in 5- to 6-bed room-45–58 zł, in 8-bed room-42–53 zł; S-120–142 zł, D-150–174 zł, Db-192–219 zł, T-180–219 zł; prices include breakfast except for dorm-dwellers—who pay 10 zł, slightly cheaper Oct–April, free Internet access and Wi-Fi, laundry service-15 zł, kitchen, lots of stairs with no elevator, plac Dąbrowskiego 3, tel. 022-826-5112, fax 022-826-8357, www.okidoki.pl, okidoki@okidoki.pl).

$ The IYHF **Szkolne Schronisko** hostel, with 110 beds and lots of school groups, is well run, bright, and clean. The downside: It's on the fifth floor, with no elevator (non-members welcome, all prices per person: dorm beds-40 zł, S-70 zł, twin D-65 zł, T-60 zł, Q-50 zł, includes sheets, 3 zł for towel, no breakfast but members' kitchen, 10 percent cheaper for hostel members, closed 10:00–16:00, curfew at 24:00, or 2:00 in the morning July–Aug; email or fax ahead to reserve limited S, D, and T rooms; good location across the street from National Museum at ulica Smolna 30, tel. & fax 022-827-8952, www.hostelsmolna30.pl, info@hostelsmolna30.pl).

$ Dom Przy Rynku is a small, friendly, charming, 40-bed hostel with two goals: housing kids from dysfunctional families, and raising money for its work by renting out beds to tourists (when it's not housing children). Located in the peaceful New Town, the cozy rooms are decorated for grade-schoolers. Beds are rented in July and August, and on Friday and Saturday nights all year (55 zł/bed in 2- to 5-bed rooms, rooms segregated by gender, bus #175 from station or airport to Franciszkańska stop, behind

the green-domed church at the corner of Kościelna and Przyrynek streets, Rynek Nowego Miasta 4, tel. & fax 022-831-5033, www.cityhostel.net, info@cityhostel.net).

Eating in Warsaw

While the Old Town has a tourist-friendly atmosphere and traditional Polish food, Varsovians know that these days, the Nowy Świat area is where it's at—with trendy international restaurants and an enticing al fresco scene on balmy summer evenings. This is especially enticing, since Warsaw offers your best break from traditional Polish food. Most restaurants are open until the "last guest," which usually means about 23:00 (sometimes later in summer).

In or near the Old Town

Rather than spending too much to eat on the Old Town Market Square, I prefer to venture a few blocks to find a place with good food and much lower prices. For locations, see the map on page 344.

At **Restauracja pod Samsonem** ("Under Samson"), dine on affordable Jewish and Polish comfort food with well-dressed locals. The ambience is pleasant, the service is playfully opinionated, and the low prices make up for the fact that you have to pay to check your coat and use the bathroom (most main dishes 15–35 zł, enjoyable outdoor seating in summer, daily 10:00–23:00, ulica Freta 3/5, tel. 022-831-1788).

Pierogarnia na Bednarskiej brags, "only our grandmothers make better pierogi." In addition to the classic Polish dumplings, the menu includes soups and a fun variety of drinks (from unusual fruit juices to *kvas,* the non-alcoholic dark beer). Order at the counter and take a seat—they'll call you when your food's ready. With mellow country decor, wooden menus, and a loyal local crowd, this is a handy spot for a quick, cheap meal along the Royal Way (13–16-zł plates of pierogi, 17-zł combo-plate includes soup and salad, daily 12:00–20:00, hiding down a quiet street behind the statue of Adam Mickiewicz at ulica Bednarska 28/30, tel. 022-828-0392).

BrowArmia is a hit with beer-lovers. This sprawling brewpub makes four different types of beer (plus special seasonal beers) and serves decent pub grub. The dark, mod, long interior fills two levels

(including a fun cellar), but in good weather I'd stake out a spot on the terrace—ideal for people-watching along the Royal Way (18–25-zł starters, 30–50-zł main dishes, daily 12:00–24:00, live music or DJ in cellar on weekends, right on Krakowskie Przedmieście near Piłsudski Square at ulica Królewska 1, tel. 022-826-5455).

On the Old Town Market Square: You'll pay triple to eat right on the square, but some visitors figure it's worth the splurge. Compare menus and views to find the spot you like best. If you want to go for the venerable old favorite—and money's no object—check out **U Fukiera.** This place offers traditional Polish and pan-European meals in a sophisticated setting with carefully designed pre-war atmosphere. In summer, sit at their tables out on the square, or find your way to the cozy courtyard garden in back (50–100-zł main dishes, daily 12:00–24:00, at #27, tel. 022-831-1013).

On or near Nowy Świat

While most Old Town eateries are traditional and cater to tourists, locals flock to the Nowy Świat neighborhood (near the National Museum and central train station) for a fun night on the town.

Fancy Eateries on Foksal Street: Foksal—the first cross street as you go down Nowy Świat from aleja Jerozolimskie—has a thriving assortment of about a half-dozen cafés and restaurants: Mexican, Italian, Asian, international, and more. Most have inviting outdoor seating that's ideal on a balmy summer evening. The clientele is young and sophisticated, and there's not a pierogi in sight. Find the place with the cuisine and ambience you like best. **Papaya** has tasty pan-Asian fare and a trendy, minimalist, black-and-white interior (30–60-zł main dishes plus pricier splurges, daily 12:00–24:00, at #16, tel. 022-826-1199). **Living Room** features pricey, healthy international fare. The outdoor seating is tops, or you can sit in the tight, stylish dining room (45–75-zł main dishes, daily 12:00–2:00 in the morning, at #18, tel. 022-826-3928).

Cheaper Milk Bars: **Sandwicz,** a colorful milk bar, serves up Polish grub (with both vegetarian and meat options) and has a self-serve salad bar (help yourself, then take to cashier to weigh and pay). Sandwiches are available only around lunchtime, but appetizing meals are sold all day long (8–16-zł main dishes, Mon–Fri 7:30–20:30, Sat–Sun 10:00–20:30, Nowy Świat 28). For a more communist-style milk bar—with lower prices, dreary decor, and grumpier service—head to **Bar Mleczny Familijny,** about a block up Nowy Świat and across the street (Mon–Fri 7:00–20:00, Sat–Sun 9:00–17:00). For more on milk bars, see page 245.

***Hungarian Cuisine*: Borpince** ("Wine Cellar") is a cozy cellar serving up very authentic Hungarian fare a long block off of Nowy Świat (toward the Palace of Culture and Science). As you

dive into spicy goulash and *paprikas*, you'll see just how different the cuisine can be on the other side of the Carpathians. If you won't be visiting Hungary on your trip, this is the next best way to sample Hungarian favorites. The restaurant also has a long list of Hungarian wines (15–25-zł soups including goulash, 30–45-zł main dishes, daily 12:00–23:00, ulica Zgoda 1, tel. 022/828-2244). For Magyar flavors at lower prices, try **Krokiecik** ("Croquette"), the simpler self-service restaurant located next door, at street level. Choose from Polish or Hungarian food, order at the counter, then take a seat (7–10-zł soups, 10–20-zł main dishes, daily 9:00–21:00, ulica Zgoda 1, 022/827-3037).

Uniquely Polish Treats

These two places are on or close to the busy Nowy Świat boulevard.

A. Blikle, Poland's most famous pastry shop, serves a wide variety of delicious treats. This is where locals shop for cakes when they're having someone special over for coffee. The specialty: *pączki* (PONCH-kee), the quintessential Polish doughnut, filled with rose-flavored jam. You can get your goodies "to go" in the shop (2.60-zł *pączki,* Mon–Sat 9:00–19:00, Sun 10:00–18:00), or pay more to enjoy them with coffee in the swanky, classic café with indoor or outdoor seating (6-zł *pączki,* Mon–Sat 9:00–22:00, Sun 10:00–22:00; both at Nowy Świat 35).

E. Wedel Pijalnia Czekolady thrills chocoholics. Emil Wedel made Poland's favorite chocolate, and today, his former residence houses this chocolate shop and genteel café (Mon–Fri 8:00–22:00, Sat 10:00–22:00, Sun 10:00–21:00, between Palace of Culture and Science and Nowy Świat at ulica Szpitalna 1, tel. 022-827-2916). This is the spot for delicious pastries and a *real* hot chocolate—*czekolada do picia* ("drinking chocolate"), a cup of actual melted chocolate, not just hot chocolate milk (11-zł). The menu describes it as, "True Wedel ecstasy for your mouth that will take you to a world of dreams and desires." Or, if you fancy chocolate mousse, try *pokusa* ("Wedel Temptation"). Wedel's was *the* Christmas treat for locals under communism. Cadbury bought the company when Poland privatized, but they kept the E. Wedel name, which is close to all Poles' hearts...and taste buds.

Warsaw Connections

Virtually all trains into and out of Warsaw go through the hulking central train station (described earlier, under "Arrival in Warsaw"; pay special attention to the "Buying Train Tickets" section). If you're heading to Gdańsk, note that the red-brick Gothic city of Toruń and the impressive Malbork Castle are on the way (though

on separate train lines, so you can't do both en route; see Gdańsk and Pomerania chapters). Also be aware that express trains to many destinations (including Kraków) require seat reservations, even if you have a railpass.

For the next few years, the duration of any train journey in Poland is likely to be in flux, as the country builds a network of new high-speed rail lines. This can result both in longer trips (due to construction delays), and—ultimately—in shorter ones (thanks to new rail lines) than those listed here. Confirm specific times online (www.rozklad-pkp.pl) or at the train station. If there is construction along your route, you'll likely experience additional delays even beyond what's scheduled.

From Warsaw by Train to: Kraków (hourly, 2.75 hrs, requires seat reservation), **Gdańsk** (nearly hourly, 5 hrs), **Toruń** (5/day, 3 hrs direct, longer with a transfer in Kutno), **Malbork** (nearly hourly, 4–4.5 hrs direct), **Prague** (2/day direct including 1 night train, more with changes, 8.5–10 hrs), **Berlin** (3/day direct, 5.75 hrs—eventually will be much shorter with construction of new high-speed rail line; plus 1 direct night train, 7.75 hrs), **Budapest** (2/day direct, including 1 night train, 10.5–11.5 hrs; or 1 each per day with transfer in Győr, Hungary, or Břeclav, Czech Republic, both 10 hrs), **Vienna** (2/day direct, including 1 night train, 7.75–8.5 hrs).

GDAŃSK and the TRI-CITY

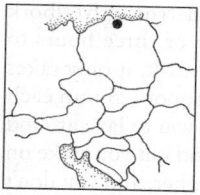

Gdańsk (guh-DAYNSK) is a true find on the Baltic Coast of Poland. You may associate Gdańsk with the images of dreary dockworkers you saw on the nightly news in the 1980s—but there's so much more to this city than shipyards, Solidarity, and smog. It's surprisingly easy to look past the urban sprawl to find one of northern Europe's most historic and picturesque cities.

Gdańsk is second only to Kraków as Poland's most appealing destination. The gem of a Main Town boasts block after block of red-brick churches and narrow, colorful, ornately decorated Hanseatic burghers' mansions. Its history is also fascinating—from its medieval Golden Age to the headlines of our own generation, big things happen here. You might even see old Lech Wałęsa still wandering the streets.

And yet, Gdańsk is also looking to its future, finally repairing some of its World War II damage after a long communist hibernation. If you sense anticipation in the air, that's because 2012 is expected to be a banner year for the city, as it will host several matches for the European soccer tournament, as well as some important EU meetings. These events have kicked off a flurry of new construction—including a futuristic new stadium shaped like a translucent glob of amber, and high-speed train lines that will more efficiently link it to the rest of Poland.

From Gdańsk, the "Tri-City" continues north along the coast, offering several day-trip opportunities. The once-faded, now-revitalized elegance of the seaside resort of Sopot beckons to tourists, while the modern burg of Gdynia sets the pace for today's Poland. Beyond the Tri-City, the sandy Hel Peninsula is a popular spot for summer sunbathing.

Planning Your Time

This region merits two days to make the trip here worthwhile. You could see Gdańsk's major sights in a day, but a second day allows you to see everything in town at a more relaxing pace, and take your pick from among several possible side-trips.

Gdańsk sightseeing has two major components: the "Royal Way" (historic main drag with good museums) and the modern shipyard where Solidarity was born (with a fascinating museum). With just one day, do one of these activities in the morning, and the other in the afternoon. With two days, do one each day, and round your time out with other attractions: art-lovers enjoy the National Museum (with a stunning painting by Hans Memling), history buffs make the pilgrimage to Westerplatte (where World War II began), and church fans might visit Oliwa Cathedral in Gdańsk's northern suburbs (on the way to Sopot).

If you have more time, consider the wide variety of side-trips. The most popular option is the half-day round-trip to Malbork Castle (40–50 min each way by train, plus two or three hours to tour the castle—see next chapter). Closer to Gdańsk, it only takes a quick visit to get a feel for the resort town of Sopot (25 min each way by train), but the town's beaches may tempt you to laze around longer. Consider a sprint through Gdynia to round out your take on the Tri-City. If you have a full day and great weather, and you don't mind fighting the crowds for a patch of sandy beach, go to Hel.

Gdańsk gets busy in late June, when school holidays begin, and it's downright crowded with mostly German tourists from July to mid-September—especially during St. Dominic's Fair (Jarmark Św. Dominika, three weeks in late July–mid-Aug), with market stalls, concerts, and other celebrations. The city is dead in the winter.

Orientation to Gdańsk

(area code: 058)

Gdańsk, with 460,000 residents, is part of a larger metropolitan area called the Tri-City (Trójmiasto, total population 750,000). But the tourist's Gdańsk is compact, welcoming, and walkable—virtually anything you'll want to see is within a 20-minute stroll of everything else.

Focus on the Main Town (Główne Miasto), home to most of the sights described, including the spectacular "Royal Way" main drag, ulica Długa. The Old Town (Stare Miasto) has a handful of

old brick buildings and faded, tall, skinny houses—but the area is mostly drab and residential, and not worth much time. Just beyond the northern end of the Old Town (about a 20-min walk from the heart of the Main Town) is the entrance to the Gdańsk Shipyard, with the excellent Solidarity museum. From here, shipyards sprawl for miles.

The second language in this part of Poland is German, not English. As this was a predominantly German city until the end of World War II, German tourists flock here in droves. But you'll win no Polish friends calling the city by its more familiar German name, Danzig.

Tourist Information

Gdańsk's TI—the only one I've seen with a tip jar—is in a red, high-gabled building across **ulica Długa** from the Town Hall. Pick up the free map and brochure, and browse through the other brochures and guidebooks (May–Sept Mon–Fri 9:00–18:00, Sat–Sun 10:00–18:00, until 20:00 during busy times; Oct–April Mon–Fri 9:00–18:00, Sat–Sun 9:00–17:00; ulica Długa 45, tel. 058-301-9151). There are also small TIs at the **main train station** (in a small kiosk out front) and the **airport.**

Busy sightseers should consider the **Tourist Card,** which includes entry to several sights in Gdańsk, Gdynia, and Sopot, discounts on others (such as 20 percent off admission to Malbork Castle), as well as free public transportation in the area. Check the list of what's covered (note that the Solidarity museum is not) and do the arithmetic. If you'll be seeing several included museums, this card could save you some money (35 zł/24 hours, 65 zł/72 hours, sold at TIs, www.gdansk4u.com/touristcard).

Arrival in Gdańsk

By Train: Gdańsk's main train station (Gdańsk Główny) is a pretty brick palace on the western edge of the old center. (To save money, architects in Colmar, France, copied this exact design to build their city's station.) Trains to other parts of Poland (marked *PKP*) use tracks 1–3; regional trains with connections to the Tri-City (marked *SKM*) use the shorter tracks 3–5 (for instructions on riding these regional SKM trains, see page 423).

Inside the terminal building, you'll find lockers, ATMs, ticket windows, and a helpful TI (just beyond the ticket windows—look for *it* sign). Outside, the pedestrian underpass by the McDonald's

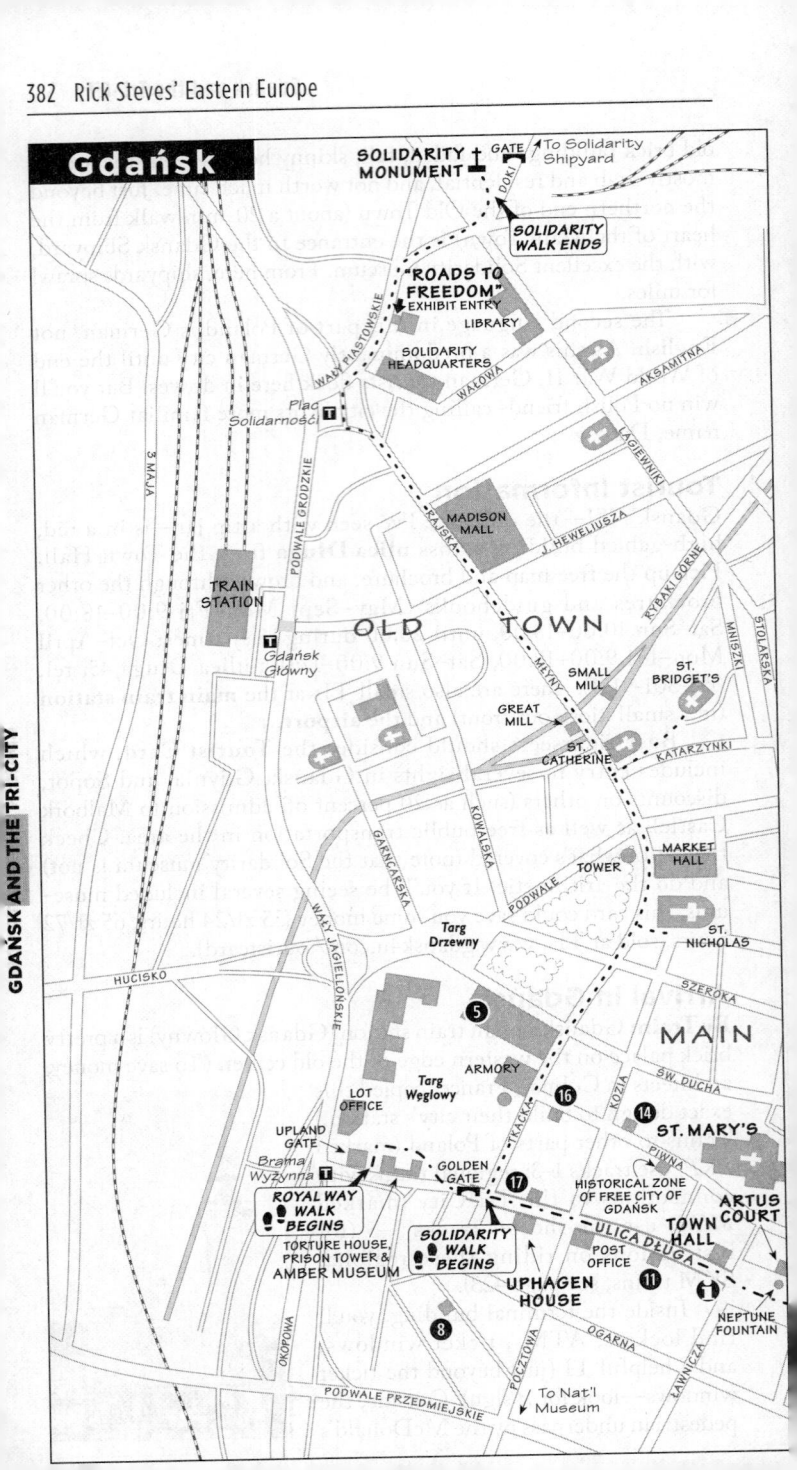
Gdańsk
SOLIDARITY MONUMENT
GATE
To Solidarity Shipyard
DOKI
SOLIDARITY WALK ENDS
"ROADS TO FREEDOM" EXHIBIT ENTRY
LIBRARY
SOLIDARITY HEADQUARTERS
WAŁY PIASTOWSKIE
WAŁOWA
AKSAMITNA
Plac Solidarności
3 MAJA
PODWALE GRODZKIE
ŁAGIEWNIKI
MADISON MALL
PAJSKA
J. HEWELIUSZA
TRAIN STATION
Gdańsk Główny
OLD TOWN
RYBAKI GÓRNE
MNISZKI
STOLARSKA
MŁYNY
SMALL MILL
ST. BRIDGET'S
GREAT MILL
ST. CATHERINE
KATARZYNKI
KOWALSKA
GAŃCARSKA
MARKET HALL
TOWER
PODWALE
Targ Drzewny
ST. NICHOLAS
WAŁY JAGIELLOŃSKIE
HUCISKO
SZEROKA
MAIN
ARMORY
Targ Węglowy
LOT OFFICE
TŁOMACKA
TOŁZIA
ŚW. DUCHA
ST. MARY'S
UPLAND GATE
Brama Wyżynna
GOLDEN GATE
PIWNA
HISTORICAL ZONE OF FREE CITY OF GDAŃSK
ARTUS COURT
ROYAL WAY WALK BEGINS
TORTURE HOUSE, PRISON TOWER & AMBER MUSEUM
SOLIDARITY WALK BEGINS
ULICA DŁUGA
TOWN HALL
POST OFFICE
UPHAGEN HOUSE
NEPTUNE FOUNTAIN
OKOPOWA
POCZTOWA
OGARNA
KAWIECZA
PODWALE PRZEDMIEJŚCIE
To Nat'l Museum

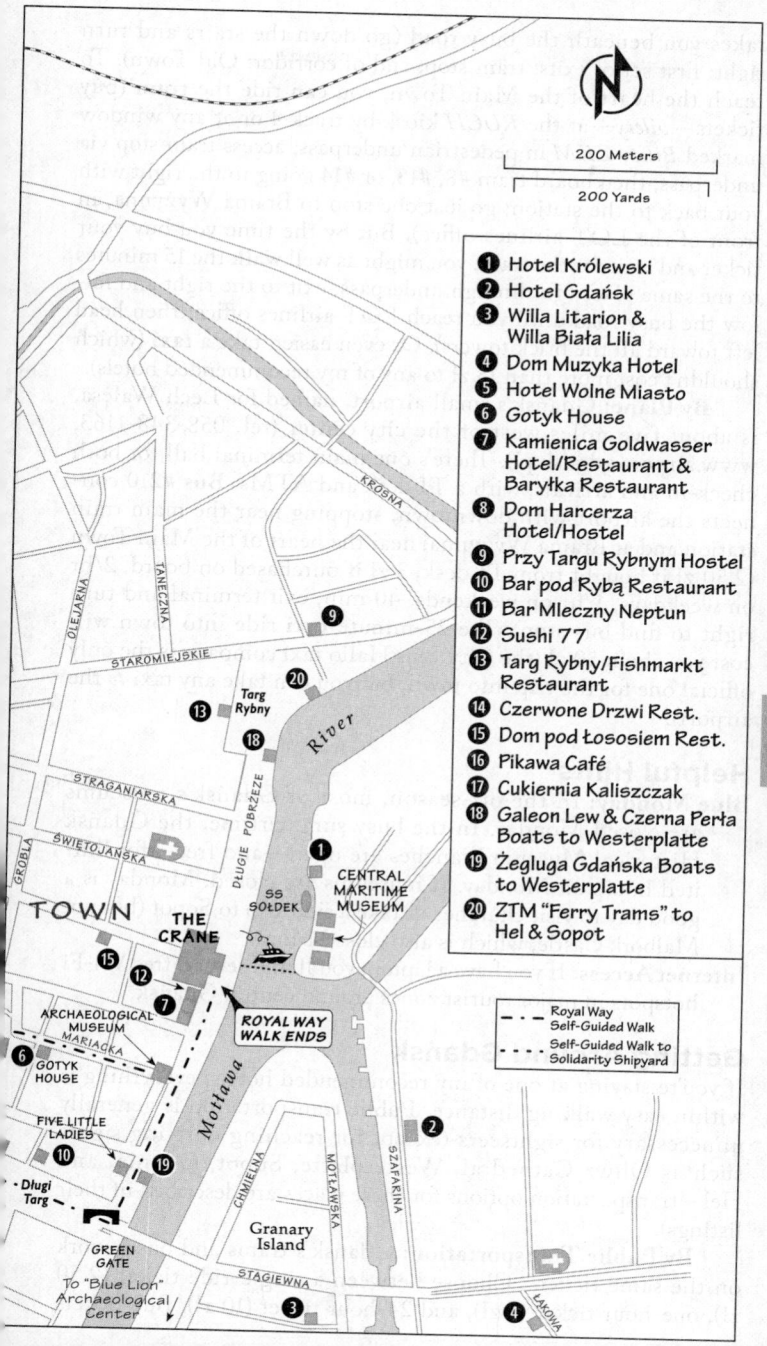
200 Meters
200 Yards
1 Hotel Królewski
2 Hotel Gdańsk
3 Willa Litarion & Willa Biała Lilia
4 Dom Muzyka Hotel
5 Hotel Wolne Miasto
6 Gotyk House
7 Kamienica Goldwasser Hotel/Restaurant & Baryłka Restaurant
8 Dom Harcerza Hotel/Hostel
9 Przy Targu Rybnym Hostel
10 Bar pod Rybą Restaurant
11 Bar Mleczny Neptun
12 Sushi 77
13 Targ Rybny/Fishmarkt Restaurant
14 Czerwone Drzwi Rest.
15 Dom pod Łososiem Rest.
16 Pikawa Café
17 Cukiernia Kaliszczak
18 Galeon Lew & Czerna Perła Boats to Westerplatte
19 Żegluga Gdańska Boats to Westerplatte
20 ZTM "Ferry Trams" to Hel & Sopot
Royal Way Self-Guided Walk
Self-Guided Walk to Solidarity Shipyard
KROSNA
OLEJARNIA
TANECZNA
STAROMIEJSKIE
Targ Rybny
River
STRAGANIARSKA
DŁUGIE POBRZEŻE
ŚWIĘTOJAŃSKA
GRÓBLA
TOWN
THE CRANE
SS SOŁDEK
CENTRAL MARITIME MUSEUM
ROYAL WAY WALK ENDS
ARCHAEOLOGICAL MUSEUM
MARIACKA
GOTYK HOUSE
FIVE LITTLE LADIES
Długi Targ
Motława
CHMIELNA
MOTŁAWSKA
SZAFARNIA
Granary Island
GREEN GATE
To "Blue Lion" Archaeological Center
STAGIEWNA
ŁAKOWA

takes you beneath the busy road (go down the stairs and turn right; first set of exits: tram stop; end of corridor: Old Town). To reach the heart of the Main Town, you can ride the **tram** (buy tickets—*bilety*—at the *RUCH* kiosk by track 4 or at any window marked *Bilety ZKM* in pedestrian underpass; access tram stop via underpass, then board tram #8, #13, or #14 going to the right with your back to the station; go just one stop to Brama Wyżynna, in front of the LOT airlines office). But by the time you buy your ticket and wait for the tram, you might as well **walk** the 15 minutes to the same place (go through underpass, exit to the right and follow the busy road until you reach LOT airlines office, then head left toward all the brick towers). Or even easier, take a **taxi** (which shouldn't cost more than 15 zł to any of my recommended hotels).

By Plane: Gdańsk's small airport, named for Lech Wałęsa, is about five miles west of the city center (tel. 058-348-1163, www.airport.gdansk.pl). There's one main terminal hall for both check-in and arrivals, with a TI desk and ATMs. **Bus** #210 connects the airport with downtown, stopping near the main train station and at Brama Wyżynna, near the heart of the Main Town (2.50 zł if bought from TI desk, 3 zł if purchased on board, 2/hr on weekdays, 1/hr on weekends, 40 min, exit terminal and turn right to find bus stop). The 25-minute **taxi** ride into town will cost you about 50 zł (the City Plus Hallo taxi company is the only official one for the trip into town, but you can take any taxi *to* the airport).

Helpful Hints

Blue Monday: In the off-season, most of Gdańsk's museums are closed Monday. In the busy summertime, the Gdańsk Historical Museum branches are open—and free—for limited hours on Monday. If museums are closed, Monday is a good day to visit churches or take a side-trip to Sopot (but not Malbork Castle, which is also closed Mon).

Internet Access: If you have a laptop, you'll find several free Wi-Fi hotspots in major tourist zones around central Gdańsk.

Getting Around Gdańsk

If you're staying at one of my recommended hotels, everything is within easy walking distance. Public transportation is generally unnecessary for sightseers (except for reaching outlying sights such as Oliwa Cathedral, Westerplatte, Sopot, Gdynia, and Hel—transportation options for these places are described in their listings).

By Public Transportation: Gdańsk's trams and buses work on the same tickets: Choose between a single-ride ticket (2.50 zł), one-hour ticket (3 zł), and 24-hour ticket (10 zł). Buy tickets

(bilety) at kiosks marked *RUCH* or *Bilety ZKM,* or on board (one-hour and 24-hour tickets only sold on board). In the city center, the stops worth knowing about are Plac Solidarnośći (near the shipyards), Gdańsk Główny (in front of the main train station), and Brama Wyżynna (near the heart of the tourist zone, in front of LOT airlines office). When buying tickets, don't confuse *ZKM* (the company that runs Gdańsk city transit) with *SKM* (the company that runs regional trains to outlying destinations).

By Taxi: Taxis cost about 7 zł to start, then 2 zł per kilometer (or 3 zł at night). Find a taxi stand, or call a cab (try Super Hallo Taxi, tel. 0800-119-191, or City Plus Hallo Taxi, tel. 19686).

Tours in Gdańsk

Walking Tours—In peak season, the TI sometimes offers a pricey three-hour English walking tour (80 zł/person, offered with demand in July–Aug only, no set schedule—ask at TI).

Private Guide—Hiring your own local guide is an exceptional value. **Agnieszka Syroka** is bubbly and personable, and also does tours of Malbork Castle (300–400 zł for up to 4 hours, more for all day, mobile 0502-554-584, www.tourguidegdansk.com, asyroka @interia.pl).

Self-Guided Walks

▲▲▲Gdańsk's Royal Way

In the 16th and 17th centuries, Gdańsk was Poland's wealthiest city, with gorgeous architecture (much of it in the Flemish Mannerist style) rivaling that in the two historic capitals, Kraków and Warsaw. During this Golden Age, Polish kings would visit this city of well-to-do Hanseatic League merchants, and gawk along the same route trod by tourists today. The following walk introduces you to the best of historic Gdańsk. It only takes about 30 minutes, not counting multiple worthwhile sightseeing stops. This stroll turns tourists into poets. On my last visit, a traveler gasped to me, "It's like stepping into a Fabergé egg."

Begin at the west end of the Main Town, between the white gate and the big brick gate (near the LOT airlines office, the busy road, and the Brama Wyżynna tram stop).

City Gates: Medieval Gdańsk had an elaborate network of

Gdańsk History

Visitors to Gdańsk are surprised at how "un-Polish" the city's history is. In this cultural melting pot of German, Dutch, and Flemish merchants (with a smattering of Italians and Scots), Poles were only a small part of the picture until the city became exclusively Polish after World War II. However, in Gdańsk, cultural backgrounds traditionally took a back seat to the bottom line. Wealthy Gdańsk was always known for its economic pragmatism—no matter who was in charge, merchants here made money.

Gdańsk is Poland's gateway to the waters of Europe—where its main river (the Vistula) meets the Baltic Sea. The town was first mentioned in the 10th century, and was seized in 1308 by the Teutonic Knights (who called it "Danzig"; for more on the Teutonic Knights, see page 434). The Knights encouraged other Germans to come settle on the Baltic coast, and gradually turned Gdańsk into a wealthy city. In 1361, Gdańsk joined the Hanseatic League, a trade federation of mostly Germanic merchant towns that provided mutual security. By the 15th century, Gdańsk was a leading member of this mighty network, which virtually dominated trade in northern Europe (and also included Toruń, Kraków, Lübeck, Hamburg, Bremen, Bruges, Bergen, Tallinn, Novgorod, and nearly a hundred other cities).

In 1454, the people of Gdańsk rose up against the Teutonic Knights, burning down their castle and forcing them out of the city. Three years later, the Polish king borrowed money from wealthy Gdańsk families to hire Czech mercenaries to take the Teutonic Knights' main castle, Malbork (described in the next chapter). In exchange, Gdańsk merchants were granted special privileges, including exclusive export rights. Gdańsk now acted as a middleman for all trade passing through the city, but paid only a modest annual tribute to the Polish king.

The 16th and 17th centuries were Gdańsk's Golden Age. Now a part of the Polish kingdom, the city had access to an enormous hinterland of natural resources to export—yet it maintained a privileged, semi-independent status. Like Amsterdam, Gdańsk became a tolerant, progressive, and booming merchant city. Its

protection for the city, including several moats and gates—among them the white **Upland Gate** (Brama Wyżynna); the red-brick **Torture House** (Wieża Więzienna); and the taller, attached red-brick **Prison Tower** (Katownia). The three gates were all connected back then, and visitors had to pass through all of them to enter the city. The Torture House/Prison Tower complex, with walls up to 15 feet thick, now holds the fine **Amber Museum** (described later, under "Sights in Gdańsk").

Now walk around the left side of the Torture House and Prison Tower. Look to your left to see a long brick building with four gables (next to the modern theater building). This is the

mostly Germanic and Dutch burghers imported Dutch, Flemish, and Italian architects to give their homes an appropriately Hanseatic flourish. At a time of religious upheaval in the rest of Europe, Gdańsk became known for its tolerance—a place that opened its doors to all visitors (many Mennonites and Scottish religious refugees emigrated here). It was also a haven for great thinkers, including philosopher Arthur Schopenhauer and scientist Daniel Fahrenheit (who invented the mercury thermometer).

Gdańsk declined, along with the rest of Poland, in the late 18th century, and became a part of Prussia (today's northern Germany) during the partitions. But the people of Gdańsk—even those of German heritage—had taken pride in their independence, and weren't enthusiastic about being ruled from Berlin. After World War I, in a unique compromise to appease its complex ethnic makeup, Gdańsk did not fall under German or Polish control, but once again became an independent city-state: the Free City of Danzig (populated by 400,000 ethnic Germans and only 15,000 Poles). The city, along with the so-called Polish Corridor connecting it to Polish lands, effectively cut off Germany from its northeastern territory. On September 1, 1939, Adolf Hitler started World War II when he invaded Gdańsk in order to bring it back into the German fold. Nearly 80 percent of the city was destroyed in the war.

After World War II, Gdańsk officially became part of Poland, and was painstakingly reconstructed (mostly replicating its Golden Age). In 1970, and again in 1980, the shipyard of Gdańsk witnessed strikes and demonstrations that would lead to the fall of European communism. Poland's great anti-communist hero and first post-communist president—Lech Wałęsa—is Gdańsk's most famous resident, and still lives here.

A city with a recent past that's both tragic and uplifting, Gdańsk celebrated its 1,000th birthday in 1997. This occasion, and preparations for the Euro 2012 soccer matches, have kicked off a wave of renovation and refurbishment that has the gables of the atmospheric Hanseatic quarter gleaming once again.

16th-century **Armory** (Zbrojownia), one of the best examples of Dutch Renaissance architecture in Europe. Though this part of the building looks like four separate house facades, it's a kind of urban camouflage to hide its real purpose from potential attackers. But there's at least one clue to what it's for: Notice the exploding cannonballs at the tops of the turrets. The round, pointy-topped tower next door is the **Straw Tower.** Gunpowder was stored here, and the roof was straw—so if it exploded, it would blow its top without destroying the walls.

• *Continue around the brick buildings until you're face-to-face with the...*

Golden Gate (Złota Brama): The other gates were defensive, but this one's purely ornamental. The four women up top represent virtues that the people of Gdańsk should exhibit toward outsiders: Peace, Freedom, Prosperity, and Fame. The inscription, a psalm in medieval German, compares Gdańsk to Jerusalem: famous and important. In the middle is one of the coats of arms of Gdańsk—two white crosses under a crown on a red shield. We'll see this symbol many times today.

• *Now go through the gate, entering the "Long Street"...*

Ulica Długa: Look back at the gate you just came through. The women on top of this side represent virtues the people of Gdańsk should cultivate in themselves: Wisdom, Piety, Justice, and Concord (if an arrow's broken, let's take it out of the quiver and fix it).

Wander this intoxicating promenade. Gdańsk was cosmopolitan and exceptionally tolerant in the Middle Ages, attracting a wide range of people, including many who were persecuted elsewhere: Jews, Scots, Dutch, Flemish, Italians, Germans, and more. Members of each group brought with them strands of their culture, which they wove into the tapestry of this city—demonstrated by the eclectic homes along this street.

This lovely street wasn't always so lively and carefree. At the end of World War II, ulica Długa was in ruins. The city was badly damaged when the Nazis first invaded, but the worst devastation came when the Soviets arrived. This was the first traditionally German city that the Red Army reached on their march toward Berlin—and the soldiers were set loose to level the place in retaliation for all of the pain the Nazis had caused. (Soviets didn't destroy nearby Gdynia—which they considered Polish, not German.) Soviet officers turned a blind eye as their soldiers raped and brutalized residents. An entire order of horrified nuns committed suicide by throwing themselves into the river. Upwards of 80 percent of this area was destroyed. It was only thanks to detailed drawings and photographs that these buildings could be so carefully reconstructed, mostly using the original brick.

During Gdańsk's Golden Age, these houses were taxed based on frontage (like the homes lining Amsterdam's canals)—so they were built skinny and deep. The widest houses belonged to the super-elite. Different as they are from the outside, every house had the same general plan inside. Each had three parts, starting with the front and moving back: First was a fancy drawing room, to show off for visitors. Then came a narrow corridor to the back

rooms—often along the side of an inner courtyard. Because the houses had only a few windows facing the outer street, this courtyard provided much-needed sunlight to the rest of the house. The residential quarters were in the back, where the family actually lived: bedroom, kitchen, office. To see the interior of one of these homes, pay a visit to the very interesting **Uphagen House** (#12, on the right, a block and a half in front of the Golden Gate; described later, under "Sights in Gdańsk").

Across the street and a little farther down are some of the most striking **facades** along all of ulica Długa. The blue-and-white house with the three giant heads is from the 19th century, when the hot style was eclecticism—borrowing bits and pieces from various architectural eras. This was one of the few houses on the street that survived World War II.

At the next corner on the right is the huge, blocky, red **post office,** which doesn't quite fit with the skinny facades lining the rest of the street. But step inside. With doves fluttering under an airy glass atrium, the interior's a class act. (To mail postcards, take a number—category C—from the machine on the left.)

Across the street and a few doors down from the post office, notice the colorful **scenes** just overhead on the facade of the cocktail bar. These are slices of life from 17th-century Gdańsk: drinking, talking, buying, fighting, playing music. The ship is a *koga,* a typical symbol of Gdańsk.

A couple of doors down from the cocktail bar is **Neptun Cinema** (marked *KINO*). In the 1980s, this was the only movie theater in the city, and locals lined up all the way down the street to get in. Young adults remember coming here with their grandparents to see a full day of cartoons. Now, as with traditional main-street cinemas in the US, this one is threatened by the rising popularity of multiplexes outside the town center.

Across the street from the theater are three houses belonging to the very influential medieval **Ferber family,** which produced many burghers, mayors, and even a bishop. On the house with the little dog over the door (#29), look for the heads in the circles. These are Caesars of Rome. At the top of the building is Mr. Ferber's answer to the constant question, "Why build such an elaborate house?"—*PRO INVIDIA,* "For the sake of envy."

A few doors down, notice the outdoor tables for Gdańsk's most popular milk bar, the recommended **Bar Mleczny Neptun.** Now you're just a few steps from the **Main Town Hall** (Ratusz

Głównego Miasta). It's closed for renovation until at least until late 2010, so you may have to just enjoy it from the outside. But if you're here after it reopens, consider climbing its observation tower and visiting its superb interior, which features ornately decorated meeting rooms for the city council (described later, under "Sights in Gdańsk"). The **TI** is across the street, on the right.

• *Just beyond the Main Town Hall, ulica Długa widens and becomes...*

Długi Targ: The centerpiece of "Long Square" is one of Gdańsk's most important landmarks, the statue of **Neptune**—god of the sea. He's a fitting symbol for a city that dominates the maritime life of Poland. Behind him is another fine museum, the **Artus Court** (described later, under "Sights in Gdańsk"). This meeting hall for various Gdańsk brotherhoods is home to the most impressive stove you've ever seen.

As you continue down Długi targ, notice the **balconies** extending out into the square, with access to cellars underneath. These were a common feature on ulica Długa in Gdańsk's Golden Age, but were removed in the 19th century to make way for a new tram system. You can find more balconies like these on Mariacka street, which runs parallel to this one (2 blocks to the left).

• *At the end of Długi targ is the...*

Green Gate (Zielona Brama): This huge gate was actually built as a residence for visiting kings...who usually preferred to stay back by Neptune instead (maybe because the river, just on the other side of this gate, stank). It might not have been good enough for kings and queens, but it's plenty fine for a former president—Lech Wałęsa's office is upstairs (see the plaque, *Biuro Lecha Wałęsy*). Other parts of the building are used for temporary exhibitions.

Notice that these bricks are much smaller than the ones we've seen earlier on this walk, which were locally made. These, however, are Dutch: Boats would come here empty, load up with goods, and take them back to Holland. For ballast, they brought bricks on the trip from Holland—which they left here to be turned into this gate.

• *Now go through the gate, and turn left along the...*

Riverfront Embankment: The Motława River—actually a side channel of the mighty Vistula—was the source of Gdańsk's phenomenal Golden Age wealth. This embankment was jam-packed in its heyday, the 14th and 15th centuries. It was so crowded with boats that you would hardly have been able see the water, and boats had to pay a time-based tax for tying up to a post. Instead of an actual embankment (which was built later), a series

of wooden piers connected the boats directly to the gates of the city. Now it's a popular place to stroll and to buy amber. Keep an eye out for old-fashioned **galleons** plying the waters here—these boats depart hourly for a fun cruise to Westerplatte and back. While kitschy, the galleons are a fun way to get out on the water (details on page 421).

Across the river is **Granary Island** (Spichrze), where grain was stored until it could be taken away by ships. Before World War II, there were some 400 granaries here; today the island is still in ruins. Three granaries have been reconstructed on the next island up, and house exhibits for the Central Maritime Museum (described later, under "Sights in Gdańsk"); two others are now recommended hotels (Hotel Gdańsk and Hotel Królewski). A big international company has bought this island, and plans to develop the prime real estate into a new city-center zone of shops, restaurants, houses, and hotels.

Continue along the embankment until you see the five big, round stones on your left. These are the **five little ladies**—mysterious ancient sculptures. If you look closely, you can make out their features, especially the chubby one on the end.

Next, the huge red-brick fort houses the **Archaeological Museum** and a tower you can climb for a good view (described later, under "Sights in Gdańsk"). The gate in the middle leads to **Mariacka street,** a calm, atmospheric drag lined with old balconies, amber shops, and imaginative gargoyles (which locals call "pukers" when it rains).

Consider taking a few minutes to window-shop your way up Mariacka street, comparison-pricing amber souvenirs. At the end of the street on the left (at #1), the recommended **Gotyk House** hotel has a characteristic little shop in the cellar that sells heavenly gingerbread from the town of Toruń. If you're not headed to Toruń (described in the next chapter), this is a good opportunity to buy some of its tasty treats. As that city was the hometown of Nicholas Copernicus—and Copernicus' former lover supposedly once lived in this very house—the shop also has a lovingly presented mini-museum dedicated to the couple. Just after Gotyk House and the gingerbread shop, you're face-to-face with **St. Mary's Church** (enter around the far side; described later, under "Sights in Gdańsk").

• *Back on the embankment, head past a few tempting eateries (including the recommended Kamienica Goldwasser and Sushi 77)—consider scouting a table here for dinner later tonight—before running right into Gdańsk's number-one symbol, and our last stop...*

The Crane (Żuraw): This monstrous 15th-century crane was once used for loading ships, picking up small crafts for repairs, and uprighting masts...beginning a shipbuilding tradition that

Gdańsk at a Gdlance

▲▲▲**Ulica Długa** Gdańsk's colorful showpiece main drag, cutting a picturesque swath through the heart of the wealthy burghers' neighborhood. **Hours:** Always open. See page 388.

▲▲▲**Solidarity Sights and Gdańsk Shipyard** The shipyard that was home to the beginning of the end of European communism, housing a towering monument and an excellent museum. **Hours:** Memorial and shipyard gate—always open. "Roads to Freedom" exhibit—May–Sept Tue–Sun 10:00–18:00, Oct–April Tue–Sun 10:00–17:00, closed Mon year-round. See page 404.

▲▲**Main Town Hall** Ornately decorated meeting rooms, exhibits of town artifacts, and climbable tower with sweeping views. **Hours:** Closed for renovation at least through 2010; once reopened, likely open mid-June–late Sept Mon 10:00–15:00, Tue–Sat 10:00–18:00, Sun 11:00–18:00; late Sept–mid-June Tue 10:00–15:00, Wed–Sat 10:00–16:00, Sun 11:00–16:00, closed Mon. See page 398.

▲▲**Artus Court** Grand meeting hall for guilds of Golden Age Gdańsk, boasting an over-the-top tiled stove. **Hours:** Mid-June–late Sept Mon 10:00–15:00, Tue–Sat 10:00–18:00, Sun 11:00–18:00; late Sept–mid-June Tue 10:00–15:00, Wed–Sat 10:00–16:00, Sun 11:00–16:00, closed Mon. See page 399.

▲▲**St. Mary's Church** Giant red-brick church crammed full of Gdańsk history. **Hours:** Mon–Sat 9:00–17:30, Sun 13:00–17:30. See page 400.

▲**Amber Museum** High-tech new exhibit of valuable golden globs of petrified tree sap. **Hours:** Mid-June–late Sept Mon 10:00–15:00, Tue–Sat 10:00–18:00, Sun 11:00–18:00; late Sept–mid-June Tue 10:00–15:00, Wed–Sat 10:00–16:00, Sun 11:00–16:00, closed Mon. See page 396.

continued to the days of Lech Wałęsa. The crane mechanism was operated by several hardworking sailors scrambling around in giant hamster wheels up top (you can see the wheels if you look up). The Crane belongs to the Central Maritime Museum (described later, under "Sights in Gdańsk"). Just beyond the Crane, they're re-building several structures that will house museum exhibits. And along here, you might see a stand selling smoked fish (7–9 zł).

▲**Uphagen House** Tourable 18th-century interior, typical of the pretty houses that line ulica Długa. **Hours:** Mid-June–late Sept Mon 10:00–15:00, Tue–Sat 10:00–18:00, Sun 11:00–18:00; late Sept–mid-June Tue 10:00–15:00, Wed–Sat 10:00–16:00, Sun 11:00–16:00, closed Mon. See page 397.

▲**Central Maritime Museum** Sprawling exhibit on all aspects of the nautical life, housed in several venues (including the landmark medieval Crane and a permanently moored steamship) connected by a ferry boat. **Hours:** July–Aug daily 10:00–18:00; Sept–Oct and March–June Tue–Sun 10:00–16:00, closed Mon; Nov–Feb Tue–Sun 10:00–15:00, closed Mon. See page 402.

Historical Zone of the Free City of Gdańsk Tiny museum examining Gdańsk's unique status as a "Free City" between the World Wars. **Hours:** Daily 11:00–18:00. See page 402.

Archaeological Museum Decent collection of artifacts from this region's past. **Hours:** July–Aug Tue–Sun 9:00–17:00, closed Mon; Sept–June Tue and Thu–Fri 8:00–16:00, Wed 10:00–17:00, Sat–Sun 10:00–16:00, closed Mon. See page 402.

National Museum in Gdańsk Ho-hum art collection with a single blockbuster highlight: Hans Memling's remarkable *Last Judgment* altarpiece. **Hours:** Tue–Sun 10:00–17:00, closed Mon. See page 412.

"Blue Lion" Archaeological Education Center New, kid-friendly exhibit about medieval Gdańsk. **Hours:** June–Aug Tue–Sun 10:00–18:00, Sept–May Tue–Sun 9:00–17:00, closed Mon year-round. See page 413.

Oliwa Cathedral Suburban church with long, skinny nave and playful organ. **Hours:** Church open long hours daily; frequent organ concerts in summer. See page 414.

• *Our orientation tour is over. Now get out there and enjoy Gdańsk... do it for Lech!*

From the Main Town to the Solidarity Shipyard

This lightly guided walk links Gdańsk's two most important sightseeing areas. Along the way, we'll see some historic landmarks, tour two of Gdańsk's more interesting red-brick churches, and wander through the city's best shopping district. The stroll takes about 20 minutes, not counting stops for sightseeing and shopping.

Begin at the top of ulica Długa, with your back to the Golden Gate. Head a few steps down the street and take a left on Tkacka. After one long block on the left, you can see the back of the **Armory** building (described in the previous self-guided walk). This pearl of Renaissance architecture recently had a striking facelift—examine the exquisite decorations.

After three short blocks, detour to the right down Świętojańska and use the side door to enter the brick **St. Nicholas Church** (Kościół Św. Mikołaja, with the ornate towers on the ends). Archaeologists have found the bodies of 3,000 Napoleonic soldiers buried here. Near the end of World War II, when the Soviet army reached Gdańsk on its march westward, they were given the order to burn all of the churches. Only this one—dedicated to Russia's patron saint—was spared. As the best-preserved church in town, today it has a more impressive interior than the others, with lavish black-and-gold Baroque altars.

Backtrack out to the main street and continue north. Immediately after the church (on the right) is Gdańsk's newly renovated **Market Hall.** Look for the coat of arms of Gdańsk over each of its four doors (two white crosses on a red shield). Inside you'll find mostly local shoppers—browsing through produce, other foods, and clothing—as well as the graves of medieval Dominican monks, which were discovered when the building was renovated (in the basement). Look up to appreciate the delicate steel-and-glass canopy.

Across the street from the Market Hall is a round, red-brick **tower,** once part of the city's protective wall. This marks the end of the Main Town, and the beginning of the Old Town.

Another long block up the street is the huge **St. Catherine's Church** (Kościół Św. Katarzyny, on the right). "Katy," as locals call it, is the oldest church in Gdańsk. In May of 2006, a carelessly discarded cigarette caused the church roof to burst into flames. Local people ran into the church and pulled everything outside, so nothing valuable was damaged; even the carillon bells were saved. However, the roof and wooden frame were totally destroyed. The people of Gdańsk were determined to rebuild this important symbol of the city. Within days of the fire, fundraising concerts were held to scrape together most of the money needed to raise the roof once more.

The church hiding behind Katy—named for Catherine's daughter Bridget—has important ties to Solidarity, and is worth a quick detour. To get there, walk up ulica Katarzynki, along the side of St. Catherine's Church, and past the monument to Pope John Paul II.

St. Bridget's Church (Kościół Św. Brygidy) was the home church of Lech Wałęsa during the tense days of the 1980s. This

church and its priest, Henryk Jankowski, were particularly aggressive in supporting the ideals of Solidarity. Jankowski became a mouthpiece for the movement, and Wałęsa named his youngest daughter Brygida in gratitude for the church's support. In the back corner, under the wall of wooden crosses, find the tomb of Solidarity martyr Jerzy Popiełuszko, a famously outspoken Warsaw priest who was kidnapped, beaten, and murdered by the communist secret police. Here, notice that his hands and feet are tied. At the front of the church, check out the enormous, unfinished altar made entirely of amber, featuring the Black Madonna of Częstochowa and a royal Polish eagle. If and when it's finished, it'll be 36 feet high, 20 feet wide, and 10 feet deep. But some locals criticize this ambitious project as an example of Father Jankowski's recent missteps. Despite his fame and contributions to Solidarity, Jankowski's public standing has taken a nosedive in the last few years—thanks to ego-driven projects like this, as well as accusations of anti-Semitism and implications of pedophilia and corruption. Because of these issues, and because of his worsening health, Jankowski has been forced to "retire."

Backtrack out past St. Catherine's Church to the main street. Just across from St. Catherine's is a red-brick building with a lot of little windows in the roof. This is the **Great Mill** (Wielki Młyn), which has been converted into a shopping mall (Mon–Fri 10:00–19:00, Sat 10:00–16:00, closed Sun). As you continue north and cross the stream, you'll also see the picturesque **Small Mill** (Mały Młyn) straddling the stream on your right.

After another block, on your right, is the modern **Madison shopping mall** (Mon–Sat 9:00–21:00, Sun 10:00–20:00). Two blocks to your left (up Heweliusza) are more shopping malls and the main train station.

But to get to the **shipyard,** keep heading straight up Rajska. After another long block, jog right (between the big, green-glass skyscraper and today's Solidarity headquarters) and head for the three tall crosses.

On the way, you'll see signs leading to the **"Roads to Freedom" exhibit** (the entrance to this underground museum is actually a freestanding kiosk by the side of the road).

But before you visit this museum, head to the shipyard to begin my self-guided tour there (see page 404). Near the entrance to the museum are two artifacts from communist times. First, parked in front of the museum is an **armored personnel carrier,** just like the ones used by the ZOMO (riot police) to terrorize Polish citizens after martial law was declared in 1981. Nearby, watch for the two big chunks of **wall:** On the left, a piece of the Berlin Wall; and on the right, a chunk of the shipyard wall Lech Wałęsa scaled to get inside and lead the strike. The message: What happened behind

one wall eventually led to the fall of the other Wall.

For the whole story, continue to the monument with the three tall crosses, and turn to page 408.

Sights in Gdańsk

Main Town (Główne Miasto)

The following sights are all in the Main Town, listed roughly in the order you'll see them on the self-guided walk of the Royal Way.

Gdańsk Historical Museum

The Gdańsk Historical Museum has four excellent branches. All have the same **cost and hours** (10 zł apiece, free Mon in summer and Tue off-season; open mid-June–late Sept Mon 10:00–15:00, Tue–Sat 10:00–18:00, Sun 11:00–18:00; late Sept–mid-June Tue 10:00–15:00, Wed–Sat 10:00–16:00, Sun 11:00–16:00, closed Mon; last entry 30 min before closing). The museums share a phone number and website (central tel. 058-767-9100, www.mhmg.gda.pl).

▲Amber Museum (Muzeum Bursztynu)—Housed in a pair of connected brick towers just outside the Main Town's Golden Gate, this museum has two oddly contradictory parts. One shows off one of Gdańsk's favorite local resources, amber, while the other focuses on implements of torture (cost and hours above, overpriced 1.5-hour audioguide-25 zł, enter at end facing Golden Gate).

Partially explained in English, the Amber Museum offers a good introduction to the globby yellow stuff. As the museum fills an old guard tower, you'll have to walk up several flights of stairs to see it all. For a primer before you go, check out the "All About Amber" sidebar.

Climb up one flight of stairs, buy your ticket, then head up to the second floor for a scientific look at amber. View inclusions (items trapped in the resin) through a magnifying glass and microscope, and see dozens of samples showing the full rainbow of amber shades. Interactive video screens explain the creation of amber. The third-floor exhibit explains the "Amber Route" (the ancient Celtic trade road connecting Gdańsk to Italy), outlines medicinal uses of the stuff, and displays a wide range of functional items made from amber—clocks, pipe stems, candlesticks, chandeliers, jewelry boxes, and much more. The fourth floor shows off more artistic items made of amber—sculptures, candelabras, beer

All About Amber

Poland's Baltic seaside is known as the Amber Coast. You can see amber *(bursztyn)* in Gdańsk's Amber Museum, in the collection at Malbork Castle (see next chapter)—and in shop windows everywhere. This fossilized tree resin originated here on the north coast of Poland 40 million years ago. It comes in as many different colors as Eskimos have words for snow: 300 distinct shades, from yellowish-white to yellowish-black, from opaque to transparent. (I didn't believe it either, until I toured Gdańsk's museum.) Darker-colored amber is generally mixed with ash and sand—making it more fragile, and generally less desirable. Lighter amber is mixed with gasses and air bubbles.

Amber has been popular since long before there were souvenir stands. Archaeologists have found graves of Roman citizens (and their coins) who were buried with crosses made of amber. Almost 75 percent of the world's amber is mined in northern Poland, and it often simply washes up on the beaches after a winter storm. Some of the elaborate amber sculptures displayed at the museum are created by joining pieces of amber with "amber glue"—made of melted-down amber mixed with an adhesive agent. More recently, amber craftsmen are combining amber with silver to create artwork—a method dubbed the "Polish School."

In addition to being good for the economy, some Poles believe amber is good for their health. A traditional cure for arthritis pain is to pour strong vodka over amber, let it set, and then rub it on sore joints. Other remedies call for mixing amber dust with honey or rose oil. It sounds superstitious, but it works—amber contains a mineral that actually can help certain health problems.

steins, chessboards, and a model ship with delicate sails made of amber. At the top floor, you'll find a modern gallery showing more recent amber craftsmanship, and displays about amber's role in fashion today.

On your way back down, detour along the upper level of the courtyard to find the museum's dark side (the Torture Museum). First is a brief exhibit about the building's history, including its chapter as a prison tower. The rest of the exhibit—with sound effects, scant artifacts, and mannequins helpfully demonstrating the grisly equipment—tries hard to make medieval torture and imprisonment interesting.

▲Uphagen House (Dom Uphagena)—This interesting place is your chance to glimpse what's behind the colorful facades lining ulica Długa (see cost and hours at top of this section; ulica Długa 12). Check out the cut-away model just inside the entry to see the

three parts you'll visit: dolled-up visitors' rooms in front, a corridor along the courtyard, and private rooms in the back. As you enter, the costumed staffers will likely usher you to the top floor, which houses temporary exhibits. Back down on the middle floor, ogle the finely decorated salon, which was used to show off for guests. Most of this furniture is original (saved from WWII bombs by locals who hid it in the countryside). Passing into the dining room, note the knee-high paintings of hunting and celebrations. Along the passage to the back, each room has a theme: butterflies in the smoking room, then flowers, then birds in the music room. In the private rooms at the back, notice how much simpler the decor is. Downstairs, you'll pass through the kitchen, the pantry, and a room with photos from the house before the war, which they used to reconstruct what you see today.

▲▲Main Town Hall (Ratusz Głównego Miasta)—This landmark building, which is closed for renovation at least until the end of 2010, contains remarkable decorations from Gdańsk's Golden Age (see cost and hours on page 392; ulica Długa 47). You can also climb to the top of the **tower** for commanding views (5 zł extra, mid-June–mid-Sept only, possibly closed during renovation).

If the building has re-opened in time for your visit, buy your ticket down below (good gift shop), then head up the stairs and inside. While the following details might be slightly different after the renovation, most of the items described here should be on display:

In the entry room, examine the photo showing this building at the end of World War II (you'll see more upstairs). The ornately carved wooden **door,** which we'll pass through in a minute, also deserves a close look. Above the door are two crosses under a crown. This seal of Gdańsk is being held—as it's often depicted—by a pair of lions. The felines are stubborn and independent, just like the citizens of Gdańsk. Close the door partway to look at the carvings of crops. Around the frame of the door are mermen, reminding us that these crops, like so many other resources of Poland, are transported on the Vistula and out through Gdańsk.

Go through the door into the **Red Hall,** where the Gdańsk city council met in the summertime. (The lavish fireplace—with another pair of lions holding the coat of arms of Gdańsk—was just for show.) City council members would sit in the seats around the room, debating city policy. The shin-level paintings depict the earth; the exquisitely detailed inlaid wood just over the seats

are animals; the paintings on the wall above represent the seven virtues the burghers meeting in this room should have; and the ceiling is all about theology. Examine that ceiling. It has 25 paintings in total, with both Christian and pagan themes—meant to inspire the decision-makers in this room to make good choices. The smaller ones around the edges are scenes from mythology and the Bible. The one in the middle (from 1607) shows God's relationship to Gdańsk. In the foreground, the citizens of Gdańsk go about their daily lives. Above them, high atop the arch, God's hand reaches down (from within clouds of Hebrew characters) and grasps the city's steeple. The rainbow arching above also symbolizes God's connection to Gdańsk. Mirroring that is the Vistula River, which begins in the mountains of southern Poland (on the right), runs through the country, and exits at the sea in Gdańsk (on the left, where the rainbow ends).

Continue into the not-so-impressive Winter Hall, with another fireplace and coat of arms held by lions. Keep going through the next room, into a room with before-and-after photos of **WWII damage.** At the foot of the destroyed crucifix is a book with a bullet hole in it. The twist of wood is all that's left of the main support for the spiral staircase (today reconstructed in the room where you entered). Ponder the inspiring ability of a city to be reborn after the tragedy of war.

Upstairs are some temporary exhibits, and several examples of **Gdańsk-style furniture.** These pieces are characterized by three big, round feet along the front, lots of ornamentation, and usually a virtually-impossible-to-find lock (sometimes hidden behind a movable decoration). You can also see a coin collection, from the days when Gdańsk had the elite privilege of minting its own currency.

▲▲Artus Court (Dwór Artusa)—In the Middle Ages, Gdańsk was home to many brotherhoods and guilds (like businessmen's clubs). For their meetings, the city provided this elaborately decorated hall, named for King Arthur—a medieval symbol for prestige and power. Just as in King Arthur's Court, this was a place where powerful and important people came together. Such halls were once common in Baltic Europe, but this is the only original one that survives (cost and hours on page 392, dry and too-thorough audioguide-5 zł; in tall, white, triple-arched building behind Neptune statue at Długi targ 43–44).

In the grand hall, various **cupboards** line the walls. Each organization that met here had a place to keep its important documents and office supplies. Suspended from the ceiling are seven giant **model ships** that depict Baltic vessels, symbolic of the city's connection to the sea.

In the far back corner is the museum's highlight: a gigantic **stove** decorated with 520 colorful tiles featuring the faces of kings, queens, nobles, mayors, and burghers. Half of these people were Protestant, and half were Catholic, mixed together in no particular order—a reminder of Gdańsk's religious tolerance. Virtually all of these tiles are original, having survived WWII bombs. But not all of the original tiles are here: three of them were recently discovered by a bargain-hunter wandering through a flea market in the southern part of the country, who returned them to their rightful home.

Notice the huge **paintings** on the walls above, with 3-D animals emerging from flat frames. Hunting is a popular theme in local artwork. Like minting coins, hunting was a privilege usually reserved for royalty, but extended in special circumstances to the burghers of special towns...like Gdańsk. If you look closely, it's obvious that these "paintings" are new, digitally generated reproductions of the originals, which were damaged in World War II.

The next room—actually in the next-door building—is a typical front room of the burghers' homes lining ulica Długa. Ogle the gorgeously carved wooden staircase. Upstairs (through the door to the right of the stairs) is a hall of knights—once again evoking Arthurian legend. If you've rented an audioguide, take it back up front to return it; otherwise, exit through the back, just down the street from St. Mary's Church; to get back to the main drag, go back around the block, to the left.

Other Museums and Churches in the Main Town

▲▲St. Mary's Church (Kościół Mariacki)—Gdańsk has so many striking red-brick churches, it's hard to keep track of them. But if you visit only one, make it St. Mary's. This is the biggest brick church in the world, accommodating up to 25,000 people. Built over 159 years in the 14th and 15th centuries, the church is an important symbol of Gdańsk (church free for individuals to enter but donation requested, audioguide-5 zł or 7 zł/2 people, open for tourists Mon–Sat 9:00–17:30, Sun 13:00–17:30).

As you enter the church, notice all of the white, empty space—unusual in a Catholic country, where frilly Baroque churches are the

norm. In the Middle Ages, Gdańsk's tolerance attracted people who were suffering religious persecution. As the Protestant population grew, they needed a place to worship. St. Mary's, like most other Gdańsk churches, eventually became Protestant—leaving these churches with the blank walls you see now. Today you'll find only one Baroque church in central Gdańsk (the domed pink-and-green chapel behind St. Mary's).

Most Gothic stone churches are built in the basilica style—with a high nave in the middle, shorter aisles on the side, and flying buttresses to support the weight. (Think of Paris' Notre-Dame.) But that design doesn't work with brick. So, like all Gdańsk churches, St. Mary's is a "hall church"—with three naves the same height, and no exterior buttresses.

Also like other Gdańsk churches, St. Mary's gave refuge to the Polish people after the communist government declared martial law in 1981. When a riot broke out and violence seemed imminent, people would flood into churches for protection. The ZOMO riot police wouldn't follow them inside.

Most of the church decorations are original. A few days before World War II broke out in Gdańsk, locals hid precious items in the countryside. Take some time now to see a few of the highlights.

Head up the right nave and find the opulent family marker to the right of the main altar, high on the pillar. Look for the falling baby (under the crown). This is Constantine Ferber. As a precocious child, Constantine leaned out his window on ulica Długa to see the king's processional come through town. He slipped and fell, but landed in a salesman's barrel of fish. Constantine grew up to become the mayor of Gdańsk.

Look on the side of the same pillar for the coat of arms with the three pigs' heads. This story relates to another member of the illustrious Ferber clan. An enemy army was laying siege to the town, and tried to starve them out. A clever Ferber decided to load the cannons with pigs' heads to show the enemy that they had plenty of food—it worked, and the enemy left.

Circle around, past the front of the beautifully carved main altar. Behind it is the biggest stained-glass window in Poland. Below the window (behind the main altar) is a huge, empty glass case. The case was designed to hold Hans Memling's *Final Judgment* painting, which used to be on display here, but is currently being held hostage by the National Museum. The museum claimed the church wasn't a good environment for such a precious work, so the priest had this display case built—but that still wasn't enough to convince the museum to give it back. You can see a smaller replica up by the main door of the church (in the little chapel on the right just before you exit), but true art fans will want to venture to the National Museum (described later) to see the much larger and far

more masterful original.

Before you head back out to the mini-Memling (and the exit), venture to the far side of the altar and check out the elaborate **astronomical clock**—supposedly the biggest wooden clock in the world. Below is the circular calendar showing the saint's day, and above are zodiac signs and the time (only one hand).

If you've got the energy, climb the 408 steps up the church's 270-foot-tall **tower.** You'll be rewarded with sweeping views of the entire city (tower climb-4 zł, Mon–Sat 9:00–17:30, Sun 13:00–17:30, entrance in back corner).

Historical Zone of the Free City of Gdańsk (Strefa Historyczna Wolne Miasto Gdańsk)—In a city so obsessed with its Golden Age and Solidarity history, this charming little collection illuminates a unique but often-overlooked chapter in the story of Gdańsk: The years between World Wars I and II, when—in an effort to find a workable compromise in this ethnically mixed city—Gdańsk was not part of Germany nor of Poland, but a self-governing "free city" *(wolne miasto).* Like a holdover from medieval fiefdoms in modern times, the city-state of Gdańsk even issued its own currency and stamps. This modest museum earnestly shows off artifacts from the time—photos, stamps, maps, flags, promotional tourist leaflets, and other items from the free city, all marked with the Gdańsk symbol of two white crosses under a crown on a red shield. The brochure explains that four out of five people living in the free city identified themselves not as German or Poles, but as "Danzigers." While some might find the subject obscure, this endearing collection is a treat for World War II history buffs (5 zł, daily 11:00–18:00, a few steps in front of St. Mary's at ulica Piwna 19-21, tel. 058-320-2828, www.tpg.info.pl).

Archaeological Museum (Muzeum Archeologiczne)—This modest museum is worth a quick peek for those interested in archaeology. The ground floor has exhibits on excavated finds from Sudan, where the museum has a branch program. Upstairs, look for the distinctive urns with cute faces, which date from the Hallstatt Period and were discovered in slate graves around Gdańsk. Also upstairs are some Bronze and Iron Age tools; before-and-after photos of WWII Gdańsk; and a reconstructed 12th-century Viking-like Slavonic longboat (6 zł; July–Aug Tue–Sun 9:00–17:00, closed Mon; Sept–June Tue and Thu–Fri 8:00–16:00, Wed 10:00–17:00, Sat–Sun 10:00–16:00, closed Mon; ulica Mariacka 25–26, tel. 058-322-2100). You can also pay 3 zł to climb the building's tower, with good views up Mariacka street toward St. Mary's Church.

▲Central Maritime Museum (Centralne Muzeum Morskie)—Gdańsk's history and livelihood are tied to the sea. This collection, spread out among several buildings on either side of the river, examines all aspects of this connection. While nautical types may

get a thrill out of the creaky, sprawling museum, most visitors find it little more than a convenient way to pass some time and enjoy a cruise across the river.

The exhibit has three parts. The first one is on the Main Town side of the river: The landmark medieval **Crane** (Żuraw)—Gdańsk's most important symbol—houses an exhibit on living in the city during its Golden Age (16th–17th centuries). You can see models of Baltic buildings (including the Crane you're inside), plus traditional tools and costumes. (For more on the Crane itself, see page 391.) A new museum building next to the Crane is in the works.

The other two parts of the museum are across the river on Ołowianka Island. You can reach the island via the little **ferry** (*prom,* 1 zł one-way, included in 18-zł museum ticket). The ferry runs about every 15 minutes in peak season (during museum hours only), but frequency declines sharply in the off-season (and it doesn't run if the river freezes). This also gives fine views back on the Crane.

Once on the island, you can visit the three rebuilt **Old Granaries** (Spichlerze). These make up the heart of the exhibit, tracing the history of Gdańsk—particularly as it relates to the sea—from prehistoric days to the present. Models of the town and region help put things into perspective. You can also see exhibits on underwater exploration, navigational aids, artifacts of the Polish seafaring tradition, peek-a-boo cross-sections of multi-level ships, and models of the modern-day shipyard where Solidarity was born. This place is home to more miniature ships than you ever thought you'd see, and the Nautical Gallery upstairs features endless rooms with paintings of boats.

Finally, crawl through the holds and scramble across the deck of a decommissioned steamship docked permanently across from the Crane, called the ***Sołdek*** (ship sometimes closed in winter). This was the first postwar vessel built at the Gdańsk shipyard. Below decks, you can see where they shoveled the coal; wander through a maze of pipes, gears, valves, gauges, and ladders; and visit the rooms where the sailors lived, slept, and ate. You can even play captain in the bridge.

Cost, Hours, Location: Individually, each of the three parts of the museum costs 8 zł, but an 18-zł ticket gets you in everywhere and also covers the ferry across the river. It's open July–Aug daily 10:00–18:00; Sept–Oct and March–June Tue–Sun 10:00–16:00, closed Mon; Nov–Feb Tue–Sun 10:00–15:00, closed Mon (ulica

Ołowianka 9–13, tel. 058-301-8611, www.cmm.pl). The museum's lack of English information is irritating; fortunately, some exhibits have descriptions you can borrow.

▲▲▲Solidarity (Solidarność) and the Gdańsk Shipyard (Stocznia Gdańska)

Gdańsk's single best experience is exploring the shipyard that witnessed the beginning of the end of communism's stranglehold on Eastern Europe. Here in the industrial wasteland that Lech Wałęsa called the "cradle of freedom," this evocative site tells the story of the brave Polish shipyard workers who took on—and ultimately defeated—an Evil Empire.

A visit to the Solidarity sights has two main parts: the memorial and gate out in front of the shipyard, and the excellent "Roads to Freedom" exhibit nearby. Allow 1.5 hours for the whole visit.

Cost, Hours, Information: Memorial and shipyard gate—free and always open; "Roads to Freedom" exhibit—6 zł, 2 zł on Wed, open May–Sept Tue–Sun 10:00–18:00, Oct–April Tue–Sun 10:00–17:00, closed Mon year-round, Wały Piastowskie 24, tel. 058-308-4428, www.fcs.org.pl and www.ecs.gda.pl.

Getting to the Shipyard: The Solidarity monument and shipyard are at the north end of the Old Town, about a 20-minute walk from ulica Długa. For the most interesting approach, follow my self-guided "From the Main Town to the Solidarity Shipyard" walk on page 393.

Background: After the communists took over Eastern Europe at the end of World War II, the oppressed people throughout the Soviet Bloc rose up in different ways. The most dramatic uprisings—Hungary's 1956 Uprising (see page 514) and Czechoslovakia's 1968 "Prague Spring" (see page 42)—were both brutally crushed under the treads of Soviet tanks. The formula for freedom that finally succeeded was a patient, decade-long series of strikes spearheaded by Lech Wałęsa and his trade union, called Solidarność—"Solidarity." (The movement also benefited from good timing, as it coincided with the *perestroika* and *glasnost* policies of the Soviet premier Mikhail Gorbachev.) While some American politicians might like to take credit for defeating communism, Wałęsa and his fellow workers were the ones fighting on the front lines, armed with nothing more than guts.

➲ **Self-Guided Tour:** First we'll visit the memorial and peek into the shipyard, then we'll backtrack to the museum. Begin at the towering monument—with three anchor-adorned crosses—near the entrance gate to the shipyard.

Monument of the Fallen Shipyard Workers: The seeds of August 1980 were sown a decade before. Since becoming part of the Soviet Bloc, the Poles staged frequent strikes, protests, and

uprisings to secure their rights, all of which were put down by the regime. But the bloodiest of these took place in December 1970—a tragic event memorialized by this monument.

The 1970 strike was prompted by price hikes. The communist government set the prices for all products. As Poland endured drastic food shortages in the 1960s and 1970s, the regime frequently announced what it called "regulation of prices." Invariably, this meant an increase in the cost of essential foodstuffs. (To be able to claim "regulation" rather than "increase," the regime would symbolically lower prices for a few select items—but these were always nonessential luxuries, such as elevators and TV sets, which nobody could afford anyway.) The regime was usually smart enough to raise prices on January 1—when the people were fat and happy after Christmas, and too hungover to complain. But on December 12, 1970, bolstered by an ego-stoking visit by West German Chancellor Willy Brandt, Polish premier Władysław Gomułka increased prices. The people of Poland—who cared more about the price of Christmas dinner than relations with Germany—struck back.

A wave of strikes and sit-ins spread along the heavily industrialized north coast of Poland, most notably in Gdańsk, Gdynia, and Szczecin. Thousands of angry demonstrators poured through the gate of this shipyard, marched into town, and set fire to the Communist Party Committee building. In an attempt to quell the riots, the government-run radio implored the people to go back to work. On the morning of December 17, workers showed up at shipyard gates across northern Poland—and were greeted by the army and police. Without provocation, the Polish army opened fire on the workers. While the official death toll for the massacre stands at 44, others say the true number is much higher. This monument, with a trio of 140-foot-tall crosses, honors those lost to the regime that December.

Go to the middle of the wall behind the crosses, to the monument of the worker wearing a flimsy plastic work helmet, attempting to shield himself from bullets. Behind him is a list—pockmarked with symbolic bullet holes—of workers murdered on that day. *Lat* means "years old"—many teenagers were among the dead. The quote at the top of the wall is from Pope John Paul II, who was elected eight years after this tragedy. The Pope was known for his clever way with words, and this very carefully phrased quote—which served as an inspiration to the Poles during

Lech Wałęsa

In 1980, the world was turned on its ear by a walrus-mustachioed shipyard electrician. Within three years, this seemingly run-of-the-mill Pole had precipitated the collapse of communism, led a massive 10 million-member trade union with enormous political impact, was named *Time* magazine's Man of the Year, and won a Nobel Peace Prize.

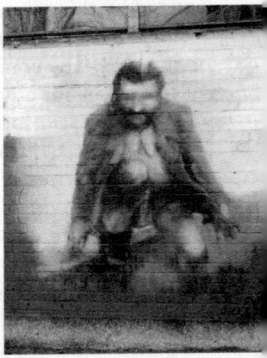

Lech Wałęsa was born in Popowo, Poland, in 1943. After working as a car mechanic and serving two years in the army, he became an electrician at the Gdańsk Shipyard in 1967. Like many Poles, Wałęsa felt stifled by the communist government, and was infuriated that a system that was supposed to be for the workers clearly wasn't serving them.

When the shipyard massacre took place in December 1970, Wałęsa was at the forefront of the protests. He was marked as a dissident, and in 1976, he was fired. He hopped from job to job and was occasionally unemployed—under communism, a rock-bottom status reserved for only the most despicable derelicts. But Wałęsa soldiered on, fighting for the creation of a trade union and building up quite a file with the secret police.

In August 1980, Wałęsa heard news of the beginnings of the Gdańsk strike, and raced to the shipyard. In an act that has since become the stuff of legend, Wałęsa scaled the shipyard wall to get inside.

Before long, Wałęsa's dynamic personality won him the unofficial role of the workers' leader and spokesman. He negotiated with the regime to hash out the August Agreements, becoming a rock star-type hero during the so-called "16 Months of Hope"...until martial law came crashing down in December of 1981. Wałęsa was arrested and interned for 11 months in a country house. After being released, Wałęsa continued to struggle

their darkest hours—skewers the regime in a way subtle enough to still be tolerated: "Let thy spirit descend, and renew the face of the earth—*this* earth" (that is, Poland). Below that is the dedication: "They gave their lives so you can live decently."

Stretching to the left of this center wall are plaques representing labor unions from around Poland—and around the world (look for the Chinese characters)—expressing solidarity with these workers. To the right is an enormous Bible verse: "May the Lord give strength to his people. May the Lord bless his people with the gift of peace" (Psalms 29:11).

More than a decade after the massacre, this monument was

underground, becoming a symbol of anti-communist sentiment.

Finally, the dedication of Wałęsa and Solidarity paid off, and Polish communism dissolved—with Wałęsa rising from the ashes as the country's first post-communist president. But the skills that made Wałęsa a rousing success at leading an uprising did not translate to the president's office. Wałęsa proved to be a stubborn, headstrong politician, frequently clashing with the parliament. He squabbled with his own party, declaring a "war at the top" of Solidarity and rotating higher-ups to prevent corruption and keep the party fresh. He also didn't choose his advisors well, enlisting several staffers who wound up immersed in scandal. His overconfidence was his Achilles' heel, and his governing style verged on authoritarian.

Unrefined and none too interested in scripted speeches, Wałęsa was a simple man who preferred playing ping-pong with his buddies to attending formal state functions. Though lacking a formal education, Wałęsa had unsurpassed drive and charisma... but that's not enough to lead a country—especially during an impossibly complicated, fast-changing time, when even the savviest politician would certainly have stumbled.

Wałęsa was defeated at the polls (by the Poles) in 1995, and when he ran again in 2000, he received a humiliating 1 percent of the vote. Since leaving office, Wałęsa has kept a lower profile, but still delivers speeches worldwide. Many poor Poles grumble that Lech, who started life simple like them, has forgotten the little people. But his fans point out that he gives much of his income to charity. And on his lapel, he still always wears a pin featuring the Black Madonna of Częstochowa—the symbol of Polish Catholicism.

Poles say there are at least two Lech Wałęsas: the young, working-class idealist Lech, at the forefront of the Solidarity strikes, who will always have a special place in their hearts; and the failed President Wałęsa, who got in over his head and tarnished his legacy.

finally constructed. It marked the first time a communist regime ever allowed a monument to be built to honor its own victims. Wałęsa called it a harpoon in the heart of the communists. Inspired by the brave sacrifice of their true comrades, the shipyard workers rose up here in August of 1980, formulating the "21 Points" of a new union called Solidarity. The demands included the right to strike and form unions, the freeing of political prisoners, and an increase in wages. These 21 Points are listed in Polish on the panel at the far end of the right wall, marked *21 X TAK Solidarność* ("21 times yes Solidarity").

• *Now continue to the gate and peer through into the birthplace of Eastern European freedom.*

Gdańsk Shipyard (Stocznia Gdańska) Gate #2: When a Pole named Karol Wojtyła was elected Pope in 1978—and visited his homeland in 1979—he inspired his 40 million countrymen to believe that impossible dreams can come true. Prices continued to go up, and the workers continued to rise up. By the summer of 1980, it was clear that the dam was about to break.

In August, Anna Walentynowicz—a Gdańsk crane operator and known dissident—was fired unceremoniously just short of her retirement. This sparked a strike in the Gdańsk Shipyard (then called the Lenin Shipyard) on August 14, 1980. An electrician named Lech Wałęsa had been fired as an agitator years before, and wasn't allowed into the shipyard. But on hearing news of the strike, Wałęsa went to the shipyard and climbed over the wall to get inside. The strike now had a leader.

Imagine being one of the 16,000 workers who stayed here for 18 days during the strike—hungry, cold, sleeping on sheets of Styrofoam, inspired by the new Polish pope, excited about finally standing up to the regime...and terrified that you might be gunned down at any moment, like your friends had been a decade before. Because you're afraid to leave the shipyard, your only way to communicate with the outside world is through this gate—your wife or brother shows up here and asks for you, and those inside spread the word until you come talk to them. Occasionally, a truck pulls up to the gate, and Lech Wałęsa stands on its cab with a megaphone and faces the thousands of people assembled outside the gate—giving them progress reports of the negotiations, and pleading for supplies. The people of Gdańsk respond, bringing armfuls of bread and other food, keeping the workers going. This truly is Solidarity.

During the strike, two items hung on the fence. One of them (which still hangs there today) was a picture of Pope John Paul II—a reminder to believe in your dreams and have faith in God (for more on the pope and his role in Solidarity, see page 270). The other item was a makeshift list of the strikers' 21 Points—demands scrawled in red paint and black pencil on pieces of plywood.

• *You'll likely see construction in the area beyond the gate.*

Today's Shipyard: This part of the shipyard, long abandoned, is gradually being redeveloped into a **"Young City"** (Młode

Miasto)—envisioned as a new city center for Gdańsk, with shopping, restaurants, and homes. Rusting shipbuilding equipment will be torn down, and old brick buildings will be converted into gentrified flats. Just behind the monument will be the new European Center of Solidarity (still an active union in some countries). The shipyard gate, monument, and other important sites from the Solidarity strikes will stay put. The ambitious project isn't due to be completed until 2030.

• *Walk to the right and peer through the gate.*

The path leading into the shipyard (which is likely closed to visitors) passes through two huge **symbolic gateways.** The first resembles the rusted hull of a ship, representing the protest of the shipbuilders. The next gateway—a futuristic, colorful tower—is a small-scale version of a 1,000-foot-tall monument planned by the prominent Soviet constructivist architect Vladimir Tatlin. This fanciful but unfulfilled design represents the misguided, failed optimism of the communist "utopia."

In the distance, squint to see the low-profile, red-brick building. This is the **BHP Conference Hall,** where the communists actually sat down across the table from Lech Wałęsa and worked out a compromise. This building is being restored, and will be a centerpiece of the "Roads to Freedom" exhibit when it moves back here in several years.

• *The museum where we'll learn the rest of the story is about 100 yards back toward the Main Town. With the main shipyard gate to your back, walk straight ahead, passing the green-and-yellow building on your right. Cross the street and walk toward the green skyscraper. After about a block, note the stairs leading underground, into the...*

"Roads to Freedom" Exhibit: Walk downstairs—startled by angry shouts from the ZOMO—and buy your ticket, which is designed to look like the communist ration coupons that all Poles had to carry and present before they could buy certain goods. Cashiers would stand with scissors at the ready, prepared to snip off a corner of your coupon after making the sale. Consider picking up a Solidarity book or other souvenir at the excellent gift shop here before moving on.

To the right of the ticket desk are some depressing reminders of the communist days. The phone booth is marked *Automat Nieczynny*—"Out of Order"—as virtually all phone booths were back then. In the humble, authentic commie WC, notice that instead of toilet paper, there's a wad of old newspapers. Actual toilet paper was cause for celebration. Notice the mannequin with several rolls on a string around her neck—time to party!

Across from the ticket desk is a typical **Polish shop** (marked *spożyw,* a truncated version of *spożywczy,* "grocery store") from the 1970s, at the worst of the food shortages. Great selection, eh?

Often the only things in stock were vinegar and mustard. Milk and bread were generally available, but they were low quality—it wasn't unusual to find a cigarette butt in your loaf. The few blocks of cheese and other items in the case weren't real—they were props, placed there so the shop wouldn't look completely empty. Sometimes they'd hang a few pitiful, phony salamis from the hooks—otherwise, people might think it was a tile shop. The only real meat in here were the flies on the flypaper. Despite the meager supplies, shoppers (mostly women) would sometimes have to wait in line literally all day long just to pick over these scant choices. People didn't necessarily buy what they needed; instead, they'd buy anything that could be bartered on the black market. On the counter, notice the little jar holding clipped-off ration coupons.

Continue into the exhibit. The first room explains the **roots** of the shipyard strikes, including the famous uprisings in Hungary and Czechoslovakia, and the December 1970 riots in Poland. (Interactive computer screens tell you more about these events.) The prison cell is a reminder of Stalin's strong-arm tactics for getting the people of Eastern Europe to sign on to his new system.

Then head into the heart of the exhibit, **August 1980.** Near the plaster statue of Lenin are several tables. These were the actual tables used (in the red-brick building back in the shipyard) when the communist authorities finally agreed to negotiate after 18 days of protests. On the afternoon of August 31, 1980, the Governmental Commission and the Inter-Factory Strike Committee (MKS) came together and signed the August Agreements, which legalized Solidarity—the first time any communist government permitted a workers' union. Photos and a video show the giddy day, as the Polish Bob Dylan laments the evils of the regime. Lech Wałęsa—sitting at the big table, with his characteristic walrus moustache—signed the agreement with a big, red, souvenir-type pen adorned with a picture of Pope John Paul II (displayed across the room). Other union reps, sitting at smaller tables, tape-recorded the proceedings, and played them later at their own factories to prove that the unthinkable had happened. Near the end of this room are replicas of the plywood boards featuring the 21 Points, which hung on the front gate we just saw.

While the government didn't take the agreements very seriously, the Poles did...and before long, 10 million of them—one out of every four Poles—joined Solidarity. So began the **16 Months of Hope**—the theme of the next room. Newly legal, Solidarity continued to stage strikes and make its opposition known. Slick Solidarity posters and children's art convey the childlike enthusiasm with which the Poles seized their hard-won kernels of freedom. The poster with a baby in a Solidarity T-shirt—one year old, just like the union itself—captures the sense of hope. The com-

munist authorities' hold on the Polish people began to slip. The rest of the Soviet Bloc looked on nervously, and the Warsaw Pact army assembled at the Polish border and glared at the uprisers. The threat of invasion hung heavy in the air.

Turn the corner to see Solidarity's progress come crashing down. On Sunday morning, December 13, 1981, the Polish head of state, General Wojciech Jaruzelski, appeared on national TV and announced the introduction of **martial law.** Solidarity was outlawed, and its leaders were arrested. Frightened Poles heard the announcement and looked out their windows to see Polish Army tanks rumbling through the snowy streets. Jaruzelski claimed that he imposed martial law to prevent the Soviets from invading. Today, many historians question whether martial law was really necessary—though Jaruzelski remains remorseless. Martial law was a tragic, terrifying, and bleak time for the Polish people. It didn't, however, kill the Solidarity movement, which continued its fight after going underground. Notice that the movement's martial law–era propaganda was produced with far more primitive printing equipment than their earlier posters.

In the next room, you see a clandestine print shop like those used to create that illegal propaganda. Surrounding the room are sobering displays of **ZOMO riot gear.** A film reveals the ugliness of martial law. Watch the footage of General Jaruzelski—wearing his trademark dark glasses—reading the announcement of martial law. Chilling scenes show riots, demonstrations, and crackdowns by the ZOMO police—including one demonstrator who's run over by a truck. An old woman is stampeded by a pack of fleeing demonstrators.

The next room shows a film tracing the whole history of **communism in Poland** (with a copy of Lech Wałęsa's Nobel Peace Prize).

For a happy ending, head into the final room, with an uplifting film about the **fall of the Iron Curtain** across Eastern Europe—right up through the 2004 "Orange Revolution" in Ukraine.

Here's how it happened in Poland: By the time the Pope visited his homeland again in 1983, martial law had finally been lifted, and Solidarity—still technically illegal—was gaining momentum, gradually pecking away at the communists. With the moral support of the Pope and the entire Western world, the brave Poles were the first European country to throw off the shackles of communism when, in the spring of 1989, the "Round Table Talks" led to the opening up of elections. The government arrogantly called for parliamentary elections, reserving 65 percent of seats for themselves. The plan backfired, as virtually every open seat went to Solidarity. This success inspired people all over Eastern Europe, and by that winter, the Berlin Wall had crumbled and

the Czechs and Slovaks had staged their Velvet Revolution. Lech Wałęsa—the shipyard electrician who started it all by jumping over a wall—became the first president of post-communist Poland. And a year later, in Poland's first true elections since World War II, 29 different parties won seats in the parliament. This celebration of democracy was brought to the Polish people by a brave electrician and the workers of Gdańsk.

South of the Main Town

A 10- to 15-minute walk south of the Main Town, these two sights are probably not worth the trek on a short visit.

National Museum in Gdańsk (Muzeum Narodowe w Gdańsku)—This art collection, housed in what was a 15th-century Franciscan monastery, is worth ▲▲ to art-lovers for one reason: Hans Memling's glorious *Last Judgment* triptych altarpiece, one of the two most important pieces of art to be seen in Poland (the other is da Vinci's *Lady with an Ermine* in Kraków's Czartoryski Museum). If you're not a purist, you can settle for seeing the much smaller replica in St. Mary's Church. But if medieval art is your bag, make the 10-minute walk here from the Main Town (10 zł, free on Fri, open Tue–Sun 10:00–17:00, last entry at 16:30, closed Mon; walk 10 min due south from ulica Długa's Golden Gate, take pedestrian underpass beneath the big cross-street, then continue down the busy street until you see signs for the museum; ulica Toruńska 1, tel. 058-301-7061, www.muzeum.narodowe.gda.pl).

From the entry, the altarpiece by Hans Memling (c. 1440–1494) is at the top of the stairs and to the right. The history of the painting is as interesting as the work itself. It was commissioned in the mid-15th century by the Medicis' banker in Florence, Angelo di Jacopo Tani. The ship delivering the painting from Belgium to Florence was hijacked by a Gdańsk pirate, who brought the altarpiece to his hometown to be displayed in St. Mary's Church. For centuries, it was admired from afar by kings, emperors, and czars, until it was seized by Napoleon in the early 19th century and taken to Paris, where it hung in the Louvre. Gdańsk finally got the painting back, only to have it exiled again—this time into St. Petersburg's Hermitage Museum—after World War II. On its return to Gdańsk in 1956, it was claimed by this museum—though St. Mary's wants it back.

Have a close look at Memling's well-traveled work. It's the end of the world, and Christ rides in on a rainbow to judge humankind. Angels blow reveille, waking the dead, who rise from their graves. The winged archangel Michael—dressed for battle and wielding the cross like a weapon—weighs the grace in each person, sending them either to the fires of hell (right panel) or up the sparkling-crystal stairway to heaven (left).

It takes all 70 square feet of paneling to contain this awesome scene. Jam-packed with dozens of bodies, a Bible's worth of symbolism, and executed with astonishing detail, the painting can keep even a non-art-lover occupied. Notice the serene, happy expressions of the righteous, as they're greeted by St. Peter (with his giant key) and clothed by angels. And pity the condemned, their faces filled with terror and sorrow as they're tortured by grotesque devils more horrifying than anything Hollywood could devise.

Tune into the exquisite details: the angels' robes, the devils' genetic-mutant features, the portrait of the man in the scale (a Medici banker), Michael's peacock wings. Get as close as you can to the globe at Christ's feet and Michael's shining breastplate, and you can just make out the whole scene in mirror reflection. Then back up and take it all in—three panels connected by a necklace of bodies that curves downward through hell, across the earth, then rising up to the towers of the New Jerusalem. On the back side of the triptych are reverent portraits of the painting's patron, Angelo Tani, and his new bride, Catarina.

Beyond the Memling, the remainder of the collection isn't too thrilling. The rest of the upstairs has more Flemish and Dutch art, as well as paintings from Gdańsk's Golden Age and various works by Polish artists. The ground floor features a cavernous, all-white cloister filled with Gothic altarpiece sculptures, gold- and silverware, majolica and Delft porcelain, and characteristic Gdańsk-style furniture.

"Blue Lion" Archaeological Education Center (Centrum Edukacji Archeologicznej "Błękitny Lew")—Hiding far from the Main Town on Granary Island, this new, kid-friendly exhibit re-creates the atmosphere of medieval Gdańsk. Occupying a rebuilt granary called the "Blue Lion," its highlight is a full-scale replica of an atmospheric medieval street, populated by mannequins whose features are based on actual human remains. Rounding out the museum are artifacts from the period, a selection of films (subtitled in English), and touchscreens that provide some background. While information is a bit sparse (especially along the medieval street), the collection tries hard not to be just another fuddy-duddy, dusty old museum, making it popular with kids on field trips (8 zł, June–Aug Tue–Sun 10:00–18:00, Sept–May Tue–Sun 9:00–17:00, closed Mon year-round, ulica Chmielna 53, tel. 058-320-3188, www.archeologia.pl).

Outer Gdańsk

These two sights—worthwhile only to those with a special interest—are each within the city limits of Gdańsk, but they take some serious time to see round-trip.

Oliwa Cathedral (Katedra Oliwska)—The suburb of Oliwa, at the northern edge of Gdańsk, is home to this visually striking church. The quirky, elongated facade hides a surprisingly long and skinny nave. The ornately decorated 18th-century organ over the main entrance features angels and stars that move around when the organ is played. While locals are proud of this place, it's hard to justify the effort it takes to get out here. Skip it unless you just love Polish churches or you're going to a concert.

Concerts: The animated organ performs its 20-minute show frequently, especially in summer (July–Aug generally at the top of each hour Mon–Fri 10:00–17:00—except at 14:00, Sat 10:00–15:00, Sun 15:00–17:00; June the same except until 16:00; May and Sept Mon–Sat at the top of each hour 10:00–13:00, Sun at 15:00 and 16:00; 1–2/day off-season). Confirm the schedule at the TI before making the trip. Note that on Sundays and holidays, there are no concerts before 15:00.

Getting There: Oliwa is about six miles northwest of central Gdańsk, on the way to Sopot and Gdynia. To get to Oliwa, you have two options: Take **tram** #6 or #12 from Gdańsk's main train station. These trams let you off right at the entrance to Oliwski Park. Go straight through to the back of the park; near the end, you can see the copper roof and two skinny, pointy spires of the cathedral on your right. Exit through the back of the park, bear right, and go one block to find the entrance to the church. Your other option is to take a **commuter SKM train** from Gdańsk's main train station 15 minutes to the "Gdańsk Oliwa" stop (see "Getting Around the Tri-City," page 423). From the Oliwa train station, it's a 15-minute walk or 10-zł taxi ride to the cathedral. Walk straight ahead out of the station and turn right when you get to the busy road. Cross the road at the light and enter the tree-filled Park Oliwski at the corner, then follow the directions above.

Westerplatte—World War II began on September 1, 1939, when Adolf Hitler sent the warship *Schleswig-Holstein* to attack this Polish munitions depot, which was guarding Gdańsk's harbor. Though it may interest serious WWII history buffs, most visitors will find little to see here aside from a modest museum, a towering monument, and some old bunkers. As it's surrounded by shipyard sprawl, it's not a particularly scenic trip, either.

Getting There: The most enjoyable approach is on a cruise—either on a modern boat, or on the fun old-fashioned galleons (45–50 min each way; see page 421). You can also take **bus** #106 from Brama Wyżynna (just outside the Main Town) to the end (about 30 min).

Shopping in Gdańsk

The big story in Gdańsk is amber *(bursztyn),* a fossil resin available in all shades, shapes, and sizes (see the "All About Amber" sidebar, earlier). While you'll see amber sold all over town, the best place to browse and buy is along the atmospheric ulica Mariacka (between the Motława River and St. Mary's Church). This pretty street, with old-fashioned balconies and dozens of display cases, is fun to wander even if you're not a shopper. Other good places to buy amber are along the riverfront embankment and on ulica Długa. To avoid rip-offs—such as amber that's been melted and reshaped—always buy it from a shop, not from someone standing on the street. (But note that most shops also have a display case and salesperson out front, which are perfectly legit.) Prices everywhere are about the same, so rather than seeking out a specific place, just window-shop until you see what you want. Styles range from gaudy necklaces with huge globs of amber, to tasteful smaller pendants in a silver setting, to cheap trinkets. All shades of amber—from near-white to dark brown—cost about the same, but you'll pay more for inclusions (bugs or other objects stuck in the amber).

Gdańsk also has several modern shopping malls, most of them in the Old Town or near the main train station. The walk between the Main Town and the Solidarity shipyard goes past some of the best malls (see page 393).

Sleeping in Gdańsk

Gdańsk's accommodation scene is booming. New hotels open every year, forcing dreary old ones to up their standards and/or lower their rates. Even with all those new rooms, many hotels are booked up (mostly with German tourists) in peak season (mid-June–mid-Sept), when prices increase—book ahead.

Across the River

These hotels are across the river from the Main Town. While that puts you a bit farther from the sightseeing action, it's a relatively short walk (no more than 10 minutes from any of these), and the prices are correspondingly lower.

$$$ Hotel Królewski, a classy hotel in a beautifully renovated red-brick granary, offers 30 stylish rooms, good rates, and a friendly staff. It's just beyond the three granaries of the Maritime Museum, across the river from the Crane (Sb-380 zł, Db-470 zł, fancier suite-like Db "plus"-500 zł, pricier apartments, lower rates mid-Oct–April, 50 zł to reserve a view room—or try asking for one when you check in for no extra charge, non-smoking rooms, elevator, free Wi-Fi, good restaurant, ulica Ołowianka 1,

Sleep Code

(3 zł = about $1, country code: 48)
S = Single, **D** = Double/Twin, **T** = Triple, **Q** = Quad, **b** = bathroom, **s** = shower only. Unless otherwise noted, breakfast is included, credit cards are accepted, and English is spoken.

To help you sort easily through these listings, I've divided the rooms into three categories, based on the price for a standard double room with bath:

$$$ Higher Priced—Most rooms 400 zł or more.
$$ Moderately Priced—Most rooms between 300–400 zł.
$ Lower Priced—Most rooms 300 zł or less.

tel. 058-326-1111, fax 058-326-1110, www.hotelkrolewski.pl, office@hotelkrolewski.pl). You can commute to your sightseeing by ferry (take the 1-zł boat trip across the river offered by the Maritime Museum). But the ferry runs only during the museum's opening hours, and is sporadic off-season. If the ferry isn't running, it's a scenic 10-minute walk along the river and over the bridge into the Main Town.

$$$ Hotel Gdańsk is a new splurge hotel over a brewpub. Also in a rehabbed granary across the river from the embankment, it's a bit closer to the Main Town than the Królewski. The 60 elegant rooms are divided between the old granary (with tiny windows and big beams) and a modern annex (Mon–Thu: Sb-490 zł, Db-590 zł, bigger "premium" Db-630 zł; Fri–Sun: Sb-460 zł, Db-560 zł, premium Db-590 zł; cheaper Nov–March, elevator, free Internet access and Wi-Fi, ulica Szafarina 9, tel. 058-300-1717, www.hotelgdansk.pl, rezerwacja@hotelgdansk.pl).

$ ***On Ulica Spichrzowa:*** Several small, similar, relatively new hotels are on the back side of a charmingly restored row of colorful houses on the island just across the river from the main drag. While they overlook a dreary vacant lot, these places (and others on the same street) offer a good value in a convenient location. As these buildings are tall and skinny, expect plenty of stairs with no elevator. **$$ Willa Litarion** is run by the eager Owsikowski family. Each of the 13 small rooms has a totally different design, but all are artsy and mod (Sb-255 zł, Db-330 zł, bigger "deluxe" Db-360 zł, 10–15 percent cheaper Oct–April, extra bed-60 zł, free cable Internet, parking garage-20 zł, ulica Spichrzowa 18, tel. 058-320-2553, fax 058-320-2563, www.litarion.pl, recepcja@litarion.pl). **$ Willa Biała Lilia** ("Villa of the White Lily"), next door, has 16 uninspired but modern and comfortable rooms (Sb-250 zł, Db-320 zł, extra bed-60 zł, slightly cheaper Oct–April, free cable

Internet, reserve ahead for parking garage-20 zł, ulica Spichrzowa 16, tel. 058-301-7074, fax 058-320-1473, www.bialalilia.pl, biala lilia@bialalilia.pl).

$ Dom Muzyka rents 87 simple, tidy rooms in a nondescript residential neighborhood. The catch: It's very difficult to find, hiding in the back of the big Academy of Music building (Akademia Muzyczna). But the prices are worth the hunt, and once you're set up, it's an easy 10-minute walk to the sights. Their "deluxe" rooms, mostly twins, are bigger and overlook the quiet courtyard; most of the standard rooms face a busy street but have good windows and air-conditioning (Sb-240 zł, standard Db-330 zł, deluxe Db-350 zł, apartment-500 zł, extra bed-100 zł, 10 zł less per person Oct–April, elevator, free Internet access and Wi-Fi, popular with tour groups, good restaurant, ulica Łąkowa 1–2, tel. 058-326-0600, fax 058-326-0601, www.dom-muzyka.pl, biuro @dom-muzyka.pl). From the Main Town's Green Gate, cross the two bridges, then walk a long block along the modern commercial building and turn right just before the park (on Łąkowa, across from the big brick church). Walk to the end of this block; before the busy road, go through the gate just before the big, yellow-brick building on the right. Once inside the gate checkpoint, the hotel is around the back of the yellow building, the farthest door down. If you get lost, just ask people, "Hotel?"

In the Main Town

You'll pay a premium to sleep in the Main Town itself, but many find it worth the extra expense.

$$$ Hotel Wolne Miasto ("Free City") offers rich, wood-carved public spaces with photos of old Gdańsk and 67 elegant, well-priced rooms on the edge of the Main Town, just two blocks from the main drag. Since it's above a popular disco that gets noisy on weekends (Thu–Sat nights), request a quieter room when you reserve (Sb-380 zł, Db-450 zł, bigger "deluxe" Db-550 zł, cheaper Oct–March, air-con in some rooms, elevator, free Internet access and Wi-Fi, ulica Świętego Ducha 2, tel. 058-322-2442, fax 058-322-2447, www.hotelwm.pl, rezerwacja@hotelwm.pl).

$$ Gotyk House, a good value, is run with warmth and pride by the Rybicki family. Owner Andrzej is an energetic armchair historian who works hard to make his little hotel comfortable while still respecting the sanctity of what's supposedly Gdańsk's oldest house. The chimes from St. Mary's Church, next door, provide a pleasant soundtrack. The cellar houses a gingerbread museum and small shrine to Copernicus (whose longtime lover may have lived here). The seven straightforward rooms share a tiny breakfast room, so you'll have to tell them what time you'd like to eat (Sb-280 zł, Db-310 zł, 30 zł less Oct–April, even cheaper

Jan–March, free Wi-Fi in most rooms, tight public spaces, ulica Mariacka 1, tel. 058-301-8567, mobile 0516-141-133, www.gotykhouse.eu, reservation@gotykhouse.eu).

$$ Kamienica Goldwasser, renting seven rooms over a good restaurant (see listing on next page), is perfectly located, right on the river embankment next door to the Crane. Each room is different, but all are thoughtfully decorated, with windows facing both the river and the back. Three of the rooms are smaller and cheaper—similar to the bigger rooms, but with cramped bathrooms, and an especially good value (small Sb-240 zł, big Sb-340 zł, small Db-340 zł, big Db-440 zł, extra bed-100 zł, lots of stairs and no elevator, free Wi-Fi, Długie Pobrzeże 22, tel. & fax 058-301-8878, www.goldwasser.pl, kamienica@goldwasser.pl).

$ Dom Harcerza is a Polish-style budget hotel/hostel with 21 old, musty, but well-maintained rooms on the second floor of a dreary office building. This institutional-feeling place won't win any prizes for personality, and communication can be difficult, but it's cheap and nicely located in a corner of the Main Town just two blocks south of the Golden Gate (S-50 zł, D-120 zł, Db-220 zł, T-150 zł, Tb-260 zł, Q-160 zł, 25 percent cheaper Oct–April, includes sheets, breakfast-9 zł, cash only, all twin beds, ground-floor café, ulica Za Murami 2–10, tel. 058-301-3621, fax 058-301-2472, www.domharcerza.pl, rezerwacje@domharcerza.pl).

$ Przy Targu Rybnym, a three-minute walk from the Crane at the north end of the embankment, is Gdańsk's most central hostel. Waldemar runs this easygoing, low-key, slightly grungy place with a spirit of fun that permeates the chummy common room. Aside from dorm beds, it offers private rooms for two to four people, most with shared bathrooms down the hall (bunk in dorm or crowded basement slumbermill-55 zł, D-200 zł, Db-250 zł, T-240 zł, Q-280 zł, cheaper Sept-April, prices include sheets and breakfast, free Internet access, 20-zł laundry service, ulica Grodzka 21, tel. 058-301-5627, www.gdanskhostel.com.pl, gdanskhostel@hotmail.com).

Eating in Gdańsk

In addition to traditional Polish fare, Gdańsk has some fine Baltic seafood. Herring *(śledź)* is popular here, as is cod *(dorsz)*. Natives brag that their salmon *(łosoś)* is better than Norway's. For a stiff drink, sample *Goldwasser* (similar to Goldschlager). This sweet and strong liqueur, flecked with gold, was supposedly invented here in Gdańsk. The following options are all in the Main Town, within three blocks of ulica Długa.

Budget Restaurants on the Main Drag

These two places are remarkably cheap, tasty, quick, and wonderfully convenient—right on ulica Długa. They're worth considering even if you're not on a tight budget.

Bar pod Rybą ("Under the Fish") is nirvana for fans of baked potatoes *(pieczony ziemniak)*. They offer more than 20 varieties, piled high with a wide variety of toppings and sauces, from Mexican beef to herring to Polish cheeses. They also offer fish dishes with salad and potatoes, making this a cheap place to sample local seafood. The tasteful decor—walls lined with old bottles, antique wooden hangers, and paintings by the owner—is squeezed into a single cozy room packed with happy eaters. In the summer, order inside, and they'll bring your food to you at an outdoor table (potatoes and fish dishes are each about 15–25 zł, daily 11:00–19:00, until 22:00 in summer, Długi Targ 35/38, tel. 058-305-1307).

Bar Mleczny Neptun is your best milk-bar option in the Main Town. A hearty meal, including a drink, runs about 15–20 zł. This popular place has more charm than your typical institutional milk bar, including outdoor seating along the most scenic stretch of the main drag, and an upstairs dining room overlooking it all. Most of the items on the counter are for display—rather than take what's there, point to what you want and they'll dish it up fresh (Mon–Fri 7:30–18:00, until 19:00 in summer, Sat 10:00–17:00, open Sun only in summer 11:00–17:00, ulica Długa 33–34, tel. 058-301-4988). For more on milk bars, see page 245.

On the Riverfront Embankment

Perhaps the most appealing dining zone in Gdańsk stretches along the riverfront embankment near the Crane. On a balmy summer evening, the outdoor tables here are enticing. As it's a popular area, consider scouting a table during your sightseeing, and reserve your choice for dinner later that night. While you have several good options along here, the following are particularly well-regarded.

Kamienica Goldwasser, which also rents rooms (see listing on previous page), offers good Polish and international cuisine at fair prices. Choose between cozy, romantic indoor seating on several levels, or scenic outdoor seating (most main dishes 40–60 zł, daily 10:00–24:00, occasional live music, Długie Pobrzeże 22, tel. 058-301-8878).

Baryłka, next door to Goldwasser, has a similar menu and outdoor seating. The elegant upstairs dining room, with windows

overlooking the river, is appealing (30–50-zł main dishes, daily 9:00–24:00, Długie Pobrzeże 24, tel. 058-301-4938).

Sushi 77, serving up a wide selection of surprisingly good sushi right next to the Crane, is a refreshing break from "ye olde" Polish food. Choose between the outdoor tables bathed in red light, or the mod interior (30–50-zł sushi sets, daily 11:00–23:00, Długie Pobrzeże 30, tel. 058-682-1823).

Targ Rybny/Fishmarkt ("The Fish Market")—run by the Goldwasser people (see listing, previous page)—is farther up the embankment, overlooking a park and parking lot. The outdoor seating isn't too scenic, but the warm, mellow-yellow nautical ambience inside is pleasant, making this a good bad-weather option. It features classy but not stuffy service, and an emphasis on fish (most main dishes 30–50 zł, plus pricier seafood splurges, daily 10:00–23:00, ulica Targ Rybny 6C, tel. 058-320-9011).

Other Restaurants in Central Gdańsk

Czerwone Drzwi ("The Red Door") serves up tasty Polish and international cuisine in a single-room, six-table restaurant. The decor is artsy, and there's live piano music nightly at 19:00; at other times, recorded jazz sets the mood (22–28-zł pierogi, big 20–25-zł salads, 30–40-zł main dishes, daily 10:00–22:00, ulica Piwna 52/53, tel. 058-301-5764).

Dom pod Łososiem ("House Under the Salmon") is a venerable old stand-by with over-the-top formality. This place will make you feel like a rich burgher's family invited you over for dinner (right down to the greeting by a stiff, bow-tied maître d'). This elegant splurge restaurant has been serving guests for more than 400 years, racking up an impressive guest list (some pictured in the lobby)—and, somewhere in there, inventing *Goldwasser.* Reservations are smart for dinner (most main dishes 40–70 zł, emphasis on fish, small portions, daily 12:00–23:00, ulica Szeroka 52–54, tel. 058-301-7652).

Coffee and Sweets

Gdańsk's Main Town is full of hip cafés that lure in young people with long menus of exotic coffee drinks and tasty cakes. Here are two good options—one new, one old.

Pikawa (as in "3.14 Coffee," pronounced "pee-kah-vah") is a trendy, atmospheric café with a wide variety of coffee drinks and herbal teas, best accompanied by the delicious *szarlotka* (Polish apple cake). The decor is cozy Old World, the outdoor seating is pleasant, and the café is packed with socializing locals (8–16-zł cakes, daily 10:00–23:00, until 24:00 in summer, ulica Piwna 5–6).

Cukiernia Kaliszczak, a bakery right on ulica Długa, is a no-frills throwback to the communist days. It's cheap but not

cheery, with delicious 3-zł cakes and ice cream and no-nonsense service—just line up and place your order, comrade. If you want ice cream, order first at the register rather than at the display case (daily 9:00–22:00, ulica Długa 74).

Gdańsk Connections

By Train

Gdańsk is well-connected to the Tri-City via the commuter SKM trains (explained later, under "Getting Around the Tri-City"). It also has frequent connections to Warsaw, and handy night trains to Berlin and Kraków. You'll likely encounter some disruptions, however, as new high-speed rail lines are being built between Gdańsk and points south, aiming to be complete by the 2012 Euro Cup. In the long term, this will reduce travel times, but in the short term, the trips noted below are prone to construction delays.

From Gdańsk by Train to: Hel (town on Hel Peninsula, 3/day direct July–Aug only, 2.25–3.25 hrs; otherwise about hourly with transfer in Gdynia), **Malbork** (about 2/hr, 40–50 min), **Toruń** (4/day direct, 3 hrs; at least hourly with a transfer in Bydgoszcz, 3–4 hrs), **Warsaw** (nearly hourly, 5 hrs), **Kraków** (4/day direct, 2 more with change in Warsaw, 7.75 hrs; plus 2 night trains, 11 hrs), **Berlin** (4/day, 8.25–9.25 hrs, transfer in Szczecin, Poznań, or Frankfurt an der Oder; plus 1 direct night train, 10 hrs).

By Boat

Various boats depart from Gdańsk's embankment to nearby destinations, including **Westerplatte** (the monument marking where World War II started) and **Hel** (the beachy peninsula, described below). While boats also run sporadically to Sopot and Gdynia, the train is better for those trips (described under "Getting Around the Tri-City," later). As these boat schedules tend to change from year to year, confirm your plans carefully at the TI. All boat trips are weather permitting, especially the faster hydrofoils. In shoulder season (April–June and Sept–Oct), even though most boats stop running from Gdańsk, several routes still run between Sopot, Gdynia, and Hel. Boats generally don't run in winter (Nov–March).

To Westerplatte: To travel by boat to the monument at Westerplatte—where World War II began—you have two options. It's more enjoyable to ride the replica **17th-century galleons,** either the *Galeon Lew* ("Lion Galleon") or the *Czerna Perła* ("Black Pearl"). These over-the-top, touristy boats depart hourly from near the Crane for a lazy 1.5-hour round-trip cruise to Westerplatte and back. (You can choose to get off at Westerplatte after 45 minutes and take a later boat back.) The *Czerna Perła* has

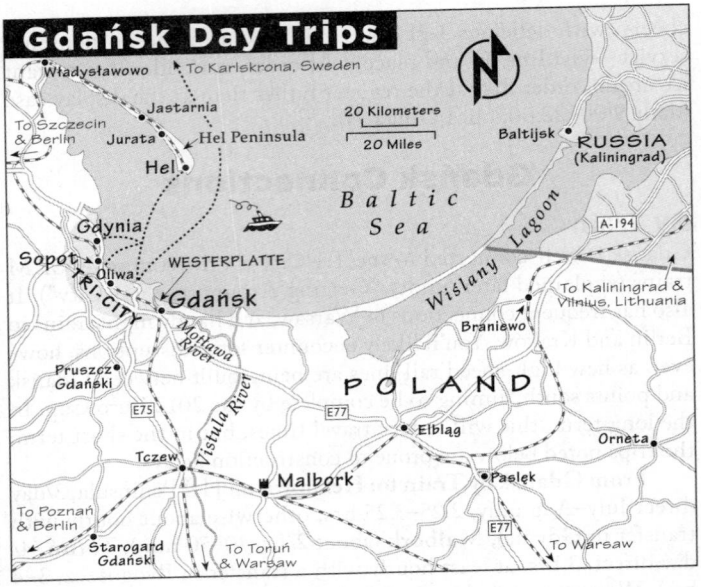

English commentary; both boats often have live nautical music on the return trip (if you've ever wanted to hear "What Shall We Do with a Drunken Sailor?" in Polish, here's your chance). It's not exactly pretty—you'll see more industry than scenery—but it's a fun excuse to set sail, even if you don't care about Westerplatte (40 zł round-trip, 27 zł one-way, the two boats take turns departing at the top of each hour 10:00–19:00 in July–Aug, fewer departures May–June and Sept, from the embankment near the Crane, mobile 0501-571-383, www.rejsyturystyczne.pl). The duller alternative is to take a modern **Żegluga Gdańska** boat (45 zł round-trip, 30 zł one-way, 50 min each way, daily April–Oct, 3–6/day in each direction).

To Hel: Various boats—mostly the ZTM "ferry trams" *(tramwaj wodny)*—zip out to Hel in two hours three times a day from June through August, with a stop in Sopot (sometimes also runs on weekends in shoulder season; 18 zł each way, carefully confirm departure point, which can change but will likely be at the north end of the embankment, past the Crane).

Near Gdańsk: The Tri-City (Trójmiasto)

Gdańsk is the anchor of the three cities that make up the metropolitan region known as the Tri-City (Trójmiasto). The other two parts are as different as night and day: a once-swanky resort town (Sopot) and a practical, nose-to-the-grindstone business center (Gdynia). The Tri-City as a whole is home to bustling industry and a sprawling university, with several campuses and plenty of well-dressed, English-speaking students. Beyond the Tri-City, the long, skinny Hel Peninsula—a sparsely populated strip of fishing villages and fun-loving beaches—arches dramatically into the Baltic Sea.

Sopot—boasting sandy beaches, tons of tourists, and a certain elegance—is clearly the most appealing day-trip option. Gdynia offers a glimpse into workaday Poland, but leaves most visitors cold. Hel, which requires the better part of a day to visit, is worthwhile only if you've got perfect summer weather and a desire to lie on the beach.

Getting Around the Tri-City

Gdańsk, Sopot, and Gdynia are connected both by regional commuter trains (*kolejka,* operated by SKM) as well as trains of Poland's national railway (operated by PKP). Trains to Hel are always operated by PKP. Tickets for one system can't be used on the other. While the two different trains chug along the same tracks, they use different (but nearby) stations. For example, at Gdańsk's main train station, national PKP trains use tracks 1–3, while regional SKM trains use tracks 3–5. And in Sopot, the SKM station is a few hundred feet before the PKP station.

Regional SKM trains are much more frequent—they go in each direction about every 10–15 minutes (less frequently after 19:30). In Gdańsk, buy tickets at the automated ticket machine marked *SKM Bilety* (near the head of platform 4, English instructions, 3.10 zł and 25 min to Sopot, or 4.50 zł and 40 min to Gdynia). If you buy your ticket from a machine, there's no need to validate it. But if you buy one from a kiosk, you'll need to stamp it in the easy-to-miss yellow or blue slots under the boards with SKM information.

Each city has multiple stops. In Gdańsk, use "Gdańsk Główny" (the end of the line); for Sopot, use the stop called simply "Sopot" (only one word); and for Gdynia, it's "Gdynia Główna" (the main station).

The bigger PKP trains are faster, but less frequent—unless you notice one that happens to be leaving at a convenient time, I'd skip them and stick with the easy SKM trains.

For a more romantic—and much slower—approach, consider the boat (see "Gdańsk Connections," earlier).

Sopot

Sopot (SOH-poht), dubbed the "Nice of the North," was a celebrated haunt of beautiful people during the 1920s and 1930s, and remains a popular beach getaway to this day.

Sopot was created in the late 19th century by Napoleon's doctor, Jean Georges Haffner, who believed Baltic Sea water to be therapeutic. By the 1890s, it had become a fashionable seaside resort. This gambling center boasted enough high-roller casinos to garner comparisons to Monte Carlo.

The casinos are gone, but the health resorts remain, and you'll still see more well-dressed people here per capita than just about anywhere in the country. While it's not quite Cannes, Sopot feels relatively high class, which is unusual in otherwise unpretentious Poland. But even so, a childlike spirit of summer-vacation fun pervades this St-Tropez-on-the-Baltic, making it an all-around enjoyable place.

Planning Your Time

You can get the gist of Sopot in just a couple of hours. Zip in on the train, follow the main drag to the sea, wander the pier, get your feet wet at the beach, then head back to Gdańsk. Why not come here in the late afternoon, enjoy those last few rays of sunshine, stay for dinner, then take a twilight stroll on the pier?

Orientation to Sopot

The main pedestrian drag, Monte Cassino Heroes street (ulica Bohaterów Monte Cassino), leads to the Molo, the longest pleasure pier in Europe. From the Molo, a broad, sandy beach stretches in each direction. Running parallel to the surf is a tree-lined, people-filled path made for strolling.

Tourist Information

Sopot's helpful TI is directly in front of the PKP train station (look for blue *it* sign). Pick up the free map, info booklet, and events schedule. They also offer a free room-booking service (daily June–mid-Sept 9:00–20:00, mid-Sept–May 10:00–18:00, ulica Dworcowa 4, tel. 058-550-3783, www.sopot.pl).

Arrival in Sopot

From the SKM station, exit to the left and walk down the street. After a block, you'll see the PKP train station on your left—detour here to find the TI (described above). Then continue on to the can't-miss-it main drag, ulica Bohaterów Monte Cassino (marked by the big red-brick church steeple). Follow it to the right, down to the seaside.

Sights in Sopot

▲Monte Cassino Heroes Street (Ulica Bohaterów Monte Cassino)—Nicknamed "Monciak" (MOHN-chak) by locals, this in-love-with-life promenade may well be Poland's most manicured street. Especially after all the suburban and industrial dreck you passed through to get here, it's easy to be charmed by this pretty drag. The street is lined with happy tourists, trendy cafés, al fresco restaurants, movie theaters, and late-19th-century facades (known for their wooden balconies).

The most popular building along here (on the left, about halfway down) is the so-called **Crooked House** (Krzywy Domek), a trippy, Gaudí-inspired building that looks like it's melting. Hard-partying Poles prefer to call it the "Drunken House," and say that when it looks straight, it's time to stop drinking.

At the bottom of the boulevard, just before the Molo, pay 4 zł to climb to the top of the Art Nouveau lighthouse for a waterfront panorama.

Molo (Pier)—At more than 1,600 feet long, this is Europe's longest wooden entertainment pier. While you won't find any amusement-park rides, you will be surrounded by vendors, artists, and Poles having the time of their lives. Buy a *gofry* (Belgian waffle topped with whipped cream and fruit) or an oversized cloud of *wata cukrowa* (cotton candy), grab your partner's hand, and stroll with gusto (4 zł, free Oct–April, open long hours daily).

Scan the horizon for sailboats and tankers. Any pirate ships? For a jarring reality check, look over to Gdańsk. Barely visible from the Molo are two of the most important sites in 20th-century history: the towering monument at Westerplatte, where World War II started; and the cranes rising up from the Gdańsk Shipyard,

where Solidarity was born and European communism began its long goodbye.

In spring and fall, the Molo is a favorite venue for pole vaulting—or is that Pole vaulting?

The Beach—Yes, Poland has beaches. Nice ones. When I heard Sopot compared to places like Nice, I'll admit that I scoffed. But when I saw those stretches of inviting sand as far as the eye can see, I wished I'd packed my swim trunks. (You could walk from Gdańsk to Gdynia on beaches like this.) The sand is finer than anything I've seen in Croatia...though the water's not exactly crystal-clear. Most of the beach is public, except for a small private stretch in front of the Grand Hotel Sopot. Year-round, it's crammed with locals. At these northern latitudes, the season for bathing is brief and crowded.

Overlooking the beach next to the Molo is the **Grand Hotel Sopot.** It was renovated to top-class status just recently, but its history goes way back. They could charge admission for room #226, a multi-room suite that has hosted the likes of Adolf Hitler, Marlene Dietrich, and Fidel Castro (but not all at the same time). With all the trappings of Sopot's belle époque—dark wood, plush upholstery, antique furniture—this room had me imagining Hitler sitting at the desk, looking out to sea, and plotting the course of World War II.

Gdynia

Compared to its flashier sister cities, straightforward Gdynia (guh-DIN-yah) has retained a more working-class vibe, still in touch with its salty, fishing-village roots. Gdynia feels much less historic than Gdańsk or Sopot, as it was mostly built in the 1920s to be Poland's main harbor after Gdańsk became a free city. Although nowhere as attractive as Gdańsk or Sopot, Gdynia has an authentic feel and a fine waterfront promenade (www.gdynia.pl).

Gdynia is a major business center, and—thanks to its youthful, progressive city government—has edged ahead of the rest of Poland in transitioning from communism. It enjoys one of the highest income levels in the country. Many of the crumbling downtown buildings have been renovated, and Gdynia is becoming known for its top-tier shopping—all the big designers have boutiques here. If a local woman has been shopping on Świętojańska street in Gdynia, it means that she's got some serious złoty.

Because Gdańsk's port is relatively shallow, the biggest cruise ships must put in at Gdynia...leaving confused tourists to poke around town looking for some medieval quaintness, before coming to their senses and heading for Gdańsk. Gdynia is also home to a major military harbor, and an important NATO base.

To get a taste of Gdynia, take the SKM train to the "Gdynia Główna" station, follow signs to *wyjście do miasta,* cross the busy street, and walk 15 minutes down Starowiejska. When you come to the intersection with the broad Świętojańska street, turn right (in the direction the big statue is looking) and walk two blocks to the tree-lined park on the left. Head through the park to the Southern Pier (Molo Południowe). This concrete slab—nowhere near as charming as Sopot's wooden-boardwalk version—features a modern shopping mall and a smattering of sights, including an aquarium and a pair of permanently moored museum boats.

Hel Peninsula (Mierzeja Helska)

Out on the edge of things, this slender peninsula juts 20 miles into the ocean, providing a sunny retreat from the big cities—even as it shelters them from Baltic winds. Trees line the peninsula, and the northern edge is one long, sandy, ever-shifting beach.

On hot summer days, Hel is a great place to frolic in the sun with Poles. Sunbathing and windsurfing are practically religions here. Small resort villages line Hel Peninsula: Władysławowo (at the base), Chałupy, Kuźnica, Jastarnia, Jurata, and—at the tip—a town also called Hel. Beaches right near the towns can be crowded in peak season, but you're never more than a short walk away from your own stretch of sand. There are few permanent residents, and the waterfront is shared by budget campgrounds and hotels hosting middle-class families, and mansions of Poland's rich and famous (former president Aleksander Kwaśniewski has a summer home here).

The easiest way to go to Hel—aside from coveting thy neighbor's wife—is by boat (see "Gdańsk Connections," earlier). Trains from Gdańsk also reach Hel (summer only), and from Gdynia, you can take a train, bus, or minibus. But overland transit is crowded and slow—especially in summer, when Hel is notorious for its hellish traffic jams.

POMERANIA

Malbork Castle • Toruń

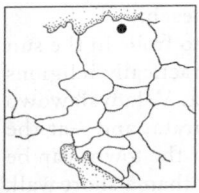

The northwestern part of Poland—known as Pomerania (Pomorze)—has nothing to do with excitable little dogs, but it does offer plenty of attractions. Two in particular are worth singling out, both conveniently located between Gdańsk and Warsaw. Malbork, the biggest Gothic castle in Europe, is one of the most interesting castles in Eastern Europe. Farther south, the Gothic town of Toruń—the birthplace of Copernicus, and a favorite spot of every proud Pole—holds hundreds of red-brick buildings (and, it seems, even more varieties of tasty gingerbread).

Planning Your Time

Malbork works well as a side-trip from Gdańsk (frequent trains, 40–50 min each way), and it's also on the main train line from Gdańsk to Warsaw. While Toruń doesn't merit a long detour, it's worth a stroll or an overnight if you want to sample a smaller Polish city. Unfortunately, Torún is on a different train line than Malbork—if you visit both in one day, it'll be a very long one. Ideally, if traveling round-trip from Warsaw, see one of these destinations coming to Gdańsk, and visit the other on the way back. Or do Malbork as a side-trip from Gdańsk, then visit Toruń on the way to Warsaw.

Malbork Castle

Malbork Castle is soaked in history. The biggest brick castle in the world, the largest castle of the Gothic period, and one of Europe's most imposing fortresses, it sits smugly on a marshy plain at the edge of the town of Malbork, 35 miles southeast of Gdańsk. This was the headquarters of the notorious Teutonic Knights, a Germanic band of ex-Crusaders who dominated northern Poland in the Middle Ages.

When the Teutonic Knights were invited to Polish lands to convert neighboring pagans in the 13th century, they found the perfect site for their new capital here, on the bank of the Nogat River. Construction began in 1274. After the Teutonic Knights conquered Gdańsk in 1308, the order moved its official headquarters from Venice to Malbork, where they remained for nearly 150 years. They called the castle Marienburg, the "Castle of Mary," in honor of the order's patron saint.

At its peak in the early 1400s, Malbork was both the imposing home of a seemingly unstoppable army, and Europe's final bastion of chivalric ideals. Surrounded by swamplands, with only one gate in need of defense, it was a tough nut to crack. Malbork Castle was never taken by force in the Middle Ages, though it had to withstand various sieges by the Poles during the Thirteen Years' War (1454–1466)—including a campaign that lasted over three years. Finally, in 1457, the Polish king gained control of Malbork by buying off Czech mercenaries guarding the castle. Malbork became a Polish royal residence for 300 years. But when Poland was partitioned in the late 18th century, this region went back into German hands. The castle became a barracks, windows were sealed up, delicate vaulting was damaged, bricks were quarried for new buildings, and Malbork deteriorated.

In the late 19th century, Romantic German artists and poets rediscovered the place. An architect named Konrad Steinbrecht devoted 40 years of his life to Malbork, painstakingly restoring the palace to its medieval splendor. A half-century later, the Nazis used the castle to house POWs, and about half of it was destroyed by the Soviet army, who saw it as a symbol of longstanding German domination. But it was restored once again, and today Malbork has been returned to its Teutonic glory.

Getting There

Malbork is on the train line between Gdańsk and Warsaw. Coming by train from Gdańsk, you'll enjoy views of the castle on your right as you cross the Nogat River. The humble, dingy Malbork train station has handy lockers (4–8 zł depending on size of bag). To get

from the station to the castle, consider taking a **taxi** (shouldn't cost more than 10 zł, though many corrupt cabbies charge twice that—keep asking until someone agrees to 10 zł). Or you can **walk** 15 minutes to the castle: Leave the station to the right, walk straight, and go through the pedestrian underpass beneath the busy road (by the red staircase). When you emerge on the other side, follow the busy road (noticing peek-a-boo views on your right of the castle's main tower) and take your first right turn (onto Kościuszki, the main shopping street). On Kościuszki, you'll pass the fancy pink building housing the TI on the right. Near the bottom of Kościuszki, at the fountain and the McDonald's, jog right, then bear left over two moats. Turn right and follow the castle wall to the end, where you'll find the ticket office (marked *kasa*).

Orientation to Malbork Castle

Cost and Hours: Castle entry costs 35 zł (ask about slightly discounted family ticket). Malbork has two seasons: high season (mid-April–mid-Sept) and low season (the rest of the year). In high season, the castle exhibits are open Tue–Sun 9:00–19:00 (last entry 17:30, grounds open until 20:00). In low season, the exhibits are open Tue–Sun 10:00–15:00 (last entry 13:00, grounds open until 16:00; in early April and late Sept, it's open until 17:00 with last entry at 15:30). On Mondays throughout the year, most of the castle is closed, with only a few sparse exhibits remaining open (you'll pay 6 zł to enter), but there's little point making the trip on a Monday. The ticket office opens 30 minutes before the castle. You'll pay an extra 15 zł for a sticker allowing you to take photos inside the buildings (photographing the grounds is free). For details, see www.zamek.malbork.pl.

Tours: You are technically required to enter the castle with a three-hour tour (Polish tour included in your ticket), but most non-Polish speakers simply split off from their guide and tour the place on their own—just enter with any tour, wander off, and explore the castle using my self-guided tour (see next page). In the future, there are plans to revamp the tour system and create several shorter tour routes.

Getting an **English tour** can be frustrating. In July and August, English tours run three times a day (likely at 11:00, 13:30, and 15:30; 6 zł extra). Year-round, you can also pay 210 zł for a private English tour (English guides are easy to arrange—even on short notice—in summer, but more difficult in winter). Ideally, contact the castle a few days ahead to reserve a guide (tel. 055-647-0978, fax 055-647-0976, kasa@zamek.malbork.pl; better to reserve by email or fax), or hire your own guide in Gdańsk (such as Agnieszka Syroka—see page 385).

Alternatively, if you show up and there's no English tour, ask if an English-speaking guide is available. Then take the initiative, play "tour guide," and get together a group of frustrated English-speakers by the cashier. On my last trip, it took me only a few minutes to gather a dozen strangers eager for some English information—bringing the per-person cost of the tour down to less than 20 zł.

Best Views: The views of massive Malbork are stunning—especially at sunset, when its red brick glows. Be sure to walk out across the bridge over the Nogat River. The most scenic part of the castle is probably the twin-turreted, riverside Bridge Gate, which used to be connected by a bridge to the opposite bank.

Sound-and-Light Show: Every night from May through mid-September, there's a sound-and-light show in the castle courtyard. Though the commentary is in Polish, the show gives you a different perspective on the mighty fortress (20 zł, buy tickets at castle drawbridge, begins after dark—which can be as late as 22:00 at these northern latitudes). Don't make a special trip (or stay late) just for this show—it really only makes sense if you're spending the night (see "Sleeping at Malbork Castle," later).

Self-Guided Tour

Malbork Castle

The official tour of Malbork lasts about three hours. And, while there's plenty to see, this self-guided tour allows you to see the highlights at your own pace. (Remember, you can split off from your group at any time.) This tour also works if you're tagging along with a Polish group, since it corresponds more or less to the route most Malbork guides take. Still, every guide is a little different, exhibits tend to move around, and entrances can be unexpectedly closed. Use the map on the next page to navigate and jump around as needed. The castle complex is a bit of a maze, with various entrances and exits for each room, often behind closed (but unlocked) doors. Don't be shy about grabbing a medieval doorknob and letting yourself in.

Lower Castle and Entrance Gate

Stand in front of the gate to one of Europe's most intimidating fortresses—home to the Grand Master, monks, and knights of the Teutonic Order. Across from the gate is the Lower Castle, which

Malbork Castle

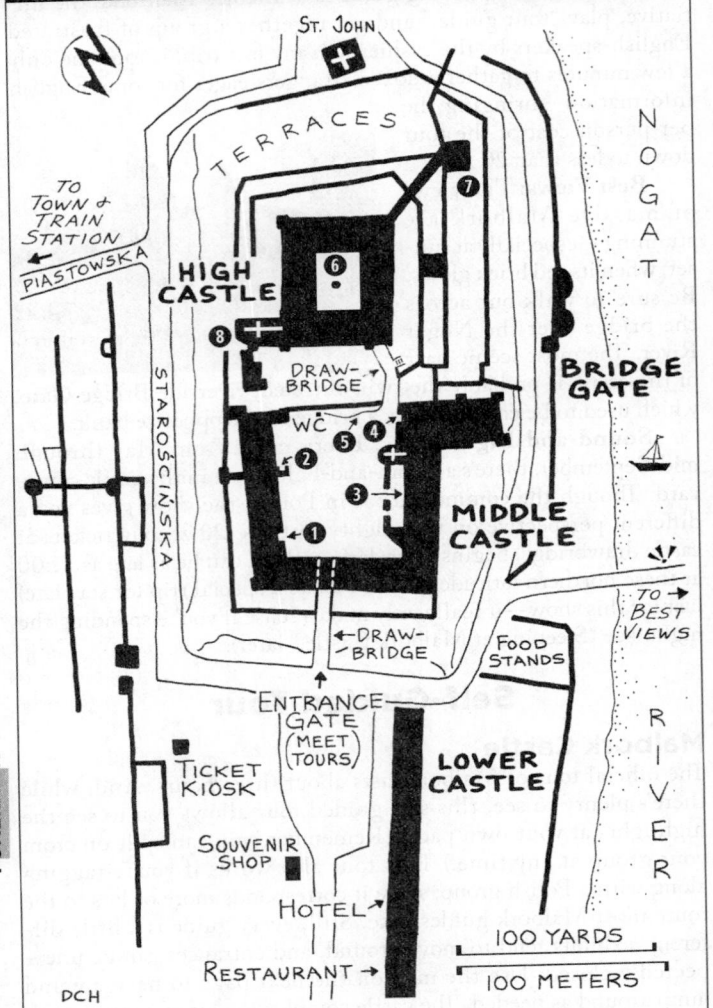

1. Amber Collection (Downstairs)
2. Armory (Upstairs) & Gothic Café (Downstairs)
3. "Boiler Room" (Downstairs) & Grand Refectory (Upstairs)
4. Grand Master's Palace
5. Grand Master Statues
6. Well
7. Dansker Tower
8. St. Mary's Church

was an infirmary and hospital for injured knights and retirees. The end closest to you is the Chapel of St. Lawrence; farther away, the former farm buildings have been converted into hotel rooms and restaurants (see "Sleeping at Malbork Castle," later).

Go up the wooden drawbridge. Above the door to the brick gate is a sculpture of St. Mary with the Baby Jesus...next to a shield and helmet. The two messages to visitors: This castle is protected by Mary, and the Teutonic Knights are here to convert pagans—by force, if necessary (or, as it turned out, even if not necessary).

Pass through this gate, into the entry area. Imagine the gate behind you closing. You look up to see wooden chutes where archers are preparing to rain arrows down on you. Your last thought: Maybe we should have left the Teutonic Knights alone, after all.

Before you're pierced by arrows, read the castle's history into its walls: The foundation is made of huge stones, which are rare in these marshy lands—they were brought from Sweden. But most of the castle, like so many other buildings in northern Poland, was built with handmade red brick. Throughout the castle, the darker-colored, rougher brick is original, and the lighter-colored, smoother brick was used for restoration (in the 19th century, and again after World War II).

Venture through two more enclosed spaces, watching for the holes in the wall (for more guards and soldiers). The Teutonic Knights connected nearby lakes to create a system of canals, forming a moat around the castle that could be crossed only by this drawbridge. Ponder the fact that you have to go through five separate, well-defended gates to reach the...

Middle Castle (Zamek Średni)

This part of Malbork, built at an uphill incline to make it even more imposing, was designed to impress. Knights and monks lived here.

Let's get oriented: To your left is the east wing, where guests would sleep. Today this houses the Amber Collection (ground floor) and the armory (upstairs). To the right (west) as you enter the main courtyard is the Grand Refectory (closer to the entrance) and the Grand Master's Palace (the taller, squarer building at the far end).

The Teutonic Knights

The Order of the Teutonic Knights began in the Holy Land in 1191, during the Third Crusade. Officially called the "Order of the Hospital of the Blessed Virgin Mary of the German House of Jerusalem," these German monks and knights took vows of poverty, chastity, and obedience. They also built hospitals and cared for injured knights. When the Crusades ended in the 12th century, the order found itself out of a job, and went back to Europe. They set up shop in Venice, and reorganized as a chivalric order of Christian mercenaries—pagan-killers for hire.

The Teutonic Knights were hired in 1226 for a gig in northern Poland, where the duke asked them to subdue a tribe of pagans who had been attacking his lands. The Teutonic Knights—claiming to be missionaries (and wearing white cloaks decorated with black crosses)—spent 60 years "saving" the pagans by turning them into serfs or brutally massacring them.

Like houseguests who didn't know when to leave, the Teutonic Knights decided they enjoyed northern Poland—and stuck around. The Knights made themselves at home, building one of Europe's biggest and most imposing fortresses: Malbork. Because they were fanatical Christians, they won the support of the pope and the Holy Roman Emperor. When the Teutonic Knights seized large parts of northern Poland in 1308, including Gdańsk—cutting off Polish access to the Baltic Sea—the Polish royals began to realize their mistake. The Teutonic Knights invited more Germans to come join them, building their numbers and tightening their grasp on the region. They grew rich from Hanseatic trade, specializing in amber, grain, and timber. The Knights conquered Estonia and Latvia, and began to threaten the Poles' pagan neighbor to the east, Lithuania. By the late 14th century, the Teutonic Knights were enjoying a Golden Age at the expense of the Poles and Lithuanians.

At about this time, Poland's long-lived Piast dynasty died out. Inspired by a mutual desire to fight back against the Teutonic

• *Before we move on, this is a good time to read up on the history of the Teutonic Knights (see sidebar). When you're ready to continue, enter the ground floor of the building on the left (remember, don't be shy about opening closed doors), and visit the...*

Amber Collection

This exhibit will make jewelry shoppers salivate. (Even as someone with zero interest in amber, I enjoyed it.) For a primer, read the "All About Amber" sidebar on page 397. Begin at the huge chunks of raw amber, and the illuminated display of inclusions (bugs stuck in the amber, à la *Jurassic Park*). Some of the ancient amber artifacts displayed here are up to 3,000 years old. These were found in graves,

Knights, the Poles and the Lithuanians decided to join their kingdoms. In 1386, Polish Princess Jadwiga married Lithuanian Prince Władysław Jagiełło (who converted to Christianity for the occasion), uniting Poland and Lithuania and kick-starting a grand new dynasty, the Jagiellonians.

Just as every American knows the date July 4, 1776, every Pole knows the date July 15, 1410—the Battle of Grunwald. King Władysław Jagiełło and Grand Duke Vytautas the Great led a ragtag army of some 40,000 soldiers—Lithuanians, Poles, other Slavs, and even speedy Tatar horsemen—against 27,000 Teutonic Knights. At the end of the day, some 18,000 Poles and Lithuanians were dead—but so were half of the Teutonic Knights (and the other half had been captured). Poland and Lithuania were victorious. Though the Teutonic Knights remained in Poland—extending their Germanic cultural influence on the region well into the 20th century—their political power waned, they pulled out of Lithuania, and they once again allowed free trade on the Vistula. A generation later, the Thirteen Years' War (1454–1466) finally put an end to the Teutonic Knights' domination of northern Poland. The order officially dissolved in 1575, when they converted to Protestantism...though some conspiracy theorists claim the Teutonic Knights are still very much active.

The Knights' influence on Poland persists today—even beyond the striking red-brick churches and castles scattered around the northern part of the country. The Polish novelist Henryk Sienkiewicz's *The Teutonic Knights* is a cultural benchmark and a favorite work of many Poles. The 19th-century Romantics who fanned the flames of Polish patriotism turned the Teutonic Knights into a symbol of Germanic oppression. Even today, Poles—and all Slavs—think of the Teutonic Knights as murderous invaders...while the Germans see them as a mere footnote in their history.

put there by people who thought amber would help the deceased enter a better world. Wandering the hall, you'll see all manner of amber creations: boxes, brooches, necklaces, chess sets, pipes, miniature ships, wine glasses, and belts for skinny-waisted, fashion-conscious women. Look for two truly exquisite pieces: a small casket and an altar. Many of the finely decorated jewelry boxes and chests have ivory, silver, or shell inlays—better for contrast than gold. The portable religious shrines and altars could be used for travel, allowing people to remain reverent on the road and still pack light. Find the amber crucifix. This is a small replica of a six-foot-tall amber and silver cross presented to Pope John Paul II by the people of Gdańsk. Another display case contains necklaces displaying the full range of

amber colors, from opaque white at the top, to transparent yellow in the middle, to virtually black at the bottom.

• *Go back outside and turn left, to the wooden staircase above the Gothic Café (worth considering for a meal, and described later, under "Eating at Malbork Castle"). Go up that staircase, and several more inside, to the top-floor...*

Armory

Browse your way through the impressive array of swords, armor, and other armaments (English descriptions). Look for the 600-year-old "hand-and-a-half" swords—too big to be held in one hand. At the end, in the display of cannons, pikes, and spears, look for the giant shield. These shields could be lined up to form a portable "wall" to protect the knights.

Head downstairs to the second room of the armory, displaying suits of armor (including one for horses). On the wall behind the first suit of armor, look for some five-foot-long "two-hand swords" even bigger than the ones upstairs. Halfway down the hall on the left, find the suit of armor from the Hussars—Polish horseback knights who had wings on their armor, which created a terrifying sound when galloping.

• *Head back outside (noticing the handy WC straight ahead) and cross the main courtyard, entering the smaller courtyard through the passage next to the dark-wood-topped tower. Find the steep steps down into the...*

"Boiler Room"

The Teutonic Knights had a surprisingly sophisticated method for heating this huge complex. You see a furnace down below, and a sort of a holding area for super-heated rocks up above. The radiant heat given off by the rocks spread through the vents without also filling them with smoke. This is one of 11 such "boiler rooms" in the castle complex. As you tour the rest of the castle, keep an eye out for little saucer-sized vents in the floor where the heat came through.

• *Head back out into the main courtyard and turn right, going uphill about 30 yards. At the upper part of this castle are two doors; take the one on the right, then climb up the stairs into the...*

Grand Master's Palace

This was one of the grandest royal residences in medieval Europe, used in later times by Polish kings and German Kaisers. (Today it's sometimes used for special exhibitions.)

• *From the top of the stairs, head down the hall to the right. Notice the troughs in the ground—anyone wanting an audience with the Grand Master had to wash both his hands and his feet.*

At the end of the hall, on the left, enter the elegant...

Summer Refectory: This was where the G. M. dined. With big stained-glass windows, and all of the delicate vaulting supported by a single pillar in the middle, this room was clearly not designed with defense in mind. In fact, medieval Polish armies focused their attacks on this room. On one legendary occasion, the attackers—tipped off by a spy—knew that an important meeting was going on here, and fired a cannonball into the room. It just missed the pillar. (You can see where the cannonball hit the wall, just above the fireplace.) The ceiling eventually did collapse during World War II.

As you continue into the **Winter Refectory,** notice that it has fewer windows (better insulation) and little manhole-like openings in the floor where the "central heating" entered the room.

• *Keep going, and you'll circle back around to where you came in. Go through the door just to the left of the stairs, into the...*

Private Rooms of the Grand Master: Though the Teutonic Order dictated that the monks sleep in dormitories, the Grand Master made an exception for himself. Near the entrance, you'll see his private bedroom (with rough original frescoes of four female martyrs). Exploring the rest of the Top Knight's residence, appreciate the show-off decor (including some 15th-century original frescoes of wine leaves and grapes). The Grand Master even had his own chapel, dedicated to St. Catherine.

• *You'll enter a small hall at the very end of these rooms. If it's open, go through the little door at the right end of this hall, and walk down to the...*

Grand Refectory: This enormous dining hall, damaged in World War II, recently re-opened after a decade-long restoration project. With remarkable palm vaulting and grand frescoes, the Grand Refectory hosted feasts for up to 400 people to celebrate a military victory or to impress visiting dignitaries.

• *Head outside. You're back by the boiler room. Go back out into the main courtyard and walk to the top. Look for the four...*

Grand Master Statues

These four statues came from a 19th-century Prussian monument that was mostly destroyed when the Soviets took Malbork at the end of World War II. Though this was a religious order, these powerful guys look more like kings than monks. From right to left, shake hands with Hermann von Salza (who was Grand Master when the Teutonic Knights came to Poland); Siegfried von Feuchtwangen (who actually moved the T. K. capital from Venice

to Malbork, and who conquered Gdańsk for the Knights—oops, can't shake his hand, which was supposedly chopped off by Soviet troops); Winrich von Kniprode (who oversaw Malbork's Golden Age, and turned it into a castle fit for a king); and Markgraf Albrecht von Hohenzollern (the last Grand Master before the order dissolved and converted to Protestantism).

• *To the right of the statues, continue over the...*

Drawbridge

As you cross, notice the extensive system of fortifications and moats protecting the innermost part of the castle. Check out the cracks in the walls—an increasing threat to this ever-settling castle set on marshy, unstable terrain. The passage is lined with holes (for surveillance), with chutes up above (to pour scalding water or pitch on unwanted visitors). It's not quite straight—so a cannon fired here would hit the side wall of the passage, rather than entering the High Castle. Which is what you're about to do now.

High Castle (Zamek Wysoki)

This is the beating heart of the castle, and its oldest section. As much a monastery as a fortress, the High Castle was off-limits to all but 60 monks of the Teutonic Order and their servants. (The knights stayed in the Middle Castle.) Here you'll find the monks' dormitories, chapels, church, and refectory. As this was the nerve center of the Teutonic Knights—the T. K. HQ—it was also their last line of defense. They stored enormous amounts of food here in case of a siege.

In the middle of the High Castle courtyard is a **well**—an essential part of any inner castle, especially one as prone to sieges as Malbork. At the top is a sculpture of a pelican. Because this noble bird was believed to kill itself to feed its young (notice that it's piercing its own chest with its beak), it was often used in the Middle Ages as a symbol for the self-sacrifice of Jesus.

• *Take some time to explore the...*

Ground Floor

Working clockwise around the courtyard from where you entered, you'll find the following: A door leads to the prison and torture chamber (with small "solitary confinement" cells near the entrance), and a long hall behind with a single tiny window. Along the back of the cloister is a post-WWII photo of Malbork. Beyond that, hiding in the far corner, is an exhibit on medieval stained-glass windows. Somewhere around here, you should see a demonstration of how medieval money was made. The Teutonic Knights minted their own coins—and you can buy your very own freshly minted replica today.

• *Continuing around the courtyard (to the right from where you entered), you'll find the most interesting exhibit on this floor, the...*

Kitchen: This exhibit really gives you a feel for medieval monastery life. The monks who lived here ate three meals a day, along with lots of beer (made here) and wine (imported from France, Italy, and Hungary). A cellar under the kitchen was used as a primitive refrigerator—big chunks of ice were cut from the frozen river in winter, stored in the basement, and used to keep food cool in summer. Behind the long table, see the big dumbwaiter (with shelves), which connects this kitchen with the refectory upstairs. Step into the giant stove and look up the biggest chimney in the castle.

• *Now go back out into the courtyard, and climb up the stairs near where you first entered.*

Middle Floor

• *From the top of the stairs, the first door on the left (with the colorfully painted arch) leads to the most important room of the High Castle, the...*

Chapter Room: Monks gathered here after Mass, and it was also the site for meetings of Teutonic Knights from around the countryside. If a Grand Master was killed in battle, the new one would be elected right here. Each monk had his own seal and a name over his seat. The big chair belonged to the Grand Master. Above his chair, notice the little windows, connecting this room to St. Mary's Church next door (described later). Church music would filter in through these windows...imagine the voices of 60 monks bouncing around with these acoustics.

While monks are usually thought to pursue simple lives, the elegant vaulting in this room is anything but plain. The 14th-century frescoes (restored in the 19th century) depict Grand Masters. In the floor are more vents for the central heating.

• *Leave the Chapter House and walk straight ahead, imagining the monk-filled corridors of Teutonic times. The first door on the right is the...*

Treasury: As you explore the rooms of the tax collector and the house administrator, notice the wide variety of safes and other lock boxes. Near the end, look for the small bed—fit for a small medieval person.

• *Continue around the cloister. At the end of the corridor, look for the little devil at the bottom of the vaulting (on the right, about eye level). He's pulling his beard and crossing his legs—pointing you down the long corridor to the...*

Dansker Tower: From the devil's grimace, you might have guessed that this tower houses the latrine.

For obvious sanitary (and olfactory) reasons, it's set apart from the main part of the castle. The toilets dropped straight down into the moat. The bins above them are filled with cabbage leaves, used by the T. K. as TP. This tower could also serve as a final measure of defense—it's easer to defend than the entire castle. Food was stored above, just in case.

• *Head back toward the main part of the High Castle. On the right-hand side of the long passage, look for a door into the...*

Church Exhibition: These rooms used to be dormitories for the monks, and today they display a wide range of relics from the church (with English descriptions). The first room features various statues, including an evocative, hands-less 15th-century Christ praying in the Garden of Gethsemane. The next room displays pictures of various eras of Malbork Castle, as well as some fragments of statues rescued from the destroyed St. Mary's Church. The huge, mangled crucifix dates from the mid-14th century. At the end of this exhibition is a replica of a Gothic altarpiece, with graphic paintings of the murder and dismemberment of Poland's patron saint, Adalbert.

• *Go back out into the main cloister, turn right, and continue down to the end, arriving at the...*

Golden Gate: This elaborate doorway—covered in protective glass—marks the entrance to St. Mary's Church. Ringed with detailed carvings from the Old Testament, and symbolic messages about how monks of the Teutonic Order should live their lives, it's a marvelous example of late-13th-century art. At the left end of the bottom of the arch, find the five wise virgins who filled their lamps with oil, conserved it wisely, and are headed to heaven. On the right, the five foolish virgins who overslept and used up all their oil are damned, much to their dismay.

• *Go through this door into...*

St. Mary's Church: This holy site was destroyed in World War II and sat for decades with no roof. After so much neglect, it's finally being renovated...slowly. Pictures of the original church with English descriptions explain some of the fragments.

• *Go through the narrow door next to the one where you entered the church, and hike up the tight spiral staircase to the final set of exhibits.*

Top Floor

Walk through the long hallway of temporary exhibits. At the end, go down the stairs into the monks' common room (on the

left). Over the fireplace is a relief depicting the Teutonic Knights fighting the pagans. To the left of that (see the stone windows) is a balcony where musicians entertained the monks after a meal. The next, very long room, with seven pillars, is the refectory, where the monks ate in silence. Along the right-hand wall are confessional-like, lockable storage boxes. At the end of this room, just beyond another decorated fireplace, notice the grated hole in the wall. This is where the dumbwaiter comes up from the kitchen (which we saw below). Beyond this room is an exhibit about the architectural renovation of the castle. On your way back out, you'll have the opportunity to pay 8 zł to climb the very tight and steep steps up to the top of the tower for a view over the castle complex.

• *Your Malbork tour ends here. When finished, you can head back the way you came. En route, you can walk around terraces lining the inner moat, between the castle walls (stairs lead down off of the drawbridge). It's hardly a must-see, but it's pleasant enough, with the Grand Master's garden, a cemetery for monks, and the remains of the small St. Anne's Chapel (with Grand Master tombs).*

Sleeping at Malbork Castle

Malbork is so well-connected by rail to Gdańsk and Warsaw that there's little sense in sleeping here. If you do stay, consider the nighttime sound-and-light show in the castle courtyard.

$$ Hotel Zamek is housed in Malbork's Lower Castle, a red-brick building that was once a hospital, just across from the main part of the fortress. The 42 rooms are overpriced, dark, musty, old-feeling, and a little creepy...but, hey—you're next door to one of

Sleep Code

(3 zł = about $1, country code: 48)
S = Single, **D** = Double/Twin, **T** = Triple, **Q** = Quad, **b** = bathroom, **s** = shower only. Unless otherwise noted, breakfast is included, credit cards are accepted, and English is spoken.

To help you sort easily through these listings, I've divided the rooms into two categories, based on the price for a standard double room with bath:

$$ Higher Priced—Most rooms 200 zł or more.
$ Lower Priced—Most rooms less than 200 zł.

Europe's grandest Gothic castles (Sb-250 zł, Db-300 zł, Tb-380 zł, cheaper mid-Sept–mid-June, elevator, ulica Starościńska 14, tel. & fax 055-272-3367, www.hotelprodus.pl).

Eating at Malbork Castle

Several cheap food stands cluster outside the castle (by the river). For a meal inside the castle complex, your best bet is the **Gothic Café,** under the stairs to the armory in the Middle Castle. Serving traditional Polish food in a nondescript cellar setting, it's handy for its 29-zł lunch deal that includes a main dish and soup (25–40-zł main dishes, Tue–Sun 9:00–17:00 or 18:00 depending on demand, tel. 050-620-8560).

Malbork Connections

From Malbork by Train to: Gdańsk (about 2/hr, 40–50 min), **Toruń** (about every 2 hrs, 3 hrs, transfer in Tczew), **Warsaw** (nearly hourly, 4–4.5 hrs direct).

Toruń

Toruń (TOH-roon) is a pretty, lazy Gothic town conveniently located about halfway between Warsaw and Gdańsk. It's worth a couple of hours to stroll the lively streets, ogle the huge red-brick buildings, and savor the flavor of Poland's most livable city.

With about 210,000 residents and 30,000 students (at Copernicus University), Toruń is a thriving burg. Locals brag that their city is a "mini-Kraków." But that sells both cities short. Toruń lacks Kraków's over-the-top romanticism, and its sights are quickly exhausted. On the other hand, Toruń may well be Poland's most user-friendly city: tidy streets with a sensible grid plan (and English signposts to keep you on track), wide pedestrian boulevards crammed with locals who greet each other like they're long-lost friends, and an easygoing ambience that seems to say, "Hey—relax." And, while it has its share of tourists, Toruń feels more off-the-beaten-path than the other Polish destinations in this book.

Toruń clings fiercely to its two claims to fame: It's the proud birthplace of the astronomer Copernicus (Mikołaj Kopernik), and home to a dizzying variety of gingerbread treats (*piernika;* pyer-NEE-kah).

Orientation to Toruń

(area code: 056)

Everything in Toruń worth seeing is in the walled Old Town, climbing up a gentle hill from the Vistula River. The broad, traffic-free main drag, ulica Szeroka (called Różana at the entrance of town) bisects the Old Town, running parallel to the river.

Arrival in Toruń

Toruń's main train station (called Toruń Główny) is about a mile away—and across the river—from the Old Town. The main hall has ticket windows, an ATM, and lockers (4–8 zł, depending on bag size).

To reach the Old Town, you have two options: If you go out the door from the main hall, you'll spot **taxis** waiting to take you into town (the trip should cost no more than 10 zł). To take the **bus,** buy a 2.40-zł ticket from the *RUCH* kiosk overlooking the tracks near the main hall. Then follow the pedestrian underpass beneath track 4 (entrance to underpass marked with low-profile *wyjście do miasta* sign and bus icon, outside main hall and to the left). When you emerge on the other side, the bus stop for bus #22 or #27 into the center is ahead and on your right. Take the bus to Plac Rapackiego, the first stop after the long bridge. To return to the station, catch bus #22 or #27 across the busy road from where you got off.

Tourist Information

The TI is on the main square, behind the Old Town Hall. Pick up the free map, and get information about hotels in town and city tours (Tue–Fri 9:00–18:00, Mon and Sat 9:00–16:00, closed Sun except May–Aug, when it's open 9:00–13:00, Rynek Staromiejski 25, tel. 056-621-0931, www.it.torun.pl).

Self-Guided Walk

Welcome to Toruń

This very lightly guided introductory stroll takes you through the heart of Toruń. With no stops, you could do it in 15 minutes.

From the Plac Rapackiego bus stop, head into the town through the passageways under the colorful buildings. Within a

block, you're at the bustling **Old Town Market Square** (Rynek Staromiejski), surrounded by huge brick buildings and outdoor restaurants buzzing with lively locals. The big building in the center is the **Old Town Hall** (Ratusz Staromiejski), with a boring museum and a climbable tower. The building with the pointy spires on the right (across from the Old Town Hall) is the **Artus Court,** where the medieval town council and merchants' guilds met (sadly, unlike the similar court in Gdańsk, it's not open to the public).

The guy playing his violin in front of the Old Town Hall is a **rafter** *(retman)*—one of the medieval lumberjacks who lashed tree trunks together and floated them down the Vistula to Gdańsk. This particular rafter came to Toruń when the town was infested with frogs. He wooed them with his violin and marched them out of town. (Hmm...sounds like a certain piper in another medieval Hanseatic city, Bremen....)

The bigger statue, at the other end of the Old Town Hall, depicts **Mikołaj Kopernik,** better known as Nicholas Copernicus (1473–1543). This Toruń-born son of aristocrats turned the world on its ear when he suggested that the sun, not the earth, is the center of the universe (an idea called the "heliocentric theory"). Toruń is serious about this local boy done good—he's the town mascot, as well as the namesake of the local university. Among its fields of study, Copernicus U. has a healthy astronomy program. There's a planetarium in the Old Town (just past the far corner of the square) and a giant radio telescope on the town outskirts. Despite all the local fuss over Copernicus, there's some dispute about his ethnicity; he was born in Toruń, all right, but at a time when it was a predominantly German town. So is he Polish or German? (For more on Copernicus, visit his birth house—now a modest museum on the astronomer—just two blocks away, and described later, under "Sights in Toruń").

What's that sweet smell in the air? For Poles, Toruń is synonymous with **gingerbread** *(piernika).* This Toruń treat can be topped with different kinds of jams or glazes, and/or dipped in chocolate. You'll see gingerbread shops all over town, mostly selling the same stuff. The shop in the Artus Court building on the Old Town Market Square is handy and atmospheric; more are around the corner on ulica Żeglarska (toward the river; the shop on the right near the end of the block has a handy bulk system—point to what looks good and get exactly the amount and types you want).

Having satisfied your ginger tooth, head back to the square and join the human stream down the appropriately named **ulica Szeroka** ("Wide Street"), an enjoyable pedestrian promenade through the heart of town. Just before the road forks at the white

Empik building, look down Przedzamcze to the right to see fragments of the town wall. This marks the border between the Old Town and the New Town (chartered only about 30 years later—both in the 13th century). While these areas are both collectively known today as the unified "Old Town," they were quite different in the Middle Ages—each with its own market square, and separated by a wall. (If you're curious to see the New Town Square and Town Hall, continue up ulica Szeroka and bear left at the fork.)

To end our walk, follow the wall to the right, down Przedzamcze, to reach the **ruins** of a castle built by the Teutonic Knights who were so influential in northern Poland in the Middle Ages (see page 434). The castle was destroyed in the 15th century by the locals—who, aside from a heap of bricks, left only the tower that housed the Teutonic toilets.

Beyond the castle ruins is the **Vistula** riverbank. The road that runs along the river here is called Bulwar Filadelfijski—for Toruń's sister city in Pennsylvania.

Sights in Toruń

Toruń is more about strolling than it is about sightseeing—the town's museums are underwhelming. Aside from its half-dozen red-brick churches (any of which are worth dropping into), the following attractions are worth considering on a rainy day.

Gingerbread Museum (Muzeum Piernika)—This fun attraction—by far Toruń's liveliest—is an actual, working gingerbread bakery of yore. Barefoot, costumed medieval bakers greet you and walk you through the traditional process of rolling, cutting out, baking, and tasting your own batch of gingerbread cookies (30–40 min, start to finish). After aging for 12 weeks to achieve the proper consistency, the dough bakes only 12 minutes—or, according to the medieval bakers, about 50 Hail Marys (10 zł, may have to wait a few minutes for an English guide to help you, daily 9:00–18:00, 2 blocks toward the river from Old Town Market Square at Rabiańska 9, www.muzeumpiernika.pl).

Copernicus House (Dom Kopernika)—Filling a pair of beautiful, gabled brick buildings, this dull and overpriced little museum celebrates the hero of Toruń. As much about medieval Toruń as about the astronomer, and sprawling over several floors in the two buildings, the exhibits loosely explain the astronomer's life and achievements. While the displays—mostly copies of important documents and paintings, models of his instruments, and English descriptions—are pretty flat, it's mildly interesting to walk around the creaky interiors. The second part of the

exhibit is an 18-minute "sound-and-light show" (slideshow with recorded commentary) about medieval Toruń, with a model of the city that lights up dramatically at appropriate moments (ask for English show when you enter; museum-10 zł, slideshow-12 zł, both-18 zł; May–Sept Tue–Sun 10:00–18:00, closed Mon; Oct–April Tue–Sun 10:00–16:00, closed Mon; Kopernika 15/17, www.muzeum.torun.pl). To get to the museum from the Old Town Market Square, head down Żeglarska and take the first right—on Kopernika, of course.

Ethnographic Park (Park Etnograficzny)—This open-air folk museum, while not ranking with Europe's best, is at least your most convenient opportunity to stroll through some traditional buildings from the region. It's in the middle of a pleasant park just outside the Old Town (14 zł; mid-April–Sept Mon, Wed, and Fri 9:00–16:00, Tue, Thu, and Sat–Sun 10:00–18:00; Oct–mid-April Tue–Fri 9:00–16:00, Sat–Sun 10:00–16:00, closed Mon; Wały Gen. Sikorskiego 19, www.etnomuzeum.pl). To get there from the Old Town Market Square, walk up Chełmińska with the river at your back and the Old Town Hall on your left. Cross the busy road, and you're in the park. Even if you're not interested in the museum, the relaxing park surrounding it is a fine place to pass some time.

Sleeping in Toruń

Toruń's Old Town has more than its share of good-value hotels (Db-200–300 zł). The TI has a brochure listing the options, and can help you find a room for no extra charge.

$$ Hotel Karczma "Spichrz" ("Granary") is a fresh, atmospheric hotel in a renovated old granary. Its 23 rooms and public spaces are a fun blend of old and new—with huge wooden beams around every corner, and the scent of the restaurant's wood-fired grill wafting through the halls. It's comfortable, central, well-priced, and a little kitschy (Sb-230 zł, Db-290 zł, 10–20 percent cheaper on weekends, tall people may not appreciate low ceilings and beams, elevator, a block off the main drag toward the river at ulica Mostowa 1, tel. 056-657-1140, fax 056-657-1144, www.spichrz.pl, hotel@spichrz.pl). The restaurant is also good (25–40-zł grilled meat dishes, daily 12:00–23:00).

$ Hotel Retman ("Rafter") has 29 older but nicely appointed rooms over a restaurant just down the street from the Gingerbread Museum (Sb-190 zł, Db-250 zł; Fri–Sun prices drop to Sb-160 zł, Db-200 zł; ulica Rabiańska 15, tel. 056-657-4460, fax 056-657-4461, www.hotelretman.pl, recepcja@hotelretman.pl).

Toruń Connections

Toruń is a handy stopover on the way between Warsaw and Gdańsk. It's on a different train line than Malbork—so visiting both Toruń and the mighty Teutonic castle in the same day is surprisingly time-consuming.

From Toruń by Train to: Warsaw (5/day, 3 hrs direct, longer with a transfer in Kutno), **Gdańsk** (4/day direct, 3 hrs; at least hourly with transfer in Bydgoszcz, 3–4 hrs), **Kraków** (1/day direct, 7.75 hrs; better to transfer at Warsaw's Zachodnia station: 4/day, 5.75–6.5 hrs).

HUNGARY

HUNGARY

Magyarország

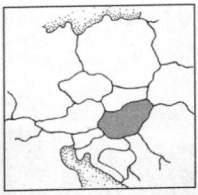

Hungary is an island of Asian-descended Magyars in a sea of Slavs. Even though the Hungarians have thoroughly integrated with their Slavic and German neighbors in the millennium-plus since they arrived, there's still something about the place that's distinctly Magyar (MUD-jar). Here in quirky, idiosyncratic Hungary, everything's a little different from the rest of Europe—in terms of history, language, culture, customs, and cuisine—but it's hard to put your finger on exactly how.

Just a century ago, this country controlled half of one of Europe's grandest realms: the Austro-Hungarian Empire. Today, perhaps clinging to their former greatness, many Hungarians remain old-fashioned and nostalgic. With their dusty museums and bushy moustaches, they love to remember the good old days. Buildings all over the country are marked with plaques boasting *MŰEMLÉK* ("historical monument").

Thanks to this focus on tradition, the Hungarians you'll encounter are generally polite, formal, and professional. Hungarians have class. Everything here is done with a proud flourish. People in the service industry seem to wear their uniforms as a badge of honor rather than a burden. When a waiter comes to your table in a restaurant, he'll say, *"Tessék parancsolni"*—literally, "Please command, sir." The standard greeting, *"Jó napot kívánok,"* means "I wish you a good day." Women sometimes hear the even more formal greeting, *"Kezét csókolom"*—"I kiss your hand." And when your train or bus makes a stop, you won't be alerted by a mindless, blaring beep or hoot—but instead, peppy music. (You'll be humming these contagious little ditties all day.) Perhaps thanks to this artful blending of elegance and formality, Hungarians have a cultural affinity for the French.

Hungarians are also orderly and tidy...in their own sometimes unexpected ways. Yes, Hungary has as much litter and graffiti—and as many crumbling buildings—as any other formerly communist country, but you'll find great reason within the chaos. My favorite town name in Hungary: Hatvan. This means "Sixty" in Hungarian...and it's exactly 60 kilometers from Budapest. You

can't argue with that kind of logic.

This tradition of left-brained thinking hasn't produced many great Hungarian painters or poets who are known outside their homeland. But the Hungarians, who are renowned for their ingenuity, have made tremendous contributions to science, technology, business, and industry. Hungarians of note include Edward Teller (instrumental in creating the A-bomb), John von Neumann (a pioneer of computer science), Andy Grove (who, as András Gróf, immigrated to the US and founded Intel), and George Soros (the billionaire investor famous—or notorious—for supporting left-wing causes). A popular local joke claims that Hungarians are so clever that they can enter a revolving door behind you and exit in front of you.

Perhaps the most famous Hungarian "scientist" invented something you probably have in a box in your basement: Ernő Rubik, creator of the famous cube. Hungarians' enjoyment of a good mind-bending puzzle is also evident in their fascination with chess, which you'll see played in cafés, parks, and baths.

Like their Viennese neighbors, Hungarians know how to enjoy the good life. Favorite activities include splashing and soaking in their many thermal baths. Locals brag that if you poke a hole in the ground anywhere in Hungary, you'll find a hot-water spring. Judging from Budapest, they might be right: The city has 123 natural springs and some two-dozen thermal baths *(fürdő)*. "Taking the waters," Hungarian-style, should be your top priority while you're here. Though public baths can sound intimidating, they're a delight. In this book I recommend my two favorite baths

Hungary Almanac

Official Name: Magyar Köztársaság (Hungarian Republic), or simply Magyarország.

Snapshot History: Settled by the Central Asian Magyars in A.D. 896, Hungary became Catholic in the year 1000, and went on to become Christian Europe's front line in fighting against the Ottomans (Muslims from today's Turkey) in the 16th–17th centuries. After serving as co-capital of the vast Austro-Hungarian Empire and losing World Wars I and II, Hungary became a Soviet satellite until achieving independence in 1989.

Population: Hungary's 10 million people (similar to Michigan) are 92 percent ethnic Hungarians who speak Hungarian. One in 50 is Roma (Gypsy). Half the populace is Catholic, with 20 percent Protestant and 25 percent listed as "other" or unaffiliated. Of the world's approximately 12 million ethnic Hungarians, one in six lives outside Hungary (mostly in areas of Romania, Slovakia, Serbia, and Croatia that were once part of Hungary).

Latitude and Longitude: 47°N and 20°E; similar latitude to Seattle, Paris, and Vienna.

Area: 36,000 square miles, similar to Indiana or Maine.

Geography: Hungary is situated in the Carpathian Basin, bound on the north by the Carpathian Mountains and on the south by the Dinaric Mountains. Though it's surrounded by mountains, Hungary itself is relatively flat, with some gently rolling hills. The Great Hungarian Plain—which begins on the east bank of the Danube in Budapest—stretches all the way to Asia. Hungary's two main rivers—the Danube and Tisza—run north–south through the country, neatly dividing it into three regions.

Biggest Cities: Budapest (the capital on the Danube, 1.7 million), Debrecen (in the east, 205,000), and Miskolc (in the north, 180,000).

in Budapest, a fine one in Eger, and another just outside of Eger. For each one, I've included careful instructions to help you enjoy the warm-water fun like a pro. (To allay your first fear: Yes, you can wear your swimsuit the entire time.)

Hungarians are also reviving an elegant, Vienna-style café culture that was dismantled by the communists. Whiling away the afternoon at a genteel coffeehouse, as you nurse a drink or a delicate dessert, is a favorite pastime.

Classical music is revered in Hungary, perhaps as nowhere else outside Austria. Aside from scientists and businessmen, the best-known Hungarians are composers: Béla Bartók, Zoltán Kodály, and Franz Liszt.

While one in five Hungarians lives in Budapest, the countryside plays an important role in Hungary's economy—this has

Economy: The Gross Domestic Product is $197 billion; the GDP per capita is $19,800. Thanks to its progressive "goulash communism," Hungary had a head start on many other former Soviet Bloc countries. But in the 1990s, many communist-era workers (especially women) lost their jobs, and in recent years, the country has suffered rampant inflation. Today, the workforce is small (only 57 percent of eligible workers) but highly skilled. Grains, metals, and machinery are major products, and nearly a third of trade is with Germany.

Currency: 200 forints (Ft, or HUF) = about $1.

Government: The single-house National Assembly (386 seats) is the only ruling branch directly elected by popular vote. The legislators in turn select the figurehead president (László Sólyom through at least 2010) and the ruling prime minister (Gordon Bajnai).

Flag: Three horizontal bands, top to bottom: red (representing strength), white (faithfulness), and green (hope). It's identical to the Italian flag, but flipped 90 degrees counterclockwise. It often includes the Hungarian coat of arms: horizontal red-and-white stripes (on the left); the patriarchal, or double-barred, cross (on the right); and the Hungarian crown (on top).

The Average János: The typical Hungarian eats a pound of lard a week (they cook with it). The average family has three members, and they spend almost three-fourths of their income on (costly) housing. According to a recent condom-company survey, the average Hungarian has sex 131 times a year (behind only France and Greece), making them Europe's third-greatest liars.

always been a highly agricultural region. You'll pass through fields of wheat and corn, but the grains are secondary to Hungarians' (and tourists') true love: wine. Hungarian winemaking standards plummeted under the communists, but many vintner families are now reclaiming their lands, returning to their precise traditional methods, and making wines worth being proud of once more. (For details, see the "Hungarian Wines" sidebar, later.)

Somehow Hungary has managed to become cosmopolitan while remaining perfectly Hungarian. In the countryside, where less cultural mixing has occurred, traditional Magyar culture is more evident. But in the cities, the Hungarians—like Hungary itself—are a cross-section of Eastern European cultures: Magyars, Germans, Czechs, Slovaks, Poles, Serbs, Jews, Ottomans, Romanians, Roma (Gypsies), and many others. Still, no matter

how many generations removed they are from Magyar stock, there's something different about a Hungarian—and not just the language. Look a Hungarian in the eye, and you'll see a glimmer of the marauding Magyar, stomping in from the Central Asian plains a thousand years ago.

Helpful Hints

First Name Last: Hungarians list a person's family name first, and the given name is last—just as in many other Eastern cultures (think of Kim Jong Il). So the composer known as "Franz Liszt" in German is "Liszt Ferenc" in his homeland. (To help reduce confusion, many Hungarian business cards list the surname in capital letters.)

Hello Goodbye: Hungarians have an endearing habit of using the English word "hello" for both "hi" and "bye," just like the Italians use "ciao." You might overhear a Hungarian end a telephone conversation with a cheery "Hello!"

Telephones: Like many things in Hungary, the telephone system is uniquely confusing. You must dial different codes whether you're calling locally, long distance within the country, or internationally to Hungary.

Dialing Fixed Lines: To dial a number in the same city, simply dial direct, with no area code.

To dial long-distance within Hungary, you have to add the prefix 06, followed by the area code (e.g., Budapest's area code is 1, so you dial 06-1, then the rest of the number).

To make an international call to Hungary, start with the international access code (00 if calling from Europe, 011 from the United States or Canada), then Hungary's country code (36), then the area code (but not the 06) and number.

To make an international call from Hungary, dial 00, the country code of the country you're calling (see chart in appendix), the area code if applicable (may need to drop initial zero), and the local number.

Dialing Mobile Phones and Other Unusual Numbers: Certain Hungarian phone numbers are particularly tricky to dial. Numbers beginning with 0620, 0630, or 0670 are mobile phones; those beginning with 0680 are toll-free; and 0681 and 0690 are expensive toll lines.

To call these numbers from within Hungary, simply dial the number direct, as it appears in this book.

To dial these numbers from outside Hungary, you need to replace the initial 06 with 011-36 (from the US) or 00-36 (from Europe). So, to call my favorite Budapest guide from a fixed line inside Hungary, you'd dial 0620-926-0557; from North America,

you'd dial 011-36-20-926-0557; and from another European country, you'd dial 00-36-20-926-0557.

Hungarian History

The Hungarian story—essentially the tale of a people finding their home—is as epic as any in Europe. Over the course of a millennium, a troublesome nomadic tribe that was the scourge of Europe gradually assimilated with its neighbors and—through stubbornness, tenacity, and diplomacy—found itself controlling a vast swath of Central and Eastern Europe. Locals toss around the names of great historical figures such as István, Kossuth, and Nagy as if they're talking about old friends. Take this crash-course so you can keep up.

The story begins long, long ago and far, far away...

Welcome to Europe

The land we call Hungary today has long been considered the place—culturally, if not geographically—where the West (Europe) meets the East (Asia). The Roman province of Pannonia extended to the final foothills of the Alps that constitute the Buda Hills, on the west side of the Danube. Across the river, Rome ended and the barbarian wilds began. From here, the Great Hungarian Plain stretches in a long, flat expanse all the way to Asia—hemmed in to the north by the Carpathian Mountains. (Geologists consider this prairie-like plain to be the westernmost steppe in Europe—resembling the terrain that covers much of Central Asia.) After Rome collapsed and Europe fell into the Dark Ages, Hungary became the territory of Celts, Vandals, Huns, and Avars...until some out-of-towners moved into the neighborhood.

The seven Magyar tribes, led by the mighty Árpád (and, according to legend, by the mythical Turul bird), thundered into the Carpathian Basin in A.D. 896. They were a mysterious, rough-and-tumble nomadic people from Central Asia who didn't like to settle down in one place. And yet, after the long and winding westward odyssey they'd been on, the Great Hungarian Plain felt comfortingly like home to the Magyars—reminiscent of the Asian steppes of their ancestors.

The Magyars would camp out in today's Hungary in the winters, and in the summers, they'd go on raids throughout Europe. They were notorious as incredibly swift horsemen, whose use of stirrups (an eastern innovation largely unknown in Europe at the

time) allowed them to easily outmaneuver foes and victims. Italy, France, Germany's Rhine, the Spanish Pyrenees, all the way to Constantinople (modern-day Istanbul)—the Magyars had the run of the Continent.

Now planted in the center of Europe, the Hungarians effectively drove a wedge in the middle of the sprawling Slavic populations of the Great Moravian Kingdom (basically today's "Eastern Europe"). The Slavs were split into two splinter groups, north and south—a division that persists today: Czechs, Slovaks, and Poles to the north; and Croats, Slovenes, Serbs, and Bosniaks to the south. (You can still hear the division caused by the Magyars in the language: While Czechs and Russians call a castle *hrad*, Croats and Serbs call it *grad*.)

For half a century, the Magyars ranked with the Vikings as the most feared people in Europe. But they were finally defeated by a German and Czech army at the Battle of Augsburg in 955. The Magyars' King Géza—realizing that if they were to survive, his people had to put down roots and get along with their neighbors—made a fateful decision that would forever shape Hungary's future: He adopted Christianity, baptized his son, Vajk, and married him to a Bavarian princess at a young age.

On Christmas Day in the year 1000, Vajk changed his name to István (Stephen) and was symbolically crowned by the pope (for more on István, see page 506). The domestication of the nomadic Magyars was difficult, thanks largely to the resistance of István's uncles, but was ultimately successful. Hungary became a legitimate Christian kingdom, welcomed by its neighbors.

The Tatars, the Ottomans, and Other Outsiders (A.D. 1000–1686)

One of Hungary's earliest challenges came at the hands of fellow invaders from Central Asia. Through the first half of the 13th century, the Tatars swept into Eastern Europe from Mongolia. They sacked and plundered Hungarian towns, laying waste to the kingdom. The Hungarian king at the time, Béla IV, was left to rebuild his ruined kingdom from the rubble—creating for the first time many of the stout hilltop castles that still line the Danube.

Each of Béla's successors left his own mark on Hungary, as the Magyar kingdom flourished. They barely skipped a beat when the original Árpád dynasty died out in 1301, as they imported French kings (from the Naples-based Anjou, or Angevin, dynasty) to

continue building their young realm. King Károly Róbert (Charles Robert) won over the Magyars, and his son Nagy Lajos (Louis the Great) expanded Hungarian holdings.

For more than 150 years, Hungary did not have a Hungarian-blooded king. This changed in the late 15th century, when a shortage of foreign kings led to the ascension to the throne of the enlightened King Mátyás (Matthias) Corvinus. The son of popular military hero János Hunyadi, King Matthias fostered the arts, sparked a mini-Renaissance, and successfully balanced foreign threats to Hungarian sovereignty (the Habsburgs to the north and west, and the Ottomans to the south and east). Under Matthias, Hungarian culture and political power reached a peak. (For more on this great Hungarian king, see page 502.)

But even before the reign of "good king Matthias," the Ottomans (from today's Turkey) had already begun slicing their way through the Balkan Peninsula toward Eastern Europe. In 1526, the Ottomans entered Hungary when Sultan Süleyman the Magnificent killed Hungary's King Lajos II at the Battle of Mohács. By 1541, they took Buda. The Ottomans would dominate Hungarian life (and history) until the 1680s—nearly a century and a half.

The Ottoman invasion divided Hungary into thirds: Ottoman-occupied "Lower Hungary" (more or less today's Hungary); rump "Upper Hungary" (basically today's Slovakia), with its capital at Bratislava (which they called "Pozsony"); and the loosely independent territories of Transylvania (in today's Romania), ruled by Hungarian dukes. During this era, the Ottomans built many of the thermal baths that you'll still find throughout Hungary.

Ottoman-occupied Hungary became severely depopulated, and many of its towns and cities fell into ruins. While it was advantageous for a Hungarian subject to adopt Islam (for lower taxes and other privileges), the Ottomans rarely resorted to forced conversion—unlike the arguably more oppressive Catholics who controlled other parts of Europe at the time (such as the monarchs of Spain, who expelled the Jews and conducted the Spanish Inquisition). Ottoman rule meant that Hungary took a different course than other parts of Europe during this time. The nation fully enjoyed the Renaissance, but missed out on other major European historical events—both good (the Age of Discovery and Age of Reason) and bad (the devastating Catholic-versus-Protestant wars that plagued the rest of Central and Eastern Europe).

Crippled by the Ottomans and lacking power and options, Hungarian nobles desperately offered their crown to the Austrian Habsburg Empire, in exchange for salvation from the invasion. The Habsburgs instead used Hungary as a kind of "buffer zone" between the Ottoman advance and Vienna. It was only the

beginning of a very troubled relationship between the Hungarians and the Austrians.

Habsburg Rule, Hungarian National Revival, and Revolution (1686–1867)

In the late 17th century, the Habsburg army, starting from Vienna, began a sustained campaign to push the Ottomans out of Hungary in about 15 years. They finally wrested Buda and Pest from the Ottomans in 1686. The Habsburgs repopulated Buda and Pest with Germans, while Magyars reclaimed the countryside.

The Habsburgs governed Hungary as an outpost of Austria. The Hungarians—who'd had enough of foreign rule—fought them tooth and nail. Countless streets, squares, and buildings throughout the country are named for the "big three" Hungarian patriots who resisted the Habsburgs during this time: Ferenc Rákóczi (who led the unsuccessful War of Independence in 1703–1711), István Széchenyi (a wealthy count who funded grand structures to give his Magyar countrymen something to take pride in), and Lajos Kossuth (who led the Revolution of 1848).

The early 19th century saw a thawing of Habsburg oppression. Here as throughout Europe, "backwards" country traditions began to trickle into the cities, gaining more respect and prominence. It was during this time of reforms that Hungarian (rather than German) became the official language. It also coincided with a Romantic Age of poets and writers, who began to use the Hungarian tongue to create literature for the first time. By around 1825, the Hungarian National Revival was underway, as the people began to embrace the culture and traditions of their Magyar ancestors. Like people across Europe—from Ireland to Italy, and from Prague to Scandinavia—the Hungarians were becoming aware of what made them a unique people.

In March of 1848, a wave of Enlightenment-fueled nationalism that began in Paris spread like wildfire across Europe, igniting a revolutionary spirit in cities such as Budapest. On March 15, the Revolution of 1848 against the Habsburgs began on the steps of the National Museum in Pest. In the spring of 1849, the Hungarians mounted a bloody but successful offensive to take over a wide swath of territory, including Buda and Pest. But in June, some 200,000 Russian reinforcements flooded into Hungary, crushing the revolution. After the final battle, the Habsburgs executed 13 Hungarian generals, then celebrated by clinking mugs of

beer. To this very day, clinking beer mugs is, for many traditional Hungarians, just bad style.

For a while, the Habsburgs cracked down on their unruly Hungarian subjects. But after an important military loss to Bismarck's Prussia in 1866, Austria began to realize that it couldn't control its rebellious Slavic holdings all by itself. And so, just 18 years after crushing the Hungarians in a war, the Habsburgs handed them the reins.

With the Compromise *(Ausgleich)* of 1867, Austria granted Budapest authority over the eastern half of their lands, creating the so-called Dual Monarchy of the Austro-Hungarian Empire. Hungary was granted their much-prized "home rule," where most matters (except finance, foreign policy, and the military) were administered from Budapest rather than Vienna. The Habsburg emperor, Franz Josef, agreed to a unique "king and emperor" *(König und Kaiser)* arrangement, where he was emperor of Austria, but only king of Hungary. In 1867, he was crowned as Hungarian king in both Buda (at Matthias Church) and Pest (on today's Roosevelt tér). The insignia "K+K" (*König und Kaiser,* king and emperor)—which you'll still see everywhere—evokes these grand days.

Budapest's Golden Age (1867–1918)

The *Ausgleich* marked an enormous turning point for the Hungarians, who once again governed their traditional holdings: large parts of today's Slovakia, Serbia, and Transylvania (northwest Romania), and smaller parts of today's Croatia, Slovenia, Ukraine, and Austria. To better govern their sprawling realm, in 1873, the cities of Buda, Pest, and Óbuda merged into one mega-metropolis: Budapest.

Serendipitously, Budapest's new prominence coincided with the 1,000th anniversary of the Hungarians' ancestors, the Magyars, arriving in Europe...one more excuse to dress things up. Budapest's longstanding rivalry with Vienna only spurred them to build bigger and better. The year 1896 saw an over-the-top millennial celebration, for which many of today's greatest structures were created (see page 480).

It was clearly Budapest's Golden Age. No European city grew faster in the second half of the 19th century than Budapest; in the last quarter of the 19th century alone, Budapest doubled in size. By 1900, the city was larger than Rome, Madrid, or Amsterdam.

It was also a period of great architectural, artistic, and creative achievement. Composers Franz Liszt (more Germanic than Magyar) and (later) Béla Bartók and Zoltán Kodály incorporated the folk and Roma (Gypsy) songs of the Hungarian and Transylvanian countryside into their music. As Magyar culture

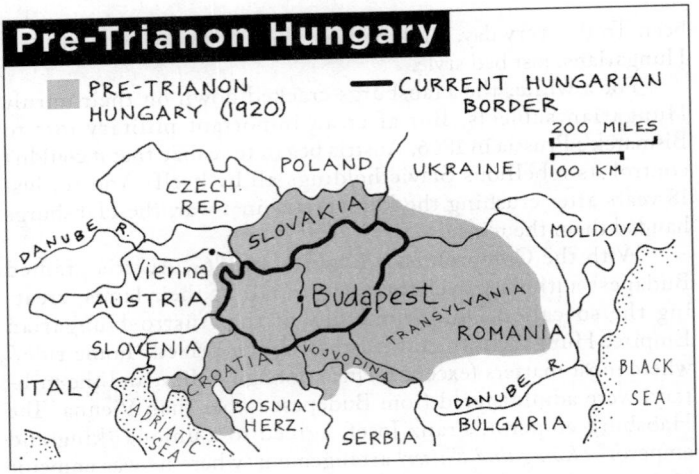

thrived, the traditions of the countryside flowed into the music salons of Budapest.

But before long, Hungarians began to make the same mistakes the Habsburgs had—limiting the rights of their minorities, and enforcing a policy of "Magyarization" that compelled subjects from all ethnic backgrounds to adopt the Hungarian language and culture. Soon the Golden Age came crashing to an end, and Hungary plunged into its darkest period.

The Crisis of Trianon (1918–1939)

World War I marked the end of the age of divine monarchs, as the Romanovs of Russia, the Ottomans of Asia Minor, and, yes, the Habsburgs of Austria-Hungary saw their empires break apart. Hungary, which had been riding the Habsburgs' coattails to power and prominence for the past half-century, now paid the price. As retribution for their role on the losing side of World War I, the 1920 Treaty of Trianon (named for the palace on the grounds of Versailles where it was signed) reassigned two-thirds of Hungary's former territory and half of its population to Romania, Ukraine, Czechoslovakia, and Yugoslavia (Slovenia, Croatia, and Serbia).

It is impossible to overstate the impact of the Treaty of Trianon on the Hungarian psyche—and on Hungarian history. Not unlike the overnight construction of the Berlin Wall, towns along the new Hungarian borders were suddenly divided down the middle. Many Hungarians found themselves unable to visit relatives or commute to jobs that were in the same country the day before. This sent hundreds of thousands of Hungarian refugees—now "foreigners" in their own towns—into Budapest, sparking an enormous but bittersweet boom in the capital.

To this day, the Treaty of Trianon is regarded as one of the greatest tragedies of Hungarian history. Like the Basques and the Serbs, the Hungarians feel separated from each other by circumstances outside their control. Today, more than two million ethnic Hungarians live outside Hungary (mostly in Romania)—and many Hungarians claim that these lands still belong to the Magyars. You'll see maps, posters, and bumper stickers with the distinctive shape of a much larger, pre-WWI Hungary...patriotically displayed by Magyars who feel as strongly about Trianon as if it happened yesterday.

After Trianon, the newly shrunken Kingdom of Hungary had to reinvent itself. The Hungarian crown sat unworn in the Royal Palace, as if waiting for someone worthy to claim it. The WWI hero Admiral Miklós Horthy had won many battles with the Austro-Hungarian navy. Though the new Hungary had no sea and no navy, Horthy retained his rank and ruled the country as a regent. A popular joke points out that during this time, Hungary was a "kingdom without a king" and a landlocked country ruled by a sea admiral. This sense of compounded deficiency pretty much sums up the morose attitude Hungarians have about those gloomy post-Trianon days.

A mounting financial crisis, and lingering resentment about the strict post-WWI reparations, made Hungary fertile ground for some bold new fascist ideas.

World War II and the Arrow Cross (1939–1945)

As Adolf Hitler rose to power, some countries that had felt unfairly treated in the aftermath of World War I—including Hungary—saw Nazi Germany as a vehicle to greater independence. Admiral Horthy joined forces with the Nazis with the hope that they might help Hungary regain the crippling territorial losses of Trianon. In June 1941, Hungary (reluctantly) declared war on the Soviet Union—and against the US and Britain in December of the same year.

Being an ally to the Nazis, rather than an occupied state, also allowed Hungary a certain degree of self-determination through the war—temporarily saving its sizeable Jewish population from immediate deportation. Winning back chunks of Slovakia, Transylvania, and Croatia in the early days of World War II also bolstered the Nazis' acceptance in Hungary.

As Nazism took hold in Germany, the Hungarian fascist movement—spearheaded by the Arrow Cross Party (Nyilaskeresztes Párt)—gained popularity within Hungary. As Germany increased its demands for Hungarian soldiers and food, Admiral Horthy resisted...until Hitler's patience wore thin. In March of 1944, the Nazis invaded and installed the Arrow Cross in power. The Arrow

Cross made up for lost time, immediately beginning a savage campaign of executing Hungary's Jews—not only sending them to death camps, but butchering them in the streets. As the end of the war neared, Hungarian Nazi collaborators resorted to more desperate measures, such as lining up Jews along the Danube and shooting them into the river. To save bullets, they'd sometimes tie several victims together, shoot one of them, and throw him into the freezing Danube—dragging the others in with him. Hungary lost nearly 600,000 Jews to the Holocaust.

The Soviet Army eventually "liberated" Hungary, but at the expense of Budapest: A months-long siege, from Christmas of 1944 to mid-February of 1945, reduced the proud city to rubble. One in 10 Hungarian citizens perished in the war.

Communism...with a Pinch of Paprika (1945–1989)

After World War II, Hungary was gradually compelled to adopt Moscow's system of government. The Soviet-puppet hardliner Mátyás Rákosi ruled Hungary with an iron fist. Everyday people were terrorized by the KGB-style secret police, called the ÁVO and ÁVH, to accept the new regime. Non-Hungarians were deported, potential and actual dissidents disappeared into the horrifying gulag system of Siberia, food shortages were epidemic, people were compelled to spy on their friends and families, and countless lives were ruined.

Beginning on October 23, 1956, the Hungarians courageously staged a monumental uprising, led by Communist Party reformer Imre Nagy. Initially, it appeared that one of the cells on the Soviet Bloc might win itself the right to semi-autonomy. But Moscow couldn't let that happen. In a Tiananmen Square–style crackdown, the Soviets sent in tanks to brutally put down the uprising and occupy the city. When the dust settled, 2,500 Hungarians were dead, and 200,000 fled to the West. (If you know any Hungarians in the US, their families more than likely fled there in 1956.) Nagy was arrested, given a sham trial, and executed in 1958. For more on these events, see the "1956" sidebar on page 514.

After the uprising, the USSR installed János Kádár—a colleague of Nagy's who was also loyal to Moscow—to lead Hungary. For a few years, things were bleak, as the secret police ratcheted up their efforts against potential dissidents. But in the 1960s, Kádár's reformist tendencies began to cautiously emerge. While still mostly cooperating with Moscow, Kádár gradually allowed the people of Hungary more freedom than citizens of neighboring countries had—a system dubbed "goulash communism." The "New Economic Mechanism" of 1968 partly opened Hungary to foreign trade. People from other Warsaw Pact countries—Czechs, Slovaks, and Poles—flocked to Budapest's Váci utca to experience

"Western evils" unavailable to them back home, such as Adidas sneakers and Big Macs. People half-joked that Hungary was the happiest barrack in the communist camp.

In the late 1980s, the Eastern Bloc began to thaw. And Hungary—which was always skeptical of the Soviets (or any foreign rule)—was one of the first satellite states that implemented real change. In February of 1989, the Hungarian communist parliament, with little fanfare, essentially voted to put an expiration date on their own regime. There were three benchmarks in that fateful year: May 2, when Hungary was the first Soviet Bloc country to effectively open its borders to the West (by removing its border fence with Austria); June 16, when communist reformer Imre Nagy and his comrades were given a proper, ceremonial reburial on Heroes' Square in Budapest; and August 19, when, in the first tentative steps toward the reunification of Europe, Hungarians and Austrians came together in a field near the town of Sopron for the so-called "Pan-European Picnic." (Some 900 East Germans seized this opportunity to make a run for the border...and slipped into the West while Hungarian border guards refused their orders to shoot defectors.) On October 23—the anniversary of the 1956 Uprising—the truly democratic Republic of Hungary triumphantly replaced the People's Republic of Hungary.

Hungary Today (1989–Present)

The transition from communism to capitalism has been rocky in Hungary. While many Hungarians were eager for the freedom to travel and pursue the interests that democracy allowed them, many others struggled to cope with the sudden reduction of government-provided services. Hungary seems to have had an even more difficult transition than some of its neighbors, as post-communist governments have attempted to preserve as many social services as possible while stepping down taxation—leaving Hungary with rampant inflation that is unmatched in Europe.

In 2004, Hungary took the monumental step of joining the European Union. But the EU hasn't solved all of Hungary's problems. The Hungarian Socialist Party, which took control of parliament in 2002, stubbornly maintained and even extended some social programs, prompting experts to worry that the mounting public debt would bankrupt the country.

Hungary made international headlines in 2006, when Prime Minister Ferenc Gyurcsány gave a secret speech to the party's leaders after his Hungarian Socialist Party won re-election in April. The intent of his shockingly frank remarks was to give his colleagues a wake-up call. But Gyurcsány's method—ranting on and on about how badly they'd fouled things up (and using very colorful language)—was ill-advised. Someone in the meeting recorded

the whole thing, waited a few months, then turned the audio tape over to the press.

On September 17, 2006, Hungarians turned on their TVs to hear their prime minister detailing the ways he and his party had driven their country to the brink of ruin, and then shamelessly lied about it to stay in power: "We have screwed up. Not a little but a lot. No country in Europe has screwed up as much as we have... We did not actually do anything for four years. Nothing...We lied morning, noon, and night."

The following night, demonstrators showed up at two strategic squares in downtown Budapest, demanding Gyurcsány's resignation. Riot police were sent in to subdue the looters with water cannons and tear gas. The violence was quickly put down, but the unrest continued to simmer for several months. Gyurcsány initially refused to resign, but finally chose to step down from his post in March of 2009, saying that he felt he was standing in the way of needed economic reforms.

Fortunately, tourists visiting today's Hungary are scarcely aware of its economic woes. The Hungarian people—relieved to be free of oppression, and allowed to pursue their lovably quirky customs with a renewed vigor—enthusiastically welcome and charm visitors. It's been a long road for the Hungarians from those distant, windblown steppes of Central Asia...but today they seem to be doing better than ever.

Hungarian Food

Hungarian cuisine—the undisputed best in Eastern Europe—delicately blends Magyar peasant cooking (with rich spices) refined by the elegance of French preparation, with a delightful smattering of flavors from the vast, multiethnic Austro-Hungarian Empire (including Germanic, Balkan, Jewish, and Carpathian). Everything is heavily seasoned: with paprika, tomatoes, and peppers of every shape, color, size, and flavor.

An *étterem* ("eatery") is a nice sit-down restaurant, while a *vendéglő* is usually more casual (similar to a tavern or an inn). A *söröző* ("beer place") is a pub that sells beer and food, ranging from a small selection of snacks to a full menu. A *kávéház* ("coffeehouse"), or café, is where Budapesters gather to meet friends, get a caffeine fix...and sometimes to have a great meal. Other cafés serve only light food, or sometimes only desserts. But if you want a wide

Paprika Primer

The quintessential ingredient in Hungarian cuisine is paprika. In Hungarian, the word *paprika* can mean both peppers (red or green) and the spice that's made with them. Peppers can be stewed, stuffed, sautéed, baked, grilled, or pickled. For seasoning, red shakers of dried paprika join the salt and pepper on tables.

Locals say paprika is best from the sunny south of Hungary. There are more than 40 varieties of paprika spice, with two main types: hot (*csípős* or *erős*) and sweet (*édesnemes* or simply *édes;* often comes in a white can). Hungarians typically cook with sweet paprika to add flavor and color. Then, at the table, they put out hot paprika so each diner can adjust the heat to their preferred taste. A can of paprika is a handy and tasty souvenir of your trip (see "Shopping in Budapest," next chapter).

On menus, anything cooked *paprikás* (PAW-pree-kash) comes smothered in a spicy, creamy red stew. To add even more kick to your food, ask for a jar of the bright-red paste called *Erős Pista* (EH-rewsh PEESH-taw). Literally "Spicy Steve," this Hungarian answer to Tabasco is best used sparingly. Or try *Édes Anna* (AY-desh AW-naw, "Sweet Anna"), a newer variation that's more sweet than spicy.

choice of cakes, look for a *cukrászda* (pastry shop—*cukr* means "sugar").

When foreigners think of Hungarian cuisine, what comes to mind is goulash. But tourists are often disappointed when "real Hungarian goulash" isn't the thick stew that they were expecting. The word "goulash" comes from the Hungarian *gulyás leves,* or "shepherd's soup"—a tasty, rustic, nourishing dish originally eaten by cowboys and shepherds on the Great Hungarian Plain. Here in its homeland, it's a clear, spicy broth with chunks of meat, potatoes, and other vegetables. Elsewhere (such as in Hungary's Germanic and Slavic neighbors), the word "goulash" does describe a thick stew.

Aside from the obligatory *gulyás,* make a point of trying another unusual Hungarian specialty: cold fruit soup *(hideg gyümölcs leves).* This sweet, cream-based treat—generally eaten before the meal, even though it tastes more like a dessert—is usually made with *meggy* (sour cherries), but you'll also see versions with *alma* (apples) or *körte* (pears). Other Hungarian soups *(levesek)* include *bableves* (bean soup), *zöldségleves* (vegetable soup), *gombaleves* (mushroom soup), *halászlé* (fish broth with paprika), *húsleves* (meat or chicken soup), and *pörkölt* (a simmered-meat soup similar to goulash but without the potatoes). The ultimate staple of traditional Hungarian home-cooking, but rarely served in restaurants, is *főzelék*—a simple but tasty wheat flour-thickened stew that can be supplemented with various vegetables and meats (served at cheap restaurants around Budapest—see Főzelékfaló Ételbár listing on page 582).

Hungarians adore all kinds of meat *(hús). Csirke* is chicken, *borjú* is veal, *kacsa* is duck, *liba* is goose, *sertés* is pork, *sonka* is ham, *kolbász* is sausage, *szelet* is schnitzel (*Bécsi szelet* means Wiener schnitzel)—and the list goes on. Meat is often covered with delicious sauces or garnishes, from rich cream sauces to spicy pastes to fruit jam. *Libamáj* is goose liver, which shows up everywhere (for example, anything prepared "Budapest style" is topped with goose liver). Lard is used extensively in cooking, making Hungarian cuisine very rich and filling.

Vegetarians have a tricky time in traditional Hungarian restaurants, many of which offer only a plate of deep-fried vegetables. They haven't quite figured out how to do a good, healthy, leafy salad; a traditional restaurant will generally offer only marinated cucumbers (listed on menus as "cucumber salad"), a plate of sliced-up pickles ("pickled cucumbers"), marinated spicy peppers, or something with cabbage—using lettuce only as a garnish.

Starches *(köretek)*—which you'll sometimes order separately from the meat course—can include *nodeli* (small potato dumplings, a.k.a. *Spätzle*), *galuska* (noodles), *burgonya* (potatoes), *krumpli* (French fries), *krokett* (croquettes), or *rizs* (rice). *Kenyér* (bread) often comes with the meal.

Sometimes your main dish will come with steamed, grilled, or deep-fried vegetables. A common side dish is *káposzta* (cabbage, often prepared like sauerkraut). You may also see *töltött káposzta* (cabbage stuffed with meat) or *töltött paprika* (stuffed peppers). Look for the traditional (and increasingly in-vogue) dish called *lescó* (LEH-chew). Basically the Hungarian answer to ratatouille, this is a mix of tomatoes, peppers, and other vegetables.

Thin, crêpe-like pancakes *(palacsinta)* are sometimes served as a main dish, typically wrapped around meat and vegetables and

smothered in creamy sauce. They also appear as desserts, stuffed and/or covered with fruit, jam, chocolate sauce, walnuts, poppy seeds, or whipped cream. Most famous is the *Gundel palacsinta,* named for *the* top-of-the-line Budapest restaurant—stuffed with walnuts and raisins in a rum sauce, topped with chocolate sauce, and flambéed.

Pastries are a big deal in Hungary. In the late 19th century, pastry-making caught on here in an attempt to keep up with the renowned desserts of rival Vienna. Today Hungary's streets are still lined with *cukrászda* (pastry shops) where you can simply point to whichever treat you'd like. Try the *Dobos torta* (a many-layered chocolate-and-caramel cream cake), *somlói galuska* (a dumpling with vanilla, nuts, and chocolate), anything with *gesztenye* (chestnuts), and *rétes* (strudel with various fillings, including *túrós,* curds). And many *cukrászda* also serve *fagylalt* (ice cream, *fagyi* for short), sold by the *gomboc* (ball).

To drink, *Kávé* (KAH-vay) and *tea* (TEH-aw) are coffee and tea. As for water (*víz,* veez) it comes as *szódavíz* (soda water, sometimes just carbonated tap water) or *ásványvíz* (spring water, more expensive).

Hungary is first and foremost wine country. For the complete run-down on Hungarian wines, see the sidebar.

Hungary isn't particularly well-known for its beer (*sör,* pronounced "shewr"), but Dreher and Borsodi are two of the better brands. *Villagos* is lager; if you prefer something darker, look for *barna* (brown).

Hungary is almost as proud of its spirits as its wines. Unicum is a unique and beloved Hungarian bitter liquor made of 40 different herbs and aged in oak casks. The flavor is powerful and unforgettable—like Jägermeister, but harsher. A swig of Unicum is often gulped before the meal, but it's also used as a cure for an upset stomach (especially if you've eaten too much rich food—not an uncommon problem in Hungary). Unicum has a history as unique and complicated as its flavor. Invented by a Doctor Zwack in the late 18th century, the drink impressed Habsburg emperor Josef II, who supposedly declared: *"Das ist ein Unikum!"* ("This is a specialty!"). The Zwack company went on to thrive during Budapest's late-19th-century Golden Age (when Unicum was the subject of many whimsical Guinness-type ads). But when the communists took over after World War II, the Zwacks fled to America—taking their secret recipe for Unicum with them. The communists continued to market the drink with their own formula, which left Hungarians (literally and figuratively) with a bad taste in their mouths. In a landmark case, the Zwacks sued the communists for infringing on their copyright...and won. In 1991,

Hungarian Wines

Wine *(bor)* is an essential part of Hungarian cuisine. Whites *(fehér)* can be sweet *(édes)*, half-dry *(félszáraz)*, or dry *(száraz)*. Whites include the standards (Riesling, Chardonnay), as well as some wines made from more typically Hungarian grapes: **Leányka** ("Little Girl"), a half-dry, fairly heavy, white table wine; **Cserszegi Fűszeres,** a spicy, light white that can be fruity; the half-dry, full-bodied **Hárslevélű** ("Linden Leaf"); and the dry **Furmint** and **Kéknyelű** ("Blue Stalk").

Reds *(vörös)* include the familiar varieties (Cabernet Sauvignon, Cabernet Franc, Merlot, Pinot Noir), and some that are less familiar. **Kekporto** is better known as Blauer Portugieser in German-speaking countries. In Eger, don't miss **Bull's Blood,** a.k.a. Egri Bikavér, a distinctive blend of reds that comes with a fun local legend (described on page 603). The spicy, medium-body **Kékfrankos** ("Blue Frankish") supposedly got its name because when Napoleonic soldiers were here, they could pay either with valuable blue-colored bank notes, or unstable white ones...and local vintners wanted the blue francs. (Like most wine origin legends, this story is untrue—Kékfránkos wasn't cultivated here until after Napoleon's time.)

Probably the most famous Hungarian wine is **Tokaji Aszú,** a sweet, late-harvest, honey-colored dessert wine made primarily

Péter Zwack—who had been living in exile in Italy—triumphantly returned to Hungary and resurrected the original family recipe. A newer version, called Unicum Next, has a softer, cherry flavor; its ads target the new generation of Hungarian drinkers. To get your own taste of this family saga, look for the round bottle with the red cross on the label (www.zwack.hu).

For a more straightforward spirit, try the local firewater, *pálinka,* a powerful schnapps made from various fruits (most often plum, *szilva;* or apricots, *barack*). Also look for the pear-flavored Vilmos brandy.

If you're drinking with some new Magyar friends, impress them with the standard toast: *Egészségedre* (EH-gehs-shay-geh-dreh; "to your health").

When the server comes to take your order, he or she might say *"Tessék"* (TEHSH-shayk), or maybe the more formal *"Tessék parancsolni"* (TEHSH-shayk PAW-rawn-chohl-nee)—"Please command, sir." When they bring the food, they will probably say,

from Furmint grapes. Known as the "wine of kings, and the king of wines," Tokaji Aszú is a D.O.C. product, meaning that to have that name, it must be grown in a particular region. Tokaj is a town in northeastern Hungary (not far from Eger), while Aszú is a "noble rot" grape. The wine's unique, concentrated flavor is made possible by a fungus *(Botrytis cinerea)* that thrives on the grapes in the late fall. The grapes are left on the vine, where they burst and wither like raisins before they are harvested in late October and November. This sucks the water out of the grape, leaving behind a very high sugar content and a deep golden color. Tokaji Aszú wines are numbered, from three to six, indicating how many eight-gallon tubs *(puttony)* of these "noble rot" grapes were added to the base wine—the higher the number, the sweeter the wine. Other variations on Tokaji can be less sweet. (This might sound like another bizarre Hungarian custom, but the French Sauterne and German Beerenauslese wines are also made from "noble rot" grapes. The similarly named French Tokay wine—which derives from the same word—is a different story altogether.)

Finally, note that, except for Bull's Blood and Tokaji Aszú, Hungarian wines are not widely available in the US. Packing home a bottle or two (in your checked luggage) is a unique souvenir.

"Jó étvágyat!" (yoh AYT-vah-yawt)—"Bon appétit." When you're ready for the bill, you can simply say, *"Fizetek"* (FEE-zeh-tehk)—"I'll pay."

Hungarian Language

Even though Hungary is surrounded by Slavs, Hungarian is not at all related to Slavic languages (such as Polish, Czech, or Croatian). In fact, Hungarian isn't related to *any* European language, except for very distant relatives Finnish and Estonian. It isn't even an Indo-European language. English is more closely related to Hindi, Russian, and French than it is to Hungarian.

Hungarian is agglutinative, which means that you start with a simple root word and then start tacking on suffixes to create meaning—sometimes resulting in a pileup of extra sounds at the end of a very long word. The emphasis always goes on the first syllable, and the following syllables are droned downhill in a kind of a monotone—giving the language a distinctive cadence that

Hungary's neighbors love to tease about.

While the language is overwhelming for tourists, one easy word is *"Szia"* (SEE-yaw), which means both hello and goodbye (like "ciao" or "aloha"). Confusingly, sometimes Hungarians simply say the English word "hello" to mean either "hi" or "bye." Another handy word that Hungarians (and people throughout Eastern Europe) will understand is *Servus* (SEHR-voos, spelled *Szervusz* in Hungarian)—the old-fashioned greeting from the days of the Austro-Hungarian Empire. If you draw a blank on how to say hello in the local language, just offer a cheery, *"Servus!"*

Hungarian pronunciation is straightforward, once you remember a few key rules. The trickiest: *s* alone is pronounced "sh," while *sz* is pronounced "s." This explains why you'll hear in-the-know travelers pronouncing Budapest as "BOO-daw-pesht." You might catch the *busz* up to Castle Hill—pronounced "boose." And "Franz Liszt" is easier to pronounce than it looks: It sounds just like "list." To review:

s sounds like "sh" as in "shirt"
sz sounds like "s" as in "saint"

Hungarian has a set of unusual palatal sounds that don't quite have a counterpart in English. To make these sounds, gently press the thick part of your tongue to the roof or your mouth (instead of using the tip of your tongue behind your teeth, as we do in English):

gy sounds like "dg" as in "hedge"
ny sounds like "ny" as in "canyon" (not "nee")
ty sounds like "tch" as in "itch"
cs sounds like "ch" as in "church"

As for vowels: The letter *a* almost sounds like o (aw, as in "hot"); but with an accent *(á),* it brightens up to the more standard "ah." Likewise, while *e* sounds like "eh," *é* sounds like "ay." An accent *(á, é, í, ó, ú)* indicates that you linger on that vowel, but not necessarily that you stress that syllable. Like German, Hungarian has umlauts *(ö, ü),* meaning you purse your lips when you say that vowel: roughly, *ö* sounds like "ur" and *ü* sounds like "ew." A long umlaut *(ő, ű)* is the same sound, but you hold it a little longer. Words ending in *k* are often plural.

Here are a few other letters than sound different in Hungarian than in English:

c and **cz** both sound like "ts" as in "cats"
zs sounds like "zh" as in "leisure"
j and **ly** both sound like "y" as in "yellow"

Okay, maybe it's not *so* simple. But you'll get the hang of it... and Hungarians will appreciate your efforts. For a list of Hungarian Survival Phrases, see page 1123.

As you navigate, remember these key Hungarian terms: ***tér*** (pronounced "tehr," square), ***utca*** (OOT-zaw, street), ***út*** (oot, boulevard), ***körút*** (KUR-root, ring road), ***híd*** (heed, bridge), and ***város*** (VAH-rohsh, town). To better match what you'll see locally, in this book I've mostly used these Hungarian terms (instead of the English equivalents).

BUDAPEST

Budapest (locals say "BOO-daw-pesht") is, in so many ways, the capital of Eastern Europe. Europe's most underrated big city, Budapest is a unique metropolis at the heart of a unique nation. You'll experience things here that you can't find anywhere else in Europe: Feel your stress ebb away as you soak in hundred-degree water, surrounded by opulent Baroque domes...and by Speedo- and bikini-clad Hungarians. Ogle some of Europe's most richly decorated interiors, which faintly echo a proud little nation's bygone glory days. Open your ears to a first-rate performance at one of the world's top opera houses—at bargain prices. Ponder the region's bleak communist era as you stroll amidst giant Soviet-style statues designed to evoke fear and obedience. Try to wrap your head around Hungary's colorful history...and your tongue around some of its notoriously difficult words. Dive into a bowl of goulash, the famous paprika-flavored peasant soup with a kick. Go for an after-dinner stroll along the Danube, immersed in a grand city that's bathed in floodlights.

Budapest is as challenging as it is enchanting. The Hungarian capital on the banks of the Danube excites good travelers...and exasperates bad ones. It's a city of nuance and paradox—cosmopolitan, complicated, and tricky for the first-timer to get a handle on. Like a full-bodied Hungarian wine, Budapest can overwhelm visitors, even as it intoxicates them with delights. But if you equip yourself with the information in this chapter, delving into the city can be an exhilarating experience.

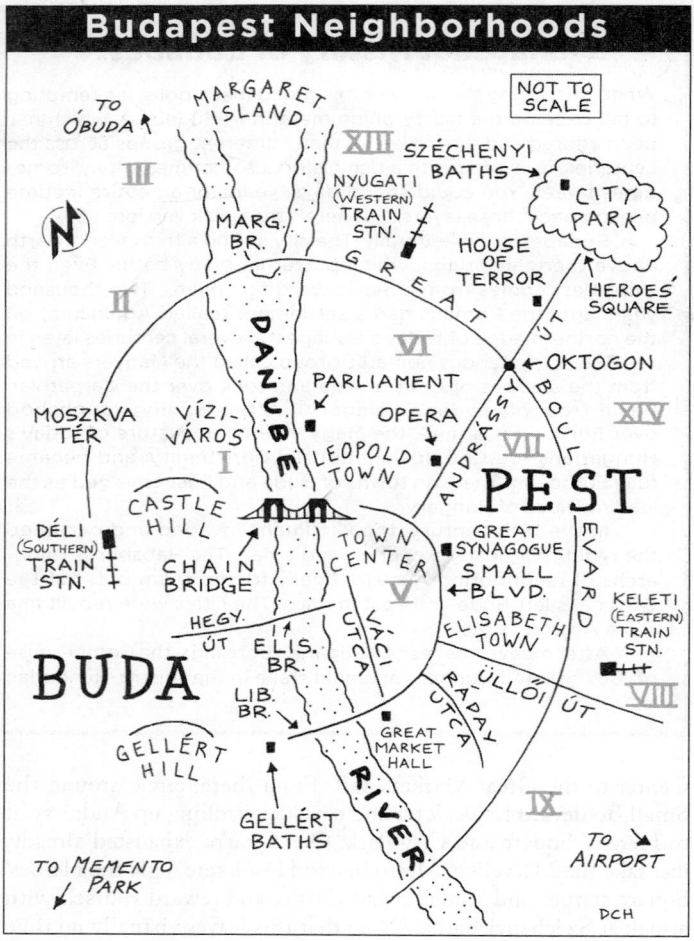

Planning Your Time

Budapest is quite decentralized, making efficient sightseeing tricky. You'll have to zig and zag, refer to your map constantly, rely on public transit, and strategize to maximize your sightseeing time.

Visitors attempting to "do" Budapest in just one day leave dazed, exhausted...and yearning for more. Two days are the bare minimum, and force you to tackle the city at a breakneck pace (and you still won't see everything). Three or four days are ideal.

If you're trying to see Budapest in **two days,** your time will be full but memorable. Spend Day 1 in Pest. Begin at the Parliament and stroll through Leopold Town, then walk through Pest Town

Snapshot History of Budapest

When describing the story of this grand metropolis, it's tempting to fall back on the trusty onion metaphor: Budapest, which has been adored and destroyed by many different groups across the centuries, is layered with a rich history...sometimes stinky, sometimes sweet. You could spend days, years, or an entire lifetime peeling back those layers. But here's the quick version:

Budapest is hot—literally. The city sits on a thin layer of earth above thermal springs, which power its many baths. Even the word Pest comes from a Slavic word for "oven." Two thousand years ago, the Romans had a settlement (called Aquincum) on the northern edge of today's Budapest. Several centuries later, in A.D. 896, a mysterious nomadic group called the Magyars arrived from the steppes of Central Asia and took over the Carpathian Basin (roughly today's Hungary). After running roughshod over Europe for a time, the Magyars—the ancestors of today's Hungarians—settled down, adopted Christianity, and became fully European. The twin towns of Buda and Pest emerged as the leading cities of Hungary.

In the 16th century, the Ottomans invaded and occupied the region for nearly a century and a half. The Habsburgs (monarchs of neighboring Austria) finally forced them out, but the Ottomans left Buda and Pest in ruins. The cities were rebuilt in a more Austrian style.

After many decades of Hungarian uprisings, the Compromise of 1867 granted Hungary an equal stake in the Austro-Hungarian

Center to the Great Market Hall. From there, circle around the Small Boulevard to Deák tér and consider strolling up Andrássy út to Heroes' Square and City Park. Or, if you're exhausted already, just take the M1/yellow Metro line to Hősök tere, ogle the Heroes' Square statues and Vajdahunyad Castle, and reward yourself with a soak at Széchenyi Baths. (Note that this leaves virtually no time for entering any museums—though you might be able to fit in one or two big sights, such as the Parliament, Opera House, Great Synagogue, or House of Terror.) On the morning of Day 2, tackle any Pest sights you didn't have time for yesterday (or take the bus out to Memento Park). After lunch, ride bus #16 from Deák tér to Castle Hill. Head back to Pest for some final sightseeing and dinner.

If you have **three or four days,** you can spread the Pest sightseeing over two (or three) days. This much time allows you to actually enter many of the sights you'd otherwise only have time to sprint past. Consider devoting one Pest day to Leopold Town, the Town Center, and the Small Boulevard sights; another day to Andrássy út and Heroes' Square/City Park; and—if you have it—

Empire. Six years later, the cities of Buda, Pest, and Óbuda united to form the capital city of Budapest, which governed a huge chunk of Eastern Europe. For the next few decades, Budapest boomed, and Hungarian culture enjoyed a Golden Age. The expansion reached its peak with a flurry of construction surrounding the year 1896—Hungary's 1,000th birthday.

But with Hungary's defeat in World War I, the city's fortunes reversed. World War II left Budapest in ruins...and in the hands of the Soviets. A bold uprising in 1956 was brutally dealt with, but before long a milder "goulash communism" emerged in Hungary. Budapest, though still oppressed, was a place where other Eastern Europeans could come to experiment with "Western evils"...from Big Macs to Nikes.

Since communism's graceful exit in 1989, Budapest has once again been forced to re-invent itself. The city clings to its past prominence even as it looks ahead to a future that promises to be much brighter than its dismal 20th century.

Through it all, Budapest—atmospherically shot through with the crumbling elegance of former greatness—remains the heart and soul of Eastern Europe. It's a rich cultural stew made up of Hungarians, Germans, Slavs, and Jews, with a dash of Turkish paprika—simmered for centuries in a thermal bath. Each group has left its mark, but through it all, something has remained that is distinctly...Budapest.

yet another day to visit Memento Park, slow down, and enter even more sights.

I've left your evenings open for your choice of activities: enjoying good restaurants, taking in an opera or concert, snuggling on a romantic floodlit river cruise, exploring the city's unique "ruin pubs," or simply strolling the Danube embankments and bridges. (Your options are outlined under "Entertainment in Budapest" on page 555.)

Orientation to Budapest

Budapest is huge, with nearly two million people. But the city is surprisingly easy to manage once you get the lay of the land and learn the excellent public transportation network (see "Getting Around Budapest," later).

Budapest is split down the center by the Danube River, with hilly Buda in the west and flat Pest in the east. All of this chapter's sightseeing, sleeping, eating, and other advice is divided between Buda and Pest. (It might help to think of these as two separate

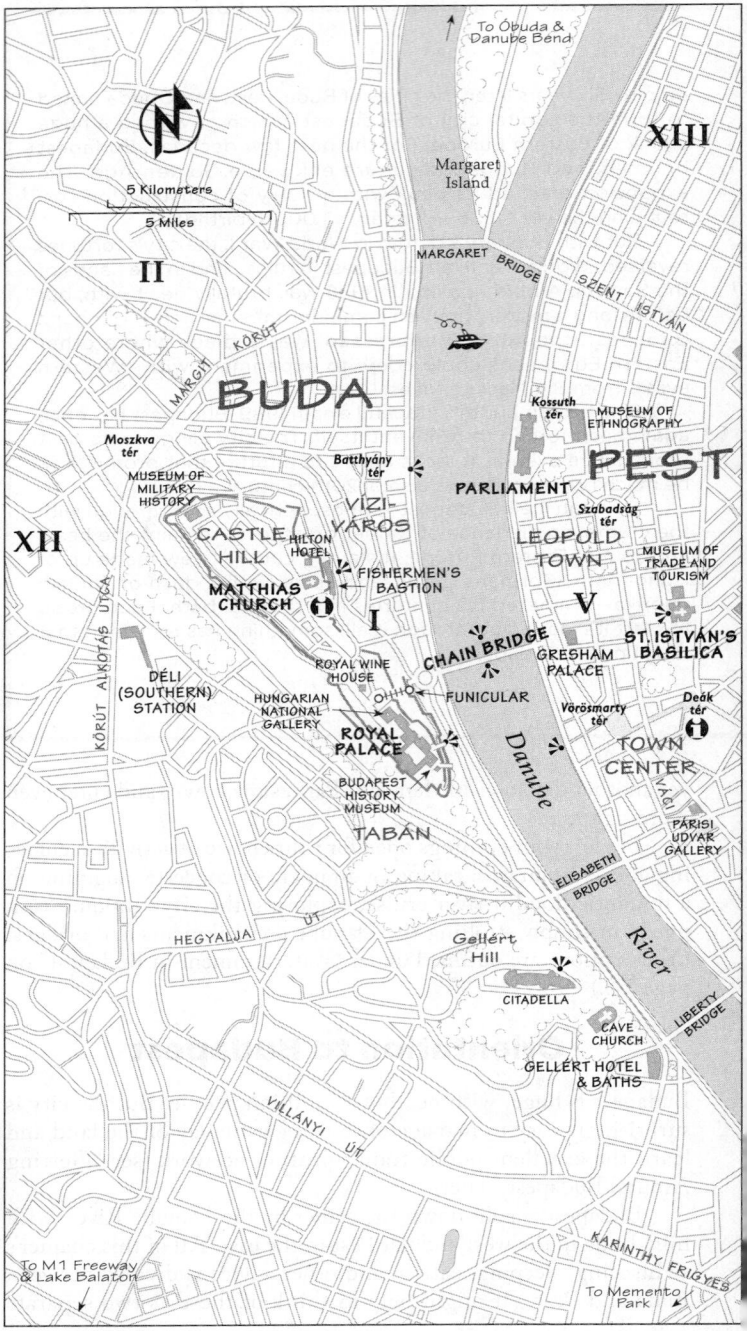
To Óbuda & Danube Bend
XIII
Margaret Island
5 Kilometers
5 Miles
II
MARGARET BRIDGE
SZENT ISTVÁN
MARGIT KÖRÚT
BUDA
Kossuth tér
MUSEUM OF ETHNOGRAPHY
Moszkva tér
Batthyány tér
PEST
MUSEUM OF MILITARY HISTORY
PARLIAMENT
VIZI-VÁROS
Szabadság tér
XII
CASTLE HILL
HILTON HOTEL
LEOPOLD TOWN
MUSEUM OF TRADE AND TOURISM
FISHERMEN'S BASTION
MATTHIAS CHURCH
I
V
CHAIN BRIDGE
ST. ISTVÁN'S BASILICA
ROYAL WINE HOUSE
GRESHAM PALACE
KÖRÚT ALKOTÁS UTCA
DÉLI (SOUTHERN) STATION
HUNGARIAN NATIONAL GALLERY
FUNICULAR
Vörösmarty tér
Deák tér
ROYAL PALACE
Danube
TOWN CENTER
BUDAPEST HISTORY MUSEUM
VÁCI
TABÁN
PÁRISI UDVAR GALLERY
ELISABETH BRIDGE
HEGYALJA ÚT
Gellért Hill
River
CITADELLA
LIBERTY BRIDGE
CAVE CHURCH
GELLÉRT HOTEL & BATHS
VILLÁNYI ÚT
KARINTHY FRIGYES
To M1 Freeway & Lake Balaton
To Memento Park

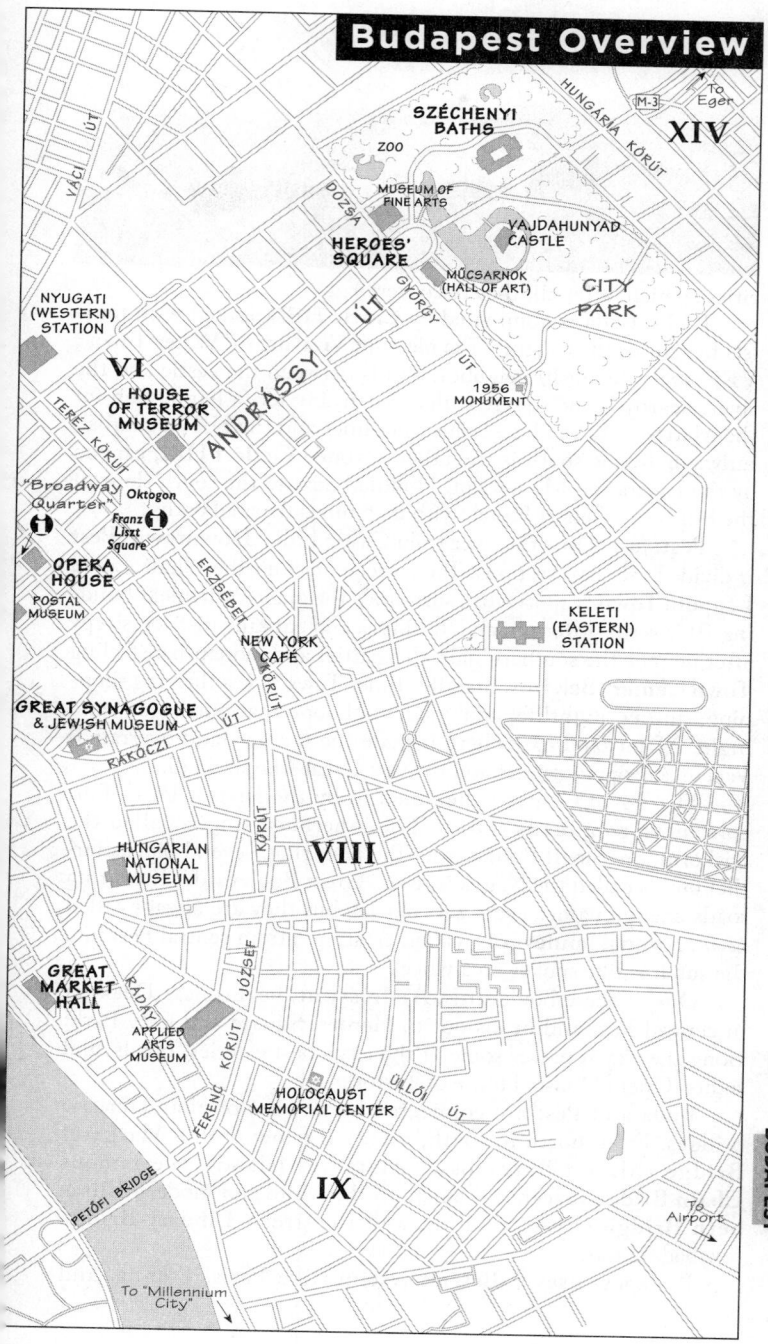
Budapest Overview
SZÉCHENYI BATHS
ZOO
HUNGÁRIA KÖRÚT
M-3
To Eger
XIV
VÁCI ÚT
DOZSA
MUSEUM OF FINE ARTS
HEROES' SQUARE
VAJDAHUNYAD CASTLE
MŰCSARNOK (HALL OF ART)
CITY PARK
GYÖRGY ÚT
NYUGATI (WESTERN) STATION
VI
ANDRÁSSY ÚT
HOUSE OF TERROR MUSEUM
1956 MONUMENT
TERÉZ KÖRÚT
"Broadway Quarter"
Oktogon
Franz Liszt Square
OPERA HOUSE
POSTAL MUSEUM
ERZSÉBET KÖRÚT
KELETI (EASTERN) STATION
NEW YORK CAFÉ
GREAT SYNAGOGUE & JEWISH MUSEUM
RÁKÓCZI ÚT
HUNGARIAN NATIONAL MUSEUM
VIII
GREAT MARKET HALL
RÁDAY
JÓZSEF KÖRÚT
APPLIED ARTS MUSEUM
FERENC KÖRÚT
HOLOCAUST MEMORIAL CENTER
ÜLLŐI ÚT
PETŐFI BRIDGE
IX
To Airport
To "Millennium City"

cities...which, after all, they once were.)

Buda: Buda is dominated by **Castle Hill** (packed with tourists by day, dead at night). The pleasant **Víziváros** ("Water Town"; VEE-zee-vah-rohsh) neighborhood is between the castle and the river; nearby is the square called Batthyány tér (a handy hub for the Metro—M2/red line—plus tram lines and the HÉV suburban railway). To the south is the taller, wooded **Gellért Hill,** capped by the Liberation Monument. Huddled next to the south slope of the hill is the Gellért Hotel, with its famous thermal baths.

Pest: Just across the river from Castle Hill, **"Downtown" Pest** is divided into two sections: The more genteel northern half, called **Leopold Town** (Lipótváros), surrounds the giant Parliament building. This is the governmental, business, and banking district (sleepy after hours). The southern half, the grittier and more urban-feeling **Town Center** (Belváros, literally "Inner Town"), is a thriving shopping, dining, nightlife, and residential zone that bustles day and night. Major landmarks here include the famous (and overrated) Váci utca shopping street and the vast Great Market Hall.

The Town Center is hemmed in by the first of Pest's four concentric **ring roads** *(körút).* The innermost ring is called the Kiskörút, or "Small Boulevard." The next ring, several blocks farther out, is called the Nagykörút, or "Great Boulevard." These ring roads change names every few blocks, but they are always called *körút.* Arterial **boulevards,** called *út,* stretch from central Pest into the suburbs like spokes on a wheel.

One of these boulevards, **Andrássy út,** begins near Deák tér in central Pest and heads out to Heroes' Square and City Park; along the way it passes some of the city's best eateries, hotels, and sights (Opera House, House of Terror).

Buda and Pest are connected by a series of characteristic bridges. From north to south, there's the low-profile **Margaret Bridge** (Margit híd, crosses Margaret Island), the famous **Chain Bridge** (Széchenyi lánchíd), the white and modern **Elisabeth Bridge** (Erzsébet híd), and the green **Liberty Bridge** (Szabadság híd).

Budapest uses a **district** system (like Paris, Vienna, and

Budapest Essentials

English	Hungarian	Pronounced
Pest's Main Pedestrian Street	Váci utca	VAHT-see OOT-zaw
Pest's Main Square	Vörösmarty tér	VOO-roosh-mar-tee tehr
Pest's Grand Boulevard	Andrássy út	AWN-drah-shee oot
City Park	Városliget	VAH-rohsh-lee-geht
(Buda) Castle	(Budai) Vár	BOO-die vahr
Castle Hill	Várhegy	VAHR-hayj
Chain Bridge	Széchenyi Lánchíd	SAY-chehn-yee LAHNTS-heed
Liberty Bridge (green, a.k.a. Franz Josef Bridge)	Szabadság híd	SAW-bawd-shahg heed
Elisabeth Bridge (white, modern)	Erzsébet híd	EHR-zay-beht heed
Margaret Bridge (crosses Margaret Island)	Margit híd	MAWR-geet heed
Danube River	Duna	DOO-naw
Eastern Train Station	Keleti pályaudvar	KEH-leh-tee PAH-yuh-uhd-vawr
Western Train Station	Nyugati pályaudvar	NYOO-gaw-tee PAH-yuh-uhd-vawr
Southern Train Station	Déli pályaudvar	DAY-lee PAH-yuh-uhd-vawr
Suburban Train System	HÉV	hayv

Prague). There are 23 districts (*kerület*), identified by Roman numerals. For example, Castle Hill is in district I and City Park is in district XIV. Notice that the district number does not necessarily indicate how central a location is: Districts II and III are to the north of Buda, where few tourists go, while the heart of Pest is district V.

Tourist Information

Budapest has several TIs (www.budapestinfo.hu, tel. 1/438-8080). The main branch is a few steps from the M2 and M3 Metro station at **Deák tér** (daily 8:00–20:00, Sütő utca 2, near the McDonald's, district V). Other locations include **Franz Liszt Square,** a block

Tonight We're Gonna Party Like It's 1896

Visitors to Budapest need only remember one date: 1896. For the millennial celebration of their ancestors' arrival in Europe, Hungarians threw a huge blowout party. In the thousand years between 896 and 1896, the Magyars had gone from being a nomadic Central Asian tribe that terrorized the Continent to sharing the throne of one of the most successful empires Europe had ever seen.

Much as the year 2000 saw a fit of new construction worldwide, Budapest used its millennial celebration as an excuse to build monuments and buildings appropriate for the co-capital of a huge empire, including:

- **Heroes' Square** and the **Millennium Monument**
- **Vajdahunyad Castle** (in City Park)
- The riverside **Parliament** building (96 meters tall, with 96 steps at the main entry)
- **St. István's Basilica** (also 96 meters tall)
- The M1 (yellow) Metro line, a.k.a. ***Földalatti*** ("Underground")—the first subway on the Continent
- The **Great Market Hall** (and four other market halls)
- **Andrássy út** and most of the fine buildings lining it
- The **Opera House**
- A complete rebuilding of **Matthias Church** (on Castle Hill)
- The **Fishermen's Bastion** decorative terrace (by Matthias Church)
- The green **Liberty Bridge** (then called Franz Josef Bridge, in honor of the ruling Habsburg emperor)

Ninety-six is the key number in Hungary—even the national anthem (when sung in the proper tempo) takes 96 seconds. But after all this fuss, it's too bad that the date was wrong: A commission—convened to establish the exact year of the Magyars' debut—determined it happened in 895. But city leaders knew they'd never make an 1895 deadline, and requested the finding be changed to 896.

south of the Oktogon on Andrássy út (June–Sept daily 10:00–19:00; Oct–April Mon–Fri 10:00–18:00, closed Sat–Sun; May Mon–Fri 10:00–18:00, Sat 10:00–16:00, closed Sun; Liszt Ferenc tér 11, district VII, M1: Oktogon, tel. 1/322-4098); on top of **Castle Hill,** across from Matthias Church (daily May–Oct 9:00–19:00, Nov–April 10:00–18:00, Szentháromság tér, district I, tel. 1/488-0475); and in both Terminals 1 and 2B at the **airport** (daily 9:00–

22:00). The helpfulness of Budapest's TIs can vary, but they do produce some free, useful publications, including a good city map, the *Budapest Panorama* events guide, and the information-packed *Budapest Guide* booklet. At all of the TIs, you can also collect a pile of other free brochures (for sights, bus tours, and more) and buy a Budapest Card.

Budapest Card: This card includes free use of all public transportation and 10–50 percent discounts on many major museums and other attractions (6,300 Ft/48 hours, 7,500 Ft/72 hours, sold at TIs and many hotels). Unfortunately, it's hard to imagine a scenario where the card might save even a very busy sightseer more than a dollar or two—I'd skip it.

Discover Budapest: Ben Frieday, an American in love with Budapest (and one of its women), runs this agency, which specializes in answering questions Americans (especially backpackers) have about Budapest. There are two locations in central Budapest: at Deák tér (Sütő utca 2, in the courtyard between the McDonald's and TI, marked "Yellow Zebra," district V, M1/M2/M3: Deák tér) and near Andrássy út (behind the Opera House at Lázár utca 16, district VI, M1: Opera). At either branch, you can use the Internet (200 Ft/15 min) or rent a bike (both offices open May–Oct daily 9:30–19:30, shorter hours off-season, tel. 1/266-8777 or 1/269-3843, www.discoverbudapest.com). Both offices also have smaller branches of the Tree Hugger Dan secondhand bookstore (described later, under "Helpful Hints"). Ben also runs Yellow Zebra bike tours, Absolute Walking Tours, and City Segway Tours (all described later).

Arrival in Budapest

By Train

Budapest has three major train stations (*pályaudvar*, abbreviated *pu.*): Keleti ("Eastern") Station, Nyugati ("Western") Station, and Déli ("Southern") Station. A century ago, the name of the station indicated which part of Europe it served. But these days, there's no correlation: Trains going to the east might leave from the Western Station, and vice-versa.

Keleti/Eastern Station and Nyugati/Western Station are both cavernous, slightly run-down, late-19th-century Erector-set masterpieces in Pest. Déli/Southern Station, behind Castle Hill in Buda, mingles its dinginess with modern flair. At all stations, access to the tracks is monitored—you might have to show your ticket to reach the platforms (though this is very loosely enforced). A few key words: *pénztár* is ticket window, *vágány* is track, *induló vonatok* is departures, and *érkező vonatok* is arrivals.

The taxi stands in front of each train station are notorious for ripping off tourists; it's better to call for a taxi. For tips on

this—and on using the Metro system to reach your destination in Budapest—see "Getting Around Budapest," later.

Here's the rundown, station by station:

Keleti/Eastern Station

Keleti train station (Keleti pu.) is just south of City Park, east of central Pest. On arrival, go to the front of long tracks 6–9 to reach the exits and services. Several travel agencies with *Tourist Information* signs cluster near the head of the tracks. None of these is an official TI, but all have a few helpful fliers. Along track 6, you'll find a left-luggage desk, an ATM (at K&H Bank), money-exchange booths (avoid Interchange, which has bad rates), and a narrow passage marked *Exit*. Following this passage leads you to a broad, beautifully renovated hallway leading (to the left) to pay WCs and (to the right) to international information and ticket windows (look for *nemzetközi pénztár,* and take a number).

Back in the main hall, domestic ticket windows are across the tracks, near track 9. The big staircase at the head of the tracks leads down to more domestic ticket windows, WCs, telephones, more ATMs, and (a few minutes' walk straight ahead, through the open-air courtyard) a passageway to the Metro station entrance (M2/red line). If you go out the front door, you'll stumble over a cluster of suspicious-looking, unmarked taxis. You can try to negotiate with these goons—the fair rate to downtown is about 1,500 Ft—but it's far more reliable and less of a hassle to phone for a taxi (buy phone card at newsstand, go to the phone bank downstairs, call 266-6666 or 211-1111, tell the English-speaking dispatcher where you are, and go out front to meet your taxi).

Nyugati/Western Station

Nyugati train station (Nyugati pu.) is the most central of Budapest's stations, on the northeast edge of downtown Pest. Most international arrivals use tracks 1–9, which are set back from the main entrance. From the head of these tracks, exit straight ahead into a parking lot with taxis and buses, or use the stairs just inside the doors to reach an underpass

and the Metro (M3/blue line). Note that the taxis here are often crooked—it's far better to call for your own cab (see instructions and phone numbers on previous page).

Ticket windows are through an easy-to-miss door across the tracks by platform 13 (marked *cassa* and *információ;* once you enter the ticket hall, international windows are in a second room at the far end—look for *nemzetközi,* daily 7:30–19:00).

From the head of tracks 10–13, exit straight ahead and you'll be on Teréz körút, the very busy Great Boulevard. (Váci utca, at the center of Pest, is dead ahead, about 20 min away by foot.) In front of the building is access to handy trams #4 and #6 (zipping all the way around Pest's great ring); to the right you'll find stairs leading to an underpass (use it to avoid crossing this busy intersection, or to reach the Metro's M3 line); and to the left you'll see the classiest Art Nouveau McDonald's on the planet. (Seriously. Take a look inside.)

Déli/Southern Station

Renovated by the heavy-handed communists, today Déli train station (Déli pu.) is dreary, dark-granite, smaller, and more modern-feeling than the others. It's tucked behind Castle Hill on the Buda side. From the tracks, go straight ahead into the vast, empty-feeling main hall, with well-marked domestic and international ticket windows at opposite ends. A left-luggage desk is outside, beyond track 1. If you head downstairs, you'll find several shops and eateries, and access to the very convenient M2/red Metro line, which connects you easily to several key points in town: Batthyány tér (on the Buda embankment, at the north end of the Víziváros neighborhood), Deák tér (the heart of Pest, with connections to other Metro lines), and Keleti train station.

By Plane at Budapest Ferihegy Airport

Budapest's airport is 10 miles southeast of the center (airport code: BUD, tel. 1/296-7000, www.bud.hu). The airport has two passenger terminals, which are about three miles from each other. Terminal 1 is used by the low-cost airlines. Terminal 2 has two adjacent parts: 2A is for flights from EU/Schengen countries (no passport control required), while 2B is for flights from other countries. (If you're flying out of Budapest, confirm which terminal your flight leaves from.) Both terminals have similar services, including ATMs and TI desks. There is no free bus between terminals. Bus #200E frequently connects Terminals 1, 2A, and 2B (covered by 300-Ft transit ticket at an automated machine, more expensive if purchased from driver), or you can connect between them with the airport shuttle minibus (700 Ft, described below).

From the Airport to Budapest: If you're using **Terminal 1,**

consider taking the handy train that heads straight to Nyugati/Western train station near downtown Pest (300 Ft, plus 520 Ft supplement for InterCity trains, 3–7/hr depending on the day and time, 25 min). Buy your ticket from the TI desk inside Terminal 1 before leaving the airport. Then, as you exit Terminal 1, bear left and follow signs to the train tracks (use colorful pedestrian overpass to reach the platform).

If you're using **Terminal 2A or 2B,** it's a hassle to get to Terminal 1 to catch the train (bus #200E to "Ferihegy 1" stop, go inside terminal to buy ticket from TI desk, then go back out to catch train). Instead, I'd consider one of these options (which also work from Terminal 1):

The fastest door-to-door option is to take a **taxi.** Zóna Taxi has a monopoly at the taxi stand out front, with a fixed off-meter price depending on where you're going (about 4,500–5,000 Ft to downtown, 1,000 Ft less from downtown to the airport, about 30 min, tel. 1/365-5555, www.zonataxi.eu). Note that you can also call any other taxi company to take you to or from the airport (see "Getting Around Budapest—By Taxi," later).

The **airport shuttle** minibus is cheaper for a solo traveler, but two people might as well take a taxi (2,600 Ft per person for minibus ride to any hotel in the city center, about 30–45 min depending on hotel location; they can also take you between terminals for 700 Ft; tel. 1/296-8555, www.airportshuttle.hu; if arranging a minibus transfer *to* the airport, call at least 24 hours in advance). Because they prefer to take several people at once, you may have to wait a while for a quorum to show up (about 15 min in busy times, up to an hour when it's slow—they can give you an estimate).

Finally, the cheapest option is to take **public bus** #200E to the Kőbánya-Kispest station on the M3/blue Metro line, and then take the Metro all the way into town (allow about an hour total for the trip to the center).

By Car

Unless you're heading to an out-of-town sight (such as Memento Park), park the car at your hotel and take public transportation. Public parking costs 150–450 Ft per hour (pay in advance at machine and put ticket on dashboard—watch locals and imitate; free parking Mon–Fri after 18:00 and all day Sat–Sun—but you'll have to pay all the time in tourist zones). Be careful to park within the lines—otherwise, your car is likely to get booted (I've seen more than one confused tourist puzzling over the giant red brace on their wheel). A guarded parking lot is safer, but more expensive (figure 3,000–4,000 Ft/day, ask your hotel or look for the blue *P*s on maps). As rental-car theft can be a problem, ask at your hotel for advice. For driving info in Budapest, visit www.fovinform.hu.

Helpful Hints

Rip-Offs: Budapest feels—and is—safe, especially for a city of its size. There's little risk of violent crime here. And, while people routinely try to rip me off in Prague, I've never had a problem in Budapest. Still, some of my readers have reported falling victim to scams and con artists here. As in any big city, it's especially important to beware of pickpockets in crowded and touristy places, particularly on the Metro and in trams. Wear a money belt and watch your valuables closely. Keep your wits about you and refuse to be bullied or distracted. Any deal that seems too good to be true...probably is.

Restaurants on the Váci utca shopping street are notorious for overcharging tourists. Here or anywhere in Budapest, don't eat at a restaurant that doesn't list prices on the menu, and always check your bill carefully.

If you're a male in a touristy area and a gorgeous local girl takes a liking to you, avoid her. She's a *konzumlány* ("consumption girl"), and the foreplay going on here will climax in your grand rip-off. You'll wind up at her "favorite bar," with astronomical prices enforced by a burly bouncer.

Budapest's biggest crooks? Unscrupulous cabbies. (For tips on outsmarting them, see page 492). Bottom line: Locals *always* call for a cab, rather than hail one on the street or at a taxi stand. If you're not comfortable making the call yourself, ask your hotel or restaurant to call for you.

Medical Help: Near Buda's Moszkva tér, **FirstMed Centers** is a private, pricey, English-speaking clinic (by appointment or urgent care, call first, Hattyú utca 14, 5th floor, district I, M2: Moszkva tér, tel. 1/224-9090, www.firstmedcenters.com).

Pharmacies: The helpful **Dorottya Gyógyszertár** pharmacy is dead-center in Pest, between Vörösmarty and Roosevelt squares. Because they cater to clientele from nearby international hotels, they have a useful directory that lists the Hungarian equivalent of US prescription medicines (Mon–Fri 8:00–20:00, likely closed Sat–Sun, Dorottya utca 13, district V, M1: Vörösmarty tér, tel. 1/317-2374). Each district has one pharmacy that stays open 24 hours (these should be noted outside the entrance to any pharmacy).

Monday Closures: Most of Budapest's museums are closed on Mondays. But you can still take advantage of these sights and activities: both major baths, Memento Park, Great Synagogue, Matthias Church and Budapest History Museum on Castle Hill, St. István's Basilica, Hungarian Museum of Trade and Tourism, Parliament tour, Great Market Hall, Opera House tour, City Park (and Zoo), Danube cruises, concerts, and bus, walking, and bike tours.

Train Tickets: Ticket-buying lines can be long at train stations, particularly for long-distance international trains. If you want to pre-buy your ticket, **MÁV** (Hungarian Railways) has a very convenient ticket office right in the heart of downtown Pest. They generally speak English and sell tickets for no additional fee (Mon–Fri 9:00–18:00, closed Sat–Sun, just up from the Chain Bridge and across from Erzsébet tér at József Attila utca 16, district V, M1: Vörösmarty tér).

Internet Access: Internet cafés are everywhere—just look for signs or ask your hotel. In Pest, I like **Discover Budapest/ Yellow Zebra,** with fast access and good prices (200 Ft/15 min; branches behind the Opera House and near Deák tér—see page 481).

Post Offices: These are marked with a smart green *posta* logo (usually open Mon–Fri 8:00–18:00, Sat 8:00–12:00, closed Sun).

Laundry: Budapest doesn't have a handy coin-op, self-serve launderette. But two places in Pest can do your laundry for a reasonable price. Your best option is **Laundromat-Mosómata,** just behind the Opera House (2,000 Ft to wash and dry a big load, generally takes 3–5 hours, Mon–Fri 9:00–19:00, Sat–Sun 10:00–16:00; walk straight behind the Opera House and turn right on Ó utca, then look left for signs at #24–26, district VI, M1: Opera; mobile 0620-392-5702). Another option—closer to the Town Center, but with more difficult communication—is **Patyolat Gyorstisztító.** They say it's "self-service," but usually you can just drop off your clothes with the monolingual laundry ladies in the morning and pick them up in the afternoon (borrow the English information sheet, allow 2,500 Ft to wash and dry a load, Mon–Fri 7:00–19:00, Sat 7:00–13:00, closed Sun, just up from Váci utca at the corner of Vármegye utca and Városház utca, district V, M3: Ferenciek tere).

English Bookstores: The **Central European University Bookshop** offers the best selection anywhere of scholarly books about this region (and beyond). They also sell guidebooks, literary fiction, and some popular American magazines—all in English (Mon–Fri 10:00–19:00, Sat 10:00–14:00, closed Sun, just down the street in front of St. István's Basilica at Zrínyi utca 12, district V, tel. 1/327-3096). **Tree Hugger Dan,** which bills itself as a "local bookstore with a global conscience," is a hole-in-the-wall crammed with a wide variety of English books, from literary fiction to leisure-reading paperbacks. They also host literary events and run a café with the "only fair-trade coffee in Hungary." The main office (where they also buy used books) is just off Andrássy út, between the House of

Terror and Oktogon (Mon–Fri 10:00–18:00, Sat 10:00–17:00, closed Sun, Csengery utca 48, district VII, M1: Vörösmarty utca, tel. 1/322-0774). Two smaller branches are in the Discover Budapest offices (one just behind the Opera House, and the other near Deák tér—see "Tourist Information," earlier). **Red Bus Bookstore** has a great selection of used books in English (also buys used books, Mon–Fri 11:00–18:00, Sat 10:00–14:00, closed Sun, Semmelweis utca 14, district V, M2: Astoria, tel. 1/337-7453).

Bike Rental: You can rent a bike at **Yellow Zebra,** part of Discover Budapest (2,500 Ft/all day, 3,500 Ft/24 hours, locations behind the Opera House and near Deák tér; for details, see "Discover Budapest" page 481).

Drivers: Friendly, English-speaking **Gábor Balázs** can drive you around the city or into the surrounding countryside (3,500 Ft/hr, 3-hour minimum in city, 4-hour minimum in countryside—good for a Danube Bend excursion, mobile 0620-936-4317, balazs.gabor@upcmail.hu). **József Király** runs a 10-car company, Artoli (20,000 Ft/4 hours within town, 40,000 Ft/8 hours to Danube Bend, these prices for up to 4 people—more for bigger groups, tel. 1/240-4050, mobile 0620-369-8890, artoli@t-online.hu). Note that these are drivers, not tour guides. For tour guides, see "Tours in Budapest," later.

Best Views: Budapest is a city of marvelous vistas. Some of the best are from the Citadella fortress (high on Gellért Hill), the promenade in front of the Royal Palace and the Fishermen's Bastion on top of Castle Hill, and the embankments or many bridges spanning the Danube (especially the Chain Bridge). Don't forget the view from the tour boats on the Danube—lovely at night.

Getting Around Budapest

Budapest is huge. Connecting your sightseeing by foot is tedious and unnecessary. It's crucial to get comfortable with the excellent public transportation system—an ingenious network of Metro lines, trams, and buses that can take you virtually anywhere you want to go.

The same tickets work for the entire system. Buy them at kiosks, Metro ticket windows, or machines. The new machines are slick and easy (with English instructions). The old orange ones are tricky: Put in the appropriate amount of money, then wait for your ticket or press the button. As it can be frustrating to find a ticket machine (especially when you see your tram or bus approaching), I generally invest in a multi-day ticket to have the freedom of hopping on at will.

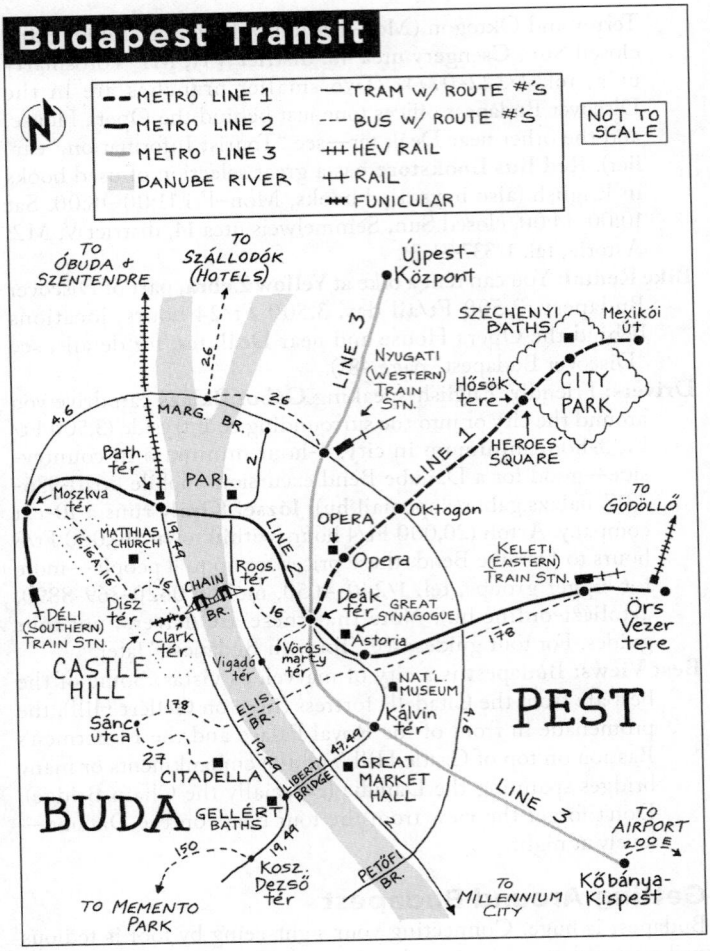

Your options are:

• **Single ticket** (*vonaljegy*, for a ride of up to an hour on any means of transit; transfers are allowed only within the Metro system)—300 Ft (or 400 Ft if bought from the driver);

• **Short single Metro ride** (*Metrószakaszjegy*, 3 stops or fewer on the Metro)—250 Ft;

• **Transfer ticket** (*átszállójegy*—allowing up to 90 minutes, including one transfer)—470 Ft;

• **Pack of 10 single tickets** (*10 darabos gyűjtőjegy*), which can be shared—2,700 Ft (that's 270 Ft per ticket, saving you 30 Ft per ticket);

• Unlimited multi-day tickets, including a **one-day ticket**

(*napijegy,* 1,550 Ft/24 hours), **three-day ticket** (*turistajegy,* 3,850 Ft/72 hours), and **weekly ticket** (*hetijegy,* 4,600 Ft/7 days, requires a photo); or

• The **Budapest Card,** which combines a multi-day ticket with sightseeing discounts (but it's generally a bad value; described earlier, under "Tourist Information").

Always validate single-ride tickets as you enter the bus, tram, or Metro station (stick it in the elbow-high box). On older buses and trams that have little red validation boxes, stick your ticket in the black slot, then pull the slot toward you to punch holes in your ticket. The multi-day tickets need be validated only once. The stern-looking people with blue-and-green armbands waiting as you enter or exit the Metro want to see your validated ticket. Cheaters are fined 6,000 Ft on the spot, and you'll be surprised how often you're checked (inspectors are most commonly seen at train stations and along the touristy M1/yellow line). All public transit runs from 4:30 in the morning until 23:10. *Végállomás* means "end of the line." A useful route-planning website is www.bkv.hu.

Construction Warning: Budapest is in the process of renovating its Metro lines and pedestrianizing much of its urban core. This can result in lots of torn-up streets, and the closures of various Metro stops and tram lines. (Unfortunately, they often do work in July and August: "low season" for business, but peak season for tourists.) If a particular stretch of a Metro line is closed, buses run the same route instead. If a tram route is interrupted, the tram is replaced by a bus; look for a bus with the same number, ending in *V* (for example, bus #47–49V would replace trams #47 and #49). For the latest on which Metro stops or tram lines are closed, ask your hotel or the TI, or check www.bkv.hu.

By Metro

Riding Budapest's Metro, you really feel like you're down in the efficient guts of the city. There are three working lines:

• **M1 (yellow)**—The oldest Metro line on the Continent, this extremely handy line runs just 20 steps below street level under Andrássy út from Vörösmarty tér (Pest's main square) to City Park. Dating from 1896, "the Underground" *(Földalatti)* is so shallow that there's no underpass for switching platforms—you must follow the signs on the street (listing end points) to gauge the right direction. Though recently renovated, the M1 line retains its 1896 atmosphere, along with fun black-and-white photos of the age.

• **M2 (red)**—Built during the communist days, it's 115 feet deep and designed to double as a bomb shelter. This line has undergone a thorough renovation, leaving its stations new and shiny. The only line going under the Danube to Buda (for now), M2 connects the Déli/Southern train station, Moszkva tér (where you catch

bus #16, #16A, or #116 to the top of Castle Hill), Batthyány tér (Víziváros and the HÉV suburban railway), Kossuth tér (behind the Parliament), Astoria (near the Great Synagogue on the Small Boulevard), and the Keleti/Eastern train station.

• **M3 (blue)**—This line makes a broad, boomerang-shaped swoop north to south on the Pest side. Key stops include the Nyugati/Western train station, Ferenciek tere (in the heart of Pest's Town Center), and Kálvin tér (near the Great Market Hall and many recommended hotels).

• **M4 (green; not yet running)**—Currently under construction, this line will go from southern Buda to the Gellért Baths, under the Danube to the Great Market Hall and Kálvin tér (where it will cross the M3/blue line), then up to Keleti/Eastern train station (where it will cross the M2/red line). As stations on this line are finished, they'll open to the public, but the whole line won't be done for several years (www.metro4.hu).

The three original lines—M1, M2, and M3—cross only once: at the **Deák tér** stop (often signed as *Deák Ferenc tér*) in the heart of Pest, near where Andrássy út begins.

Most M2 and M3 Metro stations are at intersections of ring roads and other major thoroughfares. You'll usually exit the Metro into a confusing underpass packed with kiosks, fast-food stands, and makeshift markets. Directional signs help you find the right exit. Or do the prairie-dog routine: Surface to get your bearings, then head back underground to find the correct stairs up to your destination.

The Metro stops themselves are usually very well-marked, with a list of upcoming stops on the wall behind the tracks. Digital clocks either count down to the next train's arrival, or count up from the previous train's departure; either way, you'll rarely wait more than five minutes.

You'll ride very long, steep, fast-moving escalators to access the M2 and M3 lines. Hang on tight, enjoy the gale as trains below shoot through the tunnels...and don't make yourself dizzy by trying to read the Burger King ads.

HÉV: Budapest's suburban rail system, or HÉV (pronounced "hayv"), branches off to the outskirts and beyond. The HÉV line that begins at Buda's Batthyány tér runs north to the sights in Óbuda and to the small town of Szentendre; from Örs vezér tere, a different line runs east to the royal palace at Gödöllő. However, on a short visit, it's unlikely you'll need to use the HÉV.

By Tram

Budapest's trams are handy and frequent, taking you virtually anywhere the Metro doesn't. Here are some trams you might use (note that all of these run in both directions):

Tram **#2:** Follows Pest's Danube embankment, parallel to Váci utca. From north to south, it begins at the Great Boulevard (near Margaret Bridge) and passes the Parliament, Roosevelt tér and the Chain Bridge, Vigadó tér, and the Great Market Hall.

Trams **#19** and **#41:** Run along Buda's Danube embankment from Batthyány tér (with an M2/red Metro station, and HÉV trains to Óbuda and Szentendre). From Batthyány tér, these trams run (north to south) through Víziváros to Adam Clark tér (the bottom of the Castle Hill funicular), then under Elisabeth Bridge and around the base of Gellért Hill to the Gellért Hotel and Baths.

Trams **#4** and **#6:** Zip around Pest's Great Boulevard ring road (Nagykörút), connecting Nyugati/Western train station and the Oktogon with the southern tip of Margaret Island and Buda's Moszkva tér (with M2/red Metro station). Note that these trams might be diverted in 2010 due to restoration work on Margaret Bridge.

Trams **#47** and **#49:** Connect the Gellért Baths in Buda with Pest's Small Boulevard ring road (Kiskörút), with stops at the Great Market Hall, the National Museum, the Great Synagogue (Astoria stop), and Deák tér (end of the line).

By Bus

I use the Metro and trams for most of my Budapest commuting. But some buses are useful for shortcuts within the city, or for reaching outlying sights. Note that the transit company draws a distinction between gas-powered "buses" and electric "trolley buses" (which are powered by overhead cables). Unless otherwise noted, you can assume the following are standard buses.

Buses **#16, #16A,** and **#116:** All head up to the top of Castle Hill (get off at Dísz tér, near the Royal Palace). You can catch any of these three at Moszkva tér (on M2/red Metro line). When coming from the other direction, bus #16 makes several handy stops in Pest (Deák tér, Roosevelt tér), then crosses the Chain Bridge for more stops in Buda (including Adam Clark tér, at Buda end of Chain Bridge).

Trolley buses **#70** and **#78:** Zip from near the Opera House (intersection of Andrássy út and Nagymező utca) to the Parliament (Kossuth tér).

Bus **#178:** Goes from Keleti/Eastern train station to central Pest (Astoria and Ferenciek tere Metro stops), then over the Elisabeth Bridge to Buda.

Bus **#26:** Begins at Nyugati/Western train station and heads around the Great Boulevard to Margaret Island, making several stops along the island (though in 2010, restoration work on Margaret Bridge will likely cause this service to be diverted).

Bus **#27:** Runs from Sánc utca (along Hegyalja út) up to just below the Citadella fortress atop Gellért Hill.

Bus **#150:** Goes from Kosztolányi Dezső tér (several blocks beyond Gellért Hotel and Baths, in Buda) to Memento Park.

Bus **#200E:** Connects all three terminals at Ferihegy Airport to the Kőbánya-Kispest M3/blue Metro station.

By Taxi

Budapest's public transportation is good enough that you probably won't need to take many taxis. But if you do, you're likely to run into a dishonest driver. Arm yourself with knowledge: Cabbies are not allowed to charge more than a drop rate of 300 Ft, and then 240 Ft per kilometer. (The prices go up at night, between 22:00 and 6:00 in the morning: 420 Ft drop, 350 Ft per kilometer.) The big companies charge even less than these rates. Prices are per ride, not per passenger. A 10 percent tip is expected. A typical ride within central Budapest shouldn't run more than 2,000 Ft. Despite what some slimy cabbies may tell you, there's no legitimate extra charge for crossing the river.

Instead of hailing a taxi on the street, do as the locals do and call a cab from a reputable company—it's cheaper and you're more likely to get an honest driver. Try **City Taxi** (tel. 1/211-1111), **Taxi 6x6** (tel. 1/266-6666), or **Főtaxi** (1/222-2222). Most dispatchers speak English, but if you're uncomfortable calling, you can ask your hotel or restaurant to call for you. (Request that they call a "City Taxi"—otherwise, they might call a pricier company to get a bigger kickback.)

Many cabs you'd hail on the streets are there only to prey on rich, green tourists. Avoid unmarked taxis and cabs waiting at tourist spots and train stations. If you do wave down a cab on the street, choose one that's marked with an official company logo and telephone number, and has a yellow license plate (if the plate's not yellow, it's not official). Ask for a rough estimate before you get in—if it doesn't sound reasonable, walk away. If you wind up being dramatically overcharged for a ride, simply pay what you think is fair and go inside. If the driver follows you (unlikely), your hotel receptionist will defend you.

Tours in Budapest

By Foot

Local Guides—Budapest has an abundance of enthusiastic, hardworking guides who speak perfect English and enjoy showing off their city. Given the reasonable fees and efficient use of your time, hiring your own personal expert is an excellent value. I have three favorites, any of whom can do half-day or full-day tours, and can also drive you into the countryside. **Péter Pölczman** is an exceptional guide who really puts you in touch with the Budapest you came to see (€90/4–5 hours, €150/8 hours, mobile 0620-926-0557, www.zigzagbudapest.com, peter@zigzagbudapest.com or polczman@freestart.hu). **Andrea Makkay** is also great, with a professional and polished approach (€90/4 hours, €160/8 hours, mobile 0620-962-9363, www.privateguidebudapest.com, amakkay@t-online.hu—arrange details by email; if Andrea is busy, she can arrange to send you with another guide). **Elemér Boreczky,** a university professor, leads walking tours with a scholarly approach, emphasizing Budapest's rich tapestry of architecture as "frozen music" (€25/hr, tel. 1/386-0885, mobile 0620-340-3598, www.culturaltours.mlap.hu, boreczky.elemer@gmail.com). Péter, Andrea, and Elemér were all indispensible help to me in writing this chapter.

Walking Tours—A youthful, backpacker-oriented company, **Absolute Walking Tours,** is run by Oregonian Ben Frieday. These tours are loose and informal, but informative. You can choose from a number of different itineraries, which include the following: The Absolute Walk gives you a good overview of Budapest (4,000 Ft, mid-May–Sept daily at 9:30 and 13:30, Oct–mid-May daily at 10:30, 3.5 hours). The Hammer and Sickle Tour includes a guided visit to Memento Park (you take the regular direct bus to Memento Park with other passengers), then a quick visit to a mini-museum of communist artifacts (6,500 Ft, 4/week, 3 hours). Absolute Hungro Gastro, focused on Hungarian cuisine and wine, gives you information on traditional recipes and ingredients, and a chance to taste several specialties at a local restaurant (7,000 Ft, 2/week, 1/week in winter, 3 hours). In the evening, consider the Absolute Night Stroll, which includes a one-hour cruise on the Danube (5,000 Ft, mid-April–Sept only, 4/week, 2.5 hours); or the rowdier Pub Crawl, which sometimes continues late into the night (4,500 Ft, departs 20:30, 4/week, at least 3 hours). History buffs appreciate the 1956 Uprising Walk, which visits some of the sites of those bloody but inspirational events five decades ago (6,500 Ft, 2/week, 3 hours).

All tours depart from the blocky, green-domed Lutheran church at Deák tér, near the Metro station (tel. 1/266-8777,

Budapest at a Glance

In Buda

▲▲Matthias Church Landmark Neo-Gothic church with gilded history-book interior and revered 16th-century statue of Mary and Jesus. **Hours:** Mon–Sat 9:00–17:00, Sun 13:00–17:00, sometimes closed Sat after 13:00 for weddings. See page 504.

▲▲Gellért Baths Touristy baths in historic Buda hotel. **Hours:** May–Sept daily 6:00–19:00; Oct–April Mon–Fri 6:00–19:00, Sat–Sun 6:00–17:00. See page 508.

▲▲Memento Park Larger-than-life communist statues all collected in one park, on the outskirts of town. **Hours:** Daily 10:00–sunset. See page 540.

▲Hungarian National Gallery Top works by Hungarian artists, housed in the Royal Palace. **Hours:** Tue–Sun 10:00–18:00, closed Mon. See page 500.

▲"Hospital in the Rock" Fascinating underground network of hospital and bomb-shelter corridors from WWII and the Cold War. **Hours:** Tue–Sun 10:00–19:00, closed Mon. See page 506.

In Pest

▲▲▲Széchenyi Baths Budapest's steamy soaking scene in City Park—the city's single best attraction. **Hours:** Swimming pool—daily 6:00–22:00, thermal bath—daily 6:00–19:00. See page 539.

▲▲Hungarian Parliament Vast riverside government center with remarkable interior. **Hours:** English tours usually daily at 10:00, 12:00, and 14:00; and Mon–Sat sometimes also at 16:00. See page 508.

▲▲Great Market Hall Colorful Old World mall with produce, eateries, souvenirs, and great people-watching. **Hours:** Mon 6:00–17:00, Tue–Fri 6:00–18:00, Sat 6:00–15:00, closed Sun. See page 522.

▲▲Great Synagogue The world's second-largest, with fancy interior, good museum, and memorial garden. **Hours:** April–Oct Mon–Thu 10:00–17:00, Fri 10:00–15:00, Sun 10:00–18:00; Nov–March Mon–Thu 10:00–15:00, Fri and Sun 10:00–14:00; always closed Sat and Jewish holidays. See page 525.

▲▲**Hungarian State Opera House** Neo-Renaissance splendor and affordable opera. **Hours:** Lobby/box office open Mon–Sat from 11:00 until show time—generally 19:00; Sun open 3 hours before performance—generally 16:00–19:00, or 10:00–13:00 if there's a matinee; English tours nearly daily at 15:00 and 16:00. See page 529.

▲▲**House of Terror** Harrowing remembrance of Nazis and communist secret police in former headquarters/torture site. **Hours:** Tue–Fri 10:00–18:00, Sat–Sun 10:00–19:30, closed Mon. See page 531.

▲▲**Heroes' Square** Mammoth tribute to Hungary's historic figures, fronted by art museums. **Hours:** Square always open. See page 535.

▲▲**City Park** Budapest's backyard, with Art Nouveau zoo, Transylvanian Vajdahunyad Castle replica, amusement park, and Széchenyi Baths. **Hours:** Park always open. See page 538.

▲**Szabadság Tér** Monumental square with a controversial obelisk honoring Soviet "liberators." **Hours:** Always open. See page 513.

▲**St. István's Basilica** Budapest's largest church, with a saint's withered fist and great city views. **Hours:** Mon–Fri 9:00–17:00, Sat 9:00–13:00, Sun 13:00–17:00, observation deck has shorter hours and is closed Nov–March. See page 516.

▲**Hungarian National Museum** Expansive collection of fragments from Hungary's history. **Hours:** Tue–Sun 10:00–18:00, closed Mon. See page 524.

▲**Postal Museum** Funky, charming tribute to old postal service objects in venerable old Andrássy út mansion. **Hours:** Tue–Sun 10:00–18:00, closed Mon. See page 527.

▲**Holocaust Memorial Center** Excellent memorial and museum honoring Hungarian victims of the Holocaust. **Hours:** Tue–Sun 10:00–18:00, closed Mon. See page 539.

▲**Margaret Island** Budapest's traffic-free urban playground, with spas, ruins, gardens, a game farm, and fountains, set in the middle of the Danube. **Hours:** Park always open. See page 519.

www.absolutetours.com). Travelers with this book get a 500-Ft discount on any tour, as does anyone with a student ID card.

By Boat

Danube Boat Tours—Cruising the Danube, while touristy, is fun and convenient. The most established company, **Legenda,** is a class act that runs new, glassed-in panoramic boats day and night. I've negotiated a special discount with Legenda for my readers (but you must book direct and ask for the Rick Steves price). By **day,** the one-hour cruise costs 2,300 Ft for Rick Steves readers, or pay 2,900 Ft to also include a one-hour walking tour around Margaret Island (8/day May–Aug, 7/day April and Sept, 4/day March and Oct, 1/day Nov–Feb). By **night,** the one-hour cruise (with no Margaret Island visit) costs 3,700 Ft for Rick Steves readers (3/day May–Aug, 4/day March–April and Sept–Oct, 1/day Nov–Feb). All cruises include two drinks and headphone commentary. By night, TV monitors show the interiors of the great buildings as you float by. The Legenda dock is in front of the Marriott on the Pest embankment (find pedestrian access under tram tracks just downriver from Vigadó tér, district V, M1: Vörösmarty tér, tel. 1/317-2203, www.legenda.hu). Competing river-cruise companies are nearby, but given the discount, Legenda offers the best value.

Margaret Island Shuttle—If you just want to get out on the water, but don't care for a full tour with commentary, consider Mahart's cheap hop from Vigadó tér to Margaret Island (590 Ft one-way, 890 Ft round-trip, 4/day, 45 min, June–Aug daily, Sept and May Sat–Sun only, none Oct–April, boat dock directly in front of Vigadó tér). Mahart's standard sightseeing cruises pale in comparison to Legenda's.

On Wheels

Bike Tours—A sister company of Absolute Walking Tours, **Yellow Zebra,** wheels by Budapest's major sights on a 3.5-hour tour (5,000 Ft, mid-March–mid-Oct daily at 11:00, also at 16:00 July–Aug, no tours off-season, meet at Deák tér, tel. 1/266-8777, www.yellowzebrabikes.com).

City Segway Tours—In addition to walking and bike tours, Discover Budapest also offers tours of the city by Segway (stand-up electric scooter). Although expensive, it's a unique way to see Budapest while trying out a Segway (14,500 Ft, daily at 10:00, also daily at 18:30 April–Oct, 2.5–3 hours with 30- to 45-min training beforehand, 6 people per group, must reserve and pre-pay at www.citysegwaytours.com or call the office when in Budapest—tel. 1/269-3843).

Bus Tours—Several different companies run essentially the same bus tours that glide past all the big sights (figure around 3,500

Ft for a 2-hour tour). A hop-on, hop-off bus tour by **City-Circle Sightseeing** makes 12 stops as it cruises around town on a two-hour loop (4,500 Ft for a 24-hour ticket). Most companies also offer a wide variety of other tours, including dinner boat cruises and trips to the Danube Bend. Pick up fliers about all these tours at the TI or in your hotel lobby.

RiverRide—This innovative new tour shows you Budapest by land...and from the river, using an amphibious bus (7,500 Ft, 4–5/day, 2 hours, departs from Roosevelt tér at the Pest end of the Chain Bridge, reserve online or by phone, tel. 1/332-2555, www.riverride.hu).

Sights in Budapest

A real highlight of visiting Budapest is touring the opulent interiors of its late-19th-century Golden Age buildings—an experience worth ▲▲▲. The best interiors belong to the Opera House and Parliament, and "honorable mentions" go to St. István's Basilica, the Great Synagogue, New York Café, and both the Széchenyi and the Gellért Baths.

In Buda

Nearly all of Buda's top sights are concentrated on or near its two riverside hills: Castle Hill and Gellért Hill.

Castle Hill (Várhegy)

Once the seat of Hungarian royalty, and now the city's highest-profile tourist zone, Castle Hill is a historic spit of land looming above the Buda bank of the Danube. Scenic from afar, but (frankly) a bit soulless from up close, it's best seen quickly. The major landmarks are the huge, green-domed Royal Palace at the south end of the hill (housing a pair of museums) and the frilly-spired Matthias Church near the north end (with the hill's best interior). In between are tourist-filled pedestrian streets and dull but historic buildings. Perhaps best of all are the bird's-eye views from up here across the Danube to Pest. I've listed the sights in order from south to north, and linked them together on a self-guided walk.

When to Visit: Castle Hill is packed with tour groups in the morning, but it's much less crowded in the afternoon. Castle Hill is an ideal after-lunch activity. If you want a good meal on this side of the river, head to the Víziváros neighborhood just downhill, between the castle and the river (see "Eating in Budapest" on page 574).

Getting to Castle Hill: The Metro and trams won't take you to the top of Castle Hill. Instead, you can hike, taxi, catch a bus,

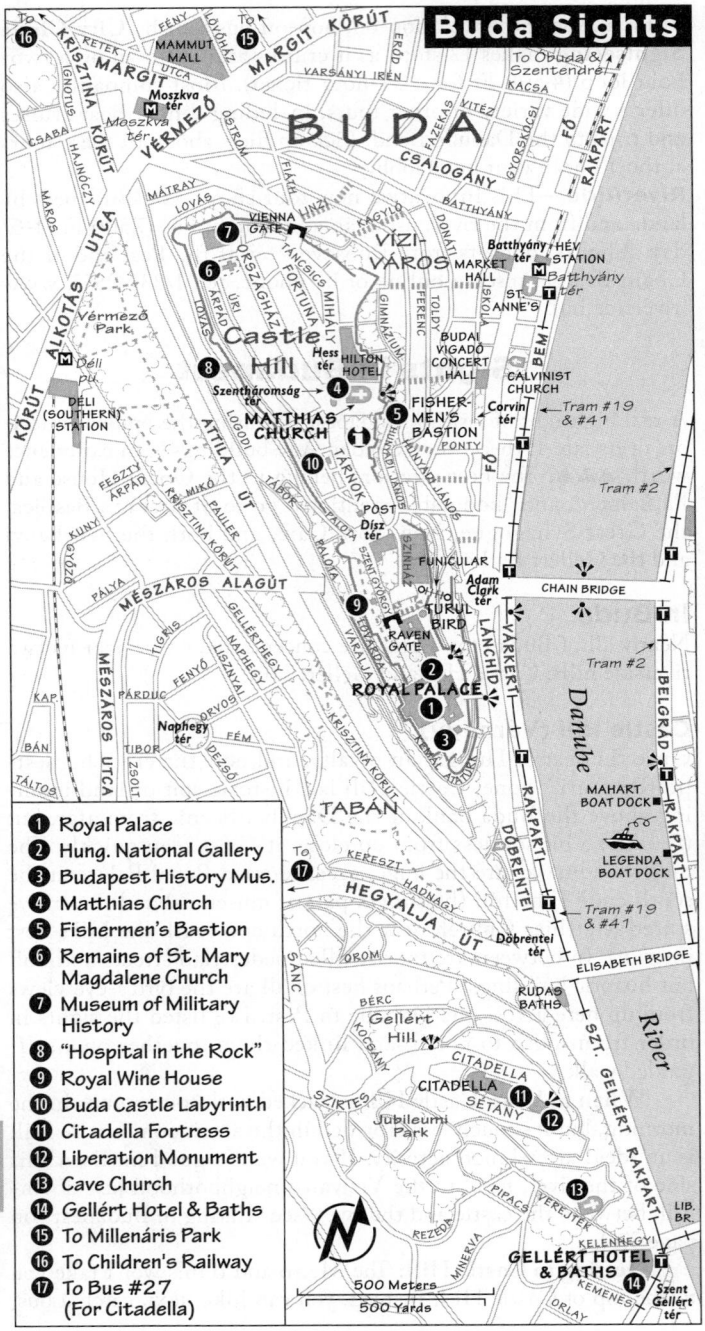
Buda Sights
BUDA
VÍZIVÁROS
Castle Hill
MATTHIAS CHURCH
FISHERMEN'S BASTION
ROYAL PALACE
TABÁN
Danube River
CHAIN BRIDGE
ELISABETH BRIDGE
MAHART BOAT DOCK
LEGENDA BOAT DOCK
GELLÉRT HOTEL & BATHS
CITADELLA
Gellért Hill
Jubileumi Park
RUDAS BATHS
MARKET HALL
ST. ANNE'S
CALVINIST CHURCH
BUDAI VIGADÓ CONCERT HALL
HILTON HOTEL
VIENNA GATE
MAMMUT MALL
DÉLI (SOUTHERN) STATION
Vérmező Park
Moszkva tér
Batthyány tér
Szentháromság tér
Hess tér
Corvin tér
Adam Clark tér
Döbrentei tér
Szent Gellért tér
Naphegy tér
Disz tér
RAVEN GATE
FUNICULAR
Tram #19 & #41
Tram #2
To Óbuda & Szentendrei
To Millenáris Park
To Children's Railway
To Bus #27 (For Citadella)
1 Royal Palace
2 Hung. National Gallery
3 Budapest History Mus.
4 Matthias Church
5 Fishermen's Bastion
6 Remains of St. Mary Magdalene Church
7 Museum of Military History
8 "Hospital in the Rock"
9 Royal Wine House
10 Buda Castle Labyrinth
11 Citadella Fortress
12 Liberation Monument
13 Cave Church
14 Gellért Hotel & Baths
15 To Millenáris Park
16 To Children's Railway
17 To Bus #27 (For Citadella)
500 Meters
500 Yards

or ride the funicular.

For most visitors, the easiest bet is to hop on **bus #16,** with handy stops in both Pest (at the Deák tér Metro hub, and at Roosevelt tér at the Pest end of the Chain Bridge) and Buda (at Adam Clark tér at the Buda end of the Chain Bridge—across the street from the lower funicular station, and much cheaper than the funicular). Or you can head up from Moszkva tér (on the M2/red Metro line); from here, bus **#16,** as well as buses **#16A** and **#116,** head up the hill (at Moszkva tér, catch the bus just uphill from Metro station—in front of red-brick, castle-looking building). All buses stop at Dísz tér, right in the middle of the hill. From Dísz tér, go past the war-damaged building (the old Ministry of War) and walk five minutes toward the giant green dome, then bear left to find the big *Turul* bird statue at the start of this walk.

The **funicular** (*sikló*, SHEE-kloh), lifting visitors from the Chain Bridge to the top of Castle Hill, is a Budapest landmark. Built in 1870 to provide cheap transportation to Castle Hill workers, today it's a pricey little tourist trip. Read the fun first-person history in glass cases at the top station (840 Ft one-way, 1,450 Ft round-trip, not covered by transit pass, daily 7:30–22:00, departs every 5 min, closed for maintenance every other Mon). It leaves you right at the *Turul* bird statue, where this walk begins.

• *Orient yourself from the top of the funicular, enjoying the views over the Danube. At the top of the nearby staircase, notice the giant bird that looks like a vulture. This is the...*

***Turul* Bird**—This mythical bird of Magyar folktales supposedly led the Hungarian migrations from the steppes of Central Asia in the ninth century. He dropped his sword in the Carpathian Basin, indicating that this was to be the permanent home of the Magyar people. While the Hungarians have long since integrated into Europe, the *Turul* remains a symbol of Magyar pride. During a surge of nationalism in the 1920s, a movement named after this bird helped revive traditional Hungarian culture. And today, the bird is invoked by right-wing nationalist politicians.

• *We'll circle back this way later. But for now, climb down the stairs by the* Turul *and walk along the broad terrace in front of the...*

Royal Palace (Királyi Palota)—The imposing palace on Castle Hill barely hints at the colorful story of this hill since the day that the legendary *Turul* dropped his sword. In the early 15th century, the Renaissance King Mátyás (Matthias) Corvinus—who we'll learn more about soon—converted a humble medieval palace on this site into one of Europe's most extravagant residences, putting

Buda—and Hungary—on the map. Just a few decades later, the invading Ottomans occupied Buda and turned the palace into a military garrison. When the Habsburgs laid siege to the hill for 77 days in 1686, gunpowder stored in the cellar exploded, destroying the palace. The Habsburgs took the hill, but Buda was deserted and in ruins. The palace was rebuilt, then damaged again during the 1848 Revolution, but was repaired. As World War II drew to a close, Budapest became the front line between the Nazis and the approaching Soviets. The Red Army laid siege to the hill for 100 days. They eventually succeeded in taking Budapest...but the city—and the hill—were devastated.

While impressive from afar, the current version of the palace—a historically inaccurate, post-WWII reconstruction—is a loose rebuilding of previous versions, lacking the style and sense of history that this important site deserves. Fortunately, the palace does house some worthwhile museums (described later), and boasts the fine terrace you're strolling on, with some of Budapest's best views.

• *Behind the big equestrian statue is the main entrance to the...*

▲Hungarian National Gallery (Magyar Nemzeti Galéria)—The best place in Hungary to appreciate the works of homegrown artists, this art museum offers a peek into the often-morose Hungarian worldview. The collection includes a remarkable group of 15th-century, wood-carved altars from Slovakia (then "Upper Hungary"); piles of gloomy canvases dating from the dark days after the failed 1848 Revolution; and several works by two great Hungarian Realist painters, Mihály Munkácsy and László Paál. Don't miss the three works by Tivadar Csontváry Kosztka, the "Hungarian Van Gogh" (for more on Csontváry, see page 620). At the second-floor landing, you see a few of this well-traveled painter's destinations: the giant canvas in the center depicts the theater at Taormina, Sicily; on the left are the waterfalls of Schaffhausen, Germany; and on the right is a cedar tree in Lebanon. Typical of Csontváry's style, these are colorful, allegorical, and expressionistic (800 Ft, may be more for special exhibitions, 1,500 Ft extra to take photos, Tue–Sun 10:00–18:00, closed Mon, required bag check for large bags, café, district I, tel. 1/201-9082, www.mng.hu).

• *Head back outside and face the palace. Go through the passage to the right of the National Gallery entrance (next to the café). You'll emerge into a courtyard decorated with a gorgeous fountain dedicated to King Matthias Corvinus (see sidebar). Go around the right side of the fountain*

and through the passage, into the palace courtyard. At the far end of this too-big space is the entrance to the...

Budapest History Museum (Budapesti Történeti Múzeum)—This earnest but dusty collection strains to bring the history of this city to life. The dimly lit fragments of 14th-century sculptures, depicting early Magyars, allow you to see how Asian those original Hungarians truly looked. The "Budapest in the Modern Times" exhibit deliberately but effectively traces the union between Buda and Pest. Rounding out the collection are exhibits on prehistoric residents and a sprawling cellar that unveils fragments from the oh-so-many buildings that have perched on this hill over the centuries (1,100 Ft, audioguide-850 Ft, some good English descriptions posted; mid-May–mid-Sept daily 10:00–18:00; March–mid-May and mid-Sept–Oct Wed–Mon 10:00–18:00, closed Tue; Nov–Feb Wed–Mon 10:00–16:00, closed Tue; last entry 30 min before closing, district I, tel. 1/487-8800, www.btm.hu).

Walk to Matthias Church—Leaving the palace courtyard, walk straight up the slight incline, passing under a gate with a raven holding a ring in its mouth (a symbol of King Matthias).

As you walk along the line of flagpoles, you'll pass a big field on your right. Look closely to spot the remains of a medieval monastery and church. Along the left side (past the flagpoles) is the ongoing excavation of the medieval Jewish quarter—more reminders that most of what you see on today's Castle Hill has been destroyed and rebuilt many times over.

After Sándor Palace is the yellow **National Dance Theater,** where Beethoven once performed. The hulking, war-damaged building beyond that (at the end of the lawn, partially covered by the huge banner) used to house the **Ministry of War.** Most of the bullet holes are from World War II, while others were left by the Soviets who occupied this hill in response to the 1956 Uprising. The building is a political hot potato—prime real estate, but nobody can decide what to do with it.

Just after the Ministry of War, at the cross street, you reach **Dísz tér** ("Parade Square"), which has a convenient bus stop for connecting to other parts of Budapest (bus #16, #16A, or #116 to Moszkva tér; or bus #16 to the Pest side of the Chain Bridge).

If you walk a few steps down the street to the left, on the left-hand side you'll find an entrance to the rampart garden between the castle walls. A short walk through this area takes you to the **Royal**

Matthias (Mátyás) Corvinus: The Last Hungarian King

The Árpád dynasty—descendants of the original Magyar tribes—died out in 1301. For more than 600 years, Hungary would be ruled by foreigners...with one exception.

In the middle of the 15th century, Hungary had bad luck hanging on to its foreign kings: Two of them died unexpectedly within seven years. Meanwhile, homegrown military general János Hunyadi was enjoying great success on the battlefield against the Ottomans. When the five-year-old László V was elected king, Hunyadi was appointed regent and essentially ruled the country.

Hunyadi defeated the Ottomans in the crucial 1456 Battle of Belgrade, which kept them out of Hungary (at least for another 70 years) and made him an even greater hero to the Hungarian people. But soon afterward, Hunyadi died from the plague, which he had contracted during that fateful battle. When the young king also died (at the tender age of 16), the nobles looked for a new leader. At first their sights settled on Hunyadi's eldest son, László. But the Habsburgs—who were trying to project their influence from afar—felt threatened by the Hunyadi family, and László was killed.

At this dark moment, the Hungarians turned to the younger Hunyadi son, Mátyás (or Matthias in English). At the time, Matthias (whose first wife was a Czech princess) was at court in Prague. According to legend, Matthias' mother sent for him with a raven with a ring in its beak. The raven supposedly flew non-stop from Transylvania to Prague. The raven-with-ring motif became part of the family crest, as well as the family name: Corvinus (Latin for "raven").

Matthias Corvinus returned to Buda, becoming the first Hungarian-descended king in more than 150 years. Progressive and well-educated in the Humanist tradition, Matthias Corvinus

Wine House and Wine Cellar Museum, where you can tour a network of old wine cellars burrowed under Castle Hill...and taste some Hungarian wines, if you choose (900 Ft for museum entry, or just 400 Ft if you also pay for a tasting, tastings cost 1,350–4,200 Ft depending on number and quality, sparkling wine and schnapps tastings also available, daily 12:00–20:00, likely shorter hours off-season, Budavár kerület, district I, tel. 1/267-1100, www.kiralyiborok.com).

Cross the street in front of the Ministry of War, noticing the handy post office on your left. On the right, behind the yellow wall, is a courtyard with an open-air Hungarian **crafts market.** While it's fun to browse, prices here are high (haggle away). The Great Market Hall has a better selection and its prices are generally lower (see page 522).

(r. 1458–1490) was the quintessential Renaissance king. A lover of the Italian Renaissance, he patronized the arts and built palaces legendary for their beauty. Also a benefactor of the poor, he dressed up as a commoner and ventured into the streets to see firsthand how the nobles of his realm treated his people.

Matthias was a strong, savvy leader. He created Central Europe's first standing army—30,000 mercenaries known as the Black Army. No longer reliant on the nobility for military support, Good King Matthias was able to drain power from the nobles and make taxation of his subjects more equitable—earning him the nickname the "people's king."

King Matthias was also a shrewd military tactician. Realizing that squabbling with the Ottomans would squander his resources, he made peace with the Ottoman sultan to stabilize Hungary's southern border. Then he swept north, invading Moravia, Bohemia, and even Austria. By 1485, Matthias moved into his new palace in Vienna, and Hungary was enjoying a Golden Age.

Five years later, Matthias died mysteriously at the age of 47, and his empire disintegrated. It is said that when Matthias died, justice died with him. To this day, Hungarians consider him the greatest of all kings, and they sing of his siege of Vienna in their national anthem. They're proud that for a few decades in the middle of half a millennium of foreign oppression, they had a truly Hungarian king—and a great one at that.

Continue straight uphill on **Tárnok utca.** This area often disappoints visitors. After being destroyed by Ottomans, it was rebuilt in sensible Baroque, lacking the romantic time-capsule charm of a medieval old town. But if you poke your head into some courtyards, you'll almost always see some original Gothic arches and other medieval features.

• *Continue on Tárnok utca up to the little park with the* ***TI*** *(on your right; pick up their handy* Castle Walks *map).*

Across the street from the park (on the left), the ***CBA grocery store*** *sells reasonably priced cold drinks, and has a coffee shop upstairs (Mon–Fri 7:00–20:00, Sat 8:00–20:00, Sun 9:00–18:00). Just beyond it, the same store runs a "grill bar" selling cheap and basic sandwiches and sides (to go, or sit at the tables out front).*

Just beyond the park, a warty plague column from 1713 marks

***Szentháromság tér** ("Holy Trinity Square"), the main square of old Buda.*

Dominating the square is the...

▲▲Matthias Church (Mátyás-Templom)—Budapest's best church has been destroyed and rebuilt several times in the 800 years since it was founded by King Béla IV. Today's version—renovated at great expense in the late 19th century and restored after World War II—is an ornately decorated lesson in Hungarian history. While it's officially named the "Church of Our Lady," everyone calls it the Matthias Church, for the popular Renaissance king who got married here—twice.

Cost, Hours, Location: 700 Ft, includes Museum of Ecclesiastical Art, 12-stop audioguide-400 Ft, Mon–Sat 9:00–17:00, Sun 13:00–17:00, may close Sat after 13:00 for weddings, Szentháromság tér 2, district I, tel. 1/355-5657, www.matyas-templom.hu.

➲ **Self-Guided Tour:** Examine the **exterior.** While the nucleus of the church is Gothic, most of what you see outside—including the frilly, flamboyant steeple—was added in 1896, for the celebrations surrounding the 1,000th anniversary of the Magyars' arrival in Europe (see sidebar on page 480). At the top of the spire facing the river, notice the raven—the ever-present symbol of King Matthias Corvinus.

The sumptuous **interior** is wallpapered with gilded pages from a Hungarian history textbook. Different eras are represented by symbolic motifs. For example, the wall immediately to the left of the entry represents the Renaissance, with a giant coat of arms of the beloved King Matthias Corvinus. (The tough guys in armor on either side are members of his mercenary Black Army, the source of his power.) Notice another raven, with a ring in its beak. Meanwhile, the wall across from the entry—with Oriental motifs—commemorates the Ottoman reign of Buda.

Work your way clockwise around the church from the entry. The first chapel (in the back corner, by the closed main doors)—the **Loreto Chapel**—holds the church's prize possession. Peer through the black iron grill to see the 1515 statue of Mary and Jesus. Anticipating Ottoman plundering, locals walled over this precious statue. The occupying Ottomans used the church as their primary mosque—oblivious to the statue plastered over in the niche. Then, a century and a half later, during the siege of Buda in 1686, gunpowder stored in the castle up the street detonated, and

the wall crumbled. Mary's triumphant face showed through, terrifying the Ottomans. Supposedly this was the only part of town taken from the Ottomans without a fight.

As you look down the **nave,** notice the banners. They've hung here since the Mass that celebrated Habsburg monarch Franz Josef's coronation at this church on June 8, 1867. In a sly political compromise to curry favor in the Hungarian part of his territory, Franz Josef was "emperor" of Austria, but only "king" of Hungary. (If you see the old German phrase "K+K"—still used today as a boast of royal quality—it refers to this *"König und Kaiser"* arrangement.) So, after F. J. was crowned emperor in Vienna, he came down the Danube and said to the Hungarians, "King me."

Along the left aisle is the entrance to the upstairs gallery, which holds the **Museum of Ecclesiastical Art** (Egyházművészeti Gyűjteménye, same ticket and hours as church). The original Hungarian crown is under the Parliament's dome—but a replica is up here, and worth a peek. The church also hosts concerts (Oct–Feb only, maybe a few in shoulder season, none in summer; ticket desk at church entry).

• *Back outside, at the end of the square next to the Matthias Church, is the...*

Fishermen's Bastion (Halászbástya)—This Neo-Romanesque fantasy rampart offers beautiful views over the Danube to Pest. In the Middle Ages, the fish market was just below here (in today's Víziváros, or "Water Town"), so this part of the rampart actually was guarded by fishermen. The current structure, however, is completely artificial—yet another example of Budapest sprucing itself up for the 1896 millennial celebrations. Its seven pointy towers represent the seven Magyar tribes. The cone-headed arcades are reminiscent of tents the nomadic Magyars called home before they moved west to Europe.

Paying 400 Ft to climb up the bastion makes little sense. Enjoy virtually the same view through the windows (left of café) for free. The café offers a scenic break if you don't mind the tour groups. Note that the grand staircase leading down from the bastion offers a handy shortcut to the Víziváros neighborhood.

• *Between the bastion and the church stands a statue of...*

St. István—Hungary's first Christian king, István (c. 967–1038), tamed the nomadic, pagan Magyars and established strict laws and the concept of private property. In the late 900s, King Géza of Hungary lost a major battle against the forces of Christian Europe—and realized that he must raise his son Vajk as a Catholic and convert his people, or they would be forcefully driven out of Europe. Vajk took the Christian name István (EESHT-vahn, "Stephen") and was baptized in the year 1000. The reliefs on this statue show the commissioners of the pope crowning St. István, bringing Hungary into the fold of Christendom. This put Hungary on the map as a fully European kingdom, forging alliances that would endure for centuries. Without this pivotal event, Hungarians believe that the Magyar nation would have been lost. A passionate evangelist—more for the survival of his Magyar nation than for the salvation of his people—István beheaded those who wouldn't convert. To make his point perfectly clear, he quartered his reluctant uncle and sent him on four separate, simultaneous tours of the country to show Hungarians that Christianity was a smart choice. Gruesome as he was, István was sainted within 30 years of his death.

• *Directly across from Matthias Church is a charming little street called...*

Szentháromság Utca—Halfway down this street on the right, look for the venerable, recommended **Ruszwurm** café—the oldest in Budapest. Then continue down the street and out to the terrace and appreciate views of the Buda Hills—the "Beverly Hills" of Budapest, draped with orchards, vineyards, and the homes of the wealthiest Budapesters.

• *If you go down the stairs here, then turn right on Lovas utca and walk 50 yards up the street, you'll reach the entrance of the...*

▲"Hospital in the Rock" Secret Military Hospital and Nuclear Bunker (Sziklakórház és Atombunker)—Sprawling beneath Castle Hill is a 25,000-square-foot labyrinthine network of hospital and fallout-shelter corridors built during the mid-20th century. And now, after decades in mothballs, it's newly open to tourists. On the required tour, your guide will lead you through the tunnels to see room after room of perfectly preserved WWII-era medical supplies and equipment, most still in working order. Wax figures engagingly bring the various hospital rooms to life: giant sick ward, operating room, and so on. On your way to the fallout shelter, you'll pass the decontamination showers, and see primitive radiation detectors and communist propaganda directing

comrades how to save themselves in case of capitalist bombs or gas attacks. In the bunker, you'll also tour the various mechanical rooms that ventilated and provided water to this sprawling underground city.

Cost and Hours: 2,000 Ft for 30-min tour of just the hospital, 3,000 Ft for 60-min tour that also includes the bunker—recommended, visits by guided tour only, Tue–Sun 10:00–19:00, English tours at the top of each hour, last tour at 18:00, closed Mon, Lovas utca 4C, district I, mobile 0630-689-8775, www.hospitalintherock.com.

• *Our Castle Hill walk is finished. If you're ready to head back down to the river (and the Víziváros neighborhood), you can make a graceful exit down the big staircase below the Fishermen's Bastion.*

If you'd like to spend more time exploring Castle Hill, poke around the northern part of the hill. In this area, you'll find several interesting sights. Next door to the Matthias Church, the modern ***Hilton Hotel*** *is built around the fragments of a 13th-century Dominican church (to see them, go inside, find the lounge, and look out the window toward Pest). A few blocks farther north stand the remains of* ***St. Mary Magdalene Church,*** *which was destroyed during the Ottoman occupation but whose bell tower has been rebuilt. Around the corner is the dusty* ***Museum of Military History.*** *And along the tree-shaded terrace at the northern tip of the hilltop, look for the* ***Turkish grave*** *of a pasha (Ottoman ruler).*

From the northern end of the hill, you can head out through the Vienna Gate and follow the road downhill to bustling Moszkva tér and its handy Metro stop (M2/red line).

Gellért Hill (Gellérthegy) and Nearby

The hill rising from the Danube just downriver from the castle is Gellért Hill. When King István converted Hungary to Christianity in the year 1000, he brought in Bishop Gellért, a monk from Venice, to tutor his son. But some rebellious Magyars had other ideas. They put the bishop in a barrel, drove long nails in from the outside, and rolled him down this hill...tenderizing him to death. Gellért became the patron saint of Budapest and gave his name to the hill that killed him. Today the hill is a fine place to commune with nature on a hike or jog, followed by a restorative splash in its namesake baths.

Citadella—This strategic, hill-capping fortress was built by the Habsburgs after the 1848 Revolution to keep an eye on their Hungarian subjects. There's not much to do up here (no museum or exhibits), but it's a good destination for an uphill hike, and provides the best panoramic view over all of Budapest.

The hill is crowned by the **Liberation Monument,** featuring a woman holding aloft a palm branch. Locals call it "the lady with the big fish" or "the great bottle opener." The heroic Soviet soldier—

who once inspired the workers with a huge red star from the base of the monument—is now in Memento Park (described later).

Getting There: It's a steep hike up from the river to the Citadella, but bus #27 cuts some time off the trip. Catch the bus along the busy highway Hegyalja út that bisects Buda, at the intersection with Sánc utca (from central Pest, you can get to this stop on bus #78 from Astoria or Ferenciek tere). From Sánc utca, ride bus #27 up to the Búsuló Juhász stop, from which it's still an uphill hike to the fortress.

Cave Church (Sziklatemplom)—Hidden in the hillside on the south end of the hill (across the street from Gellért Hotel) is Budapest's atmospheric cave church—literally burrowed into the rock face. The communists bricked up this church when they came to power, but now it's open for visitors once again (free entry, but closed to sightseers during frequent services).

▲▲Gellért Baths—Located at the famous and once-exclusive Gellért Hotel, right at the Buda end of the Liberty Bridge, this elegant bath complex has long been the city's top choice for a swanky, hedonistic soak. For details, see "Experiences in Budapest," later.

In Pest

Most of Pest's top sights cluster in four neighborhoods: **Leopold Town** and the **Town Center** (together forming the city's "downtown," along the Danube); along **Andrássy út;** and at **Heroes' Square and City Park.** Several other sights are along the **Small Boulevard** (Kiskörút), and along the boulevard called **Üllői út.**

Leopold Town (Lipótváros)

The Parliament building, which dominates Pest's skyline, is the centerpiece of a banking and business district. Called Lipótváros ("Leopold Town"), this area is one of Budapest's most genteel quarters, and features some of the best of Budapest's many monuments. I've linked up the best sights in Leopold Town as a self-guided walk, starting at the grandiose Parliament building.

▲▲Hungarian Parliament (Országház)—The Parliament was built from 1885 to 1902 to celebrate the Hungarian millennium year of 1896. Its elegant frilly spires and riverside location were inspired by its counterpart in London (where the architect who designed it studied). When completed, the Parliament was a striking and cutting-edge example of the mix-and-match Historicist style of the day—just as Frank Gehry's undulating buildings are examples of today's

bold new aesthetic. Like the Hungarian people, this building is at once grandly ambitious and a somewhat motley hodgepodge of various influences—a Neo-Gothic palace topped with a Neo-Renaissance dome, which once had a huge red communist star on top of the tallest spire. Fittingly, it's the city's top icon. The best views of the Parliament are from across the Danube—especially in the late-afternoon sunlight.

Touring the building offers the chance to stroll through one of Budapest's best interiors. On the 45-minute **tour,** you'll first pass through a security checkpoint, then climb up a 96-step staircase. Stops include the monumental entryway, the Hungarian crown (under the ornate gilded dome), and the legislative chamber of the now-disbanded House of Lords. Your guide will explain the history and symbolism of the building's intricate decorations and offer a lesson in the Hungarian parliamentary system. You'll find out why a really good speech was nicknamed a "Havana" by cigar-aficionado parliamentarians.

Cost, Hours, Location: 2,820 Ft, free for EU citizens; English tours usually daily at 10:00, 12:00, and 14:00; Mon–Sat sometimes also at 16:00—but schedule can change, so confirm in advance; Kossuth tér 1–3, district V, M2: Kossuth tér, tel. 1/441-4904, www.parlament.hu.

Getting Tickets: The ticket office opens each day at 8:00 (tickets sold for same-day tours only). On busy days, ticket-buyers line up, and tours can sell out (especially if a tour group has reserved a large block of tickets, which individuals can't do). If your heart is set on getting in, buy your tickets early (for morning tours, I'd try to arrive by 9:00; the line is longest around 10:30). Behind the Parliament, follow signs to the entry marked "X" (slightly right of center as you face the back of the giant building), and find the line at the fence marked *For Buying Tickets.* Wait for the guard to let you enter door X, pay the cashier, and return to the mob to wait for your tour.

• *The vast square behind the Parliament is...*

Kossuth Tér—This square is sprinkled with interesting monuments and packed with Hungarian history—including an **eternal flame** honoring the victims of the 1956 Uprising (near the ticket-buying line for Parliament visits); and, at the far end of the nearby park, a statue of the square's namesake, **Lajos Kossuth,** who led the 1848 Revolution against the Habsburgs. The street that leaves this square behind Kossuth is Falk Miksa utca, Budapest's

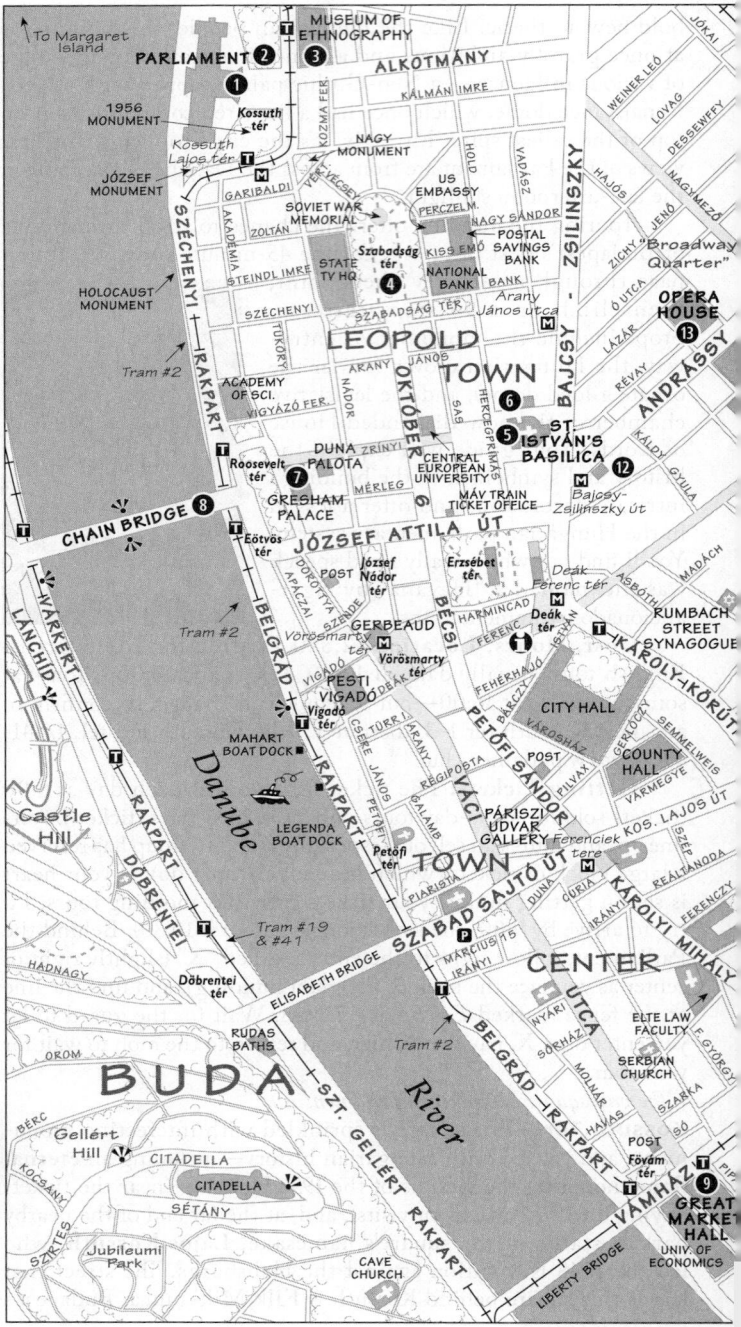
To Margaret Island
PARLIAMENT
MUSEUM OF ETHNOGRAPHY
ALKOTMÁNY
1956 MONUMENT
Kossuth tér
Kossuth Lajos tér
NAGY MONUMENT
JÓZSEF MONUMENT
GARIBALDI
SOVIET WAR MEMORIAL
US EMBASSY
PERCZEL M.
NAGY SÁNDOR
POSTAL SAVINGS BANK
Szabadság tér
STATE TV HQ.
NATIONAL BANK
HOLOCAUST MONUMENT
SZÉCHENYI
SZABADSÁG TÉR
Arany János utca
LEOPOLD TOWN
Tram #2
ACADEMY OF SCI.
VIGYÁZÓ FER.
OKTÓBER 6
BAJCSY - ZSILINSZKY
OPERA HOUSE
ANDRÁSSY
ST. ISTVÁN'S BASILICA
Roosevelt tér
DUNA PALOTA
CENTRAL EUROPEAN UNIVERSITY
GRESHAM PALACE
MÁV TRAIN TICKET OFFICE
Bajcsy-Zsilinszky út
CHAIN BRIDGE
Eötvös tér
JÓZSEF ATTILA ÚT
Erzsébet tér
Deák Ferenc tér
RUMBACH STREET SYNAGOGUE
Tram #2
GERBEAUD
Vörösmarty tér
Deák tér
KÁROLY-KÖRÚT
PESTI VIGADÓ
Vigadó tér
CITY HALL
MAHART BOAT DOCK
Danube
PETŐFI SANDOR UTCA
COUNTY HALL
Castle Hill
LEGENDA BOAT DOCK
PÁRISZI UDVAR GALLERY
Petőfi tér
TOWN
Ferenciek tere
KOS. LAJOS ÚT
KÁROLYI MIHÁLY UTCA
Tram #19 & #41
SZABAD SAJTÓ ÚT
Döbrentei tér
ELISABETH BRIDGE
CENTER
RUDAS BATHS
Tram #2
ELTE LAW FACULTY
SERBIAN CHURCH
BUDA
River
Gellért Hill
CITADELLA
SÉTÁNY
Jubileumi Park
CAVE CHURCH
SZT. GELLÉRT RAKPART
BELGRÁD RAKPART
VÁMHÁZ
POST
Fővám tér
GREAT MARKET HALL
UNIV. OF ECONOMICS
LIBERTY BRIDGE

BUDAPEST

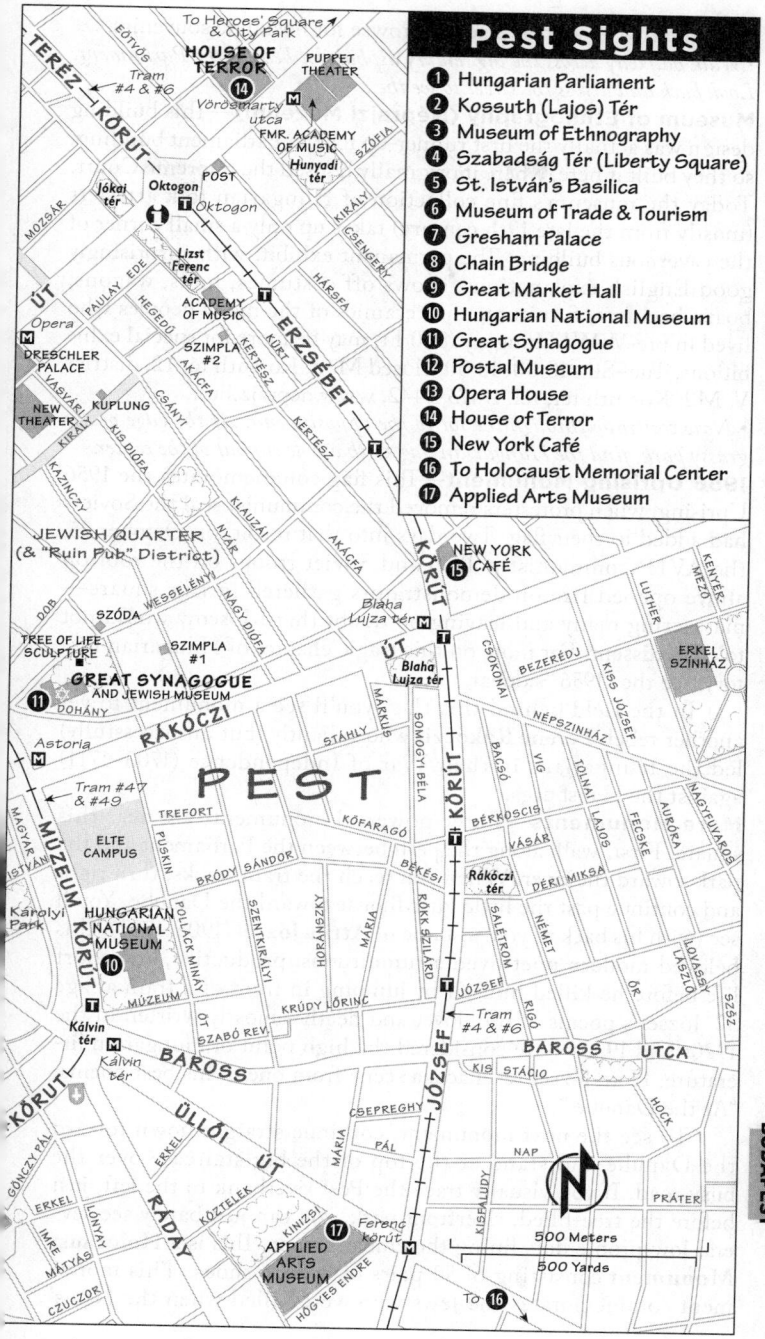
Pest Sights
1 Hungarian Parliament
2 Kossuth (Lajos) Tér
3 Museum of Ethnography
4 Szabadság Tér (Liberty Square)
5 St. István's Basilica
6 Museum of Trade & Tourism
7 Gresham Palace
8 Chain Bridge
9 Great Market Hall
10 Hungarian National Museum
11 Great Synagogue
12 Postal Museum
13 Opera House
14 House of Terror
15 New York Café
16 To Holocaust Memorial Center
17 Applied Arts Museum
To Heroes' Square & City Park
HOUSE OF TERROR
PUPPET THEATER
Tram #4 & #6
Vörösmarty utca
FMR. ACADEMY OF MUSIC
Hunyadi tér
POST
Jókai tér
Oktogon
Lizst Ferenc tér
ACADEMY OF MUSIC
Opera
DRESCHLER PALACE
SZIMPLA #2
NEW THEATER
KUPLUNG
JEWISH QUARTER (& "Ruin Pub" District)
NEW YORK CAFÉ
Blaha Lujza tér
TREE OF LIFE SCULPTURE
SZIMPLA #1
GREAT SYNAGOGUE AND JEWISH MUSEUM
ERKEL SZÍNHÁZ
Astoria
Tram #47 & #49
PEST
ELTE CAMPUS
Rákóczi tér
Károlyi Park
HUNGARIAN NATIONAL MUSEUM
Kálvin tér
Tram #4 & #6
BAROSS UTCA
APPLIED ARTS MUSEUM
Ferenc körút
To
500 Meters
500 Yards
TERÉZ KÖRÚT
ERZSÉBET ÚT
RÁKÓCZI ÚT
MÚZEUM KÖRÚT
JÓZSEF KÖRÚT
ÜLLŐI ÚT
RÁDAY
BUDAPEST

"antique row"—a great place to browse for nostalgic souvenirs.

• *Walk halfway across the big, empty asphalt lot behind the Parliament. Look back and across the street to see the...*

Museum of Ethnography (Néprajzi Múzeum)—This building design was actually the first runner-up for the Parliament building, so they built it here, where it originally housed the Supreme Court. Today the museum's fine collection of Hungarian folk artifacts (mostly from the late 19th century) takes up only a small corner of the cavernous building. The permanent exhibit, with surprisingly good English explanations, shows off costumes, tools, wagons, boats, beehives, furniture, and ceramics of the many peoples who lived in pre-WWI Hungary (800 Ft, may be more for special exhibitions, Tue–Sun 10:00–18:00, closed Mon, Kossuth tér 12, district V, M2: Kossuth tér, tel. 1/473-2442, www.neprajz.hu).

• *Now continue through the lot to the opposite end. At the edge of the grassy park, find the Hungarian flag with a hole cut out of the center.*

1956 Uprising Monument—This flag commemorates the 1956 Uprising, when protesters removed the communist seal the Soviets had added to their flag. Two days into that revolt, on October 25, the ÁVH (communist police) and Soviet troops on the rooftop above opened fire on demonstrators gathered in this square—massacring many and leaving no doubt that Moscow would not tolerate dissent. For more on this tragic chapter of Hungarian history, see the "1956" sidebar.

In the field behind this flag, you'll see a monument to yet another rebel: **Ferenc Rákóczi,** who valiantly (but unsuccessfully) led the Hungarians in their War of Independence (1703–1711) against the Habsburgs.

More Monuments—Three powerful monuments are near this square. First, walk along the path between the Parliament and the park toward the river. When you reach the tram tracks, turn right and continue past the little guardhouse toward the Danube. You'll see (with his back to you) a statue of **Attila József** (1905–1937). This beloved modern poet lived a tumultuous, productive, and short life before he killed himself by jumping in front of a train at age 32. József's poems of life, love, and death—mostly written in the 1920s and 1930s—are considered the high point of Hungarian literature. Here József re-enacts a scene from one of his best poems, "At the Danube."

To see the next monument, continue straight down toward the Danube and stand at the top of the big staircase over the busy road. If you visually trace the Pest riverbank to the left, just before the tree-filled, riverfront park, you can just barely see several low-profile dots lining the embankment. This is a **Holocaust Monument** consisting of 50 pairs of bronze shoes. This monument commemorates the Jews who were killed when the Nazis'

puppet government, the Arrow Cross, came to power in Hungary in 1944. While many Jews were sent to concentration camps, the Arrow Cross massacred some of them right here, shooting them and letting their bodies fall into the Danube.

Backtrack past Attila József, cross the tram tracks, and walk along the ugly building (with an entrance to the Metro) up to the back corner of Kossuth tér. Across the street in a little park (at Vértanúk tere), you'll see a monument to **Imre Nagy** (EEM-ray nodge, 1896–1958). When the 1956 Uprising broke out on October 23, Imre Nagy was drafted (reluctantly, some say) to become the head of the movement to soften the severity of the communist regime. Because he was a communist insider, it briefly seemed that Nagy might hold the key to finding a middle path between the suffocating totalitarian model of Moscow and the freedom of the West (represented by the bridge he's standing on). But the optimism was short-lived. The Soviets violently put down the uprising, arrested and sham-tried Nagy, executed him, and buried him face-down in an unmarked grave. The regime forced Hungary to forget about Nagy. But the Hungarians didn't oblige—and today, thanks to this monument, Nagy keeps a watchful eye on today's lawmakers in the Parliament across the way.

• *Go up the diagonal street behind Nagy, called Vécsey utca. After just one block, you emerge into...*

▲Szabadság Tér (Liberty Square)—This end of the square is dominated by a stout obelisk, a **Soviet War Memorial** commemorating "Liberation Day": April 4, 1945, when the Soviets officially forced the Nazis out of Hungary. As a very rare reminder of the Soviet days—you almost never see hammers-and-sickles in the streets of Hungary anymore—it has often been defaced, which is why a fence surrounds it.

• *Walk around the memorial and stand in the middle of Szabadság tér. Turn with your back to the obelisk, and look down to the far end of the square.*

1956

The year 1956 is etched into the Hungarian psyche. In that year, the people of Budapest staged the first major uprising against the communist regime. It also marked the first time that the Soviets implicitly acknowledged, in brutally putting down the uprising, that the people of Eastern Europe were not "communist by choice."

The seeds of revolution were sown with the death of a tyrant: Josef Stalin passed away on March 5, 1953. Suddenly the choke-hold that Moscow had held on its satellite states loosened. During this time of "de-Stalinization," Hungarian premier Imre Nagy presided over two years of mild reform, before his political opponents (and Moscow) became nervous and demoted him.

In 1955, Austria declared its neutrality in the Cold War. This thrust Hungary to the front line of the Iron Curtain, and raised the stakes both for Hungarians who wanted freedom and for Soviets who wanted to preserve their buffer zone. When Stalin's successor Nikita Khrushchev condemned Stalin's crimes in a "secret speech" to communist leaders in February of 1956, it emboldened the Soviet Bloc's dissidents. A workers' strike in Poznań, Poland, in October inspired Hungarians to follow their example.

On October 23, 1956, the Hungarian uprising began. A student union group gathered in Budapest at 15:00 to articulate a list of 16 demands against the communist regime. Then they marched toward Parliament, their number gradually swelling. One protester defiantly cut the Soviet-style insignia out of the center of the Hungarian flag, which would become the uprising's symbol.

By nightfall, some 200,000 protestors filled Kossuth tér behind Parliament, calling for Imre Nagy, the one communist leader they believed could bring change. Nagy finally appeared around 21:00. Ever the pragmatic politician, he implored patience. Following the speech, a large band of protesters took matters into their own hands, marched to City Park, and tore down the hated Stalin statue that stood there (see page 537).

Another group went to the National Radio building to read their demands on the air. The ÁVH (communist police) refused, and eventually opened fire on the protestors. The peaceful protests evolved into an armed insurrection, as frightened civilians gathered weapons and supplies.

Overnight, Moscow decided to intervene. Budapesters awoke on October 24 to find Red Army troops occupying their city. That morning, Imre Nagy—who had just been promoted again to prime minister—promised reforms and tried to keep a lid on the simmering discontent.

The next day, October 25, a huge crowd gathered on Kossuth tér behind the Parliament to hear from Nagy. In the hubbub, shots rang out, Hungarian and Soviet soldiers opened fire on the (mostly unarmed) crowd, and at least 70 protesters were killed and more than 100 injured.

The Hungarians fought back with an improvised guerilla resistance. They made use of any guns they could get their hands on, as well as Molotov cocktails, to strike against the Soviet occupiers. Many adolescents (the celebrated "Pest Youth") participated. The fighting tore apart the city, and some of the fallen were buried in impromptu graves in city parks.

Political infighting in Moscow paralyzed the Soviet response, and an uneasy ceasefire fell over Budapest. For 10 tense days, it appeared that the Soviets might allow Nagy to push through some reforms. Nagy, a firmly entrenched communist, had always envisioned a less repressive regime...but within limits. While he was at first reluctant to take on the mantle of the uprising's leadership, he gradually began to echo what he was hearing on the streets. He called for free elections, the abolishment of the ÁVH, the withdrawal of Soviet troops, and (crucially) Hungary's secession from the Warsaw Pact.

But when the uprisers attacked and killed ÁVH officers and communist leaders in Budapest, it bolstered the case of the Moscow hardliners. On November 4, the Red Army launched a brutal counterattack in Budapest that left the rebels reeling. At 5:20 that morning, Imre Nagy's voice came over the radio to beg the world for assistance. Later that morning, he sought asylum at the Yugoslav Embassy across the street from City Park. He was never seen alive in public again.

János Kádár—an ally of Nagy's who was palatable to the uprisers, yet firmly loyal to Moscow—was installed as prime minister. The fighting dragged on for about another week, but the uprising was eventually crushed. By the end, 2,500 Hungarians and more than 700 Soviets were dead, and 20,000 Hungarians were injured. Communist authorities arrested more than 15,000 people, of whom at least 200 were executed (including Imre Nagy). Anyone who had participated in the uprising was blacklisted; fearing this and other forms of retribution, some 200,000 Hungarians fled to the West.

Though the 1956 Uprising met a tragic end, within a few years Kádár did succeed in softening the regime, and the milder, so-called "goulash communism" emerged. And today, even though the communists are long gone, the legacy of 1956 pervades the Hungarian consciousness. Some Budapest buildings are still pock-marked with bullet holes from '56, and many of the Hungarians who fled the country in that year still have not returned. October 23 remains a major Hungarian holiday. In 2006, Budapest commemorated the 50th anniversary of its uprising.

On the right is the giant **Hungarian State Television** building (formerly the stock exchange). This is home to MTV—not music television, but Magyar television. The genteel open-air **café** in the middle of the park is an inviting place for a coffee break. Across the square (on the left), the yellow corner building is the **US Embassy.** This is where Cardinal József Mindszenty holed up for 15 years during the Cold War to evade arrest by the communist authorities.

• *Next we're headed for Perczel Mór utca, the street next to the US Embassy—but you'll have to detour a bit to the left (and tiptoe around some barricades) to get there. After one block on Perczel Mór utca, turn right onto Hold utca. You'll pass a* ***market hall*** *(on the left), then—on the right—Ödön Lechner's elaborate* ***Postal Savings Bank,*** *attached by a skyway to the* ***National Bank of Hungary.*** *Continue two blocks straight ahead up Hercegprimás utca. You'll emerge into a broad plaza in front of Budapest's biggest Catholic church...*

▲St. István's Basilica (Szent István Bazilika)—The church is only about 100 years old—like most Budapest landmarks, it was built around the millennial celebrations of 1896. Designed by three architects over more than 50 years, St. István's is particularly eclectic. Each architect had a favorite style: Neoclassical, Neo-Renaissance, Neo-Baroque. Construction was delayed for a while when the giant dome collapsed midway through. Though it looks like a major landmark and is packed with tour groups, the church isn't that compelling inside. Step into the dark but recently renovated interior and you'll see not Jesus, but St. István (Stephen), Hungary's first Christian king, glowing above the high altar.

The church's main claim to fame is the **"holy right hand" of St. István.** The sacred fist—a somewhat grotesque, 1,000-year-old withered stump—is in a jeweled box in the chapel to the left of the main altar (follow signs for *Szent Jobb Kápolna,* chapel often closed). Pop in a 200-Ft coin for two minutes of light, and ask the guard for tips on taking the best photo. Posted information describes the hand's unlikely journey to this spot. On your way out, in the back-right corner of the church, you'll find a small exhibit about the building's history.

The church also has a skippable **treasury** and a panoramic **observation deck.** While the views over Budapest's rooftops are pretty distant (and disappointing without a good zoom lens), it offers a good sense of the sprawl of the city. You have various options: You can walk up the entire way (302 steps); or you can take an elevator to midlevel (with WCs), where you can follow signs to another elevator (plus 42 steps) or climb 137 steps to the top.

Cost, Hours, Location: Interior—free, treasury—400 Ft, Mon–Fri 9:00–17:00, Sat 9:00–13:00 (but often closed Sat in summer for weddings), Sun 13:00–17:00; Observation deck—500 Ft, daily June–Aug 9:30–18:00, April–May 10:00–16:30, Sept–Oct 10:00–17:30, closed Nov–March; Szent István tér, district V, M1: Bajcsy-Zsilinszky út or M3: Arany János utca.

• *Hiding around the left side of the basilica is the...*

Hungarian Museum of Trade and Tourism (Magyar Kereskedelmi és Vendéglátóipari Múzeum)—This museum takes a nostalgic look at workaday 19th-century Pest commerce. Recently re-opened in a stately former bank building, the museum has a small permanent collection (one room with dusty old artifacts and minimal information), and generally well-presented temporary exhibits offering a peek into the fancy hotels, restaurants, and coffeehouses of the day (600 Ft, Wed–Mon 11:00–19:00, closed Tue, around to the left as you face St. István's Basilica at Szent István tér 15, district V, M1: Bajcsy-Zsilinszky út or M3: Arany János utca, tel. 1/375-6249, www.mkvm.hu).

• *From here, you're very close to the boulevard called* ***Andrássy út,*** *which leads to various interesting sights, including the Opera House, House of Terror, and City Park (all described later). To get there, walk around the right side of the basilica, and turn right on busy Bajcsy-Zsilinszky út; Andrássy út begins across the street, on your left.*

But for now, consider heading to the Danube for a good look at the mighty Chain Bridge. Walk straight ahead from St. István's main staircase down ***Zrínyi Utca.*** *This recently pedestrianized people zone passes (on the right)* ***Central European University,*** *a graduate school largely funded by Hungarian-American George Soros, and its good CEU Bookshop (recommended under "Helpful Hints," earlier). Later, after crossing Nádor utca, on the left you'll find* ***Duna Palota,*** *a venue and ticket office for Hungária Koncert's popular tourist shows (described later, under "Entertainment in Budapest").*

Zrínyi utca dead-ends at the big traffic circle called ***Roosevelt tér.*** *Turn left and walk a half-block to the entrance (on the left) of the...*

Gresham Palace—This was Budapest's first building in the popular Historicist style, and also incorporates elements of Art Nouveau. Budapest boomed at a time when architectural eclecticism—mashing together bits and pieces of different styles—was in vogue. But because much of the city's construction was compressed

into a short window of time, even these disparate styles enjoy an unusual harmony. Damaged in World War II, the building was an eyesore for decades. (Legend has it that an aging local actress refused to move out, so developers had to wait for her to pass on before they could reclaim the building.) In 1999, the Gresham Palace was meticulously restored to its former glory. Even if you can't afford to stay here (see "Sleeping in Budapest," later), saunter into the lobby and absorb the gorgeous details. For example, not only did they have to re-create the unique decorative tiles—they had to rebuild the original machines that made the tiles.

• *Grandly spanning the Danube from this spot is Budapest's best bridge...*

Chain Bridge (Széchenyi Lánchíd)—One of the world's great bridges connects Pest's Roosevelt tér and Buda's Adam Clark tér. This historic, iconic bridge, guarded by lions (symbolizing power), is Budapest's most enjoyable and convenient bridge to cross on foot.

Until the mid-19th century, only pontoon barges spanned the Danube between Buda and Pest. In the winter, the pontoons had to be pulled in, leaving locals to rely on ferries (in good weather) or a frozen river. People often walked across the frozen Danube, only to get stuck on the other side during a thaw, with nothing to do but wait for another cold snap.

Count István Széchenyi was stranded for a week trying to get to his father's funeral. After missing it, Széchenyi commissioned Budapest's first permanent bridge—which was also a major symbolic step toward another of Széchenyi's pet causes, the unification of Buda and Pest. The Chain Bridge was built by Scotsman Adam Clark between 1842 and 1849, and it immediately became an important symbol of Budapest. Széchenyi—a man of the Enlightenment—charged both commoners and nobles a toll for crossing his bridge, making it an emblem of equality in those tense times. Like all of the city's bridges, the Chain Bridge was destroyed by the Nazis at the end of World War II, but was quickly rebuilt.

• *As you look out to the Danube from here, to the right you can see the tip of...*

▲Margaret Island (Margitsziget)—In the Middle Ages, this island was known as the "Isle of Hares." In the 13th century, a desperate King Béla IV swore that if God were to deliver Hungary from the invading Tatars, he would dedicate his youngest daughter Margaret to the Church. Hungary was spared...and Margaret was shipped to a nunnery here. But, the story goes, Margaret embraced her new life as a castaway nun, and later refused her father's efforts to force her into a politically expedient marriage with a Bohemian king. She became St. Margaret of Hungary, and this island was named for her.

Today, Margaret Island is Budapest's playground. Budapesters come to relax in this huge, leafy park...in the midst of the busy city, but so far away (no cars are allowed on the island—just public buses). The island rivals City Park as the best spot in town for strolling, jogging, biking, and people-watching. Rounding out the island's attractions are easy bike rental options (at Bringóhintó, with branches at both ends of the island), an iconic old water tower, the remains of Margaret's convent, a rose garden, a game farm, thermal baths, and a "musical fountain" that performs to the strains of Hungarian folk tunes.

Getting There: Margaret Bridge—which connects the island to Buda and Pest—is undergoing an extensive restoration through at least late 2010. Depending on when you visit, the bridge may be closed to the trams and buses listed here. Even when the bridge is closed to transit, pedestrians should still be able to walk to the island. Inquire locally for the best approach.

When things are running normally, **bus** #26 begins at Nyugati/Western train station, crosses the Margaret Bridge, then drives up through the middle of the island—allowing visitors to easily get from one end to the other (3–6/hr). **Trams** #4 and #6, which circulate around the Great Boulevard, cross the Margaret Bridge and stop at the southern tip of the island, a short walk from some of the attractions. From Vigadó tér (along the Pest embankment), you can catch a Mahart shuttle **boat** to the island (see "Tours in Budapest—By Boat," earlier).

• *If you'd like to head for the heart of Pest, Vörösmarty tér (and the sights listed next), it's just two long blocks away: Turn left out of the Gresham Palace, and walk straight on Dorottya utca.*

Pest Town Center (Belváros)

Pest's Belváros ("Inner Town") is its gritty urban heart—simultaneously its most beautiful and ugliest district. Here you'll see fancy facades, some of Pest's best views from the Danube embankment, genteel old coffee houses that offer a whiff of the city's Golden Age, inviting oasis parks tucked between densely populated streets, and a cavernous, colorful market hall filled with Hungarian goodies.

But you'll also experience crowds, grime, and pungent smells like nowhere else in Budapest. Remember: This is a city in transition. Within a decade, all of those rough edges will be sanded off...and tourists like you will be nostalgic for the "authentic" old days.

▲Vörösmarty Tér—The central square of the Town Center, dominated by a giant statue of the revered Romantic poet Mihály Vörösmarty, is the hub of Pest sightseeing.

At the north end of the square is the landmark **Gerbeaud** café and pastry shop. Between the World Wars, the well-to-do ladies of Budapest would meet here after shopping their way up Váci utca. Today it's still *the* meeting point in Budapest (for tourists, at least). Consider stepping inside to appreciate the elegant old decor, or for a cup of coffee and a slice of cake (but meals here are overpriced—described later, under "Eating in Budapest").

The yellow **M1 Metro stop** between the Vörösmarty statue and Gerbeaud is the entrance to the shallow *Földalatti,* or "underground"—the first subway on the Continent (built for the Hungarian millennial celebration in 1896). Today, it still carries passengers to Andrássy út sights, running under that street all the way to City Park.

• *Extending straight ahead from Vörösmarty tér is a broad, bustling, pedestrianized shopping street called...*

Váci Utca—Dating from 1810–1850, Váci utca (VAHT-see OOT-zah) is one of the oldest streets of Pest. This has long been the street where the elite of Pest would go shopping, then strut their stuff for their neighbors on an evening promenade. Today, the tourists do the strutting here—and the Hungarians go to American-style shopping malls.

This boulevard—Budapest's tourism artery—was a dreamland for Eastern Bloc residents back in the 1980s. It was here that they fantasized about what it might be like to be free, while drooling over Nikes, Adidas, and Big Macs before any of these "Western evils" were introduced elsewhere in the Warsaw Pact region. In fact, partway down the street (on the right, at Régi Posta utca) is the first McDonald's behind the Iron Curtain, where people from all over the Eastern Bloc flocked to dine. Since you had to wait in a long line—stretching around the block—to get a burger, it wasn't "fast food"...but at least it was "West food."

Ironically, this street—once prized by Hungarians and other Eastern Europeans because it felt so Western—is what many Western tourists today mistakenly think is the "real Budapest."

Visitors mesmerized by this people-friendly stretch of souvenir stands, Internet cafés, and upscale boutiques are likely to miss some more interesting and authentic areas just a block or two away. Don't fall for this trap. You could have a fun and fulfilling trip to this city without setting foot on Váci utca.

• *For a more appealing people zone than Váci utca, detour from Vörösmarty tér a block toward the river, to the inviting...*

Danube Promenade (Dunakorzó)—Some of the best views in Budapest are from this walkway facing Castle Hill—especially this stretch, between the white Elisabeth Bridge (left) and the iconic Chain Bridge (right). This is a favorite place to promenade *(korzó)*, strolling aimlessly and greeting friends.

Dominating this part of the promenade is the Neo-Romantic-style **Pesti Vigadó**—built in the 1880s, and today undergoing a thorough renovation. Charmingly, the word *vigadó*—used to describe a concert hall—literally means "joyous place." In front is a playful statue of **a girl with her dog,** which captures the fun-loving spirit along this drag. At the gap in the railing, notice the platform to catch **tram #2,** which goes frequently in each direction along the promenade—a handy and scenic way to connect riverside sights in Pest. (You can ride it to the right, to the Parliament; or to the left, to the Great Market Hall.)

About 20 yards to the right, find the little statue wearing a jester's hat. She's playing on the railing with the castle behind her. The ***Little Princess*** is one of Budapest's cherished symbols and a favorite photo-op for tourists. While many of the city's monuments have interesting back-stories, this one is an exception: It's just whimsical and fun.

Look to the riverfront below. Lining the **embankment** are several long boats: Some are excursion boats for sightseeing trips up and down the Danube, while others are overpriced (but scenic) restaurants. If you're interested in taking a cruise—which is especially pleasant at night—you could cross the road here (using the tram underpass 20 yards to the left), then walk 100 yards downriver (farther left) to the Danube Legenda boat dock. For details on the cruises, see "Tours in Budapest—By Boat," earlier.

• *From here, both the promenade and Váci utca cut south through the Town Center. At the end of this zone is one of Budapest's top attractions, the Great Market Hall. Between here and there are the next two sights. While Váci utca is the most direct route, use your map to navigate the side streets in this area, and to locate these two potentially hard-to-find escapes.*

Párisi Udvar Gallery—This "Parisian Courtyard" is the grandest of Pest's many hidden galleries, once used for elegant shopping, now faded and largely unused. But first you have to find it: It's on the big square called Ferenciek tere, which is bisected by a busy road, about halfway between Vörösmarty tér and the Great Market Hall; you can enter either at Kossuth Lajos út 11, or around the corner at Petőfi Sándor utca 2.

Once inside, enjoy the delicate woodwork, fine mosaics that glitter evocatively in the low light, and breathtaking stained-glass dome. It's remarkable that such a beautiful space sits ignored, just a couple of blocks from the main shopping street. While many of the storefronts inside are abandoned, a few are still alive and kicking (including a bookstore that sells English guidebooks). This place is a reminder that if you only experience what's on the main streets in Budapest, you'll miss a big part of the story.

Károlyi Park (Károlyi Kert)—This delightful, flower-filled oasis offers the perfect break from loud and gritty urban Pest. Once the private garden of the aristocratic Károlyi family from eastern Hungary (whose mansion it's behind), it's now a public park beloved by people who live, work, and go to school in this neighborhood. The park is filled with tulips in the spring, palm trees in the summer, and rich colors in the fall. On a sunny summer day, locals escape here to read books, gossip with neighbors, or simply lie in the sun. Many schools are nearby. Teenagers hang out here after school, while younger kids enjoy the playground. You'll find the park two blocks southeast of Ferenciek tere and the gallery described above; it's a block off Károlyi Mihály utca, to the left up Ferenczy István utca.

▲▲Great Market Hall (Nagyvásárcsarnok)—"Great" indeed is this gigantic marketplace. The Great Market Hall has somehow succeeded in keeping local shoppers happy, even as it's evolved into one of the city's top tourist attractions. Goose liver, embroidered tablecloths, golden Tokaji

Aszú wine, pickled peppers, communist-kitsch T-shirts, patriotic green-white-and-red flags, kid-pleasing local candy bars, and paprika of every level of spiciness...if it's Hungarian, you'll find it here (Mon 6:00–17:00, Tue–Fri 6:00–18:00, Sat 6:00–15:00, closed Sun, Fővám körút 1–3, district IX, M3: Kálvin tér).

This market hall (along with four others) was built—like so much of Budapest—around the millennial celebration year of 1896. Appreciate the colorful Zsolnay tiles lining the roof—frostproof and harder than stone, these were an integral part of the Hungarian national style that emerged in the late 19th century.

Step inside the market and get your bearings: The cavernous interior features three levels. The ground floor has produce stands, bakeries, butcher stalls, heaps of paprika, goose liver, and salamis. Upstairs are stand-up eateries and souvenirs. And in the basement are a supermarket, a fish market, and piles of pickles.

Stroll down the "main drag," enjoying a combination of produce stands and vendors selling authentic Hungarian products. About halfway down, detour to the left to find the **Csárdi és Csárdi** stall (near the outer wall), where you can sample both types of paprika: sweet (*édes,* used for flavor) and hot (*csipós,* used sparingly to add some kick). Note the difference, choose your favorite, and buy some to take home (for more information, see "Paprika Primer" on page 465).

After you've worked your way to the far end of the hall, take the escalator to the **upper level.** You're immersed in a world of Hungarian **souvenirs** (for tips, see "Shopping in Budapest," page 560). The left wall (as you face the front) is lined with fun, cheap, stand-up, Hungarian-style fast-food joints and six-stool pubs. About two-thirds of the way along the hall (after the second bridge), the **Lángos** stand is the best eatery in the market, serving up the deep-fried snack called *lángos*—similar to elephant ears, but savory rather than sweet. The most typical version is *sajtos tejfölös*—with sour cream and cheese. You can also add garlic *(fokhagyma).* The **Fakanál Étterem** cafeteria above the main entrance is handy but pricey.

For a less glamorous look at the market, head down the escalators to the **basement.** In addition to the handy supermarket down here, the basement is pungent with tanks of still-swimming carp, catfish, and perch, and piles of pickles (along the left side). Stop at one of the pickle stands and take a look. Hungarians pickle just about anything: peppers and cukes, of course, but also cauliflower, cabbage, beets, tomatoes, garlic, and so on. Vendors are usually happy to give you a sample; consider picking up a colorful jar of mixed pickled veggies for your picnic.

• *The area in front of the Great Market Hall is a sort of transportation hub for this part of Budapest. Tram #2 runs from under the green bridge along the Danube directly back to Vigadó tér (at the promenade by Vörösmarty tér), the Chain Bridge, and the Parliament. Trams #47 and #49 (catch them directly in front of the market) zip to the right around the Small Boulevard to the Hungarian National Museum and, beyond that, the Great Synagogue (both described next)—or you can simply walk around the Small Boulevard to reach these sights in about 10–15 minutes. The green bridge leads straight to Gellért Hotel, with its famous hot-springs bath, at the foot of Gellért Hill (Gellért Baths described under "Experiences in Budapest," later).*

Along the Small Boulevard (Kiskörút)

These two major sights are along the Small Boulevard, between the Liberty Bridge/Great Market Hall and Deák tér.

▲Hungarian National Museum (Magyar Nemzeti Múzeum)—One of Budapest's biggest museums features all manner of Hungarian historic bric-a-brac, from the Paleolithic age to a more recent infestation of dinosaurs (the communists). Artifacts are explained by good, if dry, English descriptions. The first floor (one flight down from the entry) focuses on the Carpathian Basin in the pre-Magyar days, with ancient items and Roman remains. The basement features a lapidarium, with medieval tombstones and more Roman ruins. Upstairs, 20 rooms provide a historic overview from the arrival of the Magyars in 896 up to the 1989 revolution. The museum adds substance to your understanding of Hungary's story—but it helps to have a pretty firm foundation first (read "Hungarian History" on page 455). The most engaging part is room 20, with an exhibit on the communist era, featuring both pro- and anti-Party propaganda. The exhibit ends with video footage of the 1989 end of communism—demonstrations, monumental parliament votes, and a final farewell to the last Soviet troops leaving Hungarian

soil. Another uprising—the 1848 Revolution against Habsburg rule—was declared from the steps of this impressive Neoclassical building (1,000 Ft, audioguide-750 Ft/hr, Tue–Sun 10:00–18:00, closed Mon, last entry 30 min before closing, near Great Market Hall at Múzeum körút 14–16, district VIII, M3: Kálvin tér, tel. 1/327-7773, www.hnm.hu).

▲▲Great Synagogue (Zsinagóga)—Also called the "Dohány Street Synagogue," Budapest's gorgeous synagogue is the biggest in Europe and the second biggest in the world (after one in New York City). With its ornately decorated interior, attached museum offering a concise lesson in the Jewish faith, and evocative memorial garden (with its weeping-willow *Tree of Life* sculpture), it's well worth a visit.

Cost and Hours: 1,600 Ft for Great Synagogue and Jewish Museum, *Tree of Life* and memorial garden are always free; April–Oct Mon–Thu 10:00–17:00, Fri 10:00–15:00, Sun 10:00–18:00; Nov–March Mon–Thu 10:00–15:00, Fri and Sun 10:00–14:00; always closed Sat and Jewish holidays, last entry 30 minutes before closing, Dohány utca 2, district VII, M2: Astoria plus a five-minute walk, tel. 01/344-5131, www.aviv.hu.

Tours: Aviv Travel, with a well-marked kiosk just outside the synagogue entrance, leads tours of the synagogue, museum, and related sights. You have three options: A quick 45-minute tour combines the Great Synagogue and the *Tree of Life* (1,900 Ft). A longer 80-minute tour covers the above, plus a guided visit to the synagogue's museum (2,250 Ft). And the deluxe 90-minute version covers the Great Synagogue, *Tree of Life,* and the nearby synagogue on Rumbach Street, but not the museum (2,600 Ft). Since these tours include admission, you're paying a small price for the guiding—making this an affordable way to really understand the place (tours leave every 30 min April–Oct Mon–Thu and Sun 10:30–16:30, Nov–March until 13:30; year-round Fri at 10:30, 11:30, 12:30, and 13:00; no Sat tours).

➲ Self-Guided Tour: While the tours described above are worthwhile, the following commentary covers the basics.

First, go through the security checkpoint at the entrance. You can buy tickets for the synagogue interior and the museum at the end of the courtyard on the right. Then visit the sights in the following order. (Note that you can visit the *Tree of Life* and memorial garden even if you don't buy a ticket for the synagogue. Or, if the synagogue is closed, go around left side to view the monument through a fence.)

1. Great Synagogue: Before going inside, check out the synagogue's striking **facade,** and consider the rich history of the building and the people it represents: The synagogue was built in 1859 just outside what was then the city wall (where the Small Boulevard ring road is today). This was a time when Pest's Jewish community wished to prove their worth, and to demonstrate how well-integrated they were with the greater community. Building this new synagogue was an important step in impressing their Catholic neighbors. The two tall towers (designed to evoke the Temple of Solomon in Jerusalem) and the rosette (rose window) helped the synagogue resemble Christian churches of the time.

Now step **inside.** (Men will need to cover their heads, and women their shoulders; loaner yarmulkes and scarves are available at the door.) Notice that it really feels like a church with the symbols switched—with a basilica floor plan, three naves, two pulpits, and even a pipe organ. The Moorish-flavored decor—which looks almost Oriental—is a sign of the Historicist style of the time, which borrowed eclectic elements from past styles. Specifically, it evokes how Jewish culture flourished among the Sephardic Jews of Iberia. In the ark, behind the burgundy curtain, 25 original Torah scrolls are kept. Catholic priests hid these scrolls during World War II (burying them temporarily in a cemetery). The two-tiered balconies on the sides were originally for women, who worshipped separately from the men.

Ponder this building's recent history: While it survived World War II, the Great Synagogue sat neglected for 40 years. But since the thawing of communism, Hungarian Jews have taken a renewed interest in their heritage. In 1990, this synagogue was painstakingly restored, partly with financial support from Tony Curtis, an American actor of Hungarian-Jewish origin (he and his daughter Jamie Lee Curtis continue to support these causes today). Other people of Hungarian-Jewish descent include big names from every walk of life: Harry Houdini (born Erich Weisz), Elie Wiesel, Joseph Pulitzer, Estée Lauder, Goldie Hawn, Peter Lorre, and Eva and Zsa Zsa Gabor.

• *When you're finished in here, exit through the main doors, turn right, and go down the passageway to the right (across from the security checkpoint, past the gift shop).*

2. *Tree of Life* and Memorial Garden: Behind the synagogue is the ***Tree of Life,*** sculpted by renowned artist Imre Varga. The willow makes an upside-down menorah, and each of the 4,000

metal leaves is etched with the name of a Holocaust victim. In the center of the courtyard is a symbolic **grave of Raoul Wallenberg.** He was a humanitarian and diplomat who came here from Sweden to do what he could to rescue Hungary's Jews from the Nazis.

• *Go back out the way you entered. Back at the security checkpoint, turn right, go inside the building, and climb the stairs to the...*

3. Jewish Museum (Zsidó Múzeum): This small but informative museum illuminates the Jewish faith, with artifacts and succinct but engaging English explanations. You'll find descriptions of rituals and holidays, from Rosh Hashanah and Yom Kippur to Passover and Chanukah. The exhibit also explains ancient symbols (prayer shawls, the mezuzah, etc.) and traces the Jewish lifeline from birth to marriage to death. The final room holds a small exhibit about the Holocaust, with lots of old photos and newspaper clippings. Stairs lead down to a small Holocaust memorial. (For more information about this tragic chapter of the Hungarian Jewish experience, don't miss the outstanding Holocaust Memorial Center, described on page 539)

Andrássy Út

Connecting downtown Pest to City Park, Andrássy út is Budapest's main boulevard, lined with plane trees, shops, theaters, cafés, and locals living well. Budapesters like to think of Andrássy út as the Champs-Elysées and Broadway rolled into one. While that's a stretch, it is a good place to stroll, get a feel for today's urban Pest, and visit a few top attractions (most notably the Opera House and the House of Terror).

I've arranged these sights in the order you'll reach them if you walk up the boulevard from where it begins, near Deák tér. The handy M1/yellow Metro line runs every couple of minutes just under the street, making it easy to skip several blocks ahead, or to backtrack (stops marked by yellow signs).

• *Near the Bajcsy-Zsilinszky Metro stop at the beginning of Andrássy út, on the right side of the street, look for the red mailboxes flanking the entrance (at #3, dial 10 to get inside) to the...*

▲Postal Museum (Postamúzeum)—This quirky and unexpectedly enjoyable museum, in a fine old apartment from Budapest's Golden Age, features a collection of postal artifacts. You'll see post office coats of arms, 100-year-old postal furniture, antique telephone boxes, historic mailman uniforms, and all manner of

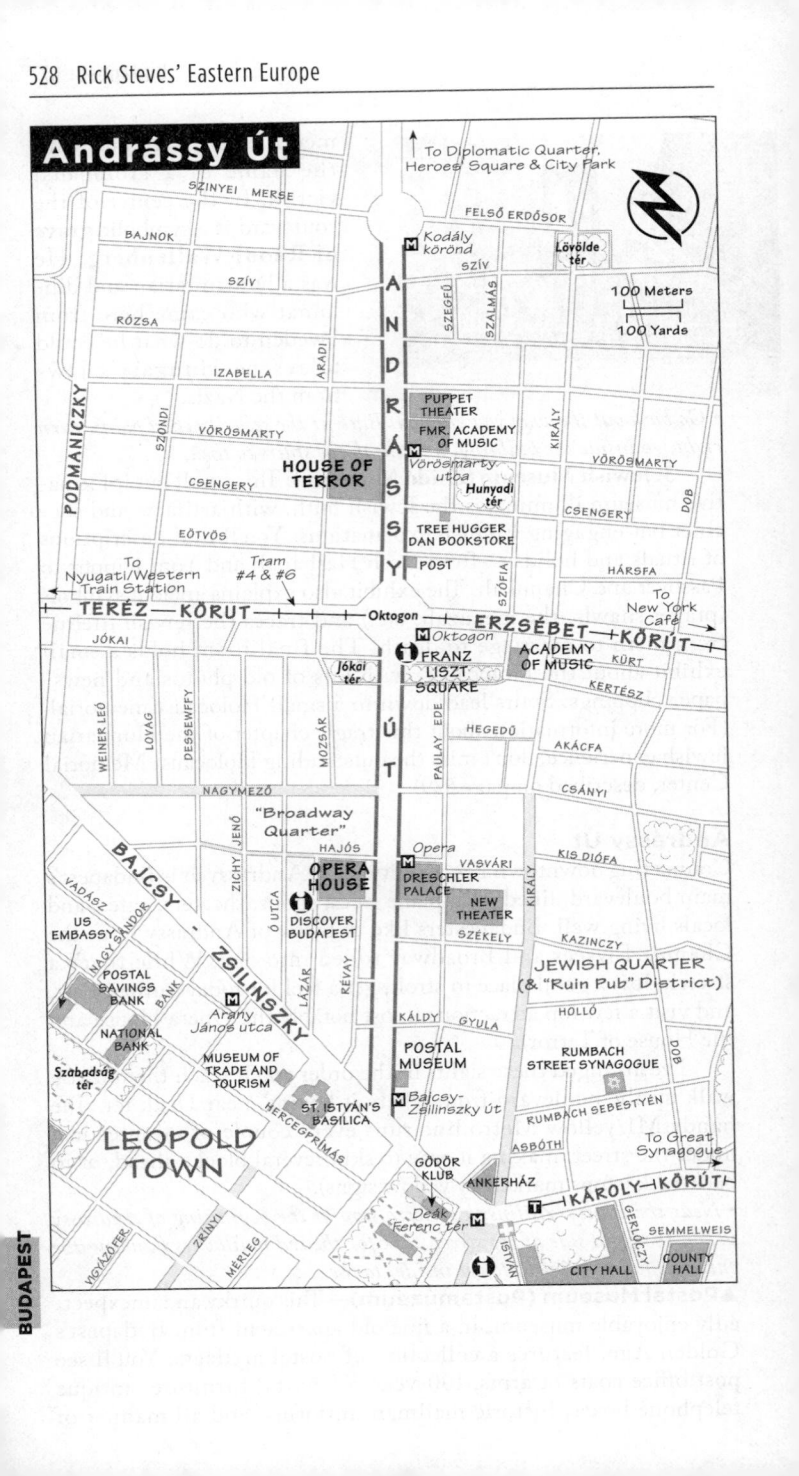
Andrássy Út
To Diplomatic Quarter, Heroes' Square & City Park
SZINYEI MERSE
FELSŐ ERDŐSOR
BAJNOK
Kodály körönd
Lövölde tér
SZÍV
RÓZSA
SZEGFŰ
SZALMÁS
100 Meters
100 Yards
ANDRÁSSY ÚT
IZABELLA
ARADI
PODMANICZKY
SZÖNDI
VÖRÖSMARTY
PUPPET THEATER
FMR. ACADEMY OF MUSIC
KIRÁLY
HOUSE OF TERROR
Vörösmarty utca
Hunyadi tér
CSENGERY
DOB
EÖTVÖS
TREE HUGGER DAN BOOKSTORE
To Nyugati/Western Train Station
Tram #4 & #6
POST
SZÓFIA
HÁRSFA
TERÉZ KÖRUT
Oktogon
ERZSÉBET KÖRÚT
To New York Café
JÓKAI
Oktogon
FRANZ LISZT SQUARE
ACADEMY OF MUSIC
KÜRT
Jókai tér
KERTÉSZ
WEINER LEÓ
LOVAG
DESSEWFFY
MOZSÁR
PAULAY ÉDE
HEGEDŰ
AKÁCFA
NAGYMEZŐ
CSÁNYI
"Broadway Quarter"
JENŐ
HAJÓS
Opera
VASVÁRI
KIS DIÓFA
BAJCSY-ZSILINSZKY
VADÁSZ
ZICHY
OPERA HOUSE
DRESCHLER PALACE
NAGY SÁNDOR
Ó UTCA
DISCOVER BUDAPEST
NEW THEATER
SZÉKELY
KAZINCZY
US EMBASSY
POSTAL SAVINGS BANK
BANK
LÁZÁR
RÉVAY
JEWISH QUARTER (& "Ruin Pub" District)
Arany János utca
KÁLDY GYULA
HOLLÓ
NATIONAL BANK
POSTAL MUSEUM
RUMBACH STREET SYNAGOGUE
Szabadság tér
MUSEUM OF TRADE AND TOURISM
Bajcsy-Zsilinszky út
RUMBACH SEBESTYÉN
ST. ISTVÁN'S BASILICA
HERCEGPRÍMÁS
LEOPOLD TOWN
ASBÓTH
To Great Synagogue
GÖDÖR KLUB
ANKERHÁZ
KÁROLY KÖRÚT
Deák Ferenc tér
GERLÓCZY
SEMMELWEIS
VIGYÁZÓ TÉR
ZRÍNYI
MÉRLEG
ISTVÁN
CITY HALL
COUNTY HALL

postal paraphernalia that was cutting-edge a century ago. The exhibits are displayed in an elegant old merchant's mansion with big Murano crystal chandeliers, all the original ornate woodwork, and creaky parquet floors. The apartment—decorated as it was when built in the 1880s—is at least as interesting as the museum's collection. If it's not too busy, one of the nostalgic women who staff the museum (and seem to be of a similar vintage as the apartment) might show you around and lovingly explain the exhibits (500 Ft, Tue–Sun 10:00–18:00, closed Mon, loaner English information in each room, just up the street from St. István's Basilica at Andrássy út 3, look for easy-to-miss sign and dial 10 to get upstairs, district VI, M1: Bajcsy-Zsilinszky út, tel. 1/269-6838, www.postamuzeum.hu).

• *Three blocks up Andrássy út on the left is the...*

▲▲Hungarian State Opera House (Magyar Állami Operaház)—The Neo-Renaissance home of the Hungarian State Opera features performances (almost daily except during outdoor music season, late June–late Sept) and delightful tours. The building dates from the 1890s, not long after Budapest had become co-capital of the Habsburg Empire. The Hungarians wanted to put their city on the map as a legitimate European capital, and that meant they needed an opera house. Emperor Franz Josef provided half the funds...on the condition that it be smaller than the opera house in his hometown of Vienna. And so, Miklós Ybl designed a building that would exceed Vienna's famous Staatsoper in opulence, if not in size. (Franz Josef was reportedly displeased.) It was built using almost entirely Hungarian materials. After being damaged in World War II, it was painstakingly restored in the early 1980s. Today, with lavish marble-and-gold-leaf decor, a gorgeous gilded interior slathered with paintings of Greek myths, and high-quality performances at bargain prices, this is one of Europe's finest opera houses.

You can drop in anytime the box office is open to ogle the ostentatious **lobby** (Mon–Sat from 11:00 until show time—generally 19:00; Sun open 3 hours before the performance—generally 16:00–19:00, or 10:00–13:00 if there's a matinee; Andrássy út 22, district VI, M1: Opera).

The 45-minute **tours** of the Opera House are a must for music-lovers, and enjoyable to anyone. With an English-speaking guide (who spouts plenty of fun if silly legends), you'll see the main entryway, the snooty lounge area, some of the cozy but plush

boxes, and the lavish auditorium. You'll find out why secret lovers would meet in the cigar lounge, how the Opera House is designed to keep the big spenders away from the nosebleed-seats rabble, and how to tell the difference between real marble and fake marble (2,600 Ft, 500 Ft to take photos, tours nearly daily at 15:00 and 16:00, tickets are easy to get—just show up right before the tour, buy ticket in opera shop—enter the main lobby and go left, shop open Mon–Fri 10:30–12:45 & 13:30–17:00, Sat–Sun 13:30–17:00, open later during performances, tel. 1/332-8197).

To see the Opera House in action, take in an excellent and refreshingly affordable **performance** (see "Entertainment in Budapest," page 555).

• *The Opera House marks the beginning of an emerging dining-and-nightlife zone dubbed the...*

"Broadway Quarter"—The street just behind the Opera House, **Hajós utca,** is newly traffic-free and a budding outdoor-dining zone with a smattering of trendy restaurants...and more soon to appear. The next major cross-street, **Nagymező utca,** features a chic cluster of restaurants, bars, and theaters. This is an enjoyable place to stroll on a summer evening. Many of my recommended restaurants described under "Eating in Budapest," later, are in this neighborhood.

• *One more, long block up the boulevard is Budapest's outdoor-dining mecca...*

Franz Liszt Square (Liszt Ferenc Tér)—This leafy square is surrounded by hip, expensive cafés and restaurants. (The best is the kitschy communist-themed restaurant Menza, described later, under "Eating in Budapest.") This is *the* scene for Budapest's yuppies. The square is named for **Franz Liszt** (pronounced "list," 1811–1886; look for his statue playing an imaginary piano in the middle of the park). This master composer, conductor, pedagogue, and (above all) pianist was prodigiously talented and traveled far and wide to share his skill ("Liszt played here" signs are plastered on buildings all over Hungary). Although Liszt was raised speaking German, he had a Hungarian surname and ancestry, and loved what he considered his homeland of Hungary.

• *One block up from Franz Liszt Square is the gigantic crossroads known as the...*

Oktogon—This vast intersection with its corners snipped off—where Andrássy út meets the Great Boulevard ring road (Nagykörút)—was called Mussolini tér during World War II, then

November 7 tér in honor of the Bolshevik Revolution. Today kids have nicknamed it American tér for the fast-food joints littering the square and streets nearby. Standing (carefully) in the center of Andrássy út, you can already see the column of Heroes' Square at the end of the boulevard.

From here, if you have time to delve into workaday Budapest, consider a trip on tram #4 or #6, which trundle in both directions around the ring road. If you've got time for a short detour to the most opulent coffee break of your life, head for **New York Café** (described on page 583): Just hop on a tram to the right (tram #6 toward Móricz Zsigmond körtér, or tram #4 toward Fehérvári út), and get off at the Wesselényi utca stop.

• *There's one more major sight between here and Heroes' Square. You can either walk two more blocks up Andrássy út, or hop on the Metro and take it one stop to Vörösmarty utca, to reach the...*

▲▲House of Terror (Terror Háza)—The building at Andrássy út 60 was home to the vilest parts of two destructive regimes: first the Arrow Cross (the Gestapo-like enforcers of Nazi-occupied Hungary), then the ÁVO and ÁVH secret police (the insidious KGB-type wing of the Soviet satellite government). Now re-envisioned as the "House of Terror," this building uses high-tech, highly conceptual, bombastic exhibits to document (if not proselytize about) the ugliest moments in Hungary's difficult 20th century. This is a powerful experience, particularly for elderly Hungarians who knew both victims and perpetrators and have personal memories of the terrors that came with Hungary's "double occupation."

Cost, Hours, Location: 1,800 Ft, 400 Ft more for special exhibitions, audioguide-1,300 Ft, Tue–Fri 10:00–18:00, Sat–Sun 10:00–19:30, closed Mon, last entry 90 min before closing, Andrássy út 60, district VI, M1: Vörösmarty utca—*not* the Vörösmarty tér stop, tel. 1/374-2600, www.terrorhaza.hu.

Audioguide and Information: The 1,300-Ft English audioguide is good but almost too thorough, and can be difficult to hear over the din of Hungarian soundtracks in each room. You can't fast-forward through the dense and sometimes long-winded commentary. As an alternative, my self-guided tour (below) covers the key points. A silver plaque in each room provides the basics (in English). For more in-depth information (very similar to what's covered by the audioguide), each room is stocked with free English fliers.

Background: In the lead-up to World War II, Hungary initially allied with Hitler—both to retain a degree of self-determination and to try to regain its huge territorial losses after World War I's devastating Treaty of Trianon (see page 460). But in March 1944, the country was taken over by the Nazi-affiliated Arrow Cross. The Arrow Cross immediately set to work exterminating Budapest's Jews (most of whom had survived until then). The Nazi surrogates deported nearly 440,000 Jewish people to Auschwitz, murdered thousands more on the streets of Budapest, and executed hundreds in the basement of this building. When the communists moved into Hungary, they took over the same building as headquarters for their secret police (the ÁVO, later renamed ÁVH). To keep dissent to a minimum, the secret police terrorized, tried, deported, or executed anyone suspected of being an enemy of the state.

➲ **Self-Guided Tour:** Buy your ticket (and rent an audioguide, if you wish) and head into the museum. The atrium features a Soviet tank and a huge wall covered with portraits of 3,200 of this building's victims.

The one-way exhibit begins two floors up, then spirals down to the cellar. To begin, you can either take the elevator (to floor 2), or walk up the red stairwell nearby, decorated with old sculptures from the communist days.

Once on the second floor, enter the exhibition. In the **Double Occupation** room, the video sets the stage for Hungary's 20th century: its territorial losses after World War I; its alliance with, then invasion by, the Nazis; and its "liberation," then occupation, by the USSR.

After passing through a room displaying uniforms and other gear belonging to Hungarian Nazis, you'll reach a room devoted to the **Gulag.** The word "gulag" refers to a network of secret Soviet prison camps, mostly in Siberia. These were hard-labor camps where potential and actual dissidents were sent to be punished, to remove their dangerous influence from society, and to make an example of those who would dare to defy the regime. On the carpet, a giant map of the USSR shows the locations of some of these camps, where an estimated 600,000–700,000 Hungarian civilians and

prisoners of war were sent...about half of whom never returned.

The **Changing Clothes** room—with rotating figures dressed alternately in Arrow Cross and communist uniforms—satirizes the readiness of many Hungarians to align with whoever was in power.

The room about **The Fifties** examines the gradual insinuation of the communist regime into the fabric of Hungary. Their methods ranged from pre-marked ballots to glossy propaganda—such as the paintings celebrating the peasants of the "people's revolution" and romanticized depictions of communist leaders (look for Lenin as the brave sailor). Behind the distorted stage is the dark underbelly of the regime: the constant surveillance that bred paranoia among the people.

The **Resistance** room features three very different kitchen tables, symbolizing the way that resistance to the regime emerged in every walk of life. The exhibit continues downstairs, where the **Resettlement and Deportation** section considers the ethnic cleansing (or, in the more pleasant parlance of the time, "mutual population exchange") that took place throughout Central and Eastern Europe in the years following World War II. In Hungary, 230,000 Germans were uprooted and deported. Meanwhile, hundreds of thousands of Hungarians who had become ethnically "stranded" in other nations after the Treaty of Trianon were sent to Hungary.

In **Surrender of Property and Land,** we learn that under the communists, the Hungarian people had to survive on increasingly sparse rations. Enter the labyrinth of pork-fat bricks, which remind old-timers of the harsh conditions of the 1950s (lard on bread for dinner). Look for the ration coupons, which people had to present before being allowed to buy even these measly staples.

The next room examines the **ÁVO**, the communist secret police who intimidated the common people of Hungary—equivalent to the KGB in the Soviet Union. Before they were finished, the ÁVO imprisoned, abused, or murdered one person from every third Hungarian family. Their power came from enlisting untold numbers of civilians as informants.

After passing through Gábor Péter's Office (he was the first director of the ÁVO), you'll reach the **"Justice"** exhibit, which explores the concept of "show trials"—high-profile, loudly publicized, and completely choreographed trials of people who had supposedly subverted the regime. The burden of proof was on the accused, not on the accuser, and coerced confessions were fair game.

From 1945 until the 1956 Uprising, more than 71,000 Hungarians were accused of political crimes, and 485 were executed.

Next you'll pass through another, more upbeat method for controlling the people: bright, cheery communist **Propaganda.** The poster about the *Amerikai Bogár* warns of the threat of the "American Beetle" (from *Kolorádó*), which threatened Hungarian crops. When the communists collectivized traditional family farm plots, they removed the trees and hedgerows that separated them—also removing birds that had kept pest populations in check. When a potato beetle epidemic hit, rather than acknowledging their own fault, the communists blamed an American conspiracy.

Rounding out this floor are sections on **"The Hungarian Silver"** (actually aluminum—lampooning the lowbrow aesthetic of the communist era) and **Religion** (those who openly practiced their faith risked being blacklisted or worse by the atheistic regime). Then you'll board an **elevator** that gradually lowers down into the cellar, while you watch a three-minute video of a guard explaining the grotesque execution process.

When the door opens, you're in the **Prison Cellar.** You'll wander through former cells used for different purposes. In the large room after the cells, you'll see a stool with a lamp; nearby are the primitive torture devices: hot pads and electrical appliances. The bucket and hose were used to revive torture victims who had blacked out. After the torture room, in a small room on the right, you'll see a gallows that was used for executions, as you just heard described in the elevator. The **Internment** exhibit explains that, while the most notorious gulag network was in Siberia, a similar system of prison camps also emerged in the Soviet satellites—including Hungary.

The room commemorating the **1956 Uprising** features a symbol of the uprising—a Hungarian flag with a hole cut out of the middle—and the slogan *Ruszkik Haza!* ("Russkies go home!"). For more on '56, see page 514.

After a sobering room displaying gallows, the **Emigration** room features a wall of postcards. More than 200,000 Hungarians simply fled the country after the uprising.

The **Hall of Tears** memorial commemorates all of the victims

of the communists from 1945 to 1967 (when the final prisoners were released from this building). The **Room of Farewell** shows several color video clips that provide a (relatively) happy ending: the festive and exhilarating days in 1991 when the Soviets departed, making way for freedom; the reburial of the Hungarian hero, Imre Nagy; Pope John Paul II's visit to Budapest; and the dedication of this museum.

The chilling finale: walls of photographs of the **Victimizers**—members and supporters of the Arrow Cross and ÁVO, many of whom are still living and who were never brought to justice. The Hungarians have a long way to go to reconcile everything they lived through in the 20th century. For many of them, this museum is an important first step.

• *While you can walk from here to Heroes' Square (visible in the distance, about a 15-minute walk), there's less to see along the rest of Andrássy út. If you prefer, hop on the Metro here and ride it three stops to Hősök tere.*

Heroes' Square and City Park

The grand finale of Andrássy út, at the edge of the city center, is also one of Budapest's most entertaining quarters. Here you'll find the grand Heroes' Square, dripping with history; the vast tree-filled expanse of City Park, dressed up with fanciful buildings; and, tucked in the middle of it all, Budapest's finest thermal spa and single best experience: the Széchenyi Baths. If the sightseeing grind gets you down, take a mini-vacation from your busy vacation like the Budapesters do...and escape to City Park. To reach this area directly, take the M1/yellow Metro line to Hősök tere (district XIV).

▲▲Heroes' Square (Hősök Tere)—Built in 1896 to celebrate the 1,000th anniversary of the Magyars' arrival in Hungary, this vast square culminates at a bold **Millennium Monument.** The granddaddy of all Magyars, Árpád, stands proudly at the bottom of the pillar, peering down Andrássy út. The 118-foot-tall pillar supports the archangel Gabriel as he offers the crown to Árpád's descendant, St. István (he accepted it and Christianized the Magyars).

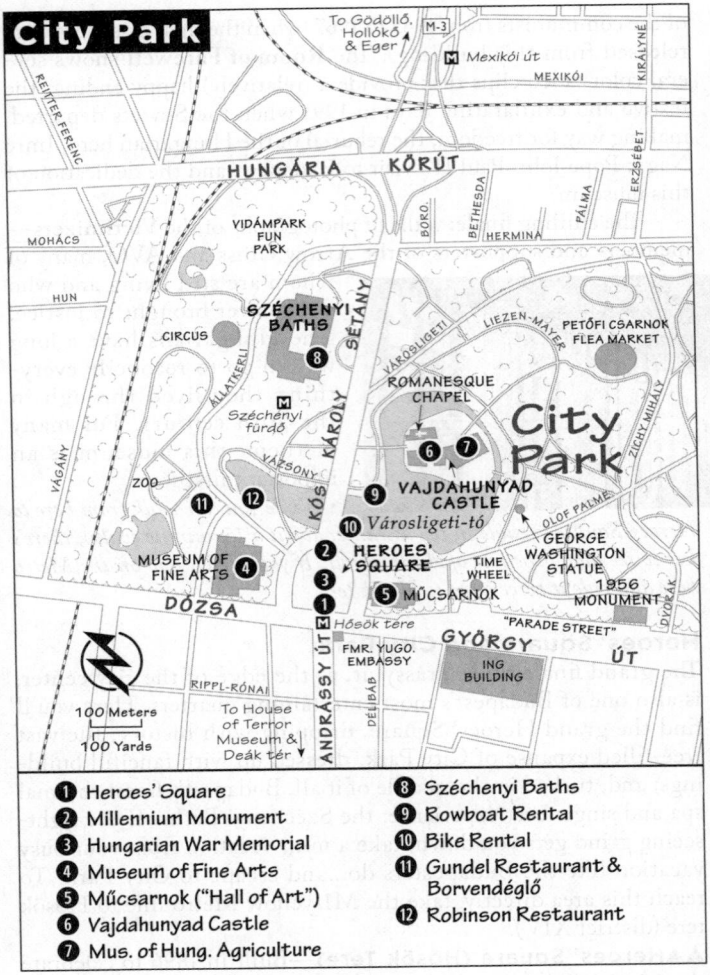

In front of the pillar is the Hungarian War Memorial (fenced in to keep skateboarders from enjoying its perfect slope). Standing stoically in the two colonnades are 14 Hungarian leaders who represent the whole span of this nation's colorful and illustrious history. Look for names you recognize: István, Béla IV, Mátyás Corvinus. The sculptures on the top corners of the two colonnades represent, in order from left to right: Work and Welfare, War, Peace, and the Importance of Packing Light. The square is also flanked by a pair of museums (described next).

Museum of Fine Arts (Szépművészeti Múzeum)—This giant collection of mostly European art is the underachieving cousin

of the famous Kunsthistorisches Museum in Vienna. Like that collection, it's strong in art from areas in the Habsburgs' cultural orbit: Germanic countries, the Low Countries, and especially Spain. If you enjoy European art (particularly from the Spanish Golden Age), consider visiting this museum. After buying your ticket, grab a floor plan and head up the stairs on the right, go to the end of the hall and through the door on the right, and do a clockwise spin through the good stuff: German and Austrian (including some works by Albrecht Dürer); early Dutch and Flemish (including paintings by both Brueghels); and finally Spanish. In the Spanish collection, you'll find works by Murillo, Zubarán, Velázquez, and more. The museum owns five El Grecos, plus several Goyas, including *The Water Carrier* (1,200 Ft, may be more for special exhibitions, audioguide-1,000 Ft, toilets and coat-check downstairs, Tue–Sun 10:00–17:30, last entry 30 min before closing, closed Mon, Dózsa György út 41, tel. 1/469-7100, www.szepmuveszeti.hu).

Műcsarnok ("Hall of Art")—Facing the Museum of Fine Arts from across Heroes' Square, the Műcsarnok shows temporary exhibits by contemporary artists—of interest only to art-lovers. The price varies depending on the exhibits and on which parts you tour. The Ernst Museum wing features up-and-coming artists (usually 1,200 Ft, or 1,400 Ft with Ernst Museum; Tue–Wed and Fri–Sun 10:00–18:00, Thu 12:00–20:00, closed Mon; Ernst Museum open Tue–Sun 11:00–19:00, closed Mon; Dózsa György út 37, tel. 1/460-7000, www.mucsarnok.hu).

• *The area along the busy street beyond the Műcsarnok was once used for communist parades. While the original communist monuments are long-gone, a new monument has taken their place...*

1956 Monument—This monument, which sits just beyond the parking lot behind the Műcsarnok, celebrates the historic uprising against the communists (see page 514). During the early days of the Soviet regime, this was the site of a giant monument to Josef Stalin that towered 80 feet high (Stalin himself was more than 25 feet tall). While dignitaries stood on a platform at Stalin's feet, military parades would march past. From the inauguration of the monument in 1951, the Hungarians saw it as a hated symbol of an unwanted regime. When the 1956 Uprising broke out, the removal of the monument was high on the protestors' list of 16 demands. The night the uprising began, October 23, some rebels decided to check this item off early. They came here to cut off Stalin just below the

knees, and toppled him from his platform. (Memento Park has a reconstruction of the monument's base, including Stalin's boots.) In 2006, to commemorate the 50th anniversary of the uprising, this new monument was erected. Symbolizing the way Hungarians came together to attempt the impossible, it begins with scattered individuals at the back (rusty and humble), gradually coming together and gaining strength and unity near the front—culminating in a silver ship's prow boldly plying the ground. To fully appreciate the monument, walk up the middle of it from the back to the front. Think about how comforting it is to realize you're not alone, as others like you gradually get closer and closer.

▲▲City Park (Városliget)—Budapest's not-so-central "Central Park," which sprawls beyond Heroes' Square, was the site of the overblown 1896 Millennium Exhibition, celebrating Hungary's 1,000th birthday. Today, the park remains endlessly entertaining. Explore the fantasy castle of Vajdahunyad (described next). Visit the animals and ogle the playful Art Nouveau buildings inside the city's zoo, ride a roller-coaster at the amusement park, or enjoy a circus under the big top. Go for a stroll, rent a rowboat, eat some cotton candy, or challenge a local Bobby Fischer to a game of chess. Or (best of all) take a dip in Budapest's ultimate thermal spa, the Széchenyi Baths (described later). This is a fine place to just be on vacation.

▲▲Vajdahunyad Castle (Vajdahunyad Vára)—Many of the buildings for Hungary's Millennial National Exhibition were erected with temporary materials, to be torn down at the end of the festival—as was the case for most world fairs at the time. But locals so loved Vajdahunyad Castle that they insisted it stay, so it was rebuilt in brick and stone. The complex actually has four parts, representing the high points of four architectural styles in Hungary: Romanesque chapel, Gothic gate, Renaissance castle, and Baroque palace (free and always open to walk around the grounds).

From this direction, the **Renaissance castle** dominates the view. It's a replica of a famous castle in Transylvania that once belonged to the Hunyadi family (János and Mátyás Corvinus—described on page 502).

Cross over the bridge and through the **Gothic gateway.** Once inside the complex, on the left you'll see a replica of a 13th-century Romanesque **Benedictine chapel.** Consecrated as an actual church, this is Budapest's most popular spot for weekend weddings in the summer. Farther ahead on the right, you'll see a big Baroque mansion—which houses the **Museum of Hungarian Agriculture** (Magyar Mezőgazdasági Múzeum). The museum brags that it's Europe's biggest agriculture museum, but most visitors will find the lavish interior more interesting than the exhibits (800 Ft; April–Oct Tue–Sun 10:00–17:00, closed Mon; Nov–March Tue–Fri 10:00–16:00, Sat–Sun 10:00–17:00, closed Mon; last entry 30 min before closing, tel. 1/363-2711).

Facing the museum entry is a monument to **Anonymous**—specifically, the Anonymous from the court of King Béla IV who penned the first Hungarian history in the Middle Ages.

▲▲▲Széchenyi Baths (Széchenyi Fürdő)—My favorite activity in Budapest, the Széchenyi Baths are an ideal way to reward yourself for the hard work of sightseeing and call it a culturally enlightening experience. You'll soak in hundred-degree water, surrounded by portly Hungarians squeezed into tiny swimsuits, while jets and cascades pound away your tension. Go for a vigorous swim in the lap pool, giggle and bump your way around the whirlpool, submerge yourself to the nostrils in water green with minerals, feel the bubbles from an underwater jet gradually caress their way up your leg, or challenge the locals to a game of chess. And it's all surrounded by an opulent yellow palace with shiny copper domes. The bright blue-and-white of the sky, the yellow of the buildings, the pale pink of the skin, the turquoise of the water...Budapest simply doesn't get any better. It's in City Park, just beyond Vajdahunyad Castle; for all the details, see "Experiences in Budapest," later.

Museums near Üllői Út

These two museums are near the city center, on the boulevard called Üllői út. You could stroll there in about 10 minutes from the Small Boulevard ring road (walking the length of the Ráday utca restaurant street gets you very close), or hop on the M3/blue Metro line to Ferenc körút (just one stop beyond Kálvin tér).

▲Holocaust Memorial Center (Holokauszt Emlékközpont)—This sight honors the nearly 600,000 Hungarian victims of the Nazis...one out of every 10 Holocaust victims. The impressive modern complex (with a beautifully restored 1920s synagogue as

its centerpiece) is a museum of the Hungarian Holocaust, a monument to its victims, a space for temporary exhibits, and a research and documentation center of Nazi atrocities. Interesting to anybody, but essential to those interested in the Holocaust, this is Budapest's best sight about that dark time. You'll pass through a security checkpoint to reach the courtyard. Once inside, a black marble wall is etched with the names of victims. Head downstairs to buy your ticket. The excellent permanent exhibit, called "From Deprivation of Rights to Genocide," traces in English the gradual process of marginalization, exploitation, and dehumanization that befell Hungary's Jews as World War II wore on. The finale is the interior of the synagogue, now a touching memorial filled with glass seats, each one etched with the image of a Jewish worshipper who once filled it (1,000 Ft, 500-Ft English audioguide repeats posted English information, Tue–Sun 10:00–18:00, closed Mon, Páva utca 39, district IX, M3: Ferenc körút, tel. 1/455-3333, www.hdke.hu). From the Ferenc körút Metro station, use the exit marked *Holokauszt Emlékközpont* and take the left fork at the exit. Walk straight ahead two long blocks, then turn right down Páva utca.

Applied Arts Museum (Iparművészeti Múzeum)—This remarkable late-19th-century building, a fanciful green-roofed castle that seems out of place in an otherwise dreary urban area, was designed by Ödön Lechner. The interior is equally striking: Because historians of the day were speculating about possible ties between the Magyars and India, Lechner decorated it with Mogul motifs (from the Indian dynasty best known for the Taj Mahal). Strolling through the forest of dripping-with-white-stucco arches and columns, you might just forget to pay attention to the exhibits. The small permanent collection displays furniture, clothes, ceramics, and other everyday items, with an emphasis on curvy Art Nouveau (all described in English). This and various temporary exhibits are displayed around a light and airy atrium. If you're visiting the nearby Holocaust Memorial Center, consider dropping by here for a look at the building (800 Ft for permanent exhibit, several temporary exhibits have separate admission costs—or buy 2,000-Ft combo-ticket for everything, Tue–Sun 10:00–18:00, closed Mon, Üllői út 33–37, district IX, M3: Ferenc körút, tel. 1/456-5100, www.imm.hu). From the Ferenc körút Metro station, follow signs to *Iparművészeti Múzeum* and bear right up the stairs.

▲▲Memento Park (a.k.a. Statue Park)

When regimes fall, so do their monuments. Just think of all those statues of Stalin and Lenin—or Saddam Hussein—crashing to the ground. Throughout Eastern Europe, people couldn't wait to get rid of these reminders of their oppressors. But some clever entrepreneur hoarded Budapest's, and has collected them in a park

in the countryside just southwest of the city. Though it can be time-consuming to visit, this collection is worth ▲▲▲ for those fascinated by Hungary's commie past. You'll see the great figures of the Soviet Bloc, both international (Lenin, Marx, and Engels) and Hungarian (local bigwig Béla Kun). And you'll see gigantic, stoic figures representing Soviet ideals.

Cost, Hours, Location: 1,500 Ft, daily 10:00–sunset, six miles southwest of city center at the corner of Balatoni út and Szabadka út, district XXII, tel. 1/424-7500, www.mementopark.hu.

Getting There: The park runs a convenient direct bus from Deák tér in downtown Budapest (bus stop is at corner of busy Bajcsy-Zsilinszky út and Harmincad utca; departs year-round daily at 11:00, July–Aug also at 15:00; round-trip takes 1.75 hours total, including a 40-min visit to the park; 3,950 Ft round-trip including park entry—which means the bus costs the equivalent of 2,450 Ft). The public-transit option is more frequent and less expensive, but also less convenient: First take tram #18, #18A, #19, #49, or #118 from Szent Gellért tér (in front of Gellért Hotel and Baths) to Kosztolányi Dezső tér. From there, catch bus #150 in the direction of Campona and ask for "Memento Park" (stop can be easy to miss—ask fellow passengers for help; 3/hr Mon–Fri, 2/hr Sat–Sun, 25-min trip, covered by one 290-Ft transit ticket or multi-day pass). Other connections are possible, but they're too complicated.

Background: Under the communists, creativity was discouraged. The primary purpose of art was to further the goals of the state, with creative expression only an afterthought. This Socialist Realistic art served two purposes: It was Realistic, breaking with the "decadent" bourgeois art that came before it (Impressionism, Post-Impressionism, and other modern -isms); and Socialistic, encouraging complicity with the brave new world the communists were forging. From 1949 until 1956, Socialist Realism was legally enforced as the sole artistic style of the Soviet Bloc.

As propaganda was an essential weapon in the Soviet arsenal, the regime made ample use of Socialist Realistic art. Aside from a few important figureheads, individuals didn't matter. Everyone was a cog in the machine—strong, stoic, doing their job well and proudly for the good of the people. Individual characteristics and distinguishing features were unimportant; people were represented

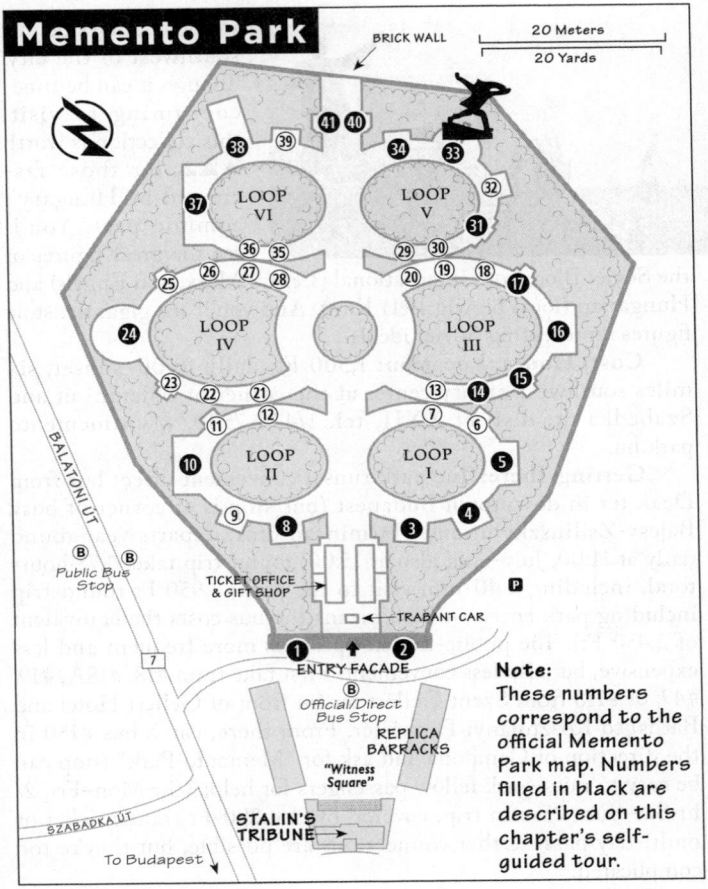

as automatons serving their nation. Artistic merit was virtually ignored. Most figures are trapped in stiff, unnatural poses that ignore the 3,000 years of artistic evolution since the Egyptians. Sculptures and buildings alike from this era were designed to evoke feelings of power and permanence.

➲ **Self-Guided Tour:** As you approach the park, you're greeted by an imposing red-brick **entry facade** featuring three of the Communist All-Stars—❶ **Lenin** and ❷ **Marx** and **Engels.** (They couldn't save the biggest "star" of all, Stalin—all statues of him were destroyed in the 1956 Uprising.) Like the rest of the park, this gate is highly conceptual in its design: It looks impressive and monumental...but, like the rotted-out pomp of communism, there's nothing behind it. It's a glossy stage-set with no substance. If you try to go through the main, central part of the gate, you'll run into

an always-locked door. Instead, as with the communist system, you have to find another way around (in this case, the smaller gate to the left).

Once inside and past the ticket-window building, notice that the main road takes you confidently toward...a dead end (the brick wall). Once again, as with life under the communists, you'll have to deviate from this main axis to actually accomplish anything. Even so, notice that the six cul-de-sacs branching off the main road all bring you right back to where you started—the futility of communism.

Work your way counterclockwise around the park.

Liberation Monuments (Loop I): Dominating this loop is a ❸ **giant soldier** holding the Soviet flag. This statue once stood at the base of the Liberation Monument that still overlooks the Danube from Gellért Hill. Typical of Socialist Realist art, the soldier has a clenched fist (symbolizing strength) and a face that shows no emotion. To the left of this soldier, see the ❹ **two comrades** stiffly shaking hands: the Hungarian worker thrilled to meet the Soviet soldier. Beyond them is a ❺ **long wall,** with a triumphant worker breaking through the left end—too busy doing his job to be very excited. Just another brick in the wall.

• *Cross "main street" to a group of statues commemorating the key communist holiday of...*

April 4, 1945 (Loop II): On this date, the Soviets forced the final Nazi soldier out of Hungary. The tall panel nearest the entrance shows a Hungarian woman and a Soviet woman setting free the ❽ **doves of peace.** According to the inscription, "Our freedom and peace is based on the enduring Hungarian-Soviet friendship." (With friends like these....) At the back of the loop, the ❿ **Hungarian worker and Soviet soldier** (who appear to be doing calisthenics) are absurdly rigid even though they're trying to be dynamic. (Even the statues couldn't muster genuine enthusiasm for communist ideals.)

• *Cross over and head up to the next loop, to pay homage to...*

Heroes of the Workers' Movement (Loop III): This loop has a ⓮ bust and a ⓯ statue of the Bulgarian communist leader **Georgi Dimitrov** (ruled 1946–1949)—one of communist Hungary's many Soviet Bloc comrades. At the back of this loop are ⓰ three blocky portraits. The middle figure is the granddaddy of Hungarian communism, **Béla Kun** (1886–1938). To the left is one of the park's

best-loved, most-photographed, and most artistic statues: ⓱ **Vladimir Lenin,** in his famous "hailing a cab" pose.

• *Cross over—passing the giant red star made of flowers—to meet...*

More Communist Heroes (Loop IV): This group is dominated by a ㉔ dramatic, unusually emotive sculpture by a genuine artist, Imre Varga. Designed to commemorate the 100th anniversary of Béla Kun's birth, this clever statue accomplishes seemingly contradictory feats. On the one hand, it reinforces the communist message: Under the able leadership of Béla Kun (safely overlooking the fray from above), the crusty, bourgeois old regime of the Habsburg Empire (on the left, with the umbrellas and fancy clothes) was converted into the workers' fighting force of the Red Army (on the right, with the bayonets). And yet, those silvery civilians in back seem more appealing than the lunging soldiers in front. And notice the lamppost next to Kun: In Hungarian literature, a lamppost is a metaphor for the gallows—reminding viewers that Kun was ultimately executed by the very communist system he espoused, during Stalin's purges of the late 1930s.

• *Zig and head up again, for a lesson in...*

Communist Concepts (Loop V): Look for a rusty pair of ㉛ **workers' hands** holding a sphere (which was once adorned with a red star). The sphere represents the hard-won ideals of communism, carefully protected by the hands—but also held out for others to appreciate. Dominating this group is a ㉝ **communist worker** charging into the future, clutching the Soviet flag. Budapesters of the time had a different interpretation: a thermal bath attendant running after a customer who'd forgotten his towel. To the left is a monument to the communist version of the Boy Scouts: the elementary school–age ㉞ **Little Drummers,** and

the older Pioneers. While these organizations existed before the communists, they were slowly infiltrated and turned into propaganda machines by the regime. These kids—with their jaunty red and blue neckerchiefs—were sent to camp to be properly raised as good little communists; today, many of them have forgotten the brainwashing, but still have fond memories of the socializing.

• *Now zag once more to learn about...*

More Communist Concepts (Loop VI): The ㊲ long, white **wall** at the back of this section tells quite a story (from left to right): The bullet holes lead up to a jumbled, frightful clutter (reminiscent of Pablo Picasso's Guernica) representing World War II. Then comes the bright light of the Soviet system, and by the end everyone's looking boldly to the future (and enjoying a bountiful crop, to boot). Next is a ㊳ **fallen hero** with arm outstretched, about to collapse to the ground—mortally wounded, yet victorious. This monument to "the Martyrs of the Counter-Revolution" commemorates those who died attempting to put down the 1956 Uprising.

• *Now continue down the main drag to, um, a....*

Dead End: Where the main path dead-ends at the wall, it's flanked by statues of two Soviet officers who negotiated with the Nazis to end the WWII siege of Budapest. ㊵ **Captain Miklós Steinmetz** (on the right) was killed by a Nazi land mine, while ㊶ **Ilja Ostapenko** (on the left) was shot under mysterious circumstances as he returned from a successful summit. Both became heroes for the communist cause. Were they killed by wayward Nazi soldiers, as the Soviets explained—or by their own Red Army, to create a pair of convenient martyrs?

Heading back out to the entry gate, peruse the fun parade of communist kitsch at the gift shop; consider picking up the good English guidebook, the CD of *Communism's Greatest Hits,*

and maybe a model of a Trabant (the classic two-stroke commie-mobile). A real Trabant is often parked just inside the gate.

• *Across the parking lot, you'll find a replica of* ***"Stalin's Tribune"****—a giant grandstand from which Hungarian and Soviet leaders would survey ceremonial processions (described on page 537). Notice the giant boots—the only part of a giant Stalin statue that survived the 1956 Uprising. Flanking the tribune are replica barracks, reminiscent of the ones where political prisoners lived in communist-era work camps. These hold special exhibits.*

Our tour is over. Now, inspired by the bold propaganda of your Hungarian comrades, march proudly into the dawn of a new day.

Near Budapest

On a visit of a few days, Budapest will keep even the most avid sightseer busy. And after Budapest, Eger and Pécs—each covered in a chapter of its own—are the best Hungarian towns. But for a longer stay, a few outlying sights are worth knowing about.

Óbuda—"Old Buda," just north of Buda, is the oldest part of Budapest, with roots going back to Celtic and Roman times. It has various sights that cluster around the Árpád híd stop of the HÉV suburban train line (catch the HÉV from the Batthyány tér Metro stop in Buda). The most interesting museum displays works by Hungarian sculptor **Imre Varga,** who worked from the 1950s through the 1990s, and created many popular sculptures in Budapest and throughout Hungary. You'll also find a museum filled with eye-popping, colorful paintings by **Victor Vasarely,** the founder of Op Art. If you ride the HÉV farther north to the Aquincum stop, you'll reach a museum at the remains of the 2,000-year-old Roman town of **Aquincum** and its amphitheater. All of these sights are closed on Mondays.

Gödöllő Royal Palace—Holding court in an unassuming town on the outskirts of Budapest, this pink Baroque palace was once the residence of Habsburg Emperor Franz Josef and his wife, Empress Elisabeth—better known to her beloved Hungarian subjects as Sisi. While the Habsburg sights in Vienna and near Prague are better, this is the best place in Hungary to learn about its former monarchs (open daily April–Oct, closed Mon Nov–March, www.kiralyikastely.hu; take the M2/red Metro line to Örs vezér tere, then catch the HÉV suburban train from to Gödöllő—figure about one hour each way from downtown Budapest).

The Danube Bend—This string of three river towns north of Budapest offers a convenient day-trip getaway for urbanites who want to commune with nature. While I find "the Bend" less than thrilling, it's undeniably convenient to reach from the capital by train or boat; these destinations make for handy stopovers if you're driving between Budapest and Bratislava or Vienna.

Szentendre is a colorful, Balkan-feeling artist colony. With a tidy main square, a few engaging art galleries, and several Orthodox churches built by the Serbs and Greeks who settled the town, it offers a relaxing escape from the city. This is the easiest pleasant small town to reach from Budapest—which means it's also deluged by tourists. To reach Szentendre, hop on the HÉV suburban train at Budapest's Batthyány tér Metro (the same one that goes to Óbuda, described above).

Visegrád offers a small riverside museum at the scant remains of a Renaissance palace built by King Matthias Corvinus, and a dramatic hilltop castle with fine views over the Bend. While you can get here by boat or by train (to the Nagymaros-Visegrád station, then boat across the river), it's not worth the trip unless you're driving.

Esztergom Basilica is Hungary's biggest and most important church, built on the site where István, Hungary's first Christian king, was crowned in A.D. 1000. Packed with history, it looms grandly above the Danube (free, daily April–mid-Oct 8:00–19:00, mid-Oct–March 8:00–16:00). The easiest way to reach it is by bus from Budapest's Újpest-Városkapu bus station (at the Metro stop of the same name); trains and other buses from Budapest take you to the far end of town, an inconvenient 45-minute walk to the basilica.

Sopron—This little Baroque town, jam-packed with historic buildings and dusty museums, is conveniently located between Budapest and Bratislava, tucked between alpine foothills. Its square—watched over by the town's symbol, the Fire Tower—might be Hungary's most romantic. While fun to explore, Sopron is small and sleepy enough that its sightseeing options are quickly exhausted.

Experiences in Budapest

Thermal Baths

Splashing and relaxing in Budapest's thermal baths is the city's top attraction. Though it might sound daunting, bathing with the Magyars is far more accessible than you'd think. The thermal baths I've described here are basically like your hometown swimming pool—except the water is 100 degrees, there are plenty of jets and bubbles to massage away your stress, and you're surrounded by scantily clad Hungarians. Overcome your jit-

Taking the Waters

American tourists often feel squeamish at the thought of bathing with Speedo-clad, pot-bellied Hungarians. Relax! It's less intimidating than it sounds—and the fun you'll have far outweighs the jitters. I was nervous on my first visit, too. But now I feel like a trip to Hungary just isn't complete without a splish-splash in the bath.

While Hungary has several mostly nude, gender-segregated Turkish baths, the places described in this book are less intimidating: Men and women are usually together, and you can keep your swimsuit on the entire time. (Even at mixed baths, there generally are a few clothing-optional, gender-segregated areas, where locals are likely to be nude—or wearing a *kötény,* a loose-fitting loincloth.)

Bring along these items, if you have them: a swimsuit, towel, flip-flops, soap and shampoo for a shower afterwards, a comb or brush, and maybe sunscreen and leisure reading. Hotels typically frown on guests taking their room towels to the baths. Try asking nicely if they have some loaner towels just for this purpose (they'll probably tell you to rent one there...but what they don't know, won't hurt them). At Budapest's baths, you can usually rent a towel, swimsuit (for men, Speedos are always available, trunks sometimes), or sandals.

Each bath complex has multiple pools, used for different purposes. Big pools with cooler water are for serious swimming, while the smaller, hotter thermal baths (*gyógyfürdő,* or simply *gőz*) are for relaxing, enjoying the jets and current pools, and playing chess. The water bubbles up from hot springs at 77° Celsius (170° Fahrenheit), then is mixed with cooler water to achieve the desired temperatures. Most pools are marked with the water temperature in Celsius (cooler pools are about 30°C/86°F; warmer pools are closer to 36°C/97°F or 38°C/100°F, about like the hot tub back home; and the hottest are 40°C/104°F... yowtch!). Locals hit the cooler pools first, then work their way up to the top temps. While the lap pools are chlorinated, most of the thermal baths are not. Unlike swimming pools in the US—where the water is recycled back into the pool—water here is slowly drained out and replaced with fresh water from the hot springs. Locals figure this means that chemicals aren't necessary.

You'll also usually find a dry sauna, a wet steam room, a cold plunge pool (for a pleasurable jolt when you're feeling overheated), and sunbathing areas (which may be segregated and clothing-optional). Some baths have fun flourishes: bubbles, whirlpools, massage jets, wave pools, and so on.

The most difficult part of visiting a Hungarian bath is the inevitably complicated entrance procedure, easily one of today's best time-travel experiences back to communist Eastern Europe. Expect monolingual staff, a complex payment and locker-rental scheme, and lengthy menus of massages and other treatments. I've carefully outlined the specifics for each bath, but be forewarned that they can change from year to year, or even from day to day. Keep track of any receipt or slip of paper you're given, as you may be asked to show it later (for a partial refund or to get your deposit back). Hang in there, go where people direct you, and enjoy this unique cultural experience. Remember, they're used to tourists—so don't be afraid to act like one. If you can make it through those first few confusing minutes, you'll soon be relaxing like a pro.

While enjoying the baths, you can leave your clothing and other belongings in your locked cabin or locker. Although I've found these to be safe, and bath employees assure me that thefts are rare (a cabin is safer than a locker), it's at your own risk. Another option is to leave valuables in a safe (generally costs 500 Ft, ask when you buy ticket). People have been known to steal rental towels from around the pools to collect the deposit—keep an eye on your towels and any other belongings you bring poolside. Many locals bring plastic shopping bags to hold their essentials: towels, leisure reading, and sunscreen.

Be aware that the jets, bubbles, waves, waterfalls, and whirlpools sometimes take turns running. For example, a current pool runs for 10 minutes, then a series of jets starts up and the current pool stops for 10 minutes, then the current pool starts up again, and so on. If a particularly fun feature of the pool doesn't seem to be working, just give it a few minutes.

If you stay less than a designated time (usually three hours), you will usually get a partial refund when you leave—if you get a receipt, take it to the ticket window on your way out and see if they'll give you anything back.

Here are some useful phrases:

English	Hungarian	Pronounced
Bath	*Fürdő*	FEWR-dur
Men	*Férfi*	FAYR-fee
Women	*Női*	NUR-ee
Changing Cabin	*Kabin*	KAH-been
Locker	*Szekrény*	SEHK-rayn
Ticket Office	*Pénztár*	PAYNZ-tar
Thermal Bath	*Gyógyfürdő, Gőz*	JODGE-fewr-dur, gorz

Please trust me, and take the plunge. My readers almost unanimously report that the thermal baths were their top Hungarian experience. If you go into it with an easygoing attitude and a sense of humor, I promise you'll have a blast.

ters, follow my instructions, and dive in...or miss out on *the* quintessential Budapest experience.

The two baths listed here are the best-known, most representative, and most convenient for first-timers: The Széchenyi Baths are more casual and popular with locals, while the Gellért Baths are touristy, famous, and genteel. To me, Széchenyi is second to none, but some travelers prefer the Gellért experience. As they're quite different, doing both is an excellent option. For more information on all of Budapest's baths, see www.spasbudapest.com.

▲▲▲Széchenyi Baths (Széchenyi Fürdő)

To soak with the locals, head for this bath complex—the big, yellow, copper-domed building in the middle of City Park. Széchenyi (SAY-chehn-yee) is the best of Budapest's many bath experiences—and, thanks to a recent renovation, it feels even classier than the famous Gellért Baths. Relax and enjoy some Hungarian good living. Magyars of all shapes and sizes stuff themselves into tiny swimsuits and strut their stuff. Housewives float blissfully in the warm water. Intellectuals and elder statesmen stand in chest-high water around chessboards and ponder their next moves. This is Budapest at its best.

Cost: 2,800 Ft for personal changing cabin, 2,400 Ft for locker in gender-segregated locker room, cheaper if you arrive within three hours of closing time, price includes thermal baths, swimming pool, and sauna. Couples can share a changing cabin: One person pays the cabin rate, the other pays the locker rate, but both use the same cabin. There's also a wide array of massages and other special treatments—find the English menu in the lobby (make an appointment as you enter). Once inside the complex, you can rent a swimsuit, towel, or sandals (about 300 Ft apiece with a 2,000- to 4,000-Ft deposit). Renting a small safe for your valuables costs 500 Ft.

Hours: Swimming pool (the best part, outdoors) generally open daily 6:00–22:00, thermal bath (less appealing, indoors) daily 6:00–19:00, last entry one hour before closing.

Location and Entrances: In City Park at Állatkerti körút 11, district XIV, M1: Széchenyi fürdő. The huge bath complex has three entrances. The busiest one—technically the **"thermal bath entrance"**—is the grand main entry, facing south (roughly toward Vajdahunyad Castle). I avoid this entrance—there's often a line during peak times, and it's a bit more confusing to find your way

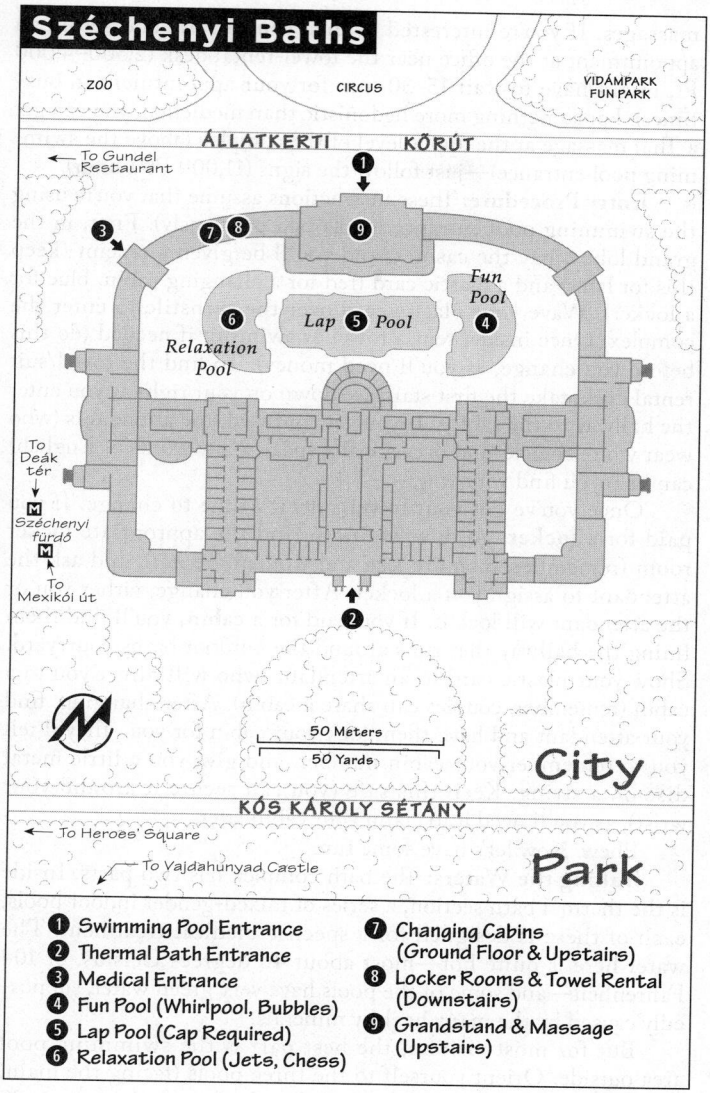

once inside. Instead, I prefer the **"swimming pool entrance,"** facing the zoo on the other side of the complex—it's faster, has shorter lines, and is open later. A third, smaller **"medical entrance,"** to the right as you face the zoo entry (near the Metro stops), provides access to either the thermal bath changing rooms or the swimming pool changing rooms, but can also have long lines.

Massage: The bath complex provides various medical

massages. If you're interested in this, you can pay and set up an appointment at the office near the towel-rental desk (2,500–4,000 Ft, might have to wait 15–30 min for your appointment in busy times). For something more hedonistic than medicinal, you can get a Thai massage at the upper level of the complex (above the swimming pool entrance)—just follow the signs (11,000 Ft/1 hour).

Entry Procedure: These instructions assume that you're using the swimming pool entrance (explained previously). First, in the grand lobby, pay the cashier, and you'll be given a receipt (keep this for later) and a plastic card (red for a changing cabin, blue for a locker). Wave your plastic card over the turnstile to enter the complex. Once inside, rent a towel or swimsuit if needed (do this before you change, as you'll need money). To find the towel/suit rental desk, take the first staircase down on your right as you enter the hallway to the cabins. If you get confused, the attendants (who wear white smocks and occasionally speak a few words of English) can help you find your way.

Once you've got your towel/suit, it's time to change. If you paid for a **locker,** go downstairs to find the appropriate locker room (remember, men are *férfi* and women are *női*), and ask the attendant to assign you a locker. After you change, either you or the attendant will lock it. If you paid for a **cabin,** you'll find them lining the hallway that runs around the outdoor baths courtyard. Show your plastic card to an attendant, who will direct you to a cabin (remember, couples can share a cabin). After changing, find your attendant and have them lock your cabin for you. They'll tell you to remember your cabin number, and give you a little metal disc on a string. Keep this safe (you can secure it around your wrist), as you'll need it to claim your cabin later.

Phew. Now let's have some fun.

Taking the Waters: The bath complex has two parts. Inside is the thermal bath section, a series of mixed-gender indoor pools; each of these is designed for a specific medical treatment. The water here is quite hot—most about 40 degrees Celsius, or 104 Fahrenheit—and some of the pools have very green water, supposedly caused by the many healthy minerals.

But for most visitors, the best part is the swimming pool area outside. Orient yourself to the three pools (facing the main, domed building): The pool to the left is for fun (cooler water—30 degrees Celsius, or 86 Fahrenheit, warmer in winter, lots of jets and bubbles, lively and often crowded, includes circular current pool); the pool on the right is for relaxation (warmer water—38 degrees Celsius, or 100 Fahrenheit, mellow atmosphere, a few massage jets, chess); and the main pool in the center is all business (the coolest water, doing laps, swimming cap required). Stairs to saunas are below the doors to the inside pools. You get extra credit

for joining the gang in a chess match.

Exit Procedure: If you rented a towel or swimsuit, return it to the desk where you got it, and present your receipt to get your deposit back. Then, as you exit the complex, insert your card into the turnstile and another receipt will print out. If you stayed shorter than three hours, the receipt will indicate the amount of your refund *(Visszatérítés: Jár* {amount} *Ft).* Present this and your original receipt at the cashier as you exit to claim your "time-proportional repayment." (If you arrived within three hours of closing time, you already got a discount and won't get a refund.) Then continue your sightseeing...soggy, but relaxed.

▲▲Gellért Baths (Gellért Fürdő)

Using the baths at Gellért (GEH-layrt) Hotel costs a bit more than the Széchenyi Baths, and you won't run into nearly as many locals; this is definitely a more upscale, touristy, spa-like scene. Because most of the warmest pools are in gender-segregated areas, it's not ideal for opposite-sex couples or families who want to spend time together. But if you want a soothing, luxurious bath experience in an elegant setting, this is the place. And if it's fun you're looking for, the Gellért Baths have something that Széchenyi doesn't: a huge, deliriously enjoyable wave pool that'll toss you around like a queasy surfer (summer only).

Cost: 3,400 Ft for personal changing cabin, 3,100 Ft for locker in gender-segregated locker room, cheaper after 16:00. When you buy your ticket, tell them if you want to buy a massage or rent a towel or a swimsuit (600 Ft each with a 4,000-Ft deposit). The 1,000-Ft visitor ticket to see—but not use—the baths is pointless, as you'll see virtually nothing more than what's visible from the ticket window.

Hours and Location: May–Sept daily 6:00–19:00; Oct–April Mon–Fri 6:00–19:00, Sat–Sun 6:00–17:00; last entry one hour before closing. It's on the Buda side of the green Liberty Bridge (trams #47 and #49 from Deák tér in Pest, or trams #19 and #41 along the Buda embankment from Víziváros below the castle). The entrance to the baths is under the white dome opposite the bridge (Kelenhegyi út 4–6, district XI, tel. 1/466-6166, ext. 165).

Entry Procedure: As you enter, a generally English-speaking information desk is dead ahead, with cashiers on either side. Beyond the cashier on the left is a window where you can deposit

valuables in the safe (500 Ft).

In the summer, they sell two different tickets based on which changing area you'll use. With a **thermal bath ticket,** you'll change in a large, gender-segregated area that connects directly to the also-segregated thermal baths (so some people walk nude directly from their cabins to the bath); this means that opposite-sex couples can't share a changing cabin. With a **swimming pool ticket,** you'll go to a mixed area where opposite-sex couples can share a cabin (this area also has gender-segregated locker rooms). Both tickets allow you to move freely between the thermal baths and swimming pool areas once you're inside.

Your entry ticket consists of two parts: a receipt-like slip of paper (which you'll surrender to get into the changing area), and a plastic card used to keep track of how long you're inside (which you'll insert in the turnstile to exit). Keep track of both of these items until you're asked for them.

A dizzying array of **massages** and **treatment options** are also sold at the ticket window. Most are available only with a doctor's note, but anyone can get a "medical massage" (with oil, 2,800 Ft/15 min, 3,800 Ft/30 min) or a "refreshing massage" (with cold soapy water, 2,500 Ft/15 min, 3,500 Ft/30 min)—both are performed in the steam-bath section. Upstairs, you can also get a Thai massage, but you have to arrange that separately.

Pay for everything you want (including massages or towel rentals), enter, and glide through the swanky lobby. The indoor swimming pool is on your right, about halfway down the main hall. Looking through the window to the pool, visualize the perfectly symmetrical bath complex: The men's thermal bath, changing cabins, and lockers are on the left, while the identical women's facilities are on the right. The two sections meet at this shared pool in the center. If you have a swimming pool ticket, you'll enter from right here: Men/*férfi* go down the stairs on the left, and women/*női* on the right (either way, you'll head down a long hallway, then up several flights of stairs and through a maze to the changing areas; for couples sharing a cabin, go to the section corresponding to the person who bought the cabin ticket). If you have a thermal bath ticket, the entrances are a bit farther away: women to the right, closer to the entrance, and men to the left, at the end of the hall. If you paid to rent a towel or swimsuit, pick it up from the attendant on your way.

Taking the Waters: Once you've changed, you can spend your time either indoors or out. Inside, the central, mixed-gender, genteel-feeling hall is home to a cool-water swimming pool (swimming cap required—free loaners available) and a crowded hot-water pool. Back toward the window and main hall are doors to the gender-segregated, clothing-optional massage rooms and thermal

baths, with nude or loincloth-wearing bathers stewing in pools at 36 and 38 degrees Celsius (97 and 100 degrees Fahrenheit). Notice that these temperatures perfectly flank that of the human body, allowing you to toggle your temp at will. You'll also find a sauna (near the showers), steam rooms (at the far end of the bath), and a cold plunge pool. If you paid for a massage, report to the massage room in this section when you're ready (no appointments—first-come, first-served; you might wait 30 min or more).

To get outside, head upstairs (which also has a fine view over the main indoor pool). Out here, you'll find several sunbathing areas and a warm thermal pool (up the stairs at the end). But the main attraction is the big, unheated wave pool in the center (generally closed Oct–April, weather-dependent). Not for the squeamish, this pool thrashes fun-loving swimmers around like driftwood. The swells in the deeper area are fun and easy to float on, but the crashing waves at the shallow end are vigorous, if not dangerous. If there are no waves, just wait around a while (you'll hear a garbled message on the loudspeaker five minutes before the tide comes in).

Exit Procedure: When you're finished, return your towel and swimsuit to reclaim your deposit, then insert your card into the machine at the exit turnstile. If you were at the bath for shorter than three hours, and it's not near the end of the day, you'll get some money back when you leave. (If the change isn't automatically dispensed when you go through the exit turnstile, take the printed receipt to the cashier.)

Aaaaahhh.

Entertainment in Budapest

Budapest is endlessly entertaining. Whether it's opera, folk music and dancing, a twilight stroll or boat trip, or holing up in one of the city's uniquely ramshackle "ruin pubs," Budapest offers something for everybody.

For **event schedules,** pick up the free, monthly *Budapest Panorama,* which makes things easy—listing performances with dates, venues, performers, and contact information for getting tickets (get it at the TI, or search from home at www.budapestpanorama.com). The English-language *Budapest Sun* newspaper also has event listings. Other helpful websites include www.wherebudapest.hu (general), www.koncertkalendarium.hu (classical), www.funzine.hu (nightlife), www.pestiest.hu and www.exit.hu (nightlife but only in Hungarian), and www.pestimusor.hu (cutting-edge arts but only in Hungarian).

To buy **tickets,** I've given strategies for the top options (Opera House and Hungária Koncert), and listed telephone numbers and (where possible) websites for others. Resources such as *Budapest*

Panorama usually explain how you can get tickets for specific performances. There are ticket offices around town, but they usually sell for only some (not all) performances. It's possible to search for and buy tickets for many Budapest events at www.kulturinfo.hu and www.jegymester.hu.

What's on can vary by **season.** For example, the Hungarian State Opera and other indoor cultural events tend to take a summer break from late June through late September (though that's prime time for outdoor music and Hungária Koncert's touristy shows).

Budapest's Music Scene

Budapest is a great place to catch a good—and inexpensive—musical performance. In fact, Viennese music lovers often make the three-hour trip here just to take in a fine, cheap opera in a luxurious setting. Options range from a performance at one of the world's great opera houses to light, touristy Hungarian folk concerts. The tourist concerts are the simplest option—you'll see the fliers everywhere—but you owe it to yourself to do a little homework and find something that really appeals to you. See the resources listed earlier, and don't miss the good classical-music schedules at www.koncertkalendarium.hu.

For the more "serious" concerts and opera, locals dress up; however, most tourists wear casual clothes (just not shorts, sneakers, or flip-flops).

A Night at the Opera—Consider taking in an opera by one of the best companies in Europe, in one of Europe's loveliest opera houses, for bargain prices. The Hungarian State Opera performs almost nightly, both at the main Opera House (Andrássy út 22, district VI, M1: Opera, described on page 529) and in the Erkel Színház theater (not nearly as impressive). Be careful to get a performance in the Opera House—not the Erkel Színház. Note that there are generally no performances from late June through late September. Most performances are in the original language with Hungarian supertitles.

Ticket prices range 1,000–17,000 Ft, but the best music deal in Europe may be the 400-Ft, obstructed-view tickets (easy to get, as they rarely run out—even when other tickets are sold out). If you buy one of these $2 opera tickets, you'll get a seat in one of two places: If you're sitting at the back of one of the boxes along the side of the theater, you can either sit comfortably, and see nothing; or

stand and crane your neck to see about half the stage. If you sit on the top of the side balcony, you can stand near the door for a view of the stage. If the seats in front of you don't fill up, scooting up to an empty seat when the show starts is less than a capital offense. Either way, you'll hear every note along with the big spenders. If a full evening of opera is too much for you, you can leave early or come late (but buy your ticket ahead of time, since the box office closes when the performance starts).

To get tickets, your best option is to order online (www.opera.hu or www.jegymester.hu), print your e-ticket, and waltz right in. Alternatively, you can call or fax the box office at the main Opera House (tel. 1/353-0170, fax 1/311-9017). In this case, you have to pick up your tickets in person the day before (or, if you fax them your credit-card number, you can pick them up just before the show). Maybe best of all, just drop by in person and see what's available during your visit. There are often a few tickets available at the door, even if it's supposedly "sold out" (box office open and phone answered Mon–Sat from 11:00 until show time—generally 19:00; Sun open 3 hours before the performance—generally 16:00–19:00, or 10:00–13:00 if there's a matinee).

Tourist Concerts by Hungária Koncert—Hungária Koncert offers a wide range of made-for-tourists performances of traditional music. These take place in one of two historic venues: the **Budai Vigadó** ("Buda Concert Hall"—on Corvin tér in Víziváros, between Castle Hill and the Danube, district I—for location, see the map on page 498); or in the former Budapest Ritz, now called the **Duna Palota** ("Danube Palace"—3 long blocks north of Vörösmarty tér in Pest, behind Roosevelt tér and the Gresham Palace at Zrínyi utca 5, district V, M1: Vörösmarty tér). The most popular options are Hungarian folk music-and-dance shows by various interchangeable troupes (3,600–6,200 Ft, June–Oct Sun–Fri at 20:00, can be at either theater) and classical "greatest hits" by the Danube Symphony Orchestra (with some traditional Hungarian instruments as well; 6,400–8,900 Ft, June–Oct Sat at 20:00, always at Duna Palota). Or you can take in an organ concert (usually mixing Bach and Mozart with Liszt or Bartók) in the Baroque **St. Anne's Church** (3,900 Ft, June–Sept Fri and Sun at 20:00, May Fri only at 20:00, on Batthyány tér at the north end of Víziváros, district I, M2: Batthyány tér). They also offer dinner cruises on the Danube and in-depth tours of the Jewish Quarter.

While highbrow classical music buffs will want a more serious concert, these shows are crowd-pleasers. If you book direct, you'll

get a 10 percent Rick Steves discount on anything they offer (must book in person, by phone, or by email—not valid if you buy your tickets on their website or through your hotel). The main office is in the Danube Palace at Zrínyi utca 5 (daily April–Dec 8:00–21:00, Jan–March 8:00–18:00, open later during concerts, tel. 1/317-2754 or 1/317-1377, www.ticket.info.hu, hunkonc@ticket.info.hu).

Nightlife in Budapest

Budapest is a young and lively city, with no shortage of after-hours fun. I've listed these roughly in increasing order of edginess, from "asleep by 10:00 (p.m.)" to "asleep by 10:00 (a.m.)."

Low-Impact Nightlife—This beautiful city is gorgeously lit after dark. Strolling along either the Buda or the Pest **promenade** along the Danube rewards you with wonderful views.

If you need some rejuvenation after a busy day of sightseeing, soak and splash at **Széchenyi Baths.** The indoor thermal baths close down at 19:00, but the outdoor pools—which are the best part anyway—stay open until 22:00 (last entry at 21:00). See "Experiences in Budapest," earlier.

Nighttime Danube Cruise—For a different angle on Budapest, consider joining one of these fun, romantic, crowd-pleasing boat trips. Danube Legenda's cruises include two drinks and evocative commentary about the floodlit buildings you pass (for details, see page 496).

Yuppie Drinking Zones—Young locals meet up for happy hour after work at the many trendy bars in two areas: on **Franz Liszt Square** (Liszt Ferenc tér, described on page 530) and along **Ráday utca** (page 576). Many of these places also serve food.

For something a bit more genteel—evocative of this city's late-19th-century Golden Age—locals pass their evenings sipping wine or nibbling dessert at a **café** (see "Budapest's Café Culture" on page 583).

In the "National Ditch"—Gödör Klub ("Ditch Club") fills the foundation for the never-completed new National Theater, in the very center of Pest at Erzsébet tér (next to Deák tér, where the three Metro lines converge). It's a café by day and a music club by night, when the sprawling subterranean art-gallery space (which is faintly visible below the surface of the park's shallow pond) hosts an eclectic range of concerts. In the summer, people fill the long, slanted approach to the club, and hang out on the lawn nearby—

creating a fun and engaging local scene (performances most nights, start at 20:00 or 21:00, Erzsébet tér, district V, M1/M2/M3: Deák tér, see Hungarian-only websites www.godorklub.hu or www.vilagveleje.hu).

"Ruin Pub" Crawl—If you're looking for memorable, lively, smoke-filled, trendy pubs crammed with twentysomething Budapesters and backpackers, explore the dingy streets of the Jewish Quarter, behind the Great Synagogue. (This area is between the Small and Great Boulevards, south of Király utca and north of Rákóczi út.) Here you'll find a funky new breed of bars, dubbed "ruin pubs." The low-profile entryways look abandoned, but once you walk back through a maze of hallways, you'll emerge into large halls and open-air courtyards filled with people huddled around ramshackle tables...rickety-chic. Note that most of these have vast outdoor zones, but small interiors—so they're better in good weather.

Szimpla ("Simple") was the first and remains the best of Budapest's "ruin pubs." This place sprawls through an old building that ought to be condemned, and spills out into an equally shoddy courtyard. It oozes nostalgia for young Budapesters who have fond memories of their communist-era childhoods. Although it's on the route of the tourist pub-crawls, Szimpla is still mostly frequented by locals (daily 12:00–4:00 in the morning, Kazinczy utca 14, district VII, M2: Astoria, tel. 1/352-4198, www.szimpla.hu). They have a second, smaller location a few blocks away (Kertész utca 48).

Kuplung is lower-profile and even rougher around the edges (if that's possible). The name means "clutch pedal"...put it into neutral. Tables are scattered around a grand hall that feels like an old hangar with a whale skeleton suspended from the ceiling, and downstairs is a hall for music acts (open nightly into the wee hours, Király utca 46, district VII, M1: Opera, www.kuplung.net). It's virtually impossible to find unless you know what to look for: Make your way to Király utca 46 (two blocks south of the Opera House), go down the parking-lot courtyard (to the right of Caesar's Sörözó) toward the *Heineken* sign, then go through the door at the far end (follow the noise). In the summer, the courtyard is also filled with outdoor seating.

Szóda (named for the seltzer bottles that line the wall) is smaller, less edgy, and more polished than the others, so it's not strictly a "ruin pub." But it's still lively and maintains a healthy reverence for the Red old days, with secondhand communist furniture and a sprawling open-air courtyard in good weather (nightly until late, Wesselényi utca 18, district VII, M2: Astoria, tel. 1/461-0007, www.szoda.com).

Shopping in Budapest

While it's not quite a shopper's mecca, Budapest does offer some enjoyable opportunities to hunt for that perfect Hungarian souvenir.

For a look at local life and a chance to buy some mementos, Budapest's single best shopping venue is the **Great Market Hall** (described on page 576). In addition to all the colorful produce downstairs, the upstairs gallery is full of fiercely competitive souvenir vendors. There's also a **folk-art market on Castle Hill** (near the bus stop at Dísz tér), but it's generally more touristy and a little more expensive. And, while **Váci utca** has been Budapest's main shopping thoroughfare for generations, today it features the city's highest prices and worst values. At touristy markets (but not established shops), haggling is common for pricier items (more than about 4,000 Ft)—but you'll likely only get the merchant to come down about 10 percent (maybe down to 20 percent for multiple items). If you pay with a credit card, you're less likely to snare a discount.

For a taste of the good old days—which somehow just feels right, here in nostalgic Budapest—wander up the city's **"antique row,"** Falk Miksa utca, just north of the Parliament (extends from Kossuth tér four blocks north to the Great Boulevard, near the end point of tram #2; also at Jászaí Mari tér stop for trams #4 and #6 around the Great Boulevard).

Budapest has several excellent **English bookstores.** For details, see page 486.

Budapesters do most of their shopping in big, American-style **shopping malls.** The biggest and most convenient options include **WestEnd City Center,** next door to Nyugati/Western train station (daily 8:00–23:00, Váci út 1–3, district VI, M3: Nyugati pu., tel. 1/374-6573, www.westend.hu); **Mammut** ("Mammoth"), two separate malls a few steps from Buda's Moszkva tér (Mon–Sat 10:00–21:00, Sun 10:00–18:00, Lövőház utca 2–6, district II, M2: Moszkva tér, tel. 1/345-8020, www.mammut.hu); and the newer **Arena Plaza,** near Keleti/Eastern train station (Mon–Sat 10:00–21:00, Sun 10:00–19:00, Kerepesi út 9, district XIV, M2: Keleti pu., tel. 1/880-7000, www.arenaplaza.hu).

Souvenir Ideas: The most popular souvenir is that quintessential Hungarian spice—**paprika.** Sold in metal cans, linen bags, or porcelain vases—and often accompanied by a tiny wooden scoop—it's a nice way to spice up your cooking with memories of your trip. (But remember that only sealed containers will make it through customs on your way back home.) For more, see "Paprika Primer" on page 465.

Special drinks are a fun souvenir, though they're tricky to

bring home (you'll have to wrap them very carefully and put them in your checked luggage—not permitted in carry-on; for customs regulations, see page 21). Consider the unique Hungarian spirit **Unicum** (described on page 467), or a bottle of Hungarian **wine** (page 468).

Another popular local item is a hand-embroidered **linen tablecloth.** The colors are often red and green—the national colors of Hungary, of course—but white-on-white designs are also available (and classy). If the thread is thick and the stitching is very even, it was probably done by machine, and therefore is less valuable.

Other handicrafts to look for include **chess sets** (most from Transylvania) and **nesting dolls.** While these dolls have more to do with Russia than with Hungary, you'll see just about every modern combination available: from classic girl dolls, to *South Park* characters, to Russian heads of state, to infamous terrorists, to American presidents. Tacky...but fun.

Fans of **communist kitsch** can look for ironic T-shirts that poke fun at that bygone era. But remember that the best selection is at the Memento Park gift shop, which also sells communist memorabilia and CDs of commie anthems.

Music-lovers can shop for a CD of **Hungarian music** at the Opera House gift shop.

Sleeping in Budapest

September is extremely tight (because of conventions), with October close behind; book as far ahead as possible for these times. The Formula 1 races (one weekend in early Aug) send rates through the roof. Most rates drop 10–25 percent in the off-season (generally Nov–March). Hoteliers know what their beds are worth, so generally you get what you pay for. Since my €100 listings are substantially nicer than my €85 listings, I'd spring for the extra expense to have a comfortable home base.

Sleep Code

(€1 = $1.40, 200 Ft = about $1, country code: 36, area code: 1)
To help you sort easily through the listings, I've divided the rooms into three categories based on the price for a standard double room with bath in high season:

$$$ Higher Priced—Most rooms €115 or more.
$$ Moderately Priced—Most rooms between €70–115.
$ Lower Priced—Most rooms €70 or less.

A flurry of new hotel construction over the last few years has flooded the market with top-end rooms. Outside of busy convention times (Sept–Oct), many of these places offer prices that are only a little more than a midrange hotel (these deals are often listed on the hotel's website; I've noted specifics in each listing).

If you're on a tight budget, consider one of Budapest's many hostels. But don't overlook the good-value Bellevue B&B (see page 573) and Mária and István (page 570).

The majority of hotels don't include the 3 percent tourist tax in their rates. Be warned that some big chains also don't include the whopping 20 percent sales tax, which can make your hotel cost nearly a quarter more than you expected. (Independent hotel rates typically do include sales tax.)

Most hotels listed here include a buffet breakfast. Some smaller budget places serve no breakfast at all, while larger chain hotels charge (too much) extra for it; in these cases, I've noted it in the listing. Consider having breakfast instead at one of three good, recommended cafés: Gerlóczy Café, Centrál Kávéház, or Callas (all described later, under "Eating in Budapest").

In Pest

Most travelers find staying in Pest more convenient than sleeping in Buda. Most sights worth seeing are in Pest, which also has a much higher concentration of Metro and tram stops, making it a snap to get around. Pest feels more lively and local than stodgy, touristy Buda, but it's also much more urban-feeling (if you don't enjoy big cities, sleep in Buda instead). I've arranged my listings by neighborhood, clustered around the most important sightseeing sectors.

Pest Town Center (Belváros), near Váci Utca

Sleeping on the very central and convenient Váci utca comes with overly inflated prices. But these less expensive options—just a block or two off Váci utca—offer some of the best values in Budapest.

$$$ Peregrinus Hotel, overpriced despite its good location, has 25 high-ceilinged, spacious, lightly renovated rooms (most of which lack air-conditioning—unusual for this price range). Because it's run by the big ELTE university, many of its guests are visiting professors and lecturers (Sb-€85, Db-€115, Tb-€150, 20 percent cheaper Nov–March, elevator, free Internet access in lobby and cable Internet in rooms, just off Váci utca at Szerb utca 3, district V; 5-min walk to M3: Kálvin tér, or tram #47 or #49 to Fövám tér; tel. 1/266-4911, fax 1/266-4913, www.peregrinushotel.hu, peregrinushotel@elte.hu).

$$ Gerlóczy Café & Rooms, which also serves good meals (recommended under "Eating in Budapest," later), is the best spot

in central Budapest for affordable elegance. The 18 rooms, around a classy old spiral-staircase atrium, recently underwent a thoughtful and stylish renovation. This gem is an exceptional value (Sb-€95, Db-€105, includes great breakfast, some restaurant noise on lower floors until 23:00, air-con, elevator planned soon, free Wi-Fi, 2 blocks from Váci utca, just off Városház utca at Gerlóczy utca 1, district V, M3: Ferenciek tere, tel. 1/501-4000, www.gerloczy.hu, info@gerloczy.hu).

$$ Kálvin-Ház, a long block up from the Great Market Hall, offers 38 big rooms with old-fashioned furnishings and squeaky parquet floors. The new top-floor rooms have a bit less classic character, but are air-conditioned and tidier than the older rooms. All things considered, it's a good value (all rooms cost the same: Sb-€70, Db-€95, apartment-€115, extra bed-€20, 15 percent cheaper Nov–March, elevator, free Internet access and Wi-Fi, Gönczy Pál utca 6, district IX, M3: Kálvin tér, tel. 1/216-4365, fax 1/216-4161, www.kalvinhouse.hu, info@kalvinhouse.hu).

$$ Leo Panzió is a peaceful oasis with 14 modern rooms in a hulking building that's seen better days. The location is central, if you can get past the dingy neighborhood. Once inside, the antique elevator is wonderfully rickety, and the double-paned windows keep out most of the noise from the busy street below. Rooms #1 and #7 overlook a quieter courtyard (Sb-€79, Db-€99, extra bed-€33, includes tax, 15 percent cheaper Nov–March, all rooms have a strange but well-marked little step down in the middle of the room, entirely non-smoking, air-con, free Wi-Fi, hiding upstairs in a giant building at Kossuth Lajos utca 2A—dial 58 at the door to call reception, district V, M3: Ferenciek tere, tel. 1/266-9041, tel. & fax 1/266-9042, www.leopanzio.hu, leo@leopanzio.hu).

$$ Ibis Hotel Budapest Centrum, with 126 rooms, is part of the no-frills chain that's sweeping Europe. Like all other Ibis branches, this place has spongy carpets, cookie-cutter predictability, and utterly no charm. But it's cheap, well-equipped for the price, and beautifully located at the start of the happening Ráday utca restaurant scene, just up the street from the Great Market Hall and Váci utca (Sb/Db-€79 April–Oct, Sb/Db-€65 Nov–March, lousy breakfast-€9/person, air-con, non-smoking rooms, elevator, pay Internet access and Wi-Fi, Ráday utca 6, district IX, M3: Kálvin tér, tel. 1/456-4100, fax 1/456-4116, www.ibis-centrum.hu, h2078@accor.com).

Near Andrássy Út

Andrássy Boulevard is handy, local-feeling, and fun. It's lined with appealing cafés, restaurants, theaters, and bars—and the living is good. The frequent Metro stations (M1/yellow line) make getting around the city easy from here. Most of the hotels listed here

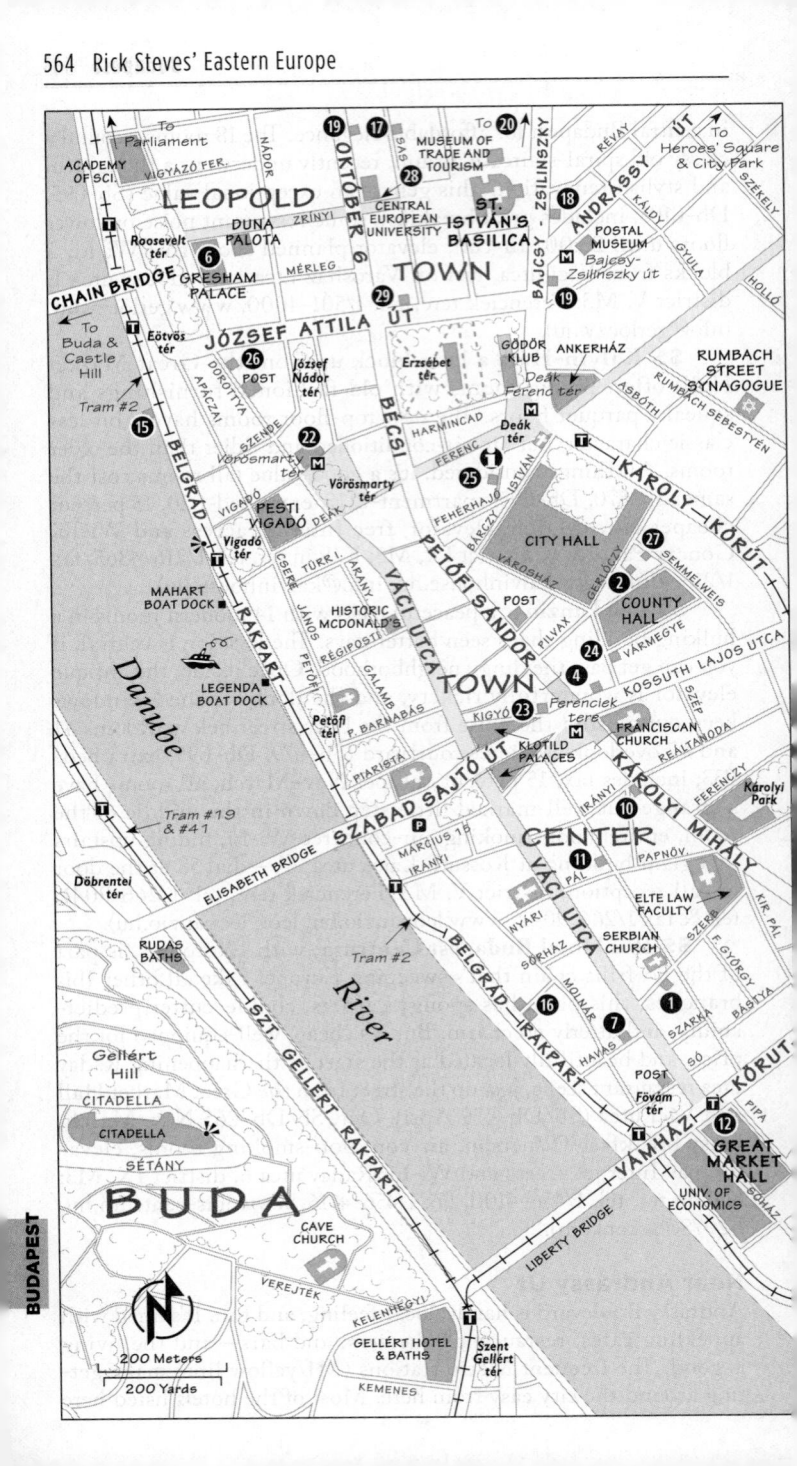
To Parliament
ACADEMY OF SCI.
VIGYÁZÓ FER.
NÁDOR
OKTÓBER 6
SAS
To
MUSEUM OF TRADE AND TOURISM
REÁY
To Heroes' Square & City Park
ANDRÁSSY ÚT
SZÉKELY
LEOPOLD TOWN
DUNA PALOTA
ZRÍNYI
CENTRAL EUROPEAN UNIVERSITY
ST. ISTVÁN'S BASILICA
BAJCSY - ZSILINSZKY
POSTAL MUSEUM
KÁLDY
GYULA
Roosevelt tér
GRESHAM PALACE
MÉRLEG
Bajcsy-Zsilinszky út
HOLLÓ
CHAIN BRIDGE
To Buda & Castle Hill
Eötvös tér
JÓZSEF ATTILA ÚT
GÓDOR KLUB
ANKERHÁZ
RUMBACH STREET SYNAGOGUE
POST
Erzsébet tér
Deák Ferenc tér
ASBÓTH
RUMBACH SEBESTYÉN
Tram #2
APÁCZAI
DOROTTYA
József Nádor tér
SZENDE
HARMINCAD
Deák tér
BECSI
FERENC
Vörösmarty tér
Vörösmarty tér
ISTVÁN
KÁROLY KÖRÚT
BELGRÁD RAKPART
VIGADÓ
PESTI VIGADÓ
DEÁK
FEHÉRHAJÓ
BÁRCZY
CITY HALL
Vigadó tér
TÜRR I.
CSERE
ARANY
VÁROSHÁZ
GERLÓCZY
SEMMELWEIS
PETŐFI SÁNDOR
VÁCI UTCA
MAHART BOAT DOCK
JÁNOS
HISTORIC MCDONALD'S
POST
COUNTY HALL
RÉGIPOSTI
FILYAX
VÁRMEGYE
Danube
PETŐFI
GALAMB
TOWN
KOSSUTH LAJOS UTCA
LEGENDA BOAT DOCK
Petőfi tér
P. BARNABÁS
KIGYÓ
Ferenciek tere
SZÉP
FRANCISCAN CHURCH
RÉÁLTANODA
PIARISTA
KLOTILD PALACES
KÁROLYI MIHÁLY
Tram #19 & #41
SZABAD SAJTÓ ÚT
IRÁNYI
FERENCZY
Károlyi Park
CENTER
MÁRCIUS 15
IRÁNYI
PAPNÖV.
Döbrentei tér
ELISABETH BRIDGE
PÁL
ELTE LAW FACULTY
KIR. PÁL
INVÁRI
VÁCI UTCA
SÖRHÁZ
SERBIAN CHURCH
SZERB
F. GYÖRGY
RUDAS BATHS
Tram #2
MOLNÁR
BÁSTYA
River
BELGRÁD RAKPART
SZAKÁ
ISZT. GELLÉRT RAKPART
HAVAS
SÓ
POST
Gellért Hill
CITADELLA
Fővám tér
PIPA
CITADELLA
VÁMHÁZ KÖRÚT
GREAT MARKET HALL
SÉTÁNY
UNIV. OF ECONOMICS
SÖRHÁZ
BUDA
CAVE CHURCH
LIBERTY BRIDGE
VEREJTÉK
KELENHEGYI
GELLÉRT HOTEL & BATHS
Szent Gellért tér
KEMENES
200 Meters
200 Yards

Pest Town Center Hotels & Restaurants
JEWISH QUARTER
(& "Ruin Pub" District)
GREAT SYNAGOGUE
AND JEWISH MUSEUM
PEST
ELTE CAMPUS
HUNGARIAN NATIONAL MUSEUM
APPLIED ARTS MUSEUM
HOLOCAUST MEMORIAL CENTER
NEW YORK CAFÉ
Tram #4 & #6
Tram #47 & #49
Astoria
Blaha Lujza tér
Kálvin tér
To Ferenc körút
To Petőfi Bridge
To Petőfi Bridge
ERZSÉBET KÖRÚT
RÁKÓCZI ÚT
MÚZEUM KÖRÚT
BAROSS
ÜLLŐI ÚT
RÁDAY
KÖZRAKTÁR UT
DOHÁNY
TREFORT
BRÓDY SÁNDOR
MÚZEUM
SZABÓ REV.
KRÚDY LŐRINC
KIRÁLY
KIS DIÓFA
CSÁNYI
KEKESZ
BARCSAY
ALMÁSSY
OSVÁT
BARÁT
KIBÉ JÓZSEF
KAZINCZY
KLAUZÁI
NYÁR
AKÁCFA
DOB
WESSELÉNYI
NAGY DIÓFA
SIP
VÁS
STÁHLY
GYULAI
PUSKIN
POLLACK MIHÁLY
SZENTKIRÁLYI
HORÁNSZKY
ÖT
ERKEL
GÖNCZY PÁL
LÓNYAY
IMRE
MÁTYÁS
CZUCZOR
KÖZTELEK
KINIZSI
BAKÁTS
KNEZICH
TÜZOLTÓ
POST
ZSIL
1 Peregrinus Hotel
2 Gerlóczy Café & Rooms
3 Kálvin-Ház Hotel
4 Leo Panzió Hotel & Főzelékfaló Ételbár
5 Ibis Hotel Budapest Centrum
6 Four Seasons Gresham Palace
7 Domino Hostel
8 Marco Polo Hostel
9 Mária & István Rooms
10 Centrál Kávéház
11 BorLabor Restaurant
12 Great Market Hall
13 Soul Café
14 Café Intenzo
15 Spoon Restaurant
16 Trattoria Toscana & Taverna Dionysos
17 Café Kör
18 Belvárosi Lugas Étterem
19 Duran Szendvics (2)
20 To Hummus Bar
21 New York Café & Deepwater Restaurant
22 Gerbeaud Café
23 Jégbüfé Snack Bar
24 Patyolat G. Laundry
25 Discover Budapest
26 Dorottya Pharmacy
27 Red Bus Bookstore
28 CEU Bookshop
29 MÁV Train Ticket Office

(except Cotton House) are within a two-block walk of this main artery. The Queen Mary and Cotton House, which are often mysteriously empty, are likely to have rooms when other hotels are full. For specific locations, see the map on page 567.

$$$ K+K Hotel Opera is wonderfully situated beside the Opera House in the fun "Broadway Quarter"—probably the handiest home-base location in Budapest. It's a regal splurge, with 206 classy rooms and helpful, professional service. The published rates are sky-high (Sb-€200, Db-€250), but most of the time you can score a better deal (often Sb-€120–140 and Db-€140–160 in summer, Sb/Db-€120 in winter, €25 more for recently renovated "executive" rooms, non-smoking floors, air-con, elevator, free Internet access and cable Internet in rooms, parking garage-€15/day, Révay utca 24, district VI, M1: Opera, tel. 1/269-0222, fax 1/269-0230, www.kkhotels.com, kk.hotel.opera@kkhotels.hu).

$$$ Kapital Inn is an upscale, new-feeling boutique B&B tucked behind the House of Terror. "Gay-owned and straight-friendly," its four rooms are pricey but perfectly stylish—there's not a pillow out of place. Albert, who lived in Boston, gives his B&B a sense of real hospitality (D-€89—a good value if you don't mind sharing a bathroom, Db-€125, 10 percent less Nov–March, air-con, free Internet access and Wi-Fi, pleasant breakfast terrace, no elevator, up several flights of stairs at Aradi utca 30, district VI, M1: Vörösmarty utca, mobile 0630-931-1023, fax 1/266-4634, www.kapitalinn.com, kapitalinn@kapitalinn.com).

$$ Hotel Pest is nicely located a block off Andrássy út (across the street from the Opera House). Its 25 newish, straightforward rooms surround a peaceful atrium with a winter-garden lounge and breakfast room. The published rates are a bit too high (Sb-€105, Db-€130), but it's worth considering if you can get a deal (often Sb-€90, Db-€110 in slower times, cheaper Nov–mid-March, air-con, elevator, free cable Internet, Paulay Ede utca 31, district VII, M1: Opera, tel. 1/343-1198, fax 1/351-9164, www.hotelpest.hu, hotelpest@hotelpest.hu).

$$ Hotel Queen Mary (named not for the British monarch, but for the owner's wife) is a good value, with 26 simple and unimaginative but new-feeling rooms. The neighborhood is dingy and gloomy, but it's on the cusp of an emerging dining zone, just two blocks beyond the end of the happening Franz Liszt Square (Sb-€70, Db-€80, Tb-€93, prices soft—ask for discount in slow times or with cash, 30 percent cheaper Nov–March, air-con, elevator, free cable Internet, Kertész utca 34, district VII, between M1: Oktogon and M2: Blaha Lujza tér, tel. 1/413-3510, fax 1/413-3511, www.hotelqueenmary.hu, info@hotelqueenmary.hu).

$$ Cotton House, a bit farther from Andrássy út than the others listed here (near the Nyugati/Western train station), is a

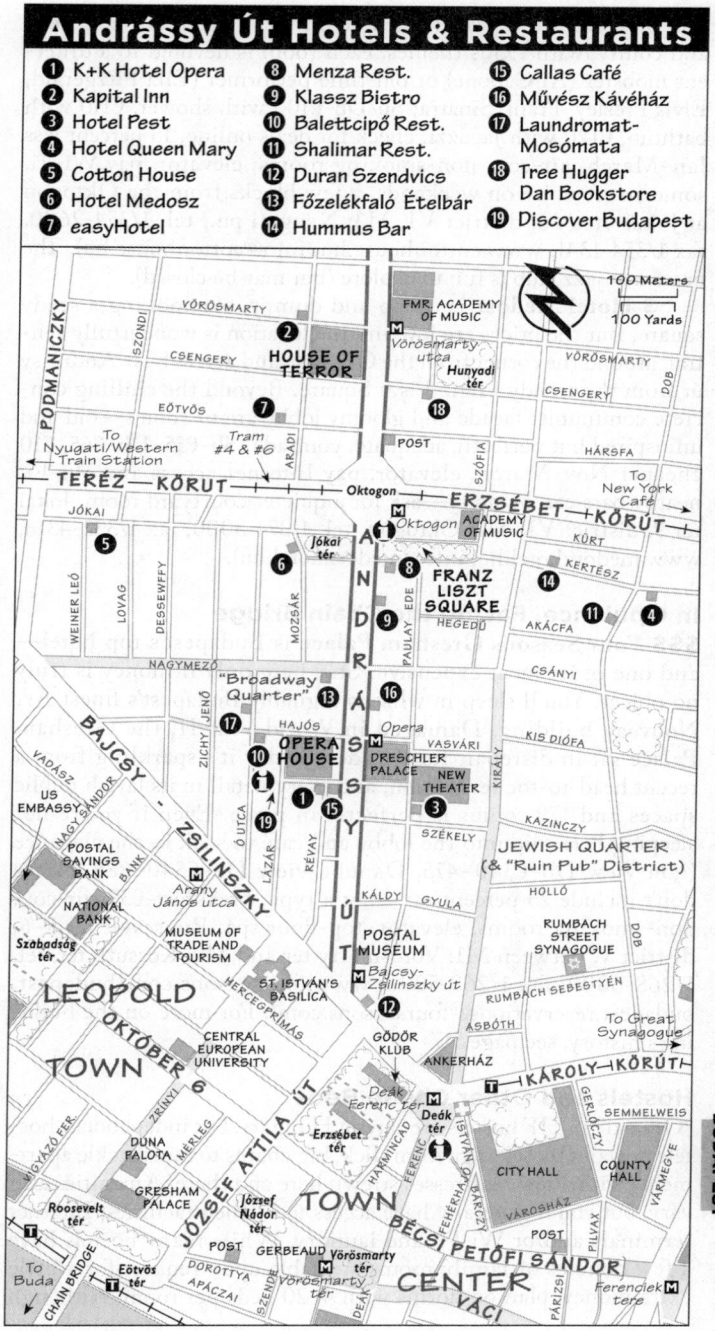
Andrássy Út Hotels & Restaurants
1 K+K Hotel Opera
2 Kapital Inn
3 Hotel Pest
4 Hotel Queen Mary
5 Cotton House
6 Hotel Medosz
7 easyHotel
8 Menza Rest.
9 Klassz Bistro
10 Balettcipő Rest.
11 Shalimar Rest.
12 Duran Szendvics
13 Főzelékfaló Ételbár
14 Hummus Bar
15 Callas Café
16 Művész Kávéház
17 Laundromat-Mosómata
18 Tree Hugger Dan Bookstore
19 Discover Budapest
100 Meters
100 Yards
VÖRÖSMARTY
CSENGERY
HOUSE OF TERROR
FMR. ACADEMY OF MUSIC
Vörösmarty utca
Hunyadi tér
EÖTVÖS
POST
HÁRSFA
To Nyugati/Western Train Station
Tram #4 & #6
TERÉZ KÖRUT
Oktogon
ERZSÉBET KÖRÜT
To New York Café
JÓKAI
Jókai tér
ACADEMY OF MUSIC
KÜRT
KERTÉSZ
FRANZ LISZT SQUARE
HEGEDŰ
AKÁCFA
NAGYMEZŐ
"Broadway Quarter"
CSÁNYI
HAJÓS
Opera
VASVÁRI
KIS DIÓFA
OPERA HOUSE
DRESCHLER PALACE
NEW THEATER
ANDRÁSSY ÚT
BAJCSY-ZSILINSZKY ÚT
US EMBASSY
SZÉKELY
KAZINCZY
JEWISH QUARTER (& "Ruin Pub" District)
POSTAL SAVINGS BANK
Arany János utca
NATIONAL BANK
KÁLDY GYULA
HOLLÓ
Szabadság tér
MUSEUM OF TRADE AND TOURISM
POSTAL MUSEUM
RUMBACH STREET SYNAGOGUE
ST. ISTVÁN'S BASILICA
Bajcsy-Zsilinszky út
LEOPOLD TOWN
HŐKEGERPRÍMÁS
RUMBACH SEBESTYÉN
OKTÓBER 6
CENTRAL EUROPEAN UNIVERSITY
GÖDÖR KLUB
ÁSBÓTH
To Great Synagogue
ANKERHÁZ
KÁROLY KÖRÚT
Deák Ferenc tér
Deák tér
SEMMELWEIS
DUNA PALOTA
Erzsébet tér
CITY HALL
COUNTY HALL
GRESHAM PALACE
Roosevelt tér
JÓZSEF ATTILA ÚT
TOWN
József Nádor tér
BÉCSI PETŐFI SÁNDOR
POST
GERBEAUD
Vörösmarty tér
VÁCI
CENTER
To Buda
CHAIN BRIDGE
Eötvös tér
DOROTTYA
APÁCZAI
SZENDY
Vörösmarty tér
DEÁK
PÁRIZSI
Ferenciek tere
PODMANICZKY
SZONDI
ARADI
SZŐFIA
DOB
WEINER LEÓ
LOVAG
DESSEWFFY
MOZSÁR
EDE
PAULAY
JENŐ
ZICHY
VADÁSZ
HAGY SÁNDOR
BANK
Ó UTCA
LÁZÁR
RÉVAY
KIRÁLY
ISTVÁN
BAKÁCSY
GERLÓCZY
VÁRMEGYE
PILVAX
VÁROSHÁZ
HAMMINCAD
FERENC
TEHERHÁZ
ZRÍNYI
MERLEG
VIGYÁZÓ FER.

fun, blast-from-the-past theme hotel. Its 23 retro rooms are fresh and comfy, with 1930s themes; each room is devoted to a different mobster (Al Capone) or old-time performer (Ella Fitzgerald, Elvis Presley, Frank Sinatra; Sb/Db-€100 with shower, €110 with bathtub, €120 with Jacuzzi, check for deals online, 15 percent less Jan–March, air-con, non-smoking rooms, elevator, pay Wi-Fi, some street noise on weekends, a few blocks from the Oktogon at Jókai utca 26, district VI, M3: Nyugati pu., tel. 1/354-2600, fax 1/354-1341, www.cottonhouse.hu, info@cottonhouse.hu). The basement jazz club is fun to explore (but may be closed).

$ Hotel Medosz is cheap and dumpy, overlooking a seedy square. But the prices are low and the location is wonderfully central, around the corner from the Oktogon and across busy Andrássy út from the trendy Franz Liszt Square. Beyond the chilling concrete communist facade and gloomy lobby are 67 rooms—old and uninspired but perfectly adequate, comrade (Sb-€55, Db-€65, €10 cheaper Nov–March, elevator, pay Internet access and Wi-Fi, nearby bars can be noisy—ask for a quieter courtyard room, Jókai tér 9, district VI, M1: Oktogon, tel. 1/374-3000, fax 1/332-4316, www.medoszhotel.hu, info@medoszhotel.hu).

In Opulence, Facing the Chain Bridge

$$$ Four Seasons Gresham Palace is Budapest's top hotel—and one of its most expensive. Stay here only if money is truly no object. You'll sleep in what is arguably Budapest's finest Art Nouveau building. Damaged in World War II, the Gresham Palace sat in disrepair for decades. Today it's sparkling from a recent head-to-toe renovation, and every detail in its lavish public spaces and 179 rooms is perfectly in place. Even if you're not sleeping here, dip into the lobby and café to soak in the elegance (non-view Db-€340–475, Danube-view Db-€540–885, prices don't include 23 percent tax—not a typo, breakfast-€35, air-con, non-smoking rooms, elevator, top-floor spa, Roosevelt tér 5–6, district V, between M1: Vörösmarty tér and M2: Kossuth tér, tel. 1/268-6000, fax 1/268-5000, www.fourseasons.com/budapest, budapest.reservations@fourseasons.com). For more on the building's history, see page 517.

Hostels and Other Cheap Beds

"Official" IYHF hostels are rare in Hungary, but independent hostels prevail. These range from slick, big chains to ramshackle apartments with a few mattresses strewn here and there. Amenities also vary, but you'll generally have access to kitchen facilities, Internet terminals and/or Wi-Fi, and laundry. While many hostels have a few doubles or family rooms available upon request for a little extra money, plan on dorms with 4–20 beds per room. Although

these hostels welcome travelers of any age, those over 30 might not enjoy bunking with the backpacker set—so I've also listed some good-value alternatives to the youth hostel scene. (Don't miss the excellent Bellevue B&B, across the river in Buda, and listed on page 573.)

$ ***Mellow Mood Hostels:*** Budapest's preeminent hostel chain has plenty of beds, but not much character. Surprisingly institutional for a non-official hostel, the Mellow Mood group is fine for predictable, crank-'em-out bunks (at both branches: cash only, prices include sheets, towel rental-300 Ft, no breakfast, guest kitchen, pay laundry, pay Internet access). There are two locations. **Domino Hostel**—with four twin rooms and 138 dorm beds in a handy location, right on Váci utca near the Great Market Hall—is more backpacker-oriented (Sb-€40, Db-€60, bunk in shared quad-€20, in 6-bed room-€18, in 8-bed room-€16, more for special events, cheaper Nov–March, 10 percent discount with ISIC card, best prices with advance online booking, lockers in room, Váci utca 77, enter at Havas utca 6, district V, M3: Kálvin tér, tel. 1/235-0492, www.dominohostel.com, info@dominohostel.com). **Marco Polo Hostel,** with a few dorm beds and 36 more twin rooms (with bathrooms) in a less convenient location, attracts a slightly older crowd (similar but slightly higher rates, Nyár utca 6, district VII, M2: Blaha Lujza tér, tel. 1/413-2555, fax 1/413-6058, www.marcopolohostel.com, sales@marcopolohostel.com). Mellow Mood also runs several budget hotels around the city, but they're not a good value.

$ ***Smaller "Indie" Hostels:*** Budapest has seemingly dozens of apartments that have been taken over by young entrepreneurs, offering basic, rough-around-the-edges hostel charm. You'll buzz in at the door and climb up a creaky, dank, and smelly staircase to a funky little enclave of fellow backpackers. Most of these places have just three rooms (one double and two small dorms) and feel more like communes than the finely tuned, high-capacity youth hostel machines in many other cities. As each of these fills a niche (party, artsy, communist-themed, etc.), it's hard to recommend just one—read reviews on a hostel site (such as www.hostels.com) and find one that suits your hosteling philosophy. Of the places I've seen, I particularly liked **Aventura Hostel,** a colorful and stylish option in a dreary urban neighborhood near the Nyugati/Western train station. Well-run by Agnes, this homey place is tastefully mod, friendly, clean, and low-key, with imaginatively decorated rooms (3 rooms, bunk in 5- or 8-bed dorm-€14–21, D-€50–60, price depends on season, includes breakfast and sheets, towel rental-500 Ft, free Internet access and Wi-Fi, pay laundry service, massage available, across the busy ring road and a very long block from Nyugati train station at 12 Visegrádi utca—dial 131 at door,

district XIII, M3: Nyugati pu., tel. 1/239-0782, www.aventurahostel.com, info@aventurahostel.com). They also rent apartments near Andrássy út (Db-€60–70).

B&B Hostel Alternative: **$ Mária and István,** your chatty Hungarian aunt and uncle, are saving a room for you in their Old World apartment. For warmth and hospitality at youth-hostel prices, consider bunking in one of their two simple, old-fashioned rooms, which share a bathroom. The smaller room is cheaper and quieter; the bigger room gets some street noise on weekends (S-€20–24, D-€30–36, T-€42–48, price depends on size of room and length of stay—longer is cheaper, no breakfast but guests' kitchen, cash only, elevator plus a few stairs, Ferenc körút 39, district IX, M3: Ferenc körút, tel. & fax 1/216-0768, www.mariaistvan.hu, mariaistvan@upcmail.hu). From the Ferenc körút Metro stop, follow signs for the *Ferenc körút 41–45* exit, bear right up the stairs, and walk straight about a block and a half, looking for #39 (on the left, after the post office; dial 19 at the door). Mária and István also rent two apartments that are two Metro stops farther from the center (Db-€50–56, Tb-€60–66, Qb-€68–80, family apartment, both near M3: Nagyvarad tér).

Institutional but Cheap and New: The **$ easyHotel** chain follows a similar model to its parent company, the no-frills easyJet airline: They charge you very little up front, then nickel-and-dime you with optional extras—so you pay only for what you want (pick up the list at entry: TV access-€7.50/24 hours; cable Internet access-€2/hr, €10/24 hours; hairdryer-€1/24 hours; room-cleaning during your stay-€10; and so on). With 59 rooms just a block off the busy Great Boulevard and around the corner from the Oktogon, the location is handy. The rooms feel popped out of a plastic mold, with a nauseating orange-and-gray color scheme, sterile quasi-linoleum floors, and tiny prefab ship's-head bathrooms. But the price is right...if you can resist the extras (Sb/Db-€15–46 depending on demand, no breakfast, 24-hour reception, non-smoking, air-con, elevator, Eötvös utca 25A, district VI, M1: Oktogon, tel. 1/411-1982, www.easyhotel.com, info@budapestoktogon.easyhotel.com).

In Buda

Víziváros

The Víziváros neighborhood—or "Water Town"—is the lively part of Buda, squeezed between Castle Hill and the Danube, where fishermen and tanners used to live. Across the river from the Parliament building, it comes with fine views. Víziváros is the most pleasant central area to stay on the Buda side of the Danube. It's expensive and a little less convenient than Pest, but also feels less urban.

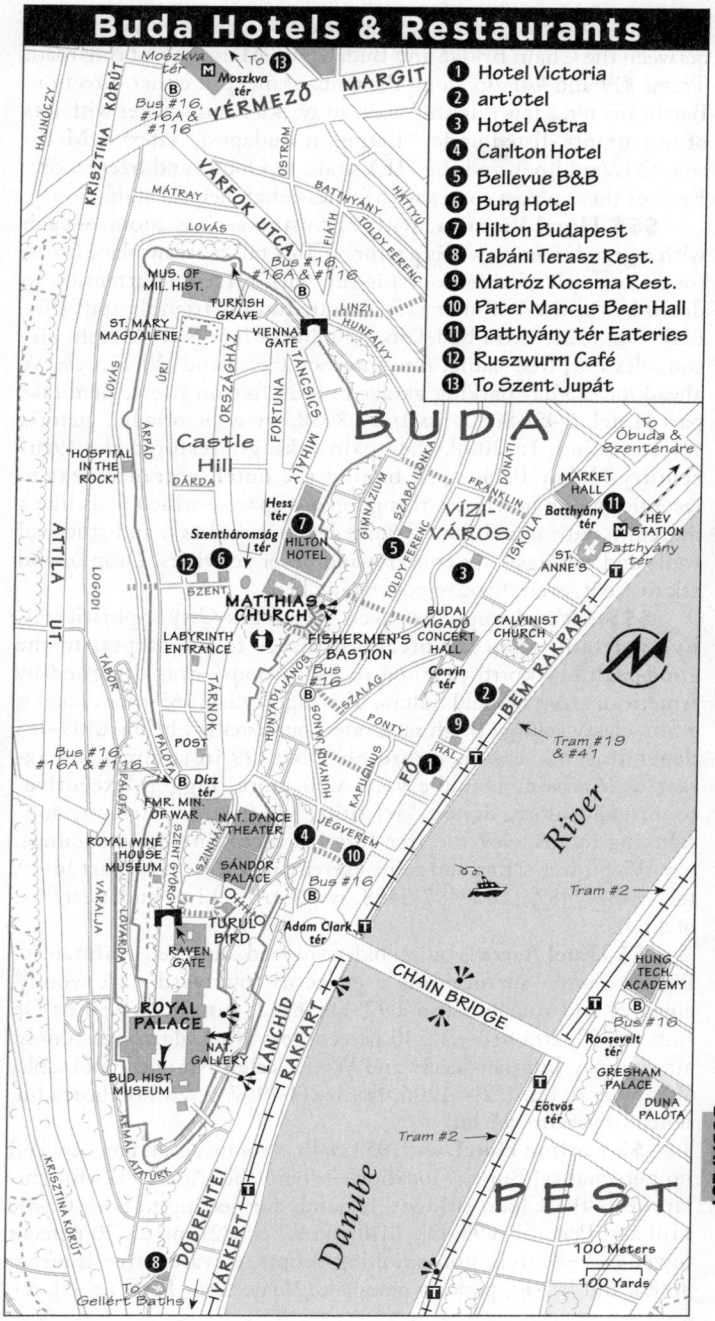
Buda Hotels & Restaurants
1 Hotel Victoria
2 art'otel
3 Hotel Astra
4 Carlton Hotel
5 Bellevue B&B
6 Burg Hotel
7 Hilton Budapest
8 Tabáni Terasz Rest.
9 Matróz Kocsma Rest.
10 Pater Marcus Beer Hall
11 Batthyány tér Eateries
12 Ruszwurm Café
13 To Szent Jupát
BUDA
PEST
Castle Hill
VÍZI-VÁROS
Danube River
Moszkva tér
VÉRMEZŐ
MARGIT
VÁRFOK UTCA
KRISZTINA KÖRÚT
HAJNÓCZY
MÁTRAY
LOVÁS
BATTHYÁNY
HÁTTYÚ
TOLDY FERENC
MUS. OF MIL. HIST.
TURKISH GRAVE
ST. MARY MAGDALENE
VIENNA GATE
LINZI
HUNFALVY
ORSZÁGHÁZ
TÁNCSICS MIHÁLY
FORTUNA
ÚRI
ÁRPÁD
"HOSPITAL IN THE ROCK"
DÁRDA
ATTILA UT.
LÓGÓDI
Hess tér
HILTON HOTEL
Szentháromság tér
SZENT
MATTHIAS CHURCH
LABYRINTH ENTRANCE
FISHERMEN'S BASTION
TÁBOR
TÁRNOK
POST
PALOTA
Díszt tér
FMR. MIN. OF WAR
ROYAL WINE HOUSE MUSEUM
SZENT GYÖRGY
SZINHÁZ
NAT. DANCE THEATER
SÁNDOR PALACE
VÁRALJA
LOVARDA
TURUL BIRD
RAVEN GATE
ROYAL PALACE
NAT. GALLERY
BUD. HIST. MUSEUM
CSÁSZÁR
KEMAL ATATÜRK
KRISZTINA KÖRÚT
DOBRENTEI
VÁRKERT
LÁNCHÍD
RAKPART
GIMNÁZIUM
SZABÓ IVÁNNA
TOLDY FERENC
HUNYADI JÁNOS
HUNYADI JÁNOS
SZALAG
PONTY
VÉGVEREM
KAPUCINUS
Adam Clark tér
CHAIN BRIDGE
FRANKLIN
ISKOLA
DONÁTI
MARKET HALL
Batthyány tér
HÉV STATION
ST. ANNE'S
BUDAI VIGADÓ CONCERT HALL
CALVINIST CHURCH
Corvin tér
BEM RAKPART
HAL
FŐ
Tram #19 & #41
Tram #2
HUNG. TECH. ACADEMY
Roosevelt tér
GRESHAM PALACE
DUNA PALOTA
Eötvös tér
To Óbuda & Szentendre
Bus #16, #16A & #116
Bus #16
To Gellért Baths
100 Meters
100 Yards

The following hotels (except the last one) are in district I, between the Chain Bridge and Buda's busy Margit körút ring road. Trams #19 and #41 zip along the embankment in either direction. Batthyány tér, a few minutes' walk away, is a handy center with lots of restaurants (listed under "Eating in Budapest," later), a Metro stop (M2/red line), and the HÉV train to Óbuda and Szentendre. Each of these places comes with professional, helpful staff.

$$$ Hotel Victoria, with 27 business-class rooms—each with a grand river view—is a winner. This tall, narrow place (three rooms on each of nine floors) is run with pride and attention to detail by on-the-ball manager Zoltán and his friendly staff (Sb-€117, Db-€123, extra bed-€46, 30 percent less Nov–March, air-con, elevator, free sauna, free Internet access and Wi-Fi, reserve ahead for €13/day parking garage or park free on street, Bem rakpart 11, tel. 1/457-8080, fax 1/457-8088, www.victoria.hu, victoria@victoria.hu). In 2008, they painstakingly restored the 19th-century Hubay Palace just behind the hotel (entrance next to reception). The hotel uses this gorgeous space—which feels like a museum, with inlaid floors, stained-glass windows, and stuccoed walls and ceilings—for concerts and other activities. Drop in and ask to see it, even if you're not staying here.

$$$ art'otel impresses even New York City sophisticates. Every detail—from the breakfast dishes to the carpets to the good-luck blackbird perched in each room—was designed by American artist Donald Sultan. This big, stylish, 165-room hotel is a fun, classy splurge (high rack rates, but usually Sb/Db-€109–165 depending on season, figure Sb/Db-€129 in summer, breakfast-€12/person, Danube view-€20 more, bigger "executive" rooms-€30 more, deluxe "art suites"-€60 more, air-con, non-smoking rooms, elevator, free Internet access in business lounge, pay Wi-Fi, free sauna and mini-exercise room, Bem rakpart 16–19, tel. 1/487-9487, fax 1/487-9488, www.artotel.hu, budapest@artotel.hu).

$$ Hotel Astra is quiet, old-fashioned, and well-maintained. Its 12 rooms—surrounding a peaceful courtyard—are woody, elegant, and spacious (Sb-€97, Db-€112, sumptuous Sb or Db suite-€139, extra bed-€20, 10 percent less Nov–March, cash only, air-con, pay Internet access and Wi-Fi, cellar bar with pool table, Vám utca 6, tel. 1/214-1906, fax 1/214-1907, www.hotelastra.hu, hotelastra@euroweb.hu).

$$ Carlton Hotel, with 95 smallish rooms, is all business and no personality. But the location—where the Castle Hill funicular meets the Chain Bridge—is handy for getting to both Castle Hill and Pest (Sb-€95, Db-€110, extra bed-€21, prices 20 percent lower Nov–March, non-smoking rooms, elevator, free Internet access and Wi-Fi, parking garage-€12/day, Apor Péter utca 3, tel.

1/224-0999, fax 1/224-0990, www.carltonhotel.hu, carltonhotel@t-online.hu).

$ Bellevue B&B, hiding in a quiet residential area on the Víziváros hillside just below the Fishermen's Bastion staircase, is easily Budapest's best deal. This gem is run by retired economists Judit and Lajos Szuhay, who lived in Canada for four years and speak flawless English. The breakfast room and some of the five straightforward, comfortable rooms have views across the Danube to the Parliament and Pest. Judit (YOO-deet) and Lajos (LIE-yosh) love to chat, and pride themselves on offering genuine hospitality and a warm welcome (let them know what time you're arriving). As this B&B is understandably popular, book ahead (Sb-€50–67, Db-€60–77, price depends on room size and view, 20–30 percent cheaper mid-Oct–mid-April, cash only, nonsmoking, air-con, free Internet access and Wi-Fi; M2: Batthyány tér plus a 10-min uphill walk, or bus #16 from Deák, Roosevelt, or Adam Clark squares to Dónati utca plus a 2-min downhill walk—they'll email you detailed directions; Szabó Ilonka utca 15/B, mobile 0630-370-8678 or 0630-951-5494, www.bellevuebudapest.com, judit@bellevuebudapest.com).

$ Hotel Papillon is farther north, in a forgettable residential area a 10-minute uphill walk past Moszkva tér. It's a cheery little place with 30 homey, pastel rooms, a garden with a tiny swimming pool, and affordable prices (Sb-€44, older Db-€54, newer "superior" Db with air-con and balcony-€64 and worth the extra money, 25 percent less Nov–March, elevator, pay Internet access, free Wi-Fi in some parts of hotel, restaurant, tram #4 or #6 from Moszkva tér to Mechwart liget stop then an uphill walk, Rózsahegy utca 3, district II, tel. 1/212-4750, fax 1/212-4003, www.hotelpapillon.hu, rozsahegy@t-online.hu).

Castle Hill

Romantics often like calling Castle Hill home (district I). These two hotels share Holy Trinity Square (Szentháromság tér) with Matthias Church. They couldn't be closer to the Castle Hill sights, but they're in a tourist zone—dead at night, and less convenient to Pest than other listings.

$$$ Burg Hotel, with 26 rooms, is simply efficient: concrete, spacious, and comfy, with a professional staff. You'll find more conveniently located hotels for less money elsewhere, but if you simply *must* stay in a modern hotel across the street from Matthias Church, this is it (Sb-€119, Db-€129, Db apartment-€149, extra bed-€39, 10 percent discount with this book unless they're very busy, cheaper for 3-night stays, prices 15 percent less Nov–March, request view room for no extra charge, no elevator, entirely nonsmoking, top-floor rooms are extremely long, family rooms, fee

for Internet access, free Wi-Fi, Szentháromság tér 7–8, tel. 1/212-0269, fax 1/212-3970, www.burghotelbudapest.com, info@burghotelbudapest.com, Lajos).

$$$ Hilton Budapest is a 322-room landmark—the first big Western hotel in town back in the gloomy days of communism. Today, while a bit faded, it still offers a complete escape from Hungary and a chance to be surrounded by rich tourists mostly from Japan, Germany, and the United States (very flexible rates, but usually about Db-€120 in slower times—a great deal, check for better prices online, best rates are for 3-week advance booking with full nonrefundable prepayment, €30 more for Danube-view rooms, prices do not include 23 percent tax, breakfast-€27/person, non-smoking floors, elevator, pay Wi-Fi, Hess András tér 1–3 on Castle Hill next to Matthias Church, tel. 1/889-6600, fax 1/889-6644, www.budapest.hilton.com, reservations.budapest@hilton.com).

Eating in Budapest

Thanks to Budapest's ever-evolving culinary scene, there's no shortage of places to dine. A few years ago, I had to scrape the bottom of the barrel to recommend eateries here. Now, I can barely keep track of what's new—and scouting new restaurants is the highlight of my research chores. The broad range of options and healthy sense of one-upmanship among local chefs keeps prices reasonable and quality high. This also means that the foodie scene here is boom-and-bust: A place quickly acquires a huge and enthusiastic following, then soon falls from grace as an even more enticing competitor opens up shop.

While you'll find the Hungarian standards, most big-city restaurants like to dabble in international cuisine. Most of my listings feature an international menu with some Hungarian flourishes. (If you want truly traditional Hungarian fare, you'll actually do a bit better in smaller towns.) The good news: Most Hungarian chefs are so skilled that any cuisine is well-executed here.

Be aware that in the city center—where you'll likely be eating—most restaurants are frequented by tourists and well-heeled local yuppies. Blue-collar Budapesters can't afford to eat out in the areas where you'll be spending your time. If you really want to eat local-style, head for the big shopping malls (like the WestEnd City Center near Nyugati train station, or Mammut near Moszkva tér). There, you can truly dine with the Budapesters...at T.G.I. Friday's and McDonald's, just like back home.

While most Hungarian restaurants are honest, rip-off joints abound in downtown Budapest's tourist zone—especially along the main walking street, Váci utca. (Frankly, I'd never eat on

Váci utca, which practically guarantees bad food and service for too-high prices.) Avoid any place with a menu that doesn't list prices, and tune in to the fine print. For example, some restaurants automatically add a 10 percent service charge to the bill. The extra charge should be noted on the menu (if it's not, complain), and appears as a line item after the subtotal on the bill (look for "service," *borravaló, felszolgálási díj,* or *szervízdíj*). In these cases, an additional tip is not necessary.

In Pest

I've listed these options by neighborhood, for easy reference with your sightseeing.

In Pest's Town Center (Belváros), near Váci Utca

When you ask natives about good places to eat on Váci utca, they just roll their eyes. Budapesters know that only rich tourists who don't know better would throw their money away on the relatively bad food and service along this high-profile pedestrian drag. But wander a few blocks off the tourist route, and you'll discover alternatives with fair prices and better food. For locations, see the map on page 564.

Gerlóczy Café is tucked on a peaceful little square next to the giant City Hall, flanked by gourmet salami and cheese shops. This classy café features international cuisine with several seating options (out on the square, in the coffee-house interior, upstairs in the non-smoking section, or down in the wine cellar). There's a good permanent menu, special themed menus that change every few months, and new specials that they try out each weekend. The clientele is a mix of tourists and upscale-urban Budapesters, including local politicians and actors from several nearby theaters. With a take-your-time ambience that's arguably more Parisian than Hungarian, this is a particularly inviting spot (2,000–2,500-Ft pastas, 1,700–4,000-Ft main dishes, good breakfasts with egg dishes for under 1,000 Ft, excellent fresh-baked pastries and bread, daily 7:00–23:00, 2 blocks from Váci utca, just off Városház utca at Gerlóczy utca 1, district V, M3: Ferenciek tere, tel. 1/501-4000). They rent good rooms, too (listed under "Sleeping in Budapest," earlier).

Centrál Kávéház, while famous as a grand, old-fashioned café, is also one of Budapest's best spots for a central, characteristic meal, and offers some good home-style Hungarian dishes you don't often find in restaurants. Since it's across the street from the university library, it's popular with students and professors. Choose between the lively, vast downstairs, or the more refined upstairs dining room—both featuring elegant, early-1900s ambience (1,000-Ft sandwiches, small but filling 1,000- to 1,500-Ft

"Zóna" plates until 16:00, larger 2,500– to 4,000-Ft main dishes anytime, daily 8:00–24:00, Károlyi Mihály utca 9, district V, M3: Ferenciek tere, tel. 1/266-2110).

BorLabor ("Wine Lab") features traditional, regional, updated Hungarian specialties at reasonable prices in a modern, romantic cellar atmosphere (2,000–3,000-Ft main dishes, daily 12:00–24:00, a block north of Váci utca at Veres Pálné utca 7, district V, M3: Ferenciek tere, tel. 1/328-0382).

Great Market Hall: At the far south end of Váci utca, you can eat a quick lunch on the upper floor of the Great Market Hall (Nagyvásárcsarnok). Fakanál Étterem—the glassed-in, sit-down cafeteria above the main entrance—is overpriced and touristy, but offers good seating (2,000–2,700-Ft main dishes). The stalls along the right side of the building are cheaper, but quality can vary (grab a bar stool or you'll stand while you munch). Locals love the Lángos stand, for deep-fried bread slathered with sour cream and cheese (add garlic for some kick). Produce and butcher stands line the main floor, and it's easy to miss the big, modern grocery store in the basement (the end nearest Váci utca; Mon 6:00–17:00, Tue–Fri 6:00–18:00, Sat 6:00–15:00, closed Sun, Fővám körút 1–3, district IX, M3: Kálvin tér).

Ráday Utca

Ráday utca is Budapest's "restaurant row." While tourists blow their budgets a few blocks away on Váci utca, Budapesters hang out at this street's trendy, inventive eateries and pubs. As this is a prime pre-dinner drink spot, many places serve no food, only drinks (find out before you sit down). The outdoor seating along here is inviting on a balmy evening. And, while the similar scene at Franz Liszt Square (described later) is becoming more touristy and snooty-upscale, locals still outnumber visitors on Ráday utca. It's worth going out of your way to come here and simply wander, choosing the place that looks best. Just take the M3/blue Metro line to Kálvin tér—a three-minute walk from the Great Market Hall—and stroll south (district IX). Most places are pretty interchangeable; survey your options and take your pick. If you can't decide, consider these:

Soul Café is one of the best-regarded eateries along this drag, with a trendy interior and international fare with some Hungarian options (1,000-Ft sandwiches before 18:00, 1,500–3,000-Ft main dishes anytime, salad options, open daily 12:00–24:00, Ráday utca 11–13, tel. 1/217-6986).

Café Intenzo hides around the corner from the start of Ráday utca, where it meets the busy ring road. Low-key and with a loyal local following, they serve Hungarian and international cuisine in a nondescript interior or out in a pleasant courtyard garden (1,100-Ft

sandwiches, 1,200–1,900-Ft pastas, 1,700–3,000-Ft main dishes, daily 10:00–1:00 in the morning, Kálvin tér 9, tel. 1/219-5243).

Danube Promenade

The riverbank facing the castle is lined with hotel restaurants and permanently moored restaurant boats. You'll find bad service, mediocre food, mostly tourists, and sky-high prices...but the atmosphere and people-watching are marvelous.

Spoon, a boat in front of the InterContinental Hotel next to the Chain Bridge, is your best Danube dining option. This hip, upscale place offers pricey, elaborately prepared international cuisine with an emphasis on seafood, plus some Hungarian standards (3,500–6,000-Ft main dishes). Choose between a dressy candlelit dining room or outdoor tables above decks. The bathrooms—Budapest's most scenic—are a must, even if you don't have to go. If you're going to pay too much to eat along the river, you might as well do it here (daily 12:00–24:00, often booked for special events—call ahead to be sure it's open and to reserve a riverside table, Vigadó tér, dock #3, district V, M1: Vörösmarty tér, tel. 1/411-0933).

For a more affordable and more local experience, head a bit farther south, near the green Liberty Bridge. Along the embankment road called Belgrád Rakpart, you'll find a cluster of fun and lively ethnic restaurants (including good Italian at **Trattoria Toscana,** #13, and a mini-Santorini with Greek fare at **Taverna Dionysos,** #16).

Various companies run **dinner cruises** along the Danube (including Hungária Koncert, which offers a 10 percent discount to Rick Steves readers; see "Entertainment in Budapest," earlier). While these can be romantic, the restaurant options in Budapest are too tempting to pass up. Instead, dine at your choice of eateries, then take the Danube Legenda nighttime cruise (see page 558).

Near St. István's Basilica

The area near St. István's Basilica—a few steps from the start of Andrássy út—has been neatly pedestrianized, and several appealing eateries have popped up here recently. For locations, see the map on pages 564.

On Sas Utca, in Front of St. István's Basilica: The street called Sas utca, running along the bottom of the grand plaza in front of St. István's, is lined with a handful of trendy, pricey, well-regarded, and somewhat snobby restaurants (such as Mokka and Dío). For something top-notch but a bit less expensive than the others, head for **Café Kör** ("Circle"). This stylish but unpretentious eatery serves up mostly Hungarian and some Mediterranean fare in a tasteful, tight one-room interior and at a few sidewalk tables. It prides itself

on being friendly and providing a good value. Because it's beloved by local foodies, reservations are smart anytime and essential on weekends (2,000–4,000-Ft main dishes, small portions for 30 percent less, good salads, daily specials, cash only, Mon–Sat 10:00–23:00, closed Sun, Sas utca 17, district V, between M3: Arany János utca and M1: Bajcsy-Zsilinszky út, tel. 1/311-0053).

Behind St. István's Basilica: **Belvárosi Lugas Étterem** is your cheap-and-central, no-frills option. *Lugas* is a Hungarian word for a welcoming garden strewn with grape vines, and the cozy dining room—with a dozen tables of happy eaters—captures that spirit. Or sit at the sidewalk tables outside on busy Bajcsy-Zsilinszky boulevard. The food is simply good Hungarian (1,300–2,800-Ft main dishes, order starches separately, daily 12:00–23:30, directly behind and across the street from St. István's Basilica at Bajcsy-Zsilinszky út 15, district VI, M1: Bajcsy-Zsilinszky út, tel. 1/302-5393).

Near Andrássy Út, Between the Oktogon and the Opera

For the locations of these eateries, see the map on page 567.

Franz Liszt Square (Liszt Ferenc Tér): Franz Liszt Square, a leafy park on the most interesting stretch of Andrássy út, boasts a stylish cluster of pricey, pretentious yuppie restaurants, many with outdoor seating (lively on a summer evening). This is the place for Budapesters to see and be seen...but only for those who can afford it (most main dishes hover around 2,500–4,000 Ft). Take the Metro to Oktogon and follow your nose. My favorite Liszt Square eatery, **Menza** (the old communist word for "School Cafeteria"), wins the "Best Design" award. Recycling 1970s furniture and an orange-and-brown color scheme, it's a postmodern parody of an old communist café—half kitschy-retro, half brand-new feeling. When locals come in here, they can only chuckle and say, "Yep. This is how it was." With tasty and well-priced updated Hungarian cuisine, embroidered leather-bound menus, brisk but efficient service, breezy jazz on the soundtrack, and indoor or outdoor seating, it's a memorable spot (1,900–2,600-Ft main dishes, daily 10:00–24:00, halfway up Andrássy út at Liszt Ferenc tér 2, district VII, tel. 1/413-1482, www.menza.co.hu). If you like the Franz Liszt Square scene, you'll find more on Kertész utca, beyond the end of the square, and in the "Broadway Quarter," near the Opera House (on Hajós utca and Nagymező utca).

Right on Andrássy út: **Klassz** is a trendy but unpretentious bistro with a similarly postmodern "eclectic-mod" aesthetic, both in its decor and its food. Serving up surprisingly affordable international/nouvelle cuisine with Hungarian flair, it's a new favorite

among Budapest's value-seeking foodies (1,500–3,000-Ft main dishes, Mon–Sat 11:30–23:00, Sun 11:30–18:00, Andrássy út 41, district VI, between M1: Opera and M1: Oktogon, no reservations possible—try to arrive by 19:00).

Behind the Opera House: **Balettcipő** ("Ballet Slipper"), with indoor and outdoor seating, boasts an affordable, very eclectic, and ever-changing menu that combines Hungarian, Asian, Mexican, Italian, and more (1,500–2,000-Ft main dishes, Mon–Fri 9:00–24:00, Sat–Sun 12:00–24:00, just behind the Opera House at Hajós utca 14, district VI, M1: Opera, tel. 1/269-3114).

Indian: Hungarians seem to have an affinity for Indian cuisines, as both enjoy smoothing together powerful spices. **Shalimar** hides in a stuffy cellar in a dreary neighborhood two blocks beyond the end of Franz Liszt Square. Everything about this place is unexceptional...except the food. This is my number-one place in Eastern Europe for a break from pork and kraut. I can never resist the *murg makhani*...and I'm never disappointed. The non-smoking section is filled with too-loud Americans, so I sit with the young locals in the smoking section (1,700–2,500-Ft main dishes, half-portions for 40 percent less, daily 12:00–16:00 & 18:00–24:00, reservations smart on weekends, Dob utca 50, district VII, between M1: Oktogon and M2: Blaha Lujza tér, tel. 1/352-0297).

In City Park

These three touristy eateries cluster around the end of the lake behind the Millennium Monument in City Park (district XIV, M1: Hősök tere). All are open for both lunch and dinner. The first one is Budapest's best-known, fanciest splurge; the other two are more reasonable and casual, but still pretty pricey. For locations, see the map on page 536.

Gundel Restaurant has been *the* dining spot for VIPs and celebrities since 1894. The pricey place is an institution—President Bill Clinton ate here. Pope John Paul II didn't, but when his people called out for dinner, they called Gundel. The elegant main room is decorated with fine 19th-century Hungarian paintings and an Art Deco flair, while the more casual garden terrace is leafy and delightful. The Hungarian cuisine flirts with sophisticated international influences (4,000–11,000-Ft main courses, 20,000–40,000-Ft fixed-price meals). At lunch, choose from the same pricey à la carte items, or opt for a more affordable fixed-price meal (4,000–5,000 Ft). Sunday brunch, with a different theme each week, is popular (6,000 Ft, served 11:30–15:00). Reserve ahead for dinner, and ask to sit either near or far from the live "Gypsy" music (12 percent service charge automatically added to bill, open daily 12:00–15:00 & 18:30–24:00, music nightly, Állatkerti út 2,

tel. 1/468-4040, www.gundel.hu). The dress code is formal: Jackets are required for men having dinner in the dining room, but not for lunch, for Sunday brunch, or if you sit outside. (You can borrow a free jacket at the door if you travel like me. Ties and dresses are not required.)

Gundel's **Borvendéglő** ("Wine Cellar") offers similar food in a more casual atmosphere at half the price. With an even more extensive wine list than the main restaurant upstairs, this option is ideal for wine lovers. In addition to full dinners, including some "home-style" dishes (2,000–6,000 Ft, pricier 10,500–13,500-Ft tasting *menus* with wine pairings), they offer wine-and-cheese tastings (4,500–7,500 Ft; Mon–Sat 18:00–23:00, closed Sun, downstairs from Gundel at Állatkerti út 2, tel. 1/468-4041).

Robinson, stranded on an island in City Park's lake, is a hip, playful, mellow theme restaurant. With island-castaway ambience and more outdoor seating than indoor, it's made to order for lazing away a sunny afternoon at the park. The upstairs café terrace has a long menu of 1,000-Ft desserts and ice-cream treats, coffee drinks, and light 2,000–2,500-Ft salads and sandwiches (daily in summer 11:00–23:00, terrace closed Oct–April). The downstairs terrace and elegant, glassed-in dining room feature pricey international and Hungarian cuisine (3,000–6,000-Ft main dishes, daily 12:00–16:00 & 18:00–24:00, reserve ahead and ask for lakefront seating, Városligeti tó, tel. 1/422-0222, www.robinsonrestaurant.hu).

In Buda

Eateries on Castle Hill are generally overpriced and touristy—as with Váci utca, locals never eat here. Instead, they head down the hill into the Víziváros ("Water Town") neighborhood. All of these (except the final one) are in district I.

Víziváros

My first listing is just beyond the southern tip of Castle Hill, near the Elisabeth Bridge. The others are in the heart of Víziváros, right between Castle Hill and the river. For locations, see the map on page 571.

Tabáni Terasz, between the castle and the big, white Elisabeth Bridge, serves tasty Hungarian food to a pleasant mix of locals and tourists. The historic 250-year-old building has several seating options: in a cozy, classy drawing-room interior; on a terrace out front; and in the inner courtyard (2,000–3,500-Ft main dishes, daily 12:00–23:00, by the single-spired yellow church at Apród utca 10, tel. 1/201-1086).

Matróz Kocsma ("Sailor Inn") features specialties from up and down the Danube—mostly Hungarian, but also German,

Transylvanian, Serbian, and more. Each dish's place of origin is noted in the menu. Very convenient to most of my recommended Víziváros hotels, this eatery has jaunty nautical decor inside and out (2,200–3,000-Ft main dishes, daily 10:00–24:00, Halász utca 1, tel. 1/212-3817).

Pater Marcus is a well-established beer hall, serving up a hundred types of Belgian beers to wash down Hungarian and international cuisine near the Chain Bridge. The outdoor alley seating is nothing special, but the cellar restaurant will transport you to Brussels (1,800–2,200-Ft main dishes, daily 12:00–24:00, Apor Péter utca 1, tel. 1/212-1612).

Batthyány Tér

This bustling square—the transportation hub for Víziváros—is overlooked by a recently renovated, late-19th-century market hall (today housing a supermarket and various shops). Several worthwhile, affordable eateries cluster around this square (all open long hours daily). Survey your options before settling in. **Nagyi Palacsintázója** ("Granny's Pancakes")—just to the right of the market hall entrance—serves up cheap and tasty crêpes *(palacsinta)* to a local crowd (300–800-Ft sweet or savory crêpes, convenient 800–1,000-Ft combo-meals, communication can be challenging—ask for English menu, open 24 hours daily, Batthyány tér 5). As you face the market hall, go up the street that runs along its left side (Markovits Iván utca) to reach more good eateries: At the end of the block on the right is **Éden Vegetarian Restaurant,** a self-service, point-and-shoot place (main dishes for less than 1,000 Ft, Mon–Thu 8:00–21:00, Fri 8:00–18:00, Sun 11:00–21:00, closed Sat, tel. 1/375-7575). And around the back side of the market hall is **Bratwursthäusle/Kolbászda,** a fun little beer hall/beer garden with specialties and blue-and-white checkerboard decor from Bavaria. Sit outside, or in the woody interior (1,000-Ft sausages, daily 11:00–23:00, Gyorskocsi utca 6, tel. 1/225-3674).

Near Moszkva Tér

Szent Jupát is a reliable choice for large portions of basic, stick-to-your-ribs, traditional Hungarian cuisine (a relative rarity in Budapest). Just a couple of blocks off Moszkva tér (the terminus for buses from the castle), near the corner of the giant Mammut shopping mall, it's a good place to head for an extremely filling meal after a busy day of Castle Hill sightseeing. Choose between the woody interior or the covered terrace beer garden out back (1,500–2,800 splittable main dishes, daily from 12:00 until very late, corner of Retek utca and Dékán utca, district II, M2: Moszkva tér, tel. 1/212-2923).

Snacks and Light Meals

When you're in the mood for something halfway between a restaurant and a picnic meal, look for take-out food stands, bakeries (with sandwiches to go), grocers willing to make you a sandwich, and simple little eateries for fast and easy sit-down restaurant food.

A popular snack is ***lángos***—a savory deep-fried doughnut (similar to an elephant ear or Native American fry-bread). Sold at stands on the street, the most typical versions are spread with cheese and sour cream, sometimes also topped with garlic. Some restaurants serve a fancier version (often with meat) as an entrée. The Lángos stand upstairs in the Great Market Hall is a local favorite (see page 576).

All around town, you'll see cheery **open-face sandwich shops,** each displaying a dozen or so tempting little treats in their front windows—thin slices of bread piled with egg salad, veggies, cold cuts, cream spreads, cheese, salmon, affordable caviar, or other toppings for around 200 Ft apiece. Two sandwiches and a drink make a quick and healthy meal for less than $5 (they'll also box things to go for a classy picnic). There are various chains, but **Duran Szendvics** is the dominant operation (convenient location near the start of Andrássy út at Bajcsy-Zsilinszky út 7, district VII, M1: Bajcsy-Zsilinszky út, tel. 1/267-9624; also in Leopold Town at Október 6 utca 15, district V, M3: Arany János utca). These shops are generally open for lunch or an early dinner (Mon–Fri 8:00–18:00, Sat 8:00–14:00, Sun 8:00–12:00).

For quick, inexpensive, and very local grub, head for the chain called **Főzelékfaló Ételbár** (roughly, "Soup Slurper Eating Bar"). This self-service cafeteria dishes up simple fare to businesspeople on their lunch break. *Főzelék,* a simple soup that's thickened with roux (wheat flour mixed into lard or butter) and can be supplemented with various vegetables, is a staple of Hungarian home cooking. Go to the counter, choose your *főzelék* soup (various flavors, 500 Ft), then choose from a variety of basic meat dishes (chicken, pork, meatballs, and more for 500–1,000 Ft apiece; some English spoken, but pointing also works). A filling meal here typically runs 1,000–2,000 Ft (usually open Mon–Fri 10:00–21:30, Sat 12:00–20:00, closed Sun, www.fozelekfalo-bartokhaz.hu). Because of the limited seating, most people get their grub to go. There are two locations in central Pest: One is just off of Andrássy út in the "Broadway Quarter" (Nagymező utca 22, a block north of the Opera House, district VI, M1: Opera), and the other is in a big building along the busy highway at Ferenciek tere (same building as the recommended Leo Panzió hotel, Kossuth Lajos utca 2A, district V, M3: Ferenciek tere). You'll also find them in the WestEnd City Center and Arena Plaza shopping malls.

Hummus Bar, while not authentically Hungarian, is a popular expat-run local chain that offers cheap Middle Eastern vegetarian meals to grateful backpackers and young locals. Their falafel is tasty (500 Ft for a pita-wrapped sandwich, combination plates for 700–1,500 Ft). I'd get it to go and enjoy it on a park bench to avoid the cramped interior (one location just beyond the end of Franz Liszt Square at Kertesz utca 39, district VII, M1: Oktogon, open daily 12:00–24:00; another in Leopold Town at Alkotmány utca 20, district V, M2: Kossuth tér, open Mon–Thu 10:00–22:00, Fri 10:00–24:00, Sat 12:00–24:00, Sun 12:00–22:00; www.hummusbar.hu).

For a fast snack, you'll see **Fornetti** stands everywhere (on street corners and Metro underpasses). This Hungary-based chain, which is becoming wildly popular across Central and Eastern Europe, sells small, tasty, freshly baked phyllo–dough–based pastries by weight. They have both sweet and savory varieties. For a bite on the go, just point to what you want and hold your fingers up for how many you'd like of each type (150 Ft per 100 grams). If you smell something heavenly in the Metro passages...it's probably a Fornetti.

Budapest's Café Culture

In the late 19th century, a vibrant café culture boomed here in Budapest, just as it did in Vienna and Paris. The *kávéház* ("coffeehouse") was a local institution. By 1900, Budapest had more than 600 cafés. In this crowded and fast-growing cityscape, a neighborhood café allowed urbanites to escape their tiny flats (or to get a jolt of caffeine to power them through a 12-hour workday). Local people, many of whom had moved to the city from the countryside, didn't want to pay to heat their homes during the day. So instead, for the price of a cup of coffee, they could come to a café to enjoy warmth, companionship, and loaner newspapers.

Realizing that these neighborhood living rooms were breeding grounds for dissidents, the communists closed the cafés or converted them into *eszpresszó*s (with uncomfortable stools instead of easy chairs) or *bisztró*s (stand-up fast-food joints with no chairs at all). Today, nostalgia is bringing back the *kávéház* culture—both as a place to get coffee and food, and as a social institution. While some serve only coffee and cakes, most serve light meals, and some serve full meals (as noted below).

On the Great Boulevard: **New York Café** makes the others listed here look like Starbucks. Originally built in 1894 as part of the "New York Palace" (and it really is palatial), this fanciful, over-the-top explosion of Neo-Baroque and Neo-Renaissance epitomizes the "mix and match, but plenty of everything" Historicist style of the day. In the early 20th century, artists, writers, and

musicians came here to sip overpriced coffee and bask in opulence. After decades of neglect, Italian investors completely restored it in 2006, and now it welcomes guests once more. Tourists and gawkers are not encouraged—you'll be stopped at the door and asked if you want a table. If you're up for a coffee break, this place might actually be worth an $8 cup of coffee or an overpriced meal. Read the fun history on the placemat. While it's a few blocks beyond the tourist zone, it's worth the trip out here for the ultimate in turn-of-the-20th-century Budapest elegance (1,000–1,500-Ft coffee and hot chocolate drinks, 1,000–2,000-Ft desserts, 3,000-Ft pastas and sandwiches, 4,000–6,000-Ft main dishes, 5,000-Ft breakfasts served 9:00–12:00, open daily 9:00–24:00, Erzsébet körút 9–11, district VII, tel. 1/886-6167). Sunken down in all that sumptuousness, in the former billiards room, is a separate restaurant called **Deepwater** (5,000-Ft pastas, 7,000-Ft main dishes, dinner only—daily 18:00–23:00). Take the M2/red Metro line to Blaha Lujza tér, and exit toward *Erzsébet körút pártalan oldal/6É Margit híd.* Bear left up the stairs, then turn right, and walk a block. You can also take tram #4 or #6 from the Oktogon (at Andrássy út) around the Great Boulevard to Wesselényi utca.

Two Blocks up from Váci utca: **Centrál Kávéház** and **Gerlóczy Café,** both listed earlier as restaurants, nicely recapture Budapest's early-1900s ambience, with elegant cakes and coffees, loaner newspapers on racks, and a management that encourages loitering. After the one listed above, these are Budapest's top two cafés.

On Vörösmarty tér: **Gerbeaud** (zhehr-BOH) isn't just a café—it's a 150-year-old landmark, the most famous gathering place in Budapest. It's touristy, but central, historic, and great for people-watching (best on a sunny day from its outdoor tables). I'd avoid the bad-value meals here, and just sip a coffee and nibble a cake (700-Ft coffee drinks, 700–1,100-Ft cakes, 1,500–3,000-Ft salads and sandwiches, daily 9:00–21:00, on Vörösmarty tér, district V, M1: Vörösmarty tér, tel. 1/429-9000). They also have a cellar pub downstairs (hearty but overpriced 2,000–4,000-Ft meals, open only in cool weather).

Near Ferenciek tere: **Jégbüfé** is where Pest urbanites get their quick, cheap, stand-at-a-counter fix of coffee and cakes. And for those feeling nostalgic for the communist days, little has changed at this typical *bisztró.* First, choose what you want at the counter. Then try to explain it to the cashier across the aisle. Finally, take your receipt back to the appropriate part of the counter (figure out

the four different zones: coffee, soft drinks, ice cream, cakes), trade your receipt for your goodie, go to the bar, and enjoy it standing up (cakes for under 300 Ft, Mon–Sat 7:00–21:30, Wed until 20:30, Sun 8:00–21:30, Ferenciek tere 10, district V, M3: Ferenciek tere). Now...back to work.

Near the Opera House: **Callas** features ideal outdoor seating facing the Opera House, and one of the finest Art Nouveau interiors in town, with gorgeous *Jugendstil* chandeliers. While their full meals are pricey (2,500–5,000 Ft), this is a wonderful spot on Andrássy út for a coffee break, tasty dessert, or breakfast (ham and eggs plus coffee for 1,800 Ft, 400–600-Ft pastries, Tue–Fri 8:30–24:00, Sat–Sun 10:00–24:00, closed Mon, Andrássy út 20, district VI, M1: Opera, tel. 1/354-0954). Across the street and a block toward the Oktogon, **Művész Kávéház** ("Artists Coffee House") is a classic café with 19th-century elegance, a hoity-toity high-ceilinged interior, outdoor seating on Andrássy út, and a wide variety of cakes. True to its name, this institution in the "Broadway Quarter" is a favorite after-rehearsal haunt of famous-to-Hungarians actors and musicians (500–700-Ft cakes, 1,000-Ft sandwiches, daily 9:00–23:45, Andrássy út 29, district VI, M1: Opera, tel. 1/352-1337).

In Buda, atop Castle Hill: **Ruszwurm** lays claim to being Budapest's oldest café (since 1827). Tiny but classy, with classic Biedermeier furnishings, it carries on its venerable reputation with pride. Its dead-central location—a block in front of St. Matthias' Church in the heart of the castle district—means that it's become a popular tourist spot. However, it remains dear to locals' hearts. Especially after the 10:00 Sunday-morning Mass at the church, you'll still see gussied-up locals chatting here (500-Ft coffees, 300–600-Ft desserts, daily 10:00–19:00, Szentháromság utca 7, district I, tel. 1/375-5284).

Budapest Connections

By Train

Remember that Budapest has three stations: Keleti/Eastern, Nyugati/Western, and Déli/Southern (for all the details, see page 481). There's no telling which station each train will use, especially since it can change from year to year—always confirm carefully which station your train leaves from. For general rail information in Hungary, call 1/461-5400; for information about international trains, call 1/461-5500.

It's best to buy your ticket in advance at the MÁV ticket office in downtown Pest (see page 486). Because ticket lines can be long—especially for international trains—it's smart to arrive at the station with plenty of time to spare if you're buying tickets there.

From Budapest by Train to: Eger (5/day direct, 2.5 hrs, more with transfer in Füzesabony, usually from Budapest's Keleti/Eastern Station), **Pécs** (8/day direct, 3 hrs; a few additional connections possible with transfer at the suburban Budapest-Kelenföld station), **Sopron** (7/day direct, 3 hrs, more with a transfer in Győr), **Visegrád** (trains arrive at Nagymaros-Visegrád station, across the river—take shuttle boat to Visegrád; hourly, 40–60 min, usually from Budapest's Nyugati/Western Station), **Esztergom** (hourly, 1.5 hrs, usually from Budapest's Nyugati/Western Station), **Bratislava** (that's ***Pozsony*** in Hungarian, 5/day direct, 2.5 hrs; more with transfers), **Vienna** (that's ***Bécs*** in Hungarian, every 2 hrs direct, 3 hrs; more with transfers), **Prague** (3/day, 7 hrs, more with 2–3 changes, 8.5 hrs; 1 night train, 7.5 hrs), **Kraków** (2/day, 9.5–11.5 hrs, transfer in Břeclav, Czech Republic, or Katowice, Poland; plus 1 direct night train/day, 10.5 hrs), **Ljubljana** (1/day direct, plus 2/day with a transfer in Zagreb, 9.5 hrs; also possible in 8.5 hrs with changes at Vienna/Wien Meidling and Maribor; no convenient night train), **Munich** (5/day direct, 7.5 hrs; plus 1 direct night train/day, 9 hrs; otherwise transfer in Vienna and Salzburg), **Berlin** (1/day direct, 11.75 hrs), and **Zagreb** (3/day direct, 6–7.5 hrs).

By Boat

In the summer, Mahart runs daily high-speed hydrofoils up the Danube to **Vienna.** It's not particularly scenic, and it's slower than the train, but it's a fun alternative for nautical types. The boat leaves Budapest late April through early October daily at 9:00 and arrives in Vienna at 15:30 (Vienna to Budapest: 9:00–14:30). The trip costs €89 one-way. On any of these boats, you can also stop in the Slovak capital, **Bratislava** (€79 one-way). To confirm times and prices, and to buy tickets, contact Mahart in Budapest (tel. 1/484-4010, www.mahartpassnave.hu) or DDSG Blue Danube in Vienna (tel. 01/58880, www.ddsg-blue-danube.at).

By Plane

For information about Budapest Ferihegy Airport, see "Arrival in Budapest—By Plane" on page 483.

Route Tips for Drivers

For pointers on driving into (and parking in) Budapest, see "Arrival in Budapest—By Car" on page 484. To get out of town, here are some pointers.

To Eger and Other Points East: Head out of the city center on Andrássy út, circling behind Heroes' Square to access Kós Károly sétány through the middle of City Park. You'll pass Széchenyi Baths on the left, then (exiting the park) go over the

Hungária körút ring road, before getting on M-3. This expressway zips you conveniently to Eger (exit #114 for Füzesabony; go north on road 33, then 3, then 25 into Eger).

To Bratislava, Vienna, and Other Points West: From central Pest, head over the Danube on the white, modern Elisabeth Bridge (Erzsébet híd). Once in Buda, the road becomes Hegyalja út; simply follow *Wien* signs to get on M-1.

EGER

Many travelers have never heard of Eger (EH-gehr). It's a county-seat town in northern Hungary, with about 60,000 people and a thriving teacher-training college. Among Hungarians, the town has various claims to fame. It's a bishopric whose powerful bishops have adorned it with gorgeous churches. It has some of the best and most beloved spas in this hot-water-crazy country (including the excellent new Salt Hill Thermal Spa in the nearby countryside). And, perhaps most of all, Eger makes Hungarians proud as the town that, against all odds, successfully held off the Ottoman advance into Europe in 1552. This stirring history makes Eger the mecca of Hungarian school field trips. If the town is known internationally for anything, it's for the surrounding wine region (its best-known red wine is Bull's Blood, or Egri Bikavér).

And yet, refreshingly, enchanting Eger remains mostly off the tourist trail. Egerites go about their daily routines amidst lovely Baroque buildings, watched over by one of Hungary's most important castles. Everything in Eger is painted with vibrant colors, and even the communist apartment blocks seem quaint. The sights are few but fun, the ambience is great, and strolling is a must. It all comes together to make Eger an ideal introduction to small-town Hungary.

Planning Your Time

Mellow Eger is the best side-trip from Budapest. It's doable round-trip in a single day (2.5 hours by train each way), but it's much more satisfying and relaxing to spend the night.

A perfect day in Eger begins with a browse through the very local-feeling market and a low-key ramble on the castle ramparts. Then head to the college building called the Lyceum to visit the library and astronomy museum, and climb up to the thrillingly low-tech camera obscura. Take in the 11:30 organ concert in the cathedral across the street from the Lyceum (mid-May–mid-Oct only). In the afternoon, unwind on the square or, better yet, at a thermal bath (in Eger, or at Salt Hill Thermal Spa in nearby Egerszalók). If you need more to do, consider a drive into the countryside (including visits to local vintners—get details at TI). Round out your day with dinner on Little Dobó Square, or a visit to Eger's touristy wine caves in the Sirens' Valley.

Orientation to Eger

(area code: 36)

Eger Castle sits at the top of the town, hovering over Dobó Square (Dobó István tér). This main square is divided in half by the Eger Creek, which bisects the town. Two blocks west of Dobó Square is the main pedestrian drag, Széchenyi utca, where you'll find the Lyceum and the cathedral. A few blocks due south from the castle (along Eger Creek) are Eger's various spas and baths.

Tourist Information

Eger's on-the-ball, eager-to-please TI (TourInform) is the most efficient place to get any Eger question answered. They give out a free brochure and town map, as well as piles of other brochures about the city and region. They can't book rooms, but they can help you find one—or anything else you're looking for (mid-June–mid-Sept Mon–Fri 9:00–18:00, Sat–Sun 9:00–13:00, possibly later; mid-Sept–mid-June Mon–Fri 9:00–17:00, Sat 9:00–13:00, closed Sun; Bajcsy-Zsilinszky utca 9, tel. 36/517-715, www.eger.hu). You can also get online here (200 Ft/30 min).

Arrival in Eger

By Train: Eger's tiny train station is a 20-minute walk south of the center. The closest ATM is at the Spar grocery store just up the street (turn left out of station, walk about 100 yards, and look for red-and-white supermarket on your right; ATM is around front). There's no official baggage storage, but sometimes workers at the train station can hold a bag for you—ask.

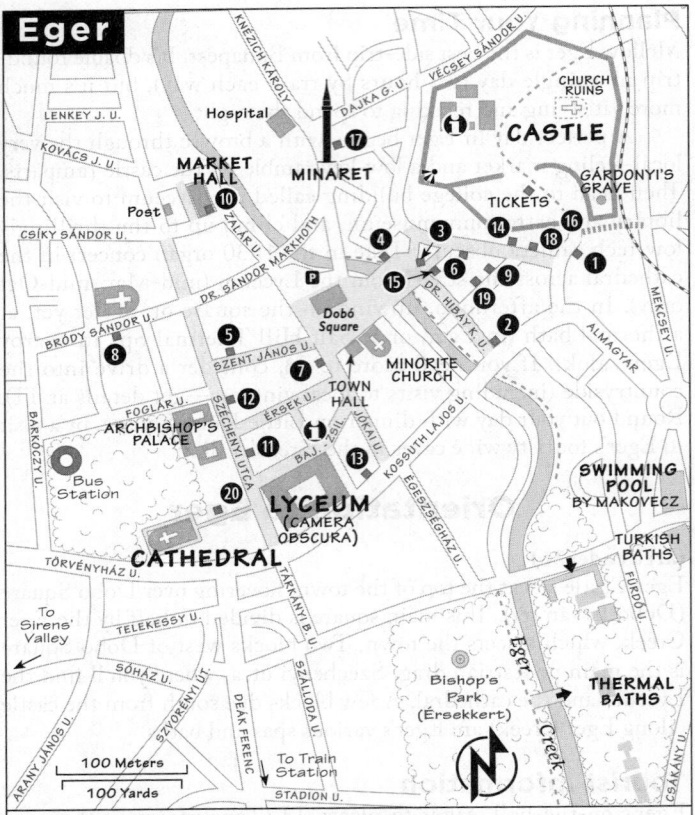

Taxis generally wait out front to take new arrivals into the center (1,000–1,400 Ft). Even in little Eger, it's always best to take a taxi with a company name and number posted.

To catch the **bus** toward the center, go straight out of the station, and when the road you're on veers right, cross it to get to the bus stop (to the left) on the busier road above it. Buses #11, #12, and #14 cut about 10 minutes off the walk into town (220 Ft, buy

ticket from driver; or 150 Ft if you buy it inside train station—ask for *helyijárat buszjegy*). Get off the bus when you reach the big yellow cathedral.

To **walk** all the way, leave the station straight ahead, turn right with the road, and then continue straight ahead (on busy Deák Ferenc utca) until you run into the cathedral. With your back to the cathedral entry, the main square is two blocks ahead of you, then a block to the left.

By Car: In this small town, most hotels will provide parking or help you find a lot. For a short visit, the most central lot is behind the department store on Dobó Square.

Getting Around Eger

Everything of interest in Eger is within walking distance. But a taxi can be helpful to reach outlying sights, including the Sirens' Valley wine caves and the Salt Hill Thermal Spa in Egerszalók (taxi meter starts at 250 Ft, then around 250 Ft/km; try City Taxi, tel. 36/555-555).

Helpful Hints

Phoning and Faxing: Confusingly, Hungary's country code is the same as Eger's city code (36). This means that if you're calling from another country, you'll have to dial 36 twice. For example, to call my favorite Eger hotel from the US, I'd dial 011-36-36-411-711.

Blue Monday: Note that the castle museums and the Lyceum are closed on Mondays. But you can still visit the cathedral (and enjoy its organ concert), swim in the thermal bath, explore the market, see the castle grounds, and enjoy the local wine.

Organ Concert: Daily from mid-May to mid-October, Hungary's second-biggest organ booms out a glorious 30-minute concert in the cathedral (500 Ft, Mon–Sat at 11:30, Sun at 12:45).

Internet Access: The TI has one terminal (200 Ft/30 min; see "Tourist Information," earlier). The town generally has other Internet cafés, but as these are prone to going out of business, ask the TI or your hotelier for current options.

Walking Tours: The TI offers an affordable town walking tour in English once weekly in summer (likely Sat at 10:00, early June–Sept only, price and schedule tend to change from year to year—confirm details at TI).

Tourist Train: A hokey little tourist train leaves the main square at the top of each hour. It does a circuit around town, then heads out to the Sirens' Valley wine caves (500 Ft, 50-min trip).

Sights in Eger

▲▲Dobó Square (Dobó István Tér)

Dobó Square is the heart of Eger. In most towns this striking, the main square is packed with postcard stalls and other tourist traps. Refreshingly, Eger's square seems mostly packed with Egerites. Ringed by pretty Baroque buildings, decorated with vivid sculptures depicting the city's noble past, and watched over by Eger's historic castle, this square is one of the most pleasant spots in Hungary.

The statue in the middle is **István Dobó** (EESHT-vahn DOH-boh), the square's namesake and Eger's greatest hero, who defended the city—and all of Hungary—from an Ottoman invasion in 1552 (see his story in the sidebar). Next to Dobó is his co-commander, István Mekcsey. And right at their side is one of the brave women of Eger—depicted here throwing a pot down onto the attackers.

Dominating the square is the exquisitely photogenic pink **Minorite Church**—often said to be the most beautiful Baroque church in Hungary. The shabby interior (free entry) is less interesting, but has some appealing details. Notice that each of the hand-carved wooden pews has a different motif. Pay close attention to the side altars that flank the nave: The first set (left and right) are 3-D illustrations, painted to replicate the wood altars that burned in a fire; the next set are real. And looking up at the faded ceiling frescoes, you'll see (in the second one from the entrance) the church's patron: St. Anthony of Padua, who's preaching God's word to the fishes after the townspeople refused to hear him.

Next to the Minorite Church is the Town Hall, then an old-fashioned pharmacy. The **monument** in front of the Town Hall also commemorates the 1552 defense of Eger: one Egerite against two Ottoman soldiers, reminding us of the townspeople's bravery despite the odds.

Use the square to orient yourself to the town. Behind the statue of Dobó is a bridge over the stream that bisects the city.

István Dobó and the Siege of Eger

In the 16th century, Ottoman invaders swept into Hungary. They easily defeated a Hungarian army—in just two hours—at the Battle of Mohács in 1526. When Buda and Pest fell to the Ottomans in 1541, all of Europe looked to Eger as the last line of defense. István Dobó and his second-in-command, István Mekcsey, were put in charge of Eger's forces. They prepared the castle (which still overlooks the square) for a siege and waited.

On September 11, 1552—after a summer spent conquering more than 30 other Hungarian fortresses on their march northward—40,000 Ottomans arrived in Eger. Only about 2,000 Egerites (soldiers, their wives, and their children) remained to protect their town. The Ottomans expected an easy victory, but the siege dragged on for 39 days. Eger's soldiers fought valiantly, and the women of Eger also joined the fray, pouring hot tar down on the Ottomans...everyone pitched in. A Hungarian officer named Gergely Bornemissza, sent to reinforce the people of Eger, startled the Ottomans with all manner of clever and deadly explosives. One of his brilliant inventions was a "fire wheel"—a barrel of gunpowder studded with smaller jars of explosives, which they'd light and send rolling downhill to wreak havoc until the final, deadly explosion. Ultimately, the Ottomans left in shame, Eger was saved, and Dobó was a national hero.

The unfortunate epilogue: The Ottomans came back in 1596 and, this time, succeeded in conquering an Eger Castle guarded by unmotivated mercenaries. The Ottomans sacked the town and controlled the region for close to a century.

In 1897, a castle archaeologist named Géza Gárdonyi moved from Budapest to Eger, where tales of the siege captured his imagination. Gárdonyi wrote a book about István Dobó and the 1552 Siege of Eger called *Egri Csillagok* ("Stars of Eger," translated into English as *Eclipse of the Crescent Moon,* available at local bookstores and souvenir stands). The book—a favorite of many Hungarians—is taught in schools, keeping the legend of Eger's heroes alive today.

Just before you reach that bridge, look to the left and you'll see the northernmost Ottoman **minaret** in Europe—once part of a mosque, it's now a tourist attraction. Across the bridge is the charming **Little Dobó Square** (Kis-Dobó tér), home to the town's best hotels, its outdoor dining zone, and a handy and atmospheric opportunity to sample local wines at the Bikavér Borház wine shop. Hovering above Little Dobó Square is Eger Castle; to get there, hang a right at the Senator Ház Hotel and go up Dobó utca. (All of these places are described in more detail later.)

Now face in the opposite direction, with the castle at your back. On your right is a handy department store (with an ATM by the door). At the bottom end of this square, various pedestrian shopping lanes lead straight ahead two short blocks to Eger's main "walking street," Széchenyi utca (with the cathedral and the Lyceum at its left end). To reach the TI, jog left at the end of this square, then right onto Bajcsy-Zsilinszky utca (TI one block ahead on right). The market hall is in the opposite direction: Leave Dobó Square to the right (on Zalár József utca, with department store on your right-hand side; you'll see the market hall on the left).

Dobó Utca—The street called Dobó utca, which leads to the entrance of the castle (up the street to the right of Senator Ház Hotel), is lined with colorful shops and attractions. Don't miss the **wine-tasting courtyard** at #18. At the **Rétesbolt** strudel shop (#10), you can watch them make mouthwatering strudel (350 Ft, daily 10:00–17:00).

Also along this street are two small, underwhelming museums—worth considering only if it's a rainy day or you have a special interest. The tiny **Palóc Folklore Museum** displays a handful of traditional tools, textiles, ceramics, costumes, and pieces of furniture (200 Ft, borrow the skimpy English information, Easter–Sept Tue–Sun 9:00–17:00, closed Mon and Oct–Easter, Dobó utca 12). The **Historical Exhibition of Weapons** (Történeti Tárház) features centuries of Eger armaments: clubs, rifles, and everything in between (300 Ft, Tue–Sun 10:00–18:00, closed Mon, 450-Ft booklet labels weapons in English, 1,600-Ft English book gives more info, Dobó utca 9, actually just down Fazola Henrik utca).

▲Eger Castle (Egri Vár)

This castle is Hungary's Alamo, where István Dobó defended Eger from the Ottomans in 1552. These days, it's usually crawling with schoolchildren on field trips from all over the country.

The great St. István—Hungary's first Christian king—founded a church on this hill a thousand years ago. The church was destroyed by Tatars in the 13th century, and this fortress was built to repel another attack.

The castle grounds feature several small museums (includ-

ing a history museum and a picture gallery), remains of a once-grand cathedral and a smaller rotunda dating from the days of St. István (10th or 11th century), underground casements (tunnels through the castle walls), Heroes' Hall (with the symbolic grave of István Dobó), and temporary exhibits. For those of us who didn't grow up hearing the legend of István Dobó, the complex is hard to appreciate, and English information is sparse. Most visitors find that the most rewarding plan is to stroll up, wander around the grounds, enjoy the view overlooking the town (find the minaret and other landmarks), maybe pay a visit to the waxworks, and then head back into town past a gaggle of colorful shops.

Cost and Tours: A 600-Ft "walking ticket" gets you into the castle grounds only (free Nov–March). To go inside all the museums (except the privately run "Other Castle Sights," described below), buy the 1,200-Ft ticket. The underground casements and Heroes' Hall are only accessible by one-hour Hungarian tour, with some posted information in English (tours depart frequently in summer, sporadically off-season). Sometimes it's possible to join an English tour for 800 Ft extra (ask at information window when you arrive; most likely in June–Aug, but there's no set schedule).

Hours: The castle **grounds** are open April–Aug daily 8:00–20:00, Sept until 19:00, March and Oct until 18:00, Nov–Feb until 17:00. The castle **museums** are open March–Oct Tue–Sun 9:00–17:00 (last entry 40 min before closing). On Monday in March–Oct, and every day in Nov–Feb, all of the official castle museums are closed except the casements, which—as usual—you can visit only with a guided tour (since most sights are closed, you'll pay a reduced price of 1,000 Ft; some of the "Other Castle Sights" described next are open Mon). General castle info: tel. 36/312-744, www.div.iif.hu.

Other Castle Sights: In addition to the official castle museums, there are other privately run exhibits, each with its own sporadic hours and prices: an **archery** exhibit (look for archers just inside inner gate in summer, and pay them for the chance to shoot old-fashioned bows and crossbows—1 arrow/100 Ft, 5 arrows/400 Ft, 10 arrows/700 Ft); the **mint,** with a display of former currencies and a chance to make your own souvenir (entry-500 Ft, souvenirs extra, in cellar of Gothic palace); **temporary exhibits** in the pink round tower; and the **waxworks,** or "Panoptikum" (500 Ft, daily April–Oct 9:00–18:00, Nov–March 9:00–16:00).

Of these, only the waxworks is worth considering. You'll see a handful of eerily realistic heroes and villains from the siege of Eger (including István Dobó himself and the leader of the Ottomans sitting in his colorful tent). Notice the exaggerated Central Asian features of the Egerites—a reminder that the Magyars were more Asian than European. Sound effects add to the fun...think of it as a very low-tech, walk-through *Ottomans of the Caribbean*. You'll also have the chance to scramble through a segment of the casements that run inside the castle walls.

Getting There: To reach the castle from Dobó Square, cross the bridge toward Senator Ház Hotel, then jog right around the hotel, turning right onto Dobó utca (with its own set of attractions, described later). Take this street a few blocks until it swings down to the right; the ramp up to the castle is across the little park to your left.

On Széchenyi Utca

You'll find Eger's best sights along its main walking street, two blocks up from Dobó Square.

▲▲Lyceum (Líceum)—In the mid-18th century, Bishop Károly Eszterházy wanted a university in Eger, but Habsburg Emperor Josef II refused to allow it. So instead, Eszterházy built the most impressive teacher-training college on the planet, and stocked it with the best books and astronomical equipment money could buy. The Lyceum still trains local teachers (enrollment: about 2,000). Since Eger is expensive by Hungarian standards, many families live in the surrounding countryside. The kids all come into Eger for school—and lots of teachers are needed. But the halls of the Lyceum are also roamed by tourists who have come to visit its classic old library (700 Ft), and its astronomy museum, with a fascinating camera obscura (covered by a separate 800-Ft ticket; both library and museum open March–mid-Oct Tue–Sun 9:30–15:30, closed Mon; mid-Oct–Feb Sat–Sun only 9:30–13:30, closed Mon–Fri; last entry 30 min before closing, Eszterházy tér 1, at south end of Széchenyi utca at intersection with Kossuth utca, enter through main door across from cathedral and buy tickets just inside and to the left).

Library: First, visit the old-fashioned library one floor up (from main entry hall, cut through the middle of the courtyard, enter the hall at the far end, turn right to find the staircase, head up one flight, then go left and look for room 223, marked *Bibliothek*). This library houses 50,000 books (here and in the two adjoining rooms, with several stacked two deep). Dr. Imre Surányi and his staff have spent the last decade cataloging these books. This is no easy task, since they're in over 100 languages—from Thai to Tagalog—and are shelved according to size, rather than topic. You'll likely meet Dr. Surányi's assistant, Dénes Szabó (if he's not away for a choral contest), or the resident tour guide, Katalin Bódi. Either of them will happily show you the library's pride and joy: a replica of a letter from Mozart. The shelves are adorned with golden seals depicting great minds of science, philosophy, and religion. Take some time to marvel at the gorgeous ceiling fresco, dating from 1778. If you want to thank the patron of this museum, say *köszönöm* to the guy in the second row up, to the right of the podium (second from left, not wearing a hat)—that's Bishop Károly Eszterházy. While the Lyceum now belongs to Eger, this library is still the property of the archbishop.

Astronomical Museum: Several flights above (continue up the same stairs you climbed to reach the library) is the **Astronomical Tower,** with some dusty old stargazing instruments, as well as a meridian line in the floor (the dot of sunlight dances along this line each day around noon). Across the hall is a fun, interactive **magic room,** where you can try out scientific experiments—such as using air pressure to make a ball levitate or sending a mini "hot-air balloon" up to the ceiling. Yet a few more flights up is the Lyceum's treasured **camera obscura.** You'll enter a dark room around a big, bowl-like canvas, and the guide will fly you around the streets of Eger (presentations about 2/hr, maybe more when busy). Fun as it is today, this camera must have astonished viewers when it was built in 1776—well before anyone had seen "moving pictures." It's a bit of a huff to get up here (nine flights of stairs, 302 steps)—but the camera obscura and the view of Eger from the outdoor terrace are worth it.

▲▲Eger Cathedral—Eger's 19th-century bishops peppered the city with beautiful buildings, including the second-biggest church in Hungary (after Esztergom's). With a quirky, sumptuous, Baroque-feeling interior, Eger's cathedral is well worth a visit (free entry, cathedral is the big, can't-miss-it yellow building at Pyrker János tér 1, just off Széchenyi utca).

Eger Cathedral was built in the 1830s by an Austrian archbishop who had previously served in Venice, and who thought Eger could use a little more class. The colonnaded Neoclassical facade, painted a pretty Habsburg yellow, boasts some fine Italian sculpture. As you walk up the main stairs, you'll pass saints István and László—Hungary's first two Christian kings—and then the apostles Peter and Paul.

Enter the cathedral and walk to the first collection box, partway down the nave. Then, facing the door, look up at the ornate **ceiling fresco:** On the left, it shows Hungarians in traditional dress, and on the right, the country's most important historical figures. At the bottom, you see this cathedral, celestially connected with St. Peter's in Rome (at the top). This symbol of devotion to the Vatican was a brave statement when it was painted in 1950. The communists were closing churches in other small Hungarian towns, but the Eger archbishop had enough clout to keep this one open.

Continue to the transept. A few years ago, the **stained-glass windows** at either end were donated to the cathedral by a rich Austrian couple to commemorate the 1,000th anniversary of Hungary's conversion to Christianity—notice the dates 1000 (when St. István converted the Magyars to Christianity) and 2000.

As you leave, notice the enormous **organ**—Hungary's second-largest—above the door. In the summer, try to catch one of the cathedral's daily half-hour organ concerts (500 Ft, mid-May–mid-Oct Mon–Sat at 11:30, Sun at 12:45, no concerts off-season).

If you walk up Széchenyi utca from here, you'll see the fancy Archbishop's Palace on your left—still home to Eger's archbishop.

Just to the right of the steps leading up to the cathedral is the entrance to the...

Town Under the Town (Város a Város Alatt)—Here you can take a guided tour of the archbishop's former wine-cellar network, which honeycombs the land behind the Archbishop's Palace (800 Ft, departs at the top of each hour, 5-person minimum, daily

April–Sept 10:00–20:00, Oct–March 10:00–17:00, last tour departs one hour before closing, www.varosavarosalatt.hu).

North of Dobó Square

▲Market Hall (Piaccsarnok)—Wandering Eger's big indoor market will give you a taste of local life—and maybe some local food, too. It's packed with Egerites choosing the very best of the fresh produce. Tomatoes and peppers of all colors and sizes are abundant—magic ingredients that give Hungarian food its kick. To reach the market, leave Dobó Square with the castle to your back; turn right on Zalár József utca, and you'll see the market on your left in two blocks, at the intersection with Dr. Sándor utca (June–Sept Mon–Fri 6:00–18:00, Sat 6:00–13:00, Sun 6:00–10:00; Oct–May Mon–Fri 6:00–17:00, Sat 6:00–13:00, Sun 6:00–10:00).

Minaret—Once part of a mosque, this slender, 130-foot-tall minaret represents the century of Ottoman rule that left its mark on Eger and all of Hungary. The little cross at the top symbolizes the eventual Christian victory over Hungary's Ottoman invaders. You can climb the minaret's 97 steps for fine views of Eger, but it's not for those scared of heights or tight spaces (200 Ft, April–Oct daily 10:00–18:00, closed Nov–March; if it's locked, ask for the key at nearby Hotel Minaret).

▲Kopcsik Marzipan Museum (Kopcsik Marcipánia)—Lajos Kopcsik is a master sculptor who's found his medium: marzipan. Kopcsik can make this delicate mixture of sugar and ground almonds take virtually any form. In this surprisingly engaging little museum, you'll see several remarkable, colorful examples of Kopcsik's skill: sword, minaret, gigantic wine bottle, suitcase, Russian stacking dolls, old-timey phonograph, grandfather clock, giant bell...and paintings galore (including Van Gogh's sunflowers and Picasso's musicians). The list literally goes on for four pages. Who'd have thought you could do so much with candy? You'll also see a video showing the master at work, and a new "Baroque room" that's furnished and decorated entirely in marzipan (400 Ft, ask for printed English information; Easter–Oct daily 10:00–18:00; Nov–Easter Tue–Sun 10:00–17:00, closed Mon; Harangöntő utca 4, tel. 36/412-626.)

Experiences in Eger

Aqua Eger

Swimming and water sports are as important to Egerites as good wine. They're proud that many of Hungary's Olympic medalists in aquatic events have come from this county. The men's water polo team took the gold for Hungary at each of the last three Olympics, and swimmer László Cseh might have been a multiple gold medal-winner at Beijing in 2008 if he hadn't been swimming next to Michael Phelps. The town's Bitskey Aladár swimming pool—arguably the most striking building in this part of Hungary—is practically a temple to water sports.

Eger also has two of the most appealing thermal bath complexes outside of Budapest: one right in town, and the other a few miles away (near the village of Egerszalók). Budapest offers classier bath experiences, but the Eger options are more modern and a bit more accessible, and allow you to save your time in Budapest for big-city sights. Before you go, be sure to read "Taking the Waters" on page 548.

In Eger

Note that you can't rent a swimsuit or a towel at either of these places; bring both with you, along with shower sandals for the locker room (if you've got them).

Bitskey Aladár Pool—This striking swimming pool was designed by Imre Makovecz, the father of Hungary's Organic architectural style. Some Eger taxpayers resented the pool's big price tag, but it left the city with a truly distinctive building befitting its love of water sports. You don't need to be an architecture student to know that the pool is special. It's worth the five-minute walk from Dobó Square just to take a look. Oh, and you can swim in it, too (750 Ft; Mon–Fri 6:00–20:00; until 21:00 on Mon, Wed, and Fri; Sat 8:00–20:00, Sun 8:00–18:00; follow Eger Creek south from Dobó Square to Frank Tivadar utca, tel. 36/511-810).

▲Eger Thermal Bath (Eger Thermálfürdő)—For a refreshing break from the sightseeing grind, consider a splash at the spa. This is a fine opportunity to try a Hungarian bath: relatively accessible (men and women are clothed and together most of the time), but frequented mostly by locals.

Cost, Hours, Location: 1,250 Ft, adventure bath included Sept–April but 700 Ft extra (and worth it) May–Aug. Open

Hungary's Organic Architecture

In recent years, a unique, eye-catching style of architecture has caught on in Hungary: Organic. The Hungarian brand of Organic was developed and championed by Imre Makovecz. After being blackballed by the communists for his nationalistic politics, Makovecz was denied access to building materials, so he taught himself to make impressive structures with nothing more than sticks and rocks. Makovecz was inspired by Transylvanian village architecture: whitewashed walls with large, overhanging mansard roofs to maximize attic space (resembling a big mushroom).

Now that the regime is dead and Makovecz is Hungary's premier architect, he still keeps things simple. He believes that a building should be a product of its environment, rather than a cookie-cutter copy. Organic buildings use indigenous materials (especially wood) and take on unusual forms—often inspired by animals or plants—that blend in with the landscape. Organic buildings look like they're rising up out of the ground, rather than plopped down on top of it. You generally won't find this back-to-nature style in big cities like Budapest; Makovecz prefers to work in small communities such as Eger (see photo on previous page), instead of working for corporations.

Organic architecture has become *the* post-communist style in Hungary. Even big supermarket chains are now imitating Makovecz—a sure sign of architectural success.

May–Sept Mon–Fri 6:00–19:30, Sat–Sun 8:00–19:00, may be open until 23:00 Thu–Sat in summer; Oct–April daily 9:00–18:30. It's at Petőfi tér 2, tel. 36/314-142, www.egertermal.hu.

Getting There: It's easy to reach, within a 10-minute walk of most hotels. From Dobó Square, follow the stream four blocks south (signs for *Strand*). You'll come first to the main entrance (on the left after crossing busy street, roughly facing the fancy swimming-pool building on Petőfi tér). However, as this entrance is a bit more confusing and farther from the best pools, I'd use the side entrance instead: Continue following the stream as it runs along the side of a park (to the right of the main entrance building). Soon you'll see the side entrance to the bath, on your left over a bridge.

Entry Procedure: You'll enter and be given a little barcode

bracelet, which acts as your ticket (keep it on until you leave). If you use the main entrance, you can change in the blocky white buildings just inside the entry (get a hanger from the desk, change in one of the free little cabins, then bring your clothes-laden hanger back for them to store it, 400 Ft extra to use safe-deposit box). At the better side entrance, you'll show your ticket/bracelet to get a key to a locker (1,000-Ft deposit per key, which will be refunded; private changing cabins available in the locker room for no extra charge). After you change and stow your stuff, put the key around your wrist, then join the fun.

Taking the Waters: There's a sprawling array of different pools, each one thoughtfully described in English and labeled with the depth and temperature. From the main entrance, you'll see them in this order: big and small warm pools, a very hot sulfur pool (where Egerites sit peacefully, ignoring the slight stink while their arthritis pains ebb away), the adventure bath, a kids' pool with splashy slide fun, and a lap pool (some of these are closed off-season). The best part is the green-domed, indoor-outdoor adventure bath, right at the side entrance. Its cascades, jets, bubbles, geysers, and powerful current pool will make you feel like a kid again.

Near Eger, in Egerszálok

▲▲Salt Hill Thermal Spa—This brand-new spa complex, in the hills about four miles outside of Eger, is the most modern and accessible thermal bath I've visited in Hungary. While it lacks the old-fashioned class of the Budapest options, it trumps them in user-friendliness and overall soggy fun.

For decades, Egerites would come to the "salt hill" (a natural terraced formation caused by mineral-rich spring water running down the hillside) in the middle of nowhere and cram together to baste in pools of hot water. Then the developers arrived. Today, those same simple pools are still used by local purists, but a giant new hotel and spa complex has been built nearby. With 12 indoor pools and five outdoor ones—many cleverly overlapping each other on several levels—these cutting-edge baths are worth the trip outside of Eger.

Ideal for kids but fun for anyone, the complex has pools with mineral water as well as plain old swimming-pool water. And the high-tech admission system is wonderfully simple: You pay and are given a watch-like bracelet to wear around your wrist, which serves as your ticket, locker key, and credit card. Press it against

a nearby computer screen to find out which locker you've been assigned. Find that locker in the common locker room (you can change in one of the private cabins), stow your stuff there, and have fun. Take some time to explore the sprawling complex. Everything is labeled in English, and each pool is clearly marked with the depth and temperature (in Celsius). You can buy food or drinks with the bracelet, too—it's keeping tabs so you can be charged when you leave.

Cost and Hours: 2,400 Ft for up to three hours, or 1,500 Ft after 17:00 on Mon–Thu, 1,000 Ft extra to access "sauna world" with five different saunas, 700 Ft for towel rental, massages and other treatments also available. Open June–Aug daily 9:00–20:00; Sept–May Mon–Fri 10:00–18:00, Sat–Sun 10:00–20:00 (as it's a new facility, these hours are subject to change—call ahead). Tel. 36/688-500, www.egerszalokfurdo.hu.

Getting There: It's about a mile outside the village of Egerszalók, which is itself about three miles from Eger. You can take a public **bus** from Eger's bus station to the baths (take bus going toward Demjén, you want the *Egerszalók Gyógyfürdő* stop—tell the bus driver "EH-gehr-sah-lohk FEWR-dur"—just after leaving the town of Egerszalók, 9/day Mon–Fri, 2/day Sat, 1/day Sun, 17-min trip, 200 Ft). Check the return bus information carefully (especially on weekends, when frequency plummets). Or you can take a **taxi** from Eger (about 2,500 Ft; tel. 36/787-761 for a return taxi from Egerszalók). A fun and very hedonistic afternoon plan: Take the bus or taxi to the spa, taxi back to Eger's Sirens' Valley for some wine-cave hopping, then taxi back to your Eger hotel.

Note: The humble little baths beside the parking lot are a whole other story—fun but very traditional (just sitting in hot water). Don't mistake these for the new complex. To find the big one, continue walking about five minutes beyond the parking lot to the hotel.

Eger Wine

Eger is at the heart of one of Hungary's best-known wine regions, internationally famous for its **Bull's Blood** (Egri Bikavér). You'll likely hear various stories as to how Bull's Blood got its name during the Ottoman siege of Eger. My favorite version: The Ottomans were amazed at the ferocity displayed by the Egerites, and wondered what they were drinking that boiled their blood and stained

their beards so red...it must be potent stuff. Local merchants, knowing that the Ottomans were Muslim and couldn't drink alcohol, told them it was bull's blood. The merchants made a buck, and the name stuck.

Creative as these stories are, they're all bunk—the term dates only from 1851. Egri Bikavér is a blend (everyone has their own recipe), so you generally won't find it at small producers. Cabernet Sauvignon, Merlot, Kékfránkos, and Kékoportó are the most commonly used grapes.

Of course, there's so much more to Hungarian wines than Bull's Blood—and the Eger region produces many fine options. For all the details, see "Hungarian Wines" on page 468.

While it would be enjoyable to drive around the Hungarian countryside visiting wineries, the most accessible way to get a quick taste of local wine is at a wine shop in town. I like the Kenyeres family's **Bikavér Borház,** right on Little Dobó Square (across from Offi Ház Hotel). In addition to a well-stocked (if slightly overpriced) wine shop, they have a wine bar with indoor and outdoor seating (six tastings and two cheeses for less than 2,000 Ft, or wine by the glass, some English spoken, menu lists basic English description for each wine, daily 10:00–22:00, Kis-Dobó tér 10, tel. 36/413-262).

Sirens' Valley (Szépasszony-völgy)—When the Ottoman invaders first occupied Eger, residents moved into the valley next door, living in caves dug into the hillside. Eventually the Ottomans were driven out, the Egerites moved back to town, and the caves became wine cellars. (Most Eger families who can afford it have at least a modest vineyard in the countryside.) There are more than 300 such caves in the valley to the southwest of Eger, several of which are open for visitors.

The best selection of these caves (about 50) is in the Sirens' Valley (sometimes also translated as "Valley of the Beautiful Women"—or, on local directional signs, the less poetic "Nice Woman Valley"). It's a fun scene—locals showing off their latest vintage, with picnic tables and tipsy tourists spilling out into the street. At some places, you'll be offered free samples; others have a menu for tastes or glasses of wine. While you're not expected to buy a bottle, it's a nice gesture to buy one if you've spent a while at one cave (and it's usually very cheap). Most caves offer something light to eat with the wine, and you'll also see lots of non-cave, full-service restaurants. Some of the caves are fancy and finished, staffed by multilingual waiters in period costume. Others feel like a dank basement, with grandpa leaning on his moped out front and a monolingual granny pouring the wine inside. (The really local places—where the decor is cement, bottles don't have labels, and food consists of potato chips and buttered Wonder Bread—can be the most fun.) This experience

is a strange mix of touristy and local, but not entirely accessible to non-Hungarian-speakers—it works best with a bunch of friends and an easygoing, social attitude. Hopping from cave to musky cave can make for an enjoyable evening, but be sure to wander around a bit to see the options before you dive in. Caves #2 (Bíró Borozó), #34, #43, and the one called "Kiss" have a particularly good reputation (cellars generally open 10:00–22:00 in summer, best June–Aug after 19:00 and good-weather weekends in the shoulder season; it's much quieter off-season, when only a handful of cellars remain open for shorter hours).

Getting to the Sirens' Valley: The valley is a 25-minute walk southwest of Eger. Figure no more than 1,000 Ft for a **taxi** between your hotel and the caves. During the summer, you can take the 500-Ft **tourist train** from Eger's main square to the caves (described earlier, under "Helpful Hints"), then catch a later one back. To **walk,** leave the pedestrian zone on the street next to the cathedral (Törvényház utca), with the cathedral on your right-hand side. Take the first left just after the back end of the cathedral (onto Trinitárius utca), go one long block, then take the first right (onto Király utca). At the fork, bear to the left. You'll stay straight on this road—crossing busy Koháry István utca—for several blocks, through some nondescript residential areas (on Szépasszony-völgy utca). When you crest the hill and emerge from the houses, you'll see the caves (and tour buses) below you on the left—go left (downhill) at the fork to get there. First you'll come to a stretch of touristy non-cave restaurants; keep going past these, and eventually you'll see a big loop of caves on your left.

Nightlife in Eger

Things quiet down pretty early in this sedate town. Youthful student bars and hangouts cluster along the main "walking street," Széchenyi utca. Older travelers feel more at home on Little Dobó Square, with schmaltzy live music until 21:00 or 22:00 in summer, or exploring the Sirens' Valley wine caves.

Sleeping in Eger

Eger is a good overnight stop, and a couple of quaint, well-located hotels in particular—Senator Ház and Offi Ház—are well worth booking in advance. The TI can help you find a room; if you're stumped, the area behind the castle has a sprinkling of cheap guesthouses *(vendégház)*. Elevators are rare (except at Panoráma)—expect to climb one or two flights of stairs to reach your room. A tax of 310 Ft per person will be added to your bill (not included in the prices listed here).

Sleep Code

(200 Ft = about $1, country code: 36, area code: 36)
S = Single, **D** = Double/Twin, **T** = Triple, **Q** = Quad, **b** = bathroom. Unless otherwise noted, English is spoken, breakfast is included, and credit cards are accepted.

To help you sort easily through these listings, I've divided the rooms into three categories, based on the price for a standard double room with bath:

$$$ Higher Priced—Most rooms 20,000 Ft or more.
$$ Moderately Priced—Most rooms between 15,000–20,000 Ft.
$ Lower Priced—Most rooms 15,000 Ft or less.

Phone Tip: Remember, if calling or faxing Eger internationally, you'll have to dial 36 twice (once for the country code, again for the area code).

$$$ Imola Udvarház rents six spacious apartments—with kitchen, living room, bedroom, and bathroom—all decorated in modern Scandinavian style (read: Ikea). They're pricey, but roomy and well-maintained, with a great location near the castle entrance (July–Aug: Sb-19,000 Ft, Db-22,000 Ft, Tb-24,000 Ft, Qb-26,000 Ft; each room 2,000 Ft less April–June and Sept–Oct and 4,000 Ft less Nov–March; air-con, free Wi-Fi, enter through restaurant courtyard at Dózsa György tér 4, tel. & fax 36/516-180, udvarhaz@imolanet.hu).

$$$ Panoráma Hotel is a good big-hotel option, still close to Dobó Square. You'll miss the quaintness of some of the other listings—its 38 faded, overpriced rooms are all business—but you get free access to its "Unicornis Thermarium" spa facility (Sb-21,500 Ft, Db-25,500 Ft, Tb-30,500 Ft, 15 percent cheaper Nov–March, apartments also available, air-con, elevator, pay Wi-Fi, free parking, Dr. Hibay K. utca 2, tel. 36/412-886, fax 36/410-136, www.panoramahotels.hu, hoteleger@panoramahotels.hu).

$$ Senator Ház Hotel is one of my favorite small, family-run hotels in all of Eastern Europe. Though the 11 rooms are a bit worn, this place is cozy and well-run by András Cseh and his right-hand man, Viktor. With oodles of character, all the right quirks, and a picture-perfect location just under the castle on Little Dobó

Square, it's a winner (July–Aug: Sb-14,200 Ft, Db-19,000 Ft; May–June and Sept–Oct: Sb-13,700 Ft, Db-18,300 Ft; cheaper Nov–April, extra bed-6,000 Ft, air-con, free Internet access and Wi-Fi, Dobó István tér 11, tel. & fax 36/411-711, www.senatorhaz.hu, info@senatorhaz.hu). The Cseh family also runs **Pátria Vendégház**—two doubles (same prices as main hotel) and four apartments (Db-20,000 Ft, Tb-27,000 Ft) with luxurious decor around a courtyard in a nearby building (same contact info as Senator Ház Hotel).

$$ Offi Ház Hotel shares Little Dobó Square with Senator Ház. Its five rooms are classy and romantic (Sb-13,500 Ft, Db-15,500 Ft, Db suite-18,500 Ft, Tb suite-23,000 Ft, extra bed-4,500 Ft, 15 percent cheaper Nov–March, non-smoking, air-con, free cable Internet, Dobó István tér 5, tel. & fax 36/518-210, www.offihaz.hu, offihaz@t-online.hu, Offenbächer family).

$$ Szent János Hotel, less charming and more business-like than the Senator Ház and Offi Ház, offers a good but less atmospheric location, 11 straitlaced rooms, and a pleasant winter garden to relax in (Sb-12,000 Ft, Db-17,500 Ft, extra bed-4,000 Ft, 15 percent cheaper Nov–April, non-smoking rooms, air-con, free cable Internet, McDonald's walk-up window across the street can be noisy at night—especially weekends—so request a quiet back room, a long block off Dobó Square at Szent János utca 3, tel. 36/510-350, fax 36/517-101, www.hotelszentjanos.hu, hotelszentjanos@hotelszentjanos.hu).

$ Dobó Vendégház, run by warm Mariann Kleszo, has seven basic but colorful rooms just off Dobó Square. Mariann speaks nothing but Hungarian, but gets simple reservation emails and faxes translated by a friend (Sb-8,500 Ft, Db-12,500 Ft, Tb-16,000 Ft, Qb-20,000 Ft, cash only, some rooms have air-con, Wi-Fi, Dobó utca 19, tel. 36/421-407, fax 36/515-715, www.dobovendeghaz.hu, dobovh@t-online.hu).

Eating in Eger

Bajor Sörház (known to locals as "HBH" for the brand of beer on tap) is favored by tourists and locals alike for its excellent Hungarian cuisine. Everything's good here. You could make a meal of the giant 750-Ft bowl of their spicy *gulyás leves* soup (that's *real* Hungarian goulash, described on page 465)—but it's fun to supplement it with some other well-prepared Hungarian dishes. This is a good place for two or more people to split several dishes. They also feature some Bavarian specialties...but with a Hungarian accent (most main dishes 1,500–3,000 Ft, daily 11:30–22:00, outdoor tables in summer, right at the bottom of Dobó Square at Bajcsy-Zsilinszky utca 19, tel. 36/515-516). If you're lucky, you may

get to meet animated István "Call Me Steve Miller" Molnár, one of my favorite Hungarians.

The recommended hotels **Senator Ház** and **Offi Ház** both have restaurants at the top end of Dobó Square that are open long hours daily (both are listed under "Sleeping in Eger," earlier). These places have fine Hungarian and international food (most main dishes 1,500–2,500 Ft) and postcard-perfect outdoor seating that shares Little Dobó Square with a gazebo featuring cheesy live music on summer evenings. This low-key scene is fun and memorable.

Szantofer Vendéglő serves traditional Hungarian food at local prices to both Egerites and tourists. The good, unpretentious, fill-the-tank grub is presented with an artistic flourish, and the creatively translated menu is good for a laugh (most main dishes 1,400–2,100 Ft, daily 11:30–22:00, Bródy Sándor utca 3, tel. 36/517-298).

Palacsintavár ("Pancake Castle"), near the ramp leading up to the castle, isn't your hometown IHOP. This cellar bar serves up inventive, artfully presented crêpe-wrapped main courses to a mostly students clientele. It's decorated with old cigarette boxes, and cutting-edge rock music plays on the soundtrack (most main dishes 1,300–1,500 Ft, daily 12:00–22:00, Dobó utca 9).

Casa della Pasta, above the market hall, has a pleasant treehouse ambience. Sit indoors or enjoy covered terrace seating that's delightful in warm weather. The menu is mostly Italian, with pasta and pizzas (900–1,400 Ft) and main dishes (1,600–2,000 Ft), and a few Hungarian standbys thrown in (1,600–2,000 Ft; daily 12:00–23:00, Katona István tér 2, tel. 36/412-452).

Fast and Cheap: **Rádi Bisztró** is a popular student hangout and a convenient spot for 200-Ft pastries and inexpensive, premade 400-Ft sandwiches (Mon–Fri 7:00–19:00, Sat 7:00–18:00, Sun 9:00–18:00, just down the street from the Lyceum at Széchenyi utca 2).

Dessert: *Cukrászda* (pastry shops) line the streets of Eger. For deluxe, super-decadent pastries of every kind imaginable—most for less than 450 Ft—drop by **Dobós Cukrászda** (daily 9:30–21:00, point to what you want inside and they'll bring it out to your table, Széchenyi utca 6, tel. 36/413-335). For a more local scene, find the tiny **Sárvári Cukrászda,** a block behind the Lyceum. Their pastries are good, but Egerites line up here after a big Sunday lunch for their homemade gelato (150 Ft/scoop, Mon–Fri 7:00–19:00, Sat–Sun 10:00–19:00, Kossuth utca 1, between Jókai utca and Fellner utca).

Eger Connections

By Train

The only major destination you'll get to directly from Eger's train station is **Budapest** (5/day direct to Budapest's Keleti/Eastern Station, 2.5 hrs; more frequent and faster with a change in Füzesabony—explained next). For most other destinations, you'll connect through Füzesabony or Budapest.

Eger is not as well-connected as the smaller, nearby junction town of **Füzesabony** (FOO-zesh-ah-boyn). Eger is connected to Füzesabony by frequent trains (13/day, 17 min). The very rustic Füzesabony station does not have lockers, but—oddly enough—does have a modest museum of local artifacts. There is no ATM at the station—exit straight from the station and walk about two blocks, and you'll find an ATM on your right.

In Füzesabony, you can transfer to Budapest (including some speedy InterCity trains—with a 900-Ft supplement—that get you to Budapest in 2 hours total).

Night Train to Kraków: If you're connecting to Poland, it's sometimes possible to use a night train between Budapest and Kraków that stops at Füzesabony. If you want to start (or end) your Hungarian trip in Eger, this allows you to sleep into (or out of) Eger with a handy change at Füzesabony, rather than backtracking to Budapest. However, recently this train has run sporadically (summer only, or maybe not at all); sometimes the Budapest–Kraków night train goes through the Czech Republic instead. If this possibility intrigues you, investigate your options carefully at http://bahn.hafas.de/bin/query.exe/en.

By Bus

From Eger to Budapest: Since Eger's bus station is more central than its train station, some travelers prefer the direct bus to **Budapest** (hourly, 2–2.25 hrs). The bus station is a five-minute uphill walk behind Eger's cathedral and Archbishop's Palace: Go behind the cathedral and through the park, and look for the modern, green, circular building. Blue electronic boards in the center of the bus station complex show upcoming departures. This bus leaves you near Budapest's Stadionok bus station (on the M2/red Metro line).

To Salt Hill Thermal Spa: Buses from the same station also connect Eger to the Salt Hill Thermal Spa near Egerszalók (see "Getting There" on page 603). However, buses marked for Egerszalók do not actually go to the spa; instead, you need a bus going *beyond* Egerszalók, marked for Demjén.

PÉCS

An established town for nearly 2,000 years, Pécs (pronounced "paych") is a historic, museum-packed, and oh-so-pretty town near Hungary's southern frontier. Cheerful, inviting Pécs, with colorful buildings dripping with lavish Zsolnay porcelain decoration, feels unusually proud and prosperous.

Owing to its illustrious history, Pécs offers surprisingly engaging sightseeing for a city of its size; museum-going is fun and enlightening here. You'll gradually peel back the many layers of Pécs' past: Walk in the footsteps of Romans through ancient crypts, stroll the medieval trade-town street plan, explore some rare surviving artifacts of the Ottoman occupation, ogle colorful Baroque and Art Nouveau buildings...and enjoy the energetic bustle of one of Hungary's leading cities. The city's symbol—a mosque-turned-church—says it all.

The Mecsek Hills gently cradle the city, protecting it from the colder northern weather. Pécs' mild Mediterranean climate is closer to Croatia's than to Budapest's. It's no surprise that this bright and invigorating city has earned a reputation as a leading art colony. Its streets are lined with museums devoted to local artists both obscure and well-known (including Vasarely and Csontváry, considered the two great figures of Hungarian art). Students love it, too. Hungary's first university was founded here in 1367, and today's U. of Pécs rivals Budapest's ELTE as the country's biggest university. More than 30,000 students give Pécs a youthful buzz.

The city's rich tradition of history and culture is ramping up for its status as a European City of Culture in 2010. Busloads of tourists are about to bust out of the Budapest rut and discover this charming city. Beat them to it.

Planning Your Time

One full day is enough to get your fill of Pécs. Like Eger, it's a long day trip from Budapest (3 hours each way by train), so it's worth spending the night. With the better part of a day in Pécs, go for a walk through town following my self-guided commentary in the "Sights in Pécs" section, dipping into the museums that appeal to you.

Orientation to Pécs

(area code: 72)

With about 170,000 people, Pécs is Hungary's fifth-largest city. But it feels like a small town, right down to the convivial strolling atmosphere that ambles along its pedestrian zone. The Belváros, or Inner Town, is hemmed in by a ring road (the site of the former town wall, some of which still stands). You can walk from one end of this central tourist zone to the other in about 15 minutes. All roads lead to the main square, Széchenyi tér, marked by the palatial yellow Town Hall and giant mosque/church. Because Pécs is nestled up against a gentle hillside, you'll go gradually uphill as you head north.

Tourist Information

The Pécs TI is right on the main square, in the ornately decorated County Hall building (mid-June–mid-Sept Mon–Fri 8:00–17:30, Sat 9:00–14:00, closed Sun; May–mid-June and mid-Sept–Oct Mon–Fri 8:00–17:30, closed Sat–Sun; Nov–April Mon–Fri 8:00–16:00, closed Sat–Sun; Széchenyi tér 9, tel. 72/213-315, www.pecs.hu).

Arrival in Pécs

By Train: The Pécs train station is three-quarters of a mile due south of the city center's Széchenyi tér. Inside, the station is long but straightforward (with ATM, lockers, and all the usual amenities). The fastest way downtown is to take the **bus:** As you exit the station, head down to the left end of the bus stops, and hop on bus #30, #32, or #33 (buy 280-Ft ticket from driver and validate in red box—stick ticket in slot, then pull the slot itself toward you; ride it three stops in about 10 minutes to Boldogsághász, just after you see the giant green-domed mosque/church on the main square). You can also **walk** there in about 15 minutes: Exit straight ahead from the station and walk up the treelined, slightly angled Jókai út, which funnels you directly to the main Széchenyi square. A **taxi** to any of my recommended hotels should cost no more than 1,000 Ft.

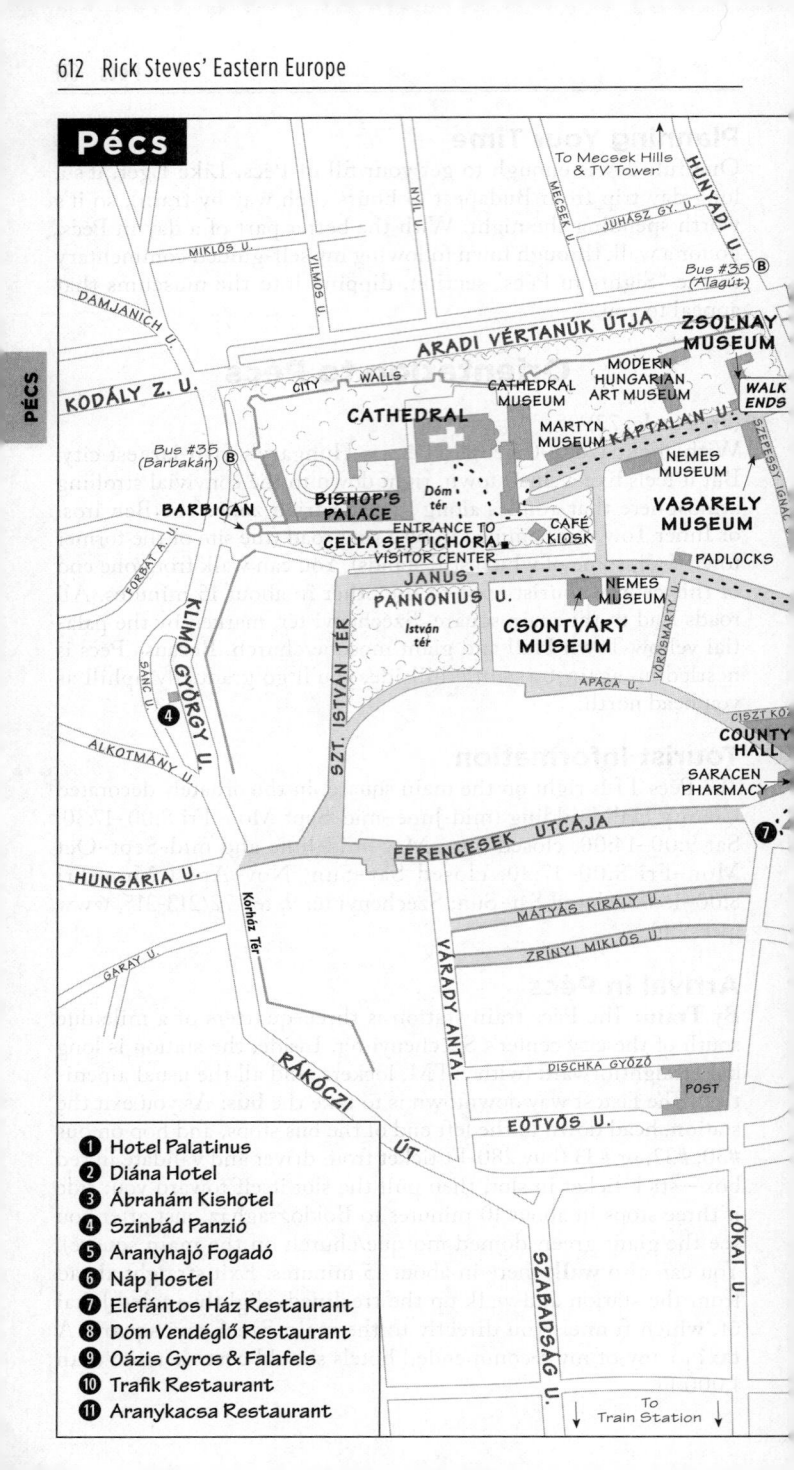
Pécs
To Mecsek Hills & TV Tower
HUNYADI U.
MECSEK U.
JUHÁSZ GY. U.
NYÁL U.
MIKLÓS U.
VILMOS U.
Bus #35 (Alagút)
DÁMJANICH U.
ARADI VÉRTANÚK ÚTJA
ZSOLNAY MUSEUM
KODÁLY Z. U.
CITY WALLS
CATHEDRAL MUSEUM
MODERN HUNGARIAN ART MUSEUM
WALK ENDS
CATHEDRAL
MARTYN MUSEUM
KÁPTALAN U.
SZÉCHENYI TÉR
Bus #35 (Barbakán)
NEMES MUSEUM
Dóm tér
BISHOP'S PALACE
BARBICAN
VASARELY MUSEUM
ENTRANCE TO CELLA SEPTICHORA
CAFÉ KIOSK
VISITOR CENTER
PADLOCKS
FORBÁT A. U.
JANUS PANNONIUS U.
NEMES MUSEUM
István tér
CSONTVÁRY MUSEUM
KLIMÓ GYÖRGY U.
SZT. ISTVÁN TÉR
VÖRÖSMARTY U.
SÁNC U.
APÁCA U.
CISZT KÖZ.
COUNTY HALL
ALKOTMÁNY U.
SARACEN PHARMACY
FERENCESEK UTCÁJA
HUNGÁRIA U.
Kórház Tér
MÁTYÁS KIRÁLY U.
ZRÍNYI MIKLÓS U.
GARAY U.
VÁRADY ANTAL
DISCHKA GYŐZŐ
POST
RÁKÓCZI ÚT
EÖTVÖS U.
JÓKAI U.
SZABADSÁG U.
To Train Station
1 Hotel Palatinus
2 Diána Hotel
3 Ábrahám Kishotel
4 Szinbád Panzió
5 Aranyhajó Fogadó
6 Náp Hostel
7 Elefántos Ház Restaurant
8 Dóm Vendéglő Restaurant
9 Oázis Gyros & Falafels
10 Trafik Restaurant
11 Aranykacsa Restaurant

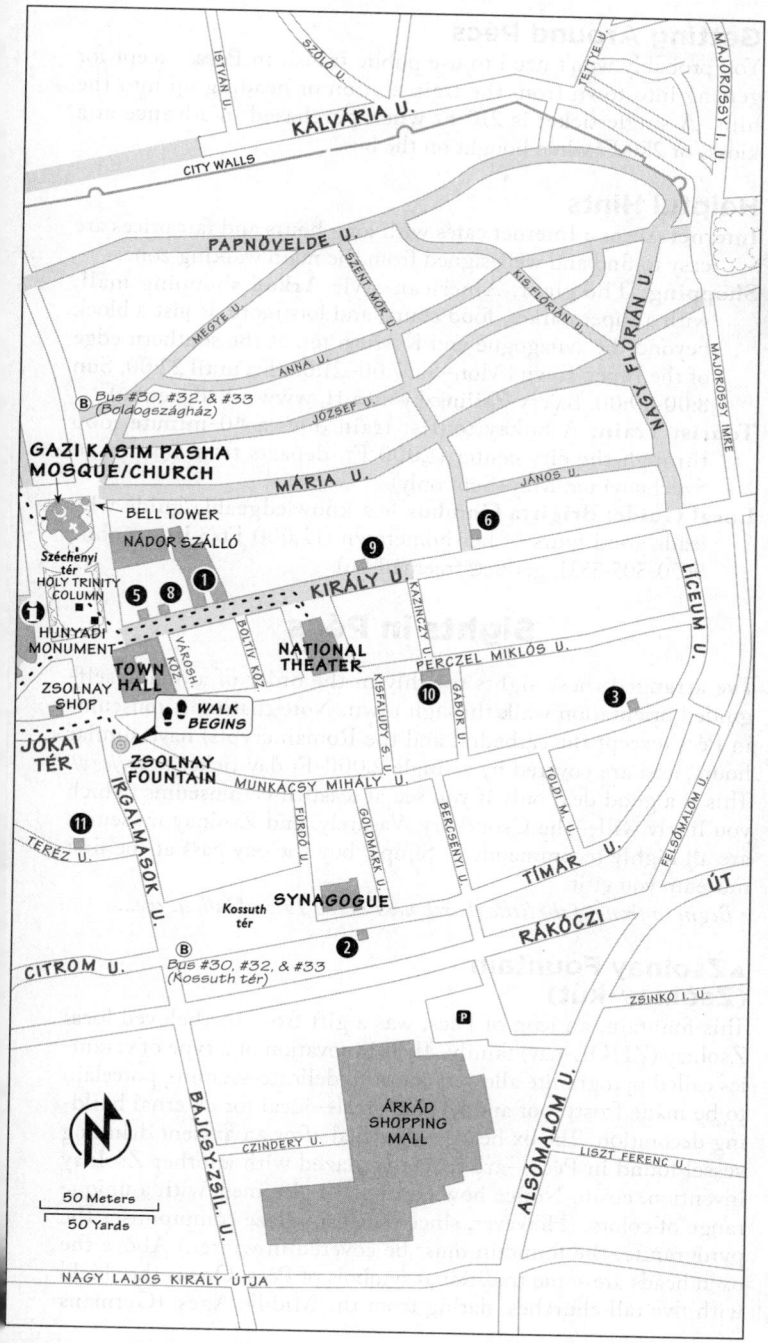
KÁLVÁRIA U.
CITY WALLS
PAPNÖVELDE U.
MEGYE U.
SZENT MÓR U.
KIS ELŐRIÁN U.
NAGY ELŐRIÁN U.
ANNA U.
JÓZSEF U.
Bus #30, #32, & #33 (Boldogszágház)
GAZI KASIM PASHA MOSQUE/CHURCH
MÁRIA U.
JÁNOS U.
BELL TOWER
NÁDOR SZÁLLÓ
Széchenyi tér
HOLY TRINITY COLUMN
HUNYADI MONUMENT
KIRÁLY U.
KÁZMÉCZY U.
LÍCEUM U.
TOWN HALL
VÁROSH. KÖZ.
BÖLTY KÖZ.
NATIONAL THEATER
PERCZEL MIKLÓS U.
ZSOLNAY SHOP
WALK BEGINS
KISFALUDY S. U.
GÁBOR U.
JÓKAI TÉR
ZSOLNAY FOUNTAIN
MUNKÁCSY MIHÁLY U.
TOLDI M. U.
IRGALMASOK U.
FÜRDŐ U.
GOLDMARK U.
BERCSÉNYI U.
TERÉZ U.
TÍMÁR U.
FELSŐMALOM U.
Kossuth tér
SYNAGOGUE
RÁKÓCZI ÚT
CITROM U.
Bus #30, #32, & #33 (Kossuth tér)
ZSINKÓ I. U.
ÁRKÁD SHOPPING MALL
BAJCSY-ZSIL. U.
CZINDERY U.
ALSÓMALOM U.
LISZT FERENC U.
50 Meters
50 Yards
NAGY LAJOS KIRÁLY ÚTJA
ISTVÁN U.
SZŐLŐ U.
TETYE U.
MAJOROSSY I. U.
MAJOROSSY IMRE

Getting Around Pécs

You probably won't need to use public transit in Pécs, except for getting into town from the train station or heading up into the hills. A single ticket is 210 Ft when purchased in advance at a kiosk, or 280 Ft when bought on the bus.

Helpful Hints

Internet Access: Internet cafés with long hours and fair prices are easy to find and well-signed from the main walking zone.

Shopping: The giant, American-style **Árkád** shopping mall, with a supermarket, food court, and lots more, is just a block beyond the synagogue and Kossuth tér, at the southern edge of the Inner Town (Mon–Sat 7:00–21:00, Fri until 22:00, Sun 8:00–19:00, Bajcsy-Zsilinszky utca 11, www.arkadpecs.hu).

Tourist Train: A hokey tourist train does a 40-minute loop through the city center (1,000 Ft, departs from bottom of Széchenyi tér, May–Sept only).

Local Guide: Brigitta Gombos is a knowledgeable guide who leads good tours of her hometown (12,000 Ft/3 hrs, mobile 0670-505-3531, gerluc@freemail.hu).

Sights in Pécs

I've arranged these sights roughly in the order of a handy self-guided orientation walk through town. Note that most museums in Pécs (except the cathedral and the Roman crypts) have similar hours, and are covered by a single 2,000-Ft day ticket *(napijegy)*. This is a good deal only if you see at least three museums (which you likely will—the Csontváry, Vasarely, and Zsolnay museums are all highly recommended). Simply buy the day pass at the first museum you visit.

• *Begin in front of the little church next to the Town Hall, at the...*

▲Zsolnay Fountain (Zsolnay-kút)

This fountain, an icon of Pécs, was a gift from the beloved local Zsolnay (ZHOL-nay) family. Their innovation of a type of ceramics called pyrogranite allowed colorful, delicate-seeming porcelain to be made frostproof and hard as steel—ideal for external building decoration. The ox heads—modeled after an ancient drinking vessel found in Pécs—are specially glazed with another Zsolnay invention, eosin. Notice how eosin glaze glimmers with a unique range of colors. (However, since the eosin glaze compromises the pyrogranite, the fountain must be covered in winter.) Above the oxen heads are some traditional symbols of Pécs. One is the shield with five tall churches, dating from the Middle Ages. (Germans

still call the town Fünfkirchen—Five Churches.) This seal was appropriated by the Zsolnay family as a symbol of their porcelain. The other seal is Pécs' coat of arms: a walled city under vineyard-strewn hills.

This is the first of many gorgeous Zsolnay decorations we'll see all over town. But Pécs isn't the only place adorned with them: In the late 19th and early 20th centuries, Budapest and cities all over Europe covered their finest buildings with decorations from this city's Zsolnay Porcelain Manufacture. (For all the details, see the "Zsolnay Porcelain" sidebar, later.)

• *Across the wide street is the entrance to an enjoyable pedestrian zone called...*

Jókai Tér

As you enter the traffic-free area, notice the **chessboards** on top of the little pillars. When this street was renovated in 2000—with funky benches and other playful elements—the designers wanted to remind locals to take the time to relax.

On the right (at #2), notice the **Zsolnay porcelain shop.** Although the company was reduced to an industrial supplier under the communists, today Zsolnay is proudly reclaiming its role as a maker of fine art. Dipping into the shop, notice that some of the decorative items use the same distinctive eosin glaze as the fountain's oxen heads...and are priced accordingly.

Continuing to the corner, look down the pedestrian street called **Ferencesek utcája.** When Pécs was a walled market town, this street—and Király utca, also now pedestrianized—made up the main east–west road. At the house on the corner, notice the elephant. This used to be a grocery store, which likely imported exotic Eastern goods, symbolized by the then-mysterious pachyderm. (Now it's a recommended Italian restaurant, Elefántos Ház—see "Eating in Pécs," later.)

Hang a right around the elephant house, noticing the former tram tracks preserved in the street. Imagine how unappealing this drag was when it was choked with tram and car traffic. On the left, look for the old-time **Saracen Pharmacy** (marked with the words *Sipöcz István* over the door). Its interior—with gorgeous woodwork, little porcelain medicine pots, and a lovely Zsolnay fountain—is protected and open to tourists (free, Mon–Fri 9:00–18:00, Sat 9:00–12:00, closed Sun, Apáca 1).

• *Continuing up the street, you'll emerge into...*

▲The Main Square: Széchenyi Tér

In the Middle Ages, Pécs was a major stop on a Byzantine trade route. At the intersection of the city's original north–south and east–west thoroughfares, Széchenyi tér was a natural meeting point and market zone. Today the market is gone, but no fewer than 12 streets converge here, and it remains the bustling city center. This is where both political demonstrations and the annual New Year's Eve festivities percolate.

Let's get oriented. Face the green-domed **Gazi Kasim Pasha Mosque** at the top of the square (described in detail later). On the right, the giant yellow-and-white building with the tower is the **Town Hall** (Városház, 1908), strategically located here since the olden days to watch over the market activities. The Town Hall's tower plays laid-back organ ditties throughout the day. Across the square (on the left) is the gorgeous, red-roofed **County Hall** (Megyháza, 1898) frosted like a wedding cake with sumptuous Zsolnay decorations (and a TI on the far corner). Because it was originally a bank, it's adorned with beehives (one at the very peak of the building, and two more between the top-floor windows)—industrious bees, who carefully collect and store away their golden deposits, are a common symbol for banking. Farther up the square on the right is the pink **Nádor Szálló.** In the early 20th century, this hotel was a popular gathering place for artists and intellectuals (but now it's awaiting a massive renovation).

The square has two monuments. On the right is an equestrian statue of **János Hunyadi,** the war hero who fended off the Ottoman invaders at the 1456 Battle of Belgrade. The Ottomans later returned, took Pécs, and built the mosque at the top of the square. But Hunyadi gets the last laugh: If you position yourself in front of the Town Hall just right, it appears that Hunyadi's club is smashing the crescent at the top of the mosque. This statue is a popular meeting point: Locals say, "I'll meet you under the horse's...tail." With perhaps unintended irony, Hunyadi—who died of the plague soon after that battle—shares the square with the **Holy Trinity Plague Column,** built to give thanks to God for surviving a nasty bout of the disease in the late 17th century. Around its base are three saints known for protecting against disease or injury: Sebastian, who was killed by arrows (on left); Rocco, with a nasty leg wound (on right); and Anthony of Padua, who offers help recovering that which is lost—including health (behind the pillar).

• *We'll visit the mosque/church soon. But first, head down the street branching off to the right, next to the Town Hall...*

▲▲The Walking Street: Király Utca

This vibrant Technicolor people zone—combined with Jókai tér and Ferencesek utcája, across the square—bisects the city center. Király utca ("Royal Street") is lined with shops, several recommended restaurants (see "Eating in Pécs," later), and gorgeous facades that continue the architectural cancan from out on the square.

A few steps down the street on the right, the big green building marked **Bazár** was the Zsolnay family home, before they moved closer to their porcelain factory just outside town. Just beyond (on the left) is the gorgeous, horseshoe-shaped **Hotel Palatinus.** Step into the lobby for a taste of genteel Secession (see "Sleeping in Pécs," later).

A few more steps take you to the square in front of the **National Theater,** built (along with most of the other houses on this square) for the Hungarian millennial celebrations of 1896 (see page 480). The decorations on the theater—including the stone-like statues—are all made of Zsolnay pyrogranite. This is a popular venue in this city of culture, sometimes hosting performances by the local philharmonic (duck into the box office to see what's showing while you're in town).

While this part of Pécs appears wealthy and manicured, the region is struggling. In the early 1950s, Pécs had only about 50,000 residents. Then coal and uranium mines kick-started the economy, and the population more than tripled over the next 50 years. However, both mines have since closed, and while the university and business center of Pécs continues to thrive, outlying communities are grappling with 30 percent unemployment.

• *Head back to Széchenyi tér to visit the...*

▲▲Gazi Kasim Pasha Mosque (Gázi Kászim Pasa Dzsámija)/Inner Town Parish Church

It's rare to find such a well-preserved Ottoman structure in Hungary. The Ottomans—who began their 150-year stay in Pécs in 1543—lived here in the Inner Town, while the dwindling Hungarian population moved to the outskirts. The Ottomans tore down the church that had stood on this spot and used the stones to build the structure you see today. After the Ottomans were

forced out, the Catholic Church reclaimed this building and turned it into a church—which is why it's still intact today. Despite renovations over the years, it remains an offbeat hybrid of Islamic and Christian faiths.

Cost and Hours: Free, but donations are requested—consider buying a postcard or booklet; mid-April–mid-Oct Mon–Sat 10:00–16:00, Sun 11:30–16:00; mid-Oct–mid-April Mon–Sat 10:00–12:00, Sun 11:30–14:00.

Self-Guided Tour: From the **outside,** notice the crescent moon of Islam capping the dome—but it's topped by the victorious Christian cross. The only decorations on the austere facade are the striped ogee arches over the windows. Before entering, notice the fig trees; locals are proud that their mild climate can support these heat-seekers.

Go **inside** and let your eyes adjust to the low light. Are you in a church, or a mosque...or both? The striped arches over the windows are inside as well. Notice the colorful Islamic-style stalactite decorations at the tops of the corners. The painting on the underside of the dome seems to combine Christian figures with the geometric designs of Islam. To the right of the main altar is a verse from the Quran, translated into Hungarian and used for Christian worship (a reminder that Islam and Christianity are founded on many of the same principles). Look for gray patches with faint Arabic script peeking through—most were whitewashed during the church-ification.

Looking back to where you entered, you'll see a large **prayer niche** (mihrab) next to the door. This niche, which faces Mecca (southeast from here), indicated to Muslim worshippers where they had to face to pray. The holy water basin in the niche and the crucifix suspended above it make it clear who's in charge now.

Mentally erase these and other Christian elements, and go back in time to the Ottoman period. There were no pews, and carpets covered the floor. Worshippers—men in front, women segregated in back—stood and knelt

as they prayed toward the mihrab. A step-stair pulpit, called a mimber, likely stood off to one side of the mihrab.

When the Christians reclaimed this building, they flipped it around, putting an altar where the entrance was, and vice versa. Much later, in 1939, they added the giant **apse** (semi-circular area behind the altar). As you explore this area, in the corners you'll see small stone basins. These once stood outside the building, where the Ottoman worshippers performed their ablution, or ritual washing before prayer. The modern paintings depict Bible scenes and events in Hungary's Christian history. And the giant organ is an Angster (made by a local Hungarian organ-maker).

Exiting the building, head around back to find the latest addition to this constantly evolving structure: the modern **bell tower,** and a concrete footprint that recalls the original church that preceded this mosque. The statue depicts St. Bartholomew, the patron of this church. Depicted (as he always is) with his skin peeling away, he steps on a serpent, representing victory over evil (in this case, probably Islam?). Every day at 12:00 and 19:00, the bell tower rises up 40 feet in the air to play a tune.

• *While interesting, this is not Pécs' main church. To see that (and a lot more), go down the street at the upper-left corner of the square...*

Janus Pannonius Utca

About a block down this street, watch (on the right) for a railing that's completely covered in **padlocks.** Nobody knows for sure how this local tradition began, back in the 1980s. Some say it was a clever way for graduating students to get rid of the padlocks from their lockers. These days, the padlocks mostly belong to lovers who want to pledge themselves to each other. You can see that many of the locks are marked (or even engraved) with couples' names. (If you're interested in early retirement, set up a padlock shop here.) Farther down the same block, the tradition continues at the padlock-covered gate.

• *Continue along the street until you emerge into the little square. In the pretty off-white building on the left (with the grey roof), you'll find Pécs' best art museum...*

▲Csontváry Museum (Csontváry Múzeum)

This small but good collection showcases the works of beloved Hungarian painter Tivadar Csontváry Kosztka. Csontváry produced only 100 paintings and 20 drawings, about half of which are

Tivadar Csontváry Kosztka
(1853–1919)

Adored by Hungarians, but virtually unknown outside his homeland, Tivadar Csontváry Kosztka had a life as interesting as his paintings. Because of the time in which he lived and his struggles with mental illness (schizophrenia)—if not for his talent—Csontváry (CHONT-vah-ree) is often compared to Van Gogh. While that's a bit of a stretch, viewing Csontváry's works give you a glimpse into the Hungarian psyche, and into his own fractured mind.

Tivadar Kosztka was born to an upper-class family, seemingly bound for a humdrum life. He didn't pick up a paintbrush until his 27th year. Then one day, while idly sketching sleeping oxen, he had a revelation (or, perhaps, a psychotic episode): A voice told him that he was destined to become "the world's greatest *plein air* painter, greater even than Raphael."

He adopted the pseudonym Csontváry and became driven by an almost pathological compulsion to prepare himself for what he believed to be his destiny. He figured it would take him 20 years, working as a pharmacist to finance his quest. At 41, he had saved enough to attend art school (in Munich and in Paris). Seeking the ideal subjects for his outdoor style, he traveled extensively around Europe and the Middle East: Italy, Croatia,

collected here. For a crash course in this enigmatic painter, read the sidebar above before visiting (700 Ft, covered by 2,000-Ft day ticket, borrow the English information sheet, April–Oct Tue–Sun 10:00–18:00, Nov–March Tue–Sun 10:00–17:00, closed Mon year-round, Janus Pannonius utca 11, tel. 72/224-255).

The museum is divided into five rooms. In Room 1, see Csontváry's art-school sketches that capture people at unguarded moments. Room 2 shows mostly scenes from around Hungary. *Storm on the Great Hortobágy* is a dynamic snapshot of life on the Great Hungarian Plain, where cowherds attend to longhorn cattle. A storm brews on the horizon as a horseman races across the bridge. Notice the balance between movement and stillness, and between the yellow sky and the deep blue clouds. In Room 3, Csontváry's most acclaimed work, *The Lonely Cedar,* depicts a windblown tree on a ridge above the sea. The tree seems boldly independent even as it longs for companionship. Rooms 3 and 4 are filled with other "postcards" of Csontváry's far-flung travels, where he found inspi-

Bosnia-Herzegovina, Greece, Egypt, Lebanon, Jerusalem, and the Tatra Mountains of his own homeland. By the time he began painting in earnest, he had only six productive years (1903–1909).

Csontváry's rough, autodidactic (self-taught) style reveals his untrained origins, but contains a depth of meaning and of composition that exceeded his technical skill. While classified as a Post-Impressionist, Csontváry forged a style all his own. Like his contemporary Marc Chagall, he worked in almost childlike bright colors and often reverted to big, bold themes. His most common subjects are the destinations he traveled to that inspired him.

After exhibitions in 1909 and 1910 failed to win him the praise he so desperately sought, he became consumed by his schizophrenia and created only bizarre, surrealistic works. He died in obscurity in 1919.

After Csontváry's death, his family planned to sell his works to wagon-makers, who wanted the valuable canvas to stretch over their wagons. Fortunately a Budapest art collector bought them instead, preserving the legacy of this important figure in Hungarian art history.

Csontváry remained largely unappreciated until the 1960s, when art-lovers began to take notice. But one discerning eye for talent knew greatness when he saw it, before many others did: Pablo Picasso reportedly discovered Csontváry's canvases at a 1949 exhibition, and proceeded to lock himself in the room with them for an hour. Finally emerging, he told his friend Marc Chagall that Chagall could never produce a work half as good as Csontváry's.

ration in the Middle East (Baalbek, Jerusalem, Nazareth) and Europe (France, Sicily, Croatia, Bosnia-Herzegovina, Greece). The last room (5) displays Csontváry's final major painting, *Riders on the Seashore.* This haunting valedictory canvas, with an equestrian party pausing by an eerily deep-blue cove, hints at the troubled depths of Csontváry's own psyche. Other works in this room date from Csontváry's final days, when—in his worsening mental state—he sketched large-scale, absurdist scenes.

• *Continue down Janus Pannonius utca, along the tree-lined path. Soon you'll see a beautiful yellow kiosk (on the right)—an inviting place for a coffee break. Just below and to the left of that, look for the modern entrance to the...*

▲▲Cella Septichora Visitor Center (Roman Crypts)

This unique, modern, well-presented museum allows visitors to take a peek inside some wonderfully preserved Roman crypts.

Cost and Hours: 1,200 Ft, April–Oct Tue–Sun 10:00–18:00, Nov–March Tue–Sun 10:00–16:00, always closed Mon, Dóm tér, tel. 72/224-755. A "joint ticket" for an extra 300 Ft gets you into another, smaller tomb nearby (at the base of the stairs up to the cathedral). It's basically more of the same, plus a marble sarcophagus.

Tours: For 300 Ft extra, you can join a 45-minute English tour. These English tours run regularly, but not according to a set schedule. If the sight isn't too busy, a guide might be able to give you a private tour; or you might have to wait up to 30 minutes in summer or 60 minutes in winter. Taking the tour is worthwhile if you really want to appreciate all the details, so consider calling ahead to check the schedule (tel. 72/224-755). For a brief visit, my self-guided tour (below)—and the good posted English descriptions—will take you through the basics.

Background: There was a Roman settlement in today's Pécs from the year A.D. 30, and by the second century it was a provincial capital called Sopinae. During that time, this part of town was a vast cemetery, which included the graves of Christian martyrs. Later, after Christianity became the state religion in the early fourth century, the tombs of these martyrs attracted pilgrims from afar. Wealthy Christian families were now free to build double-decker structures to hold the remains of their relatives: a sealed crypt below ground (painted with Bible scenes and floral motifs), with a chapel directly above for remembering and praying for the dead. About a century later, Rome fell. Nomadic invaders would live in the chapels and raid the crypts (then carefully re-cover them). Today the remains of some of these crypt-chapels have been discovered, excavated, and opened to visitors.

➲ **Self-Guided Tour:** Buy your ticket and head into the first area, the foundation of a **giant chapel with seven apses.** (The exhibit is named for this—Cella Septichora means "seven-apsed chapel.") Experts believe that the crypt of a different martyr would have been placed in each apse, and pilgrims would come here to worship. However, the structure was never finished.

Head up the stairs and go down the hall on the left. After passing a stone sarcophagus, you'll go down a steep set of stairs and through a long corridor. Unlike Rome's famous catacombs, these crypts were not originally connected underground; modern archaeologists built this tunnel to allow visitors easier access to all the tombs.

You'll emerge at the **Wine Pitcher Burial Chamber.** The model shows the two-tiered structure. Peer through the window to see the paintings that decorate the crypt. Its nickname comes from the wine jug and glass painted in the niche above the body. Romans used wine to toast to the memory of the departed (the Roman version of "pour one out for the homies who ain't here"). Climb up the stairs to what was ground level, where you can view the foundation of the chapel and look down into the crypt. From here, you'll see other paintings (representing paradise), as well as the drain at the bottom of the sarcophagus. The Romans, always clever engineers, provided a drainage system so that accumulating groundwater would not defile the body.

Retrace your steps, then follow signs to the Peter and Paul crypt. Along the way, you'll pass through an area with several **smaller crypts.** Notice that these didn't have large chapels up top; rather, worshippers would kneel and look inside a small decorative chapel. In one, a hole in the floor of the chapel indicates where tomb raiders broke in to search for valuables. Turn right into the **octagonal chapel,** which—like the seven-apsed chapel—was likely designed to be a pilgrim church. Finally you'll pass another small crypt that's more intact, showing the barrel vaulting that once covered all of these structures.

At the **Peter and Paul Burial Chamber,** kneel down to see Sts. Peter and Paul above the sarcophagus, flanking the Christogram (an ancient Christian symbol). Then head down the spiral stairs to an area below the crypt, where you can look up through Plexiglas to see more decorations. The side walls are painted with biblical scenes, while the ceiling features another Christogram, four portraits (possibly the Four Evangelists), and more nature motifs—plants and birds. (An artist's rendering of the original version is nearby.) Notice the little window above the body. Experts believe that a ribbon tied to the sarcophagus led through this window up into the chapel, so the faithful could have a tangible connection to the dead.

Retracing your steps on your way out, you'll pass through even more crypts (they've unearthed more than 20), as well as some simple brick sarcophagi used by poorer families to bury their dead.

• *Exiting the exhibit, turn right and continue down Janus Pannonius utca, which deposits you at...*

István Tér and Dóm Tér

These two squares—the lower István Square, which belonged to the people, and the upper Cathedral Square, which was the bishop's—used to be separated by a wall and moat. But the enlightened **Bishop Szepesy** turned them into one big park. In the statue that dominates the square, he's stepping down from the pulpit while clutching a Bible—a reminder that he's believed to have been the first priest to conduct services in Hungarian.

Walk up the stairs and take a closer look at Cathedral Square. The brown, Neo-Renaissance building on the left (with a yellow Baroque addition) is the Bishop's Palace. At the corner of this building, notice the engaging statue of **Franz Liszt** by popular 20th-century sculptor Imre Varga. Liszt was a friend of the bishop, and the musician's visit here in 1846 is still the stuff of legend.

• *Now turn your attention to the massive, four-towered....*

▲▲Cathedral

St. István established a bishopric in Pécs in the year 1009, and this church building grew in fits and starts from then on. By the 14th century, it had roughly the same floor plan as today, and gradually morphed with the styles that came into fashion: Romanesque, Gothic, Renaissance. The Ottomans used it as a stable, grain store, and library, and even turned one small chapel into a mosque and erected a minaret. Later, when it became the cathedral again, it got a Baroque overhaul. Finally in the 1880s, a bishop (likely hoping to be remembered as a visionary) grew tired of the architectural hodgepodge, gutted the place, and turned it into the Neo-Romanesque fortress of God before you today. The 12 apostles stand along the roofline, and the four distinctive corner towers anchor and fortify the massive structure.

Cost and Hours: 800 Ft, 300 Ft more to also visit cathedral museum and bishop's wine cellar for a tasting; April–mid-Oct Mon–Sat 9:00–17:00, Sun 13:00–17:00; mid-Oct–March Mon–Sat 10:00–16:00, Sun 13:00–16:00; can be closed for weddings Sat afternoons—especially in summer, tel. 72/513-030.

Self-Guided Tour: Get close to the entrance and inspect the highly symbolic **bronze gate** from 2000. The vines, grapes, and branches are all connected, as we are all connected to God. If you look closely, you'll find animals representing good (birds) and evil (snake, scorpion, frog). The sculpture on the left depicts St. István giving Pécs to the first bishop; on the right, Jesus offers his hand to St. Peter.

Go to church. Stepping inside, it's clear that the renovating bishop did not subscribe to the "less is more" school of church decoration. Like the Matthias Church in Budapest (see page 504)—renovated at about the same time—every square inch is covered by a thick layer of colorful paint. Along the **nave** are paintings depicting the lives of the church's patrons, Sts. Peter and Paul. Above the arches are biblical scenes. The coffered ceiling of the nave depicts the 12 apostles and (near the organ) John the Baptist.

The **altar,** with its richly decorated canopy, is a replica of the 13th-century original. The mosaic on the apse dome (behind the altar, not entirely visible from here) features Jesus flanked by Peter and Paul (on the right) and, on the left, István and Mary (the patron saint of Hungary).

To the right of the organ is the **bishop's treasury,** in the Chapel of Mary. (This is the only one of the cathedral's four such chapels open to tourists.) The vestments, goblets, and monstrances are surrounded by paintings of events from the Christian history of Hungary. At the far end of the chapel is a remarkably detailed 16th-century alabaster sculpture, done by a Dutch sculptor for an Italian family who didn't want it after all (so the Pécs bishop bought it instead).

Back in the main church, to the right of the altar are the stairs down to the **crypt.** This 11th-century forest of columns (redecorated like the rest of the church) is part of the original building on this site. The bust at the back depicts the bishop who decided to renovate the church.

• *From in front of the cathedral, if you want to take a look at part of the old* ***city wall,*** *go down the stairs and turn right at the wide path, which will take you to a barbican (round tower) that helped fortify the*

Zsolnay Porcelain

Because of the pioneering Zsolnay (ZHOL-nay) family of Pécs, buildings all over Hungary are slathered with gorgeously colorful porcelain.

Miklós Zsolnay (1800–1880) opened a porcelain factory in Pécs in 1853. His innovative son, Vilmos Zsolnay (1828–1900), experimented with glazes and additives, and revolutionized the use of porcelain in building materials. He invented a type of ceramic, called pyrogranite, that enabled the creation of porcelain decorative elements that were as resilient as steel—and weatherproof—but could still be delicately sculpted and painted any color of the rainbow. Zsolnay pyrogranite made a splash at the 1873 World Exhibition in Vienna, winning an avalanche of orders from all over Europe. The twists and curves that Zsolnay porcelain allowed for were a perfect fit for the slinky, organic Art Nouveau style of the day. Exhibits at further world fairs added to the Zsolnay family's renown and wealth.

In 1893, Vilmos Zsolnay unveiled his latest innovation: eosin, a shimmering—almost metallic—iridescent glaze. Named for the Greek word for "dawn," it has an otherworldly way of making porcelain resemble light striking a precious stone, or the surface of a soap bubble. For an example, look at the way that eosin makes Pécs' Zsolnay Fountain scintillate in the sunlight.

Boom time for the Zsolnays also coincided with the 1896 millennial celebrations in Budapest. The city's architects, who

walls. (For more on these walls, see page 628.)

Otherwise, exiting the cathedral, turn left, pass through the archway, walk over the glassed-in Roman ruins, and walk down...

Káptalan Utca: Pécs' "Museum Row"

Several museums line tranquil Káptalan Street ("Chapterhouse Street," where priests once lived), just east of the cathedral. A few of the smaller museums are skippable, but the Zsolnay and Vasarely museums are worthwhile. Remember, all of these are covered by the same 2,000-Ft day ticket (described on page 614). The website for all is www.jpm.hu. These are listed roughly in the order you reach them, coming from the cathedral.

▲Viktor Vasarely Museum (Vasarely Múzeum)—You might not know Viktor Vasarely (1908–1997), but you know his work. Think optical illusions, and the dizzying Op Art that inspired the

had ample resources and imagination, were striving to create a unique Hungarian national style. Many of them adopted colorful pyrogranite tiles and other decorations as an integral part of that style. In Budapest alone, the Great Market Hall, Matthias Church and National Archives on Castle Hill, and Ödön Lechner's Postal Savings Bank and Museum of Applied Arts are roofed with Zsolnay pyrogranite tiles. Zsolnay decorative elements also adorn the Hungarian Parliament, Gellért Baths, and many other buildings. To this day, Zsolnay tiles are synonymous with Budapest (and Hungarian) architecture.

All of that porcelain generated a lot of work for the Pécs factory. By the time World War I broke out, the Zsolnay family business was the Austro-Hungarian Empire's biggest company. But the stripped-down modern styles that emerged in the 20th century had little use for the fanciful Zsolnay decorations. The factory was nationalized by the communists, the Zsolnay name was abandoned, and quality plummeted.

In the 1990s, private investors took over and have made great strides toward rehabilitating the Zsolnay name. All over Hungary, you'll see shops selling beautiful Zsolnay tableware, some with designs as innovative as ever. But to keep up with our modern economy, Zsolnay also creates everyday items. In fact, they recently signed a big deal to make dishes for Ikea.

psychedelic 1960s. Here in his hometown, you can see a museum of Vasarely's eye-popping creations. Inspired by nature, Vasarely discovered that the repetition and slight variation of lines and forms can play with the viewer's brain to create illusions of depth and movement. In other words, black-and-white lines undulating across a canvas are trippy, baby. It's easy to get lost in Vasarely's mind-bending designs—such as, in the first room, a pair of carpets with zebras—which make you go cross-eyed before you stumble up the stairs to see him add more color to the mix (700 Ft, covered by 2,000-Ft day ticket, borrow the English information, April–Oct Tue–Sun 10:00–18:00, Nov–March Tue–Sun 10:00–17:00, closed Mon, Káptalan utca 3, tel. 72/514-040).

Modern Hungarian Art Museum (Modern Magyar Képtár)—While Hungarian art has its fans, this museum—featuring work from the late 1800s through the 1940s—feels like a house of

rip-offs of better-known French artists. Most visitors will enjoy a more focused visit to the museums dedicated to two specific artists, Vasarely and Csontváry (460 Ft, covered by 2,000-Ft day ticket, borrow the English information, April–Oct Tue–Sun 12:00–18:00, Nov–March Tue–Sun 12:00–16:00, closed Mon, Káptalan utca 4, tel. 72/514-040).

▲Zsolnay Porcelain Museum (Zsolnay Múzeum)—This museum, situated in the former mansion of the Zsolnay family, is as much a shrine to the family as a showcase of their work. (For more on the family and their legacy, see the "Zsolnay Porcelain" sidebar.) The collection is divided into two parts: architectural elements and decorative ware. In the architectural elements section, you'll see impressively detailed and colorful decorations for the many buildings the Zsolnays were involved in renovating (including Budapest's Matthias Church and Parliament). You'll also see a playful duck fountain, and some beautiful pieces of the destroyed István Stove that once warmed Budapest's Royal Palace. The decorative-ware collection displays vases, sculptures, and other objects that demonstrate the evolution of porcelain style. Watch how trends came and went over time. A spinning table allows you to inspect each place setting of Zsolnay dinnerware (700 Ft, covered by 2,000-Ft day ticket, everything well-described in English, April–Oct Tue–Sun 10:00–18:00, Nov–March Tue–Sun 10:00–17:00, closed Mon, Káptalan utca 4, tel. 72/514-040).

Other Museums—Nearby are museums that showcase the work of yet two more local artists, Ferenc Martyn and Endre Nemes.

• *From Káptalan utca, you're just a block above the main square and our starting point. If you have more time, consider some of these sights...*

Elsewhere in Pécs

City Walls—Several segments of the city walls around the northern part of Pécs are still standing (most notably around the cathedral area). Built after the Tatar invasions of the 13th century, and beefed up in the 15th century, the walls were no match for the Ottoman invaders who took the town in 1543. Still standing just west of the cathedral area is the round, stout barbican defensive gate, which you can actually climb.

Synagogue (Zsinagóga)—Just south of the old center, overlooking Kossuth tér, is Pécs' colorful synagogue. Dating from the 1860s, but recently restored, this building is a powerful reminder

of Pécs' Jewish heritage. The city had a thriving population of 4,000 Jews, of whom only a few hundred survived the Holocaust (500 Ft, May–Sept Sun–Fri 10:00–17:00, closed Sat and Oct–April, Kossuth tér, tel. 72/315-881).

Mecsek Hills—Pécs is picturesquely nestled in the Mecsek (MEH-chek) Hills, a popular place to go for a hike. To get an aerial view of Pécs, ride bus #35 about 30 minutes up to the TV tower overlooking the city and surrounding region (catch this bus at the train station, or at the northern entrance to city center). Ascend the 580-foot-tall TV tower for views over the town and region (650 Ft, daily 9:00–20:00).

Sleeping in Pécs

Most of Pécs' city-center accommodations seem to follow a similar pattern: affordable pensions with simple but sleepable rooms. Some are called *kishotel* ("small hotel"). Elevators are rare.

$$$ Hotel Palatinus is your big-hotel option, perfectly located right on the main walking street. You'll rarely find a more impressive facade, lobby, and breakfast room; the showpiece building has been painstakingly restored to its turn-of-the-20th-century glory. But many of the 100 rooms have not been renovated to a similar standard. While this makes it a bit overpriced, the location and public areas help compensate (Sb-16,000–23,000 Ft, Db-19,000–25,000 Ft, price depends on type of room—more for air-con or more recently renovated rooms, elevator, pay Wi-Fi, Király utca 5, tel. 72/889-400, www.danubiushotels.com/palatinus, palatinus.reservation@danubiushotels.com).

$$ Diána Hotel has 20 rooms just up the street from the synagogue, between the town center and the Árkád shopping mall (Sb-10,000 Ft, Db-14,000 Ft, 1,500 Ft more for bigger "deluxe" rooms, rates about 1,000 Ft cheaper if you pay cash, air-con-1,600 Ft, some street noise, Wi-Fi, Tímár utca 4a, tel. 72/328-594, www.hoteldiana.hu, rikopecs0275@t-online.hu).

$$ Ábrahám Kishotel is a Jewish-themed pension with a blue-and-white color scheme in its five tidy rooms. Ilona, who has a big personality and a little dog, doesn't speak English, but has an

Sleep Code

(200 Ft = about $1, country code: 36, area code: 72)
S = Single, **D** = Double/Twin, **T** = Triple, **Q** = Quad, **b** = bathroom. Unless otherwise noted, English is spoken, breakfast is included, and credit cards are accepted. The hotel tax (350 Ft per person, per night) is not included in these rates.

To help you sort easily through these listings, I've divided the rooms into three categories, based on the price for a standard double room with bath:

$$$ Higher Priced—Most rooms 15,000 Ft or more.
$$ Moderately Priced—Most rooms between 10,000–15,000 Ft.
$ Lower Priced—Most rooms 10,000 Ft or less.

English-speaking helper in the busy summer months (Sb-8,100 Ft, Db-11,000 Ft, Tb-13,000 Ft, 1,000 Ft extra when air-con is turned on during hot weather—typically June–Aug, one room has private bathroom across the hall, Wi-Fi, Munkácsy Mihály utca 41, tel. 72/510-422, www.abrahamhotel.hu, abrahamhotel@invitel.hu).

$$ Szinbád Panzió is on a busy street in a dull urban area just outside the city wall. But it feels more hotelesque than the other mid-range options in town: Its public areas are classy, the 27 rooms are nice, and it's a short walk from the cathedral area (Sb-8,900 Ft, Db-11,300 Ft, Tb-14,200 Ft, request quieter courtyard room, pay Internet access, free Wi-Fi in some rooms, Klimó György utca 9, tel. 72/221-110, www.szinbadpanzio.hu, szinbadpanzio@freemail.hu).

$$ Aranyhajó Fogadó ("Golden Ship Inn"), a lesser value, is ideally situated at the start of the Király utca pedestrian zone. In operation since the 18th century, the 18 rooms are old and a bit musty, with once-classy furniture (Sb-11,250 Ft, Db-14,600 Ft, Tb-17,850 Ft, pedestrian street out front can be noisy after hours—ask for quieter room in back, Király utca 3, tel. 72/210-685, www.aranyhajo.hu, hotel@aranyhajo.hu).

$ Náp Hostel ("Sun") is a colorful new hostel well-run by Tamás. Hiding upstairs in an apartment building on the main walking street, its four bedrooms share three WCs and two showers (D-11,000 Ft, bunk in 8-bed dorm-3,000 Ft, in 6-bed dorm-3,500 Ft, in 6-bed dorm with balcony-4,000 Ft, includes breakfast, Internet access and Wi-Fi, kitchen, laundry service, Király utca 23-25, tel. 72/950-684, www.naphostel.com).

Eating in Pécs

On the Pedestrian Drag

The walking streets branching off from the main square (Király utca and Ferencesek utcája) are lined with restaurants and cafés that feature outdoor tables with ideal people-watching. Window-shop for your favorite, or try one of these.

Elefántos Ház ("House at the Elephant") features good Italian fare in its ho-hum interior or outdoors at inviting tables on a delightful shopping square in the town center (1,000–1,500-Ft pizzas and pastas, 2,000–3,000-Ft meat dishes, daily 11:30–23:30, Jókai tér 6, tel. 72/216-055).

Dóm Vendéglő, wonderfully located at the head of Király utca just off the main square, serves traditional Hungarian cuisine along with pizzas and other international dishes, with indoor and outdoor seating (1,500–2,000-Ft main dishes, 1,000–1,500-Ft pizzas, 3,000-Ft steaks, daily 11:00–23:00, Király utca 3, tel. 72/210-088).

Oázis is the place for a simple, cheap, fast, and good gyro or falafel. Grab one to go, or enjoy it at their outdoor tables on the main walking street (600-Ft sandwiches, daily 10:00–23:00, Király utca 17).

Elsewhere in Pécs

Trafik, in the ground floor of the Apollo art-house cinema, offers international fare with an Italian flair, in a cool and trendy bar atmosphere (1,000–2,000-Ft main dishes, Mon–Fri 12:00–24:00, Sat 18:00–24:00, closed Sun, Perczel Miklós utca 22, tel. 72/212-672).

Aranykacsa ("Golden Duck") is in all the guidebooks thanks to its well-respected, traditional Hungarian fare, specializing in duck (1,000–2,000-Ft main dishes, pricier duck specialties, Tue–Sat 11:30–22:00, Sun 11:30–15:30, closed Mon, Teréz utca 4, tel. 72/518-860).

Pécs Connections

From Pécs by Train: For most destinations (including **Eger, Sopron,** and **Bratislava**), you'll first have to change trains in Budapest. Direct trains connect Pécs and **Budapest** (8/day, 3 hrs, a few additional connections possible with a transfer at the suburban Budapest-Kelenföld station). One handy train each afternoon follows a different route, near the Croatian border, connecting Pécs directly to **Sopron** (4.75 hrs), then **Vienna** (6 hrs).

SLOVENIA

SLOVENIA

Slovenija

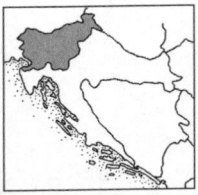

Tiny, overlooked Slovenia is one of Europe's most unexpectedly charming destinations. At the intersection of the Slavic, German, and Italian worlds, Slovenia is an exciting mix of the best of each culture. Though it's just a quick trip away from the tourist throngs in Venice, Munich, Salzburg, and Vienna, Slovenia has stayed off the tourist track—a handy detour for in-the-know Back Door travelers.

Today, it seems strange to think that Slovenia was ever part of Yugoslavia. Both in the personality of its people and in its landscape, Slovenia feels more like Austria. Slovenes are more industrious, organized, and punctual than their fellow former Yugoslavs...yet still friendly, relaxed, and Mediterranean. Locals like the balance. Visitors expecting minefields and rusting Yugo factories are pleasantly surprised to find Slovenia's rolling countryside dotted instead with quaint alpine villages and the spires of miniature Baroque churches, with breathtaking, snowcapped peaks in the distance.

Only half as big as Switzerland, but remarkably diverse for its size, Slovenia can be easily appreciated on a brief visit. Travelers can hike on alpine trails in the morning and explore some of the world's best caves in the afternoon, before relaxing with a seafood dinner on the Adriatic.

Slovenia enjoys a powerhouse economy—the healthiest of all of Europe's former communist countries. The Austro-Hungarian Empire left it with a strong industrial infrastructure, which the Yugoslav government expanded. By 1980, 60 percent of all Yugoslav industry was in little Slovenia (which had only 8 percent of Yugoslavia's population and 8 percent of its territory). With independence, Slovenia continued this trend, pushing their mighty little economy into the future. Of the 12 new nations that have joined the European Union since 2004, Slovenia was the only

one rich enough to be a net donor (with a higher per-capita income than the average), and the first one to join the euro currency zone (it adopted the euro in January 2007). Thanks to its long-standing ties to the West and can-do spirit, Slovenia already feels more "Western" than any other destination in this book.

The country has a funny way of making people fall in love with it. Slovenes are laid-back, easygoing, stylish, and fun. They won't win any world wars (they're too well-adjusted to even try)... but they're exactly the type of people you'd love to chat with over a cup of coffee. Many of today's American visitors are soldiers who participated in the conflict in nearby Bosnia and have good memories of their vacations here in Slovenia. Now they're bringing their families back with them.

The Slovenian language is as mellow as the people. While Slovenes use Serb and German curses in abundance, the worst they can say in their native tongue is, "May you be kicked by a horse." For "Darn it!" they say, "Three hundred hairy bears!"

Coming from such a small country, locals are proud of the few things that are distinctly Slovenian, such as the roofed hayrack. Foreigners think that Slovenes' fascination with these hayracks is strange...until they visit and see them absolutely

Slovenia Almanac

Official Name: Republika Slovenija, or simply Slovenija.

Snapshot History: After being dominated by Germans for centuries, Slovenian culture proudly emerged in the 19th century. In the aftermath of World War I, Slovenia merged with its neighbors to become Yugoslavia, then broke away and achieved independence for the first time in 1991.

Population: Slovenia's two million people (a count similar to Nevada's) are 83 percent ethnic Slovenes who speak Slovene, plus a smattering of Serbs, Croats, and Muslim Bosniaks. The majority of the country is Catholic.

Latitude and Longitude: 46° N and 14° E (latitude similar to Lyon, France; Quebec, Canada; or Bismarck, North Dakota).

Area: At 7,800 square miles, it's about the size of New Jersey, but with one-fourth the population.

Geography: Tiny Slovenia has three extremely different terrains and climates: the warm Mediterranean coastline (just 29 miles long—about one inch per inhabitant); the snow-capped, forested alpine mountains in the northwest (including 9,400-foot Mount Triglav); and the moderate-climate, central limestone plateau that includes Ljubljana and the cave-filled Karst region. If you look at a map of Slovenia and squint your eyes a bit, it looks like a chicken running toward the east.

Biggest Cities: Nearly one in five Slovenes lives in the two biggest cities: Ljubljana (the capital, pop. 270,000) and Maribor (in the east, pop. 115,000). Half of the population lives in rural villages.

Economy: With a Gross Domestic Product of $55 billion and a GDP per capita of $30,000, Slovenia's economy is much stronger than the average Eastern European country. Slovenia's wealth comes largely from manufactured metal products (trucks and machinery) traded with a diverse group of partners.

Currency: Slovenia uses the euro: €1 = about $1.40.

Government: The country is led by the prime minister (currently Borut Pahor), who heads the leading vote-getting party in legislative elections. He governs along with the figurehead president (currently Danilo Türk). Slovenia's relatively peaceful succession is credited largely to former Prime Minister Milan Kučan, who remains a popular figure. The National Assembly consists of about 90 elected legislators; there's also a second house of parliament, which has much less power. Despite the country's

small size, it is divided into some 200 municipalities.

Flag: Three horizontal bands of white (top), blue, and red. A shield in the upper left shows Mount Triglav, with a wavy-line sea below and three stars above.

The Average Slovene: The average Slovene skis, in this largely alpine country, and is an avid fan of team handball (yes, handball). He or she lives in a 250-square-foot apartment, earns $1,400 a month, watches 16 hours of TV a week (much of it in English with Slovene subtitles), and enjoys a drink-and-a-half of alcohol every day.

Notable Slovenes: A pair of prominent Ohio politicians—perennial presidential candidate Dennis Kucinich and Senator George Voinovich, both from the Cleveland area—are each half-Slovene. (In 1910, Cleveland had the biggest Slovenian population of any city in the world—just ahead of Trieste and Ljubljana.) Classical musicians might know composers Giuseppe Tartini and Hugo Wolf. Even if you haven't heard of architect Jože Plečnik yet, you'll hear his name a hundred times while you're in Slovenia—especially in Ljubljana (see page 672). Perhaps most famous of all is the illustrious Melania Knauss—a *GQ* cover girl who's also Mrs. Donald Trump.

Sporty Slovenes: If you follow alpine sports or team handball, you'll surely know some world-class athletes from Slovenia. NBA fans might recognize basketball players Primož Brezec and Bostjan Nachbar, as well as some lesser players. The athletic Slovenes—perhaps trying to compensate for the miniscule size of their country—have accomplished astonishing feats: Davo Karničar has skied down from the summits of some of the world's tallest mountains (including Everest, Kilimanjaro, and McKinley). Benka Pulko became the first person ever to drive a motorcycle around the world (that is, all seven continents, including Antarctica; total trip: 118,000 miles in 2,000 days—also the longest solo motorcycle journey by a woman; www.benkapulko.com). Dušan Mravlje ran across all the continents (www.dusanmravlje.si). And ultra-marathon swimmer Martin Strel has swum the entire length of several major rivers, including the Danube (1,775 miles), the Mississippi (2,415 miles), the Yangtze (3,915 miles), and the Amazon (3,393 miles; for more, see www.martinstrel.com).

everywhere (especially in the northwest). Because of the frequent rainfall, the hayracks are covered by a roof that allows the hay to dry thoroughly. The most traditional kind is the *toplar,* consisting of two hayracks connected by one big roof. It looks like a skinny barn with open, fenced sides. Hay hangs on the sides to dry; firewood, carts, tractors, and other farm implements sit on the ground inside; and dried hay is stored in the loft above. But these wooden *toplarji* are firetraps, and a stray bolt of lighting can burn one down in a flash. So in recent years, more farmers are moving to single hayracks (*enojni*); these are still roofed, but have posts made of concrete, rather than wood. You'll find postcards and miniature wooden models of both kinds of hayracks (a fun souvenir).

Another good (and uniquely Slovenian) memento is a creatively decorated front panel from a beehive *(panjske končnice).* Slovenia has a strong beekeeping tradition, and beekeepers once believed that painting the fronts of the hives made it easier for bees to find their way home. Replicas of these panels are available at gift shops all over the country. (For more on the panels and Slovenia's beekeeping heritage, see page 710.)

Slovenia is also the land of polka. Slovenes claim it was invented here, and singer/accordionist Slavko Avsenik—from the village of Begunje near Bled—cranks out popular oompah songs that make him bigger than the Beatles (and therefore, presumably, Jesus) in Germany. You'll see the Avsenik ensemble and other oompah bands on Slovenian TV, where hokey Lawrence Welk–style shows are a local institution.

To really stretch your euros, try one of Slovenia's more than 200 farmhouse B&Bs, called "tourist farms" *(turistične kmetije).* These are actual, working farms (often organic) that sell meals and/or rent rooms to tourists to help make ends meet. You can use a tourist farm as a home base to explore the entire country—remember, the farthest reaches of Slovenia are only a day trip away. A comfortable, hotelesque double with a private bathroom, plus a traditional Slovenian dinner and a hearty breakfast, costs as little as $50. Request a listing from the Slovenian Tourist Board (see page 1086), or find information at www.slovenia.info.

Most visitors to Slovenia are, in my experience, completely charmed by the place. With all it has going for it, it's hard to believe that Slovenia is not already overrun with tourists. Somehow, this little country continues to glide beneath the radar. Exploring its mountain trails and meeting its friendly locals, you'll feel like you're in on a secret.

Helpful Hints

Euro Conversion: Even though Slovenia has used the euro currency since January 2007, some locals still think in terms of the previous currency, the *tolar* (which you might see on menus or price lists). There were about 190 tolars in one dollar, and about 240 tolars in one euro.

Smoking Ban: Smoking is prohibited in public places, unless it's a specially designated (and well-ventilated) smoking room. Larger hotels still have some "smoking" rooms, but smoking isn't allowed in public areas.

Sunday Closures: Slovenia can be extremely sleepy on Sundays, even in the larger towns and cities, where virtually all shops are closed. Plan ahead. Fortunately, many restaurants remain open, plus a select few grocery stores.

Telephones: Slovenian phone numbers beginning with 080 are toll-free; 090 and 089 denote expensive toll lines. Most mobile phone numbers begin with 031, 041, 051, 040, or 070. For more details on how to dial, see page 1088.

Slovenian History

Slovenia has a long and unexciting history as part of various larger empires. Charlemagne's Franks conquered the tiny land in the eighth century, and, ever since, Slovenia has been a backwater of the Germanic world—first as a holding of the Holy Roman Empire and later, the Habsburg Empire. Slovenia seems as much German as Slavic. But even as the capital, Ljubljana, was populated by Austrians (and called Laibach by its German-speaking residents), the Slovenian language and cultural traditions survived in the countryside.

Ljubljana rose to international prominence for half a decade (1809–1813) when Napoleon named it the capital of his "Illyrian Provinces," stretching from Austria's Tirol to Croatia's Dalmatian Coast. During this time, the long-suppressed Slovene language was used for the first time in schools and the government. Inspired by the patriotic poetry of France Prešeren, national pride surged.

The last century saw the most interesting chapter of Slovenian history. Some of World War I's fiercest fighting occurred at the Soča (Isonzo) Front in northwest Slovenia—witnessed by young Ernest Hemingway, who drove an ambulance (see sidebars on pages 722 and 732). After the war, from 1918 to 1991, Slovenia was Yugoslavia's smallest, northernmost, and most affluent republic. Concerned about Serbian strongman Slobodan Milošević's nationalistic politics, Slovenia seceded in 1991. Because more than 90 percent of the people here were ethnic Slovenes, the break with Yugoslavia was simple and virtually uncontested. Its war for independence lasted just 10 days and claimed only a few

Slo-what?-ia

"The only thing I know about Slovakia is what I learned first-hand from your foreign minister, who came to Texas."

—George W. Bush, to a Slovak journalist (Bush had actually met with Dr. Janez Drnovšek, who was then Slovenia's prime minister)

Maybe it's understandable that many Americans confuse Slovenia with Slovakia. Both are small, mountainous countries that not too long ago were parts of bigger, better known, now defunct nations. But anyone who has visited Slovenia and Slovakia will set you straight—they feel worlds apart.

Slovenia, wedged between the Alps and the Adriatic, is a tidy, prosperous country with a strong economy. Until 1991, Slovenia was one of the six republics that made up Yugoslavia. Historically, Slovenia has had very strong ties with Germanic culture—so it feels like its neighbor to the north, Austria.

Slovakia—two countries away, to the northeast—is slightly bigger. Much of its territory is covered by the Carpathian Mountains, most notably the dramatic, jagged peaks of the High Tatras. In 1993, the Czechs and Slovaks peacefully chose to go their separate ways, so the nation of Czechoslovakia dissolved into the Czech Republic and the Slovak Republic (a.k.a. Slovakia).

To make things even more confusing, there's also **Slavonia.** This is the thick, inland "panhandle" that makes up the northeast half of Croatia, along Slovenia's southeast border. Much of the warfare in Croatia's 1991–1995 war took place in Slavonia (including Vukovar; see the Understanding Yugoslavia chapter).

I won't tell on you if you mix them up. But if you want to feel smarter than a former president, do a little homework and get it right.

dozen lives. (For more details, see the Understanding Yugoslavia chapter, page 1069.)

After centuries of looking to the West, Slovenia became the first of the former Yugoslav republics to join the European Union in May of 2004. The Slovenes have been practical about this move, realizing it's essential for their survival as a tiny nation in a modern world. But there are trade-offs, and "Euroskeptics" are down on EU bureaucracy. As borders disappear, Slovenes are experiencing more crime. Traditional farms are grappling with strict EU standards. Slovenian businesses are having difficulty competing with big German and other Western European firms. Before EU membership, only Slovenes could own Slovenian land. But now wealthy foreigners are buying property, driving up the cost of real estate.

In general, however, EU membership seems to be agreeing with the Slovenes. Slovenia became the first post-communist country to adopt the euro currency in January of 2007. Despite the worldwide economic crisis, business here is booming. As throughout their history, the Slovenes are adjusting to the 21st century with their characteristic sense of humor and easygoing attitude.

Slovenian Food

Slovenian cuisine offers more variety and better quality than Croatian fare. Slovenes brag that their cuisine melds the best of Italian and German cooking—but they also embrace other international influences, especially French. Like Croatian food, Slovenian cuisine also features some pan-Balkan elements: The savory phyllo-dough pastry *burek* is the favorite fast food here, and when Slovenes host a backyard barbecue, they grill up *čevapčići* and *ražnjići,* topped off with the eggplant-and-red-bell-pepper condiment *ajvar* (see "Balkan Flavors," page 753). Slovenia enjoys Italian-style fare, with a pizza or pasta restaurant on seemingly every corner. Hungarian food simmers in the northeast corner of the country (where many Magyars reside). And in most of the country, traditional Slovenian food has a distinctly Germanic vibe—including the "four S's": sausages, schnitzels, strudels, and sauerkraut.

Traditional Slovenian dishes are prepared with groats—a grainy mush made with buckwheat, barley, or corn. Buckwheat, which thrives in this climate, often appears on Slovenian menus. You'll also see plenty of *štruklji* (dumplings), which can be stuffed with cheese, meat, or vegetables. *Repa* is turnip prepared like sauerkraut. Among the hearty soups in Slovenia is *jota*—a staple for Karst peasants, made from *repa,* beans, and vegetables.

The cuisine of Slovenia's Karst region (the arid limestone plain south of Ljubljana) is notable. The small farms and wineries of this region have been inspired by Italy's Slow Food movement—their owners believe that cuisine is meant to be gradually appreciated, not rushed—making the Karst a destination for gourmet tours. Karstic cuisine is similar to France's nouvelle cuisine—several courses in small portions, with a focus on unusual combinations and preparations—but with a Tuscan flair. The Karst's tasty air-dried ham *(pršut),* available throughout the country, is worth seeking out (see sidebar). Istria (the peninsula just to the south of the Karst, in southern Slovenia and Croatia) produces truffles that, locals boast, are as good as those from Italy's Piedmont (see page 910).

Pršut

In Slovenia and Croatia, *pršut* (purr-SHOOT) is one of the essential food groups. This air-cured ham (like Italian prosciutto) is soaked in salt and sometimes also smoked. Then it hangs in open-ended barns for up to a year and a half, to be dried and seasoned by the howling Bora wind. Each region produces a slightly different *pršut*. In Dalmatia, a layer of fat keeps the ham moist; in Istria, the fat is trimmed, and the *pršut* is dryer.

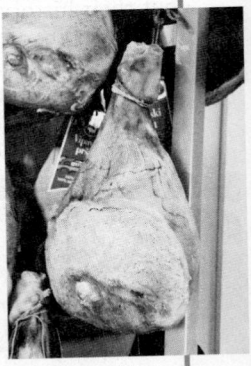

Since Slovenia joined the European Union, strict new standards have swept the land. Separate rooms must be used for the slaughter, preparation, and curing of the ham. While this seems fair enough for large producers, small family farms that want to produce just enough *pršut* for their own use—and maybe sell one or two ham hocks to neighbors—find they have to invest thousands of euros to be compliant.

Voda is water, and *kava* is coffee. Radenska, in the bottle with the three little hearts, is Slovenia's best-known brand of mineral water—good enough that the word *Radenska* is synonymous with bottled water all over Slovenia and throughout the former Yugoslavia. It's not common to ask for (or receive) tap water, but you can try requesting *voda iz pipe*.

Adventurous teetotalers should forego the Coke and sample Cockta, a Slovenian cola with an unusual flavor (which supposedly comes from berry, lemon, orange, and 11 herbs). Originally called "Cockta-Cockta," the drink was introduced during the communist period, as an alternative to the difficult-to-get Coca-Cola. This local variation developed a loyal following...until the Iron Curtain fell, and the real Coke became readily available. Cockta sales plummeted. But in recent years—prodded by the slogan "The Taste of Your Youth"—nostalgic Slovenes are drinking Cockta once more.

To toast, say, *"Na ZDROW-yeh!"*—if you can't remember it, think of "Nice driving!" The premier Slovenian brand of *pivo* (beer) is Union (OO-nee-ohn), but you'll also see a lot of Laško (LASH-koh), whose mascot is the Zlatorog (or "Golden Horn," a

mythical chamois-like animal).

Slovenia produces some fine *vino* (wine). The Celts first made wine in Slovenia; the Romans improved the process and spread it throughout the country. Slovenia has three primary wine regions. Podravje, in the northeast, is dominated by *laški* and *renski riesling*. Posavje, in the southeast, produces both white and red wines, but is known mostly for the light, russet-colored *cviček* wine. Primorska, in the southwest, has a Mediterranean climate and produces mostly reds. One of the most popular is *teran,* made from *refošk* grapes, which grow in iron-rich red soil *(terra rossa)*—infusing them with a high lactic acid content that supposedly gives the wine healing properties.

Slovenia's national dessert is *potica,* a rolled pastry with walnuts and sometimes also raisins. For more tasty treats, see the "Bled Desserts" sidebar on page 707. Locals claim that Ljubljana has the finest gelato outside of Italy—which, after all, is just an hour down the road.

Slovenian Language

Slovene is surprisingly different from languages spoken in the other former Yugoslav republics. While Serbian and Croatian are mutually intelligible, Slovene is gibberish to Serbs and Croats. Most Slovenes, on the other hand, know Serbo-Croatian because, a generation ago, everybody in Yugoslavia had to learn it.

Linguists have identified some 250 dialects of Slovene. Locals can tell which city—or sometimes even which remote mountain valley—someone comes from by their accent.

The tiny country of Slovenia borders Italy and Austria, with important historical and linguistic ties to both. For self-preservation, Slovenes have always been forced to function in many different languages. All of these factors make them excellent linguists. Most young Slovenes speak effortless, flawless English—then admit that they've never set foot in the United States or Britain, but love watching American movies and TV shows (which are always subtitled, never dubbed).

Slovene has a few letters that are pronounced differently than in English, and they add a few diacritics—little markings below and above some letters. Here are a few rules of thumb for sounding out unfamiliar words:

J / j sounds like "y" as in "yellow"
C / c sounds like "ts" as in "cats"
Č / č sounds like "ch" as in "chicken"
Š / š sounds like "sh" as in "shrimp"
Ž / ž sounds like "zh" as in "leisure"
V / v is sometimes pronounced as "u"—so the word *avto* sounds like "auto"

Slovene is notorious for its seemingly unpronounceable consonant combinations. Most difficult are **hv** (as in *hvala,* "thank you") and **nj** (as in Bohinj, a lake in Slovenia). Foreigners are notorious for over-pronouncing these combinations. In the combination hv, the h is nearly silent; if you struggle with it, simply leave off the h (for *hvala*, just say "VAH-lah"; saying "huh-VAH-lah" sounds silly). When you see nj, the j is mostly silent, with a slight "y" sound that can be omitted: for Bohinj, just say BOH-heen. Listen to locals and imitate.

The only trick: As in English, which syllable gets the emphasis is unpredictable. Slovenes use many of the same words as Croatians, but put the stress on an entirely different place.

Learn some key Slovenian phrases (see the Slovenian Survival Phrases on page 1125). You'll make more friends and your trip will go more smoothly.

A few key words are helpful for navigation: ***trg*** (pronounced "turg," square), ***ulica*** (OO-leet-sah, road), ***cesta*** (TSEH-stah, avenue), ***avtocesta*** (OW-toh-tseh-stah, expressway), and ***most*** (mohst, bridge).

LJUBLJANA

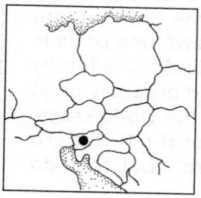

Slovenia's capital, Ljubljana (lyoob-lyee-AH-nah), with a lazy Old Town clustered around a castle-topped mountain, is often likened to Salzburg. It's an apt comparison—but only if you inject a healthy dose of breezy Adriatic culture, add a Slavic accent, and replace favorite son Mozart with local architect Jože Plečnik.

Ljubljana feels smaller than its population of 270,000. While big-league museums are in short supply, the town itself is an idyllic place that sometimes feels too good to be true. Festivals fill the summer, and people enjoy a Sunday stroll any day of the week. Fashion boutiques and al fresco cafés jockey for control of the Old Town, while the leafy riverside promenade crawls with stylishly dressed students sipping *kava* and polishing their near-perfect English. Laid-back Ljubljana is the kind of place where graffiti and crumbling buildings seem elegantly atmospheric instead of shoddy. For better or worse, Ljubljana has been sprucing up lately—be prepared for lots of torn-up streets during your visit.

Batted around by history, Ljubljana has absorbed cultural influences from all sides—most notably Prague, Vienna, and Venice. This has left the city a happy hodgepodge of cultures. Being the midpoint between the Slavic, Germanic, and Italian worlds gives Ljubljana a special spice. People often ask me: What's the "next Prague"? And I have to answer Kraków. But Ljubljana is the *next* "next Prague."

Planning Your Time

Ljubljana deserves a full day. While there are few must-see sights, the city's biggest attraction is its ambience. You'll spend much of your time strolling the pleasant town center, exploring the many

The Story of Ljubljana

In ancient times, Ljubljana was on the trade route connecting the Mediterranean (just 60 miles away) to the Black Sea (toss a bottle off the bridge here, and it can float to the Danube and, eventually, all the way to Russia). Legend has it that Jason and his Argonauts founded Ljubljana when they stopped here for the winter on their way home with the Golden Fleece. The town was Romanized (and called Emona) before being overrun by Huns, only to be resettled later by Slavs.

In 1335, Ljubljana fell under the jurisdiction of the Habsburg emperors (who called it Laibach). After six centuries of Habsburg rule, Ljubljana still feels Austrian—especially in the abundant Austrian Baroque and Viennese Art Nouveau architecture—but with a Mediterranean flair.

Napoleon put Ljubljana on the map when he made it the capital of his Illyrian Provinces, a realm that stretched from the Danube to Dubrovnik, from Austria to Albania (for only four years, 1809–1813). For the first time, the Slovene language was taught in schools, awakening a newfound pride in the Slovenian cultural heritage. People still look back fondly on this very brief era, which was the first (and probably only) time when Ljubljana rose to prominence on the world stage. After more than 600 years of being part of the Habsburg Empire, Ljubljana has no "Habsburg Square"...but they do have a "French Revolution Square."

In the mid-19th century, the railway connecting Vienna to the Adriatic (Trieste) was built through town—and Ljubljana boomed. But much of the city was destroyed by an earthquake in 1895. It was rebuilt in the Art Nouveau style so popular in Vienna, its capital at the time. A generation later, architect Jože Plečnik bathed the city in his distinctive, artsy-but-sensible, classical-meets-modern style.

In World War II, Slovenia was occupied first by the Italians, then by the Nazis. Ljubljana had a thriving resistance movement that the Nazis couldn't suppress—so they simply fenced off the entire city and made it a giant prison for three years, allowing only shipments of basic food supplies to get in. But the Slovenes—who knew their land far better than their oppressors did—continued to slip in and out of town undetected, allowing them to agitate through the end of the war.

In 1991, Ljubljana became the capital of one of Europe's youngest nations. Today the city is filled with university students, making it a very youthful-feeling town. Ljubljana has always been creative, and recent years—which have brought unprecedented freedoms—have been no exception. This city is on the cutting edge when it comes to architecture, public art, fashion, and trendy pubs. But the scintillating avant-garde culture has soft edges—hip, but also nonthreatening and user-friendly.

interesting squares and architectural gems, shopping the boutiques, and sipping coffee at sidewalk cafés along the river.

Here's the best plan for a low-impact sightseeing day: Begin on Prešeren Square, the heart of the city. Cross the Triple Bridge and wander through the riverside produce market before joining the town walking tour at 10:00 (at 11:00 in Oct-March). After the tour, wander along the Ljubljanica River to Jože Plečnik's National and University Library, French Revolution Square, and on to my favorite Ljubljana museum, the Jože Plečnik House (this sight might be closed for renovation, and even when open, it has limited hours—call or ask the TI to confirm the opening times, and plan accordingly). In the afternoon, Ljubljana is a great place to squander a few hours. Go window-shopping at colorful boutiques, commit some quality time to people-watching at a riverside café, or consider some more sightseeing: Wander through the museum zone west of Prešeren Square, dip into the Serbian Orthodox Church, and stroll through Tivoli Park (paying a visit to the good Contemporary History Museum in the park, or any others that interest you). It's also worth the 10-minute walk to visit the excellent Slovenian Ethnographic Museum, northeast of Prešeren Square.

Plenty of good day trips are a short distance from Ljubljana. With a second day, visit Lake Bled (see next chapter).

Ljubljana is dead and disappointing on Sundays (virtually all shops are closed and the produce market is quiet, but museums are generally open, a modest flea market stretches along the riverfront, and the TI's walking tour still runs). The city is also relatively quiet in August, when the students are on break and many locals head to beach resorts. They say that in August, even homeless people go to the coast.

Orientation to Ljubljana

(area code: 01)

Ljubljana—with narrow lanes, architecture that mingles the Old World and contemporary Europe, and cobbles upon cobbles of wonderful distractions—can be disorienting for a first-timer. But the charming central zone is compact, and with a little wandering, you'll quickly get the hang of it.

The Ljubljanica River—lined with cafés, restaurants, and a buzzing outdoor market—bisects the

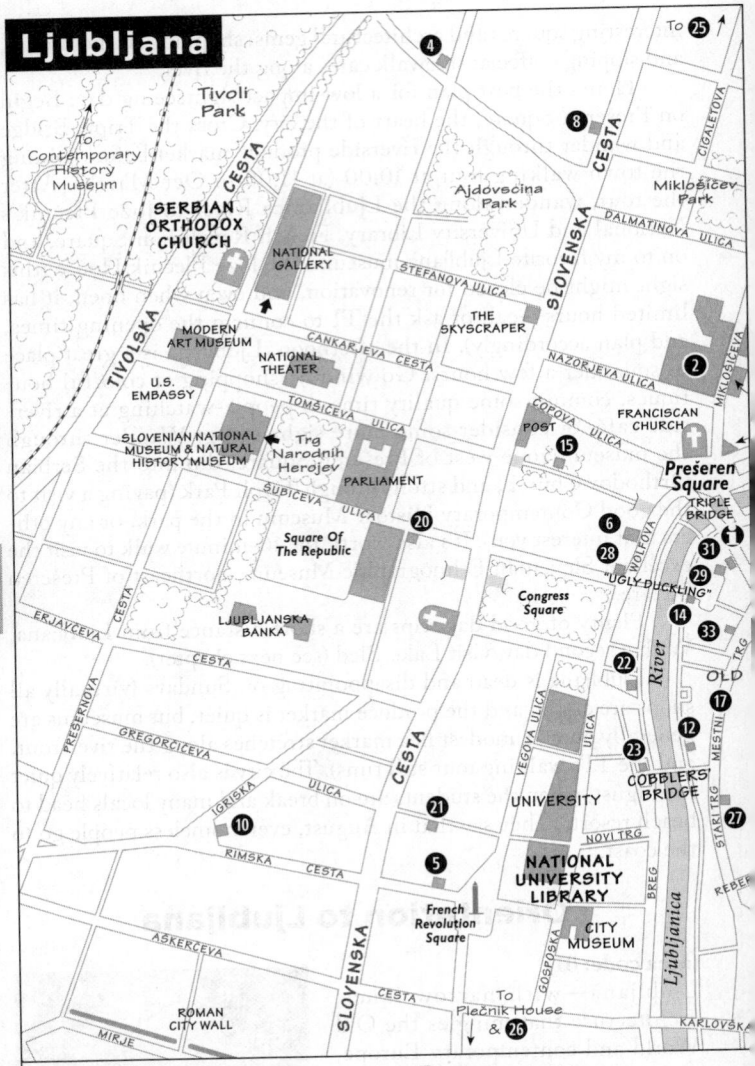

Accommodations

1. Antiq Hotel
2. Grand Hotel Union
3. Central Hotel
4. Slamič B&B
5. Pri Mraku Guesthouse
6. Hotel Emonec & Laundry
7. B&B Petra Varl
8. Hotel Center
9. Stari Tišler Rooms
10. Penzion Pod Lipo
11. Hostel Celica
12. Alibi CN27 Hostel
13. Alibi M14 Hostel

Eateries

14. Zlata Ribica Restaurant
15. Gostilna As Rest. & Lounge
16. Ribca Restaurant
17. Old Town Main-Drag Eateries

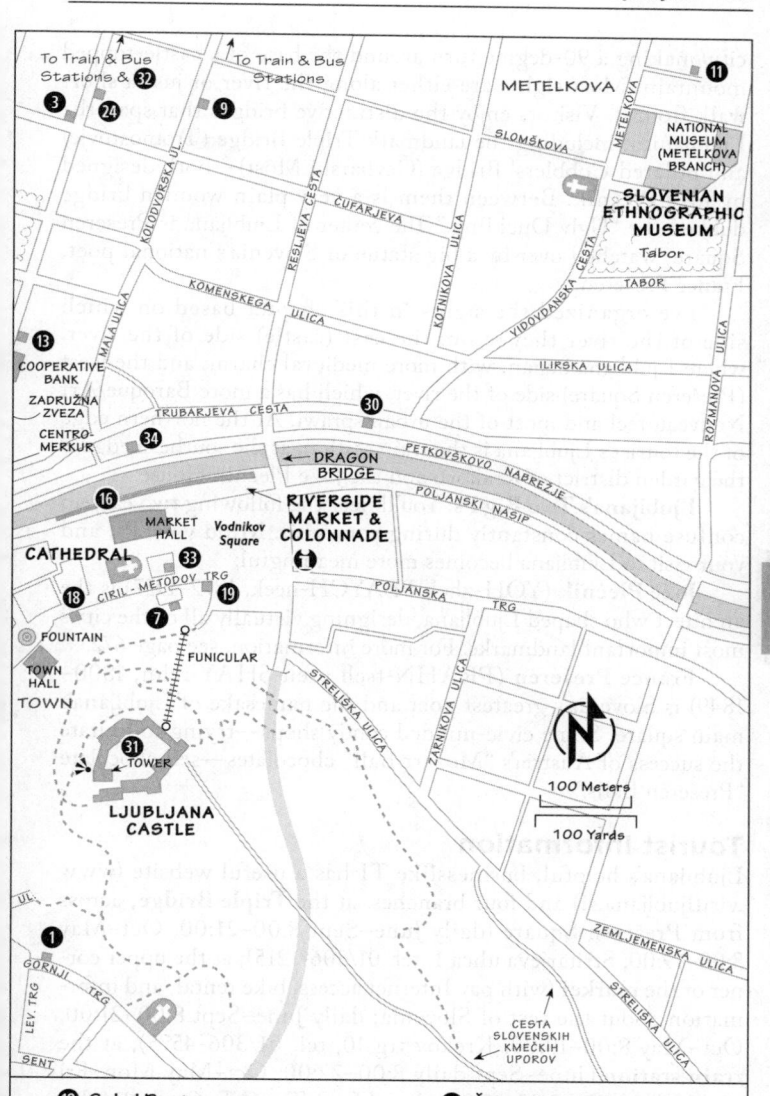

18 Sokol Restaurant
19 Vodnikov Hram
20 DaBuDa Restaurant
21 Pizzeria Foculus
22 Ljubljanski Dvor Pizzeria
23 Paninoteka Sandwiches
24 Nobel Burek
25 To Olympia Burek
26 To Pri Škofu & Harambaša
27 Čajna Hiša Teahouse
28 Zvezda Kavarna
29 Abecedarium Restaurant
30 Rustika Choc. & Ice Cream

Services

31 Rustika Gallery Shops (2)
32 To Kod & Kam Map Store
33 Dom Trgovina Shops (2)
34 Internet Café

city, making a 90-degree turn around the base of a castle-topped mountain. Most sights are either along the river or just a short walk from it. Visitors enjoy the distinctive bridges that span the Ljubljanica, including the landmark Triple Bridge (Tromostovje) and pillared Cobblers' Bridge (Čevljarski Most)—both designed by Jože Plečnik. Between them is a very plain wooden bridge dubbed the "Ugly Duckling." The center of Ljubljana is Prešeren Square, watched over by a big statue of Slovenia's national poet, France Prešeren.

I've organized the sights in this chapter based on which side of the river they're on: the east (castle) side of the river, where Ljubljana began, with more medieval charm; and the west (Prešeren Square) side of the river, which has a more Baroque/Art Nouveau feel and most of the urban sprawl. At the northern edge of the tourist's Ljubljana is the train station; at the southern edge is the garden district of Krakovo and the Jože Plečnik House.

Ljubljana's Two Big Ps: You'll hear the following two easy-to confuse names constantly during your visit. Mind your Ps, and your visit to Ljubljana becomes more meaningful:

Jože Plečnik (YOH-zheh PLAYCH-neek, 1872–1957) is the architect who shaped Ljubljana, designing virtually all of the city's most important landmarks. For more information, see page 672.

France Prešeren (FRAHN-tseh preh-SHAY-rehn, 1800–1849) is Slovenia's greatest poet and the namesake of Ljubljana's main square. Some civic-minded candy shops—trying to imitate the success of Austria's "Mozart Ball" chocolates—sell chocolate "Prešeren Balls."

Tourist Information

Ljubljana's helpful, businesslike TI has a useful website (www.visitljubljana.si) and four branches: at the **Triple Bridge,** across from Prešeren Square (daily June–Sept 8:00–21:00, Oct–May 8:00–19:00, Stritarjeva ulica 1, tel. 01/306-1215); at the upper corner of the **market** (with pay Internet access, bike rental, and information about the rest of Slovenia; daily June–Sept 8:00–21:00, Oct–May 8:00–19:00, Krekov trg 10, tel. 01/306-4575); at the **train station** (June–Sept daily 8:00–22:00; Oct–May Mon–Fri 10:00–19:00, Sat 8:00–15:00, closed Sun; Trg O.F. 6, tel. 01/433-9475); and at the **airport** (hours depend on flight schedule, generally daily 11:00–19:00).

At any TI, pick up a pile of free resources: the big city map, the Tourist Guide, the monthly *Where to?* events guide, and a wide range of informative brochures. The TI also offers a free room-finding service. Skip the **Ljubljana City Card,** which includes access to public transportation and free entry or discounts at some city museums (€13/72 hrs).

Arrival in Ljubljana

By Train: Ljubljana's modern, user-friendly train station (Železniška Postaja) is at the northern edge of the city center. Emerging from the passage up to track 1a, turn right and walk under the long canopy along the train tracks to find the yellow arrivals hall. Everything is well-signed in English, including a **TI**, the handy train-information office next door (with useful handouts outlining trips to several domestic and international destinations, daily 5:30–21:30), and—near the front of the station—a big **ticket office** with clearly marked ticket windows and an **ATM** (office open daily 5:00–22:00). Arrivals are *prihodi,* departures are *odhodi,* and track is *tir.*

The main square is an easy 10-minute **walk** from the station; you can walk to any of my recommended hotels within about 20 minutes (often less). To reach Prešeren Square at the city's center, leave the arrivals hall to the right and walk a long block along the busy Trg Osvobodilne Fronte (or "Trg O.F." for short, with the bus station in the middle). After passing all of the bus stalls, turn left across Trg O.F. and go down Miklošičeva, at the building with the round red-brick columns. This takes you past some of Ljubljana's most appealing architecture to Prešeren Square.

Unscrupulous **taxis** crouch in front of the station, waiting to take unsuspecting tourists for a ride. The fair metered rate to any of my recommended hotels is around €3 (maybe up to €4–5 in heavy traffic or after hours). But most of the train-station cabbies are crooks accustomed to charging you whatever they want without using the meter. To avoid these jerks, call for a taxi instead (dial 041-731-831 or 041-240-200; the train station TI is willing to call for you, if they're not too busy). If you do use the taxi stand, ask the price up front, and *never* pay more than €5. For more on taxis—and how to avoid rip-offs—see "Getting Around Ljubljana—By Taxi," later.

By Bus: Ljubljana's bus station (Autobusna Postaja) is a low-profile building (with ticket windows, Internet access, a bakery, and newsstands) in the middle of Trg O.F., right in front of the train station. To get into the city center, see "By Train," above.

By Car: As you approach Ljubljana on the expressway, the toll road ends. Once you're on the ring road, simply follow signs for *Center.* Once you get into the city center, you'll begin to see directional signs to individual hotels. Ask your hotel about parking—most have some available, usually for a price. If you need to gas up your rental car before returning it, you'll find a huge gas station on Tivolska Cesta (just west of the train station, near the big Union brewery). Otherwise, your options in the center are limited—it's better to look for a gas station on the expressway as you approach the city.

Ljubljana Essentials

English	Slovene	Pronounced
Ljubljana Castle	Ljubljanski Grad	lyoob-lyee-AHN-skee grahd
Prešeren Square	Prešernov trg	preh-SHEHR-nohv turg
Congress Square	Kongresni Trg	kohn-GREHS-nee turg
French Revolution Square	Trg Francoske Revolucije	turg frant-SOH-skeh reh-voh-LOOT-see-yeh
Square of the Republic	Trg Republike	turg reh-POOB-lee-keh
Triple Bridge	Tromostovje	troh-moh-STOHV-yeh
Cobblers' Bridge	Čevljarski Most	chehv-LAR-skee mohst
Dragon Bridge	Zmajski Most	ZMAY-skee mohst
Jože Plečnik, the architect	Jože Plečnik	YOH-zheh PLAYCH-neek
France Prešeren, the poet	France Prešeren	FRAHN-tseh preh-SHAY-rehn

By Plane: See "Ljubljana Connections," at the end of this chapter.

Helpful Hints

Pedestrian Safety: Many Ljubljana residents commute by bike. As a pedestrian, I've had many close calls with bikes whizzing by. Keep your eyes open and stay out of the designated bike lanes on the sidewalks (often marked in red).

Closed Days: Most Ljubljana museums (except the castle and a few less-important museums) are closed on Mondays. The recommended Jože Plečnik House is closed Sundays, Mondays, and Fridays, and might be closed entirely for restoration during your visit (for details, see page 671).

Markets: In addition to the regular **market** that sprawls along the riverfront (described under "Sights in Ljubljana"), a colorful **flea market** hops along the castle side of the Ljubljanica River (south of the TI) every Sunday from 8:00 to 14:00.

Money: Most banks are open regular hours (Mon–Fri 8:00–12:00 & 15:00–17:00, a few also open Sat 9:00–12:00, closed Sun).

Internet Access: Most hotel lobbies have Internet access for guests. The TI at the upper end of the market has several terminals (€1/30 min, see "Tourist Information," earlier). **Cyber Café Xplorer** is twice as expensive but has longer hours (Mon–Fri

10:00–22:00, Sat–Sun 14:00–22:00, across the river from the market at Petkovškovo nabrežje 23).

Post Office: The main post office *(pošta)* is in a beautiful yellow Art Nouveau building a block up Čopova from Prešeren Square, at the intersection with the busy Slovenska cesta (Mon–Fri 8:00–19:00, Sat 8:00–13:00, closed Sun).

Map Store: Kod & Kam has a huge selection of maps, English guidebooks, and other books about Slovenia (Mon–Fri 8:00–20:00, Sat 8:00–13:00, closed Sun, near the train station at Miklošičeva cesta 34).

Architecture Guidebooks: Ljubljana is a turn-on for architecture buffs. If you want to learn more about this city's quirky buildings, consider the excellent €13.50 architecture guidebook, or the €17 book about Jože Plečnik's work (sold at the Jože Plečnik House, some TIs, and many bookstores).

Laundry: Most hotels can do your laundry, but it's pricey. **Hostel Celica** serves as the town's self-serve launderette (€7/load, not very central at Metelkova 8, hostel guests have priority for using the machines; described later, under "Sleeping in Ljubljana"). Or try **Chemoexpress,** where you can drop your laundry off in the morning and pick it up in the afternoon (€4.20/kilo, figure about €20–25 for a full load, Mon–Fri 7:00–18:00, closed Sat–Sun, hiding in a courtyard at Wolfova 12, tel. 01/231-0782).

Car Rental: Figure about €60 per day (includes tax and insurance, no extra charge for drop-off elsewhere in Slovenia). Handy options include **Europcar** (in City Hotel at Dalmatinova 15, mobile 031-382-052, www.europcar.si) and **Avis** (Čufarjeva 2, tel. 01/430-8010, www.avis.si).

Best Views: If The Skyscraper's observation deck is open to visitors, it offers the best views in town (see page 668). Views from the castle are nearly as good. At street level, my favorite views are from the wooden bridge called the "Ugly Duckling" (between the Triple and Cobblers' bridges), especially at night. On sunny, blue-sky days, the colorful architecture on and near Prešeren Square pops, and you'll take photos like crazy along the river promenade.

Getting Around Ljubljana

By Bus: Virtually all of Ljubljana's sights are easily accessible by foot, so public transportation probably isn't necessary. And it's a bit of a headache: To ride a bus, you first have to buy a plastic card, called the "Urbana," for €2 (nonrefundable), which you then load with credit to pay for rides. A ride costs €0.80, but you can't pay the driver—you have to use the card (shareable by up to three people). You can buy the Urbana card at the TI, bus station, and

Ljubljana at a Glance

▲▲▲**People-Watching** Ljubljana's single best activity is sitting at an outdoor café along the river and watching the vivacious, stylish, fun-loving Slovenes strut their stuff. **Hours:** 24/7.

▲▲**Riverside Market** Lively market area in the Old Town with produce, clothing, souvenirs—even wild boar salami. **Hours:** Best in the morning, especially Sat; market hall open Mon–Fri 7:00–16:00, Sat 7:00–14:00, closed Sun.

▲▲**Serbian Orthodox Church of Sts. Cyril and Methodius** Beautifully decorated house of worship giving insight into the Orthodox faith. **Hours:** Tue–Sun 9:00–12:00 & 14:00–18:00, closed Mon.

▲▲**National and University Library** Jože Plečnik's pièce de résistance, with an intriguing facade, piles of books, and a bright reading room. **Hours:** Main stairwell open Mon–Fri 9:00–20:00, Sat 9:00–14:00, closed Sun; student reading room open to the public mid-July–mid-Aug Mon–Fri 14:00–20:00.

▲▲**Jože Plečnik House** Final digs of the famed hometown architect who shaped so much of Ljubljana, explained by an enthusiastic guide. **Hours:** English tours begin at the top of each hour Tue–Thu 10:00–18:00, Sat 9:00–15:00, last tour departs one hour before closing, closed Sun–Mon and Fri, and possibly closed at other times while undergoing renovation—call ahead.

some newsstands. Transit info: www.lpp.si.

By Taxi: While there are several companies charging different rates, taxis usually start at about €1.50, and then charge €1 per kilometer. Additional "surcharges" (such as for luggage) are bogus—and are often tacked on as a surprise after you reach your destination. Crooked cabbies are a big problem in Ljubljana (especially those hanging out at the train station). A ride within the city center (such as from the station to a hotel) should run only a few euros, generally less than €5. Your best strategy is to ask for an estimate up front. The cabbie will probably want to just take you for a flat price without using the meter. This is the easiest solution, but realize you'll probably wind up paying a euro or two more than you would if he used the meter. (If you're feeling stingy and feisty, try insisting on the meter.) Another common trick is to charge you the "Sunday and holidays" *(nedelja in počitnice)* rate even on weekdays. If you're suspicious, ask your cabbie to explain why he's chosen the tariff. Your odds of getting an honest cabbie are better if you call

▲▲**Slovenian Ethnographic Museum** Engaging, well-presented collection celebrating Slovenian culture. **Hours:** Tue–Sun 10:00–18:00, closed Mon.

▲**Dragon Bridge** Distinctive Art Nouveau bridge adorned with the city's mascot. **Hours:** Always roaring.

▲**Ljubljana Castle** Tower with good views and so-so 3-D film. **Hours:** Grounds open daily May–Sept 9:00–23:00, Oct–April 10:00–21:00; castle open daily May–Sept 9:00–21:00, Oct–April 10:00–18:00, film plays all day on the half-hour.

▲**Contemporary History Museum** Baroque mansion in Tivoli Park, with exhibit highlighting Slovenia's last 100 years. **Hours:** Tue–Sun 10:00–18:00, closed Mon.

▲**City Museum of Ljubljana** Modern, high-tech exhibit on the city's history. **Hours:** Tue–Sun 10:00–18:00, closed Mon.

▲**Cobblers' Bridge** Columned bridge that epitomizes Jože Plečnik's distinctive architectural style. **Hours:** Always open.

▲**Architectural Museum of Ljubljana** Castle with Plečnik exhibit on the edge of town. **Hours:** Mon–Fri 9:00–15:00, Sat 10:00–18:00, Sun 10:00–15:00.

for a taxi, and it's always cheaper than hailing one on the street. Don't be intimidated—dispatchers generally speak some English, and your hotel, restaurant, or maybe the TI (if they're not too busy) can call a cab for you. **Yellow Taxi** is more reputable than the norm (mobile 041-731-831); **Metro Taxi** is known for being inexpensive (mobile 041-240-200).

By Bike: Ljubljana is a cyclist's delight, with lots of well-marked bike lanes. A few hotels have rental or loaner bikes, or you can rent bikes at the market square TI (€1/2 hrs, €5/day; see "Tourist Information," earlier).

Tours in Ljubljana

Most of Ljubljana's museums are disappointing; the town's ambience, architecture, and public art are its best attraction. To help you appreciate it all, taking a walking tour—either through the TI or by hiring your own local guide—is worth ▲▲.

Walking Tour—The TI organizes excellent two-hour guided town walks of Ljubljana in English, led by knowledgeable guides. In summer, the walk also includes either a trip up to the castle (by funicular or tourist train) or a 30-minute boat ride on the river. From April through September, there are three tours daily: at 10:00, 14:00, and 17:00. From October through March, the walking tour goes daily at 11:00 (€10, meet at Town Hall around corner from Triple Bridge TI).

Local Guides—Having an expert show you around his or her hometown for two hours for €50 has to be the best value in town. Ljubljana's hardworking guides lead tours on a wide variety of topics and can tailor their tour to your interests (figure €50/2 hours, 50 percent more for same-day booking, contact TI for details, arrange at least 24 hours before). **Marijan Krišković,** who leads tours for me throughout Europe, is an outstanding guide (mobile 040-222-739, kriskovic@yahoo.com). **Barbara Jakopič,** soft-spoken and extremely knowledgeable, is also good (mobile 040-530-870, b_lucky2@yahoo.com). **Minka Kahrič,** who's traveled solo to the North Pole, also leads tours closer to home—including walks around Ljubljana and excursions into the countryside (€50/2-hour walking tour; driving: €80/up to 4 hours, €120/up to 8 hours; mobile 041-805-962, polarnimedo@yahoo.com).

Boat Cruise—Consider seeing the town from the Ljubljanica River. You have two options for your one-hour cruise: with English commentary from a live guide (€10, 2/day in summer), or unguided (€8, hourly in summer 10:00–20:00). For details, check with the TI (weather permitting, few or no cruises Nov–March, departs from near the Triple Bridge—about one block along the embankment away from the market). Because Ljubljana is a small town that's easily seen by foot, this trip is more romantic than informative.

Bike Tour—The TI offers a bike tour of the city by request (€15, 2 hours, 2-person minimum, arrange at least 24 hours ahead, get details at TI).

Self-Guided Spin-Tour

▲▲Prešeren Square

The heart of Ljubljana is lively Prešeren Square (Prešernov trg). It's always been bustling, but now it's more people-friendly than ever, since the mayor recently outlawed buses and taxis here.

The city's meeting point is the large **statue of France Prešeren,** Slovenia's greatest poet, whose works include the lyrics to the Slovenian national anthem (and whose silhouette adorns Slovenia's €2 coin). The statue shows Prešeren, an important catalyst of 19th-century Slovenian nationalism, being inspired from overhead by a Muse. This statue provoked a scandal and outraged

the bishop when it went up a century ago—a naked woman sharing the square with a church! To ensure that nobody could be confused about the woman's intentions, she's conspicuously depicted with typical Muse accessories: a laurel branch and a cloak. Even so, for the first few years they covered the scandalous statue with a tarp each night. And the model who posed for the Muse was so disgraced that no one in Slovenia would hire her—so she emigrated to South America and never returned.

Stand at the base of the statue to get oriented. The bridge crossing the Ljubljanica River is one of Ljubljana's most important landmarks, Jože Plečnik's **Triple Bridge** (Tromostovje). The middle (widest) part of this bridge already existed, but Plečnik added the two side spans to more efficiently funnel the six streets of traffic on this side of the bridge to the one street on the other side. The bridge's Venetian vibe is intentional: Plečnik recognized that Ljubljana, located midway between Venice and then-capital Vienna, is itself a bridge between the Italian and Germanic worlds. Across the bridge is the TI, WCs, ATMs, market and cathedral (to the left), and the Town Hall (straight ahead).

Now turn 90 degrees to the right, and look down the first street after the riverbank. Find the pale woman in the picture frame on the second floor of the first yellow house. This is **Julija,** the unrequited love of Prešeren's life. Tour guides spin romantic tales about how the couple met. But the truth is far less exciting: He was a teacher in her father's house when he was in his 30s and she was four. Later in life, she inspired him from afar—as she does now, from across the square—but they never got together. She may have been his muse, but when it came to marriage, she opted for wealth and status.

In 1895, a devastating earthquake destroyed half the city. While tragic, it allowed Ljubljana to rebuild in style. Today Ljubljana—especially the streets around this square—is an architecture-lover's paradise. The **Hauptmann House,** to the right of Julija, was the only building on the square to survive the quake. A few years later, the owner redecorated it in the then-trendy Viennese Art

Nouveau style you see today, using bright colors (since his family sold dyes). All that remains of the original is the little Baroque balcony above the entrance.

Just to the right of the Hauptmann House is a car-sized **model** of the city center—helpful for orientation. The street next to it (with the McDonald's) is **Čopova,** once the route of Ljubljana's Sunday promenade. A century ago, locals would put on their Sunday best and stroll from here to Tivoli Park, listening to musicians and dropping into cafés along the way. Plečnik called it the "lifeline of the city," connecting the green lungs of the park to this urban center. Today, busy Slovenska avenue and railroad tracks cross the route, making the promenade less inviting. But in the last decade, Ljubljana has been trying to recapture its golden age, and some downtown streets are pedestrian-only on weekends once again. The new evening *paseo* thrives along the river between the Triple Bridge and Cobblers' Bridge.

Continue looking to the right, past the big, pink landmark Franciscan Church of St. Mary. The characteristic glass awning marks **Centromerkur**—the first big post-quake department store, today government-protected. At the top of the building is Mercury, god of commerce, watching over the square that has been Ljubljana's commercial heart since the city began. (If you look carefully, you can see the mustachioed face of the building's owner hiding in the folds of cloth by Mercury's left foot.) Since this area was across the river from medieval Ljubljana (beyond the town's limits...and the long arm of its tax collector), it was the best place to sell and buy goods. Today it's the heart of Ljubljana's boutique culture.

The street between Centromerkur and the pink church is **Miklošičeva cesta,** which connects Prešeren Square to the train station. When Ljubljana was rebuilding after the 1895 earthquake, town architects and designers envisioned this street as a showcase of its new, Vienna-inspired Art Nouveau image.

Up Miklošičeva street and on the left is the prominent **Grand Hotel Union,** with a stately domed spire on the corner. When these buildings were designed, Prague was the cultural capital of the Slavic world. The new look of Ljubljana paid homage to "the golden city of a hundred spires" (and copied Prague's romantic image). The city actually had a law for several years that new corner buildings had to have these spires. Even the trees you'll see around town were part of the vision. When the architect Plečnik designed the Ljubljanica River embankments a generation later, he planted

tall, pointy poplar trees and squat, rounded willows—imitating the spires and domes of Prague.

Detour a block up Miklošičeva cesta to see two more architectural gems of that era (across from the Grand Hotel Union): First is a Secessionist building—marked **Zadružna Zveza**—with classic red, blue, and white colors (for the Slovenian flag). Next is the noisy, pink, zigzagged **Cooperative Bank.** The bank was designed by Ivan Vurnik, an ambitious Slovenian architect who wanted to invent a distinctive national style after World War I, when the Habsburg Empire broke up and Eastern Europe's nations were proudly emerging for the first time.

Prešeren Square is the perfect springboard to explore the rest of Ljubljana. Now that you're oriented, visit some of the areas listed next.

Sights in Ljubljana

East of the River, Under the Castle: The Market and Old Town

The castle side of the river is the city's most colorful and historic quarter, packed with Old World ambience.

▲▲Riverside Market (Tržnice)—In Ljubljana's thriving Old Town market, big-city Slovenes enjoy buying directly from the producer. Prices go down as the day gets late and as the week goes on. The market, worth an amble anytime, is best on Saturday mornings, when the townspeople take their time wandering the stalls. In this tiny capital of a tiny country, you may even see the president searching for the perfect melon.

Begin your walk through the market at the Triple Bridge (and TI). The riverside **colonnade,** which echoes the long-gone medieval city wall, was designed by (who else?) Jože Plečnik. This first stretch—nearest the Triple Bridge—is good for souvenirs: woodcarvings, miniature painted frontboards from beehives, honey products (including honey brandy), and lots of colorful candles (bubbly Marta will gladly paint a special message on your candle for no extra charge).

Farther in, the market is almost all local, and the colonnade is populated by butchers, bakers, fishermen, and lazy cafés. Peek down at the actual river and see how the architect wanted the town and river to connect. The lower arcade is a people zone, with easy access from the bridge, public WCs, inviting cafés, and a stinky fish market *(ribarnica)* offering a wide variety. The recommended restaurant just below, **Ribca,** serves fun fishy plates, beer, and coffee with great riverside seating (open Mon–Fri 8:00–16:00, Sat 8:00-14:00, closed Sun).

Across from the stairs down into the fish market, about where the souvenir stands end, you reach the first small market square. On your right, notice the 10-foot-tall concrete **cone.** Plečnik wanted to make Ljubljana the "Athens of the North" and imagined a huge hilltop cone crowning the center of a national acropolis—a complex for government, museums, and culture. This ambitious plan didn't make it off the drawing board, but part of Plečnik's Greek idea came true: this marketplace, based on an ancient Greek *agora.* Plečnik's cone still captures the Slovenes' imaginations...and adorns Slovenia's €0.10 coin.

At the top of this square, you'll find the 18th-century **cathedral** *(stolnica)* standing on the site of a 13th-century Romanesque church. The cathedral is dedicated to St. Nicholas, protector against floods and patron saint of the fishermen and boatmen who have long come to sell their catch at the market. Go under the high arch, then take a close look at the intricately decorated side door on the left. This remarkable door was created for Pope John Paul II's visit here in 1996. Buried deeply in the fecund soil of their ancient and pagan history, the nation's linden tree of life sprouts with the story of the Slovenes. The ceramic pots represent the original Roman settlement here. Just to the left, above the tree, are the Byzantine missionaries Cyril and Methodius, who came here to convert the Slavs to Christianity in the ninth century. Just above, Crusaders and Ottomans do battle. Near the top, see the Slovenes going into the cave—entering the dark 20th century (World War I, World War II, and communism). At the top is Pope John Paul II (the first Slavic pontiff, who also oversaw the fall of communism). Below him are two men who are on track for becoming Slovenia's first saints; the one on the right is Frederic Baraga, a 19th-century bishop who became a missionary in Michigan and codified Chippewa grammar (notice the Native American relief on the book he's holding). In the upper right-hand corner is a sun, which has been shining since Slovenia gained its independence in 1991. Around back of the cathedral is a similar door, carved with images of the six 20th-century bishops of Ljubljana.

The cathedral's interior is stunning Italian Baroque (free, open long hours daily but closed 12:00–15:00). The transept is sur-

rounded by sculptures of four bishops of Roman Ljubljana (when it was called Emona, or Aemon). The bust on the right depicts Anton Vovk, a 20th-century bishop who's one miracle shy of beatification. Left of the main altar, notice the distinctive chair. This was designed by the very religious Jože Plečnik, whose brother was a priest here. Look up over the nave to enjoy the recently restored, gorgeous ceiling fresco.

The building at the end of the first market square is the seminary palace. In the basement is a **market hall,** with vendors selling cheeses, meats, baked goods, dried fruits, nuts, and other goodies (Mon–Fri 7:00–16:00, Sat 7:00–14:00, closed Sun). This place is worth a graze. Most merchants are happy to give you a free sample (point to what you want, and say *probat, prosim*—"a taste, please").

When you leave the market hall, continue downstream into the big **main market square,** packed with produce and clothing stands. (The colorful flower market hides behind the market hall.) The row of vendors nearest the colonnade sell fruit from all over, but the ones located deeper in the market sell only locally grown produce. These producers go out of their way to be old-fashioned—a few of them still follow the tradition of pushing their veggies on wooden carts (called *cizas*) to the market from their garden patches in the suburbs. Once at the market, they simply display their goods on top of their cart, turning it into a sales kiosk. Tell the vendor what you want—it's considered rude for customers to touch the fruits and vegetables before they're bought. Over time, shoppers develop friendships with their favorite producers. On busy days, you'll see a long line at one stand, while the other merchants stand bored. Your choice is simple: Get in line, or eat subpar produce.

Near the market hall, look for the little **scales** in the wooden kiosks marked *Kontrolna Tehtnica*—allowing buyers to immediately check whether the producer cheated them (not a common problem, but just in case). The Habsburg days left locals with the old German saying, "Trust is good; control is better."

At the corner of this market square (toward Prešeren Square), you'll notice a big gap along the riverfront colonnade. This was to be the site of a huge, roofed **Butchers' Bridge** designed by Jože Plečnik, but those plans never materialized. Aware of Plečnik's newfound touristic currency, a few years back some town politicians dusted off the old plans and proposed building the bridge. (In fact, at one point an overzealous politician even placed a cornerstone for the project.) But after all that talk, the new bridge on

this site is based on modern designs (not Plečnik's).

• *Just beyond the end of the market colonnade is the...*

▲Dragon Bridge (Zmajski Most)—The dragon has been the symbol of Ljubljana for centuries, ever since Jason (of Argonauts and Golden Fleece fame) supposedly slew one in a nearby swamp. This is one of the few notable bits of Ljubljana architecture not by Plečnik (but by Jurij Zaninović, a fellow student of Vienna architect Otto Wagner). While the dragon is the star of this very photogenic Art Nouveau bridge, the bridge itself was officially dedicated to the 40th anniversary of Habsburg Emperor Franz Josef's reign (see the dates on the side: 1848–1888). Tapping into the emp's vanity got new projects funded—vital as the city rebuilt after its devastating earthquake of 1895. But the Franz Josef name never stuck; those dragons are just too darn memorable.

▲Town Square (Mestni Trg) and the Old Town—Ljubljana's Town Square, just across the Triple Bridge and up the street from Prešeren Square, is home to the **Town Hall** (Rotovž), highlighted by its clock tower and pillared loggia. Step inside the Renaissance courtyard to see artifacts and a map of late-17th-century Ljubljana. Studying this map, notice how the river, hill, and wall worked together to fortify the town. Courtyards like this are hidden through the city (though most are humbler). As rent in these old places is cheap, many such courtyards host funky and characteristic little businesses. Be sure to get off the main drag and poke into Ljubljana's nooks and crannies.

In the square is a recent replica of the **Fountain of Three Carniolian Rivers,** inspired in style and theme by Rome's many fountains. (The original is in a museum.) The figures with vases represent this region's three main rivers: Ljubljanica, Sava, and Krka. This is one of many works in town by Francesco Robba, an Italian who came to Ljubljana for one job, fell in love with a Slovene, and stayed here the rest of his life—decorating the city's churches with beautiful Baroque altars.

In the early 19th century, Ljubljana consisted mainly of

this single street, running along the base of Castle Hill (plus a small "New Town" across the river). Stretching south from here are two other "squares"—Stari trg (Old Square) and Gornji trg (Upper Square)—which have long since grown together into one big, atmospheric promenade lined with quaint boutiques, great restaurants, and cafés (perfect for a stroll). Virtually every house along this drag has a story to tell, of a famous resident or infamous incident. As you walk, keep your eyes open for Ljubljana's mascot dragon—it's everywhere. At the end of the pedestrian zone (at Gornji trg), look uphill and notice the village charms of some of the oldest buildings in town (four medieval houses with rooflines slanted at the ends, different from the others on this street).

▲Ljubljana Castle (Ljubljanski Grad)—The castle above town offers enjoyable views of Ljubljana and the surrounding countryside. There has probably been a settlement on this site since prehistoric times, though the first fortress here was Roman. The 12th-century version of the castle was gradually added on to over the centuries, until it fell into disrepair in the 17th century. Today's castle was rebuilt in the 1940s, renovated in the 1970s, and is still technically unfinished (subject to ongoing additions). It houses a restaurant, a gift shop, temporary exhibition halls, and a Gothic chapel with Baroque paintings of the coat of arms of St. George (Ljubljana's patron saint, the dragon-slayer). Above the restaurant are two wedding halls—Ljubljana's most popular places to get married (free for locals). While the castle and its attractions are ho-hum, the views are worth the trip.

It's free to enter the castle grounds (daily May–Sept 9:00–23:00, Oct–April 10:00–21:00, tel. 01/232-9994). Inside are two optional activities you have to pay for (€3.50 covers both, daily May–Sept 9:00–21:00, Oct–April 10:00–18:00): the **castle tower,** with 92 steps leading to one of the best views in town; and a 23-minute **3-D film** about the history of Ljubljana (touted as a "virtual museum," but barely worth your time; plays all day on the half-hour).

Tours of the castle in Slovene and English leave from the entry bridge daily June through mid–September at 10:00, 11:00, 14:00, and 16:00 (€5, tour lasts 1–1.5 hours). The castle is also home to the Ljubljana Summer Festival, with **concerts** throughout the summer (tel. 01/426-4340, www.festival-lj.si).

Getting to the Castle: A slick **funicular** whisks visitors to the top in a jiff (€1.80 one-way, €3 round-trip, every 10 min, 1-min ride, daily May–Sept 9:00–23:00, Oct–April 10:00–21:00, catch it at Krekov trg, across the street from the market square TI). From the top, you'll find free WCs and a few easy flights of stairs up into the heart of the castle complex (or take the elevator). Another sweat-free route to the top is via the **tourist train** that leaves at the top of each hour (or more frequently, with demand) from in front of the Triple Bridge TI (€3 round-trip, daily in summer 9:00–21:00, shorter hours off-season, doesn't run in snow or other bad weather). There are also two handy **trails** to the castle. The steeper-but-faster route begins near the Dragon Bridge (find Študentovska lane, just past the statue of Vodnik in the market). Slower but a bit less steep is Reber, just off Stari trg (Old Square), a few blocks south of the Town Hall. Walk up to the top of Reber; at the dead end, turn right and start climbing up the stairs. From here on out, always bear left, then go right when you're just under the castle (follow *Grad* signs).

West of the River, Beyond Prešeren Square: The Museum Zone and Tivoli Park

The Prešeren Square (west) side of the river is the heart of modern Ljubljana, and home to several prominent squares and fine museums. These sights are listed roughly in order from Prešeren Square and can be linked to make an interesting walk.

• *Leave Prešeren Square in the direction the poet is looking, bear to your left (up Wolfova, by the picture of Julija), and walk a block to...*

Congress Square (Kongresni Trg)—This grassy, tree-lined square is ringed by some of Ljubljana's most important buildings: the University headquarters, the Baroque Ursuline Church of the Holy Trinity, a classical mansion called the Kazina, and the Philharmonic Hall. At the top end of the square, by the entry to a pedestrian underpass, a Roman sarcophagus sits under a gilded statue of a **Roman citizen**—a replica of an artifact from 1,700 years ago, when this town was called Emona. The busy street above you has been the main trading route through town since ancient Roman times. This square hosts the big town events. Locals remember how, when President Clinton visited, tens of thousands packed the square.

• *Take the underpass beneath busy Slovenska avenue (the town's main traffic thoroughfare), then continue straight through the shopping mall into the...*

▲Square of the Republic (Trg Republike)—This unusual square is essentially a parking lot ringed by an odd collection of buildings. While hardly quaint, the Square of the Republic gives you a good taste of a modern corner of Ljubljana. And it's his-

toric—this is where Slovenia declared its independence in 1991.

The **twin office towers** (with the world's biggest digital watch, flashing the date, time, and temperature) were designed by Plečnik's protégé, Edvard Ravnikar. As harrowing as these seem, imagine if they had followed the original plans—twice as tall as they are now, and connected by a bridge, representing the gateway to Ljubljana. These buildings were originally designed as the Slovenian parliament, but they were scaled back when Tito didn't approve (since it would have made Slovenia's parliament bigger than the Yugoslav parliament in Belgrade). Instead, the **Slovenian Parliament** is across the square, in the strangely low-profile office building with the sculpted entryway. The carvings are in the Socialist Realist style, celebrating the noble Slovenian people conforming to communist ideals for the good of the entire society. Completing the square are a huge conference center (Cankarjev Dom, the white building behind the skyscrapers), a shopping mall, and some public art.

• *Just a block north, through the grassy park (Trg Narodni Herojev), you'll find the...*

Slovenian National Museum (Narodni Muzej Slovenije) and Slovenian Museum of Natural History (Prirodoslovni Muzej Slovenije)—These two museums share a single historic building facing a park behind the Parliament. While neither collection is particularly good, they're both worth considering if you have a special interest or if it's a rainy day (€3 for each museum, or €5 for both, some English descriptions, daily 10:00–18:00, Thu until 20:00, Muzejska 1, tel. 01/241-4400, www.narmuz-lj.si and www.pms-lj.si).

The **National Museum** occupies the ground floor, featuring a lapidarium with carved-stone Roman monuments and exhibits on Egyptian mummies. (Temporary exhibits are also on this level.) Upstairs and to the right are more exhibits of the National Museum, with archaeological findings ranging from old armor and pottery to the museum's two prized possessions: a fragment of a 45,000-year-old Neanderthal flute, supposedly the world's oldest musical instrument; and the "figural situla," a beautifully decorated bronze bucket from 500 B.C. (The National Museum also has a newer branch in the Metelkova district, described later.)

Upstairs and to the left is the **Natural History** exhibit, featuring the flora and fauna of Slovenia. You'll see partial skeletons of a mammoth and a cave bear, plenty of stuffed reptiles, fish, and

birds, and an exhibit on "human fish" (*Proteus anguinus*—long, skinny, pale-pink amphibians).

• *At the far end of the building is a glassed-in annex displaying Roman stone monuments (free). Turning left around the museum building and walking one block, you'll see the...*

US Embassy—This pretty yellow chalet (with brown trim and a red roof, at Prešernova cesta 31) wins my vote for quaintest embassy building in the world. Resist the urge to snap a photo... those guards are all business.

• *Just up Prešernova street from the embassy are two decent but skippable art museums.*

National Gallery (Narodna Galerija)—This museum has three parts: European artists, Slovenian artists, and temporary exhibits. Find the work of Ivana Kobilca, a late-19th-century Slovenian Impressionist. Art-lovers enjoy her self-portrait in *Summer.* If you're going to Bled, you can get a sneak preview with Marko Pernhart's huge panorama of the Julian Alps (€7, more for special exhibits, permanent collection free first Sun of the month, open Tue–Sun 10:00–18:00, closed Mon, enter through old-fashioned facade at Cankarjeva 20, another entrance is at big glass box between two older buildings at Prešernova 24, tel. 01/241-5418, www.ng-slo.si).

Museum of Modern Art (Moderna Galerija Ljubljana)—This museum has a ho-hum permanent collection of modern and contemporary Slovenian artists, as well as temporary exhibits by both Slovenes and international artists. Having recently undergone an extensive renovation, it might be open in time for your visit (if open: likely €4, Tue–Sun 10:00–18:00, closed Mon, Tomšičeva 14, tel. 01/241-6800, www.mg-lj.si).

• *By the busy road near the art museums, look for the distinctive Neo-Byzantine design (tall domes with narrow slits) of the...*

▲▲Serbian Orthodox Church of Sts. Cyril and Methodius—Ljubljana's most striking church interior isn't Catholic, but Orthodox. This church was built in 1936, soon after the Slovenes joined a political union with the Serbs. Wealthy Slovenia attracted its poorer neighbors from the south—so it built this church for that community. Since 1991, the Serb population continues to grow, as people from the struggling corners of the former Yugoslavia flock to prosperous Slovenia.

Step inside for the best glimpse of the Orthodox faith this side of Dubrovnik (free, Tue–Sun 9:00–12:00 & 14:00–18:00, closed Mon). The church is colorfully decorated without a hint

of the 21st century, mirroring a very conservative religion. You'll see Cyrillic script in this building, which evokes Moscow more than Rome. Notice that there are no pews, because worshippers stand throughout the service. On the left, find the little room with tubs of water, where the faithful light tall, skinny beeswax candles (purchased at the little window in the back corner). The painted screen, or iconostasis, is believed to separate our material world from the spiritual realm behind it. Ponder the fact that several centuries ago, before the Catholic Church began to adapt to a changing world, all Christians worshipped this way. For more on the Orthodox faith, see the sidebar on page 789.

• *On the other side of the busy street is...*

Tivoli Park (Park Tivoli)—This huge park, just west of the center, is where Slovenes relax on summer weekends. The easiest access is through the graffiti-covered underpass from Cankarjeva cesta (between the Serbian Orthodox Church and the Museum of Modern Art). As you emerge, the Neoclassical pillars leading down the promenade clue you in that this part of the park was designed by Jože Plečnik. Along this "main boulevard" of the park, various changing photographic exhibitions are displayed.

• *Aside from taking a leisurely stroll, the best thing to do in the park is visit the...*

▲Contemporary History Museum (Muzej Novejše Zgodovine)—In a Baroque mansion (Cekinov Grad) in Tivoli Park, a well-done exhibit called "Slovenians in the 20th Century" traces the last hundred years of Slovenia—essentially from the end of World War I to independence in 1991. Out front is a T-55 Yugoslav tank that was commandeered by the Slovenes during their war for independence. Inside, the ground floor displays temporary exhibits, and upstairs you'll find several rooms using models, dioramas, and light-and-sound effects to creatively tell the story of one of Europe's youngest nations. It's a little difficult to fully appreciate, even with the good English descriptions. But the creativity and spunky spirit of the place are truly enjoyable. The "Slovenia 1945–1960" exhibit outlines both the good and the bad of the early Tito years (including a photo album with Tito's visits to Slovenia). But the most evocative room has artifacts from the Slovenes' brave declaration of independence from a hostile Yugoslavia in 1991. The well-organized Slovenes had only to weather a 10-day skirmish to gain their freedom. Camouflage-clad mannequins represent the two sides that stared each other down during this tense standoff—

the ragtag but determined Slovenian militia (on the left) and the well-equipped but unmotivated Yugoslav National Army (on the right). It's chilling to think that bombers were en route to level this gorgeous city. The planes were called back at the last minute, by a Yugoslav National Army officer with allegiances to Slovenia (€3.50, permanent exhibit free first Sun of the month, open Tue–Sun 10:00–18:00, closed Mon, in Tivoli Park at Celovška cesta 23, tel. 01/300-9610, www.muzej-nz.si).

Getting There: The museum is a 20-minute walk from the center, best combined with a wander through Tivoli Park. The fastest approach: As you emerge from the Cankarjeva cesta underpass into the park, climb up the stairs, then turn right and go straight ahead for five minutes. You'll continue straight up the ramp, then turn left after the tennis courts and look for the big pink-and-white mansion on the hill.

• *Hungry? Straight ahead and down the stairs from the museum, look for the "Hot Horse" food kiosk, selling €4 horseburgers (no joke). A local institution, this is a popular place to get together with friends and neighbors. The giant, modern, blocky, light-blue building across the busy road is the Pivovarna Union—the brewery for Ljubljana's favorite beer.*

On your way back to the center, consider stopping by...

The Skyscraper (Nebotičnik)—This 1933 Art Deco building was the first skyscraper in Slovenia, for a time the tallest building in Central Europe, and one of the earliest European buildings that was clearly influenced by American architecture. The Skyscraper's observation deck offers the best view of Ljubljana's skyline; unfortunately, it's been closed to the public for years. However, an investor is carrying out an extensive renovation project, and hopes to open it to visitors in early 2010 (ask TI for details; The Skyscraper is 2 blocks from Prešeren Square at Štefanova ulica 1).

• *A few blocks south, near several Jože Plečnik sights (see next section) at the river end of French Revolution Square, you'll find the...*

▲City Museum of Ljubljana (Mestni Muzej Ljubljana)—This thoughtfully presented museum, located in the recently restored Auersperg Palace, offers a high-tech, in-depth look at the "Faces of Ljubljana." You'll begin your visit in the cellar, with Roman ruins (including remains of the original Roman road and sewer system, found right here and displayed *in situ*) and layers of medieval artifacts. Touchscreens provide more information.

Then you'll head up to the first floor, which traces the social history of Ljubljana through the eyes of its participants: men (see the creatively painted shooting targets, from the "country clubs" of the late-18th-century aristocracy); women (with stories and artifacts of six women who've had an impact on the city); children (who were hidden from the authorities during the Nazi occupation); and youth (specifically in the 1960s and 1970s, when Ljubljana's Šumi

bar was Yugoslavia's answer to the Haight-Ashbury).

Various themed exhibits fill the second floor. One traces how the city's role has evolved over time. In another room, pay close attention to Slovenia's short-lived currency, the *tolar* (1991–2006). Rather than heads of state and generals, all of the notables pictured on these bills were artists and scientists. The most interesting exhibit ("From State to State") explains how Ljubljana has belonged to 10 different states over the last 200 years, ranging from the genteel Habsburg Empire to the oppressive Nazi regime to membership in the benevolent EU. Another exhibit examines the modern woes of traffic, including noise and air pollution, and gives you the opportunity to sit in a mustard-yellow, communist-era Fiat Fičko car.

Rounding out the collection is a relaxing 15-minute movie and a range of special exhibits on the ground floor. Though everything is well-described in English, a student on the museum's staff might be able to show you around if it's not too busy—ask (entry-€4, Tue–Sun 10:00–18:00, closed Mon, kid-friendly, Gosposka 15, tel. 01/241-2500, www.mestnimuzej.si).

• *If visiting the museum, don't miss the nearby National University Library and French Revolution Square—both described in the next section.*

South of Prešeren Square: Jože Plečnik's Architecture

Jože Plečnik is to Ljubljana what Antoni Gaudí is to Barcelona: a homegrown and amazingly prolific genius who shaped his town with a uniquely beautiful vision. And, as in Barcelona, Ljubljana has a way of turning people who couldn't care less about architecture into huge Plečnik fans. There's plenty to see. In addition to the Triple Bridge, the riverside market, and the sights listed here, Plečnik designed the embankments along the Ljubljanica and Gradaščica Rivers in the Trnovo neighborhood; the rebuilt Roman wall along Mirje street, south of the center; the Church of St. Francis, with its classicist bell tower; St. Michael's Church on the Marsh; Orel Stadium; Žale Cemetery; and many more buildings throughout Slovenia.

Some of the best Plečnik sights are near the river, just south of Congress and Prešeren squares. I've linked them up in the order of a short self-guided walk.

• *From Prešeren Square, stroll south along the river. After the plain wooden bridge called the "Ugly Duckling," you'll come to the...*

▲Cobblers' Bridge (Čevljarski Most)—Named for the actual cobblers (shoemakers) who set up shop along the river in olden times, the bridge encapsulates Plečnik's style perhaps better than any other structure: simple, clean lines adorned with classical

columns. Ideal for people-watching (with the castle hovering scenically overhead), this is one of Ljubljana's most appealing spots.

• *Continue past the Cobblers' Bridge on the right side of the river. After about a block, turn right up the parked-up street called Novi trg. At the top of this street, on the left, is a red-brick building embedded with gray granite blocks in an irregular checkerboard pattern. This is the...*

▲▲National and University Library (Narodna in Univerzitetna Knjižnica, or NUK)—Widely regarded as Plečnik's masterpiece, this building is a bit underwhelming...until an understanding of its symbolism brings it to life. On the surface, the red-and-gray color scheme evokes the red soil and chunks of granite of the Karst region, south of Ljubljana. But on a deeper level, the library's design evokes the beauty of overcoming obstacles to attain knowledge. The odd-sized and -shaped blocks in the facade represent a complex numerological pattern that suggests barriers on the path to enlightenment. The sculpture on the river side is Moses—known for leading his people through 40 years of hardship to the Promised Land. On the right side of the building, find the horse-head doorknobs—representing the winged horse Pegasus (grab hold, and he'll whisk you away to new levels of enlightenment). Step inside. The main staircase is dark and gloomy—modeled after an Egyptian tomb. But at the top, through the door marked *Velika Čitalnica,* is the bright, airy main reading room: the ultimate goal, a place of learning. The top-floor windows are shaped roughly like open books.

Aside from being a great work of architecture, the building also houses the most important library in Slovenia, with more than two million books (about one per Slovene). The library is supposed to receive a copy of each new book printed in the country. In a freaky bit of bad luck, this was the only building in town damaged

in World War II, when a plane crashed into it. But the people didn't want to see their books go up in flames—so hundreds of locals formed a human chain, risking life and limb to get the books out of the burning building.

You can easily duck into the main stairwell (free, Mon–Fri 9:00–20:00, Sat 9:00–14:00, closed Sun). The quiet student reading room is officially open for visitors during very limited hours, when it's technically closed to students (mid-July–mid-Aug Mon–Fri 14:00–20:00). If you're not here during that one-month span, and you're really determined to see the room, you can try sticking close to a student going inside—but note that the guards frown on uninvited visitors. To get out, follow another student—or push gently on the door (it'll likely open easily).

• *Directly behind the library is a mellow square with an obelisk in the middle. This is...*

French Revolution Square (Trg Francoske Revolucije)—Plečnik designed the **obelisk** in the middle of the square to commemorate Napoleon's short-lived decision to make Ljubljana the capital of his Illyrian Provinces. It's rare to find anything honoring Napoleon outside of Paris, but he was good to Ljubljana. Under his rule, Slovenian culture flourished, schools were established, and roads and infrastructure were improved. The monument contains ashes of the unknown French soldiers who died in 1813, when the region went from French to Austrian control.

The Teutonic Knights of the Cross established the nearby **monastery** (Križanke, ivy-capped wall and gate, free entry) in 1230. The adaptation of these monastery buildings into the Ljubljana Summer Theatre was Plečnik's last major work (1950–1956).

• *From here, it's a scenic 10-minute walk to the next sight. From the obelisk, walk down Emonska toward the twin-spired church. You'll pass (on the left) the delightful Krakovo district—a patch of green countryside in downtown Ljubljana. Many of the veggies you see in the riverside market come from these carefully tended gardens. When you reach the Gradaščica stream, head over the bridge (also designed by Plečnik) and go around the left side of the church to find the house.*

▲▲Jože Plečnik House (Plečnikova Zbirka)—Ljubljana's favorite son lived here from 1921 until his death in 1957. He added on to an existing house, building a circular bedroom for himself and filling the place with bric-a-brac he designed, as well as artifacts, photos, and gifts from around the world that inspired him as he shaped

Jože Plečnik
(1872–1957)

There is probably no other single architect who has shaped one city as Jože Plečnik (YOH-zheh PLAYCH-neek) shaped Ljubljana. From libraries, office buildings, cemeteries, and stadiums to landscaping, riverside embankments, and market halls, Plečnik left his mark everywhere. While he may not yet register very high on the international Richter scale of important architects, the Slovenes' pride in this man's work is understandable.

Plečnik was born in Ljubljana and trained as a furniture designer before his interest turned to architecture. He studied in Vienna under the Secessionist architect Otto Wagner. His first commissions, done around the turn of the 20th century in Vienna, were pretty standard Art Nouveau stuff. Then Tomáš Masaryk, president of the new nation of Czechoslovakia, decided that the dull Habsburg design of Prague Castle could use a new look to go with its new independence. But he didn't want an Austrian architect; it had to be a Slav. In 1921, Masaryk chose Jože Plečnik, who sprinkled the castle grounds with his distinctive touches. By now, Plečnik had perfected his simple, eye-pleasing style, which mixes modern and classical influences, with lots of

Ljubljana. Living a simple, almost monastic lifestyle, Plečnik knew what he liked, and these tastes are mirrored in his house.

Today the house is decorated exactly as it was the day Plečnik died, containing much of his equipment, models, and plans. The house can be toured only with a guide, whose enthusiasm brings the place to life. There are very few barriers, so you are in direct contact with the world of the architect. Still furnished with unique, Plečnik-designed furniture, one-of-a-kind inventions, and favorite souvenirs from his travels, the house paints an unusually intimate portrait of an artist.

While the house initially underwhelms some visitors, it's worth ▲▲▲ for those who get caught up in Ljubljana's idiosyncratic sense of style. As you tour the place, be patient. Listen to its stories. Appreciate the subtle details. Notice how reverently your guide (and other Slovenes) speak of this man. Contrast the humbleness of Plečnik's home with the dynamic impact he had on the cityscape of Ljubljana and the cultural heritage of Slovenia. Wandering Plečnik's hallways, it's hard not to be tickled by this man's sheer creativity and by the unique world he forged for him-

columns and pyramids—simultaneously austere and playful.

By the time Plečnik finished in Prague, he had made a name for himself. His prime years were spent creating for the Kingdom of Yugoslavia (before the ideology-driven era of Tito). Plečnik returned home to Ljubljana and set to work redesigning the city, both as an architect and as an urban planner. He lived in a humble house behind the Trnovo Church (now a tourable and recommended museum), and on his walk to work every day, he pondered ways to make the city even more livable. Wandering through town, notice how thoughtfully he incorporated people, nature, the Slovenian heritage, town vistas, and symbolism into his works—it's feng shui on a grand urban scale.

An astounding number of Plečnik's ideas became reality, but even more did not. After World War II, the very religious Plečnik fell out of favor with the new communist government and found it more difficult to get his projects completed. (It's fun to imagine how this city might look if Plečnik had always gotten his way.) After his death in 1957, Plečnik was virtually forgotten by Slovenes and scholars alike. His many works in Ljubljana were taken for granted.

But in 1986, an exposition about Plečnik at Paris' Pompidou Center jump-started interest in the architect. Within a few years Plečnik was back in vogue. Today, scholars laud him as a genius who was ahead of his time...while locals and tourists enjoy the elegant simplicity of his works.

self to live in. As a visitor to his home, you're in good company. He invited only his closest friends here—except during World War II, when Ljubljana was occupied by Nazis, the university was closed, and Plečnik allowed his students to work with him here.

Possible Closure: As the house is slated to be closed for restoration sometime soon, it's important to ask the TI, check the website, or call the museum to be sure it's open before making the trek out here.

Cost, Hours, Information: €4, Tue–Thu 10:00–18:00, Sat 9:00–15:00, 30-min English tours begin at the top of each hour, last tour departs one hour before closing, closed Sun–Mon and Fri, tel. 01/280-1600, www.aml.si, pz@aml.si. It's well-run by Ana and Natalija, who sometimes lead the tours.

Getting There: It's directly behind the twin steeples of the Trnovo Church, at Karunova ulica 4. The 15-minute stroll from the center—the same one Plečnik took to work each day—is nearly as enjoyable as the house itself. You can either walk south along the river, then turn right onto Gradaška and stroll along the stream to the church; or, from French Revolution Square, head

south on Emonska. Either way, you'll pass through the garden-patch district of Krakovo, where pea patches and characteristic Old World buildings gracefully cohabitate. On the way to or from the museum, consider getting a meal in Krakovo (two great restaurants—Pri Škofu and Harambaša—are described later, under "Eating in Ljubljana").

• *The final sight is on the outskirts of town.*

▲Architectural Museum of Ljubljana (Arhitekturni Muzej Ljubljana)—If your visit to Ljubljana has infected you with Plečnik fever, you can trek out to this interesting museum, located in Fužine Castle on the outskirts of Ljubljana. The permanent exhibit features parts of the 1986 Paris exhibition that made Plečnik famous all over again. Downstairs is a display of plans and photos from Plečnik's earlier works in Vienna and Prague, and upstairs, you'll find an exhibit on his works in Slovenia, including some detailed plans and models for ambitious projects he never completed (like the huge, cone-shaped parliament building atop Castle Hill). It's worthwhile, but a bit of a hassle to reach—only true enthusiasts should pay a visit (€3, Mon–Fri 9:00–15:00, Sat 10:00–18:00, Sun 10:00–15:00, last entry 30 min before closing, Pot na Fužine 2, tel. 01/540-9798, www.aml.si). Take bus #20 or #22 from near Congress Square (direction: Fužine) to the end of the line (about 20 min).

Museums in Metelkova, Northeast of Prešeren Square

These two museums, in the dull but up-and-coming district of Metelkova, face each other on a slick modern plaza next to the park called Tabor. They are about a 10-minute walk northeast of Prešeren Square.

▲▲Slovenian Ethnographic Museum (Slovenski Etnografski Muzej)—Housed in a brand-new facility, this delightful museum is Ljubljana's most underrated attraction. At the core of the collection is an exhibit that strives to explain what it is to be Slovene, with well-presented and well-described cultural artifacts from around the country (many English descriptions posted, others are borrowable). A good but slow-moving film visits the four major regions of Slovenia. One exhibit ponders how people half a world away—in Slovenia and in North America—simultaneously invented a similar solution (snowshoes) for a common problem. Another exhibit deconstructs Slovenian clichés (including this country's odd fascination with its traditional hayracks). The collection is displayed to emphasize the evolution of an increasingly complicated civilization, from basic farming tools to ceramics to modern technology. The children's section features an A-to-Ž array of engaging, hands-on activities. The museum also houses a collec-

tion of non-European cultures (with more photos and prose and fewer artifacts), as well as high-quality temporary exhibits. The newest permanent exhibit, called "I, We, and Others," encourages visitors to examine their place in the world. If you've caught the Slovenian folk culture itch, this is the place to scratch it (€4.50, free last Sun of month, Tue–Sun 10:00–18:00, closed Mon, great café, Metelkova 2, tel. 01/300-8745, www.etno-muzej.si).

Slovenian National Museum-Metelkova (Narodni Muzej Slovenije)—Having decided to bring its collection out of storage, Slovenia's National Museum recently moved the contents of its attics and cellars to two floors of this brand-new facility, right next to the Ethnographic Museum. This very pretty historical bric-a-brac is neatly presented without much context—it's just an excuse to get a bunch of interesting stuff out into public view. Each room has a different collection: furniture, pottery and ceramics, church vestments, weapons and armor, and more. The painting gallery is nicely organized by century and style. Everything's labeled in English, and on weekday afternoons and all day on weekends, a guide on their staff can show you around, if they're not too busy (€3, Tue–Sun 10:00–18:00, closed Mon, Maistrova 1, tel. 01/241-4400).

Shopping in Ljubljana

Ljubljana, with its easygoing ambience and countless boutiques, is made to order for whiling away an afternoon shopping. It's also a fun place to stock up on souvenirs and gifts for the folks back home. Popular items include wood carvings and models (especially of the characteristic hayracks that dot the countryside), different flavors of schnapps (the kind with a whole pear inside—cultivated to actually grow right into the bottle—is considered a particularly classy gift), honey-mead brandy (*medica*—sweet and smooth), and those adorable painted frontboard panels from beehives (described on page 710). Rounding out the list of traditional Slovenian items are wrought-iron products from Kropa, crystal from Rogaska, lace from Idrija, salt from Piran, and Peko shoes (similar to high-fashion Italian models, but cheaper; the name is an abbreviation of its founder's name: Peter Kozina).

Souvenirs: The most atmospheric trinket-shopping is in the first stretch of the **market colonnade,** along the riverfront next to the Triple Bridge (described earlier, under "Sights in Ljubljana"). A souvenir shop with a wide variety is **Dom Trgovina,** with two locations: One is a block across the Triple Bridge from Prešeren Square and facing the Town Hall (Mon–Fri 9:00–19:00, Sat 9:00–15:00, closed Sun, Mestni trg 24, tel. 01/241-8390), and the other is across from the TI on the main market square (Mon–Fri 8:00–19:00, Sat 8:00–15:00, closed Sun, Ciril-Metodov trg 5). If

you're looking for serious handicrafts rather than trinkets, drop by the **Rustika** gallery, just over the Triple Bridge (on the castle side). In addition to beehive panels, they also have lace, painted chests and boxes, and other tasteful local-style mementos (Mon–Fri 9:00–19:00, Sat 10:00–19:00, Sun 10:00–14:00, Stritarjeva ulica 9, mobile 031-459-509). There's another location up at the castle courtyard.

Boutiques and Galleries: Of the many fun and funky boutique streets in town, my two favorites are along the main drag through the **Old Town** (Mestni trg/Stari trg/Gornji trg), and along **Trubarjeva street,** a block up from the river (easy to find from Prešeren Square).

Sleeping in Ljubljana

Ljubljana has a good range of accommodations in all price ranges. I've focused my listings in or within easy walking distance of the city center. To get the best value, book ahead. The most expensive hotels raise their prices even more during conventions (Sept–Oct, and sometimes also June). The TI can give you a list of cheap private rooms *(sobe)*. To locate the following accommodations, see the map on page 648.

$$$ Antiq Hotel is a family-run boutique hotel idyllically situated on a cobbled square in Ljubljana's Old Town. Its 16 overpriced, idiosyncratically decorated rooms sprawl through two buildings with lots of stairs and a mazelike floor plan (small S-€61, Sb-€113–133, small D-€77, Db-€144–168, price depends on size, air-con, free Internet access and Wi-Fi, some rooms have low beams and doors, Gornji trg 3, tel. 01/421-3560, fax 01/421-3565, www.antiqhotel.si, info@antiqhotel.si).

$$$ Grand Hotel Union is Ljubljana's top address, as much an Art Nouveau landmark as a hotel. You'll pay dearly for its Old World elegance, hundred years of history, professional staff, big pool, and perfect location (right on Prešeren Square). While their rack rates are outrageously high, you can often snare a great deal in the summer (July–Aug), winter, and on many weekends. The 194 plush "Executive" rooms are in the main building (official rates: Sb-€194, Db-€224; in slow times maybe as low as Sb-€110, Db-€120; air-con, non-smoking floors, elevator, free cable Internet, Miklošičeva cesta 1, tel. 01/308-1270, fax 01/308-1015, www.gh-union.si, hotel.union@gh-union.si). Its 133 "Business" rooms next door are less luxurious, almost as expensive, and a lesser value (official rates: Sb-€178, Db-€208; same potential deals as "Executive" rooms, air-con, non-smoking floors, elevator, free cable Internet, Miklošičeva cesta 3, tel. 01/308-1170, fax 01/308-1914, www.gh-union.si, hotel.business@gh-union.si). Both have access to a pool

Sleep Code

(€1 = about $1.40, country code: 386, area code: 01)
S = Single, **D** = Double/Twin, **T** = Triple, **Q** = Quad, **b** = bathroom. Unless otherwise noted, credit cards are accepted, breakfast is included, and the modest tourist tax (€1.01 per person, per night) is not. Everyone speaks English.

To help you easily sort through these listings, I've divided the rooms into three categories based on the price for a standard double room with bath:

$$$ Higher Priced—Most rooms €110 or more.
$$ Moderately Priced—Most rooms between €70–110.
$ Lower Priced—Most rooms €70 or less.

and sauna in the Business branch, and a free Internet terminal and parking (€17/day) in the Executive branch. Because of a noisy nearby disco, request a quieter room at either building if you're here on a weekend.

$$$ Central Hotel, technically part of the Grand Hotel Union up the street, has 74 rooms similar to (but slightly smaller than) the "Business" rooms at the main hotel, but cheaper and in a friendlier, less-pretentious package. The hotel is conveniently situated between Prešeren Square and the train station (official rates: Sb-€139, Db-€167; much lower prices likely July–Aug, in winter, and on weekends—maybe as low as Sb-€75, Db-€90; extra bed-€27, non-smoking rooms, elevator, free Internet access and cable Internet, parking garage-€19/day, Miklošičeva cesta 9, tel. 01/308-4300, fax 01/230-1181, www.centralhotel.si, central.hotel@gh-union.si).

$$ Slamič B&B has 11 modern rooms with hardwood floors and tasteful decor. Over an upscale café in a nondescript neighborhood, this is a fine spot for affordable elegance (Sb-€65–75, Db-€95–99, price depends on size; suite: Sb-€135, Db-€165; free Wi-Fi, no elevator, Kersnikova 1, tel. 01/433-8233, fax 01/433-8022, www.slamic.si, info@slamic.si). As the café hours are limited (Mon–Thu 7:30–22:00, Fri 7:30–21:00, Sat 9:00–16:00, closed Sun), clearly communicate your arrival time.

$$ Pri Mraku Guesthouse has 36 comfortable, slightly overpriced rooms in a pleasant neighborhood near French Revolution Square. While it's a bit rough around the edges and not without its quirks, this trusty old place is my sentimental favorite in Ljubljana (Sb-€70–74, Db-€106, ground-floor and top-floor rooms have air-con and cost about €15 more, 8 percent discount for Rick Steves readers if you reserve ahead, extra bed-€20,

cheaper mid-Oct–March, non-smoking floor, free Internet access and Wi-Fi, lunch restaurant with terrace under an old vine, Rimska 4, tel. 01/421-9650, fax 01/421-9655, www.daj-dam.si, mrak@daj-dam.si).

$$ Hotel Emonec (eh-MOH-nets), with some of the most centrally located cheap beds in Ljubljana, hides just off Wolfova lane between Prešeren and Congress squares. Its 41 sleek rooms—in two buildings across a courtyard from each other—feel institutional and characterless, with cramped bathrooms, but the price is right. As it's near a noisy disco, light sleepers should try requesting a quiet room (Sb-€64, small Db-€69, bigger "standard" Db-€77, Tb-€96, Qb-€111, pay Internet access, free Wi-Fi, free loaner bikes for guests, Wolfova 12, tel. 01/200-1520, fax 01/200-1521, www.hotel-emonec.net, hotelemonec@siol.net).

$ B&B Petra Varl offers comfortable, affordable, nicely appointed rooms on a courtyard across from the bustling riverside market. Petra, who's an artist and speaks good English, will help you feel at home. This place is an appealing budget option for non-hostelers, so book early (Db-€60, extra bed-€10, includes kitchenette with basic do-it-yourself breakfast, cash only, air-con, free cable Internet, go into courtyard at Vodnikov trg 5 and look for *B&B* sign at 5A, mobile 041-389-470, petra@varl.si).

$ Hotel Center (not to be confused with "Hotel Central," above) is a particularly good value. Marko's eight new, small, modern rooms deliver on his promise of "three-star furnishings at two-star prices," and the location—just across the busy Slovenska road from the main part of town—is convenient for the price (Db-€66, breakfast-€3, free Wi-Fi, some traffic noise on streetside rooms—ask for quieter courtyard room, down the passage at Slovenska cesta 51 and around back, mobile 041-263-347, www.hotelcenter.si, info@hotelcenter.si).

$ Stari Tišler ("Old Carpenter") is a good budget option in a characteristically old, time-warp house immersed in a commercial zone a 10-minute walk from Prešeren Square. Its four modern rooms—which are nicely appointed for this price range—share two toilets and one shower, keeping prices low. It's above a restaurant that's popular at lunchtime with local businesspeople (D-€44, T-€66, breakfast-€5, up 2 flights of stairs, free Wi-Fi, Kolodvorska 8, tel. 01/430-3370, www.stari-tisler.com, info@stari-tisler.com, Sandra).

$ Penzion Pod Lipo, a lesser value, has 10 rooms above a restaurant in a mostly residential area about a 12-minute walk from Prešeren Square. While the rooms are old and simple, this is an acceptable budget option (Db-€58, Tb-€69, Qb-€92, breakfast in restaurant-€3.50 extra, cash only, reception open 8:00–24:00, non-smoking, guest kitchen, free Internet access, free cable Internet,

tel. 01/251-1683, mobile 031-809-893, www.penzion-podlipo.com, ko.mar2@siol.net, Marjan).

Hostels

Ljubljana has several good hostels. The ones listed here are particularly well-established.

$ Hostel Celica, a proud, innovative, and lively place, is funded by the city and run by a nonprofit student organization. This former military prison's 20 cells *(celica)* have been converted into hostel rooms—each one unique, decorated by a different designer (tours of the hostel daily at 14:00). The top floor features more typical hostel rooms (each with its own bathroom, for 3–12 people). The building also houses an art gallery, tourist information, Internet access and Wi-Fi, self-serve laundry (€7/load), good restaurant, and shoes-off "Oriental café" (all prices listed are per person—cell rooms: S-€47, D-€28, T-€23; bed in top-floor rooms with bathrooms: 3- to 5-bed room-€26, 6- to 7-bed dorm-€23, 12-bed dorm-€21; includes breakfast, sheets, towels, and tax; no curfew, non-smoking, bike and car rental, active excursions around Slovenia, Metelkova 8, a dull 15-min walk to Prešeren Square, 8 min to the train station, tel. 01/230-9700, fax 01/230-9714, www.hostelcelica.com, recepcija@souhostel.si). Light sleepers take note: The hostel hosts live music events about two nights per week until around 24:00, but otherwise maintains "quiet time" after 23:00. However, the surrounding neighborhood—a bit run-down and remote, but safe—is a happening nightlife zone, which can make for noisy weekends.

$ Alibi Hostel, an official IYHF hostel creatively run by Gorazd, has two very different branches. For a grungy, funky backpacker scene, head for **Alibi CN27,** with 100 beds (including five private rooms). The rooms are colorful and scruffy, and it's ideally located right on Ljubljana's main riverfront-café drag. The imaginative graffiti murals—featuring a stripper with memorable piercings and a certain cowboy president—are guaranteed to offend just about anyone over 30 (dorm bed-€17, or €19 Fri–Sat; D-€50, or €60 Fri–Sat; includes sheets and tax, cheaper Oct–May, no breakfast, lockers, free Internet access and Wi-Fi, Cankarjevo nabrežje 27, tel. 01/251-1244, www.alibi.si). When backpackers grow a bit older and more sedate, they're more interested in comfort than socializing—and it's time to head for **Alibi M14,** across the street from Grand Hotel Union, a few steps off Prešeren Square. With five small but well-appointed private rooms, a 10-bed dorm (sharing one bathroom), and a pleasant kitchen—but not a lot of rowdy hangout areas—it's a good compromise (dorm bed-€18, or €20 Fri–Sat; D-€50, or €60 Fri–Sat; Db-€60, or €70 Fri–Sat; cheaper Oct–May, includes sheets and towels, coin-op laundry,

lockers, free Internet access and Wi-Fi, Miklošičeva cesta 14, tel. 01/232-2770, www.alibi.si, m14@alibi.si).

Eating in Ljubljana

At this crossroads of cultures (and cuisines), Italian and French flavors are just as "local" as meat-and-starch Slovenian food. This cosmopolitan city also dabbles in other cuisines; you'll find Thai, Indian, Chinese, Mexican, and more. To locate these restaurants, see the map on page 648.

Zlata Ribica ("Golden Fish") is along the castle side of the embankment, with pricey food but the best riverfront view in town. The menu features modern and traditional Slovenian cuisine and delicious pastas, especially the gnocchi (€9–15 pastas, €12–24 main dishes, daily 9:00–24:00, between the Triple and Cobblers' bridges at Cankarjevo nabrežje 5–7, tel. 01/241-2680).

Gostilna As ("Ace"), tucked into a courtyard just off Prešeren Square, offers fish-lovers the best blowout in town. It's dressy, pricey, and pretentious (waiters ignore the menu and recommend what's fresh). Everything is specially prepared each day and beautifully presented. It's loosely based on the Slow Food model: Servings are small, and you're expected to take your time and order two or three courses (mostly fish and Italian, €11-22 starters, €22–45 main dishes, daily 12:00–24:00, reservations smart, Čopova ulica 5A, or enter courtyard with *As* sign near image of Julija on Wolfova ulica, tel. 01/425-8822). For cheaper food from the same kitchen, eat at their attached **As Lounge.** This much livelier, more casual spot features drinks, €8-11 salads and sandwiches, €7–10 pastas, and €11–19 main dishes. You'll sit in the leafy courtyard or the glassed-in winter garden (food served daily 12:00–23:00, longer hours for drinks). The courtyard also has a couple of other fun eateries—and, in the summer only, live music and a much-loved gelato stand.

Ribca ("Fish")—not to be confused with Zlata Ribica, described earlier—hides under the first stretch of market colonnade near the Triple Bridge. This is your best bet for a relatively quick and cheap riverside lunch. Choose between the two straightforward menus: grilled fillets or fried small fish. With the fragrant fish market right next door, you know it's fresh. If you just want to enjoy sitting along the river below the bustling market, this is also a fine spot for a coffee or beer (€6 salads, €5–8 main dishes, Mon–Fri 8:00–16:00, Sat 8:00–14:00, closed Sun).

In the Old Town: The main drag through the Old Town (which starts at the Town Hall and changes names as it goes: Mestni trg, then Stari trg, then Gornji trg) is lined with inviting eateries. Tables spill into the cobbled pedestrian street, filled with happy diners. While I list no specific restaurants here, it's

only because I've tried several and they're uniformly good. (The across-the-street duet of Romeo and Julija, about halfway along this stretch, are both excellent; I've also enjoyed a great salad lunch at the Čajna Hiša tea house—described later, under "Coffee, Tea, and Treats.") If you're at a loss for where to eat, stroll here to survey your options, then pick your favorite menu and ambience.

Traditional Slovenian: Two restaurants in central Ljubljana serve up stick-to-your-ribs Slovenian fare. Because Slovenes head into the countryside when they want this sort of food, both of these places cater mostly to tourists—so don't expect top quality or a great value. But if you want a taste of traditional Slovenia, these are your handiest options in town. **Sokol,** with brisk, traditionally clad waiters, fills a fun, sprawling Slovenian-village interior with jaunty polka on the soundtrack and a very central location. It's in all the guidebooks and deluged by tourists, so don't expect an authentic experience (€8–22 main dishes, veggie options, Mon–Sat 7:00–23:00, Sun 10:00–23:00, on castle side of Triple Bridge at Ciril-Metodov trg 18, tel. 01/439-6855). A few blocks away, across from the main market square, **Vodnikov Hram** has an Old World interior and outdoor tables overlooking a parking lot. While a variation on the same theme as Sokol, it's marginally less touristy, and has slightly lower prices (€7–8 pastas, €7–25 main dishes, Mon–Sat 9:00–24:00, Sun 18:00–24:00, Vodnikov trg 2, tel. 01/234-5260).

Asian Fusion: **DaBuDa** is the best spot in Ljubljana for Asian cuisine, featuring good Thai dishes (salads, curries, wok meals, and noodles) in a very mod, dark-wood, split-level setting frequented by hip young professionals (good-value €6–7 lunch specials, €8–13 main dishes at dinner, Mon–Fri 11:00–23:00, Sat–Sun 12:00–23:00, also a few outdoor tables, between Congress Square and Square of the Republic at Šubičeva 1A, tel. 01/425-3060).

Pizzerias

Ljubljana has lots of great sit-down pizza places. Expect to pay €5–10 for an average-sized pie (wide variety of toppings).

Pizzeria Foculus, tucked in a boring alleyway a few blocks up from the river, has a loyal local following, a happening atmosphere, an innovative leafy interior, a few outdoor tables, and Ljubljana's best pizza (over 50 types for €5–9, €4–6 salads, Mon–Fri 10:00–24:00, Sat–Sun 12:00–24:00, just off French Revolution Square

across the street from Plečnik's National and University Library at Gregorčičeva 3, tel. 01/251-5643).

Ljubljanski Dvor enjoys the most convenient and scenic location of any pizzeria in town. On a sunny summer day, the outdoor riverside terrace is unbeatable. The interior has a simple pizza parlor downstairs (€5–11 pizzas and pastas), with a more refined dining room upstairs (selling the same pizzas and pastas, plus €12–20 Italian main dishes; pizza parlor open daily 10:00–24:00, upstairs restaurant opens at 12:00 and is closed Sun in winter, just 50 yards from Cobblers' Bridge at Dvorni trg 1, tel. 01/251-6555). They also have a cheap pizza take-out window (listed in the next section).

Fast and Cheap

Paninoteka serves tasty €3-4 grilled sandwiches, €4–6 wraps, and €6–7 salads right along the river. The outdoor seating—a prime people-watching vantage point, with the Cobblers' Bridge and the castle above—is particularly inviting on a sunny day (order at the display case for take-away, or sit at a table to be waited on; great vegetarian options, casual service, Mon–Sat 8:00–1:00 in the morning, Sun 9:00–23:00, fine outdoor seating, Jurčičev trg 3, mobile 059-018-455).

Burek, the typical Balkan phyllo-dough snack (see "Balkan Flavors" on page 753), can be picked up at street stands around town. Most are open 24 hours and charge about €2 for a hearty portion. An easy choice is **Nobel Burek,** next to Miklošičeva cesta 30; but many locals prefer **Olympia Burek,** around the corner at Pražakova ulica 14 (across from the post office).

Pizza Slices: **Ljubljanski Dvor,** listed earlier, has a walk-up window selling cheap pizza by the slice; from the riverfront, go around back to the walk-up window on Congress Square (€2 slices to go, picnic in the park or down on the river—plenty of welcoming benches, Mon–Sat 9:00–24:00, closed Sun).

In Krakovo

The Krakovo district—just south of the city center, where garden patches nearly outnumber simple homes—is a pleasant area to wander. It's also home to a pair of tasty restaurants. Consider combining a meal here with your trip to the Jože Plečnik House (which is just beyond Krakovo).

Pri Škofu ("By the Bishop") is a laid-back, informal place with mostly outdoor seating and a focus on freshness, serving international cuisine with a Slovenian flair. There's no menu—the waiter tells you what's good today...and it is. They'll ask what kind of pasta or meat you want, then help you narrow down your options (sauces, sides, etc.) to get to your ideal meal. This hidden

gem is deliciously memorable and worth seeking out. Reservations are essential (creative €3 soups, €7–8 lunches, €7–17 main dishes at dinner, homemade €3 desserts, Mon–Fri 10:00–24:00, Sat–Sun 12:00–24:00, Rečna 8, tel. 01/426-4508).

Harambaša is the closest thing to a ticket to Sarajevo. Serving Balkan grilled meats, this popular-with-students eatery has Bosnian-flavored decor, old pictures, and cuisine reminiscent of the Bosnian capital. For a refresher on the meat dishes, see "Balkan Flavors" on page 753. The menu is limited, which makes ordering easy. Their handy €6.50 *pola-pola* combo-plate—with lotsa meat combined with chopped onions, *kajmak* (a buttery spread), and *lepinja* (bread)—makes for a simple but filling lunch. Also consider the Turkish coffee (a high-octane brew with "mud" at the bottom) and baklava. Vegetarians need not apply (€5–7 main dishes, Mon–Fri 10:00–22:00, Sat 12:00–22:00, Sun 12:00–18:00, Vrtna ulica 8, mobile 041-843-106).

Coffee, Tea, and Treats

Riverfront Cafés: Enjoying a coffee, beer, or ice-cream cone along the Ljubljanica River embankment (between the Triple and Cobblers' bridges) is Ljubljana's single best experience—worth ▲▲▲. Tables spill into the street, and some of the best-dressed, best-looking students on the planet happily fill them day and night. (A common question from first-time visitors to Ljubljana: "Doesn't anybody here have a job?") This is some of the top people-watching in Europe. Rather than recommend a particular place (they're all about the same), I'll leave you to explore and find the spot with the breezy ambience you like best. When ordering, the easiest choice is a *bela kava*—"white coffee," basically a caffè latte.

Tea House: If coffee's not your cup of tea, go a block inland to the teahouse **Čajna Hiša.** They have a shop (called "Cha") with over 100 varieties of tea, plus porcelain teapots and cups from all over (Mon–Fri 9:00–20:00, Sat 9:00–13:30, closed Sun). The café serves about 50 different types of tea, light food (including great salads), and desserts (€3 cakes and sandwiches, €5–8 salads, Mon–Fri 9:00–22:30, Sat 9:00–15:00 & 18:00–22:00, closed Sun, on the atmospheric main drag in the Old Town a few steps from Cobblers' Bridge at Stari trg 3, tel. 01/252-7010).

Cakes: **Zvezda Kavarna,** a trendy, central place at the bottom of Congress Square, is a local favorite for cakes, pastries, and ice cream (decadent €3–4 cakes, Mon–Sat 7:00–23:00, Sun

10:00–20:00, a block up from Prešeren Square at Wolfova 14, tel. 01/421-9090). **Abecedarium** (ah-beh-tseh-dah-ree-oom, like the alphabet) serves up delicious €4 Nutella-banana cake (and other food) with indoor or outdoor seating near the Triple Bridge. It's located in the oldest house in town, named for a work by one of Slovenia's greatest thinkers, who also lived in the house (daily 8:00–24:00, Ribji trg 2, tel. 01/426-9514).

Chocolates and Ice Cream: **Rustika** is a local chain that sells tasty homemade chocolates (€3.50/100 grams), cookies (including one with three different kinds of chocolate), and a wide variety of unusual and delicious artisan ice cream flavors. The menu changes from day to day, but highlights can include balsamic vinegar with vanilla or strawberry, very dark chocolate, Kanada (with maple syrup and walnuts), and Greek yogurt with honey and nuts. The handiest location is about an eight-minute walk from Prešeren Square, and comes with a delightful stroll along colorful Trubarjeva street (€1/scoop, Mon–Fri 8:00–20:00, Sat 9:00–14:00, closed Sun, Trubarjeva 44, mobile 059-935-730).

More Ice Cream: Ljubljana is known for its Italian gelato–style ice cream. You'll see fine options all along the Ljubljanica River embankment. Favorites include the courtyard garden at **Gostilna As** (summer only) and **Zvezda Kavarna** (both described above).

Ljubljana Connections

As Slovenia's transportation hub, Ljubljana is well-connected to both domestic and international destinations. When checking schedules, be aware of name variations: In Slovene, Vienna is "Dunaj" and Budapest is "Budimpešta."

Getting to Croatia

To reach **Istria** by public transportation, you have two relatively straightforward options: In summer (June–late Sept), a direct bus departs Ljubljana for Rovinj each day (around 13:45, 5.5 hrs, €22, no buses off-season; also stops en route in Piran and Poreč). Mondays through Fridays year-round, there's also a train connection to Pula (departs around 13:20, 3.5 hrs, changes in Divača, Slovenia, and Buzet, Croatia); once in Pula, you can connect by bus to other Istrian destinations. On off-season weekends, you might have to get creative (try connecting through Rijeka).

If connecting directly to Croatia's **Dalmatian Coast,** you have three options: Train to Zagreb (2.5 hrs), where you can catch a cheap Croatia Air flight or a bus (see "Zagreb Connections" on page 932); take the long, once-daily train connection from Ljubljana to Split (8 hrs, requires a change in Zagreb); or, much slower, take the train to Rijeka, then cruise on a boat down the

coast from there. (For specifics on flights, buses, and boats, see "Getting to the Dalmatian Coast," page 745.)

By Train

From Ljubljana by Train to: Lesce-Bled (roughly hourly, 40–60 min—but bus is better because it goes right to Bled town center), **Postojna** (nearly hourly, 1 hr), **Divača** (close to Škocjan caves and Lipica, nearly hourly, 1.75 hrs), **Piran** (direct bus is better—see below; otherwise allow 4 hours, train to Koper, 5/day, 2.5 hrs; then bus to Piran, 7/day, 30 min), **Maribor** (hourly, 2–3 hrs, more with a transfer in Zidani Most), **Ptuj** (3/day, 2.5 hrs, more with transfer in Pragersko), **Zagreb** (8/day, 2.5 hrs), **Rijeka** (2–3/day direct, 2.5 hrs), **Pula** (1/day Mon–Fri, none Sat–Sun, 3.5 hrs, transfer in Divača, Slovenia, and Buzet, Croatia), **Split** (1/day, 9 hrs, transfer in Zagreb), **Vienna** (that's ***Dunaj*** in Slovene, 1/day direct, 6 hrs; otherwise 6/day with transfer in Villach, Maribor, or Graz, 6–7 hrs), **Budapest** (that's ***Budimpešta*** in Slovene; 6/day, 8–9 hrs, 1–2 changes, night train departs Ljubljana around 2:00 in the morning), **Venice** (1/day direct, 4 hrs; plus 1/day with a change to a bus in Villach, 6.75 hrs), **Salzburg** (4/day direct, 5 hrs), **Munich** (3/day direct, 6 hrs, including 1 night train; otherwise transfer in Salzburg). Train info: tel. 01/291-3332, www.slo-zeleznice.si.

By Bus

The bus station is a low-profile building in front of the train station. Buses depart from the numbered stalls in the middle of the street. For any bus, you have to buy tickets at the bus station ticket windows, not from the driver. Bus info: www.ap-ljubljana.si, tel. 090-4230 (toll number—about €0.75/min).

By Bus to: Bled (Mon–Sat hourly—usually at the top of each hour, fewer on Sun, 1.25 hrs, €6.30), **Postojna** (at least hourly, 1 hr, €6), **Divača** (close to Škocjan caves and Lipica, about every 2 hrs, 1.5 hrs, €7.90), **Piran** (6/day, 2.5 hrs, €12), over the **Vršič Pass** to **Bovec** (1/day July–Aug, departs Ljubljana 6:30, arrives Bovec 10:45, €13.10; off-season only Sat–Sun), **Rovinj** (1/day June–late Sept, departs Ljubljana around 13:45, 5.5 hrs, €22, no buses off-season), **Rijeka** (2/day, 2.5 hrs).

By Plane

Slovenia's only **airport** (airport code: LJU) is 14 miles north of Ljubljana, about halfway to Bled. Confusingly, the airport goes by three names: Ljubljana Airport (the international version); Brnik (for the town that it's near); and Jože Pučnik Airport (a politician for whom it was controversially renamed in 2007). Most flights are operated by Slovenia's national airline, Adria Airways

(www.adria-airways.com), but others are run by easyJet (www.easyjet.com), Wizz Air (www.wizzair.com), Czech Airlines (www.csa.cz), and others. There's a TI in the airport's arrivals hall. If you're killing time here, follow signs (around to the right as you face the outside of the terminal) to *Razgledna Terasa* and ride the elevator up to the rooftop terrace (with a café). Here you can sip a coffee while you watch planes land and take off. Airport info: tel. 04/206-1000, www.lju-airport.si.

Getting Between Downtown Ljubljana and the Airport: Two kinds of buses connect the airport with Ljubljana's bus station: **public bus** #28 (to the right as you exit the airport; Mon–Fri hourly until 20:00, only 7/day Sat–Sun, 45 min, €4.10), and a **minibus** (to the left as you exit the airport, scheduled to depart after various arriving flights—look for schedule posted near bus stop). Two different companies run the minibus transfers, which take about 30 minutes: Markun (€5 to train station, €9 to your hotel, mobile 041-792-865) and Marko Nowotny (€8 regardless of your destination, mobile 040-771-771, www.airport-shuttle.si). I'd take whichever one is departing first. For a transfer *to* the airport, your hotel can make arrangements with one of these companies a day or so in advance (same price). Unfortunately, certain evening arrivals don't coordinate well with either the bus or the minibus, so you might have to wait a while or take a costly **taxi** (figure €20–25 to the airport, but more like €42 *from* the airport—since you have to use the pricey taxi stand out front).

The Austrian Alternative: Since Ljubljana's airport is the only one in the country and thus charges extremely high taxes and airport fees, many Slovenes prefer to fly out of Austria. The airport in **Klagenfurt** (airport code: KLU, also known as "Alpe-Adria Airport"), just over the Austrian border to the north, is subsidized by the local government to keep prices low and compete with Ljubljana's airport. Especially if you're connecting to Bled, it's somewhat handy to reach (from Ljubljana or Bled, take the train to Villach, then to Klagenfurt's Annabichl station, which is a 5-min walk from the airport; total trip 3 hrs from Ljubljana, or 2 hrs from Bled; www.klagenfurt-airport.com). A taxi transfer to Bled runs a hefty €120 and takes about an hour (see "By Taxi" on page 693). Austrian Airlines (www.aua.com) flies from Klagenfurt, as do low-cost carriers such as Ryanair (www.ryanair.com), TUIfly (www.tuifly.com), Germanwings (www.germanwings.com), and Air Berlin (www.airberlin.com).

LAKE BLED

Lake Bled—Slovenia's leading mountain resort—comes complete with a sweeping alpine panorama, a fairy-tale island, a cliff-hanging medieval castle, a lazy lakeside promenade, and the country's most sought-after desserts. While Bled has all the modern resort-town amenities, its most endearing qualities are its stunning setting, its natural romanticism, and its fun-loving wedding parties.

Since the Habsburg days, Lake Bled (locals pronounce it "blayd") has been *the* place where Slovenes wow visiting diplomats. Tito had one of his vacation homes here (today's Hotel Vila Bled), and more recent visitors have included Prince Charles, Madeleine Albright, and Laura Bush. But above all, Lake Bled feels like a place that Slovenes enjoy alongside their visitors.

Lake Bled has plenty of ways to idle away an afternoon. While the lake's main town, also called Bled, is more functional than quaint, it offers postcard views of the lake and handy access to the region. Hike up to Bled Castle for intoxicating vistas. Make a wish and ring the bell at the island church. Wander the dreamy path around the lake. Sit on a dock, dip your feet in the water, and feed some of the lake's resident swans. Then dive into some of Bled's famous cakes while you take in the view of Triglav, Slovenia's favorite mountain (see "Mount Triglav" sidebar on page 720). Bled quiets down at night—no nightlife beyond a handful of pubs—giving hikers and other holiday-makers a chance to recharge. Bled is also a great jumping-off point for a car trip through the Julian Alps (see next chapter).

Bled and the Julian Alps Essentials

English	Slovene	Pronounced
Slovenia's Biggest Mountain	Triglav	TREE-glahv
Lake Bled	Blejsko Jezero	BLAY-skoh YAY-zay-roh
The Island	Otok	OH-tohk
Bled Castle	Blejski Grad	BLAY-skee grahd
Town near Bled with Train Station	Lesce	lest-SEH
Town with Bee Museum	Radovljica	rah-DOH-vleet-suh
Gorge near Bled	Vintgar	VEENT-gar
Rustic Lake near Bled	Bohinj	BOH-heen
Scenic High-Mountain Pass	Vršič	vur-SHEECH
Historic River Valley	Soča	SOH-chah

Planning Your Time

Bled and its neighboring mountains deserve two days. With one day, spend it in and around Bled (or, to rush things, spend the morning in Bled and the afternoon day-tripping). With a second day and a car, drive through the Julian Alps using the self-guided tour in the next chapter. The circular route takes you up and over the stunning Vršič Pass, then down the scenic and historic Soča River Valley. Without a car, skip the second day, or spend it doing nearby day trips: Bus or bike to Radovljica to see the bee museum, hike to Vintgar Gorge, or visit the more rustic Lake Bohinj (all described under "Near Lake Bled," at the end of this chapter).

Orientation to Lake Bled

(area code: 04)

The town of Bled is on the east end of 1.5-mile-long Lake Bled. The lakefront is lined with cafés and resort hotels. A 3.5-mile path meanders around the lake. As no motorized boats are allowed, Lake Bled is particularly peaceful.

The tourists' center of Bled is a cluster of big resort hotels, dominated by the giant, red Hotel Park (dubbed the "red can"). The

busy street called **Ljubljanska cesta** leads out of Bled town toward Ljubljana and most other destinations. Just up from the lakefront, across Ljubljanska cesta from Hotel Park, is the modern **commercial center** (Trgovski Center Bled), with a travel agency, grocery store, ATM, shops, and a smattering of lively cafés. Nicknamed "Gaddafi" by the people of Bled, the commercial center was designed for a Libyan city, but the deal fell through—so the frugal Slovenes built it here instead. Just up the road from the commercial center, you'll find the post office and library (with Internet access).

Bled's less-touristy Old Town is under the castle, surrounding the pointy spire of St. Martin's Church. There you'll find the bus station, some good restaurants, a few hostels, and more locals than tourists.

The mountains poking above the ridge at the far end of the lake are the Julian Alps, crowned by the three peaks of Mount Triglav. The big mountain behind the town of Bled is Stol ("Chair"), part of the Karavanke range that defines the Austrian border.

Tourist Information

Bled's helpful TI is in the long, lakefront casino building across the street from the big, red Hotel Park (as you face the lake, the TI is hiding around the front at the far left end, overlooking the lake). Pick up the good map (with the lake on one side and the whole region on the other) and the free Bled information booklet. Get advice on hikes and day trips, confirm transit schedules, and if you're doing any serious hiking, spring for a good regional map (July–Aug Mon–Sat 8:00–21:00, Sun 9:00–17:00; May–June and Sept Mon–Sat 8:00–19:00, Sun 11:00–17:00; Oct–April Mon–Sat 8:00–18:00, Sun 8:00–13:00; Cesta Svobode 10, tel. 04/574-1122, www.bled.si). The TI can give you a list of accommodations, but they can't find you a room (book direct or use Kompas Bled Travel Agency's room-booking service—see "Helpful Hints," later).

For more details on hiking in Triglav National Park, pay a visit to the new **Triglav National Park Information Center** on the main road out of town (free information, maps and guidebooks for sale, possible charge for exhibition, Tue–Sun 10:00–18:00, closed Mon, Ljubljanska cesta 27, tel. 04/578-0200, www.tnp.si).

Arrival in Bled

By Train: Two train stations have the name "Bled." The **Bled Jezero** ("Bled Lake") station is across the lake from Bled town and is used only by infrequent, slow, tourist-oriented trains into the mountains. You're much more likely to use the **Lesce-Bled** station in the nearby village of Lesce. The Lesce-Bled station is on the main line and has far better connections to Ljubljana and international destinations. So if you're buying a train ticket or checking

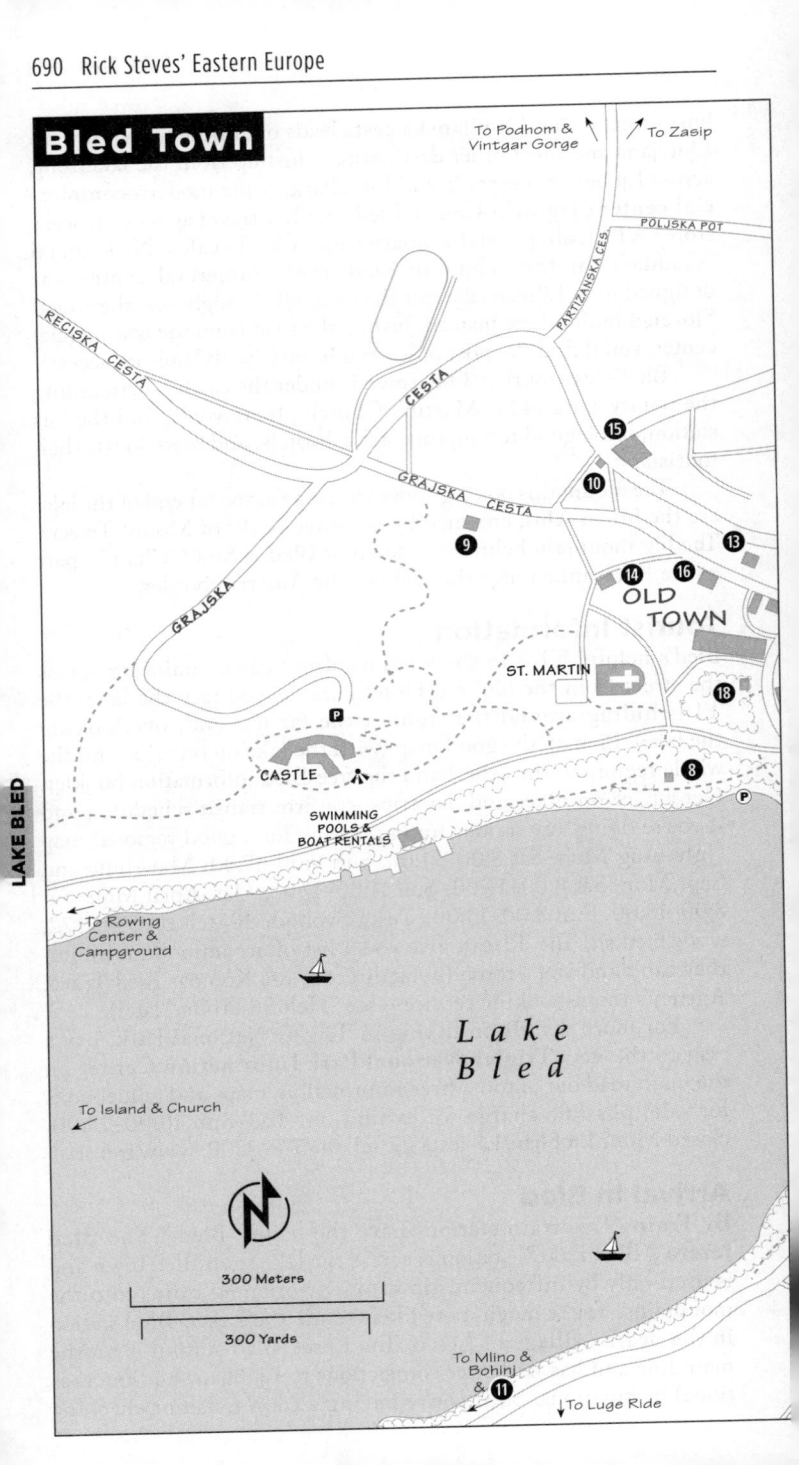
Bled Town
To Podhom & Vintgar Gorge
To Zasip
POLJSKA POT
PARTIZANSKA CES.
RECIŠKA CESTA
CESTA
GRAJSKA CESTA
GRAJSKA
15
10
9
13
14
16
OLD TOWN
ST. MARTIN
18
P
CASTLE
8
P
SWIMMING POOLS & BOAT RENTALS
LAKE BLED
To Rowing Center & Campground
Lake Bled
To Island & Church
N
300 Meters
300 Yards
To Mlino & Bohinj &
11
To Luge Ride

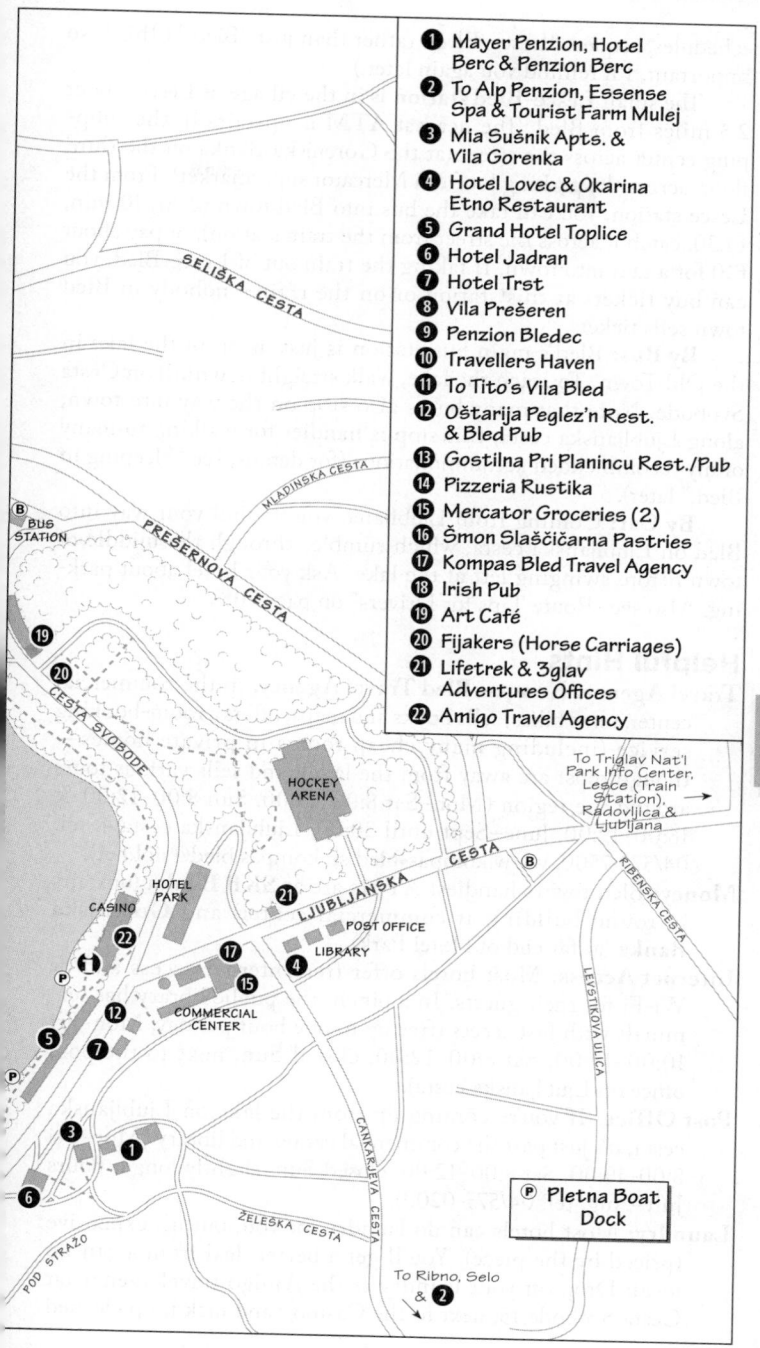
1 Mayer Penzion, Hotel Berc & Penzion Berc
2 To Alp Penzion, Essense Spa & Tourist Farm Mulej
3 Mia Sušnik Apts. & Vila Gorenka
4 Hotel Lovec & Okarina Etno Restaurant
5 Grand Hotel Toplice
6 Hotel Jadran
7 Hotel Trst
8 Vila Prešeren
9 Penzion Bledec
10 Travellers Haven
11 To Tito's Vila Bled
12 Oštarija Peglez'n Rest. & Bled Pub
13 Gostilna Pri Planincu Rest./Pub
14 Pizzeria Rustika
15 Mercator Groceries (2)
16 Šmon Slaščičarna Pastries
17 Kompas Bled Travel Agency
18 Irish Pub
19 Art Café
20 Fijakers (Horse Carriages)
21 Lifetrek & 3glav Adventures Offices
22 Amigo Travel Agency
SELIŠKA CESTA
MLADINSKA CESTA
BUS STATION
PREŠERNOVA CESTA
CESTA SVOBODE
HOCKEY ARENA
To Triglav Nat'l Park Info Center, Lesce (Train Station), Radovljica & Ljubljana
LJUBLJANSKA CESTA
RIBENSKA CESTA
HOTEL PARK
CASINO
POST OFFICE
LIBRARY
COMMERCIAL CENTER
LEVSTIKOVA ULICA
CANKARJEVA CESTA
ŽELEŠKA CESTA
POD STRAŽO
Pletna Boat Dock
To Ribno, Selo & 2

schedules, request "Lesce-Bled" rather than just "Bled." (This is so important, I'll remind you again later.)

The small **Lesce-Bled station** is in the village of Lesce, about 2.5 miles from Bled. The nearest ATM is upstairs in the shopping center across the street (at the Gorenjska Banka on the third floor, across the parking lot from Mercator supermarket). From the Lesce station, you can take the bus into Bled town (2/hr, 10 min, €1.30, catch it across the street from the train station); or pay about €10 for a taxi into town. If taking the train out of Lesce-Bled, you can buy tickets at this station or on the train—nobody in Bled town sells tickets.

By Bus: Bled's main bus station is just up from the lake in the Old Town. To reach the lake, walk straight downhill on Cesta Svobode. Note that many buses also stop on the way into town, along Ljubljanska cesta; this stop is handier for walking to many of my recommended accommodations (for details, see "Sleeping in Bled," later).

By Car: Coming from Ljubljana, you'll wind your way into Bled on Ljubljanska cesta, which rumbles through the middle of town before swinging left at the lake. Ask your hotel about parking. Also see "Route Tips for Drivers" on page 708.

Helpful Hints

Travel Agency: Kompas Bled Travel Agency, in the commercial center, rents bikes, sells books and maps, offers a room-booking service (including many cheap rooms in private homes—though most are away from the lake), and sells various tours around the region (Mon–Sat 8:00–19:00, Sun 8:00–12:00 & 16:00–19:00, June–Sept until 20:00, Ljubljanska cesta 4, tel. 04/572-7500, www.kompas-bled.si, kompas.bled@siol.net).

Money: Bled town's handiest ATMs are at **SKB Banka** (upstairs in round building at commercial center) and **Gorenjska Banka** (at far end of Hotel Park).

Internet Access: Most hotels offer free Internet access and/or Wi-Fi for their guests. In a pinch, the public library has terminals with fast access (free up to one hour per day, Mon–Fri 10:00–19:00, Sat 8:00–12:00, closed Sun, next to the post office on Ljubljanska cesta).

Post Office: If you're coming up from the lake on Ljubljanska cesta, it's just past the commercial center and library (Mon–Fri 8:00–19:00, Sat 8:00–12:00, closed Sun, slightly longer hours July–Aug, tel. 04/575-0200).

Laundry: Most hotels can do laundry for you, but it's expensive (priced by the piece). You'll get a better deal from a can-do local: Drop off your laundry at the Amigo travel agency (at Cesta Svobode 15, next to the Casino), and pick it up cleaned

and folded 24 hours later (€15/load, €5 more for same-day express service, Anže Štalc, call first to arrange, mobile 041-575-522).

Car Rental: The Julian Alps are ideal by car. Several big chains rent cars in Bled—figure €60 per day, including tax, insurance, and unlimited mileage (generally no extra charge for drop-off elsewhere in Slovenia). Various major companies have branches in Bled, including **Europcar** (mobile 031-382-055), **Budget** (tel. 04/578-0320), **National** (mobile 041-400-980), and **Sixt** (tel. 04/578-0120), but as the offices tend to move around, inquire in Bled about the current locations.

Massage: If you're here to relax, consider a massage at the **Essense** wellness center at the recommended Alp Penzion. This modern, classy facility—hiding in the countryside about a 15-minute walk or five-minute taxi ride above the lake—offers a wide range of spa treatments, including pedicure, Thai massage, and Indian ayurveda massage (with warm oils). A standard 50-minute massage will run you about €30 (call first to arrange, Cankarjeva cesta 20A, tel. 04/576-7450, www.alp-penzion.com).

Getting Around Lake Bled (Literally)

By Bike: You can rent a mountain bike at the TI or at Kompas Bled Travel Agency (both listed earlier) for the same rates (€3.50/hr, €6/3 hrs, €8/half-day, €11/day). While walking around the lake is slo-mo bliss, biking around it is also enjoyable. For a longer pedal, ask for the TI's excellent biking map, with various great bike trips clearly marked and described. The bike path to the nearby town of Radovljica (and its bee museum) is about four miles one-way (get details at the TI).

By Horse and Buggy: Buggies called *fijakers* are the romantic, expensive, and easy way to get around the lake. You'll see them along the lakefront between Hotel Park and the castle (around the lake-€30, one-way up to castle-€30, round-trip to castle with 30-min wait time-€40, mobile 041-710-970).

By Tourist Train: A little train makes a circuit around the lake every 40 minutes in summer (€3, daily 9:00–21:00 in peak season, shorter hours off-season, weather-dependent, mobile 051-337-478).

By Tourist Bus: A handy shuttle bus passes through Bled once daily in summer. It leaves the bus station at 10:00, stops at a few hotels (including Grand Hotel Toplice), then goes up to the castle and on to the Vintgar Gorge entrance (€3.50, mid-June–Sept only, confirm schedule at TI or bus station).

By Taxi: Your hotel can call a taxi for you. Or contact **Bled Tours,** run by friendly, English-speaking driver Sandi Demšar

and his girlfriend Cvetka (€10 to the castle or to Lesce-Bled train station, €14 to Radovljica, €50 to Ljubljana airport, €120 to Klagenfurt airport in Austria, mobile 031-205-611, info@bledtours.si).

By Boat: For information on renting your own boat, see "Boating," page 700. For details on riding the characteristic *pletna* boats, see "Getting to the Island," page 697.

By Private Plane: If you have deep pockets and the weather is perfect, there's no more thrilling way to experience Slovenia's high-mountain scenery than from a small propeller plane soaring over the peaks. Flights depart from a grass airstrip near the village of Lesce, a 10-minute drive or taxi ride from Bled. Expensive...but unforgettable (€75 for 15-min hop over Lake Bled only, €135 for 30-min flight that also buzzes Lake Bohinj, €195 for deluxe 45-min version around the summit of Triglav, arrange at least a day in advance, tel. 04/532-0100, www.alc-lesce.si, info@alc-lesce.si).

Tours at Lake Bled

Local Guides—**Tina Hiti** and **Sašo Golub** are excellent guides who enjoy sharing the town and region they love with American visitors. Hiring one of them can add immeasurably to your enjoyment and understanding of Bled (€30/2 hrs, arrange several days in advance; Tina: mobile 040-166-554, tinahiti@gmail.com; Sašo: mobile 040-524-774, sasogolub@gmail.com). Either one can drive you in their car on a long day tour into the Julian Alps—or anywhere in Slovenia—for €120. (This price is for two people; it's more expensive for three or more people, since they have to rent a van.) I've spent great days with both Tina and Sašo and was thankful they were behind the wheel. If these two are busy, they might send Tina's father, Gorazd—a former Yugoslav Olympian (in ice hockey) who brings the older generation's perspective to the trip (and speaks fine English).

Excursions—To hit several far-flung day-trip destinations in one go, you could take a package tour from Bled. Destinations range from Ljubljana and the Karst region to the Austrian Lakes to Venice. For example, an all-day Julian Alps trip to the Vršič Pass and Soča Valley runs about €35 (sold by various agencies, including Kompas Bled). This tour is handy, but two people can rent a car for the day for about the same price and do it at their own pace using the self-guided driving tour in the next chapter.

Adventure Trips—Various Bled-based companies specialize in taking tourists on active, outdoorsy excursions into the surrounding countryside and mountains. One popular, all-day trip is white-water rafting on the Soča River (around €90). Other

options include canyoning, river tubing, mountain biking, paragliding, rock climbing, and more. Various outfits cluster near the commercial center; these include **3glav Adventures** (just above commercial center at Ljubljanska cesta 1, mobile 041-683-184, www.3glav-adventures.com), **Lifetrek Adventures** (next to 3glav at Ljubljanska cesta 1, mobile 040-508-853, www.lifetrek-slovenia.com), and **Amigo** (next to the Casino at Cesta Svobode 15, tel. 05/597-3250, www.amigo.si). Note that these companies tend to attract a young, sometimes rowdy crowd that enjoys lubricating their adventures with plenty of alcohol.

Sights at Lake Bled

Bled doesn't have many "sights," but there are plenty of rewarding and pleasant activities.

▲▲▲Walk Around the Lake—Strolling the 3.5 miles around the lake is enjoyable, peaceful, and scenic. At a leisurely pace, it takes about an hour and a half...not counting stops to snap photos of the ever-changing view. On the way, you'll pass some great villas, mostly from the beginning of the 19th century. The most significant one was a former residence of Marshal Tito—today the Hotel Vila Bled, a great place to stop for a coffee and pretend Tito invited you over for a visit (described next). For the more adventurous, hiking paths lead up into the hills surrounding the lake (ask TI for details and maps; or hike to Vintgar Gorge, described on page 712).

▲Tito's Vila Bled—Before World War II, this villa on Lake Bled was the summer residence for the Yugoslav royal family. When Tito ran Yugoslavia, the part-Slovene communist leader took over the place and had it renovated using plans from the architect Jože Plečnik. During his heyday, Tito entertained international guests here (big shots from the communist and non-aligned world, from Indira Gandhi to Nikita Khrushchev to Kim Il Sung to Raúl Castro). Since 1984, it's been a classy hotel and restaurant, offering guests grand Lake Bled views and ambience worthy of James Bond. The garden surrounding the villa is filled with exotic trees, brought here by Tito's guests from distant lands.

The terrace has a restaurant that welcomes visitors to drop in for a meal, a piece of cake, or just a cup of coffee. Tito fans might want to splurge for an overnight (standard Db-€210, tel. 04/579-1500, www.vila-bled.com). But even if you're not a guest here, the hotel's staff is generally tolerant of curious tourists poking around

the public areas inside. From the marbled lobby, head upstairs. This is where Tito fans have a nostalgic opportunity to send an email from Tito's desk, sip tea in his lounge, and gawk at his **Socialist Realist wall murals.** Those murals, decorating the upper walls of a vast ballroom on the second floor, are a fascinating peek at the propaganda of the time. Follow the rousing story of the origins of postwar Yugoslavia, starting on the upper left as you enter: First you see the Nazi destruction of Belgrade in 1941, a dark moment that inspired the South Slavs to band together to fight these foreign occupiers. See Tito raising his ragtag army, then leading them into pivotal battles in Bosnia-Herzegovina (notice the minaret and the destroyed bridge over the Neretva River), followed by a winter spent enduring hardship. At the end of this long wall, Tito's victorious Partisans crush the final vestiges of the Nazis; in the upper-right corner, the spring blossoms represent a promising future for the people of Yugoslavia. The large panel at the end of the room trumpets the idealized postwar world that Tito envisioned: proud workers from all walks of life coming together for the betterment of Yugoslavia. In the shadow of a mighty factory—a symbol of heavy industry, which communists embraced as the way of the future—notice that the ironworker and the farmer are literally holding hands in unity. The room's focal point is the mother hoisting a young child with one arm, and the flag of the nascent Socialist Federal Republic of Yugoslavia with the other.

Getting There: The villa is a 20-minute lakeside walk from the town of Bled at Cesta Svobode 26 (it's the big, white villa with the long staircase at the southern end of the lake, just beyond the village of Mlino). You can also ask your *pletna* gondolier to drop you off here after visiting the island. Those hiking around the lake will pass the gate leading up through Tito's garden to the restaurant and lobby.

▲▲The Island (Otok)—Bled's little island—capped by a supercute church—nudges the lake's quaintness level over the top. Locals call it simply "The Island" *(Otok)*. While it's pretty to look at from afar, it's also fun to visit.

The island has long been a sacred site with

a romantic twist. On summer Saturdays, a steady procession of brides and grooms, cheered on by their entourages, heads for the island. Ninety-nine steps lead from the island's dock up to the Church of the Assumption on top. It's tradition for the groom to carry—or try to carry—his bride up these steps. About four out of five are successful (proving themselves "fit for marriage"). During the communist era, the church was closed, and weddings were outlawed here. But the tradition re-emerged—illegally—even before the regime ended, with a clandestine ceremony in 1989.

An eighth-century Slavic pagan temple dedicated to the goddess of love and fertility once stood here; the current Baroque version (with Venetian flair—the bell tower separate from the main church) is the fifth to occupy this spot. Go inside (€3, daily May–Sept 9:00–19:00, Oct and April until 18:00, Nov–March until 16:00) and find the rope for the church bell, hanging in the middle of the aisle just before the altar. A local superstition claims that if you can get this bell to ring three times with one big pull of the rope, your dreams will come true. Worth a try.

If you're waiting for a herd of tourists to ring out their wishes, pass the time looking around the front of the church. When the church was being renovated in the 1970s, workers dug up several medieval graves (you can see one through the glass under the bell rope). They also discovered Gothic frescoes on either side of the altar, including, above the door on the right, an unusual ecclesiastical theme: the *bris* (Jewish circumcision ritual) of Christ.

A café (with a WC) and souvenir shop (with an exhibit of nativity scenes) are near the church at the top of the steps.

To descend by a different route, walk down the trail behind the church, then follow the path around the island's perimeter back to where your *pletna* boat awaits.

Getting to the Island: The most romantic route to the island is to cruise on one of the distinctive ***pletna*** boats (€12 per person round-trip, includes 30-min wait time at the island; catch one at several spots around the lake—most convenient from in front of Grand Hotel Toplice or just below Hotel Park, might have to wait for more passengers to fill the boat, generally run from dawn until around 20:00 in summer, stop earlier off-season, replaced by enclosed electric boats in winter—unless the lake freezes—mobile 031-316-575). For more on these characteristic little vessels, see the "*Pletna* Boats" sidebar. You can also **rent your own boat** to row to the island (see "Boating," later). It's even possible to **swim** to the

Pletna Boats

The *pletna* is an important symbol of Lake Bled. In addition to providing a pleasant way to reach the island, these boats also carry on a tradition dating back for generations. In the 17th century, Habsburg Empress Maria Theresa granted the villagers from Mlino—the little town along the lakefront just beyond Bled—special permission to ferry visitors to the island. (Since Mlino had very limited access to farmland, the people needed another source of income.) Mlino residents built their *pletnas* by hand, using a special design passed down from father to son for centuries—like the equally iconic gondolas of Venice. Eventually, this imperial decree and family tradition evolved into a modern union of *pletna* oarsmen, which continues to this day.

Today *pletna* boats are still hand-built according to that same centuries-old design. There's no keel, so the skilled oarsmen work hard to steer the flat-bottomed boat with each stroke—boats piloted by an inexperienced oarsman can slide around on very windy days. There are 21 official *pletnas* on Lake Bled, all belonging to the same union. The gondoliers dump all of their earnings into one fund, give a cut to the tourist board, and divide the rest evenly among themselves. Occasionally a new family tries to break into the cartel, underselling their competitors with a "black market" boat that looks the same as the official ones. While some see this as a violation of a centuries-old tradition, others view it as good old capitalism. Either way, competition is fierce.

island, especially from the end of the lake nearest the island (see "Swimming," later), but you're not allowed into the church in your swimsuit.

▲Bled Castle (Blejski Grad)—Bled's cliff-hanging castle, dating in one form or another from 1,000 years ago, was the seat of the Austrian Bishops of Brixen, who controlled Bled in the Middle Ages. Your castle admission includes a newly spruced-up castle museum (with interesting videos, creaky rooms, and good

English descriptions); a small theater continuously showing a fun 20-minute movie about Bled (under the restaurant); a tiny chapel with 3-D frescoes that make it seem much bigger than it is; and a rampart walk with an "herbal gallery" (gift shop of traditional-meets-modern herbal brandies, cosmetics, and perfumes). While these attractions are nothing exciting, the real reason to come up here is to bask in the sweeping views over Lake Bled and the surrounding mountainscapes (€7, daily May–Oct 8:00–20:00, Nov–April 9:00–17:00, tel. 04/572-9782).

In addition, the castle is home to a pair of interesting, old-fashioned shops: You can visit a working replica of a **printing press** *(grajska tiskarna)* from Gutenberg's time and print your own custom-made souvenir certificate for €5–10 (in the castle's oldest tower—from the 11th century). Or, at the **wine cellar** *(grajska klet de Adami),* bottle and cork your own bottle of wine (€10–15). These attractions are manned by a pair of gregarious guys, one dressed as a medieval printer and the other as a monk. Both men happen to be named Andrej (they switch costumes sometimes for a change of pace). Both shops are generally open daily in summer 10:00–18:00 (less off-season; if one of the shops is closed, the other should be open).

Eating at the Castle: The **restaurant** at the castle is fairly expensive, but your restaurant reservation gets you into the castle grounds for free (international cuisine and some local specialties, €10–20 main dishes, tel. 04/579-4424). Better yet, there's a scenic little **picnic spot** in the castle courtyard, with fine tables and views (buy sandwiches at the Mercator grocery store in the commercial center before you ascend—described later, under "Eating in Bled").

Getting to the Castle: To really earn those views, you can **hike** up the steep hill (20–30 min). The handiest trails are behind big St. Martin's Church: Walk past the front door of the church with the lake at your back, and look left after the first set of houses for the *Grad* signs marking the steepest route up (on this trail, bear uphill—or right—at the benches); or, for a longer but less steep route, continue past the church on the same street about five minutes, bearing uphill (left) at the fork, and find the *Grad* sign just after the Pension Bledec hostel on the left. Once you're on this second trail, don't take the sharp-left uphill turn at the fork (instead, continue straight up, around the back of the hill). If you'd rather skip the hike, you can take the 10:00 **tourist bus** (see "Getting Around Lake Bled," earlier), your **rental car,** a **taxi** (around €10), or—if you're wealthy and romantic—a **horse and buggy** (€30, €10 extra to wait 30 min and bring you back down). However, these options take you only to the parking lot, from which it's a steep and slippery-when-wet five-minute hike up to the castle itself.

Boating—Bled is the rowing center of Slovenia. Town officials even lengthened the lake a bit so it would perfectly fit the standard two-kilometer laps, with 100 meters more for the turn. Three world championships have been held here. The town has produced many Olympic medalists, who won gold in Sydney and silver in Athens. You'll notice that local crew team members are characters—with a tradition of wild and colorful haircuts. You'll likely see them running or rowing. This dedication to rowing adds to Bled's tranquility, since no motorized boats are allowed on the lake.

If you want to get into the action, you'll find **rental rowboats** at the swimming pool under the castle (small 3-person boat: first hour-€12, additional hours-€6.50 each; bigger 5-person boat: first hour-€14, additional hours-€7.50 each; daily in summer 10:00–18:00). Two other places farther from Bled town also rent rowboats (4-person boat-€10/hr, closed in bad weather and off-season): Pension Pletna in Mlino (a 15-minute walk around the lake past Grand Hotel Toplice) and the campground on the far end of the lake.

Swimming—Lake Bled has several suitable spots for a swim. The swimming pools under the castle are filled with lake water and routinely earn the "blue flag," meaning the water is top-quality (swim all day-€6.50, less for afternoon only, June–Sept daily 8:00–19:00, closed Oct–May and in bad weather, tel. 04/578-0528). Bled's two beaches are at the far end of the lake. Both are free; the one at the campground (southwest corner) has lots of tourists, while locals prefer the one at the rowing center (northwest corner). If you swim to the island, remember that you can't get into the church in your swimsuit.

Luge Ride (Polento Sankanje)—Bled's "summer toboggan" luge ride, atop Mount Straža overlooking the lake, allows you to scream down a steep, curvy metal rail track on a little plastic sled. A chairlift takes you to the top of the track, where you'll sit on your sled, take a deep breath, and remind yourself: Pull back on the stick to slow down, push forward on the stick to go faster. You'll drop 480 feet in altitude on the 570-yard-long track, speeding up to about 25 miles per hour as you race toward the lake. You'll see the track on the hillside just south of town, beyond the Grand Hotel Toplice (€6/ride, cheaper for multiple rides, chairlift only-€3, weather-dependent—if it rains, you can't go; mid-June–Aug daily 11:00–20:00; May–mid-June and Sept Sat–Sun only 11:00–18:00, closed Mon–Fri; Oct Sat–Sun only 11:00–16:30; most of April Sat-Sun only 11:00-17:00; closed Nov–early April).

Day Trips—For details on some easy and enjoyable nearby side-trips—including a quirky bee museum, a scenic gorge hike, and a more remote lake experience—see "Near Lake Bled" at the end of this chapter.

Nightlife in Bled

Bled Pub Crawl

Bled is quiet after hours. However, the town does have a few fun bars that are lively with a young crowd (all open nightly until 2:00 in the morning). Since many young people in Bled are students at the local tourism school, they're likely to speak English...and eager to practice with a native speaker. Try a "Smile," a Corona-type Slovenian lager. *Šnops* (schnapps) is a local specialty—popular flavors are plum *(slivovka),* honey *(medica),* blueberry *(borovničevec),* and pear *(hruškovec).*

Kick things off with the fun-loving local gang at **Gostilna Pri Planincu** near the bus station (described later, under "Eating in Bled"). Then head down Cesta Svobode toward the lake; just below Hotel Jelovica, you'll find the rollicking **Irish Pub** (a.k.a. "The Pub"), with Guinness and indoor or outdoor seating. For a more genteel atmosphere, duck across the street and wander a few more steps down toward the lake to find the **Art Café,** with a mellow ambience reminiscent of a Van Gogh painting. Around the lake near the commercial center, **Bled Pub** (a.k.a. "The Cocktail Bar" or "Troha"—for the family that owns it) is a trendy late-night spot where bartenders sling a dizzying array of mixed drinks to an appreciative crowd (between the commercial center and the lake, above the recommended Oštarija Peglez'n restaurant). If you're still standing, several other, more low-key bars and cafés percolate in the commercial center.

Sleeping in Bled

Bled is dominated by a few giant, gradually decaying, communist-era convention hotels. Some have been nicely renovated, but most are stale, outmoded, and overpriced. (It's a strange, incestuous little circle—the majority of the town's big hotels and restaurants are owned by the same company.) Instead, I prefer staying in smaller, countryside, pension-type accommodations—many of them just a short walk above the lake. These quaint little family-run pensions book up early with Germans and Brits; reserve as far ahead as possible. I've listed the high-season prices (May–Oct). Off-season, prices are typically 10–20 percent lower. For even cheaper beds, consider one of the many *sobe* (rooms in private homes) scattered around the lake (about €25 per person in peak season, often with

Sleep Code

(€1 = about $1.40, country code: 386, area code: 04)
S = Single, **D** = Double/Twin, **T** = Triple, **Q** = Quad, **b** = bathroom. Unless otherwise noted, credit cards are accepted. Everyone speaks English, and all of these accommodations include breakfast. Bled levies a €1.01 tourist tax per person, per night (not included in below prices unless noted).

To help you sort easily through these listings, I've divided the rooms into three categories based on the price for a standard double room with bath:

$$$ Higher Priced—Most rooms €100 or more.
$$ Moderately Priced—Most rooms between €60–100.
$ Lower Priced—Most rooms €60 or less.

a hefty 30 percent surcharge for stays shorter than three nights). Kompas Bled Travel Agency can book you a *soba* (see page 692), but be sure the location is convenient before you accept.

Above the Lake

These friendly, cozy, characteristic accommodations are Bled's best values. The only catch is that they're perched on a hilltop a steep five- to ten-minute climb up from the lake (easier than it sounds). There are two ways to find them from the town center: Walk around the lake to Grand Hotel Toplice, then go up the stairs around the right side of the Hotel Jadran (on the hill across the street from Grand Hotel Toplice). Or, from the main road into town (Ljubljanska cesta), take the small service road just above the commercial center (in front of Hotel Lovec), and loop up around the big Kompas and Golf hotels. Some buses (including those to Ljubljana) stop at a bus stop higher up on Ljubljanska cesta, just above the traffic light. This stop is handier to these hotels than Bled's main bus station. From the bus stop, you can walk down Ljubljanska cesta and take the road just above the post office, which leads up to this area. If you're sleeping up here, Mayer Penzion's restaurant is the easiest choice for dinner (described later, under "Eating in Bled").

$$ Mayer Penzion, thoughtfully run by the Trseglav family, comes with 13 great-value rooms, a helpful staff, a tasty restaurant, an atmospheric wine-tasting cellar, and beautifully handcrafted Slovenian woodwork inside and out. They book up fast in sum-

mer with return clients, so reserve early (Sb-€55, Db-€80, €5 less for 3 nights or more, extra bed-€20, family deals, elevator, Wi-Fi, Želeška cesta 7, tel. 04/576-5740, fax 04/576-5741, www.mayer-sp.si, penzion@mayer-sp.si). They also rent a cute, newly restored two-story Slovenian farm cottage next door (Db-€120, Tb/Qb-€150).

$$ Hotel Berc and **Penzion Berc** (pronounced "berts"), run by the Berc brothers, are next door to Mayer Penzion. Both have cozy public spaces, free Internet access and Wi-Fi, and free loaner bikes, and are worth reserving ahead (both cash only, www.berc-sp.si). The new hotel building has 15 rooms with pleasantly woody decor (Sb-€40–50, Db-€70-80; price depends on size, season, and length of stay; all rooms have balconies, Pod Stražo 13, tel. 04/576-5658, fax 04/576-5659, hotel@berc-sp.si, run by Luka). The older, adjacent *penzion* offers 11 cheaper, older, but nearly-as-nice rooms (Sb-€35, Db-€60, €5 more for 1-night stays, 10 percent cheaper off-season, most rooms have balconies, closed in Nov and sporadically off-season, Želeška cesta 15, tel. 04/574-1838, fax 04/576-7320, penzion@berc-sp.si, run by Miha).

$$ Alp Penzion is in a tranquil countryside setting amid hayfields. It's a long hike beyond the others listed here, but still within a 15-minute walk of the lake (better for drivers or for those who don't mind the walk). With 11 rooms, this place is enthusiastically run by the Sršen family, who offer lots of fun extras, including a tennis court and summer barbecue grill/outdoor pub (Sb-€55, Db-€80–85—higher price is for balcony, Tb-€100, 3 percent cheaper if you pay cash, cheaper Oct-April, family rooms, half-board for just €5 extra per person, free Internet access and Wi-Fi, free loaner bikes, Cankarjeva cesta 20A, tel. 04/574-1614, fax 04/574-4590, www.alp-penzion.com, bled@alp-penzion.com). Just next door is the relaxing Essense spa (described earlier, under "Helpful Hints").

$ Mia Sušnik, who is friendly and speaks English, rents out two comfortable apartments. Modern, tidy, and equipped with kitchens, these are a good budget choice for families (Db-€57, 20 percent extra for fewer than 3 nights, no breakfast, cash only, laundry service-€10, free Wi-Fi, free parking, Želeška cesta 3, tel. 04/574-1731, www.bled-holiday.com, susnik@bled-holiday.com). It's just toward the lake from the bigger pensions, with a big crucifix out front. Her sister Ivanka also rents apartments, but they're farther from the lake.

$ Tourist Farm Mulej, farther out of town than my other listings and better for drivers, is a new but traditional farmhouse in a tranquil valley about a half-mile from the lake (1.5 miles from Bled town). Damjana and Jože, who run a working farm, rent out eight modern rooms and four apartments—all with balconies—and serve breakfasts and dinners made with food they produce

(Db-€60, or €80 with dinner; €30 per extra person in apartments, or €40 with dinner; 20 percent extra for 1- or 2-night stays in June-Aug, cash only, family rooms, free cable Internet, free loaner bikes, horseback riding, Selo pri Bledu 42a, tel. & fax 04/574-4617, www.mulej-bled.com, info@mulej-bled.com). It's in the farm village of Selo—drive along the lakeside road south from Bled, then turn off in Mlino toward Selo, and look for the signs (to the right) once in the village.

$ Vila Gorenka is your non-hostel, low-budget option. The Žerovec family's old-fashioned house has 10 basic, faded, musty rooms sharing two bathrooms upstairs from their home (S-€20, D-€36, cash only, no extra charge for 1-night stays, no breakfast, free Internet access and Wi-Fi, just below the bigger pensions at Želeška cesta 9, mobile 051-369-070, http://freeweb.siol.net/mz2, vila.gorenka@siol.net, Martin).

Near the Lake

You'll pay a premium to be closer to the lake—but it's hard to argue with the convenience.

$$$ Hotel Lovec (LOW-vets), a Best Western Premier, sits in a convenient (but non-lakefront) location just above the commercial center. Gorgeously renovated inside and out, and run by a helpful and friendly staff, it's a welcoming, cheery, well-run alternative to Bled's many old, dreary communist hotels. Its 60 plush rooms come with all the comforts (Sb-€128, Db-€151, €20 more for a lake-view balcony, very soft rates fluctuate with demand—email to ask for best price, cheaper Nov–Feb, family and "executive" suites available, delicious breakfast, elevator, free Internet access and cable Internet, indoor pool, free parking garage for guests, Ljubljanska cesta 6, tel. 04/620-4100, fax 04/576-8625, www.lovechotel.com, booking@kompas-lovec.eu).

$$$ Grand Hotel Toplice (TOHP-leet-seh) is the grande dame of Bled, with 87 high-ceilinged rooms, parquet floors, an elegant view lounge, posh decor, all the amenities, and a long list of high-profile guests—from Madeleine Albright to Jordan's King Hussein to Slovene-by-marriage Donald Trump (ask to see their "wall of fame"). Rooms in the back are cheaper, but have no lake views and overlook a noisy street—try to get one as high up as possible (non-view: Sb-€150, Db-€170; lake view: Sb-€180, Db-€220; suites with lake views-€280; 15–20 percent less Nov–April, elevator, air-con, free one-hour boat rental for guests, free Internet access and cable Internet, free parking, Cesta Svobode 12, tel. 04/579-1000, fax 04/574-1841, www.hotel-toplice.com, ghtoplice@hotelibled.com). The hotel's name—*toplice*—means "spa"; guests are free to use the hotel's swanky, natural-spring-fed indoor swimming pool (a chilly 72 degrees Fahrenheit). This hotel also runs

two smaller, far less luxurious hotels nearby with very dated and faded rooms and lower rates (Hotel Trst and Hotel Jadran, details at Toplice's website).

$$$ Vila Prešeren has eight stylish, pricey rooms above a popular restaurant right on the lake (Sb-€112, Db-€150, apartment-€200–214 depending on size, cheaper mid-Oct–early May, no reception—check in at the restaurant, air-con, free Wi-Fi, Veslaška promenada 14, tel. 04/575-2510, www.vilapreseren.si, vilapreseren@sportinaresorts.si).

$ Penzion Bledec (BLED-ets), an official IYHF hostel, is just below the castle at the top of the Old Town. Each of the 13 rooms has its own bathroom, and some can be rented as doubles (though "doubles" are actually underutilized triples and quads, with separate beds pushed together—so they might not be reservable July–Aug or at other busy times). The friendly staff is justifiably proud of the bargain they offer (bed in 4- to 7-bed dorm-€21, Db-€54, Tb-€63, cheaper Nov–April, members pay 10 percent less, includes sheets and breakfast, great family rooms, free Internet access and Wi-Fi, full-service laundry for guests-€9/load, restaurant, Grajska 17, tel. 04/574-5250, fax 04/574-5251, www.mlino.si, bledec@mlino.si).

$ Travellers Haven is a low-key hostel run by Mirjam and Karmen. The 27 beds fill six rooms in a nicely renovated hundred-year-old villa in the Old Town (€19 for a bunk in a 4–6-bed room, D-€48, no breakfast but guest kitchen, tight bathrooms offer little privacy, reception open 8:00–13:00 & 16:00–23:00; free Internet access, Wi-Fi, laundry machines, and loaner bikes; Riklijeva cesta 1, mobile 031-704-455 or 041-396-545, www.travellers-haven.si, travellers-haven@t-2.net).

Eating in Bled

Bled has several good restaurants, but most everything is quite similar. For variety, wait for Ljubljana.

Okarina Etno, run by charming, well-traveled Leo Ličof, serves a diverse array of cuisines, all of them well-executed: international fare, traditional Slovenian specialties, and Indian (Himalayan) dishes. Leo has a respect for salads and vegetables and a passion for fish. Creative cooking, fine presentation, friendly service, and an atmosphere as tastefully eclectic as the food make this place a great splurge (€9–14 pastas, €10–22 main dishes, plus a few pricier splurges, Mon–Fri 18:00–24:00, Sat–Sun 12:00–24:00, next to Hotel Lovec at Ljubljanska cesta 8, tel. 04/574-1458). In the back of the menu, look for the copy of the guest book page with Paul McCartney's visit from May 2005. Around the left side of the building is **Leo's Balkan Grill**, serving up typical grilled

meat dishes (see "Balkan Flavors" on page 753; €6–10 dishes, open summer only).

Oštarija Peglez'n ("The Old Iron"), conveniently located on the main road between the commercial center and the lake, cooks up tasty Slovenian and Mediterranean meals, with an emphasis on fish. Choose between the delightful Slovenian cottage interior or the shady streetside terrace. Reservations are smart in summer (€7–9 salads and pastas, €12–25 main dishes, daily 12:00–23:00, fun family-style shareable plates, Cesta Svobode 19A, tel. 04/574-4218).

Vila Prešeren is the best choice for lakeside dining, with a giant terrace reaching all the way down to the lakefront path. Featuring mod decor and international cuisine, this is a great spot for a meal, a drink, or a classic Lake Bled dessert (€9–11 salads, €7–10 pastas, €12–28 main dishes, daily 7:00–23:00, Veslaška promenada 14, tel. 04/575-2510).

Mayer Penzion, just up the hill from the lakefront, has a dressy restaurant with good traditional cooking that's worth the short hike. This is where a Babel of international tourists come to swap hiking tips and day-trip tales. As this is the only real restaurant in the pension neighborhood, it can be very busy—reserve ahead (main dishes €8–21, Tue–Sun 18:00–24:00, closed Mon, indoor or outdoor seating, above Hotel Jadran at Želeška cesta 7, tel. 04/576-5740).

Gostilna Pri Planincu ("By the Mountaineers") is a homey, informal bar coated with license plates and packed with fun-loving and sometimes rowdy natives. A larger dining area sprawls behind the small, local-feeling pub, and there's outdoor seating out front and on the side patio. The menu features huge portions of stick-to-your-ribs Slovenian pub grub, plus Balkan grilled-meat specialties (€7–16 main dishes, fish splurges up to €25). Ask about their €5–7 daily specials—huge, home-style traditional dishes. Upstairs is a timbered pizzeria selling €4–8 wood-fired pies (daily 9:00–23:00, pizzeria open from 11:00, Grajska cesta 8, tel. 04/574-1613). The playful cartoon mural along the outside of the restaurant shows different types of mountaineers (from left to right): thief, normal, mooch ("gopher"), climber, and naked (...well, almost).

Pizzeria Rustika, in the Old Town, offers good wood-fired pizzas and salads. Its upstairs terrace is relaxing on a balmy evening (€5–8 pizzas, Tue–Sun 12:00–22:00, Mon 15:00–22:00—but opens at 12:00 in peak season, service can be slow when it's busy, Riklijeva cesta 13, tel. 04/576-8900).

The **Mercator** grocery store, in the commercial center, has the makings for a bang-up picnic. They sell pre-made sandwiches for about €3, or will make you one to order (point to what you want). This is a great option for hikers and budget travelers (Mon–Fri 7:00–19:00, Sat 7:00–15:00, Sun 8:00–12:00). There's another

Bled Desserts

While you're in Bled, be sure to enjoy the town's specialty, a cream cake called ***kremna rezina*** (KRAYM-nah ray-ZEE-nah; often referred to by its German-derived name, ***kremšnita,*** KRAYM-shnee-tah). It's a layer of cream and a thick layer of vanilla custard artfully sandwiched between sheets of delicate, crispy crust. Heavenly. Slovenes travel from all over the country to sample this famous dessert.

Slightly less renowned—but just as tasty—is ***grmada*** (gur-MAH-dah, "bonfire"). This dessert was developed by Hotel Jelovica as a way to get rid of their day-old leftovers. They take yesterday's cake, add rum, milk, custard, and raisins, and top it off with whipped cream and chocolate syrup.

Finally, there's *prekmurska gibanica*—or just ***gibanica*** (gee-bah-NEET-seh) for short. Originating in the Hungarian corner of the country, *gibanica* is an earthy pastry filled with poppy seeds, walnuts, apple, and cheese, and drizzled with rum.

These desserts are typically enjoyed with a lake-and-mountains view—the best spots are the terrace at Vila Prešeren, the Panorama restaurant by Grand Hotel Toplice, and the terrace across from the Hotel Park (figure around €5 for cake and coffee at any of these places). For a more local (but non-lake view) setting, consider Šmon Slaščičarna (only slightly cheaper; see below).

location closer to the Old Town and castle.

Dessert: While tourists generally gulp down their cream cakes on a hotel restaurant's lakefront terrace, local residents know the best desserts are at **Šmon Slaščičarna** (a.k.a. the "Brown Bear," for the bear on the sign). It's nicely untouristy, but lacks the atmosphere of the lakeside spots (€2–3 cakes, daily 7:30–21:00, near bus station at Grajska cesta 3, tel. 04/574-1616).

Lake Bled Connections

The most convenient train connections to Bled leave from the Lesce-Bled station, about 2.5 miles away (see details under "Arrival in Bled," earlier). Remember, when buying a train ticket to Lake Bled, make it clear that you want to go to the Lesce-Bled station (not the Bled Jezero station, which is poorly connected to the main line). No one in the town of Bled sells train tickets; buy them at the station just before your train departs (open Mon–Fri

5:30–21:00, Sat 7:00–14:00, Sun 13:30–19:30). If the ticket window there is closed, buy your ticket on board from the conductor (who will likely waive the €2.50 additional fee).

Note that if you're going to **Ljubljana,** the bus (which leaves from Bled town itself) is better than the train (which leaves from the Lesce-Bled train station).

From Lesce-Bled by Train to: Ljubljana (roughly hourly, 40–60 min—but bus is better since it leaves from Bled town), **Salzburg** (5/day, 4 hrs), **Munich** (3/day, 6 hrs), **Vienna** (that's ***Dunaj*** in Slovene, 5/day, 6 hrs, transfer in Villach, Austria), **Venice** (3/day with transfer in Villach, 6 hrs), **Zagreb** (5/day, 3.5 hrs).

By Bus to: Ljubljana (Mon–Sat hourly—usually at :30 past the hour, fewer on Sun, 1.25 hrs, €6.30), **Radovljica** (Mon–Fri at least 2/hr, Sat hourly, Sun almost hourly, 15 min, €1.60), **Lesce-Bled train station** (2/hr, 10 min, €1.30), **Lake Bohinj** (hourly, 40 min and €3.60 to Bohinj Jezero stop, 50 min and €4.10 to Bohinj Vogel or Bohinj Zlatorog stop), **Podhom** (15-min hike away from Vintgar Gorge, Mon–Fri 5/day in the morning, 1/day Sat, none Sun, 15 min, €1.30), **Spodnje Gorje** (also 15-min hike from Vintgar Gorge, take bus in direction of Krnica, hourly, 15 min, €1.30). Confirm times at the TI or using the schedules posted at the unstaffed Bled bus station. Buy tickets on the bus.

By Plane: Ljubljana Airport is between Lake Bled and Ljubljana, about a 45-minute drive from Bled. Connecting by taxi costs around €50 (set price up front—since it's outside of town, they don't use the meter). The bus connection from Bled to the airport is cheap (total cost: about €5) but complicated and time-consuming: First, go to Kranj (Mon–Fri 12/day, Sat–Sun 8/day, 35 min), then transfer to a Brnik-bound bus (at least hourly, 20 min). Many Bled residents prefer to fly from Klagenfurt, Austria. For details on both the Ljubljana and Klagenfurt airports, see page 685.

Route Tips for Drivers: Bled is less than an hour north of Ljubljana. The new A-2 expressway zips you almost all the way there; a bridge and a tunnel might not yet be completed for your visit (due to be done by sometime in 2011). Watch for signs to *Bled;* the Bled exit will take you directly to the lake (where the road becomes Ljubljanska cesta).

To reach Radovljica (bee museum) or Lesce (train station), drive out of Bled on Ljubljanska cesta toward the expressway. Watch for the turnoff to those two towns on the right. They're on the same road: Lesce first (to reach train station, divert right when entering town), then Radovljica.

Near Lake Bled

The countryside around Bled offers several day trips that can be done easily without a car (bus connection information is described in each section). The three listed here are the best (one small-town/museum experience, two hiking/back-to-nature options). They're more convenient than can't-miss, but each is worthwhile on a longer visit, and all give a good taste of the Julian Alps. For a self-guided driving tour through farther-flung (and even more striking) parts of the Julian Alps, see the next chapter.

Radovljica

The town of Radovljica (rah-DOH-vleet-suh) is larger than Bled, perched on a plateau above the Sava River. The town itself is nothing exciting, though its old center pedestrian zone, Linhartov trg, makes for a pleasant stroll (TI tel. 04/531-5300). But the town is home to a fascinating and offbeat beekeeping museum—which, with only a few rooms, still ranks as one of Europe's biggest on the topic. Skip the town on Mondays, when the museum is closed (and be aware that the museum closes for a three-hour lunch break in shoulder season).

Getting to Radovljica: Buses to Radovljica generally leave Bled every half-hour (fewer on weekends, €1.60, buy ticket from driver, trip takes about 15 min). **Drivers** leave Bled on Ljubljanska cesta, then turn right at the sign for *Radovljica* and go through the village of Lesce; the road dead-ends at Radovljica's pedestrian zone, where you'll find a parking lot and rustic garage. From here, it's a short walk to the bee museum (see directions below). A handy **bike** path scenically and peacefully connects Bled with Radovljica (about 4 miles, get details at TI).

Arrival in Radovljica: To reach the old town square and the bee museum from the bus station, leave the station going straight ahead, cross the bus parking lot and the next street, then turn left down the far street (following brown sign for *Staro Mesto*). In five minutes, you'll get to the pedestrianized Linhartov trg (TI on right just before you enter pedestrian zone). At the end of this square on the left is the big, yellow Baroque mansion that houses the bee museum (upstairs).

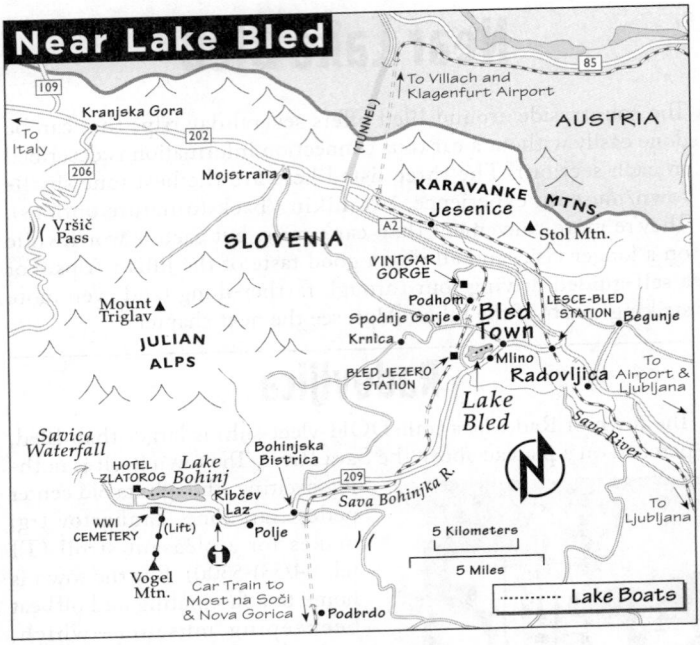

Sights in Radovljica

▲Apicultural Museum (Čebelarski Muzej)

This museum celebrates Slovenia's long beekeeping heritage. Since the days before Europeans had sugar, Slovenia has been a big honey producer. Slovenian farmer Anton Janša is considered the father of modern beekeeping and was Europe's first official teacher of beekeeping (in Habsburg Vienna).

The first two rooms of the museum trace the history of beekeeping, from the time when bees were kept in hollowed-out trees to the present day. Notice the old-fashioned **tools** in the second room. When a new queen bee is born, the old queen takes half the hive's bees to a new location. Experienced beekeepers used the long, skinny instrument (a beehive stethoscope) to figure out when the swarm would fly the coop. Then, once the bees had moved to a nearby tree, the beekeeper used the big spoons to retrieve the queen—surrounded by an angry ball of her subjects—from her new home before she could get settled in. The beekeeper transported the furious gang into a manmade hive designed for easier, more sanitary collection of the honey. You can also see the tools beekeepers used to create smoke, which makes bees less aggressive. Even today, some of Slovenia's old-fashioned beekeepers simply light up a cigarette and blow smoke on any bees that get ornery.

The third room features the museum's highlight: whimsically painted beehive **frontboards** (called *panjske končnice*). Nineteenth-century farmers, believing these paintings would help the bees find their way home, developed a tradition of decorating their hives with religious, historical, and satirical folk themes (look for the devil sharpening a woman's tongue on a wheel). The depiction of a hunter's funeral shows all the animals happy...except his dog. There's everything from portraits of Habsburg emperors, to a "true crime" sequence of a man murdering his family as they sleep, to proto-"Lockhorns" cartoons of marital strife, to 18th-century erotica (one with a woman showing some leg and another with a flip-up, peek-a-boo panel).

The life-size wooden statues were used to "guard" the beehives—and designed to look like fearsome Ottoman and Napoleonic soldiers.

You'll also find an interactive multimedia exhibit, a good video in English, temporary exhibitions, and—in the summer only—an actual, functioning beehive (try to find the queen). The gift shop is a good place for souvenirs, with hand-painted replicas of frontboards, honey brandy, candles, ornaments, and other bee products (museum entry-€2.50, good English descriptions, free sheet of English info, €1.60 English guidebook is a nice souvenir; May–Oct Tue–Sun 10:00–18:00, closed Mon; March–April and Nov–Dec Wed and Sat–Sun 10:00–12:00 & 15:00–17:00, Tue and Thu–Fri 8:00–15:00, closed Mon; Jan–Feb Tue–Fri 8:00–15:00, closed Sat–Mon; upstairs at Linhartov trg 1, tel. 04/532-0520, www.muzeji-radovljica.si).

Eating in Radovljica

Several Radovljica restaurants near the bee museum have view terraces overlooking the surrounding mountains and valleys.

Lectar offers pricey, hearty Slovenian fare in a rural-feeling setting with a user-friendly, super-traditional menu. Its several heavily decorated rooms are often filled with tour groups, but in good weather, don't miss the terrace out back. The restaurant is known for its heart-shaped gingerbread cookies (called *lect*), inscribed with messages of love. In the cellar is a €1 "museum" where you can watch costumed bakers make and decorate these hearts according to the traditional recipe (€9–18 main dishes, Wed–Mon 12:00–22:00, closed Tue, family-friendly, Linhartov trg 2, tel. 04/537-4800).

The cheaper **Grajska Gostilnica** dishes up good, basic pub grub (salads, pizza, pastas, open long hours daily, across from the bus station and to the left, inside Hotel Grajski Dvor at Kranjska 2, tel. 04/531-5585).

Vintgar Gorge

Just north of Bled, the river Radovna has carved this mile-long, picturesque gorge into the mountainside. For hikers, Vintgar (VEENT-gar) Gorge is worth ▲▲. Boardwalks and bridges put you right in the middle of the action of this "poor man's Plitvice." You'll cross over several waterfalls and marvel at the clarity of the water. The easy hike is on a boardwalk trail with handrails (sometimes narrow and a bit slippery). At the end of the gorge, you'll find a snack stand, WCs, and a bridge with a fine view. Go back the way you came, or take a prettier return to Bled (see "Scenic Hike Back to Bled," later). The gorge is easily reachable from Bled by bus or foot and is the best option for those who are itching for a hike but don't have a car (€4 to enter gorge, open daily May–late Oct 8:00–19:00 or until dusk, June–Aug maybe until 20:00, closed late Oct–April, tel. 04/572-5266).

Getting to Vintgar Gorge: The gorge is 2.5 miles north of Bled. You can walk (at least one hour) or bus (15-min ride plus 15-min walk, or 30-min ride on summer tourist bus) to the gorge entrance.

Walkers leave Bled on the road between the castle and St. Martin's Church and take the uphill (left) road at the fork. Just after the little yellow chapel, turn right on the road with the big tree, then immediately left at the Mercator grocery store. When the road swings left, continue straight onto Partizanska (marked for *Podhom* and a walking sign for *Vintgar*; ignore the bus sign for *Vintgar* pointing left). At the fork just after the little bridge, go left for Podhom, then simply follow signs for *Vintgar*.

In summer, the easy **tourist bus** takes you right to the gorge entrance in 30 minutes (see "Getting Around Lake Bled," page 693). Otherwise, you can take a **local bus** to one of two stops: Podhom (Mon–Fri 5/day in the morning, 1/day Sat, none Sun, 15 min, €1.30) or Spodnje Gorje (take bus in direction of Krnica, hourly, 15 min, €1.30). From either the Podhom or the Spodnje Gorje bus stop, it's a 15-minute walk to the gorge (follow signs for *Vintgar*).

Drivers follow signs to *Podhom,* then *Vintgar* (see walking instructions, above).

Scenic Hike Back to Bled: If you still have energy once you reach the end of the gorge, consider this longer hike back with panoramic views. Behind the snack stand, find the trail marked *Katarina Bled.* You'll go uphill for 25 strenuous minutes (following the red-and-white circles and arrows) before cresting the hill and enjoying beautiful views over Bled town and the region. Continue straight down the road 15 minutes to the typical, narrow, old village of Zasip, then walk (about 30 min) or take the bus back to Bled.

Lake Bohinj

The pristine alpine Lake Bohinj (BOH-heen), 16 miles southwest of Bled, enjoys a quieter scene and (in clear weather) even better vistas of Triglav and the surrounding mountains. This is a real back-to-nature experience, with just a smattering of hotels and campgrounds, rather than the well-oiled resort machine of Bled. Some people adore Bohinj; others are bored by it. If you think Bled is too touristy to allow you to really enjoy the nature, go to Bohinj.

Getting to Lake Bohinj: From Bled, hourly **buses** head for Bohinj, stopping at three different destinations: Bohinj Jezero (the village of Ribčev Laz, 40 min, €3.60), then Bohinj Vogel (a 10-minute walk from the base of the Vogel Mountain cable car, 50 min, €4.10), and finally a few hundred yards more to Bohinj Zlatorog (Hotel Zlatorog and the one-hour hike to the Savica waterfall trailhead, 50 min, €4.10). Off-season, there are fewer buses—confirm times before you depart. **Drivers** leave Bled going south along the lakefront road, Cesta Svobode; in the village of Mlino, you'll peel off from the lake and follow signs to *Boh Bistrica* (a midsize town near Lake Bohinj). Once in the town of Bohinjska Bistrica, turn right, following *Bohinj Jezero* signs. The road takes you to the village of Ribčev Laz and along the lakefront road with all the attractions.

Sights at Lake Bohinj

A visit to Bohinj has three parts: a village, a cable car (and nearby cemetery), and a waterfall hike. I've listed them as you'll reach them along the main road from Bled, which runs along the south side of the lake.

Ribčev Laz Village—Coming from Bled, your first views of Bohinj will be from the little village called Ribčev Laz (loosely translated as "Good Fishin' Hole") at the southeast corner of the lake. Here you'll find a TI, a handful of hotels and ice-cream stands, and the Bohinj Jezero bus stop. The town's main landmark is its church, **St. John the Baptist** (to your right as you face the lake, past the distinctive stone bridge; not open to visitors).

In the other direction, a five-minute stroll down the lakefront road, is a dock where you can catch an electric **tourist boat** to make a silent circuit around the lake (€10 round-trip, €7 one-way, daily 10:00–18:00, 2/hr, less off-season). The boat stops at the far end of the lake, at Camp Zlatorog—a 10-minute walk from the Vogel cable car (see below). Across from the Ribčev Laz dock is a fun concrete 3-D model of Triglav (compare to the real thing, hovering across the lake). Finally, a few more steps down the road, just beyond a boat rental dock, you'll see a statue of Zlatorog, the "Golden Horn"—a mythical chamois-like creature native to the Julian Alps. Continuing down the road, you'll reach the next attraction.

Vogel Mountain Cable Car—For a mountain climb without the sweat, take the cable car up to Vogel Mountain, which offers impressive panoramic views of Mount Triglav and the Julian Alps (€13 round-trip, runs every 30 min, daily 7:00–19:00 in summer, 8:00–18:00 in winter, shorter hours and less frequent departures in spring and fall—confirm schedule before you make the trip, closed Nov, www.vogel.si). The top is a ski-in-winter, hike-in-summer area with fine views and a chairlift experience. The alpine hut Merjasec ("Wild Boar") offers tasty strudel and a wide variety of local brandies (including the notorious "Boar's Blood"—a concoction of several different flavors guaranteed to get you snorting). To reach the cable-car station, drivers follow signs to *Vogel* (to the left off the main lakefront road); by bus, get off at the Bohinj Vogel stop (request this stop from driver) and hike about 10 minutes up the steep road on the left (away from the lake).

World War I Cemetery—Back down below the cable car, on the main road just beyond the cable-car station and Bohinj Vogel bus stop, look for the metal gate on the left marking a World War I cemetery—the final resting place for some Soča Front soldiers (see sidebar on page 732). While no fighting occurred here (it was mostly on the other side of these mountains), injured soldiers were brought to a nearby hospital. Those who didn't recover ended

up here. Notice that many of the names are not Slovenian, but Hungarian, Polish, Czech, and so on—a reminder that the entire multiethnic Austro-Hungarian Empire was involved in the fighting. If you're walking down from the cable-car station, the cemetery makes for a poignant detour on your way to the main road (look for it through the trees).

Savica Waterfall (Slap Savica)—Up the valley beyond the end of the lake is Bohinj's final treat, a waterfall called Slap Savica (sah-VEET-seh). Hardy hikers enjoy following the moderate-to-strenuous uphill trail (including 553 stairs) to see the cascade, which dumps into a remarkably pure pool of aquamarine snowmelt (€2.40, daily in summer from 8:00 until dusk, allow about 90 min for the round-trip hike). Drivers follow the lakefront road to where it ends, right at the trailhead. Without a car, getting to the trailhead is a hassle. If you take the public bus from Bled, or the boats on the lake, they'll get you only as far as the Bohinj Zlatorog stop—the end of the line, and still a one-hour hike from the trailhead (from the bus stop, follow signs to *Slap Savica*). In summer, a sporadic shuttle bus takes you right to the trailhead. But frankly, it's not worth it if you don't have a car.

THE JULIAN ALPS

Vršič Pass • Soča River Valley • Bovec • Kobarid

The countryside around Lake Bled is plenty spectacular. But to crescendo your Slovenian mountain experience, head for the high hills. The northwestern corner of Slovenia—within yodeling distance of Austria and Italy—is crowned by the Julian Alps (named for Julius Caesar). Here, mountain culture has a Slavic flavor.

The Slovenian mountainsides are laced with hiking paths, blanketed in a deep forest, and speckled with ski resorts and vacation chalets. Beyond every ridge is a peaceful alpine village nestled around a quaint Baroque steeple. And in the center of it all is Mount Triglav—ol' "Three Heads"—Slovenia's national symbol and tallest mountain.

The single best day in the Julian Alps is spent driving up and over the 50 hairpin turns of the breathtaking Vršič Pass (vur-SHEECH, open May–Oct) and back down via the Soča (SOH-chah) River Valley, lined with offbeat nooks and Hemingway-haunted crannies. As you curl on twisty roads between the cut-glass peaks, you'll enjoy stunning high-mountain scenery, whitewater rivers with superb fishing, rustic rest stops, thought-provoking World War I sights, and charming hamlets.

A pair of Soča Valley towns holds watch over the region. Bovec is all about good times (it's the whitewater adventure-sports hub), while Kobarid attends to more serious matters (WWI history). Though neither is a destination in itself, both Bovec and Kobarid are pleasant, functional, and convenient home bases for exploring this gloriously beautiful region.

Getting Around the Julian Alps

The Julian Alps are best by **car.** Even if you're doing the rest of your trip by train, consider renting a car here for maximum day-trip flexibility. I've included a self-guided driving tour incorporating the best of the Julian Alps (Vršič Pass and Soča Valley).

It's difficult to do the Vršič Pass and Soča Valley without your own wheels. Hiring a **local guide** with a car can be a great value, making your time not only fun, but also informative. Cheaper but less personal, you could join a day-trip **excursion** from Bled. (Both options are explained under "Tours at Lake Bled," page 694.) A public **bus** follows more or less this same route, leaving Ljubljana each morning at 6:30, arriving in Bovec at 10:45 (daily July–Aug, Sat–Sun only Sept–June). Or stay closer to Bled, and get a taste of the Julian Alps by taking advantage of easy and frequent bus connections to more convenient day-trip destinations (Radovljica, the Vintgar Gorge, and Lake Bohinj—all described under "Near Lake Bled" in the previous chapter).

Julian Alps Self-Guided Driving Tour

This all-day, self-guided driving tour, rated ▲▲▲, takes you over the highest mountain pass in Slovenia, with stunning scenery and a few quirky sights along the way. From waterfalls to hiking trails, World War I history to queasy suspension bridges, this trip has it all.

Orientation to the Julian Alps

Most of the Julian Alps are encompassed by the Triglav National Park (Triglavski Narodni Park). (Some sights near Lake Bled—such as Lake Bohinj and the Vintgar Gorge—are also part of this park, but are covered in the previous chapter.) This drive is divided into two parts: the Vršič Pass, and the Soča River Valley. While not for stick-shift novices, all but the most timid drivers will agree that the scenery is worth the many hairpin turns. Frequent pull-outs offer plenty of opportunity to relax, stretch

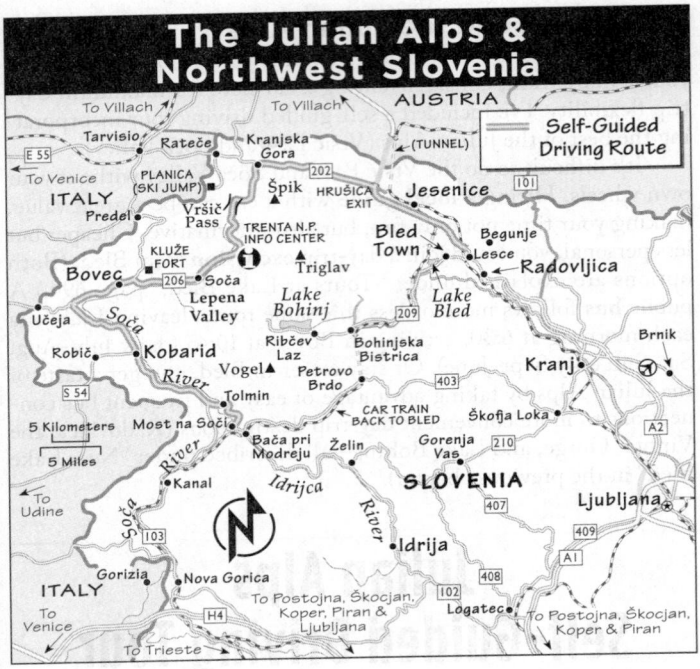

your legs, and enjoy the vistas.

Planning Your Time: This drive can be done in a day, but consider spending the night along the way for a more leisurely pace. You can start and end in Bled or Ljubljana. For efficient sightseeing, I prefer to begin in Bled (after appreciating the mountains from afar for a day or two) and end in the capital.

Length of This Tour: These rough estimates do not include stops: Bled to the top of Vršič Pass—1 hour; Vršič Pass to Trenta (start of Soča Valley)—30 min; Trenta to Bovec—30 min; Bovec to Kobarid—30 min; Kobarid to Ljubljana or Bled—2 hours (remember, it's an hour between Ljubljana and Bled). In other words, if you started and ended in Bled and drove the entire route without stopping, you'd make it home in less than five hours...but you'd miss so much. It takes at least a full day to really do the region justice.

Tourist Information: The best sources of information are the Bled TI (see page 689), the Triglav National Park Information Centers in Trenta (page 723) and Bled (page 689), and the TIs in Bovec and Kobarid (both listed in this chapter).

Maps: Pick up a good map before you begin (available at local TIs, travel agencies, and gas stations). The all-Slovenia *Autokarta Slovenija* or the TI's *Next Exit: Goldenhorn Route* map both include

all the essential roads, but several more detailed options are also available. The 1:50,000 Kod & Kam *Posoče* map covers the entire Vršič Pass and Soča Valley (but doesn't include the parts of the drive near Bled and Ljubljana).

OK...let's ride.

Part 1: Vršič Pass

From Bled or Ljubljana, take the A-2 expressway north, enjoying views of Mount Triglav on the left as you drive. About 10 minutes past Bled, you'll approach the industrial city of **Jesenice,** whose iron- and steelworks—once called the "Detroit of Yugoslavia"—filled this valley with multicolored smoke until most of them closed in the 1980s. The city plans to convert these old factories into a sort of theme park.

Just after the giant smokestack with the billboards, the little gaggle of colorful houses on the right (just next to the freeway) is **Kurja Vas** ("Chicken Village"). This unassuming place is locally famous for producing hockey players: 18 of the 20 players on the 1971 Yugoslav hockey team—which went to the World Championships—were from this tiny hamlet.

As you zip past Jesenice, keep your eye out for the exit marked *Jesenice-zahod, Trbiž/Tarvisio, Kr. Gora,* and *Hrušica* (it's after the gas station, just before the tunnel to Austria). When you exit, turn left toward *Trbiž/Tarvisio* and *Kranjska Gora* (yellow sign).

Just after the exit, the big, blue building surrounded by tall lights was the former border station (the overpass you'll go under leads into Austria). Locals have fond memories of visiting Austria during the Yugoslav days, when they smuggled home forbidden Western goods. Some items were simply not available back home (VCRs, Coca-Cola, designer clothes); other goods were simply better over there (chocolate, coffee, dishwasher soap).

Slovenes brag that their country—"with 56 percent of the land covered in forest"—is Europe's second-greenest. As you drive toward Kranjska Gora, take in all this greenery...and the characteristic Slovenian hayracks (recognized as part of the national heritage and now preserved; see page 635). The Vrata Valley (on the left) is a popular starting point for climbing Mount Triglav. Paralleling the road on the left is a rails-to-trails bike path that loops from here through Italy and Austria, allowing bikers to connect three countries in one day. On the right, watch for the statue of Jakob Aljaž, who actually bought Triglav, back when such a

Mount Triglav

Mount Triglav ("Three Heads") stands watch over the Julian Alps and all of Slovenia. Slovenes say that its three peaks are the guardians of the water, air, and earth. This mountain defines Slovenes, even adorning the nation's flag: Look for the national seal, with three peaks. The two squiggly lines under it represent the Adriatic. Or take a look at one of Slovenia's €0.50 coins.

From the town of Bled, you'll see Triglav peeking up over the ridge on a clear day. (You'll get an even better view from nearby Lake Bohinj.)

It's said that you're not a true Slovene until you've climbed Triglav. One native took these words very seriously and climbed the mountain 853 times...in one year. Climbing to the summit—at 9,396 feet—is an attainable goal for any hiker in decent shape. If you're here for a while and want to become an honorary Slovene, befriend a local and ask if he or she will take you to the top.

If mountain climbing isn't your style, relax at an outdoor café with a piece of cream cake and a view of Triglav. It won't make you a Slovene...but it's close enough on a quick visit.

thing was possible (he's pointing at his purchase). Ten minutes later, in Gozd Martuljek, you'll cross a bridge and enjoy a great head-on view of Špik Mountain.

Entering Kranjska Gora (once Yugoslavia's leading winter resort, still popular with Croatian skiers), you'll see a turnoff to the left marked for *Bovec* and *Vršič*. This leads up to the pass, but winter sports fanatics may first want to take a 15-minute detour to see the biggest ski jump in the world, a few miles ahead (stay straight through Kranjska Gora, then turn left at signs for **Planica,** the last stop before the Italian border). Every year, tens of thousands of sports fans flock here to watch the ski-flying world championships. This is where a local boy was the first human to fly more than 100 meters (328 feet) on skis. Today's competitors routinely set new world records (currently 784 feet—that's 17 seconds in the air). From the ski jump, you're a few minutes' walk from Italy or Austria. This region—spanning three nations—lobbied unsuccessfully under the name Senza Confini (Italian for "without borders") to host the 2006 Winter Olympics. This philosophy is in tune with the European Union's vision for a Europe of regions, rather than nations.

Back in Kranjska Gora, follow the signs for *Vršič*. Before long, you'll officially enter **Triglav National Park** and come to the first of this road's 50 hairpin turns (24 up, then 26 down)—each one numbered and labeled with the altitude in meters. Notice that they're cobbled to provide better traction. If the drive seems daunting, remember that 50-seat tour buses routinely conquer this pass... if they can do it, so can you. (Better yet, imagine the bicyclists who routinely pedal to the top. The best can do it in less than 30 minutes—faster than driving.)

After switchback #8, with the cute waterfall, park your car on the right and hike up the stairs on the left to the little **Russian chapel**. This road was built during World War I by at least 10,000 Russian POWs (of the Austro-Hungarian Empire) to supply the front lines of the Soča Front. The POWs lived and worked in terrible conditions, and several hundred died of illness and exposure. On March 8, 1916, an avalanche thundered down the mountains, killing hundreds more workers. This chapel was built where the final casualty was found. Take a minute to pay your respects to the men who built the road you're enjoying today. Because it's a Russian Orthodox chapel, notice that the crosses topping the steeples have three crossbars. (For more on the Orthodox faith, see page 789.)

Back on the road, after #17, look as high as you can on the cliff face to see sunlight poking through a **"window"** in the rock. This natural formation, a popular destination for intrepid hikers, is big enough for the Statue of Liberty to crawl through.

After #22, at the pullout for Erjavčeva Koča restaurant, you may see tour-bus groups making a fuss about the mountain vista. They're looking for a ghostly face in the cliff wall, supposedly belonging to the mythical figure **Ajda.** This village girl was cursed by the townspeople after correctly predicting the death of the Zlatorog (Golden Horn), a magical, beloved, chamois-like animal. Her tiny image (with a Picasso nose) is just above the tree line, a little to the right—try to get someone to point her out to you (you can see her best if you stand at the signpost near the road).

After #24, you reach the **summit** (5,285 feet). Consider getting out of the car to enjoy the views (in peak season,

Hemingway in the Julian Alps

It was against the scenic backdrop of the Slovenian Alps that a young man from Oak Park, Illinois, first came to Europe—the continent with which he would forever be identified. After graduating high school in 1917 and working briefly as a newspaper reporter, young Ernest Hemingway wanted to join the war effort in Europe. Bad vision kept him out of the army, but he craved combat experience—so he joined the Red Cross Ambulance Corps instead.

After a short detour through Paris, Hemingway was sent to the Italian Front. On his first day, he was given the job of retrieving human remains—gruesomely disfigured body parts—after the explosion of a munitions factory. Later he came to the Lower Piave Valley, not far from the Soča Front. In July 1918, his ambulance was hit by a mortar shell. Despite his injuries, he saved an Italian soldier who was also wounded. According to legend, he packed his own wound with cigarette butts to stop the flow of blood.

Sent to Milan to recuperate, Hemingway fell in love with a nurse, but she later left him for an Italian military officer. A decade later, Hemingway wrote about Kobarid (using its Italian name, Caporetto), the war, and his case of youthful heartbreak in the novel *A Farewell to Arms*.

you'll pay an attendant to park here). Hike up to the hut for a snack or drink on the grand view terrace. On the right, a long gravel chute gives hikers a thrilling glissade down. (From the pullout just beyond #26, it's easy to see hikers "skiing" down.)

As you begin the descent, keep an eye out for old WWI debris. A lonely guard tunnel stands after #28, followed by a tunnel marked *1916* (on the left) that was part of the road's original path. Then you'll see abandoned checkpoints from when this was the border between Italy and the Austro-Hungarian Empire. At #48 is a statue of **Julius Kugy,** an Italian botanist who wrote books about alpine flora.

At #49, the road to the right (marked *Izvir Soče*) leads to the **source of the Soča River.** If you feel like stretching your legs after all that shifting, drive about five minutes down this road to a restaurant parking lot. From here, you can take a challenging 20-minute uphill hike to the Soča source. This is also the starting point for a new, well-explained Soča Trail (Soška Pot) that leads all the way to the town of Bovec, mostly following the road we're driving on today. With plenty of time and a hankering to hike rather than drive, consider taking this trail (about 12 miles one-way).

Nearing the end of the switchbacks, follow signs for Bovec. Crossing the Soča River, you begin the second half of this trip.

Part 2: Soča River Valley

During World War I, the terrain between here and the Adriatic made up the Soča (Isonzo) Front. As you follow the Soča River south, down what's nicknamed the "Valley of the Cemeteries," the scenic mountainsides around you tell the tale of this terrible warfare. Imagine a young Ernest Hemingway driving his ambulance through these same hills (see sidebar).

But it's not all so gloomy. There are plenty of other diversions—interesting villages and churches, waterfalls and suspension bridges, and lots more. Perhaps most impressive is the remarkable clarity and milky-blue color of the Soča itself, which Slovenes proudly call their "emerald river."

The last Vršič switchback (#50) sends you into the village of **Trenta.** You'll pass a church and a botanical garden of alpine plants (Alpinum Juliana), then go over a bridge. Immediately after the bridge on the right is the parking lot for the Mlinarica Gorge. While the gorge is interesting, the bridge leading to it was damaged in a severe storm and hasn't yet been rebuilt—so it's best left to hardy hikers.

As you get to the cluster of buildings in Trenta's "downtown," look on the left for the **Triglav National Park Information Center,** which also serves as a regional TI (daily May–Oct 10:00–18:00, Dec–April 10:00–14:00, closed Nov, tel. 05/388-9330, www.tnp.si). The humble €4 museum here provides a look (with English explanations) at the park's flora, fauna, traditional culture, and mountaineering history. A poetic 15-minute slideshow explains the wonders and fragility of the park (included in museum entry, ask for English version as you enter).

After Trenta, you'll pass through a tunnel; then, on the left, look for a classic **suspension bridge.** Pull over and get out, enjoying the river's crystal-clear water and the spectacular mountain panorama as you bounce on the bridge.

About five miles beyond Trenta, in the town of Soča, is the **Church of St. Joseph** (with red onion dome, hiding behind the big tree on the right). The church was damaged in the earthquakes of 1998 and 2004, so the interior is likely covered with scaffolding. But if it's not covered, you'll see some fascinating art. During World War II, an artist hiding out in the mountains filled this church with patriotic symbolism. The interior is bathed in Yugoslav red, white, and blue—a brave statement made when such nationalistic sentiments were dangerous. On the ceiling is St. Michael (clad in Yugoslav colors) with Yugoslavia's

three WWII enemies at his feet: the eagle (Germany), the wolf (Italy), and the serpent (Japan). The tops of the walls along the nave are lined with saints, but these are Slavic, not Catholic. Finally, look carefully at the Stations of the Cross and find the faces of hated Yugoslav enemies: Hitler (fourth from altar on left) and Mussolini (first from altar on right). Behind the church, the stylized cross on the hill marks a World War I **cemetery**—the final resting place of some 600 Austro-Hungarian soldiers who were killed in action.

For another good example of how the Soča River cuts like God's band saw into the land, stop about two minutes past the church at the small gravel lot (on the left) marked ***Velika Korita Soče*** ("Grand Canyon of Soča"). Venture out onto the suspension bridge over the gorge...and bounce if you dare. Just beyond this bridge is the turnoff (on the left) to the Lepena Valley, home of the recommended Pristava Lepena pension—and their Lipizzaner horses (described later, under "Sleeping in Bovec").

Roughly five miles after the town of Soča, you exit the National Park, pass a WWI graveyard (on the left), and come to a fork in the road. The main route leads to the left, through Bovec. But first, take a two-mile detour to the right (marked *Trbiž/Tarvisio* and *Predel/Kluže*), where the WWI **Kluže Fort** keeps a close watch over the narrowest part of a valley leading to Italy (€3; July–Aug daily 9:00–20:00; June and Sept Sun–Fri 9:00–17:00, Sat 9:00–18:00; May and Oct Sat–Sun 10:00–18:00, closed Mon–Fri; closed Nov–April). In the 15th century, the Italians had a fort here to defend against the Ottomans. Half a millennium later, during World War I, it was used by Austrians to keep Italians out of their territory. Notice the ladder rungs fixed to the cliff face across the road from the fort—allowing soldiers to quickly get up to the mountaintop.

Back on the main road, continue to **Bovec.** This town, which saw some of the most vicious fighting of the Soča Front, was hit hard by earthquakes in 1994 and 1998 (and another tremor in 2004). Today, it's been rebuilt and remains the adventure-sports capital of the Soča River Valley—also known as the "Adrenaline Valley," famous for its whitewater activities. (Since the water comes

from high-mountain runoff, the temperature of the Soča never goes above 68 degrees Fahrenheit.) For a good lunch stop in Bovec, take the turnoff as you first reach the town, and you'll pass a pair of inviting restaurant terraces on the right (Martinov Hram, then Letni Vrt; for details, see "Eating in Bovec," later). But if you're not eating or spending the night in Bovec, you could skip the town (continue along the main road to bypass the town center).

Heading south along the river—with water somehow both perfectly clear and spectacularly turquoise—watch for happy kayakers. When you pass the intersection at Žaga, you're just four miles from Italy. Along the way, you'll also pass a pair of waterfalls: the well-known Boka ("Slovenia's second-longest waterfall," on the right just before Žaga) and the hidden gem Veliki Kozjak (unmarked, on the left just before Kobarid). For either, you'll have to park your car and hike uphill to see the falls.

Signs lead to the town of **Kobarid,** home to a sleepy main square and some fascinating WWI sights. Even if you don't think you're interested in the Soča Front, consider dropping in the Kobarid Museum. Driving up to the Italian mausoleum hovering over the town is a must. (These sights are described later, under "Sights in Kobarid.")

Leaving Kobarid, continue south along the Soča to **Tolmin.** Before you reach Tolmin, decide on your route back to civilization...

Finishing the Drive

To Ljubljana: From Tolmin, you have two possible driving routes to the capital. Either option brings you back to the A-1 expressway south of Ljubljana, and will get you to the city in about two hours (though the second route has fewer miles).

The option you'll encounter first (turnoff to the right before Tolmin) is the smoother, longer route southwest to **Nova Gorica.** This fairly dull city is divided in half by the Italian border (the Italian side is called "Gorizia"). Because Italians aren't allowed to gamble in their home towns, Nova Gorica is packed with casinos catering to Italian gamblers. In fact, it's home to Europe's biggest casino. Rocks spell out the name "TITO" on a hillside above town—a strange relic of an earlier age. From Nova Gorica, you can hop on the H-4 expressway, which links easily to the main A-1 expressway back to Ljubljana.

I prefer the more rural second option: Continue through Tolmin, then head southeast through the hills back toward Ljubljana. Along the way, you could stop for a bite and some sightseeing at the town of **Idrija** (EE-dree-yah), known to all Slovenes for three things: its tourable mercury mine, fine delicate lace, and tasty *žlikrofi* (like ravioli). Back at the expressway (at Logatec), head north to Ljubljana or on to Bled.

To Bled: The fastest option is to load your car onto a **"Car Train"** (Autovlak) that cuts directly through the mountains. The train departs at 18:30 from Most na Soči (just south of Tolmin, along the Idrija route described above) and arrives at Bohinjska Bistrica, near Lake Bohinj, at 19:14 (€12 for the car; confirm schedule at the Bled TI before making the trip). From Bohinjska Bistrica, it's just a half-hour drive back to Bled. No reservations are necessary, but arrive at the train station about 30 minutes before the scheduled departure to allow time to load the car.

To **drive** all the way back, the fastest route (about 2 hours) is partially on a twisty, rough, very poor-quality road (go through Tolmin, turn off at Bača pri Modreju to Podbrdo, then from Petrovo Brdo take a very curvy road through the mountains into Bohinjska Bistrica and on to Bled). For timid drivers, it's more sane and not too much longer to start out on the Idrija route toward Ljubljana (described above), but turn off in Želin (before Idrija) toward Skofja Loka and Kranj, then on to Bled. Or take one of the two routes described above for Ljubljana, then continue on the expressway past Ljubljana and back up to Bled (allow 3 hours).

Bovec

The biggest town in the area, Bovec (BOH-vets) has a happening main square and all the tourist amenities. It's best known as a hub for whitewater adventure sports. While not exactly quaint, Bovec is charming enough to qualify as a good lunch stop or overnight home base. If nothing else, it's a nice jolt of civilization wedged between the alpine cliffs.

Orientation to Bovec

(area code: 05)

Tourist Information

The helpful TI on the main square offers fliers on mountain biking and water sports (flexible hours, generally June–Sept daily 8:30–20:30, shorter hours off-season, Trg Golobarskih Žrtev 8, tel. 05/389-6444, www.bovec.si).

Arrival in Bovec

The main road skirts Bovec, but you can turn off (watch for signs on the right) to take the road that goes through the heart of town, then rejoins the main road farther along. As you approach the city center, you can't miss the main square, Trg Golobarskih Žrtev,

with the TI and a pair of good restaurants (described later, under "Eating in Bovec").

Sleeping in Bovec

$$$ Dobra Vila is a gorgeous hotel with classy, traditional-meets-contemporary decor that feels out of place in remote little Bovec. Not that I'm complaining. Its 12 rooms are swanky, and the public spaces (including a sitting room/library, breakfast room/restaurant, wine cellar, winter garden porch, and terrace with cozy mountain-view chairs) are welcoming. Enthusiastically run by Andreja and Sebastian Kovačič, it's a winner (high season: Db-€127–134, Db with balcony-€137–172; low season: Db-€112–119, Db with balcony-€122–157; Sb-€20 less than Db rate, price depends on size of room, 10 percent extra for 1-night stays, includes breakfast and dinner, fun old-fashioned elevator, on the left just as you enter town on the main road from the Vršič Pass at Mala Vas 112, tel. 05/389-6400, fax 05/389-6404, www.dobra-vila-bovec.com, welcome@dobra-vila-bovec.com).

$$ Martinov Hram has 11 nondescript modern rooms over a popular restaurant a few steps from Bovec's main square. While the rooms are an afterthought to the busy restaurant (reception at the bar), they're comfortable (very flexible rates, in peak season figure Sb-€40, Db-€70, a few euros less off-season, no extra charge for 1-night stays, Trg Golobarskih Žrtev 27, tel. 05/388-6214, sara.berginc@volja.net).

Near Bovec

$$$ Pristava Lepena is a relaxing oasis hiding out in the Lepena Valley just north of Bovec. Well-run by Milan and Silvia Dolenc,

Sleep Code

(€1 = about $1.40, country code: 386, area code: 05)
S = Single, **D** = Double/Twin, **T** = Triple, **Q** = Quad, **b** = bathroom. Unless otherwise noted, breakfast is included and credit cards are accepted. Everyone speaks English and all of these accommodations include breakfast. These prices don't include the €1.01 tourist tax per person, per night.

To help you sort easily through these listings, I've divided the rooms into three categories based on the price for a standard double room with bath:

$$$ Higher Priced—Most rooms €100 or more.
$$ Moderately Priced—Most rooms between €50–100.
$ Lower Priced—Most rooms €50 or less.

this place is its own little village: a series of rustic-looking cabins, a restaurant, and a sauna/outdoor swimming pool. Hiding behind the humble split-wood shingle exteriors is surprising comfort: 13 cozy apartments (with wood-burning stoves, TV, telephone, and all the amenities) that make you feel like relaxing. This place whispers "second honeymoon" (July–Aug: Db-€138; May–June and Sept: Db-€122; early Oct and late April: Db-€106; closed in winter, multi-night stays preferred, 1-night stays may be possible for 20 percent extra, dinner-€19, lunch and dinner-€31, nonrefundable 30 percent advance payment when you reserve; just before Bovec, turn left off the main road toward Lepena, and follow the white horses to Lepena 2; tel. 05/388-9900, fax 05/388-9901, www.pristava-lepena.com, pristava.lepena@siol.net). The Dolences also have three Welsh ponies and four purebred Lipizzaner horses (two mares, two geldings) that guests can ride (in riding ring-€16/hr, on trail-€20/hr, riding lesson-€24; non-guests may be able to ride for a few euros more—call ahead and ask).

$ Tourist Farm Pri Plajerju, on a picturesque plateau at the edge of Trenta (the first town at the bottom of the Vršič Pass road), is your budget option. Run by the Pretner family, this organic farm raises sheep and goats, and rents four apartments and one room in three buildings separate from the main house. While not quite as tidy as other tourist farms I recommend, it's the best one I found in the Soča Valley (July–Aug: Db-€38–50; Sept–June: Db-€34–45; price depends on size of room or apartment, breakfast-€6, dinner-€10, watch for signs to the left after passing through the village of Trenta, Trenta 16a, tel. & fax 05/388-9209, www.eko-plajer.com, info@eko-plajer.com).

Eating in Bovec

Martinov Hram, run by the Berginc family, has an inviting outdoor terrace under a grape trellis. Inside, the nicely traditional decor goes well with Slovenian specialties focused on sheep (good homemade bread, €6–9 pastas, €9–15 main courses, closed Mon, on the main road through Bovec, just before the main square on the right at Trg Golobarskih Žrtev 27, tel. 05/388-6214).

Letni Vrt Pizzeria, dominating the main square, is the busiest place in town—with pizzas, pastas, salads, and more (closed Sun, Trg Golobarskih Žrtev 12, tel. 05/388-6335).

Kobarid

Kobarid (KOH-bah-reed) feels older, and therefore a bit more appealing, than its bigger neighbor Bovec. This humble settlement was immortalized by a literary giant, Ernest Hemingway, who drove an ambulance in these mountains during World War I. He described Kobarid as "a little white town with a campanile in a valley. It was a clean little town and there was a fine fountain in the square." Sounds about right. Even though Kobarid loves to tout its Hemingway connection, historians believe that Papa did not actually visit Kobarid until he came back after the war to research his book.

Aside from its brush with literary greatness, Kobarid is known as a hub of Soča Front information (with an excellent WWI museum, a hilltop Italian mausoleum, and walks that connect the nearby sights). You won't find the fountain Hemingway wrote about—it's since been covered up by houses (though the town government hopes to excavate it as a tourist attraction). You will find a modern statue of Simon Gregorčič (overlooking the main intersection), the beloved Slovenian priest-poet who came from and wrote about the Soča Valley.

Orientation to Kobarid

(area code: 05)

The main road cuts right through the heart of little Kobarid, bisecting its main square (Trg Svobode). The Kobarid Museum is along this road, on the left before the square. To reach the museum from the main square, simply walk five minutes back toward Bovec.

Tourist Information

The TI has good information on the area and Internet access (daily July–Sept 9:00–19:00, Oct–April 10:00–13:00 & 14:00–15:00, May–June 9:00–13:00 & 14:00–18:00, tel. 05/380-0490, on the main square at Trg Svobode 16, www.lto-sotocje.si and www.kobarid.si).

Sights in Kobarid

▲▲▲Kobarid Museum (Kobariški Muzej)—This modest but world-class museum, offering a haunting look at the tragedy of the Soča Front, was voted Europe's best museum in 1993. The tasteful exhibits, with fine English descriptions and a pacifist tone, take an even-handed approach to the fighting—without getting hung up on identifying the "good guys" and the "bad guys." The museum's focus is not on the guns and heroes, but on the big picture of the front and on the stories of the common people who fought and died here.

Cost, Hours, Location: €4, good €8 *Soča Front* book; April–Sept Mon–Fri 9:00–18:00, Sat–Sun 9:00–19:00; Oct–March Mon–Fri 10:00–17:00, Sat–Sun 9:00–18:00; Gregorčičeva 10, tel. 05/389-0000, www.kobariski-muzej.si.

➲ Self-Guided Tour: The entry is lined with hastily made cement and barbed-wire gravestones, flags representing all the nationalities involved in the fighting, and pictures of soldiers and nurses from diverse backgrounds who were brought together here (for example, the men wearing fezzes were from Bosnia-Herzegovina, annexed by the Austro-Hungarian Empire shortly before the war).

Buy your ticket and ask to watch the English version of the 19-minute film on the history of the Soča Front (informative but dry, plays on top floor).

The first floor up is divided into several rooms. The White Room, filled with rusty crampons, wire-cutters, pickaxes, and shovels, explains wintertime conditions at the front. What looks like a bear trap was actually used to trap enemy soldiers. The Room of the Rear shows the day-to-day activities away from the front line, from supplying troops to more mundane activities (milking cows, washing clothes, getting a shave, playing with a dog). The Black Room is the museum's most somber room, commemorating the more than one million casualties of the Soča Front. These heartbreaking exhibits honor the common people whose bodies fertilized the battlefields of Europe. Horrific images of war injuries are juxtaposed with a display of medals earned by soldiers such as these—prompting the question, was it worth it? The little altar was donated by schoolchildren, who sent it to the front to offer the troops some solace.

Through the door marked *Room of the Krn Range* (also on the first floor up), find your way to the Kobarid Rooms, which trace

the history of this region from antiquity to today. High on the wall, look for the timelines explaining the area's turbulent history. The one in the second room shows wave after wave of invaders (including Ottomans, Habsburgs, and Napoleon). In the next room, above a display case with military uniforms, another timeline shows the many flags that flew over Kobarid's main square in the 20th century.

On the top floor, across from the room where the film plays (described above), you'll see a giant model of the surrounding mountains, painstakingly tracing the successful Austrian-German *Blitzkrieg* attack during the Battle of Kobarid.

▲▲Italian Mausoleum (Kostnica)—The 55 miles between here and the Adriatic are dotted with more than 75 cemeteries, reminders of the countless casualties of the Soča Front. One of the most dramatic is this mausoleum, overlooking Kobarid. The access road, across Kobarid's main square from the side of the church, is marked by stone gate towers (with the word *Kostnica*—one tower is topped with a cross and the other with a star for the Italian army).

Take the road up Gradič Hill—passing Stations of the Cross—to the mausoleum. Built in 1938 (when this was still part of Italy) around the existing Church of St. Anthony, this octagonal pyramid holds the remains of 7,014 Italian soldiers. The stark, cold, Neoclassical architecture is pure Mussolini. Names are listed alphabetically, along with mass graves for more than 1,700 unknown soldiers *(militi ignoti)*.

Walk behind the church and enjoy the **view.** Find the WWI battlements high on the mountain's rock face (with your back to church, they're at 10 o'clock). Incredibly, the fighting was done on these treacherous ridges; civilians in the valleys only heard the distant battles. Looking up and down the valley, notice the "signal churches" evenly spaced on hilltops, each barely within view of the next—an ancient method for spreading messages or warnings across long distances quickly.

If the **church** is open, go inside and look above the door to see a brave soldier standing over the body of a fallen comrade and fending off enemies with nothing but rocks.

When Mussolini came to dedicate the mausoleum, local revolutionaries plotted an assassination attempt that couldn't fail. A young man planned to suicide-bomb Mussolini as he came back into town from this hilltop. But as Mussolini's car drove past,

The Soča (Isonzo) Front

The valley in Slovenia's northwest corner—called Soča in Slovene and Isonzo in Italian—saw some of World War I's fiercest fighting. While the Western Front gets more attention, this eastern border between the Central Powers and the Allies was just as significant. In a series of 12 battles involving 22 different nationalities along a 60-mile-long front, 300,000 soldiers died, 700,000 were wounded, and 100,000 were declared MIA. In addition, tens of thousands of civilians died. A young Ernest Hemingway, who drove an ambulance for the Italian army in nearby fighting, would later write the novel *A Farewell to Arms* about the battles here (see "Hemingway in the Julian Alps" sidebar on page 722).

On April 26, 1915, Italy joined the Allies. A month later, it declared war on the Austro-Hungarian Empire (which included Slovenia). Italy unexpectedly invaded the Soča Valley, quickly taking the tiny town of Kobarid, which it planned to use as a home base for attacks deeper into Austro-Hungarian territory. For the next 29 months, Italy launched 10 more offensives against the Austro-Hungarian army on the mountaintops. All of these Italian offensives were unsuccessful, even though the Italians outnumbered their opponents three to one. This was unimaginably difficult warfare—Italy had to attack uphill, waging war high in the mountains, in the harshest of conditions. Trenches were carved into rock instead of mud, and many unprepared conscripts—brought here from faraway lands and unaccustomed to the harsh winter conditions atop the Alps—froze to death. During one winter alone, some 60,000 soldiers were killed by avalanches.

Visitors take a look at this tight valley, hemmed in by seemingly impassible mountains, and wonder: Why would people fight so fiercely over such inhospitable terrain? At the time, Slovenia was the natural route from Italy to the Austro-Hungarian capital

the would-be assassin looked at his fellow townspeople around him, realized the innocent blood he would also spill, and had a last-minute change of heart. Mussolini's trip was uneventful, and fascism continued to thrive in Italy.

World War I Walks—At the Kobarid Museum (and local TIs), you can pick up a free brochure outlining the **"Kobarid Historical Walk"** tracing WWI sites in town and the surrounding countryside (3 miles, mostly uphill, allow 3–5 hours; or you can just do a shorter stretch along the river, 1–2 hours). A newer **"Walk of**

at Vienna. The Italians believed that if they could hold this valley and push over the mountains, Vienna—and victory—would be theirs. Once committed, they couldn't turn back, and the war devolved into one of attrition—who would fall first?

In the fall of 1917, Austro-Hungarian Emperor Karl appealed to his ally, Germany, and the Germans agreed to assemble an army for a new attack to retake Kobarid and the Soča Valley. In an incredible logistical feat, they spent just six weeks building and supplying this new army by transporting troops and equipment high across the mountaintops under cover of darkness... over the heads of their oblivious Italian foes dozing in the valley.

On October 24, Austria-Hungary and Germany launched a downhill attack of 600,000 soldiers into the town of Kobarid. This crucial 12th battle of the Soča Front, better known as the Battle of Kobarid, was the turning point—and saw the introduction of battlefield innovations that are commonplace in the military today. German field commanders were empowered to act independently on the battlefield, reacting immediately to developments rather than waiting for approval. Also, for the first time ever, the Austrian-German army used elements of a new surprise-attack technique called *Blitzkrieg*. (One German officer, Erwin Rommel, made great strides in the fighting here, and later climbed the ranks to become famous as Hitler's "Desert Fox" in North Africa.)

The attack caught the Italian forces off-guard, quickly breaking through three lines of defense. Within three days, the Italians were forced to retreat. (Because the Italian military worked from the top down, the soldiers were sitting ducks once they were cut off from their commanders.) The Austrians called their victory the "Miracle at Kobarid." But Italy felt differently. The Italians saw the battle of Caporetto (the Italian name for Kobarid) as their Alamo. To this day, when an Italian finds himself in a mess, he says, "At least it's not a *Caporetto*."

A year later, Italy came back—this time with the aid of British, French, and US forces—and easily retook this area. On November 4, 1918, Austria-Hungary conceded defeat. After more than a million casualties, the fighting at Soča was finally over.

Peace" links several WWI sights all along the Soča Valley (details and map at TI). History buffs can also call ahead to arrange a private guide (€15/hr, tel. 05/389-0000).

Sleeping in Kobarid

(€1 = about $1.40, country code: 386, area code: 05)

My first listing is right on the main square. The other two hide on side-streets about a block off the main road through town, between

the museum and the main square (about a 3-min walk to either).

$$$ Hotel Hvala is the only real hotel in town. Run by the Hvala family, its 31 contemporary rooms are comfortable, and the location can't be beat. The mural on the wall in the elevator shaft tells the story of the Soča Valley as you go up toward the top floor (mid-July–Aug: Sb-€76, Db-€112; April–mid-July and Sept–mid-Nov: Sb-€72, Db-€104; cheaper off-season; pricier superior Db with air-con and sleek new decor-€160–200, hotel closed Feb and most of Nov, elevator, Trg Svobode 1, tel. 05/389-9300, fax 05/388-5322, www.hotelhvala.si, topli.val@siol.net).

$ Picerija Fedrig is a pizzeria that rents five simple but fine rooms upstairs (Db-€40, less for more than 1 night, 10 percent more in Aug, between the main square and the Kobarid Museum at Volaričeva 11, tel. 05/389-0115, jernej.grahli@volja.net).

$ Apartma-Ra has four rooms and three apartments in a cozy, family-friendly house (D-€30, Db-€40–50, apartment-€80–110, cash only, also runs a rafting company, Gregorčičeva 6C, mobile 041-641-899, apartma-ra@siol.net).

Eating in Kobarid

Topli Val ("Heat Wave"), Hotel Hvala's restaurant, is pricey but good, with a menu that emphasizes fish (€9–15 pastas, €10–30 main dishes, lengthy list of Slovenian wines, daily 12:00–15:00 & 18:00–23:00, Trg Svobode 1, tel. 05/389-9300).

Kotlar Restaurant, across the square from Hotel Hvala, is similarly priced and well-regarded (Thu–Mon 12:00–23:00, closed Tue–Wed, Trg Svobode 11, tel. 05/389-1110). Kotlar also rents rooms if you're in a pinch.

Picerija Fedrig (also listed under "Sleeping in Kobarid," above) serves up good €5–7 pizzas (Tue–Sun 12:00–22:00, closed Mon, Volaričeva 11, tel. 05/389-0115).

CROATIA

CROATIA

Hrvatska

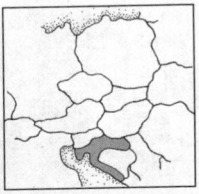

Sunny beaches, succulent seafood, and a taste of *la dolce vita*...in Eastern Europe?

With thousands of miles of seafront and more than a thousand islands, Croatia's coastline is Eastern Europe's Riviera. Holidaymakers love its pebbly beaches, predictably balmy summer weather, and melt-in-your-mouth seafood. Croatia is also historic. From ruined Roman arenas and Byzantine mosaics to Venetian bell towers, Habsburg villas, and even communist concrete, past rulers have left their mark.

Croatia feels more Mediterranean than "Eastern European." Historically, Croatia has more in common with Venice and Rome than Vienna or Budapest. Especially on the coast, it's sometimes difficult to distinguish this lively, chaotic place from Italy. If you've become accustomed to the Germanic efficiency of Slovenia, Croatia's relaxed and unpredictable style can come as a shock.

Aside from its fun-in-the-sun status, Croatia is also known as one of the sites, just over a decade and a half ago, of the most violent European war in generations. Thankfully, the bloodshed is in the past. While a trip to Croatia offers thoughtful travelers the opportunity to understand a complicated chapter of recent history, most visitors focus instead on its substantial natural wonders: mountains, waterfalls, sun, sand, and sea.

Croatia's 3,600 miles of coastline—its main draw for visitors—is loosely divided into three regions. Most people flock to the Dalmatian Coast, in the south—where dramatic limestone cliffs rise from the deep and islands are scattered just offshore (Korčula is the most appealing). Here you'll find Croatia's top tourist town, Dubrovnik, and the big city of Split, with its impressive Roman ruins. Way up at the northern corner of the country is the wedge-

shaped peninsula called Istria, which has less dramatic scenery but arguably even more romantic towns—including my favorite, the Venetian-flavored Rovinj—along with the city of Pula (more great Roman ruins) and a hilly interior blanketed with vineyards and topped with hill towns (Motovun is the best).

Enjoy the coast, but don't ignore the interior. The bustling capital of Zagreb is urban, engaging, and full of great museums. And Croatia's single best natural wonder (in this country that's so full of them) are the stunning waterfalls at Plitvice Lakes National Park.

If you want to blow through a lot of money here, you can. Croatian hotels, especially on the coast, are a terrible value, and there are plenty of touristy restaurants happy to overcharge you. But if you know where to look, you can find some wonderful budget alternatives—foremost among them *sobe* (rooms in private

Croatia Almanac

Official Name: Republika Hrvatska, or just Hrvatska for short.

Snapshot History: After losing its independence to Hungary in 1102, Croatia watched as most of its coastline became Venetian and its interior was conquered by Ottomans. Croatia was "rescued" by the Habsburgs, but after World War I it became part of Yugoslavia—a decision many Croats regretted until they finally gained independence in 1991 through a bitter war with their Serbian neighbors.

Population: Of the country's 4.5 million people, 90 percent are ethnic Croats (Catholic) and 4.5 percent are Serbs (Orthodox). (The Serb population was more than double that before the ethnic cleansing of the 1991–1995 war.) About 1.3 percent of Croatians are Bosniak (Muslim). "Croatians" are citizens of Croatia; "Croats" are a distinct ethnic group made up of Catholic South Slavs. So Orthodox Serbs living in Croatia can be Croatians, but they can't be Croats (since they're not Catholic).

Latitude and Longitude: 45°N and 15°E (similar latitude to Venice, Italy; Ottawa, Canada; or Portland, Oregon).

Area: 22,000 square miles, similar to West Virginia.

Geography: This boomerang-shaped country has two terrains: Stretching north to south is the long, rugged Mediterranean coastline (3,600 miles of beach, including more than 1,100 offshore islands), which is warm and dry. Rising up from the sea are the Dinaric Mountains (which also cover virtually all of neighboring Bosnia-Herzegovina). To the northeast, beginning at about Zagreb, Croatia's flat, inland "panhandle" (called Slavonia) has hot summers and cold winters.

Biggest Cities: The capital, Zagreb (in the northern interior), has 780,000 people; Split (along the Dalmatian Coast) has 189,000; and Rijeka (on the northern coast) has 150,000.

Economy: Much of the country's wealth ($70 billion GDP, $18,300 GDP per capita) comes from tourism, banking, and trade with Italy. Unemployment is a stiff 14 percent.

homes). *Sobe* are a comfortable compromise: new-feeling, fresh, hotelesque doubles with a private bathroom and TV, for half the cost of a moldy room in a crumbling resort hotel just down the beach (for details, see the "Croatian Accommodation" sidebar, later).

Europeans are reverent sun-worshippers, and on sunny days, virtually every square inch of coastal Croatia is occupied by a sunbather on a beach towel. Nude beaches are a big deal, especially for vacationing Germans and Austrians. If you want to work on an all-around tan, seek out a beach marked *FKK* (from the German

Currency: 1 kuna (kn, or HRK) = about 20 cents, and 5 kunas = about $1. One kuna is broken down into 100 lipa. *Kuna* is Croatian for "marten" (a foxlike animal), recalling the long-ago era when fur pelts were used as currency. A *lipa* is a linden tree.

Government: The country's prime minister (currently Jadranka Kosor, head of the majority party in parliament) is conservative, while the directly elected (but more figurehead) president—Stipe Mesić through 2010—is left-of-center. The single-house assembly (Sabor) of 152 legislators is elected by popular vote.

Flag: The flag has three horizontal bands (red on top, white, and blue) with a traditional red-and-white checkerboard shield in the center.

The Average Croatian: The average Croatian will live to age 74 and have 1.4 children. One in four uses the Internet. The average Croatian absolutely adores the soccer team Dinamo Zagreb and absolutely despises Hajduk Split...or vice versa.

Notable Croatians: A pair of big-league historical figures was born in Croatia: Roman Emperor Diocletian (A.D. 245–313) and explorer Marco Polo (1254?–1324). More recently, many Americans whose name ends in "-ich" have Croatian roots, including actor John Malkovich and Ohio politicians Dennis Kucinich and John Kasich, not to mention baseball legend Roger Marich...I mean, Maris. More Croatian athletes abound: NBA fans might recognize Toni Kukoč or Gordan Giricek, and at the 2002 and 2006 Winter Olympic Games, the women's downhill skiing events were dominated by Janica Kostelić. Actor Goran Višnjić (from TV's *ER*) was born and raised in Croatia, and served in the army as a paratrooper. You've likely never heard of the beloved Croatian sculptor Ivan Meštrović, but you'll see his expressive works all over the country (see page 832). Inventor Nikola Tesla (1856–1943)—who, as a rival of Thomas Edison's, invented alternating current (AC)—was a Croatian-born Serb. And a band of well-dressed 17th-century Croatian soldiers stationed in France gave the Western world a new fashion accessory—the *cravate*, or necktie (for the full story, see page 830).

Freikörper Kultur, or "free body culture"). First-timers get comfortable in a hurry, finding they're not the only pink novices on the rocks. But don't get too excited—these beaches are most beloved by people you'd rather see with their clothes on.

Perhaps because sunshine is so important to the economy, Croatians often seem particularly affected by weather. They complain that the once-predictable climate has become erratic, with surprise rainy spells or heat waves in the once perfectly consistent, balmy summer months. Historically, the Dubrovnik senate was legally forbidden from making any major decision if the hot,

humid Jugo wind was blowing, as that wind tended to make people cranky and ill-tempered. And today, the weather report includes a *biometeorološka prognoza* that indicates how the day's weather will affect your mood. Weather maps come with smiley or frowny faces, and forecasts predict, "People will be tired in the afternoon and not feel like working." Hmm...good excuse.

Every Croatian coastal town has two parts: The time-warp old town, and the obnoxious resort sprawl. Main drags are clogged with gift shops selling shell sculptures and tasteless T-shirts. While European visitors enjoy this tacky-trinket tourism, Americans are generally more interested in Old World charm. Fortunately, it's relatively easy to ignore the touristy scene and instead poke your way into twisty old medieval lanes, draped with drying laundry and populated by gossiping housewives, humble fishermen's taverns, and soccer-playing kids.

Croatian popular music, the mariachi music of Europe, is the ever-present soundtrack of a Dalmatian vacation. Oliver Dragojević—singing soulful Mediterranean ballads with his gravelly, passionate voice—is the Croatian Tom Jones. Known simply as "Oliver," this beloved crooner gets airplay across Europe and has spawned many imitators (such as the almost-as-popular Gibonni).

More traditional is the hauntingly beautiful *klapa* music—men's voices harmonizing a cappella, like barbershop with a soothing Adriatic flavor. Typically the leader begins the song, and the rest of the group (usually 3 to 12 singers) follow behind him with a slight delay. You'll see mariachi-style *klapa* groups performing in touristy areas; a CD of one of these performances (or of a professional group—Cambi is great) is a fun souvenir.

Croatia may be Europe's second most ardently Catholic country (after Poland). Under communism, religion was downplayed and many people gave up the habit of attending Mass (or mosque) regularly. But as the wars raged in the early 1990s, many Croatians rediscovered their religion. You may be surprised by how many people you see worshipping in Croatia's churches today.

In the Yugoslav era, Croatia was flooded with tourists—both European and American—who fell in love with its achingly beau-

tiful beaches and coves. In its heyday, Croatia hosted about 10 million visitors a year, who provided the country with about a third of its income. But then, for several years after the war, Croatia floundered. Just a decade ago, the streets of Dubrovnik were empty, lined with souvenir shops tended by desperate-looking vendors. But in the last few years, locals are breathing a sigh of relief as the number of visitors returns to pre-war highs. With astonishing speed, Croatia is becoming one of Europe's top destinations.

Even so, the standards for service (at restaurants, hotels, and so on) are lower than you might expect. While you'll meet plenty of wonderfully big-hearted Croatians, many of my readers have characterized the Croatian waiters or hotel receptionists they've encountered as "rude." Be prepared for two universal gestures: the classic eye-roll, directed at anyone asking someone to do something that's not precisely in their job description—or, all too often, something that is; and the "Croatian Shrug"—a simple gesture meaning, "Don't know, don't care."

Maybe this attitude is understandable, even forgivable. After all, how would you like it if a tidal wave of sweaty, ill-behaved, clueless tourists took over your entire town for the nicest months of each year? The one-two punch of several decades of communism, followed by a devastating war, wasn't exactly the best preparation for being the perfect host. On the other hand, it can be a bit jarring in a place so dependent upon tourism to find such a stubborn disregard for some of the fundamentals of hospitality. My advice: Expect the worst, then be pleasantly surprised by the positive interactions you have, rather than getting hung up on the frustrating ones.

Today's Croatia is crawling with a Babel of international guests speaking German, French, Italian, every accent of English...and a smattering of Croatian. And yet, despite the tourists, this place remains distinctly and stubbornly Croatian. You'd have to search pretty hard to find a McDonald's.

Helpful Hints

Stow Your Euros: Tourists are notorious for confusing euro bills with Croatian kuna bills (both modeled after the old German *Deutschmark* and therefore similar). Make a point of deep-storing all euros while outside the euro zone, or you'll pay about seven times more than you should to enjoy Croatia.

Hotel Prices: In some towns, most accommodations tend to list prices in euros; in others, it's in kunas; and in Dubrovnik, it's a pretty even mix of both. No matter how hotels list their prices, they generally prefer payment in kunas. To make it easier for you to compare your options, in a few cases I've converted the rates they gave me into the other currency, so you might notice some

Croatian Accommodations

For most travelers, Croatian hotels are a bad value. You basically have two options: Over-the-top, fancy, overpriced splurge hotels catering to the international jet set crowd; or run-down, communist-era, overpriced resort hotels desperate for a renovation. Whether old or new, Croatian hotels all seem to carry on the old Yugoslav aesthetic of mass tourism: crowded "beach" access (often on a concrete pad), typically surly staff, a travel-agency desk selling excursions in the lobby, corny live music a few nights each week, and a seaview apéritif bar. More money buys you a friendlier, more polished staff and newer decor. These hotels are just fine with the busloads of European tourists who head south for a week-long summer holiday. But Americans are appalled at how much you have to spend for such low quality.

Fortunately, the void of mid-range sleeps is filled perfectly by what locals call "private accommodations": a rented apartment *(apartman)* or a room in a private home (*soba,* pronounced SOH-bah; plural *sobe*, SOH-bay). Private accommodations offer travelers a characteristic and money-saving alternative for a fraction of the price of a hotel.

Often run by empty-nesters, private accommodations are similar to British bed-and-breakfasts...minus the breakfast (ask your host about the best nearby breakfast spot). Generally the more you pay, the more privacy and amenities you get: private bathroom, TV, air-conditioning, kitchenette, and so on. The simplest *sobe* allow you to experience Croatia on the cheap, at nearly youth-hostel prices, while giving you a great opportunity to connect with a local family. The fanciest *sobe* are downright swanky and offer near-hotel anonymity. Apartments are bigger and cost more than *sobe,* but they're still far cheaper than hotels.

Registered *sobe* are rated by the government, using a system that assigns stars based on amenities. Three or more stars means that you'll have your own bathroom, two stars means that the bathroom's down the hall, and one star is rock-bottom basic. If you don't like the idea of sharing a toilet with strangers, look for three stars and you'll do fine. (Apartments always have private bathrooms, plus modest kitchen facilities.) Many, but not all, three-star *sobe* also have TV and air-conditioning (but usually no telephone). The prices for private accommodations generally

fluctuate with the seasons, and remember that stays of fewer than three nights usually come with a 20–50 percent surcharge (though this is often waived outside of peak season).

You can reserve most *sobe* in advance by email or by phone. In fact, since the best-value *sobe* deservedly book up early, reservations are highly recommended. But keep in mind that holding you a room represents a major financial risk for your host, who loses money if you don't show up. For this reason, some hosts may ask for your credit card number to secure the reservation. (They'll generally ask for payment in cash when you're there; your credit card won't be charged, and is used only as a convenience to secure your reservation.) Other hosts might ask you to wire or mail money to them as a deposit. Because wiring money can come with substantial fees—which you (rather than the *sobe* host) will incur—it usually works better to mail them a check or travelers check. Ask your *sobe* host which options they accept. If their request seems too complicated for you, reserve elsewhere.

If you like to travel spontaneously, during most of the year you'll have no problem finding *sobe* as you go (though August can be extremely crowded). Locals hawking rooms meet each arriving boat, bus, and train. Many of these *sobe* have not been classified by the government, but they can sometimes turn out to be a good deal. The person generally shows photos of her place, you haggle for a price, then she escorts you to your new home. Be sure you understand exactly where it's located (i.e., within easy walking distance of the attractions) before you accept—ask to see the location on a map, and find out how long it takes to walk into town.

You can also keep an eye out for rooms as you walk or drive through town—you'll see blue *sobe* and *apartman* signs everywhere. It's actually fun to visit a few homes and make a deal. While it takes nerve to just show up without a room, this is standard operating procedure for backpackers.

As a last resort, you can enlist the help of a travel agency to find you a room—but you'll pay 10–30 percent extra (various agencies are listed in this book; to search from home, try www.dubrovnikapartmentsource.com for Dubrovnik, or www.adriatica.net for all of Croatia).

I'm accustomed to staying in hotels. But a few years ago, I found all of the hotels in Dubrovnik booked up. With some trepidation, I stayed in a *soba*...and I'll never go back to a Croatian resort hotel again. I've made it my mission to convince you to sleep in *sobe*, too.

variation between the actual prices and those listed in this book. If you need to convert prices between kunas and euros (7 kunas = about €1), it's simple: just divide the kuna price by 7 to get euros, or multiply the euro price by 7 to get kunas.

Seasonality: Croatia is the most seasonal destination in this book. In a little coastal resort village, a few weeks can mean the difference between being a ghost town or being deluged with crowds. Peak season is July and August, though late June and most of September are becoming nearly as popular. During these busy times, accommodations, boats, and beaches are jam-packed. Shoulder season—the most appealing time to travel here—is late May through mid-June, and late September through early October. During the off-season (mid-October–mid-May), many small towns close down entirely, with only one hotel and one restaurant remaining open during the lean winter months.

Be aware that even in peak season, schedules are made to be broken, and opening times can change suddenly based on demand. The hours I've listed *should* be right...but if you have your heart set on a certain sight, confirm times with the TI on your arrival.

Telephones: Croatian mobile phone numbers begin with 091, 098, or 099. Numbers beginning with 060 are pricey toll lines. For more details on how to dial, see page 1088.

Free Tourist Help by Phone: The "Croatian Angels" service gives free information in English over a toll-free line (tel. 062-999-999, daily June–Aug 8:00–24:00, April–May and Sept–mid-Oct 9:00–17:00, closed mid-Oct–March).

Addresses: Addresses listed with a street name and followed by "b.b." have no street number. In most small towns, locals ignore not only street numbers but also street names—navigate with a map or by asking for directions.

Slick Pavement: Old towns, with their well-polished pavement stones and many slick stairs, can be quite treacherous, especially after a rainstorm. (On a recent trip, one of your co-authors almost broke his arm slipping down a flight of stairs.) Tread with care.

Beaches: Croatia is known for its glimmering beaches. However, most are pebbly or rocky rather than sandy—and spiny sea urchins are not uncommon. In addition to your swimsuit, you may want to pack (or buy in Europe) a pair of water shoes for wading. Bring good sunscreen, and—if you'll be hiking on Croatia's many scenic coastal trails, which can be rugged and often lack shade—a sun hat and sturdy shoes.

Siesta: Croatians eat their big meal at lunch, then take a traditional Mediterranean siesta. This means that many stores, museums, and churches are closed in the mid-afternoon.

Business Closures on Sundays: During the busier tourist

months, from June through December, stores are allowed to be open on Sundays. Off-season, from January through May, most shops are legally required to close.

Dalmatian Coast Practicalities

Although it's a long haul from the other destinations in this book, the Dalmatian Coast is well worth it: It's the cherry on top of your grand Eastern European adventure. The following tips are useful for those traveling to Dubrovnik, Split, and Korčula (covered in the next three chapters).

Getting to the Dalmatian Coast

Three recent developments help make the long trip down to Dalmatia nearly painless: an expressway, a high-speed train line, and budget flights.

By Car or Bus: Thanks to Croatia's new A-1 super-expressway, the road trip from Zagreb to Split—which used to take seven hours—now takes less than five. Travelers who used to opt for an all-day journey or a bleary-eyed night bus can now leave Zagreb after an early dinner and arrive in Split before bedtime.

By Train: Croatian Railways' "tilting train" line connects Zagreb to Split three times a day (2/day off-season, www.hznet.hr). These trains can reach high speeds because the tracks are banked and the cars are designed to tilt slightly, allowing you to make it from the capital to the Dalmatian Coast in just five and a half hours.

By Plane: Several low-cost airlines connect Dalmatia to northern Croatia and the rest of Europe. Even the national carrier, Croatia Airlines, often has surprisingly cheap tickets between Zagreb and Dubrovnik or Split. For more details, see page 1105.

By Boat: Overnight boats sail in each direction between Rijeka (on the northern Croatian coast—4 hours by train from Zagreb and 2.5 hours by train from Ljubljana) and Split. But this option is much slower than the alternatives mentioned above.

Getting Around the Dalmatian Coast

There are no trains along the Dalmatian Coast (the southernmost station is in Split). Once here, you'll rely on ferries, buses, or a rental car. I've listed the most useful boat and bus departures in the "Connections" section for each destination.

By Boat: Plodding car ferries and speedy catamarans inexpensively shuttle tourists between major coastal cities and quiet island towns. Boat rides are cheap for deck passengers. A short hop, such as from Split to the island of Korčula, costs around $5–10; for a longer trip, such as from Split to Dubrovnik, figure $20–25. Most of the ferries are run by Jadrolinija, which conveniently

connects the three destinations in this book, plus many more (www.jadrolinija.hr). Advance reservations are not necessary for deck passengers; you can almost always find a seat on the deck or in the on-board café. You can't reserve a space for a car, so in peak season, drivers will want to arrive at the boat early (ask the local TI what time you should arrive). The faster, passenger-only catamarans are run by smaller companies. These include the *Krilo* between Split, Hvar, and Korčula (www.krilo.hr); and the *Nona Ana* between Dubrovnik and Korčula (www.gv-line.hr). Because space is limited on the catamarans, it's smart to buy your tickets early in the day (ask the local TI or boat ticket office what time they recommend; catamaran tickets generally go on sale the morning of the day the boat departs, except in Korčula, where they're sold the night before). Then, to get a good seat on board, it's wise to show up 30–60 minutes before departure time.

By Bus: Buses can be a good way to connect destinations when there are gaps in the boat schedule, even for islands. Confusingly, a single bus route can be operated by a variety of different companies, making it difficult to find comprehensive schedules (though Split has a handy online timetable: www.ak-split.hr). Confirm schedules with a local TI or bus station. Prices vary among companies, even for identical journeys. For popular routes during peak season, drop by the station to buy your ticket a few hours—or even days—in advance to ensure getting a seat (ask the bus station ticket office or the local TI how far ahead you should arrive). You'll pay about $2 per bag to stow your luggage under the bus. If you're headed south along the coast, sitting on the right side comes with substantially better scenery (sit on the left for northbound buses).

By Car: Considering the long distances, cheap and frequent buses, long ferry lines for cars (as opposed to quick and fun connections for walk-ons), and worthlessness of a car in Dubrovnik or Split, those simply lacing together the major sights are better off without a car. Drivers should be prepared for twisty seaside roads, wonderful views, and plenty of tempting stopovers. As you approach any town, follow the signs to *Centar* (usually also signed with a bull's-eye symbol). Note that south of Split, the new super-expressway is still under construction; to check the progress, see www.hac.hr or www.hak.hr. For detailed route tips on driving in Dalmatia, see page 1103.

Croatian History

For nearly a millennium, bits and pieces of what we today call "Croatia" were batted back and forth between foreign powers: Hungarians, Venetians, Ottomans, Habsburgs, and Yugoslavs. Only in 1991 did Croatia regain its independence—violently.

Early History

Croatia's first inhabitants were the Illyrians (ancestors of today's Albanians). During antiquity, the Greeks and Romans both sailed ships up and down the strategic Dalmatian Coast, founding many towns that still exist today, and littering the Adriatic seabed with shipwrecks. Romans built larger settlements on the Dalmatian Coast as early as 229 B.C., and in the fourth century A.D., Emperor Diocletian built his retirement palace in the coastal town of Split. When Rome fell in the fifth century, Slavs (the ancestors of today's Croatians) and other barbarians flooded Europe. The northern part of Croatia's coast fell briefly under the Byzantines, who slathered churches with shimmering mosaics (the best are in the Euphrasian Basilica in Poreč, Istria).

Beginning in the seventh century, Slavic Croats began to control most of the land that is today's Croatia. In A.D. 925, the Dalmatian Duke Tomislav united the disparate Croat tribes into a single kingdom. By consolidating and extending Croat-held territory and centralizing power, Tomislav created the first "Croatia."

Loss of Independence

By the early 12th century, the Croatian kings had died out, and neighboring powers (Hungary, Venice, and Byzantium) threatened the Croats. For the sake of self-preservation, Croatia entered an alliance with the Hungarians in 1102, and for the next 900 years, Croatia was ruled by foreign states. The Hungarians gradually took more and more power from the Croats, exerting control over the majority of inland Croatia. Meanwhile, the Venetian Republic conquered most of the coast and peppered the Croatian Adriatic with bell towers and statues of St. Mark. Through it all, the tiny Republic of Dubrovnik flourished—paying off whomever necessary to maintain its independence and becoming one of Europe's most important shipbuilding and maritime powers.

The Ottomans conquered most of inland Croatia in the 15th century and challenged the Venetians—unsuccessfully—for control of the coastline. Most of the stout walls, fortresses, and other fortifications you'll see all along the Croatian coast date from this time, built by the Venetians to defend against Ottoman attack. In the 17th century, the Habsburgs forced the Ottomans out of inland Croatia. Then, after Venice and Dubrovnik fell to Napoleon in the early 19th century, the coast also went to the Habsburgs—beginning a long tradition of Austrians basking on Croatian beaches.

The Yugoslav Era, World War II, and the Ustaše

When the Austro-Hungarian Empire broke up at the end of World War I, Croats banded together with the Serbs, Bosniaks, and

Slovenes in the union that would become Yugoslavia. But virtually as soon as Yugoslavia was formed, many Croats began to fear that the Serbs would rule Yugoslavia with their own betterment the top priority. So when the Nazis invaded and installed a puppet government—run by the homegrown fascist Ustaše party—many Croats supported them, believing that fascism could provide them with greater independence from Serbia. The Ustaše operated one of the most brutal Nazi puppet states during World War II. Ustaše concentration camps were used to murder not only Jews and Roma (Gypsies), but also Serbs. Hot-tempered debate rages even today about how many Serbs died at the hands of the Ustaše—estimates vary wildly, from 25,000 to over a million, but most legitimate historians put the number in the hundreds of thousands.

Cardinal Alojzije Stepinac was one Croat who made the mistake of backing the Ustaše. By most accounts, Stepinac was a mild-mannered, extremely devout man who didn't agree with the extremism of the Ustaše...but also did little to fight it. When Tito came to power, he arrested, tried, and imprisoned Stepinac, who died under house arrest in 1960. In the years since, Stepinac has become a martyr for Catholics and Croat nationalists. But even though he's the single most revered figure of Croatian Catholicism, Stepinac remains highly controversial and unpopular among Serbs.

At the end of World War II, the Ustaše were forced out by Yugoslavia's homegrown Partisan Army, led by a charismatic war hero named Josip Broz, who went by his nickname, "Tito." Tito became "president for life," and Croatia once again became part of a united Yugoslavia. The union would hold together for more than 40 years, until it broke apart under Serbian President Slobodan Milošević and Croatian President Franjo Tuđman.

For all the details on Yugoslavia and its breakup, see the Understanding Yugoslavia chapter.

Independence Regained

Croatia's declaration of independence from Yugoslavia in 1991 was met with fear and anger on the part of its more than half-million Serb residents. Even before independence, the first volleys of a bloody war had been fired. The war had two phases: First, in 1991, Croatian Serbs declared independence from the new nation of Croatia, forming their own state and forcing out or murdering any Croats in "their" territory (with the thinly disguised support of Slobodan Milošević). Then a tense cease-fire fell over the region until 1995, when the second phase of the war ignited: Croatia pushed back through the Serb-dominated territory, reclaiming it for Croatia and forcing out or murdering Serbs living there. For details on this bloody war, see the Understanding Yugoslavia chapter.

After the War

Some Americans shy away from Croatia, clinging to outdated memories of wartime images on the nightly news. But those who venture here are, without exception, amazed by how peaceful and stable today's Croatia feels. Croatia's primary tourist region—the coast—was barely touched by the war (except Dubrovnik, which has been painstakingly restored). The interior is sprinkled with destroyed homes and churches, but even these villages are gradually being refurbished.

The only actual danger is that much of the Croatian interior was once full of landmines. Most of these mines have been removed, and fields that may be dangerous are usually clearly marked. As a precaution, stay on roads and paths, and don't go wandering through overgrown fields and deserted villages.

The biggest impact from the war has been on the people. Throughout the country, but especially in the war-torn interior, sadness and resentment hang heavy in the air. Though the country is repairing itself admirably, the Croatians' souls will take the longest to heal.

For more on Croatia during and after the war, see the Understanding Yugoslavia chapter.

Imagine becoming an independent nation after nine centuries of foreign domination. The Croatians seized their hard-earned freedom with a nationalist fervor that bordered on fascism. This was a heady and absurd time, which today's Croatians recall with disbelief, sadness...and maybe a tinge of nostalgia.

In the Croatia of the early 1990s, even the most bizarre notions seemed possible. Croatia's first post-Yugoslav president, the extreme nationalist Franjo Tuđman (see sidebar), proposed implausible directives for the new nation—such as privatizing all of the nation's resources and handing them over to 200 super-elite families (which, thankfully for everyone else, never happened). The government began calling the language "Croatian" rather than "Serbo-Croatian" and creating new words from specifically Croat roots. The Croats even briefly considered replacing the Roman alphabet with the ninth-century Glagolitic script to invoke Croat culture and further differentiate Croatian from Serbia's Cyrillic alphabet. Fortunately for tourists, this plan didn't take off.

After Tuđman's death in 1999, Croatia began the new millennium with a more truly democratic leader, Stipe Mesić. The popular Mesić, who was once aligned with Tuđman, had split off and formed his own political party when Tuđman's politics grew too extreme. Tuđman spent years tampering with the constitution to give himself more and more power, but when Mesić took over,

Franjo Tuđman
(1922–1999)

Independent Croatia's first president was the controversial Franjo Tuđman (FRAHN-yoh TOOJ-mahn). Tuđman began his career fighting for Tito on the left, but later had a dramatic ideological swing to the far right. His anticommunist, highly nationalistic HDZ party was the driving force for Croatian statehood, making him the young nation's first hero. But even as he fought for independence from Yugoslavia, his own ruling style grew more and more authoritarian. Today Tuđman remains a polemical figure.

Before entering politics, Tuđman was a historian. He revered the Ustaše, Croatia's Nazi-affiliated government during World War II, who murdered hundreds of thousands of Serbs and Jews in concentration camps. (Because the Ustaše governed the first "independent" Croatian state since the 12th century, Tuđman figured that these quasi-Nazis were the original Croatian "freedom fighters.") When Croatia voted for independence and Tuđman was elected president in 1990, he immediately reintroduced many Ustaše symbols, including their currency (the kuna, still used today). His actions raised eyebrows worldwide and raised alarms in Croatia's Serb communities.

Tuđman espoused many of the same single-minded attitudes about ethnic divisions as the ruthless Serbian leader Slobodan Milošević. Croat forces—which may or may not have been acting under Tuđman's orders—carried out wide-scale ethnic cleansing, targeting Serb and Muslim minorities. Tuđman and Milošević had secret, Hitler-and-Stalin-esque negotiations even as they were ripping into each other rhetorically. According to some reports, at one meeting they drew a map of Bosnia-Herzegovina on a

he reversed those changes and handed more authority back to the parliament.

Croatia Today

In 2003, Croatia applied for membership in the European Union. It's officially an EU candidate country, and may join as early as 2011.

Initially, Croatia's biggest hurdle to EU membership was its human-rights record during the recent war. Several Croatian officers were indicted for war crimes by the International Criminal Tribunal for the Former Yugoslavia (ICTY) in The Hague, Netherlands. But many Croatians feel that the soldiers branded as "war criminals" by The Hague are instead heroes of their war of independence. The highest-profile Croatian figure to be arrested was Ante Gotovina, a lieutenant general accused of atrocities against Serb civilians. After four years in hiding, Gotovina was

cocktail napkin, then drew lines divvying up the country between themselves. When Tuđman's successor moved into the president's office, he discovered a top-secret hotline to Milošević's desk.

To ensure that he stayed in power, Tuđman played fast and loose with his new nation's laws. He was notorious for changing the constitution as it suited him. By the late 1990s, when his popularity was slipping, Tuđman extended Croatian citizenship to anyone in the world who had Croatian heritage—a ploy aimed at getting votes from Croats living in Bosnia-Herzegovina, who were sure to line up with him on the far right.

Through it all, Tuđman kept a tight grip on the media, making it illegal to report anything that would disturb the public—even if true. When Croatians turned on their TV sets and saw the flag flapping in the breeze to the strains of the national anthem, they knew something was up...and switched to CNN to get the real story. In this oppressive environment, many bright, young Croatians fled the country, causing a "brain drain" that hampered the postwar recovery.

Tuđman died of cancer at the end of 1999. While history will probably judge him harshly, the opinion in today's Croatia is qualified. Most agree that Tuđman was an important and even admirable figure in the struggle for Croatian statehood, but he ultimately went too far and got too greedy. Tuđman's political party is still active, frequently naming streets, squares, and bridges for this "hero" of Croatian nationalism. But if he were alive, Tuđman would be standing trial before the International Criminal Tribunal in The Hague.

found and arrested in Spain in December 2005 and sent to stand trial in The Hague. As a sign of support, photos of Gotovina appeared in towns throughout Croatia. Gotovina's name means "cash." Many Croatians grouse, "To get into the EU, we have to pay cash *(gotovina)*!"

Some Croatians remain skeptical about joining the EU for other reasons. One Croatian said to me, "We were just badly divorced. We're not ready to be married again." For the other countries that recently joined the EU, a concern with EU membership was that the new members' citizens would flood to the West. Some Croatians are worried about the opposite: Westerners buying up Adriatic beachfront property.

Perhaps not surprisingly for a post-communist country, Croatia's government can be excessively bureaucratic. Expats who want to work here find it a tough place to do business. Laws tend to be implemented, then quickly overturned. In the last few years, a ban on shops being open on Sundays, a smoking ban, and a zero blood-alcohol limit for drivers have all come and gone. (The last one was contested by priests, who pointed out that if the blood-alcohol limit is zero, their parishioners can't take the wine at communion.)

Despite the country's false starts, pro-EU President Stipe Mesić's re-election in 2005 is a clear signal that most Croatians are optimistic about becoming a part of a united Europe. Mesić is viewed both by most Croatians and by international observers as precisely the kind of moderate, modern, European-minded leader a fledgling country needs to lead it into the 21st century. When Mesić's second—and, constitutionally, last—term is up in 2010, Croatia will need to decide which direction to take in the future.

Croatian Food

Croatian food is good, but tends to be fairly expensive and unimaginative—and all too often comes with less than cheerful service. The country's tourist board has gone to great lengths to promote its cuisine and wines as major components of any trip. This seems to have backfired, as many visitors find themselves disappointed by Croatian restaurants. Adjust your expectations and you'll eat well here—it ain't Tuscany, but it ain't bad, either.

Like its people, the food in Croatia's different regions has been shaped by various influences—predominantly Italian, Turkish, and Hungarian. Choosing between strudel and baklava on the same menu, you're constantly reminded that this is a land where East meets West. And yet, the cuisine here is surprisingly uniform: 90 percent of coastal restaurants have a similar menu of seafood, pasta, and pizza. Because it's so easy to get into a culinary rut here, I've also tried to recommend a few more exotic alternatives.

Two staples of Croatian food, as in most Mediterranean lands, are wine and olive oil. You'll see vineyards and olive groves blanketing the Croatian countryside and islandscapes. Croatians joke that grapes are like a new bride—they demand a lot of attention, while olives are like a mother—low-maintenance. Another major part of the local diet is the air-dried ham called *pršut* (a.k.a. prosciutto—see sidebar on page 642).

Balkan Flavors

All of the countries of the Balkan Peninsula—basically from Slovenia to Greece—have several foods in common. The Ottomans from today's Turkey, who controlled much of this territory for centuries, imported some goodies that remained standard fare here long after they left town. Whether you're in Slovenia, Croatia, Bosnia-Herzegovina, Montenegro, Serbia, Kosovo, or Albania, here are some local tastes worth seeking out.

A popular, cheap fast food you'll see everywhere is ***burek*** (BOO-rehk)—phyllo dough filled with meat, cheese, spinach, or apples. The more familiar ***baklava*** is phyllo dough layered with honey and nuts.

Grilled meats are a staple of Balkan cuisine. You'll most often see ***čevapčići*** (cheh-VAHP-chee-chee), or simply ***čevap*** (cheh-VAHP)—minced meat formed into a sausage-link shape, then grilled; and ***ražnjići*** (RAZH-nyee-chee)—small pieces of steak on a skewer, like a shish kebab. Sometimes you'll come across ***pljeskavica*** (plehs-kah-VEET-suh)—similar to *čevapčići,* except the meat is in the form of a hamburger-like patty.

While Balkan cuisine favors meat, a nice veggie complement is ***đuveđ*** (JOO-vedge)—a spicy mix of stewed vegetables, flavored with tomatoes and peppers.

And you just can't eat any of this stuff without the ever-present condiment ***ajvar*** (EYE-var). Made from red bell pepper and eggplant, *ajvar* is like ketchup with a kick. Many Americans pack a jar of this distinctive, savory sauce to remember the flavors of the Balkans when they get back home. And these days, you can often find it at specialty grocery stores in the US (look for "eggplant/red pepper spread").

On the coast, seafood is a specialty, and the Italian influence is obvious. According to Dalmatians, "Eating meat is food; eating fish is pleasure." They also say that a fish should swim three times: first in the sea, then in olive oil, and finally in wine—when you eat it.

You can get all kinds of seafood: fish, scampi, mussels, squid, octopus, you name it. At fish restaurants, seafood is often priced by weight—either by kilogram or by hectogram (100 grams, or one-tenth of a kilogram). A one-kilogram portion feeds two hungry people or three light eaters. When ordering, be prepared for surprises. For example, *škampi* (shrimp) often come still in their

shells (sometimes with crayfish-like claws), which can be messy and time-consuming to eat. Before you order shrimp, ask if it's shelled. The menu item called "small fried fish" is generally a plate of deep-fried minnows. If you're not clear on exactly what something is, feel free to ask for clarification (though some waiters are more forthcoming than others).

Sometimes it's a pleasant surprise. Many menu items that don't sound appetizing can be delicious. Jump at the chance to sample a good, fresh anchovy—which, when done right, has a pleasant flavor and a melt-in-your-mouth texture that's a world away from the salty, withered little fish you might find topping a pizza back home. Those not accustomed to eating octopus might want to try octopus salad—a flavorful mix of octopus, tomatoes, onions, and spices. In the interior, trout is popular.

If you're not a seafood-eater, there are plenty of meat options. A Dalmatian specialty is *pašticada*—braised beef in a slightly sweet wine-and-herb sauce, usually served with gnocchi. Dalmatia is also known for its mutton. Since the lambs graze on salty seaside herbs, the meat—often served on a spit—has a distinctive flavor. The most widely available meat dish is the "mixed grill"—a combination of various Balkan grilled meats, best accompanied by the eggplant-and-red-pepper condiment *ajvar* (see "Balkan Flavors" on page 753).

The best meat dish in Croatia is veal or lamb prepared under a *peka*—a metal baking lid that's covered with red-hot coals, to allow the meat to gradually cook to tender perfection. Available only in traditional restaurants, this dish typically must be ordered in advance and for multiple people. You'll also find a break from seafood in the north (Zagreb) and east (Slavonia), where the food has more of a Hungarian flavor—heavy on meat served with cabbage, noodles, or potatoes.

Many tourists reserve meat and fish for splurge dinners and mostly dine on cheaper and faster pastas and pizzas. You'll see familiar dishes, such as spaghetti Bolognese (with meat sauce) and spaghetti carbonara (with an egg, parmesan, and bacon sauce), gnocchi (*njoki,* potato dumplings), and lasagna. Risotto (a rice dish) is popular here, often mixed with squid ink and various kinds of seafood.

There are many good local varieties of cheese made with sheep's or goat's milk. Pag, an island in the Kvarner Gulf, produces a famous, very salty, fairly dry sheep's-milk cheese *(paški sir),* which is said to be flavored by the herbs the sheep eat.

A common side dish is boiled potatoes and mangold *(blitva),* similar to Swiss chard. When ordering salad, choose between mixed (typically shredded cabbage, tomatoes, and maybe some beets and a little lettuce) or green (mostly lettuce). Throughout

Croatian Wine

The quality of Croatia's wine declined under the communists, as much of the industry was state-run and focused on mass production. Now that the communists are gone, vintner families are returning to their roots—literally—and bringing quality back to Croatian wine.

The northern part of the country primarily produces whites *(bijelo vino)*, usually dry *(suho)* but sometimes semi-dry *(polusuho)* or sweet *(slatko)*. The sunny mountains just north of Zagreb are covered with vineyards producing whites. From Slavonia (Croatia's inland panhandle), you'll find *graševina*—crisp, dry, and acidic (like Welsh Riesling); Krauthaker and Enjingi are well-respected brands. The Istrian Peninsula corks up some good whites, including *malvazija*, a very popular, light, midrange wine (Muscat is also popular).

As you move south, along the Dalmatian Coast, the wines turn red—which Croatians actually call "black wine" *(crno vino)*. The most common grape here is *plavac mali* ("little blue")—a distant ancestor of Californian Zinfandel grapes. Generally speaking, the best coastal reds are produced on the long Pelješac Peninsula, across from Korčula (the most well-respected regions are Dingač—literally, "Donkey"—and Postup). But each island also produces its own good wines. Korčula makes *pošip* (near the town of Čara), *grk*, and *korčulanka*, and Hvar has *bogdanuša*.

Miljenko Grgić (a.k.a. "Mike Grgich"), a Croatian-American who has started a Croatian branch of his California wine empire, is putting Croatian wines on the map. Grgić grows his red wines (*plavac mali* grapes) at Postup and Dingač on the Pelješac Peninsula, and his white wines on Korčula Island. The prices for Grgić's wines match his reputation; for producers that are comparable but a bit more affordable, look for these red-wine alternatives: Madirazza (they make a great Postup), Frano Miloš (try the full-bodied Stagnum), and Matuško and Skaramuća (good Dingač).

Croatia, salad is typically served with the main dish unless you request that it be brought beforehand.

For dessert, look no further than the mountains of delicious, home-made ice cream *(sladoled)* that line every street in Dalmatia. I've worked hard to sample and recommend the best ice-cream parlors in each town. (Poor me.) Dalmatia's typical dessert is a flan-like crème caramel custard, which they call *rozata*. *Prošek* is a sweet dessert wine.

Water is *voda,* and mineral water is *mineralna voda.* Jamnica is the main Croatian brand of bottled water, but you'll also see Bistra and Studenac. Many restaurants—especially fancier ones—might not want to bring you a glass of tap water, but you can try asking for *voda iz slavine.* For coffee *(kava),* the easiest choice is *bijela kava* (BEE-yeh-lah KAH-vah)—"white coffee," or espresso with lots of milk (similar to a caffè latte). To get it black, ask for *crna kava.*

The most popular Croatian beers *(pivo)* are Ožujsko and Karlovačko, but you'll also see the Slovenian brand Laško (which is also brewed here in Croatia). Fans of dark beer *(crno pivo)* enjoy Tomislav.

Even more beloved in Croatia is wine (*vino;* see "Croatian Wine" sidebar). Along the coast, locals find it refreshing to drink wine mixed with mineral water (called, as in English, *špricer*). When toasting with some new Croatian friends, raise your glass with a hearty *"Živjeli!"* (ZHEE-vyeh-lee).

To request a menu, say, *"Meni, molim"* (MEH-nee, MOH-leem; "Menu, please"). To get the attention of your waiter, say *"Konobar"* (KOH-noh-bahr; "Waiter"). When he brings your food, he'll likely say, *"Dobar tek!"* ("Enjoy your meal!"). When you're ready for the bill, ask for the *račun* (RAH-choon).

Croatian Language

Croatian was once known as "Serbo-Croatian," the official language of Yugoslavia. Most Yugoslav republics—including Croatia, Serbia, and Bosnia-Herzegovina—spoke this same language (though Slovene is quite different). And while each of these countries has tried to distance its language from that of its neighbors since the war, the languages spoken in all of these places are still very similar. The biggest difference is in the writing: Croatians and Bosniaks use our Roman alphabet, while Serbs use Cyrillic letters.

In recent years, Croatia has attempted to artificially differentiate its vocabulary from Serbian. A decade ago, you'd catch a plane at the *aerodrom.* Today, you'll catch that same flight at the *zračna luka*—a new coinage that combines the old Croatian words for "air" and "port." These new words, once created, are immediately injected into the lexicon. Croatians watching their favorite TV show will suddenly hear a character use a word they've never heard before...and think, "Oh, we have another new word."

Here are some tips for Croatian pronunciation:

J / j sounds like "y" as in "yellow"
C / c sounds like "ts" as in "cats"
Č / č and **Ć / ć** sound like "ch" as in "chicken"
Š / š sounds like "sh" as in "shrimp"
Ž / ž sounds like "zh" as in "leisure"

Đ / đ is like the "dj" sound in "jeans" (often replaced with **dj** in English)

Croatian has the same tricky consonant combinations as in Slovene, most notably hv (as in *hvala,* "thank you") and nj (as in Rovinj). Don't over-pronounce these. For **hv,** the h is nearly silent—it's easiest just to omit the h (for *hvala*, just say "VAH-lah," not "huh-VAH-lah"). In the combination **nj,** the j is mostly silent, with a slight "y" sound that can be omitted: Rovinj sounds like roh-VEEN.

When attempting to pronounce an unfamiliar word, remember that the accent is usually on the first syllable (and never on the last). Confusingly, Croatian pronunciation—even of the same word—can vary in different parts of the country. This is because modern Croatian has three distinct dialects, called Kajkavian, Shtokavian, and Chakavian—based on how you say "what?" (*kaj?, što?,* and *ča?,* respectively). That's a lot of variety for a language with only five million speakers.

For a smoother trip, take some time to learn a few Croatian Survival Phrases (listed on page 1127).

As you navigate through Croatia, these words might help: ***trg*** (pronounced "turg," square), ***ulica*** (OO-leet-sah, road), ***cesta*** (TSEH-stah, avenue), ***autocesta*** (OW-toh-tseh-stah, expressway), ***most*** (mohst, bridge), ***otok*** (OH-tohk, island), ***trajekt*** (TRAH-yehkt, ferry), and ***Jadran*** (YAH-drahn, Adriatic).

DUBROVNIK

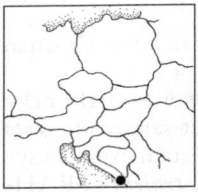

Dubrovnik is a living fairy tale that shouldn't be missed. It feels like a small town today, but 500 years ago Dubrovnik was a major maritime power, with the third-biggest navy in the Mediterranean. Still jutting confidently into the sea and ringed by thick medieval walls, Dubrovnik deserves its nickname: the Pearl of the Adriatic. Within the ramparts, the traffic-free Old Town is a fun jumble of quiet, cobbled back lanes; low-impact museums; narrow, steep alleys; and kid-friendly squares. After all these centuries, the buildings still hint at old-time wealth, and the central promenade (Stradun) remains the place to see and be seen. If I had to pick just one place to visit in Croatia, this would be it.

The city's sleepy charm is the result of its no-nonsense past. Busy merchants, the salt trade, and shipbuilding made Dubrovnik rich. But the city's most valued commodity was always its freedom—even today, you'll see the proud motto *Libertas* displayed all over town (see *"Libertas"* sidebar).

Dubrovnik flourished in the 15th and 16th centuries, but an earthquake destroyed nearly everything in 1667. Most of today's buildings in the Old Town are post-quake Baroque, although the few surviving palaces, monasteries, and convents from Dubrovnik's earlier Golden Age display a rich mix of Gothic and Renaissance styles.

Dubrovnik remained a big tourist draw through the Tito years, bringing in much-needed hard currency from Western visitors. Consequently, it never acquired the hard socialist patina of other Yugoslav cities (such as the nearby Montenegrin capital Podgorica, then known as "Titograd").

As Croatia violently separated from Yugoslavia in 1991,

Libertas

Libertas—liberty—has always been close to the heart of every Dubrovnik citizen. Dubrovnik was a proudly independent republic for centuries, even as most of Croatia became Venetian and Hungarian. Dubrovnik believed so strongly in *libertas* that it was the first foreign state in 1776 to officially recognize an upstart, experimental republic called the United States of America.

In the Middle Ages, the city-state of Dubrovnik (then called Ragusa) bought its independence from whoever was strongest—Byzantium, Venice, Hungary, the Ottomans—sometimes paying off more than one at a time. Dubrovnik's ships flew whichever flags were necessary to stay free, earning the nickname "Town of Seven Flags." As time went on, Europe's big-league nations were glad to have a second major seafaring power in the Adriatic to balance the Venetian threat. A free Dubrovnik was more valuable than a pillaged, plundered Dubrovnik.

In 1808, Napoleon conquered the Adriatic and abolished the Republic of Dubrovnik. After Napoleon was defeated, the fate of the Continent was decided at the Congress of Vienna. But Dubrovnik's delegate was denied a seat at the table. The more powerful nations, no longer concerned about Venice and fed up after years of being sweet-talked by Dubrovnik, were afraid that the delegate would play old alliances off each other to re-establish an independent Republic of Dubrovnik. Instead, the city became a part of the Habsburg Empire and entered a long period of decline.

Libertas still hasn't died in Dubrovnik. In the surreal days of the early 1990s, when Yugoslavia was reshuffling itself, a movement for the creation of a new Republic of Dubrovnik gained some momentum (led by a judge who, in earlier times, had convicted others for the same ideas). Another movement pushed for Dalmatia to secede as its own nation. But now that the dust has settled, today's locals are content and proud to be part of an independent Republic of Croatia.

Dubrovnik became the only coastal city to be pulled into the fighting (see "The Siege of Dubrovnik" sidebar, later). Imagine having your youthful memories of good times spent romping in the surrounding hills replaced by visions of tanks and warships shelling your hometown. The city was devastated, but Dubrovnik has been repaired with amazing speed. The only physical reminders of the war are lots of new, bright-orange roof tiles. Locals,

relieved the fighting is over but forever hardened, are often willing to talk openly about the experience with visitors—offering a rare opportunity to grasp the harsh realities of war from an eyewitness perspective.

Though the war killed tourism in the 1990s, today the crowds are most decidedly back. In fact, Dubrovnik's biggest downside is the overwhelming midday crush of multinational tourists who converge on the Old Town when their cruise ships dock. But locals—relieved that all these visitors are finally helping them get their economy back on track—appreciate that the numbers are about back to prewar levels. While Europeans and Australians have been flocking here for years, Americans have only just begun to rediscover Dubrovnik.

Planning Your Time

While Dubrovnik's museums are nothing special, the town is one of those places that you never want to leave. The real attraction here is the Old Town and its relaxing, breezy ambience. While Dubrovnik could easily be "seen" in a day, a second or third day to unwind (or even more time, for side-trips) makes the long journey here more worthwhile.

To hit all the key sights in a single day, start at the Pile Gate, just outside the Old Town. Walk around the city's walls to get your bearings (before it gets too hot and crowded), then work your way down the main drag (following my "Welcome to Dubrovnik" self-guided walk). As you explore, drop in at any museums or churches that appeal to you. To squeeze the most into a single day (or with a second day), consider a boat excursion from the Old Port (Lokrum Island, just offshore, requires the least brainpower).

Orientation to Dubrovnik

(area code: 020)

Nearly all of the sights worth seeing are in Dubrovnik's traffic-free, walled **Old Town** (Stari Grad) peninsula. The main pedestrian promenade through the middle of town is called the **Stradun**; from this artery, the Old Town climbs steeply uphill in both directions to the walls. The Old Town connects to the mainland through three gates: the **Pile Gate,** to the west; the **Ploče Gate,** to the east; and the smaller **Buža Gate,** at the top of the stepped lane called Boškovićeva. The **Old Port** (Gradska Luka), with leisure boats to nearby destinations, is at the east end of town. While greater Dubrovnik has about 50,000 people, the local population within the Old Town is just a few thousand in the winter—and even smaller in summer, when many residents move out to rent their apartments to tourists.

Dubrovnik Essentials

English	Croatian	Pronounced
Old Town	Stari Grad	STAH-ree grahd
Old Port	Stara Luka	STAH-rah LOO-kah
Pile Gate	Gradska Vrata Pile	GRAHD-skah VRAH-tah PEE-leh
Ploče Gate	Gradska Vrata Ploče	GRAHD-skah VRAH-tah PLOH-cheh
Main Promenade	Stradun	STRAH-doon
Adriatic Sea	Jadran	YAH-drahn

The **Pile** (PEE-leh) neighborhood, a pincushion of tourist services, is just outside the western end of the Old Town (through the Pile Gate). In front of the gate, you'll find a TI and Internet café (sharing an office), ATMs, a post office, taxis, buses (fanning out to all the outlying neighborhoods), a cheap Konzum grocery store, and the Atlas Travel Agency (described later, under "Helpful Hints"). Just off this strip are some good *sobe* (rooms in private homes—described under "Sleeping in Dubrovnik"). This is also the starting point for my "Welcome to Dubrovnik" self-guided walk.

A mile or two away from the Old Town are beaches peppered with expensive resort hotels. The closest area is **Boninovo Bay** (a 20-min walk or 5-min bus trip from the Old Town), but most cluster on the lush **Lapad Peninsula** to the west (a 15-min bus trip from the Old Town); I've recommended accommodations in each of these areas. Across the bay from the Lapad Peninsula is **Port Gruž,** with the main bus station, ferry terminal, and cruise-ship port.

Tourist Information

Dubrovnik's TI has several branches (www.tzdubrovnik.hr), with hours that tend to fluctuate depending on demand. Plans to consolidate smaller TIs into one larger office just outside the Pile Gate (near the main bus stop) might lead to the closure of some of these branches. Until then, you'll find TIs at the following locations (note that only the Old Town and Port Gruž TIs are likely to stay open through the winter):

• In the **Old Town,** a few steps off the main drag at Široka 1 (July–mid-Sept daily 8:00–22:00; mid-Sept–Oct Mon–Fri 8:00–19:00, Sat–Sun 9:00–14:00; Nov–March Mon–Sat 9:00–19:00, Sun 9:00–14:00; April–June Mon–Sat 9:00–21:00, Sun 9:00–14:00; tel. 020/323-587).

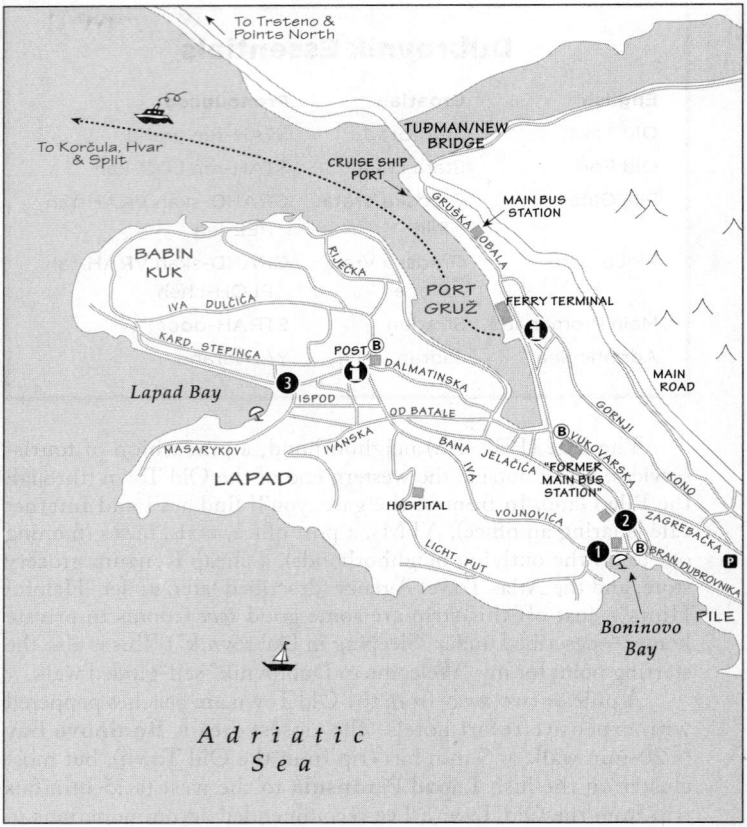

• In the **Pile** neighborhood just outside the Old Town, 100 yards up the street from the Pile Gate (July–mid-Sept daily 8:00–21:00; June and mid-Sept–Oct Mon–Fri 8:00–19:00, Sat 9:00–14:00, closed Sun; April–May Mon–Fri 8:00–15:00, Sat 9:00–14:00, closed Sun; likely closed Nov–March; Branitelja Dubrovnika 7, tel. 020/427-591; Internet access in the same office).

• At **Port Gruž,** across the street from the Jadrolinija ferry dock (July–mid-Sept daily 8:00–20:00; mid-Sept–Oct Mon–Fri 8:00–19:00, Sat–Sun 9:00–14:00; Nov–March Mon–Fri 9:00–16:00, Sat 9:00–14:00, closed Sun; April–May Mon–Fri 8:00–15:00, Sat 9:00–14:00, closed Sun; June Mon–Fri 8:00–20:00, Sat–Sun 9:00–14:00; Gruška obala, tel. 020/417-983).

• In the **Lapad** resort area, at the head of the main drag (July–mid-Sept daily 8:00–21:00; mid-Sept–Oct Mon–Fri

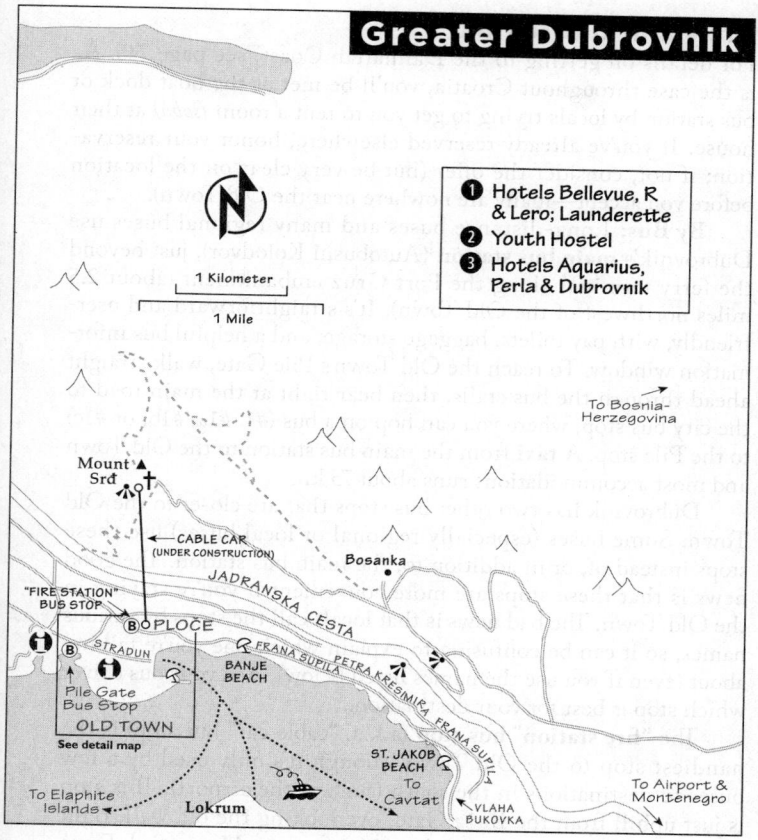

8:00–12:30 & 17:00–19:00, Sat 9:00–14:00, closed Sun; April–May Mon–Fri 9:00–20:00, Sat 9:00–14:00, closed Sun; June Mon–Fri 9:00–20:00, Sat 9:00–14:00, closed Sun; likely closed Nov–March; Šetalište Kralja Zvonimira 25, tel. 020/437-460).

All the TIs are government-run and legally can't sell you anything—but they can answer questions and give you a copy of the free town map and monthly information booklet *The Best in Dubrovnik Riviera,* which contains helpful maps, bus and ferry schedules, museum prices and hours, a current schedule of events and performances, specifics on side-trip destinations, and more. If you need a room and the TI isn't busy, they might be willing to unofficially call around to find a place for you.

Skip the combo-ticket that the TIs sell. A different combo-ticket, sold at participating sights, is a better deal (both described later, under "Sights in Dubrovnik").

Arrival in Dubrovnik

For details on getting to the Dalmatian Coast, see page 745. As is the case throughout Croatia, you'll be met at the boat dock or bus station by locals trying to get you to rent a room *(soba)* at their house. If you've already reserved elsewhere, honor your reservation; if not, consider the offer (but be very clear on the location before you accept—many are nowhere near the Old Town).

By Bus: Long-distance buses and many regional buses use Dubrovnik's **main bus station** (Autobusni Kolodvor), just beyond the ferry terminal along the Port Gruž embankment (about 2.5 miles northwest of the Old Town). It's straightforward and user-friendly, with pay toilets, baggage storage, and a helpful bus information window. To reach the Old Town's Pile Gate, walk straight ahead through the bus stalls, then bear right at the main road to the city bus stop, where you can hop on a bus (#1, #1a, #1b, or #1c) to the Pile stop. A **taxi** from the main bus station to the Old Town and most accommodations runs about 75 kn.

Dubrovnik has two other bus stops that are closer to the Old Town. Some buses (especially regional or local buses) use these stops instead of, or in addition to, the main bus station. The good news is that these stops are more convenient if you're staying in the Old Town. The bad news is that locals call the stops by various names, so it can be confusing to explain which one you're talking about (even if you use the names listed below). Ask your bus driver which stop is best for your destination.

The **"fire station" bus stop** (a.k.a. "cable car" bus stop) is the handiest stop to the Old Town, though it's only used by a few buses to destinations in the south (such as the airport). This stop is just uphill from the Buža Gate, overlooking the old wall, right next to the bottom station of the cable car up to Mount Srđ. From this bus stop, simply walk downhill (and through the pedestrian underpass)—you'll be inside the Old Town walls within a few minutes.

Another transit point is roughly between the Old Town and the main bus station. It's confusingly nicknamed the **"former main bus station"** (locals also call this the "old main bus station," "water polo pool," or "Lapad Stanica"). This station is mostly served by regional, numbered buses (such as bus #10 to Cavtat, or bus #12 or #15 to Trsteno Arboretum). This station is connected to the Pile Gate by local buses #1, #1a, #1b, and #1c (which also go in the opposite direction, to the main bus station), as well as by bus #6.

By Car Ferry or Catamaran: The big car ferries arrive at Port Gruž, two miles northwest of the Old Town. On the road in front of the ferry terminal, you'll find a bus stop (#1, #1a, #1b, and #1c go to the Old Town's Pile Gate; wait on the embankment side of the street) and a taxi stand (figure 70 kn to the Old Town and most

accommodations). Across the street is the Jadrolinija office (with an ATM out front) and a TI. You can book a private room *(soba)* at Atlas Travel Agency (room-booking desk in boat terminal building, May-Sept only) or at Gulliver Travel Agency (behind TI). The fast *Nona Ana* catamaran from Mljet and Korčula also arrives near this big ferry dock.

By Cruise Ship: Some ships moor just offshore from the Old Port, then send their passengers into the Old Town on transfer boats. Others actually put in at Port Gruž, generally just beyond the bus station. To reach the Old Town, take a public bus or pay 80 kn for a taxi (described earlier, under "By Bus.")

By Plane: Dubrovnik's small airport (Zračna Luka) is in a place called Ćilipi, 13 miles south of the city. A Croatia Airlines bus meets arriving flights for most major airlines at the airport, and brings you to the main bus station (35 kn, 40 min). Legitimate cabbies charge around 220 kn for the ride between the airport and the center (though some cabbies are charging as much as 300 kn; consider arranging your transfer in advance with one of the drivers listed on page 771, or through your *soba* host). Airport info: tel. 020/773-333, www.airport-dubrovnik.hr.

To get *to* the airport, you can take the same Croatia Airlines bus, which typically leaves from Dubrovnik's main bus station 1.5 hours before each Croatia Airlines or Austrian Airlines flight, or two hours before other airlines' international flights (but confirm this schedule at the TI). If you're staying in or near the Old Town, you'll find it more convenient to catch the airport bus at the "fire station" bus stop just above the Old Town. From the Old Town's main drag, hike up steep Boškovićeva lane and go through the wall at the Buža Gate. Once outside, continue straight under the arch and up the stairs, then swing right at the fire station onto the busy Krešimira street; the bus stop is a few steps up the road, by the cable-car station. The airport bus reaches this stop a few minutes after leaving the main bus station—wave it down or it might pass you by. While it's theoretically possible that the bus will be full and not pick you up, locals assure me that it almost always works (and I've done this many times without a problem; in a pinch, call a taxi at tel. 020/970).

By Car: Coming from the north, you'll drive over the super-modern Tuđman Bridge (which most locals, mindful of their former president's tarnished legacy, call simply "the New Bridge"). Immediately after crossing the bridge, you have two options: To get to the main bus station, ferry terminal (with some car-rental drop-off offices nearby), and Lapad Peninsula, take the left turn just after the bridge, wind down to the waterfront, then turn left and follow this road along the Port Gruž embankment. Or, to head for the Old Town, continue straight after the bridge. You'll

Dubrovnik at a Glance

▲▲▲ **Stradun Stroll** Charming walk through Dubrovnik's vibrant Old Town, ideal for coffee, ice cream, and people-watching. **Hours:** Always open. See page 772.

▲▲▲**Town Walls** Scenic mile-long walk along top of 15th-century fortifications encircling the city. **Hours:** July-Aug daily 8:00-19:30, progressively shorter hours off-season until 10:00-15:00 in mid-Nov-mid-March. See page 779.

▲**Franciscan Monastery Museum** Tranquil cloister, medieval pharmacy-turned-museum, and a century-old pharmacy still serving residents today. **Hours:** Daily April-Oct 9:00-18:00, Nov-March 9:00-17:00. See page 782.

▲**Cathedral** Eighteenth-century Roman Baroque cathedral and treasury filled with unusual relics such as a swatch of Jesus' swaddling clothes. **Hours:** Church—daily 8:00-20:00, treasury—generally open same hours as church, both have shorter hours off-season. See page 784.

▲**Dominican Monastery Museum** Another relaxing cloister with precious paintings, altarpieces, and manuscripts. **Hours:** Daily May-Sept 9:00-18:00, Oct-April 9:00-17:00. See page 785.

▲**Synagogue Museum** Europe's second-oldest synagogue and Croatia's only Jewish museum, with 13th-century Torahs and Holocaust-era artifacts. **Hours:** May-mid-Nov daily 10:00-20:00; mid-Nov-April Mon-Fri 10:00-13:00, closed Sat-Sun. See page 787.

▲**Institute for the Restoration of Dubrovnik** Photos and videos of the recent war and an exhibit on restoration work. **Hours:** June-Sept Mon-Fri 10:00-14:00, closed Sat-Sun; rotating exhibits Oct-May. See page 788.

pass above the Port Gruž area, then take the right turn-off marked *Dubrovnik* (with the little bull's-eye). You'll go through a tunnel, then turn left for *Centar*, and begin following the brown signs for *Grad* (Old Town); individual big hotels are also signed from here. You'll pass the Old Town parking garage (described next), then wind up just above the walls.

If you're sleeping in or near the Old Town, **parking** is tricky. The handiest place to park long-term is the Old Town garage, which you'll pass on the right as you head toward the Old Town

▲Serbian Orthodox Church and Icon Museum Active church serving Dubrovnik's Serbian Orthodox community and museum with traditional religious icons. **Hours:** Church—daily May–Sept 8:00–20:00, Oct–April 8:00–15:00, short services daily at 8:30 and 19:00, longer liturgy Sun at 9:00; museum—May–Oct Mon–Sat 9:00–14:00, closed Sun; Nov–April Mon–Fri 9:00–14:00, closed Sat–Sun. See page 788.

▲Rupe Granary and Ethnographic Museum Good folk museum with tools, jewelry, clothing, and painted eggs above immense underground grain stores. **Hours:** Wed–Mon 9:00–16:00, closed Tue. See page 790.

▲Mount Srđ Napoleonic fortress capping the mountain above Dubrovnik, now hosting a modest museum to the recent war. **Hours:** Mountaintop—always open; museum—daily 10:00–18:30, maybe until 20:00 in summer. See page 791.

Rector's Palace Sparse antiques collection in the former home of rectors who ruled Dubrovnik in the Middle Ages. **Hours:** Daily May–Oct 9:00–18:00, Nov–April 9:00–16:00. See page 783.

Maritime Museum Contracts, maps, paintings, and models from Dubrovnik's days as a maritime power and shipbuilding center. **Hours:** Vary with demand, usually March–Oct Tue–Sun 9:00–18:00, closed Mon, shorter hours Nov–Feb. See page 787.

Aquarium Tanks of local sea life housed in huge, shady old fort. **Hours:** Daily July–Aug 9:00–21:00, progressively shorter hours off-season until 9:00–13:00 Nov–March. See page 787.

War Photo Limited Thought-provoking photographic look at contemporary warfare. **Hours:** June–Sept daily 9:00–21:00; May and Oct Tue–Sat 9:00–15:00, Sun 10:00–14:00, closed Mon; closed Nov–April. See page 788.

(10 kn/hr, 120 kn/day, half-price Oct-May). From here, it's about a 10-minute downhill walk to the Old Town, or you can take a shuttle bus (2/hr, free if you're paying to park here). If you'd like to be closer to the Old Town, you can take your chances on finding a spot—either on the street directly behind and above the town walls (pay at meter), or in the convenient but often-crammed pay lot nicknamed "the tennis court," just behind the wall (10 kn/hr). Another option is to drive to this area near the Old Town to unload your bags, then leave your car at the Old Town garage (or a

cheaper, more distant one) for the duration of your visit. When in doubt, ask your *soba* host or hotel for parking tips.

If you're sleeping at Lapad or Boninovo Bay, you'll have an easier time finding parking at or near your hotel—ask.

Helpful Hints

Festivals: Dubrovnik is most crowded during its Summer Festival, a month and a half of theater and musical performances held annually from July 10 to August 25 (www.dubrovnik-festival.hr). This is quickly followed by the "Rachlin & Friends" classical music festival in September (www.julianrachlin.com). For other options, see "Entertainment in Dubrovnik," later.

Crowd-Beating Tips: Dubrovnik has been discovered—especially by cruise ships (800 of which visit each year). Cruise-ship crowds descend on the Old Town on most summer days, roughly between 8:30 and 14:00 (the streets are most crowded 9:00–13:00). In summer, try to avoid the big sights—especially walking around the wall—during these peak times, and hit the beach or take a siesta midday, when the town is hottest and most crowded. On very busy days, as many as 9,000 cruise-ship day-trippers deluge Dubrovnik (three big ships' worth). If you're caught off-guard, it can be miserable. For others, it's entertaining to count the dozens of tour guides toting numbered paddles through the Old Town, and to watch the blocky orange transfer boats going back and forth to the ships moored offshore.

Travel Agency: You'll see travel agencies all over town. At any of them, you can buy seats on an excursion, rent a car, book a room, buy Jadrolinija ferry tickets, and pick up a pile of brochures. The most established company is **Atlas,** with an office just outside the Pile Gate from the Old Town—though the location might change (June–Sept Mon–Sat 8:00–21:00, Sun 8:00–13:00; Oct–May Mon–Fri 8:00–20:00, Sat 8:00–15:00, closed Sun; down the little alley at Sv. Đurđa 4, otherwise look for signs to new location around the bus-stop area, tel. 020/442-574, fax 020/323-609, www.atlas-croatia.com, atlas.pile@atlas.hr). They also have an office at the ferry terminal building at Port Gruž (May-Sept only).

Internet Access: You'll see signs all over town for Internet cafés with similar rates (around 5 kn/10 min). In the Old Town, my favorite is the modern **Netcafé,** with several speedy terminals right on Prijeko street, the "restaurant row" (daily 9:00–24:00, Prijeko 21, tel. 020/321-025). When staying in the Pile neighborhood, I use the **Dubrovnik Internet Centar** inside the Pile TI (May–Sept daily 8:00–24:00; Oct–April Mon–Sat 8:00–21:00, closed Sun; Branitelja Dubrovnika 7). There are plans

to provide free Wi-Fi throughout the Old Town—if you're traveling with a laptop, ask the TI or your *sobe* host about this. Otherwise, Dubrovnik Internet Centar sells vouchers to get online at hotspots around the Old Town (including the Stradun and Old Port; 50 kn/1 day, 100 kn/3 days).

Laundry: Hotels charge a mint to wash your clothes; *sobe* hosts are cheaper, but often don't have the time (ask). The best affordable option is the full-service **launderette** near the hotels at Boninovo Bay, a 20-minute uphill walk or five-minute bus trip from the Pile Gate (90 kn for wash and dry in about 3 hours, no self-service, Mon–Fri 9:00–13:00 & 15:00–18:00, Sat 9:00–15:00, closed Sun, across from the big seafront Hotel Bellevue at Pera Čingrije 8, tel. 020/333-347).

English Bookstore: The **Algoritam** shop, right on the Stradun, has a wide variety of guidebooks (including this one), nonfiction books about Croatia and the former Yugoslavia, novels, and magazines—all in English (July–Aug Mon–Sat 9:00–23:00, Sun 10:00–13:00 & 18:00–22:00; June and Sept Mon–Sat 9:00–21:00, Sun 10:00–13:00; Oct–May Mon–Fri 9:00–20:30, Sat 9:00–15:00, Sun 9:00–13:00; Placa 8).

Wine Shop: For the best wine-tasting selection in a cool bar atmosphere, don't miss **d'vino Wine Bar** (described on page 796). If you want to shop rather than taste, **Vinoteka Miličić** offers a nice variety of local wines and helpful advice for choosing one—though they do tend to push their own wines (daily 9:00–23:00 in peak season, shorter hours off-season, near the Pile end of the Stradun, tel. 020/321-777).

Car Rental: The big international chains, such as **Avis** (tel. 020/313-633), have offices both at the airport and near the Port Gruž embankment where the big boats come in. In addition, the many travel agencies closer to the Old Town also have a line on rental cars. Figure €50–60 per day, including taxes, insurance, and unlimited mileage (at the bigger chains, there's usually no extra charge for drop-off elsewhere in Croatia). Be sure the agency knows if you're crossing a border (such as Bosnia-Herzegovina or Montenegro) to ensure you have the proper paperwork.

Best Views: Walking the **Old Town walls** late in the day, when the city is bathed in rich light, is a treat. The **Fort of St. Lawrence,** perched above the Pile neighborhood cove, has great views over the Old Town. A stroll up the road east of the city walls offers nice views back on the Old Town (best light is early in the day).

Better yet, if you have a car, head south of the city in the morning for gorgeously lit Old Town views over your right shoulder; various turn-offs along this road are ideal photo

stops. The best one, known locally as the **"panorama point,"** is where the road leading up and out of Dubrovnik meets the main road that passes above the town (look for the pull-out on the right, with tour buses). Even if you're heading north, in good weather it's worth a quick detour south for this view. For the highest vantage point without wings, head up to the fortress atop **Mount Srđ,** directly above the Old Town, which also houses a museum about the recent war (described later, under "Sights in Dubrovnik").

Getting Around Dubrovnik

If you're staying in or near the Old Town, everything is easily walkable. But those sleeping on Boninovo Bay or the Lapad Peninsula will want to get comfortable using the buses. Once you understand the system, commuting to the Old Town is a breeze.

By Bus: Libertas runs Dubrovnik's public buses. Tickets, which are good for an hour, are cheaper if you buy them in advance from a newsstand or your hotel (8 kn, ask for *autobusna karta,* ow-toh-BOOS-nah KAR-tah) than if you buy them from the bus driver (10 kn). A 24-hour ticket costs 25 kn, and a ticket for 20 rides costs 120 kn (only sold at special bus-ticket kiosks, such as the one near the Pile Gate bus stop).

When you enter the bus, validate your ticket in the machine next to the driver (orange arrow in, white side up). Because most tourists can't figure out how to validate their tickets, it can take a long time to load the bus (which means drivers are understandably grumpy, and locals aren't shy about cutting in line).

All buses stop near the Old Town, just in front of the Pile Gate (buy tickets at the newsstand or bus-ticket kiosk right by the stop). From here, they fan out to just about anywhere you'd want to go (hotels on Boninovo Bay, Lapad Peninsula, and the ferry terminal and long-distance bus station). You'll find bus schedules and a map in the TI booklet (for more information, visit www.libertasdubrovnik.hr).

By Taxi: Taxis start at 25 kn, then charge 8 kn per kilometer. The handiest taxi stand for the Old Town is just outside the Pile Gate. The biggest operation is Radio Taxi (tel. 020/970).

Tours in Dubrovnik

Walking Tours—Two companies—**Dubrovnik Walking Tours** and **Dubrovnik Walks**—offer similar one-hour walking tours of the Old Town daily at 10:00, and sometimes again in the afternoon (90 kn, also other departures and topics—look for fliers at TI). These tours are pricey and brief, touching lightly on the same basic information explained in this chapter.

Local Guide—For an in-depth look at the city, consider hiring your own local guide. **Štefica Curić** really knows her stuff and can give you an insider's look at the city (480 kn/2 hours, mobile 091-345-0133, dugacarapa@yahoo.com). If Štefica is busy, she can refer you to another good guide for the same price. The TI can also suggest guides.

Bus-Plus-Walking Tours—Two big companies (**Atlas** and **Elite**) offer expensive tours of Dubrovnik (about 220 kn, 2 hours).

From Dubrovnik

Package Excursions—The big **Atlas Travel Agency** in Dubrovnik offers guided excursions (by bus and/or boat) to nearby destinations, including Mostar, Korčula, Montenegro, islands and villages near Dubrovnik, Albania, and others (figure €30-100/person, depending on the itinerary; book tickets at Atlas in Dubrovnik—listed earlier, under "Helpful Hints"—or at other travel agencies; Atlas tel. 020/442-574, www.atlas-croatia.com). While these excursions can be a convenient way to see otherwise difficult-to-reach destinations, the experience is generally disappointing: The buses are packed, the guides are uninspired (reading from a dull script—often in multiple languages), and quality time at the destinations is short. If you have no other way to reach a place you're dying to visit, guided excursions can still be worth considering. But I'd exhaust my other options first—consider renting a car for the day, or hiring your own driver (described next).

Hire Your Own Driver—I enjoy renting my own car to see the sights around Dubrovnik (see "Helpful Hints," earlier). But if you're more comfortable having someone else do the driving, consider hiring a driver. While the drivers listed here are not official tour guides, they speak great English and offer ample commentary as you roll, and can help you craft a good day-long itinerary to Mostar, Montenegro, Korčula, or anywhere else near Dubrovnik (typically departing around 8:00 and returning in the early evening). Friendly **Pepo Klaić,** a veteran of the 1991 war, enjoys surprising my readers with worthwhile detours—go along with his suggestions (€250/day, €125 for half-day trip to nearer destinations, airport transfer for about 200 kn—cheaper than a taxi, these prices for up to 4 people—more expensive for bigger groups, mobile 098-427-301, http://pepoklaic.pondi.hr, pepoklaic@yahoo.com). For €70, Pepo can drive you to the fortress at Mount Srđ up above the Old Town, with sweeping views of the entire area (about 1–1.5 hours round-trip). **Petar Vlašić** can do similar tours for similar prices, and specializes in wine tours to the Pelješac Peninsula, with stops at various wineries along the way (220-kn airport transfers, mobile 091-580-8721, www.dubrovnikriviera tours.com, meritum@du.t-com.hr). **Pero Carević,** who runs the

recommended Villa Ragusa guest house, also drives travelers on excursions (similar prices, mobile 098-765-634, villa.ragusa@du.t-com.hr; see "Sleeping in Dubrovnik," later).

Self-Guided Walk

▲▲▲Welcome to Dubrovnik: Strolling the Stradun

Running through the heart of Dubrovnik's Old Town is the 300-yard-long Stradun promenade—packed with people and lined with sights. This walk offers an ideal introduction to Dubrovnik's charms. It takes about a half-hour, not counting sightseeing stops.

• *Begin at the busy square in front of the west entrance to the Old Town, the Pile (PEE-leh) Gate.*

Pile Neighborhood

This bustling area is the nerve center of Dubrovnik's tourist industry—it's where the real world meets the fantasy of Dubrovnik (for details on services offered here, see "Orientation to Dubrovnik," earlier). Near the modern, mirrors-and-TV-screens monument is a leafy café terrace. Wander over to the edge of the terrace and take in the imposing walls of the Pearl of the Adriatic. The huge, fortified peninsula just outside the city walls is the **Fort of St. Lawrence** (Tvrđava Lovrijenac), Dubrovnik's oldest fortress and one of the top venues for the Dubrovnik Summer Festival. Shakespearean plays are often performed here, occasionally starring Goran Višnjić, the Croatian actor who became an American star on the TV show *ER*. You can climb this fortress for great views over the Old Town (20 kn, or covered by same ticket as Old Town walls on the same day).

• *Cross over the moat (now a shady park) to the round entrance tower in the Old Town Wall. This is the...*

Pile Gate (Gradska Vrata Pile)

Just before you enter the gate, notice the image above the entrance of **St. Blaise** (Sveti Vlaho in Croatian) cradling Dubrovnik in his arm. You'll see a lot more of Blaise during your time here—we'll find

out why later on this walk.

Inside the outer wall of the Pile Gate and to the left, a white **sign** shows where each bomb dropped on the Old Town in the recent war. Once inside town, you'll see virtually no signs of the war—a testament to the townspeople's impressive resilience in rebuilding so well, and so quickly.

Passing the rest of the way through the gate, you'll find a lively little square surrounded by landmarks. To the left, a steep stairway leads up to the imposing **Minčeta Tower**. This is a good starting point for Dubrovnik's best activity, walking around the top of the wall (described later, under "Sights in Dubrovnik").

Next to the stairway is the small **Church of St. Savior** (Crkva Svetog Spasa). Appreciative locals built this votive church to thank God after Dubrovnik made it through a 1520 earthquake. When the massive 1667 quake destroyed the city, this church was one of the only buildings left intact. And during the recent war, the church survived another close call when a shell exploded on the ground right in front of it (you can still see faint pockmarks from the shrapnel).

The giant, round structure in the middle of the square is **Onofrio's Big Fountain** (Velika Onofrijea Fontana). In the Middle Ages, Dubrovnik had a complicated aqueduct system that brought water from the mountains seven miles away. The water ended up here, at the town's biggest fountain, before continuing through the city. This plentiful supply of water, large reserves of salt (from the town of Ston, a key source of Dubrovnik's wealth), and a massive granary (now the Rupe Ethnographic Museum, described under "Sights in Dubrovnik") made little, independent Dubrovnik very siege-resistant.

The big building on the left just beyond the small Church of St. Savior is the **Franciscan Monastery Museum.** This building, with a delightful cloister and one of Europe's oldest pharmacies, is worth touring (described later, under "Sights in Dubrovnik").

• *When you're finished taking in the sights on this square, continue along...*

The Stradun

Dubrovnik's main promenade—officially called the Placa, but better known as the Stradun—is alive with locals and tourists alike. This is the heartbeat of the city: an Old World shopping mall by day and sprawling cocktail party after dark, when everybody

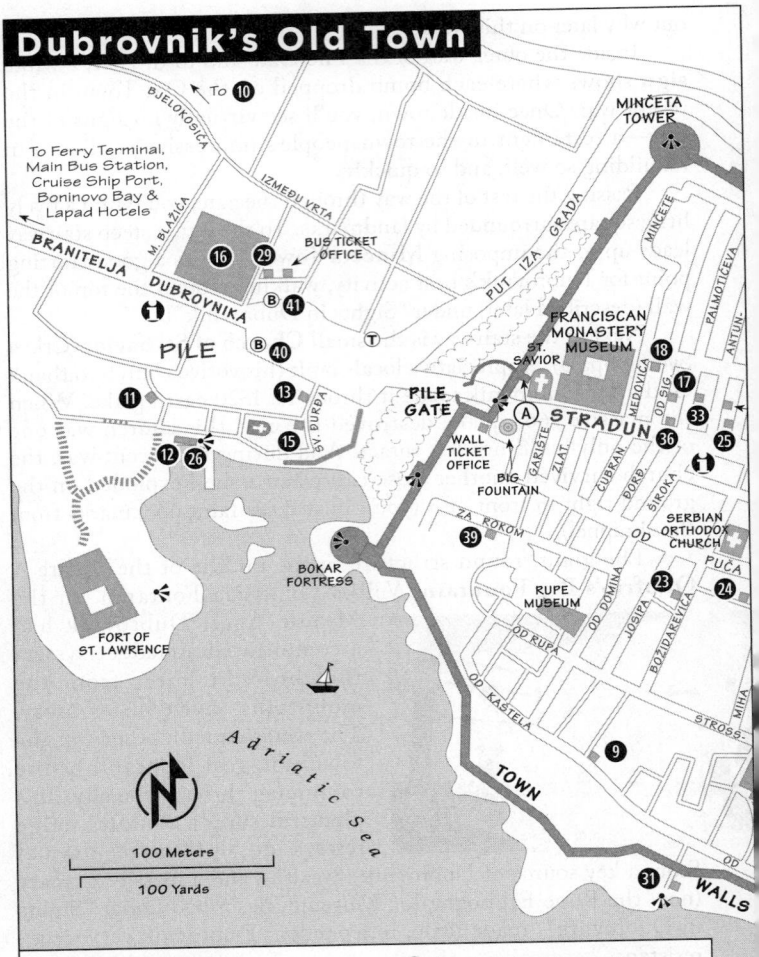

Accommodations

1. Villa Ragusa & Apts. Paviša
2. Apartments Martecchini
3. Raič Apartments
4. Plaza Apartments
5. Karmen Apartments
6. Apartments Amoret (3)
7. Apartments Placa
8. Renata Zijadić Rooms
9. Fresh Sheets Hostel
10. To Jadranka Benussi Rooms
11. Paulina Čumbelić Rooms
12. Rest. Orhan Guest House
13. Nedjeljka Benussi Rooms
14. Villa Adriatica
15. Atlas Travel Agency
16. Hilton Imperial Dubrovnik
17. Hotel Stari Grad

Restaurants, Bars & Groceries

18. Nishta Restaurant
19. Dubrovački Kantun
20. Konoba Kamenice
21. Lokanda Peskarija

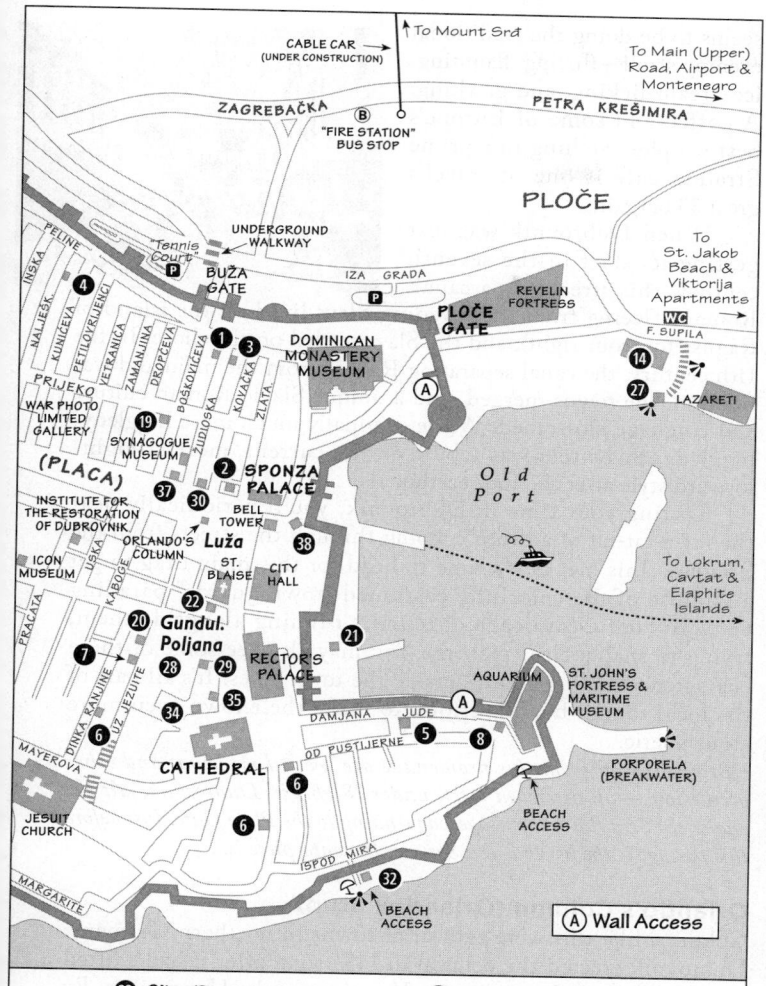

22 Oliva Pizzeria
23 Spaghetteria Toni
24 Taj Mahal Restaurant
25 Dolce Vita Ice Cream
26 Orhan Restaurant
27 Komarda Restaurant
28 Produce Market
29 Konzum Groceries (2)
30 Dubrava Bistro
31 Cold Drinks "Buža" II
32 Cold Drinks "Buža" I
33 d'vino Wine Bar
34 Jazz Caffè Troubadour
35 Nonenina Cocktail Bar

Other

36 Vinoteka Miličić Wine Shop
37 Algoritam Bookshop
38 Sloboda Cinema
39 Jadran Cinema
40 Arriving Bus Stop
41 Departing Bus Stop

seems to be doing the traditional evening stroll—flirting, flaunting, ice-cream-licking, and gawking. A coffee and some of Europe's best people-watching in a prime Stradun café is one of travel's great $3 bargains.

When Dubrovnik was just getting its start in the seventh century, this street was a canal. Romans fleeing from the invading Slavs lived on the island of Ragusa (on your right), and the Slavs settled on the shore. In the 11th century, the canal separating Ragusa from the mainland was filled in, the towns merged, and a unique Slavic-Roman culture and language blossomed. While originally much more higgledy-piggledy, this street was rebuilt in the current, more straightforward style after the 1667 earthquake.

During your time in Dubrovnik, you'll periodically hear the rat-a-tat-tat of a drum echoing through the streets from the Stradun. This means it's time to head for this main drag to get a glimpse of the colorfully costumed "town guards" parading through (and a cavalcade of tourists running alongside them, trying to snap a clear picture). You may also see some of these characters standing guard outside the town gates. It's all part of the local tourist board's efforts to make their town even more atmospheric.

• *Branching off from this promenade are several museums and other attractions—all described later, under "Sights in Dubrovnik." At the end of the Stradun is a passageway leading to the Ploče Gate. Just before this passage is the lively Luža Square. Its centerpiece is...*

Orlando's Column (Orlandov Stup)

Columns like this were typical of towns in northern Germany. Dubrovnik erected the column in 1417, soon after it had shifted allegiances from the oppressive Venetians to the Hungarians. By putting a northern European symbol in the middle of its most prominent square, Dubrovnik decisively distanced itself from Venice. Anytime a decision was made by the Republic, the town crier came to Orlando's Column and announced the news. The step he stood on indicated the importance of his message—the higher up, the more important the news. It was also used as the pillory, where people were publicly punished. The thin line on the top step in front of Orlando is exactly as long as the statue's forearm. This mark was Dubrovnik's standard measurement—not for a foot, but for an "elbow."

• *Now stand in front of Orlando's Column and orient yourself with a...*

Luža Square Spin-Tour

Orlando is looking toward the **Sponza Palace** (Sponza-Povijesni Arhiv). This building, from 1522, is the finest surviving example of Dubrovnik's Golden Age in the 15th and 16th centuries. It's a combination of Renaissance (ground-floor arches) and Venetian Gothic (upstairs windows). Houses up and down the main promenade used to look like this, but after the 1667 earthquake, they were replaced with boring uniformity. This used to be the customs office *(dogana),* but now it's an exhaustive archive of the city's history, with temporary art exhibits and a war memorial. The poignant **Memorial Room of Dubrovnik Defenders** (on the left as you enter) has photos of dozens of people from Dubrovnik who were killed fighting Yugoslav forces in 1991. A TV screen and images near the ceiling show the devastation of the city. Though the English descriptions are (perhaps unavoidably) slanted to the Croat perspective, it's compelling to look in the eyes of the brave young men who didn't start this war...but were willing to finish it (free, long hours daily in peak season, shorter hours off-season). Beyond the memorial room, the impressive **courtyard,** which generally displays temporary exhibits, is worth a peek (20 kn).

To the right of Sponza Palace is the town's **Bell Tower** (Gradski Zvonik). The original dated from 1444, but it was rebuilt when it started to lean in the 1920s. The big clock may be an octopus, but only one of its hands tells time. Below that, the circle shows the phase of the moon. At the bottom, the old-fashioned digital readout tells the hour (in Roman numerals) and the minutes (in five-minute increments). At the top of each hour (and again three minutes later), the time is clanged out on the bell up top by two bronze bell ringers, Maro and Baro. (If this all seems like a copy of the very similar clock on St. Mark's Square in Venice, locals are quick to point out that this clock predates that one by several decades.) The clock still has to be wound every two days. Notice the little window between the moon phase and the "digital" readout: The clock-winder opens this window to get some light. During the 1991–1992 siege, the clock-winder's house was destroyed—with the winding keys inside. For days, the clock bell didn't run. But then, miraculously, the keys were discovered lying in the street. Excited Dubrovnik citizens came together in this square and cheered as the clock was wound and the bell chimed, signaling to the soldiers surrounding their city that they hadn't won yet.

The big building to the right of the Bell Tower is the **City Hall** (Vijećnica). Next to that is **Onofrio's Little Fountain** (Mala Onofrijea Fontana), the little brother of the one at the other end of the Stradun. Beyond that is the **Gradska Kavana,** or "Town Café." This hangout—historically Dubrovnik's favorite spot for gossiping and people-watching—has pricey drinks and seating all the way through the wall to the Old Port. Just down the street from the Town Café is the Rector's Palace, and then the cathedral (for more on each, see "Sights in Dubrovnik").

Behind Orlando is **St. Blaise's Church** (Crkva Sv. Vlaha), dedicated to the patron saint of Dubrovnik. You'll see statues and paintings of St. Blaise all over town, always holding a model of the city in his left hand. According to legend, a millennium ago St. Blaise came to a local priest in a dream and warned him that the up-and-coming Venetians would soon attack the city. The priest alerted the authorities, who prepared for war. Of course, the prediction came true. St. Blaise has been a Dubrovnik symbol—and locals have resented Venice—ever since.

• *Your tour is finished. From here, you've got plenty of sightseeing options (all described in the next section, "Sights in Dubrovnik"). As you face the Bell Tower, you can go up the street to the right to reach the Rector's Palace and cathedral; you can walk through the gate straight ahead to reach the Old Port; or you can head through the gate and jog left to find the Dominican Monastery Museum. Even more sights—including an old synagogue, an Orthodox church, two different exhibits of war photography, and the medieval granary—are in the steep streets between the Stradun and the walls.*

Sights in Dubrovnik

Nearly all of Dubrovnik's sights are inside the Old Town's walls.

Combo-Tickets: The Rector's Palace, Maritime Museum, and Rupe Granary and Ethnographic Museum—which normally cost 40 kn apiece—are covered by a combo-ticket (45 kn to visit any two, 50 kn to visit all three, tickets sold at all three sights, valid for three days). If you're visiting any one of these sights, you might as well buy the three-sight ticket and poke into the others, since it costs just slightly more than an individual entry. The TI's bigger combo-ticket—which covers the same three sights, plus the City Walls and a few lesser attractions—won't save the casual sightseer any money (100 kn for 1 day).

▲▲▲Town Walls (Gradske Zidine)

Dubrovnik's single best attraction is strolling the scenic mile-and-a-quarter around the city walls. As you meander along this lofty perch—with a sea of orange roofs on one side, and the actual sea on the other—you'll get your bearings and snap pictures like mad of the ever-changing views. Bring your map, which you can use to pick out landmarks and get the lay of the land.

There have been walls here almost as long as there's been a Dubrovnik. As with virtually all fortifications on the Croatian Coast, these walls were beefed up in the 15th century, when the Ottoman navy became a threat. Around the perimeter are several substantial forts, with walls rounded so that cannonballs would glance off harmlessly. These stout forts intimidated would-be invaders during the Republic of Dubrovnik's Golden Age, and protected local residents during the 1991–1992 siege.

Walking the walls also offers the best illustration of the damage Dubrovnik sustained during the recent siege. It's easy to see that nearly two-thirds of Dubrovnik's roofs were replaced after the bombings (notice the new, bright-orange tiles—and the way some buildings salvaged the old tiles, but have new ones underneath). Looking over this gorgeous panorama, ponder that the pristine-seeming Old Town was rebuilt using exactly the same materials and methods with which it was originally constructed.

The highest point is the empty Minčeta Tower, above the Pile Gate at the west end of town. The tower rewards those who climb to its top with a fine view.

Posted signs send wall-walkers counterclockwise. Therefore, if you begin at the main Pile Gate entrance, you'll reach the Minčeta Tower last. Speed demons with no cameras can walk the walls in about an hour; strollers and shutterbugs should plan on longer. Because it can be very hot up top, with almost no shade, it's essential to bring sunscreen, a hat, and water. Take your time: There are several steep stretches, and you'll be climbing up and down the whole way around. A few scant shops and cafés along the top of

The Siege of Dubrovnik

In June 1991, Croatia declared independence from Yugoslavia. Within weeks, the nations were at war (for more on the war, see the Understanding Yugoslavia chapter). Though warfare raged in the Croatian interior, nobody expected that the bloodshed would reach Dubrovnik.

As refugees from Vukovar (in northeastern Croatia) arrived in Dubrovnik that fall, telling horrific stories of the warfare there, local residents began fearing the worst. Warplanes from the Serb-dominated Yugoslav National Army buzzed threateningly low over the town, as if to signal an impending attack.

Then, at 6:00 in the morning on October 1, 1991, Dubrovnik residents awoke to explosions on nearby hillsides. The first attacks were focused on Mount Srđ, high above the Old Town. First the giant cross was destroyed, then a communications tower (both have been rebuilt and are visible today). This first wave of attacks cleared the way for Yugoslav land troops—mostly Serbs and Montenegrins—who surrounded the city. The ragtag, newly formed Croatian Army quickly dug in at the old Napoleonic-era fortress at the top of Mount Srđ, where just 25 or 30 soldiers fended off a Yugoslav takeover of this highly strategic position.

At first, the shelling targeted military positions on the outskirts of town. But soon, Yugoslav forces began bombing residential neighborhoods, then the Pearl of the Adriatic itself: Dubrovnik's Old Town. Defenseless townspeople took shelter in their cellars, and sometimes even huddled together in the city wall's 15th-century forts. It was the first time in Dubrovnik's long history that the walls were actually used to defend against an attack.

Dubrovnik resisted the siege better than anyone expected. The Yugoslav forces were hoping that residents would flee the town, but the people of Dubrovnik stayed. Though severely outgunned and outnumbered, Dubrovnik's defenders managed to hold the fort atop Mount Srđ, despite Yugoslav forces controlling the nearby mountaintops. All supplies had to be carried up to the fort by foot or by donkey. Dubrovnik wasn't prepared for war, so they had to improvise their defense. Many brave young locals lost their lives when they slung old hunting rifles over their shoulders and, under cover of darkness, climbed the hills above Dubrovnik to meet Yugoslav soldiers face-to-face.

the wall (mostly on the sea side) sell water and other drinks, but it's safest to bring what you'll need with you. Because your ticket is electronically scanned as you enter, you can't leave and re-enter the wall later.

Cost and Entrance: 50 kn to enter walls, also includes the St. Lawrence Fort outside the Pile Gate. The main entrance to the walls is just inside the Pile Gate: As you enter the Old Town

After eight months of bombing, Dubrovnik was liberated by the Croatian Army, which attacked Yugoslav positions from the north. By the end of the siege, 100 civilians were dead, as well as more than 200 Dubrovnik citizens who lost their lives actively fighting for their hometown (much revered today as "Dubrovnik Defenders"). More than two-thirds of Dubrovnik's buildings had been damaged, and more than 30,000 people had to flee their homes—but the failed siege was finally over.

Why was Dubrovnik—so far from the rest of the fighting—dragged into the conflict? Yugoslavia wanted to catch the city and surrounding region off-guard, gaining a toehold on the southern Dalmatian Coast so they could push north to Split. They also hoped to ignite pro-Serb (and pro-Yugoslav) passions in the nearby Serb-dominated areas of Bosnia-Herzegovina and Montenegro. But perhaps most of all, Yugoslavia wanted to hit Croatia where it hurt—its proudest, most historic, and most beautiful city, the tourist capital of a nation dependent on tourism. (It seems their plan backfired. Locals now say, "When Yugoslavia attacked Dubrovnik, they lost the war"—because images of the historic city under siege swayed international public opinion *against* Yugoslavia.)

The war initially devastated the tourist industry. Now, to the casual observer, Dubrovnik seems virtually back to normal. Aside from a few pockmarks and many bright, new roof tiles, there are scant reminders of what happened here nearly two decades ago. But even though the city itself has been repaired, the people of Dubrovnik are forever changed. Imagine living in an idyllic paradise, a place that attracted and awed visitors from around the world...and then watching it gradually blown to bits. It's understandable if Dubrovnik citizens are a little less in love with life than they once were.

Dubrovnik has various low-key attractions related to its recent war, including the Memorial Room of Dubrovnik Defenders in the Sponza Palace on Luža Square; the Institute for the Restoration of Dubrovnik, a few blocks away across the Stradun; and the museum in the ruined fortress atop Mount Srđ. Another sight, War Photo Limited, expands the scope to war photography from around the world. All of these sights are described in this chapter.

through the gate, the stairs up to the top of the wall are directly to your left; but first, you have to buy your ticket at the office, tucked in the corner to your right. You can also buy tickets and enter the walls at two other points: near the Dominican Monastery north of the Ploče Gate, and by the Maritime Museum south of the Old Port.

Hours: July–Aug daily 8:00–19:30, progressively shorter

hours off-season until mid-Nov–mid-March 10:00–15:00. Since the hours change with the season, confirm them by checking signs posted at the entrance (essential if you want to time your wall walk to avoid the worst crowds—explained below). Note that posted closing time indicates when the walls shut down, *not* the last entry—ascend at least an hour before this time if you want to make it all the way around. Attendants begin circling the walls about 30 minutes after the posted closing time to lock the gates. There's talk of eventually illuminating the walls at night, in which case the hours would be extended until after dark.

Audioguide: You can rent a 40-kn audioguide, separate from the admission fee, for a dryly narrated circular tour of the walls (look for vendors near the entry points). But I'd rather just enjoy the views and lazily pick out the landmarks with my map.

Crowd Control: Because this is Dubrovnik's top attraction, it's extremely crowded. Your best strategy is to avoid the walls during the times when the cruise ships are in town. On days when the walls open at 8:00, try to get started around that time. The walls are the most crowded from about 8:30 until 11:00, when the cruise ships are docked. There's generally an afternoon lull in the crowds (11:00–15:00), but that's also the hottest time to be atop the walls. Crowds pick up again in the late afternoon (starting around 15:00), peaking about an hour before closing time (18:30 in high season). So your options are either early, crowded, or hot.

The "Other" Wall Climb: Your ticket for the Old Town Walls also includes the Fort of St. Lawrence just outside the Old Town (valid same day only; fort described on page 772). If you've already bought a 20-kn ticket there, show it when buying your main wall ticket and you'll pay only the difference.

Near the Pile Gate

This museum is just inside the Pile Gate.

▲Franciscan Monastery Museum (Franjevački Samostan-Muzej)—In the Middle Ages, Dubrovnik's monasteries flourished. While all you'll see here are a fine cloister and a one-room museum in the old pharmacy, it's a delightful space. Enter through the gap between the small church and the big monastery (30 kn, daily April–Oct 9:00–18:00, Nov–March 9:00–17:00, Placa 2, www.malabraca.hr). Just inside the door (before the ticket-seller), a century-old pharmacy still serves residents.

Explore the peaceful, sun-dappled **cloister.** Examine the capitals at the tops of the 60 Romanesque-Gothic double pillars. Each one is different. Notice that some of the portals inside the courtyard are made with a lighter-colored stone—these had to be repaired after being hit during the 1991–1992 siege. The damaged 19th-century frescoes along the tops of the walls depict

the life of St. Francis, who supposedly visited Dubrovnik in the early 13th century.

In the far corner stands the monastery's original medieval **pharmacy.** Part of the Franciscans' mission was to contribute to the good health of the citizens, so they opened this pharmacy in 1317. The monastery has had a pharmacy in continual operation ever since. On display are jars, pots, and other medieval pharmacists' tools. The sick would come to get their medicine at the little window (on left side), which limited contact with the pharmacist and reduced the risk of passing on disease. Around the room, you'll also find some relics, old manuscripts, and a detailed painting of early 17th-century Dubrovnik.

Near Luža Square

These sights are at the far end of the Stradun (nearest the Old Port). As you stand on Luža Square facing the Bell Tower, the Rector's Palace and cathedral are up the wide street called Pred Dvorom to the right, and the Dominican Monastery Museum is through the gate by the Bell Tower and to the left.

Rector's Palace (Knežev Dvor)—In the Middle Ages, the Republic of Dubrovnik was ruled by a rector (similar to a Venetian doge), who was elected by the nobility. To prevent any one person from becoming too powerful, the rector's term was limited to one month. Most rectors were in their 50s—near the end of the average life span and when they were less likely to shake things up. During his term, a rector lived upstairs in this palace. Because it's been plundered twice, this empty-feeling museum isn't as interesting as most other European palaces—but it does offer a glimpse of Dubrovnik in its glory days (40 kn, covered by 45-kn or 50-kn combo-ticket, daily May–Oct 9:00–18:00, Nov–April 9:00–16:00, some posted English information, 6-kn English booklet is helpful, Pred Dvorom 3).

The **exterior** is decorated in the Gothic-Renaissance mix (with particularly finely carved capitals) that was so common in Dubrovnik before the 1667 earthquake.

Standing at the main door, you can generally get a free peek into the palace's impressive **courtyard**—a venue for the Summer Festival, hosting music groups ranging from the local symphony to the Vienna Boys' Choir. In the courtyard (and also visible from the door) is the only secular statue created during the centuries-long Republic. Dubrovnik republicans, mindful of the dangers

of hero-worship, didn't believe that any one citizen should be singled out. They made only one exception—for Miho Pracat (a.k.a. Michaeli Prazatto), a rich citizen who donated vast sums to charity and willed a fleet of ships to the city. But notice that Pracat's statue is displayed in here, behind closed doors, not out in public.

The palace collection, which requires a ticket, is skippable. But if you'd like to go **inside**, proceed to the ticket desk, then tour a few ground-floor exhibits. You'll see some old prison cells, which supposedly were placed within earshot of the rector's quarters, so he would hear the moans of the prisoners...and stay honest. Leaving the prison, you'll enter the courtyard described earlier, where you can get a better look at the Pracat statue.

On the mezzanine level (stairs near the main entrance), you'll find a decent display of furniture, a wimpy gun exhibit, a ho-hum coin collection, and an interesting painting of "Ragusa" in the early 17th century—back when it was still bisected by a canal.

Head back down to the courtyard and go to the upper floor (using the staircase across from mezzanine stairs, near the Pracat statue—notice the "hand" rails). Upstairs, you'll explore old apartments that serve as a painting gallery. The only vaguely authentic room is the red room in the corner, decorated more or less as it was in 1500, when it was the rector's office. Mihajlo Hamzić's exquisite *Baptism of Christ* painting, inspired by Italian painter Andrea Mantegna, is an early Renaissance work from the "Dubrovnik School" (see "Dominican Monastery Museum" listing, later).

▲Cathedral (Katedrala)—Dubrovnik's original 12th-century cathedral was funded largely by the English King Richard the Lionhearted. On his way back from the Third Crusade, Richard was shipwrecked nearby. He promised God that if he survived, he'd build a church on the spot where he landed—which happened to be on Lokrum Island, just offshore. At Dubrovnik's request, Richard agreed to build his token of thanks inside the city instead. It was the finest Romanesque church on the Adriatic...before it was destroyed by the 1667 earthquake. This version is 18th-century Roman Baroque. Inside, you'll find a painting from the school of Titian *(Assumption of the Virgin)* over the stark contemporary altar, and a quirky treasury *(riznica)* packed with 187 relics (church: free, daily 8:00–20:00; treasury: 15 kn, generally open same hours as church; both have shorter hours off-season).

Examining the **treasury** collection, notice that there are three locks on the treasury door—the stuff in here was so valuable, three different VIPs (the rector, the bishop, and a local aristocrat) had to agree before it could be opened. On the table near the door are several of St. Blaise's body parts (pieces of his arm, skull, and leg—all encased in gold and silver). In the middle of the wall directly opposite the door, look for the crucifix with a piece of the "true cross." On a dig in Jerusalem, St. Helen (Emperor Constantine's mother) discovered what she believed to be the cross that Jesus was crucified on. It was brought to Constantinople, and the Byzantine czars doled out pieces of it to Balkan kings. Note the folding three-paneled altar painting (underneath the cross). Dubrovnik ambassadors packed this on road trips (such as their annual trip to pay off the Ottomans) so they could worship wherever they traveled. On the right side of the room, the silver casket supposedly holds the actual swaddling clothes of the Baby Jesus (or, as some locals call it somewhat less reverently, "Jesus' nappy"). Dubrovnik bishops secretly passed these clothes down from generation to generation... until a nun got wind of it and told the whole town. Pieces of the cloth were cut off to miraculously heal the sick, especially new mothers recovering from a difficult birth. No matter how often it was cut, the cloth always went back to its original form. Then someone tried to use it on the wife of a Bosnian king. Since she was Muslim, it couldn't help her, and it never worked again. True or not, this legend hints at the prickly relationships between faiths (not to mention the male chauvinism) here in the Balkans.

▲Dominican Monastery Museum (Dominikanski Samostan-Muzej)—You'll find many of Dubrovnik's art treasures—paintings, altarpieces, and manuscripts—gathered around the peaceful Dominican Monastery cloister inside the Ploče Gate (20 kn, art buffs enjoy the 50-kn English book, daily May–Sept 9:00–18:00, Oct–April 9:00–17:00). Historically, this was the church for wealthy people, while the Franciscan Church (down at the far end of the Stradun) was for poor people. Services were staggered by 15 minutes to allow servants to drop off their masters here, then rush down the Stradun for their own service.

Work your way clockwise around the cloister. The room in the far corner from the entry contains paintings from the **"Dubrovnik School,"** the Republic's circa-1500 answer to the art boom in Florence and Venice. Though the 1667 earthquake

destroyed most of these paintings, about a dozen survive, and five of those are in this room. Don't miss the triptych by Nikola Božidarović with St. Blaise holding a detailed model of 16th-century Dubrovnik (left panel)—the most famous depiction of Dubrovnik's favorite saint. You'll also see reliquaries shaped like the hands and feet that they hold.

Continuing around the courtyard, duck into the next room. Here you'll see a painting by **Titian** depicting St. Blaise, Mary Magdalene, and the donor.

At the next corner of the courtyard is the entrance to the striking **church** at the heart of this still-active monastery. Step inside. The interior is decorated with modern stained glass, a fine 13th-century stone pulpit that survived the earthquake (reminding visitors of the intellectual approach to scripture that characterized the Dominicans), and a precious 14th-century Paolo Veneziano crucifix hanging above the high altar. The most memorable piece of art in the church is the *Miracle of St. Dominic,* showing the founder of the order bringing a child back to life (over the altar to the right, as you enter). It was painted in the Realist style (late 19th century) by Vlaho Bukovac.

Near the Old Port (Stara Luka)

The picturesque Old Port, carefully nestled behind St. John's Fort, faces away from what was Dubrovnik's biggest threat, the Venetians. The long seaside building across the bay on the left is the Lazareti, once the medieval quarantine house. In those days, all visitors were locked in here for 40 days before entering town. (Today it hosts folk-dancing shows—described later, under "Entertainment in Dubrovnik.")

A bench-lined harborside walk leads around the fort to a breakwater, providing a peaceful perch. From the breakwater, rocky beaches curl around the outside of the wall.

Excursions—At the port, you can haggle with captains selling excursions. The basic option is a 50-minute "panorama cruise" out into the water and back again (75 kn, departures every hour). Among your vessel choices is the ***Sv. Ivan,*** a cargo boat dating from 1878. other popular trips are to **Lokrum Island,** just offshore (40 kn round-trip, 10 kn for a map, runs April-Sept, 2/hr, 9:00–17:00, mid-June–Aug until 19:00, none Oct–March); and to the archipelago called the **Elaphite Islands,** with visits to three different islands (about 250 kn with lunch, 180 kn without, several boats depart daily around 10:30–11:00, return around 18:00–18:30;

so they can buy enough food, companies prefer that you reserve and pay a 50-kn deposit the day before).

Maritime Museum (Pomorski Muzej)—By the 15th century, when Venice's nautical dominance was on the wane, Dubrovnik emerged as a maritime power and the Mediterranean's leading shipbuilding center. The Dubrovnik-built "argosy" boat (from "Ragusa," an early name for the city) was the Cadillac of ships, frequently mentioned by Shakespeare. This small museum traces the history of Dubrovnik's most important industry with contracts, maps, paintings, and models—all well-described in English. The main floor takes you through the 18th century, and the easy-to-miss upstairs covers the 19th and 20th centuries. Boaters will find the museum particularly interesting (40 kn, covered by 45-kn or 50-kn combo-ticket, 5-kn English booklet, hours depend on demand—usually March–Oct Tue-Sun 9:00–18:00, closed Mon, shorter hours Nov–Feb, upstairs in St. John's Fort, at far/south end of Old Port, tel. 020/323-904).

Aquarium (Akvarij)—Dubrovnik's aquarium, housed in the cavernous St. John's Fort, is an old-school place, with 31 tanks on one floor. A visit here allows you a close look at the local marine life and provides a cool refuge from the midday heat (30 kn, kids-10 kn, English descriptions, daily July–Aug 9:00–21:00, progressively shorter hours off-season until 9:00–13:00 Nov–March, ground floor of St. John's Fort, enter from Old Port).

Between the Stradun and the Mainland

These two museums are a few steps off the main promenade toward the mainland.

▲Synagogue Museum (Sinagoga-Muzej)—When Jews were forced out of Spain in 1492, a steady stream of them passed through here en route to today's Turkey. Finding Dubrovnik to be a flourishing and relatively tolerant city, many stayed. Židioska ulica ("Jewish Street"), just inside Ploče Gate, became the ghetto in 1546. It was walled at one end and had a gate (which would be locked at night) at the other end. Today, the same street is home to the second-oldest continuously functioning synagogue in Europe (after Prague's), which contains Croatia's only Jewish museum. The top floor houses the synagogue itself. Notice the lattice windows that separated the women from the men (according to Orthodox Jewish tradition). Below that, a small museum with good English descriptions gives meaning to the various Torahs (including a 14th-century one from Spain) and other items—such as the written orders *(naredba)* from Nazi-era Yugoslavia, stating that Jews were to identify their shops as Jewish-owned and wear armbands. (The Ustaše—the Nazi puppet government in Croatia—interned and executed not only Jews and Roma/Gypsies, but also Serbs

and other people they considered undesirable; see page 748.) Of Croatia's 24,000 Jews, only 4,000 survived the Holocaust. Today Croatia has about 2,000 Jews, including 12 Jewish families who call Dubrovnik home (15 kn, 10-kn English booklet; May–mid-Nov daily 10:00–20:00; mid-Nov–April Mon–Fri 10:00–13:00, closed Sat–Sun; Žudioska ulica 5, tel. 020/321-028).

War Photo Limited—If the tragic story of wartime Dubrovnik has you in a pensive mood, drop by this gallery with images of warfare from around the world. The brainchild of photojournalist Wade Goddard, this thought-provoking museum—with well-displayed exhibits on two floors—attempts to show the ugly reality of war through raw, often disturbing photographs taken in the field. A permanent exhibit depicts the wars in the former Yugoslavia through photography and video footage. Each summer, the gallery also houses two different temporary exhibits. Note that the focus is not solely on Dubrovnik, but on war anywhere and everywhere (30 kn; June–Sept daily 9:00–21:00; May and Oct Tue–Sat 9:00–15:00, Sun 10:00–14:00, closed Mon; closed Nov–April; Antuninska 6, tel. 020/322-166, www.warphotoltd.com).

Between the Stradun and the Sea

▲Institute for the Restoration of Dubrovnik (Zavod za Obnovu Dubrovnika)—This small photo gallery is the closest thing Dubrovnik has to a museum about the eight-month siege of the city from late 1991 to mid-1992 (see "The Siege of Dubrovnik" sidebar, earlier). The front two rooms display images of bombed-out Dubrovnik, each one juxtaposed with an image of the same building after being restored. The back room offers rotating exhibits about efforts to restore Dubrovnik to its pre-siege glory. The photos are too few, but still illuminating. The highlight of the exhibit is a video showing a series of breathless news reports from a British journalist stationed here during the siege. As you watch shells devastating this glorious city, and look in the eyes of its desperate citizens at their darkest hour, you might just begin to grasp what went on here not so long ago (free; June–Sept Mon–Fri 10:00–14:00, closed Sat–Sun; Oct–May the same space is used for rotating exhibits on other topics; Zuzorić 6, tel. 020/324-060).

▲Serbian Orthodox Church and Icon Museum (Srpska Pravoslavna Crkva i Muzej Ikona)—Round out your look at Dubrovnik's faiths (Catholic, Jewish, and Orthodox) with a visit to this house of worship—one of the most convenient places in Croatia to learn about Orthodox Christianity. Remember that people from the former Yugoslavia who follow the Orthodox faith are, by definition, ethnic Serbs. With all of the (perhaps understandably) hard feelings about the recent war, this church serves as an important reminder that all Serbs aren't bloodthirsty killers.

The Serbian Orthodox Church

While most of the former Yugoslav destinations covered in this book are in the Catholic areas (Slovenia and Croatia), don't overlook the rich diversity of faiths in this region. Dubrovnik's Serbian Orthodox Church offers an invaluable opportunity to learn about a faith that's often unfamiliar to visitors (there's also one in Ljubljana; see page 666).

As you explore an Orthodox church, keep in mind that these churches carry on the earliest traditions of the Christian faith. Orthodox and Catholic Christianity came from the same roots, so the oldest surviving early-Christian churches (such as the stave churches of Norway) have many of the same features as today's Orthodox churches.

Notice that there are no pews. Worshippers stand through the service, as a sign of respect (though some older parishioners sit on the seats along the walls). Women stand on the left side, men on the right (equal distance from the altar—to represent that all are equal before God). The Orthodox Church uses essentially the same Bible as Catholics, but it's written in the Cyrillic alphabet, which you'll see displayed around any Orthodox church. Following Old Testament Judeo-Christian tradition, the Bible is kept on the altar behind the iconostasis, the big screen in the middle of the room covered with curtains and icons (golden paintings of saints), which separates the material world from the spiritual one. At certain times during the service, the curtains or doors are opened so the congregation can see the Holy Book.

Unlike many Catholic church decorations, Orthodox icons are not intended to be lifelike. Packed with intricate symbolism, and cast against a shimmering golden background, they're meant to remind viewers of the metaphysical nature of Jesus and the saints rather than their physical form, which is considered irrelevant. You'll almost never see a statue, which is thought to overemphasize the physical world...and, to Orthodox people, feels a little too close to violating the commandment, "Thou shalt not worship graven images." Orthodox services generally involve chanting (a dialogue that goes back and forth between the priest and the congregation), and the church is filled with the evocative aroma of incense.

The incense, chanting, icons, and standing up are all intended to heighten the experience of worship. While many Catholic and Protestant services tend to be more of a theoretical and rote consideration of religious issues (come on—don't tell me you've never dozed through the sermon), Orthodox services are about creating a religious experience. Each of these elements does its part to help the worshipper transcend the physical world and enter communion with the spiritual one.

Dubrovnik never had a very large Serb population (an Orthodox church wasn't even allowed inside the town walls until the mid-19th century). During the recent war, most Serbs fled, created new lives for themselves elsewhere, and saw little reason to return. But some old-timers remain, and Dubrovnik's dwindling, aging Orthodox population is still served by this church. The candles stuck in the sand and water (to prevent fire outbreaks) represent prayers: The ones at knee level are for the deceased, while the ones higher up are for the living. The gentleman selling candles encourages you to buy and light one, regardless of your faith, so long as you do so with the proper intentions and reverence (free entry, good 20-kn English book explains the church and the museum, daily May–Sept 8:00–20:00, Oct–April 8:00–15:00, short services daily at 8:30 and 19:00, longer liturgy Sundays at 9:00, Od Puča 8).

A few doors down, you'll find the **Icon Museum** (10 kn; May–Oct Mon–Sat 9:00–14:00, closed Sun; Nov–April Mon–Fri 9:00–14:00, closed Sat–Sun). This small collection features 78 different icons (stylized paintings of saints, generally on a golden background—a common feature of Orthodox churches) from the 15th through the 19th centuries, all identified in English. In the library—crammed with old shelves holding some 12,000 books—look for the astonishingly detailed calendar, with portraits of hundreds of saints. The gallery on the ground floor, run by Michael, sells original icons and reproductions (open longer hours than museum).

▲Rupe Granary and Ethnographic Museum (Etnografski Muzej Rupe)—This huge, 16th-century building was Dubrovnik's biggest granary. *Rupe* means "holes"—and it's worth the price of entry just to peer down into these cavernous underground grain stores, designed to maintain the perfect temperature to preserve the seeds (63 degrees Fahrenheit). When the grain had to be dried, it was moved upstairs—where today you'll find a surprisingly well-presented Ethnographic Museum, with tools, jewelry, clothing, instruments, painted eggs, and other folk artifacts from Dubrovnik's colorful history. Borrow the free English information guide at the entry (40 kn, covered by 45-kn or 50-kn combo-ticket, Wed–Mon 9:00–16:00, closed Tue). The museum hides several blocks uphill from the main promenade, toward the sea (climb up Široka—the widest side street from the Stradun—which becomes Od Domina on the way to the museum).

Above Dubrovnik

▲Mount Srđ—After adding Dubrovnik to his holdings, Napoleon built a fortress atop the hill behind the Old Town to keep an eye on his new subjects (in 1810). During the city's 20th-century tourism heyday, a cable car was built to effortlessly whisk visitors to the top so they could enjoy the fine views from the fortress and the giant cross nearby. But when war broke out in the 1990s, Mount Srđ became a crucial link in the defense of Dubrovnik—the only high land that locals were able to hold. The fortress was shelled and damaged, and the cross and cable car were destroyed. Minefields and unexploded ordnance left the hilltop a dangerous no-man's land.

But today, with the landmines cleared (see "Warning," later) and reconstruction of the cable car underway, Mount Srđ is reclaiming its status as a major tourist attraction. There are two reasons to visit: for the sweeping views, and for a ragtag new museum about the war. However, until the cable car starts running again, this trip is only worth it for those who have a healthy interest and plenty of time (given the expense and/or time it takes to summit the mountain—explained later, under "Getting There").

The bird's-eye **view** is truly spectacular, looking straight down to the street plan of Dubrovnik's Old Town. From this lofty perch, you can see north to the Dalmatian islands (the Elaphite, Mljet, and beyond); south to Montenegro; and east into Bosnia-Herzegovina.

The **cross** was always an important symbol in this very Catholic town. After it was destroyed, a temporary wooden one was erected to encourage the townspeople who were waiting out the siege below. During a visit in 2003, Pope John Paul II blessed the rubble from the old cross; those fragments are now being used in the foundations of the city's newest churches.

The **fortress** houses a humble but interesting exhibit called "Dubrovnik During the Homeland War (1991–1995)." Photos, video clips, documents, and artifacts tell the story (with some English descriptions) of the overarching war with Yugoslavia and how the people defended this fortress. You'll see actual items used

in the fighting: basic, rusty rifles that the Croatians used for their improvised defense, and mortar shells and other projectiles that Yugoslav forces hurled at the fortress and the city. Look for the wire-guided Russian rockets. After being launched at their target, the rockets would burrow into a wall, waiting to be detonated until their operators saw the opportunity for maximum destruction. The explanations are, perhaps unavoidably, slanted to the Croat perspective—with talk of "Serb-Montenegrin aggression" and statements such as, "This senseless attack...showed the full hate towards the Croatian people." Though the museum feels hastily assembled and a bit basic, it's fascinating to learn about this historical moment in a place that played such a major role in the events (15 kn, daily 10:00–18:30, maybe until 20:00 in summer).

After seeing the exhibit, climb up a few flights of stairs to the **rooftop** for the view. The giant communications tower overhead flew the Croatian flag during the war, to inspire the besieged residents below. At the other end of the fortress are the haunting remains of a simpler time: a badly damaged, light-up dance floor from the disco era, back when the fortress hosted not Napoleonic or Croatian soldiers, but a popular dance club for locals and tourists. You might see some charred trees around here—these were claimed not by the war, but more recently, by forest fires. (Fear of landmines and other explosives prevented locals from fighting the wildfires as aggressively as they might have done otherwise, making these fires more dangerous than ever.)

Warning: While this area has officially been cleared of landmines, nervous locals remind visitors that this was a war zone. Be sure to stay on clearly defined paths and roads.

Getting There: Work has begun to rebuild the **cable car**, which will conveniently zip visitors up to the fortress from just above the Buža Gate at the top of the Old Town. Ask around—if the cable car is running, it's easily the best option (www.dubrovnikcablecar.com). Until then, summiting Mount Srđ is a bit of a hassle.

If you have a **car**, you can drive up. From the high road above the Old Town, watch for the turnoff to Bosanka, which leads you to that village, then up to the fortress and cross—follow signs for *Srđ* (it's twisty but not far—figure a 20-minute drive from the Old Town area). If you're coming south from the Old Town, once you reach the main road above, you'll have to turn left and backtrack a bit to reach the Bosanka turnoff.

An easier option is to hire a **taxi**, but it's very expensive (figure €50–70 round-trip, including some waiting time at the top). Some cabbies will provide a little informal commentary during your visit. Or for €70, recommended driver Pepo Klaić will take you to the summit while sharing his firsthand experiences defending the fortress (listed on page 771).

Public **bus** #17 brings you from outside the Old Town's Ploče Gate most of the way up, but the frequency is limited (roughly every 2 hours, 25 min). From the bus stop, you'll still have to hike nearly a mile uphill, with almost no shade. For **hikers,** a switchback trail (used to supply the fortress during the siege) connects the Old Town to the mountaintop—but it's very steep and provides minimal shade. (If you're in great shape and it's not too hot, you could ride the bus up, then hike down.)

Activities in Dubrovnik

Swimming and Sunbathing—If the weather's good and you've had enough of museums, spend a sunny afternoon at the beach. There are no sandy beaches on the mainland near Dubrovnik, but there are lots of suitable pebbly options, plus several concrete perches. The easiest and most atmospheric place to take a dip is right off the Old Town. From the Old Port and its breakwater, uneven steps clinging to the outside of the wall lead to a series of great sunbathing and swimming coves (and even a showerhead sticking out of the town wall). Another delightful rocky beach hangs onto the outside of the Old Town's wall (at the bar called Cold Drinks "Buža" I; for more on this bar, and how to find it, see page 795). Locals prefer to swim on Lokrum Island, because there are fewer tourists there; for details on taking a boat to Lokrum, see page 786. Other convenient public beaches are Banje (just outside Ploče Gate, east of Old Town) and the beach in the middle of Lapad Bay (near Hotel Kompas).

My favorite hidden beach—**St. Jakob**—takes a lot longer to reach, but if you're up for the hike, it's worth it to escape the crowds. Figure about a 25-minute walk (each way) from the Old Town. Go through the Ploče Gate at the east end of the Old Town, and walk along the street called Frana Supila as it climbs uphill above the waterfront. At Hotel Argentina, take the right (downhill) fork and keep going on Vlaha Bukovca. Eventually you'll reach the small church of St. Jakob. You'll see the beach—in a cozy protected cove—far below. Curl around behind the church and keep an eye out for stairs going down on

the right. Unfortunately, these stairs are effectively unmarked, so it might take some trial and error to find the right ones. (If you reach the rusted-white gateway of the old communist-era open-air theater, you've gone too far.) Hike down the very steep stairs to the gentle cove, which has rentable chairs and a small restaurant for drinks (and a WC). Enjoy the pebbly beach and faraway views of Dubrovnik's Old Town.

Shopping in Dubrovnik

Most souvenirs sold in Dubrovnik—from lavender sachets to plaster models of the Old Town—are pretty tacky. Whatever you buy, prices are much higher along the Stradun than on the side-streets.

A classy alternative to the knickknacks is a type of local jewelry called *Konavoske puce* ("Konavle buttons"). Sold as earrings, pendants, and rings, these distinctive and fashionable filigree-style pieces consist of a sphere with several small posts. Though they're sold around town, it's least expensive to buy them on Od Puča street, which runs parallel to the Stradun two blocks toward the sea (near the Serbian Orthodox Church). The high concentration of jewelers along this lane keeps prices reasonable. You'll find the "buttons" in various sizes, in both silver (affordable) and gold (pricey).

You'll also see lots of jewelry made from red coral, which can only be legally gathered in small amounts from two small islands in northern Dalmatia. If you see a particularly large chunk of coral, it's likely imported. To know what you're getting, shop at an actual jeweler instead of a souvenir shop.

Entertainment in Dubrovnik

Musical Events

Dubrovnik annually hosts a full schedule of events for its Summer Festival (July 10–Aug 25, www.dubrovnik-festival.hr). Lovers of classical music enjoy the "Rachlin & Friends" festival in September (www.julianrachlin.com), and historians delight in the Renaissance-oriented Historical Festival in late September (www.ragvsevm.hr). But the town also works hard to offer traditional music outside of festival time. Spirited folk-music concerts are performed for tourists twice weekly in the Lazareti (old quarantine building) just outside the Old Town's Ploče Gate (80 kn, usually at 21:30). About one night per week through the winter, you can

watch the Dubrovnik Symphony Orchestra (usually at the Rector's Palace in good weather, or Dominican Monastery in bad weather). And since Dubrovnik is trying to become a year-round destination, the city also offers tourist-oriented musical events most nights throughout the winter (often at a hotel). For the latest on any of these festivals and concerts, check the events listings in the *Best in Dubrovnik Riviera* brochure, or ask the TI.

Nightlife

Dubrovnik's Old Town is one big, romantic parade of relaxed and happy people out strolling. The main drag is brightly lit and packed with shops, cafés, and bars, all open late. This is a fun scene. And if you walk away from the crowds or out on the port, you'll be alone with the magic of the Pearl of the Adriatic. Everything feels—and is—very safe after dark.

If you're looking for a memorable bar after dark, consider these:

▲▲▲Drinks with a View—Either **Cold Drinks "Buža"** offers, without a doubt, the most scenic spot for a drink in Dubrovnik. Perched on a cliff above the sea, clinging like a barnacle to the outside of the city walls, this is a peaceful, shaded getaway from the bustle of the Old Town...the perfect place to watch cruise ships disappear into the horizon. *Buža* means "hole in the wall"—and that's exactly what you'll have to go through to get to this place. There are actually two different Bužas, with separate owners. My favorite is Buža II (which is actually the older and bigger of the pair). Filled with mellow tourists and bartenders pouring wine from tiny screw-top bottles into plastic cups, Buža II comes with castaway views and Frank Sinatra ambience. This is supposedly where Bill Gates hangs out when he visits Dubrovnik (25–40-kn drinks, summer daily 9:00–into the wee hours, closed mid-Nov–Jan). Buža I is more casual, plays hip rather than romantic music, and has concrete stairs leading down to a beach on the rocks below (18–45-kn drinks). If one Buža is full, check the other.

Getting There: Both Bužas are high above the bustle of the

main drag, along the seaward wall. To reach them from the cathedral area, hike up the grand staircase to St. Ignatius' Church, then go left to find the lane that runs along the inside of the wall. To find the classic Buža II, head right along the lane and look for the *Cold Drinks* sign pointing to a literal hole in the wall. For the hipper Buža I, go left along the same lane, and locate the hole in the wall with the *No Topless No Nudist* graffiti.

Wine Tasting—d'vino Wine Bar, just a few steps off the main drag, is the handiest place in Dalmatia to taste and learn about Croatian wines. Run by Canadian transplant Cameron Wilson, this cozy bar (with a few outdoor tables) sells more than 50 wines by the glass and lots more by the bottle. The emphasis is on Croatian wines, but they also have vintages from Italy, France, Spain, the US, Australia, and South America. Each wine is well-described on the menu, and the staff is happy to guide you through your options—just tell them what you like (18–80-kn glasses—most around 25–35 kn, 40-kn wine flights, daily June–Sept 12:00–24:00, Oct–May 17:00–24:00, Palmotićeva 4a, tel. 020/321-223).

Cocktails and People-Watching—Jazz Caffè Troubadour is a cool place, owned by a former member of the Dubrovnik Troubadours—Croatia's answer to the Beatles (or, perhaps more accurately, the Turtles). On balmy evenings, 50 chairs with tiny tables are set up theater-style in the dreamy alley facing the musicians. Step inside to see old 1970s photos of the band (40–65-kn cocktails, daily 9:00–24:00, live jazz nightly from about 22:00 or whenever the boss shows up, often live piano at other times, next to cathedral at Bunićeva Poljana 2, tel. 020/323-476).

Nonenina, a few steps from the cathedral on Pred Dvorom, is an outdoor lounge with big, overstuffed chairs at a fine vantage point for people-watching. They brag that they serve 180 different types of cocktails (50–80 kn, daily 9:00–2:00 in the morning, shorter hours off-season, across from Rector's Palace).

Movies

The Old Town has a pair of movie theaters showing American blockbusters (usually in English with Croatian subtitles, unless the film's animated or for kids). The **Sloboda** cinema, right under the Bell Tower on Luža Square, is nothing special. But in good weather, head for the fun outdoor **Jadran** cinema, where you can lick ice cream (B.Y.O.) while you watch a movie with a Dubrovnik-mountaintop backdrop. This is a cheap, casual, and very Croatian scene, where people smoke and chat, and the neighbors sit in their windowsills to watch the movie (most nights in summer only, shows begin shortly after sundown; in the Old Town near the Pile Gate). To find out what's playing, look for posters around town.

Sleeping in Dubrovnik

You basically have two options in Dubrovnik: a centrally located room in a private home *(soba);* or a resort hotel on a distant beach, a bus ride away from the Old Town. Since Dubrovnik hotels are generally a poor value, I highly recommend giving the *sobe* a careful look. For locations, see the map on page 774.

Be warned that the Old Town is home to many popular discos. My listings are quieter than the norm, but if you're finding a place on your own, you may discover you have a late-night soundtrack—particularly if you're staying near the Stradun.

No matter where you stay, prices are much higher mid-June through mid-September, and highest in July and August. Reserve ahead for these peak times, especially during the Summer Festival (July 10–Aug 25 every year). Some accommodations prefer to list their rates in euros (and I've followed suit), but you'll pay in kunas.

Sobe (Private Rooms): A Dubrovnik Specialty

In Dubrovnik, you'll almost always do better with a *soba* than with a hotel. Before you choose, carefully read "Croatian Accommodation" on page 742. All of my favorite *sobe* are run by friendly English-speaking Croatians and are inside or within easy walking distance of the Old Town. There's a range of places, from simple and cheap rooms where you'll share a bathroom, to downright fancy places with private facilities and satellite TV, where you can be as anonymous as you like. Most *sobe* don't include breakfast, so I've listed some suggestions later, under "Eating in Dubrovnik."

Sleep Code

(€1 = about $1.40, 5 kn = about $1, country code: 385, area code: 020)

S = Single, **D** = Double/Twin, **T** = Triple, **Q** = Quad, **b** = bathroom. The modest tourist tax (7 kn or €1 per person, per night, lower off-season) is not included in these rates. Hotels generally accept credit cards and include breakfast in their rates, while most *sobe* accept only cash and don't offer breakfast. Everyone listed here speaks English.

To help you sort easily through these listings, I've divided the rooms into three categories based on the price for a standard double room with bath in peak season:

$$$ Higher Priced—Most rooms 700 kn (€95) or more.
$$ Moderately Priced—Most rooms between 400–700 kn (€55–95).
$ Lower Priced—Most rooms 400 kn (€55) or less.

Book direct—middleman agencies tack on fees, making it more expensive for both you and your host. Note that many Dubrovnik *sobe* hosts might ask you to send them a deposit to secure your reservation. Sometimes they'll accept your credit-card number; others might want you to mail them a check or traveler's check (the better option), or wire them the money (which can be expensive). While it's a bit of a hassle, this request is reasonable and part of the experience of sleeping at a *soba*. Remember that you'll usually need to pay your bill in cash, not with a credit card.

In the Old Town, Above the Stradun Promenade

These are some of my favorite accommodations in Dubrovnik. All are located at the top of town, high above the Stradun, and all are excellent values. The first three are within a few steps of each other, along a little block dubbed by some "Rickova ulica." If you don't mind the very steep hike up, you'll find this to be a wonderful enclave of hospitality. When one of these places is full, they work together to find space for you. The last listing is a few blocks over, and equally nice (and equally steep). Because all of these hosts live off-site, be sure to let them know when you'll arrive so they can let you in.

$$ Villa Ragusa offers my favorite rooms for the price in the Old Town. Pero and Valerija Carević have renovated a 600-year-old house at the top of town that was damaged during the war. The five comfortable, modern rooms come with atmospheric old wooden beams, antique furniture, and thoughtful touches. There are three doubles with bathrooms (including a top-floor room with breathtaking Old Town views for no extra charge—request when you reserve) and two singles that share a bathroom (July–Aug: S-€40, Db-€80; May–June and Sept–Oct: S-€30, Db-€70; Nov–April: S-€25, Db-€50; 30 percent more for 1- or 2-night stays, €8 breakfast can be eaten here or at nearby Stradun café, cash only, air-con, lots of stairs with no elevator, Žudioska ulica 15, tel. 020/453-834, mobile 098-765-634, http://villaragusa.netfirms.com, villa.ragusa@du.t-com.hr). Pero offers his guests airport transfers for a reasonable €30, and can drive you on an all-day excursion (such as to Montenegro or Mostar) for €250—if you can split this cost with other guests, it's a good value (same price for up to 6 people).

$$ Apartments Paviša, next door to Villa Ragusa and run by Pero and Davorka Paviša, has three good rooms at the top of the Old Town (July–Aug: Db-€100; May–June and Sept–Oct: Db-€70; Nov–April Db-€50; 10 percent discount if you book

direct with this book, no breakfast, cash only, air-con, lots of stairs, Žudioska ulica 19, mobile 098-427-399 or 098-175-2342, www.apartmentspavisa.com, davorka.pavisa@du.t-com.hr). They have two more rooms in the **Viktorija** neighborhood, about a 20-minute mostly uphill walk beyond the Ploče Gate east of the Old Town. While it's a long-but-scenic walk into town, the views from these apartments are spectacular (same prices as in-town rooms, Frana Supila 59, bus stop nearby). Pero and Davorka also manage three more apartments. Called the **Apartments Martecchini,** these are a bit closer to the main drag in the Old Town (July–Aug: small apartment-€100, bigger apartment-€110, biggest apartment-€120; May–June and Sept–Oct: small apartment-€70, bigger apartment-€80, biggest apartment-€90; Nov–April: small apartment-€50, bigger apartment-€50, biggest apartment-€60; 10 percent less if you book direct with this book, prices depend on size and views, www.apartmentsmartecchini.com).

$$ Anita and Ivana Raič are sisters renting three new-feeling apartments with kitchenettes and air-conditioning (July–Aug: Db-€90; June and Sept–Oct: Db-€70; Nov–May: Db-€50–60; no extra charge for 1- or 2-night stays, no breakfast, cash only, air-con, Žudioska ulica 16, mobile 098-996-0858, www.apartments-raic.com, ivanaraic@gmail.com).

$$ Plaza Apartments, run by Lidija and Maro Matić, rents three clean, well-appointed apartments on a plant-filled lane—the steepest and most appealing stretch of stairs leading up from the Stradun. Lidija's sweet personality is reflected in the cheerful rooms, which are a great value if you don't mind the hike (July–Aug: Db-€70; May–June and Sept: Db-€55; Oct: Db-€50; Nov–April: Db-€40; these special prices for Rick Steves readers, no breakfast, cash only, air-con, free Wi-Fi, climb the stairs past Dolce Vita gelato shop to Nalješkovićeva 22, tel. 020/321-493, mobile 091-517-7048, www.dubrovnik-online.com/apartment_plaza, lidydu@yahoo.com).

In the Old Town, near the Cathedral and St. John's Fort

The following places are south of the Stradun, mostly clustering around the cathedral and St. John's Fort, at the end of the Old Port. To find the Karmen and Zijadić apartments from the cathedral, walk toward the big fort tower along the inside of the wall (follow signs for *akvarji*).

$$$ Karmen Apartments are well-run by a Brit named Marc and his Croatian wife Silva, who offer four apartments just inside the big fort. The prices are very high, and they're in all the guidebooks, but the apartments are big, well-equipped, and homey-feeling, each with a bathroom and kitchen. The decor is eclectic but

tasteful, and Marc and Silva are good hosts (May–Sept: smaller apartment-€90, bigger apartment-€145; April and Oct–Nov: smaller apartment-€70, bigger apartment-€110; less Dec–March, 20 percent more for 1- or 2-night stays, no breakfast, cash only, air-con, free Wi-Fi, near the aquarium at Bandureva 1, tel. 020/323-433, www.karmendu.com, apartments@karmendu.tk).

$$$ Apartments Amoret, run by Branka Dabrović and her husband Ivica, are in all the guidebooks. The pricey but good apartments are in three different buildings: two over Amoret Restaurant in front of the cathedral (at Restićeva 2); eight more sharing an inviting terrace on a quiet, untouristy lane a few blocks east (at Dinka Ranjine 5); and two more nearby (at Ilije Sarake 4). The furnishings are a tasteful mix of traditional and modern. Since Branka doesn't live on-site, arrange a meeting time and place when you reserve (July–Aug: Db-€90–120; June and Sept: Db-€80–110; May and Oct: Db-€70–90; Nov–April: Db-€50–80; price depends on size, 30 percent more for 1-night stays, 20 percent more for 2-night stays, 10 percent more for 3-night stays, no breakfast, cash only, air-con, free Wi-Fi, mobile 091-530-4910, tel. & fax 020/324-005, www.dubrovnik-amoret.com, dubrovnik@post.t-com.hr).

$$ Apartments Placa (PLAH-tsah; not to be confused with Apartments Plaza, described earlier) is run by Tonči (TOHN-chee). He rents three apartments overlooking the market square in the heart of the Old Town. You might get some early-morning noise from the market set-up, but the double-paned windows help, and the location is wonderfully central (July–Aug: Db-€90; June and Sept: Db-€80; May and Oct: Db-€70; Nov–April: Db-€60; no breakfast, cash only, no extra charge for 1- or 2-night stays, several flights of stairs, air-con, Gundulićeva poljana 5, mobile 091-721-9202, www.dubrovnik-online.com/apartments_placa, tonci.korculanin@du.t-com.hr).

$$ Renata Zijadić, a friendly mom who speaks good English, offers four well-located rooms with slanting floors, funky colors, and over-the-top antique furniture. A single and a double (both with great views) share one bathroom; another double features an ornate old cabinet, air-conditioning, and its own bathroom; and the top-floor apartment comes with low ceilings, air-conditioning, and fine vistas (July–Aug: S-220 kn, D-330 kn, Db-440 kn, apartment-600 kn; June and Sept: S-200 kn, D-300 kn, Db-365 kn, apartment-550 kn; cheaper Oct–May, no extra charge for 1- or 2-night stays, no breakfast, cash only, free Wi-Fi, follow signs for wall access and walk up the steps marked *ulica Stajeva* going over the street to find Stajeva 1; tel. 020/323-623, www.dubrovnik-online.com/house_renata, renatadubrovnik@yahoo.com).

$ Fresh Sheets, a bright, stylish, and appealingly funky hostel run by the former owners of Dubrovnik's hippest (now-closed)

expat bar, is your best youth hostel option in the Old Town. The 22 bunks (four beds per room, two rooms and one bathroom per floor, plus one double room) sit above a tight but enjoyable common area. Located at the very top of town just inside the town walls, it's a steep hike up from the main drag, but worth it if you enjoy youthful backpacker bonding (€25/bed, likely open only April–mid-Nov, free breakfast, free Internet access and Wi-Fi, lockers, kitchen, laundry service, Smokvina 15, mobile 091-799-2086, www.igotfresh.com, beds@igotfresh.com).

In the Pile Neighborhood, Just Outside the Old Town

There's a concentration of good *sobe* just outside the Old Town's Pile Gate. The Pile (PEE-leh) neighborhood offers all the conveniences of the modern world (grocery store, bus stop, post office, travel agency, etc.), just steps from Dubrovnik's magical Old Town. The first place is up the hill (away from the water) from the Pile Gate's bus stop; the rest cluster around a quiet, no-name cove near Restaurant Orhan. From the bus stop area in front of Pile Gate, various lanes lead down toward this cove.

$$ Jadranka and Milan Benussi, a middle-aged professional couple, rent four rooms in a quiet, traffic-free neighborhood. Their stony-chic home, complete with a leafy terrace, is a steep 10-minute hike above the Old Town—close enough to be convenient, but far enough to take you away from the bustle and into a calm residential zone. Jadranka speaks good English, enjoys visiting with her guests, and gives her place a modern Croatian class unusual for *sobe* (July–Aug: small Db-440 kn, big Db-520 kn, small apartment-680 kn, big apartment with balcony-740 kn; June and Sept: small Db-400 kn, big Db-480 kn, small apartment-630 kn, big apartment-700 kn; cheaper Oct–May, 20 percent more for stays less than 4 nights, no breakfast, cash only, all rooms have air-con and kitchenettes, Miha Klaića 10, tel. 020/429-339, mobile 098-928-1300, www.dubrovnik-benussi.com, jadranka@dubrovnik-benussi.com). To find the Benussis, go to the big Hilton Hotel just outside the Pile Gate (across from the TI). Walk up the little stepped lane called Marijana Blažića at the upper-left corner of the Hilton cul-de-sac. When that lane dead-ends, go left up ulica Don Iva Bjelokosića (more steps) until you see a little church on the left. The Benussis' house is just before this church.

$ Paulina Čumbelić is a kind, gentle woman renting four old-fashioned rooms in her homey, clean, and peaceful house (July–Sept: S-200 kn, D-300 kn, T-450 kn; shoulder season: S-170 kn, D-260 kn, T-350 kn; 20 percent more for 1- or 2-night stays, no breakfast, cash only, closed in winter, Od Tabakarije 2, tel. 020/421-327, mobile 091-530-7985).

$ Restaurant Orhan Guest House allows hotel anonymity at *sobe* prices. Its 11 simple rooms—in a couple of different buildings around the corner from the restaurant—are well-located and quiet, with modern bathrooms (some also have air-con). As the rooms are an afterthought to the restaurant, don't expect a warm welcome (Sb or Db-400 kn, 100 kn more for 1-night stays, breakfast-50 kn, cash only, Od Tabakarije 1, tel. & fax 020/414-183, www.restaurant-orhan.com, restoran.orhan@yahoo.com). Their restaurant is also a good spot for a scenic meal (described later, under "Eating in Dubrovnik").

$ Nedjeljka Benussi, the sister-in-law of Jadranka Benussi (listed earlier), rents three modern, straightforward rooms sharing two bathrooms and a pretty view (May–Oct: D-400 kn, T-550 kn; Nov–April: D-300, T-450 kn; no extra charge for 1-night stays, no breakfast, cash only, fans but no air-con, Sv. Đurđa 4, tel. 020/423-062, mobile 098-170-5699).

Beyond the Ploče Gate, East of the Old Town

To reach these options, you'll go through the Ploče Gate and walk along the road stretching east from the Old Town (with fine views back on the Old Port). This area is shared by giant waterfront luxury hotels and residential areas, so it has a bit less character than the Pile and Old Town listings (which I prefer).

$$ Apartments Paviša, described on page 798, has two fine apartments in the Viktorija neighborhood about a 20-minute walk or short bus ride from town.

$$ Villa Adriatica has four old-fashioned rooms above a travel agency and a family home just outside the Ploče Gate, a few steps from the Old Town. The rooms share a terrace with priceless Old Port views (the main reason to consider staying here), plus a common living room and kitchen furnished with museum-piece antiques. Likeable Teo manages the rooms; ask for him at the Perla Adriatic travel agency, just outside the Ploče Gate (July–Aug: Db-€85–95; June and Sept: Db-€80–90; May and Oct: Db-€75–85; Nov–April: Db-€55–60; price depends on size and view, 20 percent more for 1- or 2-night stays, no breakfast, cash only, air-con, free Wi-Fi in some areas, Frana Supila 4, mobile 098-377-954, tel. 020/411-962, fax 020/422-766, www.dubrovnik-online.com/villa_adriatica, miroslav.tomsic@du.t-com.hr, Tomšić family).

Sobe-Booking Websites and Agencies

Several websites put you in touch with Dubrovnik's *sobe* and apartments. Of course, you'll save yourself and your host money if you book direct, but these sites are convenient. For example, www.dubrovnikapartmentsource.com, run by an American couple, offers a range of carefully selected, well-described accommodations. You can browse a variety of options, then reserve your choice and pay a nonrefundable deposit by credit card. Another, bigger operation—with a wider selection but less personal attention—is www.adriatica.net.

If you arrive without a reservation and the TI isn't too busy, they might be able to call around and find you a *soba* for no charge. Otherwise, just about any travel agency in town can help you, on the spot or in advance...for a fee. **Atlas** is the biggest company (figure Db-€50 and apartment-€60–80 in June–Sept, €10 less in shoulder season; for more on Atlas, see page 768).

Hotels

If you must stay in a hotel, you have only a few good options. There are just two hotels inside the Old Town walls—and one of them charges $500 a night (Pucić Palace, www.thepucicpalace.com). Any big, resort-style hotel within walking distance of the Old Town will run you at least €200. These inflated prices drive most visitors to Boninovo Bay or the Lapad Peninsula, a bus ride west of the Old Town. In the mass-tourism tradition, many European visitors choose to take the half-board option at their hotel (i.e., dinner in the hotel restaurant). This can be convenient and a good value—especially considering the relatively low quality of Dubrovnik's restaurants (explained later, under "Eating in Dubrovnik")—but the Old Town is a much more atmospheric place to dine.

In and near the Old Town

$$$ Hilton Imperial Dubrovnik, sitting regally just outside the Pile Gate, is the closest big hotel to the Old Town. This grand 19th-century building was recently overhauled to create 147 plush rooms. If you want predictable Hilton comfort a short walk from the Old Town, this is the place (July–Aug: Db-€300, actual rate generally closer to Db-€200; less off-season, €55 extra for sea view, €65 extra for balcony but no view, €120 extra for balcony and view, includes breakfast but not the 10 percent tax, elevator, air-con, pay cable Internet, parking-200 kn/night, Marijana Blažića 2, tel. 020/320-320, fax 020/320-220, www.hilton.com, sales.dubrovnik@hilton.com).

$$$ Hotel Stari Grad knows it's the only real hotel option inside the Old Town—and charges accordingly. It has eight modern yet nicely old-fashioned rooms a half-block off the Old

Town's main drag. The rooftop breakfast terrace (summer only) enjoys a grand view over orange tiles. This place books up fast, so reserve early (July–Sept: Sb-€165, Db-€221; April–June and Oct: Sb-€125, Db-€180; Nov–March: Sb-€91, Db-€130; plus silly "insurance" charge of 8 kn/person per night, 10 percent more for 1- or 2-night stays, air-con, lots of stairs with no elevator, pay Wi-Fi in lobby, Od Sigurate 4, tel. 020/322-244, fax 020/321-256, www.hotelstarigrad.com, info@hotelstarigrad.com).

Near Boninovo Bay

Boninovo Bay is your best bet for an affordable and well-located hotel. Above this bay are Dubrovnik's only three-star hotels within walking distance of the Old Town (not to mention the city's only official youth hostel). These places offer slightly better prices and closer proximity to the Old Town than the farther-out Lapad Bay resorts. Boninovo Bay is an uphill 20-minute walk or five-minute bus ride from the Old Town (straight up Branitelja Dubrovnika). Once you're comfortable with the buses, the location is great: Any bus that leaves the Pile Gate stops first at Boninovo Bay. You'll see the bay on your left as you climb the hill, then get off at the stop after the traffic light (or stay on bus #4, which stops even closer to the hotels). To reach the hotels from the Boninovo bus stop, go up Pera Čingrije (the busy road running along the top of the cliff overlooking the sea). There's a super little bakery, Pekarnica Klas, on the right (across the street from Hotel Bellevue).

$$$ Hotel Bellevue has a striking location, with its back against the cliff rising up from Boninovo Bay and an elevator plunging directly to its own pebbly beach. Completely gutted and rebuilt just a few years ago, its 93 top-notch rooms—all with sea views, many with balconies—offer upscale wood-grain elegance (July-Aug: standard Db-generally €250; less off-season, very flexible rates, €50 more for balcony, air-con, elevator, free Wi-Fi, Pera Čingrije 7, tel. 020/330-000, fax 020/330-100, www.hotel-bellevue.hr, welcome@hotel-bellevue.hr).

$$$ Hotel R, a homey enclave with just 10 rooms, feels friendlier and less greedy than all the big resort hotels. Well-run by the Rešetar family, it's a good small-hotel value (June–Sept: Sb-€70, Db-€107; May and Oct: Sb-€56, Db-€84; Easter–April: Sb-€48, Db-€74; closed Nov–Easter, 10 percent more for balcony, half-board-€13, air-con, free Wi-Fi, just beyond the big Hotel Lero at Iva Vojnovića 16, tel. 020/333-200, fax 020/333-208, www.hotel-r.hr, helpdesk@hotel-r.hr).

$$$ Hotel Lero, 250 yards up the street from the bus stop, has 140 recently renovated rooms. Choose between sea views with some road noise, or quieter back rooms (soft rates, but generally early July–late Sept: Sb-€110, Db-€140; May–early July and late

Sept–mid-Oct: Sb-€85, Db-€106; even less in winter; in busy times, you may be quoted more than these rates—try asking for a better deal; air-con, elevator, pay Internet access, free Wi-Fi in lobby, half-board-€6, Iva Vojnovića 14, tel. 020/341-333, fax 020/332-123, www.hotel-lero.hr, sales@hotel-lero.hr).

$ Dubrovnik's official **Youth Hostel** is quiet, modern, and well-run by proud manager Laura. It's institutional, with 82 beds in 19 fresh, woody dorms and few extra hostel amenities (bunk in 4- to 6-bed dorm—July–Aug: 125 kn; June and Sept: 115 kn; May and Oct: 105 kn; Nov–April: 95 kn; 10 kn more for nonmembers, includes sheets, breakfast-5 kn; reception open daily June–Oct 7:00–2:00 in the morning, Nov–May 8:00–14:00 & 18:00–20:00; 2:00 a.m. curfew in summer, none in winter; up the steps at ulica bana Jelačića 15–17, tel. 020/423-241, fax 020/412-592, www.hfhs.hr, dubrovnik@hfhs.hr). From the Boninovo bus stop, go down Pera Čingrije toward Hotel Bellevue, but take the first right uphill onto ulica bana Jelačića and look for signs up to the hostel on your left, on ulica Vinka Sagrestana. Several houses nearby rent rooms to those who prefer a double...and pick off would-be hostelers as they approach.

In Lapad

For a real resort-style vacation (at premium prices), many travelers call the touristy area around Lapad Bay home. The main drag running through the middle of this scene, called Šetalište Kralja Zvonimira, is a nicely pedestrianized people zone buzzing with tourists, restaurants, cafés, and mild diversions. From the bus stop, the main drag leads to a pleasant pebble beach good for swimming and a romantic bayside path. While I much prefer sleeping near the Old Town, this is an appealing place to be on vacation (even if the Old Town wasn't just a short bus ride away). To get here from the Old Town's Pile Gate, pile onto bus #6 with all the other tourists and get off at the Pošta Lapad stop (poorly marked—after bus turns left away from the big harbor, watch for low-profile yellow *pošta* sign on left; 4–6 buses/hr until 24:30, 15 min). A taxi costs about 60 kn.

$$$ ***Small Hotels in Lapad:*** In this area, I like three newish, interchangeable small hotels. While not affiliated with each other, each one has similar amenities—air-con, elevator (except Hotel Dubrovnik), Internet access either in lobby or in room—and similar prices (July–Sept: around Db-1,000–1,400 kn, but prices are very soft and can flex with demand, season, and length of stay; check online for the latest, and ask for a deal when you reserve). **Hotel Aquarius,** hiding a block off the main drag, has 24 comfortable, plush-feeling rooms and an inviting terrace out front (Mata Vodopića 8, tel. 020/456-111, fax 020/456-100,

www.hotel-aquarius.net, stjepanka@hotel-aquarius.net). **Hotel Perla,** right on the main drag, has 25 modern rooms (tel. 020/438-244, fax 020/438-245, www.perla-dubrovnik.com, info@perla-dubrovnik.com). **Hotel Dubrovnik,** two doors up from the Perla, has 25 simpler rooms (tel. 020/435-030, fax 020/435-999, www.hoteldubrovnik.hr, info@hoteldubrovnik.com).

Eating in Dubrovnik

Dubrovnik disappoints diners with high prices, surly service, and mediocre quality. With the constant influx of deep-pocketed tourists corrupting greedy restaurateurs, places here tend to go downhill faster than a game of marbles on the *Titanic*. Promising new restaurants open all the time, but most quickly fade, and what's great one year can be miserable the next. Therefore, lower your expectations, take my suggestions with a grain of salt, and ask around locally for what's good this month. Don't bother looking for a "local" favorite anywhere near the Old Town—people who live here eat out at restaurants in the 'burbs. The good news is that it's atmospheric. Anywhere you dine, breezy outdoor seating is a no-brainer, and scrawny, adorable kittens beg for table scraps. In general, seafood restaurants are good only at seafood; if you want pasta, go to a pasta place.

In the Old Town

Nishta, featuring a short menu of delicious vegetarian fusion cuisine with Asian flair, offers a welcome change of pace from the Dalmatian seafood-pasta-pizza rut. Busy Swiss owner/chef Gildas cooks, while his wife Ruža serves. This tiny place—which, in my experience, is the only reliably good eatery in town—has just a few indoor and outdoor tables. Even if you're not a vegetarian, it's worth a visit (55–80-kn main dishes, Mon–Sat 12:00–15:00 & 18:00–22:00, closed Sun, on the restaurant-clogged Prijeko street—near the Pile Gate end of the street, mobile 098-186-7440).

Dubrovački Kantun ("Dubrovnik's Nook") serves up typical, traditional Dalmatian specialties in a cozy eight-table interior that's ideal on rainy days. For now, this is one of the Old Town's more reputable options for good food. Despite its lack of outdoor seating, I'd give it a serious look (hearty 25-kn soups, 65–70-kn pastas, 70–120-kn main dishes, daily 12:00–16:00 & 18:00–24:00,

near the corner of Boškovićeva and Prijeko, tel. 020/331-911, Andrej).

Konoba Kamenice, a no-frills fish restaurant, is a local institution offering inexpensive, fresh, and good meals on a charming market square, as central as can be in the Old Town. On the limited menu, the seafood dishes are excellent (try their octopus salad, even if you don't think you like octopus), while the few non-seafood dishes are uninspired. Some of the waitstaff are notorious for their playfully brusque service, but loyal patrons happily put up with it. Arrive early, or you'll have to wait (35–70-kn main dishes, daily 8:00–23:00, until 22:00 off-season, Gundulićeva poljana 8, tel. 020/323-682).

Lokanda Peskarija enjoys an enticing setting, with a sea of tables facing the Old Port. Servings are hearty and come in a pot, "home-style." The 60-kn seafood risotto easily feeds two, and sharing is no problem. The menu's tiny—with only seafood options, and not much in the way of vegetables. Locals complain that the quality has taken a nosedive ever since the restaurant's following has grown and its idyllic setting expanded to the hilt. But for reasonably priced seafood dishes on the water, this remains an acceptable option (most main dishes 55–80 kn, daily 12:00–24:00, very limited indoor seating fills up fast, plenty of outdoor tables—which can also fill up, tel. 020/324-750, no reservations taken in summer). Notice that the tables farthest from the main restaurant have a different menu, focused on Balkan-style grilled meats; if that's what you want, skip this place and head for Taj Mahal instead (described below).

Pizza: Dubrovnik seems to have a pizzeria on every corner. Little separates the various options—just look for a menu and outdoor seating option that appeals to you. I've eaten well at **Oliva Pizzeria,** just behind St. Blaise's Church (35–65-kn pizzas, Lučarica 5, daily 10:00–24:00, tel. 020/324-594). Around the side is a handy take-out window for a bite on the go.

Pasta: **Spaghetteria Toni** is popular with natives and tourists. While nothing fancy, they offer good pastas at reasonable prices. Choose between the cozy 10-table interior, or the long alley filled with outdoor tables (45–80-kn pastas, 40–60-kn salads, daily in summer 11:00–23:00, closed Sun in winter, closed Jan, Nikole Božidarevića 14, tel. 020/323-134).

Bosnian Cuisine: For a break from Croatian fare, consider the grilled meats and other tasty Bosnian dishes at the misnamed **Taj Mahal.** Though the service can be lacking, the menu offers an enticing taste of the Turkish-flavored land to the east. Choose between the tight interior, which feels like a Bosnian tea house, or tables out on the alley (50-kn salads, 45–115-kn main dishes, daily 10:00–24:00, Nikole Gučetića 2, tel. 020/323-221). For a primer on

Bosnian food, see "Balkan Flavors" on page 753.

Ice Cream: Dubrovnik has lots of great *sladoled*, but locals swear by the stuff at **Dolce Vita** (daily 9:00–24:00, a half-block off the Stradun at Nalješkovićeva 1A, tel. 020/321-666).

The Old Town's "Restaurant Row," Prijeko Street: The street called Prijeko, a block toward the mainland from the Stradun promenade, is lined with outdoor, tourist-oriented eateries—each one with a huckster out front trying to lure in diners. (Many of them aggressively try to snare passersby down on the Stradun, as well.) Don't be sucked into this vortex of bad food at outlandish prices. The only place worth seeking out here is Nishta (described earlier); the rest are virtually guaranteed to disappoint. Still, it can be fun to take a stroll along here—the atmosphere is lively, and the sales pitches are entertainingly desperate.

Just Outside the Old Town, with a View

Orhan Restaurant, overlooking the tranquil cove at the Pile neighborhood outside the Old Town, feels just beyond the tourist crush. It features disinterested service and unremarkable food, but great views on a large terrace (reserve a seat here in advance). Watch the people walk the Old Town walls across the cove (55–105-kn pastas, 80–180-kn main dishes, daily 10:00–23:00, basic breakfast from 9:00, cash only, Od Tabakarije 1, tel. 020/414-183).

Komarda serves up forgettable food on a memorably romantic terrace, with views of Dubrovnik's walls and Old Port. Tables are scattered around a tranquil garden just above the sea and a concrete beach. As there's no point eating here unless you have a good view, consider dropping by early in the day to pick out and reserve the table of your choice for dinner (50–80-kn pastas, 65–120-kn main dishes, 60-kn lunch special, daily 7:00–2:00 in the morning, reservations essential in summer, mobile 098-428-239). To find it, exit the Old Town through the Ploče Gate (east). After walking through the final fortification, you'll reach a block of travel agencies. Once you pass these, look for the stairs down to Komarda, on the right.

Picnic Tips

Dubrovnik's lack of great restaurant options makes it a perfect place to picnic. You can shop for fresh fruits and veggies at the open-air produce market (each morning near the cathedral, on the square called Gundulićeva Poljana). Supplement your picnic with grub from the cheap Konzum grocery store (one location near the bus stop just outside Pile Gate: Mon–Sat 7:00–21:00, Sun 8:00–14:00; another on the market square near the produce-vendors:

Mon–Sat 7:00–21:00, Sun 7:00–13:00). Good picnic spots include the shaded benches overlooking the Old Port; the Porporela breakwater (beyond the Old Port and fort—comes with a swimming area, sunny no-shade benches, and views of Lokrum Island); and the green, welcoming park in what was the moat just under the Pile Gate entry to the Old Town.

Breakfast

If you're sleeping in a *soba,* you'll likely be on your own for breakfast. Fortunately, you have plenty of cafés and pastry shops to choose from, and your host probably has a favorite she can recommend. In the Pile neighborhood, I like **Restaurant Orhan,** right on the cove (described earlier; 50 kn for omelet or continental breakfast, served daily 9:00–11:00). In the Old Town, **Dubrava Bistro**—nicknamed "Snack Bar" by locals—has great views and fine outdoor seating at the most colorful end of the Stradun (basic 35–45-kn egg dishes, 18-kn caffè lattes; you'll pay a few extra kunas to sit outside—listed on the menu as *taraci*—but it's worth it; daily 8:00–24:00, Placa 6, tel. 020/321-229). Some of the other restaurants listed in this section (including Kamenice) also serve breakfast. Not many places serve before 9:00 or 10:00; if you'll be departing early, stock up on groceries the night before.

On Lapad Bay

If you want a break from the Old Town, consider venturing to Lapad Bay. The ambience is pleasant and Lapad is worth an evening stroll (for details on getting here, see page 805 under "Sleeping in Dubrovnik"). This area's main drag, **Šetalište Kralja Zvonimira,** is an amazingly laid-back pedestrian lane where bars have hammocks, Internet terminals are scattered through a forested park, and a folksy Croatian family ambience holds its own against the better-funded force of international tourism. Stroll from near Hotel Zagreb to the bay, marked by Hotel Kompas. From Hotel Kompas, a romantic walk—softly lit at night—leads past some splurge restaurants along the bay through the woods, with plenty of private little stone coves for lingering.

Dubrovnik Connections

Note that the boats listed here leave from Dubrovnik's Port Gruž, a bus ride away from the Old Town (described earlier, under "Arrival in Dubrovnik—By Boat").

From Dubrovnik by Big Jadrolinija Car Ferry: The big boats leave Dubrovnik in the morning and go to **Korčula** (5/week July–Sept, 4/week June, 2/week Oct–May, 3–4 hrs), **Stari Grad**

on Hvar Island (2/week year-round, 6.5 hrs), **Split** (2/week year-round, 8–9.25 hrs), and **Rijeka** (2/week year-round, 21 hrs including overnight from Split to Rijeka). Boat schedules are subject to change—confirm your plans at a local TI, or see www.jadrolinija.hr.

From Dubrovnik by Speedy *Nona Ana* Catamaran: This handy service connects Dubrovnik to popular islands to the north (Mljet, Korčula, and Lastovo). This schedule is subject to change from year to year, so carefully confirm the details before planning your trip. In the summer (June–Sept), the boat departs Dubrovnik each morning and heads for **Sobra** and **Polače** (1.75 hrs, 50 kn one-way) on Mljet Island. In the peak months of July and August, it sometimes continues on to **Korčula** (4/week, 2.75 hrs, 55 kn) and **Lastovo Island** (2/week, 4 hrs, 60 kn). In the winter (Oct–May), the boat goes daily to **Sobra** on Mljet (but not to Polače, Korčula, or Lastovo). The catamaran leaves from Dubrovnik's Port Gruž (buy tickets at the kiosk next to the boat, ticket window opens 1 hour before departure; in peak season, it's smart to show up about an hour ahead to be sure you get on the boat). Confirm schedules at the Dubrovnik TI, or check www.gv-line.hr.

By Bus to: Split (almost hourly, generally at the top of each hour, less off-season, 5 hrs), **Korčula** (peak season: 2/day, 3.5 hrs; off-season: Mon–Sat 1/day, Sun 2/day; also consider the shuttle-bus service described below), **Rijeka** (2/day, 12 hrs), **Zagreb** (7/day including some overnight options, 10 hrs), **Mostar** in Bosnia-Herzegovina (2–5/day depending on season, 4–5 hrs), **Kotor** in Montenegro (2–3/day, 2.5 hrs), **Pula** and **Rovinj** (nightly, 15 hrs to Pula, 16 hrs to Rovinj). For bus information, call 060-305-070 (a pricey toll line, but worth it).

By Shuttle Bus to Korčula: Korčula-based Korkyra Travel Agency runs a handy door-to-door shuttle service from your Dubrovnik accommodations to Korčula (125 kn one-way plus 10 kn/bag; departs Mon–Fri at 14:00 year-round, Sat–Sun by request only; 2 hrs, reserve ahead, mobile 091-571-4355, www.korkyra.info, info@korkyra.info).

By Plane: To quickly connect remote Dubrovnik with the rest of your trip, consider a cheap flight (see "Getting to the Dalmatian Coast," page 745.) For information on Dubrovnik's airport, see "Arrival in Dubrovnik," earlier.

By Car: For tips on driving along the Dalmatian Coast between Dubrovnik and Split, see page 848 in the Split chapter.

Can I Get to Greece from Dubrovnik?: Not easily. Your best bet is to fly (though there are no direct flights, aside from the occasional charter flight from Dubrovnik to Athens—you'll generally have to transfer elsewhere in Europe). Even though Croatia and Greece are nearly neighbors, no direct boats connect them, and the

overland connection is extremely long and rugged.

What About Italy?: Flying is the easiest option, though there are only two direct flights (on Croatia Airlines to Rome, or on easyJet to Milan). You can take a direct night boat from Dubrovnik to Bari, or head to Split for more boat connections (for more on all of these boats, see page 846). The overland connection is overly long (figure 5 hrs to Split, then 5 hrs to Zagreb, then 7 hrs to Venice).

SPLIT

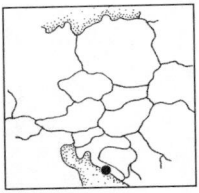

Dubrovnik is the darling of the Dalmatian Coast, but Split (pronounced as it's spelled) is Croatia's "second city" (after Zagreb), bustling with 189,000 people. If you've been hopping along the coast, landing in urban Split feels like a return to civilization. While most Dalmatian coastal towns seem made for tourists, Split is real and vibrant—a shipbuilding city with ugly sprawl surrounding an atmospheric Old Town, which teems with Croatians living life to the fullest.

Though today's Split throbs to a modern, young beat, its history goes way back—all the way to the Roman Empire. Along with all the trappings of a modern city, Split has some of the best Roman ruins this side of Italy. In the fourth century A.D., the Roman Emperor Diocletian (245–313) wanted to retire in his native Dalmatia, so he built a huge palace here. Eventually, the palace was abandoned. Then locals, fleeing seventh-century Slavic invaders, moved in and made themselves at home, and a medieval town sprouted from the rubble of the old palace. In the 15th century, the Venetians took over the Dalmatian Coast. They developed and fortified Split, slathering the city with a new layer of Gothic-Renaissance architecture.

But even as Split grew, the nucleus remained the ruins of Diocletian's Palace. To this day, 2,000 people live or work inside the former palace walls. A maze of narrow alleys is home to fashionable boutiques and galleries, wonderfully atmospheric cafés, and Roman artifacts around every corner.

Today's Split is struggling to decide how it fits into Croatia's new tourist-mecca image: Is it a big, drab metropolis; a no-

nonsense transit point; an impressive destination in its own right, with sights to rival Dubrovnik's...or all three?

Planning Your Time

Split is Dalmatia's hub for bus, boat, train, and flight connections to other destinations in the country and abroad. This means that many visitors to Dalmatia stop in Split only long enough to change boats. But the city is the perfect real-life contrast to the lazy, prettified Dalmatian beach resorts—it deserves a full day. Begin by strolling the remains of Diocletian's Palace, then have a coffee break along the Riva promenade or lunch in the Old Town. After lunch, browse the shops or visit a couple of Split's museums (the Meštrović Gallery, which is a long walk or short bus or taxi ride from the Old Town, is tops). Promenading along the Riva with the natives is *the* evening activity.

Orientation to Split

(area code: 021)

Split sprawls, but almost everything of interest to travelers is around the City Harbor (Gradska Luka). At the top of this harbor is the Old Town (Stari Grad). Between the Old Town and the sea is the Riva, a waterfront pedestrian promenade lined with cafés and shaded by palm trees. The main ferry terminal (Trajektni Terminal, a.k.a. Trajektna Luka) juts into the harbor from the east side. Along the harborfront embankment between the ferry terminal and the Old Town are the long-distance bus station (Autobusni Kolodvor) and the forlorn little train station (Željeznička Stanica). West of the Old Town, poking into the Adriatic, is the lush and hilly Marjan peninsula.

Split's domino-shaped Old Town is made up of two square sections. The east half was once Diocletian's Palace, and the west half is the medieval town that sprang up next door. The shell of Diocletian's ruined palace provides a checkerboard street plan, with a gate at each end. But the streets built since are anything but straight, making the Old Town a delightfully convoluted maze (double-decker in some places). At the center of the former palace is a square called the Peristyle (Peristil), where you'll find the TI, cathedral, and highest concentration of Roman ruins.

Tourist Information

Split's TI is on the square called the Peristyle, in the very center of Diocletian's Palace (Easter–mid-Oct Mon–Sat 8:00–21:00, Sun 8:00–13:00; mid-Oct–Easter Mon–Fri 8:00–20:00, Sat 8:00–13:00, closed Sun; exact location might change due to restoration—ask around, tel. 021/345-606, www.visitsplit.com). Pick up the free town map, monthly *Visit Split* booklet (with information on museums, events, restaurants, and more), and other brochures.

The TI also sells the **Splitcard,** which includes free admission to several sights (including the City Museum, Ethnographic Museum, and cathedral), a 50 percent discount at other sights (including the Meštrović Gallery and Archaeological Museum), and minor discounts at other attractions, shops, and restaurants around town (35 kn/72 hrs). This card might save busy sightseers some money—do the arithmetic. The Splitcard is free if you're staying at least three nights in town; to claim yours, bring a note from your hotel to the TI.

Arrival in Split

For all the details on getting to the Dalmatian Coast, see page 745.

By Boat, Bus, or Train: The **Jadrolinija passenger catamaran** to and from Hvar and Korčula docks at the Obala Lazareta embankment, right in front of the Old Town. The ***Krilo*** **passenger catamaran** to those destinations uses pier #11, the shorter pier halfway along the harbor. Bigger **car ferries** use various docks along the east side of the harbor (the main terminal, Trajektni Terminal, is at the far end). If you arrive at this ferry terminal, wade through the *sobe* hawkers to the main terminal building, where you'll find ATMs, WCs, a grocery store, and offices for all of the main ferry companies. The large Jadrolinija ticket and information office at the main terminal, which is open long hours daily, generally has a helpful English-speaking staff.

Split's **car ferry** terminal, **main bus station** (Autobusni Kolodvor), and **train station** (Željeznička Stanica) all share a busy and very practical strip of land called Obala Kneza Domagoja, on the east side of the City Harbor. From any of them, you can see the Old Town and Riva; just walk around the harbor toward the big bell tower (about a 10-min walk). Along the way, you'll pass travel agencies, left-luggage offices, locals trying to rent rooms, a post office, Internet cafés, shops, and cafés. Arriving or leaving from

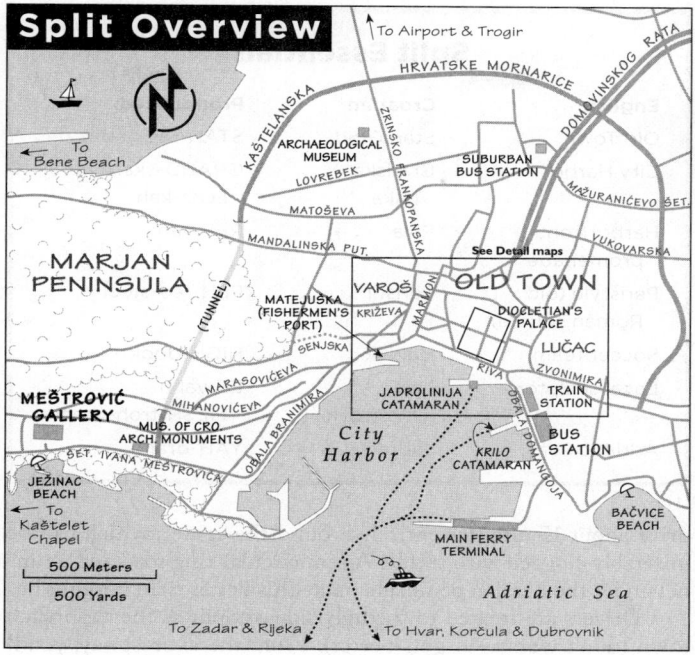

this central location, you never need to deal with the concrete, exhaust-stained sprawl of outer Split.

By Plane: Split's airport (Zračna Luka Split-Kaštela) is across the big bay, 15 miles northwest of the center, near the town of Trogir (tel. 021/203-305, www.split-airport.hr). A handy airline bus connects the airport with downtown Split (30 kn, 40 min). This bus meets most arriving flights at the airport; to use it to get *to* the airport, catch it at the small "Air Terminal" near the southeast corner of Diocletian's Palace (departs 1.5 hours before each Croatia Airlines flight and some other companies' flights). Cheaper long-distance buses also run regularly between the airport and Split's main bus station on their way to other destinations (15 kn, 7/day Mon–Fri, none Sat–Sun, 40 min). Yet another option is to take public bus #37 (20 kn, 3/hr Mon–Fri, 2/hr Sat–Sun, 45 min); the catch is that bus #37 uses the suburban bus station, which is a dreary 10-minute walk north of downtown Split. The most expensive option is a taxi, which costs a hefty 300 kn between the airport and downtown Split.

By Car: Driving around the city center can be tricky—Split is split by its Old Town, which is welded to the harbor by the pedestrian-only Riva promenade. This means drivers needing to get 300 yards from one side of the Old Town to the other must

Split Essentials

English	Croatian	Pronounced
Old Town	Stari Grad	STAH-ree grahd
City Harbor	Gradska Luka	GRAHD-skah LOO-kah
Harborfront promenade	Riva	REE-vah
Peristyle (old Roman square)	Peristil	PEH-ree-steel
Soccer team	Hajduk	HIGH-dook
Local sculptor	Ivan Meštrović	EE-vahn MESH-troh-veech
Adriatic Sea	Jadran	YAH-drahn

drive about 15 minutes entirely around the center, which can be miserably clogged with traffic. A semicircular ring road and a tunnel under the Marjan peninsula make this better than it might be.

Drivers are treated to the ugly side of Split as they approach town (don't worry—it gets better). From the expressway, you'll pass through an industrial zone, then curl through a few tunnels as you twist your way down into Split's striking, bowl-like setting. While you're still quite a distance from downtown, you'll come to a fork where you'll have to make a decision about which side of town you want to drive to (east or west); ask your hotel in advance for directions, and be ready for your turn. (While many hotels are individually signposted at the fork, it's a long list and hard to read quickly as you zip past.)

At the main fork, turning to the right (marked with *Centar* signs) takes you to the **west end** of the Old Town, including the Varoš neighborhood. Or, if you continue straight (marked *Trajekt*—"ferry"), you'll eventually reach other *Centar* signs and the **east end** of the Old Town, with the ferry terminal and the bus and train stations and the Lučac neighborhood. You'll pop out right at the southeast corner of Diocletian's Palace (by the Green Market). For handy (but expensive) parking, when the road swings left to the ferry terminal, continue straight and you'll drive right into a parking lot just outside the palace walls (10 kn/hr).

Helpful Hints

Internet Access: Internet cafés are plentiful in the Old Town; look for signs, especially around the Peristyle. Closer to the stations and ferry terminal is **Backpacker C@fé,** which

has Internet access, coffee and drinks with outdoor seating, and used paperbacks for sale (30 kn/hr, daily July–Aug 6:00–23:00, shoulder season 6:30–22:00, even shorter hours off-season, near the beginning of Obala Kneza Domagoja, tel. 021/338-548). **Modrulj Launderette** (described below) also has Internet access.

Post Office: A modern little post office is next to the bus station (Mon–Fri 7:30–19:00, Sat 7:30–14:30, closed Sun, on Obala Kneza Domagoja).

Laundry: Modrulj Launderette, a rare coin-operated launderette, is well-run by an Australian couple, Shane and Julie (self-service-50 kn/load, full-service-75 kn/load, air-con, Internet access, left-luggage service; April–Oct daily 8:00–20:00; Nov–March Mon–Sat 9:00–17:00, closed Sun; Šperun 1, tel. 021/315-888). It's conveniently located in the Varoš neighborhood at the west end of the Old Town, near several recommended restaurants—handy if multitasking is your style.

Travel Agencies: Travel49, run by gregarious Josip, is a jack-of-all-trades agency buried deep in the Old Town. Josip offers walking tours (see "Tours in Split," later), bike tours, excursions, a room-booking service, bike and car rental, Internet access, luggage storage, and other services (May–Nov daily 8:00–22:00, shorter hours off-season, mornings only in winter, on Nepotova street, tel. 021/572-772, www.travel49.com). **Turistički Biro,** between the two halves of the Old Town on the Riva, books *sobe* and hotels, sells guidebooks and maps, and sells tickets for excursions (mid-June–Sept Mon–Fri 8:00–21:00, Sat 8:00–20:00, closed Sun except mid-July–mid-Sept Sun 8:00–13:00; Oct–mid-June Mon–Fri 8:00–20:00, Sat 8:00–13:00, closed Sun; Riva 12, tel. & fax 021/347-100, turist.biro.split@st.t-com.hr).

Luggage Storage: The train station and adjacent bus station both have safe and efficient left-luggage services *(garderoba)*. If one has a long line, check the other to see if the line is shorter. You can also store your luggage at several places in and near the Old Town, including Modrulj Launderette and Travel49 (both listed earlier).

Wine Shop: At **Vinoteka Bouquet,** at the west end of the Riva (near the restaurants and launderette on Šperun street), knowledgeable Denis can help you pick out a bottle of Croatian wine to suit your tastes (Mon–Fri 8:30–12:30 & 17:00–20:30, Sat 9:00–13:30, closed Sun, Obala Hrvatskog Narodnog Preporoda 3, tel. 021/348-031). For a wine primer before you visit, see page 755.

Who's Hajduk?: You'll see the word *Hajduk* (HIGH-dook), and a distinctive red-and-white checkerboard circle design (or

red-and-blue stripes), all over town and throughout northern Dalmatia. Hajduk Split is the fervently supported local soccer team, named for a band of highwaymen bandits who rebelled against Ottoman rule in the 17th–19th centuries. Most locals adore Hajduk as much as they loathe their bitter rivals, Dinamo Zagreb.

G'day, *Gospod*: You may notice a surprising concentration of Australians in Split. Many of them are actually Australian-born Croats, returning to the cosmopolitan capital city of their parents' Dalmatian homeland.

Getting Around Split

Most of what you'll want to see is within walking distance, but some sights (such as the Meštrović Gallery) are more easily reached by bus or taxi.

By Bus: Local buses, run by Promet, cost 10 kn per ride (or 9 kn if you buy a ticket from a newsstand or Promet kiosk, ask for a *putna karta;* zone I is fine for any ride within Split). For a round-trip within the city, buy a 16-kn transfer ticket, which works like two individual tickets (must buy at kiosk). Validate your ticket in the machine or with the driver as you board the bus. Suburban buses to towns near Split generally use the suburban bus station (Prigradski Autobusni Kolodvor), a 10-minute walk due north of the Old Town on Domovinskog rata. Bus information: www.promet-split.hr.

By Taxi: Taxis start at 20 kn, then cost around 10 kn per kilometer. Figure 50 kn for most rides within the city (for example, from the ferry terminal to most hotels)—but if going from one end of the Old Town to the other, it can be faster to walk. To call for a taxi, try Radio Taxi (tel. 021/970).

Tours in Split

Walking Tours—Various companies offer walking tours of Split's Old Town. The most established is **Unique Walking Tours,** which is part of Travel49. Their 1.5-hour tours depart from the Peristyle daily at 10:30, 12:00, and 19:00 (80 kn, tours run May–Nov only, no reservations needed, www.travel49.com).

Local Guides—Consider hiring an insider to show you around. **Maja Benzon** is a smart and savvy local guide who leads good walking tours through the Old Town (500 kn/up to 2 hours, 600 kn/3 hours, mobile 098-852-869, maja.benzon@gmail.com). You can also hire a guide through the **guide association,** which has an office at the Peristyle (525 kn/1.5-2 hours; June–Aug Mon–Fri 9:00–13:00 & 15:00–19:00, Sat 9:00–14:00, closed Sun; May and Sept Mon–Fri 9:00–17:00, Sat 9:00–15:00, closed Sun; Oct–April

generally open mornings only but closed Sun; tel. 021/360-058, tel. & fax 021/346-267, mobile 098-361-936, www.guides.hr, info @guides.hr).

Beyond Split

Lifejacket Adventures, run by Australian couple Shane and Julie, works hard to come up with culturally meaningful excursions that connect travelers to the Croatia they came to see. Many of their trips involve a cruise on an authentic, old-fashioned fishing boat. Options include a sunset cruise, a swim and a picnic on a nearby island, a Jewish-themed walking tour of Split, a cooking trip to Hvar, and longer excursions to Plitvice Lakes National Park. They also arrange custom excursions, with a focus on kayaking, hiking, wine, history, and archaeological sites. Because their schedule is based on demand, get the latest by checking their website (www.lifejacketadventures.com), calling 098-931-6400, or stopping by their office in Split (around the corner from Modrulj Launderette, which Shane and Julie also run; see "Helpful Hints," earlier).

Atlas Travel offers a variety of excursions from Split (mostly full-day, about 300–700 kn). Itineraries include a tour of Split and Trogir, whitewater rafting on the nearby Cetina River, the island of Brač, the island of Hvar, Brač and Hvar together, Međugorje, Krka National Park, Dubrovnik, and Plitvice Lakes National Park. While the guiding is generally disappointing, this can be a quick, convenient way to get to places that are time-consuming to reach by public transportation. Get information and tickets at any travel agency, such as the Turistički Biro on the Riva (see "Helpful Hints," earlier).

Travel49, listed earlier under "Helpful Hints," also runs excursions.

Self-Guided Walk

▲▲▲Diocletian's Palace (Dioklecijanova Palača)

Split's top activity is visiting the remains of Roman Emperor Diocletian's enormous retirement palace, sitting on the harbor in the heart of the city. This monstrous complex was two impressive structures in one: luxurious villa and fortified Roman town. Since the ruins themselves are now integrated with the city's street plan, exploring them is free (though you'll pay to enter a few parts, such as the cellars and the cathedral/mausoleum). Fragments of the palace are poorly marked, and there are no good guidebooks or audioguides for tracking down the remains, making Split a good place to take a walking tour or hire a local guide (see "Tours in Split," earlier). This self-guided tour provides enough information

for most visitors. To begin the tour, stand in front of the palace (at the east end of the Riva) to get oriented.

Background: Diocletian grew up just inland from Split, in the town of Salona (Solin in Croatian), which was then the capital of the Roman province of Dalmatia. He worked his way up the Roman hierarchy and ruled as emperor for the unusually long tenure of 20 years (A.D. 284–305). Despite all of his achievements, Diocletian is best remembered for two questionable legacies: dividing the huge empire among four emperors (which helped administer it more efficiently, but began a splintering effect that arguably led to the empire's decline); and torturing and executing Christians, including thousands right here on the Dalmatian Coast.

As Diocletian grew older, he decided to return to his homeland for retirement. Since he was in poor health, the medicinal sulfur spring here was another plus. His massive palace took only 11 years to build—and this fast pace required a big push (more than 2,000 slaves died during construction). Huge sections of his palace still exist, modified by medieval and modern developers alike. To get a sense of the original palace, check out the big illustration posted across from the palace entry. Across the street at the end of the Riva, notice the big car-size model of today's Old Town, which is helpful for orientation. (Both the sign and the model are usually crowded with tour groups.)

Palace Facade

The "front" of today's Split—facing the harbor—was actually the back door of Diocletian's Palace. There was no embankment in front of the palace back then, so the water came right up to this door—sort of an emergency exit by boat. Looking out to the water, appreciate the palace's strategic location, in a place easy to fortify and to watch for enemies approaching either by land or by sea.

Visually trace the outline of the gigantic palace, which was more than 600 feet long on each side. On the corner to the right stands a big, rectangular guard tower (one of the original 16). To the left, the tower is gone and the corner is harder to pick out (look for the beginning of the newer-looking buildings). Mentally erase the ramshackle two-story buildings added 200 years ago, which obscure the grandness of the palace wall.

Halfway up the facade, notice the row of 42 arched window frames (mostly filled in today). Diocletian and his family lived in the seaside half of the palace. Imagine him strolling back and forth

along this fine arcade, enjoying the views of his Adriatic homeland. The inland, non-view half of the palace was home to 700 servants, bodyguards, and soldiers.

• *Now go through the door in the middle of the palace (known as the "Brass Gate," located under the* Substructure of Diocletian's Palace *banner). Just inside the door and to the left is the entrance to...*

Diocletian's Cellars (Podromi)

Since the palace was built on land that sloped down to the sea, these chambers were built to level out a foundation for the massive structure above (like a modern "daylight basement"). These cellars were filled with water from three different sources: a freshwater spring, a sulfur spring, and the sea. Later, medieval residents used them as a dump. Rediscovered only in the last century, the cellars enabled archaeologists to derive the floor plan of some of the palace's long-gone upper sections. Today, these underground chambers are used for art exhibits and a little strip of souvenir stands. But before you go shopping, explore the cellars at this end (25 kn, short and dry 10-kn guidebook, some posters inside explain the site; opens daily at 9:00 and closes June–Aug at 21:00, Sept at 20:00, May and Oct at 18:00, April at 17:00; Nov–March Mon–Sat 9:00–14:00, closed Sun).

➲ **Self-Guided Tour:** Use the free map you get at the entry to navigate this labyrinthine complex of cellars. First visit the **western cellars** (to the left as you enter). Near the ticket-seller, notice the big **topographical map** of the Split area, clearly showing the city's easily defensible location—with a natural harbor sheltered by tall mountains. You'll see the former Roman city of Salona, Diocletian's birthplace, just inland.

Then head into the main part of the cellars by going through the door on the right, just past the ticket-seller. This takes you into the complex's vast, vaulted **main hall**—the biggest space in the cellars, with stout pillars to support everything upstairs. When those first villagers took refuge in the abandoned palace from the rampaging Slavs in 641, the elite lived upstairs, grabbing what was once the emperor's wing. They carved the rough holes you see in the ceiling to dump their garbage and sewage. Over the generations, the basement (where you're standing) filled up with layers of waste that solidified, ultimately becoming a once-stinky, then-precious bonanza for 19th- and 20th-century archaeologists. Today this hall is used for everything from flower and book shows to fashion catwalks.

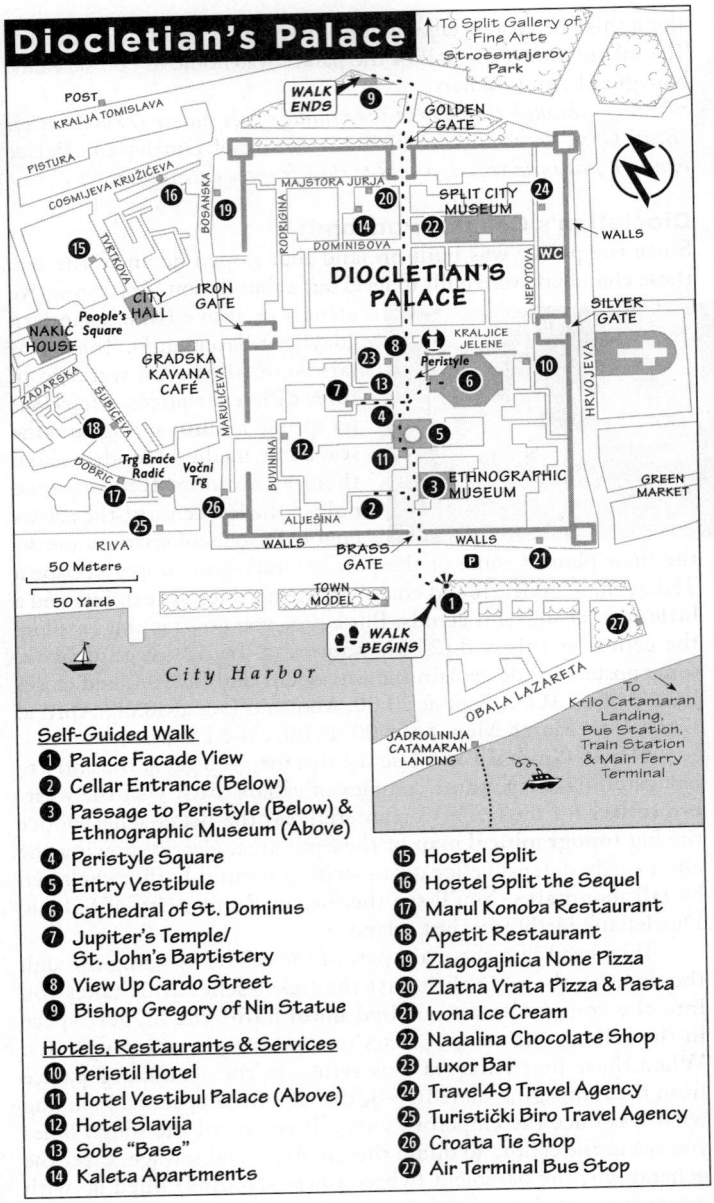

Self-Guided Walk

1. Palace Facade View
2. Cellar Entrance (Below)
3. Passage to Peristyle (Below) & Ethnographic Museum (Above)
4. Peristyle Square
5. Entry Vestibule
6. Cathedral of St. Dominus
7. Jupiter's Temple/ St. John's Baptistery
8. View Up Cardo Street
9. Bishop Gregory of Nin Statue

Hotels, Restaurants & Services

10. Peristil Hotel
11. Hotel Vestibul Palace (Above)
12. Hotel Slavija
13. Sobe "Base"
14. Kaleta Apartments
15. Hostel Split
16. Hostel Split the Sequel
17. Marul Konoba Restaurant
18. Apetit Restaurant
19. Zlagogajnica None Pizza
20. Zlatna Vrata Pizza & Pasta
21. Ivona Ice Cream
22. Nadalina Chocolate Shop
23. Luxor Bar
24. Travel49 Travel Agency
25. Turistički Biro Travel Agency
26. Croata Tie Shop
27. Air Terminal Bus Stop

Exit the main hall through either of the doors on the left, turn right down the narrow corridor, and then turn left at the end of the corridor. In this room you'll see a stone olive-oil press. Continue through a small room and into a round room, which has a headless, pawless black granite sphinx—one of 13 that Diocletian brought home from Egypt (only four survive, including a mostly intact one we'll see soon on the Peristyle). Look up to admire the circular brickwork. Then continue straight ahead into the long room, which displays two petrified beams. Looking just overhead, you'll see the holes that once held these beams to support floorboards, making this a two-story cellar.

Exit through the door at the far-right corner (near the mound of ancient garbage) to another round room, featuring a bust of Diocletian (or is it Sean Connery?). Continue straight ahead (near the public WCs), then turn left, left, and right into the second grand hall, with more beam holes and a giant replica of a golden Diocletian coin at the far end. Exiting this hall at the end opposite the coin, you'll find an unexcavated wing—a compost pile of ancient lifestyles, awaiting the tiny shovels and toothbrushes of future archaeologists. Here you'll also see original Roman sewer pipes—square outside and round inside—designed to fit into each other to create long pipes.

From here, head back out to the exit. If you'd like to see more cellars—mostly with their ceilings missing, so they're open to the air—cross over into the **eastern cellars** (same ticket). This section is less interesting than the western part, but worth a quick visit.

• *When you're finished, head back to the main gallery. Ignore the tacky made-in-Malaysia trinket shops as you head down the passage and up the stairs into the...*

Peristyle (Peristil)

This square was the centerpiece of Diocletian's Palace. As you walk up the stairs, the entry vestibule into the residence is above your head, Diocletian's mausoleum (today's Cathedral of St. Dominus) is to your right, and the street to Jupiter's Temple is on your left. On this square, you'll find the TI (because the old structures on the square are being restored, its exact location might vary). Straight ahead, beyond the little chapel, is the narrow street to the former main entrance to the palace, the Golden Gate.

Go to the middle of the square and take it all in. The red granite pillars—which you'll see all over Diocletian's Palace—are

from Egypt, where Diocletian spent many of his pre-retirement years. Imagine the pillars defining fine arcades—now obscured by medieval houses. (As the Peristyle is undergoing a lengthy restoration, you may notice that many of the ruins are lighter-colored than others, and scaffolding may block your view.) The black sphinx is the only one of Diocletian's collection of 13 that's still (mostly) intact.

• *Climb the stairs (above where you came in) into the domed, open-ceilinged...*

Entry Vestibule: Impressed? That's the idea. This was the grand entry to Diocletian's living quarters, meant to wow visitors. Emperors were believed to be gods. Diocletian called himself "Jovius"—the son of Jupiter, the most powerful of all gods. Four times a year (at the change of the seasons), Diocletian would stand here and overlook the Peristyle. His subjects would lie on the ground in worship, praising his name and kissing his scarlet robe. Notice the four big niches at floor level, which once held statues of the four tetrarchs who ruled the unwieldy empire after Diocletian retired. The empty hole in the ceiling was once capped by a dome (long since collapsed), and the ceiling itself was covered with frescoes and mosaics.

In this grand space, you're likely to run into an all-male band of ***klapa*** singers, performing traditional a cappella harmonies. Just stand and enjoy a few glorious tunes—you'll rarely find a better group or acoustics. A 100-kn *klapa* CD is the perfect souvenir.

Wander out back to the harbor side through medieval buildings (some with seventh-century foundations), which evoke the way local villagers came in and took over the once-spacious and elegant palace. Back in this area, you'll find the beautifully restored home of the **Ethnographic Museum** (described later, under "Sights in Split").

• *Now go back into the Peristyle and turn right, climbing the steps to the...*

Cathedral of St. Dominus (Katedrala Sv. Duje)

The original octagonal structure was Diocletian's elaborate mausoleum, built in the fourth century. But after the fall of Rome, it was converted into the town's cathedral. Construction of the bell tower began in the 13th century and took 300 years to complete. Before you go inside, notice the sarcophagi ringing the cathedral. In the late Middle Ages, this was prime post-mortem real estate,

since being buried closer to a cathedral improved your chances of getting to heaven. On the 13th-century main doors, notice the 14 panels on each of the two wings—showing 28 scenes from the life of Christ.

Various parts of the cathedral are covered by separate tickets: 15 kn for the "treasury" (actually the fee to enter the cathedral), another 10 kn to climb the tower, and yet another 5 kn for the crypt below. All the sights are open similar hours, but can be closed unexpectedly for services (generally open daily in summer 7:00–19:00, often closed Sat afternoons for weddings and Sun mornings for Mass; in winter daily 7:00–12:00, maybe later on request; Kraj Sv. Duje 5, tel. 021/344-121).

Buy your treasury/cathedral ticket and step inside the oldest—and likely smallest—building used as a cathedral anywhere in Christendom. Imagine the place in pre-Christian times, with Diocletian's tomb in the center. The only surviving decor from those days are the granite columns and the relief circling the base of the dome (about 50 feet up)—a ring of carvings heralding the greatness of the emperor. The small red-marble pillars around the top of the pulpit (near the entry) were scavenged from Diocletian's sarcophagus. These pillars are all that remain of Diocletian's remains.

Diocletian brutally persecuted his Christian subjects. Just before he moved to the Dalmatian Coast, he had Bishop Dominus of Salona killed, along with several thousand Christians. When Diocletian died, there were joyful riots. In the seventh century, his mausoleum became a cathedral dedicated to the martyred bishop. The extension behind the altar was added in the ninth century. The sarcophagus of St. Dominus (to the right of the altar, with early-Christian carvings) was once the cathedral's high altar. To the left of today's main altar is the impressively detailed, Renaissance-era altar of St. Anastasius, who is lying on a millstone that is tied to his neck. On Diocletian's orders, this Christian martyr was drowned in A.D. 302. To the left of St. Anastasius' altar is the "new" altar of St. Dominus; his relics lie in the 18th-century Baroque silver reliquary, decorated with a relief showing him being beheaded. Posthumous poetic justice:

Now Christian saints are entombed in Diocletian's mausoleum... and Diocletian is nowhere to be found.

For another 10 kn, you can climb 183 steep steps to the top of the 200-foot-tall **bell tower.** You'll be rewarded with sweeping views of Split, but it's not for claustrophobes or those scared of heights.

If you circle down and around the right side of the cathedral, you'll find the entrance to the **crypt** (separate 5-kn ticket). This musty, domed cellar (with eerie acoustics) was originally used to level the foundation of Diocletian's mausoleum. Later, Christians turned it into another chapel. The legend you'll likely hear about Diocletian torturing and murdering Christians in this very crypt, which began about the same time this became a church, is probably false.

Jupiter's Temple/St. John's Baptistery

Remember that Diocletian believed himself to be Jovius (that's Jupiter, Jr.). On exiting the mausoleum of Jovius, worshippers would look straight ahead to the temple of Jupiter. (Back then, all of these medieval buildings weren't cluttering up the view.) Make your way through the narrow alley (directly across from the cathedral entry), past another headless, pawless sphinx, to explore the small temple (5 kn, same hours as cathedral; if it's locked, go ask the guy at the cathedral to let you in).

About the time the mausoleum became a cathedral, this temple was converted into a baptistery. The big 12th-century baptismal font—large enough to immerse someone (as was the tradition in those days)—is decorated with the intricate, traditional *pleter* design also used around the border of Croatia's current passport stamp. On the font, notice the engraving: a bishop (on the left) and the king on his throne (on the right). At their feet (literally under the feet of the bishop) is a submissive commoner—neatly summing up the social structure of the Middle Ages. Standing above the font is a statue of St. John the Baptist counting to four, done by the great Croatian sculptor Ivan Meštrović (see page 832). The half-barrel vaulted ceiling, completed later, is considered the best-preserved of its kind anywhere. Every face and each patterned box is different.

• *Back at the Peristyle, stand in front of the little chapel with your back to the entry vestibule. The little street just beyond the chapel (going left to right) connects the east and west gates. If you've had enough Roman history, head right (east) to go through the "Silver Gate" and find Split's busy, open-air Green Market. Or, head to the left (west), which takes you to the "Iron Gate" and People's Square (see "Sights in Split," later) and, beyond that, the fresh-and-smelly fish market. But if you want to see one last bit of Roman history, continue straight ahead up the...*

Cardo

A traditional Roman street plan has two roads: Cardo (the north–south axis) and Decumanus (the east–west axis). Split's Cardo street was the most important in Diocletian's Palace, connecting the main entry with the heart of the complex. As you walk, you'll pass several noteworthy sights: in the first building on the right, a bank with modern computer gear all around its exposed Roman ruins (look through window); at the first gate on the left, the courtyard of a Venetian merchant's palace (a reminder that Split was dominated by Venice from the 15th century on); on the right, an alley to the **City Museum** (described later, under "Sights in Split"); and, on the right, the **Nadalina** chocolate shop, a local artisan chocolatier selling mostly dark chocolate creations with some innovative Dalmatian flavors (30 kn/100 grams, 13-kn chocolate bars, Mon–Fri 9:00–21:00, Sat 9:00–12:00, closed Sun).

• *Before long, you'll pass through the...*

Golden Gate (Zlatna Vrata)

This great gate was the main entry of Diocletian's Palace. Its name wasn't literal—the "gold" instead suggests the importance of this gateway to Salona, the Roman provincial capital at the time. Standing inside the gate itself, you can appreciate the double-door design that kept the palace safe. Also notice how this ancient building is now being used in very different ways from its original purpose. Above, on the outer wall, you can see the bricked-in windows that contain part of a Dominican convent. At the top of the inner wall, notice somebody's garden terrace.

Go outside the gate, where you'll get a much clearer feel for the way the palace looked before so many other buildings were grafted on. Straight ahead from here is Salona (Solin), which was a major city of 60,000 (and Diocletian's hometown) before there was a Split. The big statue by Ivan Meštrović is

Bishop Gregory of Nin, a 10th-century Croatian priest who tried to convince the Vatican to allow sermons during Mass to be said in Croatian, rather than Latin. People rub his toe for good luck (though only nonmaterial wishes are given serious consideration). The big building beyond the statue houses Split's new **Gallery of Fine Arts** (described later, under "Sights in Split").

• *Your tour is finished. Now enjoy the rest of Split.*

Sights in Split

In or near the Old Town

In addition to the palace, cellars, and cathedral described on my self-guided walk, you can also enjoy these attractions.

▲People's Square (Narodni Trg)—The lively square at the center of the Old Town is called by locals simply *Pjaca,* pronounced the same as the Italian *piazza* (PYAH-tsah). Stand in the center and enjoy the bustle. Look around for a quick lesson in Dalmatian history. When Diocletian lived in his palace, a Roman village popped up here, just outside the wall. Face the former wall of Diocletian's Palace (behind and to the right of the 24-hour clock tower). This was the western entrance, or so-called "Iron Gate." By the 14th century, a medieval town had developed, making this the main square of Split.

On the wall just to the right of the lane leading to the Peristyle, look for the life-size relief of **St. Anthony.** Notice the creepy "mini-me" clutching the saint's left leg—depicting the sculptor's donor, who didn't want his gift to be forgotten. Above this strange statue, notice the smaller, faded relief of a man and a woman arguing.

Turn around and face the square. On your left is the city's grand old café, **Gradska Kavana,** which has been the Old Town's venerable meeting point for generations. Today it's both a café and a restaurant with disappointing food but the best outdoor ambience in town (30-kn breakfasts, 50–75-kn pastas, 70–130-kn main dishes, daily 7:00–24:00, Narodni trg 1, tel. 021/317-835).

Across the square, the white building jutting into the square was once the **City Hall,** and now houses temporary exhibitions. The loggia is all that remains of the original Gothic building.

At the far end of the square is the out-of-place **Nakić House,** built in the early-20th-century Viennese Secession style—a reminder that Dalmatia was part of the Habsburg Empire, ruled

by Vienna, from Napoleon's downfall through World War I.

The lane on the right side of the Nakić House leads to Split's **fish market** (Ribarnica), where you can see piles of the still-wriggling catch of the day. No flies? It's thanks to the sulfur spring in the nearby spa building (with the gray statues, on the corner). Just beyond the fish market is the pedestrian boulevard Marmontova.

Ethnographic Museum (Etnografski Muzej)—This museum uses well-presented temporary exhibits to show off the culture, costumes, furniture, tools, jewelry, weapons, and paintings of Dalmatia. It's all displayed in a gorgeously renovated early-medieval palace with a confusing treehouse floor plan. You'll find it in the upper level of the Old Town, behind Diocletian's entry vestibule. Check out the artsy "golden fleece" entry door. The ground floor sports the remains of a seventh-century church, and the exhibits usually include a good look at traditional folk dress. Your ticket also includes access to the roof of the vestibule (find the stairs at the far end of the museum); while it's not high enough to be thrilling, and you can't actually see down into the vestibule, it's a nice view over the rooftops of Split (10 kn, some English explanations; July–mid-Sept Mon–Fri 9:00–21:00, Sat 9:00–13:00, closed Sun; June Mon–Fri 9:00–14:00 & 17:00–20:00, Sat 9:00–13:00, closed Sun; mid-Sept–May Mon–Fri 9:00–14:00, Sat 9:00–13:00, closed Sun; Severova 7, tel. 021/344-164, www.etnografski-muzej-split.hr).

Split City Museum (Muzej Grada Splita)—This museum traces how the city grew over the centuries. It's a bit dull, but it can help you appreciate a little better the layers of history you're seeing in the streets. The ground floor displays Roman fragments (including coins from the days of Diocletian) and temporary exhibits. The upstairs focuses on the Middle Ages (find the terrace displaying carved stone monuments), and the top floor goes from the 16th century to the present (10 kn, some English descriptions, 75-kn guidebook is overkill; May–Sept Tue–Fri 9:00–21:00, Sat–Mon 9:00–16:00; Oct–April Tue–Fri 9:00–16:00, Sat–Sun 10:00–13:00, closed Mon; Papalićeva 1, tel. 021/360-171, www.mgst.net).

The 15th-century Papalić Palace, which houses the City Museum, is a sight all its own. At the end of the palace, near Cardo street, look up to see several typical Venetian-style Gothic-Renaissance windows. The stone posts sticking out of the wall next to them were used to hang curtains.

Radić Brothers Square (Trg Braće Radića)—Also known as Voćni Trg ("Fruit Square") for the produce that was once sold here, this little piazza is just off the Riva between the two halves of the Old Town. Overhead is a **Venetian citadel.** After Split became part of the Venetian Republic, there was a serious danger of attack by the Ottomans, so octagonal towers like this were built all

along the coast. But this imposing tower had a second purpose: to encourage citizens of Split to forget about any plans of rebellion.

In the middle of the square is a studious sculpture by Ivan Meštrović of the 16th-century poet **Marko Marulić,** who is considered the father of the Croatian language. Marulić was the first to write literature in the Croatian vernacular, which before then had generally been considered a backward peasants' tongue.

On the downhill (harbor) side of the square is **Croata,** a necktie boutique that loves to explain how Croatian soldiers who fought with the French in the Thirty Years' War (1618–1648) had a distinctive way of tying their scarves. The French found it stylish, adopted it, and called it *à la Croate*—or eventually, *cravate*—thus creating the modern necktie that many people wear to work every day throughout the world. Croata's selection includes ties with traditional Croatian motifs, such as the checkerboard pattern from the flag or writing in the ninth-century Glagolitic alphabet. Though pricey, these ties make nice souvenirs (250–700 kn, Mon–Fri 8:00–20:30, Sat 8:00–13:00, closed Sun, shorter hours off-season). There's also a bigger, second location of this shop on the Peristyle.

Green Market—This lively open-air market bustles at the east end of Diocletian's Palace. Locals shop for produce and clothes here, and there are plenty of tourist souvenirs as well. Browse the wide selection of T-shirts, and ignore the creepy black-market tobacco salesmen who mutter at you: *"Cigaretta?"*

Split Gallery of Fine Arts (Galerija Umjetnina Split)—This collection, beautifully displayed in a finely restored old hospital just behind Diocletian's Palace, features mostly Croatian artwork from the 14th to the 21st centuries. It's basically a hodgepodge with few highlights—best reserved for art-lovers. Cross through the courtyard, climb up the stairs, and follow the one-way route through the chronologically displayed collection, which is heavy on the 20th century (20 kn, Tue–Sat 11:00–19:00, Sun 10:00–13:00, closed Mon, mod café, go straight out the Golden Gate and a bit to the left—behind the statue of Gregory of Nin—to Kralja Tomislava 15, tel. 021/350-110, www.galum.hr).

Archaeological Museum (Arheološki Muzej)—If you're intrigued by all the "big stuff" from Split's past (buildings and ruins), consider paying a visit to this collection of its "little stuff." A good exhibit of artifacts (mostly everyday domestic items) traces this region's history chronologically, from its Illyrian beginnings through its notable Roman period (items from Split and Salona) to the Middle Ages. About a 10-minute walk north of the Old Town, it's worth the trip for archaeology fans (20 kn; June–Sept Mon–Sat 9:00–14:00 & 16:00–20:00, closed Sun; Oct–May Mon–Fri 9:00–14:00 & 16:00–20:00, Sat 9:00–14:00, closed Sun; Zrinsko

Frankopanska 25, tel. 021/329-340, www.mdc.hr/split-arheoloski). Don't confuse this with the less-interesting Museum of Croatian Archaeological Monuments, on the way to the Ivan Meštrović Gallery.

Ivan Meštrović Sights, West of the Old Town

The excellent Meštrović Gallery and nearby Kaštelet Chapel just outside the Old Town can be reached by foot, bus, or taxi.

▲▲Meštrović Gallery (Galerija Meštrović)—Split's best art museum is dedicated to the sculptor Ivan Meštrović, the most important of all Croatian artists (see sidebar). Many of Meštrović's finest works are housed in this palace, designed by the sculptor himself to serve as his residence, studio, and exhibition space. If you have time, it's worth the 25-minute walk or short bus or taxi ride from the Old Town.

Cost, Hours, Location: 30 kn, includes Kaštelet Chapel entry, free guide booklet, 80-kn guidebook is overkill for most visitors, pricey mobile-phone audioguides available; May–Sept Tue–Sun 9:00–19:00, closed Mon; Oct–April Tue–Sat 9:00–16:00, Sun 10:00–15:00, closed Mon; hours can be sporadic—call to confirm it's open before making the trip, Šetalište Ivana Meštrovića 46, tel. 021/340-800, www.mdc.hr/mestrovic.

Getting There: To get to the gallery, you can take **bus** #12 from the little cul-de-sac at the west end of the Riva (departs hourly, get off at the stop in front of the gallery—just after your bus passes a museum prominently marked *Muzej Hrvatskih Arheoloških Spomenika*). Or you can **walk** about 25 minutes: Follow the harbor west of town toward the big marina, swing right with the road, and follow the park until you see the gallery on your right. A **taxi** from the west end of the Old Town to the gallery costs about 50 kn (much more from the east end of the Old Town).

➲ Self-Guided Tour: After buying your ticket (and asking about the time for your return bus to the Old Town), climb the stairs toward Meštrović's house, pausing in the **garden** to admire a smattering of sculptures (including several female nudes, Cyclops hurling a giant shotput, and an eagle).

Climbing another set of stairs, you reach the **Entrance Hall,** displaying sculptures mostly of Carrara marble, which was Michelangelo's favorite medium. Notice the black sculptures by the two staircases: on the left, representing birth, and on the right, representing death—Meštrović strove to capture the full range of human experience in his work.

Ivan Meštrović
(1883–1962)

Ivan Meštrović (EE-vahn MESH-troh-veech), who achieved international fame for his talents as a sculptor, was Croatia's answer to Rodin. You'll see Meštrović's works everywhere, in the streets, squares, and museums of Croatia.

Meštrović came from humble beginnings. He grew up in a family of poor, nomadic farm workers just inland from Split. At an early age, his drawings and wooden carvings showed promise, and a rich family took him in and made sure he was properly trained. He eventually went off to school in Vienna, where he fell in with the Secession movement and found fame and fortune. He lived in Prague, Paris, and Switzerland, fully engaged in the flourishing European artistic culture at the turn of the 20th century (he counted Rodin among his friends). After World War I, Meštrović moved back to Croatia, where he had an atelier, or workshop, in Zagreb (now a museum—see page 926).

Later in life—like Diocletian before him—Meštrović returned to Split and built a huge seaside mansion (today's Meštrović Gallery). The years between the World Wars were Meštrović's happiest and most productive. It was during this time that he sculpted his most internationally famous works, a pair of giant Native American warriors on horseback in Chicago's Grant Park. But when World War II broke out, Meštrović—an outspoken supporter of the ideals of a united Yugoslavia—was briefly imprisoned by the anti-Yugoslav Ustaše (Croatia's Nazi puppet government). After his release, Meštrović fled to Italy, then the US, where he lectured at prominent universities such as Notre Dame and Syracuse. After the war, the Yugoslav dictator Tito invited Meštrović to return, but the very religious artist refused to cooperate with an atheist regime. (Meštrović was friends with the Archbishop Alojzije Stepinac, who was imprisoned by Tito.) Meštrović died in South Bend, Indiana.

Meštrović worked in wood, plaster, marble, and bronze, and dabbled in painting. His sculptures depict biblical, mythological, political, and everyday themes. Meštrović's figures typically have long, angular fingers, arms, and legs. Whether whimsical or emotional, Meštrović's expressive, elongated faces—often with a strong-profile nose—powerfully connect with the viewer.

Go to the left, and enter the **Dining Room** at the end of the main floor. It's decorated with portraits of Meštrović's wife, mother, and children. Meštrović often used his mother as a model for older women and his second wife Olga as a model for younger women. Also look for the self-portrait and two painted portraits of Meštrović (one as a young man, another shortly before his death). A painting of the *Last Supper* hangs in virtually every Dalmatian dining room. Meštrović's is no exception—he painted this version himself. At the end of the room are two giant caryatids carved from Dalmatian stone (embedded with fragments of seashells).

Now climb the stairs and go to the right, into the **Secession Room.** Some of these works—including the girl singing and the intimate portrait of a family—show the influence of Meštrović's contemporary, Rodin.

Pass through the room of drawings into the **Long Hall,** lined with life-size figures and a view terrace. The woman sitting with her knees apart and feet together is demonstrating a favorite pose of Meštrović's.

At the end of the hall is the **Study Room,** filled with miniature sculptures Meštrović created to prepare for larger-scale works. Notice the small study of *Job*, then go into the small side-room to see the much larger final version. One of Meštrović's most powerful works, *Job*—howling with an agony verging on insanity—was carved by the artist in exile, as his country was turned upside-down by World War II. Meštrović sketched his inspiration for this piece (displayed on the wall) while he was imprisoned by the Ustaše.

Head down the stairs and turn left into the **Sacral Room.** Meštrović was very religious, and here you can see some of his many works depicting biblical figures. The giant, wood-carved *Adam* and *Eve* dominate the room, but don't miss the smaller side-room, with another of the gallery's highlights: the quietly poignant *Roman Pietà*. Meštrović follows the classical pyramid form, with Joseph of Arimathea (top), Mary (left), and Mary Magdalene (right) surrounding the limp body of Christ. But the harmony is broken by the painful angles of the mourning faces. While this sculpture is plaster, Meštrović also completed a marble version for the campus of Notre Dame in the US.

▲Kaštelet Chapel—If you enjoy the gallery, don't miss the nearby Kaštelet Chapel ("Chapel of the Holy Cross"). Meštrović bought this 16th-century fortified palace to display his 28 wood reliefs of Jesus' life. Because he carved these over a nearly 30-year

span (completing the last 12 when he was in the US), you can watch Meštrović's style change over time. (However, note that he didn't carve the reliefs in chronological order—ask for a booklet identifying the topic and year for each one.) While the earlier pieces are well-composed and powerful, the later ones seem more hastily done, as Meštrović rushed to complete his opus. Work clockwise around the room, tracing the life of Christ. Notice that some of the Passion scenes are out of order (a side-effect of Meštrović's nonlinear schedule). The beautiful *pietà* near the end still shows some of the original surface of the wood, demonstrating the skill required to create depth and emotion in just a few inches of medium. Dominating the chapel is an extremely powerful wooden crucifix, with Christ's arms, legs, fingers, and toes bent at unnatural angles—a typically expressionistic flair Meštrović used to exaggerate suffering.

Cost and Hours: The chapel is covered by the same 30-kn ticket as the gallery, and open the same hours.

Getting There: It's a five-minute walk past the gallery down Šetalište Ivana Meštrovića (on the left, in an olive grove).

Activities in Split

▲▲Strolling the Riva (Obala Hrvatskog Narodnog Preporoda)—The official name for this seaside pedestrian drag is the "Croatian National Revival Embankment," but locals just call it "Riva" (Italian for "harbor"). This is the town's promenade, an integral part of Mediterranean culture. After dinner, Split residents collect their families and friends for a stroll on the Riva. It offers some of the best people-watching in Croatia; make it a point to be here for an hour or two after dinner. At the west end of the Riva, the people-parade of Croatian culture turns right and heads away from the water, up Marmontova. The stinky smell that sometimes accompanies the stroll isn't a sewer. It's sulfur—a reminder that the town's medicinal sulfur spas have attracted people here since the days of Diocletian.

The Riva recently underwent an extensive, costly, and controversial renovation. The old potholed pavement and scrubby gardens were torn up and replaced with a broad, sleek, carefully landscaped people zone. A clean, synchronized line of modern white lampposts and sun screens sashays down the promenade. But many locals miss the colorful quirks of the old version. For example,

each café used to have its own tables and umbrellas; now they're forced to buy identical tables and chairs to make everything match. (In protest, some cafés have chosen to offer no outdoor seating at all.) Some locals think that the starkly modern strip is at odds with the rest of the higgledy-piggledy Old Town, while others see this as simply the early-21st century's contribution to the architectural hodgepodge that is Split.

Exploring Matejuška Fishermen's Port—While Split's harborfront Riva is where the beautiful people stroll, the city's fishermen roots still thrive just to the west. The neighborhood called Matejuška—at the little harbor where the Varoš district hits the water (a five-minute walk beyond the end of the Riva, with the water on your left)—has long been Split's working fishermen's harbor. While the area has received a facelift to match the one along the Riva, it still retains its striped-collar character. You'll notice that the enclosed harbor area is filled with working fishing boats and colorful dinghies that bob in unison. Along the breakwater, notice the new fishermen's lockers, where people who earn their living from the Adriatic still keep their supplies. You'll see the most fishing action here in the mornings.

The far side of the breakwater—all glitzy white marble—is another world, with a pebbly beach, inviting plaza, and some of the best views looking back on the Riva. After its recent facelift, this jetty has become a popular open-air, after-hours hangout spot for local young people. Like Split itself, these two worlds—that of grizzled fishermen mending nets, and that of teenagers living it up—coexist more smoothly than you might expect.

Hiking the Marjan Peninsula—This long, hilly peninsula extends west from the center of Split. With out-of-the-way beaches and lots of hiking trails, this is where Split goes to relax. Ask at the TI (or ask any local) for tips on how to enjoy this area. You can walk around the mostly level perimeter of the peninsula, passing the Meštrović Gallery and two of the beaches (Ježinac and Bene) that are described next. Or, if you're up for a serious hike, hoof it up to the top of the peninsula for views back over the city. You can take the slower, more gradual route up through the lanes of the Varoš neighborhood, or find the steeper steps that lead up from the salty Matejuška harbor. If you're in great shape, figure about an hour hike up to the top (third) viewpoint, then another 45 minutes back down.

Hitting the Beach—Since it's more of a big city than a resort, Split's beaches aren't as scenic (and the water not as clear) as small towns elsewhere along the coast. The beach that's most popular—and crowded—is **Bačvice**, in a sandy cove just a short walk east of the main ferry terminal. As it's very shallow, it's especially popular with kids. After dark, it becomes a hopping meat-market nightlife zone for older "kids." You'll find less crowded beaches just to the east of Bačvice.

Or head in the other direction to Marjan, the peninsular city park, which is ringed with several sunbathing beaches. Along the southern edge of Marjan, just below the Meštrović Gallery, is a rocky but more local-feeling and less crowded beach called **Ježinac** (Croatian for "sea urchin"...be sure to wear water shoes). **Bene Beach** is along the northern edge of Marjan—reachable on bus #12 (the same one that goes to the Meštrović Gallery), by bike, or by foot (about a 45-minute walk from the Old Town).

Nightlife in Split

Strolling the Riva—Every night in Split, the sea of Croatian humanity laps at the walls of Diocletian's Palace along the town's pedestrian promenade. Choose a bench and watch life go by, or enjoy a drink at one of the many outdoor cafés.

Visiting Old Town Pubs—Wander the labyrinthine lanes of the Old Town to find the pub of your choice. The **Luxor** bar, right on the Peristyle, often features live music in the evening, with cushions filling the steps surrounding Diocletian's entry hall (if you sit on a cushion, you're expected to order a drink, but you can sit or stand elsewhere for free). Several atmospheric bars cluster along Majstora Jurja (just inside the Golden Gate and—facing outside—to the left about a block) and near Radić Brothers Square (Trg Braće Radića; from the square's statue of Marulić, enter the Old Town and bear right, following the beat).

Clubbing at Bačvice Beach—This family-friendly beach by day becomes a throbbing party area for young locals late at night. Since all Old Town bars have to close by 1:00 in the morning, night owls hike on over to the Bačvice crescent of clubs. The three-floor club complex is a cacophony of music, with the beat of each club melting into the next—all with breezy terraces overlooking the harbor.

Sleeping in Split

Split's sleeps are expensive. Since there aren't enough beds in peak season, many hoteliers are shameless about gouging their customers. Lower your expectations. Split also suffers from perhaps the worst nighttime noise of any destination in this book—bring earplugs, and always ask for a quiet room (if available). For locations, all of these are on the "Split Hotels & Restaurants" map on page 838; some also appear on the more detailed "Diocletian's Palace" map on page 822.

Near the Old Town

These good values are within a five-minute walk of the Old Town. They're nearly as convenient as the Old Town options, but cheaper. Note that none of these places has a full-time reception desk; call ahead to arrange your arrival time.

In the Lučac Neighborhood, East of the Old Town

The drab and dull Lučac neighborhood—which lines up along the busy street called Kralja Zvonimira—feels urban and a bit gritty, but it's handy to the Old Town. You'll find more Old World atmosphere (and the recommended Black Cat Bistro) on Petrova street, a block below the main road.

$$$ Villa Diana has six overpriced, mostly small rooms in a stone house over a restaurant (July–Aug: Sb-760 kn, Db-900 kn; May–June and Sept: Sb-630 kn, Db-765 kn; Oct: Sb-560 kn, Db-670 kn; cheaper Nov–April; pricier apartment also available, air-con, free Wi-Fi, Kuzmanića 3, tel. & fax 021/482-460, www.villadiana.hr, info@villadiana.hr).

Sleep Code

(5 kn = about $1, country code: 385, area code: 021)
S = Single, **D** = Double/Twin, **T** = Triple, **Q** = Quad, **b** = bathroom. The modest tourist tax (7 kn per person, per night, lower off-season) is not included in these rates. Hotels generally accept credit cards and include breakfast in their rates, while most *sobe* accept only cash and don't offer breakfast. English is spoken at all my recommended accommodations.

To help you sort easily through these listings, I've divided the rooms into three categories based on the price for a standard double room with bath in peak season:

$$$ Higher Priced—Most rooms 800 kn or more.
$$ Moderately Priced—Most rooms between 550–800 kn.
$ Lower Priced—Most rooms 550 kn or less.

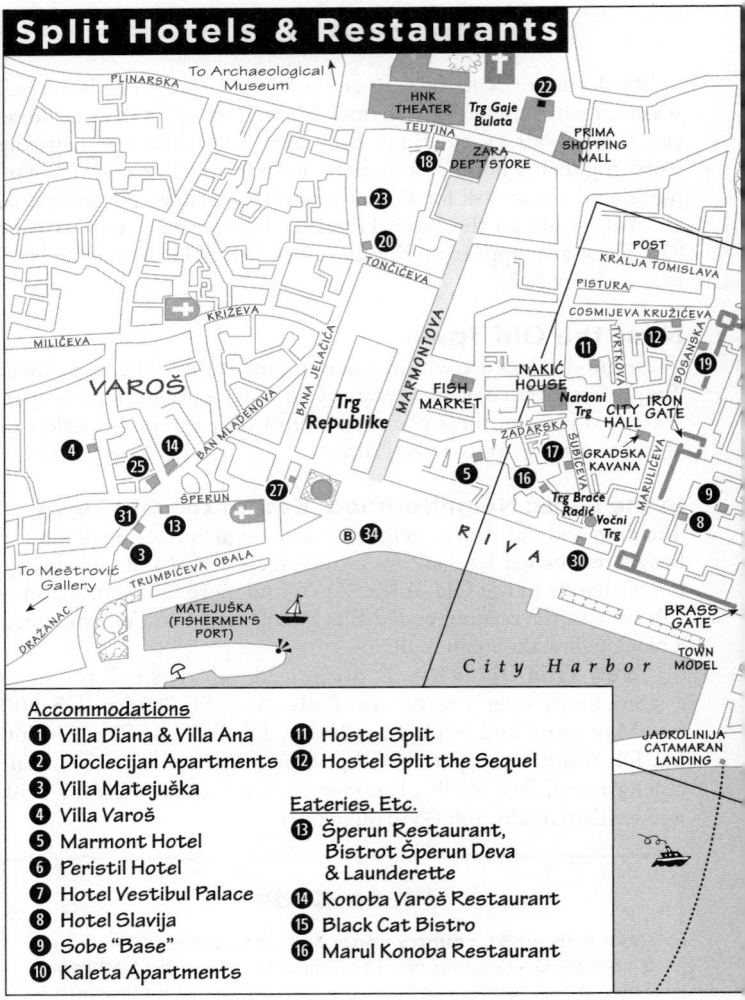

$$ Villa Ana, my favorite small hotel in Split, has five modern, comfortable rooms in a smart little freestanding stone house. If they're full, try another one of my listings (April–Oct: Sb-600 kn, Db-750 kn, Tb-850 kn; Nov–March: roughly 150 kn less; includes breakfast, air-con, free Wi-Fi, reception open sporadically 7:00–22:00, may be closed mid-Dec–mid-Jan, a few tight free parking spots out front; 2 long blocks east of Old Town up busy Kralja Zvonimira, follow the driveway-like lane opposite Koteks skyscraper to Vrh Lučac 16; tel. 021/482-715, fax 021/482-721,

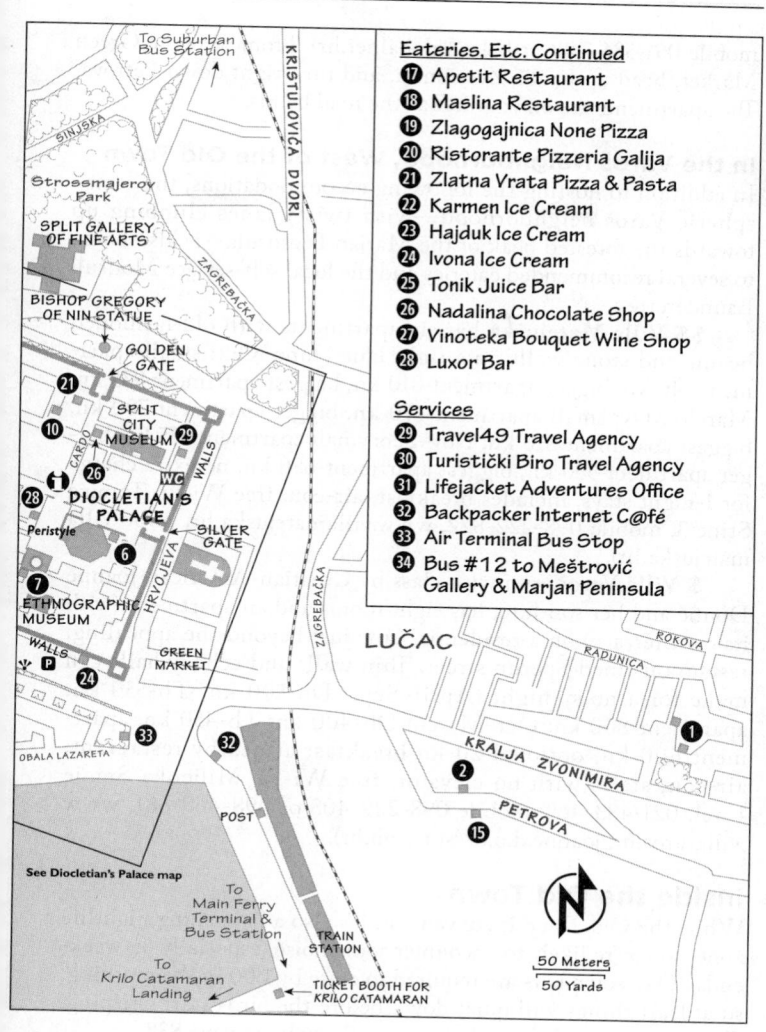

www.villaana-split.hr, info@villaana-split.hr, Danijel Bilobrk and helpful Branka).

$ Dioclecijan Apartments, run by Tomislav Skalić and his wife Ivana, has two small rooms and one apartment in a pleasant local neighborhood. The decor is a tasteful mix of new and traditional (April–Sept: Db-400 kn, apartment-590 kn; Oct–March: Db-280 kn, apartment-480 kn; 1-night stays cost 40 kn more in rooms or 75 kn more in apartment, prices soft, cash only, no breakfast, air-con, Petrova 19, Tomislav's mobile 091-537-1826, Ivana's

mobile 091-536-7486, tskalic@globalnet.hr). From near the Green Market, head up Kralja Zvonimira, and turn right down Petrova. The apartments are on your left as the road bends.

In the Varoš Neighborhood, West of the Old Town

In addition to hosting the following accommodations, the atmospheric Varoš neighborhood—with twisty lanes climbing up towards the forested peak of the Marjan Peninsula—is also home to several recommended eateries and the local self-service Modrulj Launderette.

$$ Villa Matejuška has six apartments with old-fashioned beams and stone walls on a tight lane (June–Oct: small apartment-740 kn, bigger apartment-810 kn, biggest apartment-935 kn; March–May: small apartment-670 kn, bigger apartment-700 kn, biggest apartment-810 kn; Nov–Feb: small apartment-555 kn, bigger apartment-590 kn, biggest apartment-680 kn; no extra charge for 1-night stays, includes breakfast, air-con, free Wi-Fi, Tomića Stine 3, mobile 098-222-822, www.villamatejuska.hr, info@villamatejuska.hr).

$ Villa Varoš, run with class by Croatian-American Joanne Đonlić and her son Jure, has eight rooms and an apartment (with its own terrace) on a residential lane just beyond the appealing, restaurant-lined Šperun street. Thin walls and echoey halls can make for a noisy night (April–Sept: Db-500 kn, Tb-550 kn, apartment-800 kn; Oct–March: Db-400 kn, Tb-450 kn, apartment-600 kn; optional 20-kn breakfast at nearby restaurant, air-con, stairs with no elevator, free Wi-Fi, Miljenka Smoje 1, tel. 021/483-469, mobile 098-229-408 or 098-469-681, www.villavaros.hr, joanne.d.o.o@st.t-com.hr).

Inside the Old Town

While the Old Town is convenient, it's also a happening nightlife zone, so you're likely to encounter some noise (especially on weekends). Old Town bars are required to close by 1:00 in the morning, so at least things will quiet down before the birds start chirping. To locate these accommodations, see the map on page 838.

$$$ Marmont Hotel is a very inviting new place offering four-star comfort, with 21 mod-feeling rooms in a relatively quiet corner of the Old Town (July–Sept: Sb-1,250 kn, Db-1,670 kn; April–June: Sb-1,070 kn, Db-1,530 kn; Oct–March: Sb-850 kn, Db-1,300 kn; breakfast-75 kn per person, air-con, elevator, free Wi-Fi, sun terrace, Zadarska 13, tel. 021/308-060, fax 021/308-070, www.marmonthotel.com, booking@marmonthotel.com).

$$$ Peristil Hotel has 12 classy rooms over a restaurant just steps from the couldn't-be-more-central square of the same name. Run by the Caktaš family, it's homey and convenient, if pricey

(May–Sept: Sb-1,000 kn, Db-1,200 kn; April and Oct: Sb-800 kn, Db-1,000 kn; Nov–March: Sb-700 kn, Db-900 kn; extra bed-100 kn, air-con, stairs with no elevator, free Wi-Fi, some noise from nearby bars, just behind TI and inside the Silver Gate at Poljana Kraljice Jelene 5, tel. 021/329-070, fax 021/329-088, www.hotelperistil.com, hotel.peristil@email.t-com.hr).

$$$ Hotel Vestibul Palace is the swankiest splurge in Split's Old Town, with modern decor in an old shell. Tucked in a corner just behind the entry vestibule on the upper level of Diocletian's Palace, this plush place offers seven rooms with maximum comfort and style for maximum prices. Throughout the day, you'll hear the harmonious voices of the *klapa* singers echoing up from the vestibule below (July–Sept: Sb-1,200–1,420 kn, Db-1,420–1,950 kn; April–June: Sb-1,050–1,250 kn, Db-1,250–1,800 kn; cheaper Oct–March, prices depend on room size and amenities, pricier suites also available, air-con, no elevator, free Internet access and Wi-Fi, valet parking-100 kn, Iza Vestibula 4, tel. 021/329-329, fax 021/329-333, www.vestibulpalace.com, info@vestibulpalace.com). They also have four more rooms in a nearby annex, called Villa Dobrić.

$$$ Hotel Slavija is a lesser value sharing a tiny square with some very popular late-night discos and cafés, so it can be noisy—especially on weekends (double-paned windows attempt, with only some success, to keep out the throbbing dance beat; try requesting a quieter back room). Each of its 25 stark, unimaginative rooms is a little different (June–Sept: Sb-800 kn, Db-1,000 kn, Tb-1,200 kn; March–May and Oct: 100 kn less per room; even cheaper Nov–Feb; 50–250 kn more for balcony or terrace, suites and huge family rooms available, air-con, pay Wi-Fi, a block from Radić Brothers Square at Buvinina 2—look for the low-profile sign at the top of a white staircase, tel. 021/323-840, fax 021/323-868, www.hotelslavija.com, info@hotelslavija.com).

$ Sobe "Base" has three of the nicest rooms in the Old Town. Tina and her dad Ivo offer many amenities unusual for this price range, including free Wi-Fi and Internet terminals in each room. You can't be more central: All of the colorful rooms—located over a gift shop—overlook the front steps of the cute little Jupiter's Temple (July–Aug: Db-510 kn; Sept–June: Db-450 kn; no extra charge for 1- or 2-night stays, cash only, no breakfast, air-con, Kraj Svetog Ivana 3, tel. 021/317-375, Tina's mobile 098-234-855, Ivo's mobile 098-361-387, www.base-rooms.com, mail@base-rooms.com). Because some bustling bars are just around the corner, expect some nighttime noise (even though the double-paned windows do their darnedest to provide silence).

$ Kaleta Apartments consists of two modern, stylish apartments run by the Raić family in a building squeezed between cafés

along a tight alley at the back of the Old Town. While it's a lively area, the good windows do a heroic job of keeping the noise to a minimum (June–Sept: Db-500 kn; Oct–May: Db-425 kn; cash only, no breakfast, air-con, free Wi-Fi and Internet terminal in each room, Majstora Jurja 4, mobile 099-509-4299, www.kaletaapartments.hr, kaletaapartments@email.t-com.hr).

$ *Other* Sobe: Though there are very few *sobe* inside Split's Old Town, there are plenty within a 10-minute walk. As in any coastal town, you can simply show up at the boat dock or bus station, be met by locals trying to persuade you into their rooms, and check out the best offer (about 250 kn for a double). Or you can try booking through a travel agency, such as **Travel49** or **Turistički Biro** (both listed earlier, under "Helpful Hints").

$ Hostel Split is centrally located just off Narodni Trg in the very heart of town. This small, youthful hostel has 23 beds in four cramped rooms, and a shared outdoor terrace to give everyone some much-needed breathing room. Run by a pair of Croat-Aussie women with the simple slogan "booze & snooze," it's Split's most central hostel option (bunk in 6-bed room—June–Sept: 150 kn; mid-April–May: 125 kn; Oct–mid-April: 110 kn; cash only, no breakfast, free Internet access and Wi-Fi, laundry service, excursions, 8 Narodni Trg, tel. 021/342-787, www.splithostel.com, info@splithostel.com). Their second location—"Hostel Split the Sequel"—has the same prices and a downstairs bar; it's a short walk away, still inside the Old Town (at Kružićeva 5).

Eating in Split

Split's Old Town has oodles of atmosphere, but the street called Šperun, just a couple of blocks west of the Old Town, has several characteristic *konoba*s (traditional restaurants) with good prices (including my first two listings, below). Service in Split's restaurants tends to be a bit grouchy, and you may be unceremoniously turned away if they're very busy (reservations are wise, especially for dinner). All of these eateries are marked on the "Split Hotels & Restaurants" map on page 838; some also appear on the more detailed "Diocletian's Palace" map on page 822.

Šperun Restaurant has a classy, cozy Old World ambience and a passion for good Dalmatian food. Animated owner Zdravko Banović and his son Damir serve a mix of Croatian and "eclectic Mediterranean," specializing in seafood. A "buffet" table of antipasti (starters) in the lower dining room shows you what you're getting, so you can select your ideal meal (not self-service—order from the waiter). This place distinguishes itself by offering a warm welcome and good food for reasonable prices (35–70-kn pastas, 50–120-kn meat and seafood dishes, daily 9:00–23:00, air-

con interior, a few sidewalk tables, reservations wise in summer, Šperun 3, tel. 021/346-999). Their annex across the street, **Bistrot Šperun Deva,** has a simpler and cheaper menu, lots of outdoor seating, and a handy à la carte breakfast for *sobe*-dwellers (30–40-kn salads, 50–60-kn plates, daily 8:00–23:00, Šperun 2).

Konoba Varoš, though bigger and more impersonal than Šperun, is beloved by natives and tourists alike for its great food. Serious waiters serve a wide range of Croatian cooking (including pastas, seafood, and meat dishes) under droopy fishnets in a slightly gloomy throwback interior (50–80-kn pastas, 60–110-kn main dishes, daily 9:00–24:00, lots of groups, reservations smart—busiest 20:00–22:00, Ban Mladenova 7, tel. 021/396-138).

Black Cat Bistro, popular with expats, is an innovative eatery offering a range of eclectic flavors, including Tex-Mex, Indian, and Thai—and all are reasonably well-executed. The menu also features several hearty salads that go beyond the cabbage-and-lettuce rut, and breakfast for *sobe*-dwellers (7–16-kn continental breakfast, 16–30-kn cooked breakfast). Choose between the inviting covered terrace out on a local-feeling lane, or the nondescript interior (45–65-kn salads and main dishes, 30–35-kn sandwiches and wraps, Mon–Sat 8:00–23:00, closed Sun, corner of Petrova and Šegvića, tel. 021/490-284). It's about a five-minute walk beyond the Old Town: From the Green Market, walk up Kralja Zvonimira and take the first right down Petrova (just past the big, white building); you'll see the restaurant on your right just after the road curves to the left.

Apetit is a new place serving up traditional, home-cooked Dalmatian cuisine in an appealingly modern, second-floor dining room. As there's no outdoor seating, this is a good option in bad weather (45–70-kn pastas, 60–110-kn main dishes; 90-kn daily special in summer includes soup, salad, and main dish; daily 9:00–24:00, Šubićeva 5, tel. 021/332-549).

Marul Konoba offers traditional Dalmatian cuisine with delightful outdoor seating on a fine Old Town square, or in an atmospheric, oak-and-stone interior (45–65-kn pastas, 65–110-kn main dishes, daily 8:00–24:00, Trg Braće Radića 2, tel. 021/339-068).

Maslina ("Olive"), an unpretentious family-run spot filled with locals, hides behind a shopping mall on the busy Marmontova pedestrian street. They serve a wide range of 40–70-kn pizzas and pastas, plus 65–110-kn meat and fish dishes (Tue–Sat 10:00–24:00, Sun–Mon 12:00–24:00, Teutina 1A, tel. 021/314-988, Pezo family). Approaching the top of Marmontova from the harbor, look for the low-profile wooden archway on the left beyond the café tables (just before the big Zara department store).

Take-Away Pizza: **Zlagogajnica None** ("Grandma's") is a stand-up or take-away pizza joint handy for a quick bite in the Old

Town. In addition to pizzas and bruschettas with various toppings, they serve up a pair of traditional pizza-like specialties (with crust on bottom and top, like a filled pizza): *viška pogača,* with tomatoes, onion, and anchovy; and *soparnik,* with a thin layer of spinach, onion, and olive oil. They can also make you a grilled sandwich—just point to what you want (10–30 kn, Mon–Sat 7:00–23:00, closed Sun, just outside Diocletian's Palace on the skinny street that runs along the wall at Bosanska 4, tel. 021/347-252).

Pizzerias: **Ristorante Pizzeria Galija,** at the west end of the Old Town, has a boisterous local following and good wood-fired pizza, pasta, and salads (35–50 kn, Mon–Sat 9:00–24:00, Sun 12:00–24:00, air-con, just a block off of the pedestrian drag Marmontova at Tončićeva 12, tel. 021/347-932; the recommended Hajduk ice-cream shop is nearby). **Zlatna Vrata** ("Golden Gate"), right in the Old Town, offers wood-fired pizzas and pasta dishes. The food and interior are nothing special, but there's wonderful outdoor seating in a tingle-worthy Gothic courtyard with pointy arches and lots of pillars (40–60 kn, Mon–Sat 7:00–24:00, closed Sun, just inside the Golden Gate and—as you face outside—up the skinny alley to the left, on Majstora Jurja, tel. 021/345-015).

Gelato: Split has several spots for delicious ice cream (*sladoled).* Most ice-cream parlors *(kuća sladoleda)* are open daily 8:00–24:00. To my taste buds, the following three spots are much better than the other options in town. Locals swarm to a pair of places near Trg Gaje Bulata (the modern shopping square—with the big Prima mall and modern-looking church—at the top end of the Marmontova pedestrian drag, just beyond the northwest corner of the Old Town): **Karmen** (hides behind the building in the middle of the square, facing the modern church on Kačićeva) and **Hajduk** (named for Split's soccer team; ask them to dip your cone in milk chocolate for no extra charge; a block west from the top of Marmontova and around the corner from Pizzeria Galija at Matošićeva 4). More central, at the east end of the Riva, look for **Ivona** (near entrance to Diocletian's cellars at Kaštelanska cesta 65).

Smoothies and Fruit Juices: For a healthier energy boost, head for **Tonik Juice Bar,** run by Croat-Aussie Stefanie. You can select from the diverse smoothie menu (25–30 kn), or they'll custom-make a juice combo to your liking (15–40 kn). In summer, they also serve light meals (25-kn wraps and salads, 25-kn muesli for breakfast, June–Sept daily 7:00–23:00, shoulder season 8:00–21:00, less in winter, near the launderette and Šperun street restaurants at Ban Mladenova 5, mobile 098-641-376).

Split Connections

Boat Connections

As the transport hub for the Dalmatian Coast, Split has good boat connections to most anywhere you want to go. Big car ferries use the main ferry terminal at the end of the harbor. The fast passenger catamarans dock a bit closer to the Old Town: The *Krilo* catamaran uses dock #11, which is along the pier halfway between the main ferry terminal and the Old Town. The Jadrolinija catamaran arrives and departs at the handy Obala Lazareta embankment just in front of the Old Town.

Schedules: Be warned that the following boat information is subject to change—always confirm before you make your plans. To check Jadrolinija schedules, see www.jadrolinija.hr; for *Krilo* catamaran schedules, see www.krilo.hr. Split's helpful Jadrolinija boat ticket office is in the main ferry terminal (open 24/7 in summer, daily 4:15–24:00 off-season, tel. 021/338-333; see "Arrival in Split," page 814), several smaller branch offices are scattered between there and the Old Town. You can buy *Krilo* tickets at the small Jadrolinija kiosk halfway along the harbor, near where that catamaran departs.

Buying Tickets: Tickets for the fast passenger catamarans (either *Krilo* or Jadrolinija) are not sold until 6:00 in the morning on the day of departure. As these boats can sell out quickly in peak season, buy your tickets in the morning (for the 11:30 boat, try to get your tickets by 9:30; for afternoon boats, buy your tickets by noon). If you're a passenger walking onto a car ferry, there's no need to buy tickets in advance. However, if you're driving onto a car ferry, it's smart to buy your tickets and line up early—ask locally about the best advice for your particular boat. For the connections below, I've listed the passenger fare.

Big Jadrolinija Car Ferries: These hulking boats depart twice weekly year-round; they leave Split early in the morning (at 6:30 or 7:00) and head south, stopping at **Stari Grad** on Hvar Island (20-min bus ride from Hvar town; 1.75 hrs, 40 kn; the catamarans described below are faster and take you right to Hvar town), **Korčula town** (5–6 hrs, 97 kn; the catamarans described next are faster and cheaper), and **Dubrovnik** (8–9.25 hrs, 115 kn). You can also sleep on the boat as it heads north to **Rijeka** (2/week, 11 hrs overnight, 162-kn deck passage, more if you want a bed). Fares are cheaper off-season.

Sailing Between Croatia and Italy

Many travelers are tempted to splice a little bit of Croatia into their Italian itinerary, or vice versa. But zipping across the Adriatic isn't as effortless as it seems. Most sea crossings involve an overnight on the boat, and the Italian towns best connected to Croatia—Ancona, Pescara, and Bari—are far from Italy's top sights. Plan thoughtfully. For example, if you're in northern Italy and want to sample Croatia, it's much easier to dip into Istria than it is to get all the way down to Croatia's Dalmatian Coast.

If you decide to set sail, you have several options, run by various companies. Split is the primary hub, but you can also go from other cities (usually Dubrovnik or Zadar; some international ferries also call at the small Dalmatian islands). Almost all boats go to Ancona, Italy, which is about two-thirds of the way up the Italian coast (on the calf of Italy's "boot"). Others go to Pescara, about 100 miles south of Ancona; and to Bari, near the southern tip of Italy (the "heel"). Most trips are overnight and last 8–10 hours, but there are faster daytime catamarans. Note that these connections are highly subject to change from year to year—consider doing an Internet search on your own to be confident you know all of your options.

Slow Night Boats: Figure about €55 per person for one-way deck passage (about 10–20 percent more in peak season, roughly July–Aug; sometimes even more on weekends). Onboard accommodation costs extra (about €20 per person for a *couchette* in a 4-berth compartment, €60–75 per person in 2-bed compartment with private shower and WC). Three different companies operate night boats to Italy:

Jadrolinija goes from Split to Ancona, from Zadar to Ancona, and from Dubrovnik to Bari (tel. 051/211-444 or 021/338-333, www.jadrolinija.hr).

Blue Line sails from Split to Ancona; on weekends in late July-Aug, it stops en route at either Stari Grad (on Hvar Island)

Other Boats to Hvar Island: Ideally, catch a boat heading to Hvar town, the most interesting part of the island. Speedy **Jadrolinija catamarans** run daily year-round from Split to Hvar town (June–Sept: 2/day, departing Split at 11:30 and 15:00, costs 42 kn in the morning or 22 kn in the afternoon; Oct–May: 1/day, departing Split at 14:00, 50–60 min to Hvar town, 22 kn; occasionally stops at Milna on Brač Island). A different company runs the similar ***Krilo*** **catamaran** directly from Split to Hvar town (June–Sept: departs Split daily at 17:00; Oct–May: departs Split daily at 16:00, 50–60 min to Hvar town, 22 kn). You can also reach Hvar Island on the **local car ferries** from Split; these are frequent but more expensive and less convenient, since they take you to the town of Stari Grad, across the island from Hvar town (3-7/day, 1.75

or Vis Island (can book at Split Tours travel agency in Split, tel. 021/352-533, www.blueline-ferries.com).

Azzurraline goes between Bari and Dubrovnik, and between Bari and Kotor, Montenegro (Croatian tel. 020/313-178, Montenegrin tel. 085/313-617, Italian tel. 080-592-8400, www.azzurraline.com).

Other companies serving these routes come and go each year—ask the Split TI or poke around Split's main terminal building to discover the latest.

Fast Daytime Boats: Some speedier crossings are available. But because these boats are faster and smaller, they're also weather-dependent—so they don't run off-season. In 2009, due to decreased demand, these boats ran only in August—check online for the 2010 schedule. **SNAV** connects Split and Ancona in just 4.5 hours; they also zip from Split to Stari Grad (on Hvar Island), then on to the Italian town of Pescara (6 hours total; either trip €60–100 one-way, depending on season; Croatian tel. 021/322-252, Italian tel. 081-428-5555, www.snav.it).

Trains Within Italy: From **Ancona,** you can catch a train to Venice (almost hourly, 4.25–5.25 hrs, most transfer in Bologna), Florence (almost hourly, 3–4.25 hrs, most transfer in Bologna), or Rome (8/day direct, 3–4.5 hrs). From **Pescara,** trains head to Rome (6/day direct, 3.75–4.25 hrs) and Florence (almost hourly, 4.5–5.25 hrs, transfer in Bologna). From **Bari,** you can hop a train to Naples (6/day, 3.75–6 hrs, most transfer in Caserta), Rome (3/day direct, 4.75 hrs), or Florence (8/day, 6.75–8.5 hrs, transfer in Rome or Bologna). For timetables, check www.ferroviedellostato.it or http://bahn.hafas.de/bin/query.exe/en (Germany's excellent all-Europe website).

Note that in Italian, Split is called "Spalato" (which is also the sound you hear if seasickness gets the best of you).

hrs, 38 kn; from Stari Grad, it's an easy 20-minute bus trip into Hvar town).

Other Boats to Korčula Island: Many of the same boats that go to Hvar town (described above) continue on to Korčula Island. The most convenient is the ***Krilo* catamaran,** which takes you right to Korčula town (June–Sept: departs Split daily at 17:00; Oct–May: departs Split daily at 16:00; 2.5–2.75 hrs to Korčula, 55 kn; in summer, it also stops en route at Prigradica on Korčula Island). The other boats leave you at Vela Luka, at the far end of Korčula Island from Korčula town (buses meet arriving boats to take passengers on the one-hour trip into Korčula town). The **Jadrolinija catamaran** goes from Split to Hvar town, then to Vela Luka (departs Split at 15:00 June–Sept, at 14:00 Oct–May, 1.75 hrs

to Vela Luka, 27 kn, occasionally stops at Mlina on Brač Island). Jadrolinija's slower **local car ferries** also go from Split to Vela Luka (1–2/day, 2.75 hrs, 46 kn).

Sailing to Italy: See the sidebar on previous pages.

Overland Connections

By Bus to: Zagreb (at least hourly, 5–8 hrs, depending on route, about 175–200 kn), **Dubrovnik** (almost hourly, less off-season, 4-5 hrs, 105–155 kn), **Korčula** (1 night bus leaves at 1:00 in the morning and arrives at 6:00, 125 kn), **Trogir** (at least hourly, 30 min, about 20 kn), **Zadar** (at least hourly, 3 hrs, about 75 kn), **Mostar** in Bosnia-Herzegovina (7/day, 4–4.5 hrs), **Međugorje** in Bosnia-Herzegovina (4/day, 3.5 hrs), **Rijeka** (10/day including some night buses, 8.5 hrs). Zagreb-bound buses sometimes also stop at **Plitvice** (confirm with driver and ask him to stop at the national park entrance; about 5/day, 4–6 hrs, 130–155 kn). Each of these routes is served by multiple companies, which charge slightly different rates, so the prices listed here are rough estimates. Reservations for buses are generally not necessary, but always ask about the fastest option—which can save hours of bus time. On busy peak-season days, it's smart to arrive about 30 minutes before your bus departs to buy tickets (or, better yet, come to the station to buy them earlier in the day). The generally English-speaking staff at Split's bus station gives out handy little schedules for popular journeys. Bus info: www.ak-split.hr, toll tel. 060-327-777.

By Train to: Zagreb (3/day, 2/day off-season, 5.5 hrs, plus 1 direct night train, 8 hrs), **Ljubljana** (1/day, 8.25 hrs, transfer in Zagreb). Train info: tel. 021/338-525 or toll tel. 060-333-444, www.hznet.hr.

Route Tips for Drivers: Driving in Dalmatia

If you're connecting Split with destinations to the north, the plan is simple: Just drive up out of the city's bowl-like setting and follow signs to the A-1 expressway north (toward Zagreb).

If you're heading south—such as to Dubrovnik, other Dalmatian Coast destinations, or Mostar—it's a bit more complicated, as the expressway southbound from Split is only partially completed. You have two options. The main **coastal road** twists slowly but picturesquely along some fantastic scenery, in an area dubbed the "Makarska Riviera." From the town of Drvenik, a ferry plods across to Sućuraj on the island of Hvar, where a surprisingly long and twisty road traverses the length of the island to Hvar town at the opposite end (taking a car ferry directly from Split to Stari Grad on Hvar island is a much faster and less stressful option). Continuing south, you'll wind up in the town of Ploče (described below).

To save some time, most travelers prefer to take the **expressway** at least part of the way. To do this, as you leave Split, follow blue expressway signs to *Dubrovnik*. You can take A-1 south as far as it goes; it cuts inland from the sea, running behind the tall coastal mountain range, near the Bosnian border. As of early 2010, A-1 was complete to the remote town of Vrgorac, about 100 km (60 miles) south of Split; a small section around the coastal town of Ploče, about 25 km (15 miles) south of Vrgorac, was also complete. To connect Vrgorac to Ploče, you'll transfer to rough and rugged surface roads, or—once A-1 is finished—stay on the expressway the entire way. (Note that if you're headed to Mostar, the fastest way from here is to pass into Bosnia-Herzegovina just south of Vrgorac, at Veliki Prolog, then follow signs to *Mostar* from there.)

Ploče has a ferry that runs to the town of Trpanj, on the landward side of the Pelješac Peninsula—not far from Orebić, where another boat plods across to Korčula town. If you're headed to Korčula and plan your timing to catch this ferry, it could save you some driving.

Just south of Ploče is the dramatic Neretva River Delta, a scenic and lush zone of farmland—and, likely, the end of the A-1 expressway. Here you'll hop on the main Dalmatian coastal road. Halfway along the delta, you'll see the turnoff to Metković, the gateway town on the main, heavily touristed road between Croatia and Mostar.

South of the Neretva River Delta—after twisting up to a high perch overlooking the delta—you'll reach a border crossing. Here begins an odd little stretch of coastline that's technically in Bosnian rather than Croatian territory. Have your passport ready, but don't panic—the border is generally a quick wave-through. You'll drive along the tiny Bosnian coast, then through the large town of Neum. Its giant concrete hotels are a clue to Neum's reputation as a cut-rate seaside destination that undersells its nearby Croatian coastal competitors. (Age-old tensions combined with pragmatic economic concerns have prompted some Croatian politicians to push for the construction of a bridge from the coastal road to the Pelješac Peninsula, allowing drivers to bypass Bosnia-Herzegovina entirely; you might see some work already going on for this project.)

After a few more miles, you'll cross back into Croatia, and shortly come to a crossroads where, if you like, you can turn right and detour a few minutes to the impressively walled little villages

of Ston and Mali Ston, at the base of the Pelješac Peninsula. If you're headed to Korčula, continue beyond Ston to the far end of the peninsula, where the ferry goes from Orebić to Dominče, near Korčula town.

After Ston, you're only about an hour from Dubrovnik. Along the way, you'll have fine views of Mljet and the Elaphite Islands. As you're getting close to Dubrovnik, you'll pass through the town of Trsteno, which has a good arboretum. When you cross the giant, modern bridge, you'll know Dubrovnik is just around the bend; for arrival tips, see "Arrival in Dubrovnik," on page 764.

KORČULA

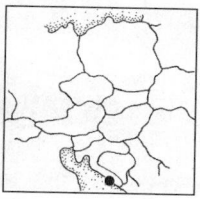

The island town of Korčula (KOHR-choo-lah) boasts an atmospheric Old Town, some surprisingly engaging museums, and a dramatic, fjord-like mountain backdrop. Korčula—while certainly on the tourist trail—has an often-appealing, occasionally frustrating backwater charm. All things considered, Korčula is the most enjoyable Back Door stopover on the Dalmatian Coast.

Like so many other small Croatian coastal towns, Korčula was founded by the ancient Greeks. It became part of the Roman Empire and was eventually a key southern outpost of the Venetian Republic. Four centuries of Venetian rule left Korčula with a quirky Gothic-Renaissance mix and a strong siesta tradition. Korčulans take great pride in the fact that Marco Polo was born here in 1254—the explorer remains the town's poster boy. Korčula is also known for its traditional *Moreška* sword dance.

You'll discover that there are two Korčulas: the tacky seaside resort and the historic Old Town. Savvy visitors ignore the tourist sprawl and focus on Korčula's medieval quarter, a mini-Dubrovnik poking into the sea on a picture-perfect peninsula. Tiny lanes branch off the humble main drag like ribs on a fishbone. This street plan is designed to catch both the breeze and the shade. All in all, this laid-back island village is an ideal place to take a vacation from your busy vacation.

Planning Your Time

Korčula deserves the better part of a day, but you'll quickly exhaust the town's sightseeing options. With a single day, spend the morning wandering the medieval Old Town and exploring the handful of tiny museums (many close for siesta in the early afternoon,

especially outside of peak season). In the afternoon, kick back at a café or restaurant and bask on the beach. If you're here on a Thursday, be sure to catch the performance of the *Moreška* dance (also Mon July–Aug). With a second day, really be on vacation.

Orientation to Korčula

(area code: 020)

The long, skinny island of Korčula runs alongside the even longer, skinnier Pelješac Peninsula. The main town and best destination on the island—just across a narrow strait from Pelješac—is also called Korčula.

Korčula town is centered on its compact **Old Town** (Stari Grad) peninsula, which is connected to the mainland at a big staircase leading to the Great Land Gate. In the area in front of this staircase, you'll find ATMs, travel agencies, the Jadrolinija ferry office, Internet cafés, the Konzum supermarket, a colorful outdoor produce market, and other handy tourist services.

Stretching to the south and east of the Old Town is **"Shell Bay,"** surrounded by a strip of tacky tourist shops and resort hotels. This seamier side of Korčula—best avoided—caters mostly to Brits and Germans here to worship the sun for a week or two.

To the west of Old Town is the serene waterfront street **Put Sv. Nikola,** where you'll find a few *sobe* (including Rezi Depolo's—see "Sleeping in Korčula," later), some inviting swimming areas, great views back on the Old Town, and more locals than tourists.

Tourist Information

Korčula's TI, run by Stanka Kraljević, is next to Hotel Korčula on the west side of the Old Town waterfront. Ask about the Korčula brochure and map (mid-June–Sept Mon–Sat 8:00–15:00 & 16:00–22:00, Sun 9:00–13:00; Oct–mid-June Mon–Sat 8:00–14:00, closed Sun, may be open Sun in shoulder season; tel. 020/715-701, www.korcula.net).

Arrival in Korčula

For all the details on getting to the Dalmatian Coast, see page 745.

By Boat: The big Jadrolinija ferries can arrive on either side of the Old Town peninsula, depending on the wind. (The Orebić passenger ferry and the fast catamarans generally dock at the west side of town.) From either side of the peninsula, it's just a two-minute

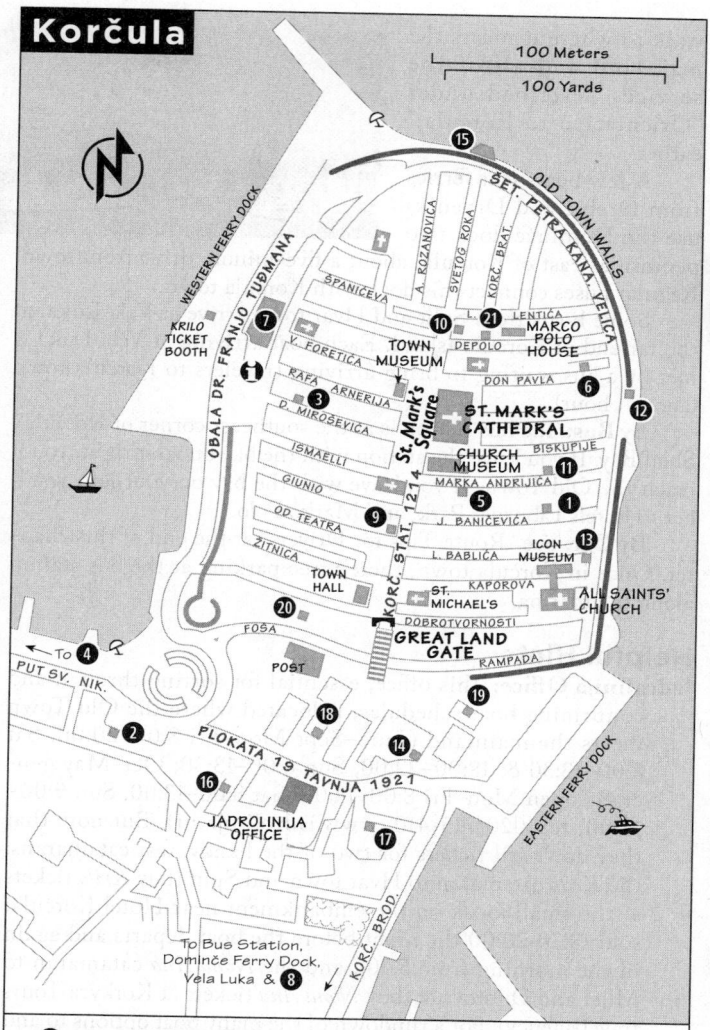

1. Apartments Lenni
2. Royal Apartments
3. Vitaić Family Rooms
4. To Depolo Rooms
5. Marco Polo Apartments
6. Portolan Rooms
7. Hotel Korčula
8. To Hotels Marko Polo, Liburna, Park & Bon Repos
9. Pizzeria Amfora
10. Adio Mare Restaurant
11. Konoba Marinero Rest.
12. Konoba Morski Konjic Rest.
13. Pizzeria Tedeschi
14. Konzum Supermarket
15. Buffet "Massimo"
16. Cukarin Sweet Shop
17. Kiwi Ice Cream
18. Atlas Travel
19. Korkyra Travel Agency
20. Moreška Outdoor Theater
21. Marco Polo Gift Shop

walk to where it meets the mainland and all of the services described under "Orientation to Korčula," earlier.

A few boats (car ferries from Orebić and Drvenik) use the Dominče dock two peninsulas east of Korčula, about a five-minute drive from town. Regular buses connect this dock with Korčula town.

Some boats from Split and Hvar town arrive at Vela Luka, at the far end of Korčula Island. Each boat arriving at Vela Luka is met by a bus waiting to bring arriving travelers to Korčula town (about 1 hour).

By Bus: The bus station is at the southeast corner of Korčula's Shell Bay. If you leave the station with the bay on your right, you'll reach the Old Town. If you leave with the bay on your left, you'll get to hotels Liburna, Park, and Marko Polo.

By Car: See "Route Tips for Drivers" at the end of this chapter. Once in Korčula town, there's free parking at the bus station along the marina.

Helpful Hints

Jadrolinija Office: This office, essential for sorting through and confirming boat schedules, is located where the Old Town meets the mainland (June–Sept Mon–Fri 8:00–20:00, Sat 8:00–13:30 & 18:00–22:00, Sun 6:00–13:30; Oct–May generally open Mon–Fri 8:00–14:00, Sat 8:00–13:00, Sun 9:00–13:00; tel. 020/715-410, www.jadrolinija.hr). But note that they don't sell tickets for two of the handy, fast catamarans: the *Krilo* catamaran to Hvar town and Split (buy *Krilo* tickets at the small kiosk on the embankment near Hotel Korčula; sold 18:30-20:00 the night before the boat departs and again in the morning from 5:30), and the *Nona Ana* catamaran to Mljet and Dubrovnik (buy *Nona Ana* tickets at Korkyra Tours travel agency). For a rundown of the many boat options to and from Korčula, see the end of this chapter.

Travel Agencies: Korčula has several travel agencies where you can book an excursion, browse shelves of books and souvenirs, and get information about car rental and other activities. The most established option is **Atlas Travel** (long hours daily in summer, closed for mid-afternoon break and sometimes closed Sun in shoulder season, open Mon–Sat mornings and closed Sun in winter; a few steps down from the Great Land Gate at Trg 19 Travnja, tel. 020/711-231; main office closed in winter, but second office around the corner stays open).

Korkyra Tours travel agency is also good (just outside the Great Land Gate, mobile 091-571-4355, www.korkyra.info, info@korkyra.info).

Festivals: Korčula has a couple of fun annual festivals. The Marco Polo Festival is in late June and early July, with lots of exhibitions, concerts, dances, and a parade with a costumed Marco Polo returning to his native Korčula after his long visit to China (www.marcopolofest.hr). And for several days at the beginning of September, Korčula remembers the great 1298 naval battle that took place just offshore, when the Genoese captured Marco Polo. The festivities culminate in a 14-ship reenactment, complete with smoke and sound effects.

Sights in Korčula

Korčula's few sights cluster within a few yards of each other in the Old Town. I've listed them roughly in order from the Great Land Gate (the Old Town's main entry) to the tip of the Old Town peninsula. All museums are officially "closed" November through April, but most will usually open by request (ask the TI to call for you...or just try knocking on the door).

▲▲*Moreška* Dance—Lazy Korčula snaps to life when locals perform a medieval folk dance called the *Moreška* (moh-REHSH-kah). The plot helps Korčulans remember their hard-fought past: A bad king takes the good king's bride, the dancing forces of good and evil battle, and there's always a happy ending (100 kn, June–mid-Oct every Thu at 21:00, July–Aug also Mon at 21:00, in outdoor theater next to the Great Land Gate—to the left as you face the gate, or in a nearby congress center if bad weather; buy tickets from travel agency, at your hotel, or at the door).

▲Great Land Gate (Veliki Revelin)—A noble staircase leads up to the main entrance to the Old Town. Like all of the town's towers, it's adorned with the Venetian winged lion and the coats of arms of the doge of Venice (left) and the rector of Korčula (right; the offset coat of arms below was the rector who later renovated the gate). Climb the tower to visit a small exhibit with costumes and photos from the *Moreška* dance, then head up to the top level to enjoy panoramic town views (15 kn, daily 10:00–16:00, until 19:00 in summer, generally closed Nov–May, English descriptions).

Just inside the gate is **Franjo Tuđman Square,** renamed in 2001 for the first president of an independent Croatia (see

page 750). During the war, Tuđman was considered a hero. In later years, it was revealed that he had held secret negotiations with the Serbian leader Slobodan Milošević about the postwar division of Bosnia-Herzegovina. As the key figure of a recent-but-bygone era that combined both joy and terror, Tuđman remains controversial in today's Croatia. But members of his party are still in power and hold local offices throughout the country, and they sometimes adorn a square or street with his name.

On the left inside the gate is the 16th-century **Town Hall and Rector's Palace.** The seal of Korčula (over the center arch) symbolizes the town's importance as the southernmost bastion of the Venetian Republic: St. Mark standing below three defensive towers. The little church on the other side of the square is dedicated to **St. Michael** (Crkva Sv. Mihovila). Throughout Croatia, many towns have churches dedicated to St. Michael just inside the town gates, as he is believed to offer saintly protection from enemies. Notice that a passageway connects the church to the building across the street—home to the Brotherhood of St. Michael, one of Korčula's many religious fraternal organizations (see "Icon Museum," later).

• *Now begin walking up the...*

Street of the Korčulan Statute of 1214 (Ulica Korčulanskog Statuta 1214)—This street is Korčula's backbone—in more ways than one: While most medieval towns slowly evolved with twisty, mazelike lanes, Korčula was carefully planned to resemble a fish skeleton. The streets to the west (left) of this one are straight, to allow the refreshing northwesterly Maestral winds into town. To the east (right), they're curved (notice you can't see the sea) to keep out the bad-vibe southeasterly Jugo winds.

The street's complicated name honors a 1214 statute—the oldest known written law in Central Europe—with regulations about everyday life and instructions on maintaining the city walls, protecting nature, keeping animals, building a house, and so on. As you head up the street, look up to notice some interesting decorations on the houses' upper floors.

• *If you continue up the street, you'll reach St. Mark's Square (Trg Sv. Marka). From here, you're a few steps from the next four sights.*

▲St. Mark's Cathedral (Katedrala Sv. Marka)—Korčula became a bishopric in the 14th century. In the 19th century—36 bishops later—the Habsburgs decided to centralize ecclesiastical power in their empire, and they removed Korčula's bishop. The town still has this beautiful "cathedral"—but no bishop. On the ornately decorated tympanum above the main door, you'll see another Venetian statue of St. Mark (flanked by Adam and Eve). Inside, above the main altar, is an original Tintoretto painting (recently restored in Zagreb). At the altar to the left, find the statue

of St. Rok (better known by his Italian name, San Rocco) pointing to a wound on his leg. This popular-in-Croatia French saint is believed to help cure disease. As you leave, notice the weapons on the back wall, used in some of the pivotal battles that have taken place near strategically situated Korčula (free, May–Oct daily 9:00–14:00 & 17:00–19:00, may be open all day long in peak season, closed during church services, generally closed Nov–April but may be open Mon–Fri 9:00–12:00 after Easter).

▲Church Museum (Opatska Riznica)—This small museum has an eclectic and fascinating collection. Go on a scavenger hunt for the following items: a ceremonial necklace from Mother Teresa (who came from Macedonia, not far from here—she gave this necklace to a friend from Korčula), some 12th-century hymnals, two tiny drawings by Leonardo da Vinci, a coin collection (including a 2,400-year-old Greek coin minted here in Korčula), some Croatian modern paintings, three amphora jugs, and two framed reliquaries with dozens of miniscule relics (20 kn; July–Aug daily 9:00–19:00, sometimes later; May–June and Sept–Oct Mon–Sat 9:00–14:00 & 17:00–20:00, closed Sun except sometimes open in the morning; generally closed Nov–April but may be open Mon–Fri 9:00–12:00 after Easter).

▲Town Museum (Gradski Muzej)—Housed in an old mansion, this museum does a fine job of bringing together Korčula's various claims to fame. It's arranged like a traditional Dalmatian home: shop on the ground floor, living quarters in the middle floors, kitchen on top. Notice that some of the walls near the entry have holes in them. Archaeologists are continually doing "digs" into these walls to learn how medieval houses here were built.

On the ground floor is a lapidarium, featuring fragments of Korčula's stone past (see the first-century Roman amphora jugs). Upstairs is a display on Korčula's long-standing shipbuilding industry, including models of two modern steel ships built here (the town still builds ship parts today). There's also a furnished living room and, in the attic, a kitchen. This was a smart place for the kitchen—if it caught fire, it was less likely to destroy the whole building. Notice the little WC in the corner. A network of pipes took kitchen and other waste through town and out to sea (20 kn, limited posted English information—pick up the free English brochure at entry; mid-June–Aug Mon–Sat 9:30–21:00, closed Sun; Sept–mid-June Mon–Fri 8:00–15:00—if it's locked, try knocking, closed Sat–Sun; tel. 020/711-420).

Marco Polo's House (Kuća Marka Pola)—Korčula's favorite son is the great 13th-century explorer Marco Polo. Though Polo sailed under the auspices of the Venetian Republic, and technically was a Venetian (since the Republic controlled this region), Korčulans proudly claim him as their own. Marco Polo was the first Westerner to sail to China, bringing back amazing stories and exotic goods (like silk) that Europeans had never seen before. After his trip, Marco Polo fought in an important naval battle against the Genoese near Korčula. He was captured, taken to Genoa, and imprisoned. He told his story to a cellmate, who wrote it down, published it, and made the explorer a world-class and much-in-demand celebrity. To this day, kids in swimming pools around the world try to find him with their eyes closed.

Today, Korčula is the proud home to "Marco Polo's House"—actually a more recent building on the site of what may or may not have been his family's property. The house is in poor repair, but most of the building has been purchased by the city to open to visitors. Currently you can just climb the stubby tower (for an uninspiring view), but in the future, the town hopes to turn the complex into a world-class museum about the explorer (15 kn, daily July–Aug 9:00–21:00, Easter–June and Sept–Oct 9:00–13:30 & 15:30–19:00, closed Nov–Easter, just north of cathedral on—where else?—ulica Depolo).

Across the street from the house's entrance, you'll find a clever **Marco Polo gift shop** selling various items relating to the explorer—herbs, brandies, honey, ice cream, and so on. Each one comes with a little tag telling a legend about M.P.—for example, how the word "million" was based on his middle name, Emilio (because no existing word was superlative enough for his discoveries). There's even a life-size Marco Polo and Kublai Khan keeping an eye on the cash register (daily in summer 9:00–24:00, progressively shorter hours and closed for mid-afternoon break off-season, closed in winter, ulica Depolo 1A, mobile 091-189-8048).

▲Icon Museum (Zbirka Ikona)—Korčula is known for its many brotherhoods—centuries-old fraternal organizations that have sprung up around churches. The Brotherhood of All Saints has been meeting every Sunday after Mass since the 14th century, and they run a small but interesting museum of icons. Maja, who lives upstairs, speaks no English but will point out what's worth seeing. These golden religious images were brought back from Greece in the 17th century by Korčulans who had been fighting the Ottomans on a Venetian warship (12 kn, hours depend on demand, but generally May–Oct daily 10:00–14:00 & 17:00–20:00, may be open all day long in peak season, closed Nov–April—but try ringing the bell, on Kaprova ulica at the Old Town's southeast tip).

Brotherhoods' meeting halls are often connected to their

church by a second-story walkway. Use this one to step in to the Venetian-style **All Saints' Church** (Crkva Svih Svetih). Under the loft in the back of the church, notice the models of boats and tools—donated by Korčula's shipbuilders. Look closely at the painting to the right of the altar. See the guys in the white robes kneeling under Jesus? That's the Brotherhood, who commissioned this painting.

▲Old Town Walls—For several centuries, Korčula held a crucial strategic position as one of the most important southern outposts of the Venetian Republic (the Republic of Dubrovnik started at the Pelješac Peninsula, just across the channel). The original town walls around Korčula date from at least the 13th century, but the fortifications were extended (and new towers built) over several centuries to defend against various foes of Venice—mostly Ottomans and pirates.

The most recent tower dates from the 16th century, when the Ottomans attacked Korčula. The rector and other VIPs fled to the mainland, but a brave priest remained on the island and came up with a plan. All of the women of Korčula dressed up as men, and then everybody in town peeked over the wall—making the Ottomans think they were up against a huge army. The priest prayed for help, and the strong northerly Bora wind blew. Not wanting to take their chances with the many defenders and the weather, the Ottomans sailed away, and Korčula was saved.

By the late 19th century, Korčula was an unimportant Habsburg beach town, and the walls had no strategic value. The town decided to quarry the top half of its old walls to build new homes (and to improve air circulation inside the city). Though today's walls are half as high as they used to be, the town has restored many of the towers, giving Korčula its fortified feel. Each one has a winged lion—a symbol of Venice—and the seal of the rector of Korčula when the tower was built.

Activities in Korčula

Swimming—The water around Korčula is clean and suitable for swimming. You'll find pebbly beaches strewn with holiday-goers all along Put Sv. Nikola, the street that runs west from the Old Town. While this shoreline doesn't have much flat land for sunning yourself, you can generally find a relatively comfy rock to recline on. Another good swimming spot is at the very end of the Old Town peninsula. Or trek to the beaches near Lumbarda (described next).

Lumbarda—For a break from Korčula town, venture about three miles southeast to Lumbarda, a tranquil end-of-the-road village. Lumbarda is known for its wine (the sweet *grk* dessert wine) and

for its beaches: the pebbly Bilin Žal, just east of town; and the sandy Vela Pržina, about a 20-minute walk through vineyards to the south. While not worth going out of your way for, Lumbarda and its beaches are fun to explore on a lazy vacation day. From Korčula town, you can get to Lumbarda by water taxi (50 kn) or by bus (hourly Mon–Sat, fewer buses Sun, 15 min, 10 kn).

Excursions—Various companies offer day-long excursions to nearby destinations (generally available June–Oct, each itinerary offered 2–4 times per week). The most popular options are Dubrovnik and the national park on Mljet Island. The biggest, most established operation is Atlas (see "Helpful Hints," earlier). Several new, more active tour companies have popped up recently, offering canoe trips, snorkeling, kayaking, and other "adventures"—look for fliers around town (Sokol is well-regarded, www.korcula-adventures.com).

Other Activities—You'll see travel agencies all over town where you can rent a car, bike, scooter, boat, sea kayak, or anything else you want for some vacation fun. Local captains take tourists on cruises to nearby bays and islands to get out on the water, swim, and enjoy a local-style "fish picnic." Inquire at any travel agency, or simply talk to a captain at the harbor (near the eastern ferry dock, at Shell Bay; figure about 200 kn per hour regardless of number of people). If you're a wine-lover, consider hiring a driver to take you on a tour of Korčula Island, including stops at some wineries (ask at TI or travel agency).

Sleeping in Korčula

Korčula has only five hotels—all owned by the same company (which is, in turn, government-run). The lack of competition keeps quality low and prices ridiculously high—which makes *sobe* a particularly good alternative.

Sobe

My favorite *sobe* in Korčula offer similar comfort to the hotels at far lower prices—and most of them have TVs and air-conditioning, to boot. These are your best *sobe* options, well worth reserving ahead.

$$ Apartments Lenni is run by Lenni and Periša (Peter) Modrinić, both of whom are outgoing and speak good English. They rent three tight, modern, comfortable rooms (one with a private bathroom across the hall) and three apartments in a nicely

Sleep Code

(€1 = about $1.40, country code: 385, area code: 020)
S = Single, **D** = Double/Twin, **T** = Triple, **Q** = Quad, **b** = bathroom. The modest tourist tax (€1 per person, per night, lower off-season) is not included in these rates. Unless otherwise noted, hotels accept credit cards and include breakfast in their rates, while most *sobe* accept only cash and don't offer breakfast. The accommodations quote their prices in euros, but you'll pay in kunas. Everyone listed here speaks at least enough English to make a reservation (or knows someone nearby who can translate).

To help you sort easily through these listings, I've divided the rooms into three categories based on the price for a standard double room with bath in peak season:

$$$ Higher Priced—Most rooms €100 or more.
$$ Moderately Priced—Most rooms between €55–100.
$ Lower Priced—Most rooms €55 or less.

renovated house right in the heart of the Old Town. Since they live off-site, confirm your reservation the day before and let them know your arrival time (July–Aug: Db-€60, apartment-€80; shoulder season: Db-€45, apartment-€60; cheaper off-season, 2-night minimum unless it's not too busy, cash only, air-con, near Konoba Marko Polo restaurant at Jakova Baničevića 13, tel. 020/711-400, mobile 091-551-6592, www.ikorcula.net/lenni, perisa.modrinic@du.t-com.hr).

$$ Royal Apartments are some of the most hotelesque (and most expensive) rooms in town. The five apartments are classy and new-feeling, making the place feel more like a small hotel with no real reception desk—arrange your arrival time carefully (July–Aug: small apartment-€80, big apartment-€90; June and Sept: small apartment-€70, big apartment-€80; closed Oct–May, no extra charge for 1- or 2-night stays, cash only, air-con, well-marked with green awning just west of Old Town at Trg Petra Šegedina 4, mobile 098-184-0444, royalapt@ica.net, Jelavić family—Annamaria speaks English, but Marko doesn't).

$$ The **Vitaić family** is a father-and-sons operation renting three rooms in the Old Town (July–Aug: Db-€65; Sept–June: Db-€45; 10 percent more for 1- or 2-night stays, cash only, air-con, pay Wi-Fi, Dinko Mirošević 8, tel. 020/715-312, mobile

098-932-7670, www.familyvitaic.com, info@familyvitaic.com).

$ Rezi and Andro Depolo, probably distant relatives of Marco, rent four comfy rooms on the bay west of the Old Town. Three of the rooms offer beautiful views to the Old Town, and the five-minute stroll into town is pleasant and scenic. English-speaking Rezi is very friendly and works to make her guests feel welcome (July–Aug: Db-€40; Sept–June: Db-€35; room with kitchen-€5 more, 30 percent more for 1-night stays, continental breakfast-€4, big breakfast-€5, cash only, air-con, Put Sv. Nikola 43; walk along waterfront from Old Town with bay on your right, look for *Apartments Depolo* sign at the yellow house set back from the street, just before the two monasteries; tel. 020/711-621, mobile 098-964-3687, tereza.depolo@du.t-com.hr).

$ Anka Portolan, with her helpful English-speaking granddaughter Vesna, rents four fine, older-feeling rooms perfectly located near the wall in the Old Town (July–Aug: Db-€35, small apartment-€45, bigger apartment-€50; Sept–June: Db-€30, small apartment-€35, bigger apartment-€40; 30 percent more for 1- or 2-night stays, cash only, air-con, ulica Don Pavla Poše 7, tel. 020/711-711, vesna.stankovic.14@gmail.com).

$ Marco Polo Apartments has four apartments in the Old Town (July–Aug: Db-€50; Sept-June: Db-€40; cash only or pay online through PayPal, air-con, ulica Marka Andrijica, mobile 099-686-3717, British tel. +44-794-620-8177, www.marcopolo-apartments.com, booking@marcopolo-apartments.com).

$ *Booking* Sobe *Through an Agency:* While you can walk along Put Sv. Nikola and generally find a fine deal on a private room, you can also book one through one of Korčula's travel agencies for an additional 20 percent (figure Db-€35–50 in high season, €20–35 off-season, 30 percent more for 1- or 2-night stays). For information on two agencies—Atlas and Korkyra—see "Helpful Hints," earlier.

Hotels

All five of Korčula's hotels are owned by HTP Korčula. If you don't want to stay in a *soba,* these are the only game in town. You can reserve rooms at any of them through the main office (tel. 020/726-336, fax 020/711-746, www.korcula-hotels.com, marketing@htp-korcula.hr). I've listed peak-season prices with breakfast only; rates are progressively lower the further you get into off-season. You can pay €10 more per person for half-board (dinner at the hotel). It's much cheaper to stay a week or longer. There's a long-term plan to renovate all of these hotels, but so far the Marko Polo is the only one that's seen any progress (and the only one that has air-conditioning).

$$$ Hotel Korčula has by far the best location, right on the waterfront alongside the Old Town. It has a fine seaside terrace restaurant and friendly staff, even if the 20 rooms are outmoded and waaay overpriced. The rooms are on two floors: The more expensive "first-floor" rooms (actually on the third floor) have big windows and sea views; the cheaper "second-floor" rooms (actually on the fourth floor) have tiny windows and no views (July–Aug: Sb-€120, Db-€160; mid-May–June and Sept-mid-Oct: Sb-€85–105, Db-€120–140; cheaper off-season, reception tel. 020/711-078).

$$$ Hotel Marko Polo, the only one of the chain that has been renovated, has 94 crisp rooms, air-conditioning, and an elevator. All of this makes it the town's only real "splurge"...and it's priced accordingly (July–Aug: Sb-€150, Db-€200; mid-May-June and Sept–mid-Oct: Sb-€105–130, Db-€150–170; cheaper off-season, reception tel. 020/726-004).

$$$ ***Other Hotels:*** Three more hotels cluster a 15-minute walk away, around the far side of Shell Bay. All are rough around the edges, overpriced, and relatively inconvenient to the Old Town, but they share a nice beach. **Hotel Liburna,** with a clever split-level design that reflects the skyline of the Old Town, has 109 rooms, most of them accessible by elevator; half the rooms face the sea and cost an additional 10 percent (July–Aug: Sb-€120, Db-€160; mid-May–June and Sept–mid-Oct: Sb-€85–105, Db-€120–140; cheaper off-season; reception tel. 020/726-006). Dreary **Hotel Park** has 153 cheaper rooms (reception tel. 020/726-100). The fifth hotel, **Hotel Bon Repos**—another 15 minutes by foot from the Old Town—is, in every sense, the last resort.

Eating in Korčula

Korčula is awash in interchangeable seafood restaurants. These are all good options, but everything in town is pretty similar—make your decision based on atmosphere and what looks best to you. The price ranges listed below don't include top-end seafood splurges (which are normally listed in menus by the 100-gram unit or by the kilogram). Note that almost all of these eateries close from about November to Easter.

Pizzeria Amfora, on a side lane off the people-parade up Korčula's main drag in the Old Town, features delicious and well-priced pastas and pizzas. Squeeze into the small dining room or enjoy the sidewalk tables (50–70-kn pizzas and pastas, 60–100-kn main dishes, daily 11:00–24:00, closed 15:00–18:00 and Sun dinner in shoulder season, ulica od Teatra 4, tel. 020/711-739).

Adio Mare, with fine seafood, may have the best decor in town: a cavernous stone dining room with long, shared tables and

a thick vine scaling one wall. Or climb the stairs and cross the little bridge to the delightful rooftop garden terrace (50–110-kn main dishes, well-described menu, daily 17:30–24:00, sometimes also 12:00–14:00 in peak season, on the main drag just past Marco Polo's House, tel. 020/711-253).

Konoba Marinero has pleasantly nautical decor, outdoor tables on an atmospherically tight lane, and a simple menu of Dalmatian specialties (60–110-kn main dishes, Easter–Oct daily 11:00–24:00, Marka Andrijića 13, tel. 020/711-170).

Along the Seawall: Various restaurants line up scenically along the Old Town's eastern seawall, offering al fresco dining with salty views. Their tables, spilling out along the seafront, are ideal for romantic harborside meals. For traditional fare, consider **Konoba Morski Konjic** ("Moorish Seahorse")—though the crank-'em-out food is disappointing and the service can be jaded (60–110-kn main dishes, 10-kn cover, daily 8:00–24:00). For something more affordable, try **Pizzeria Tedeschi,** which serves up good pizzas closer to the base of the peninsula (long hours daily, tel. 020/711-586).

Cheaper Options Around Shell Bay: Prices inside the Old Town are the highest in Korčula. But several cheaper eateries lie just outside the Old Town. Window-shop menus along the harbor, then hang a left at the bus station and continue up the road toward the big resort hotels. You'll find plenty of cafés, pizzerias, and *konoba*s (traditional restaurants), most with outdoor seating.

Picnics: Just outside the main gate, you'll find a lively produce market and a big, modern, air-conditioned **Konzum** supermarket (Mon–Sat 7:00–20:30, Sun 8:00–20:00). A short stroll from there down Put Sv. Nikola takes you to rocky seafront perches with the best Korčula views. Otherwise, there are many inviting picnic spots along the Old Town embankment.

A Scenic Drink: The best setting for drinks is at **Buffet "Massimo,"** a youthful-feeling cocktail bar in a city-wall tower at the very tip of the Old Town peninsula. You can have a drink on one of three levels: the downstairs bar, the main-floor lounge, or climb the ladder (at your own risk) to the tower-top terrace (terrace is only for cocktail-sippers—no beer or wine). If you're up top, notice the simple dumbwaiter for hauling up drinks (35–60-kn cocktails, daily in summer 18:00–2:00 in the morning, shoulder season 17:30–1:00 in the morning, closed Nov–April, tel. 020/715-073).

Sweet Shop: For some good (if pricey) local sweets, stop by **Cukarin,** which sells tasty traditional cookies such as the *amareta* almond cake and the walnut-cream-filled *klašun*. They also sell homemade wine, liqueur, honey, and jam (Mon–Sat 8:30–12:00 & 17:30–20:00, closed Sun and Jan–Feb, a block behind the Jadrolinija office on ulica Hrvatske Bratske Zajednice, tel. 020/711-055).

Ice Cream: My favorite *sladoled* in Korčula is at **Kiwi** (just up the lane across from Konzum supermarket, open long hours daily).

Korčula Connections

Korčula is reasonably well-connected to the rest of the Dalmatian Coast by boat, but service becomes sparse in the off-season. If you're here during a lull in the sailing schedule, buses are your ticket out of town (making the short crossing to the Pelješac Peninsula on the Dominče–Orebić ferry). No matter when you travel, it's smart to carefully study current boat schedules, as they are always subject to change.

Boat Connections

Boats big and small depart from the embankment surrounding Korčula's Old Town peninsula. Which side of the peninsula a boat uses can depend on the weather—be flexible and inquire locally about where to meet your boat. Some boats leave from other parts of the island, most notably the town of Vela Luka (at the opposite tip of the island, a 1-hour bus ride from Korčula town—described later). Other boats, including the car ferry to Orebić (described later, under "Route Tips for Drivers"), leave from the Dominče dock, about a five-minute drive east of Korčula town.

Big Jadrolinija Car Ferries: From Korčula town, these huge, handy vessels go north, to **Stari Grad** on Hvar Island (20-min bus ride from Hvar town; 2/week, 3.5 hrs; the catamaran described next is faster and takes you right to Hvar town) and **Split** (2/week, 5–6 hrs—catamaran described next is faster and cheaper); or south, to **Sobra** on Mljet Island (1.25-hr bus ride from the national park, 2-3/week June–Sept, none Oct–May, 2 hrs) and **Dubrovnik** (5/week July–Sept, 4/week June, 2/week Oct–May, 3–4 hrs).

Speedy *Krilo* Catamaran from Korčula Town to Hvar Town and Split: A speedy catamaran called *Krilo* leaves Korčula town at 6:00 in the morning every day year-round, and zips to Hvar town and Split (to Hvar: 1.5 hrs, 33 kn; to Split: 2.5–2.75 hrs, 55 kn; in summer, it also stops en route at Prigradica on Korčula Island). In Korčula, tickets for the *Krilo* are sold at a small waterfront kiosk near Hotel Korčula—not at the Jadrolinija office. While you can buy *Krilo* tickets starting a half-hour before the boat departs (at 5:30), they can sell out—it's much better to buy them the night before (they're sold at the kiosk between 18:30 and 20:00). Since it returns from Split and Hvar the same afternoon, this extremely handy catamaran allows you to effortlessly day-trip to either place (see "Split Connections" on page 845). For the latest schedule, see www.krilo.hr.

Speedy *Nona Ana* Catamaran to Mljet and Dubrovnik: In July and August, this convenient boat zips travelers from Korčula to Polače (on Mljet Island, handy to the national park there), then to Sobra (a less-appealing spot on Mljet) and on to Dubrovnik (4/week, generally departs Korčula at 16:00; to Polače: 1 hr, 30 kn; to Dubrovnik: 2.75 hrs, 55 kn). Unfortunately, the boat doesn't serve Korčula at other times (Sept–June). Confirm schedules at www.gv-line.hr, and buy tickets at Korkyra Tours travel agency (see "Helpful Hints," earlier).

From Vela Luka to Hvar Town and Split: There are additional boats to points north, but they usually require a very early bus from Korčula town (departing at 4:00 in the morning) to the port at Vela Luka, an hour away at the other end of the island. A Jadrolinija **fast catamaran** goes daily from Vela Luka to both Hvar town and Split (Mon–Sat departs at 5:30, Sun at 8:00; to Hvar: 45 min, 22 kn; to Split: 1.75 hrs, 27 kn). A much slower **car ferry** also travels daily from Vela Luka to Split (1–2/day, 2.75 hrs, 46 kn, does not stop at Hvar town). Since reaching Vela Luka from Korčula town is a hassle, carefully confirm these boat schedules and understand all your options (at the Korčula TI or Jadrolinija office) before you get up early to make the trip.

Bus Connections

All buses from Korčula town (except those to Vela Luka) first drive to Dominče, where they meet the car ferry to cross over to Orebić, on the Pelješac Peninsula. Don't be surprised if you have to get off the bus, walk onto the ferry, and meet a different bus across the channel. It takes just over an hour to drive the length of the Pelješac Peninsula and meet the main coastal road.

From Korčula Town by Bus to: Dubrovnik (peak season: 2/day, 3.5 hrs; off-season: Mon–Sat 1/day with an early departure, Sun 2/day; about 100 kn), **Zagreb** (1/day, 9–13.5 hrs depending on route), **Split** (1/day, 5 hrs, same bus goes to Zagreb), **Vela Luka** (at far end of island, Mon–Fri 7/day, Sat 6/day, Sun 4/day, 1 hr, first bus at 4:00 gets you to the early-morning ferries—see above).

Shuttle Bus to Dubrovnik: Korkyra Tours travel agency runs a handy minibus that costs only slightly more than the bus and takes you right to your accommodations in Dubrovnik (125 kn one-way plus 10 kn/bag, runs Mon–Fri at 8:00 year-round, Sat–Sun by request only, 2 hrs, includes light breakfast and room-finding help if needed, reserve ahead, mobile 091-571-4355, www.korkyra.info, info@korkyra.info).

Route Tips for Drivers: Between Korčula and the Mainland

The island of Korčula is connected to the mainland by a small car ferry that runs between Dominče—about a mile east of Korčula town—and Orebić, across the channel on the Pelješac Peninsula (58 kn/car, 12 kn/passenger, 15-min crossing, departs Dominče at the top of most but not all hours—check carefully in Korčula, departs Orebić at :30 past most hours).

If you're driving via the mainland, you'll first cross on this car ferry to Orebić on the vineyard-strewn Pelješac Peninsula. The Pelješac Peninsula is extremely long and narrow, and the roads are very rough, so it can take longer than you'd expect to reach the main coastal road (figure 1–1.5 hrs from Orebić). Where the peninsula meets the mainland, you'll see the cute little "Great Wall of Croatia" town of Ston.

If you're heading south to **Dubrovnik,** the coastal road zips you right there (about an hour from Ston). If you're heading north to **Split,** soon after joining the coastal road you'll actually pass through Bosnia-Herzegovina for a few miles (around the town of Neum—just stop and flash your passport as you enter and exit the country; for more details, see page 849).

Because of the ferry crossing and the long drive along the Pelješac Peninsula, driving **between Split and Korčula** is time-consuming and tiring. Instead, I prefer to take the longer car ferry the whole way between Split and Vela Luka, at the far end of Korčula Island (described above; allow 1 hour for the drive from Korčula town to Vela Luka, about 300 kn per car). The scenic and relaxing 2.75-hour boat ride from Vela Luka to Split saves you more than that much driving time.

ROVINJ and ISTRIA

Pula • Motovun

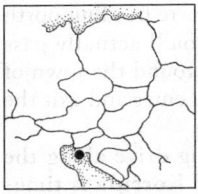

Rising dramatically from the Adriatic as though being pulled up to heaven by its grand bell tower, Rovinj (roh-VEEN; Rovigno/roh-VEEN-yoh in Italian) is a welcoming Old World oasis in a sea of tourist kitsch. Among the villages of Croatia's coast, there's something particularly romantic about Rovinj—the most Italian town in Croatia's most Italian region. Rovinj's streets are delightfully twisty, its ancient houses are characteristically crumbling, and its harbor—lively with real-life fishermen—is as salty as they come. Like a little Venice on a hill, Rovinj is the stage set for your Croatian seaside dreams.

Rovinj was prosperous and well-fortified in the Middle Ages. It boomed in the 16th and 17th centuries, when it was flooded with refugees fleeing both the Ottoman invasions and the plague. Because the town was part of the Republic of Venice for five centuries (13th to 18th centuries), its architecture, culture, and even language are strongly Venetian. The local folk groups sing in a dialect actually considered more Venetian than what the Venetians themselves speak these days. (You can even see Venice from Rovinj's church bell tower on a very clear day.)

After Napoleon seized the region, then was defeated, Rovinj became part of Austria. The Venetians had neglected the town, but the Austrians invested in it, bringing the railroad, gas lights, and a huge Ronhill tobacco factory. (This factory—recently replaced by

an enormous, state-of-the-art facility you'll pass on the highway farther inland—is one of the town's most elegant structures, and is slated for extensive renovation in the coming years.) The Austrians chose Pula and Trieste to be the empire's major ports—cursing those cities with pollution and sprawl, while allowing Rovinj to linger in its trapped-in-the-past quaintness.

Before long, Austrians discovered Rovinj as a handy escape for a beach holiday. Tourism arrived in the late 1890s, when a powerful Austrian baron bought one of the remote, barren islands offshore and brought it back to life with gardens and a grand villa. Before long, another baron bought another island...and a tourist boom was underway. In more recent times, Rovinj has become a top destination for nudists. The resort of Valalta, just to the north, is a popular spot for those seeking "southern exposure"... as a very revealing brochure at the TI illustrates (www.valalta.hr). Whether you want to find PNBs (pudgy nude bodies), or avoid them, remember that the German phrase *FKK* (*Freikörper Kultur,* or "free body culture") is international shorthand for nudism.

Rovinj is the star attraction of Croatia's wedge-shaped Istrian Peninsula. With more time in Istria (EE-stree-ah; "Istra" in Croatian), visit the striking Roman ruins in urban Pula and the laid-back hill town of Motovun (both described later in this chapter; for more on Istria, see page 892).

Rovinj is the most atmospheric of all of Croatia's small coastal towns. Maybe that's because it's always been a real town, where poor people lived. You'll find no fancy old palaces here—just narrow streets lined with skinny houses that have given shelter to humble families for generations. While it's becoming known on the tourist circuit, Rovinj retains the soul of a fishermen's village; notice that the harbor is still filled not with glitzy yachts, but with a busy fishing fleet.

Planning Your Time

While you can reach Rovinj by bus (see "Rovinj Connections," later), it's most worthwhile by car (which allows you to easily visit nearby destinations, such as Pula and Motovun). For drivers, Rovinj fits neatly between Slovenia and Croatia (for example, on a Ljubljana-Lake Bled-Julian Alps-Rovinj-Plitvice-Split itinerary).

Rovinj is hardly packed with diversions. You can get the gist of the town in a one-hour wander. The rest of your time is for enjoying the ambience or pedaling a rental bike to a nearby beach.

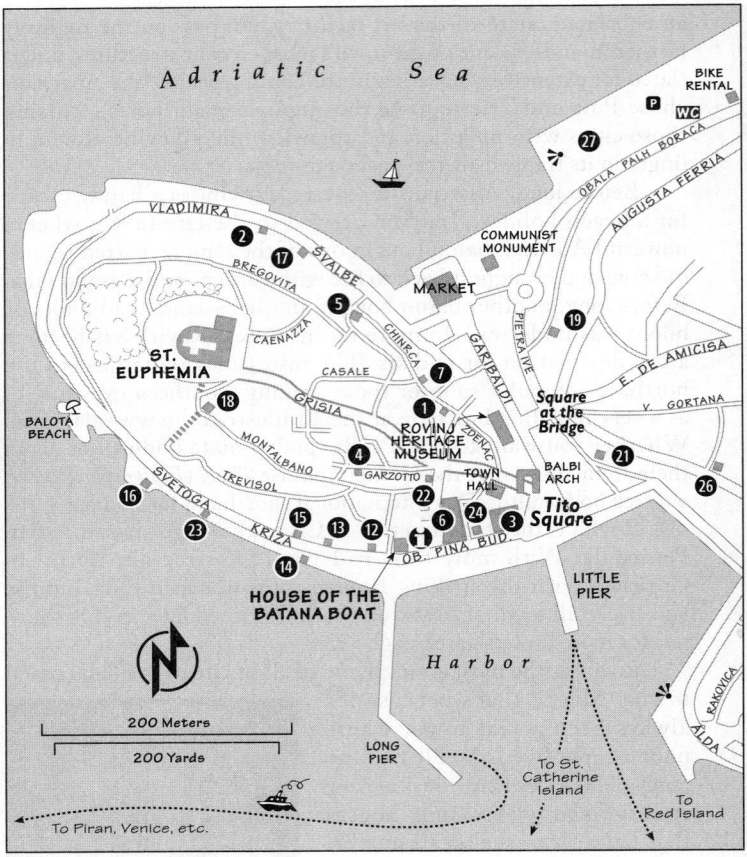

With a second day, side-trip to Pula and Motovun; to fill a lazy afternoon on a single day, choose just one of these attractions. Be aware that much of Rovinj closes down from November through Easter.

Orientation to Rovinj

(area code: 052)

Rovinj, once an island, is now a peninsula. The Old Town is divided in two parts: a particularly charismatic chunk on the oval-shaped peninsula, and the rest on the mainland (with similarly time-worn buildings, but without the commercial cuteness that comes with lots of tourist money). Where the mainland meets the peninsula is a broad, bustling public space called Tito Square (Trg Maršala Tita). The Old Town peninsula—traffic-free except for

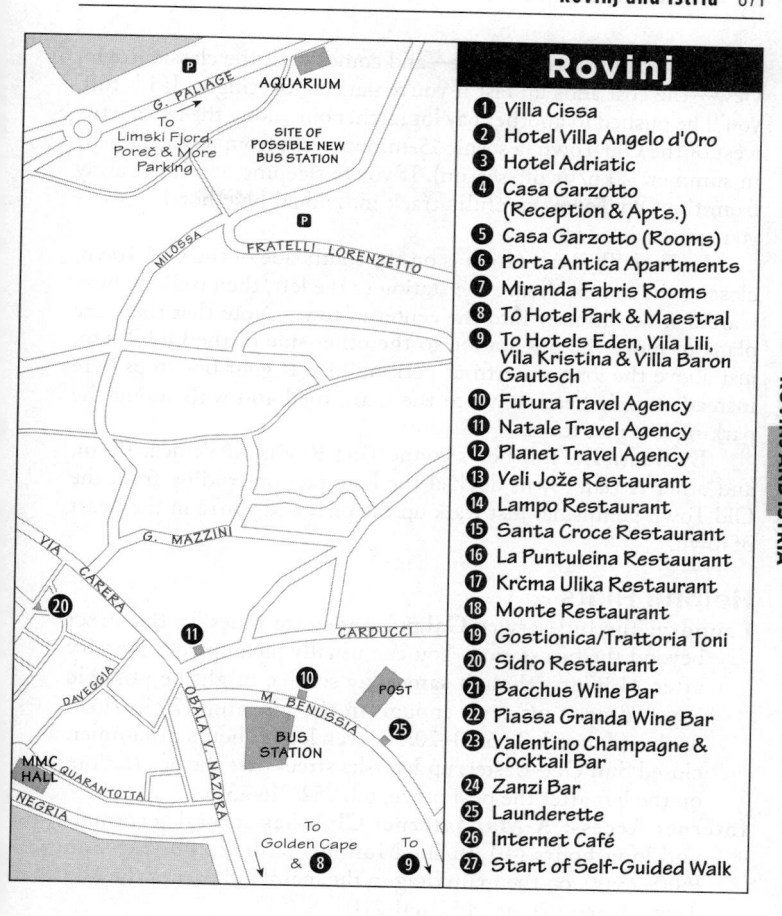

the occasional moped—is topped by the massive bell tower of the Church of St. Euphemia. At the very tip of the peninsula is a small park.

Tourist Information

Rovinj's helpful TI, facing the harbor, has several handy, free materials, including a town map and an info booklet (June-Sept daily 8:00–22:00; Oct–May Mon–Fri 8:00–15:00, Sat 8:00–13:00, closed Sun; along the embankment at Obala Pina Budičina 12, tel. 052/811-566, www.tzgrovinj.hr).

Arrival in Rovinj

By Car: To make a beeline to the Old Town, follow *Centar* signs through the little roundabout to the big parking lot on the waterfront (5 kn/hr, or 4 kn/hr from 1:00–6:00 in the morning). While

this lot is the most convenient—and comes with the classic Rovinj view—the cost adds up fast if you're parking overnight. If it's full, you'll be pushed to another pay lot farther out, along the bay northwest of the Old Town (a scenic 15-minute walk from town; 5 kn/hr in summer, 2 kn/hr off-season). If you're sleeping at a hotel away from the Old Town, carefully track individual blue hotel signs as you approach town.

By Bus: The bus station is on the south side of the Old Town, close to the harbor. Leave the station to the left, then walk on busy Carera street directly into the center of town. Note that there are plans to move the bus station to the other side of the Old Town, just above the long waterfront parking lots. If your bus stops here instead, simply head down to the main road and walk along the parking lots into town.

By Boat: The few boats connecting Rovinj to Venice, Piran, and other Istrian towns dock at the long pier protruding from the Old Town peninsula. Just walk up the pier, and you're in the heart of town.

Helpful Hints

Laundry: The full-service **Galax** launderette hides up the street beyond the bus station. You can usually pick up your laundry after 24 hours, though same-day service might be possible if you drop it off early enough in the morning (70 kn/load wash and dry, daily 6:00–20:00, even longer hours in summer, closed Sun Oct–Easter, up Istarska street past the bus station, on the left after the post office, tel. 052/816-130).

Internet Access: **A-Mar Internet Club** has several terminals and long hours (40 kn/hr, Mon–Fri 8:00–22:00, Sat–Sun 9:00–23:00, on the main drag in the mainland part of the Old Town, Carera 26, tel. 052/841-211).

Local Guides: **Vukica Palčić** is a very capable guide who knows her town intimately and loves to share it with visitors (€50 for a 2-hour tour, mobile 098-794-003, vukica.palcic@pu.t-com.hr). **Renato Orbanić** is a laid-back musician (sax) who also enjoys wandering through town with visitors. While light on heavy-hitting facts, his casual tour somehow suits this easy-going little town (€60 for a 2-hour tour, mobile 091-521-6206, rorbanic@inet.hr).

Best Views: The town is full of breathtaking views. Photography buffs will be busy in the "magic hours" of early morning and evening, and even by moonlight. The postcard view of Rovinj is from the parking lot embankment at the north end of the Old Town (at the start of the "Self-Guided Walk," below). For a different perspective on the Old Town, head for the far side of the harbor on the opposite (south) end of town. The

church bell tower provides what amounts to an aerial view of the town and a grand vista of the outlying islands.

Self-Guided Walk

▲▲▲Rovinj Ramble

This orientation walk introduces you to Rovinj in about an hour. Begin at the parking lot just north of the Old Town.

Old Town View

Many places offer fine views of Rovinj's Old Town, but this is the most striking. Boats bob in the harbor, and behind them Venetian-looking homes seem to rise from the deep. (For an aerial perspective, notice the big billboard overhead and to the left.)

The Old Town is topped by the church, whose bell tower is capped by a weathervane in the shape of Rovinj's patron saint, Euphemia. Local fishermen look to this saintly weathervane for direction: When Euphemia is looking out to sea, it means the stiff, fresh Bora wind is blowing, bringing dry air from the interior...a sailor's delight. But if she's facing the land, the humid Jugo wind will soon bring bad weather from the sea. After a day or so, even a tourist learns to look to St. Euphemia for the weather report.

As you soak in this scene, ponder how the town's history created its current shape. In the Middle Ages, Rovinj was an island, rather than a peninsula, and it was surrounded by a double wall—a protective inner wall and an outer seawall. Because it was so well-defended against pirates and other marauders (and carefully quarantined from the plague), it was extremely desirable real estate. And yet, it was easy to reach from the mainland, allowing it to thrive as a trading town. With more than 10,000 residents at its peak, Rovinj became immensely crowded, explaining today's pleasantly claustrophobic Old Town.

Over the centuries—as demand for living space trumped security concerns—the town walls were converted into houses, with windows grafted on to their imposing frame. Gaps in the wall, with steps that seem to end at the water, are where fishermen would pull in to unload their catch directly into the warehouses on the bottom level of the houses. (Later you can explore some of these lanes from inside the town.) Today, if you live in one of these houses, the Adriatic is your backyard.

• *Now head into town. In the little park near the sea, just beyond the end of the parking lot, look for the big, blocky...*

Communist-Era Monument

Dating from the time of Tito, this celebrates the Partisan Army's victory over the Nazis in World War II and commemorates the victims of fascism. The minimalist reliefs on the ceremonial tomb show a slow prisoners' parade of victims prodded by a gun in the back from a figure with a Nazi-style helmet. Notice that one side of the monument is in Croatian, and the other is in Italian. With typical Yugoslav grace and subtlety, this jarring block shatters the otherwise harmonious time-warp vibe of Rovinj. Fortunately, it's the only modern structure anywhere near the Old Town.

• *Now walk a few more steps toward town, stopping to explore the covered...*

Market

The front part of the market, near the water, is for souvenirs. But natives delve deeper in, to the local produce stands. Separating the gifty stuff from the nitty-gritty produce is a line of merchants aggressively pushing free samples. Everything is local and mostly homemade. Consider this snack-time tactic: Loiter around, joking with the farmers while sampling their various tasty walnuts, figs, cherries, grapes, olive oils, honey, *rakija* (the powerful schnapps popular throughout the Balkans), and more. If the sample is good, buy some more for a picnic. In the center of the market, a delightful and practical fountain from 1908 reminds locals of the infrastructure brought in by their Habsburg rulers a century ago. The hall labeled *Ribarnica/Pescheria* at the back of the market is where you'll find fresh, practically wriggling fish. This is where locals gather ingredients for their favorite dish, *brodet*—a stew of various kinds of seafood mixed with olive oil and wine...all of Istria's best bits in one delicious bowl. It's slowly simmered and generally served with polenta (unfortunately, it's rare in restaurants).

• *Continue up the broad street, named for* ***Giuseppe Garibaldi****—one of the major players in late-19th-century Italian unification. Imagine: Even though you're in Croatia, Italian patriots are celebrated in this very Italian-feeling town (see the "Italo-Croatia" sidebar). After one long block, you'll come to the wide cross-street called...*

Italo-Croatia

Apart from its tangible attractions, one of the Istrian Peninsula's hallmarks is its biculturalism: It's an engaging hybrid of Croatia and Italy. Like most of the Croatian Coast, Istria has variously been controlled by Illyrians, Romans, Byzantines, Slavs, Venetians, and Austrians. After the Habsburgs lost World War I, most of today's Croatia joined Yugoslavia—but Istria became part of Italy. During this time, the Croatian vernacular was suppressed, while Italian linguistic and cultural influences were predominant. This extra chapter of Italian rule left Istrians with an identity crisis. After World War II, Istria joined Yugoslavia, and Croatian culture and language returned. But many people here found it difficult to abandon their ties to Italy.

Today, depending on who you ask, Istria is the most Italian part of Croatia...or the most Croatian part of Italy. Istria pops up on Italian weather reports. A few years ago, Italy's Prime Minister Silvio Berlusconi declared that he still considered Istria part of Italy—and he wanted it back. When I wrote an article about Istria for a newspaper recently, some Italian readers complained that I made it sound "too Croatian," while some Croatians claimed my depiction was "too Italian."

People who actually live here typically don't worry about the distinction. Locals insist that they're not Croatians and not Italians—they're Istrians. They don't mind straddling two cultures. Both languages are official (and often taught side-by-side in schools), street signs are bilingual, and most Istrians dabble in each tongue—often seeming to foreign ears as though they're mixing the two at once.

As a result of their tangled history, Istrians have learned how to be mellow and take things as they come. They're gregarious, open-minded, and sometimes seem to thrive on chaos. A twentysomething local told me, "My ancestors lived in Venice. My great-grandfather lived in Austria. My grandfather lived in Italy. My father lived in Yugoslavia. I live in Croatia. My son will live in the European Union. And we've all lived in the same town."

Square at the Bridge (Trg na Mostu)

This marks the site of the medieval bridge that once connected the fortified island of Rovinj to the mainland (as illustrated in the small painting above the door of the Kavana al Ponto—"Bridge Café"). Back then, the island was populated mostly by Italians, while the mainland was the territory of Slavic farmers. But as Rovinj's strategic importance waned, and its trading status rose, the need for easy access became more important than the canal's protective purpose—so in 1763, it was filled in. The two populations integrated, creating the bicultural mix that survives today.

Notice the breeze? Via Garibaldi is nicknamed Val de Bora ("Valley of the Bora Wind") for the constant cooling wind that blows here. On the island side of Trg na Mostu is the Rovinj Heritage Museum (described later, under "Sights in Rovinj"). Next door, the town's cultural center posts lovingly hand-lettered signs in Croatian and Italian announcing upcoming musical events (generally free, designed for locals, and worth noting and enjoying).

Nearby (just past Kavana al Ponto, on the left), the Viecia Batana Café—named for Rovinj's unique, flat-bottomed little fishing boats—has a retro interior with a circa-1960 fishermen mural that evokes an earlier age. The café is popular for its chocolate cake and "Batana" ice cream.

• *Now proceed to the little fountain in the middle of the square (near Hotel Adriatic).*

Tito Square (Trg Maršala Tita)

This wide-open square at the entrance to the Old Town is the crossroads of Rovinj. The **fountain,** with a little boy holding a water-spouting fish, celebrates the government-funded water system that finally brought running water to the Old Town in 1959. Walk around the fountain, with your eyes on the relief, to see a successful socialist society at the inauguration of this new water system. Despite the happy occasion, the figures are pretty stiff—conformity trumped most other virtues in Tito's world.

Now walk out to the end of the concrete pier, called the **Mali Molo ("Little Pier").** From here, you're surrounded by Rovinj's crowded harbor, with fishing vessels and excursion boats that shuttle tourists out to the offshore islands. If the weather's good, a **boat trip** can be a memorable way to get out on the water for a different angle on Rovinj. In Rovinj's own little archipelago, the two most popular islands to visit are St. Catherine (Sv. Katarina—the lush, green island just across the harbor, about a 5-min trip, boats run about hourly in summer, 20 kn) and Red Island (Crveni Otok—farther out, about a 15-min trip, boats run hourly in summer, 30 kn). Each island has a hotel and its own share of beaches. If you're more interested in the boat trip than the destination, it's also fun to simply go for a cruise to the various coves and islands around Rovinj. Your two basic options are a straightforward 1.5-hour loop trip around the offshore islands for around 100 kn; or a four-hour, 150-kn sail north along the coast and into the disappointing "Limski Canal" (a.k.a. "Limski Fjord"), where you'll have two hours of free time. To sort through your options, chat with the captains nearby hawking excursions.

Scan the **harbor.** On the left is the MMC, the local meeting and concert hall (described later, under "Nightlife in Rovinj").

Above and behind the MMC, the highest bell tower inland marks the Franciscan monastery, which was the only building on the mainland before the island town was connected to shore. Along the waterfront to the right of the MMC is Hotel Park, a typical monstrosity from the communist era, now tastefully renovated on the inside. A recommended bike path starts just past this hotel, leading into a nature preserve and the best nearby beaches (which you can see in the distance; for more on bike rental, see "Activities in Rovinj," later).

Now head back to the base of the pier. If you were to walk down the **embankment** between the harbor and the Old Town (past Hotel Adriatic), you'd find the TI and a delightful "restaurant row" with several tempting places for a drink or a meal. Many fishermen pull their boats into this harbor, then simply carry their catch across the street to a waiting restaurateur. (This self-guided walk finishes with a stroll down this lane.)

Backtrack 10 paces past the fountain and face the Old Town entrance gate, called the **Balbi Arch.** The winged lion on top is a reminder that this was Venetian territory for centuries.

• *Head through the gate into the Old Town. Inside and on the left is the red...*

Town Hall

On the old Town Hall, notice another Venetian lion, as well as other historic crests embedded in the wall. The town hall actually sports an Italian flag (along with ones for Croatia and Rovinj) and faces a square named for Giacomo Matteotti, a much-revered Italian patriot.

Continue a few more steps into town. Gostionica/Trattoria Cisterna faces another little square, which once functioned as a cistern (collecting rainwater, which was pulled from a subterranean reservoir through the well you see today). On your left, the building with a *batana* boat out front is the Italian Union—yet another reminder of how Istria has an important bond with Italy.

• *Now begin walking up the street to the left of Gostionica/Trattoria Cisterna.*

Grisia Street

The main "street" (actually a tight lane) leading through the middle of the island is choked with tourists during the midday rush and

lined with art galleries. This inspiring town has attracted many artists, some of whom display their works along this colorful stretch. Notice the rusty little nails speckling the walls—each year in August, an art festival invites locals to hang their best art on this street. With paintings lining the lane, the entire community comes out to enjoy each other's creations.

As you walk, keep your camera cocked and ready, as you can find delightful scenes down every side lane. Remember that, as crowded as it is today, little Rovinj was even more packed in the Middle Ages. Keep an eye out for arches that span narrow lanes (such as on the right, at Arsenale street)—the only way a walled city could grow was up. Many of these additions created hidden little courtyards, nooks, and crannies that make it easy to get away from the crowds and claim a corner of the town for yourself. Another sign of Rovinj's overcrowding is the distinctive chimneys poking up above the rooftops. These chimneys, added long after the buildings were first constructed, made it possible to heat previously underutilized rooms...and squeeze in even more people.

• *Continue up to the top of Grisia. Capping the town is the can't-miss-it...*

▲Church of St. Euphemia (Sv. Eufemija)

Rovinj's landmark Baroque church dates from 1754. It's watched over by an enormous 190-foot-tall campanile, a replica of the famous bell tower on St. Mark's Square in Venice. The tower is topped by a copper weathervane with the weather-predicting St. Euphemia, the church's namesake.

Go inside (free, generally open May–Sept daily 10:00–18:00, Easter–April and Oct–Nov open only for Mass and with demand, generally closed Dec–Easter). The vast, somewhat gloomy interior boasts some fine altars of Carrara marble (a favorite medium of Michelangelo's). Services here are celebrated using a combination of Croatian and Italian, suiting the town's mixed population.

To the right of the main altar is the church's highlight: the chapel containing the relics of St. Euphemia. Before stepping into the chapel, notice the altar featuring Euphemia—depicted, as she

usually is, with her wheel (a reminder of her torture) and a palm frond (symbolic of her martyrdom), and holding the fortified town of Rovinj, of which she is the protector.

St. Euphemia was the virtuous daughter of a prosperous early-fourth-century family in Chalcedon (near today's Istanbul). Euphemia used her family's considerable wealth to help the poor. Unfortunately, her pious philanthropy happened to coincide with anti-Christian purges by the Roman Emperor Diocletian. When she was 15 years old, Euphemia was arrested for refusing to worship the local pagan idol. She was brutally tortured, her bones broken on a wheel. Finally she was thrown to the lions as a public spectacle. But, the story goes, the lions miraculously refused to attack her—only nipping her gently on one arm. The Romans murdered Euphemia anyway, and Christians later rescued her remains. In the year 800, a gigantic marble sarcophagus containing St. Euphemia's relics somehow found its way into the Adriatic and floated all the way up to Istria, where Rovinj fishermen discovered it bobbing in the sea. They towed it back to town, where a crowd gathered. The townspeople realized what it was and wanted to take it up to the hilltop church (an earlier version of the one we're in now). But nobody could move it...until a young boy with two young calves showed up. He said he'd had a dream of St. Euphemia—and, sure enough, he succeeded in dragging her relics to where they still lie.

The small chapel behind the altar is dominated by Euphemia's famous sarcophagus. The front panel (with the painting of Euphemia) is opened with much fanfare every September 16, St. Euphemia's feast day, to display the small, withered, waxen face of Rovinj's favorite saint. The sarcophagus is flanked by frescoes depicting her most memorable moment (protected by angels, as a bored-looking lion tenderly nibbles at her right bicep) and her arrival here in Rovinj (with burly fishermen looking astonished as the young boy succeeds in moving the giant sarcophagus). Note the depiction of Rovinj fortified by a double crenellated wall—looking more like a castle than like the creaky fishing village of today. At the top of the hill is an earlier version of today's church.

• *If you have time and energy, consider climbing the...*

Bell Tower

Scaling the church bell tower's creaky wooden stairway requires an enduring faith in the reliability of wood. It rewards those who brave the climb with a commanding view of the town and surrounding islands

(10 kn, same hours as church, enter from inside church—to the left of the main altar). The climb doubles your altitude, and from this perch you can also look down—taking advantage of the quirky little round hole in the floor to photograph the memorable staircase you just climbed.

• *Leave the church through the main door. A peaceful café on a park terrace (once a cemetery) is a bit to your right. Farther to the right, a winding lane leads down toward the water, then forks. A left turn zigzags you past a WWII pillbox and leads along the "restaurant row," where you can survey your options for a drink or a meal (see "Eating in Rovinj," later). A right turn curls you down along the quieter northern side of the Old Town peninsula. Either way, Rovinj is yours to enjoy.*

Sights in Rovinj

▲House of the Batana Boat (Kuća o Batani)—Rovinj has a long, noble shipbuilding tradition, and this tiny but interesting museum gives you the story of the town's distinctive *batana* boats. Locals say this museum puts you in touch with the soul of this town.

The flat-bottomed vessels are favored by local fishermen for their ability to reach rocky areas close to shore that are rich with certain shellfish. The museum explains how the boats are built, with the help of an entertaining elapsed-time video showing a boat built from scratch in five minutes. You'll also meet some of the salty old sailors who use these vessels (find the placemat with wine stains, and put the glass in different red circles to hear various seamen talk in the Rovinj dialect). Another movie shows the boats at work. Upstairs is a wall of photos of *batana* boats still in active use, a tiny library (peruse photos of the town from a century ago), and a video screen displaying *bitinada* music—local music with harmonizing voices that imitate instruments. Sit down and listen to several (there's a button for skipping ahead). The museum has no posted English information, so pick up the comprehensive English flier as you enter (5 kn; June–Sept daily 9:00–13:00 & 19:00–22:00; Oct–Dec and March–May Tue–Sun 10:00–13:00 & generally also 15:00–17:00, closed Mon; closed Jan–Feb; Obala Pina Budicina 2, tel. 052/812-593, www.batana.org).

The museum, which serves as a sort of cultural heritage center for the town, also presents a variety of engaging *batana*-related **activities**. On some summer evenings, you can take a boat trip on a *batana* from the pier near the museum. The trip, which is accompanied by traditional music, circles around the end of the Old Town peninsula and docks on the far side, where a traditional wine cellar has a fresh fish dinner ready, with local wine and more live music (June–mid-Sept, generally 2 days per week—likely Tue

and Thu at 20:30, boat trip-50 kn, dinner-120 kn extra, visit or call the museum the day before to reserve). Also on some summer evenings, you can enjoy an outdoor food market with traditional Rovinj foods and live *bitinada* music. The centerpiece is a *batana* boat being refurbished before your eyes (in front of museum, 20–30-kn light food, mid-June–early Sept generally Tue and Sat 20:00–23:00—but confirm details at museum). Even if you're here off-season, ask at the museum if anything special is planned.

Rovinj Heritage Museum (Zavičajni Muzej Grada Rovinja)—This ho-hum museum combines art old (obscure classic painters) and new (obscure contemporary painters from Rovinj) in an old mansion. Rounding out the collection are some model ships and a small archaeological exhibit (15 kn; summer Tue–Fri 9:00–15:00 & 19:00–22:00, Sat–Sun 9:00–14:00 & 19:00–22:00, closed Mon; winter Tue–Sat 9:00–15:00, closed Sun–Mon; Trg Maršala Tita 11, tel. 052/816-720, www.muzej-rovinj.com).

Aquarium (Akvarij)—This century-old collection of local sea life is one of Europe's oldest aquariums. Unfortunately, it's also tiny (with three sparse rooms holding a few tanks of what you'd see if you snorkeled here), disappointing, and overpriced (20 kn, daily June–Aug 9:00–21:00, Sept 9:00–20:00, Oct–May 10:00–16:00 or longer depending on demand, across the street from the end of the waterfront parking lot at Obala G. Paliage 5, tel. 052/804-712).

Activities in Rovinj

▲Swimming and Sunbathing—The most central spot to swim or sunbathe is at **Balota Beach,** on the rocks along the embankment on the south side of the Old Town peninsula (no showers, but scenic and central). For bigger beaches, go to the wooded **Golden Cape** (Zlatni Rt) south of the harbor (past the big, waterfront Hotel Park). This cape is lined with walking paths and beaches, and shaded by a wide variety of trees and plants. For a scenic and memorable sunbathing spot, choose a perch facing Rovinj on the

north side of the Golden Cape. Another beach, called **Kuvi,** is beyond the Golden Cape. To get away from it all, take a boat to an island on Rovinj's little archipelago (described earlier, on my self-guided walk).

▲Bike Ride—The TI's free, handy biking map suggests a variety of short and long bike rides. The easiest and most scenic is a quick loop around the Golden Cape (Zlatni Rt, described above). You can do this circuit and return to the Old Town in about an hour (without stops). Start by biking south around the harbor and past the waterfront Hotel Park, where you leave the cars and enter the wooded Golden Cape. Peaceful miniature beaches abound (see above). The lane climbs to a quarry (much of Venice was paved with Istrian stone), where you're likely to see beginning rock climbers inching their way up and down. Cycling downhill from the quarry and circling the peninsula, you hit the Lovor Grill (open daily in summer 10:00–16:00 for drinks and light meals)—a cute little restaurant housed in the former stables of the Austrian countess who planted what today is called "Wood Park." From there, you can continue farther along the coast or return to town (backtrack two minutes and take the right fork through the woods back to the waterfront path).

Bike Rental: Bikes are rented at subsidized prices from the city parking lot kiosk (5 kn/hr, open 24 hours daily except no rentals in winter, fast and easy process; choose a bike with enough air in its tires or have them pumped up, as the path is rocky and gravelly). Various travel agencies around town rent bikes for quadruple the price (20 kn/hr); look for signs or ask around.

Nightlife in Rovinj

Rovinj After Dark

Rovinj is a delight after dark. Views that are great by day become magical by moonlight and floodlight. The streets of the Old Town are particularly inviting when empty and under stars.

Concerts—Lots of low-key, small-time music events take place right in town (ask at the

TI, check the events calendar at www.tzgrovinj.hr, and look for handwritten signs on Garibaldi street near the Square at the Bridge). Groups perform at various venues around town: right along the harborfront (you'll see the bandstand set up); in the town's churches (especially St. Euphemia and the Franciscan church); in the old cinema/theater by the market; at the House of the Batana Boat (described earlier, under "Sights in Rovinj"); and at the Multi-Media Center (a.k.a. the "MMC," which locals call "Cinema Belgrade"—its former name), in a cute little hall above a bank across the harbor from the Old Town.

Wine Bars—Rovinj has two good places to sample Istrian and Croatian wines, along with light, basic food—such as prosciutto-like *pršut*, truffles, and olive oil. Two popular local wines worth trying are *malvazija* (mahl-VAH-zee-yah, sometimes spelled Malvasia in English—a light white wine that can be either sweet/*slatko* or dry/*suho*) and *teran* (a heavy red). At **Bacchus Wine Bar,** owner Paolo is happy to explain how local wines have improved since communist times, when wine production stagnated (15–40 kn per deciliter, most cost around 20–30 kn, 70–250-kn bottles, daily 7:00–23:00, Carera 5, tel. 052/812-154). **Piassa Granda,** on a charming little square right in the heart of the Old Town, has a classy, cozy interior and 140 types of wine (18–25-kn glasses, 30–70-kn Istrian small plates, more food than Bacchus, daily 10:00–24:00, Veli trg 1, mobile 098-824-322, Helena).

Lounging—Valentino Champagne and Cocktail Bar is a memorable, romantic, justifiably pretentious place for a late-night waterfront drink with jazz. Fish, attracted by its underwater lights, swim by from all over the bay...to the enjoyment of those nursing a cocktail on the rocks (literally—you'll be given a small seat cushion and welcomed to find your own seaside niche). Or you can choose to sit on one of the terraces. Classy candelabras twinkle in the twilight, as couples cozy up to each other and the view. Patricia opens her bar nightly from 19:00 until whenever the action stops. While the drinks are extremely pricey, this place is unforgettably cool (50–65-kn cocktails, 50-kn non-alcoholic drinks, Via Santa Croce 28, tel. 052/830-683). **La Puntuleina**—next door and listed later, under "Eating in Rovinj"—has a similarly rocky ambience, with lower prices (30–40-kn drinks) but a bit less panache than Valentino. **Zanzi Bar,** while named for an African archipelago, has a Havana ambience. Stepping over its threshold, you enter a colonial Caribbean world, with seating indoors or out on the tropical veranda (80 different

cocktails for 45–60 kn each, nightly until 1:00 in the morning, near the TI on Obala Pina Budicina).

Batana Boat Activities—In summer, the House of the Batana Boat often hosts special events such as a boat trip and traditional dinner, and an outdoor food court. For details, see the listing earlier, under "Sights in Rovinj."

Sleeping in Rovinj

Most Rovinj accommodations (both hotels and *sobe*) prefer longer stays of at least four or five nights, so in peak season (mid-July–mid-Sept), you'll likely run into strict minimum-stay requirements or high surcharges for shorter stays. Unfortunately, you'll probably have to simply eat this extra cost for a short stay. Hoteliers and *sobe* hosts are somewhat more flexible in the shoulder season. Don't just show up here without a room in August—popular Rovinj is packed during that peak month.

In the Old Town

All of these accommodations are on the Old Town peninsula, rather than the mainland section of the Old Town. Rovinj has no real hostel, but *sobe* are a good budget option.

$$$ Hotel Villa Angelo d'Oro is your Old Town splurge. The location—on a peaceful street just a few steps off the water—is ideal, and the public spaces (including a serene garden bar and sauna/whirlpool area) are rich and inviting. The 23 rooms don't quite live up to the fuss, but if you want your money to talk your way into the Old Town, this is the place (mid-July–Aug: Sb-950

Sleep Code

(5 kn = about $1, country code: 385, area code: 052)
S = Single, **D** = Double/Twin, **T** = Triple, **Q** = Quad, **b** = bathroom. The modest tourist tax (7 kn per person, per night, lower off-season) is not included in these rates. Hotels accept credit cards and include breakfast in their rates, while most *sobe* accept only cash and don't offer breakfast. Everyone listed here speaks at least enough English to make a reservation (or knows someone nearby who can translate).

To help you sort easily through these listings, I've divided the rooms into three categories based on the price for a standard double room with bath in peak season:

$$$ Higher Priced—Most rooms 800 kn or more.
$$ Moderately Priced—Most rooms between 500–800 kn.
$ Lower Priced—Most rooms 500 kn or less.

kn, Db-1,600 kn; June–mid-July and Sept: Sb-860 kn, Db-1,450 kn; cheaper Oct–Dec and March–May, closed Jan–Feb, pricier suites also available, no extra charge for 1-night stays, no elevator, air-con, free Wi-Fi in lobby, bike rental for guests, Vladimira Švalbe 38–42, tel. 052/840-502, fax 052/840-111, www.angelodoro.hr, hotelangelo@vip.hr).

$$$ Porta Antica rents 15 comfortable, nicely decorated apartments in five different buildings around the Old Town (two houses—Porta Antica and Marco Polo—are on the peninsula, while the others are on the mainland). Review your options on their website and be specific in your request—though in busy times (July–Aug), they might not be able to guarantee a particular apartment. The underwhelming sea views aren't worth the extra expense. You'll pay less per night the longer you stay; I've listed rates per night for two-night stays, but you can check specific rates on their website (most of Aug: Db-1,000 kn; July: Db-920 kn; late May–June and late Aug–late Sept: Db-675 kn; rest of year: Db-570 kn; sea views-70–140 kn extra, extra person-180 kn, no breakfast, air-con, tries to be non-smoking, open year-round, reception and main building next door to TI on Obala Pina Budičina, tel. 052/812-548, mobile 099-680-1101, www.portaantica.com, portaantica@yahoo.it).

$$$ Hotel Adriatic, a lightly renovated holdover from the communist days, features 27 rooms overlooking the main square, where the Old Town peninsula meets the mainland. The quality of the drab, worn rooms doesn't justify the outrageously high prices... but the location might. Of the big chain of Maistra hotels, this is the only one in the Old Town (rates flex with demand, in top season figure Sb-1,125 kn, Db-1,700 kn; these prices are per night for 1- or 2-night stays—cheaper for 3 nights or more, all Sb are non-view, most Db are twins and have views—otherwise 150 kn less, closed mid-Oct–March, no elevator, air-con, pay Wi-Fi, some nighttime noise—especially on weekends, Trg Maršala Tita, tel. 052/803-520, fax 052/813-573, www.maistra.hr, adriatic@maistra.hr).

$$ Villa Cissa, run by Zagreb transplant Veljko Despot, has three apartments with tastefully modern, artistic decor above an art gallery in the Old Town. Kind, welcoming Veljko—who looks a bit like Robin Williams—is a fascinating guy who had an illustrious career as a rock-and-roll journalist (he was the only Eastern Bloc reporter to interview the Beatles) and record-company executive. Now his sophisticated, artistic style is reflected in these comfortable apartments. Because the place is designed for longer stays, you'll pay a premium for a short visit (50 percent extra for 2-night stays, prices double for 1-night stays), and it comes with some one-time fees, such as for cleaning. Veljko lives off-site, so be sure to clearly communicate your arrival time (July–early Sept: Db-700

kn; most of Sept: Db-625 kn; May–June and late Sept–Oct: Db-550 kn; April: Db-480 kn; rest of the year: Db-410 kn; about 650–700 kn more for bigger apartment; cash only, air-con, free Wi-Fi, some night noise from café across the street, Zdenac 14, tel. 052/813-080, www.villacissa.com, info@villacissa.com).

$$ Casa Garzotto is an appealing mid-range option, with four apartments, four rooms, and one large family apartment in three different Old Town buildings. These classy and classic lodgings have modern facilities but old-fashioned charm, with antique furniture and historic family portraits on the walls. Thoughtfully run by a friendly staff, it's a winner (rooms—mid-June–late Sept: Sb-370 kn, Db-520 kn; rest of year: Sb-300 kn, Db-450 kn; apartments—mid-July–Aug: 1,030 kn, mid-June–mid-July and Sept: 920 kn, mid-May–mid-June and early Oct: 780 kn, less off-season; 2-bedroom family apartment—mid-June–Sept: Db-890–1,030 kn, Tb-1,110 kn, Qb-1,470 kn; mid-May–mid-June and early Oct: Db-780 kn, Tb-960 kn, Qb-1,180; includes breakfast, off-site parking, loaner bikes, and other thoughtful extras; no extra charge for 1-night stays, air-con, lots of stairs, free Wi-Fi in main building, reception and most apartments are at Garzotto 8, others are a short walk away, tel. 052/811-884, mobile 098-616-168, www.casa-garzotto.com, casagarzotto@gmail.com).

$ Miranda Fabris is an outgoing local teacher who rents four cheap, basic, tight apartments with kitchenettes. While rough around the edges, the rooms are affordable and pleasantly located in the thick of the Old Town (July–Aug: Db-370 kn; Sept–June: Db-300 kn; no extra charge for 1- or 2-night stays, cash only, no breakfast, lots of steep stairs, across from Villa Val de Bora at Chiurca 5, mobile 091-881-8881, miranda_fabris@yahoo.com).

$ *Other* Sobe: Try looking for your own room online (www.inforovinj.com is helpful). Several agencies rent private rooms in the Old Town for good prices (figure Db-150–300 kn, depending on season, location, and size). But remember that in peak season, you'll pay about 70 percent extra for a one-night stay, and 30 percent extra for a two- or three-night stay. Just about everyone in town has a line on rooms. These two agencies are English-friendly and handy to the bus station (open sporadic hours, based on demand): **Futura Travel** (across from bus station at Benussi 2, tel. 052/817-281, fax 052/817-282, www.futura-travel.hr) and **Natale** (Carducci 4, tel. & fax 052/813-365, www.rovinj.com). In the Old Town, try **Planet,** near the TI (Sv. Križa 1, tel. 052/840-494, www.planetrovinj.com).

On the Mainland

To escape the high prices of Rovinj's Old Town, consider the resort neighborhood just south of the harbor. While the big hotels

themselves are an option, I prefer cheaper alternatives in the same area. The big hotels are signposted as you approach town (follow signs for *hoteli,* then your specific hotel). Once you're on the road to Hotels Eden and Park, the smaller ones are easy to reach: Villa Baron Gautsch is actually on the road to Hotel Park (on the right, brown *pansion* sign just before Hotel Park itself); Hotel Vila Lili and Vila Kristina are a little farther on the main road toward Eden (to the left just after turnoff for Hotel Park, look for signs). All of these options are about a 15-minute uphill walk from the Old Town.

$$$ ***Maistra Hotels:*** The local hotel conglomerate, Maistra, has several hotels in the lush parklands just south of the Old Town. Most of my readers—looking for proximity to the Old Town rather than predictable rooms, a big lounge, and hotel-based activities—will prefer to save money and stay at one of my other listings. These hotels have extremely slippery pricing, based on the hotel, the type of room, the season, and how far ahead you book (for starters, in July–Aug figure non-view Sb-925 kn, non-view Db-1,240 kn, view Db-1,450 kn, more for 1- or 2-night stays, cheaper off-season), but you'll have to call or check the website for specifics (www.maistra.hr). **Hotel Park** has 202 thoroughly renovated but dull rooms in a colorized communist-era hull, and a seaside swimming pool with sweeping views to the Old Town. From here, you can walk in about 15 minutes along the scenic harborfront promenade into town (tel. 052/811-077, fax 052/816-977, park@maistra.hr). **Hotel Eden** offers 325 upscale, imaginatively updated rooms with oodles of contemporary style behind a brooding communist facade. This flagship hotel is the fanciest one in the Maistra chain, but it's a bit farther from the Old Town—frustrating without a car (10 percent extra for fancier rooms, tel. 052/800-400, fax 052/811-349, eden@maistra.hr). Both hotels have air-conditioning, elevators, free parking, and pay Internet access. The Maistra chain also has several other properties (including the Old Town's Hotel Adriatic, described earlier, and other more distant, cheaper options). Only one branch of the Maistra chain remains open through the winter.

$$$ Hotel Vila Lili, a lesser value, is a family-run hotel with 20 overpriced rooms above a restaurant on a quiet, leafy lane (April–Oct: Sb-450 kn, Db-800 kn; shoulder season: Sb-370 kn, Db-550 kn; cheaper off-season, pricier suites also available, 10 percent discount with this book except in July–Aug, no extra charge for 1-night stays, elevator, air-con, parking-30 kn/day, Mohorovičića 16, tel. 052/840-940, fax 052/840-944, www.hotel-vilalili.hr, info@hotel-vilalili.hr, Petričević family).

$$ Vila Kristina, run by friendly Kristina Kiš and her family, has 10 rooms and five apartments along a busy road (July–Aug:

Db-590 kn, extra bed-295 kn; Sept–June: Db-520 kn, extra bed-260 kn; includes breakfast, air-con, no elevator, free Wi-Fi, Luje Adamovića 16, tel. 052/815-537, www.kis-rovinj.com, kristinakis@mail.inet.hr).

$$ Villa Baron Gautsch, named for a shipwreck, is a German-owned pension with 17 comfortable rooms and an inviting, shared terrace with a view (late July–early Sept: Db-570 kn; late June–late July and early Sept–early Oct: Db-500 kn; off-season: Db-400–440 kn; they also have two Sb for half the Db price, 20 percent more for 1- or 2-night stays, 35 kn less without balcony, non-balcony rooms have air-con, closed Nov–Easter, cash only, no elevator, free Wi-Fi, Ronjgova 7, tel. 052/840-538, fax 052/840-537, www.baron-gautsch.com, baron.gautsch@gmx.net).

Eating in Rovinj

It's expensive to dine in Rovinj—don't expect great value for your money. Interchangeable restaurants cluster where Rovinj's Old Town peninsula meets the mainland, and all around the harbor. Be warned that most eateries—like much of Rovinj—close for the winter (roughly November to Easter).

Along Rovinj's "Restaurant Row"

The easiest dining option is to stroll the Old Town embankment overlooking the harbor (Obala Pina Budičina), which changes its name to Svetoga Križa and cuts behind the buildings after a few blocks. Window-shop the pricey but scenic eateries along here, each of which has its own personality (all open long hours daily). I've listed these in the order you'll reach them. You'll pay top dollar, but the ambience is memorable.

Veli Jože, with a few outdoor tables and a rollicking, folksy interior decorated to the hilt, is in all the guidebooks but still delivers on its traditional, if overpriced, Istrian cuisine (35–80-kn pastas, 60–120-kn main dishes, Sv. Križa 1, tel. 052/816-337).

Lampo is simpler, with scenic seating right on the water—fine for a big salad, pizza, or pasta at a reasonable price (30–45-kn pastas, 60–100-kn main dishes, Sv. Križa 22).

Santa Croce, with tables scenically scattered along a terraced incline that looks like a stage set, is well-respected for its pricey seafood and pastas (50–70-kn pastas, 70–160-kn main dishes, daily

18:00–24:00, Sv. Križa 11, tel. 052/842-240).

La Puntuleina, at the end of the row, is the most scenic option. This upscale restaurant/cocktail bar/wine bar features pricey Italo-Mediterranean cuisine served in the contemporary dining room, or outside—either on one of the many terraces, or at tables literally scattered along the rocks overlooking a swimming hole. The menu is small, and the selection each day is even smaller, since Miriam and Giovanni insist on serving only what's fresh in the market. I wouldn't pay these prices unless I got a nice table out on a terrace. Reservations are recommended (80–100-kn pastas, 100–160-kn main dishes, Thu–Tue 12:00–15:00 & 18:00–22:00, closed Wed except in peak season, closed Nov–Easter, on the Old Town embankment past the harbor at Sv. Križa 38, tel. 052/813-186). You can also order just a drink to sip while sitting down on the rocks.

Just before La Puntuleina, don't miss the inviting **Valentino Champagne and Cocktail Bar**—with no food but similar "drinks on the rocks" ambience (described earlier, under "Nightlife in Rovinj"). If you're on a tight budget, dine cheaply elsewhere, then come here for an after-dinner finale.

International Fare in the Old Town Peninsula

Offering upscale, international (rather than strictly Croatian) food and presentation, these options are expensive but memorable.

Krčma Ulika, a classy hole-in-the-wall run by Inja Tucman, has a mellow, cozy, art-strewn interior. Inja enjoys surprising diners with unexpected flavor combinations. While the lack of a real kitchen in the back makes this less than a gourmet experience, the food preparation area in a corner of the tight, six-table dining room adds to the ambience. The food is a bit overpriced and can be hit-or-miss, but the experience feels like an innovative break from traditional Croatian fare. Explore your options with Inja's help before ordering (12-kn cover, 100–130-kn main dishes, daily 19:00–1:00 in the morning, Sun–Thu also 13:00–15:00, until 23:00 in shoulder season, closed Nov–Easter, cash only, Vladimira Švalbe 34, tel. 052/818-089, mobile 098-929-7541).

Monte Restaurant is your upscale, white-tablecloth splurge—made to order for a memorable dinner out. With tables strewn around a covered terrace just under the town bell tower, this atmospheric place features inventive cuisine that melds Istrian products with international techniques. Come here only if you value a fine dining experience, polished service, and the chance to learn about local food and wines more than the price tag (plan to spend 300–500 kn per person for dinner, daily 12:00–14:30 & 18:30–23:00, reserve ahead in peak season, Montalbano 75, tel. 052/830-203, Đekić family).

Affordable Alternatives on the Mainland

These options are a bit less expensive than those described above. I've listed them as you'll reach them as you walk around Rovinj's harbor.

Gostionica/Trattoria Toni is a hole-in-the-wall serving up small portions of good Istrian and Venetian fare. Choose between the cozy interior (tucked down a tight lane), or out on their terrace on a bustling, mostly pedestrian street (40–60-kn pastas, 50–120-kn main dishes, Thu–Tue 12:00–15:00 & 18:00–22:30, closed Wed, just up ulica/via Driovier on the right, tel. 052/815-303).

Sidro offers a break from pasta, pizza, and fish; it's well-respected for its Balkan meat dishes such as *čevapčići* (see "Balkan Flavors" on page 753) and a spicy pork-and-onion stew called *mućkalica*. With unusually polite service and a long tradition (run by three generations of the Paoletti family since 1966), it's a popular local hangout (45–70-kn pastas, 55–90-kn grilled meat dishes, 75–140-kn steaks and fish, daily 11:00–23:00, closed Nov–Feb, harborfront at Rismondo 14, tel. 052/813-471).

Maestral combines affordable, straightforward pizzas and seafood with Rovinj's best view. If you want an outdoor table overlooking bobbing boats and the Old Town's skyline—without breaking the bank—this is the place. It fills a big building surrounded by workaday shipyards about a 10-minute walk from the Old Town, around the harbor toward Hotel Park (30-kn sandwiches, 45–60-kn pizzas and pastas, 45–100-kn fish and meat dishes, May–Sept open long hours daily, Oct–April drinks only and open until 20:00, obala N. Nazora b.b., look for *Bavaria* beer sign).

Breakfast

Most rental apartments come with a kitchenette handy for breakfasts (stock up at a neighborhood grocery shop). Cafés and bars along the waterfront serve little more than an expensive croissant with coffee. The best budget breakfast (and a fun experience) is a picnic. Within a block of the market, you have all the necessary stops: the Brionka bakery (fresh-baked cheese or apple strudel); mini-grocery stores (juice, milk, drinkable yogurt, and so on); market stalls (cherries, strawberries, walnuts, and more, as well as an elegant fountain for washing); an Albanian-run bread kiosk/café between the market and the water...plus benches with birds chirping, children playing, and fine Old Town views along the water. For a no-fuss alternative, you can shell out 60 kn for the buffet breakfast at Hotel Adriatic (daily 7:00–10:00, until 11:00 July–Aug; described earlier, under "Sleeping in Rovinj").

Rovinj Connections

From Rovinj by Bus to: Pula (about hourly, 45 min), **Poreč** (6–9/day, 1 hr), **Umag** (5/day, 1.5 hrs), **Rijeka** (4–7/day, 3 hrs), **Zagreb** (6–9/day, 5–8 hrs), **Venice** (1/day Mon–Sat departing very early in the morning, none Sun, 5 hrs). In the summer, you can reach Slovenia—including **Piran** (2.5 hrs) and **Ljubljana** (5.5 hrs)—by hopping on the 8:00 bus from Rovinj (June–late Sept only, no buses off-season). You can also reach Piran (and other Slovenian destinations) with a transfer in Umag and Portorož. A bus departs Rovinj every evening at 19:00 for the Dalmatian Coast, arriving in **Split** at 6:00 and **Dubrovnik** at 11:00. (If this direct bus isn't running, you might have to take an earlier bus to Pula, from where this night bus leaves at 20:00; also note that Pula has two daytime connections to Split.) As always, confirm these times before planning your trip. Bus information: tel. 052/811-453.

Pula

Pula (POO-lah, Pola in Italian) isn't quaint. Istria's biggest city is an industrial port town with traffic, smog, and sprawl...but it has the soul of a Roman poet. Between the shipyards, you'll discover some of the top Roman ruins in Croatia, including a stately amphitheater—a fully intact mini-Colosseum that marks the entrance to a seedy Old Town with ancient temples, arches, and columns.

Strategically situated at the southern tip of the Istrian Peninsula, Pula has long been a center of industry, trade, and military might. In 177 B.C., the city became an important outpost of the Roman Empire. It was destroyed during the wars following Julius Caesar's death and rebuilt by Emperor Augustus. Many of Pula's most important Roman features—including its amphitheater—date from this time (early first century A.D.). But as Rome fell, so did Pula's fortunes. The town changed hands repeatedly, caught in the crossfire of wars between greater powers—Byzantines, Venetians, and Habsburgs. After being devastated by Venice's enemy, Genoa, in the 14th century, Pula gathered dust as a ghost town...still militarily strategic, but otherwise abandoned.

In the mid-19th century, Italian unification forced the Austrian Habsburgs—whose navy had been based in Venice—to

Istria

Rovinj is just one of many worthwhile attractions on the peninsula called Istria. In Istria, pungent truffles, Roman ruins, cute hill towns, quaint coastal villages, carefully cultivated food and wine, and breezy Italian culture all compete for your attention.

While you could spend days exploring Istria, two destinations outside Rovinj are especially worthwhile (each one deserves a half-day side-trip). Down at the tip of Istria is big, industrial Pula, offering a bustling urban contrast to the rest of the time-passed coastline, plus some remarkable Roman ruins (including an amphitheater so intact, you'll marvel that you haven't heard of it before). The charming hill town of Motovun—with sweeping views over the surrounding terrain, including a truffle-packed forest—is one of the country's most appealing reasons to head inland.

Getting Around Istria

Istria is a cinch for **drivers,** who find distances short and roads and attractions well-marked (though summer traffic can be miserable, especially on weekends). While Istria has no four-lane expressways, it is neatly connected by a speedy two-lane highway nicknamed "the *ipsilon*" (the Croatian word for the letter Y, which is what the highway is shaped like). One branch of the "Y" (A-9) runs roughly parallel to the coast from Slovenia to Pula, about six miles inland; the other branch (A-8) cuts diagonally northeast to the Učka Tunnel (leading to Rijeka). You'll periodically come to toll booths, where you'll pay a modest fee for using the *ipsilon*. Following road signs here is easy (navigate by town names), but if you'll be driving a lot, pick up a good map to more easily navigate the back roads. My favorite is the Kod & Kam 1:100,000 *Istra* map (available in local bookstores and some TIs).

If you're relying on **public transportation,** Istria is frustrating. While it may be possible to patch together some of the better sights (such as Rovinj and Motovun) by bus, it's probably

not worth the hassle. Even if you're doing the rest of your trip by public transportation, consider renting a car for a day or two in Istria.

By Boat to Venice: Venezia Lines connects Venice with Rovinj and Pula, as well as Poreč (in Istria), Piran (in Slovenia), and other Adriatic destinations. While designed for day-trippers from Istria to Venice, this service can also be used one-way. Since the schedule tends to change from year to year, check their website for details: www.venezialines.com.

look for a new home for their fleet. In 1856, they chose Pula, and over the next 60 years, the population grew thirtyfold. (Despite the many Roman and Venetian artifacts littering the Old Town, most of modern Pula is essentially Austrian.) By the dawn of the 20th century, Pula's harbor bristled with Austro-Hungarian warships, and it had become the crucial link in a formidable line of imperial defense that stretched from here to Montenegro. As one of the most important port cities of the Austro-Hungarian Empire, Pula attracted naval officers, royalty...and a young Irishman named James Joyce on the verge of revolutionizing the literary world.

Today's Pula, while no longer quite so important, remains a vibrant port town and the de facto capital of Istria. It offers an enjoyably urban antidote to the rest of this stuck-in-the-past peninsula.

Planning Your Time

Pula's sights, while top-notch, are quickly exhausted. Two or three hours should do it: Visit the amphitheater, stroll the circular Old Town, and maybe see a museum or two. As it's less than an hour from Rovinj, there's no reason to spend the night.

Orientation to Pula

(area code: 052)

Although it's a big city, the tourist's Pula is compact: the amphitheater and, beside it, the ring-shaped Old Town circling the base of an old hilltop fortress. The Old Town's main square, the Forum, dates back to Roman times.

Tourist Information

Pula's well-organized TI overlooks the Old Town's main square, the Forum. It offers a free map and information on the town and all of Istria (May–Oct daily 9:00–21:00, July–Aug until 22:00; Nov–April Mon–Sat 9:00–18:00 or 19:00, Sun 10:00–16:00; Forum 3, tel. 052/219-197, www.pulainfo.hr).

Arrival in Pula

By Car: Pula is about a 45-minute drive south of Rovinj. Approaching town, follow *Centar* signs, then look for the amphitheater. You'll find a large pay lot just below the amphitheater, toward the waterfront (4 kn/hr, 20 kn/all day).

By Bus: As you exit the bus station, walk toward the yellow mansion, then turn left onto the major street (ulica 43 Istarske Divizije); at the roundabout, bear left again, and you'll be headed for the amphitheater (about a 10-min walk total).

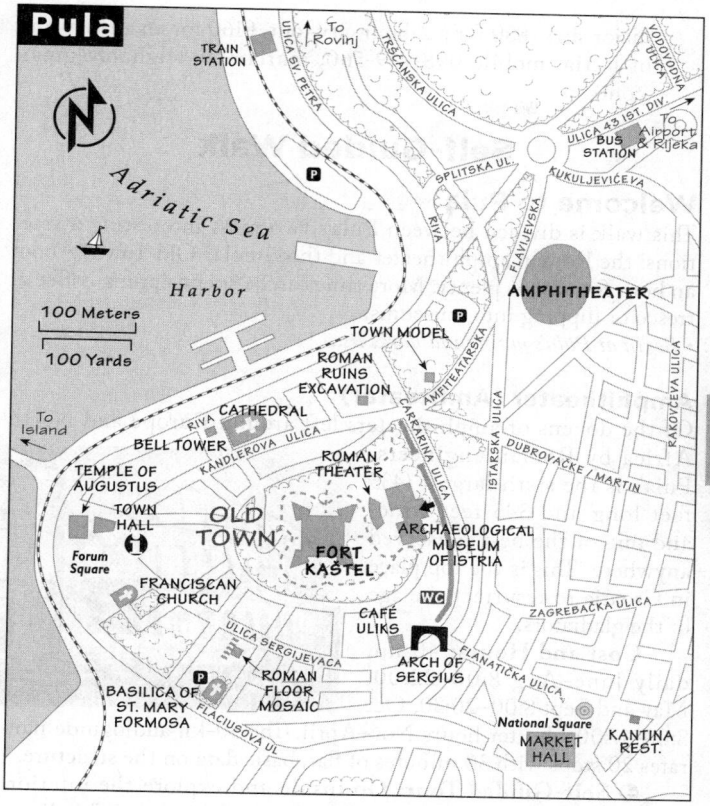

By Train: The train station is a 15-minute walk from the amphitheater, near the waterfront (in the opposite direction from the Old Town). Walk with the coast on your right until you see the amphitheater.

By Plane: Pula's small airport, which is served by various low-cost airlines, is about 3.5 miles northeast of the center. Since there's no convenient public bus option, count on paying 100 kn for the taxi ride into town. Airport info: tel. 052/530-105, www.airport-pula.com.

Helpful Hints

Car Rental: To rent a car in Pula, **Avis** is the most central (Riva 14, tel. 052/224-350). Several other companies have offices at the airport, which is a 100-kn taxi ride outside of town (see "Arrival in Pula," above).

Local Guide: If you'd like a local guide to help you uncover the story of Pula, **Mariam Abdelghani** leads great tours of the

major sites (€80 for a 2-hour city tour, €160 for an all-day tour of Istria, mobile 098-419-560, mariam.abdelghani@gmail.com).

Self-Guided Walk

Welcome to Pula

This walk is divided between Pula's two most interesting attractions: the Roman amphitheater and the circular Old Town. About an hour for each is plenty. More time can be spent sipping coffee al fresco or dipping into museums.

• *Begin at Pula's main landmark, its...*

Amphitheater (Amfiteatar)

Of the dozens of amphitheaters left around Europe and North Africa by Roman engineers, Pula's is the sixth-largest (435 feet long and 345 feet wide) and one of the best-preserved anywhere. This is the top place in Croatia to resurrect the age of the gladiators.

Cost and Hours: 40 kn, daily June–Aug 8:00–22:00, May and Sept 8:00–20:30, Oct 8:00–17:00, shorter hours Nov–April. The 30-kn audioguide narrates 20 stops with 30 minutes of flat, basic data on the structure.

➲ **Self-Guided Tour:** Go inside and explore the interior, climbing up the seats as you like. An "amphi-theater" is literally a "double theater"—imagine two theaters, without the back wall behind the stage, stuck together to maximize seating. Pula's amphitheater was built over several decades (first century A.D.) under the reign of three of Rome's top-tier emperors: Augustus, Claudius, and Vespasian. It was completed around A.D. 80, about the same time as the Colosseum in Rome. It remained in active use until the beginning of the fifth century, when gladiator battles were outlawed. The location is unusual but sensible: It was built just outside town (too big for tiny Pula, with just 5,000 people) and near the sea (so its giant limestone blocks could more easily be transported here from the quarry six miles away).

Notice that the amphitheater is built into the gentle incline of a hill. This economical plan, unusual for Roman amphitheaters, saved on the amount of stone needed, and provided a natural foundation for some of the seats (notice how the upper seats incorporate the slope). It may seem like the architects were cutting corners, but they actually had to raise the ground level at the lower end of the

Amphorae

In museums, hotels, and restaurants all along the Croatian coast, you'll see amphorae. An amphora is a jug that was used to transport goods when the ancient Greeks ruled the seas, through about the second century B.C. Later, the Romans also used their own amphorae. These tall and skinny ceramic jugs—many of them lost in ancient shipwrecks—litter the Adriatic coastline.

Amphorae were used to carry oil, wine, and fish on long sea journeys. They're tapered at the bottom because they were stuck into sand (or placed on a stand) to keep them upright in transit. They also have a narrow neck at the top, often with two large handles. In fact, the name comes from the Greek *amphi pherein,* "to carry from both sides." The taller, skinnier amphorae were generally used for wine, while the fat, short ones were for olive oil. Because amphorae differ according to their purpose and nationality, archaeologists find them to be a particularly useful clue for dating shipwrecks and determining the country of origin of lost ships. This is made easier by later Roman amphorae, which are actually stamped with the place they came from and what they held.

amphitheater to give it a level foundation. The four rectangular towers anchoring the amphitheater's facade are also unique (two of them are mostly gone). These once held wooden staircases for loading and unloading the amphitheater more quickly. At the top of each tower was a water reservoir, used for powering fountains that sprayed refreshing scents over the crowd to mask the stench of blood.

And there was plenty of blood. Imagine this scene in the days of the gladiators. More than 25,000 cheering fans from all social classes filled the seats. The Romans made these spectacles cheap or even free—distracting commoners with a steady diet of mindless entertainment prevented discontent and rebellion. (Hmm... *American Idol,* anyone?) Canvas awnings rigged around the top of the amphitheater shaded many seats. The fans surrounded the

"slaying field," which was covered with sand to absorb blood spilled by man and beast, making it easier to clean up after the fight. This sand *(harena)* gave the amphitheater its nickname...arena.

The amphitheater's "entertainers" were gladiators (named for the *gladius,* a short sword that was tucked into a fighter's boot). Some gladiators were criminals, but most were prisoners of war from lands conquered by Rome, who dressed and used weapons according to their country of origin. A colorful parade kicked off the spectacle, followed by simulated fights with fake weapons. Then the real battles began. Often the fights represented stories from mythology or Greek or Roman history. Most ended in death for the loser. Sometimes gladiators fought exotic animals—gathered at great expense from far corners of the empire—which would enter the arena from the two far ends (through the biggest arches). There were female gladiators, as well, but they always fought other women.

While the life of a gladiator seems difficult, consider that it wasn't such a bad gig—compared to, say, being a soldier. Gladiators were often better paid than soldiers, enjoyed terrific celebrity (both in life and in death), and only had to fight a few times each year.

Ignore the modern seating, and imagine when the arena (sandy oval area in the center) was ringed with two levels of stone seating and a top level of wooden bleachers. Notice that the outline of the arena is marked by a small moat—just wide enough to keep the animals off the laps of those with the best seats, but close enough so that blood still sprayed their togas.

After the fall of Rome, builders looking for ready-cut stone picked apart structures like this one—scraping it as clean as a neat slice of cantaloupe. Sometimes the scavengers were seeking the iron hooks that were used to connect the stone; in those oh-so "Dark Ages," the method for smelting iron from ore was lost. Most of this amphitheater's interior structures—such as steps and seats—are now in the foundations and walls of Pula's buildings...not to mention palaces in Venice, across the Adriatic. In fact, in the late 16th century, the Venetians planned to take this entire amphitheater apart, stone by stone, and reassemble it on the island of Lido on the Venetian lagoon. A heroic Venetian senator—still much revered in Pula—convinced them to leave it where it is.

Despite these and other threats, the amphitheater's exterior has been left gloriously intact. The 1999 film *Titus* (with Anthony

Hopkins and Jessica Lange) was filmed here, and today the amphitheater is still used to stage spectacles—from Placido Domingo to Marilyn Manson—with seating for about 5,000 fans. Recently, the loudest concerts were banned, because the vibrations were damaging the old structure.

Before leaving, don't miss the museum exhibit (in the "subterranean hall," down the chute marked #17). This takes you to the lower level of the amphitheater, where gladiators and animals were kept between fights. When the fight began, gladiators would charge up a chute and burst into the arena, like football players being introduced at the Super Bowl. As you go down the passage, you'll walk on a grate over an even lower tunnel. Pula is honeycombed with tunnels like these, originally used for sewers and as a last-ditch place of refuge in case of attack. Inside, the exhibit—strangely dedicated to "viniculture and olive-oil production in Istria in the period of antiquity" instead of, you know, gladiators—is surprisingly interesting. Browse the impressive collection of amphorae (see sidebar), find your location on the replica of a fourth-century A.D. Roman map (oriented with east on top), and ogle the gigantic grape press and two olive-oil mills.

• *From the amphitheater, it's a few minutes' walk to Pula's Old Town, where more Roman sights await. Exit the amphitheater to the left and walk one long block up the busy road (Amfiteatarska ulica) along the small wall, bearing right at the fork. When you reach the big park on your right, look for the little, car-sized...*

Town Model

Use this handy model of Pula to get oriented. Next to the amphitheater, the little water cannon spouting into the air marks the blue house nearby, the site of a freshwater spring (which makes this location even more strategic). The big star-shaped fortress on the hill is Fort Kaštel, designed by a French architect but dating from the Venetian era (1630). Read the street plan of the Roman town into this model: At the center (on the hill) was the *castrum,* or military base. At the base of the hill (the far side from the amphitheater) was the forum, or town square. During Pula's Roman glory days, the hillsides around the *castrum* were blanketed with the villas of rich merchants. The Old Town, which clusters around the base of the fortress-topped hill, still features many fragments of the Roman period, as well as Pula's later occupiers. We'll take a counterclockwise stroll around the fortified old hill through this ancient zone.

The huge anchor across the street from the model celebrates Pula's number-one employer—its shipyards.

• *Continue along the street. At the fork, again bear right (on Kandlerova ulica—level, not uphill). Notice the* ***Roman ruins*** *on your right. Just*

about any time someone wants to put up a new building, they find ruins like these. Work screeches to a halt while the valuable remains are excavated. In this case, they've discovered three Roman houses, two churches, and 2,117 amphorae—the largest stash found anywhere in the world. (Notice the harbor just behind, which suggests this might have been a storehouse for off-loaded amphorae.) I guess the new parking garage will have to wait.

After about three more blocks strolling through gritty, slice-of-life Pula, on your right-hand side, you'll see Pula's...

Cathedral (Katedrala)

This church combines elements of the two big Italian influences on Pula: Roman and Venetian. Dating from the fifth century A.D., the Romanesque core of the church (notice the skinny, slitlike windows) marks the site of an early-Christian seafront settlement in Pula. The Venetian Baroque facade and bell tower are much more recent (early 18th century). Typical of the Venetian style, notice how far away the austere bell tower is from the body of the church. The bell tower's foundation is made of stones that were scavenged from the amphitheater. On the square is an instructive poster illustrating the physical development of the town through the ages. The church's interior features a classic Roman-style basilica floor plan, with a single grand hall—the side naves were added in the 15th century, after a fire (free, generally open daily 7:00–12:00 & 16:00–18:00, but often closed).

• *Keep walking through the main pedestrian zone, past all the tacky souvenir shops and Albanian-run fast-food and ice-cream joints. After a few more blocks, you emerge into the...*

Forum

Every Roman town had a forum, or main square. Twenty centuries later, Pula's Forum not only serves the same function but has kept its old Roman name.

Two important buildings front the north end of the square, where you enter. The smaller building (on the left, with the columns) is the first-century A.D. Roman **Temple of Augustus** (Augustov Hram). Built during the reign of, and dedicated to, Augustus Caesar, this temple took a direct hit from an Allied bomb in World War II. After the war, the Allied occupiers rebuilt it as a sort of mea culpa—notice the patchwork repair job. It's the only

one remaining of three such temples that once lined this side of the square. Inside the temple is a single room with fragments of ancient sculptures (10 kn, daily June–Aug 9:00–22:00, Sept 9:00–20:00, early to mid-Oct 9:00–19:30, May 9:00–21:00, closed mid-Oct–April, sparse English labels). The statue of Augustus, which likely stood on or near this spot, dates from the time of Christ. Other evocative chips and bits of Roman Pula include the feet of a powerful commander with a pathetic little vanquished barbarian obediently at his knee (perhaps one of the Histri—the indigenous Istrians that the Romans conquered in 177 B.C.).

Head back out on to the square. As Rome fell, its long-subjugated subjects in Pula had little respect for the former empire's symbols, and many temples didn't survive. Others were put to new use: Part of an adjacent temple (likely dedicated to Diana) was incorporated into the bigger building on the right, Pula's medieval **Town Hall** (Gradska Palača). If you circle around behind this building, you can still see Roman fragments embedded in the back. The Town Hall encapsulates many centuries of Pula architecture: Romanesque core, Gothic reliefs, Renaissance porch, Baroque windows...and a few Roman bits and pieces. Notice the interesting combination of flags above the door: Pula, Croatia, Istria (with its mascot goat), Italy (for the large ethnic minority here), and the European Union (since Croatia is a candidate country).

• *Consider dropping by the* ***TI*** *on this square before continuing our circular stroll down the main drag, Sergijevaca. You'll pass by a small park on your right, then a block of modern shops. Immediately after the Kenvelo shop on the right (with a red-and-black* K *sign), turn right into the white, unmarked doorway. Emerging on the other side, turn left, walk to the metal grill, and look down to see the...*

Roman Floor Mosaic (Rimski Mozaik)

This hidden mosaic is a great example of the Roman treasures that lie below the old center of Pula. Uncovered by locals who were cleaning up from World War II bombs, this third-century floor was carefully excavated and cleaned up for display right where it was laid nearly two millennia ago. (Notice that the Roman floor level was about six feet below today's.) The centerpiece of the mosaic depicts the punishment of Dirce. According to the ancient Greek legend, King Lykos of Thebes was bewitched by Dirce and abandoned his pregnant queen. The queen gave birth to twin

boys (depicted in this mosaic), who grew up to kill their deadbeat dad and tie Dirce to the horns of a bull to be bashed against a mountain. This same story is famously depicted in the twisty *Toro Farnese* sculpture, partly carved by Michelangelo, on display in Naples' Archaeological Museum.

• *For an optional detour to Byzantine times, walk into the parking lot just beyond the mosaic. Near the end of the lot, on the left-hand side, is a fenced-off grassy field. At the far end of the field is the small...*

Basilica of St. Mary Formosa (Kapela Marije Formoze)

We've seen plenty of Roman and Venetian bric-a-brac, but this chapel survives from the time of another Istrian occupier: Byzantium. For about 170 years after Rome fell (the sixth and seventh centuries A.D.), this region came under the control of the Byzantine Empire and was ruled from Ravenna (now in Italy, across the Adriatic, south of Venice). Much of this field was once occupied by a vast, richly decorated basilica. This lonely chapel is all that's left, but it still gives a feel for the architecture of that era—including the Greek cross floor plan (with four equal arms) and heavy brick vaulting. An informational sign posted nearby outlines the original basilica and floor plan.

• *Back on the main drag (Sergijevaca), continue a few more blocks through Pula's most colorful and most touristy neighborhood, until you arrive at the...*

Arch of Sergius (Slavoluk Sergijevaca)

This triumphal arch, from the first century B.C., was Michelangelo's favorite Roman artifact in Pula. Marking the edge of the original Roman town, it was built to honor Lucius Sergius Lepidus. He fought on the side of Augustus in the civil wars that swept the empire after Julius Caesar's assassination. The proto-feminist inscription proudly explains, "Silvia of the Sergius family paid for this with her own money." Statues of Silvia's husband, Lucius, plus her son and her brother-in-law, once stood on the three blocks at the top of the arch. (Squint to see the *Sergivs* name on each block.) On the underside of the arch is a relief of an eagle (Rome) clutching an evil snake in its talons.

• *Before going under the arch, look to your left to see a famous Irishman appreciating the view from the terrace of...*

Café Uliks

In October 1904, a young writer named James Joyce moved from Dublin to Pula with his girlfriend, Nora Barnacle. By day, he taught English to Austro-Hungarian naval officers at the Berlitz language school (in the yellow building just behind). By night, he imagined strolling through his hometown as he penned short stories that would eventually become the collection *Dubliners*. But James and Nora quickly grew bored with little Pula and moved to Trieste in March 1905. Even so, Pula remains proud of its literary connections.

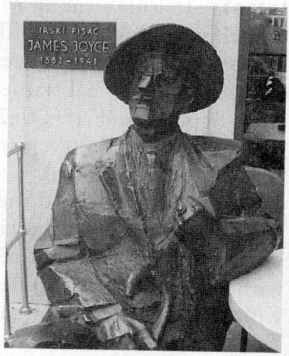

• *Now pass through the arch, into a square next to remains of the town wall. Continue straight ahead (up two bustling blocks, along the in-love-with-life Flanatička street) to...*

National Square (Nardoni Trg) and Market Hall

Pula's market hall was an iron-and-glass marvel when inaugurated in the 19th century. This structure is yet another reminder of the way the Austro-Hungarian Empire modernized Pula with grace and gentility. You'll find smelly fish on the ground floor (Mon–Sat 7:00–13:30, Sun 7:00–12:00) and an inviting food circus upstairs (Mon–Fri 7:00–15:00, Sat 7:00–14:00, Sun 7:00–12:00). All around is a busy and colorful farmers' market that bustles until about 13:00, when things quiet down.

• *Our tour is finished. If you're ready for lunch, consider one of the cheap options inside the market hall, or walk one block to Kantina (see "Eating in Pula," later).*

When you're done here, backtrack to the town wall. As you face the Arch of Sergius, take a right and walk under the leafy canopy next to the wall. Keep an eye out (mostly on your left, along the wall) for more Roman remains. Among these are the ***Twin Gates*** *(Porta Gemina), marking the entrance to a garden that's home to the* ***Archaeological Museum of Istria*** *(described next, under "Sights in Pula"). With more time, you can also consider a trip to the hilltop fortress,* ***Fort Kaštel.*** *Otherwise, we've completed our circular tour—the amphitheater is just around the corner.*

Sights in Pula

Archaeological Museum of Istria (Arheološki Muzej Istre)—If Pula's many ruins intrigue you, here's the place to scratch your Roman itch. This museum, over a century old, shows off some of what you've seen in the streets, plus lots more—stone monuments, classical statues, ancient pottery...you name it (20 kn; May–Sept Mon–Fri 9:00–20:00, Sat–Sun 9:00–15:00; Oct–April Mon–Fri 9:00–14:00, closed Sat–Sun; Carrarina 3, tel. 052/351-301, www.mdc.hr/pula).

On the hill behind the museum (and free to visit even if you don't buy a museum ticket) is its highlight, the remains of a **Roman Theater** (Rimsko Kazalište). Part of the stage is still intact, along with the semicircle of stone seats (some of which are still engraved with the names of the wealthy theatergoers who once sat there). To find it, go up the hill around the right side of the museum. This was the smaller of the two theaters in Roman Pula; the second was south of the center (and is no longer intact).

Fort Kaštel—For a bird's-eye view over the town, head up to its centerpiece fortress. This deserted-feeling place, hosting the Historical Museum of Istria, is worth visiting only for the chance to wander the ramparts. While neither the museum nor the fortress is worth the hike up here, it's a good way to kill some extra time in Pula and sample the views over the town and amphitheater (various trails lead up from the streets below).

Eating in Pula

The best lunch options are in and near the town's **market hall** (which is also where my self-guided walk ends). The top floor of the market is a food circus with a number of cheap and tempting eateries with both indoor and terrace seating (Mon–Fri 7:00–15:00, Sat 7:00–14:00, Sun 7:00–12:00). Upstairs in the back, look for **Laterna**, with unusually classy decor and fish specialties. Back outside, **Pekarna Corona**—a bakery across from the right side of the market (as you face the main entrance)—serves up good, fresh, cheap *burek,* the phyllo-dough pastry (Mon–Fri 6:30–18:00, Sat 6:30–15:00, closed Sun).

Kantina Restaurant, a block away, serves good lunches (including veggie options) and hearty, creative 35-kn salads in both an elegant vaulted cellar and on a lazy shady terrace. The service can be slow—if you're in a rush, eat at the market hall instead (50–75-kn pastas, 90–130-kn meat dishes, daily 12:00–23:00, at the end of the pedestrian zone at Flanatička 16, tel. 052/214-054). They also have a smaller café (drinks only, no food) directly across from the market hall.

Pula Connections

By Bus from Pula to: Rovinj (about hourly, 45 min), **Poreč** (12/day, 1.5 hrs), **Opatija** (almost hourly, 2 hrs), **Rijeka** (nearly hourly, 2–2.5 hrs), **Zagreb** (almost hourly, 3.75–6 hrs), **Split** (2/day, 10 hrs, plus 1 night bus—described below), **Venice** (1/day departing at 5:30, 5 hrs). A night bus departs Pula at 20:00, going to **Split** (arrives 6:00) and **Dubrovnik** (arrives 11:00). To reach destinations in **Slovenia** (including Piran and Ljubljana), you'll first transfer in Umag; or, in the summer, you can take the 8:00 bus from Rovinj (described on page 891). Be aware that bus connections are more frequent on weekdays (fewer departures Sat–Sun). Bus info: tel. 060-300-800.

By Train to: Zagreb (3/day, 6 hrs, transfer in Rijeka; in summer also 1 night train with very early arrival in Zagreb, 8 hrs), **Ljubljana** (1/day Mon–Fri, none Sat–Sun, 3.5 hrs, transfer in Buzet, Croatia, and Divača, Slovenia).

Motovun

Most tourists in Croatia focus on the coast. For a dash of variety, head inland. Some of the best bits of the Croatian interior lie just a short drive from Rovinj. Dotted with picturesque hill towns, speckled with wineries and olive-oil farms, embedded with precious truffles, and grooved by meandering rural roads, the Istrian interior is worth a visit.

Dramatically situated high above vineyards and a truffle-filled forest, Motovun (moh-toh-VOON; Montona in Italian, pop. 593) is the best-known and most-touristed of the Istrian hill towns. And for good reason: Its hilltop Old Town is particularly evocative, with a colorful old church and a rampart walk with the best spine-tingling vistas in the Istrian interior. It's hard to believe that race-car driver Mario Andretti was born in such a tranquil little traffic-free hamlet. Today Motovun's quiet lanes are shared by locals, tourists, and artists—who began settling here a generation ago, when it was nearly deserted.

Getting to Motovun

While it's possible to reach Motovun by public transportation (by bus from Pazin), the rewards are not worth the headaches. Drivers

find it worth a quick detour from the Istrian coast: From Rovinj or Pula, take the fast *ipsilon* highway north to Buje (between the *ipsilon* and Buje, consider stopping for a meal in Brtonigla—described later, under "Eating in Motovun"). From Buje, continue eastward through Krasica and take road #44, which follows the Mirna River Valley farther eastward, to Motovun (well-signed off the main road).

Orientation to Motovun

(area code: 052)

Motovun is steep. Most everything of interest to tourists is huddled around its tippy-top. The main, upper entrance gate into town deposits you at the main square, with the church on your left and Hotel Kaštel on your right. From there, you're just about two blocks in every direction from a sheer drop-off. This hilltop zone is circled by an old rampart that today offers Motovun's most scenic stroll.

Tourist Information

Motovun doesn't have an official TI, but the gang at Hotel Kaštel dispenses tourist information. During the day, you can drop into their travel agency on the main square, called Istria Magica (Mon–Fri 8:00–16:00, closed Sat–Sun, to the right as you face Hotel Kaštel, at Trg Andrea Antico 8, tel. 052/681-750); at other times, ask at the hotel reception desk (listed later, under "Sleeping in Motovun").

Arrival in Motovun

Motovun's striking hilltop setting comes with a catch: Visitors usually have to hike up part of the way. A steep, twisty road connects the base of the hill with the Old Town up top. If it's not too crowded, drive as far up this road as possible until you're directed to park in the lot partway up (near the lower church, a steep 10-min uphill walk to the main square, 15 kn/day). In busier peak times, this lot might be full, so you may have to wait a few minutes for a car to leave; or you can park in the big lot at the foot of the hill and walk all the way up (during very busy times, such as the film festival, a shuttle bus may be taking visitors up the hill). If you're staying at Hotel Kaštel, follow the procedure explained under "Sleeping in Motovun," later. If staying elsewhere, ask your hotelier for advice.

Self-Guided Walk

Welcome to Motovun

The following commentary will bring some meaning to your Motovun hilltop stroll. The walk begins at the traffic barrier half-

way up the hill (the highest you can drive unless you're sleeping up top).

The main drag leading up into town is lined with wine-and-truffle shops. My favorite is the Lanča family's **Etnobutiga ČA** (just above the parking lot on the right, at Gradiziol 33). This restored 17th-century house has a beautiful view terrace and a wide selection of local wines, brandies, and truffle products (most of them from the Zigante company, just across the valley). Like many people around here, Livio Lanča makes his own mistletoe brandy laced with honey (daily in season 10:00–20:00, slightly shorter hours in shoulder season, closed Nov–mid-March, tel. 052/681-767).

Hike several more steep minutes up the hill. Soon you'll pass yet another traffic barrier and reach the base of the town's wall (and the recommended Mondo Konoba restaurant). Circling up and around, you'll go through the first of two **defensive gateways.** Inside this passage (under the fortified gate), notice the various insignias from Motovun's history lining the walls—look for the Venetian lion, the Latin family tombstone, and the seal of Motovun (with five towers being watched over by an angel). The area above the gate was a storehouse for weapons in the 15th century, when Motovun first flourished.

Emerging from the gateway, you're greeted by sweeping views of the valley below on your right-hand side. (A coffee or light meal with this view is unforgettable; the town's lone ATM is to your left.) Just up and to the left, you'll find another defensive gateway, which is the main entrance into the heart of the **Old Town.** (Inside this gateway, notice the recommended Konoba pod Voltom restaurant.)

To your left as you come through the main gate is the yellow town church, **St. Stephen's.** The crenellated tower is a reminder of a time when this hilltop town needed to be defended. While unassuming from the outside, this austere house of worship has an impressive pedigree: It was designed by the famous Venetian architect Andrea Palladio (1508–1580), who greatly influenced the Neoclassical architecture of Washington, DC. The interior is a little gloomy but refreshingly lived-in—used more by locals than by tourists. On the left, notice a painting of the heart of Jesus, its eyes following you around the church (free, generally open daily 10:00–18:00 and during frequent services).

As you stand on the square in front of the church, imagine

Motovun during its annual **film festival,** when it's filled with 20,000 movie-lovers from throughout the region and around the world—often including a minor celebrity or two. This square fills to capacity, and films are projected on a giant screen at the far end (generally late July or early Aug, www.motovunfilmfestival.com).

Facing the church is the **Italian Cultural Center,** which fills an important role in this very Italian corner of Croatia. While the building is not open to the public, if your timing is right you'll enjoy beautiful music spilling out from its windows and filling the square. The local *klapa* music troupe—with men's voices harmonizing a cappella—practices here twice weekly (usually Mon and Fri evenings, at 21:00 in summer and 20:00 in winter, www.klapamotovun.com). If you hear them, find a bench and enjoy the show.

At the other end of the square is a leafy little piazza dominated by the big **Hotel Kaštel**—the main industry in town. In addition to its rooms and restaurant, Hotel Kaštel serves as the town TI. This is also where bigwigs in town for the local film festival call home—ask the staff about recent star-sightings of B-, C-, and D-list celebrities. (For example, if you're staying here, you may be showering in the same bathroom once graced by Jason Biggs, star of *American Pie.* Lucky you.) In the fall, they can also arrange truffle-finding excursions for tourists (about 700 kn/person).

Between the church and Hotel Kaštel, follow the lane to the **ramparts.** Take the five-minute stroll around the Old Town on these fortifications. While most of Croatia is overrun by stray cats, Motovun seems populated by dog lovers. If you see or hear dogs in people's backyards, it's a safe bet that they are trained to hunt for truffles in the surrounding forest.

As you breathe in the stunning panorama, notice that well-defended Motovun has been fortified three times—two layers of wall up top, and a third down below.

Sleeping in Motovun

Unlike most small Croatian towns, Motovun's accommodations don't charge extra for one- or two-night stays. In fact, if you're staying for three or more nights, try to score a discount.

$$ Hotel Kaštel, dominating Motovun's hilltop (and its tourist industry), is can-do, ideally located, and the only real hotel in this little burg. Most of the 32 colorful rooms have views. True to its name, the building used to be a castle, so the floor plan can be

confusing (July–Aug: Sb-410 kn, Db-690 kn, Tb-950 kn; June and Sept: Sb-380 kn, Db-635 kn, Tb-875 kn; May and Oct: Sb-355 kn, Db-585 kn, Tb-800 kn; 10 percent discount with this book, pricier apartments available, cheaper off-season, elevator, air-con in some rooms, laundry service is handy and affordable if you do it by the kilo, pay Internet access and Wi-Fi, Trg Andrea Antico 7, tel. 052/681-607, fax 052/681-652, www.hotel-kastel-motovun.hr, info@hotel-kastel-motovun.hr). Guests have free access to the new spa facility, with a beautiful indoor pool and a spa offering a wide range of massages (starting at 150 kn/30 min). Guests with cars should tell the attendant at the traffic barrier that you're staying here. If there's room on top, he'll let you drive up. Otherwise he'll tell you where to park and call the hotel, which will send down a free car to shuttle you up.

$ At **Bella Vista,** just below the lower town gate (a five-minute uphill walk to the main square), the Kotiga family rents five apartments with cute decor and balconies that offer sweeping views across the countryside (Db-360 kn, no breakfast, cash only, Gradiziol 1, check in at gift shop, clearly communicate arrival time if coming after 20:00, tel. & fax 052/681-724, mobile 091-523-0321, www.apartmani-motovun.com, info@apartmani-motovun.com, Mirjana).

$ Café Antico rents five simple rooms above a lively café/bar, a few steps around the corner from the main square (Db-300 kn, apartment with air-con-400 kn, no breakfast, cash only, some rooms get late-night noise from the café—try requesting a quieter one, Pietra Kandlera 2, tel. 052/681-697, mobile 098-173-0019, antico_motovun@hi.t-com.hr, Tomislav and Sandra).

$ Sobe Nena, run by sweet Doris, is a good budget option at the very bottom of Motovun's hill. It's a steep hike up into town, but you can try catching the shuttle bus from the lower parking lot, or Doris can give you a ride (Sb-215 kn, Db-285 kn, cash only, Kanal 32, tel. 052/681-719, mobile 098-937-2060, sobe.nena@gmail.com).

Eating in Motovun

Considering this is a small hill town with just three real restaurants, all of them are impressively good; the first two listings are particularly notable. Every menu is topped by pricey (but tasty) truffle dishes—but keep in mind that these are a better investment when truffles are in season and the flavors are pungent (see sidebar); otherwise you'll get older, blander truffles.

Mondo Konoba, run by a typical Croatian-Italian hybrid family and located just below the lower town gate (on the left, at the base of the wall), serves up Sicilian-Istrian fusion cuisine. Most

Truffle Mania

A mysterious fungus with a pungent, unmistakable flavor has been all the rage in Istria for the last decade or so. Called *tartufi* in both Croatian and Italian, these precious tubers have been gathered here since Roman times and were favored by the region's Venetian and Austrian rulers. More recently, local peasants ate them as a substitute for meat (often mixed with polenta) during the lean days after World War II.

In 1999, local entrepreneur Giancarlo Zigante discovered a nearly three-pound white truffle. In addition to making Giancarlo Zigante a very wealthy man, this giant truffle legitimized Istria on the world truffle scene. Today, Istria is giving France's Provence and Italy's Piedmont a run for their money in truffle production. Most of Istria's truffles are concentrated in the Motovun Forest, the damp, oak-tree-filled terrain surrounding Motovun, Livade, and Buzet.

A truffle is a tuber that grows entirely underground, usually at a depth of eight inches, near the roots of oak trees. Since no part of the plant grows aboveground, they're particularly difficult to find...and, therefore, valuable. Traditionally, Istrian truffle-gatherers use specially trained dogs to find truffles. This is most productive at night, when the darkness forces the dog to rely more on its sense of smell rather than sight.

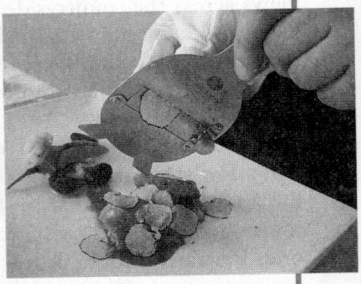

There are two general types of truffles: white (more valuable and with a milder flavor—*Tuber magnatum,* known as the "Queen of the Truffles") and black. Each type of truffle has a "season"—a specific time of year when its scent is released, making it easier to find (May–Nov for black, Oct–Jan for white). Once dug up, they look pretty unassuming—like a tough, dirty pinecone.

Truffles can be eaten in a variety of ways. Thanks to their powerful and distinctive kick, they're often used sparingly for flavor—grated like parmesan cheese, or as truffle oil sprinkled over a dish. But you'll also find them in cheese, salami, olive oil, pâté, and even ice cream. Some people find that the pungent, musty aftertaste follows them around all day... and all night, when its supposed aphrodisiac qualities kick in. Because they're so rare and difficult to find, truffles are incredibly expensive—but many people are more than happy to pay royally for that inimitable flavor.

If you're a truffle nut, you'll find yourself in heaven here; if not, you may still appreciate the chance to sample a little taste of truffle. While you do that, ponder how one giant tuber changed the economy of an entire region.

diners skip the forgettable dining room in favor of the inviting little outdoor terrace. The Mondo family's pack of five truffle-hunting dogs occasionally pays a visit (60–100-kn pastas, 90–170-kn main dishes, Wed–Mon 12:00–15:30 & 18:00–22:00, closed Tue, tel. 052/681-791).

Konoba pod Voltom is actually inside the town's upper, main gate (on the right, with the *Taberna* sign above the door). Motovun's most traditional eatery serves excellent, well-presented Istrian food in a cozy dining room. In good weather (June–Sept only), it's hard to beat their view loggia, just below and outside the gate (40–60-kn pastas, 60–110-kn main dishes, 140–220-kn truffle splurges, Thu–Tue 12:00–22:00, closed Wed, tel. 052/681-923).

Hotel Kaštel has its own restaurant, with good food and delightful seating right on the leafy main square (also listed under "Sleeping in Motovun," earlier; daily 7:00–10:00 & 13:00–15:00 & 19:00–21:00).

The simple **Montona Gallery** café, with tables along the rampart between the two gates, serves drinks and ice cream with mammoth views (open long hours daily).

In Brtonigla, Between Motovun and Rovinj

Brtonigla (bur-toh-NEEG-lah, Verteneglio in Italian, literally "black soil") is a tiny wine village surrounded by vineyards. Brtonigla is well-marked off the main *ipsilon* highway (coming north from Rovinj, but still south of Buje). Once in town, you'll find just a handful of haphazard streets, and this fine restaurant.

Konoba Astarea is a local favorite for traditional, take-your-time Istrian cuisine with a focus on fish and lamb. Anton and Alma Kernjus don't print an English menu, but they'll explain your options. Choose between the warmly cluttered, borderline-kitschy dining room huddled around the blazing open fire, where Alma does a lot of the cooking, or the cool and welcoming terrace with faraway sea views. It's smart to reserve ahead (70–120-kn meals, daily 11:00–23:00, closed Nov, tel. 052/774-384).

ZAGREB

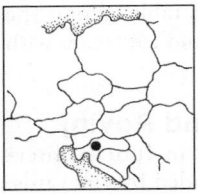

In this land of time-passed coastal villages, Zagreb (ZAH-grehb) offers a welcome jolt of big-city sophistication. You can't get a complete picture of modern Croatia without a visit here—away from the touristy resorts, in the lively and livable city that is home to one out of every six Croatians (pop. 780,000). In Zagreb, you'll find historic neighborhoods, worthwhile museums, a thriving café culture, my favorite urban people-watching in Croatia, and virtually no tourists.

Zagreb began as two walled medieval towns, Gradec and Kaptol, separated by a river. As Croatia fell under the control of various foreign powers—Budapest, Vienna, Berlin, and Belgrade—the two hill towns that would become Zagreb gradually took on more religious and civic importance. Kaptol became a bishopric in 1094, and it's still home to Croatia's most important church. In the 16th century, the Ban (Croatia's governor) and the Sabor (parliament) called Gradec home. The two towns officially merged in 1850, and soon after, the railroad connecting Budapest with the Adriatic port city of Rijeka was built through the city. Zagreb prospered.

After centuries of being the de facto religious, cultural, and political center of Croatia, Zagreb officially became a European capital when the country declared its independence in 1991. In the ensuing war with Yugoslavia, Zagreb was hardly damaged—Yugoslav bombs hit only a few strategic targets. Today, just a decade and a half later, Zagreb has long since repaired the minimal damage, and the capital is safe, modern, lively, and fun.

Planning Your Time

Most visitors just pass through Zagreb, but the city is worth a longer look. Throw your bag in a locker at the station and zip into the center for a quick visit—or consider spending the night.

You can get a decent sense of Zagreb in just a few hours. With whatever time you have, make a beeline for Jelačić Square to visit the TI and get oriented. Take the funicular up to Gradec, visit the excellent Museum of Naive Art, and stroll St. Mark's Square. Then wander down through the Stone Gate to the lively Tkalčićeva scene (good for a drink or meal), through the market (closes at 14:00), and on to Kaptol and the cathedral.

With more time, visit some of Zagreb's museums, or wander the series of parks called the "Green Horseshoe."

If you're moving on from Zagreb to Plitvice Lakes National Park (see next chapter), be warned that the last bus leaves in the mid-afternoon (usually 16:00); confirm your bus departure carefully to ensure that you don't get stranded in Zagreb.

Orientation to Zagreb

(area code: 01)

Zagreb, just 30 minutes from the Slovenian border, stretches from the foothills of Medvednica ("Bear Mountain") to the Sava River. In the middle of the sprawl, you'll find the modern **Lower Town** (Donji Grad, centered on **Jelačić Square**) and the historic **Upper Town** (Gornji Grad, comprising the original hill towns of **Gradec** and **Kaptol**). To the south is a U-shaped belt of parks, squares, and museums that make up the "Green Horseshoe." The east side of the U is a series of three parks, with the train station at the bottom (south) and Jelačić Square at the top (north).

Zagrebians have devised a brilliant scheme for confusing tourists: Street names can be depicted several different ways. For example, the street that is signed as ulica Kralja Držislava ("King Držislav Street") is often called by locals simply Držislavova ("Držislav's"). So if you're looking for a street, don't search for an exact match—be willing to settle for something that just has a lot of the same letters.

Tourist Information

Zagreb has Croatia's best-organized TI, right on Jelačić Square (Mon–Fri 8:30–20:00, until 21:00 in summer, Sat 9:00–17:00, Sun

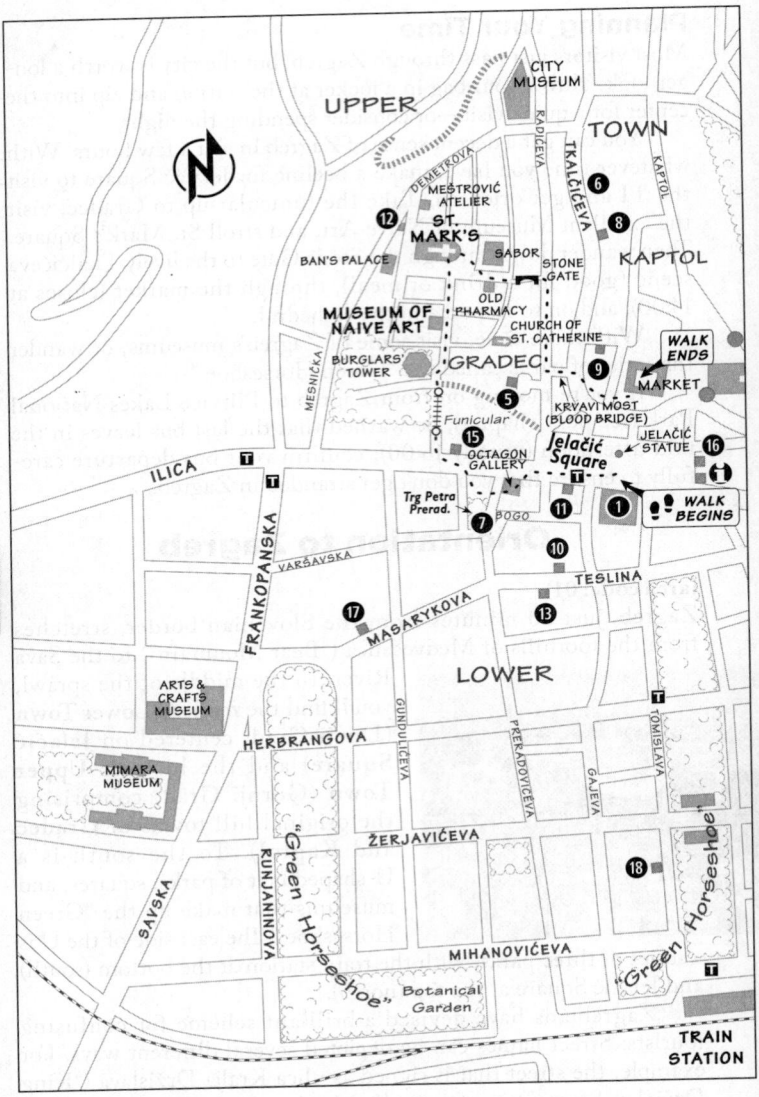

10:00–14:00, Trg bana Jelačića 11, tel. 01/481-4052, www.zagreb-touristinfo.hr). The TI offers piles of free, well-produced tourist brochures; highlights include the one-page city map (with handy transit map and regional map on back), the *Zagreb Info* booklet (including accommodations and restaurant listings), the monthly events guide, and the great *City Walks* brochure (with a couple of mildly diverting self-guided walking tours). I'd skip the TI's

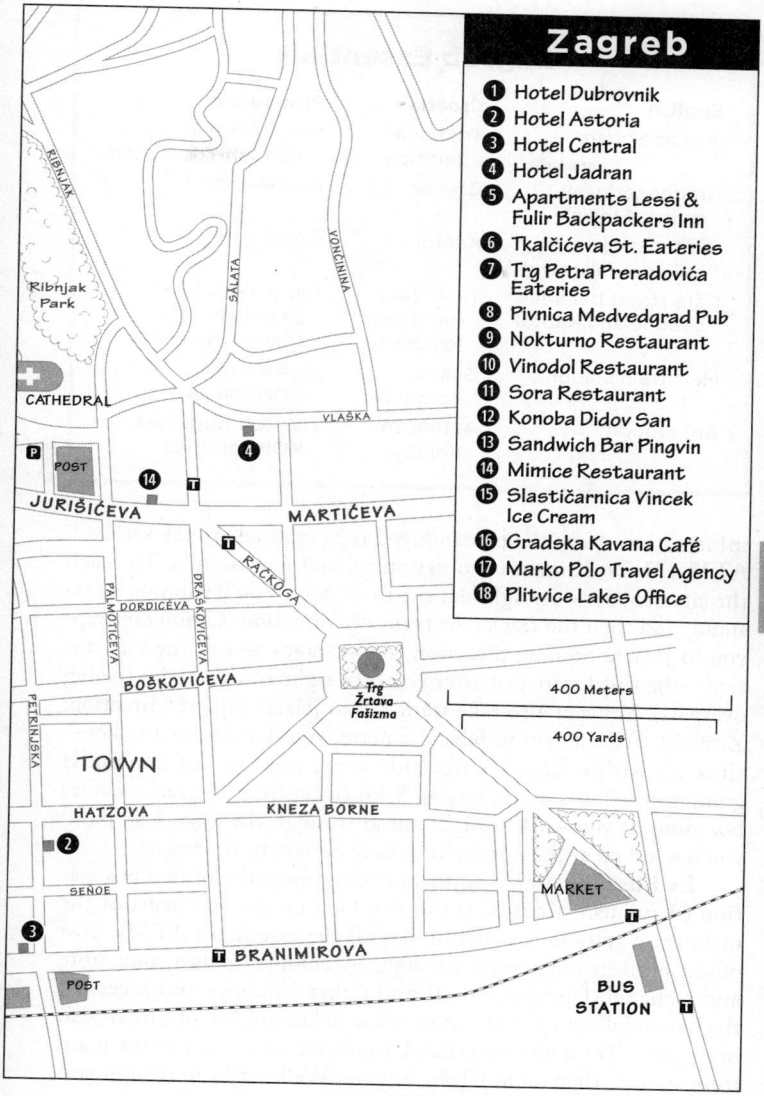

Zagreb Card (free transportation and discounts at most Zagreb museums, 60 kn/24 hrs, 90 kn/72 hrs).

Arrival in Zagreb

By Train: Zagreb's main train station (Glavni Kolodvor) is conveniently located a few blocks south of Jelačić Square on the Green Horseshoe. The straightforward arrivals hall has a train

Zagreb Essentials

English	Croatian	Pronounced
Jelačić Square	Trg bana Jelačića	turg BAH-nah YEH-lah-chee-chah
Gradec (original civic hill town)	Gradec	GRAH-dehts
Kaptol (original religious hill town)	Kaptol	KAHP-tohl
Café street between Gradec and Kaptol	Tkalčićeva (or "Tkalči" for short)	tuh-KAHL-chee-chay-vah (tuh-KAHL-chee)
Main train station	Glavni Kolodvor	GLAHV-nee KOH-loh-dvor
Bus station	Autobusni Kolodvor	OW-toh-boos-nee KOH-loh-dvor

information desk, ticket windows, luggage lockers (15 kn/day), ATMs, WCs, Konzum grocery store, and newsstands. To reach the city center, go straight out the front door. You'll run into a taxi stand, and then the tracks for **tram** #6 (direction: Črnomerec zips you to Jelačić Square; direction: Sopot takes you to the bus station—the third stop, just after you turn right and go under the big overpass). You can also take tram #13 to Jelačić Square (direction: Žitnjak). For the trip to Jelačić Square, you don't need a ticket—since it's within Zagreb's free-ride zone, you can just hop on. If going to the bus station, buy an 8-kn ticket from the kiosk before boarding. If you **walk** straight ahead through the long, lush park, you'll wind up at the bottom of Jelačić Square in 10 minutes.

By Bus: The user-friendly but inconveniently located bus station (Autobusni Kolodvor) is a few long blocks southeast of the main train station. The station has all the essentials: ATMs, post office, mini-grocery store, left-luggage counter...plus a smut store and a chapel. Upstairs, you'll find ticket windows and access to the buses (follow signs to *perone;* wave ticket in front of turnstile to open gate). Tram #6 (direction: Črnomerec) takes you to the main train station, then on to Jelačić Square. Walking from the bus station to Jelačić Square takes about 25 minutes.

By Plane: Zagreb's small airport is 10 miles south of the center (tel. 01/626-5222, www.zagreb-airport.hr). Once you get through security, your only food and drink option is one very expensive bar. While a shuttle bus connects the airport to the bus station (2/hr, 30 min, 30 kn), it's more convenient to pay for a taxi right to your hotel (30 min; the fair metered rate is around 180–200 kn, but some crooked cabbies might try to charge you more).

Getting Around Zagreb

The main mode of public transportation is the **tram,** operated by ZET (Zagreb Electrical Transport). You can ride free for up to two stops in any direction from Jelačić Square (including the train station); people over age 65 can ride free anywhere. For longer rides, a single ticket (good for 90 min in one direction, including transfers) costs 10 kn if you buy it from the driver (8 kn at kiosk, ask for *ZET karta*—zeht KAR-tah). A day ticket *(dnevna karta)* costs 25 kn. The most useful tram for tourists is #6, connecting Jelačić Square with the train and bus stations.

Taxis start at 19 kn, then run 7 kn per kilometer (20 percent more Sun and 22:00–5:00, 3 kn extra for each piece of baggage; beware of corrupt cabbies—ask for an estimate up front, or call Radio Taxi, tel. 01/661-0200 or 060-800-800). A typical ride within the city center shouldn't run more than about 30 kn, and the trip to the airport should cost no more than 200 kn (agree on a price first).

Helpful Hints

Schedule Quirks: Virtually all of Zagreb's museums are closed on Sunday afternoon and all day Monday. Some museums stay open late one night a week in summer (usually Thu). On Sunday morning, the city is bustling—but by afternoon, it's extremely quiet.

Ferry Tickets: If you're heading for the coast, you can reserve and buy Jadrolinija ferry tickets at the **Marko Polo** travel agency (Mon–Fri 9:00–17:00, Sat 9:00–13:00, closed Sun, Masarykova 24, tel. 01/481-5216).

Plitvice Lakes Office: If you're going to Plitvice Lakes National Park, you can get a preview and ask any questions at their information office in Zagreb (Mon–Fri 8:00–16:00, closed Sat–Sun, a block in front of main train station at Trg Kralja Tomislava 19, tel. 01/461-3586).

Tours in Zagreb

Local Guide—Dijana Bebek Miletić is an energetic, knowledgeable guide who helps visitors appreciate Zagreb's charms (500 kn/3-hour walking tour, mobile 091-303-3979, dijana.bebek@vip.hr).

Bus-plus-Walking Tours—This option, which combines a two-hour town walk with a one-hour bus tour, is a good way to get your bearings in this city. Unfortunately, there's no set schedule, so you'll have to ask for details at the TI (165 kn, www.ibus.hr).

Self-Guided Walk

▲▲Zagreb's Upper Town

The following one-way circular orientation walk begins at Jelačić Square. The entire route takes about an hour at a leisurely pace (not counting museum stops).

▲Jelačić Square (Trg bana Jelačića)

The "Times Square" of Zagreb bustles with life. Watching the crowds pile in and out of trams and seeing the city buzz with activity, you feel the energy of an on-the-rise capital of a vibrant new nation. The city's busy pedestrian scene, sense of style, and utter lack of tourists make it arguably Croatia's best people-watching destination.

Believe it or not, this frenetic Donji Grad ("lower town") once held the townspeople's farm fields. Today, it features a prominent equestrian statue of national hero **Josip Jelačić** (YOH-seep YEH-lah-cheech, 1801–1859), a 19th-century governor who extended citizens' rights and did much to unite the Croats within the Habsburg Empire. In Jelačić's time, the Hungarians were exerting extensive control over Croatia, even trying to make Hungarian the official language. Meanwhile, Budapesters revolted against Habsburg rule in 1848. Jelačić, ever mindful of the need to protect Croatian cultural autonomy, knew that he'd have a better shot at getting his way from Austria than from Hungary. Jelačić chose the lesser of two evils and fought alongside the Habsburgs to put down the Hungarian uprising. In the Yugoslav era, Jelačić was considered a dangerously nationalistic symbol, and this statue was dismantled and stored away. But when Croatia broke away in 1991, Croatian patriotism was in the air, and Jelačić returned. Though

Jelačić originally faced his Hungarian foes to the north, today he's staring down the Serbs to the south.

Get oriented. As you face Jelačić's statue, down a long block to your left is a funicular that takes you up to one of Zagreb's original villages, Gradec. To the right, look for the TI. At the top-right corner of the square is the **Gradska Kavana**, Zagreb's top café (with an elegant white-and-purple Art Deco interior that was recently renovated in gleaming style). If you leave the square ahead and to the right, you'll reach the other original village, Kaptol, and the cathedral (you can't miss its huge, pointy, Neo-Gothic spires—visible from virtually everywhere in Zagreb). The small street behind Jelačić and a little to the left leads to the market (Dolac) and the lively café street, Tkalčićeva.

For now, we'll head up to Gradec. Go a long block down the busy Ilica, then enter the big "**Octagon" shopping gallery** on the left (at #5, enter under *Privedna Banka Zagreb* sign). This was the ultimate in iron-and-glass shopping elegance a century ago, and still features a few of the city's top shops (including Croata, the tie store that loves to explain how Croatians invented the necktie; for the whole story, see page 830).

Walk all the way through the gallery, exiting into the inviting café-lined square called **Trg Petra Preradovića.** Survey your options for a coffee break, then turn right and head back out to Ilica street, where you'll turn left and continue the way you were headed before (noticing, at #18, the popular and recommended ice cream and cake shop Slastičarnica Vincek).

After another block, cross the tram tracks and turn right up Tomičeva, where you'll see a small **funicular** (ZET Uspinjača) crawling up the hill. Dating from the late 19th century, this funicular is looked upon fondly by Zagrebians—both as a bit of nostalgia and as a way to avoid some steps. You can walk up if you want, but the ride is more fun and takes only 55 seconds (4 kn, validate ticket in orange machine before you board, leaves every 10 min daily 6:30–21:00).

Gradec

From the top of the funicular, you'll enjoy a fine panorama over Zagreb. The tall tower you face as you exit is one of Gradec's original watchtowers, the **Burglars' Tower** (Kula Lotršćak). After the Tatars ransacked Central Europe in the early 13th century, King Béla IV decreed that towns be fortified—so Gradec built a wall and guard towers (just like Kraków and Budapest did). Look for the little cannon in the top-floor window. Every day at noon, this cannon fires a shot, supposedly to commemorate a 15th-century victory over the besieging Ottomans. Zagrebians hold on to other traditions, too—the lamps on this hill are still gas-powered, lit by

a city employee every evening.

Head up the street next to the tower. Little remains of medieval Gradec. When the Ottomans overran Europe, they never managed to take Zagreb, but the threat was enough to scare the nobility into the countryside. When the Ottomans left, the nobles came back, and they replaced the medieval buildings here with Baroque mansions. At the first square, to the right, you'll see the Jesuit **Church of St. Catherine.** It's not much to look at from the outside, but the interior is intricately decorated. The same applies to several mansions on Gradec. This simple-outside, ornate-inside style is known as "Zagreb Baroque."

As you continue up the street, notice that the old-timey **street signs** are a holdover from the Austro-Hungarian era: in both Croatian (Gospodska ulicza) and German (Herren Gasse).

On the left you'll see the **Croatian Museum of Naive Art**—Zagreb's best museum, and well worth a visit (listed later, under "Sights in Zagreb"). In the next block, on the left, look for the monument to Nikola Tesla (1856–1943), a prominent Croatian-born Serb scientist who moved to America and championed alternating current as a better electrical system than Thomas Edison's direct current.

At the end of the block, you'll come to **St. Mark's Square** (Markov trg), centered on the **Church of St. Mark.** The original church here was from the 13th century, but only a few fragments remain. The present church's colorful tile roof, from 1880, depicts two coats of arms. On the left, the red-and-white checkerboard symbolizes north-central Croatia, the three lions' heads stand for the Dalmatian Coast, and the marten (*kuna,* like the money) running between the two rivers (Sava and Drava) represents Slavonia—Croatia's northern, inland panhandle. On the right is the seal of Zagreb, featuring a walled city. (The seal typically shows wide-open doors—to demonstrate that Zagreb is strong, but still welcoming to visitors—but on this seal, the doors are closed.) The church interior (open sporadically) features frescoes with Bible scenes, and was redecorated in the early 20th century by local artists. Sculptures by the talented artist Ivan Meštrović flank the main altar: a *pietà* on the left, and Madonna and Child on the right (sitting cross-legged, in a typical Meštrović pose). He also sculpted the crucifix over the main altar. If you like these works, consider visiting Meštrović's nearby former home, which is now a museum of his works (it's about a block away: go

down the street behind the church on the left-hand side, and you'll see the museum on the right; see Ivan Meštrović Atelier listing later, under "Sights in Zagreb").

As you face the church, to the right is the **Sabor,** or parliament. From the 12th century, Croatian noblemen would gather here to make important decisions regarding their territories. This gradually evolved into today's modern parliament. (If you walk along the front of the Sabor and continue straight ahead two blocks, you'll run into the excellent Zagreb City Museum, described later, under "Sights in Zagreb.")

Across the square from the Sabor (to your left as you face the church) is the **Ban's Palace** (Banski Dvori), today the offices for the prime minister. This was one of the few buildings in central Zagreb damaged in the war following Croatia's independence. In October of 1991, Yugoslav forces shelled it from afar, knowing that Croatian President Franjo Tuđman was inside...but Tuđman survived. (Notice the different-colored tiles where the roof had to be patched.)

Walk from Gradec to Kaptol

For an interesting stroll from St. Mark's Square to the cathedral, head down the street (Kamenita ulica) to the right of the parliament building. Near the end of the street, on the right, you'll see the oldest **pharmacy** in town—recently restored and gleaming (c. 1355, marked *gradska ljekarna*).

Just beyond, you'll reach Gradec's only surviving town gate, the **Stone Gate** (Kamenita Vrata). Inside is an evocative chapel.

The focal point is a painting of Mary that miraculously survived a major fire in the adjoining house in 1731. When this medieval gate was reconstructed in the Baroque style, they decided to turn it into a makeshift chapel. The candles (purchased in the little shop and lit in the big metal bin) represent Zagrebians' prayers. Notice the soot-blackened ceiling over the forest fire of blazing candles in the bin. The stone plaques on the wall give thanks *(hvala)* for prayers that were answered. You may notice people making the sign of the cross as they walk through here, and often a crowd of worshippers gathers, gazing intently at the painting. Mary was made the official patron saint of Zagreb in 1990.

As you leave the Stone Gate and come to Radićeva, turn right and walk downhill. Take the next left, onto the street called **Krvavi Most**—"Blood Bridge." At the end of Krvavi Most, you'll

come to Tkalčićeva. This lively café-and-restaurant street used to be a river—the natural boundary between Gradec and Kaptol. The two towns did not always get along, and sometimes fought against each other. Blood was spilled, and the bridge that once stood here between them became known as Blood Bridge. By the late 19th century, the towns had united, and the polluted river began to stink—so they covered it over with this street.

As you cross the pedestrian drag called **Tkalčićeva,** you enter the old town of Kaptol. Consider taking a detour up delightful, in-love-with-life Tkalčićeva to scout your options for a coffee, beer, or meal (I've listed a few recommendations under "Eating in Zagreb," later).

Just beyond Tkalčićeva is the **market** *(dolac),* packed with colorful stalls selling produce of all kinds (Mon–Sat 7:00–14:00, Sun 7:00–13:00). At the back-left corner is the fragrant fish market *(ribarnica),* and under your feet is an indoor part of the market *(tržnica),* where farmers sell farm-fresh eggs and dairy products (same hours as outdoor market, entrance below in the direction of Jelačić Square).

Your walk is over. On the other side of the market, you can visit the cathedral (described later, under in "Sights in Zagreb").

Sights in Zagreb

▲▲▲Croatian Museum of Naive Art (Hrvatski Muzej Naivne Umjetnosti)

This remarkable spot, founded in 1952 as the "Peasant Art Gallery," is one of the most enjoyable little museums in Croatia. It features expressionistic paintings by untrained peasant artists (called "autodidacts" because they are self-taught). On one easy floor, the museum displays 80 paintings made mostly by Croatians from the 1930s to the 1980s.

Cost, Hours, Location: 20 kn, pick up the English explanations as you enter, Tue–Fri 10:00–18:00, Sat–Sun 10:00–13:00, closed Mon, ulica Sv. Čirila i Metoda 3, tel. 01/485-1911, www.hmnu.org.

Background: Starting in the late 19th century, the art world began to broaden its definition of great art, seeking out worthy art originating outside the esteemed academies and salons of the day. Their goal: to demonstrate that art was not simply a trained skill, but an inborn talent. Intellectuals began to embrace an "anti-intellectual" approach to art. Interest grew in

the indigenous art of Africa, Mesoamerica, and Polynesia (Picasso went through an African mask phase, and Gauguin went to live in Tahiti); composer Béla Bartok collected traditional folk melodies from the Hungarian countryside; the "art brut" movement preserved artwork by people deemed "insane" by mainstream society; the self-taught painter Grandma Moses became well-known in the US and Europe; and art by children gained acclaim.

Here in Croatia in the 1930s, the focus was on art by untrained peasants. At that time, as in much of rural Europe, 85 percent of Croatians lived virtually medieval lifestyles—with no electricity or other modern conveniences—and about 60 percent were illiterate and uneducated. These artists captured this humble reality, creating figurative works in an increasingly abstract age. By the 1950s and 1960s, Croatian "naive art" had emerged at the forefront of a Europe-wide phenomenon.

This museum presents an easily digestible sampling of the top names from this movement. Viewing these evocative works, it's important to remember that this isn't considered "folk art" or "amateur art"—but top-quality works by great artists who were, by fluke of fate, never formally trained.

➲ **Self-Guided Tour:** Buy your ticket and follow the one-way route through the five numbered rooms, which you'll circle counter-clockwise.

Room 1: Immediately to the right as you enter is the first of many paintings by **Ivan Generalić** (1914–1992), the founder and star of Croatian naive art (his self-portrait, with a blue background, dominates the room). Generalić was discovered in the 1930s by a Paris-trained Croatian artist. The first few paintings show his evolution as an artist (and the evolution of Croatian naive art in general): While his early works came with a social or political agenda (such as *The Requisition,* where two policemen repo a cow from an impoverished couple), he eventually mellowed his focus to simply show typical village scenes. These start out as purely representational of peasant life *(Village Dance),* gradually become more and more fantastical *(Harvesters),* and eventually strip away people entirely to focus on the land (1939's *Landscape*). In 1953, Generalić—still relatively unknown outside his homeland—did a show in Paris, sold everything, and came home rich. This put Croatian naive art on the international map and kick-started a new vigor in the movement. *Woodcutters* (see photo on top of next page), from 1959, shows the next phase, as Generalić's works became even more

rich with fantasy—the peacock, the men clinging to tree tops, and the trademark "coral trees." Instead of showing, Generalić is evoking; naive art strove to capture the spirit and emotion of peasant life. Paintings such as this one inspired Generalić's followers (called the "Hlebine School," for the village where Generalić lived).

Flanking the door are works by the next generation of naive art—two big-name followers who were inspired (if not trained) by Generalić: on the left, the gruesome *Evangelists at Cavalry* crucifix, by **Ivan Večenaj,** who focused on religious scenes; and on the right, *Winter Landscape with Woman,* by **Mijo Kovačić,** who specialized in peasant landscapes.

Room 2: The next room features more works by Večenaj and Kovačić. Studying Kovačić's many landscapes, notice how he took a style of painting pioneered by Generalić and brought it to the next level. Winter scenes were most common, because the peasant artists were busy working the fields the rest of the year. (Early on, such artists were sometimes called "Sunday painters," because they had to work their "real" jobs from Monday to Saturday.) Kovačić also enjoyed winter scenes for the evocative black-and-white contrast they allowed. Like Dalí, Magritte, and other surrealists, Kovačić juxtaposed super-realism (look at each individual hair on the swine in his painting *Swineherd*) with fantastical, almost otherworldly settings. Also in this room are some landscapes by **Dragan Gaži,** a friend and neighbor of Generalić's.

You may notice that these supposedly "untrained" artists seem to borrow from other painters—most notably, the countryside peasant scenes often feel ripped from a Pieter Bruegel canvas. While not formally schooled, there's no doubt that these artists were aware of, and often inspired by, their artistic forebears.

Also notice that naive artists frequently painted on glass. It was cheaper and more readily available in rural areas than art canvases, and—because it required no special technique—was an easier medium for the untrained naive artists to work on.

Room 3: On the right, find the portraits of Roma (Gypsy) people by **Martin Mehkek.** For the one depicting his cross-eyed neighbor Steve, Mehkek mostly painted with his fingers, using brushes only for fine details (such as the Hitler-style moustache). On the other side of the door is *Guiana '78*—by **Josip Generalić,** the founder's less-talented son—showing the gruesome aftermath of the Jim Jones mass suicide, with a pair of monkeys surveying the smiling corpses. (While vivid, this painting doesn't reflect the Croatian peasant experience, and the curator admits it's not the best representative of naive art.) Filling out the room are more of those distinctive coral-style trees that pervade naive works, these by **Ivan Lacković.**

Room 4: This room shows off two big names from the latter part of the movement. On the left are lyrical landscapes by **Ivan Rabuzin,** arguably second only to Ivan Generalić in importance to this movement. Like a visual haiku, Rabuzin's dreamlike world of hills, trees, and clouds is reminiscent of Marc Chagall. Rabuzin's works are especially popular among the museum's many Japanese visitors. On the right are **Emerik Feješ**'s colorful scenes of famous monuments from around Europe—Paris, Venice, Vienna, Milan, and more. In fact, Feješ never traveled to any of these places—his paintings are based on romantic black-and-white postcards of the era, which Feješ "colorized" in his unique style.

Rooms 5 and 6: Room 5 displays works mostly by naive artists from other countries. And Room 6 features pencil sketches used by naive artists to create their works. After the sketch was complete, the artist would put it against a pane of glass to paint the scene—small details first, gradually filling in more and more of the background. Then the glass painting would literally be flipped over to be viewed. All of the works on glass you've seen in this collection were actually painted backwards.

Other Museums in Gradec

▲Ivan Meštrović Atelier—Ivan Meštrović—Croatia's most famous artist—designed, built, and decorated this house, and lived here from 1922 until 1942 (before he fled to the US after World War II). The house has been converted into a delightful gallery of the artist's works, displayed in two parts: residence and studio. Split's Meštrović Gallery (described on page 831) is the definitive museum of the 20th-century Croatian sculptor, but if you're not going there, Zagreb's gallery is a convenient place to gain an appreciation for this prolific, thoughtful artist (30 kn, 20-kn English catalog, Tue–Fri 10:00–18:00, Sat–Sun 10:00–14:00, closed Mon, behind St. Mark's Square at Mletačka 8, tel. 01/485-1123, www.mdc.hr/mestrovic). For more on Meštrović, see page 832.

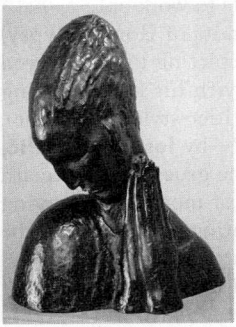

▲Zagreb City Museum (Muzej Grada Zagreba)—This collection, with a modern, well-presented exhibit that sprawls over two floors of an old convent, traces the history of the city through town models, paintings, furniture, clothing, and lots of fascinating artifacts. After buying your ticket, head through the door and turn left, then work your way up through the ages. Each display has a fine English description. The 19th-century wing is like a folk museum. Find the giant map on the floor, punctuated with models of key buildings. The coverage of the tumultuous 20th century is perhaps most engaging, with an understandably bad attitude about the Serb-dominated first Yugoslav period, followed by stirring videos, a hall of propaganda posters, and artifacts from World War II and the Tito period (when Croatia was a player in Belgrade). The finale is a room dedicated to the creation of independent Croatia, including an exhibit on damage sustained during the warfare (20 kn, Tue–Fri 10:00–18:00, Thu until 22:00, Sat 11:00–19:00, Sun 10:00–14:00, closed Mon, at north end of Gradec at Opatička 20, tel. 01/485-1361, www.mgz.hr).

▲Cathedral (Katedrala)

By definition, Croats are Catholics. Before the recent war, relatively few people practiced their faith. But as the Croats fought against their Orthodox and Muslim neighbors, Catholicism took on a greater importance. Today, more and more Croats are

attending Mass. This is Croatia's single most important church.

In 1094, when a diocese was established at Kaptol, this church quickly became a major center of high-ranking church officials. In the mid-13th century, the original cathedral was destroyed by invading Tatars, who actually used it as a stable. It was rebuilt, only to be destroyed again by an earthquake in 1880. The current version—undergoing yet another renovation for the last several years—is Neo-Gothic (about a hundred years old inside and out). Surrounding the church are walls with pointy-topped towers (part of a larger archbishop's palace) that were built for protection against the Ottomans. The full name is the Cathedral of the Assumption of the Blessed Virgin Mary and the Saintly Kings Stephen and Ladislav (whew!)—but most locals just call it "the cathedral."

As you stand out front, appreciate the stately facade and modern tympanum (carved semicircular section over the door). Then step inside and wander down the nave (free, Mon–Sat 10:00–17:00, Sun 13:00–17:00). Look closely at the silver relief on the main **altar:** a scene of the Holy Family doing chores around the house (Mary sewing, Joseph and Jesus building a fence...and angels helping out).

In the front-left corner (on the wall, between the confessionals), find the modern tombstone of **Alojzije Stepinac.** He was the Archbishop of Zagreb during World War II, when he shortsightedly supported the Ustaše (Nazi puppet government in Croatia)—thinking, like many Croatians, that this was the ticket to greater independence from Serbia. When Tito came to power, he put Stepinac on trial and sent him to jail for five years. But Stepinac never lost his faith, and he remains to many the most important inspirational figure of Croatian Catholicism. (He's also respected in the US, where some Catholic schools bear his name. But many Serbs today consider Stepinac a villain who cooperated with the brutal Ustaše.)

Facing the nearby altar, on the right look for the grave of **Josip Jelačić,** the statesman whose statue adorns Zagreb's main square.

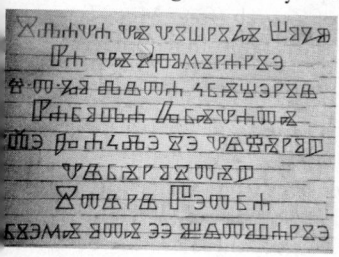

As you leave the church, look high on the wall to the left of the door. This strange script is the **Glagolitic alphabet** *(glagoljca),* invented by Byzantine missionaries Cyril and Methodius in the ninth century to translate the Bible into

Slavic languages. Though these missionaries worked mostly in Moravia (today's eastern Czech Republic), their alphabet caught on only here, in Croatia. (Glagolitic was later adapted in Bulgaria to become the Cyrillic alphabet—still used in Serbia, Russia, and other parts east.) In 1991, when Croatia became its own country and nationalism surged, the country flirted with the idea of making this the official alphabet.

The Green Horseshoe

With extra time, stroll around the Green Horseshoe (the U-shaped belt of parks and museums in the city center). The museums here aren't nearly as interesting as those on Gradec, but may be worth a peek on a rainy day.

Mimara Museum (Muzej Mimara)—This grand, empty-feeling building displays the eclectic collection of a wealthy Dalmatian, ranging from ancient artifacts to paintings by European masters. While the names are major—Rubens, Rembrandt, Velázquez, Renoir, Manet—the paintings themselves are minor. Still, art buffs may find something to get excited about (40 kn, 90-kn English guidebook, otherwise virtually no English, Tue–Sat 10:00–17:00, Thu until 19:00, Sun 10:00–14:00, closed Mon, Rooseveltov trg 5, tel. 01/482-8100).

Arts and Crafts Museum (Muzej za Umjetnost i Obrt)—This decorative arts collection of furniture, ceramics, and clothes is well-displayed. From the entry, go upstairs, then work your way clockwise and up to the top floor—passing through each artistic style, from Gothic to the present. It's mostly furniture, with a few paintings and other items thrown in (30 kn, some rooms have laminated English descriptions to borrow, otherwise very limited English, Tue–Sat 10:00–19:00, Thu until 22:00, Sun 10:00–14:00, closed Mon, Trg Maršala Tita 10, tel. 01/488-2111, www.muo.hr).

Botanical Garden (Botanički Vrt)—For a back-to-nature change of pace from the urban cityscape, wander through this relaxing garden, run by the University of Zagreb (free, Mon–Tue 9:00–14:30, Wed–Sun 9:00–18:00—or until 19:00 in summer, at southwest corner of the Green 'Shoe).

Sleeping in Zagreb

Hotels in central Zagreb are very expensive. I prefer sleeping in Ljubljana or at Plitvice Lakes National Park, both of which offer better values. But if you must stay in Zagreb, these are the best

Sleep Code

(5 kn = about $1, country code: 385, area code: 01)
S = Single, **D** = Double/Twin, **T** = Triple, **Q** = Quad, **b** = bathroom. English is spoken at each place. Unless otherwise noted, credit cards are accepted, breakfast is included, and the modest tourist tax (7 kn per person, per night) is not.

To help you sort easily through these listings, I've divided the rooms into three categories based on the price for a standard double room with bath:

$$$ Higher Priced—Most rooms 800 kn or more.
$$ Moderately Priced—Most rooms between 500–800 kn.
$ Lower Priced—Most rooms 500 kn or less.

deals right in the main tourist zone. If you show up without a reservation, the TI can help you find a hotel room or *soba* for no fee.

$$$ Hotel Dubrovnik is a professional-feeling, business-class hotel with 268 rooms, ideally located at the bottom of Jelačić Square (small Sb-820 kn, bigger Sb-980 kn, Db with 1 big bed-1,200 kn, twin Db-1,300 kn, suite-1,500–1,600 kn, extra bed-250 kn, rooms overlooking the square don't cost extra but come with some tram noise, often cheaper on weekends, prices soft, air-con, non-smoking floors, elevator, free Internet access and Wi-Fi, Gajeva 1, tel. 01/486-3555, fax 01/486-3506, www.hotel-dubrovnik.hr, reservations@hotel-dubrovnik.hr).

$$$ Hotel Astoria, a Best Western, offers 100 smallish but plush, recently renovated rooms and a high-class lobby. It's on a grimy street near the train station, so I wouldn't splurge here unless I was in town on a weekend, when rates drop by a third (Sb-880–900 kn, Db-1,140 kn; Fri–Sun: Sb-610–690 kn, Db-785 kn; rates can be soft on some weekdays, various discounts offered—including military—fancier suites also available, air-con, elevator, free Internet access and Wi-Fi, Petrinjska 71, tel. 01/480-8900, fax 01/480-8908, www.bestwestern.com, recepcija@hotelastoria.hr).

$$ InZagreb, run by Ivana and Ksandro Kovačić, rents nine well-furnished, mostly one-bedroom apartments in various buildings around the city. While locations vary, most are within a 10- to 15-minute walk of the main square. Visit their website, find the apartment that appeals to you, and make a reservation. Clearly communicate your arrival time, and they'll pick you up at the train or bus station (no extra charge) or at the airport (150 kn extra) and take you to your home-away-from-home in Zagreb (Db-475–625 kn depending on apartment and location, no 1-night stays, 50 percent extra for 2-night stays, no breakfast, kitchenettes, air-con,

free Wi-Fi, laundry machine, mobile 091-652-3201, fax 01/652-3201, www.inzagreb.com, info@inzagreb.com).

$$ Hotel Central's 76 overly perfumed rooms are comfortable and modern, and the price is right. This place seems to get a little better every year, and the location—right across from the main train station—is convenient for rail travelers (Sb-530 kn, larger Sb-660 kn, Db with one big bed-800 kn, twin Db-870 kn, Tb-1,100 kn, air-con, elevator, free Wi-Fi, Branimirova 3, tel. 01/484-1122, fax 01/484-1304, www.hotel-central.hr, info@hotel-central.hr).

$$ Hotel Jadran has 49 outdated, throwback rooms two urban blocks from the cathedral, and about a 10-minute walk east of Jelačić Square (Sb-520 kn, Db-730 kn, Tb-900 kn, some street noise—request quiet room, air-con, elevator, pay Wi-Fi, Vlaška 50, tel. 01/455-3777, fax 01/461-2151, www.hup-zagreb.hr, jadran@hup-zagreb.hr).

$ Apartments Lessi, run by youthful and English-speaking Tin, are three rooms that share a centrally located courtyard with a bar and the Fulir Backpackers Inn (see next listing). The rooms (one of which is up a tight spiral staircase) have pleasantly rustic decor with modern comforts (smaller room: Sb-200 kn, Db-360 kn; apartments: Sb-350 kn, Db-450 kn, Tb-550 kn, Qb-600 kn; cash only, no breakfast, air-con, free Wi-Fi, tucked down the courtyard at Radićeva 3a, mobile 091-288-8858, www.lessi.com.hr, info@lessi.com.hr).

$ Fulir Backpackers Inn, a funky slumbermill named for a legendary Zagrebian bon vivant, is loosely run by Davor and Leo, a pair of can-do Croats who lived in Ohio. It's colorful, friendly, and youthful, with a big 10-bunk dorm, three six-bed rooms, and a quad. Just a few steps from Jelačić Square, this hostel puts you in the heart of Zagreb (130–145 kn/bunk depending on season—cheaper Oct-April, includes sheets, no breakfast, free lockers, free Internet access and Wi-Fi, self-service laundry, upstairs at the end of the courtyard at Radićeva 3a, tel. 01/483-0882, mobile 098-193-0552, www.fulir-hostel.com).

Eating in Zagreb

People-Watching and Coffee-Sipping

One of my favorite Zagreb pastimes is nursing a drink along its thriving people zones, watching an endless parade of fashionable locals saunter past, and wondering why they don't create such an inviting space in my hometown. The best place is on **Tkalčićeva street,** Zagreb's main café street and urban promenade rolled into one. It's a parade of fashionable locals and *the* place to see and be seen (starts a block behind Jelačić Square, next to the market). I've

listed my favorite Tkalčićeva eateries below. Honorable mention goes to **Trg Petra Preradovića,** an inviting square just a short walk from Jelačić Square (up Ilica street) that bustles with appealing outdoor cafés and bars.

Eating on or near Tkalčićeva Street

Most places along Tkalčićeva serve only drinks. For a meal, consider these options.

Pivnica Medvedgrad is a brewpub serving five different in-house beers and heavy, stick-to-your-ribs pub grub that feels closer to Prague than to Dubrovnik. The food offers a welcome break from the pizzas-pastas-and-seafood rut you'll encounter on the coast, and the outdoor seating right on Tkalčićeva's most colorful stretch will seduce you into staying for another beer (25–50-kr meals, daily 10:00–24:00, food served until 22:00, Tkalčićeva 36, tel. 01/492-9613).

Nokturno, just off of Tkalčićeva, serves up good pizza and pasta in a lively interior and has ample outdoor seating on a terrace cascading down the street (cheap 20–30-kn pizzas, pastas, and salads; 30–50-kn meat and fish dishes; daily 9:00–1:00 in the morning, Skalinska 4, tel. 01/481-3394).

***At the Market* (Dolac):** Zagreb's busy market offers plenty of options (Mon–Sat 7:00–14:00, Sun 7:00–13:00). Assemble a fresh picnic direct from the producers. Or, for something already prepared, duck into one of the many cheap restaurants and cafés on the streets around the market. The middle level of the market, facing Jelačić Square, is home to a line of places with cheap food and indoor or outdoor seating.

Elsewhere in Zagreb

Vinodol is your white-tablecloth classy dinner spot, with a peaceful covered terrace and a smartly appointed dining room under an impressive vaulted ceiling. The good, reasonably priced cuisine includes veal prepared *peka*-style, in a pot covered with hot coals (*peka* portion costs 80 kn, served only at certain times—generally at 12:30 and 18:30; 60–100-kn main dishes, open daily 10:00–24:00, Teslina 10, tel. 01/481-1427).

Sky-High Asian: To dine on trendy Japanese fare atop a skyscraper with Zagreb's best view, ride up to the 16th floor of the Ilica Tower (just a block off Jelačić Square) and grab a table at **Sora**. The restaurant has mod, air-conditioned, jazzy ambience and enjoys

fantastic views over the rooftops of Zagreb, though the stout security bars shatter some of the appeal (35–50-kn sushi, 30–70-kn light dishes, 70–90-kn noodles, 80–170-kn main dishes, Mon–Sat 11:30–1:00 in the morning, closed Sun, reservations smart, Ilica 1a, tel. 01/482-8940).

In the Upper Town (Gradec): For a lunch or dinner break from sightseeing in the upper town, **Konoba Didov San** serves up traditional food from the Dalmatian hinterland. You'll find the normal Dalmatian specialties, plus eel, frogs, and snails. Choose between the homey, traditional interior and the outdoor tables (25–40-kn starters, 60–100-kn main dishes, daily 10:00–24:00, a few steps up from the Ivan Meštrović Atelier at Mletačka 11, tel. 01/485-1154).

Fast and Cheap: **Sandwich Bar Pingvin,** busy with locals dropping by for take-away, is a favorite for quick, cheap, tasty sandwiches with chicken, turkey, steak, fish, and even salmon. They'll wrap it all in a piece of grilled bread and top it with your choice of veggies and sauces to go—or, to eat here, sit at one of the few tiny tables or stools. There are so many options that ordering can be tricky, but the menu is in English, and the staff generally speaks English, too (20–30 kn, open long hours daily, about a block below Jelačić Square at Teslina 7).

Fried and Fishy: **Mimice** is a local institution and an old-habits-die-hard favorite of the older generation. While a bit tired and dreary, it's a cheap and memorable time-warp serving up simple fish dishes (15–35 kn, order starches and sauces separately). Choose what you want from the limited menu (if confused, survey the room for a plate that looks good and ask what it is), pay, and take your receipt to the next counter to claim your food. Order the smelt to get a plate of tiny deep-fried fish (Mon–Fri 7:00–22:00, Sat 7:00–18:00, closed Sun, Jurišićeva 21). As Zagreb is a Catholic town, you'll have to wait in line if you're here on a Friday.

Dessert: As the long line out front suggests, Zagreb's favorite *sladoled* (Italian gelato-style ice cream) is at **Slastičarnica Vincek,** two blocks west of Jelačić Square. Choose from a wide variety of flavors (6 kn/scoop), giving special consideration to the Vincek flavor—chocolate and walnuts. They also have other desserts, including *Zagrebačka kremšnita*—a variation on the famous cream-and-custard cake from Lake Bled (see page 707), but with chocolate (Mon–Sat 8:00–23:00, closed Sun, on the busy tram-lined Ilica street at #18).

Zagreb Connections

From Zagreb by Train to: Rijeka (3/day, 4 hrs), **Pula** (3/day, 6 hrs, transfer in Rijeka; in summer also 1 night train, 8 hrs), **Split** (3/day, 2/day off-season, 5.5 hrs, plus 1 direct night train, 8 hrs), **Mostar**

(1/day, 12 hrs, bus is faster), **Ljubljana** (8/day, 2.5 hrs), **Vienna** (4/day, 5.5–7 hrs, 2 direct, others with 1–2 changes), **Budapest** (2/day, 5 or 7 hrs), **Lake Bled** (via Lesce-Bled, 5/day, 3.5 hrs).

By Bus to: Plitvice Lakes National Park (about hourly until around 16:00, 2–2.5 hrs), **Rijeka** (hourly, 3.5 hrs), **Rovinj** (6–9/day, 5–8 hrs), **Pula** (almost hourly, 3.75–6 hrs), **Split** (about 2/hr, 5–9 hrs), **Mostar** (1/day, 8 hrs, plus 1 night bus, 9.5 hrs), **Dubrovnik** (7/day including some overnight options, 10 hrs), **Korčula** (1/night, 13.5 hrs).

Bus schedules can be sporadic (e.g., several departures clustered around the same time, then nothing for hours)—confirm your plans carefully (inquire locally, or use the good online schedules at www.akz.hr). The TI is very helpful with providing bus information. Popular buses, such as the afternoon express to Split, can fill up quickly in peak season. Unfortunately, it's impossible to buy bus tickets anywhere in the center, so to guarantee a seat, you'll have to get to the station early (locals suggest even two hours in advance). Better yet, call the central number for the bus station to check schedules and reserve the bus you want, ideally at least 24 hours ahead: tel. 060-313-333 (from abroad, dial +385-1-611-2789). If you can't get an English-speaker on the line, and the TI isn't too busy, they might be willing to call for you.

PLITVICE LAKES NATIONAL PARK

Nacionalni Park Plitvička Jezera

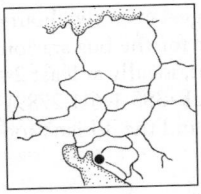

Plitvice (PLEET-veet-seh) is one of Europe's most spectacular natural wonders. Imagine Niagara Falls diced and sprinkled over a heavily forested Grand Canyon. There's nothing like this lush valley of 16 terraced lakes, laced together by waterfalls and miles of pleasant plank walks. Countless cascades and water that's both strangely clear and full of vibrant colors make this park a misty natural wonderland. Years ago, after eight or nine visits to Europe, I thought I really knew the place. Then I discovered Plitvice and realized you can never exhaust Europe's surprises.

Planning Your Time

Plitvice deserves at least a few good hours. Since it takes some time to get here (two hours by car or bus from Zagreb), the most sensible plan is to spend the night in one of the park's hotels (no character, but comfortable and convenient) or a nearby private home (cheaper, but practical only if you're driving). If you're coming from the north (e.g., Ljubljana), you can take the train to Zagreb in the morning, spend a few hours seeing the Croatian capital, then take the bus (generally no buses after about 16:00) or drive to Plitvice in the late afternoon to spend the night at the park. Get up early and hit the trails (ideally by 8:30); by early afternoon, you'll be ready to move on (by bus to the coast, or back to Zagreb). The

most interesting and accessible part of the park can be seen very efficiently, in a three- to four-hour hike; while there are other hiking opportunities, they pale in comparison to this "greatest hits" section. Therefore, two nights and a full day at Plitvice is probably overkill for all but the most avid hikers.

Crowd-Beating Tips: Plitvice is swamped with international tour groups, many of whom aren't shy about elbowing into position for the best photos. The park's trails are most crowded between 10:00 and 15:00. It's essential to get an early start to get in front of the hordes. I try to hit the trails by 8:30; that way, the crowds are moving in just as I'm finishing up.

Getting to Plitvice

Plitvice Lakes National Park, a few miles from the Bosnian border, is two hours by car south of Zagreb on the old highway #1 (a.k.a. D-1).

By **car** from Zagreb, you'll take the A-1 expressway south for about an hour, exiting at Karlovac (marked for *1* and *Plitvice*). From here, D-1 takes you directly south about another hour to the park. If you're staying at the park hotels, you can park for free at the hotel lot; to park at the lots at Entrance 1 or Entrance 2, you'll have to pay (7 kn/hr). For information about driving onward from Plitvice, see "Route Tips for Drivers" at the end of this chapter.

Buses leave from Zagreb's main bus station in the direction of Plitvice. Various bus companies handle the route; just go to the ticket window and ask for the next departure (about 75–95 kn depending on company, trip takes 2–2.5 hours). Buses run from Zagreb about hourly until about 16:00; while sporadic buses run late at night, they'll get you to the park extremely late and should be avoided. Confirm that your bus will actually stop at Plitvice. (The official Plitvice bus stop is along the main road, about a five- to ten-minute walk beyond the hotels.) Confirm the schedule online (www.akz.hr) or at the Plitvice tourism office in Zagreb (Mon–Fri 8:00–16:00, closed Sat–Sun, Trg Kralja Tomislava 19, tel. 01/461-3586).

By car or bus, you'll see some thought-provoking terrain between Zagreb and Plitvice. As you leave Karlovac, you'll pass through the village of **Turanj,** part of the war zone from almost two decades ago. The destroyed, derelict houses belonged to Serbs who have not come back to reclaim and repair them. Farther along, about 25 miles before Plitvice, you'll pass through the striking village of **Slunj,** perched picturesquely on travertine formations (like Plitvice's) and surrounded by sparkling streams and waterfalls. If you're in a car, this is worth a photo stop. This town, too, looks very different than it did before the war—when it was 30 percent Serb.

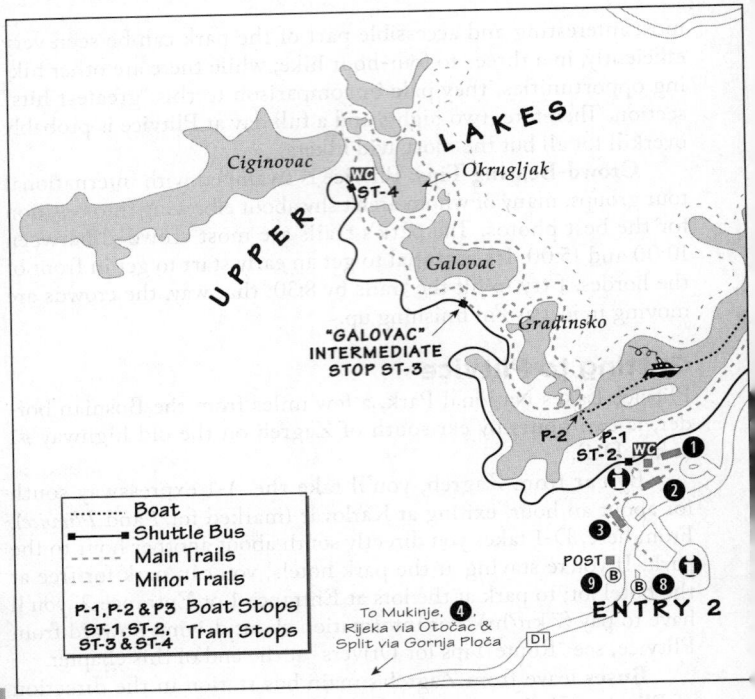

As in countless other villages in the Croatian interior, the Orthodox church has been destroyed...and locals still seethe when they describe how occupying Serbs "defiled" the town's delicate beauty.

Orientation to Plitvice

(area code: 053)

Plitvice's 16 lakes are divided into the Upper Lakes (Gornja Jezera) and the Lower Lakes (Donja Jezera). The park officially has two entrances *(ulaz)*, each with ticket windows and snack and gift shops. Entrance 1 is at the bottom of the Lower Lakes, across the busy D-1 road from the park's best restaurant, Lička Kuća (described later, under "Eating in Plitvice"). Entrance 2 is about 1.5 miles south, below the cluster of Plitvice's three hotels (Jezero, Plitvice, and Bellevue; see "Sleeping in Plitvice," later). There is no town at Plitvice. The nearest village, Mukinje, is a residential community mostly for park workers (boring for tourists, but has some good private room options).

Cost: The price to enter the park during peak season (April–Oct) is 110 kn (80 kn Nov–March; covers park entry, boat, and

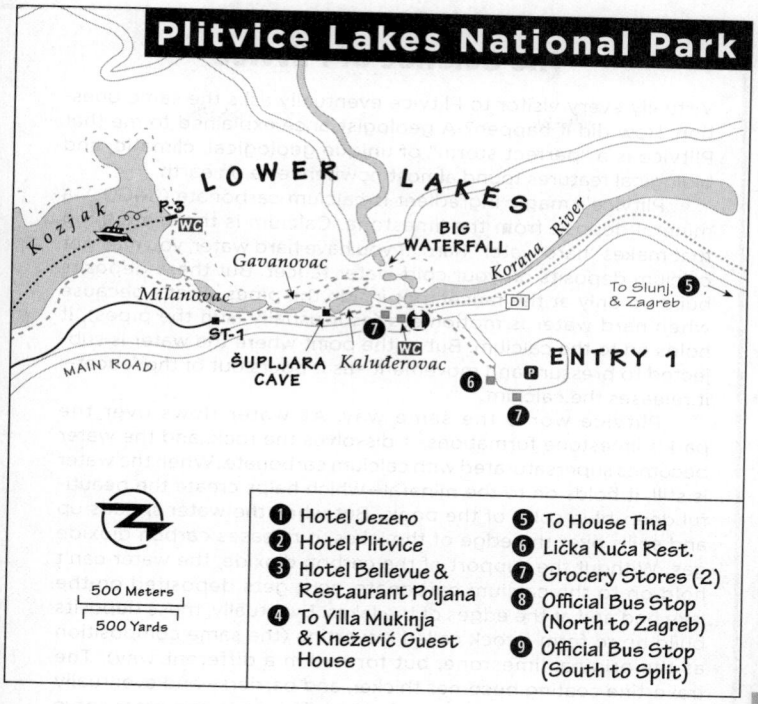

shuttle bus). Park hotel guests pay the entry fee only once for their entire stay; if you're staying off-site and want to visit the park on several days, you'll have to buy separate tickets each day.

Hours: The park is open every day, but the hours vary by season. In summer, it's generally open 7:00–20:00 (last ticket sold at 16:00); in spring and fall, 8:00–18:00 (last ticket sold at 14:00); and in winter, 8:00–16:00 (last ticket sold at 12:00). Night owls should note that the park never really "closes"; these hours are for the ticket booths and the boat and shuttle bus system. You can just stroll right into the park at any time, provided that you aren't using the boat or bus. Again, for fewer tour-group crowds, visit early or late in the day.

Tourist Information

A handy map of the trails is on the back of your ticket, and big maps are posted all over the park. Purchasing your own copy of the big map is a good idea; the various English-language guidebooks are generally poorly translated and not very helpful (both sold at entrances, hotels, and shops throughout the park). The park has a good website: www.np-plitvicka-jezera.hr.

The Science of Plitvice

Virtually every visitor to Plitvice eventually asks the same question: How did it happen? A geologist once explained to me that Plitvice is a "perfect storm" of unique geological, climatic, and biological features found almost nowhere else on earth.

Plitvice's magic ingredient is calcium carbonate ($CaCO_3$), a mineral deposit from the limestone. Calcium is the same thing that makes "hard water" hard. If you have hard water, you may get calcium deposits on your cold-water faucet. But these deposits build up only at the faucet, not inside the pipes. That's because when hard water is motionless (as it usually is in the pipes), it holds on to the calcium. But at the point where the water is subjected to pressure and movement—as it pours out of the faucet—it releases the calcium.

Plitvice works the same way. As water flows over the park's limestone formations, it dissolves the rock, and the water becomes supersaturated with calcium carbonate. When the water is still, it holds on to the mineral—which helps create the beautiful deep-blue color of the pools. But when the water speeds up and spills over the edge of the lakes, it releases carbon dioxide gas. Without the support of the carbon dioxide, the water can't hold on to the calcium carbonate, so it gets deposited on the lake bed and at the edges of the lakes. Eventually, these deposits build up to form a rock called travertine (the same composition as the original limestone, but formed in a different way). The travertine coating becomes thicker, and barriers—and eventually dams and new waterfalls—are formed. The moss and grass serve

Getting Around Plitvice

Of course, Plitvice is designed for hikers. But the park has a few ways (included in entry cost) to help you connect the best parts.

By Shuttle Bus: Buses connect the hotels at Entrance 2 (stop ST2, below Hotel Jezero) with the top of the Upper Lakes (stop ST4) and roughly the bottom of the Lower Lakes (stop ST1, a 10-min walk from Entrance 1). Between Entrance 2 and the top of the Upper Lakes is an intermediate stop (ST3, at Galovac Lake)—designed for tour groups, available to anyone, and offering a convenient way to skip the less interesting top half of the Upper Lakes. Buses start running early and continue until late afternoon (frequency depends on demand—generally 3–4/hr; buses run from March until the first snow—often Dec). Note that the park refers to its buses as "trains," which confuses some visitors. Also note that no local buses take you along the major road (D-1) that connects the entrances. The only way to get between them without a car is by shuttle bus (inside the park) or by foot (about a 40-min walk).

as a natural foundation for the calcification. In other words, the stone hangs down like the foliage because the foliage guides the growth of the stone. Because of this ongoing process, Plitvice's landscape is always changing.

And why is the water so clear? For one thing, it comes directly from high-mountain runoff, giving it little opportunity to become polluted or muddy. And because the water calcifies everything it touches, it prevents the creation of mud—so the bottoms of the lakes are made entirely of stone. Also, a different mineral in the water, magnesium carbonate, both gives the water its special color (which, park rangers brag, changes based on the direction of the sunshine) and makes it extremely pure, preventing the growth of plant life (such as certain algae) that could cloud the water.

The park contains nearly 1,300 different species of plants. Wildlife found in the park include deer, wolves, wildcats, lynx, wild boar, voles, otters, 350 species of butterflies, 42 types of dragonflies, 21 species of bats, and more than 160 species of birds (including eagles, herons, owls, grouse, and storks). The lakes (and local menus) are full of trout, and you'll also see smaller, red-finned fish called *klen* ("chub" in English). Perhaps most importantly, Plitvice is home to about 40 or 50 brown bears—a species now extremely endangered in Europe. You'll see bears, the park's mascot, plastered all over the tourist literature (and in the form of a scary representative in the lobby of Hotel Jezero).

By Boat: Low-impact electric boats ply the waters of the biggest lake, Kozjak, with three stops: below Hotel Jezero (stop P1), at the bottom of the Upper Lakes (P2), and at the far end of Kozjak, at the top of the Lower Lakes (P3). From Hotel Jezero to the Upper Lakes, it's a quick five-minute ride; the boat goes back and forth continuously. The trip from the Upper Lakes to the Lower Lakes takes closer to 20 minutes, and the boat goes about twice per hour—often at the top and bottom of every hour. (With up to 10,000 people a day visiting the park, you might have to wait for a seat on this boat.) Unless the lake freezes (about every five years), the boat also runs in the off-season—though frequency drops to hourly, and it stops running earlier.

Sights in Plitvice

Plitvice is a refreshing playground of 16 terraced lakes, separated by natural travertine dams and connected by countless waterfalls. Over time, the water has simultaneously carved out, and, with the help of mineral deposits, built up this fluid landscape.

Plitvice became Croatia's first national park in 1949, and was a popular destination during the Yugoslav period. On Easter Sunday in 1991, the first shots of Croatia's war with Yugoslavia were fired right here—in fact, the war's first casualty was a park policeman, Josip Jović. The Serbs occupied Plitvice until 1995, and most of the Croatians you'll meet here were evacuated and lived near the coastline as refugees. During those five years, the park saw virtually no tourists, and was allowed to grow wild—allowing the ecosystem to recover from the impact of so many visitors. Today, the war is a fading memory, and the park is again a popular tourist destination, with nearly a million visitors each year (though relatively few are from the US).

▲▲▲Hiking the Lakes

Plitvice's system of trails and boardwalks makes it possible for visitors to get immersed in the park's beauty. (In some places, the path leads literally right up the middle of a waterfall.) The official park map and signage recommend a variety of hikes, but there's no need to adhere strictly to these suggestions; invest in the big map and create your own route.

Most visitors stick to the main paths and choose between two basic plans: uphill or downhill. Each one has pros and cons. Park officials generally recommend hiking uphill, from the Lower Lakes to the Upper Lakes, which offers slightly better head-on views of the best scenery (this is the route described below). It also saves the most scenic stretch of lakes and falls—the Upper Lakes—for last. Hiking downhill, from Upper to Lower, is easier (though you'll have to hike steeply up out of the canyon at the end), and since most groups go the opposite way, you'll be passing—but not stuck behind—the crowds. Either way you go, walking briskly and with

a few photo stops, figure on an hour for the Lower Lakes, an hour for the Upper Lakes, and a half-hour to connect them by boat.

Lower Lakes (Donja Jezera)—The lower half of Plitvice's lakes are accessible from Entrance 1. If you start here, the route marked *G2* (intended for groups, but doable for anyone) leads you along the boardwalks to Kozjak, the big lake that connects the Lower and the Upper Lakes (see below).

From the entrance, you'll descend a steep path with lots of **switchbacks,** enjoying thrilling views over the canyon of the Lower Lakes. As you reach the lakes and begin to follow the boardwalks, you'll have great up-close views of the travertine formations that make up Plitvice's many waterfalls. Count the trout. If you're tempted to throw in a line, don't. Fishing is strictly forbidden. (Besides, they're happy.)

After you cross the path over the first lake, an optional 10-minute detour (to the right) takes you down to the **Big Waterfall** (Veliki Slap). It's the biggest of Plitvice's waterfalls, where the Plitvica River plunges 250 feet over a cliff into the valley below. Depending on recent rainfall, the force of the Big Waterfall varies from a light mist to a thundering deluge.

If you're a hardy hiker, consider climbing the steep steps from the Big Waterfall up to a **viewpoint** at the top of the canyon (marked *Sightseeing Point/ Vidikovac*; it's a strenuous 10-min hike to the top). Take the stairs up, bearing to the right at the top (near the shelter) to find a nice viewpoint overlooking the Big Waterfall. From here, you can carry on along the road that actually goes up over the top of the Big Waterfall, offering more views over the park. (Go as far as you like, then return the way you came.) The giant mill perched at the top of the Big Waterfall was used to grind grains; this very poor part of Croatia was traditionally inhabited by farmers.

After seeing the Big Waterfall, backtrack up to the main trail and continue on the boardwalks. After you pass another bank of waterfalls, a smaller trail branches off (on the left) toward **Šupljara Cave.** You can actually climb through this slippery cave all the way up to the trail overlooking the Lower Lakes (though it's not recommended). This unassuming cavern is a surprisingly big draw. In the 1960s, several German and Italian "Spaghetti Westerns" were filmed at Plitvice and in other parts of Croatia (which, to European eyes, has terrain similar to the American West). The most famous, *Der Schatz im Silbersee (The Treasure in Silver Lake),* was filmed here

at Plitvice, and the treasure was hidden in this cave. The movie—complete with *Deutsch*-speaking "Native Americans"—is still a favorite in Germany, and popular theme tours bring German tourists to movie locations here in Croatia. (If you drive the roads near Plitvice, keep an eye out for strange, Native American–sounding names such as Winnetou—fictional characters from these beloved stories of the Old West, by the German writer Karl May.)

After Šupljara Cave, you'll stick to the east side of the lakes, then cross over one more time to the west, where you'll cut through a comparatively dull forest. You'll emerge at a pit-stop-perfect clearing with WCs, picnic tables, a souvenir shop, and a self-service restaurant. Here you can catch the shuttle boat across Lake Kozjak to the bottom of the Upper Lakes (usually every 30 min).

Lake Kozjak (Jezero Kozjak)—The park's biggest lake, Kozjak, connects the Lower and Upper Lakes. The 20-minute boat ride between Plitvice's two halves offers a great chance for a breather. You can hike between the lakes along the west side of Kozjak, but the scenery's not nearly as good as in the rest of the park.

Upper Lakes (Gornja Jezera)—Focus on the lower half of the Upper Lakes, where nearly all the exotic beauty is. From the boat dock, signs for *C* and *G2* direct you up to Gradinsko Lake through the most striking scenery in the whole park. Enjoy the stroll, taking your time...and lots of photos.

After Gradinsko Lake, when you reach the top of Galovac Lake, you'll have three options:

1. Make your hike a loop by continuing around the lake (following *H* and *G1* signs back to the P2 boat dock), then take the boat back over to the hotels (P1 stop).

2. Hike a few steps up to the ST3 bus stop to catch the shuttle bus back to the hotels (more efficient, but doesn't give you a second look at the lakes).

3. Continue hiking to the top of the Upper Lakes; you'll get away from the crowds and feel like you've covered the park thoroughly. From here on up, the scenery is less stunning, and the waterfalls are fewer and farther between. At the top, you'll finish at shuttle bus stop ST4 (with food stalls and a WC), where the bus zips you back to the entrances and hotels.

Nice work!

Sleeping in Plitvice

At the Park

The most convenient way to sleep at Plitvice is to stay at the park's lodges, which are run by the same office (reservation tel. 053/751-015, fax 053/751-013, www.np-plitvicka-jezera.hr, info

Sleep Code

(€1 = about $1.40, country code: 385, area code: 053)
English is spoken, credit cards are accepted, and breakfast is included at each place. The tourist tax (€1 per person, per day) is not included in these prices.

To help you sort easily through these listings, I've divided the rooms into three categories based on the price for a standard double room with bath in peak season:

$$$ Higher Priced—Most rooms €100 or more.
$$ Moderately Priced—Most rooms between €50–100.
$ Lower Priced—Most rooms €50 or less.

@np-plitvicka-jezera.hr; reception numbers for each hotel listed below). Warning: Because of high volume in peak season, the booking office often doesn't respond to emails. Instead, to make a reservation, use the park's website to book your room (look for the "Online booking" box). In a pinch, try calling the booking office or the hotel directly (they speak English), or emailing the park information office in Zagreb (np.zg.info@np-plitvicka-jezera.hr), which is more likely to respond in the busy summer months.

$$$ Hotel Jezero is big and modern, with all the comfort—and charm—of a Holiday Inn. It's well-located right at the park entrance and offers 200 rooms that feel newish, but generally have at least one thing that's broken. Rooms facing the park have big glass doors and balconies (July–Aug: Sb-€83, Db-€118; May–June and Sept–Oct: Sb-€76, Db-€108; Nov–April: Sb-€61, Db-€86; elevator, reception tel. 053/751-400).

$$ Hotel Plitvice, a better value than Jezero, offers 50 rooms and mod, wide-open public spaces on two floors with no elevators. For rooms, choose from economy (fine, older-feeling; July–Aug: Sb-€72, Db-€96; May–June and Sept–Oct: Sb-€65, Db-€82; Nov–April: Sb-€50, Db-€70), standard (just a teeny bit bigger; July–Aug: Sb-€77, Db-€106; May–June and Sept–Oct: Sb-€70, Db-€96; Nov–April: Sb-€55, Db-€74), or superior (bigger still, with a sitting area; July–Aug: Sb-€82, Db-€116; May–June and Sept–Oct: Sb-€75, Db-€106; Nov–April: Sb-€60, Db-€84, reception tel. 053/751-100).

$$ Hotel Bellevue is simple and bare-bones (no TVs or elevator). It has an older feel to it, but the price is right and the 80 rooms are perfectly acceptable (July–Aug: Sb-€55, Db-€74; May–June and Sept–Oct: Sb-€50, Db-€68; Nov–April: Sb-€40, Db-€54, reception tel. 053/751-700).

Sobe near the Park

While the park's lodges are the easiest choice for non-drivers, those with a car should consider sleeping at a *soba* (room in a private home). You'll see *sobe* signs for miles on either side of the park. A few that have good reputations include **Villa Mukinja** (in the village of Mukinje just south of the park, tel. 01/652-1857, www.plitvice-lakes.com, info@plitvice-lakes.com), **House Tina** (just north of the park in the village at Grabovac, tel. 04/778-4197), and **Knežević Guest House** (also in the village of Mukinje, tel. 053/774-081, mobile 098-168-7576, www.knezevic.hr, guest_house@vodatel.net, daughter Kristina speaks English).

Eating in Plitvice

The park runs all of the restaurants at Plitvice. These places are handy, and the food is affordable and decent. If you're staying at the hotels, you have the option of paying for half-board with your room (lunch or dinner, €12 each). This option is designed for the restaurants inside hotels Jezero and Plitvice, but you can also use the voucher at other park eateries (you'll pay the difference if the bill is more). The half-board option is worth doing if you're here for dinner, but don't lock yourself in for lunch—you'll want more flexibility as you explore Plitvice (excellent picnic spots and decent food stands abound inside the park).

Hotel Jezero and **Hotel Plitvice** both have big restaurants with adequate food and friendly, professional service (half-board for dinner, described above, is a good deal; or order à la carte; both open daily until 23:00).

Lička Kuća, across the pedestrian overpass from Entrance 1, has a wonderfully dark and smoky atmosphere around a huge open-air wood-fired grill (pricey, daily 11:00–24:00, tel. 053/751-024).

Restaurant Poljana, behind Hotel Bellevue, has the same boring, park-lodge atmosphere in both of its sections: cheap, self-service cafeteria and sit-down restaurant with open wood-fired grill (same choices and prices as the better-atmosphere Lička Kuća, above; both parts open daily but closed in winter, tel. 053/751-092).

For **picnic** fixings, there's a small grocery store at Entrance 1 and another one with a larger selection across road D-1 (use the pedestrian overpass). At the P3 boat dock, you can buy grilled meat and drinks. Friendly old ladies sell homemade goodies (such as strudel or hunks of cheese) throughout the park, including at Entrance 1.

Plitvice Connections

To reach the park, see "Getting to Plitvice," earlier in this chapter. Moving on from Plitvice is trickier. Buses pass by the park in each direction—northbound (to **Zagreb,** 2–2.5 hrs) and southbound (to coastal destinations such as **Split,** 4–6 hrs).

There is no bus station—just a low-profile *Plitvice Centar* bus stop shelter. To reach it from the park, go out to the main road from either Hotel Jezero or Hotel Plitvice, then turn right; the bus stops are just after the pedestrian overpass. The one on the hotel side of the road is for buses headed for the coast (southbound); the stop on the opposite side is for Zagreb (northbound). Try to carefully confirm the bus schedule with the park or hotel staff, then head out to the bus stop and wave down the bus. (It's easy to confuse public buses with private tour buses, so don't panic if a bus doesn't stop for you—look for a bus with your final destination marked in the windshield.)

But here's the catch: If the bus is full, they won't stop to pick you up at Plitvice. This is most common on days when the buses are jammed with people headed to or from the coast. For example, on Fridays—when everyone is going from Zagreb to Split—you'll have no luck catching a southbound bus at Plitvice after about 12:00, as they are likely to be full. Similarly, on Sunday afternoons, northbound buses are often full.

While this sounds risky, and there is a chance that you'll miss a bus and have to wait for the next one, in practice it usually works...if you're patient.

Route Tips for Drivers

Plitvice's biggest disadvantage is that it's an hour away from the handy A-1 expressway that connects northern Croatia to the Dalmatian Coast. You have three ways to access this expressway from Plitvice, depending on which direction you're heading.

Going North: If you're heading north (to Zagreb or Slovenia), you'll get on the expressway at **Karlovac:** From Plitvice, drive about one hour north on D-1 to the town of Karlovac, where you can access A-1 northbound. Alternatively, you can take A-1 southbound to A-6, which leads west to Rijeka, Opatija, and Istria (though this route is more boring and only slightly faster than the route via Otočac, below).

Going to Central Croatia: If you're going to central destinations, such as Istria, get on the expressway at **Otočac.** From Plitvice, go south on D-1, then go west on road #52 to the town of Otočac (about an hour through the mountains from Plitvice to Otočac). After Otočac, you can get on A-1 (north to Zagreb, south to the Dalmatian Coast); or continue west and twist down

the mountain road to the seaside town of Senj, on the main coastal road of the Kvarner Gulf. From Senj, it's about an hour north along the coast to Rijeka, then on to Istria.

During the recent war, the front line between the Croats and Serbs ran just east of **Otočac** (OH-toh-chawts), and bullet holes still mar the town's facades. (Watch for minefield warning signs just east of Otočac, but don't be too nervous—it's safe to drive here, but not safe to get out of your car and wander through the fields.) Today Otočac is putting itself back together, and it's a fine place to drop into a café for a coffee, or pick up some produce at the outdoor market. The Catholic church in the center of town, destroyed in the war but now rebuilt, has a memorial out back with its damaged church bells. Notice that the crucifix nearby is made of old artillery shells. Just up the main street, beyond the big, grassy park, is the Orthodox church. Otočac used to be about one-third Serbian, but the Serbs were forced out during the war, and this church fell into disrepair. But, as Otočac and Croatia show signs of healing, about two dozen Serbs have returned to town and reopened their church (for more on the Serbian Orthodox Church, see page 789).

Going South: If you're heading south (to Split and the rest of Dalmatia) from Plitvice, catch the expressway at **Gornja Ploča.** Drive south from Plitvice on D-1, through Korenica, Pećane, and Udbina, then follow signs for the A-1 expressway (and *Lovinac*) via Kurjak to the Gornja Ploča on-ramp. Once on A-1, you'll twist south through the giant Sveti Rok tunnel to Dalmatia.

BOSNIA-HERZEGOVINA

MOSTAR

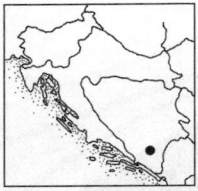

The early 1990s weren't kind to Bosnia-Herzegovina: War. Bloodshed. Destruction. But apart from its tragic separation from Yugoslavia, the country has long been—and still remains—a remarkable place, with ruggedly beautiful terrain, a unique mix of cultures and faiths, kind and welcoming people who pride themselves on their hospitality, and some of the most captivating sightseeing in southeastern Europe. After all, little Bosnia-Herzegovina—with fewer than four million people—is a country with three faiths, three languages, and two alphabets.

There's so much to see in this country. But for the scope of this book, I've selected just one destination: Mostar. Safe, stable, and within easy reach of the Dalmatian Coast, Mostar (MOH-star) is worth considering as a detour—both geographical and cultural—from the Croatian mainstream. In Mostar's cobbled Old Town, you can poke into several mosques, tour old-fashioned Turkish-style houses, shop your way through a bazaar of souvenir stands, and hear the call to prayer echoing across the rooftops. For me, it's the single best side-trip from Dubrovnik.

Mostar represents the best and the worst of Yugoslavia. During the Tito years, it was an idyllic mingling of cultures—Catholic Croats, Orthodox Serbs, and Muslim Bosniaks living together in harmony, their differences spanned by an Old Bridge that epitomized an optimistic vision of a Yugoslavia where ethnicity didn't matter. And yet, as the country unraveled in the early 1990s, Mostar was gripped by a gory three-way war among those same peoples...and that famous bridge crumbled into the Neretva River.

More than any other destination in this book, Mostar rearranges your mental furniture. Most startling are the vivid and thought-provoking signs of the war. A few years ago, much of the city was destroyed; today, while still easy to find, the ruins aren't quite as in your face. Still, especially outside of the tourist zone, burned-out husks of buildings, unmistakable starburst patterns in the pavement, and bullet holes in walls are a constant reminder that the city is still recovering—physically and psychologically. In an age when we watch TV news coverage of conflicts abroad with the same detachment we give Hollywood blockbusters, Mostar provides an unpleasant but essential reminder of how real and how destructive war truly is.

Western visitors may also be struck by the immediacy of the Muslim culture that permeates Mostar. Located along the fault line separating the Christian and Muslim worlds, Mostar's skyline is shared by minarets and church steeples. During the Ottomans' 400-year control of this region, many Slavic subjects converted to Islam (see "The Muslims of Mostar" sidebar, later). And, although they retreated in the late 19th century, the Ottomans left behind a rich architectural, cultural, and religious legacy that has forever shaped Mostar. Five times each day, loudspeakers on minarets crackle to life, the call to prayer warbles through the streets, and Mostar's Muslim residents flock into the mosques. In many parts of the city, you'd swear you were in Turkey.

If these factors intrigue you, read on—Mostar has so much more to offer. Despite the scars of war, its setting is stunning: straddling the banks of the gorgeous Neretva River, with tributaries and waterfalls carving their way through the rocky landscape. The sightseeing—mosques, old Turkish-style houses, and that spine-tingling Old Bridge—is more engaging than much of what you'll find in Croatia or Slovenia. And it's cheap—hotels, food, and museums are less than half the prices you'll pay in Croatia.

While a visit to Mostar just a few years ago was depressing, these days, more and more, it's uplifting. The city is rebuilding at an impressive pace, and local entrepreneurs are working hard to make Mostar tourist-friendly. Before long, Mostar will reclaim its status as one of the premier destinations in the former Yugoslavia. Visit now, while it still has its rough-around-the-edges charm—and you'll get to see it before it really takes off.

Bosnia-Herzegovina Almanac

Official Name: Bosna i Hercegovina (abbreviated "BiH"); the *i* means "and"—Bosnia *and* Herzegovina (the country's two regions). The tongue-twisting name "Herzegovina" (hert-seh-GOH-vee-nah) comes from the German word for "dukedom" (*Herzog* means "duke").

Snapshot History: Bosnia-Herzegovina's early history is similar to the rest of the region: Illyrians, Romans, and Slavs (oh, my!). The country's story parts ways with Croatia's in the late 15th century, when Turkish rulers from the Ottoman Empire began a 400-year domination of the country. Many of the Ottomans' subjects converted to Islam, and their descendants remain Muslims today. After the Habsburgs forced out the Ottomans in 1878, Bosnia-Herzegovina became part of the Austro-Hungarian Empire, then Yugoslavia, until it declared independence in October of 1991. The bloody war that ensued came to an end in 1995. (For details, see the Understanding Yugoslavia chapter.)

Population: About 4.6 million. (There were about 100,000 identified casualties of the war, but many estimates of total casualties are double that number.) Someone who lives in Bosnia-Herzegovina, regardless of ethnicity, is called a "Bosnian." A southern Slav who practices Islam is called a "Bosniak." Today, about half of all Bosnians are Bosniaks (Muslims), a little more than a third are Orthodox Serbs, and about 15 percent are Catholic Croats. Traditionally, Bosniaks lived in the towns and cities, while Serbs and Croats farmed the countryside.

Political Divisions: As a part of the Dayton Peace Accords that ended the conflict here in 1995, the nation is divided into three separate regions: the Federation of Bosnia and Herzegovina (FBiH, shared by Bosniaks and Croats, very roughly in the western and central parts of the country), the Republika Srpska (RS, dominated by Serbs, generally to the north and east), and the Brčko District (BD, a tiny corner of the country, with a mix of the ethnicities). For the most part, each of the three native ethnic groups stays in "their" part of this divided country, but tourists can move freely between them.

Language: Technically, Bosnia-Herzegovina has three languages—Bosnian, Serbian, and Croatian. But all three are mutually intelligible dialects of what was until recently considered a single language: Serbo-Croatian. Bosniaks and Croats use basically the same Roman alphabet we do, while Serbs generally use the Cyrillic alphabet. You'll see both alphabets on currency and other official documents. Many people also speak English.

Area: 19,741 square miles (like Vermont and New Hampshire combined, or slightly larger than Slovakia).

Geography: Bosnia and Herzegovina are two distinct regions that share the same mountainous country. Bosnia constitutes the majority of the country (in the north, with a continental climate), while Herzegovina is the southern tip (about a fifth of the total area, with a hotter Mediterranean climate). Mostar is the biggest city and unofficial capital of Herzegovina—so saying you're in "Bosnia" while you're here is technically incorrect.

Red Tape: To enter Bosnia-Herzegovina, Americans and Canadians need only a passport (no visa required).

Economy: The country's economy has struggled since the war—the per capita GDP is $6,500, and the official unemployment rate is around 29 percent.

Currency: The official currency is the Convertible Mark (Konvertibilna Marka, abbreviated KM locally, BAM internationally). The official exchange rate is $1 = about 1.30 KM. But merchants in these destinations are willing to take euros or Croatian kunas, roughly converting prices with a simple formula:

2 KM = €1 = 8 kunas (= about $1.40)

Even though you can get by without Convertible Marks, consider making a small withdrawal to get a sense of them. Notice that to satisfy the country's various factions, the currency uses both the Roman and the Cyrillic alphabets, and bills have different figureheads and symbols (some bills feature Bosniaks, others Serbs).

Telephones: Bosnia-Herzegovina's country code is 387. If calling from another country, first dial the international access code (00 in Europe, 011 in the US), then 387, then the area code (minus the initial zero), then the number.

Flag: The flag of Bosnia-Herzegovina, adopted after the recent war, is a blue field with a yellow triangle along the top edge. The three points of the triangle represent Bosnia-Herzegovina's three peoples (Bosniaks, Croats, Serbs), and the triangle also resembles the physical shape of the country. A row of white stars underscores the longest side of the triangle. These stars—and the yellow-and-blue color scheme—resemble the flag of the European Union (a nod to the EU's efforts to bring peace to the region). While this compromise flag sounds like a nice idea, almost no Bosnian embraces it as his or her own; each group has its own unofficial but highly prized symbols and flags (such as the fleur-de-lis for the Bosniaks, the red-and-white checkerboard shield for the Croats, and the cross with the four S's for the Serbs)—many of which offend the other groups.

Planning Your Time

Because of its cultural hairiness, a detour into Bosnia-Herzegovina feels like a real departure from a Dalmatian vacation. But actually, Mostar is easier to reach from Dubrovnik or Split than many popular Dalmatian islands (it's within a three-hour drive or bus ride from either city).

The vast majority of tourists in Mostar are day-trippers from the coast, which means the Old Town is packed midday, but empty in the morning and evening. You can get a good feel for Mostar in just a few hours, but a full day gives you time to linger and ponder.

You have three basic options: take a package tour from Dalmatia; rent a car for a one-day side-trip into Mostar; or (my favorite) spend the night here en route between Croatian destinations. To work a Mostar overnight into your itinerary, consider a round-trip plan that takes you south along the coast, then back north via Bosnia-Herzegovina (for example, Split–Korčula–Dubrovnik–Mostar–back to Split).

Getting to Mostar

By Car: Coming with your own car gives you maximum flexibility, but you may find Mostar—which has poor signage—stressful to drive in. For specific route information, see "Route Tips for Drivers" at the end of this chapter. If you do plan to drive here, let your car-rental company know in advance to ensure you have the appropriate paperwork for crossing the border. If you're not up for driving yourself, consider splurging on a driver to bring you here (for drivers based in Dubrovnik, see page 771; for a Mostar-based driver, see page 955).

By Bus: Especially if you're spending the night in Mostar, bus connections with destinations on the Dalmatian Coast (especially Split and Dubrovnik) are workable. For details, see "Mostar Connections," later.

By Package Tour: Taking a package excursion from a Dalmatian resort town seems like an efficient way to visit Mostar. Unfortunately, in reality it can be less rewarding than doing it on your own—count on lots and lots of hours on a crowded bus, listening to a lackluster, multilingual tour guide reading from a script, and relatively little time in the destinations themselves. But if you just want a quick one-day look at these places, it's worth considering. These all-day tours are sold from Split, Hvar, Korčula, Dubrovnik, and other Croatian coastal destinations for about €50–60. The best tours max out their time in Mostar itself (it still won't be enough); avoid the tours that include a pointless boat trip on the Neretva River. Those that add a quick visit to the worthwhile town of Počitelj are a better deal. Atlas is the biggest

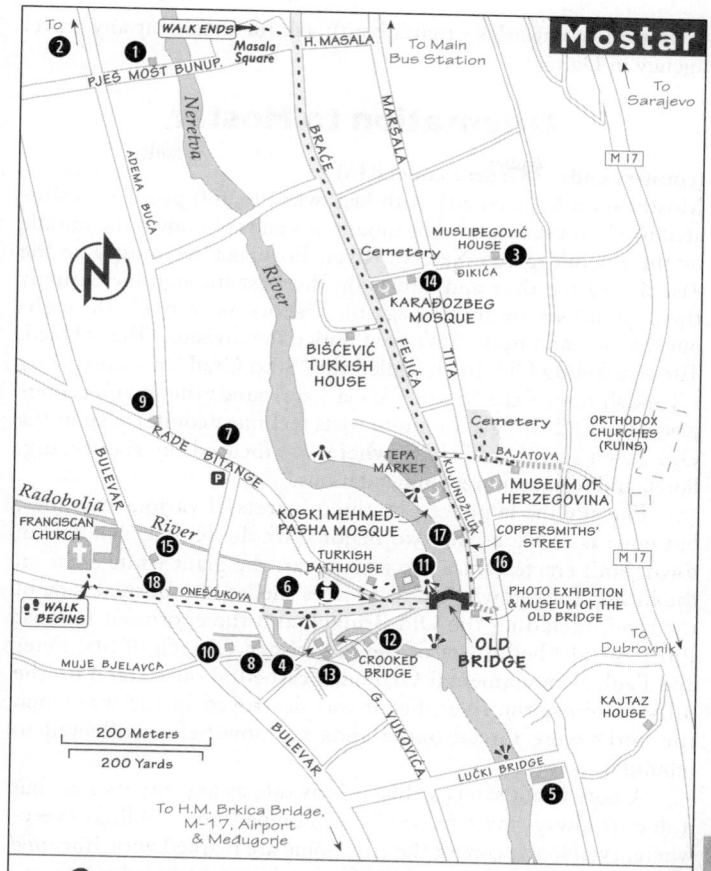

1. Hotel Bristol
2. To Hotel Ero
3. Muslibegović House
4. Motel Kriva Ćuprija
5. Hotel Kriva Ćuprija II
6. Motel Emen
7. Villa Fortuna B&B
8. Pansion Botticelli
9. Pansion Most
10. Dika Kasumačić Rooms
11. Bridge View Eateries
12. Restoran Hindin Han
13. Konoba Dvije Pećine
14. Saray Restaurant
15. Bistro Verona
16. Ali Baba Nightclub
17. Fortuna Tours
18. Future Synagogue Site

operation (www.atlas-croatia.com); ask for details at any travel agency in Dalmatia.

Orientation to Mostar

(country code: 387; area code: 036)
Mostar—a mid-sized city with just over 100,000 people—is situated in a basin surrounded by mountains and split down the middle by the emerald-green Neretva River. Bosniaks live mostly on the east side of the river and Croats on the west (though increasingly the populations are mixing again). Visitors move freely throughout the city, and most don't even notice the division. The cobbled, Turkish-feeling Old Town (called the "Stari Grad" or—borrowing a Turkish term—the "Stara Čaršija") surrounds the town's centerpiece, the Old Bridge. Timid tourists feel most comfortable in the Old Town sector, and that's where I've focused my sightseeing, hotel, and restaurant recommendations.

The skyline is pierced by the minarets of various mosques, but none is as big as the two major Catholic (Croat) symbols in town, both erected since the recent war: the giant white cross on the hilltop (placed where Croat forces shelled the Bosniak side of the river, including the Old Bridge); and the enormous (almost 100-foot-tall) bell tower of the Franciscan Church of Sts. Peter and Paul. A monumental Orthodox cathedral once stood on the hillside across the river, but it was destroyed in the war when the Serbs were forced out. Funds are now being collected to rebuild it.

A note about safety: Mostar is as safe as any city its size, but it doesn't always *feel* safe. You'll see bombed-out buildings everywhere, even in the core of the city. Some are marked with *Warning! Dangerous Ruin* signs, but for safety's sake, never wander into any building that appears damaged or deserted.

Tourist Information

The virtually worthless TI shares a building with a tour office, but it does give out a free town map and a few other brochures on Mostar and Herzegovina (sporadic hours, generally open June–Oct daily 9:00–17:00, maybe later in busy times, likely closed Nov–May, just a block from the Old Bridge on Rade Bitange street, tel. 036/580-275, www.bhtourism.ba).

Arrival in Mostar

By Bus or Train: As with many things in Mostar, bus service is divided; most Bosniak (Muslim) buses, and some Croat ones, use the main bus station on the east side of town, while other Croat buses use a different stop, on the west side of town. (For details on

this confusing system, see "Mostar Connections," later.)

The main bus station, which is combined with the train station, is north of the Old Town on the east side of the river (about a 10-KM taxi trip). At the station, you'll find ticket windows in the lobby facing the bus stalls. But you're better off visiting the English-speaking and generally helpful Autoprevoz "tourist agency" (to the left as you face the station, tel. 036/551-900, www.autoprevoz-bus.ba; note that they have good information for Bosniak bus companies, but not necessarily for Croat ones). To find your way to town center, walk through the bus stalls and parking lot and turn left at the big road, which leads you to the Old Town area in about 15 minutes.

By Car: For tips on driving to Mostar from the Dalmatian Coast, see page 974.

Helpful Hints

Local Cash: Need Convertible Marks? The most convenient ATM in town is to the left of Fortuna Tours' door, right at the top of Coppersmiths' Street (but remember that Croatian kunas and euros are also accepted here).

Travel Agency: The handy **Fortuna Tours** travel agency, right in the heart of the Old Town (at the top of Coppersmiths' Street), sells all the tourist stuff, can book you a local guide, and answers basic questions (open long hours daily, Kujundžiluk 2, tel. 036/551-887, main office tel. 036/552-197, fax 036/551-888, www.fortuna.ba, fortuna_mostar1@bih.net.ba).

Local Guides: Hiring a guide is an excellent investment to help you understand Mostar. I've enjoyed working with **Alma Elezović,** a warm-hearted Bosniak who loves sharing her city with visitors (€20 per person up to €70 per group for 2–3-hour tour, includes entries into a Turkish house and a mosque, tel. 036/550-514, mobile 061-467-699, aelezovic@gmail.com). If Alma is busy, various companies around town can arrange for a local guide at extremely reasonable prices (€40/2-hour tour); try **Fortuna Tours,** listed above.

If someone approaches you offering to be your guide, ask the price in advance (they often charge ridiculously high rates). If they seem cagey or overpriced, decline politely. The official guides are better anyway.

Local Driver: Ermin Elezović, the husband of local guide Alma Elezović, is a friendly, English-speaking driver who enjoys taking visitors on day trips from Mostar. You can also hire him for a transfer between Mostar and destinations anywhere in Croatia (small car for up to 3 people: €100 for transfer to Split, Dubrovnik, or Sarajevo, or €150 for an all-day excursion; bigger van for up to 8 people: €150 for transfer to Split,

Dubrovnik, or Sarajevo, or €200 for all day; tel. 036/550-514, mobile 061-908-597, elezovicermin@gmail.com).

Sights in Mostar

Mostar's major sights line up along a handy L-shaped axis. I've laced them together as an enjoyable orientation walk: From the Franciscan Church, you'll walk straight until you cross the Old Bridge. Then you'll turn left and walk basically straight (with a couple of detours) to the big square at the far end of town.

• *Begin at the...*

▲Franciscan Church of Sts. Peter and Paul

In a town of competing religious architectural exclamation points, this spire is the tallest. The church, which adjoins a working Franciscan monastery, was built after the fighting subsided in 1997 (the same year as the big cross on the hill). The tower, which looks at first glance like a minaret on steroids, is actually modeled after the typical Croatian/Venetian *campanile* bell towers. Step inside to see how the vast and coarse concrete shell awaits completion. In the meantime, the cavernous interior is already hosting services. (Sunday Mass here is an inspiration.)

• *The church fronts the busy boulevard called...*

▲Bulevar

This "Boulevard" was once the modern main drag of Mostar. In the early 1990s, this city of Bosniaks, Croats, and Serbs began to fracture under the pressure of politicians' propaganda. In October 1991, Bosnia-Herzegovina—following Croatia's and Slovenia's example, but without the blessing of its large Serb minority—declared independence from Yugoslavia. Soon after, the Serb-dominated Yugoslav National Army invaded. Mostar's Bosniaks and Croats joined forces to battle the Serbs and succeeded in claiming the city as their own, forcing out the Serb residents.

But even as they defended their city from the final, distant bombardments of Serb forces, the Bosniaks and Croats began

to squabble. Neighbors, friends, and even relatives took up arms against each other. As fighting raged between the Croat and Bosniak forces, this street became the front line—and virtually all of its buildings were destroyed. Then as now, Bosniaks held the area to the east of here (toward the river), while Croats controlled the western part of town.

While many of the buildings along here have been rebuilt, some damage is still evident. Stroll a bit, imagining the hell of a split community at war. Mortar craters in the asphalt leave poignant scars. (In Sarajevo, these have been filled with red resin to create monuments called "Sarajevo roses.") During those dark war years, the Croats on this side of the city laid siege to the Bosniaks on the other side, cutting off electricity, blocking roads, and blaring Croatian rabble-rousing pop music and Tokyo Rose–type propaganda speeches from loudspeakers. Through '93 and '94, when the Bosniaks dared to go out, they sprinted past exposed places, for fear of being picked off by a sniper. Local Bosniaks explain, "Night was time to live" (in black clothes). When people were killed along this street, their corpses were sometimes left here for months (because it wasn't safe to retrieve the bodies). Tens of thousands fled their homeland, some to the Scandinavian countries (first to open their doors), others to destinations in Europe, the US, and Canada.

The stories are shocking, and it's difficult to remain impartial. But looking back on this complicated war, I try not to broadly cast one side as the "aggressors" and another as the "victims." The Bosniaks were victimized in Mostar, just as the Croats were victimized during the siege of Dubrovnik (explained on page 780). And, as the remains of a destroyed Orthodox cathedral on the hillside above Mostar (not quite visible from here) attest, the Serbs also took their turn as victims. Every conflict has many sides, and tragically it's the civilians who often pay the highest toll—no matter their affiliation.

Cross the boulevard and head down Onešćukova street. A few steps down on the left, the vacant lot with the menorah-ornamented metal fence will someday be the Mostar Synagogue. While the town's Jewish population has dwindled to a handful of families since World War II, many Jews courageously served as aid workers and intermediaries when Croats and Bosniaks were killing each other. In recognition of their loving help, the community of Mostar gave them this land for a new synagogue.

• *Continue past the synagogue site, entering the Old Town and following the canyon with the small river...*

Radobolja River Valley

The creek called Radobolja winds over waterfalls and several mills on its way to join the Neretva. As you step upon cobbles,

you suddenly become immersed in the Turkish heritage of Mostar. From the arrival of the Ottomans all the way through the end of World War II, Mostar had fewer than 15,000 residents. This compact central zone was pretty much all there was to the city until it became industrialized and grew like crazy during the Tito years. The historic core is cobbled with smooth, ankle-twisting river stones. Until 2004, the stones were simply embedded in loose sand, but now they're held together with concrete. As you explore, survey the atmospheric eateries clinging to the walls of this canyon—and choose one for a meal or drink later in the day (I've noted a couple under "Eating in Mostar," later).

Walk straight ahead until you reach a square viewpoint platform on your right. It's across from a charming little mosque and above a stream. The mosque is one of 10 in town. Before the recent war, there were 36. Many mosques were actually damaged or destroyed in World War II, but were never repaired or replaced (since Tito's communist Yugoslavia discouraged religion). But the recent war inspired Muslims to finally rebuild. Each of the town's newly reconstructed mosques has been financed by a Muslim nation or organization (this one was a gift from an international association for the protection of Islamic heritage). Around you are several fine examples of Mostar's traditional heavy limestone-shingled roofs.

• *Spanning the river below the mosque is the...*

▲Crooked Bridge (Kriva Ćuprija)

This miniature Old Bridge was built nearly a decade before its more famous sibling, supposedly to practice for the real deal. Damaged—but not destroyed—during the war, the bridge was swept away several years later by floods. The bridge you see today is a recent reconstruction.

• *Continue deeper on the same street into the city center. After a few steps, a street to the left (worth a short detour) leads to the* **TI**, *then a copper-domed* hammam, *or Turkish bathhouse, which was destroyed in World War II and only recently rebuilt. A happening nightlife and restaurant scene tumbles downhill toward the river from here, offering spectacular views of the Old Bridge.*

Back on the main drag, continue along the main shopping zone, past several market stalls, to the focal point of town, the...

▲▲▲Old Bridge (Stari Most)

One of the most evocative sights in the former Yugoslavia, this iconic bridge confidently spanned the Neretva River for more than four centuries. Mostarians of all faiths love the bridge and speak of "him" as an old friend. Traditionally considered the point where East meets West, the Old Bridge is as symbolic as it is beautiful. Dramatically arched and flanked by two boxy towers, the bridge is striking—even if you don't know its history.

Before the Old Bridge, the Neretva was spanned only by a rickety suspension bridge, guarded by *mostari* ("watchers of the bridge"), who gave the city its name. Commissioned in 1557 by the Ottoman Sultan Süleyman the Magnificent, and completed just nine years later, the Old Bridge was a technological marvel for its time..."the longest single-span stone arch on the planet." (In other words, it's the granddaddy of the Rialto Bridge in Venice.) Because of its graceful keystone design—and the fact that there are empty spaces inside the structure—it's much lighter than it seems. And yet, nearly 400 years after it was built, the bridge was still sturdy enough to support the weight of the Nazi tanks that rolled in to occupy Mostar. Over the centuries, it became the symbol for the town and region—a metaphor in stone for the way the diverse faiths and cultures here were able to bridge the gaps that divided them.

All of that drastically changed in the early 1990s. When the city became engulfed in war, the Old Bridge frequently got caught in the crossfire. Old tires were slung over its sides to absorb some of the impact from nearby artillery or shrapnel. In November 1993, Croats began shelling the bridge from the top of the mountain (where the cross is now—you can just see its tip peeking over the hill from the top of the bridge). Several direct hits caused the venerable Old Bridge to lurch, then tumble in pieces into the river. The mortar inside, which contained pink bauxite, turned the water red as it fell in. Locals said that their old friend was bleeding.

The decision to destroy the bridge was partly strategic—to cut off a Bosniak-controlled strip on the west bank from Bosniak forces on the east. (News footage from the time shows Bosniak soldiers scurrying back and forth over the bridge.) But there can be no doubt that, like the siege of Dubrovnik, the attack was also partly symbolic: the destruction of a bridge representing the city's Muslim legacy.

After the war, city leaders decided to rebuild the Old Bridge. Chunks of the original bridge were dredged up from the river. But the stone had been compromised by soaking in the water for so long, so it couldn't be used (you can still see these pieces of the old Old Bridge on the riverbank below). Staying true to their pledge to do it authentically, restorers quarried new stone (a limestone called *tenelija*) from the original quarry, and each stone was hand-carved. Then they assembled the stones with the same technology used by the Ottomans 450 years ago: Workers erected wooden scaffolding and fastened the stones together with iron hooks cast in lead. The project cost over $13 million, funded largely by international donors and overseen by UNESCO.

It took longer to rebuild the bridge in the 21st century than it did to build it in the 16th century. But on July 23, 2004, the new Old Bridge was inaugurated with much fanfare and was immediately embraced by both the city and the world as a sign of reconciliation. Feel the shivers run down your spine as you walk over the Old Bridge today, and ponder its troubled yet inspirational past.

On a lighter note: One of Mostar's favorite traditions is for young men to jump from the bridge 75 feet down into the Neretva (which remains icy cold even in summer). Done both for the sake of tradition and to impress girls, this custom was carried on even during the time when the destroyed bridge was temporarily replaced by a wooden one. Now the tower on the west side of the bridge houses the office of the local "Divers Club," a loosely run organization that carries on this long-standing ritual. On hot summer days, you'll see divers making a ruckus and collecting donations at the top of the bridge. They tease and tease, standing up on the railing and pretending they're about to jump...then getting down and asking for more money. (If he's wearing trunks rather than Speedos, he's not a diver—just a teaser.) Once they collect about €30, one of them will take the plunge.

Before moving on, see how many of the town's ten mosques you can spot from the top of the bridge (I counted eight minarets).

• *If you'd like to see one of the best* ***views*** *in town—looking up at the Old Bridge from the riverbank below—backtrack the way you came into the shopping zone, take your first left (at Šadran restaurant—a good place to try the powerful "Bosnian coffee"), then find the steps down to the river on the left.*

When you're ready to continue, hike back up to the Old Bridge and cross to the other side. After the bridge on the right are two different

exhibits that are worth a quick visit. First is a good, free ***photo exhibition*** *of powerful images of war-torn Mostar, displayed inside a former mosque for soldiers who guarded the bridge. Just beyond that, tucked into the corner on the right, look for the stairs leading up to the...*

Museum of the Old Bridge (Muzej Stari Most)

Located within one of the Old Bridge's towers, this museum features a film and photos about the reconstruction of the bridge, archaeological findings, and a few other paltry exhibits about the history of the town and bridge, all in English (5 KM, daily 10:00–18:00, lots of stairs, Bajatova 4, tel. 036/551-602). First you'll climb up the stairs just after the bridge and buy your ticket, before hiking the rest of the way up to the top of the tower, where you'll enjoy fine views through grubby windows. Then you'll go around below to the archaeological exhibit. The museum offers more detail than most casual visitors need; consider just dropping into the free, smaller photo exhibition described above, then moving along.

• *After the Old Bridge, the street swings left and leads you along...*

▲▲Coppersmiths' Street (Kujundžiluk)

This lively strip, with the flavor of a Turkish bazaar, offers some of the most colorful shopping this side of Istanbul. You'll see Mostar's characteristic bridge depicted in every possible way, along with blue-and-white "evil eyes" (believed in the Turkish culture to keep bad spirits at bay), old Yugoslav army kitsch, and hammered-copper decorations (continuing the long tradition that gave the street its name). Partway up, the homes with the colorfully painted facades double as galleries for local artists. The artists live and work upstairs, then sell their work right on this street. Pop into the *atelier d'art* ("Đul Emina") on the right to meet Sead Vladović and enjoy his impressive iconographic work (daily 9:00–20:00). This is the most touristy street in all of Bosnia-Herzegovina, so don't expect any bargains. Still, it's fun. As you stroll, check out the fine views of the Old Bridge.

• *Continue uphill. About halfway along this street, on the left-hand side, look for the entrance to the...*

▲Koski Mehmed-Pasha Mosque (Koski Mehmed-Paša Džamija)

Mostar's Bosniak community includes many practicing Muslims. Step into this courtyard for a look at one of Mostar's many mosques (4 KM to enter mosque, 4 KM more to climb minaret,

The Muslims of Mostar

While recent Muslim immigrants are becoming a fixture in most European cities, Bosnia-Herzegovina is one place where Muslims have continuously been an integral part of the cultural tapestry for centuries.

During the more than 400 years that Mostar was part of the Ottoman Empire, the Muslim Turks (unlike some Catholic despots at the time) did not forcibly convert their subjects. However, it was advantageous for non-Turks to adopt Islam (for lower taxes and better business opportunities), so many Slavs living here became Muslims. In fact, within 150 years of the start of Ottoman rule, half of the population of Bosnia-Herzegovina was Muslim.

The Ottomans became increasingly intolerant of other faiths as time went on, and uprisings by Catholics and Orthodox Christians eventually led to the end of Ottoman domination in the late 19th century. But even after the Ottomans left, many people in this region continued practicing Islam, as their families had been doing for centuries. These people constitute an ethnic group called "Bosniaks," and many of them are still practicing Muslims today (following the Sunni branch of the Muslim faith). Keep in mind that most Bosniaks are Slavs—of the same ethnic stock as Croats and Serbs—and look pretty much the same as their neighbors, although some Bosniaks have ancestors who married into Turkish families, and they may have some Turkish features.

Due to the recent actions of a small but attention-grabbing faction of Muslim extremists, Islam is

daily April–Oct 9:00–18:00, until 19:00 at busy times, Nov–March 9:00–15:00). This mosque, dating from the early 17th century, is notable for its cliff-hanging riverside location, and because it's particularly accessible for tourists. The information here generally applies to the other mosques in Mostar, as well:

The fountain *(šadrvan)* in the courtyard allows worshippers to wash before entering the mosque, as directed by Islamic law. This practice, called ablution, is both a literal and a spiritual cleansing in preparation for being in the presence of Allah. It's also refreshing in this hot climate, and the sound of running water helps worshippers concentrate.

The minaret—the slender needle jutting up next to the dome—is the Islamic equivalent of the Christian bell tower, used

burdened with a bad reputation in the Western world. But judging Islam based on Osama bin Laden and al-Qaeda is like judging Christianity based on Timothy McVeigh and the Ku Klux Klan. Visiting Mostar is a unique opportunity to get a taste of a fully Muslim society, made a bit less intimidating because it wears a more-familiar European face.

Here's an admittedly basic and simplistic outline (written by a non-Muslim) designed to help travelers from the Christian West understand a very rich but often misunderstood culture worthy of respect:

Muslims, like Christians and Jews, are monotheistic. They call God "Allah." The most important person in the Islamic faith is Muhammad, Allah's most important prophet, who lived in the sixth and seventh centuries A.D.

The "five pillars" of Islam are the same among Muslims in Bosnia-Herzegovina, Turkey, Iraq, Indonesia, the US, and everywhere else. Followers of Islam should:

1. Say and believe, "There is only one God, and Muhammad is his prophet."

2. Pray five times a day, facing Mecca. Modern Muslims explain that it's important for this ritual to include several elements: washing, exercising, stretching, and thinking of God.

3. Give to the poor (one-fortieth of your wealth, if you are not in debt).

4. Fast during daylight hours through the month of Ramadan. Fasting is a great social equalizer and helps everyone to feel the hunger of the poor.

5. Visit Mecca. This is interpreted by some Muslims as a command to travel. Muhammad said, "Don't tell me how educated you are, tell me how much you've traveled."

Good advice for anyone, no matter what—or if—you call a higher power.

to call people to prayer. In the old days, the *muezzin* (prayer leader) would climb the tower five times a day and chant, "There is only one God, and Muhammad is his prophet." In modern times, loudspeakers are used instead. Climbing the minaret's claustrophobic staircase is a memorable experience, rewarding you with a grand view at the top (entrance to the right of mosque entry).

Because this mosque is accustomed to tourists, you don't need to take off your shoes to enter (there's a special covering on the floor), women don't need to wear scarves, and it's fine to take photos inside. Near the front of the mosque, you may see some of the small, overlapping rugs that are below this covering (reserved for shoes-off worshippers).

Once inside, notice the traditional elements of the mosque.

The niche *(mihrab)* across from the entry is oriented toward Mecca (the holy city in today's Saudi Arabia)—the direction all Muslims face to pray. The small stairway *(mimber)* that seems to go nowhere is symbolic of the growth of Islam—Muhammad had to stand higher and higher to talk to his growing following. This serves as a kind of pulpit, where the cleric gives a speech, similar to a sermon or homily in Christian church services. No priest ever stands on the top stair, which is symbolically reserved for Muhammad.

The balcony just inside the door is traditionally where women worship. For the same reason I find it hard to concentrate on God at aerobics classes, Muslim men decided prayer would go better without the enjoyable but problematic distraction of bent-over women between them and Mecca. These days, women can also pray on the main floor with the men, but they still must avoid physical contact.

Muslims believe that capturing a living creature in a painting or a sculpture is inappropriate. (In fact, depictions of Allah and the prophet Muhammad are strictly forbidden.) Instead, mosques are filled with ornate patterns and calligraphy (of the name "Muhammad" and important prayers and sayings from the Quran). Some of the calligraphy is in Arabic, and some is in Bosnian. You'll also see some floral and plant designs, which you'd never see in a more conservative, Middle Eastern mosque.

Before leaving, ponder how progressive the majority of Mostar's Muslims are. Most of them drink alcohol, wear modern European clothing (you'll see virtually no women wearing head scarves or men with beards), and almost never visit a mosque to pray. In so many ways, these people don't fit our preconceived notions of Islam...and yet, they consider themselves Muslims all the same.

The mosque's courtyard is shared by several merchants. When you're done haggling, head to the terrace behind the mosque for the best view in town of the Old Bridge.

• *Just beyond this mosque, the traffic-free cobbles of the Old Town end. Take a right and leave the cutesy tourists' world. Walk up one block to the big...*

▲▲New Muslim Cemetery

In this cemetery, which was a park before the war, every tomb is dated 1993, 1994, or 1995. As the war raged, more exposed cemeteries were unusable. But this tree-covered piece of land was relatively safe from Croat snipers. As the casualties mounted,

locals buried their loved ones here under cover of darkness. Many of these people were soldiers, but some were civilians. Strict Muslim graves don't display images of people, but here you'll see photos of war dead who were young, less-traditional members of the Muslim community. The fleur-de-lis shape of many of the tombstones is a patriotic symbol for the nation of Bosnia. The Arabic squiggles are the equivalent of an American having Latin on his or her tombstone—old-fashioned and formal.

• *Go up the wide stairs to the right of the cemetery (near the mosque). At #4 on the right, just before and across from the bombed-out tower, you'll find the...*

Museum of Herzegovina (Muzej Hercegovine)

This humble but worthwhile little museum holds fragments of this region's rich history, including historic photos and several items from its Ottoman period. There are sparse English descriptions, but without a tour guide the exhibits are a bit difficult to appreciate. Topics include the Turkish period, Herzegovina under the Austro-Hungarian Empire, village life, and local archaeology. One small room commemorates the house's former owner, Dzemal Bijedić, who was Tito's second-in-command during the Yugoslav period until he was killed in a mysterious plane crash in 1977. (If Bijedić had lived, many wonder whether he might have succeeded Tito... and succeeded in keeping Yugoslavia together.)

But the museum is made worthwhile by a deeply moving **film,** rated ▲▲, that traces the history of the town through its Old Bridge: fun circa-1957 footage of the diving contests; harrowing scenes of the bridge being pummeled, and finally toppled, by artillery; and a stirring sequence showing the bridge's reconstruction and grand reopening on that day in 2004—with high-fives, Beethoven's *Ode to Joy*, fireworks, and more divers (5-KM museum entry includes 12-min film, no narration—works in any language, ask about "film?" as you enter, daily 8:00–16:00, Bajatova 4—walking up these stairs, it's the second door that's marked for the museum, under the overhanging balcony, www.muzejhercegovine.com).

• *Backtrack to where you left the Old Town. Notice the* ***Tepa Market****, with locals buying produce, in the area just beyond the pedestrian zone. Now walk (with the produce market on your left) along the lively street called* ***Braće Fejića.*** *(There's no sign, but the street is level and busy with cafés.) You're in the "new town," where locals sit out in front of*

boisterous cafés sipping coffee while listening to the thumping beat of distinctly Eastern-sounding music.

Stroll down this street for a few blocks. At the palm trees (about 50 yards before the minaret), you can side-trip a block to the left to reach...

▲Bišćević Turkish House (Bišćevića Kuća)

Mostar has three traditional Turkish-style homes that are open for tourists to visit. The Bišćević House is the first and most convenient for a quick visit, but two others are described at the end of this listing. Dating from 1635, the Bišćević House is typical of old houses in Mostar, which mix Oriental style with Mediterranean features (4 KM, daily March–Oct 8:00–20:00, Nov–Feb 9:00–15:00, Bišćevića 13).

A high wall surrounds the house, offering protection from the sun's rays, from thieves...and from prying eyes. First you'll step through the outer (or animals') garden, then into the inner (or family's) garden. Notice how the smooth river stones are set in geometrical forms in the floor (for example, the five-sided star), and keep an eye out for the house's pet turtles. It's no coincidence that the traditional fountain *(šadrvan)* resembles those at the entrance to a mosque—a reminder of the importance of running water in Muslim culture. The little white building is a kitchen—cleverly located apart from the house so that the heat and smells of cooking didn't permeate the upstairs living area.

Buy your ticket and take off your shoes before you climb up the wooden staircase. Imagine how a stairway like this one could be pulled up for extra protection in case of danger. The cool, shady, and airy living room is open to the east—from where the wind rarely blows. The overhanging roof also prevented the hot sun from reaching this area. The loom in the corner was the women's workplace—the carpets you're standing on would have been woven there. The big chests against the wall were used to bring the dowry when the homeowner took a new wife. Study the fine wood carving and the heavy stonework of the roof.

Continue back into the main gathering room *(divanhan)*. This space—whose name comes from the word "talk"—is designed in a circle so people could face each other, cross-legged, for a good conversation while they enjoyed a dramatic view overlooking the Neretva. The room comes with a box of traditional costumes—great for photo fun. Put on a pair of baggy pants and a fez and really lounge.

Other Turkish Houses: If you're intrigued by this, consider

dropping by Mostar's two other Turkish houses. The **Muslibegović House** (Muslibegovića Kuća) feels newer because it dates from 1871, just a few years before the Ottomans left town. This homey house—which also rents out rooms to visitors (see "Sleeping in Mostar," later)—has many of the same features as the Bišćević House. If she's not too busy, Sanela can give you an English tour (4 KM, mid-April–mid-Oct daily 10:00–18:00, closed to visitors off-season, just two blocks uphill from the Karađozbeg Mosque at Osman Dikica 41, tel. 036/551-379, www.muslibegovichouse.com). To find it, go up the street between the Karađozbeg Mosque and the cemetery, cross the busy street, and continue a long block uphill on the alley. The wall with the slate roof on the left marks the house.

The **Kajtaz House** (Kajtazova Kuća), hiding up a very residential-feeling alley a few blocks from the Old Bridge, feels lived-in because it still is (in the opposite direction from most of the other sights, at Gaše Ilića 21).

• *Go back to the main café street and continue to the...*

▲Karađozbeg Mosque (Karađozbegova Džamija)

The city's main mosque was completed in 1557, the same year work began on the Old Bridge. This mosque, which welcomes visitors, feels less touristy than the one back in the Old Town (4 KM to enter mosque, 4 KM more to climb minaret, daily May–Sept 9:00–19:30, Oct–April 10:00–15:00). Before entering the gate into the complex, look for the picture showing the recent war damage sustained by this mosque (which has since been repaired). You'll see that this mosque has most of the same elements as the Koski Mehmed-Pasha Mosque (described earlier). But here, some of the decorations are original. Across the street is another cemetery with tombstones from that terrible year, 1993.

• *Now continue into modern, urban Mostar along the street in front of the Karađozbeg Mosque. This grimy, mostly traffic-free street is called...*

▲Braće Fejića

Walking along the modern town's main café strip, enjoy the opportunity to observe this workaday Bosniak town. You'll see the humble offices of the ragtag B&H Airlines; a state-run gambling office taxing its less-educated people with a state lottery; and lots of cafés that serve drinks but no food. People generally eat at home

before going out to nurse an affordable drink. (Café ABC has good cakes and ice cream; the upstairs is a popular pizza hangout for students and families.)

Obituary announcements are tacked to trees by the mosque, listing the bios and funeral times for locals who have recently died. A fig tree grows out of the minaret in the small mosque—just an accident of nature, illustrating how that plant can thrive with almost no soil.

Walking farther, you see a few ruins—still ugly nearly two decades after the war. There's a messy confusion about who owns what. Surviving companies have no money. Yugo Bank, which held the mortgages, is defunct. No one will invest until clear ownership is established. Until then, the people of Mostar sip their coffee and rip up their dance clubs in the shadow of these jagged reminders of the warfare that wracked this town not so long ago.

Near the end of the pedestrian zone, through the parking lot on the right, look for the building with communist-era reliefs of Bogomil tomb decor from the 12th century—remembering the indigenous culture before the arrival of the Ottomans.

When you finally hit the big street (with car traffic), head left one block to the big **Masala Square** (literally, "Place for Prayer"). Historically this was where pilgrims gathered before setting off for Mecca on their hajj. This is a great scene on balmy evenings, when it's a rendezvous point for the community.

• *For a finale, you can continue one block more out onto the bridge to survey the town you just explored. From here, you can backtrack to linger in the places you found most inviting.*

Nightlife in Mostar

Be sure to enjoy the local scene after dark in Mostar. Though the town is touristy, it's also a real urban center with a young population interested in the same things as young people everywhere else; just for fun, watch them cavort in the local "meat market" (in the courtyard next to the old Turkish bathhouse, near the TI). The Old Bridge is a popular meeting place for locals as well as tourists (and pickpockets). A stroll from the Old Bridge down the Braće Fejića café-lined boulevard, to the modern Masala Square at the far end of town (described earlier), gives a great peek at Mostarians socializing.

Ali Baba is an actual cave featuring a fun, atmospheric, and youthful party scene. Order a cocktail or try a Turkish-style

hubbly-bubbly (*šiša*, SHEE-shah). Ask to have one of these big water pipes fired up for you and choose your flavored tobacco: apple, cappuccino, banana, or lemon (20 KM per pipe per group, 8-KM cocktails, open late daily; look for low-profile, cave-like entrance along Coppersmiths' Street, just down from the Old Bridge—watch for *Open Sesame* sign tucked down a rocky alley).

Sleeping in Mostar

My first two listings are big, full-service hotels, but a bit farther from the charming Old Town. The rest are small, friendly, accessible, affordable guest houses in or very near the Old Town. Mostar's Old Town can be very noisy on weekends, with nightclubs and outdoor restaurants rollicking into the wee hours. If you're a light sleeper, consider Villa Fortuna and the Muslibegović House, which are quieter than the norm.

$$$ Hotel Bristol is the only business-class place near central Mostar, overlooking the river a 10-minute walk from the heart of the Old Town. While it's on a busy street, the windows in its 47 rooms are good (Sb-€60, Db-€100, apartment-€115, extra bed-€16, air-con, elevator, pay Internet access, Mostarskog Bataljona, tel. 036/500-100, fax 036/500-502, www.bristol.ba, info@bristol.ba).

$$$ Hotel Ero, a 20-minute walk north of the Old Town, is a good big-hotel option, with 140 fine rooms and a professional staff. This was one of the only big buildings in the center not damaged during the war, since it hosted journalists and members of

Sleep Code

(€1 = about $1.40, country code: 387, area code: 036)
S = Single, **D** = Double/Twin, **T** = Triple, **Q** = Quad, **b** = bathroom. Unless otherwise noted, prices include breakfast. To help you sort easily through these listings, I've divided the rooms into three categories based on the price for a standard double room with bath in peak season:

$$$ Higher Priced—Most rooms €80 or more.
$$ Moderately Priced—Most rooms between €40–80.
$ Lower Priced—Most rooms €40 or less.

the international community and was therefore off-limits (Sb-€50, Db-€85, suite-€110, air-con, elevator, some traffic noise, ulica Dr. Ante Starčevića, tel. 036/386-777, fax 036/386-700, www.ero.ba, hotel.ero@tel.net.ba).

$$ The **Muslibegović House,** a Bosnian national monument that also invites tourists in to visit during the day, is in an actual Turkish home dating from 1871. The complex houses nine homey rooms and two suites, all of which combine classic Turkish style (elegant old beds, old floors, carpets, sofas; guest remove shoes at the outer door) with modern comforts (air-con, free Wi-Fi). Situated on a quiet residential lane just above the bustle of Mostar's main pedestrian drag and Old Town zone, this is the most enticing deal in town and a memorable experience (Sb-€50, Db-€70, "pasha suite"-€95, all prices €15 more in July–Aug, price includes tour of house, 2 blocks uphill from the Karađozbeg Mosque at Osman Dikica 41, tel. 036/551-379, www.muslibegovichouse.com).

$$ Motel Kriva Ćuprija ("Crooked Bridge"), by the bridge of the same name, is tucked between waterfalls in a picturesque valley a few steps from the Old Bridge. It's an appealing oasis with seven rooms, three apartments, and a restaurant with atmospheric outdoor seating (Sb-€39, Db-€65, apartment-€70, extra bed-€20, 10 percent discount with this book, can be noisy, air-con, free Wi-Fi, Kriva Ćuprija 2, tel. 036/550-953, mobile 061-135-286, www.motel-mostar.ba, info@motel-mostar.ba, Sami). Their second location—called **Hotel Kriva Ćuprija II**—offers 10 rooms in a Habsburg-style building overlooking the river in a modern neighborhood about 200 yards to the south (same prices, discount, amenities, and contact information as main hotel; Maršala Tita 186, next to the Lučki Bridge).

$$ Motel Emen has six modern, sleek rooms overlooking a busy café street a few cobbled blocks from the Old Bridge (Sb-€40, Db-€60, bigger Db with balcony-€70, air-con, free Internet access and Wi-Fi, Onešćukova 32, tel. 036/581-120, www.motel-emen.com, info@motel-emen.com).

$ Villa Fortuna B&B, in a nondescript urban neighborhood a few minutes' walk farther away from the Old Bridge, has nine tasteful, modern, air-conditioned rooms. The rooms are just above the main office of Fortuna Tours, and you'll reserve through them. There's free, secure parking on the courtyard in front, and a pleasant garden in back (Sb-€30, Db-€40, breakfast-€5, tel. 036/552-197, mobile 063-315-017, fax 036/551-888,

fortuna_headoffice@bih.net.ba). Fortuna Tours can also put you in touch with locals renting rooms and apartments.

$ Pansion Botticelli, overlooking a charming waterfall garden just up the valley from the Crooked Bridge, has five colorful rooms (Sb-€30, Db-€40, Tb-€60, breakfast-€3, air-con, Muje Bjelavca 6, enter around back along the alley, mobile 063-319-057, botticelli@bih.net.ba, Snježana and Zoran).

$ Pansion Most rents eight small, older-feeling rooms a few minutes' walk farther from the Old Bridge, above a sports book and a travel agency. I'd consider this a last resort for budget travelers (Sb-€25, Db-€38, air-con, Adema Buća 100, tel. 036/552-528, www.pansionmost.dzaba.com, pansion_most@yahoo.com).

$ Dika Kasumačić has five basic, inexpensive rooms on a quiet lane just above the Crooked Bridge action (S-€15, D-€30, cash only, air-con, follow green *pansion* signs from near Pansion Botticelli to Kapetanovina 16, mobile 061-506-443, sanjink @hotmail.com).

Eating in Mostar

Most of Mostar's tourist-friendly restaurants are conveniently concentrated in the Old Town. If you walk anywhere that's cobbled, you'll stumble onto dozens of tempting restaurants charging about the same reasonable prices and serving rustic, traditional Bosnian food. In my experience, the menu at most places is about the same—though quality and ambience can vary greatly. Grilled meats are especially popular—read "Balkan Flavors," on page 753, before you dine. Another specialty here is *dolma*—a pepper stuffed with minced meat, vegetables, and rice. Sarajevsko Pivo beer is on tap.

On the Embankment, with Old Bridge Views

For the best atmosphere, find your way into the several levels of restaurants that clamber up the riverbank with perfect views of the Old Bridge. To reach these, go over the Old Bridge to the west side of the river, and bear right on the cobbles until you get to the old Turkish bathhouse, or *hammam* (with the copper domes on the roof). To the right of the bathhouse is the entrance to a lively courtyard surrounded with cafés and restaurants. Continuing toward the river from the courtyard, stairs lead down to several riverfront terraces. While you'll have menus pushed in your face as

you walk, don't hesitate—poke around to find your favorite bridge view before settling in for a drink or a meal. If you want a good perch, it's fun and smart to drop by earlier in the day and personally reserve the table of your choice. In terms of the setting and views, this is the most memorable place to dine in Mostar—but be warned that the quality of the food along here is uniformly low.

Away from the Old Bridge

While they lack the Old Bridge views, these places serve food that's generally a step up. The first two places are in the atmospheric Old Town, while the last two are in the modern part of town.

Restoran Hindin Han is pleasantly situated on a woody terrace over a rushing stream. It's respected locally for its good cooking and fair prices (big 10–15-KM salads, 6–12-KM grilled dishes, 10–20-KM fish and other main dishes, Sarajevsko beer on tap, daily 11:00–24:00, Jusovina 10, tel. 036/581-054). To find it, walk west from the Old Bridge, bear left at the Šadrvan restaurant, cross the bridge, and you'll see it on the left.

Konoba Dvije Pećine ("The Two Caves") is a mom-and-pop place woven into a tangle of terraces over a rushing little stream facing the Crooked Bridge. It's known for its home-cooking (*domaća*—"homemade"—is the key word), and the food does taste a cut above the norm (6–18-KM plates, splittable mixed grill for 16 KM, daily 11:00–24:00, on Jusovina street at the end of the Crooked Bridge, mobile 061-558-228, Nuna and Jusa Dizdarević and Cako the charming head waiter).

Saray is a nondescript little eatery just uphill from the Karađozbeg Mosque in the modern part of town. They have a basic menu of very tasty grilled meats—specializing in the classic *čevapčići* (little sausage-shaped meat patties)—and outdoor seating overlooking a playground that offers good people- and kid-watching while you eat (5–8-KM grilled meat dishes, big 6–7-KM salads, daily 9:00–17:00, mobile 061-529-320).

Bistro Verona sits along the bombed-out but increasingly revitalized Bulevar, in the shadow of the towering Franciscan Church. While as charming as a strip-mall diner, it's a great chance to eat—indoors or out—surrounded by a humble, friendly, and perfectly local scene without a hint of tourism (6–10-KM grilled meat dishes and pastas, Husnije Rebca 3, mobile 062-432-260).

Mostar Connections

By Bus

Not surprisingly for a divided city, Mostar has two different bus terminals, each served by different companies. On the east (Bosniak/Muslim) side of the river, you'll find the main bus station

(called "Autobusna Stanica"; about a 15-minute walk north of the Old Town—for details, see "Arrival in Mostar," earlier). On the west (Croat/Catholic) side, the situation is less predictable: Some buses leave from a bus stop near the Franciscan Church, while others use a bus station (called "Kolodvor") on Vukovarska street.

Most Bosniak buses are operated by Autoprevoz (tel. 036/551-900, www.autoprevoz-bus.ba). Many Croat buses are run by Globtour (www.globtour.com). And local or regional buses are operated by Mostar Bus, whose buses depart from across the street from the main bus station (www.mostarbus.ba).

Tracking down reliable **schedule** information in Mostar is next to impossible. There's still tension between the Bosniak and Croat companies, which means there's often a lack of communication and therefore no single, reliable place where you can go to be sure you know all of your options. Start by checking the websites above, but realize that schedules can change unexpectedly. The Autoprevoz "tourist agency" at the main bus station (described earlier, under "Arrival in Mostar") is English-speaking and generally helpful, but they don't have dependable information about Croat-run buses. It's not unheard-of for someone to ride a bus here in the morning from Dubrovnik, expecting to take a late-afternoon bus back the same day—only to find that the day's last departure leaves just a few minutes after they arrive. While this sounds intimidating, it's workable. Just do your best to double-check schedules at both ends to be sure your connection lines up—especially if you'll be cutting it close. Note that buses to seasonal destinations (such as along the Dalmatian Coast) run more frequently in peak season, roughly June through mid-September.

From Mostar by Bus to: Međugorje (7/day Mon–Fri, 3/day Sat, none Sun, 50 min, mostly from the west side, 3 KM), **Sarajevo** (about hourly, 2.5 hrs, from main bus station, 15 KM), **Zagreb** (daily at about 9:00, 8 hrs, plus 1 night bus/day, 9.5 hrs, 70 KM), **Split** (4–7/day depending on season, 4–4.5 hrs, can be from either side—ask locally about your specific bus, 20–30 KM), **Dubrovnik** (2–5/day depending on season, 4–5 hrs, from main bus station, 20–30 KM—but note that except for some weekends, most Dubrovnik buses leave early in the day, making an afternoon return from Mostar to Dubrovnik impossible). Service to **Korčula** is sporadic—sometimes once per week, sometimes none at all.

By Train

Mostar is on the train line that runs from Ploče (on the Croatian coast between Split and Dubrovnik) to Zagreb, via Mostar and Sarajevo. This train—which leaves from next to the main bus station—generally runs once daily, leaving **Ploče** soon after 6:00 in the morning, with stops at **Mostar** (1.5 hours), **Sarajevo** (4.25

hours), and **Zagreb** (13.5 hours; bus is faster). Going the opposite direction, the train leaves Zagreb at about 9:00 in the morning.

Route Tips for Drivers

You have two ways to drive between Mostar and Dubrovnik: easy and straightforward, or adventurous and off the beaten path.

Between Mostar and the Main Coastal Road

The most convenient entry point into Bosnia-Herzegovina from the Dalmatian Coast is the town of **Metković,** about halfway between Dubrovnik and Split. (If you're driving there from Dubrovnik or Korčula, you'll actually cross into Bosnia-Herzegovina twice—including the short stretch of coastline that Bosnia-Herzegovina still controls, with the town of **Neum.** For more details, see page 849.)

Near Metković, the main coastal road jogs away from the coast and around the striking **Neretva River Delta**—the extremely fertile "garden patch of Croatia," which produces a significant portion of Croatia's fruits and vegetables. The Neretva is the same river that flows under Mostar's Old Bridge upstream—but in Metković, it spreads out into 12 branches as it enters the Adriatic, flooding a vast plain and creating a bursting cornucopia in the middle of an otherwise rocky and arid region. Enjoying some of the most plentiful sunshine on the Croatian coast, as well as a steady supply of water for irrigation, the Neretva Delta is as productive as it is beautiful.

After passing through Metković, you'll cross the border into **Bosnia-Herzegovina,** then continue straight on the main road (M-17) directly into Mostar. As you drive, you'll see destroyed buildings and occasional roadside memorials bearing the likenesses of fresh-faced soldiers who died in the recent war.

Along the way are a few interesting detours: In Čapljina, you can turn off toward **Međugorje**. At this popular Catholic pilgrimage site, six residents have reported seeing visions of the Virgin Mary. While this can be a powerful experience for pilgrims, nonbelievers generally find it underwhelming (aside from the thriving zone of kitschy restaurants, hotels, and rosary shops surrounding the town church).

Soon after, a mountaintop castle tower on the right side of the road marks the medieval town of **Počitelj** (pictured at right)—an artists' colony with a compelling mix of Christian and Muslim architecture, including a big mosque and a multi-domed bathhouse. It's well worth

pulling over and strolling around this steep village.

With extra time, just before Mostar (in Buna), you can detour a few miles along the Buna River into **Blagaj**—the historical capital of the region until the arrival of the Ottomans. This is the site of a mountain called Hum, which is topped by the ruins of a hilltop castle that once belonged to Herzog ("Duke") Stjepan, who gave Herzegovina its name. Deep in Blagaj is an impressive cliff face with a scenic house marking the source of the Buna River. The building, called the Tekija, is actually a former monastery for Turkish dervishes (an order that emphasizes poverty and humility, and is famous for the way they whirl when in a worshipful trance); inside is a modest museum with the graves of two important dervishes. Today the area is surrounded by gift shops and a big restaurant with fine views over the river and cliff.

Approaching **Mostar** on M-17, you'll pass the airport, then turn left at your first opportunity to cross the river. After crossing the bridge, bear right onto Bulevar street, and continue on that main artery for several blocks (passing several destroyed buildings). At the street called Rade Bitange (just after the giant church bell tower), turn right to find the public parking lot—less than a 10-minute walk from the Old Bridge. Be warned that signage is poor; if you get lost, try asking for directions to "Stari Most" (STAH-ree most)—the Old Bridge.

Rugged-but-Scenic Backcountry Route Through Serbian Herzegovina

If you're visiting Mostar round-trip from Dubrovnik, consider coming back a different route, mostly through Herzegovina. This feels much more remote and takes an hour or two longer, but the roads are good and the occasional gas station and restaurant break up the journey. Since this route takes you through the Republika Srpska part of Herzegovina, most road signs are exclusively in the Cyrillic alphabet—though, interestingly, much of the advertising you'll see uses the more familiar Roman alphabet. (Because this road goes through the Serbian part of Herzegovina, it's not popular among Bosniaks or Croats—in fact, locals might tell you this road "does not exist." It does.)

This route is narrated from Dubrovnik to Mostar, but you can do it in reverse—just hold the book upside-down. If you want a little taste of Republika Srpska, consider just day-tripping into Trebinje—especially on Saturday, when the produce market is at its liveliest.

From Dubrovnik, head south toward Cavtat, the airport, and Montenegro. Shortly after leaving Dubrovnik, watch for signs on the left directing you to *Gornji Brgat*. Follow this road to the border of Bosnia-Herzegovina, cross the border, and carry on about 20

minutes into **Trebinje** (Требиње). Consider stopping for a break in Trebinje, a pleasant and relatively affluent town with a leafy main square that hosts a fine Saturday market. Overlooking the town from its hilltop perch is the striking Orthodox Church of Nova Gračanica, built to resemble the historically important Gračanica Monastery in Kosovo. If you have time, drive up to the church's viewpoint terrace for great views over Trebinje and the valley.

From Trebinje, you have two options. One is to drive along the very pretty valley via **Ljubinje** (Љубиње) and **Stolac** (Столац), on the Serb-Muslim boundary, then to **Počitelj** (described earlier) and on to Mostar.

Or, for a longer, more remote, middle-of-nowhere adventure, consider this alternate route: From Trebinje, drive north toward **Bilećko Lake**—a vast, aquamarine lake you'll see on your right (the Vikiovac Restaurant offers a great viewpoint). Then you'll go through the town of **Bileća** (Билећа), turning west at the gloomy industrial town of **Gacko** (Гацко, with a giant coal mine), and onward to the humble but proud little town of **Nevesinje** (Невесиње). From Nevesinje, it's a quick drive up over the mountains, then down into Mostar—passing more familiar Roman-alphabet road signs, then spectacular views of Herzog Stjepan's imposing castle over the town of Buna. Follow signs on into Mostar.

AUSTRIA

VIENNA

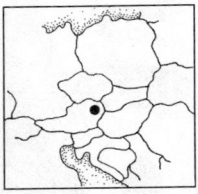

Vienna is the capital of Austria, the cradle of classical music, the home of the rich Habsburg heritage, and one of Europe's most livable cities. The city center is skyscraper-free, pedestrian-friendly, dotted with quiet parks, and traversed by quaint electric trams. Many buildings still reflect 18th- and 19th-century elegance, when the city was at the forefront of the arts and sciences. Compared with most modern European urban centers, the pace of life is slow.

Vienna has always been considered the easternmost city of the West. For 640 years, Vienna was the capital of the enormous Austrian Empire (a.k.a. the Austro-Hungarian Empire, a.k.a. the Habsburg Empire). Stretching from the Alps of northern Italy to the rugged Carpathians of Romania, and from the banks of the Danube to sunny Dubrovnik, this multiethnic empire was arguably the most powerful European entity since Rome. And yet, of its 60 million people, only eight million were Austrian; Vienna was a kind of Eastern European melting pot. Today, the truly Viennese person is not Austrian, but a second-generation Habsburg cocktail, with grandparents from the distant corners of the old empire—Hungary, the Czech Republic, Slovakia, Poland, Slovenia, Croatia, Bosnia-Herzegovina, Serbia, Romania, and Italy.

The city reached its peak in the 19th century. After Napoleon's defeat and the

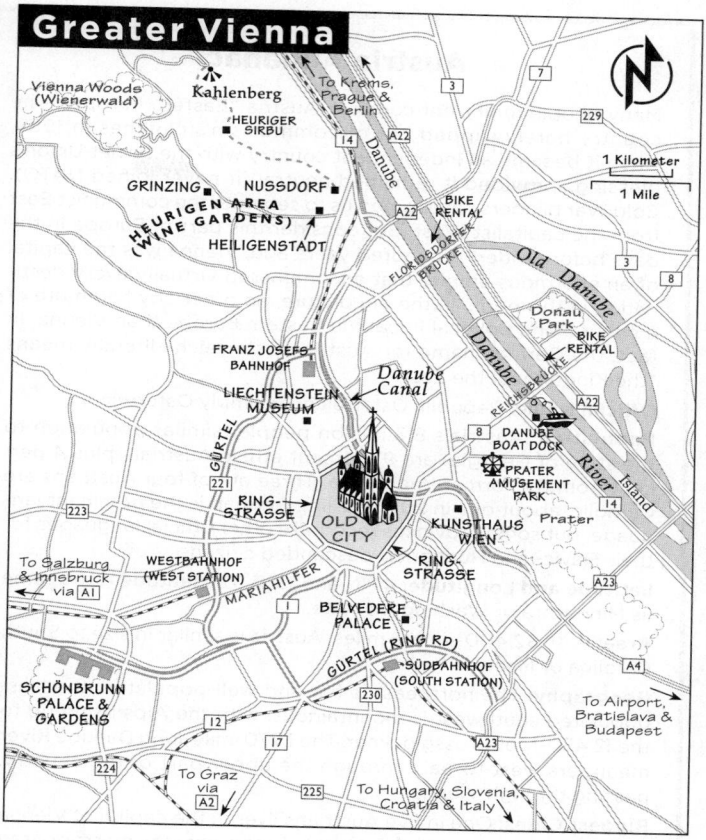

Congress of Vienna in 1815 (which shaped 19th-century Europe), Vienna enjoyed its violin-filled belle époque, giving us our romantic image of the city: fine wine, chocolates, cafés, waltzes, and the good life. In 1900, Vienna's 2.2 million inhabitants made it the world's fifth-largest city—after New York, London, Paris, and Berlin. Vienna sat on the cusp between stuffy Old World monarchy and subversive modern trends.

However, after starting and losing World War I, the Habsburgs lost their far-flung holdings. Then came World War II: While Vienna's old walls had long held out would-be invaders—Germanic barbarians (in Roman times), Mongol hordes (13th century), Ottoman Turks (the sieges of 1529 and 1683)—they were no match for WWII bombs, which destroyed nearly a quarter of the city's buildings. In the Cold War, neutral Austria took a big bite out of the USSR's Warsaw Pact buffer zone—and

Austria Almanac

Many people might not consider Austria "Eastern Europe." The country barely slipped out of communism's clutches in 1955, when it became an independent country with the Soviet Union's blessing...provided it remained neutral (it never joined NATO). Cold War blinders have forced us to separate the communist East from the capitalist West. But consider this part of Europe in the days before Hitler: A hundred years ago, Vienna was the capital of an enormous empire that encompassed virtually every destination in this book. In the big picture, no other city had more of a cultural and political impact in Eastern Europe than Vienna. In fact, the German name for Austria—Österreich—literally means "the Kingdom of the East."

Official Name: Republik Österreich, or simply Österreich.

Population: Austria's 8.3 million people (similar population to the state of Georgia) are 91 percent ethnic Austrian, plus 4 percent from the former Yugoslavia. Three out of four Austrians are Catholic; about one in 20 is Muslim. German is the dominant language, but some provinces recognize other official languages for their Slavic- and Hungarian-descended citizens.

Latitude and Longitude: 47°N and 13°E. The latitude is the same as Minnesota or Washington state.

Area: With 32,400 square miles, Austria is similar in size to South Carolina or Maine.

Geography: The northeast is flat and well-populated; the less-populated southwest is mountainous, with the Alps rising up to the 12,450-foot Grossglockner. The 1,770-mile-long Danube River meanders west-to-east through the upper part of the country, passing through Vienna.

Biggest Cities: One in five Austrians lives in the capital of Vienna (1.7 million in the city; 2.2 million in the greater metropolitan area). Graz has 255,000, and Linz has 189,000.

Economy: Bordered by eight countries, Austria is well-integrated into the EU economy. The Gross Domestic Product is $330 billion (similar to Massachusetts'). It has a GDP per capita of $40,000—among Europe's highest. One of its biggest moneymakers is tourism. Austria produces wood, paper products (nearly half the

Vienna became, for a time, a den of spies.

Today, Vienna has settled down into a somewhat sleepy, pleasant place where culture is still king. Its once-grand empire having collapsed, Vienna is now a head without a body. But culturally, historically, and from a sightseeing point of view, this city is the sum of its illustrious past. Classical music is everywhere. People nurse a pastry and coffee over the daily paper at small cafés. It's a city of world-class museums, big and small. Anyone with an interest

land is forested)...and Red Bull Energy Drink. The country has an aging population that increasingly collects social security—a situation that will strain the national budget in years to come.

Government: Austria has been officially neutral since 1955 and its citizens take a dim view of European unity. Although right-leaning parties made substantial gains in recent elections, the government continues to be a center-left coalition, currently headed by Federal President Heinz Fischer and Chancellor Werner Faymann (both Social Democrats). The resurgent right—buoyed by anti-immigrant and anti-EU sentiment—was dealt a blow in October 2008 when its "yuppie fascist" leader Jörg Haider died in a car accident. Austria is the only EU nation that lets 16- and 17-year-olds vote.

Flag: Three horizontal bands of red (top), white, and red.

Cuisine: Austrian treats include Wiener schnitzel (breaded veal cutlet), *Knödel* (dumplings), *Apfelstrudel* (apple strudel), *Kaiserschmarr'n* (fluffy, caramelized pancake strips), and fancy desserts like the Sacher torte, Vienna's famous chocolate cake.

Language: Austria's official language is German. It's important to greet people in the breakfast room and those you pass on the streets or meet in shops. The Austrian version of "Hi" is a cheerful *"Grüss Gott."* You'll get the correct pronunciation after the first volley—listen and copy. For German Survival Phrases, see page 1129.

Gemütlichkeit: The Austrians are not Germans—and they cherish their distinct cultural and historical traditions. Austria is mellow and relaxed compared to Deutschland. *Gemütlichkeit* is the word most often used to describe this special Austrian cozy-and-easy approach to life. On the other hand, Austria feels relatively stiff and formal compared to most of Eastern Europe (except maybe Hungary).

The Average Austrian: A typical Austrian is 41 years old, has 1.36 children, and will live to be 79. He or she inhabits a 900-square-foot home, and spends leisure time with a circle of a few close friends. Chances are high that someone in that closely knit circle is a smoker—Austrians smoke more cigarettes per day than any other Europeans.

in painting, music, architecture, beautiful objects, or Sacher torte with whipped cream will feel right at home.

From a practical standpoint, Vienna serves as a prime "gateway" city. The location is central and convenient to most major Eastern European destinations. Actually farther east than Prague, Ljubljana, and Zagreb, and just upstream on the Danube from Budapest and Bratislava, Vienna is an ideal launchpad for a journey into the East.

Planning Your Time

For a big city, Vienna is pleasant and laid-back. Packed with sights, it's worth two days and two nights on the speediest trip. If you're visiting Vienna as a part of a longer trip, you could sleep in and sleep out on the train—Kraków, Warsaw, Berlin, Venice, Rome, the Swiss Alps (via Zürich), Paris, and the Rhine Valley are all just a handy night train away.

The Hofburg and Schönbrunn are both world-class palaces, but seeing both is redundant—with limited time or money, I'd choose just one. The Hofburg comes with the popular Sisi Museum and is right in the town center, making for an easy visit. With more time, a visit to Schönbrunn—set outside town amid a grand and regal garden—is also a great experience.

If you have two days for Vienna, here's a good way to spend them:

Day 1

9:00 Drop by the TI for any planning and ticket needs, then see the sights in Vienna's old center (following my self-guided walk); consider breaking en route to take in St. Stephen's Cathedral (nave closed 11:30–13:30) and climb its south tower.

12:00 Lunch of finger sandwiches at Buffet Trzesniewski.

13:00 Tour the Hofburg Palace and Treasury.

16:00 Hit one more museum, or shop, browse, and people-watch.

19:30 Choose classical music (concert or opera), Haus der Musik, a *Heuriger* wine garden, or visit a museum—many of Vienna's sights are open late at least one night a week.

Day 2

Morning Choose between Schönbrunn Palace (which could be redundant if you've seen the Hofburg Palace yesterday) or the Lipizzaner stallions. If you choose Schönbrunn Palace, arrive by 9:00 and return to central Vienna by noon. The Spanish Riding School's Lipizzaner stallions begin their practice at 10:00 (about March–June and mid-Aug–Dec Tue–Sat 10:00–12:00, no practice Sun–Mon or July–mid-Aug).

12:00	Have lunch at the Naschmarkt, and consider ducking into one or two sights (such as the Secession) on nearby Karlsplatz.
13:00	Tour the Opera (check red sign on door for today's schedule).
14:00	Visit the Kunsthistorisches Museum.
16:00	Choose from the many sights left to see in Vienna.
Evening	See Day 1 evening options. In summer, hit the City Hall food circus for dinner or a drink (on Rathausplatz).

Orientation to Vienna

(area code: 01)

Vienna sits between the Vienna Woods (Wienerwald) and the Danube (Donau, DOH-now). To the southeast is industrial sprawl. The Alps, which arc across Europe from Marseille, end at Vienna's wooded hills, providing a popular playground for walking and sipping new wine. This greenery's momentum carries on into the city. More than half of Vienna is parkland, filled with ponds, gardens, trees, and statue-maker memories of Austria's glory days.

Think of the city map as a target with concentric sections: The bull's-eye is St. Stephen's Cathedral, the towering cathedral south of the Danube. Surrounding that is the old town, bound tightly by the circular road known as the Ringstrasse, marking what used to be the city wall. The Gürtel, a broader ring road, contains the rest of downtown. Outside the Gürtel lies the (uninteresting) sprawl of modern Vienna.

Addresses start with the district, or *Bezirk,* followed by the street and building number. The Ringstrasse (a.k.a. the Ring) circles the first *Bezirk*. Any address higher than the ninth *Bezirk* is beyond the Gürtel, far from the center.

Nearly all your sightseeing will be in the old town, located inside (and along) the Ringstrasse. To walk across this circular district takes about 30 minutes. St. Stephen's Cathedral sits in the center, at the intersection of the two main (pedestrian-only) streets: Kärntner Strasse runs north–south and Graben runs east–west. Within a few blocks of the cathedral is the Hofburg, a sprawling complex of palaces and museums.

Several sights lie on or just outside the Ringstrasse. A branch of the Danube River borders the Ring to the north. On the south

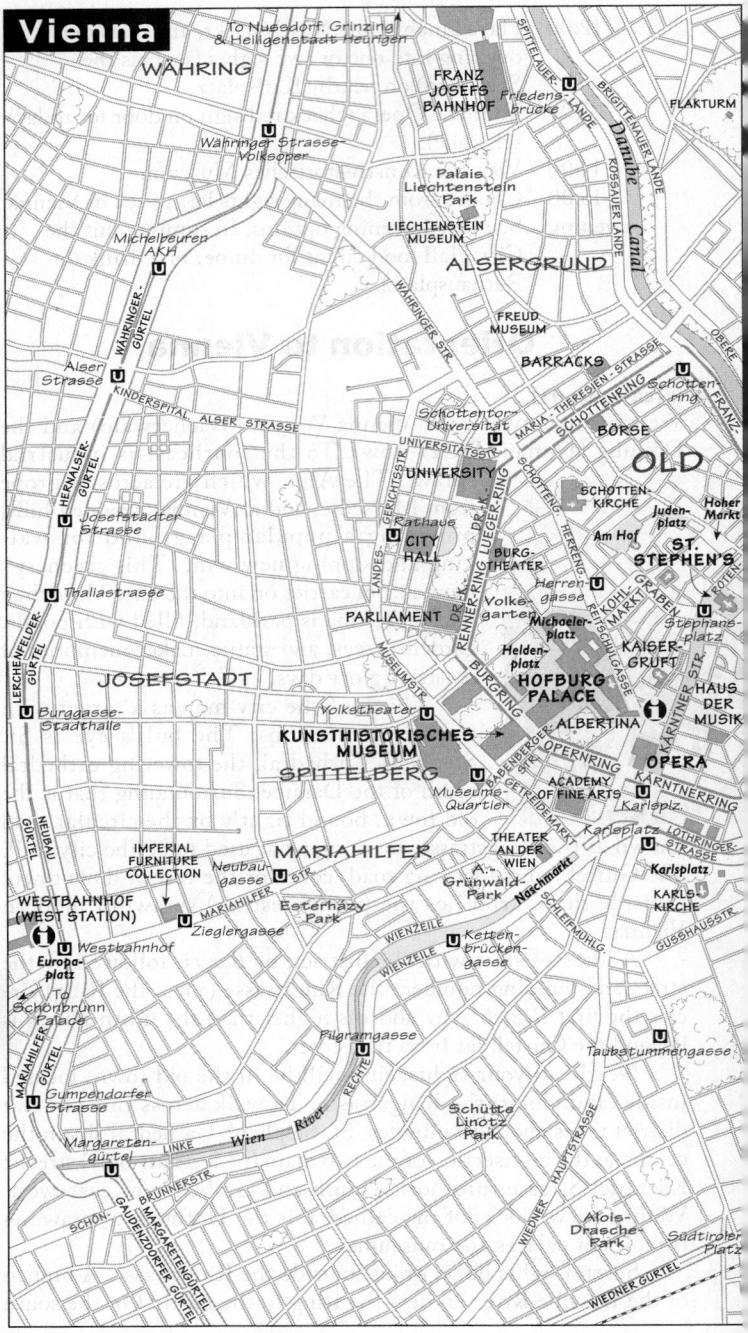
Vienna
To Nussdorf, Grinzing & Heiligenstadt Heurigen
WÄHRING
FRANZ JOSEFS BAHNHOF
Friedens-brücke
SPITTELAUER LANDE
BRIGITTEAUER LANDE
FLAKTURM
Danube Canal
KOSSAUER LANDE
Währinger Strasse Volksoper
Palais Liechtenstein Park
LIECHTENSTEIN MUSEUM
Michelbeuren AKH
ALSERGRUND
WÄHRINGER STR.
FREUD MUSEUM
WÄHRINGER-GÜRTEL
Alser Strasse
KINDERSPITAL
ALSER STRASSE
BARRACKS
THERESIEN-STRASSE
SCHOTTENRING
Schotten-ring
OBERE
FRANZ
Schottentor-Universität
UNIVERSITÄTSSTR.
MARIA
BÖRSE
OLD
UNIVERSITY
GERICHTSSTR.
SCHOTTEN-KIRCHE
Juden-platz
Hoher Markt
HERNALSER-GÜRTEL
Josefstädter Strasse
Rathaus
CITY HALL
LANDES-
DR.-KARL-RENNER-RING
LUEGER-RING
BURG-THEATER
Am Hof
ST. STEPHEN'S
Thaliastrasse
Herren-gasse
KOHL-MARKT
GRABEN
ROTEN
Volke-garten
PARLIAMENT
Michaeler-platz
Stephans-platz
Helden-platz
KAISER-GRUFT
LERCHEFELDER-GÜRTEL
JOSEFSTADT
MUSEUMSTR.
HOFBURG PALACE
KÄRNTNER STR.
HAUS DER MUSIK
Burggasse-Stadthalle
Volkstheater
ALBERTINA
KUNSTHISTORISCHES MUSEUM
OPERNRING
OPERA
SPITTELBERG
Museums-Quartier
ACADEMY OF FINE ARTS
KÄRNTNERRING
Karlsplz.
Karlsplatz
LOTHRINGER-STRASSE
NEUBAU-GÜRTEL
IMPERIAL FURNITURE COLLECTION
MARIAHILFER
Neubau-gasse
STR.
THEATER AN DER WIEN
Karlsplatz
A.-Grünwald-Park
Naschmarkt
KARLS-KIRCHE
WESTBAHNHOF (WEST STATION)
MARIAHILFER
Esterházy Park
SCHLEIFMÜHLG.
Zieglergasse
WIENZEILE
Ketten-brücken-gasse
GUSSHAUSSTR.
Westbahnhof
Europa-platz
To Schönbrunn Palace
Filgramgasse
Taubstummengasse
MARIAHILFER-GÜRTEL
Gumpendorfer Strasse
RECHTE
Schütte Linotz Park
Margareten-gürtel
LINKE
Wien River
HAUPTSTRASSE
B.-BRUNNERSTR.
SCHÖN-
B.-MARGARETENGÜRTEL
GAUDENZDORFER GÜRTEL
WIEDNER
Alois-Drasche-Park
Südtiroler Platz
WIEDNER GÜRTEL

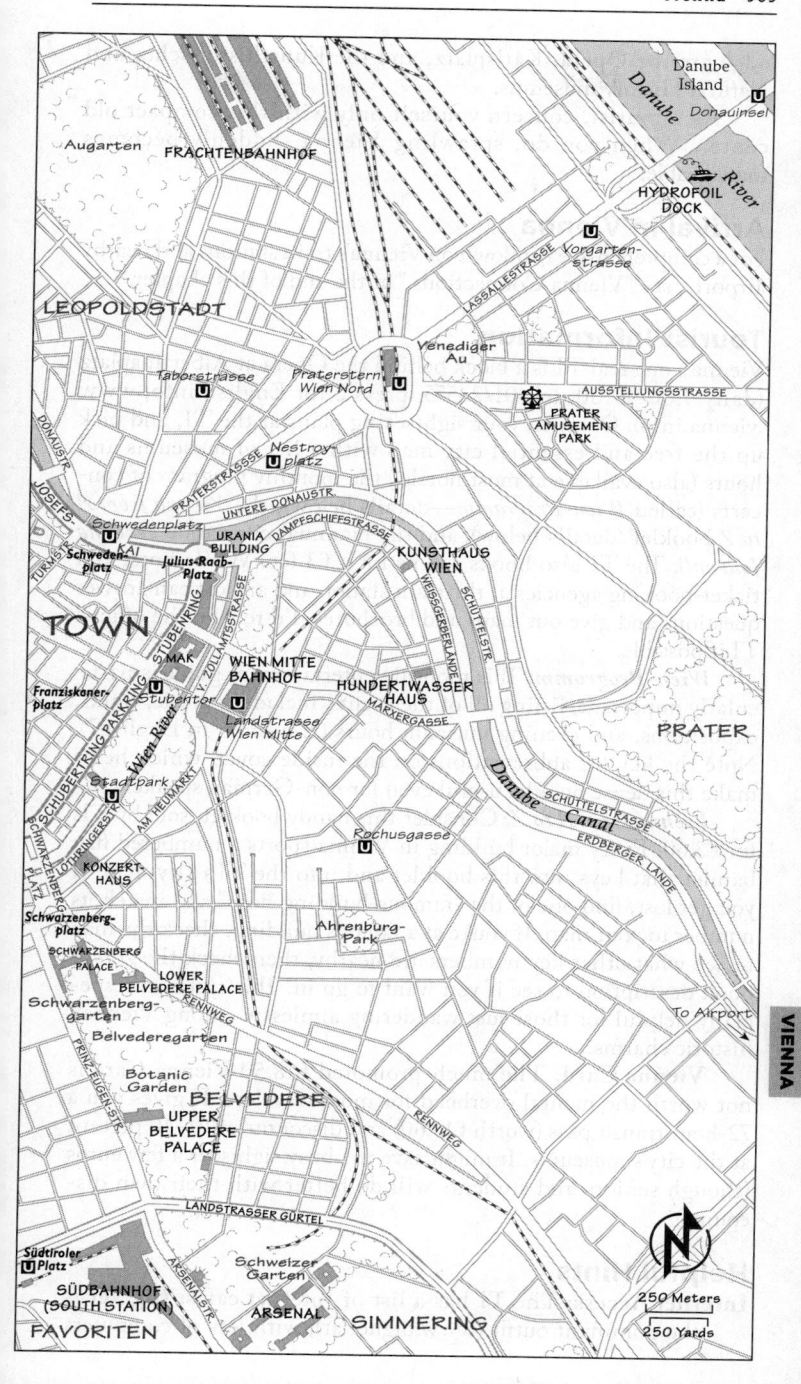
Danube Island
Donauinsel
Danube River
Augarten
FRACHTENBAHNHOF
HYDROFOIL DOCK
Vorgarten-strasse
LASSALLESTRASSE
LEOPOLDSTADT
Venediger Au
Taborstrasse
Praterstern Wien Nord
AUSSTELLUNGSSTRASSE
PRATER AMUSEMENT PARK
DONAUSTR
Nestroy-platz
PRATERSTRASSE
JOSEFS-KAI
UNTERE DONAUSTR
Schwedenplatz
URANIA BUILDING
DAMPFSCHIFFSTRASSE
KUNSTHAUS WIEN
Schweden-platz
Julius-Raab-Platz
TURMSTR
STUBENRING
V. ZOLLAMTSSTRASSE
WEISSGERBERLANDE
SCHUTTELSTR
TOWN
STMAK
WIEN MITTE BAHNHOF
Franziskaner-platz
Stubentor
HUNDERTWASSER HAUS
MARXERGASSE
Wien River
Landstrasse Wien Mitte
PRATER
SCHUBERTRING PARKRING
Stadtpark
AM HEUMARKT
Danube Canal
SCHUTTELSTRASSE
LOTHRINGERSTR
Rochusgasse
ERDBERGER LANDE
SCHWARZENBERG PLATZ
KONZERT-HAUS
Schwarzenberg-platz
Ahrenburg-Park
SCHWARZENBERG PALACE
LOWER BELVEDERE PALACE
Schwarzenberg-garten
RENNWEG
To Airport
Belvederegarten
PRINZ-EUGEN-STR
Botanic Garden
BELVEDERE
UPPER BELVEDERE PALACE
RENNWEG
LANDSTRASSER GÜRTEL
Südtiroler Platz
ARSENALSTR
Schweizer Garten
SÜDBAHNHOF (SOUTH STATION)
ARSENAL
SIMMERING
FAVORITEN
250 Meters
250 Yards

edge are the Opera, Karlsplatz, and the Kunsthistorisches and Natural History museums.

As a tourist, concern yourself only with this compact old center. When you do, sprawling Vienna suddenly becomes manageable.

Arrival in Vienna

For a comprehensive rundown on Vienna's train stations and nearby airports, see "Vienna Connections," at the end of this chapter.

Tourist Information

Vienna's one real TI is a block behind the Opera at Albertinaplatz (daily 9:00–19:00, tel. 01/24555, press 2 for English info, www.vienna.info). Confirm your sightseeing plans at the TI, and pick up the free and essential city map with a list of museums and hours (also available at most hotels), the monthly program of concerts (called *Wien-Programm*—details below), the *Vienna from A to Z* booklet (details below), and the biannual city guide *(Vienna Journal)*. The TI also books rooms for a €3 fee. While hotel and ticket-booking agencies at the train station and airport can answer questions and give out maps and brochures, I'd rely on the official TI if possible.

***Wien-Programm*:** This monthly entertainment guide is particularly important, listing all of the events, including music, walks, expositions, and evening museum hours (*E* means "in English"). Note the key for abbreviations on the inside cover, which helps make this dense booklet useful even for non-German speakers.

Vienna from A to Z: Consider this handy booklet, sold by TIs for €3.60. Every major building in Vienna sports a numbered flag banner that keys into this booklet and into the TI's city map. If you get lost, find one of the "famous-building flags" and match its number to your map. If you're at a famous building, check the map to see what other key numbers are nearby, then check the *A to Z* book description to see if you want to go in. This system is especially helpful for those just wandering aimlessly among Vienna's historic charms.

Vienna Card: The much-promoted €18.50 Vienna Card is not worth the mental overhead for most travelers. It gives you a 72-hour transit pass (worth €13.60) and discounts of 10–40 percent at the city's museums. It might save the busy sightseer a few euros (though seniors and students will do better with their own discounts).

Helpful Hints

Internet Access: The TI has a list of Internet cafés. **BigNet** is the dominant outfit (www.bignet.at), with lots of computers

at Hoher Markt 8–9 (daily 9:00–23:00). **Surfland Internet Café** is near the Opera (daily 10:00–23:00, Krugerstrasse 10, tel. 01/512-7701), and **Netcafe** is close to many of my recommended hotels (Mon–Fri 9:00–22:00, Sat 10:00–22:00, Sun 12:00–22:00, Mariahilfer Strasse 103, tel. 01/595-5558).

Post Offices: The main post office is near Schwedenplatz at Fleischmarkt 19 (Mon–Fri 7:00–22:00, Sat–Sun 9:00–22:00). Branch offices are at the Westbahnhof (Mon–Fri 7:00–22:00, Sat–Sun 9:00–20:00), near the Opera (Mon–Fri 7:00–19:00, closed Sat–Sun, Krugerstrasse 13), and scattered throughout town.

English Bookstore: Stop by the woody and cool **Shakespeare & Co.** (Mon–Sat 9:00–19:00 and sometimes later, generally closed Sun, north of Hoher Markt at Sterngasse 2, tel. 01/535-5053). Also inside the Ring is **The British Bookshop** (Mon–Fri 9:30–18:30, Sat 9:30–18:00, closed Sun, between Franziskaner Platz and the Ring at Weihburggasse 24, tel. 01/512-194-522).

Keeping Up with the News: Don't buy newspapers. Read them for free in Vienna's marvelous coffee houses. It's much classier.

Travel Agency: Intropa is convenient, with good service for flights and train tickets. They'll waive the service charge for my readers (Mon–Fri 9:00–18:00, Sat 10:00–13:00, closed Sun, Spiegelgasse 15, tel. 01/513-4000).

Getting Around Vienna

By Public Transportation: Take full advantage of Vienna's simple, cheap, and super-efficient transit system, which includes trams (a.k.a streetcars), buses, U-Bahn (subway), and S-Bahn (faster suburban trains). The smooth, modern trams are Porsche-designed, with "backpack technology" that locates the engines and mechanical hardware on the roofs for a lower ride and easier entry. I generally stick to the tram to zip around the Ring and take the U-Bahn to outlying sights or hotels. Trams #1, #2, and #D all travel partway around the Ring.

The free Vienna map, available at TIs and hotels, includes a smaller schematic map of the major public transit lines, making

the too-big €2.50 transit map unnecessary. (Transit maps are also posted conveniently on U-Bahn station walls.) As you study the map, note that tram lines are marked with numbers (such as #38). Buses have numbers followed by an *A* (such as #38A). U-Bahn lines begin with U (e.g., U-1), and the directions are designated by the end-of-the-line stops. Blue lines are the speedier S-Bahns (transit info tel. 01/790-9100).

Trams, buses, the U-Bahn, and the S-Bahn all use the same tickets. Buy your tickets from *Tabak-Trafik* shops, station machines, marked *Vorverkauf* offices in the station, or—for trams only—on board (tickets only, more expensive). You have lots of choices:

- Single tickets (€1.80, €2.20 if bought on tram, good for one journey with necessary transfers);
- 24-hour transit pass (€5.70);
- 48-hour transit pass (€10);
- 72-hour transit pass (€13.60);
- 7-day transit pass (*Wochenkarte,* €14, pass always starts on Mon); or
- 8-day card *(Acht Tage Karte),* covering eight full days of free transportation for €28.80 (can be shared—for example, 4 people for 2 days each). With a per-person cost of €3.60/day (compared to €5.70/day for a 24-hour pass), this can be a real saver for groups.

Kids under 15 travel free on Sundays and holidays; kids under 6 always travel free.

Stamp a time on your ticket as you enter the Metro system, tram, or bus (stamp it only the first time for a multiple-use pass). Cheaters pay a stiff €70 fine, plus the cost of the ticket. Rookies miss stops because they fail to open the door. Push buttons, pull latches—do whatever it takes. Before you exit a U-Bahn station, study the wall-mounted street map. Choosing the right exit—signposted from the moment you step off the train—saves lots of walking.

Cute little electric buses wind through the tangled old center. Bus #1A is best for a joyride—hop on and see where it takes you.

By Taxi: Vienna's comfortable, civilized, and easy-to-flag-down taxis start at €2.50. You'll pay about €10 to go from the Opera to the Westbahnhof. Pay only what's on the meter—any surcharges (other than the €2 fee added to fares when you telephone them, or €10 for the airport) are just crude cabbie rip-offs.

By Bike: Vienna is a great city for biking, though cheap bike-rental options are scarce in the city center (see recommendations below and get a list at the TI). The bike path along the Ring is wonderfully entertaining. Your best biking is likely up and down the traffic-free and people-filled Donauinsel (Danube Island).

Weather permitting from March through October, you can

rent a bike all day (about 9:30 until dusk) from one of two shops near these bridges: **Floridsdorferbrücke** (€3.60/hr, €18/day, near tram #31 stop, tel. 01/278-8698) and **Reichsbrücke** (€5.40/hr, €27/day, tel. 01/263-5242).

American Rick Watts runs **Pedal Power,** and will deliver your bike to your hotel and pick it up when you're done (€32/day including delivery, Ausstellungsstrasse 3, tel. 01/729-7234, www.pedalpower.at). Rick also operates guided city tours on Segway scooters (2/day, see website for details) and by bike (see "Bike Tours," later).

Crazy Chicken bike rental, a short tram ride from the Westbahnhof, is less convenient, but a lot cheaper (€3/hr, €12/day, daily 8:30–19:00, near recommended Pension Fünfhaus at Grangasse 8—see pension listing on page 1056 for directions, tel. 01/892-2134, mobile 0664-421-4789).

Citybikewien, which has bikes parked in public racks all over town, is a clever program that works fine for locals, but can be headachy for tourists to figure out. The bikes lock in their stalls (50 of which are scattered through the city center) and are released when you insert a Citybike Tourist Card, sold for €2 at Pedal Power (listed earlier) and at Royal Tours (Herrengasse 1–3). Bikes cost €2 per hour (first hour free, fliers explain the process in English, www.citybikewien.at).

Tours in Vienna

Walking Tours—The TI's *Walks in Vienna* brochure describes Vienna's many guided walks. The basic 1.5-hour "Vienna at First Glance" introductory walk is offered daily throughout the summer (€13, leaves at 14:00 from near the Opera, in English and German, tel. 01/876-7111, mobile 0664-260-4388, www.wienguide.at). Various specialized tours go once a week and are listed on their website.

Bike Tours—Several companies offer city tours. **Pedal Power** runs two different three-hour tours daily from May to September (€23 per tour includes bike, €40 for both tours, departs at 9:45 and 14:15 in front of Opera at corner of Operngasse and the Kärntner Ring, also rents bikes, tel. 01/729-7234, www.pedalpower.at). **Wolfgang Höfler** leads bike tours as well as walking tours (€135/2 hrs, office @vienna-aktivtours.com; listed later, under "Private Guides").

Hop-On, Hop-Off Bus Tour—Vienna Sightseeing operates hop-on, hop-off bus tours (departures from the Opera 2–3/hr April–Oct 10:00–18:00, at top of each hour Nov–March 10:00–17:00, recorded commentary). The schedule is posted curbside (three different routes, €13 for one hour, €16 for two). You could pay much more to get 24 hours of hop-on and hop-off privileges,

Vienna at a Glance

▲▲▲**St. Stephen's Cathedral** Enormous, historic Gothic cathedral in the center of Vienna. **Hours:** Church doors open Mon–Sat 6:00–22:00, Sun 7:00–22:00; nave open for tourists only Mon–Sat 9:00–11:30 & 13:30–16:30, Sun 13:00–16:30. South tower climbable daily 9:00–17:30; elevator up shorter north tower runs daily July–Aug 8:30–18:00, April–June and Sept–Oct 8:30–17:30, Nov–March 8:30–17:00. See page 1003.

▲▲▲**Opera** Dazzling, world-famous opera house. **Hours:** Visit the Opera by guided 50-minute tour only, nearly daily in English; generally July–Aug at 11:00, 13:00, 14:00, 15:00, and often at 10:00 and 16:00; Sept–June fewer tours, afternoon only; call ahead to confirm tour times or check out daily schedule in red on door. Opera Museum open Tue–Sun 10:00–18:00, closed Mon. See page 1005.

▲▲▲**Hofburg Palace's Imperial Apartments** Lavish main residence of the Habsburgs. **Hours:** Daily July–Aug 9:00–18:00, Sept–June 9:00–17:00. See page 1008.

▲▲▲**Hofburg Palace's Treasury** The Habsburgs' collection of jewels, crowns, and other valuables—the best on the Continent. **Hours:** Wed–Mon 10:00–18:00, closed Tue. See page 1013.

▲▲▲**Kunsthistorisches Museum** World-class exhibit of the Habsburgs' art collection, including Raphael, Titian, Caravaggio, Bosch, and Brueghel. **Hours:** Tue–Sun 10:00–18:00, Thu until 21:00, closed Mon. See page 1022.

▲▲▲**Schönbrunn Palace's Royal Apartments** Spectacular summer residence of the Habsburgs, similar in grandeur to Versailles. **Hours:** Daily July–Aug 8:30–18:00, April–June and Sept–Oct 8:30–17:00, Nov–March 8:30–16:30, reservations recommended. See page 1035.

▲▲**Hofburg's New Palace Museums** Uncrowded collection of armor, musical instruments, and ancient Greek statues, in the elegant halls of a Habsburg palace. **Hours:** Wed–Mon 10:00–18:00, closed Tue. See page 1015.

▲▲**Albertina Museum** Habsburg residence with decent apartments and world-class temporary exhibits. **Hours:** Daily 10:00–18:00, Wed until 21:00. See page 1016.

▲▲**Kaisergruft** Crypt for the Habsburg royalty. **Hours:** Daily 10:00–18:00. See page 1016.

▲▲**Haus der Musik** Modern museum with interactive exhibits on Vienna's favorite pastime. **Hours:** Daily 10:00–22:00. See page 1020.

▲▲**Belvedere Palace** Elegant palace of Prince Eugene of Savoy, with a collection of 19th- and 20th-century Austrian art (including Klimt). **Hours:** Daily 10:00–18:00. See page 1032.

▲**Spanish Riding School** Prancing white Lipizzaner stallions. **Hours:** Spring and fall only, performances Sun at 11:00 and either Sat at 11:00 or Fri at 19:00, practice sessions Tue–Sat 10:00–12:00. See page 1018.

▲**Natural History Museum** Big building facing Kunsthistorisches Museum, featuring the ancient *Venus of Willendorf*. **Hours:** Wed–Mon 9:00–18:30, Wed until 21:00, closed Tue. See page 1025.

▲**Karlskirche** Baroque church with close-up look at restoration. **Hours:** Mon–Sat 9:00–18:00, Sun 13:00–18:00. See page 1027.

▲**Academy of Fine Arts** Small but exciting collection by Bosch, Botticelli, Rubens, Guardi, and Van Dyck. **Hours:** Tue–Sun 10:00–18:00, closed Mon. See page 1029.

▲**The Secession** Art Nouveau exterior and Klimt paintings *in situ*. **Hours:** Tue–Sun 10:00–18:00, Thu until 20:00, closed Mon. See page 1030.

▲**Naschmarkt** Sprawling, lively, people-filled outdoor market. **Hours:** Mon–Fri 6:00–18:30, Sat 6:00–17:00, closed Sun, closes earlier in winter. See page 1030.

▲**Imperial Furniture Collection** Eclectic collection of Habsburg furniture. **Hours:** Tue–Sun 10:00–18:00, closed Mon. See page 1032.

▲**Liechtenstein Museum** Impressive Baroque collection. **Hours:** Fri–Tue 10:00–17:00, closed Wed–Thu. See page 1033.

▲**KunstHausWien** Modern art museum dedicated to zany local artist/environmentalist Hundertwasser. **Hours:** Daily 10:00–19:00. See page 1033.

▲**Prater** Beloved amusement park with landmark Ferris wheel. **Hours:** Rides operate daily until late. See page 1037.

but given the city's excellent public transportation and this outfit's meager frequency, I'd take this not to hop on and off, but only to get the narrated orientation drive through town.

Ring Tram Tour—The **Vienna Ring Tram,** a made-for-tourists streetcar, runs along the entire Ringstrasse (€6 for one loop, €9 for 24-hour hop-on, hop-off privileges, runs twice hourly 10:00–18:00, July–Aug until 19:00, recorded narration).

City Bus Tour—Vienna Sightseeing offers a basic three-hour city tour, including a tour of Schönbrunn Palace (€36, 3/day April–Oct, 2/day Nov–March, call 01/7124-6830 or go to www.viennasightseeingtours.com, which also lists their many other tours).

Horse and Buggy Tour—These traditional horse-and-buggies, called *Fiakers*, take rich romantics on clip-clop tours lasting 20 minutes (€40-old town), 40 minutes (€65-old town and the Ring), or one hour (€95-all of the above, but more thorough). You can share the ride and cost with up to five people. Because it's a kind of guided tour, talk to a few drivers before choosing a carriage, and pick a driver who's fun and speaks English (tel. 01/401-060).

Driver—Consider the luxury of having your own car and driver. Johann (a.k.a. John) Lichtl is a kind, honest, English-speaking cabbie who can take up to four passengers in his car (€27/1 hour, €22/hr for 2 or more hours, €27 to or from airport, mobile 0676-670-6750).

Private Guides—The tourist board's website (www.vienna.info) has a long list of local guides with their specialties and contact information. **Lisa Zeiler** is an excellent English-speaking guide (two-hour walks for €130—if she's booked up, she can set you up with another guide, tel. 01/402-3688, lisa.zeiler@gmx.at). **Ursula Klaus**—an art scholar specializing in turn-of-the-20th-century Vienna, music, art, and architecture—also offers two-hour tours for €130 (mobile 0676-421-4884, ursula.klaus@aon.at). Lisa and Ursula are both top-notch, bring art museums to life masterfully, and can tailor tours to your interests. **Wolfgang Höfler** focuses on Vienna's 20th-century history (€135/2 hrs, also leads bike tours—described earlier, www.vienna-aktivtours.com, office@vienna-aktivtours.com).

Self-Guided Walk

Vienna City Walk

This walk connects the top three sights in Vienna's old center: the Opera, St. Stephen's Cathedral, and the Hofburg Palace. Along the way, you'll see sights covered elsewhere in the book (to find

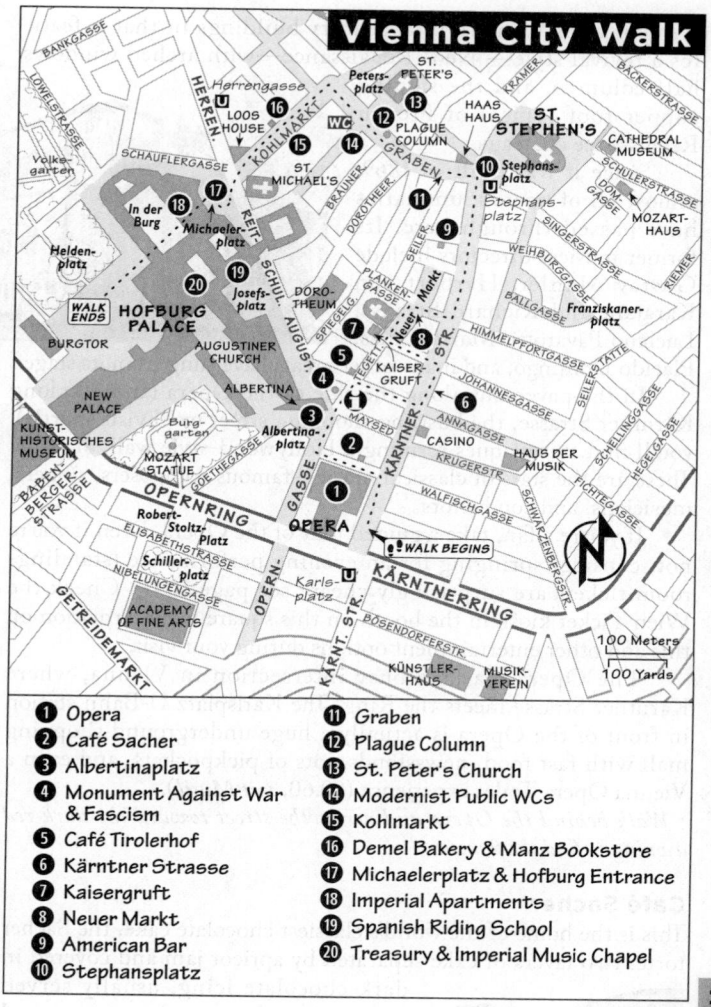

the full descriptions, flip to "Sights in Vienna," later), and get an overview of Vienna's past and present. Allow one hour, and more time if you plan to stop into any of the major sights along the way.

• *Begin at the square outside Vienna's landmark Opera House. (The Opera's entrance faces the Ringstrasse; we're starting at the busy pedestrian square that's to the right of the entrance as you're facing it.)*

Opera

If Vienna is the world capital of classical music, this building is its throne room, one of the planet's premier houses of music.

It's typical of Vienna's 19th-century buildings in that it features a revival style—"Neo"-Renaissance—with arched windows, half-columns, and the sloping copper roof typical of French Renaissance châteaux.

Since it was built in 1869, almost all of opera's luminaries have passed through here. Its former musical directors include Gustav Mahler, Herbert von Karajan, and Richard Strauss. Luciano Pavarotti, Maria Callas, Placido Domingo, and many other greats have sung from its stage.

In the pavement along the side of the Opera (and all along Kärntner Strasse, the bustling shopping street we'll visit shortly), you'll find star plaques forming a Hollywood-style walk of fame. These are the stars of classical music—famous composers, singers, musicians, and conductors.

If you're a fan, take a guided tour of the Opera. Even if you're not, consider springing for an evening performance (standing-room tickets are surprisingly cheap; see page 1041). Check the Wien Ticket kiosk in the booth on this square for information on this and other entertainment options during your visit.

The Opera marks a busy intersection in Vienna, where Kärntner Strasse meets the Ring. The Karlsplatz U-Bahn station in front of the Opera is actually a huge underground shopping mall with fast food, newsstands, lots of pickpockets, and even a Vienna Opera Toilet experience (€0.60, *mit Musik*).

• *Walk behind the Opera and across the street toward the dark red awning to find the famous...*

Café Sacher

This is the home of the world's classiest chocolate cake, the Sacher torte: two layers of cake separated by apricot jam and covered in dark-chocolate icing, usually served with whipped cream. It was invented in a fit of improvisation in 1832 by Franz Sacher, dessert chef to Prince Metternich (the mastermind diplomat who redrew the map of post-Napoleon Europe). The cake became world-famous when the inventor's son served it next door at his hotel (you may have noticed the fancy doormen). Some locals complain that the cakes have gone downhill, and many tourists

are surprised by how dry they are—you really need that dollop of *Schlagobers*. Still, coffee and a slice of cake here can be €8 well invested for the historic ambience alone. While the café itself is grotesquely touristy, the adjacent Sacher Stube has ambience and natives to spare. For maximum elegance, sit inside.

• *Head to the left of Hotel Sacher (as you face the café). At the end of the street is a small square where you'll find the TI (see "Tourist Information," earlier), an equestrian statue, and a building with a huge modern overhang.*

Albertinaplatz

The tan-and-white Neoclassical building with the statue alcoves marks the tip of the Hofburg Palace—the sprawling complex of buildings that was long the seat of Habsburg power (we'll end this walk at the palace's center). The balustraded terrace up top was originally part of Vienna's defensive rampart. Later, it was the balcony of Empress Maria Theresa's daughter Maria Christina, who lived at this end of the palace. And today, her home houses the **Albertina Museum,** topped by a sleek, controversial titanium canopy (called the "diving board" by critics). Most of the museum's stunning permanent collection isn't on display, but visitors can enjoy first-rate temporary exhibits.

Albertinaplatz is filled with statues that make up the powerful, thought-provoking **Monument Against War and Fascism,** which remembers the dark years when Austria came under Nazi rule (1938–1945).

The statue group has four parts. The split white monument, *The Gates of Violence,* remembers victims of all wars and violence. Standing directly in front of it, you're at the gates of a concentration camp. Step into a montage of wartime images: clubs and WWI gas masks, a dying woman birthing a future soldier, and chained slave laborers sitting on a pedestal of granite cut from the infamous quarry at Mauthausen Concentration Camp in the Danube Valley. The hunched-over figure on the ground behind is a Jew forced to scrub anti-Nazi graffiti off a street with a toothbrush. The statue with its head buried in the stone is Orpheus entering the underworld, meant to remind Austrians (and the rest of us) of the victims of Nazism...and the consequences of

not keeping our governments on track. Behind that, the 1945 declaration that established Austria's second republic—and enshrined human rights—is cut into the stone.

The experience gains emotional impact when you realize this monument stands on the spot where several hundred people were buried alive when the cellar they were hiding in was demolished during a WWII bombing attack (see photo to right of park, English description of memorial on the left).

Austria was led into World War II by Germany, which annexed the country in 1938, saying Austrians were wannabe Germans anyway. But Austrians are not Germans—never were, never will be. They're quick to tell you that while Austria was founded in the 10th century, Germany wasn't born until 1870. For seven years just before and during World War II (1938–1945), there was no Austria. In 1955, after 10 years of joint occupation by the victorious Allies, Austria regained total independence on the condition that it would be forever neutral (and never join NATO or the Warsaw Pact). To this day, Austria is outside of NATO (and Germany).

Behind the monument is **Café Tirolerhof,** a classic Viennese cafe full of things that time has passed by: chandeliers, marble tables, upholstered booths, waiters in tuxes, and newspapers. For more on Vienna's cafés, see page 1043.

• *From the café, turn right on Führichsgasse, passing the recommended cafeteria-style Rosenberger Markt Restaurant. Walk one block until you hit...*

Kärntner Strasse

This grand, mall-like street (traffic-free since 1974) is the people-watching delight of this in-love-with-life city. Today's Kärntner Strasse (KAYRNT-ner SHTRAH-seh) is mostly a crass commercial pedestrian mall—its famed elegant shops long gone. But locals know it's the same road Crusaders marched down as they headed off from St. Stephen's Cathedral for the Holy Land in the 12th century. Its name indicates that it leads south, toward the region of Kärnten (Carinthia, a province divided between Austria and Slovenia). Today it's full of shoppers and street musicians.

Where Führichsgasse meets Kärntner Strasse, note the city **Casino** (across the street and a half-block to your right, at #41)—once venerable, now tacky, it exemplifies the worst of the street's evolution. Turn left to head up Kärntner Strasse, going away from the Opera. As you walk along, be sure to look up, above the modern storefronts, for glimpses of the street's former glory. On the left at #26, **J & L Lobmeyr Crystal** ("Founded in 1823") still has its impressive brown storefront with gold trim, statues, and the Habsburg double-eagle. Inside, breathe in the classic Old World ambience as you climb up to the glass museum.

In the market for some $400 napkin rings? Lobmeyr's your place.
• *At the end of the block, turn left on Marco d'Aviano Gasse to make a short detour to the square called Neuer Markt. Straight ahead is an orange-ish church with a triangular roof and cross, the Capuchin Church. In its basement is the...*

Kaisergruft

Under the church sits the Imperial Crypt, filled with what's left of Austria's emperors, empresses, and other Habsburg royalty. For centuries, Vienna was the heart of a vast empire ruled by the Habsburg family, and here is where they lie buried in their fancy coffins. You'll find all the Habsburg greats, including Maria Theresa, her son Josef II (Mozart's patron), Franz Josef, and "Sisi." Before moving on, consider paying your respects here.

Neuer Markt

In the center of Neuer Markt square is the **four rivers fountain,** which shows Lady Providence surrounded by figures symbolizing the rivers that flow into the Danube. The statues, originally nude, were replaced with more modest versions by Maria Teresa. The buildings all around you were rebuilt after World War II. Half of the city's inner center was intentionally destroyed by Churchill to demoralize the Viennese, who were disconcertingly enthusiastic about the Nazis.

• *Lady Providence's one bare breast points back to Kärntner Strasse (50 yards away). Before you head back to the busy shopping street, you could stop for a sweet treat at the heavenly Kurkonditorei Oberlaa (look for the vertical sign at the far corner of the square; described later, under "Eating in Vienna"). Leave the square by returning to Kärntner Strasse and turn left. Two blocks along, on the left, is the...*

American Bar

Over the door, the jutting American-flag sign (in red, white, and blue glass) is one of the few ornaments on this minimalist building. This is the first of several structures along this walk designed by the architect Adolf Loos (Vienna's answer to Frank Lloyd Wright).

Inside it's dark, plush, and small, with great €8 cocktails (note that gawkers are discouraged in this still-hip bar).

• *Continue down Kärntner Strasse to the main square. As you approach the cathedral, you're likely to first see it as a reflection in the round-glass windows of the modern Haas Haus. Pass the U-Bahn station (which has WCs), where the street spills into...*

Stephansplatz

The cathedral's massive spire looms overhead, worshippers and tourists pour inside the church, and shoppers and top-notch street entertainers buzz around the outside. You're at the center of Vienna.

The Gothic church (c. 1300–1450) is known for its 450-foot south tower, its colorful roof, and its place in Viennese history. When it was built, it was a huge church for what was then a tiny town, and it helped put the fledgling city on the map.

At this point, you may want to take a break from the walk to tour the church. Even if you don't go inside, you can check out some of the exterior sights: the south tower, remnants of earlier churches (underground in the U-Bahn station, follow *Virgilkapelle* signs), the old facade, and World War II-era photos that show the destruction during the war (to the right of the church). If the weather's clear, consider heading up the cathedral's spire for the view over Vienna's rooftops.

Surrounding the church are buildings featuring centuries of architectural styles. Start at the cathedral and pan the square clockwise. To the right of the Gothic cathedral, the upper floors of the **International Building/Bank of Austria** have decorative Art Nouveau elements. Where Kärntner Strasse hits Stephansplatz (at #3), the **Equitable Building** (filled with lawyers, bankers, and insurance brokers) is a fine example of Neoclassicism from the turn of the 20th century. Look up and imagine how slick Vienna must have felt in 1900.

Facing St. Stephen's is the sleek concrete-and-glass **Haas Haus,** a postmodern building by noted Austrian architect Hans Hollein (finished in 1990). The curved facade is supposed to echo the Roman fortress of Vindobona (its ruins were found near here). The Viennese initially protested having this stark modern tower right next to their beloved cathedral, but since then, it's become a fixture of Vienna's main square. Notice how the smooth, rounded glass reflects St. Stephen's pointy architecture, providing a great photo opportunity. The café and pricey restaurant inside offer a

nice perch, complete with a view of Stephansplatz below.

At the north end of the square is the (somewhat run-down) Modernist **J. F. Kennedy Haus,** named for the popular American president who came to Vienna for a summit hoping (but failing) to halt the construction of the Berlin Wall.

To the left of the church, the **Manner** store is known for its wafer cookies with the church logo. For a quick detour, turn right at the Manner store and walk past the touristy horse carts to the doorway at #6. This leads to a picturesque **lane** lined with shops and restaurants. Behind the church, a block away (but not worth the detour) is **Mozarthaus,** where the composer lived while writing the opera *The Marriage of Figaro.*

• *Exit the square with your back to the cathedral entrance. Walk past the Haas Haus, down the street called...*

Graben

This was once a *Graben,* or ditch—originally the moat for the Roman military camp. Back during Vienna's 19th-century heyday, there were nearly 200,000 people packed into the city's inner center (inside Ringstrasse), walking through dirt streets. Today this area houses 20,000. Graben was a busy street with three lanes of traffic until the 1970s, when it was turned into one of Europe's first pedestrian-only zones.

As you walk down Graben, you'll reach Dorotheergasse (two blocks on your left after leaving Stephansplatz), which leads to the **Dorotheum** auction house (consider poking your nose in here later for some fancy window-shopping).

In the middle of this pedestrian zone is the extravagantly blobby **Holy Trinity plague column** *(Pestsäule).* The 70-foot pillar of clouds sprouts angels and cherubs, with the wonderfully gilded Father, Son, and Holy Ghost at the top.

In 1679, Vienna was hit by a massive epidemic of bubonic plague. Around 75,000 Viennese died—about a third of the city. Emperor Leopold I dropped to his knees (something emperors never did in public) and begged God to save the city. (Find Leopold about a quarter of the way up the monument. Hint: The typical inbreeding of royal families left him with a gaping underbite.) His prayer was heard by Lady Faith (the statue below Leopold, carrying a cross). With the help of a heartless little cupid, she tosses an old naked woman—symbolizing the plague—into the abyss and saves the city. In gratitude, Leopold vowed to erect

this monument, which became a model for other cities ravaged by the same plague.

• *Just past the plague monument, look down the short street to the right, which frames a Baroque church with a stately green dome.*

St. Peter's Church

Leopold I also ordered this church to be built as a thank-you for surviving the 1679 plague. The church stands on the site of a much older church that may have been Vienna's first (or second) Christian church. Inside, St. Peter's shows Vienna at its Baroque best.

• *Continue west on Graben, where you'll immediately find some stairs leading underground to two...*

Public WCs

In about 1900, a local chemical-maker needed a publicity stunt to prove that his chemicals really got things clean. He purchased two wine cellars under Graben and had Adolf Loos turn them into classy WCs in the Modernist style, complete with chandeliers and finely crafted mahogany (that's right—they're Loos' loos). The restrooms remain clean to this day—in fact, they're so inviting that they're used for poetry readings. Locals and tourists happily pay €0.50 for a quick visit.

• *Graben dead-ends at the aristocratic supermarket Julius Meinl am Graben (described later, under "Eating in Vienna"). From here, turn left. In the distance is the big green and gold dome of the Hofburg, where we'll end this walk. The street leading up to the Hofburg is...*

Kohlmarkt

This is Vienna's most elegant and unaffordable shopping street—Tiffany, Cartier, Giorgio Armani—with the emperor's palace at the end. Strolling Kohlmarkt, daydream about the edible window displays at **Demel** (#14, daily 10:00–19:00). Demel is the ultimate Viennese chocolate shop. The room is filled with Art Nouveau boxes of Empress Sisi's choco-dreams come true: *Kandierte Veilchen* (candied violet petals), *Katzenzungen* (cats' tongues), and so on. The cakes here are moist (compared to the dry Sacher tortes). The enticing window displays change monthly, reflecting current happenings in Vienna. Inside, an impressive cancan of cakes is displayed to tempt visitors into springing for the €10 cake-and-coffee deal (point to the cake you

want). You can sit inside, with a view of the cake-making, or outside, with the street action. (Upstairs is less crowded.) Shops like this boast "K.u.K."—signifying that during the Habsburgs' heyday, it was patronized by the *König und Kaiser* (king of Hungary and emperor of Austria—same guy).

Next to Demel, the **Manz Bookstore** has a Loos-designed facade. Just beyond Demel and across the street, at #1152, you can pop in to a charming little Baroque **carriage courtyard,** with the surviving original carriage garages.

• *Kohlmarkt ends at the square called...*

Michaelerplatz

This square is dominated by the impressive facade of the Hofburg Palace. Opposite the facade, notice the modern **Loos House** (now a bank) built at about the same time as the palace's grandiose facade. In the center of this square, a scant bit of Roman Vienna lies exposed just beneath street level. On the left is the fancy Loden Plankl shop, with traditional Austrian formal wear. Next door (at #6), pop through the passageway to find a quiet courtyard with a big wooden carving of Jesus praying in Gethsemane. Across Augustinerstrasse, to the left of the Hofburg entrance, is the wing of the palace that houses the **Spanish Riding School** and its famous white Lipizzaner stallions. Farther down this street lies Josefsplatz, with its **Augustinian Church,** and at the end of the street, Albertinaplatz and the Opera (where we started this walk).

• *We'll finish up our tour where Austria's glorious history began—at the...*

Hofburg

This is the complex of palaces where the Habsburg emperors lived (except in summer, when they lived out at Schönbrunn Palace).

Study the grand entry facade to the Hofburg Palace—it's Neo-Baroque from about 1900. The four heroic giants illustrate Hercules wrestling with his great challenges (much like the late-empire Habsburgs, I'm sure).

Enter the Hofburg through the gate, where you immediately find yourself beneath a big rotunda (the netting is there to keep birds from perching). The doorway on the right is the entrance to the **Imperial Apartments,** where the Habsburg emperors once lived in chandeliered elegance. Today you can tour its lavish rooms, as well as a museum on Empress Sisi, and a porcelain and silver

collection. To the left is the ticket office for the **Spanish Riding School**.

Continuing on, you emerge from the rotunda into the main courtyard of the Hofburg, called **In der Burg.** The Caesar-like statue is of Habsburg Emperor Franz II (1768–1835), grandson of Maria Theresa, grandfather of Franz Josef, and father-in-law of Napoleon. Behind him is a tower with three kinds of clocks (the yellow disk shows the phase of the moon tonight). To the right of Franz are the Imperial Apartments, and to the left are the offices of Austria's mostly ceremonial president (the more powerful chancellor lives in a building just behind this courtyard).

Franz faces the oldest part of the palace. The colorful red, black, and gold gateway (behind you), which used to have a drawbridge, leads to the 13th-century Swiss Court (Schweizerhof), named for the Swiss mercenary guards once stationed there. Here you'll find the **Treasury** (Schatzkammer) and the **Imperial Music Chapel** (Hofmusikkapelle) where the Boys' Choir sings the Mass.

Back at In der Burg, face Franz and turn left, passing through the **tunnel,** with a few tourist shops and restaurants (for recommendations, see page 1007).

The tunnel spills out into spacious **Heldenplatz** (Heroes' Square). On the left is the impressive curved facade of the **New Palace** (Neue Burg). This vast wing was built in the early 1900s to be the new Habsburg living quarters (and was meant to have a matching building facing it). But in 1914, the heir-to-the-throne Archduke Franz Ferdinand—while waiting politely for his long-lived uncle, Emperor Franz Josef, to die—was assassinated in Sarajevo. The archduke's death sparked World War I and the eventual end of eight centuries of Habsburg rule (for more on Franz Ferdinand, see page 167).

This impressive building saw even sadder days a few decades later, when Adolf Hitler addressed adoring throngs from the New Palace balcony in 1938, after Austria had been annexed.

Inside the building nowadays are the **New Palace Museums,** an eclectic collection of weaponry, suits of armor, musical instruments, and ancient Greek statues. The two equestrian statues are Prince Eugene of Savoy (1663–1736), who battled the Ottoman Turks, and Archduke Charles (1771–1847), who battled Napoleon. Eugene gazes to the far distance at the prickly Neo-Gothic spires of Vienna's City Hall.

The Hofburg's **Burggarten** (with the much-photographed Mozart statue) is not visible from here, but it's just behind the New Palace. If you were to continue on through the Greek-columned passageway (the Äussere Burgtor), you'd reach the Ringstrasse, the Kunsthistorisches Museum, and the MuseumsQuartier.

• *Our walk is finished. You're in the heart of Viennese sightseeing. The*

Hofburg contains some of Vienna's best sights and museums (described in detail on page 1006). From the Opera to the Hofburg, from chocolate to churches, from St. Stephen's to Sacher torte—Vienna waits for you.

Sights in Vienna

The sights listed below are arranged by neighborhood for handy sightseeing.

Inside the Ring

▲▲▲St. Stephen's Cathedral (Stephansdom)

This massive church is the Gothic needle around which Vienna spins. According to the medieval vision of its creators, it stands like a giant jeweled reliquary, offering praise to God from the center of the city. The church and its towers, especially the 450-foot south tower, give the city its most iconic image. (Check your pockets for 10-cent euro coins; ones minted in Austria feature the south tower on the back.) The cathedral has survived Vienna's many wars and today symbolizes the city's freedom.

Cost: Entering the church is free (except July–mid-Oct, when it's €3 to get past the rear of the nave). Going up the towers costs €3 (by stairs, south tower) or €4.50 (by elevator, north tower).

Hours: The church doors are open Mon–Sat 6:00–22:00, Sun 7:00–22:00, but the nave is only open for tourists Mon–Sat 9:00–11:30 & 13:30–16:30, Sun 13:30–16:30. During services, you can't enter the main nave (unless you're attending Mass), but you can go into the back of the church to reach the north tower elevator (described later, under "Ascending the North Tower").

Information: Tel. 01/515-523-526, www.stephanskirche.at.

Tours: The €4 tours in English are entertaining (daily April–Oct at 15:45, check information board inside entry to confirm schedule). The €2 audioguide is well done, but for most, the tour below will be enough.

➲ **Self-Guided Tour:** Find a spot in the square where you can take in the sheer magnitude of this massive church, with its skyscraping spire. The church we see today dates mainly from 1300–1450, when builders expanded on an earlier structure and added two huge towers at the end of each transept. The impressive 450-foot south tower took two generations to build (65 years), and was finished in 1433. Consider climbing the tower now, or wait until after your cathedral visit (details at the end of this tour).

This is the third church to stand on this spot. You can see the footprint of the **earlier church** in the pavement, to the right of the main entrance. Nearby (along the building with the Austrian flags and *Churhaus* plaque) are **old photos** showing the destruction the church suffered at the end of World War II. In 1945, Vienna was

caught in the chaos between the occupying Nazis and the approaching Soviets. Allied bombs sparked fires in nearby buildings. The embers leapt to the cathedral rooftop. The original timbered Gothic roof burned and collapsed into the nave, the cathedral's huge bell crashed to the ground, and the fire raged for two days.

The church's **main entrance** is the oldest part of the church (c. 1240), done in the Romanesque style. Before Christians occupied Vienna, there was a pagan Roman temple here, and the facade pays homage to that ancient heritage. Roman-era statues are embedded in the facade, and the two octagonal towers are dubbed the "heathen towers" because they're built with a few Roman stones (flipped over to hide the pagan inscriptions and expose the smooth sides).

Stepping inside, find a spot to look down the immense **nave**—more than a football field long and nine stories tall. Stylistically, the nave is Gothic with a Baroque overlay. The nave's columns are richly populated with 77 life-size stone and ceramic statues, making a saintly parade to the high altar.

Start down the nave toward the altar. At the second pillar on the left is the Gothic sandstone **pulpit** (c. 1515), a masterpiece carved from three separate blocks (see if you can find the seams). The pulpit is as crammed with religious meaning as it is with beautifully realistic carvings. The top of the stairway's railing swarms with lizards (as animals of light), and toads (as animals of darkness). The "Dog of the Lord" stands at the top, making sure none of those toads pollutes the sermon. Below the toads, wheels with three parts (the Trinity) roll up, while wheels with four spokes (the four seasons, symbolizing mortal life) roll down.

Find the guy peeking out from under the stairs. This may be a self-portrait of the artist. In medieval times, art was done for the glory of God, and artists worked anonymously. But this pulpit was carved as humanist Renaissance ideals were creeping in from Italy—and individual artists were becoming famous. So the artist included what may be a rare self-portrait bust in his work. He leans out from a window, sculptor's compass in hand, to observe the world and his work.

During World War II, many of the city's top art treasures were hidden safely in cellars and salt mines—hidden by both the Nazi occupiers (to protect against war damage) and by citizens (to protect against Nazi looters). The **stained-glass windows** behind the high altar were meticulously dismantled and packed away. The pulpit was encased in a shell of brick. As the war was drawing to a close, it appeared St. Stephen's would escape major damage. But as the Nazis were fleeing, the bitter Nazi commander in charge of the city ordered that the church be destroyed. Fortunately, his underlings disobeyed. Unfortunately, the church accidentally caught fire during Allied bombing shortly thereafter, and the roof collapsed. Among the other losses, the nave's precious stained-glass windows were blown out in the big fire, and had to be replaced with lesser-quality, Tupperware-colored glass. Before the fire, the entire church was lit with windows like the richly colored ones behind the altar.

Ascending the North Tower: This tower, reached from inside the church (look for the *Aufzug zur Pummerin* sign), holds the famous "Pummerin" bell and is easier to ascend than the south tower (described next), but it's much shorter and not as exciting, with lesser views (no stairs, elevator-€4.50, daily July–Aug 8:30–18:00, April–June and Sept–Oct 8:30–17:30, Nov–March 8:30–17:00, last elevator ascends 20 min before closing, entrance on the left side of the nave). The Pummerin is supposedly the second biggest bell in the world that rings by swinging. A physical symbol of victory over the Ottoman Turks in 1683, it was cast from cannons (and cannon balls) captured from the Ottomans when Vienna was liberated from the siege. During the WWII fire that damaged the church, the Pummerin fell to the ground and cracked. It had to be melted down and recast. These days, locals know the Pummerin as the bell that rings in the New Year.

Climbing the South Tower: The iconic south tower offers a far better view than the north one, but you'll earn it by climbing 343 tightly wound steps up the spiral staircase (€3, daily 9:00–17:30, this hike burns about one Sacher torte of calories). To reach the entrance, exit the church and make a U-turn to the left. Note: If the top is still surrounded by scaffolding on your visit, views may be obscured. This tower, once key to the city's defense as a lookout point, is still dear to Viennese hearts. (It's long been affectionately nicknamed "Steffl," Viennese for "Stevie.") No church spire in (what was) the Austro-Hungarian Empire is taller—by Habsburg decree. From the top, use your city map to locate the famous sights.

▲▲▲Opera (Staatsoper)

The Opera, facing the Ring and near the TI, is a central point for any visitor. Vienna remains one of the world's great cities for

classical music, and this building still belts out some of the finest opera, both classic and cutting-edge. While the critical reception of the building 130 years ago led the architect to commit suicide, and though it's been rebuilt since its destruction by WWII bombs, it's still a sumptuous place. The interior has a chandeliered lobby and carpeted staircases perfect for making the scene. The theater itself features five wrap-around balconies, gold and red decor, and a bracelet-like chandelier.

Depending on your level of tolerance for opera, you can: simply admire the Neo-Renaissance building from the outside; take a guided tour of the lavish interior; visit the Opera Museum; or attend a performance.

Tours: Unless you're attending a performance, you can enter the Opera only with a guided 50-minute tour, offered nearly daily in English (€6.50; generally July–Aug at 11:00, 13:00, 14:00, 15:00, and often at 10:00 and 16:00; Sept–June fewer tours, afternoons only; tel. 01/514-442-624). Tour times are often changed or cancelled due to rehearsals and performances. The opera posts a monthly schedule (blue, on the wall), but the more accurate schedule is the daily listing (red, posted on the door on the Operngasse side of building, farthest from St. Stephen's Cathedral). Tour tickets include the tiny and disappointing Opera Museum (across the street toward the Hofburg), except on Monday, when the museum is closed.

Opera Museum: New and included in your opera tour ticket (whether you like it or not), the Opera Museum is a let-down, with descriptions only in German and rotating six-month-long special exhibits (€3, or included in the €6.50 tour ticket, Tue–Sun 10:00–18:00, closed Mon, a block away from the Opera, near Albertina Museum, tel. 01/514-442-100).

Performances: For information on attending a performance, see page 1041.

Habsburg Sights in and near the Hofburg Palace

The complex, confusing, and imposing Imperial Palace, with 640 years of architecture, demands your attention. This first Habsburg residence grew with the family empire from the 13th century until 1913, when the last "new wing" opened. The winter residence of the Habsburg rulers until 1918, it's still the home of the Spanish Riding School, the Vienna Boys' Choir, the Austrian president's office, 5,000 government workers, and several important museums. For an over-

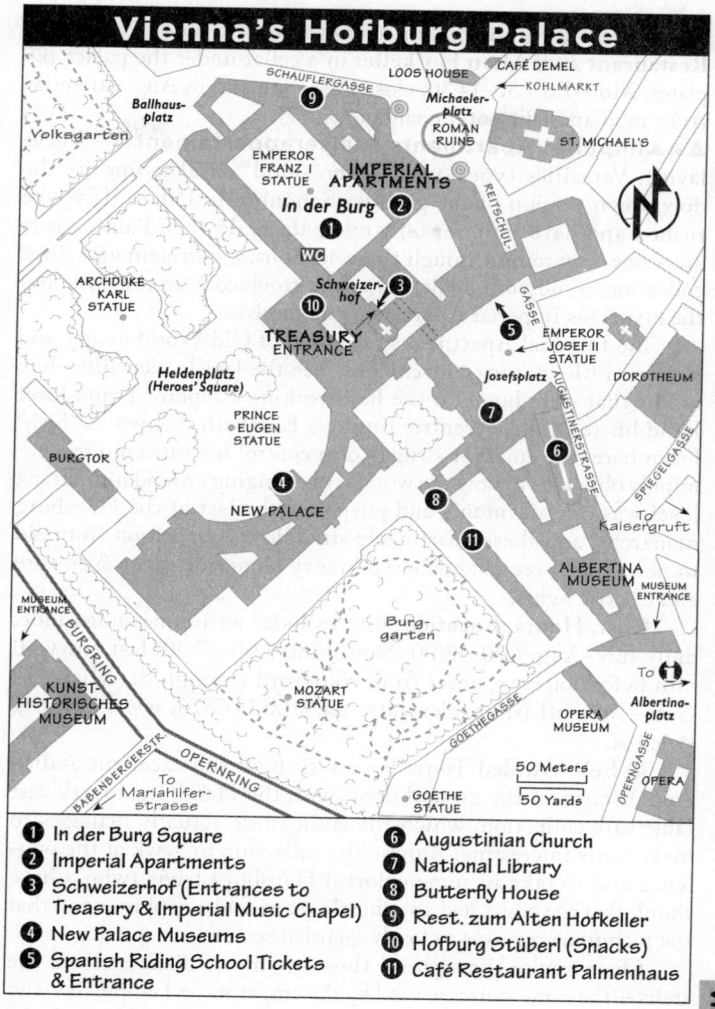

view of the palace layout, see above. Don't get confused by the Hofburg's myriad courtyards and many museums. Focus on three sights: the Imperial Apartments, Treasury, and the museums at the New Palace (Neue Burg).

The section below also covers Habsburg sights located near—but not actually inside—the Hofburg (including the Albertina Museum, Kaisergruft, and Augustinian Church).

Eating at the Hofburg: Down the tunnel to Heroes' Square is a tiny but handy sandwich bar called **Hofburg Stüberl** (same €2.50 sandwich price whether you sit or go, Mon–Fri 7:00–18:00,

Sat–Sun 10:00–16:00). For a cheap, quick meal, duck into **Restaurant zum Alten Hofkeller** in a cellar under the palace (€5 plates, Mon–Fri 7:30–14:30, closed Sat–Sun and in Aug, cafeteria-style, mod and efficient, Schauflergasse 7).

▲▲▲Imperial Apartments (Kaiserappartements)—These lavish, Versailles-type, "wish-I-were-God" royal rooms are the downtown version of the grander Schönbrunn Palace. If you're rushed and have time for only one palace, do this. Palace visits are a one-way romp through three sections: a porcelain and silver collection, a museum dedicated to the troubled Empress Sisi, and the luxurious Imperial Apartments themselves.

The Imperial Apartments are a mix of Old World luxury and modern 19th-century convenience. See the lavish, Versailles-like rooms that were home to the hardworking Emperor Franz Josef I and his reclusive, eccentric Empress Elisabeth, known as "Sisi." From here, the emperor struggled to control his vast empire, seemingly oblivious to how the world was changing around him. Franz Josef was (for all intents and purposes) the last of the Habsburg monarchs, and these apartments straddle the transition from old to new. You'll see chandeliered luxury alongside office furniture and electric lights.

Cost, Hours, Location: €10, includes well-done audioguide, daily July–Aug 9:00–18:00, Sept–June 9:00–17:00, last entry 30 min before closing, enter from courtyard through St. Michael's Gate—just off Michaelerplatz, tel. 01/533-7570, www.hofburg-wien.at.

➲ Self-Guided Tour: Your visit (and the excellent audioguide) starts on the ground floor, with the Habsburg court's vast tableware collection, which the audioguide actually manages to make fairly interesting. Browse the collection to gawk at the opulence and to take in some colorful Habsburg trivia (who'd have thunk that the court had an official way to fold a napkin—and that the technique remains a closely guarded secret?).

Once you're through all those rooms of dishes, climb the stairs—the same staircase used by the emperors and empresses who lived here. At the top is a timeline of Sisi's life. Pass through the turnstile, consider the WC, and enter the room with the **model of the Hofburg.** Circle to the far side to find where you're standing right now, near the smallest of the Hofburg's three domes.

The Hofburg was the epicenter of one of Europe's great political powers. Six hundred years of Habsburgs lived here in the winter and at Schönbrunn Palace in the heat of summer. The Hofburg started as a 13th-century medieval castle (near where you are right now) and expanded over the centuries to today's 240,000-square-meter (60-acre) complex, now owned by the state.

To the left of the dome (as you face the facade) is the steeple

Sisi
(1837–1898)

Empress Elisabeth was the 19th-century equivalent of Princess Diana. Known as "Sisi" since childhood, she became an instant celebrity when she married Franz Josef at the age of 16.

Sisi's main goals in life seem to have been preserving her reputation as a beautiful empress, maintaining her Barbie-doll figure, and tending to her fairy-tale, ankle-length hair. In the 1860s, she was considered one of the most beautiful women in the world. But, in spite of severe dieting and fanatic exercise, age took its toll. After turning 30, she refused photographs and portraits and was generally seen in public with a delicate fan covering her face (and bad teeth).

Complex and influential, Sisi was adored by Franz Josef, whom she respected. Although Franz Josef was supposed to have married her sister Helene (in an arranged diplomatic marriage), he fell in love with Sisi instead. It was one of the Habsburgs' few marriages for love.

Sisi's personal mission and political cause was promoting Hungary's bid for autonomy within the empire. Her personal tragedy was the death of her son Rudolf, the crown prince, in an apparent suicide (an incident often dramatized as the "Mayerling Affair," after the royal hunting lodge where it happened). Disliking Vienna and the confines of the court, Sisi traveled more and more frequently. (She spent so much time in Budapest, and with Hungarian statesman Count Andrássy, that many believe her third daughter to be the count's.) As the years passed, the restless Sisi and her hardworking husband became estranged. In 1898, while visiting Geneva, Switzerland, she was murdered by an Italian anarchist.

Sisi's beauty, bittersweet life, and tragic death helped create her larger-than-life legacy. However, her importance is often inflated by melodramatic accounts of her life. The Sisi Museum seeks to tell a more accurate story.

of the Augustiner church. It was there, in 1854, that Franz Josef married 16-year-old Elisabeth of Bavaria, and their story began.

Sisi Museum: Empress Elisabeth was Franz Josef's mysterious, beautiful, and narcissistic wife. This museum traces her fabulous but tragic life. The exhibit starts where her life ended and her legend began (see her death mask, and pictures of her funeral procession). You'll read bits of her poetic writing, see exact copies of her now-lost jewelry, and learn about her escapes, dieting

Emperor Franz Josef
(1830–1916)

Franz Josef I—who ruled for 68 years (1848–1916)—was the embodiment of the Habsburg Empire as it finished its six-century-long ride. Born in 1830, Franz Josef had a stern upbringing that instilled in him a powerful sense of duty and—like so many men of power—a love of things military.

His uncle, Ferdinand I, suffered from profound epilepsy, which prevented him from being an effective ruler. As the revolutions of 1848 rattled royal families throughout Europe, the Habsburgs forced Ferdinand to abdicate and put 18-year old Franz Josef on the throne. Ironically, as one of his first acts as emperor, Franz Josef—whose wife would later become closely identified with Hungarian independence—put down the 1848 revolt in Hungary with bloody harshness. He spent the first part of his long reign understandably paranoid, as social discontent simmered.

Franz Josef was very conservative. But worse, he wrongly believed that he was a talented military tactician, and led Austria into catastrophic battles against Italy (which was fighting for its unification and independence) in the 1860s. As his army endured severe, avoidable casualties, it became clear: Franz Josef was a disaster as a general.

Wearing his uniform to the end, he never saw what a dinosaur his monarchy was becoming, and never thought it strange that the majority of his subjects didn't even speak German. Franz Josef had no interest in democracy and pointedly never set foot in Austria's parliament building. But, like his contemporary Queen Victoria, he was a microcosm of his empire—old-fashioned but sacrosanct. His passion for low-grade paperwork earned him the nickname "Joe Bureaucrat." Mired in these petty details, he missed the big picture. In 1914, he helped start a Great War that ultimately ended the age of monarchs. The year 1918 marked the end of Europe's big royal families: Hohenzollerns (Prussia), Romanovs (Russia), and Habsburgs (Austria).

mania, and chocolate bills. Admire Sisi's hard-earned thin waist (20 inches at age 16, 21 inches at age 50...after giving birth to four children). The black statue in the dark room represents the empress after the suicide of her son—aloof, thin, in black, with her back to the world. At the end, ponder the crude knife that killed Sisi.

Imperial Apartments—Emperor's Rooms: After the Sisi Museum, a one-way route takes you through a series of royal rooms. The first room—as if to make clear that there was more to the Habsburgs than Sisi—shows a family tree tracing the Habsburgs from 1273 to their messy WWI demise. From here, you enter the

private apartments of the royal family (Franz Josef's first, then Sisi's). These were the private apartments and public meeting rooms for the emperor and empress. Franz Josef I lived here from 1857 until his death in 1916. (He had hoped to move to new digs in the New Palace, but that was not finished until after his death.)

Franz Josef was the last great Habsburg ruler. In these rooms, he presided over defeats and liberal inroads, as the world was changing and the monarchy became obsolete. Here he met with advisors and welcomed foreign dignitaries, hosted lavish, white-gloved balls and stuffy formal dinners, and raised three children. He slept (alone) on his austere bed while his beloved wife Sisi retreated to her own rooms. He suffered through the assassination of his brother, the suicide of his son and heir, the murder of his wife, and the assassination of his nephew, Archduke Ferdinand, which sparked World War I and spelled the end of the Habsburg monarchy.

In the **waiting room for the Audience Room,** mannequins from the many corners of the Habsburg realm illustrate the multiethnic nature of the vast empire. (Also see the map of the empire, by the window.) Every citizen had the right to meet privately with the emperor, and people traveled fairly far to do so. While they waited nervously, they had these three huge paintings to stare at—propaganda showing crowds of commoners enthusiastic about their Habsburg rulers.

The **Audience Room** is where Franz Josef received commoners from around the empire. They came from far and wide to show gratitude or to make a request. Imagine you've traveled for days to have your say before the emperor. You're wearing your new fancy suit—Franz Josef required that men coming before him wear a tailcoat, women a black gown with a train. You've rehearsed what you want to say. You hope your hair looks good.

Suddenly, you're face-to-face with the emp himself. (The portrait on the easel shows Franz Josef in 1915, when he was more than 80 years old.) Despite your efforts, you probably weren't in this room long. He'd stand at the high table (far left) as the visiting commoners had their say. (Standing kept things moving.) You'd hear a brief response from him (quite likely the same he'd given all day), and then you'd back out of the room while bowing (also required). On the table, you can read a partial list of 56 appointments he had on January 3, 1910 (three columns: family name, meeting topic, and *Anmerkung*—the emperor's "action log").

In the **conference room,** the emperor presided over the equivalent of cabinet meetings. An ongoing topic was what to do with unruly Hungary. After 1867, Franz Josef granted Hungary a measure of independence (thus creating the "Austro-Hungarian Empire"). Hungarian diplomats attended meetings here, watched over by paintings on the wall showing Austria's army suppressing

the popular Hungarian uprising...subtle.

Next, Franz Josef's **study** evokes how seriously the emperor took his responsibilities as the top official of a vast empire. The walls between the rooms are wide enough to hide servants' corridors (the hidden door to his valet's room is in the back left corner).

Moving on to the emperor's **bedroom,** note his famously no-frills iron bed. He typically rose at 3:30, and started his day in prayer, kneeling at the prayer stool against the far wall. While he had a typical emperor's share of mistresses, his dresser was always well-stocked with photos of Sisi.

The **Large Salon** was for royal family gatherings, and went unused after Sisi's death. The **Small Salon,** used as a smoking room (no women allowed), is dedicated to the memory of Franz Josef's brother (see the bearded portrait), the Emperor Maximilian of Mexico, who was assassinated in 1867. After the birth of their last child in 1868, Franz Josef and his wife Sisi began to drift farther apart. Left of the door is a small button the emperor had to buzz before entering his estranged wife's quarters. You, however, can go right in.

Imperial Apartments—Empress' Rooms: Sisi's **bedroom/drawing room** was refurbished in the Neo-Rococo style in 1854. There's the red carpet, covered with oriental rugs. Sisi kept this room filled with fresh flowers. She not only slept here, but also lived here—the bed was rolled in and out daily—until her death in 1898.

Next comes Sisi's **dressing/exercise room.** Servants worked three hours a day on Sisi's famous hair, while she passed the time reading. She'd exercise on the wooden structure and on the rings suspended from the doorway to the left. Afterward, she'd get a massage on the red-covered bed.

Detour into the behind-the-scenes palace. In the narrow passageway, you'll walk by Sisi's hand-painted porcelain, dolphin-head WC (on the right). In the main **bathroom,** you'll see her huge copper tub (with the original wall coverings behind it) where servants washed her hair—an all-day affair. Sisi was the first Habsburg to have running water in her bathroom (notice the hot and cold faucets).

Next, enter the **servants' quarters,** with hand-painted tropical scenes. Take time to enjoy the playful details. As you leave these rooms and re-enter the imperial world, look back to the room on the left.

The empress' **Great Salon** is painted with Mediterranean escapes, the 19th-century equivalent of travel posters. A print shows how Franz Josef and Sisi would—on their good days—share breakfast in this room.

The portrait in the **Small Salon** is of Crown Prince Rudolf,

Franz Josef and Sisi's only son. On the morning of January 30, 1889, 30-year-old Rudolf and a beautiful baroness were found shot dead in his hunting lodge in Mayerling. An investigation never came up with a complete explanation, but Rudolf had obviously been cheating on his wife, and the affair ended in an apparent murder-suicide. The scandal shocked the empire and tainted the Habsburgs, Sisi retreated further into her fantasy world, and Franz Josef carried on stoically—with a broken heart.

Alexander Apartments: Leaving Sisi's wing, turn the corner into the white-and-gold rooms, used for formal occasions and public functions. In the **Red Salon,** the Gobelin wall hangings were a 1776 gift from Marie-Antoinette and Louis XVI in Paris to their Viennese counterparts.

The tour ends in the **dining room.** It's dinnertime, and Franz Josef has called his extended family together. The settings are modest...just silver. Gold was saved for formal state dinners. Next to each name card was a menu naming the chef responsible for each dish. (Talk about pressure.) While the Hofburg had tableware for 4,000, feeding 3,000 was a typical day. The cellar was stocked with 60,000 bottles of wine. The kitchen was huge—50 birds could be roasted on the hand-driven spits at once.

The emperor sat in the center of the long table. "Ladies and gentlemen" alternated in the seating. Franz Josef enforced strict protocol at mealtime: No one could speak without being spoken to by the emperor, and no one could eat after he was done. While the rest of Europe was growing democracy and expanding personal freedoms, the Habsburgs preserved their ossified worldview to the bitter end.

In 1918, World War I ended, Austria was created as a modern nation-state, the Habsburgs were tossed out...and the Hofburg Palace was destined to become a museum.

▲▲▲Hofburg Treasury (Weltliche und Geistliche Schatzkammer)—This "Secular and Religious Treasure Room" contains the best jewels on the Continent. Slip through the vault doors and reflect on the glitter of 21 rooms filled with scepters, swords, crowns, orbs, weighty robes, double-headed eagles, gowns, gem-studded bangles, and a unicorn horn. Not only are the objects beautiful, they're also historic—some crowns and scepters date back to the time of Charlemagne.

Cost, Hours, Information: €10, €18 combo-ticket with Kunsthistorisches Museum, Wed–Mon 10:00–18:00, closed Tue;

from the Hofburg's central courtyard, follow *Schatzkammer* signs to the Schweizerhof; tel. 01/525-240, www.khm.at. While no English descriptions are provided within the Treasury, the well-produced, €3 audioguide provides a wealth of information and is worth renting.

Self-Guided Tour: Here's a rundown of the highlights (the audioguide is much more complete).

Room 2: The personal crown of Rudolf II has survived since 1602—it was considered too well-crafted to cannibalize for other crowns. It's a big deal because it's the adopted crown of the Austrian Empire, established in 1806 after Napoleon dissolved the Holy Roman Empire (an alliance of Germanic kingdoms so named because it wanted to be considered the continuation of the Roman Empire). Pressured by Napoleon, the Austrian Francis II—who had been Holy Roman Emperor—became Francis I, Emperor of Austria (the stern guy on the wall, near where you entered). Look at the crown. Its design symbolically merges the typical medieval king's crown and a bishop's miter.

Rooms 3 and 4: These rooms contain some of the coronation vestments and regalia needed for the new Austrian (not Holy Roman) emperor. There was a different one for each of the emperor's subsidiary titles, e.g., King of Hungary or King of Lombardy. So many crowns and kingdoms in the Habsburg's vast empire!

Room 5: Ponder the Cradle of the King of Rome, once occupied by Napoleon's son, who was born in 1811 and made King of Rome. While pledging allegiance to democracy, Napoleon in fact crowned himself Emperor of France and hobnobbed with Europe's royalty. When his wife Josephine could not bear him a male heir, Napoleon divorced her and married into the Habsburg family. With the birth of the baby King of Rome, Napoleon and Marie Louise (Francis I/II's daughter) were poised to start a new dynasty of European rulers...but then Napoleon met his Waterloo, and the Habsburgs remained in power.

Room 7: These jewels are the true "treasures," a cabinet of wonders used by Habsburgs to impress their relatives (or to hock when funds got low).

Room 8: The eight-foot-tall, 500-year-old "unicorn horn" (a narwhal tusk), was considered to have magical healing powers bestowed from on high. This one was owned by the Holy Roman Emperor—clearly a divine monarch.

Room 10: The next few rooms contain some of the oldest and most venerated objects in the Treasury—the robes, crowns, and

sacred objects of the Holy Roman Emperor.

Room 11: The collection's highlight is the 10th-century **crown of the Holy Roman Emperor.** It was probably made for the first king to call himself Holy Roman Emperor, Otto I (c. 960). The Imperial Crown swirls with symbolism "proving" that the emperor was both holy and Roman: The cross on top says the HRE ruled as Christ's representative on earth, and the jeweled arch over the top is reminiscent of the parade helmet of ancient Romans. The crown's eight sides represent the celestial city of Jerusalem's eight gates. The jewels on the front panel symbolize the 12 apostles. Imagine the impression this priceless, glittering crown must have made on the emperor's medieval subjects.

The nearby 11th-century **Imperial Cross** preceded the emperor in ceremonies. Encrusted with jewels, it had a hollow compartment (its core is wood) that carried substantial chunks thought to be from *the* **cross** and *the* **Holy Lance** used to pierce the side of Jesus when he was crucified (both pieces are displayed in the same glass case). Holy Roman Emperors actually carried the lance into battle in the 10th century. Look behind the cross to see how it was a box that could be clipped open and shut, used for holding holy relics. You can see bits of the "true cross" anywhere, but this is a prime piece—with the actual nail hole.

Another glass case contains objects that may have belonged to Charlemagne (a.k.a. Karl der Grosse). On the wall nearby, the **tall painting** depicts Charlemagne modeling the Imperial Crown—although the crown was actually made a hundred years after he died.

Room 12: Now picture all this regalia used together. The painting shows the coronation of Maria Theresa's son Josef II as Holy Roman Emperor in 1764. Set in a church in Frankfurt (filled with the bigwigs—literally—of the day), Josef is wearing the same crown and royal garb that you've just seen.

Room 16: This last room contains the **royal vestments** (15th century), which display perhaps the most exquisite workmanship in the entire Treasury. Look closely—they're "painted" with gold and silver threads. But after seeing so much bling, by the time you view these vestments, they can seem downright understated—just another example of the pomp and circumstance of the majestic Habsburgs.

▲▲Hofburg New Palace Museums: Armor, Music, and Ancient Greek Statues—The New Palace (Neue Burg) houses

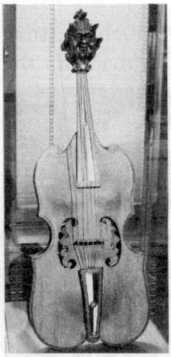

three separate collections, all included in a single ticket price—an armory (with a killer collection of medieval weapons), historical musical instruments, and classical statuary from ancient Ephesus (in modern-day Turkey). The included audioguide brings the exhibits to life and lets you actually hear the collection's fascinating old instruments being played. An added bonus is the chance to wander alone among the royal Habsburg halls, stairways, and painted ceilings (€8, Wed–Mon 10:00–18:00, closed Tue, last entry 30 min before closing, almost no tourists, tel. 01/525-240, www.khm.at).

▲▲Albertina Museum—This building, at the southern tip of the Hofburg complex (near the Opera), was the residence of Maria Teresa's favorite daughter: Maria Christina, who was the only one allowed to marry for love rather than political strategy. Her many sisters were jealous. (Marie-Antoinette had to marry the French king...and lost her head over it.) Maria Christina's husband, Albert of Saxony, was a great collector of original drawings, and amassed an enormous assortment of works by Dürer, Rembrandt, Rubens, Schiele, and others. Today, reproductions of some of these works hang in the Albertina's elegant French Classicist–style state rooms *(Prunkräume)*. Head here first—this offers a great opportunity to wander freely under the chandeliers of a Habsburg palace, unconstrained by velvet ropes. Then browse the modern galleries, which hold a rotating exhibit from the museum's Batliner collection of modern art (with minor works by major artists—Monet, Picasso, Chagall, Matisse), along with temporary exhibits. Though the entry fee is a bit steep, the Albertina's temporary exhibits are often top-notch—if you're unsure whether it's worth the admission fee, check fliers and posters around town to see what's on (€9.50, price can vary based on special exhibits, audioguide-€4, daily 10:00–18:00, Wed until 21:00, overlooking Albertinaplatz across from the TI and Opera, tel. 01/534-830, www.albertina.at).

▲▲Kaisergruft, the Remains of the Habsburgs—Visiting the imperial remains is not as easy as you might imagine. These original organ donors left their bodies—about 150 in all—in the unassuming Kaisergruft (the Imperial Crypt at the Capuchin Church), their hearts in the Augustinian Church (described later; church open long hours daily), and their entrails in the crypt below St. Stephen's Cathedral. Don't tripe.

Cost, Hours, Location: €4, daily 10:00–18:00, last entry at 17:40, behind the Opera on Neuer Markt, tel. 01/512-6853. As you enter, be sure to buy the €0.50 map with a Habsburg family tree and a chart locating each coffin.

Empress Maria Theresa (1717–1780) and Her Son, Emperor Josef II (1741–1790)

Maria Theresa was the only woman to officially rule the Habsburg Empire in that family's 640-year reign. She was a strong and effective empress (r. 1740–1780). People are quick to remember Maria Theresa as the mother of 16 children (10 survived)—imagine that the most powerful woman in Europe either was pregnant or had a newborn for most of her reign. Maria Theresa ruled after the Austrian defeat of the Ottomans, when Europe recognized Austria as a great power. (Her rival, the Prussian emperor, said, "When at last the Habsburgs get a great man, it's a woman.")

The last of the Baroque imperial rulers, and the first of the modern rulers of the Age of Enlightenment, Maria Theresa marked the end of the feudal system and the beginning of the era of the grand state. She was a great social reformer. During her reign, she avoided wars and expanded her empire by skillfully marrying her children into the right families. For instance, after daughter Marie-Antoinette's marriage into the French Bourbon family (to Louis XVI), a country that had been an enemy became an ally. (Unfortunately for Marie-Antoinette, Maria Theresa's timing was slightly off.)

Maria Theresa was a great reformer and in tune with her age. She taxed the Church and the nobility, provided six years of obligatory education to all children, and granted free health care to all in her realm. Maria Theresa also welcomed the boy genius Mozart into her court.

The empress' legacy lived on in her son, Josef II, who ruled as emperor himself for a decade (1780–1790). He was an even more avid reformer, building on his mother's accomplishments. An enlightened monarch, Josef mothballed the too-extravagant Schönbrunn Palace, secularized the monasteries, established religious tolerance within his realm, freed the serfs, made possible the founding of Austria's first general hospital, and promoted relatively enlightened treatment of the mentally ill. Josef was a model of practicality (for example, reusable coffins à la *Amadeus,* and no more than six candles at funerals)—and very unpopular with other royals. But his policies succeeded in preempting the revolutionary anger of the age, enabling Austria to avoid the turmoil that shook so much of the rest of Europe.

Highlights: The double coffin of **Maria Theresa** (1717–1780) and her husband, **Franz I** (1708–1765), is worth a close look for its artwork. Maria Theresa outlived her husband by 15 years—which she spent in mourning. Old and fat, she installed a special lift enabling her to get down into the crypt to be with her dear, departed Franz (even though he had been far from faithful). The couple recline—Etruscan-style—atop their fancy lead coffin. At each corner are the crowns of the Habsburgs—the Holy Roman Empire, Hungary, Bohemia, and Jerusalem. Notice the contrast between the Rococo splendor of Maria Theresa's tomb and the simple box holding her more modest son, **Josef II** (at his parents' feet).

Franz Josef (1830–1916) is nearby, in an appropriately austere military tomb. Flanking Franz Josef are the tombs of his son, the archduke **Rudolf,** and Empress Elisabeth. Rudolf and his teenage mistress supposedly committed suicide together in 1889 at Mayerling hunting lodge and—since the Church figured he forced her and was therefore a murderer—it took considerable legal hair-splitting to win Rudolf this spot (after examining his brain, it was determined that he was mentally disabled and therefore incapable of knowingly killing himself and his girl). *Kaiserin* Elisabeth (1837–1898), a.k.a. **Sisi,** always gets the "Most Flowers" award.

In front of those three are the two most recent Habsburg tombs. **Empress Zita** was laid to rest here in 1989, followed by her son, **Karl Ludwig,** in 2007. The funeral procession for Karl Ludwig, the fourth son of the last Austrian emperor, was probably the last such Old Regime event in European history. The monarchy died hard in Austria. Today there are about 700 living Habsburg royals, mostly living in exile. When they die, they get buried in their countries of exile.

Body parts and ornate tombs aside, the real legacy of the Habsburgs is the magnificence of this city. Step outside. Pan up. Watch the clouds glide by the ornate gables of Vienna.

▲Spanish Riding School and Lipizzaner Stallions—While the famous court horses of the Habsburg emperors were originally from Spain, by the 16th century they were moved closer to Vienna (to the Slovenian town of Lipica, then part of the Habsburg Empire). For four centuries, the "Lipizzaner stallions" have been bred, raised, and trained in Lipica. They actually have "surnames" that can be traced to the original six 16th-century stallions that made the trip from Spain.

The dressage movements of the stallions originated as battle

moves, and include the *pirouette* (quick turns for surviving in the thick of battle), *levade* (rearing on hind legs, to make a living shield for the knight), and the *capriole* (a strong back-kick that could floor any enemy). After tanks replaced horses on the battlefield, these equestrian military moves morphed into court entertainment. Lipizzaner fans have a warm spot in their hearts for US General George Patton. At the end of World War II—knowing that the Soviets were about to take control of Vienna—he ordered a raid on the stables to save the horses and ensure the survival of their fine old bloodlines.

Seats for performances book up months in advance, but standing room is sometimes available the same day (tickets-€35–165, standing room-€20–28, March–June and Sept–Dec Sun at 11:00 and either Sat at 11:00 or Fri at 19:00, no shows July–Aug, fewer Feb, none in Jan, tel. 01/533-9031, www.srs.at). Luckily for the masses, training sessions with music in a chandeliered Baroque hall are open to the public (€12 at the door, roughly March–June and mid-Aug–Dec Tue–Sat 10:00–12:00—but only when the horses are in town).

Tourists line up early at Josefsplatz (the large courtyard between Michaelerplatz and Albertinaplatz), at the door marked *Spanische Hofreitschule*. If you want to hang out with tour groups, get there early and wait for the doors to open at 10:00. Better yet, simply show up late. Almost no one stays for the full two hours—except for the horses. As people leave, new tickets are printed continuously, so you can just prance in with no wait at all. Don't have high expectations, as the horses often do little more than trot and warm up.

▲Augustinian Church (Augustinerkirche)—This is the Gothic and Neo-Gothic church where the Habsburgs latched, then buried, their hearts (weddings took place here, and the royal hearts are in the vault). Don't miss the exquisite, tomb-like Canova memorial (Neoclassical, 1805) to Maria Theresa's favorite daughter, Maria Christina, with its incredibly sad white-marble procession. The church's 11:00 Sunday Mass is a hit with music-lovers—both a Mass and a concert, often with an orchestra accompanying the choir. To pay, contribute to the offering plate and buy a CD afterwards. Programs are posted by the entry (church open long hours daily, Augustinerstrasse 3).

The church faces Josefsplatz, with its statue of the great reform emperor Josef II. Next to the Augustinian Church, the **National Library** and its State Hall are impressive (€7, Tue–Sun

10:00–18:00, Thu until 21:00, closed Mon).

Burggarten (Palace Garden)—This greenbelt, once the backyard of the Hofburg and now a people's park, welcomes people to loiter on the grass. On nice days, it's lively with office workers enjoying a break. The statue of Mozart facing the Ringstrasse is popular. The iron-and-glass pavilion now houses the recommended Café Restaurant Palmenhaus and a small but fluttery butterfly exhibit (€5.50; April–Oct Mon–Fri 10:00–16:45, Sat–Sun 10:00–18:15; Nov–March daily 10:00–15:45). The butterfly zone is delightfully muggy on a brisk off-season day, but trippy any time of year. If you tour it, notice the butterflies hanging out on the trays with rotting slices of banana. They lick the fermented banana juice as it beads, and then just hang out there in a stupor...or fly giddy loop-de-loops.

More Sights Inside the Ring

▲▲Haus der Musik—Vienna's "House of Music" has a small first-floor exhibit on the Vienna Philharmonic, and upstairs you'll enjoy fine audiovisual exhibits on each of the famous hometown boys (Haydn, Mozart, Beethoven, Strauss, and Mahler). But the museum is unique for its effective use of interactive touchscreen computers and headphones to actually explore the physics of sound. You can twist, dissect, and bend sounds to make your own musical language, merging your voice with a duck's quack or a city's traffic roar. Wander through the "sonosphere" and marvel at the amazing acoustics—I could actually hear what I thought only a piano tuner could hear. Pick up a virtual baton to conduct the Vienna Philharmonic Orchestra (each time you screw up, the musicians put their instruments down and ridicule you). Really experiencing the place takes time. It's open late and makes a good evening activity (€10, €15 combo-ticket with Mozarthaus, daily 10:00–22:00, last entry one hour before closing, 2 blocks from the Opera at Seilerstätte 30, tel. 01/51648, www.hdm.at).

▲Vienna's Auction House, the Dorotheum—For an aristocrat's flea market, drop by Austria's answer to Sotheby's, the Dorotheum. Its five floors of antique furniture and fancy knick-knacks have been put up either for immediate sale or auction, often by people who inherited old things they don't have room for. Wandering through here, you feel like you're touring a museum with exhibits you can buy (Mon–Fri 10:00–18:00, Sat 9:00–17:00, closed Sun, classy little café on second floor, between the Graben pedestrian street and Hofburg at Dorotheergasse 17, tel. 01/51560,

www.dorotheum.com). The info desk at the ground floor has a building map and schedule of upcoming auctions. Labels on each item predict the auction value. Continue your hunt for the perfect curio on the streets around the Dorotheum, lined with many fine antique shops.

St. Peter's Church (Peterskirche)—Baroque Vienna is at its best in this gem, tucked away a few steps from the Graben.

Admire the rose-and-gold, oval-shaped Baroque interior, topped with a ceiling fresco of Mary kneeling to be crowned by Jesus and the Father, while the dove of the Holy Spirit floats way up in the lantern. Taken together, the church's elements—especially the organ, altar painting, pulpit, and coat of arms (in the base of the dome) of church founder Leopold I—make St. Peter's one of the city's most beautiful and ornate churches.

To the right of the altar, a dramatic golden statue shows the martyrdom of St. John Nepomuk (c. 1340–1393). The Czech saint defied the heretical King Wenceslaus, so he was tossed to his death off the Charles Bridge in Prague. In true Baroque style, we see the dramatic peak of his fall, when John has just passed the point of no return. The Virgin Mary floats overhead in a silver cloud. (For more on this saint, see page 81.)

The present church (from 1733) stands atop earlier churches, dating back 1,600 years. On either side of the nave are glass cases containing skeletons of Christian martyrs from Roman times. Above the relic on the left is a painting of the modern saint Josemaria Escriva, founder of the conservative Catholic organization Opus Dei, of *Da Vinci Code* notoriety (free, church open Mon–Fri 7:00–19:00, Sat–Sun 9:00–19:00; organ concert Mon–Fri at 15:00, Sat–Sun at 20:00; just off the Graben between the Plague Monument and Kohlmarkt, tel. 01/533-6433).

Mozarthaus—Opened in 2006 to commemorate Wolfgang's 250th birthday, this museum is easy to get excited about, but it disappoints. Exhibits fill the only surviving Mozart residence in Vienna, where he lived from 1784 to 1787, when he had lots of money. You'll learn his life story, with an emphasis on his most creative years...when he lived here. Included is a rundown on the Vienna music scene during the Mozart years, a quirky look at his gambling habits and his interest in crudely erotic peep shows, and a four-minute montage of his most famous arias in a mini-theater. Unfortunately, visiting the museum is like reading a book standing up—rather than turning pages, you climb stairs. There are

almost no real artifacts. Wolfie would have found the audioguide dreadful. I enjoy the Haus der Musik much more (€9, €15 combo-ticket with Haus der Musik, daily 10:00–19:00, a block behind the cathedral, go through arcade at #5 and walk 50 yards to Domgasse 5, tel. 01/512-1791, www.mozarthausvienna.at).

Judenplatz Memorial and Museum—The classy square called Judenplatz marks the location of Vienna's 15th-century Jewish community, one of Europe's largest at the time. The square, once filled with a long-gone synagogue, is now dominated by a blocky memorial to the 65,000 Austrian Jews killed by the Nazis. The memorial—a library turned inside out—symbolizes Jews as "people of the book" and causes viewers to ponder the huge loss of culture, knowledge, and humanity that took place between 1938 and 1945.

The nearby Judenplatz Museum, while sparse, has displays on medieval Jewish life and a well-done video recreating the ghetto as it looked five centuries ago. (If you're skipping the museum, at least pop into its entry hall to check the model of Vienna as it was in the 1500s.) Wander the scant remains of the medieval synagogue below street level—discovered during the construction of the Holocaust memorial. This was the scene of a medieval massacre. Since Christians weren't allowed to lend money, Jews were Europe's moneylenders. As so often happened in Europe, when Viennese Christians fell too deeply into debt, they found a convenient excuse to wipe out the local ghetto—and their debts at the same time. In 1421, 200 of Vienna's Jews were burned at the stake. Others who refused a forced conversion committed mass suicide in the synagogue (€4, Sun–Thu 10:00–18:00, Fri 10:00–14:00, closed Sat, Judenplatz 8, tel. 01/535-0431, www.jmw.at).

Kunsthistorisches Museum and Nearby

▲▲▲Kunsthistorisches Museum—This exciting museum, across the Ring from the Hofburg Palace, showcases the grandeur and opulence of the Habsburgs' collected artwork in a grand building (built as a museum in 1888). There are European masterpieces galore, all well-hung on one glorious floor, plus a fine display of Egyptian, classical, and applied arts.

Cost, Hours, Location: €10, €18

combo-ticket with the Hofburg Treasury, audioguide-€3, Tue–Sun 10:00–18:00, Thu until 21:00, closed Mon, on the Ringstrasse at Maria-Theresien-Platz, U-2 or U-3: Volkstheater/Museumsplatz, tel. 01/525-240, www.khm.at.

➲ Self-Guided Tour: The Kunsthistorwhateveritis Museum—let's just say "Koonst"—houses some of the most beautiful, sexy, and fun art from two centuries (c. 1450–1650). The collection reflects the *joie de vivre* of Austria's luxury-loving Habsburg rulers. At their peak of power in the 1500s, the Habsburgs ruled Austria, Germany, northern Italy, the Netherlands, and Spain—and you'll see a wide variety of art from all these places and beyond.

If you're short on time, focus on the Painting Gallery *(Gemäldegalerie)* on the first floor. Climb the main staircase, featuring Antonio Canova's statue of *Theseus Clubbing the Centaur.* Italian Art is in the right half of the building (as you face Theseus), and Northern Art to the left. Notice that the museum labels the largest rooms with Roman numerals (Saal I, II, III), and the smaller rooms around the perimeter with Arabic (Rooms 1, 2, 3).

Saals I–III cover the Venetian renaissance. The first spans the long career of **Titian,** who painted

portraits, Christian Madonnas, and sexy Venuses with equal ease. Next comes Paolo **Vernese,** whose colorful works reflect the wealth of Venice, the funnel through which luxury goods from the exotic East flowed into northern Europe. And **Tintoretto**'s many portraits give us a peek at the movers and shakers of the Venetian Empire.

Rooms 1–4 hold some of the museum's most important works: **Mantegna**'s *St. Sebastian,* **Correggio**'s *Jupiter and Io,* and **Raphael**'s *Madonna of the Meadow (Die Madonna im Grünen),* a geometrically perfect masterpiece of the High Renaissance, painted when Raphael was just 22.

Farther along, through the small rooms along the far end of this wing, find the cleverly deceptive portraits by Giuseppe **Arcimboldo.** His *Summer*—a.k.a "Fruit Face"—is one of four paintings the Habsburg court painter did showing the seasons (and elements) as people. With a pickle nose, pear chin, and corn-husk ears, this guy literally is what he eats.

Caravaggio (in Saal V) shocked the art world with brutally honest reality. Compared with Raphael's super-sweet *Madonna of the Meadow,* Caravaggio's *Madonna of the Rosary* (*Die Rosenkranzmadonna,* the biggest canvas in the room) looks perfectly ordinary, and the saints kneeling around her have dirty feet. In *David with the Head of Goliath (David mit dem Haupt des Goliath)* Caravaggio turns a third-degree-interrogation light on a familiar Bible story. David shoves the dripping head of the slain giant—the artist's self portrait—right in our noses.

When the Habsburgs ruled both Austria and Spain, cousins kept in touch through portraits of themselves and their kids. Diego **Velázquez** (in Room 10) was the greatest of Spain's "photojournalist" painters: heavily influenced by Caravaggio's realism, capturing his subjects without passing judgment, flattering, or glorifying them.

The half of this floor features works of the "Northern Renaissance," which was more secular and Protestant than Catholic-funded Italian art (that means fewer Madonnas, saints, and Greek gods and more peasants, landscapes, and food). Paintings are smaller and darker, full of down-to-earth objects. Northern artists sweated the details, encouraging the patient viewer to appreciate the beauty in everyday things.

Don't miss the slice-of-village-life scenes by Pieter **Breugel** the Elder (the Normal Rockwell of the 16th century), **Rubens**'

large, lush canvases; **Vermeer**'s *The Art of Painting (Die Malkunst);* and **Rembrandt**'s frank, defiant self-portraits.

▲Natural History Museum—In the twin building facing the Kunsthistorisches Museum, you'll find moon rocks, dinosaur stuff, and the fist-sized *Venus of Willendorf*—at 25,000 years old, the world's oldest sex symbol, found in the Danube Valley. Even though the museum is not glitzy or high-tech, it's a hit with children and scientifically curious grown-ups (€8, Wed–Mon 9:00–18:30, Wed until 21:00, closed Tue, on the Ringstrasse at Maria-Theresien-Platz, U-2 or U-3: Volkstheater/Museumsplatz, tel. 01/521-770, www.nhm-wien.ac.at).

For a quick visit, head first to the *Venus of Willendorf*—she's on the mezzanine level, in Room 11 (from the entrance lobby, climb the stairs, head for the back, and turn left). The 4-inch-tall, chubby stone statuette is a generic female (no face or feet) resting her hands on her ample breasts. The statue's purpose is unknown, but she may have been a symbol of fertility for our mammoth-hunting ancestors. In Room 10 nearby are big dinosaur skeletons.

For a more chronological visit, start upstairs on the first floor (in Room 21), and follow hundreds of millions of years of evolution—from single cells to sea creatures, reptiles, birds, mammals, and primates. Finish with the hairless primate—man—downstairs in Rooms 11–14.

The collection of rocks (mezzanine, Rooms 1–5, to the right of the entrance lobby) is also impressive, and includes one of the largest collections of meteorites in the world. Of the museum's 20 million objects, you're sure to find something interesting.

MuseumsQuartier—The vast grounds of the former imperial stables now corral several impressive, cutting-edge museums. Walk into the complex from the Hofburg side, where the main entrance (with visitors center) leads to a big courtyard with cafés, fountains, and ever-changing "installation lounge furniture," all surrounded by the quarter's various museums (behind Kunsthistorisches Museum, U-2 or U-3: Volkstheater/Museumsplatz). Various combo-tickets are available for those interested in more than just the Leopold and Modern Art museums (visit www.mqw.at).

Gustav Klimt
(1862–1918)

Klimt, a noted womanizer, made a career painting the female form as beautiful, seductive, and dangerous. A founding member of the Secessionist artists who "seceded" from bourgeois constraints, his erotic paintings scandalized official Vienna. He dedicated his later years to works commissioned by the liberal elite.

Klimt explored multimedia. Besides oil paints, he painted with gold leaf or applied bright objects to the canvas/panel for decorative effect. He often worked in a square-frame format. (He occasionally made the frames themselves, in collaboration with his brother, a gold engraver.) There's no strong 3-D in his paintings; the background and foreground are merged together into a decorative pattern. His women are clearly drawn, emerging from the complex design. With their come-hither looks and erotic poses, they capture the overripe beauty and edgy decadence of turn-of-the-century Vienna.

The **Leopold Museum** features several temporary exhibits of modern Austrian art, and a top floor that holds the largest collection of works by Egon Schiele (1890–1918; these works make some people uncomfortable—Schiele's nudes are *really* nude) and a few paintings by Gustav Klimt, Kolo Moser, and Oskar Kokoschka (€10, €3 audioguide—worth it only for enthusiasts, daily 10:00–18:00, Thu until 21:00, tel. 01/525-700, www.leopoldmuseum.org). Note that for these artists, you'll do better in the Belvedere Palace (described on page 1032).

The **Museum of Modern Art** (Museum Moderner Kunst Stiftung Ludwig, a.k.a. "MUMOK") is Austria's leading modern-art gallery. It's the striking lava-paneled building—three stories tall and four stories deep, offering seven floors of far-out art that's hard for most visitors to appreciate. This huge, state-of-the-art museum displays revolving exhibits showing off art of the last generation—including Paul Klee, Pablo Picasso, and Pop artists (€9, €2 audioguide has more than you probably want to hear, daily 10:00–18:00, Thu until 21:00, tel. 01/52500, www.mumok.at).

Rounding out the sprawling MuseumsQuartier are an architecture museum, Transeuropa, Electronic Avenue, children's museum, and the Kunsthalle Wien—an exhibition center for

contemporary art (€7.50, daily 10:00–19:00, Thu until 22:00, tel. 01/521-8933, www.kunsthallewien.at).

Karlsplatz and Nearby

These sights cluster around Karlsplatz, just southeast of the Ringstrasse (U-1, U-2, or U-4: Karlsplatz). From the U-Bahn station's passageway, it's a 30-minute walk around the sights on Karlsplatz: the Karlskirche, Secession, and Naschmarkt (allow more time to actually visit these sights).

Karlsplatz—This picnic-friendly square, with its Henry Moore sculpture in the pond, is ringed with sights. The massive, domed Karlskirche and its twin spiral columns dominate the square. The small green, white, and gold pavilions near the church are from the late 19th-century municipal train system *(Stadtbahn)*. One of Europe's first subway systems, this precursor to today's U-Bahn was built with a military purpose in mind: to move troops quickly in time of civil unrest—specifically, out to Schönbrunn Palace. With curvy iron frames, decorative marble slabs, and painted gold trim, these are pioneering works in the *Jugendstil* style, designed by Otto Wagner, who influenced Klimt and the Secessionists. One of the pavilions is open as an exhibit on Otto Wagner (€2, April–Oct Tue–Sun 9:00–18:00, closed Mon and Nov–March, near the Ringstrasse).

▲Karlskirche (St. Charles' Church)—Charles Borromeo, a 16th-century bishop from Milan, was an inspiration during plague times. This "votive church" was dedicated to him in 1713, when an epidemic spared Vienna. The recently restored church offers the best Baroque in Vienna, with a unique combination of columns (showing scenes from the life of Charles Borromeo, à la Trajan's Column in Rome), a classic pediment, and an elliptical dome. Inside, the fresco in the dome shows Signor Borromeo (in red and white bishops' robes) gazing up into heaven, spreading his arms wide and pleading with Christ to spare Vienna from the plague. The colorful 13,500-square-foot fresco was painted in the 1730s by Johann Michael Rottmayr. Give yourself a minute to take it in: Faith, Hope, and Charity triumph and inspire. Borromeo lobbies heaven for plague relief. Meanwhile, a Protestant's Lutheran Bible is put to the torch by angels. At the very top, you'll see the tiny dove representing the Holy Ghost, surrounded by a cheering squad of nipple-lipped cupids (€6, includes audioguide and skippable

Art Nouveau (a.k.a. *Jugendstil* or the Vienna Secession), c. 1896–1914

As Europe approached the dawn of a new *(nouveau)* century, it embraced a new art: Art Nouveau.

On the one hand, it was very forward-looking and modern, embracing the new technology of iron and glass. But Art Nouveau was also a reaction against the sheer ugliness of the mass-produced, boxy, rigidly geometrical art of the Industrial Age. Art Nouveau artists returned to nature (which abhors a straight line), and were inspired by the curves of plants. And as in nature, no two objects are exactly the same, leaving the artist free to make his work unique.

Art Nouveau street lamps twist and bend like flower stems. Ironwork fountains sprout buds that squirt water. Dining rooms are paneled with leafy garlands of carved wood. Advertising posters feature flowery typefaces and beautiful young women rendered in pure, curving lines. A hit with interior decorators, Art Nouveau was a total "look" that could be applied to furniture, jewelry, paintings, and the building itself.

Though the Art Nouveau movement began in Paris and Belgium, each country gave it its own spin. In German-speaking lands (including Austria), Art Nouveau was called *Jugendstil* (YOO-gend-shteel, meaning "youth style").

The innovators in Vienna called their particular *Jugendstil* movement The Secession, named for the daring artists who "seceded" from tradition. They turned their backs on Vienna's centuries-long love affair with Baroque, Rococo, and Neoclassical styles. They preferred buildings that were simple and geometrically pure, which they then decorated with a few unadulterated Art Nouveau touches. Various artists were part of this movement. Architects, painters, and poets had no single unifying style, except a commitment to what was new. The Secessionist motto was: "To each age its art, and to art its liberty."

The TI has a brochure laying out Vienna's 20th-century architecture. Here are some of the best of Vienna's scattered *Jugendstil* sights:

one-room museum, Mon–Sat 9:00–18:00, Sun 13:00–18:00, last entry 30 min before closing).

Wien Museum Karlsplatz—This underappreciated museum walks you through the history of Vienna with fine historic artifacts. You'll work your way up, chronologically: The ground floor exhibits Roman artifacts and original statues from St. Stephen's Cathedral (c. 1350), with various Habsburgs showing off the slinky hip-hugging fashion of the day. The first floor features old city maps, booty from an Ottoman siege, and an 1850 city model showing the town just before the wall was replaced by the Ring.

The Secession: This clean-lined building at the Ring end of the Naschmarkt was the headquarters of the group of artists calling themselves The Secession. It's nicknamed the "golden cabbage" for its bushy gilded rooftop (actually, those are the laurel leaves of Apollo, the God of Poetry) designed by the painter Gustav Klimt. It was here that young artists first exhibited their "youth-style" art in 1897. In the basement is Klimt's *Beethoven Frieze*.

Belvedere Palace: This museum's collection includes work by Secessionist leader and poster boy Gustav Klimt (1862–1917). He gained fame painting slender young women entwined together in florid embrace, exploring the highly charged erotic terrain of his contemporary, Sigmund Freud. Klimt took the decorative element of Art Nouveau to extremes. In many of his paintings, only the face and bits of body show through gilded ornamental friezes. The two lovers of *The Kiss* are wrapped up in the colorful gold-and-jeweled cloak of bliss.

The Anchor Clock on Hoher Markt: This mosaic-decorated clock (1911–1917) spans two buildings and does a musical act at noon. The clock honors 12 great figures from Vienna's history, from Marcus Aurelius to Joseph Haydn. While each gets his own top-of-the-hour moment, all parade by at high noon. A plaque on the left names each figure. Notice the novel way to mark the time.

Karlsplatz: Otto Wagner (1841–1918), Vienna's premier *Jugendstil* architect, designed several structures for Vienna's subway system, including the original arched entrances.

Finally, the second floor displays a city model from 1898 (with the new Ringstrasse), sentimental Biedermeier paintings and objets d'art, and early 20th-century paintings (including some by Gustav Klimt). The museum is worth the €6 admission (free Sun, open Tue–Sun 9:00–18:00, closed Mon, www.wienmuseum.at).

▲Academy of Fine Arts (Akademie der Bildenden Künste)—This small but exciting collection includes works by Bosch, Botticelli, and Rubens (quick, sketchy cartoons used to create his giant canvases); a Venice series by Guardi; and a self-portrait by a 15-year-old Van Dyck. It's all magnificently lit and

well-described by the €2.50 audioguide, and comes with comfy chairs (€7; Tue–Sun 10:00–18:00, closed Mon, 3 blocks from the Opera at Schillerplatz 3, tel. 01/588-162-222, www.akademiegalerie.at).

The fact that this is a working art academy gives it a certain realness. As you wander the halls of the academy, ponder how history might have been different if Hitler—who applied to study architecture here but was rejected—had been accepted as a student. Before leaving, peek into the ground floor's central hall—textbook Historicism, the Ringstrasse style of the late 1800s.

▲The Secession—This little building, behind the Academy of Fine Arts, was created by the Vienna Secession movement, a group of nonconformist artists led by Gustav Klimt, Otto Wagner, and friends. The young trees carved into the walls and its bushy "golden cabbage" rooftop are symbolic of a renewal cycle. The Secessionist motto, under the cabbage, reads: "To each age its art, and to art its liberty." Today, the Secession continues to showcase cutting-edge art, as well as one of Gustav Klimt's most famous works (€3.50, but temporary exhibits often boost the price to €6, Tue–Sun 10:00–18:00, Thu until 20:00, closed Mon, Friedrichstrasse 12, tel. 01/587-5307, www.secession.at).

While the staff hopes you take a look at the temporary exhibits (and the ticket price includes this section whether you like it or not), most tourists head directly for the **basement,** home to a small exhibit about the history of the building and the museum's highlight: Klimt's classic *Beethoven Frieze* (a.k.a. the "Searching Souls"). The piece features floating female figures yearning for happiness, who drift and weave and search—like we all do—through internal and external temptations and forces, falling victim to base and ungodly temptations, and losing their faith. Then, they become inspired by poetry, music, and art to carry on, and they finally reach true happiness, represented by Mr. Poetry. At the climax of the frieze, a naked couple embraces in ecstasy as a heavenly choir sings the "Ode to Joy" from the Ninth Symphony: "Joy, you beautiful spark of the gods...under thy gentle wings, all men shall become brothers."

Glass cases show sketches Klimt did in preparation for this work. Klimt embellished the painting with painted-on gold (his brother and colleague was a goldsmith), and by gluing on reflecting glass and mother-of-pearl for the ladies' dresses and jewelry. The adjacent room tells the history of this masterpiece (transferred from screens to the Secession walls), and how the building was damaged in World War II.

▲Naschmarkt—In 1898, the city decided to cover up its Vienna River. The long, wide square they created was filled with a lively produce market that still bustles most days (closed Sun). It's long

been known as *the* place to get exotic, faraway foods. In fact, locals say, "From here start the Balkans."

From near the Opera, the Naschmarkt (roughly, "Munchies Market") stretches along Wienzeile street. This "Belly of Vienna" comes with two parallel lanes—one lined with fun and reasonable eateries, and the other featuring the town's top-end produce and gourmet goodies. This is where top chefs like to get their ingredients. At the gourmet vinegar stall, you sample the vinegar like perfume—with a drop on your wrist. Farther from the center, the Naschmarkt becomes likeably seedy and surrounded by sausage stands, Turkish *Döner Kebab* stalls, cafés, and theaters. At the market's far end is a line of buildings with fine Art Nouveau facades. Each Saturday, the Naschmarkt is infested by a huge flea market where, in olden days, locals would come to hire a monkey to pick little critters out of their hair (Mon–Fri 6:00–18:30, Sat 6:00–17:00, closed Sun, closes earlier in winter; U-1, U-2, or U-4: Karlsplatz). For a picnic in the park, pick up your grub here and walk over to Karlsplatz (described previously).

On the Ring's Eastern Edge

Museum of Applied Art (Österreichisches Museum für Angewandte Kunst)—The "MAK," as it's called, is Vienna's answer to London's Victoria and Albert Museum. It shows off the fancies of local aristocratic society, including a fine *Jugendstil* collection. The MAK is more than just another grand building on the Ringstrasse. It was built to provide models of historic design for Ringstrasse architects, and is a delightful space in itself (many locals stop in to enjoy a coffee on the plush couches in the main lobby). Each wing is dedicated to a different era. Exhibits, well-described in English, come with a playful modern flair—notable modern designers were assigned various spaces (€8, €10 includes a hefty English guidebook, free on Sat, open Tue–Sun 10:00–18:00, Tue until 24:00, closed Mon, Stubenring 5, tel. 01/711-360, www.mak.at).

The associated **Restaurant Österreicher im MAK** is named for a chef renowned for his classic and modern Viennese cuisine. Classy and mod, it's trendy for locals (open daily, reserve for evening, €10–15 plates).

Beyond the Ring

The following museums are located outside the Ringstrasse but inside the Gürtel, or outer ring road.

▲▲Belvedere Palace—This is the elegant palace of Prince Eugène of Savoy (1663–1736), the still-much-appreciated conqueror of the Ottomans. Eugène, a Frenchman considered too short and too ugly to be in the service of Louis XIV, offered his services to the Habsburgs. While he was indeed short and ugly, he became the greatest military genius of his age and the toast of Viennese society. When you conquer cities, as Eugène did, you get really rich.

He had no heirs, so the state got his property and Emperor Josef II established the Belvedere as Austria's first great public art gallery. Today you can tour the lavish palace, see sweeping views of the gardens and the Vienna skyline, and enjoy world-class art starring Gustav Klimt, French Impressionism, and a grab-bag of other 19th- and early-20th-century artists (€9.50 for Upper Belvedere Palace only, €12.50 for Upper and Lower palaces—not worth it, audioguide-€3, daily 10:00–18:00, no photos allowed inside, entrance at Prinz-Eugen-Strasse 27, tel. 01/7955-7134, www.belvedere.at). The palace is a 15-minute walk south of the Ring. To get there from the center, catch tram #D at the Opera (direction Südbahnhof; it stops at the palace gate).

The Belvedere Palace is actually two grand buildings—the Upper Palace and Lower Palace—separated by a fine garden. For our purposes, the Upper Palace is what matters. The Lower Palace exhibits a less-interesting collection of Austrian Baroque and medieval art. *Belvedere* means "beautiful view." From the Upper Palace's **Marble Hall,** look over the Baroque gardens, the Lower Palace, and the city.

The Upper Palace's eclectic collection, arranged chronologically, is tailor-made for browsing. Skip the second floor, and focus instead on the first floor, where you'll find Historicism, Romanticism, Impressionism, Realism, tired tourism, Expressionism, Art Nouveau, and early Modernism. Each room tries to pair Austrian works from that period with much better-known European works.

In the two rooms full of sumptuous paintings by Klimt you can get caught up in his fascination with the beauty and danger he saw in women. To Klimt, all art was erotic art. Be sure to see his famous *Judith I* (holding the head of her biblical victim, she's the modern femme fatale) and his glowingly radiant masterpiece, *The Kiss.*

▲Imperial Furniture Collection (Kaiserliches Hofmobiliendepot)—Bizarre, sensuous, eccentric, or precious, this collection is your peek at the Habsburgs' furniture—from grandma's wheel-

chair to the emperor's spittoon—all thoughtfully described in English. The Habsburgs had many palaces, but only the Hofburg was permanently furnished. The rest were furnished on the fly—set up and taken down by a gang of royal roadies called the "Depot of Court Movables" (Hofmobiliendepot). When the monarchy was dissolved in 1918, the state of Austria took possession of the Hofmobiliendepot's inventory—165,000 items. Now this royal storehouse is open to the public in a fine and sprawling museum. Don't go here for the *Jugendstil* furnishings. The older Baroque, Rococo, and Biedermeier pieces are the most impressive and tied most intimately to the royals. Combine a visit to this museum with a stroll down the lively shopping boulevard, Mariahilfer Strasse (€7, Tue–Sun 10:00–18:00, closed Mon, Mariahilfer Strasse 88, U-3: Zieglergasse, tel. 01/5243-3570).

▲Liechtenstein Museum—The noble Liechtenstein family (who own only a tiny country, but whose friendship with the Habsburgs goes back generations) amassed an incredible private art collection. Their palace was long a treasure for Vienna art lovers. Then, in 1938—knowing Hitler was intent on plundering artwork to create an immense "Führer Museum"—the family fled to their tiny homeland with their best art. Attendance has been disappointing since the museum reopened in 2004, but the problem is its location (and perhaps its steep price)...not its worthiness. The Liechtensteins' "world of Baroque pleasures" includes the family's rare "Golden Carriage" which was used for their grand entry into Paris in 1738. It was carted to the edge of town and assembled there. It's a rare example of the French Rococo style, as nearly all such carriages were destroyed in the French Revolution. The museum also has a plush Baroque library, an inviting English Garden, and an impressive collection of paintings, including a complete cycle of early Rubens (€10, audioguide-€1, Fri–Tue 10:00–17:00, last entry 30 min before closing, closed Wed–Thu, tram #D to Bauernfeldplatz, Fürstengasse 1, tel. 01/319-5767-252, www.liechtensteinmuseum.at). The gardens are free and open until 20:30 (but aren't worth the trip on their own).

▲KunstHausWien: Hundertwasser Museum—This "make yourself at home" museum and nearby apartment complex are a hit with lovers of modern art, mixing the work and philosophy of local painter/environmentalist Friedensreich Hundertwasser (1928–2000). Stand in front of the colorful checkerboard building and consider Hundertwasser's style. He was against "window racism": Neighboring houses allow only one kind of window, but 100H_2O's windows are each different—and he encouraged residents in the Hundertwasserhaus (a 5–10 minute walk away, described next) to personalize them. He recognized "tree tenants" as well as human tenants. His buildings are spritzed with a forest and topped with

dirt and grassy little parks—close to nature and good for the soul.

Floors and sidewalks are irregular—to "stimulate the brain" (although current residents complain it just causes wobbly furniture and sprained ankles). Thus 100H_2O waged a one-man fight—during the 1950s and 1960s, when concrete and glass ruled—to save the human soul from the city. (Hundertwasser claimed that "straight lines are godless.")

Inside the museum, start with his interesting biography. His fun paintings are half psychedelic *Jugendstil* and half just kids' stuff. Notice the photographs from his 1950s days as part of Vienna's bohemian scene. Throughout the museum, keep an eye out for the fun philosophical quotes from an artist who believed, "If man is creative, he comes nearer to his creator" (€9 for Hundertwasser Museum, €12 combo-ticket includes special exhibitions, half-price on Mon, open daily 10:00–19:00, extremely fragrant and colorful garden café, Untere Weissgerberstrasse 13, tram #1: Hetzgasse or U-3: Landstrasse—but the tram stop is much closer than the U-Bahn stop, tel. 01/712-0491, www.kunsthauswien.com).

Hundertwasserhaus: The KunstHausWien provides by far the best look at Hundertwasser, but for an actual lived-in apartment complex by the green master, walk five minutes to the one-with-nature Hundertwasserhaus (at Löwengasse and Kegelgasse). This complex of 50 apartments, subsidized by the government to provide affordable housing, was built in the 1980s as a breath of architectural fresh air in a city of boring, blocky apartment complexes. While not open to visitors, it's worth visiting for its fun and colorful patchwork exterior and the Hundertwasser festival of shops across the street. Don't miss the view from Kegelgasse to see the "tree tenants" and the internal winter garden that residents enjoy.

Hundertwasser detractors—of which there are many—remind visitors that 100H_2O was a painter, not an architect. They describe the Hundertwasserhaus as a "1950s house built in the 1980s," and colorfully painted with no real concern about the environment, communal living, or even practical comfort. Almost all of the

original inhabitants got fed up with the novelty and moved out.

Sigmund Freud Museum—Freud enthusiasts enjoy seeing the humble apartment and workplace of the man who fundamentally changed our understanding of the human psyche. Dr. Sigmund Freud (1856-1939), a graduate of Vienna University, established his practice here in 1891. For the next 47 years, he received troubled patients who hoped to find peace by telling him their dreams, life traumas, and secret urges. It was here that he wrote his influential works, including the landmark *Interpretation of Dreams* (€7, audioguide-€2, daily July–Sept 9:00–18:00, Oct–June 9:00–17:00, cool shop, half a block downhill from the Schlickgasse tram #D stop, Berggasse 19, tel. 01/319-1596, www.freud-museum.at).

Schönbrunn Palace (Schloss Schönbrunn)

Among Europe's palaces, only Schönbrunn rivals Versailles. This former summer residence of the Habsburgs is big, with 1,441 rooms. But don't worry—only 40 rooms are shown to the public.

Of the plethora of sights at the palace, the highlight is a tour of the Royal Apartments—the chandeliered rooms where the Habsburg nobles lived. You can also stroll the gardens, tour the coach museum, and visit a handful of lesser sights nearby.

Getting There: Take U-4 to Schönbrunn and walk 400 yards (just follow the crowds). The main entrance is in the left side of the palace as you face it.

▲▲▲Royal Apartments—While the exterior is Baroque, the interior was finished under Maria Theresa in let-them-eat-cake Rococo. The chandeliers are either of Bohemian crystal or of hand-carved wood with gold-leaf gilding. Thick walls hid the servants as they ran around stoking the ceramic stoves from the back, and attending to other behind-the-scenes matters. When WWII bombs rained on the city and the palace grounds, the palace itself took only one direct hit. Thankfully, that bomb, which crashed through three floors—including the sumptuous central ballroom—was a dud. Most of the public rooms are decorated in Neo-Baroque, as they were under Franz Josef (r. 1848–1916). The rest of the palace has been converted to simple apartments and rented to the families of 260 civil servants, who enjoy rent control and governmental protections so they can't be evicted.

Cost: The admission price is based on which route you select (each one includes an audioguide): the 22-room **Imperial Tour**

(€9.50, 45 min, Grand Palace rooms plus apartments of Franz Josef and Elisabeth—mostly 19th-century and therefore least interesting) or the 40-room **Grand Tour** (€13, 60 min, includes Imperial tour plus Maria Theresa's apartments—18th-century Rococo). A combo-ticket called the **Schönbrunn Pass Classic** includes the Grand Tour, as well as other sights on the grounds: the Gloriette viewing terrace, maze, privy garden, and court bakery—complete with *Apfelstrudel* demo and tasting (€16, available April–Oct only). I'd go for the Grand Tour.

Hours: Daily July–Aug 8:30–18:00, April–June and Sept–Oct 8:30–17:00, Nov–March 8:30–16:30. Information: www.schoenbrunn.at.

Crowd-Beating Tips: Schönbrunn suffers from crowds. It can be a jam-packed sauna in the summer. It's busiest from 9:30 to 11:30, especially on weekends and in July and August; it's least crowded from after 14:00, when there are no groups. To avoid the long delays in summer, make a reservation by telephone a few days in advance (tel. 01/8111-3239, answered daily 8:00–17:00, wait through the long message for the operator). You'll get an appointment time and a ticket number. Check in at least 30 minutes early. Upon arrival, go to the "Group and Reservations" desk (immediately inside the gate on the left at the gate house—long before the actual palace), give your number, pick up your ticket, and jump in ahead of the masses. If you show up in peak season without calling first, you deserve the frustration. (In this case, you'll have to wait in line, buy your ticket, and wait until the listed time to enter—which could be tomorrow.) If you have any time to kill, spend it exploring the gardens or Wagenburg Coach Museum.

Palace Gardens—Unlike the gardens of Versailles, meant to shut out the real world, Schönbrunn's park was opened to the public in 1779 while the monarchy was in full swing. It was part of Maria Theresa's reform policy, making the garden a celebration of the evolution of civilization from autocracy into real democracy.

Most of the park itself is free, as it has been since the 1700s (open daily sunrise to dusk, entrance on either side of the palace). The small side gardens are the most elaborate. The Kammergarten on the left was a fancy private garden for the Habsburgs (now restored and with a fee). The so-called Sisi Gardens on the right are free. Inside are several other sights, including a **palm house** (€4, daily May–Sept 9:30–18:00, Oct–April 9:30–17:00, last entry 30 min before closing); Europe's oldest **zoo,** or *Tiergarten,* built by Maria Theresa's husband for the entertainment and education of the court in 1752 (€12, April–Sept daily 9:00–18:30, closes earlier off-season, tel. 01/877-9294); and—at the end of the gardens—the **Gloriette,** a purely decorative monument celebrating an obscure Austrian military victory and offering a fine city view (viewing

terrace-€2, included in €16 Schönbrunn Pass Classic, daily April–Sept 9:00–18:00, July–Aug until 19:00, Oct 9:00–17:00, closed Nov–March). A touristy choo-choo train makes the rounds all day, connecting Schönbrunn's many attractions.

Wagenburg Coach Museum—The Schönbrunn coach museum is a 19th-century traffic jam of 50 impressive royal carriages and sleighs. Highlights include silly sedan chairs, the death-black hearse carriage (used for Franz Josef in 1916, and most recently for Empress Zita in 1989), and an extravagantly gilded imperial carriage pulled by eight Cinderella horses. This was rarely used other than for the coronation of Holy Roman Emperors, when it was disassembled and taken to Frankfurt for the big event (€4.50; daily April–Oct 9:00–18:00; Nov–March 10:00–16:00; last entry 30 min before closing, 200 yards from palace, walk through right arch as you face palace, tel. 01/525-24-3470).

Activities in Vienna

People-Watching and Strolling

These activities allow you to take it easy and enjoy the Viennese good life.

▲Stadtpark (City Park)—Vienna's major park is a waltzing world of gardens, memorials to local musicians, ponds, peacocks, music in bandstands, and Viennese escaping the city. Notice the *Jugendstil* entrance at the Stadtpark U-Bahn station. The Kursalon, where Strauss was the violin-toting master of waltzing ceremonies, hosts daily touristy concerts in three-quarter time.

▲Prater—Since the 1780s, when the reformist Emperor Josef II gave his hunting grounds to the people of Vienna as a public park, this place has been Vienna's playground. While tired and a bit run-down these days, Vienna's sprawling amusement park still tempts visitors with its huge 220-foot-tall, famous, and lazy Ferris wheel *(Riesenrad),* roller coaster, bumper cars, Lilliputian railroad, and endless eateries. Especially if you're traveling with kids, this is a fun, goofy place to share the evening with thousands of Viennese (rides run May–Sept 9:00–24:00—but quiet after 22:00, March–April and Oct 10:00–22:00, Nov–Dec 10:00–20:00, grounds always open, U-1: Praterstern). For a local-style family dinner, eat at Schweizerhaus (good food, great Czech Budvar—the original "Budweiser"—beer, classic conviviality).

Donauinsel (Danube Island)—In the 1970s, the city dug a canal parallel to the mighty Danube River, creating both a flood barrier and a much-loved island escape from the city (easy U-Bahn access on U-1 to Donauinsel). This skinny, 12-mile-long island provides a natural wonderland. All along the traffic-free, grassy park you'll find locals—both Viennese, and especially immigrants and those

who can't afford their own cabin or fancy vacation—at play. The swimming comes tough, though, with rocky entries rather than sand. The best activity here is a bike ride (see page 988). Note that if you venture far from the crowds, you're likely to encounter nudists on Rollerblades.

Shopping

Traditional Austrian Clothing—If you're interested in picking up a classy felt suit or dirndl, you'll find shops all over town. Most central is the fancy **Loden Plankl** shop (across from the Hofburg, at Michaelerplatz 6). But the **Tostmann Trachten** shop is the ultimate for serious shopping. Frau Tostmann powered the resurgence of this style. Her place is like a shrine to traditional Austrian and folk clothing (called *Tracht*)—handmade and very expensive (Schottengasse 3A, 3-min walk from Am Hof, tel. 01/533-5331, www.tostmann.at).

Artsy Gifts—Vienna's museum shops are some of Europe's best. The design store in the Museum of Applied Art (MAK) is a delight; the shops of the Albertina Museum, Kunsthistorisches Museum, Belvedere Palace, KunstHausWien, and the MuseumsQuartier museums are also particularly good.

Window-Shopping—The narrow streets north and west of the cathedral are sprinkled with old-fashioned shops that seem to belong to another era, carrying a curiously narrow range of items for sale (old clocks, men's ties, gloves, and so on). Dedicated window-shoppers will enjoy the Dorotheum auction house (see page 1020).

Experiences in Vienna

Vienna—the birthplace of what we call classical music—still thrives as a music capital. On any given evening, you'll have your choice of opera, Strauss waltzes, Mozart chamber concerts, the famous Boys' Choir, and lighthearted musicals.

Live Music

As far back as the 12th century, Vienna was a mecca for musicians—both sacred and secular (troubadours). The Habsburg emperors of the 17th and 18th centuries were not only generous supporters of music, but fine musicians and composers themselves. (Maria Theresa played a mean double bass.) Composers such as Haydn, Mozart, Beethoven, Schubert, Brahms, and Mahler gravitated to this music-friendly environment. They taught each other, jammed together, and spent a lot of time in Habsburg palaces. Beethoven was a famous figure, walking—lost in musical thought—through Vienna's woods. In the city's 19th-century belle époque, "Waltz

King" Johann Strauss and his brothers kept Vienna's 300 ballrooms spinning.

This musical tradition continues into modern times, leaving some prestigious Viennese institutions for today's tourists to enjoy: the Opera, the Boys' Choir, and the great Baroque halls and churches, all busy with classical and waltz concerts. As you poke into churches and palaces, you may hear groups practicing. You're welcome to sit and listen.

Vienna is Europe's music capital. It's music *con brio* (with brilliance) from October through June, reaching a symphonic climax during the Vienna Festival each May and June. Sadly, in July and August, the Boys' Choir, the Opera, and many more music companies are—like you—on vacation. But Vienna hums year-round with live classical music. Except for the Boys' Choir, the musical events listed below are offered in summer.

The best-known entertainment venues are the Staatsoper (for straight-up opera), the Volksoper (for musicals and "operettas"), the Wiener Musikverein (home of the Vienna Philharmonic Orchestra), and the Wiener Konzerthaus (various events).

Vienna Boys' Choir—The boys sing (from a high balcony, where they are heard but not seen) at the 9:15 Sunday Mass from September through June in the Hofburg's Imperial Music Chapel (Hofmusikkapelle). The entrance is at Schweizerhof; you can get there from In der Burg square or go through the tunnel from Josefsplatz.

Reserved seats must be booked two months in advance (€5–29; reserve by fax, email, or mail: fax from the US 011-431-533-992-775, whmk@chello.at, or write Hofmusikkapelle, Hofburg-Schweizerhof, 1010 Wien; call 01/533-9927 for information only—they can't book tickets at this number).

Much easier, standing room inside is free and open to the first 60 who line up. Even better, rather than line up early, you can simply swing by and stand in the narthex just outside, where you can hear the boys and see the Mass on a TV monitor.

Boys' Choir concerts are also given Fridays at 16:00 in late April, May, June, September, and October on stage at the Musikverein, near the Opera and Karlskirche (€36–56, around 30 standing-room tickets go on sale at 15:30 for €15, Karlsplatz 6; U-1, U-2, or U-4: Karlsplatz; tel. 01/5880-4173).

They're talented kids, but, for my taste, not worth all the commotion. Remember, many churches have great music during Sunday Mass. Just 200 yards from the Boys' Choir chapel, Augustinian Church has a glorious 11:00 service each Sunday (see page 1019).

Touristy Mozart and Strauss Concerts—If the music comes to you, it's touristy—designed for flash-in-the-pan Mozart fans.

Powdered-wig orchestra performances are given almost nightly in grand traditional settings (€25–50). Pesky wigged-and-powdered Mozarts peddle tickets in the streets. They rave about the quality of the musicians, but you'll get second-rate chamber orchestras, clad in historic costumes, performing the greatest hits of Mozart and Strauss. These are casual, easygoing concerts with lots of tour groups. While there's not a Viennese person in the audience, the tourists generally enjoy the evening.

To sort through all your options, check with the ticket office in the TI (same price as on the street, but with all venues to choose from). Savvy locals suggest getting the cheapest tickets, as no one seems to care if cheapskates move up to fill unsold pricier seats. Critics explain that the musicians are actually very good (often Hungarians, Poles, and Russians working a season here to fund an entire year of music studies back home), but that they haven't performed much together so aren't "tight."

Of the many fine venues, the **Mozarthaus** might be my favorite—a small room richly decorated in Venetian Renaissance style with intimate chamber-music concerts (€35–42, Thu–Fri at 19:30, Sat at 18:00, near St. Stephen's Cathedral at Singerstrasse 7, tel. 01/911-9077).

Strauss Concerts in the Kursalon—For years, Strauss concerts have been held in the Kursalon, where the "Waltz King" himself directed wildly popular concerts 100 years ago (€39–56, concerts nightly generally at 20:15, just east of the Ringstrasse in the Stadtpark, tel. 01/512-5790 to reserve). Shows last 1.75 hours and are a mix of ballet, waltzes, and a 15-piece orchestra. It's touristy—tour guides holding up banners with group numbers wait out front after the show. Even so, the performance is playful, visually fun, fine quality for most, and with a tried-and-tested, crowd-pleasing format. The conductor welcomes the crowd in German (with a wink) and English; after that...it's English only.

Serious Concerts—These events, including the Opera, are listed in the monthly *Wien-Programm* (available at TI). Most tickets run €40–55 (plus a stiff booking fee when booked in advance or

through a box office like the one at the TI). A few venues charge as little as €25; look around if you're not set on any particular concert. While it's easy to book tickets online long in advance, spontaneity is also workable, as there are invariably people selling their extra tickets at face value or less outside the door before concert time. If you call a concert hall directly, they can advise you on the availability of (cheaper) tickets at the door. Vienna takes care of its starving artists (and tourists) by offering cheap standing-room tickets to top-notch music and opera (generally an hour before each performance).

The Opera—The Vienna State Opera (Staatsoper)—with musicians provided by the Vienna Philharmonic Orchestra in the pit—is one of the world's top opera houses. They put on 300 performances a year, but in July and August the singers rest their voices (or go on tour). Since there are different operas nearly nightly, you'll see big trucks out back and constant action backstage—all the sets need to be switched each day. Even though the expensive seats normally sell out long in advance, the opera is perpetually in the red and subsidized by the state.

Opera Tickets: To buy tickets in advance, call 01/514-440 or 01/513-1513 (phone answered daily 10:00–21:00, www.wiener-staatsoper.at). The theater's box office is open from 9:00 until two hours before each performance. Unless Placido Domingo is in town, it's easy to get one of 567 **standing-room tickets** (*Stehplätze,* €3 up top or €4 downstairs). While the front doors open one hour before the show starts, a side door (middle of building, on the Operngasse side) opens 80 minutes before curtain time, giving those in the know an early grab at standing-room tickets (tickets sold until 20 min after curtain time). Just walk straight in, then head right until you see the ticket booth marked *Stehplätze* (tel. 01/514-447-880). If fewer than 567 people are in line, there's no need to line up early. If you're one of the first 160 in line, try for the "Parterre" section and you'll end up dead-center at stage level, directly under the Emperor's Box (otherwise, you can choose between the third floor—*Balkon,* or the fourth floor—*Galerie*). Dress is casual (but do your best) at the standing-room bar. Locals save their spot along the rail by tying a scarf to it.

The excellent "electronic libretto" translation screens help make the experience worthwhile for opera newbies. (Press the button to turn yours on; press again for English.)

Rick's Crude Tips: For me, three hours is a lot of opera.

But just to see and hear the Opera in action for half an hour is a treat. You can buy a standing-room spot and just drop in for part of the show. Ending time is posted in the lobby—you could stop by for just the finale. If you go at the start or finish, you'll see Vienna dressed up. Of the 567 people with cheap standing-room tickets, invariably many will not stand through the entire performance. If you drop by after showtime, you can wait for tourists to leave and bum their tickets off them—be sure to ask them for clear directions to your spot. (While it's perfectly legal to swap standing-room spots, be discreet if finding your spot mid-performance—try to look like you know where you're going.) Even those with standing-room tickets are considered "ticket-holders," and are welcome to explore the building. As you leave, wander around the first floor (fun if leaving early, when halls are empty) to enjoy the sumptuous halls (with prints of famous stage sets and performers) and the grand entry staircase. The last resort (and worst option) is to drop into the Café Oper Vienna inside the Opera, and watch the opera live on TV screens (reasonable menu and drinks).

Vienna Volksoper: For less-serious operettas and musicals, try Vienna's other opera house, located along the Gürtel, west of the city center (see *Wien-Programm* brochure or ask at TI for schedule, Währinger Strasse 78, tel. 01/5144-4360, www.volksoper.at).

Theater an der Wien—Considered the oldest theater in Vienna, this venue was designed in 1801 for Mozart operas—intimate, with just a thousand seats. Reopened in 2006 for Mozart's 250th birthday, it treats Vienna's music lovers to a different opera every month—generally Mozart with a contemporary setting and modern interpretation—with the excellent Vienna Radio Orchestra in the pit. With the reopening of Theater an der Wien, Vienna now supports three opera companies. This one is the only company playing through the summer (facing the Naschmarkt at Linke Wienzeile 6, tel. 01/5883-0660 for information, tickets available at www.theater-wien.at).

Musicals—The Wien Ticket pavilion sells tickets to contemporary American and British musicals performed in the German language (€10–100, €5 standing-room tickets available 2 hours before curtain time), and offers these tickets at half-price from 14:00 until 17:00 the day of the show. Or you can reserve (full-price) tickets for the musicals by phone (call Wien Ticket at tel. 01/58885).

Dance Evening—If you'd like to actually dance (waltz and ballroom), or watch people who are really good at it, consider the Dance Evening at the Tanz Café in the Volksgarten (€5–6, May–Sept, Sat from 19:00 and Sun from 18:00, www.volksgarten.at).

Films of Concerts—To see free films of great concerts in a lively, outdoor setting near City Hall, see "Nightlife in Vienna," later.

Viennese Coffee: From Ottomans to Starbucks

The story of coffee in Vienna is steeped in legend. In the 17th century, the Ottomans (invaders from the Turkish Empire) were laying siege to Vienna. A spy working for the Austrians who infiltrated the Ottoman ranks got to know the Turkish lifestyle...including their passion for a drug called coffee. After the Austrians persevered, the ecstatic Habsburg emperor offered the spy anything he wanted. The spy asked for the Ottomans' spilled coffee beans, which he gathered up to start the first coffee shop in town. (It's a nice story. But actually, there was already an Armenian in town running a coffeehouse.)

In the 18th century, coffee boomed as an aristocratic drink. In the 19th-century Industrial Age, people were expected to work 12-hour shifts, and coffee became a hit with the working class, too. By the 20th century, the Vienna coffee scene became so refined that old-timers remember when waiters brought a sheet with various shades of brown (like paint samples) so a customer could make clear exactly how milky she wanted her coffee.

In 2003, Vienna's first Starbucks boldly opened next to the Opera—across the street from the ultimate Old World coffeehouse, the Café Sacher. The locals like the easy-chair ambience and quality of Starbucks coffee, but think it's overpriced. Viennese coffee connoisseurs aren't impressed by quantity, can't relate to flavored coffee, and think drinking out of a paper cup is really trashy. The consensus: For the same price, you can have an elegant and traditional experience in a top Vienna-style coffee shop instead. While the "coffee-to-go" trend has been picked up by many bakeries and other joints, the Starbucks invasion has stalled, with nowhere near as many outlets as the Seattle-based coffee empire had planned.

Classical Music to Go—To bring home Beethoven, Strauss, or the Wiener Philharmonic on a top-quality CD, shop at Gramola on the Graben or EMI on Kärntner Strasse.

Vienna's Cafés

In Vienna, the living room is down the street at the neighborhood coffee house. This tradition is just another example of Viennese expertise in good living. Each of Vienna's many long-established (and sometimes even legendary) coffee houses has its individual character (and characters). These classic cafés are a bit tired, with a shabby patina and famously grumpy waiters who treat you like an uninvited guest invading their living room. Still, it's a welcoming

place. They offer newspapers, pastries, sofas, quick and light workers' lunches, elegant ambience, and "take all the time you want" charm for the price of a cup of coffee. Order it *melange* (like a cappuccino), *brauner* (strong coffee with a little milk), or *schwarzer* (black). Americans who ask for a latte are mistaken for Italians and given a cup of hot milk. Rather than buy the *International Herald Tribune* ahead of time, spend the money on a cup of coffee and read the paper for free, Vienna-style, in a café.

These are my favorites:

Café Hawelka has a dark, "brooding Trotsky" atmosphere, paintings by struggling artists who couldn't pay for coffee, a salo-on-wood flavor, chalkboard menu, smoked velvet couches, an international selection of newspapers, and a phone that rings for regulars. Mrs. Hawelka died just a couple weeks after Pope John Paul II. Locals suspect the pontiff wanted her much-loved *Buchteln* (marmalade-filled doughnuts) in heaven. Mr. Hawelka, now alone and understandably a bit forlorn, still oversees the action (Wed–Mon 8:00–2:00 in the morning, Sun from 10:00, closed Tue, just off the Graben, Dorotheergasse 6).

Café Sperl dates from 1880, and is still furnished identically to the day it opened—from the coat tree to the chairs (Mon–Sat 7:00–23:00, Sun 11:00–20:00 except closed Sun July–Aug, just off Naschmarkt near Mariahilfer Strasse, Gumpendorfer 11, tel. 01/586-4158).

Café Bräunerhof, between the Hofburg and the Graben, offers a classic ambience with no tourists and live music on weekends (light classics, no cover, Sat–Sun 15:00–18:00), and a practical menu with daily specials (open long hours daily, Stallburgasse 2).

Other Classics in the Old Center: All of these places are open long hours daily: **Café Pruckel** (at Dr.-Karl-Lueger-Platz, across from Stadtpark at Stubenring 24); **Café Tirolerhof** (2 blocks from the Opera, behind the TI on Tegetthoffstrasse, at Führichgasse 8); and **Café Landtmann** (directly across from the City Hall on the Ringstrasse at Dr.-Karl-Lueger-Ring 4). The Landtmann is unique, as it's the only grand café built along the Ring, with all the other grand buildings.

Wein in Wien: Vienna's Wine Gardens (*Heurigen*)

The *Heuriger* (HOY-rih-gur) is a uniquely Viennese institution. When the Habsburgs let Vienna's vintners sell their own new wine (called *Sturm*) tax-free, several hundred families opened *Heurigen* (HOY-rih-gehn)—wine-garden restaurants clustered around the edge of town. A tradition was born. Today, they do their best to maintain the old-village atmosphere, serving the homemade new wine (the last vintage until November 11, when a new vintage year

The *Heurigen* Experience

Within Vienna's city limits are more than 1,700 acres of vineyards, and countless *Heuriger* taverns. For a *Heuriger* evening, rather than go to a particular place, take a tram to the wine-garden district of your choice and wander around, choosing the place with the best ambience.

At any *Heuriger,* fill your plate at a self-serve cold cut buffet (€6–9 for dinner). Food is sold by the *"10 dag"* unit. (A *dag* is a decigram, so *10 dag* is 100 grams—about a quarter-pound.)

Dishes to look for...or look out for: *Stelze* (grilled knuckle of pork), *Fleischlaberln* (fried ground-meat patties), *Schinkenfleckerln* (pasta with cheese and ham), *Schmalz* (a spread made with pig fat), *Blunzen* (black pudding...sausage made from blood), *Presskopf* (jellied brains and innards), *Liptauer* (spicy cheese spread), *Kornspitz* (whole-meal bread roll), and *Kummelbraten* (crispy roast pork with caraway).

Waitresses will then take your wine order (€2.50 per quarter-liter, about 8 oz). Many locals claim it takes several years of practice to distinguish between the *Sturm* wine and vinegar.

begins) with small meals and strolling musicians. Most *Heurigen* are decorated with enormous antique presses from their vineyards. Wine gardens might be closed on any given day; call ahead to confirm if you have your heart set on a particular place. (For a near-*Heuriger* experience in downtown Vienna, drop by Gigerl Stadtheuriger, listed at the top of "Eating in Vienna," later.)

I've listed three good *Heuriger* neighborhoods, plus one rural *Heuriger,* on the outskirts of Vienna (see map on page 979). To reach the neighborhoods from downtown Vienna, it's best to use public transportation (cheap, 30 min, runs late in the evening, directions given per listing below), or you can take a 15-minute taxi ride from the Ring.

Nussdorf—An untouristy district, characteristic and popular with the Viennese, Nussdorf has plenty of *Heuriger* ambience. Right at the last stop on tram #D's route (Beethovengang), you'll find three long and skinny places side by side. Of these, **Schübel-Auer Heuriger** is my favorite (Tue–Sat 16:00–24:00, closed Sun–Mon, Kahlenberger Strasse 22, tel. 01/370-2222). Also consider **Heuriger Kierlinger** (daily 15:30–24:00, Kahlenberger Strasse

20, tel. 01/370-2264) and **Steinschaden** (daily 15:00–24:00, Kahlenberger Strasse 18, tel. 01/370-1375). Walk through any of these and you pop out on Kahlenberger Strasse, where a walk 20 yards uphill takes you to some more eating and drinking fun: **Bamkraxler** ("Tree Jumper"), the only *Biergarten* amid all these vineyards. It's a fun-loving, youthful place with fine keg beer and a regular menu—traditional, ribs, veggie, kids' menu—rather than the *Heuriger* cafeteria line (€8–12 meals, kids' playground, Tue–Sat 16:00–24:00, Sun 11:00–24:00, closed Mon, Kahlenberger Strasse 17, tel. 01/318-8800).

***Getting to the Nussdorf* Heurigen:** Take tram #D from the Ringstrasse (stops include the Opera, Hofburg/Kunsthistorisches Museum, and City Hall) to its endpoint (the stop labeled *Nussdorf* isn't the end—stay on for one more stop to Beethovengang). If you're not starting from somewhere near tram #D's route, take the U-4 to Heiligenstadt, then catch tram #D from in front of the U-Bahn station. Tram #D runs every 5–10 minutes (fewer trams after 23:00, last tram around 24:30).

Grinzing—Of the many *Heuriger* suburbs, Grinzing is the most famous, lively...and touristy. If you're looking to avoid tour groups, head elsewhere.

***Getting to the Grinzing* Heurigen:** From the Heiligenstadt U-4 station, take bus #38A and get off at Himmelstrasse, just past the green onion-top dome (runs every 10–20 minutes, 2/hr after 21:00, last bus around 22:30).

Don't confuse bus #38A with tram #38—which also goes to Grinzing, but starts at the Ring (at Schottentor). From the Grinzing tram stop, follow Himmelgasse uphill toward the green onion-top dome. You'll pass plenty of wine gardens—and tour buses—on your way up. Just past the dome, you'll find the heart of the *Heurigen.*

Heiligenstadt (Pfarrplatz)—Between Nussdorf and Grinzing, this neighborhood features several decent spots, including the famous and touristy **Mayer am Pfarrplatz** (a.k.a Beethovenhaus, Mon–Sat 16:00–24:00, Sun 11:00–23:00, Pfarrplatz 2, tel. 01/370-1287). This place has a charming inner courtyard with an accordion player and a sprawling backyard with a big children's play zone. Beethoven lived—and began work on his Ninth Symphony—here in 1817; he'd previously written his Sixth Symphony *(Pastorale)* while staying in this then-rural district. He hoped the local spa would cure his worsening deafness. **Weingut and Heuriger Werner Welser,** a block uphill from Beethoven's place, is lots of fun, with music nightly from 19:00 (open daily 15:30–24:00, Probusgasse 12, tel. 01/318-9797).

***Getting to the Heiligenstadt* Heurigen:** From the Heiligenstadt U-4 station, take bus #38A (runs every 10–20 min, 2/hr after

21:00, last bus around 22:30). Get off at Fernsprechamt/Heiligenstadt, walk uphill, and take the first right onto Nestelbachgasse, which leads to Pfarrplatz and the Beethovenhaus.

Heuriger Sirbu—This option is actually in the vineyards, high above Vienna with great city and countryside views, a top-notch buffet, a glass veranda, and a traditional interior for cool weather. It's a bit touristy, and dinner reservations are often required, since it's more upmarket and famous as "the ultimate setting" (May–mid-Oct from 15:00, closed Sun, big play zone for kids, Kahlenberger Strasse 210, tel. 01/320-5928). It's high above regular transit service, but fun to incorporate with a little walking. Ideally, ride bus #38A to Kahlenberg, and walk behind the buildings to find Kahlenberger Strasse—then follow it downhill for 15 minutes. (If you're starting with Nussdorf, then going on to Sirbu, follow directions to Bamkraxler—see Nussdorf listing, earlier—then follow Kahlenberger Strasse uphill for 35 min).

Nightlife in Vienna

If old music and new wine aren't your thing, Vienna has plenty of alternatives. For an up-to-date rundown on fun after dark, check www.viennahype.at.

City Hall Open-Air Classical-Music Cinema and Food Circus—A thriving people scene erupts each evening in summer (July–early Sept) at the park in front of City Hall (Rathaus, on the Ringstrasse). Thousands of people keep a food circus of 24 simple stalls busy. There's not a plastic cup anywhere, just real plates and glasses—Vienna wants the quality of eating to be as high as the music that's about to begin. About 3,000 folding chairs face a 60-foot-wide screen up against the City Hall's Neo-Gothic facade. When darkness falls, an announcer explains the program, and then the music starts. The program is different every night—mostly movies of opera and classical concerts, with some films. The TI has the schedule (programs generally last about two hours, starting when it's dark—between 21:30 in July and 20:30 in Aug and early Sept).

Since 1991, the city has paid for 60 of these summer event nights each year. Why? To promote culture. Officials know that the City Hall Music Festival is mostly a "meat market" where young people come to hook up. But they believe many of these people will develop a little appreciation of classical music and

high culture on the side.

English Cinema—Two great theaters offer three or four screens of English movies nightly (€6–9): **English Cinema Haydn,** near my recommended hotels on Mariahilfer Strasse (Mariahilfer Strasse 57, tel. 01/587-2262, www.haydnkino.at); and **Artis International Cinema,** right in the town center a few minutes from the cathedral (Schultergasse 5, tel. 01/535-6570).

***The Third Man* at Burg Kino**—This movie, voted the best British film ever by the British Film Institute, takes place in 1949 Vienna—when it was divided, like Berlin, between the four victorious Allies. With a dramatic Vienna cemetery scene, coffee-house culture surviving amid the rubble, and Orson Welles being chased through the sewers, the tale of a divided city about to fall under Soviet rule and rife with smuggling is an enjoyable two-hour experience while in Vienna (€8, in English with German subtitles; three or four showings weekly: Fri at 22:45, Tue and Sun afternoons depending on other film times; Opernring 19, tel. 01/587-8406, www.burgkino.at).

Sleeping in Vienna

As you move out from the center, hotel prices drop. My listings are in the old center (figure at least €100 for a decent double), along the likeable Mariahilfer Strasse (about €90), and near the Westbahnhof (about €70).

Book ahead for Vienna if you can, particularly for holidays. Business hotels have their highest rates in September and October, when it's peak convention time. Prices are also high right around New Year's Eve.

While few accommodations in Vienna are air-conditioned, you can generally get fans on request. Places with elevators often have a few stairs to climb, too.

These hotels lose big and you pay more if you find a room through Internet booking sites. Book direct by phone, fax, or email and save. For tips on reaching these hotels upon arrival in Vienna, see "Vienna Connections," at the end of this chapter.

Within the Ring, in the Old City Center

You'll pay extra to sleep in the atmospheric old center, but if you can afford it, staying here gives you the best classy Vienna experience.

$$$ Hotel am Stephansplatz is a four-star business hotel with 56 rooms. It's plush but not over-the-top, and reasonably priced for its incredible location—literally facing the cathedral—and sleek comfort. Every detail is modern and quality; breakfast is superb, with a view of the city waking up around the cathedral;

Sleep Code

(€1 = about $1.40, country code: 43, area code: 01)
S = Single, **D** = Double/Twin, **T** = Triple, **Q** = Quad, **b** = bathroom, **s** = shower only. English is spoken at each place. Unless otherwise noted, credit cards are accepted, rooms have no air conditioning, and breakfast is included.

To help you sort easily through these listings, I've divided the rooms into three categories, based on the price for a standard double room with bath:

$$$ Higher Priced—Most rooms €120 or more.
$$ Moderately Priced—Most rooms between €75–120.
$ Lower Priced—Most rooms €75 or less.

and the staff is always ready with a friendly welcome (Sb-€160–180, Db-€210–250, prices vary with season and room size, prices shoot up during conventions—most often in Sept–Oct, €20 less July–Aug and in winter, €15 less Fri–Sun, extra bed-€50, children free or very cheap, air-con, free Internet access, Wi-Fi in lobby, sauna, elevator, Stephansplatz 9, U-1 or U-3: Stephansplatz, tel. 01/534-050, fax 01/5340-5710, www.hotelamstephansplatz.at, office@hotelamstephansplatz.at).

$$$ Hotel Pertschy, circling an old courtyard, is big and hotelesque. Its 56 huge rooms are elegantly creaky, with chandeliers and Baroque touches. Those on the courtyard are quietest (Sb-€95–114, Db-€139–169 depending on room size, €20–30 cheaper off-season, extra bed-€36, non-smoking rooms, free Internet terminal in lobby, free Wi-Fi, elevator, Habsburgergasse 5, U-1 or U-3: Stephansplatz, tel. 01/534-490, fax 01/534-4949, www.pertschy.com/cms/index.html, pertschy@pertschy.com).

$$$ Pension Aviano is another peaceful place, with 17 comfortable rooms on the fourth floor above lots of old-center action (Sb-€104, Db-€148–169 depending on size, roughly €20 cheaper per room in July–Aug and Nov–March, extra bed-€33, non-smoking rooms, fans, elevator, between Neuer Markt and Kärntner Strasse at Marco d'Avianogasse 1, tel. 01/512-8330, fax 01/5128-3306, www.secrethomes.at, aviano@secrethomes.at).

$$$ Hotel Schweizerhof is classy, with 55 big rooms, all the comforts, shiny public spaces, and a formal ambience. It's centrally located midway between St. Stephen's Cathedral and the Danube Canal (Sb-€80–100, Db-€115–150, Tb-€135–175, extra bed-€35, low prices are for July–Aug and slow times, with cash and this book get your best price and then claim a 10 percent discount, free Wi-Fi, elevator, Bauernmarkt 22, U-1 or U-3: Stephansplatz,

Hotels in Central Vienna

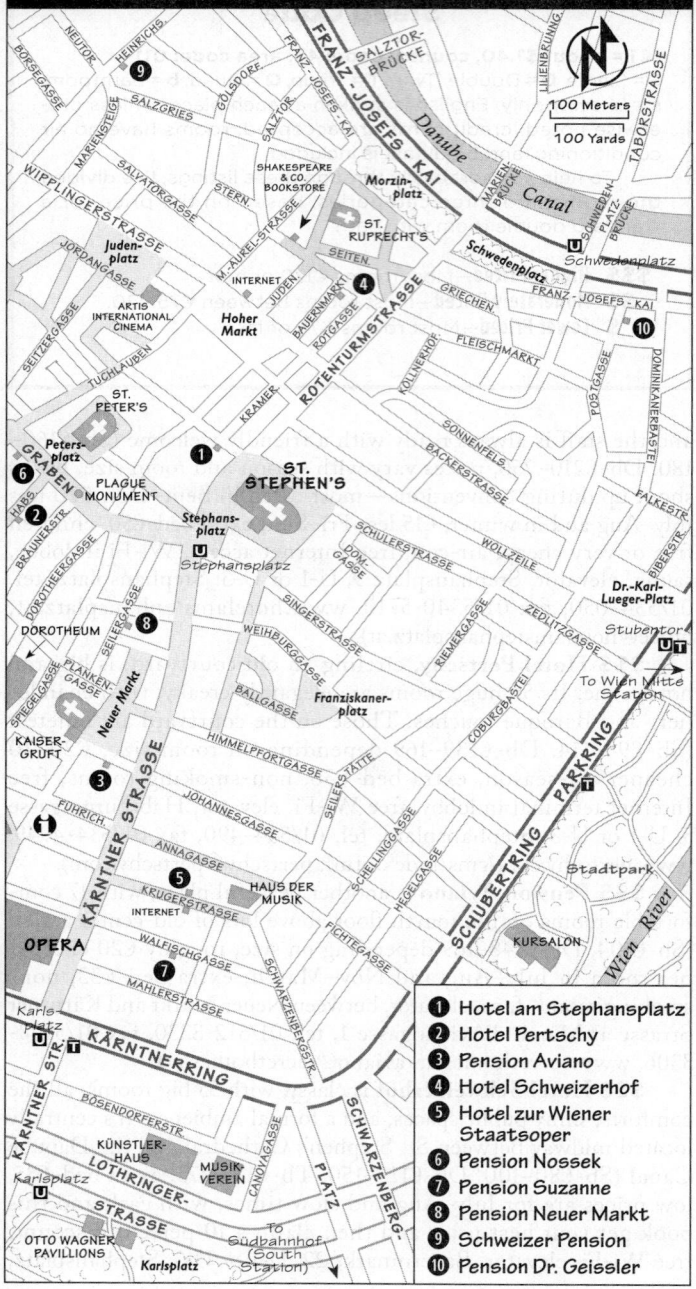

VIENNA

tel. 01/533-1931, fax 01/533-0214, www.schweizerhof.at, office @schweizerhof.at). Since this is in a busy nightclub area, it can be noisy on weekends (Thu–Sat). If you'll be here then, ask for a quiet room when you reserve.

$$$ Hotel zur Wiener Staatsoper, the Schweizerhof's sister hotel, is quiet, with a more traditional elegance. Its 22 tidy rooms come with high ceilings, chandeliers, and fancy carpets on parquet floors (tiny Sb-€80–100, Db-€113–150, Tb-€135–175, extra bed-€25, cheaper prices are for July–Aug and Dec–March, fans on request, elevator, a block from the Opera at Krugerstrasse 11; U-1, U-2, or U-4: Karlsplatz; tel. 01/513-1274, fax 01/513-127-415, www.zurwienerstaatsoper.at, office@zurwienerstaatsoper.at, manager Claudia).

$$ At **Pension Nossek,** an elevator takes you above any street noise into Frau Bernad's and Frau Gundolf's world, where the children seem to be placed among the lace and flowers by an interior designer. With 30 rooms right on the wonderful Graben, this is a particularly good value (S-€52–60, Ss-€62, Sb-€76–80, Db-€120, €30 extra for sprawling suites, extra bed-€35, cash only, elevator, Graben 17, U-1 or U-3: Stephansplatz, tel. 01/5337-0410, fax 01/535-3646, www.pension-nossek.at, reservation@pension-nossek.at).

$$ Pension Suzanne, as Baroque and doily as you'll find in this price range, is wonderfully located a few yards from the Opera. It's small, but run with the class of a bigger hotel. The 25 rooms are packed with properly Viennese antique furnishings and paintings (Sb-€81, Db-€103–124 depending on size, 4 percent discount with this book and cash, extra bed-€25, spacious apartment for up to 6 also available, discounts in winter, fans on request, elevator, free Internet access, free Wi-Fi, Walfischgasse 4; U-1, U-2, or U-4: Karlsplatz and follow signs for Opera exit; tel. 01/513-2507, fax 01/513-2500, www.pension-suzanne.at, info@pension-suzanne.at, manager Michael).

$$ Pension Neuer Markt is family-run, with 37 quiet, comfy rooms in a perfectly central locale. Its hallways have the ambience of a cheap cruise ship (Ss-€60–77, Sb-€90–130, smaller Ds-€80–96, Db-€110–135, prices vary with season and room size, extra bed-€20, request a quiet room when you reserve, fans, fee to use lobby Internet terminal, elevator, Seilergasse 9, tel. 01/512-2316, fax 01/513-9105, www.hotelpension.at/neuermarkt, neuermarkt @hotelpension.at).

$$ Schweizer Pension has been family-owned for three generations. Anita runs an extremely tight ship, offering 11 homey rooms for a great price, with parquet floors and lots of tourist info (S-€42–51, big Sb-€65–78, D-€60–75, Db-€82–93, Tb-€105–119, prices depend on season and room size, cash only, entirely non-smoking, elevator, laundry-€18/load, Heinrichsgasse 2, U-2

or U-4: Schottenring, tel. 01/533-8156, fax 01/535-6469, www.schweizerpension.com, schweizer.pension@chello.at). She also rents a quad with bath (€125–132—too small for 4 adults but great for combos of 2 adults/2 kids or 3 adults/1 kid).

$$ Pension Dr. Geissler has 23 plain-but-comfortable rooms in a modern, nondescript apartment building about 10 blocks northeast of St. Stephen's, near the canal (S-€48, Ss-€68, Sb-€76, D-€65, Ds-€77, Db-€95, 20 percent less in winter, elevator, Postgasse 14, U-1 or U-4: Schwedenplatz—Postgasse is to the left as you face Hotel Capricorno, tel. 01/533-2803, fax 01/533-2635, www.hotelpension.at/dr-geissler, dr.geissler@hotelpension.at).

Hotels and Pensions on and near Mariahilfer Strasse

Lively Mariahilfer Strasse connects the Westbahnhof (West Station) and the city center. The U-3 line, starting at the Westbahnhof, goes down Mariahilfer Strasse to the cathedral. This tourist-friendly, vibrant area is filled with shopping malls, simpler storefronts, and cafés. Its smaller hotels and private rooms are generally run by people from the non-German-speaking part of the former Habsburg Empire (i.e., Eastern Europe). Most hotels are within a few steps of a U-Bahn stop, just one or two stops from the Westbahnhof (direction from the station: Simmering). The nearest place to do laundry is **Schnell & Sauber Waschcenter** (wash-€4.50 for small load or €9 for large load, plus a few euros to dry, daily 6:00–23:00, a few blocks north of Westbahnhof on the east side of Urban-Loritz-Platz).

$$$ NH Hotels, a Spanish chain, runs two stern, stylish-but-passionless business hotels a few blocks apart on Mariahilfer Strasse. Both rent ideal-for-families suites, each with a living room, two TVs, bathroom, desk, and kitchenette (rack rate: Db suite-€118–237, going rate usually closer to €130, plus €16 per person for optional breakfast, apartments for 2–3 adults, 1 kid under 12 free, non-smoking rooms, elevator, free Internet access, pay Wi-Fi). The 78-room **NH Atterseehaus** is at Mariahilfer Strasse 78 (U-3: Zieglergasse, tel. 01/524-5600, fax 01/524-560-015, nhattersee haus@nh-hotels.com), and the slightly pricier **NH Wien** has 106 rooms at Mariahilfer Strasse 32 (usually around Db-€145, U-3: Neubaugasse—follow *Stiftgasse* signs to exit and turn left from top of escalator; from Mariahilferstrasse, enter through shop passageway between Nordsee and Edusco—or from Lindengasse 9, tel. 01/521-720, fax 01/521-7215, nhwien@nh-hotels.com). The website for both is www.nh-hotels.com.

$$ Hotel Pension Corvinus is bright, modern, and proudly and warmly run by a Hungarian family: Miklós, Judit, Anthony,

and Zoltan. Its 12 comfortable rooms are spacious, and some are downright sumptuous (Sb-€59–69, Db-€95–105, Tb-€109–119, get these special Rick Steves prices with this book, extra bed-€26, also has apartments with kitchens, most rooms non-smoking, air-con, elevator, free Internet access and Wi-Fi, parking garage-€15/day with this book, on the third floor at Mariahilfer Strasse 57–59, U-3: Neubaugasse, tel. 01/587-7239, fax 01/587-723-920, www.corvinus.at, hotel@corvinus.at).

$$ Hotel Pension Mariahilf's 12 rooms are clean, well-priced, and good-sized (if outmoded), with a slight Art Deco flair. Book direct and ask for a Rick Steves discount (Sb-€60–75, twin Db-€78–98, Db-€88–115, Tb-€110–138, 5- to 6-person apartment with kitchen-€115–160, lower prices are for off-season or longer stays, elevator, free Wi-Fi, parking-€15, Mariahilfer Strasse 49, U-3: Neubaugasse, tel. 01/586-1781, fax 01/586-178-122, www.mariahilf-hotel.at, office@mariahilf-hotel.at).

$$ K&T Boardinghouse rents spacious, comfortable, good-value rooms at both of its two locations. The first has three bright and airy rooms three flights above lively Mariahilfer Strasse (no elevator). The second location, just across the street, has five newly-furnished units on the first floor (Db-€79, Tb-€99, Qb-€119, 2-night minimum, no breakfast, air-con-€10/day, cash only but reserve with credit card, non-smoking, free Internet access and Wi-Fi, coffee in rooms, first location: Mariahilfer Strasse 72, second location: Chwallagasse 2; for either, get off at U-3: Neubaugasse; tel. 01/523-2989, mobile 0676-553-6063, fax 01/522-0345, www.ktboardinghouse.at, k.t@chello.at, Tina). To reach the Chwallagasse location from Mariahilfer Strasse, turn left at Café Ritter and walk down Schadekgasse one short block; tiny Chwallagasse is the first right.

$$ Haydn Hotel is big and formal, with masculine public spaces and 50 spacious rooms (Sb-€80–90, Db-€110–120, suites and family apartments, extra bed-€30, ask for 10 percent Rick Steves discount, all rooms non-smoking, air-con, elevator, free Internet access, pay Wi-Fi, parking-€15/day, Mariahilfer Strasse 57–59, U-3: Neubaugasse, tel. 01/5874-4140, fax 01/586-1950, www.haydn-hotel.at, info@haydn-hotel.at, Nouri).

$$ Hotel Kugel is run with pride and attitude. "Simple quality and good value" is the motto of the hands-on owner, Johannes Roller. It's a big 34-room hotel with simple Old World charm, offering a fine value (Db-€85, supreme Db with canopy beds-€105–115, cash only, completely non-smoking, Siebensterngasse 43, at corner with Neubaugasse, U-3: Neubaugasse, tel. 01/523-3355, fax 01/5233-3555, www.hotelkugel.at, office@hotelkugel.at). Herr Roller also offers several cheaper basic rooms for backpackers.

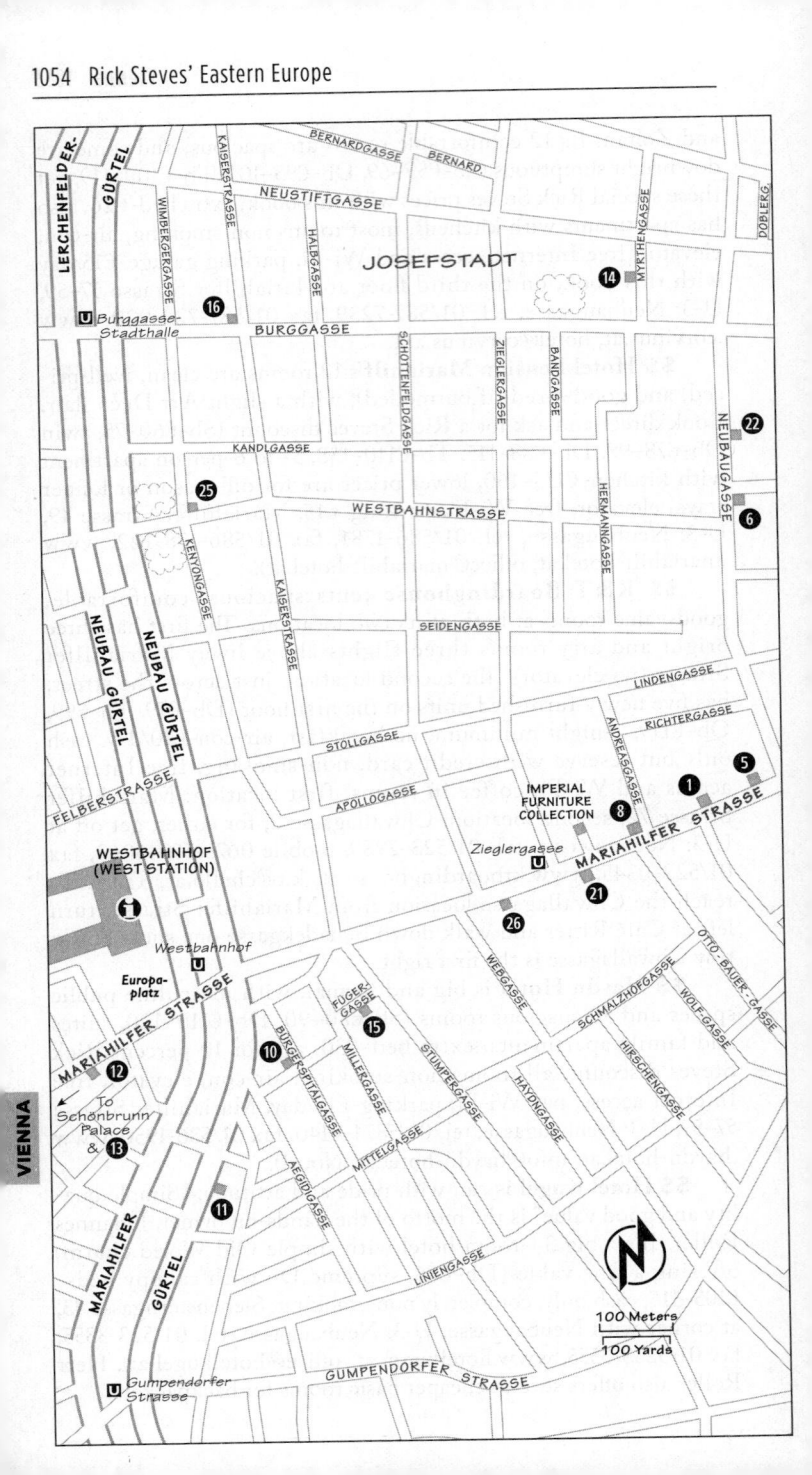
LERCHENFELDER-GÜRTEL
WIMBERGERGASSE
KAISERSTRASSE
BERNARDGASSE
BERNARD.
NEUSTIFTGASSE
HALBGASSE
JOSEFSTADT
MYRTHENGASSE
DOBLERG.
Burggasse-Stadthalle
BURGGASSE
SCHOTTENFELDGASSE
ZIEGLERGASSE
BANDGASSE
NEUBAUGASSE
KANDLGASSE
WESTBAHNSTRASSE
HERMANNGASSE
KENYONGASSE
KAISERSTRASSE
SEIDENGASSE
NEUBAU GÜRTEL
NEUBAU GÜRTEL
LINDENGASSE
RICHTERGASSE
STOLLGASSE
ANDREASGASSE
FELBERSTRASSE
APOLLOGASSE
IMPERIAL FURNITURE COLLECTION
MARIAHILFER STRASSE
Zieglergasse
WESTBAHNHOF (WEST STATION)
Westbahnhof
Europa-platz
WEBGASSE
OTTO-BAUER-GASSE
SCHMALZHOFGASSE
WOLF-GASSE
FUGERI-GASSE
MARIAHILFER STRASSE
BÜRGERSPITALGASSE
MILLERGASSE
STUMPERGASSE
HAYDNGASSE
HIRSCHENGASSE
To Schönbrunn Palace &
MITTELGASSE
AEGIDIGASSE
LINIENGASSE
MARIAHILFER GÜRTEL
100 Meters
100 Yards
Gumpendorfer Strasse
GUMPENDORFER STRASSE

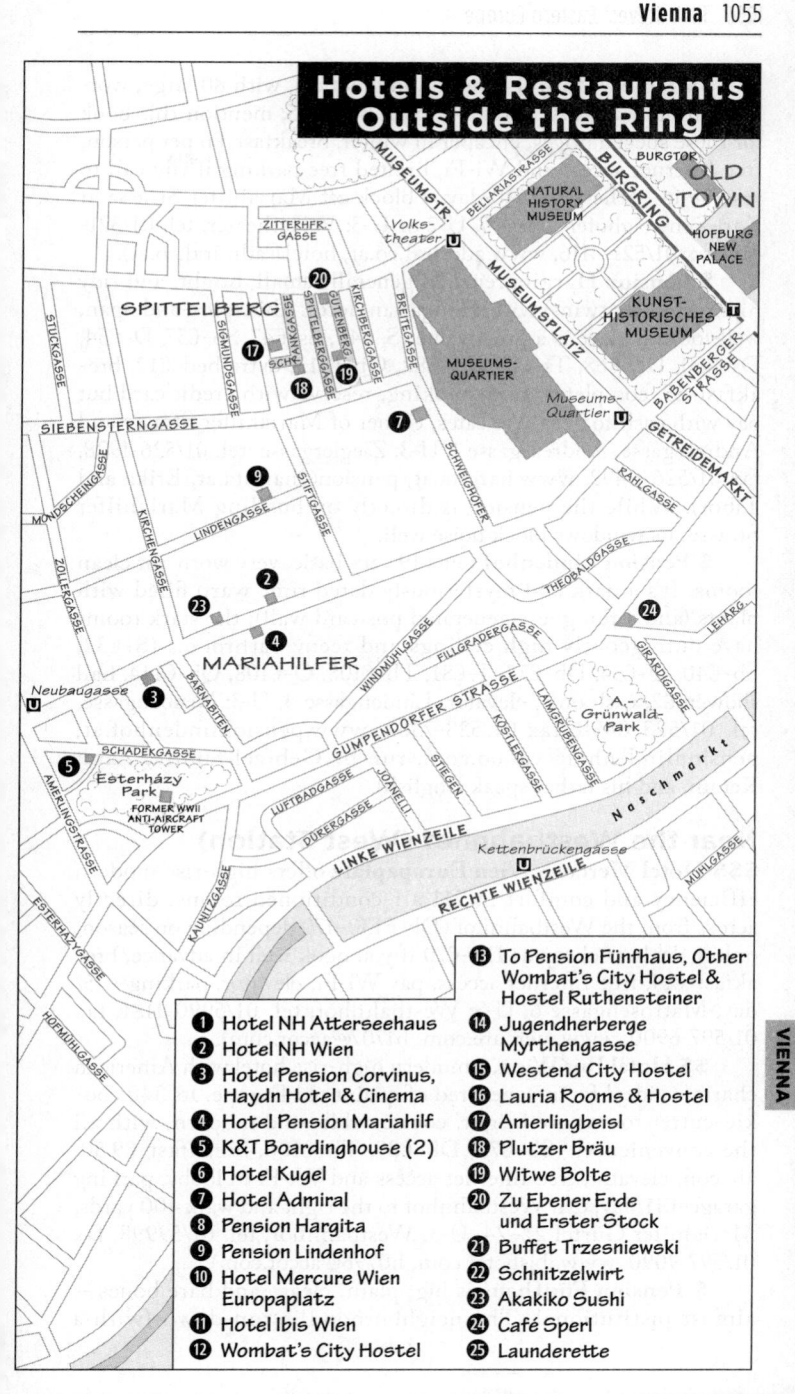
Hotels & Restaurants Outside the Ring
MUSEUMSTR.
BELLARIASTRASSE
BURGRING
BURGTOR
OLD TOWN
NATURAL HISTORY MUSEUM
HOFBURG NEW PALACE
ZITTERHFR.-GASSE
Volks-theater
MUSEUMSPLATZ
KUNST-HISTORISCHES MUSEUM
SPITTELBERG
STUCKGASSE
SIGMUNDSGASSE
FRANKGASSE
SPITTELBERGGASSE
GUTENBERGGASSE
KIRCHBERGGASSE
BREITEGASSE
MUSEUMS-QUARTIER
Museums-Quartier
BABENBERGER-STRASSE
SIEBENSTERNGASSE
GETREIDEMARKT
SCHNEIGHOFER
RAHLGASSE
MONDSCHEINGASSE
KIRCHENGASSE
LINDENGASSE
STIFTGASSE
THEOBALDGASSE
ZOLLERGASSE
LEHARG.
WINDMÜHLGASSE
FILLGRADERGASSE
MARIAHILFER
Neubaugasse
BARNABITEN
GIRARDIGASSE
GÜMPENDORFER STRASSE
LAIMGRUBENGASSE
A.-Grünwald-Park
SCHADEKGASSE
KÖSTLERGASSE
Esterházy Park
FORMER WWII ANTI-AIRCRAFT TOWER
LUFTBADGASSE
JOANELLI
STIEGEN
Naschmarkt
AMERLINGSTRASSE
DÜRERGASSE
LINKE WIENZEILE
Kettenbrückengasse
RECHTE WIENZEILE
MÜHLGASSE
KAUNITZGASSE
ESTERHÁZYGASSE
HÖFMÜHLGASSE
1 Hotel NH Atterseehaus
2 Hotel NH Wien
3 Hotel Pension Corvinus, Haydn Hotel & Cinema
4 Hotel Pension Mariahilf
5 K&T Boardinghouse (2)
6 Hotel Kugel
7 Hotel Admiral
8 Pension Hargita
9 Pension Lindenhof
10 Hotel Mercure Wien Europaplatz
11 Hotel Ibis Wien
12 Wombat's City Hostel
13 To Pension Fünfhaus, Other Wombat's City Hostel & Hostel Ruthensteiner
14 Jugendherberge Myrthengasse
15 Westend City Hostel
16 Lauria Rooms & Hostel
17 Amerlingbeisl
18 Plutzer Bräu
19 Witwe Bolte
20 Zu Ebener Erde und Erster Stock
21 Buffet Trzesniewski
22 Schnitzelwirt
23 Akakiko Sushi
24 Café Sperl
25 Launderette

$$ Hotel Admiral is huge and practical, with 80 large, workable rooms (Sb-€70, Db-€94, extra bed-€25, mention this book for these special prices, cheaper in winter, breakfast-€6 per person, free Internet access and Wi-Fi, limited free parking if you call to reserve it—otherwise €10/day, a block off Mariahilfer Strasse at Karl-Schweighofer-Gasse 7, U-2 or U-3: Volkstheater, tel. 01/521-410, fax 01/521-4116, www.admiral.co.at, hotel@admiral.co.at).

$ Pension Hargita rents 24 generally small, bright, and tidy rooms (mostly twins) with Hungarian decor. This spick-and-span, well-located place is a great value (S-€40, Ss-€47, Sb-€57, D-€54, Ds-€60, Db-€68, Ts-€75, Tb-€82, Qb-€112, extra bed-€12, breakfast-€5, completely non-smoking, reserve with credit card but pay with cash to get these rates, corner of Mariahilfer Strasse and Andreasgasse, Andreasgasse 1, U-3: Zieglergasse, tel. 01/526-1928, fax 01/526-0492, www.hargita.at, pension@hargita.at, Erika and Tibor). While the pension is directly on bustling Mariahilfer Strasse, its windows block noise well.

$ Pension Lindenhof rents 19 very basic, very worn but clean rooms. It's a dark and mysteriously dated time warp filled with plants (and a fun guest-generated postcard wall); the stark rooms have outrageously high ceilings and teeny bathrooms (S-€32, Sb-€40, D-€54, Db-€72, T-€81, Tb-€108, Q-€108, Qb-€144, hall shower-€2, cash only, elevator, Lindengasse 4, U-3: Neubaugasse, tel. 01/523-0498, fax 01/523-7362, www.pensionlindenhof.at, pensionlindenhof@yahoo.com, run by Gebrael family; Zara, Keram, and his father speak English).

Near the Westbahnhof (West Station)

$$$ Hotel Mercure Wien Europaplatz offers high-rise modern efficiency and comfort in 211 air-conditioned rooms, directly across from the Westbahnhof (Db-€130–170 depending on season, online deals as cheap as Db-€70 if you book well in advance, breakfast-€14, free Internet access, pay Wi-Fi, elevator, parking-€15/day, Matrosengasse 6, U-3: Westbahnhof, tel. 01/5990-1181, fax 01/597-6900, www.mercure.com, h1707@accor.com).

$$ Hotel Ibis Wien, a modern high-rise hotel with American charm, is ideal for anyone tired of quaint old Europe. Its 340 cookie-cutter rooms are bright, comfortable, and modern, with all the conveniences (Sb-€72, Db-€89, Tb-€106, breakfast-€9.50, air-con, elevator, free Internet access and Wi-Fi in lobby, parking garage-€11/day; exit Westbahnhof to the right and walk 400 yards, Mariahilfer Gürtel 22–24, U-3: Westbahnhof; tel. 01/59998, fax 01/597-9090, www.ibishotel.com, h0796@accor.com).

$ Pension Fünfhaus is big, plain, clean, and bare bones—almost institutional. The neighborhood is run-down (with a

few ladies loitering late at night) and the floors are tile, but this 47-room pension offers the best doubles you'll find for about €50 (S-€37, Sb-€45, D-€50–53, Db-€60–63, T-€73–79, Tb-€88–94, 4-person apartment-€100–110, cash only, closed mid-Nov–Feb, Sperrgasse 12, U-3: Westbahnhof, tel. 01/892-3545 or 01/892-0286, fax 01/892-0460, www.pension5haus.at, pension5haus@tiscali.at, Frau Susi Tersch). Half the rooms are in the main building and half are in the annex, which has good rooms but is near the train tracks and a bit scary on the street at night. From the station, ride tram #52 or #58 two stops down Mariahilfer Strasse away from center, and ask for Sperrgasse. Crazy Chicken bike rental, listed on page 989, is just a block farther down Sperrgasse.

Cheap Dorms and Hostels near Mariahilfer Strasse

$ Jugendherberge Myrthengasse is your classic huge and efficient youth hostel, with 260 beds (€17–21 per person in 2- to 6-bed rooms, includes sheets and breakfast, non-members pay €3.50 extra, pay Internet access, free Wi-Fi, always open, no curfew, lockers and lots of facilities, Myrthengasse 7, tel. 01/523-6316, fax 01/523-5849, hostel@chello.at).

$ Westend City Hostel, just a block from the Westbahnhof and Mariahilfer Strasse, is well-run and well-located, with 180 beds in 4- to 12-bed dorms (€21–25 per person, depending on how many in the room, D-€62–68, €4 cheaper Nov–mid-March—except around New Year's, includes sheets, breakfast, and locker; cash only, pay Internet access, free Wi-Fi, laundry-€7, Fügergasse 3, tel. 01/597-6729, fax 01/597-672-927, www.westendhostel.at, info@westendhostel.at).

$ Lauria Rooms and Hostel is a creative little place run by friendly Gosha, with two 10-bed coed dorms with lockers for travelers ages 17 to 30 (€16/bed), plus several other rooms sleeping two to four each (any age, €22–25/bed, Ds-€62, Ts-€78, Qs-€96; Kaiserstrasse 77, tram #5 or a 10-min walk from Westbahnhof, tel. 01/522-2555, www.lauria-vienna.at, lauria_vienna@hotmail.com).

$ ***More Hostels:*** Other hostels with €17–19 beds and €50 doubles near Mariahilfer Strasse are **Wombat's City Hostel** (2 locations: one near tracks behind the station at Grangasse 6, another even closer to station at Mariahilfer Strasse 137, tel. 01/897-2336, www.wombats-hostels.com, office@wombats-vienna.at) and **Hostel Ruthensteiner** (smoke-free; leave the Westbahnhof to the right and follow Mariahilfer Strasse behind the station, then left on Haidmannsgasse for a block, then turn right and find Robert-Hamerling-Gasse 24; tel. 01/893-4202, www.hostelruthensteiner.com, info@hostelruthensteiner.com).

Eating in Vienna

The Viennese appreciate the fine points of life, and right up there with waltzing is eating. The city has many atmospheric restaurants. As you ponder the Eastern European specialties on menus, remember that while Vienna's diverse empire may be no more, its flavor still lingers.

While cuisines are routinely named for countries, Vienna claims to be the only *city* with a cuisine of its own: Viennese soups come with fillings (semolina dumpling, liver dumpling, or pancake slices). *Gulasch* is a beef ragout of Hungarian origin (spiced with onion and paprika). Of course, Wiener schnitzel is traditionally a breaded and fried veal cutlet (though pork is more common these days). Another meat specialty is boiled beef *(Tafelspitz).* While you're sure to have *Apfelstrudel,* try the sweet cheese strudel, too (*Topfenstrudel*—wafer-thin strudel pastry filled with sweet cheese and raisins).

On nearly every corner, you can find a colorful *Beisl* (BYE-zul). These uniquely Viennese taverns are a characteristic cross between an English pub and a French brasserie—filled with poetry teachers and their students, couples loving without touching, housewives on their way home from cello lessons, and waiters who enjoy serving hearty food and drinks at an affordable price. Ask at your hotel for a good *Beisl.*

Two other don't-miss Viennese institutions, its cafés and wine gardens, are covered under "Experiences in Vienna," earlier.

Near St. Stephen's Cathedral

Each of these eateries is within about a five-minute walk of the cathedral.

Gigerl Stadtheuriger offers a friendly near-*Heuriger* wine cellar experience (à la Grinzing—see "*Wein* in Wien," page 1044), often with accordion or live music, without leaving the city center. Just point to what looks good. Food is sold by the weight; 100 grams *(10 dag)* is about a quarter-pound (cheese and cold meats cost about €3 per 100 grams, salads are about €2 per 100 grams; price sheet is posted on the wall to right of buffet line). The *Karree* pork with herbs is particularly tasty and tender. They also have menu entrées, spinach strudel, quiche, *Apfelstrudel,* and, of course, casks of new and local wines (sold by the *Achtel*—eighth-liter glass). Meals run €7–12 (daily 15:00–24:00, indoor/outdoor seating, behind cathedral, a block off Kärntner Strasse, a few cobbles off Rauhensteingasse on Blumenstock, tel. 01/513-4431).

Zu den Drei Hacken, another fun and typical wine cellar, is famous for its local specialties (€10 plates, Mon–Sat 11:00–23:00, closed Sun, indoor/outdoor seating, Singerstrasse 28, tel. 01/512-

Wieners in Wien

For hardcore Viennese cuisine on a budget, drop by a *Würstelstand*. The local hot-dog stand is a fixture on city squares throughout the old center, serving a variety of hot dogs and pickled side dishes with a warm corner-meeting-place atmosphere. You'll find particularly good stands on Hoher Markt, the Graben, and in front of the Albertina Museum.

The *Wiener* we know is named for Vienna, but the guy who invented the weenie studied in Frankfurt. Out of nostalgia for his school years, he named his fun fast food for that city...a Frankfurter. Only in Vienna are *Wieners* called *Frankfurters*. (Got that?)

The many varieties of hot dogs cost €2–3 each. Explore the fun menus. Be adventurous: Generally, the darker the weenie, the spicier it is. Key words: *Weisswurst*—boiled white sausage; *Bosna*—with onions and curry; *Käsekrainer*—with melted cheese inside; *Debreziner*—spicy Hungarian; *Frankfurter*—our weenie; *frische*—fresh; *Kren*—horseradish; and *Senf*—mustard (ask for *süss*—sweet; or *scharf*—sharp). Note: Only a tourist puts the sausage in a bun like a hot dog. Munch alternately between the meat and the bread ("that's why you have two hands"), and you'll look like a native.

5895). A third recommended *Stadtheuriger*, the Melker Stiftskeller, sits between Am Hof square and the Ring (listed later in this section).

Buffet Trzesniewski is an institution—justly famous for its elegant and cheap finger sandwiches and small beers (€1 each). Three different sandwiches and a *kleines Bier (Pfiff)* make a fun, light lunch. Point to whichever delights look tasty (or grab the English translation sheet and take time to study your 22 sandwich options). The classic favorites are *Geflügelleber* (chicken liver), *Matjes mit Zwiebel* (herring with onions), and *Speck mit Ei* (bacon and eggs). Pay for your sandwiches and a drink. Take your drink tokens to the lady on the right. Sit on the bench and scoot over to a tiny table when a spot opens up. Trzesniewski has been a Vienna favorite for a century...and many of its regulars seem to have been here for the grand opening (Mon–Fri 8:30–19:30, Sat 9:00–17:00, closed Sun; 50 yards off the Graben, nearly across from brooding Café Hawelka, Dorotheergasse 2; tel. 01/512-3291). In the fall, this is a good opportunity to try the fancy grape juices—*Most* or *Traubenmost*. Their other location, at Mariahilfer Strasse 95, serves the same sandwiches with the same menu in the same ambience, and is near many recommended hotels (Mon–Fri 8:30–19:00, Sat 9:00–18:00, closed Sun).

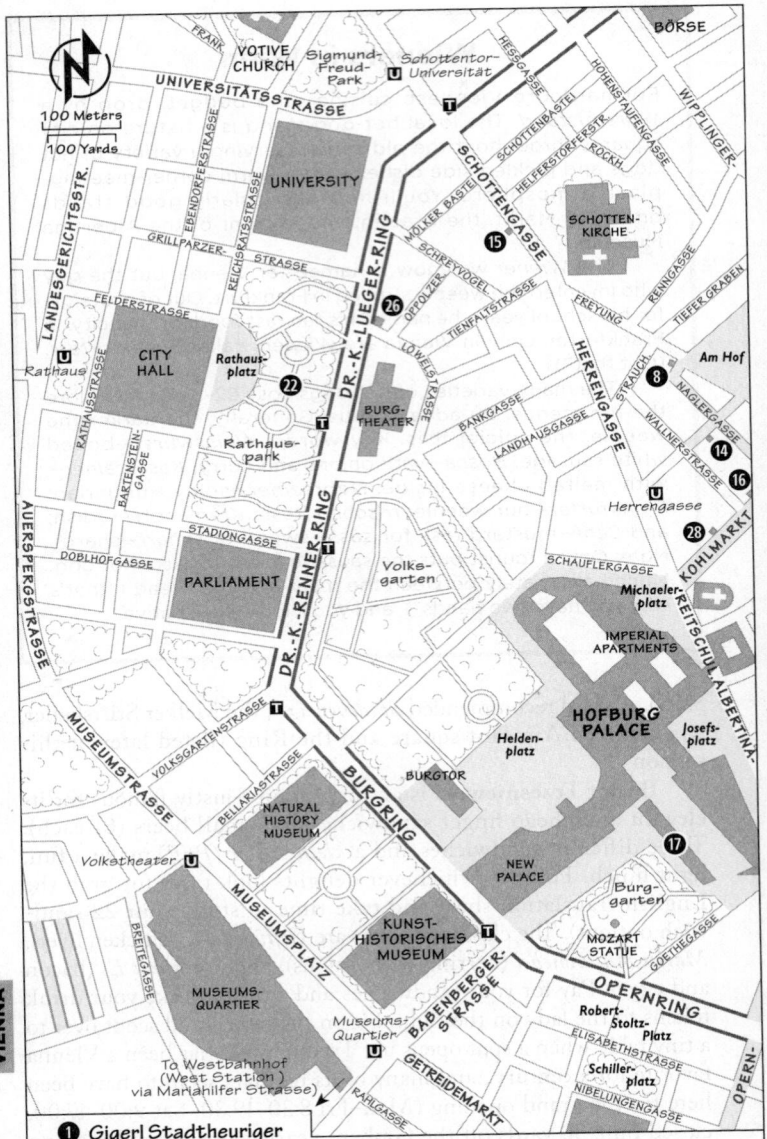

1. Gigerl Stadtheuriger
2. Zu den Drei Hacken
3. Buffet Trzesniewski
4. Reinthaler's Beisl & Café Hawelka
5. Plachutta Restaurant
6. Cantinetta La Norma
7. Gyros
8. Akakiko Sushi (3)
9. Zanoni & Zanoni Gelateria
10. Zum Schwarzen Kameel
11. Restaurant Ofenloch
12. Brezel-Gwölb
13. Beisl zum Scherer
14. Esterhazykeller

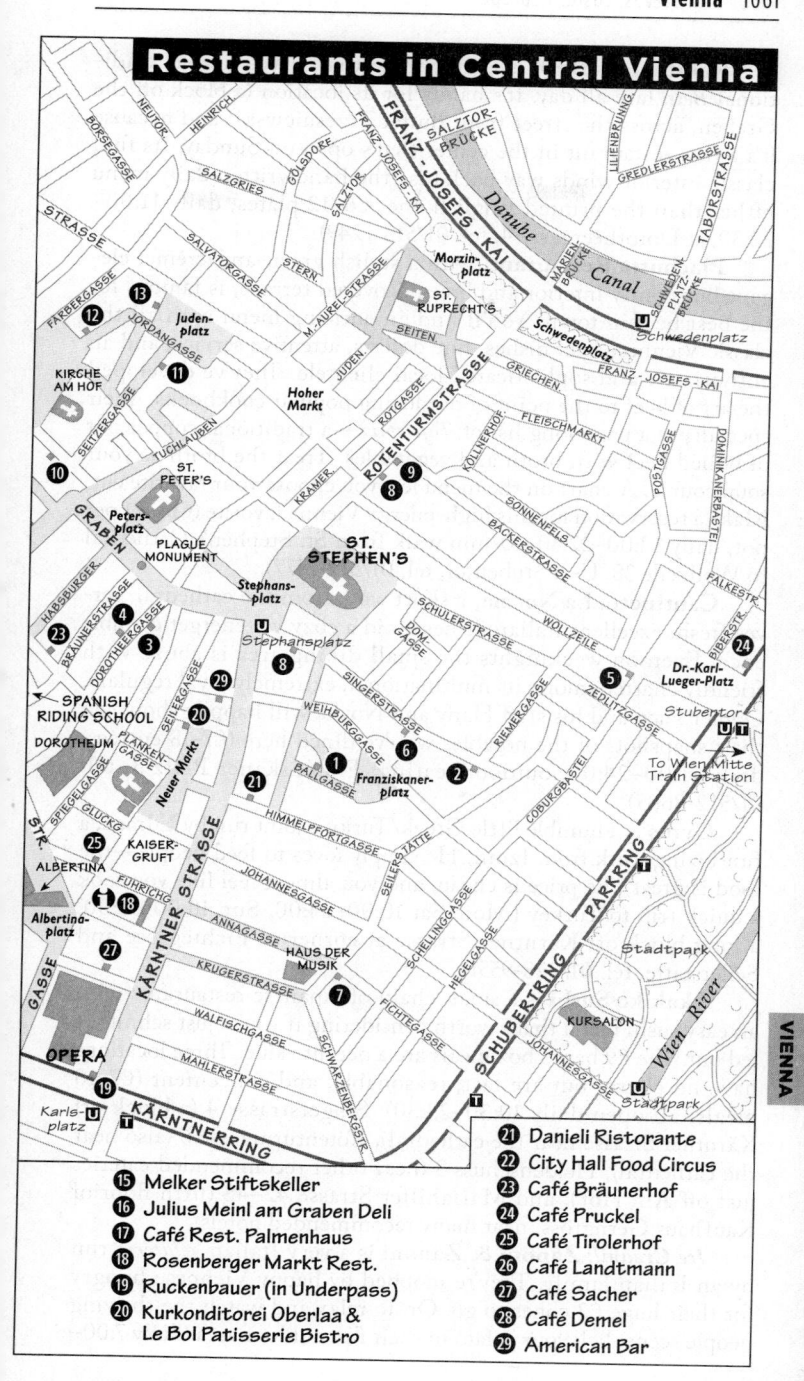
Restaurants in Central Vienna
FRANZ-JOSEFS-KAI
SALZTOR-BRÜCKE
Danube
Canal
LILIENBRUNNGG.
GREDLERSTRASSE
TABORSTRASSE
MARIEN-BRÜCKE
SCHWEDEN-PLATZ-BRÜCKE
Schwedenplatz
Morzin-platz
ST. RUPRECHT'S
NEUTOR
HEINRICH
BORSGASSE
SALZGRIES
GÖLSDORF
SALZTOR
STRASSE
SALVATORGASSE
STERN
M.-AUREL-STRASSE
SEITEN
FARBERGASSE
JORDANGASSE
Juden-platz
KIRCHE AM HOF
SEILERGASSE
JUDEN
Hoher Markt
ROTGASSE
GRIECHEN
FRANZ-JOSEFS-KAI
FLEISCHMARKT
KOLLNERHOF
TUCHLAUBEN
ST. PETER'S
KRAMER
ROTENTURMSTRASSE
POSTGASSE
DOMINIKANERBASTEI
GRABEN
Peters-platz
PLAGUE MONUMENT
ST. STEPHEN'S
SONNENFELS
BÄCKERSTRASSE
HABSBURGER
BRÄUNERSTRASSE
DOROTHEERGASSE
Stephans-platz
Stephansplatz
SCHULERSTRASSE
DOM-GASSE
WOLLZEILE
FALKESTR.
BIBERSTR.
Dr.-Karl-Lueger-Platz
SPANISH RIDING SCHOOL
SEILERGASSE
SINGERSTRASSE
WEIHBURGGASSE
ZEDLITZGASSE
RIEMERGASSE
Stubentor
DOROTHEUM
PLANKENGASSE
Neuer Markt
BÄLLGASSE
Franziskaner-platz
To Wien Mitte Train Station
SPIEGELGASSE
GLUCKG.
HIMMELPFORTGASSE
COBURGBASTEI
KAISER-GRUFT
ALBERTINA
SEILERSTÄTTE
FUHRICHG.
JOHANNESGASSE
PARKRING
Albertina-platz
ANNAGASSE
SCHELLINGGASSE
HEGELGASSE
Stadtpark
KÄRNTNER STRASSE
HAUS DER MUSIK
KRUGERSTRASSE
GASSE
WALFISCHGASSE
FICHTEGASSE
SCHUBERTRING
KURSALON
Wien River
OPERA
MAHLERSTRASSE
SCHWARZENBERGSTR.
JOHANNESGASSE
Stadtpark
Karls-platz
KÄRNTNERRING
VIENNA
15 Melker Stiftskeller
16 Julius Meinl am Graben Deli
17 Café Rest. Palmenhaus
18 Rosenberger Markt Rest.
19 Ruckenbauer (in Underpass)
20 Kurkonditorei Oberlaa & Le Bol Patisserie Bistro
21 Danieli Ristorante
22 City Hall Food Circus
23 Café Bräunerhof
24 Café Pruckel
25 Café Tirolerhof
26 Café Landtmann
27 Café Sacher
28 Café Demel
29 American Bar

Reinthaler's Beisl is a time warp that serves simple, traditional *Beisl* fare all day. It's handy for its location (a block off the Graben, across the street from Buffet Trzesniewski) and because it's a rare restaurant in the center that's open on Sunday. Its fun, classic interior winds way back (use the handwritten daily menu rather than the printed English one, €6–12 plates, daily 11:00–22:30, at Dorotheergasse 4, tel. 01/513-1249).

Plachutta Restaurant, with a stylish green-and-crème, elegant-but-comfy interior and breezy covered terrace, is famous for the best beef in town. You'll find an enticing menu with all the classic Viennese beef dishes, fine deserts, attentive service, and an enthusiastic and sophisticated local clientele. They've developed the art of beef to the point of producing popular cookbooks. Their specialty is a page-long list of *Tafelspitz*—a traditional copper pot of boiled beef with broth and vegetables. Treat the broth as your soup course. A chart on the menu lets you choose your favorite cut. Make a reservation for this high-energy Vienna favorite (€16–21 per pot, daily 12:00–22:30, 10-min walk from St. Stephen's Cathedral to Wollzeile 38, U-3: Stubentor, tel. 01/512-1577).

Cantinetta La Norma, a short walk from the cathedral, serves fresh, excellent Italian dishes amid a cozy yet energetic ambience. Even on weeknights the small dining area is abuzz with friendly chatter among its multinational, extremely loyal regulars. Owner Paco and his staff Hany and Novka will happily show you their snapshots of the notables who've dined here (€7–18 entrées, daily 11:00–24:00, outdoor seating, Franziskaner Platz 3, tel. 01/512-8665).

Gyros is a humble little Greek/Turkish joint run by Yilmaz, a fun-loving Turk from Izmir. He simply loves to feed people—the food is great, the price is cheap, and you almost feel like you took a quick trip to Turkey (Mon–Sat 10:00–24:00, Sun 10:00–18:00, a long block off Kärntner Strasse at corner of Fichtegasse and Seilerstätte, tel. 01/228-9551).

Akakiko Sushi is a small chain of Japanese restaurants with an easy sushi menu that's worth considering if you're just schnitzeled out. The €9 bento box meals are a decent value. Three locations have no charm but are fast, reasonable, and convenient (€7–10 meals, all open daily 10:30–23:30): Singerstrasse 4 (a block off Kärntner Strasse near the cathedral), Rotenturmgasse 6 (also near the cathedral), Heidenschuss 3 (near other recommended eateries just off Am Hof), and Mariahilfer Strasse 42–48 (fifth floor of Kaufhaus Gerngross, near many recommended hotels).

***Ice Cream!:* Zanoni & Zanoni** is a very Italian *gelateria* run by an Italian family. They're mobbed by happy Viennese hungry for their huge €2 cones to go. Or, to relax and watch the thriving people scene, lick your gelato in their fun outdoor area (daily 7:00–

24:00, 2 blocks up Rotenturmstrasse from cathedral at Lugeck 7, tel. 01/512-7979).

Near Am Hof Square

The square called Am Hof (U-3: Herrengasse) is surrounded by a maze of atmospheric medieval lanes; the following eateries are all within a block of the square.

Zum Schwarzen Kameel ("The Black Camel") is popular for its two classy but very different scenes: a tiny, elegant restaurant and a trendy wine bar. The small, dark-wood, 12-table, Art Nouveau restaurant serves fine gourmet Viennese cuisine (three-course dinner-€60–75 plus pricey wine). The wine bar is filled with a professional local crowd enjoying small plates from the same kitchen at a better price. This is *the* place for horseradish and thin-sliced ham (*Beinschinken mit Kren,* €7 a plate, *Achtung*—the horseradish is *hot*). I'd order the *Vorspeisenteller* (a great antipasti dish that comes with ham and horseradish) and their *Tafelspitz* (€16). Stand, grab a stool, or sit anywhere you can—it's customary to share tables in the wine-bar section. Fine Austrian wines are listed on the board; Aussie bartender Karl can help you choose. They also have a buffet of tiny €1–2 sandwiches (daily 8:30–24:00, Bognergasse 5, tel. 01/533-8125).

Restaurant Ofenloch serves good, old-fashioned Viennese cuisine with friendly service, both indoors and out. This 300-year-old eatery, with great traditional ambience, is dressy (with white tablecloths) but intimate and woodsy. It's central but not overrun with tourists (€13–19 main dishes, Mon–Sat 11:00–22:30, closed Sun, Kurrentgasse 8, tel. 01/533-8844).

Brezel-Gwölb, a Tolkienesque wine cellar with outdoor dining on a quiet square, serves delicious light meals, fine *Krautsuppe* (cabbage soup), and old-fashioned Viennese dishes. It's ideal for a romantic late-night glass of wine (daily 11:30–23:30; leave Am Hof on Drahtgasse, then take first left to Ledererhof 9; tel. 01/533-8811).

Beisl zum Scherer, around the corner, is untouristy and serves traditional plates for €10–15. Sitting outside, you'll face a stern Holocaust memorial. Inside comes with a soothing woody atmosphere and intriguing decor (Mon–Sat 11:30–22:00, closed Sun, Judenplatz 7, tel. 01/533-5164).

Esterhazykeller, both ancient and popular, has traditional fare deep underground. For a cheap and sloppy buffet, climb down to the lowest cellar. For table service on a pleasant square, sit outside (Mon–Sat 11:00–23:00, Sun 16:00–23:00, may close for lunch in Aug–Sept and/or in bad weather, just below Am Hof at Haarhof 1, tel. 01/533-3482).

Melker Stiftskeller is an untouristy *Stadtheuriger* in a deep

and rustic circa-1626 cellar with hearty, inexpensive meals and new wine (Tue–Sat 17:00–24:00, closed Sun–Mon and mid-July–mid-Aug, between Am Hof and Schottentor U-Bahn stop at Schottengasse 3, tel. 01/533-5530).

Julius Meinl am Graben, a posh supermarket right on the Graben, has been famous since 1862 as a top-end delicatessen with all the gourmet fancies. Along with the picnic fixings on the shelves, there's a café with light meals and great outdoor seating, a stuffy and pricey restaurant upstairs, and a take-away counter (shop open Mon–Fri 8:00–19:30, Sat 9:00–18:00, closed Sun; restaurant open Mon–Sat until 24:00, closed Sun; Am Graben 19, tel. 01/532-3334).

Near the Opera

Café Restaurant Palmenhaus overlooks the Burggarten (Palace Garden, described earlier, under "Sights in Vienna"). Tucked away in a green and peaceful corner two blocks behind the Opera in the Hofburg's back yard, this is a world apart. If you want to eat modern Austrian cuisine surrounded by palm trees rather than tourists, this is it. And, since it's at the edge of a huge park, it's great for families. Their fresh fish with generous vegetables specials are on the board (€8.50 two-course lunches available Mon–Fri, €15–18 entrées, open daily 10:00–24:00, serious vegetarian dishes, fish, extensive wine list, indoors in greenhouse or outdoors, tel. 01/533-1033).

Rosenberger Markt Restaurant is mobbed with tour groups. Still, if you don't mind a freeway-cafeteria ambience in the center of the German-speaking world's classiest city, this self-service eatery is fast and easy. It's just a block toward the cathedral from the Opera. The best cheap meal here is a small salad or veggie plate stacked high (daily 10:30–23:00, lots of fruits, veggies, fresh-squeezed juices, addictive banana milk, ride the glass elevator downstairs, Maysedergasse 2, tel. 01/512-3458).

Ruckenbauer, a favorite for a quick bite, is a fast-food kiosk in a transit underpass under the street in front of the Opera, between the entryways marked *U2/U4* and *U1* (Mon–Fri 6:00–20:00, Sat–Sun 9:00–20:00). Their €1.60 *Tramezzini* sandwiches and fine pastries make a classy, quick picnic lunch or dinner before the Opera, just 100 yards away.

Kurkonditorei Oberlaa may not have the royal and plush fame of Demel, but this is where Viennese connoisseurs serious about the quality of their pastries go to get fat. With outdoor seating on Neuer Markt, it's particularly nice on a hot summer day (€10 daily three-course lunches, great selection of cakes, daily 8:00–20:00, Neuer Markt 16, other locations about town, including the Naschmarkt, tel. 01/5132-9360). Next door, **Le Bol Patisserie**

Bistro satisfies your need for something French. The staff speaks to you in French, serving fine €8 salads, baguette sandwiches, and fresh croissants (Mon–Sat 8:00–22:00, Sun 10:00–20:00, Neuer Markt 14).

Danieli Ristorante is your best classy Italian bet in the old center. White-tablecloth dressy, but not stuffy, it has reasonable prices (€10–18 pizza and pastas, fresh fish, open daily, 30 yards off Kärntner Strasse opposite Neuer Markt at Himmelpfortgasse 3, tel. 01/513-7913).

City Hall (Rathausplatz) Food Circus

During the summer, scores of outdoor food stands and hundreds of picnic tables are set up in the park in front of the City Hall. Local mobs enjoy mostly ethnic meals for decent-but-not-cheap prices, and classical entertainment on a big screen (see page 1047). The fun thing here is the energy of the crowd, and a feeling that you're truly eating as the Viennese do...not schnitzel and quaint traditions, but trendy "world food" with young people out having fun in a fine Vienna park setting (July–mid-Sept daily from 11:00 until late, in front of City Hall on the Ringstrasse).

Spittelberg Quarter

A charming cobbled grid of traffic-free lanes and Biedermeier apartments has become a favorite neighborhood for Viennese wanting a little dining charm between the MuseumsQuartier and Mariahilfer Strasse (handy to many recommended hotels; take Stiftgasse from Mariahilfer Strasse, or wander over here after you close down the Kunsthistorisches Museum). Tables tumble down sidewalks and into breezy courtyards filled with appreciative natives enjoying dinner or a relaxing drink. It's only worth the trip on a balmy summer evening, as it's dead in bad weather. Stroll Spittelberggasse, Schrankgasse, and Gutenberggasse and pick your favorite. Don't miss the vine-strewn wine garden at Schrankgasse 1. To locate these restaurants, see the map on pages 1054–1055.

Amerlingbeisl, with a casual atmosphere both on the cobbled street and in its vine-covered courtyard, is a great value (€7 plates, €6–8 daily specials, salads, veggie dishes, traditional specialties, daily 9:00–2:00 in the morning, Stiftgasse 8, tel. 01/526-1660).

Plutzer Bräu, next door, is also good (ribs, burgers, traditional dishes, Tirolean beer from the keg, daily 11:00–2:00 in the morning, food until 24:00, Schrankgasse 4, tel. 01/526-1215).

Witwe Bolte is classier and a good choice for uninspired Viennese cuisine with tablecloths. Its tiny square has wonderful leafy ambience (daily 11:30–23:30 except closed 15:00–17:30 mid-Jan–mid-March, Gutenberggasse 13, tel. 01/523-1450).

Zu Ebener Erde und Erster Stock is a charming little restaurant with a near-gourmet menu. The upstairs is Biedermeier-style, with violet tablecloths and seating for about 20. The downstairs is more casual and woody. Reservations are smart (traditional three-course fixed-price meal-€30, Mon–Fri 7:00–20:30, closed Sat–Sun, Burggasse 13, tel. 01/523-6254).

Near Mariahilfer Strasse

Mariahilfer Strasse (see map on pages 1060–1061) is filled with reasonable cafés serving all types of cuisine. For a quick yet traditional bite, consider the venerable **Buffet Trzesniewski** sandwich bar at Mariahilfer Strasse 95 (see page 1059).

Schnitzelwirt is an old classic with a 1950s patina and a clientele to match. In this once-smoky, still-working-class place, no one finishes their schnitzel ("to-go" for the dog is wrapped in newspaper, "to-go" for you is wrapped in foil). You'll find no tourists, just cheap €6 schnitzel meals (Mon–Sat 10:00–23:00, closed Sun, Neubaugasse 52, tel. 01/523-3771).

The **Naschmarkt** (described on page 1030) is Vienna's best Old World market, with plenty of fresh produce, cheap local-style eateries, cafés, *Döner Kebab* and sausage stands, and the best-value sushi in town (Mon–Fri 6:00–18:30, Sat 6:00–17:00, closed Sun, closes earlier in winter; U-4: Karlsplatz, follow *Karlsplatz* signs out of the station). Survey the lane of eateries at the end of the market nearest the Opera. The circa-1900 pub is inviting. Picnickers can buy supplies at the market and eat on nearby Karlsplatz (plenty of chairs facing the Karlskirche).

Vienna Connections

By Train

Long home to two bustling main train stations, Vienna is currently building one central station (Hauptbahnhof) that will replace both by 2013. Until then, the Westbahnhof (West Station) continues to serve trains to/from Germany, Switzerland, and Hungary, but the Südbahnhof (South Station)—the locus of the new central station—is mostly closed (though trains to/from Bratislava now run from a provisional eastern "Ostbahn" section of the Südbahnhof). Most other international trains are now served by the Wien-Meidling Bahnhof (southbound trains to/from Slovenia, Croatia, and Italy, as well as northbound trains to/from the Czech Republic and Poland). Trains don't always adhere to these generalizations, so be sure to confirm which station your train leaves from. For general train information in Austria, call 051-717 (to get an operator, dial 2, then 2).

Westbahnhof: The Reisebüro am Bahnhof desk has maps,

books hotels (for a pricey fee), sells the Vienna Card (described on page 986), and answers questions (Mon–Fri 8:00–19:00, Sat 8:00–13:00, closed Sun). This station is also under construction, so its many services are now scattered throughout a provisional hall—including a train info desk (daily 7:30–21:00), a grocery store (daily 5:30–23:00), ATMs, change offices, a post office, and storage facilities. To reach airport buses and taxis, from the platforms head outside and left.

To get to the city center (and most likely, your hotel), take the U-Bahn (subway) on the U-3 line (buy your ticket or transit pass from a machine). Follow *U-3* signs down to the tracks (for Mariahilfer Strasse hotels or the center, direction: Simmering). If your hotel is along Mariahilfer Strasse, your stop is on this line (see page 1052). If you're sleeping in the center or just can't wait to start sightseeing, ride five stops to Stephansplatz, escalate to the exit (direction: Stephansplatz), and you'll hit St. Stephen's Cathedral. From the cathedral, the TI is a five-minute stroll down the busy Kärntner Strasse pedestrian street.

Wien-Meidling Bahnhof: This once-small suburban station has been souped up to accommodate the traffic that once passed through the Südbahnhof. It has a train info desk, ATMs, luggage lockers (underground, near track 7), as well as airport bus services. To reach the hotels on Mariahilfer Strasse, or to head to Stephansplatz, take the U-Bahn on the U-6 line (direction: Floridsdorf) to the Westbahnhof, then change to the U-3 line (see "Westbahnhof," above). If you're staying near the Opera, you can catch the direct tram #62 (direction: Karlsplatz); to Schwedenplatz, take the U-6 (direction: Floridsdorf) two stops to Längenfeldgasse, then change to the U-4 (direction: Heiligenstadt). To get here from the center, take the U-Bahn or tram to Philadelphiabrücke.

Südbahnhof (Ostbahn): If you're coming from Bratislava, you'll find yourself at the busy construction zone that was once the Südbahnhof. To reach the city center from here, you can take tram #D to the Ring (departs every 5 min, stops right at the Opera). Bus #13A goes to Mariahilfer Strasse, where many of my recommended hotels are located.

From Vienna by Train to: Bratislava (2/hr, 1–1.5 hrs), **Budapest** (every 2 hours direct, 3 hrs; more with transfers), **Prague** (5/day direct, 4–4.5 hrs; more with 1 change, 5–6 hrs), **Český Krumlov** (5/day, 5–6 hrs, 1–2 changes, connections from all three Vienna stations depending on time of day), **Kraków** (3 decent daytime options, 6.25 hrs direct or 7–8.5 hrs with 1–3 changes, plus a night train), **Warsaw** (2/day direct including 1 night train, 7.75–8.5 hrs), **Ljubljana** (1 convenient early-morning direct train, 6 hrs; otherwise 6/day with change in Villach, Maribor, or Graz, 6–7 hrs), **Zagreb** (4/day, 5.5–7 hrs, 2 direct, others with 1–2

changes), **Salzburg** (1–2/hr, 2.5–3 hrs), **Hallstatt** (hourly, 4 hrs, change in Attnang-Puchheim), **Innsbruck** (every 2 hrs, 5 hrs), **Munich** (4/day direct, 4.25 hrs; otherwise about hourly, 5 hrs, transfer in Salzburg), **Berlin** (8/day, most with 1 change, 9.5 hrs, some via Czech Republic; longer on night train), **Zürich** (2 direct morning trains, 8 hrs; 2 more/day with changes, plus 1 direct night train, all 9 hrs), **Rome** (3/day, 13–15 hrs, plus several overnight options), **Venice** (3/day, 8–10 hrs with changes—some may involve bus connection; plus 1 direct night train, 12 hrs), **Frankfurt** (7/day direct, 7 hrs), **Paris** (7/day, 12–17 hrs, 1–3 changes, night train), **Amsterdam** (3/day, 11.25–12.5 hrs, 1–2 changes; longer night-train options via Hannover).

By Plane

Vienna International Airport, 12 miles from the center, has easy connections to Vienna's various train stations (airport tel. 01/700-722-233, www.viennaairport.com).

To get from the airport to the center of town, your cheapest option is taking the S-Bahn commuter train to the central Wien-Mitte Bahnhof, on the east side of the Ring (S-7 yellow, buy 2-zone ticket from machines on the platform, price includes any bus or S- or U-Bahn transfers, 2/hr, 24 min, €3.40, generally departs at :09 and :39). You can also take the newer City Airport Train to the Wien-Mitte Bahnhof (CAT, follow green signs, 2/hr, usually departs at :05 and :35, 16 min, €10, www.cityairporttrain.com). From Wien-Mitte you can take the U-Bahn to Mariahilfer Strasse or other neighborhoods.

Express airport buses (parked immediately in front of the arrival hall, €6, 2/hr, 30 min, buy ticket from driver, note time to destination on curbside TV monitors) go conveniently to the Schwedenplatz U-Bahn station (for city-center hotels), the Westbahnhof (for Mariahilfer Strasse hotels), and the Wien-Meidling Bahnhof, where it's easy to continue by taxi or public transportation (see "By Train," earlier).

Taxis into town cost about €35 (including the €11 airport surcharge); taxis also wait at the downtown terminus of each airport transit service. Hotels arrange for fixed-rate car service to the airport (€30, 30-min ride).

For details on arriving at the airport in nearby **Bratislava**, Slovakia—just an hour away from Vienna, and a hub for some low-cost flights—see page 219.

UNDERSTANDING YUGOSLAVIA

Americans struggle to understand the complicated breakup of Yugoslavia—especially when visiting countries that rose from its ashes, such as Croatia and Slovenia. Talking to the locals can make it even more confusing: Everyone in the former Yugoslavia seems to have a slightly different version of events. A very wise Bosniak told me, "Listen to all three sides—Muslim, Serb, and Croat. Then decide for yourself what you think." That's the best advice I can offer. But since you likely won't have time for that on your brief visit, here's an admittedly oversimplified, as-impartial-as-possible history to get you started.

Balkan Peninsula 101

For starters, it helps to have a handle on the different groups who've lived in the Balkans—the southeastern European peninsula between the Adriatic and the Black Sea, stretching from Hungary to Greece. The Balkan Peninsula has always been a meeting place of diverse cultures. The Illyrians, Greeks, and Romans had settlements here before the Slavs moved into the region from the north around the seventh century. During the next millennium and a half, the western part of the peninsula—which would become Yugoslavia—was divided by a series of cultural, ethnic, and religious fault lines.

The most important influences were three religions: **Western Christianity** (i.e., Roman Catholicism, first brought to the western part of the region by Charlemagne and later reinforced by the Austrian Habsburgs), **Eastern Orthodox Christianity** (brought to the east from the Byzantine Empire), and **Islam** (in the south, from the Ottomans).

Two major historical factors made the Balkans what they are today: The first was the **split of the Roman Empire** in the fourth

century A.D., dividing the Balkans down the middle into Roman Catholic (west) and Byzantine Orthodox (east)—roughly along today's Bosnian-Serbian border. The second was the **invasion of the Islamic Ottomans** in the 14th century. The Ottoman victory at the Battle of Kosovo Polje (1389) began five centuries of Islamic influence in Bosnia-Herzegovina and Serbia, further dividing the Balkans into Christian (north) and Muslim (south).

Because of these and other events, several distinct ethnic identities emerged. Confusingly, the major "ethnicities" of Yugoslavia are all South Slavs—they're descended from the same ancestors and speak essentially the same language, but they practice different religions. Catholic South Slavs are called **Croats** or **Slovenes** (mostly west of the Dinaric Mountains: Croats along the Adriatic coast and Slovenes farther north, in the Alps); Orthodox South Slavs are called **Serbs** (mostly east of the Dinaric range); and Muslim South Slavs are called **Bosniaks** (whose ancestors converted to Islam under the Ottomans, mostly living in the Dinaric Mountains). To complicate matters, the region is also home to

Who's Who in Yugoslavia

Yugoslavia was made up of six republics, which were inhabited by eight different ethnicities (not counting small minorities such as Jews, Germans, and Roma). This chart shows each ethnicity, and in which republic(s) they were most concentrated. Not coincidentally, the more ethnically diverse a region was, the more conflict it experienced.

	Serbia*	Croatia	Bosnia-Herz.	Slovenia	Montenegro	Macedonia
Serbs (Orthodox)	X	X	X		X	
Croats (Catholic)		X	X			
Bosniaks (Muslims)			X			
Slovenes (Catholic)				X		
Macedonians (like Bulgarians)						X
Montenegrins (like Serbs)					X	
Albanians	X		X			X
Hungarians	X	X		X		

*Within Serbia were two "autonomous provinces," each of which was dominated by a non-Slavic ethnic group: Hungarians in Vojvodina and Albanians in Kosovo. Tito intentionally set up these two autonomous provinces to prevent Serbia from becoming too powerful. Tito was right: Slobodan Milošević's annexation of Kosovo is precisely what tipped the balance of power in Yugoslavia, sparking the Balkan wars of the 1990s.

several non-Slavic minority groups, including **Hungarians** (in the northern province of Vojvodina) and **Albanians,** concentrated in the southern state of Kosovo (descended from the Illyrians, who lived here long before the Greeks and Romans).

Of course, these geographic divisions are extremely general. The groups overlapped a lot—which is exactly why the breakup of Yugoslavia was so contentious. One of the biggest causes of this ethnic mixing came in the 16th century. The Ottomans were threatening to overrun Europe, and the Austrian Habsburgs wanted a buffer zone—a "human shield." The Habsburgs encouraged Serbs who were fleeing from Ottoman invasions to settle

along today's Croatian-Bosnian border (known as *Vojna Krajina,* or "Military Frontier"). The Serbs stayed after the Ottomans left, establishing homes in predominantly Croat communities.

After the Ottoman threat subsided in the late 17th century, some of the Balkans (basically today's Slovenia and Croatia) became part of the Austrian Habsburg Empire. The Ottomans stayed longer in the south and east (today's Bosnia-Herzegovina and Serbia)—making the cultures in these regions even more different. Serbia finally gained its independence from the Ottomans in the mid-19th century, but it wasn't long before World War I erupted...after a disgruntled Bosnian Serb nationalist killed the Austrian archduke and heir to the Habsburg throne.

South Slavs Unite

When the Austro-Hungarian Empire fell at the end of World War I, the European map was redrawn for the 20th century. After centuries of being governed by foreign powers, the South Slavs began to see their shared history as more important than their differences. A tiny country of a few million Croats or Slovenes couldn't have survived on its own. Rather than be absorbed by a non-Slavic power, the South Slavs decided that there was safety in numbers, and banded together as a single state—first called the "Kingdom of the Serbs, Croats, and Slovenes" (1918), later known as the Kingdom of Yugoslavia ("Land of the South Slavs"—*yugo* means "south"). "Yugoslav unity" was in the air, but this new union was fragile and ultimately bound to fail (not unlike the partnership between the Czechs and Slovaks, formed at the same time and for much the same reasons).

From the very beginning, the various ethnicities struggled for power within the new union of Yugoslavia. The largest group was the Serbs (about 45 percent), followed by the Croats (about 25 percent). Croats often felt they were treated as lesser partners under the Serbs. For example, many Croats objected to naming the country's official language "Serbo-Croatian"—why not "Croato-Serbian?" Serbia already had a very strong king, Alexander Karađorđević, who immediately attempted to give his nation a leading role in the federation. A nationalistic Croatian politician named Stjepan Radić, pushing for a more equitable division of powers, was shot by a Serb during a parliament session in 1928. Karađorđević abolished the parliament and became dictator. Six years later, infuriated Croatian separatists killed him.

Many Croat nationalists sided with the Nazis in World War II in the hopes that it would be their ticket to independence from Serbia. The Nazi puppet government in Croatia (under the Ustaše party) conducted an extermination campaign, murdering hundreds of thousands of Serbs (along with Jews and Roma) living in

Croatia; other Serbs were forced to flee the country or convert to Catholicism. Most historians consider the Ustaše concentration camps to be the first instance of "ethnic cleansing" in the Balkans, and the Serbs' long memory of it may go far in explaining their own harsh ethnic cleansing of the Croats in the 1990s.

At the end of World War II, the rest of Eastern Europe was "liberated" by the Soviets, but the Yugoslavs regained their independence on their own, as their communist Partisan Army forced out the Nazis. After the short but rocky Yugoslav union between the World Wars, it seemed that no one could hold the southern Slavs together in a single nation. But there was one man who could, and did: Tito.

Tito's Yugoslavia

Communist Party president and war hero Josip Broz (a.k.a. Tito) emerged as a political leader after World War II. With a Slovene for a mother, a Croat for a father, a Serb for a wife, and a home in Belgrade, Tito was a true Yugoslav. Tito had a compelling vision that this fractured union of the South Slavs could function. And, under him, it did.

Tito's new incarnation of Yugoslavia aimed for a more equitable division of powers. It was made up of six republics, each with its own parliament and president: **Croatia** (mostly Catholic Croats), **Slovenia** (mostly Catholic Slovenes), **Serbia** (mostly Orthodox Serbs), **Bosnia-Herzegovina** (the most diverse—mostly Muslim Bosniaks, but with very large Croat and Serb populations), **Montenegro** (mostly Serb-like Montenegrins), and **Macedonia** (with about 25 percent Albanians and 75 percent Macedonians—who share similarities with both Bulgarians and Serbs). Within Serbia, there were also two autonomous provinces, each one dominated by an ethnicity that was a minority in greater Yugoslavia: Albanians in **Kosovo** (to the south) and Hungarians in **Vojvodina** (to the north). Tito hoped that by allowing these two provinces some degree of independence—including voting rights—they could balance the political clout of Serbia, preventing a single republic from dominating the union.

Each republic managed its own affairs...but always under the watchful eye of president-for-life Tito, who said that the borders between the republics should be "like white lines in a marble column." Nationalism was strongly discouraged, and Tito's tight control—though sometimes oppressive—kept the country from unraveling. For more on Tito, see the sidebar.

Tito's Yugoslavia was communist, but it wasn't Soviet communism; you'll find no statues of Lenin or Stalin here. Despite strong pressure from Moscow, Tito refused to ally himself with the Soviets—and therefore received good will (and $2 billion) from the

Tito
(1892–1980)

The Republic of Yugoslavia was the vision of a single man, who made it reality. Josip Broz—better known as Maršal Tito—presided over the most peaceful and prosperous era in this region's long and troubled history. Nearly three decades after his death, Tito is beloved by many of his former subjects...and yet, he was a communist dictator known for torturing and executing his political enemies. This love-him-and-hate-him autocrat is one of the most complex and quixotic figures in the history of this very complicated land.

Josip Broz was born in 1892 to a Slovenian mother and a Croatian father in the northern part of today's Croatia, which then belonged to the Austro-Hungarian Empire. After growing up in the rural countryside, Tito was trained as a metalworker. He was drafted into the Austro-Hungarian army, went to fight on the Eastern Front during World War I, and was captured and sent to Russia as a prisoner of war. Freed by Bolsheviks, Broz fell in with the Communist Revolution... and never looked back.

At war's end, Broz returned home to the newly independent Kingdom of Yugoslavia, where he worked in conjunction with the Soviets to build a national Communist Party. As a clandestine communist operative, he adopted the code name with which he would always be associated: Tito. (Some people half-joke that the name came from Tito's authoritarian style: *"Ti, to!"* means "You, do this!")

When the Nazis occupied Yugoslavia, Tito became the commander of a homegrown, communist Partisan Army. Through guerilla tactics, Tito's clever maneuvering, and sheer determination, the Partisans liberated their country. And because they did so mostly without support from the USSR's Red Army, Yugoslavia could set its own course after the war.

The war hero Tito quickly became the "president for life" of postwar Yugoslavia. But even as he introduced communism to his country, he retained some elements of a free-market economy—firmly declining to become a satellite of Moscow. He also led the creation of the worldwide Non-Aligned Movement, joining with nations in Africa, the Middle East, Asia, and Latin America in refusing to ally with the US or USSR. Stubborn but suitably cautious, Tito expertly walked a tightrope between East and West.

There was a dark side to Tito. In the early years of his regime, Tito resorted to brutal, Stalin-esque tactics to assert his control. Immediately following World War II, the Partisan Army massacred tens of thousands of soldiers who had supported the Nazis. Then Tito ruthlessly and systematically routed out other

Nazi supporters, arresting, trying, torturing, or executing those who did not accept his new regime. One of his highest-profile enemies was the Croatian archbishop Alojzije Stepinac, whom Tito imprisoned for five years (see page 927).

But once he had gained full control, Tito moved away from strong-arm tactics and into a warm-and-fuzzy era of Yugoslav brotherhood. Tito believed that the disparate peoples of Yugoslavia could live in harmony...and, under him, they did. For example, every Yugoslav male had to serve in the National Army, and Tito made sure that each unit was a microcosm of the complete Yugoslavia—with equal representation from each ethnic group. This meant that Yugoslavs from diverse backgrounds were forced to work together and socialize, and as a result, they became friends.

Tito's reign is a case study in the power of the cult of personality. Rocks on hillsides throughout Yugoslavia were rearranged to spell "TITO," and his portrait hung over every family's dinner table. Each of the six republics renamed one of its cities for their dictator (such as "Titograd" for Montenegro's Podgorica, or "Titovo Velejne" in Slovenia). The main street and square in virtually every town was renamed for Tito (and many have kept the name). Tito also had vacation villas in all of Yugoslavia's most beautiful areas, including Lake Bled, Croatia's Brijuni Islands, and the Montenegrin Coast. People sang patriotic anthems to their Druža (Comrade) Tito: "Comrade Tito, we bow to you."

Tito died in 1980 in a Slovenian hospital. His body was loaded onto his Blue Train and went on a grand tour of the Yugoslav capitals: Ljubljana, Zagreb, Sarajevo, and Belgrade, where he was buried before hundreds of thousands of mourners, including more heads of state than any other funeral in history.

The genuine outpouring of support at Tito's death might seem unusual for a man who was, on paper, an authoritarian communist dictator. But even today, many former Yugoslavs—especially Slovenes—have forgiven him for governing with an iron fist, believing that this was a necessary evil to keep the country strong and united. The eventual balance Tito struck between communism and capitalism, and between the competing interests of his ethnically diverse nation, led to this region's most stable and prosperous era. Pictures of Tito still hang in many Croatians' homes. In a recent poll in Slovenia, Tito had a higher approval rating than any present-day politician, and 80 percent of Slovenes said they had a positive impression of him.

And yet, the Yugoslavs' respect for their former leader was not enough to keep them together. Tito's death began a long, slow chain reaction that led to the end of Yugoslavia. As the decades pass, the old joke seems more and more appropriate: Yugoslavia had eight distinct peoples in six republics, with five languages, three religions (Orthodox, Catholic, and Muslim), and two alphabets (Roman and Cyrillic), but only one Yugoslav—Tito.

United States. Tito's vision was for a "third way," where Yugoslavia could work with both East and West, without being dominated by either. Yugoslavia was the most free of the communist states: While large industry was nationalized, Tito's system allowed for small businesses. This experience with a market economy benefited Yugoslavs when Eastern Europe's communist regimes eventually fell. And even during the communist era, Yugoslavia remained a popular tourist destination for visitors from both East and West, keeping its standards more in line with Western Europe than the Soviet states. Meanwhile, Yugoslavs were in a unique position among communist countries of being allowed to travel to Western countries. In fact, because Yugoslavs were able to travel relatively hassle-free in both East and West, their "red passports" were worth even more on the black market than American ones.

Things Fall Apart

With Tito's death in 1980, Yugoslavia's six constituent republics gained more autonomy, with a rotating presidency. But before long, the fragile union Tito had held together started to unravel.

The breakup began in the late 1980s, with squabbles in the province of Kosovo between the Serb minority and the ethnic-Albanian majority. While technically part of Serbia, Kosovo had been awarded partial autonomy by Tito. But, even though nine out of every 10 Kosovars were Albanian, the region remained important to the Serbs, who consider Kosovo the cradle of their civilization—the site of their most important monasteries and historic sites. Most significantly, it was the location of the Battle of Kosovo Polje ("Field of Blackbirds"), an epic 14th-century battle that is considered the foundation of Serbian cultural identity...even though the Serbs lost to the Ottoman invaders (sort of the Serbian Alamo). One Serb told me, "Kosovo is the Mecca and Medina of the Serb people."

Serbian politician Slobodan Milošević saw how the conflict could be used to Serbia's (and his own) advantage. Milošević went to Kosovo, where he delivered a rabble-rousing speech, pledging that Serbia would come to the aid of their Kosovar-Serb brothers. In this one visit, Milošević upset the delicate balance that Tito had so carefully sought to attain. (He had also set the stage for his own rise to the Serbian presidency.) The end of Yugoslavia was near.

When Milošević-led Serbia annexed Kosovo soon after, other republics (especially Slovenia and Croatia) feared that he would gut their nation to create a "Greater Serbia," instead of a friendly coalition of diverse Yugoslav republics. Some of the leaders—most notably Milan Kučan of Slovenia—tried to avoid warfare by suggesting a plan for a loosely united Yugoslavia, based on the Swiss model of independent yet confederated cantons. But other parties,

who wanted complete autonomy, refused. Over the next decade, Yugoslavia broke apart, with much bloodshed.

The Slovene Secession

Slovenia was the first Yugoslav republic to hold free elections, in the spring of 1990. The voters wanted the communists out—and their own independent nation. Along with being the most ethnically homogeneous of the Yugoslav nations, Slovenia was also the most Western-oriented, most prosperous, and most geographically isolated—so secession just made sense. But that didn't mean that there was no violence.

After months of stockpiling weapons, Slovenia closed its borders and declared independence from Yugoslavia on June 25, 1991. Belgrade sent in the Yugoslav National Army to take control of Slovenia's borders with Italy and Austria, figuring that whoever controlled the borders had a legitimate claim on sovereignty. Fighting broke out around these borders. Because the Yugoslav National Army was made up of soldiers from all republics, many Slovenian soldiers found themselves fighting their own countrymen. (The army had cut off communication between these conscripts and the home front, so they didn't know what was going on—and often didn't realize they were fighting their friends and neighbors until they were close enough to see them.)

Slovenian civilians bravely entered the fray, blockading the Yugoslav barracks with their own cars and trucks. Most of the Yugoslav soldiers—now trapped—were young and inexperienced, and were terrified of the ragtag (but relentless) Slovenian militia, even though their own resources were far superior.

After 10 days of fighting and fewer than a hundred deaths, Belgrade relented. The Slovenes stepped aside and allowed the Yugoslav National Army to take all of the weapons with them back into Yugoslavia and destroy all remaining military installations. When the Yugoslav National Army cleared out, they left the Slovenes with their freedom.

The Croatian Conflict

In April 1990, a historian named Franjo Tuđman—and his highly nationalistic, right-wing party, the HDZ (Croatian Democratic Union)—won Croatia's first free elections (for more on Tuđman, see page 750). Like the Slovenian reformers, Tuđman and the HDZ wanted more autonomy from Yugoslavia. But Tuđman's methods were more extreme than those of the gently progressive Slovenes. Tuđman invoked the spirit of the last group that led an "independent" Croatia—the Ustaše, who had ruthlessly run Croatia's puppet government under the Nazis. Tuđman reintroduced historical symbols that had previously been embraced by

the Ustaše, including the red-and-white checkerboard flag and the kuna currency. The 600,000 Serbs living in Croatia, mindful of their grandparents, who had been massacred by the Ustaše, saw the writing on the wall and began to rise up.

The first conflicts were in the Serb-dominated Croatian city of Knin. Among Tuđman's reforms was the decree that all of Croatia's policemen wear a new uniform, which bore a striking resemblance to Nazi-era Ustaše uniforms. Infuriated by this slap in the face, and prodded by Slobodan Milošević's rhetoric, Serb police officers in Knin refused. Over the next few months, tense negotiations ensued. Serbs from Knin and elsewhere began the so-called "tree trunk revolution"—blocking important tourist roads to the coast with logs and other barriers. Meanwhile, the Croatian government—after being denied support from the United States—illegally purchased truckloads of guns from Hungary. Tensions escalated, and the first shots of the conflict were fired on Easter Sunday 1991 at Plitvice Lakes National Park, between Croatian policemen and Serb irregulars from Knin.

By the time Croatia declared its independence (on June 25, 1991—the same day as Slovenia), it was already embroiled in the beginnings of a bloody war. Croatia's more than half-million Serb residents immediately declared their own independence from Croatia. The Serb-dominated Yugoslav National Army swept in, supposedly to keep the peace between Serbs and Croats—but it soon became obvious that they were there to support the Serbs. The ill-prepared Croatian resistance, made up mostly of policemen and a few soldiers who defected from the Yugoslav National Army, were quickly overwhelmed. The Serbs gained control over the parts of inland Croatia where they were in the majority: a large swath around the Bosnian border (including Plitvice) and Croatia's inland panhandle (the region of Slavonia). They called this territory—about a quarter of Croatia—the **Republic of Serbian Krajina** (*krajina* means "border"). This new "country" (hardly recognized by any other nations) minted its own money and raised its own army, much to the consternation of Croatia—which was now worried about the safety of Croats living in Krajina.

As the Serbs advanced, hundreds of thousands of Croats fled to the coast and lived as refugees in resort hotels. The Serbs began a campaign of ethnic cleansing, systematically removing Croats from contested territory—often by murdering them. The bloodiest siege was at the town of **Vukovar,** which the Yugoslav Army surrounded and shelled relentlessly for three months. By the end of the siege, thousands of Croat soldiers and civilians had mysteriously disappeared. Many of these people were later discovered in mass graves; hundreds are still missing, and bodies are still being found. In a surprise move, Serbs also attacked the tourist resort

of **Dubrovnik** (see page 758). By early 1992, both Croatia and the Republic of Serbian Krajina had established their borders, and a tense ceasefire fell over the region.

The standoff lasted until 1995, when the now well-equipped Croatian Army retook the Serbian-occupied areas in a series of two offensives—**"Lightning"** *(Blijesak),* in the northern part of the country, and **"Storm"** *(Oluja),* farther south. Some Croats retaliated for earlier ethnic cleansing by doing much of the same to Serbs—torturing and murdering them, and dynamiting their homes. Croatia quickly established the borders that exist today, and the Erdut Agreement brought peace to the region. But most of the 600,000 Serbs who once lived in Croatia/Krajina were forced into Serbia or were killed. While Serbs have long since been legally invited back to their ancestral Croatian homes, relatively few have returned—afraid of the "welcome" they might receive from the Croat neighbors who killed their relatives or blew up their houses just a few years ago.

The War in Bosnia-Herzegovina

Bosnia-Herzegovina declared its independence from Yugoslavia four months after Croatia and Slovenia did. But Bosnia-Herzegovina was always at the crossroads of Balkan culture, and therefore even more diverse than Croatia, as it was populated predominantly by Muslim Bosniaks (mostly in the cities) but also by large numbers of Serbs and Croats (many of them farmers).

The fighting in Bosnia-Herzegovina began for similar reasons as fighting in Croatia did: As soon as Bosnia-Herzegovina declared independence, the Bosnian Serb minority seceded as their own "state," called the Republic of the Serb People of Bosnia-Herzegovina. To legitimize their claim on this land, the Serbs began a campaign of ethnic cleansing against Bosniaks and Croats in the spring of 1992.

At first, the Bosniaks and Croats teamed up to fight against the Serbs. But even before the first wave of fighting had subsided, Croats and Bosniaks turned their guns on each other. The Croats split off their own mini-state, which they called the Croatian Republic of Herzeg-Bosnia. A bloody war raged for years between the three groups: the Serbs (with support from Serbia proper), the Croats (with support from Croatia proper), and—squeezed between them—the internationally recognized Bosniak (Muslim) government, led by President Alija Izetbegović, who desperately

worked for peace.

Bosnia-Herzegovina was torn apart. Even the many mixed families were forced to choose sides. If you had a Serb mother and a Croat father, you were expected to pick one ethnicity or the other—and your brother might choose the opposite. As families and former neighbors trained their guns on each other, proud and beautiful cities such as Sarajevo and Mostar were turned to rubble, and people throughout Bosnia-Herzegovina lived in a state of constant terror.

Serb sieges of Bosnian Muslim cities—such as the notorious siege of Srebrenica in July 1995, which ended with a massacre of about 8,000 Bosniak civilians—brought the ongoing atrocities to the world's attention. The methods of the aggressors were intentionally gruesome and violent. Perhaps most despicable was the establishment of so-called "rape camps"—concentration camps where Bosniak women were imprisoned and systematically raped by Serb soldiers. It was the aggressors' goal not only to remove people from "their" land (which could have been done more peacefully), but to ensure that the various groups could never tolerate living together again.

While there were many villains in this conflict, the two men considered most responsible for the worst atrocities in Bosnia-Herzegovina were the Bosnian Serb President Radovan Karadžić and his general, Ratko Mladić.

The United Nations Protection Force (UNPROFOR)—dubbed "Smurfs" both for their light-blue helmets and for their ineffectiveness—exercised their very limited authority to try to suppress the violence. But because they were not allowed to use force, even in self-defense, they became impotent witnesses to atrocities. This ugly situation was brilliantly parodied in the film *No Man's Land* (which won the Oscar for Best Foreign Film in 2002), a very dark comedy about the absurdity of the Bosnian war.

Finally, in 1995, the Dayton Peace Accords carefully divided Bosnia-Herzegovina among the different ethnicities. According to this compromise, the country is split into three different units: the Federation of Bosnia and Herzegovina (shared by Bosniaks and Croats), the Serb-dominated Republika Srpska, and the Brčko District (a tiny corner of the country, with a mix of the ethnicities).

The Fall of Milošević

After years of bloody conflicts, public opinion among Serbs had decisively swung against their president. The transition began gradually in early 2000, spearheaded by Otpor, a nonviolent, grassroots, student-based opposition movement, and aided by similar groups. These organizations used clever PR strategies to

gain support and convince Serbians that real change was possible. As anti-Milošević sentiments gained momentum, opposing political parties banded together and got behind one candidate, Vojislav Koštunica. Public support for Koštunica mounted, and when the arrogant Milošević called an early election in September 2000, he was soundly defeated. Though Milošević tried to claim that the election results were invalid, determined Serbs streamed into their capital, marched on their parliament, and—like the Czechs and Slovaks a decade before—peacefully took back their nation.

In 2001, Milošević was arrested and sent to The Hague, in the Netherlands, to stand trial before the International Criminal Tribunal for the Former Yugoslavia (ICTY). Milošević served as his own attorney as his trial wore on for five years, frequently delayed due to his health problems. Then, on March 11, 2006—as his trial was coming to a close—Milošević was found dead in his cell. Ruled a heart attack, Milošević's death, like his life, was controversial. His supporters alleged that Milošević had been denied suitable medical care, some speculated that he'd been poisoned, and others suspected that he'd intentionally worsened his heart condition to avoid the completion of his trial. Whatever the cause, in the end Milošević avoided coming to justice—he was never found guilty of a thing.

The Strange Tale of Dr. Dragan David Dabić

On July 18, 2008, Serbian police announced that they had captured Radovan Karadžić, the former leader of the Bosnian Serb state who is considered one of the worst culprits in the Serbs' brutal ethnic cleansing during the war.

Karadžić, who went into hiding shortly after the war (in 1996), had been living for part of that time in a residential neighborhood of Belgrade, posing as an alternative-medicine healer named Dr. Dragan David Dabić. (Karadžić had previously received training as a psychiatrist.) This expert on what he called "Human Quantum Energy" had his own website and even presented at conferences.

How did one of the world's most wanted men effectively disappear in plain sight for 12 years? He had grown a very full beard and wore thick glasses as a disguise, and frequented a neighborhood bar where a photo of him, in his earlier life, hung on the wall...and yet, he was undetected even by those who saw him every day. It's alleged that at least some Serb authorities knew of his whereabouts, but, considering him a hero, refused to identify or arrest him.

After his arrest, Karadžić was taken to stand trial in The Hague for war crimes including genocide. He insisted on defending himself, then boycotted the start of his trial twice until the judge appointed a defense attorney for him. As his trial wears on, at

the time of this writing, Karadžić's military leader, General Ratko Mladić, is still at large—and now individually holds the title of world's most wanted man (after, perhaps, Osama bin Laden).

Montenegro and Kosovo: Europe's Newest Nations

After the departures of Croatia, Slovenia, Bosnia-Herzegovina, and Macedonia (which peacefully seceded in 1991), by the late 1990s only two of the original six republics of Yugoslavia remained united: Serbia (which still included the provinces of Kosovo and Vojvodina) and Montenegro. But in 2003, Montenegro began a gradual, tiptoe secession process that ended when it peacefully gained its independence in 2006.

The Yugoslav crisis concluded in the place where it began: the Serbian province of Kosovo. Kosovo's majority Albanians rebelled in 1998, only to become victims of Milošević's ethnic cleansing (until US General Wesley Clark's NATO warplanes forced the Serbian Army out). For nearly a decade, Kosovo remained a UN protectorate within Serbia—still nominally part of Serbia, but for all practical purposes separate and self-governing (under the watchful eye of the UN).

The long-term plan was for Kosovo to eventually become independent. But on Sunday, February 17, 2008, Kosovo's provisional government unilaterally declared its independence as the "Republic of Kosovo"— without going through proper UN channels. (It had grown impatient that its UN bid for independence was being stalled by Russia.) The Republic of Kosovo was quickly recognized by the US, UK, France, Germany, and several other countries, but not officially endorsed by the UN. Serbia was backed in its opposition by several large countries who are involved in their own internal disputes with ethnic regions that would like to secede: Russia (areas of Georgia), China (Taiwan), and Spain (Catalunya, the Basque Country, and others).

The new Kosovo government very carefully stated it would protect the rights of its minorities, including Serbs. But the Serbs deeply believed that losing Kosovo would also mean losing their grip on their own history and culture. They also feared for the safety of the Serb minority there (and potential retribution from Albanians who had so long been oppressed themselves). For a few tense months, international observers watched nervously, worrying that war might erupt in the region once more. There were a few scuffles, especially in some of the large Serb settlements. But as of this writing, Kosovo independence appears to be successful—representing, perhaps, the final chapter of a long and ugly Yugoslav succession. Kosovo is the seventh country to emerge from the break-up of Yugoslavia.

Finding Their Way: The Former Yugoslav Republics

Today, Slovenia and Croatia are as stable as Western Europe, Bosnia-Herzegovina has made great strides in putting itself back together, Macedonia feels closer to Bulgaria than to Belgrade, and the sixth and seventh countries to emerge from "Yugoslavia"—Montenegro and Kosovo—are fledgling democracies.

And yet, nagging questions remain. Making the wars even more difficult to grasp is the fact that there were no clear-cut "good guys" and "bad guys"—just a lot of ugliness on all sides. When considering specifically the war between the Croats and the Serbs, it's tempting for Americans to take Croatia's "side" because we saw them in the role of victims first; because they're Catholic, so they seem more "like us" than the Orthodox Serbs; and because we admire their striving for an independent nation. But in the streets and the trenches, it was never that straightforward. The Serbs believe that *they* were the victims first—back in World War II, when their grandparents were executed in Croat-run Ustaše concentration camps. And when Croatians retook the Serb-occupied areas in 1995, they were every bit as brutal as the Serbs had been a few years before. Both sides resorted to ethnic cleansing, both sides had victims, and both sides had victimizers.

Even so, many can't help but look for victims and villains. During the conflict in Bosnia-Herzegovina, several prominent and respected reporters began to show things from one "side" more than the others—specifically, depicting the Bosniaks (Muslims) as victims. This reawakened an old debate in the journalism community: Should reporters above all be impartial, even if "showing all sides" might make them feel complicit in ongoing atrocities?

As for villains, it's easy to point a finger at Slobodan Milošević, Radovan Karadžić, Ratko Mladić, and other military leaders who are wanted or standing trial at The Hague. Others condemn the late Croatian President Franjo Tuđman, who, it's becoming increasingly clear, secretly conspired with Milošević to redraw the maps of their respective territories throughout the course of the war.

Visitors traveling in this region quickly realize that the vast majority of people they meet here never wanted these wars. And so finally comes the inevitable question: Why did any of it happen in the first place?

Explanations tend to gravitate to two extremes. Some observers say that in this inherently warlike part of the world, deep-seated hatreds and age-old tribal passions between the various ethnic groups have flared up at several points throughout history. According to these people, there's an air of inevitability about the recent wars...and about the potential for future conflict.

Others believe that this theory is an insulting oversimplification. Sure, animosity has long simmered in this region, but it takes a selfish leader to exploit it to advance his own interests. It wasn't until Milošević, Tuđman, and others expertly manipulated the people's grudges that the country fell into war. By vigorously fanning the embers of ethnic discord, and carefully controlling media coverage of the escalating violence, these leaders turned what could have been a healthy political debate into a holocaust.

Tension still exists throughout the former Yugoslavia—especially in the areas that were most war-torn. Croatians and Slovenes continue to split hairs over silly border disputes, and Serbs ominously warn that they'll take up arms to reclaim Kosovo. When the people of this region encounter other Yugoslavs in their travels, they immediately evaluate each other's accent to determine: Are they one of us, or one of them?

But, with time, these hard feelings are fading. The younger generations don't look back—teenaged Slovenes no longer learn Serbo-Croatian, can't imagine not living in an independent little country, and get bored (and a little irritated) when their old-fashioned parents wax nostalgic about the days of a united Yugoslavia. A middle-aged Slovene friend of mine thinks fondly of his months of compulsory service in the Yugoslav National Army, when his unit was made up of Slovenes, Croats, Serbs, Bosniaks, Albanians, Macedonians, and Montenegrins—all of them countrymen, and all good friends. To these young Yugoslavs, ethnic differences didn't matter. He still often visits with his army buddy from Dubrovnik—600 miles away, not long ago part of the same nation—and wishes there had been a way to keep it all together. But he says, optimistically, "I look forward to the day when the other former Yugoslav republics also join the European Union. Then, in a way, we will all be united once again."

APPENDIX

Contents

Tourist Information 1085
Communicating 1086
Transportation 1096
Resources 1106
Holidays and Festivals 1111
Conversions and Climate. 1114
Essential Packing Checklist. 1117
Hotel Reservation Form. 1118
Czech Survival Phrases 1119
Slovak Survival Phrases 1120
Polish Survival Phrases 1121
Hungarian Survival Phrases 1123
Slovenian Survival Phrases 1125
Croatian Survival Phrases 1127
German Survival Phrases. 1129
Pronouncing Eastern European
Place Names 1132

Tourist Information

In the US

Each country's national tourist office in the US is a wealth of information. Before your trip, get the free general information packet and request any specifics you may want (such as regional and city maps and festival schedules).

Czech Republic: Basic information and a map are free; additional materials are $4 (prepaid by Czech...er, check). Call 212/288-0830 or visit www.czechtourism.com (info-usa@czechtourism.com).

Poland: Ask for Warsaw and Kraków information, regional brochures, maps, and more. Call 201/420-9910 or visit www.poland.travel (info.na@poland.travel).

Hungary: Request the free *Budapest Guide*. They also have regional and topical brochures. Call 212/695-1221 or visit www.gotohungary.com (info@gotohungary.com).

Slovakia: Call 212/679-7045 or visit www.cometoslovakia.com (slovakoffice@nyc.rr.com).

Slovenia: They have a *Slovenia Invigorates* brochure, map, and information on various regions, hiking, biking, winter travel, and tourist farms. From the US, call Slovenian tel. 011-386-1-589-8550 or visit www.slovenia.info (info@slovenia.info).

Croatia: Ask for their free brochures and maps. In the US, call 800-829-4416 or visit http://us.croatia.hr (cntony@earthlink.net).

Austria: They have maps and information on festivals, hiking, the wine country, and more. Call 212/944-6880 or visit www.austria.info.

In Eastern Europe

Your best first stop in any town is generally the local tourist information office—abbreviated **TI** in this book. You'll find local TIs are usually well-organized and always have an English-speaking staff.

A TI is a great place to get a city map, advice on public transportation (including bus and train schedules), walking-tour information, tips on special events, and recommendations for nightlife. Many TIs have information on the entire country or at least the region, so try to pick up maps for destinations you'll be visiting later in your trip. If you're arriving in town after the TI closes, call ahead or pick up a map in a neighboring town.

Most TIs in Eastern Europe are run by the government, which means their information isn't colored by a drive for profit. They're not allowed to make money by running a room-booking service—though they can almost always give you a list of local hotels and private rooms. And, if they're not too busy, they might be willing to call around for you to check on availability. While most towns have at least one travel agency with a room-booking service, even if there's no "fee," you'll save yourself and your host money by going direct with the listings in this book.

Communicating

Hurdling the Language Barrier

The language barrier in Eastern Europe is no bigger than in Western Europe. In fact, I find that it's much easier to communi-

cate in Hungary or Croatia than in Italy or Spain.

Since the Eastern European countries are small and not politically powerful, their residents realize that it's unreasonable to expect visitors to learn Hungarian (with only 12 million speakers worldwide), Croatian (5 million), or Slovene (2 million). It's essential to find a common language with the rest of the world—so they learn English early and well. In Croatia, for example, all schoolchildren start learning English in the third grade. (I've had surprisingly eloquent conversations with Croatian grade-schoolers.)

Of course, not everyone speaks English. You'll run into the most substantial language barriers in situations when you need to deal with a clerk or service person aged 40 or above (train-station and post-office counters, maids, museum guards, bakers, and so on). Be reasonable in your expectations. Czech post-office clerks and Polish museum ticket-sellers are every bit as friendly, cheery, and multilingual as their American counterparts.

Luckily, it's relatively easy to get your point across in these situations. I've often bought a train ticket simply by writing out the name of my destination (preferably with the local spelling—for example, "Praha" instead of "Prague"); the time I want to travel (using the 24-hour clock); and, if I'm not traveling on the same day I'm buying the ticket, I include the date I want to leave (day first, then the month as a Roman numeral, then the year). Here's an example of what I'd show a ticket-seller at a train station: "Warszawa, 17:30, 15.VII.10."

Eastern Europeans, realizing that their language intimidates Americans, often invent easier nicknames for themselves—so Šárka goes by "Sara," András becomes "Andrew," and Jaroslav tells you, "Call me Jerry."

Most of the destinations in this book—the Czech Republic, Slovakia, Poland, Slovenia, Croatia, and Bosnia-Herzegovina—speak Slavic languages. These languages are closely related to each other and to Russian, and are, to varying degrees, mutually intelligible (though many spellings change—for example, Czech *hrad*, or "castle," becomes Croatian *grad*). Slavic languages have simple vocabularies but are highly inflected—that is, the meaning of a sentence depends on complicated endings that are tacked onto the ends of the words (as in Latin).

Slavic words are notorious for their seemingly unpronounceable, long strings of consonants. Slavic pronunciation can be tricky. In fact, when the first Christian missionaries, Cyril and Methodius, came to Eastern Europe a millennium ago, they invented a whole new alphabet to represent these strange Slavic sounds. A modified version of that alphabet—called Cyrillic—is still used today in the eastern Slavic countries (such as Serbia and Russia).

Fortunately, the destinations covered in this book all use the same Roman alphabet we do, but they add lots of different diacritics—little markings below and above some letters—to represent a wide range of sounds (for example, č, ą, ó, đ, ł). I explain each of these diacritics in this book's various country introductions.

Hungarian is another story altogether—it's completely unrelated to Slavic languages, German, or English. For more on the challenging Magyar tongue, see page 469.

German is spoken in Vienna. As part of the same language family as English, German sounds noticeably more familiar to American ears than the Slavic languages. Throughout Eastern Europe, speaking German can come in handy, especially if you're interacting with somebody over age 40 (while few people under communism learned English, German ranked right up there with Russian as a popular second language). A few words of Italian can come in handy in Slovenia and Croatia.

There are certain universal English words all Eastern Europeans know: hello, please, thank you, super, pardon, stop, menu, problem, and no problem. Another handy word that people throughout the region will understand is *Servus* (SEHR-voos)—the old-fashioned greeting from the days of the Austro-Hungarian Empire. If you draw a blank on how to say hello in the local language, just offer a cheery, *"Servus!"*

Get an ear for the local language (see the language section in each of this book's country introductions), learn the key phrases (you'll find survival phrases for each language starting on page 1120), and travel with a phrase book. Consider Lonely Planet's good *Eastern Europe Phrasebook,* which covers all of the destinations in this book (except Vienna).

Don't be afraid to interact with locals. Eastern Europeans can initially seem shy or even brusque—a holdover from the closed communist society—but often a simple smile is the only icebreaker you need to make a new friend. You'll find that doors open a little more quickly when you know a few words of the language. Give it your best shot. The locals will appreciate your efforts.

Telephones

Smart travelers learn the phone system and use it daily to reserve or reconfirm rooms, get tourist information, reserve restaurants, confirm tour times, or phone home. This section covers dialing instructions, phone cards, and types of phones. (If you need more in-depth information than I provide below, see www.ricksteves.com/phoning.)

How to Dial

Calling from the US to Europe, or vice versa, is simple—once you

break the code. The European calling chart in this chapter will walk you through it.

Dialing Domestically within Eastern Europe

About half of all European countries use area codes; the other half use a direct-dial system without area codes.

In countries that use area codes (such as Slovakia, Slovenia, Croatia, and Austria), you dial the local number when calling within a city, and add the area code (which starts with a zero) if calling long distance within the same country. For example, Dubrovnik's area code is 020, and the number of one of my recommended Dubrovnik B&Bs is 453-834. To call the B&B within Dubrovnik, just dial 453-834. To call it from Split, dial 020/453-834.

Hungary, which also uses area codes, is a special case: To call within the same city, just dial the local number. But for long distance within Hungary, you have to dial "06," followed by the area code and number. For example, to call a hotel in Eger, I'd dial 411-711 if I'm calling from within Eger; but from Budapest, I'd have to dial 06, then 36 (Eger's area code), then 411-711. For more on the confusing Hungarian phone system, see page 454.

To make calls within a country that uses a direct-dial system (such as the Czech Republic or Poland), you dial the same number whether you're calling across the country or across the street.

Don't be surprised that in some countries, local phone numbers have different numbers of digits within the same city, or even the same hotel (e.g., a hotel can have a 6-digit phone number, a 7-digit mobile phone number, and an 8-digit fax number).

Dialing Internationally to or from Eastern Europe

If you want to make an international call, follow these steps:

1. Dial the international access code (00 if you're calling from Europe, 011 from the US or Canada).

2. Dial the country code of the country you're calling (see the European calling chart in this chapter).

3. Dial the area code (if applicable) and the local number, keeping in mind that calling many countries requires dropping the initial zero of the phone number (the calling chart lists specifics per country).

Here are some examples:

Calling from the US to Croatia: To call from the US to the Dubrovnik B&B from the US, dial 011, 385 (Croatia's country code), 20 (Dubrovnik's area code without the initial zero), and 453-834.

Calling from any European country to the US: To call my office in Edmonds, Washington, from anywhere in Europe, I dial 00 (Europe's international access code), 1 (the US country code),

425 (Edmonds' area code), and 771-8303.

Note: You might see a + in front of a European number. When dialing the number, replace the + with the international access code of the country you're calling from (00 from Europe, 011 from the US or Canada).

Public Phones and Hotel-Room Phones

To make calls from public phones, you'll need a prepaid phone card. There are two different kinds of phone cards: insertable (usable only in pay phones) and international (usable from any phone, but hard to find). Coin-op phones are virtually extinct.

Insertable phone cards: This type of card is a convenient way to pay for calls from public pay phones and can be purchased at post offices, newsstands, and tobacco shops. Simply take the phone off the hook, insert the prepaid card, wait for a dial tone, and dial away. The price of the call (local or international) is automatically deducted while you talk. These cards only work in the country where you buy them (so your Czech phone card is worthless in Poland). Insertable phone cards are a good deal for calling within Europe, but calling the US can be pricey (at least 50 cents/min). Be aware that with the prevalence of mobile phones, public phones are getting harder to find.

International phone cards: Although common throughout much of Western Europe, international phone cards are still relatively rare (and more expensive) in the East. You're more likely to find them in the Czech Republic than in other countries in this book (in Prague, look for the Smartcall brand—with a black-and-orange ad). Try looking for fliers advertising long-distance rates, or ask about the cards at Internet cafés, newsstands, exchange bureaus, souvenir shops, and youth hostels. I'd buy a low denomination in case the card turns out to be a dud. These cards generally work only in the country where you buy them.

If you can snare one of these cards, your calls to the US will generally cost around 25–50 cents per minute (and you can also use them for domestic calls). They work from any type of phone, including the one in your hotel room (but ask at the front desk if there are any fees for calling the access number). To use the card, you'll dial a toll-free access number, then type in your scratch-to-reveal PIN number. But a few of the cards I've tried have an access number that's not toll-free—which means that you pay both for the call, and for the time being deducted from your card.

Hotel Room Phones: Calling from your hotel room can be cheap for local calls (ask for the rates at the front desk first), but is often a rip-off for long-distance calls. Incoming calls are free, making this an inexpensive way for friends and family to stay in touch (provided they have a good long-distance plan for calls to

Europe—and a list of your hotels' phone numbers). If you're staying at a private room—such as Croatia's *sobe*—be aware that you're unlikely to have a telephone in your room.

Metered Phones: These are available in phone offices and sometimes in bigger post offices. You can talk all you want, then pay the bill when you leave—but be sure you know the rates before you have a lengthy conversation.

US Calling Cards: These cards, such as the ones offered by AT&T, Verizon, or Sprint, are the worst option. You'll nearly always save a lot of money by using a pay phone and a locally purchased, insertable phone card instead.

Mobile Phones

Many travelers enjoy the convenience of traveling with a mobile phone.

Using Your Mobile Phone: Your US mobile phone works in Europe if it's GSM-enabled, tri-band or quad-band, and on a calling plan that includes international calls. For example, with a T-Mobile phone, you'll pay $1 to $1.50 per minute to make or receive a call, and about $0.35 apiece for text messages.

You can save money if your phone is electronically "unlocked"—then you can simply buy a **SIM card** (a fingernail-sized chip that stores the phone's information) in Europe. SIM cards, which give you a European phone number, are sold at mobile-phone stores and some newsstand kiosks for about $5–10; this usually includes some calling time (enough for a few minutes' worth of calls in that country). Simply insert the SIM card in your phone (usually in a slot behind the battery), and it'll work like a European mobile phone. When buying a SIM card, always ask about fees for domestic and international calls, roaming charges, and how to check your credit balance and buy more time.

Many **smartphones**, such as the iPhone or BlackBerry, work in Europe—but beware of sky-high fees, especially for data downloading (checking email, browsing the Internet, watching videos, and so on). Ask your provider in advance how to avoid unwittingly "roaming" your way to a huge bill. Some applications allow for cheap or free smartphone calls over a Wi-Fi connection (see "Calling over the Internet," below).

Using a European Mobile Phone: Local mobile-phone shops all over Europe sell basic phones for around $50–100. You'll also need to buy a SIM card (explained above) and prepaid credit for making calls. If you remain in the phone's home country, domestic calls are reasonable, and incoming calls are free. You'll pay more if you're "roaming" in another country. If your phone is "unlocked," you can swap out its SIM card for a new one in other countries.

European Calling Chart

Just smile and dial, using this key:
AC = Area Code, LN = Local Number.

European Country	Calling long distance within...	Calling from the US or Canada to...	Calling from a European country to...
Austria	AC + LN	011 + 43 + AC (without the initial zero) + LN	00 + 43 + AC (without the initial zero) + LN
Belgium	LN	011 + 32 + LN (without initial zero)	00 + 32 + LN (without initial zero)
Bosnia-Herzegovina	AC + LN	011 + 387 + AC (without initial zero) + LN	00 + 387 + AC (without initial zero) + LN
Britain	AC + LN	011 + 44 + AC (without initial zero) + LN	00 + 44 + AC (without initial zero) + LN
Croatia	AC + LN	011 + 385 + AC (without initial zero) + LN	00 + 385 + AC (without initial zero) + LN
Czech Republic	LN	011 + 420 + LN	00 + 420 + LN
Denmark	LN	011 + 45 + LN	00 + 45 + LN
Estonia	LN	011 + 372 + LN	00 + 372 + LN
Finland	AC + LN	011 + 358 + AC (without initial zero) + LN	999 (or other 900 number) + 358 + AC (without initial zero) + LN
France	LN	011 + 33 + LN (without initial zero)	00 + 33 + LN (without initial zero)
Germany	AC + LN	011 + 49 + AC (without initial zero) + LN	00 + 49 + AC (without initial zero) + LN
Gibraltar	LN	011 + 350 + LN	00 + 350 + LN
Greece	LN	011 + 30 + LN	00 + 30 + LN
Hungary	06 + AC + LN	011 + 36 + AC + LN	00 + 36 + AC + LN
Ireland	AC + LN	011 + 353 + AC (without initial zero) + LN	00 + 353 + AC (without initial zero) + LN

European Country	Calling long distance within...	Calling from the US or Canada to...	Calling from a European country to...
Italy	LN	011 + 39 + LN	00 + 39 + LN
Montenegro	AC + LN	011 + 382 + AC (without initial zero) + LN	00 + 382 + AC (without initial zero) + LN
Morocco	LN	011 + 212 + LN (without initial zero)	00 + 212 + LN (without initial zero)
Netherlands	AC + LN	011 + 31 + AC (without initial zero) + LN	00 + 31 + AC (without initial zero) + LN
Norway	LN	011 + 47 + LN	00 + 47 + LN
Poland	LN	011 + 48 + LN (without initial zero)	00 + 48 + LN (without initial zero)
Portugal	LN	011 + 351 + LN	00 + 351 + LN
Slovakia	AC + LN	011 + 421 + AC (without initial zero) + LN	00 + 421 + AC (without initial zero) + LN
Slovenia	AC + LN	011 + 386 + AC (without initial zero) + LN	00 + 386 + AC (without initial zero) + LN
Spain	LN	011 + 34 + LN	00 + 34 + LN
Sweden	AC + LN	011 + 46 + AC (without initial zero) + LN	00 + 46 + AC (without initial zero) + LN
Switzerland	LN	011 + 41 + LN (without initial zero)	00 + 41 + LN (without initial zero)
Turkey	AC (if there's no initial zero, add one) + LN	011 + 90 + AC (without initial zero) + LN	00 + 90 + AC (without initial zero) + LN

- The instructions above apply whether you're calling a land line or mobile phone.
- The international access codes (the first numbers you dial when making an international call) are 011 if you're calling from the US or Canada, or 00 if you're calling from virtually anywhere in Europe (except Finland, where it's 999 or another 900 number, depending on the phone service you're using).
- To call the US or Canada from Europe, dial 00, then 1 (the country code for the US and Canada), then the area code and number. In short, 00 + 1 + AC + LN = Hi, Mom!

Calling over the Internet

Some things that seem too good to be true...actually are true. If you're traveling with a laptop, you can make calls using **VoIP** (Voice over Internet Protocol). With VoIP, two computers act as the phones, and the Internet-based calls are free (or you can pay a few cents per minute to call from your computer to a telephone). The major providers are Skype (www.skype.com) and Google Talk (www.google.com/talk).

Useful Phone Numbers

Emergencies

For medical or other emergencies, dial 112 in any of the countries in this book (except Bosnia-Herzegovina, where it's 124). For police, dial 112 in Slovakia, Hungary, Poland, or Austria; dial 158 in the Czech Republic; dial 113 in Slovenia; dial 92 in Croatia; and dial 122 in Bosnia-Herzegovina.

US Embassies

In Austria: Parkring 12a, Vienna, passport services available Mon–Fri 8:00–11:30, tel. 01/313-390, www.usembassy.at.

In Bosnia-Herzegovina: Alipašina 43, Sarajevo, passport services available Mon–Fri 14:00–15:30 plus Fri 8:00–10:30, tel. 033/445-700, on weekends and after hours call the same number and press 0 after the recording, http://sarajevo.usembassy.gov. There's also a branch office in Mostar (Mostarskog Bataljona b.b., tel. 036/580-580).

In Croatia: ulica Thomasa Jeffersona 2, Zagreb, passport services available Mon–Thu 13:00–15:00 plus Wed 9:00–11:00, tel. 01/661-2200, after business-hours tel. 01/661-2400, consular services tel. 01/661-2300, http://zagreb.usembassy.gov.

In the Czech Republic: Tržiště 15, Prague, passport services available Mon–Fri 9:00–11:30, tel. 257-022-000, www.usembassy.cz.

In Hungary: Szabadság tér 12, Budapest, passport services available Mon–Thu 13:00–16:00, Fri 9:00–12:00 & 13:00–16:00, tel. 1/475-4400, after-hours emergency tel. 1/475-4703 or 1/475-4924, www.usembassy.hu.

In Poland: ulica Piękna 12, Warsaw, passport services available Mon–Fri 9:00–12:00, tel. 022-625-1401, www.usinfo.pl; also a US Consulate in Kraków at ulica Stolarska 9, passport services available Mon–Fri 8:30–15:00, tel. 012-424-5183.

In Slovakia: Hviezdoslavovo námestie 4, Bratislava, passport services available Mon–Fri 8:00–11:45 & 14:00–15:15, tel. 02/5443-0861, http://slovakia.usembassy.gov.

In Slovenia: Prešernova 31, Ljubljana, passport services available Mon–Fri 9:00–11:30 & 13:00–15:00, tel. 01/200-5595, after business hours tel. 01/200-5500, www.usembassy.si.

Canadian Embassies

For after-hours emergencies, Canadian citizens can call collect to the Foreign Services Office in Ottawa, Canada at 613/996-8885.

In Austria: Laurenzerberg 2, Vienna, passport services available Mon–Fri 8:30–12:30 & 13:30–15:30, tel. 01/313-83000, toll-free emergency tel. 800-2326-6831, www.austria.gc.ca.

In Bosnia-Herzegovina: Services provided by Canadian Embassy in Budapest, Hungary (listed below).

In Croatia: Prilaz Đjure Deželića 4, Zagreb, passport services available Mon–Thu 10:00–12:00 & 13:00–15:00, Fri 10:00–13:00, tel. 01/488-1200, www.croatia.gc.ca.

In the Czech Republic: Muchova 6, Prague, passport services available Mon–Fri 8:30–12:30 & 13:30–16:30, tel. 272-101-800, www.czechrepublic.gc.ca; also provides services for Slovakia.

In Hungary: Ganz ulica 12–14, Budapest, passport services available Mon–Thu 8:00–16:30, Fri 8:00–13:30, tel. 1/392-3360, www.hungary.gc.ca; also provides services for Bosnia-Herzegovina and Slovenia.

In Poland: ulica Jana Matejki 1–5, Warsaw, passport services available Mon–Fri 8:30–16:30, tel. 022-584-3100, toll-free emergency tel. 800-111-4319, www.canada.pl.

In Slovakia: Mostova 2, Bratislava, passport services available Mon–Fri 8:30–12:00 & 13:30–16:30, tel. 02/5920-4031; some services provided through Canadian Embassy in Prague, Czech Republic (listed above).

Canadian Consulate in Slovenia: Trg Republike 3, 12th floor, Ljubljana, passport services available Mon–Fri 9:00–13:00, tel. 01/252-4444; some services provided through Canadian Embassy in Budapest, Hungary (listed above).

Travel Advisories

US Department of State: tel. 202/647-5225, www.travel.state.gov

Canadian Department of Foreign Affairs: Canadian tel. 800-267-6788, www.dfait-maeci.gc.ca

US Centers for Disease Control and Prevention: tel. 800-CDC-INFO (800-232-4636), www.cdc.gov/travel

Directory Assistance

Dial 1188 in the Czech Republic, 913 in Poland, 198 in Hungary, 988 in Croatia or Slovenia, 1181 in Slovakia, and 16 in Austria.

The Internet

The Internet can be an invaluable tool for planning your trip (researching and booking hotels, checking bus and train schedules, and so on). It's also useful to get online periodically as you travel—to reconfirm your trip plans, check the weather, catch up

on email, blog or post photos from your trip, or call folks back home (explained earlier, under "Calling over the Internet").

Some hotels offer a computer in the lobby with Internet access for guests. Smaller places may sometimes let you sit at their desk for a few minutes just to check your email, if you ask politely.

Internet connections for laptop users are becoming commonplace at most hotels and B&Bs. Many accommodations that offer this do so for free, but some (especially fancier chain hotels) charge by the minute. You'll either access the hotel's wireless Internet (Wi-Fi), sometimes using a password provided by the hotelier; or plug your computer directly into an Internet wall socket (they can usually loan you a cable). On my last trip, I was able to get online at most hotels in this book.

If your hotel doesn't have access, ask your hotelier to direct you to the nearest place to get online. You can generally find a café with Wi-Fi or an Internet hotspot in most towns.

Mail

Get stamps at the neighborhood post office, newsstands within fancy hotels, and some mini-marts and card shops. While you can arrange for mail delivery to your hotel (allow 10 days for a letter to arrive), phoning and emailing are so easy that I've dispensed with mail stops altogether.

Transportation

By Car or Public Transportation?

In Eastern Europe, I travel mostly by public transportation. For long distances between big cities (such as Prague to Kraków, Warsaw to Budapest, or Vienna to Dubrovnik), I prefer to take a cheap flight or a night train. For shorter distances (like Gdańsk to Warsaw or Ljubljana to Zagreb), I take a daytime train or bus. In areas with lots of exciting day-trip possibilities, such as the Czech or Slovenian countryside, I rent a car for a day or two—or hire a local with a car to drive me around (which can be cheaper than you might think; in this book, I recommend several drivers and tour guides with cars).

If you're debating between public transportation and car rental, consider these factors: Cars are best for three or more traveling together (especially families with small kids), those packing heavy, and those scouring the countryside. Trains, buses, and boats are best for solo travelers, blitz tourists, and city-to-city travelers; those with an ambitious, multi-country itinerary; and those who don't want to drive in Europe. While a car gives you more freedom—enabling you to search for hotels more easily and carrying your bags for you—trains, buses, and boats zip you effortlessly

and scenically from city to city, usually dropping you in the center, often near a TI. Cars are great in the countryside, but a worthless headache in places like Prague, Budapest, and Dubrovnik.

Public Transportation

Throughout this book, I'll suggest whether trains, buses, or boats are better for a particular destination (in the "Connections" section at the end of each chapter).

Trains

Trains are punctual and cover cities well, but frustrating schedules make a few out-of-the-way recommendations difficult—or impossible—to reach (usually the bus will get you there instead; see "Buses," later).

Schedules: Pick up train schedules from stations as you go, or print them out from an online source. To study ahead on the Web, check http://bahn.hafas.de/bin/query.exe/en (Germany's excellent all-Europe timetable). Individual countries also have their own train timetable websites:

- **Czech Republic:** www.idos.cz
- **Slovakia:** www.cp.sk
- **Poland:** www.rozklad-pkp.pl
- **Hungary:** www.elvira.hu
- **Slovenia:** www.slo-zeleznice.si
- **Croatia:** www.hznet.hr
- **Austria:** www.oebb.at

Tickets: Buy tickets at the train station (or on board, if the station is unstaffed). In many big-city train stations, it can be tricky to find the correct line (you'll see separate ticket windows for domestic trips, international journeys, and other concerns—all of them poorly marked). Before getting in line, confirm with fellow travelers that you've chosen the right one. Many ticket-sellers speak limited (or no) English—be prepared to write out your destination and time. Bigger cities have train-ticket offices, either downtown (such as in Prague, Budapest, and Kraków) or in the station (such as in Warsaw and Ljubljana) where you can take a number to wait for an English-speaking clerk to sort through your options; I've listed these in this book. Especially if you have a complicated request (such as reserving a night-train berth a few days ahead), these offices can save you some frustration, and—in some cases—a needless trip to the station. While most short-haul journeys do not require a reservation, you are required to reserve on some high-speed trains (such as the Warsaw-Kraków express). It's also smart to reserve a sleeping berth if you're taking a night train.

Night Trains: To cover the long distances between the major destinations in this book, consider using night trains (or taking

Public Transportation in Eastern Europe
To Copenhagen
To Rødby (Denmark)
To Ystad (Sweden)
To Ystad & Copenhagen
Baltic Sea
LITH.
KALININGRAD (RUSSIA)
Gdynia
Gdańsk
Sopot
To Vilnius & Riga
Lübeck
Puttgarten
Hamburg
To Amsterdam
Swinoujście
Tczew
Malbork
Szczecin
Toruń
To Brest & Moscow
Frankfurt an der Oder
Berlin
Poznań
Warsaw
To Amsterdam
Forst
GERMANY
POLAND
Leipzig
Görlitz
Dresden
Zgor.
Wrocław
Częstochowa
Schona
Opole
Katowice
Oświęcim (Auschwitz)
Karlovy Vary
Lichkov
To Frankfurt
Prague
CZECH. REP.
Zeb.
Kraków
Medyka
Cheb
Plzeň
Žil.
Zak.
Plaveč
To L'viv
Furth
Nürnberg
Český Krumlov
České Bud.
Brno
SLOVAKIA
Levoča
UKR.
To Frankfurt
Sum.
Břeclav
Spišská Nova Ves
Košice
Passau
Gmünd
Bratislava
Munich
Linz
Vienna
Eger
Cana
Miskolc
Heg.
Salzburg
Füzesabony
Inns.
Graz
Sopron
Győr
Budapest
To Zürich
AUSTRIA
Siófok
Curtici
Villach
Klag
Spiel.
Tarvisio
Jes.
Mar.
Hodos
HUNGARY
To Bucharest
ITALY
Bled
SLOVENIA
Ljub.
Kop.
Pécs
To Milan
Trieste
V.O.
Zagreb
Subotica
Verona
ROMANIA
Venice
Rijeka
Koper
CROATIA
Šid
Piran
Zadar
Plitvice
Belgrade
Rovinj
Pula
BOSNIA-HERZ.
SERBIA
Bologna
Adriatic Sea
Split
Sarajevo
BULG.
Niš
Kalotina
ITALY
Mostar
Ploče
Florence
Ancona
Korčula
MONT.
Pres.
KOS.
To Sofia & Istanbul
Dubrovnik
Skopje
MACE-DONIA
Rome
Kotor
Bar
ALB.
To Athens
To Naples
Not to Scale
Bari
Bus Route
Ferry Route
Railway
Border Station

an inexpensive flight—see "Cheap Flights," later). Each night on the train saves a day for sightseeing. Fortunately, most of Eastern Europe's big cities are connected by night trains. I appreciate the convenience of night trains, and take them routinely. Still, some of my readers have complained that Eastern European night trains aren't as new, plush, and comfy as those they've used in the West. Expect a bumpy, noisy ride and gross WCs. In general, if you're accustomed to a higher degree of comfort, fly or take a day train.

One more thing: No matter how many times you hear "totally true" stories of train cars being "gassed" with a sleep-inducing drug by thieves, it's an urban legend, most likely invented by travelers who felt foolish for sleeping through a theft. But as on Western European night trains, thefts do occur, so lock the door and secure your belongings (to make it difficult—or at least noisy—for thieves to rip you off). When sleeping on a night train, I wear my money belt.

Railpasses: While railpasses can be a good deal in Western Europe, they aren't necessarily the best option in the East for two reasons: Point-to-point tickets are cheap and simple here, and most railpasses don't conveniently combine Eastern European countries. For example, with the Eurail Selectpass, you can buy unlimited travel for up to 15 travel days (within a two-month period) in three, four, or five adjacent countries; but of the countries in this book, only Hungary, Austria, the Czech Republic, and Slovenia/Croatia are eligible. A more popular option is the European East Pass, covering the Czech Republic, Hungary, Poland, Slovakia, and Austria—but not Slovenia or Croatia. Each country except Bosnia-Herzegovina has its own individual railpass, valid for trips only within that country. Various pre-selected two- and three-country options are also available. Again, none of these passes is likely to save you much money, but if a pass matches your itinerary, give it a look and crunch the numbers. For options, including approximate point-to-point train fares, see www.ricksteves.com/rail.

Buses

While the train can get you most places faster than a bus can, this book covers a few areas where buses are worth considering. For example, Ljubljana and Lake Bled are connected by both train and bus—but the bus station is right in the town center of Bled, while the train station is a few miles away. And a few destinations, including Croatia's Plitvice Lakes National Park and Rovinj, are accessible only by bus. In general, trains are best in Poland and Hungary; buses are often better in Slovakia and Croatia; and it's a toss-up in the Czech Republic and Slovenia. When in doubt, ask at the local TI for advice.

Boats

Once you get to the Croatian coast, boats can be your best option. For details, see "Getting Around the Dalmatian Coast" on page 745.

Renting a Car

Bring your US driver's license. Given the language barrier, it can be helpful (and, in fact, is required by some countries) to get an International Driving Permit ahead of time at your local AAA office ($15 plus two passport-type photos, www.aaa.com). However, I've frequently rented cars in Eastern Europe and traveled problem-free with just my US license.

Drivers under the age of 25 may incur a young-driver surcharge, and some rental companies do not rent to anyone 75 and over. If you're considered too old, look into leasing (explained later), which has less stringent age restrictions.

Research car rentals before you go. It's cheaper to arrange long-term European car rentals in the US than in Europe. For short rentals of a day or two, I've had pretty good luck finding an affordable car on the spot (I've listed car-rental companies in this book)—but if your itinerary is set, it doesn't hurt to book ahead. All of the big American companies have offices throughout Eastern Europe. Two reputable consolidators among many are Auto Europe (www.autoeurope.com) and Europe by Car (www.ebctravel.com). Comparison-shop on the Web to find the best deal, or ask your travel agent. For a longer trip, look into leasing (described later).

Expect to pay about $300–450 to rent a small economy car for two weeks with unlimited mileage, basic insurance, gas, and tolls. Note that short rentals cost significantly more per day. I normally rent a small, inexpensive model like a Ford Fiesta or Škoda Fabia. You'll pay extra for Collision Damage Waiver (CDW) insurance (described later). Be warned that dropping a car off in a different country—say, picking up in Prague and dropping in Dubrovnik—can be prohibitively expensive (depends on distance, but the extra fee averages a few hundred dollars, and can exceed $1,000). If you're doing a multi-country trip by car, find out what the international drop-off fee will be. If it's exorbitant, consider instead doing a round-trip itinerary, renting a car per country...or using public transportation. Again, I prefer to connect long distances by train or bus, then rent cars for a day or two where they're most useful. But be aware that some companies have a minimum rental period (generally three days); you can keep the car for fewer days, but you'll pay for the minimum period anyway. If you want the car for just a day or two, try to find a company that allows short rentals.

Almost all rentals are manual by default, so if you need an automatic, you must request one in advance; be aware that these

Driving: Distance & Time
Not to Scale
To Gdańsk
GERMANY
POLAND
CZECH REPUBLIC
SLOVAKIA
AUSTRIA
HUNGARY
SLOVENIA
ITALY
SERBIA
CROATIA
BOSNIA-HERZEGOVINA
MONT.
Adriatic Sea
Berlin
Poznań
Toruń
Warsaw
Dresden
Terezín
Prague
Karlštejn Castle
Kutná Hora
Częstochowa
Auschwitz
Kraków
Zakopane
Poprad
Brno
Český Krumlov
Vienna
Bratislava
Eger
Munich
Salzburg
Budapest
Pécs
Bled
Ljubljana
Zagreb
Trieste
Venice
Rovinj
Rijeka
Pula
Plitvice
Zadar
Split
Mostar
Ston
Korčula
Dubrovnik
120m 2.5h
215m 5h
220m • 3.5h
180m • 3.75h
190m • 4h
120m 2.25h
365m • 8h
140m • 3.5h
185m • 4.5h
390m • 9.5h
65m 1.5h
65m 1.75h
80m • 2h
40m 1.25h
290m • 5.5h
40m 1h
25k • .75h
40m 1.25h
100m • 2.25h
100m • 2.75h
175m • 3.5h
130m • 2.5h
180m • 4h
45m 1.5h
80m 2h
200m • 4h
200m • 3.5h
115m • 3.5h
240m • 4h
135m • 3.25h
80m 1.5h
240m • 5.5h
40m 1h
140m • 3h
125m • 2h
125m • 2h
80m • 2h
90m 1.5h
150m • 2.5h
240m 4h
235m • 4h
275m • 5h
145m • 2.5h
130m • 2.75h
125m • 3.5h
30m 1h
90m • 2h
60m 1.5h
140m • 2h
240m • 5h
75m 2h
100m • 1.75h
100m • 4h
50m • 1.5h
85m • 2h
90m • 2.5h
30m • .75h
55m 1.5h
140m • 3h
85m 1.75h
125m • 4.5h
65m 2h
110m • 5h
105m • 2.5h
35m 1h
35m • 1h
3.4h
Note: Your times may vary based on traffic, construction, and road conditions.
m = miles
h = hours
--- = car ferry

cars are usually larger models (not as maneuverable on narrow, winding roads). An automatic transmission adds about 50 percent to the car-rental cost over a manual transmission.

As a rule, always tell your car-rental company up front exactly which countries you'll be entering. Some companies levy extra insurance fees for trips taken with certain types of cars (such as BMWs, Mercedes, and convertibles) in certain countries. Or the company may prohibit driving the car in off-the-beaten-track destinations, such as Bosnia-Herzegovina. As you cross borders, you may need to show the proper paperwork, such as proof of insurance (called a "green card"). Double-check with your rental agent that you have all the documentation you need before you drive off.

When picking up the car, check it thoroughly and make sure any damage is noted on your rental agreement. Find out how your car's lights, turn signals, wipers, and gas cap function, and be sure you know what type of fuel your car takes.

If you drop off your car early or keep it longer, you'll be credited or charged at a fair, prorated price. But always keep your receipts in case any questions arise about your billing.

Before returning your car, make sure you understand where the office is located (and get directions), and what time it's open. As gas stations can be sparse in some cities, begin looking for a chance to fill up long before you reach your drop-off point (ideally at an expressway stop on the way into town). When you turn in the car, be sure the agent verifies its condition with you.

Car Insurance Options

Accidents can happen anywhere, but when you're on vacation, the last thing you need is stress over car insurance. When you rent a car, you are liable for a very high deductible, sometimes equal to the entire value of the car. Limit your financial risk in case of an accident by choosing one of these three options: Buy Collision Damage Waiver (CDW) coverage from the car-rental company, get coverage through your credit card (free, but more complicated), or buy coverage through Travel Guard.

While each rental company has its own variation, the basic **CDW** costs $15–25 a day (figure roughly 25 percent extra) and reduces your liability, but does not eliminate it. When you pick up the car, you'll be offered the chance to "buy down" the basic deductible to zero (for an additional $10–30/day; sometimes called "super CDW").

If you opt for **credit-card coverage,** there's a catch. You'll technically have to decline all coverage offered by the car-rental company, which means they can place a hold on your card for the full deductible amount. In case of damage, it can be time-consuming to resolve the charges with your credit-card company. Before

you decide on this option, quiz your credit-card company about how it works and ask them to explain the worst-case scenario.

Finally, you can buy CDW-type insurance from **Travel Guard** ($9/day plus a one-time $3 service fee covers you up to $35,000, $250 deductible, tel. 800-826-4919, www.travelguard.com). It's valid everywhere in Europe except for the Republic of Ireland, and some Italian car-rental companies refuse to honor it. Oddly, residents of Washington State aren't allowed to buy this coverage.

For more fine print about car-rental insurance, see www.ricksteves.com/cdw.

Leasing

For trips of two and a half weeks or more, leasing (which automatically includes zero-deductible collision and theft insurance) is the best way to go. By technically buying and then selling back the car, you save lots of money on tax and insurance, but you may have to pick up and drop off the car in Germany or Italy. Leasing provides you a new car with unlimited mileage and a 24-hour emergency assistance program. You can lease for as little as 17 days to as long as six months. Car leases must be arranged from the US. One of many companies offering affordable lease packages is Europe by Car (US tel. 800-223-1516, www.ebctravel.com).

Driving

On the Road: Learn the universal road signs. Bring your driver's license. Seat belts are required, and two beers under those belts are enough to land you in jail. More and more European countries—including the Czech Republic, Poland, Hungary, Slovenia, Croatia, and Bosnia-Herzegovina—require you to have your headlights on whenever you're driving, even in broad daylight. The lights on many newer cars automatically turn on and off with the engine, but others are manually controlled—ask when you pick up your car. Many countries prohibit using handheld mobile phones while driving.

Fuel: Gas is expensive—often about $6 per gallon. Diesel cars are more common in Europe than back home, so be sure you know what type of gas your car takes before you fill up. Gas pumps are color-coded for unleaded or diesel.

Road Conditions: Throughout Eastern Europe, superhighways are being rolled out like crazy. Since construction is ongoing, it's not unusual to discover that a not-yet-finished expressway ends, requiring a transfer to an older, slower road. Likewise,

you'll sometimes discover that a much faster road has been built between major destinations since your three-year-old map was published. (This is another good reason to travel with the most up-to-date maps available and study them before each drive.) Over the last several years, new superhighways opened between Dresden and Prague (A17), and from Zagreb to Budapest (to the north) and Zagreb to Split (to the south). As soon as a long-enough section is completed, the roads are opened to the public.

Occasionally back-country roads are the only option (especially in Poland and Slovakia). These can be bumpy and slow, but they're almost always paved (or, at least, they once were). In Poland, where the network of new expressways is far from complete, locals travel long distances on two-lane country roads. Since each lane is about a lane and a half wide, passing is commonplace. Slower drivers should keep to the far-right of their lane, and not be surprised when faster cars zip past them.

Tolls: In many countries, driving on highways requires a toll sticker (generally available at the border, post offices, gas stations, and sometimes car-rental agencies): the **Czech Republic** (*dálnični známka,* 200 Kč/15 days, 300 Kč/2 months); **Slovakia** (*úhrada,* €4.90/week, €9.90/month, www.ndsas.sk/vignettes); **Hungary** (*autópálya matrica,* 1,170–1,530 Ft/4 days depending on season, 2,550 Ft/10 days, 4,200 Ft/month, www.motorway.hu); **Slovenia** (*vinjeta,* €15/week, €30/month); and **Austria** (*Vignette,* €7.90/10 days, €22.90/2 months). Fines for not having a toll sticker can be stiff. Note that you don't need a toll sticker if you'll be dipping into the country on minor roads—only for major highways. Your rental car may already come with the necessary sticker—ask. In **Croatia,** you'll take a toll-ticket as you enter the expressway, then pay when you get off, based on how far you've traveled (figure about $8/hr). In **Poland,** drivers also pay tolls to use completed expressway segments.

Parking: Parking is a costly headache in big cities. You'll pay

about $10–25 a day to park safely. Rental-car theft can be a problem in cities (especially Prague), so ask at your hotel for advice.

Cheap Flights

Low-cost airlines allow you to cheaply connect many of the destinations in this book. Two well-established budget airlines are based in Eastern Europe: **Wizz Air** (www.wizzair.com, with hubs in Budapest, Prague, Warsaw, Gdańsk, and Katowice, near Kraków) and **Smart Wings** (www.smartwings.net, based in Prague). Several Western European budget airlines also fly to Eastern European destinations. These include **easyJet** (www.easyjet.com), **Ryanair** (www.ryanair.com), **Air Berlin** (www.airberlin.com), and **Norwegian Air** (www.norwegian.no).

A visit to **www.skyscanner.net** sorts through the numerous options offered by the many discount airlines, enabling you to see the best schedules for your trip and come up with the best deal. Other good search engines include www.mobissimo.com and www.wegolo.com.

Be aware of the potential drawbacks of flying on the cheap: nonrefundable and nonchangeable tickets, minimal customer assistance, and pricey baggage fees. Especially if you're traveling with lots of luggage, a cheap flight can quickly become a bad deal. To avoid unpleasant surprises, read the small print—especially baggage policies—before you book. Also be aware that you'll sometimes fly out of less convenient, secondary airports. For example, Wizz Air's flights from "Kraków" actually depart from Katowice, 50 miles away.

Now that the established airlines in Eastern Europe face more competition, they've been forced to adapt. Many national carriers charge reasonable fares for short-distance trips. For example, check out Croatia Airlines (www.croatiaairlines.com) and Poland's LOT Airlines (www.lot.com). On recent trips, I've flown affordably on LOT between Kraków and Ljubljana, and between Kraków and Budapest, avoiding lengthy overland journeys.

Europe by Air offers a Flight Pass, charging $99 per leg (plus taxes and airport fees) for flights within Europe. They partner with various well-established airlines, providing good coverage for low prices (most useful for Croatia Airlines flights to and from the Dalmatian Coast; tickets can be purchased only in US, www.europebyair.com, US tel. 888-321-4737).

Resources

Resources from Rick Steves

Rick Steves' Eastern Europe is one of more than 30 titles in my series of **books** on European travel, which includes country guidebooks, city and regional guidebooks, and my budget-travel skills handbook, *Rick Steves' Europe Through the Back Door.* Some of my books are available in electronic format, and selected chapters from my guidebooks are reprinted as easy-to-pocket Snapshot books. My phrase books—for German, French, Italian, Spanish, and Portuguese—are practical and budget-oriented. My other books are *Europe 101* (a crash course on art and history, newly expanded and in full color), *Travel as a Political Act* (a travelogue sprinkled with advice for bringing home a global perspective), *European Christmas* (on traditional and modern-day celebrations), and *Postcards from Europe* (a fun memoir of my travels over 25 years). For a complete list of my books, see the inside of the last page of this book.

My **TV series,** *Rick Steves' Europe,* covers European destinations in 70 shows, including several episodes that explore Eastern Europe. My weekly public **radio show,** *Travel with Rick Steves,* features interviews with travel experts from around the world, including many from Eastern Europe. All the TV scripts and radio shows (which are easy and free to download to an iPod or other MP3 player) are at www.ricksteves.com.

Maps

The black-and-white maps in this book, designed by my well-traveled staff, are concise and simple. The maps are intended to help you locate recommended places and get to local TIs, where you can pick up more in-depth maps of towns or regions (usually free).

Better maps are sold at newsstands and bookstores in Europe—take a look before you buy to be sure the map has the level of detail you want. Train travelers can usually manage fine with the freebies they get at the local tourist offices. Hikers will find no shortage of excellent, very detailed maps locally. For drivers, I'd recommend a 1:200,000- or 1:300,000-scale map for each country. Since new expressways are constantly being built in these

Begin Your Trip at www.ricksteves.com

At our travel website, you'll find a wealth of free information on European destinations, including fresh monthly news and helpful tips from thousands of fellow travelers. You'll also find my latest guidebook updates (www.ricksteves.com/update) and my travel blog.

Our **online Travel Store** offers travel bags and accessories specially designed by Rick Steves to help you travel smarter and lighter. These include Rick's popular carry-on bags (roll-aboard and rucksack versions), money belts, totes, toiletries kits, adapters, other accessories, and a wide selection of guidebooks, planning maps, and DVDs.

Choosing the right **railpass** for your trip—amidst hundreds of options—can drive you nutty. We'll help you choose the best pass for your needs, plus give you a bunch of free extras.

Rick Steves' Europe Through the Back Door travel company offers **tours** with more than three dozen itineraries and more than 300 departures reaching the best destinations in this book...and beyond. Our 17-day Best of Eastern Europe tour visits the Czech Republic, Poland, Hungary, Croatia, and Slovenia, while our 14-day Adriatic tour that focuses on Slovenia, Croatia, and a bit of Bosnia-Herzegovina. We also offer an 8-day tour that covers Prague and Budapest, and a 12-day tour of Berlin, Prague, and Vienna. You'll enjoy great guides, a fun bunch of travel partners (with small groups of generally around 28), and plenty of room to spread out in a big, comfy bus. You'll find European adventures to fit every vacation length. For all the details, and to get our Tour Catalog and a free Rick Steves Tour Experience DVD (filmed on location during an actual tour), visit www.ricksteves.com or call the Tour Department at 425/608-4217.

countries, an up-to-date map is essential—it can mean the difference between choosing an old, slow road or saving an hour by finding the brand-new highway. In Croatia and Slovenia, my favorite maps of the region are by the Slovenian cartographer Kod & Kam (they have a store in Ljubljana—see page 653—but you can find these maps everywhere).

Other Guidebooks

If you're heading beyond my recommended destinations, $40 for extra maps and books is money well spent. For several people traveling by car, the extra weight and expense of a small trip library are negligible.

The following books are worthwhile, though not updated annually; check the publication date before you buy. The Rough Guides, which individually cover the countries in this book, are packed with historical and cultural insight. The Lonely Planet guides are similar, but are designed more for travelers than for intellectuals. If choosing between these two titles, I'd buy the one that was published most recently. Lonely Planet's fat, far-ranging *Eastern Europe* overview book gives you little to go on for each destination, though their country- and city-specific guides are more thorough.

Students, backpackers, and nightlife-seekers should consider the Let's Go guides (by Harvard students, with the best hostel listings). Dorling Kindersley publishes snazzy Eyewitness Guides, covering Prague, the Czech Republic, Slovakia, Budapest, Hungary, Kraków, Warsaw, Poland, Dubrovnik and the Dalmatian Coast, Croatia, and Vienna. While pretty to look at, these books weigh a ton and are skimpy on written content.

In Your Pocket publishes regularly updated magazines on major Eastern European cities (especially useful in Poland, including editions for Kraków, Warsaw, and Gdańsk). These handy guides are particularly good for their up-to-date hotel, restaurant, and nightlife recommendations (available locally, usually for a few dollars, but often free; condensed versions available free online at www.inyourpocket.com). The British entertainment publication *Time Out* sells a similarly well-researched annual magazine with up-to-date coverage on Croatia (look for it at newsstands, www.timeout.com).

For more extensive coverage of this region and neighboring countries, consider *Rick Steves' Prague & the Czech Republic, Rick Steves' Budapest, Rick Steves' Croatia & Slovenia,* and *Rick Steves' Vienna, Salzburg & Tirol.*

Recommended Books and Movies

To learn about Eastern Europe past and present, check out a few of these books and films.

Non-Fiction

Lonnie Johnson's *Central Europe: Enemies, Neighbors, Friends* is the best historical overview of the countries in this book. Timothy Garton Ash has written several good "eyewitness account" books analyzing the fall of communism in Eastern Europe, including *History of the Present* and *The Magic Lantern*. Michael Meyer's *The Year that Changed the World* intimately chronicles the exciting events of 1989, culminating in the fall of the Berlin Wall. Tina Rosenberg's dense but thought-provoking *The Haunted Land* asks how those who actively supported communism in Eastern Europe should be treated in the post-communist age.

Patrick Leigh Fermor's *Between the Woods and the Water* is the vivid memoir of a young man who traveled by foot and on horseback across the Balkan Peninsula (including Hungary) in 1933. Rebecca West's classic, bricklike *Black Lamb and Grey Falcon* is the definitive travelogue of the Yugoslav lands (written during a journey between the two World Wars). For a more recent take, Croatian journalist Slavenka Drakulić has written a trio of insightful essay collections from a woman's perspective: *Café Europa: Life After Communism; The Balkan Express;* and *How We Survived Communism and Even Laughed.*

For a thorough explanation of how and why Yugoslavia broke apart, read *Yugoslavia: Death of a Nation* (by Laura Silber and Allan Little). Joe Sacco's powerful graphic novel *Safe Area Goražde* describes the author's actual experience living in a mostly Muslim town in Bosnia-Herzegovina while it was surrounded by Serb forces during the wars of the 1990s.

For information on Eastern European Roma (Gypsies), consider the textbook-style *We Are the Romani People* by Ian Hancock, and the more literary *Bury Me Standing* by Isabel Fonseca.

Fiction

The most prominent works of Eastern European fiction have come from the Czechs. These include *I Served the King of England* (Bohumil Hrabal), *The Unbearable Lightness of Being* (Milan Kundera), and *The Good Soldier Švejk* (Jaroslav Hašek). The Czech existentialist writer Franz Kafka wrote many well-known novels, including *The Trial* and *The Metamorphosis*. Bruce Chatwin's *Utz* is set in communist Prague.

James Michener's *Poland* is a hefty look into the history of the Poles. *Zlateh the Goat* (Isaac Bashevis Singer) includes seven folktales of Jewish Eastern Europe. Joseph Roth's *The Radetzky*

March details the decline of an aristocratic family in the Austro-Hungarian Empire.

Imre Kertész, a Hungarian-Jewish Auschwitz survivor who won the Nobel Prize for Literature in 2002, is best known for his semi-autobiographical novel *Fatelessness (Sorstalanság)*, which chronicles the experience of a young concentration-camp prisoner. Márai Sándor's reflective *Embers* paints a rich picture of cobblestoned, gaslit Vienna just before the empire's glory began to fade.

Arthur Phillips' confusingly titled 2002 novel *Prague* tells the story of American expats negotiating young-adult life in post-communist Budapest, where they often feel one-upped by their compatriots doing the same in the Czech capital (hence the title).

Films

Each of these countries has produced fine films. Here are a few highlights:

Czech Republic: *I Served the King of England* (2006); *Czech Dream* (2004); *Divided We Fall* (2000); *Kolya* (1996); *The Trial* (1993); *Kouř* (*Smoke*, 1991); *The Unbearable Lightness of Being* (1988); *The Firemen's Ball* (1967); *Closely Watched Trains* (1966); *The Loves of a Blonde* (1965).

Poland: *Katyń* (2007); *Karol: A Man Who Became Pope* (2005); *The Decalogue* (1989); *The Wedding* (1972).

Hungary: *Children of Glory* (*Szabadság, Szerelem*, 2006); *Fateless* (2005); *Kontroll* (2003); *Csinibaba* (1997); *Time Stands Still* (1981); *The Witness* (1969).

Croatia: *How the War Started on My Island* (1996); *Underground* (1995); *Tito and Me* (1992); *When Father Was Away on Business* (1985).

Slovenia: *No Man's Land* (2002, Slovenian-produced, but deals with Bosnian war; Oscar winner for Best Foreign Film).

Other Movies: Two recent German movies are excellent for their insight into the surreal and paranoid days of the Soviet Bloc. The Oscar-winning *The Lives of Others* (2006) chronicles the constant surveillance that the communist regime employed to keep potential dissidents in line. For a darkly funny and nostalgic look at post-communist Europe's fitful transition to capitalism, *Good Bye Lenin!* (2003) can't be beat.

Schindler's List (1993) and *The Pianist* (2002)—both of which won multiple Oscars—chronicle the plight of Jewish Holocaust victims in Kraków and Warsaw, respectively.

Sunshine (1999, starring Ralph Fiennes, directed by István Szabó; not to be confused with Danny Boyle's 2007 film of the same name) somewhat melodramatically traces three generations of an aristocratic Jewish family in Budapest, from the Golden Age, through the Holocaust, to the Cold War.

Documentaries about this region are also worth looking for. The BBC produced a remarkable (but difficult-to-find) six-hour documentary series called *The Death of Yugoslavia,* featuring interviews with all of the key players (the book *Yugoslavia: Death of a Nation,* noted above, was a companion piece to this film). The 1998 Oscar-winning documentary *The Last Days* recounts the fate of Jews when the Nazis took over Hungary in 1944.

Holidays and Festivals

This is a partial list of holidays and festivals—in these countries, holidays can strike without warning. Catholic holidays are celebrated in Poland, Slovakia, Croatia, and Slovenia (and to a lesser extent in Hungary and the Czech Republic). Before planning a trip around a festival, make sure to verify the dates by checking the festival's website or contacting that country's national tourist office (listed at the beginning of this chapter). They can also provide specifics and a more comprehensive list of festivals.

Jan 1 New Year's Day, all countries

Jan 6 Epiphany, Catholic countries

Jan 19 Anniversary of Jan Palach's Death, Prague (flowers in Wenceslas Square)

Feb 8 National Day of Culture, Slovenia (celebrates Slovenian culture and national poet France Prešeren)

Early March One World International Human Rights Film Festival, Prague (1 week, www.oneworld.cz)

March 15 National Day, Hungary (celebrates 1848 Revolution)

Late March Budapest Spring Festival (2 weeks, www.festivalcity.hu); last weekend is also Budapest Fringe Festival

Late March Ski Flying World Championships, Planica, Slovenia (3 days, www.planica.info)

Easter (April 4 in 2010, April 24 in 2011) all countries

April 27 National Resistance Day, Slovenia

April 30 Witches' Night, Czech Republic (similar to Halloween, with bonfires)

May Vienna Festival of Arts and Music (www.festwochen.or.at)

May 1 Labor Day, all countries

May 3 Constitution Day, Poland (celebrates Europe's first constitution)

May 8	Liberation Day, Czech Republic and Slovakia
Ascension	(May 13 in 2010, June 2 in 2011) Catholic countries
Pentecost/ Whitsunday	(May 23 in 2010, June 12 in 2011) Catholic countries
Whitmonday	(May 24 in 2010, June 13 in 2011) Hungary
Mid-May	Prague International Marathon (www.pim.cz)
Mid- to Late May	"Prague Spring" Music Festival (3 weeks, www.festival.cz)
Corpus Christi	(June 3 in 2010, June 23 in 2011) Catholic countries
Early June	Dance Week Festival, Zagreb, Croatia (www.danceweekfestival.com)
Mid-June	Celebration of the Rose, Český Krumlov, Czech Republic (3 days, medieval festival, music, theater, dance, knights' tournament)
June 22	Antifascist Struggle Day, Croatia
June 25	National Day, Slovenia; Statehood Day, Croatia
Late June	Floating of the Wreaths Midsummer Festival, Kraków, Poland (1 weekend, wreaths on rafts in Vistula River, fireworks, music)
Late June	Jewish Culture Festival, Kraków, Poland (1 week, www.jewishfestival.pl)
Late June	Midsummer Eve Celebrations, Austria
July 5	Sts. Cyril and Methodius Day, Czech Republic and Slovakia
July 6	Jan Hus Day, Czech Republic
July 10–Aug 25	(every year) Dubrovnik Summer Festival, Croatia (www.dubrovnik-festival.hr)
Early July–late Aug	Ljubljana Summer Festival, Slovenia (www.ljubljanafestival.si)
Mid-July–mid-Aug	International Music Festival, Český Krumlov, Czech Republic (www.festivalkrumlov.cz)
Late July	Marco Polo Festival, Korčula, Croatia (3 days, www.marcopolofest.hr)
Late July	International Folklore Festival, Zagreb, Croatia (5 days, costumes, songs, dances from all over Croatia, www.msf.hr)

July–Aug	Prague Proms, Prague (music festival, www.prague proms.cz)
Aug 5	National Thanksgiving Day, Croatia
Early Aug	Sziget Festival, Budapest (1 week, rock and pop music, www.sziget.hu)
Aug 15	Assumption of Mary, Catholic countries
Aug 20	Constitution Day and St. Stephen's Day, Hungary (fireworks, celebrations)
Aug 29	National Uprising Day, Slovakia (commemorates uprising against Nazis)
Late Aug	Formula 1 races, Budapest (1 day, www.hungaroinfo.com/formel1)
Late Aug–early Sept	Jewish Summer Festival, Budapest (2 weeks, www.jewishfestival.hu)
Aug-Sept	Dvořák's Prague Music Festival, Prague (www.dvorakovapraha.cz)
Sept	Radio Autumn, Prague (international music festival of radio orchestras)
Early Sept	Marco Polo Naval Battle Reenactment, Korčula, Croatia
Sept 1	Constitution Day, Slovakia
Late Sept	Prague Autumn Music Festival (2 weeks, www.pragueautumn.cz)
Sept 28	St. Wenceslas Day, Czech Republic (celebrates national patron saint and Czech statehood)
Oct	International Jazz Festival, Prague
Oct 8	Independence Day, Croatia
Mid-Oct	Budapest Autumn Festival (1 week, music, www.festivalcity.hu)
Oct 23	Republic Day, Hungary (remembrances of 1956 Uprising)
Oct 26	National Day, Austria
Oct 28	Independence Day, Czech Republic
Oct 31	Reformation Day, Slovenia
Nov 1	All Saints' Day/Remembrance Day, Catholic countries (religious festival, some closures)
Nov 11	Independence Day, Poland; St. Martin's Day (official first day of wine season), Slovenia and Croatia
Nov 17	Velvet Revolution Anniversary, Czech Republic and Slovakia
Dec 5	St. Nicholas Eve, Prague (St. Nick gives gifts to children in town square)

Dec 24–25 Christmas Eve and Christmas Day, all countries
Dec 26 Boxing Day/St. Stephen's Day; Independence and Unity Day, Slovenia
Dec 31 St. Sylvester's Day, Prague and Vienna (fireworks)

Conversions and Climate

Numbers and Stumblers

- Europeans write a few of their numbers differently than we do. 1 = 1, 4 = 4, 7 = 7.
- In Europe, dates appear as day/month/year, so Christmas is 25/12/11.
- Commas are decimal points and decimals commas. A dollar and a half is 1,50, and there are 5.280 feet in a mile.
- When counting with fingers, start with your thumb. If you hold up your first finger to request one item, you'll probably get two.
- What Americans call the second floor of a building is the first floor in Europe.
- On escalators and moving sidewalks, Europeans keep the left "lane" open for passing. Keep to the right.

Metric Conversions (Approximate)

A kilogram is 2.2 pounds, and 1 liter is about a quart, or almost four to a gallon. A kilometer is six-tenths of a mile. I figure kilometers to miles by cutting them in half and adding back 10 percent of the original (120 km: 60 + 12 = 72 miles, 300 km: 150 + 30 = 180 miles).

1 foot = 0.3 meter	1 square yard = 0.8 square meter
1 yard = 0.9 meter	1 square mile = 2.6 square kilometers
1 mile = 1.6 kilometers	1 ounce = 28 grams
1 centimeter = 0.4 inch	1 quart = 0.95 liter
1 meter = 39.4 inches	1 kilogram = 2.2 pounds
1 kilometer = 0.62 mile	32°F = 0°C

Clothing Sizes

When shopping for clothing, use these US-to-European comparisons as general guidelines (but note that no conversion is perfect).

- Women's dresses and blouses: Add 30 (US size 10 = European size 40)
- Men's suits and jackets: Add 10 (US size 40 regular = European size 50)
- Men's shirts: Multiply by 2 and add about 8 (US size 15 collar = European size 38)

- Women's shoes: Add about 30 (US size 8 = European size 38½)
- Men's shoes: Add 32–34 (US size 9 = European size 41; US size 11 = European size 45)

Climate

First line is the average daily high temperature; second line, average daily low; third line, average number of rainy days. For more detailed weather statistics for destinations in this book (as well as the rest of the world), check www.worldclimate.com.

J	F	M	A	M	J	J	A	S	O	N	D
AUSTRIA • Vienna											
34°	38°	47°	58°	67°	73°	76°	75°	68°	56°	45°	37°
25°	28°	30°	42°	50°	56°	60°	59°	53°	44°	37°	30°
15	14	13	13	13	14	13	13	10	13	14	15
CROATIA • Dubrovnik											
53°	55°	58°	63°	70°	78°	83°	82°	77°	69°	62°	56°
42°	43°	57°	52°	58°	65°	69°	69°	64°	57°	51°	46°
13	13	11	10	10	6	4	3	7	11	16	15
CZECH REPUBLIC • Prague											
31°	34°	44°	54°	64°	70°	73°	72°	65°	53°	42°	34°
23°	24°	30°	38°	46°	52°	55°	55°	49°	41°	33°	27°
13	11	10	11	13	12	13	12	10	13	12	13
HUNGARY • Budapest											
34°	39°	50°	62°	71°	78°	82°	81°	74°	61°	47°	39°
25°	28°	35°	44°	52°	58°	62°	60°	53°	44°	38°	30°
13	12	11	11	13	13	10	9	7	10	14	13
POLAND • Kraków											
32°	34°	45°	55°	67°	72°	76°	73°	66°	56°	44°	37°
22°	22°	30°	38°	48°	54°	58°	56°	49°	42°	33°	28°
16	15	12	15	12	15	16	15	12	14	15	16
SLOVENIA • Ljubljana											
36°	41°	50°	60°	68°	75°	80°	78°	71°	59°	47°	39°
25°	25°	32°	40°	48°	54°	57°	57°	51°	43°	36°	30°
13	11	11	13	16	16	12	12	10	14	15	15

Temperature Conversion: Fahrenheit and Celsius

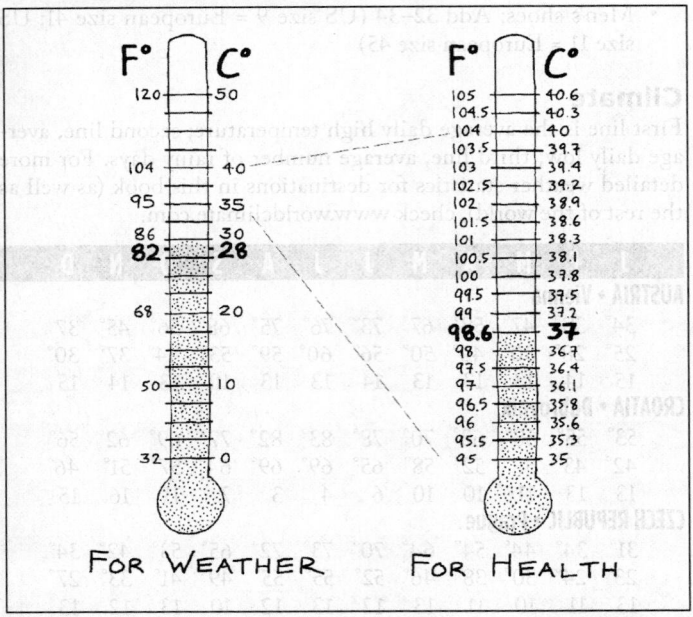

Europe takes its temperature using the Celsius scale, while we opt for Fahrenheit. For a rough conversion from Celsius to Fahrenheit, double the number and add 30. For weather, remember that 28°C is 82°F—perfect. For health, 37°C is just right.

Essential Packing Checklist

Whether you're traveling for five days or five weeks, here's what you'll need to bring. Remember to pack light to enjoy the sweet freedom of true mobility. Happy travels!

- ❑ 5 shirts
- ❑ 1 sweater or lightweight fleece jacket
- ❑ 2 pairs pants
- ❑ 1 pair shorts
- ❑ 1 swimsuit (women only—men can use shorts)
- ❑ 5 pairs underwear and socks
- ❑ 1 pair shoes
- ❑ 1 rainproof jacket
- ❑ Tie or scarf
- ❑ Money belt
- ❑ Money—your mix of:
  - ❑ Debit card for ATM withdrawals
  - ❑ Credit card
  - ❑ Hard cash in US dollars ($20 bills)
- ❑ Documents (and back-up photocopies)
- ❑ Passport
- ❑ Printout of airline e-ticket
- ❑ Driver's license
- ❑ Student ID and hostel card
- ❑ Railpass/car rental voucher
- ❑ Insurance details
- ❑ Daypack
- ❑ Sealable plastic baggies
- ❑ Camera and related gear
- ❑ Empty water bottle
- ❑ Wristwatch and alarm clock
- ❑ Earplugs
- ❑ First-aid kit
- ❑ Medicine (labeled)
- ❑ Extra glasses/contacts and prescriptions
- ❑ Sunscreen and sunglasses
- ❑ Toiletries kit
- ❑ Soap
- ❑ Laundry soap
- ❑ Clothesline
- ❑ Small towel
- ❑ Sewing kit
- ❑ Travel information
- ❑ Necessary map(s)
- ❑ Address list (email and mailing addresses)
- ❑ Postcards and photos from home
- ❑ Notepad and pen
- ❑ Journal

If you plan to carry on your luggage, note that all liquids must be in three-ounce or smaller containers and fit within a single quart-size baggie. For details, see www.tsa.gov/travelers.

Hotel Reservation

To: _____ _____
hotel ***email or fax***

From: _____ _____
name ***email or fax***

Today's date: _____ /_____ /_____
day ***month*** ***year***

Dear Hotel _____,
Please make this reservation for me:

Name: _____

Total # of people: _____ # of rooms: _____ # of nights: _____

Arriving: _____ /_____ /_____ My time of arrival (24-hr clock): _____
day ***month*** ***year*** (I will telephone if I will be late)

Departing: _____ /_____ /_____
day ***month*** ***year***

Room(s): Single___ Double ___ Twin___ Triple___ Quad___

With: Toilet ___ Shower___ Bath___ Sink only___

Special needs: View___ Quiet___ Cheapest___ Ground Floor___

Please email or fax confirmation of my reservation, along with the type of room reserved and the price. Please also inform me of your cancellation policy. After I hear from you, I will quickly send my credit-card information as a deposit to hold the room. Thank you.

_____
Name

_____
Address

_____
City ***State*** ***Zip Code*** ***Country***

Before hoteliers can make your reservation, they want to know the information listed above. You can use this form as the basis for your email, or you can photocopy this page, fill in the information, and send it as a fax (also available online at www.ricksteves.com/reservation).

Czech Survival Phrases

Two Czech letters are particularly difficult to pronounce: **ř** (as in "Dvořák") sounds like a cross between a rolled "r" and "zh." And **ň** is pronounced roughly "ny" (as in "canyon"). As these sounds are notoriously challenging for foreigners to duplicate, it's generally easiest just to replace them with simple "r" and "n" sounds.

Hello. (formal)	**Dobrý den.**	DOH-bree dehn
Hi. / Bye. (informal)	**Ahoj.**	AH-hoy
Do you speak English?	**Mluvíte anglicky?**	MLOO-vee-teh ANG-lits-kee
Yes. / No.	**Ano. / Ne.**	AH-no / neh
Please. / You're welcome. / Can I help you?	**Prosím.**	PROH-zeem
Thank you.	**Děkuji.**	DYACK-khuyi
I'm sorry. / Excuse me.	**Promiňte.**	PROH-meen-teh
Good.	**Dobře.**	DOHB-zhay
Goodbye.	**Na shledanou.**	nah SKLEH-dah-now
one / two	**jeden / dva**	YAY-dehn / dvah
three / four	**tři / čtyři**	tree / chuh-TEE-ree
five / six	**pět / šest**	pyeht / shehst
seven / eight	**sedm / osm**	SEH-dum / OH-sum
nine / ten	**devět / deset**	DEHV-yeht / DEH-seht
hundred	**sto**	stoh
thousand	**tisíc**	TYEE-seets
How much?	**Kolik?**	KOH-leek
local currency	**koruna (Kč)**	koh-ROO-nah
Where is...?	**Kde je...?**	gday yeh
...the toilet	**...vécé**	vayt-SAY
men	**muži**	MOO-zhee
women	**ženy**	ZHAY-nee
water / coffee	**voda / káva**	VOH-dah / KAH-vah
beer / wine	**pivo / víno**	PEE-voh / VEE-noh
Cheers!	**Na zdraví!**	nah zdrah-VEE
the bill	**účet**	OO-cheht
I'll pay.	**Zaplatím.**	zah-plah-TEEM

Slovak Survival Phrases

Hello. (formal)	**Dobrý deň.**	DOH-bree dyehn
Hi. / Bye. (informal)	**Ahoj.**	AH-hoy
Do you speak English?	**Hovoríte po anglicky?**	hoh-VOH-ree-teh poh ANG-lits-kee
Yes. / No.	**Áno. / Nie.**	AH-no / nyeh
Please. / You're welcome. / Can I help you?	**Prosím.**	PROH-seem
Thank you.	**Ďakujem.**	DYAH-koo-yehm
I'm sorry. / Excuse me.	**Prepáčte.**	preh-PAHCH-teh
Good.	**Dobro.**	DOH-broh
Goodbye.	**Do videnia.**	doh vih-DAY-neeah
one / two	**jeden / dva**	YAY-dehn / dvah
three / four	**tri / štyri**	tree / SHTEE-ree
five / six	**päť / šesť**	peht / shehst
seven / eight	**sedem / osem**	SEH-dyehm / OH-sehm
nine / ten	**deväť / desať**	DYEH-veht / DYEH-saht
hundred	**sto**	stoh
thousand	**tisíc**	TYEE-seets
How much?	**Koľko?**	KOHL-koh
local currency	**euro (€)**	YOO-roh
Where is...?	**Kde je...?**	gday yeh
...the toilet	**...záchod**	ZAH-khohd
men	**muži**	MOO-zhee
women	**ženy**	ZHAY-nee
water / coffee	**voda / káva**	VOH-dah / KAH-vah
beer / wine	**pivo / víno**	PEE-voh / VEE-noh
Cheers!	**Na zdravie!**	nah ZDRAH-vyeh
the bill	**účet**	OO-cheht

Polish Survival Phrases

Keep in mind a few Polish pronunciation tips: **w** sounds like "v," **ł** sounds like "w," **ch** is a back-of-your-throat "kh" sound (as in the Scottish "loch"), and **rz** sounds like the "zh" sound in "pleasure." The "shch" sound (indicated by various combinations, including *ść* and *szcz*) is easier than it seems—just say the two sounds in rapid succession (think of the phrase "fresh cheese"). The "khch" sound (denoted by *chci*) is similar: the guttural "kh" sound quickly followed by ch. The vowels with a tail (**ą** and **ę**) have a slight nasal "n" sound at the end, similar to French; depending on the word, this can have a strong n sound, or be nearly silent—just follow the phonetics below.

Hello. (formal)	**Dzień dobry.**	jehn DOH-brih
Hi. / Bye. (informal)	**Cześć.**	cheshch
Do you speak English? (asked of a man)	**Czy Pan mówi po angielsku?**	chih pahn MOO-vee poh ahn-GYEHL-skoo
Do you speak English? (asked of a woman)	**Czy Pani mówi po angielsku?**	chih PAH-nee MOO-vee poh ahn-GYEHL-skoo
Yes. / No.	**Tak. / Nie.**	tahk / nyeh
I (don't) understand.	**(Nie) rozumiem.**	(nyeh) roh-ZOO-myehm
Please. / You're welcome. / Can I help you?	**Proszę.**	PROH-sheh
Thank you (very much).	**Dziękuję (bardzo).**	jehn-KOO-yeh (BARD-zoh)
Excuse me. / I'm sorry.	**Przepraszam.**	psheh-PRAH-shahm
(No) problem.	**(Żaden) problem.**	(ZHAH-dehn) PROH-blehm
Good.	**Dobrze.**	DOHB-zheh
Goodbye.	**Do widzenia.**	doh veed-ZAY-nyah
one / two	**jeden / dwa**	YEH-dehn / dvah
three / four	**trzy / cztery**	tzhih / CHTEH-rih
five / six	**pięć / sześć**	pyench / sheshch
seven / eight	**siedem / osiem**	SHYEH-dehm / OH-shehm
nine / ten	**dziewięć / dziesięć**	JEH-vyench / JEH-shench
hundred / thousand	**sto / tysiąc**	stoh / TIH-shants
How much?	**Ile?**	EE-leh
local currency	**złoty (zł)**	ZWOH-tih
Write it.	**Napisz to.**	NAH-peesh toh
Is it free?	**Czy to jest za darmo?**	chih toh yehst zah DAR-moh
Is it included?	**Czy jest to wliczone?**	chih yehst toh vlee-CHOH-neh
Where can I find / buy...?	**Gdzie mogę dostać / kupić...?**	guh-DYEH MOH-geh DOH-statch / KOO-peech
I'd like...(said by a man)	**Chciałbym...**	KHCHAW-beem
I'd like...(said by a woman)	**Chciałabym...**	KHCHAH-wah-beem
We'd like...	**Chcielibyśmy...**	KHCHEHL-ee-bish-mih
...a room.	**...pokój.**	POH-kooey
...a ticket to ___.	**...bilet do ___.**	BEE-leht doh ___
Is it possible?	**Czy jest to możliwe?**	chih yehst toh mohzh-LEE-veh
Where is...?	**Gdzie jest...?**	guh-DYEH yehst
...the train station	**...dworzec kolejowy**	DVOH-zhehts koh-leh-YOH-vih
...the bus station	**...dworzec autobusowy**	DVOH-zhehts ow-toh-boos-OH-vih
...the tourist information office	**...informacja turystyczna**	een-for-MAHT-syah too-ris-TITCH-nah
...the toilet	**...toaleta**	toh-ah-LEH-tah
men / women	**męska / damska**	MEHN-skah / DAHM-skah
left / right	**lewo / prawo**	LEH-voh / PRAH-voh
straight	**prosto**	PROH-stoh
At what time...	**O której godzinie...**	oh kuh-TOO-ray gohd-ZHEE-nyeh
...does this open / close?	**...będzie otwarte / zamknięte?**	BEND-zheh oht-VAHR-teh / zahm-KNYEHN-teh
Just a moment.	**Chwileczkę.**	khvee-LETCH-keh
now / soon / later	**teraz / niedługo / później**	TEH-rahz / nyed-WOO-goh / POOZH-nyey
today / tomorrow	**dzisiaj / jutro**	JEE-shigh / YOO-troh

In the Restaurant

I'd like to reserve... (said by a man)	**Chciałbym zarezerwować...**	KHCHAW-beem zah-reh-zehr-VOH-vahch
I'd like to reserve... (said by a woman)	**Chciałabym zarezerwować...**	KHCHAH-wah-beem zah-reh-zehr-VOH-vahch
We'd like to reserve...	**Chcielibyśmy zarezerwować...**	KHCHEHL-ee-bish-mih zah-reh-zehr-VOH-vahch
...a table for one person / two people.	**...stolik na jedną osobę / dwie osoby.**	STOH-leek nah YEHD-now oh-SOH-beh / dvyeh oh-SOH-bih
Non-smoking.	**Niepalący.**	nyeh-pah-LOHNT-sih
Is this table free?	**Czy ten stolik jest wolny?**	chih tehn STOH-leek yehst VOHL-nih
Can I help you?	**W czym mogę pomóc?**	vchim MOH-geh POH-moots
The menu (in English), please.	**Menu (po angielsku), proszę.**	MEH-noo (poh ahn-GYEHL-skoo) PROH-sheh
service (not) included	**usługa (nie) wliczona**	oos-WOO-gah (nyeh) VLEE-choh-nah
cover charge	**wstęp**	vstenp
"to go"	**na wynos**	nah VIH-nohs
with / without	**z / bez**	z / behz
and / or	**i / lub**	ee / loob
milk bar (cheap cafeteria)	**bar mleczny**	bar MLETCH-nih
fixed-price meal (of the day)	**zestaw (dnia)**	ZEHS-tahv (dih-NYAH)
specialty of the house	**specjalność zakładu**	speht-SYAHL-nohshch zah-KWAH-doo
half portion	**pół porcji**	poow PORTS-yee
daily special	**danie dnia**	DAH-nyeh dih-NYAH
appetizers	**przystawki**	pshih-STAHV-kee
bread	**chleb**	khlehb
cheese	**ser**	sehr
sandwich	**kanapka**	kah-NAHP-kah
soup	**zupa**	ZOO-pah
salad	**sałatka**	sah-WAHT-kah
meat	**mięso**	MYEHN-soh
poultry	**drób**	droob
fish	**ryba**	RIH-bah
seafood	**owoce morza**	oh-VOHT-seh MOH-zhah
fruit	**owoce**	oh-VOHT-seh
vegetables	**warzywa**	vah-ZHIH-vah
dessert	**deser**	DEH-sehr
(tap) water	**woda (z kranu)**	VOH-dah (SKRAH-noo)
mineral water	**woda mineralna**	VOH-dah mee-neh-RAHL-nah
carbonated / not carbonated	**gazowana / niegazowana**	gah-zoh-VAH-nah / NYEH-gah-zoh-vah-nah
milk	**mleko**	MLEH-koh
(orange) juice	**sok (pomarańczowy)**	sohk (poh-mah-rayn-CHOH-vih)
coffee	**kawa**	KAH-vah
tea	**herbata**	hehr-BAH-tah
wine	**wino**	VEE-noh
red / white	**czerwone / białe**	chehr-VOH-neh / bee-AH-weh
sweet / dry / semi-dry	**słodkie / wytrawne / półwytrawne**	SWOHT-kyeh / vih-TRAHV-neh / poow-vih-TRAHV-neh
glass / bottle	**szklanka / butelka**	SHKLAHN-kah / boo-TEHL-kah
beer	**piwo**	PEE-voh
vodka	**wódka**	VOOD-kah
Cheers!	**Na zdrowie!**	nah ZDROH-vyeh
Enjoy your meal.	**Smacznego.**	smatch-NEH-goh
More. / Another.	**Więcej. / Inny.**	VYEHNT-say / EE-nih-nih
The same.	**Taki sam.**	TAH-kee sahm
the bill	**rachunek**	rah-KHOO-nehk
I'll pay.	**Ja płacę.**	yah PWAHT-seh
tip	**napiwek**	nah-PEE-vehk
Delicious!	**Pyszne!**	PISH-neh

Hungarian Survival Phrases

Remember, the letter *a* is pronounced "aw," while *á* is a brighter "ah." In the phonetics, *dj* is pronounced like the j in "jeans."

Hello. (formal)	**Jó napot kívánok.**	yoh NAH-pot KEE-vah-nohk
Hi. / Bye. (informal)	**Szia.** or **Hello.**	SEE-yaw, "Hello"
Do you speak English?	**Beszél angolul?**	BEH-sayl AWN-goh-lool
Yes. / No.	**Igen. / Nem.**	EE-gehn / nehm
I (don't) understand.	**(Nem) értem.**	(nehm) AYR-tehm
Please.	**Kérem.**	KAY-rehm
You're welcome.	**Szívesen.**	SEE-veh-shehn
Thank you (very much).	**Köszönöm (szépen).**	KUR-sur-nurm (SAY-pehn)
Excuse me. / I'm sorry.	**Bocsánat.**	BOH-chah-nawt
No problem.	**Semmi gond.**	SHEH-mee gohnd
Good.	**Jól.**	yohl
Goodbye.	**Viszontlátásra.**	VEE-sohnt-lah-tahsh-raw
one / two	**egy / kettő**	edj / KEH-tur
three / four	**három / négy**	HAH-rohm / naydj
five / six	**öt / hat**	urt / hawt
seven / eight	**hét / nyolc**	hayt / nyolts
nine / ten	**kilenc / tíz**	KEE-lehnts / teez
hundred / thousand	**száz / ezer**	sahz / EH-zehr
How much?	**Mennyi?**	MEHN-yee
local currency	**forint (Ft)**	FOH-reent
Where is it?	**Hol van?**	hohl vawn
Is it free (no charge)?	**Ingyen van?**	een-JEHN vawn
Is it included?	**Benne van az árban?**	BEH-neh vawn oz AHR-bawn
Where can I find / buy...?	**Hol találok / vehetek...?**	hohl TAW-lah-lohk / VEH-heh-tehk
I'd like...	**Kérnék...**	KAYR-nayk
We'd like...	**Kérnénk...**	KAYR-naynk
...a room	**...egy szobát**	edj SOH-baht
...a ticket (to ___)	**...egy jegyet (___-ig)**	edj YEHDJ-eht (___-ig)
Is it possible?	**Lehet?**	leh-HEHT
Where is the...?	**Hol van a...?**	hohl vawn aw
big train station (in Budapest)	**pályaudvar**	PAH-yood-vawr
small train station (elsewhere)	**vasútállomás**	VAW-shoot-ah-loh-mahsh
bus station	**buszpályaudvar**	BOOS-pah-yood-vawr
tourist information office	**turista információ**	TOO-reesh-taw EEN-for-maht-see-yoh
toilet	**toalet** or **WC**	TOH-aw-leht, VAYT-say
men	**férfi**	FAYR-fee
women	**női**	NUR-ee
left / right	**bal / jobb**	bawl / yohb
straight	**egyenesen** or **előre**	EDJ-eh-neh-shehn, EH-lew-reh
At what time...	**Mikor...**	MEE-kohr
...does this open / close?	**...nyit / zár?**	nyit / zahr
Just a moment.	**Egy pillanat.**	edj PEE-law-nawt
now / soon / later	**most / hamarosan / később**	mohsht / HAW-maw-roh-shawn / KAY-shurb
today / tomorrow	**ma / holnap**	maw / HOHL-nawp

In the Restaurant

I'd like to reserve a table for one / two people.	**Szeretnék foglalni egy asztalt egy / két fő részére.**	SEH-reht-nayk FOG-lawl-nee edj AWS-tawlt edj / kayt few RAY-say-reh
Non-smoking.	**Nem dohányzó.**	nehm DOH-hayn-zoh
Is this table free?	**Ez az asztal szabad?**	ehz oz AWS-tawl saw-BAWD
Can I help you?	**Tessék.**	TEHSH-shayk
The menu (in English), please.	**Kérem az (angol) étlapot.**	KAY-rehm oz (AWN-gohl) AYT-law-poht
service (not) included	**a számla a felszolgálási díjat (nem) tartalmazza**	aw SAHM-law aw FEHL-sohl-gah-lah-shee DEE-yawt (nehm) TAWR-tawl-maw-zaw
cover charge	**belépő**	BEH-lay-pur
"to go"	**elvitelre**	EHL-vee-tehl-reh
with / without	**___-val / nélkül**	___-vawl / NAYL-kewl
and / or	**és / vagy**	aysh / vawdj
fixed-price meal (of the day)	**(napi) menü**	(NAW-pee) MEH-new
specialty of the house	**a ház specialitása**	aw hahz SHPEHT-see-aw-lee-tah-shaw
half portion	**fél adag**	fayl AW-dawg
daily special	**napi ajánlat**	NAW-pee AW-yahn-lawt
fixed-price meal (for tourists)	**(turista) menü**	(TOO-reesh-taw) MEH-new
main courses	**főételek**	FUR-ay-teh-lehk
appetizers	**előételek**	EH-lur-ay-teh-lehk
bread / cheese	**kenyér / sajt**	KEHN-yayr / shayt
sandwich	**szendvics**	SEND-veech
soup / salad	**leves / saláta**	LEH-vehsh / SHAW-lah-taw
meat / poultry	**hús / szárnyasok**	hoosh / SAHR-nyaw-shohk
fish	**halak**	HAW-lawk
seafood	**tengeri halak**	TEHN-geh-ree HAW-lawk
fruit	**gyümölcs**	JEWM-urlch
vegetables	**zöldség**	ZULRD-shayg
dessert	**desszert**	DEH-sehrt
vegetarian	**vegetáriánus**	VEH-geh-tah-ree-ah-noosh
(tap) water	**(csap) víz**	(chawp) veez
mineral water	**ásványvíz**	ASH-vawn-veez
milk	**tej**	TAYee
(orange) juice	**(narancs) lé**	(NAW-rawnch) lay
coffee / tea	**kávé / tea**	KAH-vay / TEH-aw
beer / wine	**sör / bor**	shohr / bohr
red / white	**vörös / fehér**	VUR-rursh / FEH-hayr
sweet / dry / semi-dry	**édes / száraz / félszáraz**	AY-dehsh / SAH-rawz / FAYL-sah-rawz
glass / bottle	**pohár / üveg**	POH-hahr / EW-vehg
Cheers!	**Egészségedre!**	EH-gehs-shay-geh-dreh
More. / Another.	**Még. / Másikat.**	mayg / MAH-shee-kawt
The same.	**Ugyanazt.**	OODJ-aw-nawst
Bill, please. (literally, "I'll pay.")	**Fizetek.**	FEE-zeh-tehk
tip	**borravaló**	BOH-raw-vaw-loh
Bon appétit!	**Jó étvágyat!**	yoh AYT-vah-yawt
Delicious!	**Finom!**	FEE-nohm

Slovenian Survival Phrases

When using the phonetics, pronounce ī / Ī as the long I sound in "light." The vowel "eh" sometimes sounds closer to "ay" (depending on the speaker).

Hello. (formal)	**Dober dan.**	DOH-behr dahn
Hi. / Bye. (informal)	**Živjo.**	ZHEEV-yoh
Do you speak English?	**Ali govorite angleško?**	AH-lee goh-voh-REE-teh ahn-GLEHSH-koh
Yes. / No.	**Ja. / Ne.**	yah / neh
I (don't) understand.	**(Ne) razumem.**	(neh) rah-ZOO-mehm
Please. / You're welcome.	**Prosim.**	PROH-seem
Thank you (very much).	**Hvala (lepa).**	HVAH-lah (LEH-pah)
Excuse me. / I'm sorry.	**Oprostite.**	oh-proh-STEE-teh
problem	**problem**	proh-BLEHM
No problem.	**Ni problema.**	nee proh-BLEH-mah
Good.	**Dobro.**	DOH-broh
Goodbye.	**Na svidenje.**	nah SVEE-dehn-yeh
one / two	**ena / dve**	EH-nah / dveh
three / four	**tri / štiri**	tree / SHTEE-ree
five / six	**pet / šest**	peht / shehst
seven / eight	**sedem / osem**	SEH-dehm / OH-sehm
nine / ten	**devet / deset**	deh-VEHT / deh-SEHT
hundred / thousand	**sto / tisoč**	stoh / TEE-sohch
How much?	**Koliko?**	KOH-lee-koh
local currency	**euro**	EE-oo-roh
Write it?	**Napišite?**	nah-PEESH-ee-teh
Is it free?	**Ali je brezplačno?**	AH-lee yeh brehz-PLAHCH-noh
Is it included?	**Ali je vključeno?**	AH-lee yeh vuk-LYOO-cheh-noh
Where can I find / buy...?	**Kje lahko najdem / kupim...?**	kyeh LAH-koh NĪ-dehm / KOO-peem
I'd / We'd like...	**Želel / Želeli bi...**	zheh-LEEoo / zheh-LEH-lee bee
...a room.	**...sobo.**	SOH-boh
...a ticket to ___.	**...vozovnico do ___.**	voh-ZOHV-neet-soh doh
Is it possible?	**Ali je možno?**	AH-lee yeh MOHZH-noh
Where is...?	**Kje je...?**	kyeh yeh
...the train station	**...železniška postaja**	zheh-LEHZ-neesh-kah pohs-TĪ-yah
...the bus station	**...avtobusna postaja**	OW-toh-boos-nah pohs-TĪ-yah
...the tourist information office	**...turistično informacijski center**	too-REES-teech-noh een-for-maht-SEE-skee TSEHN-tehr
...the toilet	**...vece (WC)**	VEHT-SEH
men	**moški**	MOHSH-kee
women	**ženski**	ZHEHN-skee
left / right	**levo / desno**	LEH-voh / DEHS-noh
straight	**naravnost**	nah-RAHV-nohst
At what time...	**Ob kateri uri...**	ohb kah-TEH-ree OO-ree
...does this open / close?	**...se odpre / zapre?**	seh ohd-PREH / zah-PREH
(Just) a moment.	**(Samo) trenutek.**	(sah-MOH) treh-NOO-tehk
now / soon / later	**zdaj / kmalu / pozneje**	zuh-DĪ / kuh-MAH-loo / pohz-NEH-yeh
today / tomorrow	**danes / jutri**	DAH-nehs / YOO-tree

In the Restaurant

I'd like to reserve...	**Rezerviral bi...**	reh-zehr-VEE-rahl bee
We'd like to reserve...	**Rezervirali bi...**	reh-zehr-VEE-rah-lee bee
...a table for one / two.	**...mizo za enega / dva.**	MEE-zoh zah EH-neh-gah / dvah
Non-smoking.	**Za nekadilce.**	zah NEH-kah-deelt-seh
Is this table free?	**Ali je ta miza prosta?**	AH-lee yeh tah MEE-zah PROH-stah
Can I help you?	**Izvolite?**	eez-VOH-lee-teh
The menu (in English), please.	**Jedilni list (v angleščini), prosim.**	yeh-DEEL-nee leest (vuh ahn-GLEHSH-chee-nee) PROH-seem
service (not) included	**postrežba (ni) vključena**	post-REHZH-bah (nee) vuk-LYOO-cheh-nah
cover charge	**pogrinjek**	poh-GREEN-yehk
"to go"	**za s sabo**	zah SAH-boh
with / without	**z / brez**	zuh / brehz
and / or	**in / ali**	een / AH-lee
fixed-price meal (of the day)	**(dnevni) meni**	(duh-NEW-nee) meh-NEE
specialty of the house	**specialiteta hiše**	speht-see-ah-lee-TEH-tah HEE-sheh
half portion	**polovična porcija**	poh-loh-VEECH-nah PORT-see-yah
daily special	**dnevna ponudba**	duh-NEW-nah poh-NOOD-bah
fixed-price meal for tourists	**turistični meni**	too-REES-teech-nee meh-NEE
appetizers	**predjedi**	prehd-yeh-DEE
bread	**kruh**	krooh
cheese	**sir**	seer
sandwich	**sendvič**	SEND-veech
soup	**juha**	YOO-hah
salad	**solata**	soh-LAH-tah
meat	**meso**	meh-SOH
poultry	**perutnina**	peh-root-NEE-nah
fish	**riba**	REE-bah
seafood	**morska hrana**	MOHR-skah HRAH-nah
fruit	**sadje**	SAHD-yeh
vegetables	**zelenjava**	zeh-lehn-YAH-vah
dessert	**sladica**	slah-DEET-sah
(tap) water	**voda (iz pipe)**	VOH-dah (eez PEE-peh)
mineral water	**mineralna voda**	mee-neh-RAHL-nah VOH-dah
milk	**mleko**	MLEH-koh
(orange) juice	**(pomarančni) sok**	(poh-mah-RAHNCH-nee) sohk
coffee	**kava**	KAH-vah
tea	**čaj**	chī
wine	**vino**	VEE-noh
red / white	**rdeče / belo**	ahr-DEH-cheh / BEH-loh
sweet / dry / semi-dry	**sladko / suho / polsuho**	SLAHD-koh / SOO-hoh / POHL-soo-hoh
glass / bottle	**kozarec / steklenica**	koh-ZAH-rehts / stehk-leh-NEET-sah
beer	**pivo**	PEE-voh
Cheers!	**Na zdravje!**	nah ZDROW-yeh
More. / Another.	**Še. / Še eno.**	sheh / sheh EH-noh
The same.	**Isto.**	EES-toh
Bill, please.	**Račun, prosim.**	rah-CHOON PROH-seem
tip	**napitnina**	nah-peet-NEE-nah
Delicious!	**Odlično!**	ohd-LEECH-noh

Croatian Survival Phrases

When using the phonetics, pronounce ī / Ī as the long I sound in "light."

Hello. (formal)	**Dobar dan.**	DOH-bahr dahn
Hi. / Bye. (informal)	**Bog.**	bohg
Do you speak English?	**Govorite li engleski?**	GOH-voh-ree-teh lee EHN-glehs-kee
Yes. / No.	**Da. / Ne.**	dah / neh
I (don't) understand.	**(Ne) razumijem.**	(neh) rah-ZOO-mee-yehm
Please. / You're welcome.	**Molim.**	MOH-leem
Thank you (very much).	**Hvala (ljepa).**	HVAH-lah (LYEH-pah)
Excuse me. / I'm sorry.	**Oprostite.**	oh-PROH-stee-teh
problem	**problem**	proh-BLEHM
No problem.	**Nema problema.**	NEH-mah proh-BLEH-mah
Good.	**Dobro.**	DOH-broh
Goodbye.	**Do viđenija.**	doh veed-JAY-neeah
one / two	**jedan / dva**	YEH-dahn / dvah
three / four	**tri / četiri**	tree / CHEH-teh-ree
five / six	**pet / šest**	peht / shehst
seven / eight	**sedam / osam**	SEH-dahm / OH-sahm
nine / ten	**devet / deset**	DEH-veht / DEH-seht
hundred / thousand	**sto / tisuća**	stoh / TEE-soo-chah
How much?	**Koliko?**	KOH-lee-koh
local currency	**kuna**	KOO-nah
Write it?	**Napišite?**	nah-PEESH-ee-teh
Is it free?	**Da li je besplatno?**	dah lee yeh BEH-splaht-noh
Is it included?	**Da li je uključeno?**	dah lee yeh OOK-lyoo-cheh-noh
Where can I find / buy...?	**Gdje mogu pronaći / kupiti...?**	guh-DYEH MOH-goo PROH-nah-chee / KOO-pee-tee
I'd like / We'd like...	**Želio bih / Željeli bismo...**	ZHEH-lee-oh beeh / ZHEH-lyeh-lee BEES-moh
...a room.	**...sobu.**	SOH-boo
...a ticket to ___.	**...kartu do ___.**	KAR-too doh
Is it possible?	**Da li je moguće?**	dah lee yeh MOH-goo-cheh
Where is...?	**Gdje je...?**	guh-DYEH yeh
...the train station	**...željeznička stanica**	ZHEH-lyehz-neech-kah STAH-neet-sah
...the bus station	**...autobusna stanica**	OW-toh-boos-nah STAH-neet-sah
...the tourist information office	**...turističko informativni centar**	TOO-ree-steech-koh EEN-for-mah-teev-nee TSEHN-tahr
...the toilet	**...vece (WC)**	VEHT-SEH
men	**muški**	MOOSH-kee
women	**ženski**	ZHEHN-skee
left / right	**lijevo / desno**	LEE-yeh-voh / DEHS-noh
straight	**ravno**	RAHV-noh
At what time...	**U koliko sati...**	oo KOH-lee-koh SAH-tee
...does this open / close?	**...otvara / zatvara?**	OHT-vah-rah / ZAHT-vah-rah
(Just) a moment.	**(Samo) trenutak.**	(SAH-moh) treh-NOO-tahk
now / soon / later	**sada / uskoro / kasnije**	SAH-dah / OOS-koh-roh / KAHS-nee-yeh
today / tomorrow	**danas / sutra**	DAH-nahs / SOO-trah

In the Restaurant

I'd like to reserve...	**Rezervirao bih...**	reh-zehr-VEER-ow beeh
We'd like to reserve...	**Rezervirali bismo...**	reh-zehr-VEE-rah-lee BEES-moh
...a table for one / two.	**...stol za jednog / dva.**	stohl zah YEHD-nog / dvah
Non-smoking.	**Za nepušače.**	zah NEH-poo-shah-cheh
Is this table free?	**Da li je ovaj stol slobodan?**	dah lee yeh OH-vī stohl SLOH-boh-dahn
Can I help you?	**Izvolite?**	EEZ-voh-lee-teh
The menu (in English), please.	**Jelovnik (na engleskom), molim.**	yeh-LOHV-neek (nah EHN-glehs-kohm) MOH-leem
service (not) included	**posluga (nije) uključena**	POH-sloo-gah (NEE-yeh) OOK-lyoo-cheh-nah
cover charge	**couvert**	KOO-vehr
"to go"	**za ponjeti**	zah POHN-yeh-tee
with / without	**sa / bez**	sah / behz
and / or	**i / ili**	ee / EE-lee
fixed-price meal (of the day)	**(dnevni) meni**	(duh-NEHV-nee) MEH-nee
specialty of the house	**specijalitet kuće**	speht-see-yah-LEE-teht KOO-cheh
half portion	**pola porcije**	POH-lah PORT-see-yeh
daily special	**jelo dana**	YEH-loh DAH-nah
fixed-price meal for tourists	**turistički meni**	TOO-ree-steech-kee MEH-nee
appetizers	**predjela**	PREHD-yeh-lah
bread	**kruh**	krooh
cheese	**sir**	seer
sandwich	**sendvič**	SEND-veech
soup	**juha**	YOO-hah
salad	**salata**	sah-LAH-tah
meat	**meso**	MAY-soh
poultry	**perad**	PEH-rahd
fish	**riba**	REE-bah
seafood	**morska hrana**	MOHR-skah HRAH-nah
fruit	**voće**	VOH-cheh
vegetables	**povrće**	POH-vur-cheh
dessert	**desert**	deh-SAYRT
(tap) water	**voda (od slavine)**	VOH-dah (ohd SLAH-vee-neh)
mineral water	**mineralna voda**	MEE-neh-rahl-nah VOH-dah
milk	**mlijeko**	mlee-YEH-koh
(orange) juice	**sok (od naranče)**	sohk (ohd NAH-rahn-cheh)
coffee	**kava**	KAH-vah
tea	**čaj**	chī
wine	**vino**	VEE-noh
red / white	**crno / bijelo**	TSEHR-noh / bee-YEH-loh
sweet / dry / semi-dry	**slatko / suho / polusuho**	SLAHT-koh / SOO-hoh / POH-loo-soo-hoh
glass / bottle	**čaša / boca**	CHAH-shah / BOHT-sah
beer	**pivo**	PEE-voh
Cheers!	**Živjeli!**	ZHEE-vyeh-lee
More. / Another.	**Još. / Još jedno.**	yohsh / yohsh YEHD-noh
The same.	**Isto.**	EES-toh
Bill, please.	**Račun, molim.**	RAH-choon MOH-leem
tip	**napojnica**	NAH-poy-neet-sah
Delicious!	**Izvrsno!**	EEZ-vur-snoh

German Survival Phrases

When using the phonetics, pronounce ī as the long I sound in "light."

Good day.	**Guten Tag.**	**goo**-tehn tahg
Do you speak English?	**Sprechen Sie Englisch?**	**shprehkh**-ehn zee **ehng**-lish
Yes. / No.	**Ja. / Nein.**	yah / nīn
I (don't) understand.	**Ich verstehe (nicht).**	ikh fehr-**shtay**-heh (nikht)
Please.	**Bitte.**	**bit**-teh
Thank you.	**Danke.**	**dahng**-keh
I'm sorry.	**Es tut mir leid.**	ehs toot meer līt
Excuse me.	**Entschuldigung.**	ehnt-**shool**-dig-oong
(No) problem.	**(Kein) Problem.**	(kīn) proh-**blaym**
(Very) good.	**(Sehr) gut.**	(zehr) goot
Goodbye.	**Auf Wiedersehen.**	owf **vee**-der-zayn
one / two	**eins / zwei**	īns / tsvī
three / four	**drei / vier**	drī / feer
five / six	**fünf / sechs**	fewnf / zehkhs
seven / eight	**sieben / acht**	**zee**-behn / ahkht
nine / ten	**neun / zehn**	noyn / tsayn
How much is it?	**Wieviel kostet das?**	**vee**-feel **kohs**-teht dahs
Write it?	**Schreiben?**	**shrī**-behn
Is it free?	**Ist es umsonst?**	ist ehs oom-**zohnst**
Included?	**Inklusive?**	in-kloo-**zee**-veh
Where can I buy / find...?	**Wo kann ich kaufen / finden...?**	voh kahn ikh **kow**-fehn / **fin**-dehn
I'd like / We'd like...	**Ich hätte gern / Wir hätten gern...**	ikh **heh**-teh gehrn / veer **heh**-tehn gehrn
...a room.	**...ein Zimmer.**	īn **tsim**-mer
...a ticket to ___.	**...eine Fahrkarte nach ___.**	ī-neh **far**-kar-teh nahkh
Is it possible?	**Ist es möglich?**	ist ehs **mur**-glikh
Where is...?	**Wo ist...?**	voh ist
...the train station	**...der Bahnhof**	dehr **bahn**-hohf
...the bus station	**...der Busbahnhof**	dehr **boos**-bahn-hohf
...tourist information	**...das Touristen-informationsbüro**	dahs too-**ris**-tehn-in-for-maht-see-**ohns**-**bew**-roh
...toilet	**...die Toilette**	dee toh-**leh**-teh
men	**Herren**	**hehr**-rehn
women	**Damen**	**dah**-mehn
left / right	**links / rechts**	links / rehkhts
straight	**geradeaus**	geh-**rah**-deh-**ows**
When is this open / closed?	**Um wieviel Uhr ist hier geöffnet / geschlossen?**	oom **vee**-feel oor ist heer geh-**urf**-neht / geh-**shloh**-sehn
At what time?	**Um wieviel Uhr?**	oom **vee**-feel oor
Just a moment.	**Moment.**	moh-**mehnt**
now / soon / later	**jetzt / bald / später**	yehtst / bahld / **shpay**-ter
today / tomorrow	**heute / morgen**	**hoy**-teh / **mor**-gehn

In the Restaurant

I'd like / We'd like...	**Ich hätte gern / Wir hätten gern...**	ikh **heh**-teh gehrn / veer **heh**-tehn gehrn
...a reservation for...	**...eine Reservierung für...**	**ī**-neh reh-zer-**feer**-oong fewr
...a table for one / two.	**...einen Tisch für ein / zwei.**	**ī**-nehn tish fewr īn / tsvī
Non-smoking.	**Nichtraucher.**	**nikht**-rowkh-er
Is this seat free?	**Ist hier frei?**	ist heer frī
Menu (in English), please.	**Speisekarte (auf Englisch), bitte.**	**shpī**-zeh-kar-teh (owf **ehng**-lish) **bit**-teh
service (not) included	**Trinkgeld (nicht) inklusive**	**trink**-gehlt (nikht) in-kloo-**zee**-veh
cover charge	**Eintritt**	**īn**-trit
to go	**zum Mitnehmen**	tsoom **mit**-nay-mehn
with / without	**mit / ohne**	mit / **oh**-neh
and / or	**und / oder**	oont / **oh**-der
menu (of the day)	**(Tages-) Karte**	**(tah**-gehs-) **kar**-teh
set meal for tourists	**Touristenmenü**	too-**ris**-tehn-meh-**new**
specialty of the house	**Spezialität des Hauses**	**shpayt**-see-ah-lee-**tyt** dehs **how**-zehs
appetizers	**Vorspeise**	**for**-shpī-zeh
bread	**Brot**	broht
cheese	**Käse**	**kay**-zeh
sandwich	**Sandwich**	**zahnd**-vich
soup	**Suppe**	**zup**-peh
salad	**Salat**	zah-**laht**
meat	**Fleisch**	flīsh
poultry	**Geflügel**	geh-**flew**-gehl
fish	**Fisch**	fish
seafood	**Meeresfrüchte**	**meh**-rehs-**frewkh**-teh
fruit	**Obst**	ohpst
vegetables	**Gemüse**	geh-**mew**-zeh
dessert	**Nachspeise**	**nahkh**-shpī-zeh
mineral water	**Mineralwasser**	min-eh-**rahl**-vah-ser
tap water	**Leitungswasser**	**lī**-toongs-vah-ser
milk	**Milch**	milkh
(orange) juice	**(Orangen-) Saft**	(oh-**rahn**-zhehn-) zahft
coffee	**Kaffee**	kah-**fay**
tea	**Tee**	tay
wine	**Wein**	vīn
red / white	**rot / weiß**	roht / vīs
glass / bottle	**Glas / Flasche**	glahs / **flah**-sheh
beer	**Bier**	beer
Cheers!	**Prost!**	prohst
More. / Another.	**Mehr. / Noch ein.**	mehr / nohkh īn
The same.	**Das gleiche.**	dahs **glīkh**-eh
Bill, please.	**Rechnung, bitte.**	**rehkh**-noong **bit**-teh
tip	**Trinkgeld**	**trink**-gehlt
Delicious!	**Lecker!**	**lehk**-er

For more user-friendly German phrases, check out *Rick Steves' German Phrase Book and Dictionary* or *Rick Steves' French, Italian & German Phrase Book.*

Pronouncing Eastern European Place Names

Remember that in all of these languages, **j** is pronounced as "y," and **c** is pronounced "ts." Diacritical markings over most consonants (such as **č, š, ś,** or **ž**) have the same effect as putting an *h* after it in English; for example, č is "ch," š or ś is "sh," ž is "zh."

Name	Pronounced
Auschwitz (Concentration Camp, Poland)	OWSH-vits
Birkenau (Concentration Camp, Poland)	BEER-keh-now
Bled (Slovenia)	bled (as it's spelled); locals say "blayd"
Bohinj (Slovenia)	BOH-heen
Bovec (Slovenia)	BOH-vets
Bratislava (Slovakia)	brah-tee-SLAH-vah
Brtonigla (Croatia)	bur-toh-NEEG-lah
Budapest (Hungary)	BOO-dah-pest in English, BOO-daw-pesht in Hungarian
Český Krumlov (Czech Republic)	CHESS-key KROOM-loff
Dubrovnik (Croatia)	doo-BROHV-nik
Dunajec (River Canyon, Slovakia)	DOO-nah-yets
Eger (Hungary)	EH-gehr
Egerszalók (Hungary)	EH-gehr-sah-lohk
Esztergom (Hungary)	EHS-tehr-gohm
Füzesabony (Hungary)	FOO-zesh-ah-boyn
Gdańsk (Poland)	guh-DAYNSK
Gdynia (Poland)	guh-DIN-yah
Gödöllő (Palace, Hungary)	GER-der-ler
Herzegovina (Bosnia-Herzegovina)	hert-seh-GOH-vee-nah
Istria (Croatia)	EE-stree-ah
Jadrolinija (Croatian Ferry Company)	yah-droh-LEE-nee-yah
Karlštejn (Castle, Czech Republic)	KARL-shtayn
Kazimierz (Poland)	kah-ZHEE-mezh
Kobarid (Slovenia)	KOH-bah-reed
Konopiště (Castle, Czech Republic)	KOH-noh-peesh-tyeh
Korčula (Croatia)	KOHR-choo-lah

Kraków (Poland)	KRACK-cow in English, KROCK-oof in Polish
Křivoklát (Castle, Czech Republic)	KREE-vohk-laht
Kutná Hora (Czech Republic)	KOOT-nah HO-rah
Levoča (Slovakia)	LEH-voh-chah
Ljubljana (Slovenia)	lyoob-lyee-AH-nah
Malbork (Castle, Poland)	MAHL-bork
Mostar (Bosnia-Herzegovina)	MOH-star
Motovun (Croatia)	moh-toh-VOON
Nowa Huta (Poland)	NOH-vah HOO-tah
Oświęcim (Poland)	ohsh-VEENCH-im
Pécs (Hungary)	paych
Plitvice (National Park, Croatia)	PLEET-veet-seh
Praha (Czech name for Prague, Czech Republic)	PRAH-hah
Pula (Croatia)	POO-lah
Radovljica (Slovenia)	rah-DOH-vleet-suh
Rijeka (Croatia)	ree-YAY-kah
Rovinj (Croatia)	roh-VEEN
Soča (River Valley, Slovenia)	SOH-chah
Sopot (Poland)	SOH-poht
Sopron (Hungary)	SHOH-prohn
Spiš (Region, Slovakia)	speesh
Split (Croatia)	split (as it's spelled)
Szentendre (Hungary)	SEHN-tehn-dreh
Terezín (Concentration Camp, Czech Republic)	TEH-reh-zeen
Toruń (Poland)	TOH-roon
Vintgar (Gorge, Slovenia)	VEENT-gar
Visegrád (Hungary)	VEE-sheh-grahd
Vršič (Pass, Slovenia)	vur-SHEECH
Warszawa (Polish name for Warsaw, Poland)	vah-SHAH-vah
Wieliczka (Salt Mine, Poland)	veel-EECH-kah
Wien (German name for Vienna, Austria)	veen
Zagreb (Croatia)	ZAH-grehb

INDEX

A

A. Blikle (Warsaw): 347, 377
Academy of Fine Arts (Vienna): 991, 1029–1030
Accommodation: *See* Sleeping; *and specific destinations*
Airlines (airfares): 8, 1105; carry-on restrictions, 12
Airports: Bratislava, 219; Budapest, 483–484; Dubrovnik, 765; Gdańsk, 384; Klagenfurt, 686; Kraków, 254–255; Ljubljana, 685–686, 708; Prague, 57–58; Pula, 895; Split, 815; Vienna, 1068; Warsaw, 340; Zagreb, 916
Albertina Museum (Vienna): 990, 995, 1016
Albertinaplatz (Vienna): 995–996
Alchemy Museum (Kutná Hora): 153–154
All Saints' Church (Korčula): 859
Alps, the: *See* Julian Alps
Amber: 397; shopping for, 300, 391, 415
Amber Collection (Malbork Castle): 434–436
Amber Museum (Gdańsk): 392, 396–397
American Bar (Vienna): 997–998
Amphitheater (Pula): 896–899
Amphorae: about, 897
Andrássy út: Budapest, 478, 517, 527–531; eating, 578–579; map, 528, 567; sleeping, 563, 566–568
Apicultural Museum (Radovljica): 710–711
Applied Arts Museum: Budapest, 540; Vienna, 1031
Apponyi House (Bratislava): 212
Aquariums: 287, 767, 787, 881
Aquincum (Budapest): 474, 546
Archaeological Museums: Gdańsk, 391, 393, 402; Pula, 904; Split, 830–831
Archbishop's Palace (Kraków): 271–272
Archdiocesan Museum (Kraków): 273, 287
Architectural Museum of Ljubljana: 655, 674
Arch of Sergius (Pula): 902
Armory: Gdańsk, 387, 394; Kraków, 281; Malbork Castle, 436
Art Nouveau: Krakow, 262, 266; Ljubljana, 657–658; Prague, 85, 93–96, 143; Vienna, 1028–1029, 1030
Arts and Crafts Museum (Zagreb): 928
Artus Court: Gdańsk, 390, 392, 399–400; Toruń, 444
Astronomical Clock: Gdańsk, 402; Prague, 74–75
Astronomical Museum (Eger): 597
ATM machines: 15–16. *See also specific destinations*
Attitude adjustment: 5
Auction house, in Vienna: 999, 1020–1021
Augustinian Church (Vienna): 1001, 1019
Auschwitz-Birkenau: 317–333; guided tours, 257, 319–321; maps, 322, 329; self-guided tour, 321–331
Austria: 978–1068; almanac, 980–981; information, 1086. *See also* Vienna
Austrian Museum of Applied Art (Vienna): 1031

B

Back Door travel philosophy: 32
Bačvice Beach (Split): 836
Balota Beach (Rovinj): 881
Barber's Bridge (Český Krumlov): 180
Barbican: Kraków, 261; Warsaw, 357

Barbie Museum (Prague): 67, 120
Bar Mleczny: *See* Milk bars, in Poland
Baroque Theater (Český Krumlov): 182
Batana boats: 880–881, 884
Baths: Budapest, 547–555; Eger, 600–602; Egerszálok, 602–603
Batthyány tér (Budapest): 581
Beaches: Bled Lake, 700; Croatia, 744; Dubrovnik, 793–794; Hel Peninsula, 427; Korčula, 859; Lumbarda, 859–860; Prague, 99; Rovinj, 881–882; Sopot, 424, 426; Split, 836
Bear Pits (Český Krumlov): 181
Beekeeping: 638, 710–711
Beer: Croatia, 756, 931; Czech Republic, 46, 174, 176; Hungary, 464, 467, 581; Poland, 246, 312, 375; Slovenia, 668; Vienna, 1037, 1059, 1065
Beethovenhaus (Heiligenstadt): 1046
Belvedere Palace (Vienna): 991, 1029, 1032
Bene Beach (Split): 836
Beneš, Edvard: 178–179
Berlin Wall (Gdańsk): 395–396
Bertramka Villa (Prague): 123
Bethlehem Chapel (Prague): 111
Big Jadrolinija Car Ferry: *See* Jadrolinija
Biking: Bled, 693; Budapest, 487, 496; Kraków, 257, 260; Ljubljana, 655, 656; Prague, 59; Rovinj, 882; Vienna, 988–989
Bilećko Lake: 976
Birkenau: *See* Auschwitz-Birkenau
Biščević Turkish House (Mostar): 966
Bishop Erazm Ciołek Palace (Kraków): 273, 285
Bitskey Aladár Pool (Eger): 600
Black Light Theater (Prague): 122
Black Madonna (Czestochowa): 356, 395
Black Madonna House (Prague): 77–78
Blagaj: 975
Bled: 687–708; eating, 705–707; information, 689; map, 690–691; nightlife, 701; sights/activities, 695–701; sleeping, 701–705; tours, 694–695; transportation, 689, 692, 693–694, 707–708
Bled, Lake: 687, 688–689, 695–700; boating, 697–698, 700; swimming, 700
Bled Castle: 698–699
"Blood Bridge" (Zagreb): 921–922
"Blue Lion" Archaeological Education Center (Gdańsk): 393, 413
Boat travel and cruises: Bled Lake, 697–698; Bohinj Lake, 714; Bratislava, 218–219; Budapest, 496, 558, 577, 586; Dalmatian Coast, 745–746; Danube River, 218–219, 496, 558, 577, 586; Dubrovnik, 764–765, 786–787, 809–811; Gdańsk, 421–422; Korčula, 852, 854, 865–866; Ljubljana, 656; Plitvice Lakes, 939; Prague, 69; Rovinj, 872; Split, 814–815, 845–848
Bohemia: 48, 52–53, 56. *See also* Český Krumlov; Prague
Bohinj, Lake: 713–715; boating, 714
Bone Church (Sedlec): 156–157
Boninovo Bay: 761; sleeping, 804–805
Books, recommended: 1109–1110
Border crossing: 13
Bosnia-Herzegovina: 948–976; almanac, 950–951; currency, 15, 951. *See also* Mostar
Bosnian convertible marks: 15, 951
Bovec: 724–725, 726–728
Boznańska, Olga: 266, 362
Braće Fejića (Mostar): 967–968
Bratislava: 200–219; eating, 217–218; information, 201; map, 202–203; sights/activities, 205–215; sleeping, 216–217; tours, 205; transportation, 201, 204, 218–219
Bratislava Airport: 219
Bratislava Castle: 213–214

Bratislava City History Museum: 212
Broz, Josip: *See* Tito
Brtonigla: 911
Buda (Budapest): 478, 494, 497–508; eating, 580–583; maps, 498, 571; sleeping, 570–574
Budapest: 472–587; baths, 547–555; cafés, 583–585; eating, 574–585; entertainment, 555–558; helpful hints, 485–487; history of, 474–475; information, 479–481; layout of, 475, 478–479; nightlife, 558–559; planning tips, 473–475; rip-offs, 485; shopping, 560–561; sights/activities, 497–555; sleeping, 561–574; tours, 493, 496–497; transportation, 481–484, 487–492, 585–587. *See also specific neighborhoods*
Budapest City Park: 495, 508, 538; eating, 579–580; map, 536
Budapest Ferihegy Airport: 483–484
Budapest Great Synagogue: 494, 525–527
Budapest History Museum: 501
Budapest Museum of Ecclesiastical Art: 505
Budapest Uprising (1956): *See* Hungarian Uprising
Budgeting: 5, 8–9
Bulevar (Mostar): 956–957
Bull's Blood (wine): 603–605
Burggarten (Vienna): 1002, 1020
Burglars' Tower (Zagreb): 919–920
Bus travel: 1099; Auschwitz, 332–333; Bled, 692, 693, 708; Budapest, 491–492, 496–497; Český Krumlov, 174, 189–190; Dalmatian Coast, 746; Dubrovnik, 764, 770, 771, 810; Eger, 590, 609; Gdańsk, 384–385; Korčula, 854, 866; Kraków, 254, 256–257, 260; Ljubljana, 651, 653–654, 685; Mostar, 952, 954–955, 972–973; Pécs, 611; Plitvice Lakes, 935, 938; Prague, 56–57, 68–69, 148–149; Pula, 894, 905; Rovinj, 872, 891; Split, 818, 848; Vienna, 987–989, 992; Warsaw, 340–341; Zagreb, 916, 933
Butchers' Bridge (Ljubljana): 661–662

C

Cabs: tipping, 19. *See also specific destinations*
Café Sacher (Vienna): 994–995
Café Uliks (Pula): 903
Camera obscura: 589, 597
Canaletto Room (Warsaw): 354
Cardo (Split): 827
Car insurance: 1102–1103
Car leasing: 1103
Carpathian Mountains, High Tatras: 229–230
Car rentals: 8, 12, 1100, 1102. *See also specific destinations*
Car travel: 1096–1097, 1103–1105; map, 1101; Bled, 692, 726; Budapest, 484, 586–587; Dalmatia, 848–850; Dalmatian Coast, 745, 746; Dubrovnik, 765–768, 810; Eger, 591; Korčula, 867; Kraków, 254; Ljubljana, 651; Mostar, 952, 974–975; Plitvice Lakes, 935, 945–946; Pula, 894; Rovinj, 871–872; Serbian Herzegovina, 975–976; Split, 815–816; Warsaw, 340
Casinos: 725, 996
Castle Hill (Budapest): 478, 497, 499; sleeping, 573–574
Castle Quarter (Prague): 64, 67, 106–121; eating, 146–147; map, 108–109
Castle Square (Prague): 112–114
Castle Square (Warsaw): 342, 352–353
Cave Church (Budapest): 508
Celetná street (Prague): 73, 77–78, 124–125
Cella Septichora Visitor Center (Pécs): 621–623
Cell (mobile) phones: 1091
Central European University (Budapest): 517
Central Maritime Museum (Gdańsk): 393, 402–404

Centromerkur (Ljubljana): 658
Ceremonial Hall (Prague): 86
Červený Kláštor: 228
Český Krumlov: 171–190; eating, 187–189; festivals, 174; history of, 172–173; information, 173; map, 175; sights/activities, 176–184; sleeping, 184–187; tours, 174, 176; transportation, 173–174, 189–190
Český Krumlov Castle: 180–182
Český Krumlov Museum of Regional History: 176–177
Chain Bridge (Budapest): 518
Charles Bridge (Prague): 66, 79–82
Charles Square (Prague): 100
Chocolate: 206, 246, 377, 684, 827, 1000
Chopin, Fryderyk: 286, 347–348, 363; Museum (Warsaw), 342, 362–363
Chopin International Airport (Warsaw): 340
Cimrman, Jára: 41, 104–105; Museum (Prague), 106
Citadella (Budapest): 507–508
City Museum of Ljubljana: 655, 668–669
Climate: 9, 1115
Cloth Hall (Kraków): 258, 267–268, 300
Coach Museum Wagenburg (Vienna): 1037
Cobblers' Bridge (Ljubljana): 655, 669–670
Coffee, Viennese: 1043
Collegium Maius (Kraków): 259, 286–287
Comenius, John Amos: 41, 105
Communism: Croatia, 740, 874; Czech Republic, 35, 42, 90, 91–92, 96–97, 106; Hungary, 462–463, 531–535, 540–546; Poland, 239–242, 297–300, 346, 348–349, 395–396, 406–407, 411–412
Communism Museum (Prague): 66, 96–97
Concentration camps: 295; Auschwitz-Birkenau, 317–333; Terezín, 158–165
Congress Square (Ljubljana): 664
Contemporary History Museum (Ljubljana): 655, 667–668
Copernicus, Nicholas: 235, 286, 347, 391, 417, 443, 444; House (Toruń), 445–446
Coppersmiths' Street (Mostar): 961
Costs of trip: 5, 8–9
Cracow: *See* Kraków
Crane (Gdańsk): 391–392, 403
Credit cards: 12, 16, 18
Croatia: 736–946; almanac, 738–739; currency, 15, 739, 741; at a glance, 7; information, 1086; map, 737; overview, 736–757. *See also* Dubrovnik; Istria; Korčula; Plitvice Lakes National Park; Split; Zagreb
Croatian kunas: 15, 739
Croatian Museum of Naive Art (Zagreb): 920, 922–925
Croatian Parliament (Zagreb): 921
Crooked Bridge (Mostar): 958
Crooked House (Sopot): 425
Cruises: *See* Boat travel and cruises
Csontváry (Tivadar) Museum (Pécs): 619–621
Cuisine: *See* Eating; *and specific destinations*
Curie, Marie: 235, 358
Currency and exchange: 14–15; Bosnia-Herzegovina, 15, 951; Croatia, 15, 739, 741; Czech Republic, 15, 37; Hungary, 15, 453; Poland, 15, 235; Slovakia, 194; Slovenia, 15, 636, 639
Customs regulations: 21
Czartoryski Museum (Kraków): 259, 281–283
Czech crowns: 15, 37
Czech Cubism Museum (Prague): 77–78
Czech Museum of Silver (Kutná Hora): 153
Czech National Library (Prague): 66, 79
Czech Philharmonic (Prague): 123
Czech Railways: 148
Czech Republic: 34–190; almanac, 36–37; currency, 15, 37; at a

glance, 6; information, 1085; map, 35; overview, 34–48. *See also* Český Krumlov; Prague
Czech State Opera (Prague): 124

D

Dalmatian Coast: Istrian Peninsula, 868–905; transportation, 745–746, 845–850. *See also* Dubrovnik; Korčula; Split
Dancing House (Prague): 99–100
Danube Bend: 546–547
Danube Island (Vienna): 1037–1038
Danube Promenade (Budapest): 521, 577
Danube River: 475, 478, 518–519, 983, 986; bridges, in Bratislava, 210–211, 214–215; cruises, 218–219, 496, 558, 577, 586
Da Vinci, Leonardo: 282–283, 857
Debit cards: 12, 16, 18
Demel (Vienna): 1000
Dining: *See* Eating; *and specific destinations*
Diocletian: 739, 747, 812, 819–829; Palace (Split), 819–824; map, 822
Discounts: 14; Bratislava, 201; Budapest, 481, 489; Dubrovnik, 778; Gdańsk, 381; Kraków, 253; Ljubljana, 650; Split, 814; Vienna, 986; Warsaw, 338
Długi Targ (Gdańsk): 390
Dobó, István: 592, 593, 594–595
Dobó Square (Eger): 592, 594
Dobó utca (Eger): 594
Dominican Monastery Museum (Dubrovnik): 766, 785–786
Donauinsel (Vienna): 1037–1038
Dorotheum (Vienna): 999, 1020–1021
Dragon Bridge (Ljubljana): 655, 662
Dragon's Den (Kraków): 279
Driving: *See* Car travel
Dubrovnik: 758–811; eating, 806–809; entertainment, 794–795; helpful hints, 768–770; history of, 780–781; information, 761–763; layout of, 760–761; maps, 762–763, 774–775; nightlife, 795–796; planning tips, 760; shopping, 794; sights/activities, 772–794; sleeping, 797–806; tours, 770–772; transportation, 764–768, 770, 809–811; walking tour, 772–778
Dubrovnik Aquarium: 767, 787
Dubrovnik Bell Tower: 777
Dubrovnik Cathedral: 766, 784–785
Dubrovnik City Hall: 778
Dubrovnik Ethnographic Museum: 767, 790
Dubrovnik Maritime Museum: 767, 787
Dubrovnik Serbian Orthodox Church: 767, 788, 790
Dubrovnik Synagogue Museum: 766, 787–788
Dubrovnik Town Walls: 766, 769, 779–782
Dunajec Canyon: 228
Dunajec River: rafting, 227–228
Duna Palota (Budapest): 517, 557
Dürer, Albrecht: 114, 537
Dvořák, Antonín: 41, 122, 124

E

"Eastern Europe:" use of term, 2
Eating: 29–31; budgeting, 8; tipping, 19; Austria, 981; Croatia, 752–756; Czech Republic, 44–45, 47; Hungary, 464–469; Poland, 244–247; Slovakia, 198; Slovenia, 641–643. *See also specific destinations*
Ecclesiastical Art Museum (Budapest): 505
Economy: Austria, 980–981; Bosnia-Herzegovina, 951; Croatia, 738; Czech Republic, 36–37; Hungary, 453; Poland, 234; Slovakia, 194; Slovenia, 636
Eger: 588–609; eating, 607–608; information, 589; map, 590; nightlife, 605; sights/activities, 592–605; sleeping, 605–607; transportation, 589–591, 609

Eger Castle: 594–596
Eger Cathedral: 597–598
Eger Lyceum: 596–597
Eger Market Hall: 599
Eger Minaret: 599
Egerszálok: 602–603
Eger Thermal Bath: 600–602
Eger wine: 603–605
Egon Schiele Art Center (Český Krumlov): 180
Egri Bikavér: *See* Bull's Blood
Elaphite Islands: 786–787
Electricity: 13–14
Elisabeth, Empress: *See* Sisi, Empress
E-mail: *See* Internet access
Embassies: 1094–1095
Entertainment: budgeting, 8. *See also* Music; *and specific destinations*
Equitable Building (Vienna): 998
Estates Theater (Prague): 78, 123–124
Esztergom Basilica: 547
Ethnographic Museums: Budapest, 512; Dubrovnik, 767, 790; Kraków, 259, 293–294; Ljubljana, 655, 674–675; Split, 829
Ethnographic Park (Toruń): 446
Euphemia, Saint: 873, 878–879
Euro currency: 15, 194
European Union (EU): 17, 28, 242–243, 463, 640–641, 750–751
Events: *See* Festivals
Exchange rates: *See* Currency and exchange

F

Ferihegy Airport (Budapest): 483–484
Ferries: *See* Jadrolinija
Festivals: 1111–1114; Český Krumlov, 174; Dubrovnik, 768, 794–795; Korčula, 855; Prague, 124; Vienna, 1039
Fishermen's Bastion (Budapest): 505
Flag: Austria, 981; Bosnia-Herzegovina, 951; Croatia, 739; Czech Republic, 37; Hungary, 453; Poland, 235; Slovakia, 194; Slovenia, 637
Florian Gate (Kraków): 261
Floriańska street (Kraków): 262–263
Food: *See* Eating; *and specific destinations*
Fort Kaštel (Pula): 904
Franciscan Garden (Prague): 93
Franciscan Monastery Museum (Dubrovnik): 766, 773, 782–783
Frank, Anne: 324–325
Franz Ferdinand, Archduke: 166, 167
Franz Josef, Emperor: 95, 459, 505, 529, 546, 1008–1013, 1018, 1035–1036
Franz Liszt Square (Budapest): 530, 558, 578
"Fred and Ginger" house (Prague): 99–100
French Revolution Square (Ljubljana): 671
Freud (Sigmund) Museum (Vienna): 1035
Fryderyk Chopin International Airport (Warsaw): 340
Fürstenberg Gardens (Prague): 120–121
Füzesabony: 609
Fužine Castle (Ljubljana): 674

G

Gacko: 976
Galicia Jewish Museum (Kraków): 293
Gallery of 19th-Century Polish Art (Kraków): 259, 268, 284–285
Galovac Lake: 938, 942
Garnets, shopping for: 125
Gazi Kasim Pasha Mosque (Pécs): 616, 617–619
Gdańsk: 379–422; eating, 418–421; excursion areas, 423–427; information, 381; layout of, 380–381; maps, 382–383, 422; planning tips, 380; shopping, 415; sights/activities, 385–414; sleeping, 415–418; tours, 385;

INDEX

transportation, 381, 384–385, 421–422; walking tour, 385–396
Gdańsk, Historical Zone of the Free City of: 393, 402
Gdańsk Archaeological Museum: 391, 393, 402
Gdańsk Central Maritime Museum: 393, 402–404
Gdańsk Historical Museum: 396–397
Gdańsk Main Town: *See* Main Town
Gdańsk Shipyard: 392, 395, 404–409
Gdynia: 426–427
Gehry, Frank: 99–100
Gellért Baths (Budapest): 494, 508, 553–555
Gellért Hill (Budapest): 478, 507–508
Geography: Austria, 980; Bosnia-Herzegovina, 951; Croatia, 738; Czech Republic, 36; Hungary, 452; Poland, 234; Slovakia, 194; Slovenia, 636
Ghetto Heroes Square: Kraków, 294; Warsaw, 365
Gingerbread Museum (Toruń): 445
Ginz, Petr: 159
Gödöllo Royal Palace: 546
Golden Cape (Rovinj): 881–882
Golden Gate: Gdańsk, 388; Split, 827–828
Golden Lane (Prague): 120
Gotyk House (Gdańsk): 391, 417–418
Government: Austria, 981; Croatia, 739, 750–751; Czech Republic, 37, 42, 44; Hungary, 453, 463–464; Poland, 235, 243–244; Slovakia, 194, 196–198; Slovenia, 636–637
Graben (Vienna): 999–1000
Gradec (Zagreb): 919–921, 926–928
Granary Island (Gdańsk): 391, 413
Grand Hotel Union (Ljubljana): 658, 676–677
Great Land Gate (Korčula): 855–856
Great Market Hall (Budapest): 494, 522–524, 560
Great Mill (Gdańsk): 395
Great Synagogue (Budapest): 494, 525–527
Greece: transportation, 810–811
Green Gate (Gdańsk): 390
Green Horseshoe (Zagreb): 928
Green Market (Split): 830
Gresham Palace (Budapest): 517–518
Grinzing: 1046
Grisia street (Rovinj): 877–878
Grodzka street (Kraków): 272–273, 313
Guidebooks: 1108; Rick Steves, 1106
Gundel (Budapest): 579–580
Gypsies: *See* Roma

H

Haas Haus (Vienna): 998–999
Hajós utca (Budapest): 530
Hašek, Jaroslav: 37, 1109
Hauptmann House (Ljubljana): 657–658
Haus der Musik (Vienna): 991, 1020
Havel, Václav: 37, 41, 42, 92
Havelská Market (Prague): 66, 78
Havlíček Square (Kutná Hora): 155–156
Heiligenstadt: 1046–1047
Heldenplatz (Vienna): 1002
Hel Peninsula: 421, 422, 427
Hemingway, Ernest: 639, 722, 729, 732
Heroes' Square (Budapest): 495, 535–536
Heurigen, in Vienna: 1044–1047
High Synagogue (Kraków): 292
High Tatras: 229–230
Hiking: Bled, 695; Bohinj, 715; Český Krumlov, 184; High Tatras, 229–230; Kobarid, 732–733; Marjan Peninsula, 835; Plitvice Lakes, 940–942; Slovak Paradise, 227; Srbsko, 169; Vintgar Gorge, 712–713
Hill of the Cross (Český Krumlov): 184

Historical Exhibition of Weapons (Eger): 594
Historical Zone of the Free City of Gdańsk: 393, 402
History: 1069–1084; Bosnia-Herzegovina, 950, 1079–1080; Croatia, 746–750, 780–781, 1077–1079; Czech Republic, 38–42, 172–173; Hungary, 455–463, 474–475, 593; Poland, 237–242, 364, 368, 386–387, 406–407; Slovakia, 193, 195–197, 222; Slovenia, 639–641, 646, 1077. *See also* Communism; World War I; World War II
Hockey: 43
Hofburg Palace (Vienna): 1001–1003, 1006–1020; eating, 1007–1008; Imperial Apartments, 990, 1001–1002, 1008–1013; map, 1007; New Palace Museums, 990, 1002, 1015–1016; Treasury, 990, 1002, 1013–1015
Holidays: 13, 1111–1114
Holocaust Memorial Center (Budapest): 495, 539–540
Holocaust Monument (Budapest): 512–513
Holy Cross Church (Warsaw): 347–348
Holy Trinity Plague Column: Pécs, 616; Vienna, 999–1000
Horní Bridge (Český Krumlov): 176
Horses, Lipizzaner stallions (Vienna): 991, 1018–1019
"Hospital in the Rock" (Budapest): 494, 506–507
Hostels: overview, 26. *See also specific destinations*
Hotel Růže (Český Krumlov): 177
Hotels: overview, 24–25; reservations, 26–27, 29; reservations form, 1118. *See also specific destinations*
Hot springs: *See* Baths
House of Terror (Budapest): 495, 531–535
House of the Batana Boat (Rovinj): 880–881, 884
Hradčany (Prague): *See* Castle Quarter
Hrádek (Kutná Hora): 153
Hundertwasser Museum (Vienna): 991, 1033–1035
Hungarian Agriculture Museum (Budapest): 539
Hungarian forints: 15, 453
Hungarian Museum of Trade and Tourism (Budapest): 517
Hungarian National Gallery (Budapest): 494, 500
Hungarian National Museum (Budapest): 495, 524–525
Hungarian Parliament (Budapest): 494, 508–509
Hungarian State Opera House (Budapest): 495, 529–530, 556–557
Hungarian Uprising (1956): 462, 509, 512–515, 534; Monument (Budapest), 512, 537–538
Hungary: 450–631; almanac, 452–453; currency, 15, 453; at a glance, 6–7; information, 1086; map, 451; overview, 450–471. *See also* Budapest; Eger; Pécs
Hus, Jan: 39–40, 41, 71, 75; Memorial (Prague), 71–72
Hvar Island: 846–847
Hviezdoslav Square (Bratislava): 210

I

Icon Museum: Dubrovnik, 767, 790; Korčula, 858–859
Idrija: 725
Imperial Apartments (Vienna): 990, 1001–1002, 1008–1013
Imperial Furniture Collection (Vienna): 991, 1032–1033
Imperial Music Chapel (Vienna): 1002, 1039
Infant of Prague: 104–105
Information: 1085–1086. *See also specific destinations*
Institute for the Restoration of Dubrovnik: 766, 788
International Building/Bank of Austria (Vienna): 998

Internet access: 1095–1096; Bled, 692; Bratislava, 204; Budapest, 486; Český Krumlov, 174; Dubrovnik, 768–769; Eger, 591; Gdańsk, 384; Kraków, 255; Ljubljana, 652–653; Pécs, 614; Prague, 59; Rovinj, 872; Split, 816–817; Vienna, 986–987
Isaac Synagogue (Kraków): 292–293
Istria: 868–905; map, 892; transportation, 892–893. *See also* Rovinj
Istria Archaeological Museum (Pula): 904
István (Stephen), Saint: 506, 516–517, 547, 594, 624
István tér (Pécs): 624
Italian Court (Kutná Hora): 154–155
Italian Cultural Center (Motovun): 908
Italian Mausoleum (Kobarid): 731–732
Italo-Croatia: 875
Italy: transportation, 811, 846–847

J

Jadrolinija: Dalmatian Coast, 745–746, 845–848; Dubrovnik, 809–810; Korčula, 852, 854, 865; Split, 814, 845
Jadwiga, Saint: 238, 276, 435
Jagiellonian University Museum (Kraków): 259, 286–287
J & L Lobmeyr Crystal (Vienna): 996–997
Jan Hus Memorial (Prague): 71–72
Janus Pannonius utca (Pécs): 619
Jelačić Square (Zagreb): 918–919
Jerusalem Synagogue (Prague): 95
Jesenice: 719
Jewish Cemeteries (Kraków): 258, 291–292
Jewish Ghetto (Dubrovnik): 787–788
Jewish Ghetto (Warsaw): 343, 364, 365–366
Jewish Historical Institute of Poland (Warsaw): 366
Jewish Museum (Budapest): 527
Jewish Quarter (Kraków): *See* Kazimierz
Jewish Quarter (Prague): 64, 66, 73, 82–88; map, 83; sleeping, 142; tours, 65, 68
Ježinac Beach (Split): 836
John Paul II, Pope (Karol Wojtyła): 77, 226, 235, 270–272, 277, 299–300, 408; Archdiocesan Museum (Kraków), 273, 287
John Paul II Kraków-Balice Airport (Kraków): 254–255
Jókai tér (Pécs): 615
Josef II, Emperor: 84, 467, 596, 1015, 1017–1019, 1032, 1037
Josefov (Prague): *See* Jewish Quarter
Joyce, James: 894, 903
Jože Plecnik House (Ljubljana): 654, 671–674
Judenplatz Memorial and Museum (Vienna): 1022
Julian Alps: 716–734; car rentals, 693; map, 718; self-guided driving tour, 717–726; tours, 694, 717. *See also* Bled
Jupiter's Temple (Split): 826

K

Kafka, Franz: 38, 41, 120, 1109
Kaiserappartements (Vienna): 990, 1001–1002, 1008–1013
Kaisergruft (Vienna): 990, 997, 1016, 1018
Kajtaz House (Mostar): 967
Kampa Island (Prague): 100, 145–146
Kanonicza street (Kraków): 273
Kaptol (Zagreb): 921–922
Karadozbeg Mosque (Mostar): 967
Karlova street (Prague): 78–79
Karlskirche (Vienna): 991, 1027–1028
Karlsplatz (Vienna): 1027, 1029
Karlštejn Castle: 168–169
Karlův Most (Prague): 66, 79–82
Kärntner Strasse (Vienna): 996–997
Károlyi Park (Budapest): 522
Kaštelet Chapel (Split): 833–834

Kazimierz (Kraków): 287–294; eating, 314–315; map, 288; nightlife, 301; sleeping, 309–310
Kazimierz (the Great): 238, 267, 272, 276–279, 296; biographical sketch, 265
Kazimierz Market Square (Kraków): 293
Kennedy (John F.) Haus (Vienna): 999
Király utca (Pécs): 617
Klaus Synagogue (Prague): 86
Klementinum (Prague): 66, 79
Klezmer music: 314–215
Klimt, Gustav: 1026, 1029, 1030, 1032
Kluže Fort: 724
Kobarid: 725, 729–734
Kobarid Museum: 730–731
Kohlmarkt (Vienna): 1000–1001
Konopište Castle: 166–168
Kopcsik Marzipan Museum (Eger): 599
Korčula: 851–867; eating, 863–865; information, 852; map, 853; sights/activities, 855–860; sleeping, 860–863; transportation, 852, 854, 865–867
Korčula Old Town Walls: 859
Korčula Town Hall: 856
Korčula Town Museum: 857
Košciuszko, Tadeusz: 239, 274, 277, 285
Košciuszko Mound (Kraków): 279
Koski Mehmed-Pasha Mosque (Mostar): 961–964
Kossuth tér (Budapest): 509, 512
Kozjak, Lake: 942
Krakovo (Ljubljana): eating, 682–683
Kraków: 248–316; eating, 310–315; entertainment, 300–301; helpful hints, 255–256; information, 253; layout of, 252–253; planning tips, 252; shopping, 300; sights/activities, 260–300; sleeping, 302–310; tours, 257–260; transportation, 253–255, 256–257, 316; walking tour, 260–274
Kraków Aquarium: 287
Kraków City Walls: 261–262
Kraków Main Market Square: 258, 264–267, 313–314
Kraków Old Synagogue: 292
Krakowskie Przedmieście (Warsaw): 347–351
Kraków Town Hall Tower: 268–269
Kranjska Gora: 719–721
Křivoklát Castle: 169–170
Křížový Vrch (Český Krumlov): 184
Krumlov Castle (Český Krumlov): 180–182
Krvavi Most (Zagreb): 921–922
Kubicki Arcades (Warsaw): 354–355
Kundera, Milan: 37, 41, 1109
KunstHausWien (Vienna): 991, 1033–1035
Kunsthistorisches Museum (Vienna): 990, 1022–1025; map, 1023
Kupa Synagogue (Kraków): 293
Kurja Vas: 719
Kursalon (Vienna): 1040
Kutná Hora: 150–158; map, 154–155
Kuvi Beach (Rovinj): 882

L

Lady with an Ermine (da Vinci): 282–283
Lake Bled region: 687–708
Language: 1086–1088; Austria, 981; Bosnia-Herzegovina, 950; Croatia, 756–757; survival phrases, 1127–1128; Czech Republic, 47–48; survival phrases, 1119; German survival phrases, 1129–1130; Hungary, 469–471; survival phrases, 1123–1124; Poland, 247, 249; survival phrases, 1120–1122; Slovakia, 198–199; Slovenia, 635, 643–644; survival phrases, 1125–1126
Lapad Peninsula: 761, 793; eating, 809; sleeping, 805–806

Laundry: Bled, 692–693; Budapest, 486; Český Krumlov, 174; Dubrovnik, 769; Kraków, 256; Ljubljana, 653; Prague, 59; Rovinj, 872; Split, 817
Łazienki Park (Warsaw): 343, 363, 365
Lennon Wall (Prague): 100–102
Leopold Museum (Vienna): 1026
Leopold Town (Budapest): 478, 508–519
Lesnica: 228
Levoča: 221–229
Levoča Town Hall: 226
Liberation Monument (Budapest): 487, 507–508
Libertas: 759
Liberty Bridge (Budapest): 478, 480
Liechtenstein Museum (Vienna): 991, 1033
Lipizzaner stallions (Vienna): 991, 1018–1019
Liszt, Franz: 459, 530, 624
Little Quarter (Prague): 64, 67, 100–106; eating, 145–146; maps, 101, 130; sleeping, 129–131
Little Quarter Square (Prague): 102
Ljubinje: 976
Ljubljana: 645–686; eating, 680–684; helpful hints, 652–653; history of, 646; information, 650; layout of, 647, 650; map, 648–649; planning tips, 645, 647; shopping, 675–676; sights/activities, 656–675; sleeping, 676–680; tours, 655–656; transportation, 651, 653–655, 684–686
Ljubljana Airport: 685–686, 708
Ljubljana Architectural Museum: 655, 674
Ljubljana Castle: 655, 663–664
Ljubljana Cathedral: 660–661
Ljubljana City Museum: 655, 668–669
Ljubljana Contemporary History Museum: 655, 667–668
Ljubljana Riverside Market: 654, 659–660
Ljubljana Skyscraper: 653, 668
Ljubljana Town Hall: 662
Ljubljana Town Square: 662–663
Ljubljanica River: 647, 650, 657; cruises, 656
Lobkowicz Palace (Prague): 120
Lokrum Island: 786, 793
Loos, Adolf: 997–998, 1000, 1001; House (Vienna), 1001
Lord's Ark Church (Kraków): 299–300
Loreta Church (Prague): 111–112
Loreto Chapel (Budapest): 504–505
Lost Wawel (Kraków): 281
Lucerna Gallery (Prague): 92–93
Luges: 700
Lumbarda: 859–860
Luther, Martin: 39, 71
Luža Square (Dubrovnik): 777–778, 783
Lyceum (Eger): 596–597

M

Mail: *See* Post offices
Main Market Square (Kraków): 258, 264–267, 313–314
Main Town (Gdańsk): 380, 396–404; eating, 419–421; sleeping, 417–418
Main Town Hall (Gdańsk): 389–390, 392, 398–399
Maisel Synagogue (Prague): 87–88
Maksymilian Kolbe, Saint: 270, 326, 327
Malbork Castle: 429–442; map, 432; self-guided tour, 431–441
Maps: about, 1106, 1108; legend, 3. *See also specific destinations*
Marco Polo Festival (Korčula): 855, 1112
Margaret Island (Budapest): 495, 496, 519
Mariánska Hora (Levoča): 226
Maria Theresa, Empress: 158, 208, 213, 1016–1019, 1035–1036
Marjan Peninsula: 835
Markets: Budapest, 494, 502, 522–524, 560; Český Krumlov, 174; Dubrovnik, 808–809; Eger, 599; Gdańsk, 394, 400; Kraków, 265,

267–268, 293, 300, 315; Kutná Hora, 156; Ljubljana, 652, 654, 659–660, 661, 675; Mostar, 965; Pécs, 616; Prague, 66, 78; Pula, 903, 904; Rovinj, 874; Split, 829, 830; Vienna, 991, 1030–1031; Zagreb, 922, 931
Mary Magdalene Square (Kraków): 273
Masaryk, Tomáš Garrigue: 41, 112–113, 114, 156
Master Pavol of Levoča: 222, 223, 226
Matejko, Jan: 237, 264, 269, 284, 285, 354, 360–362; House (Kraków), 286
Matejuška Fishermen's Port (Split): 835
Matthias Church (Budapest): 494, 504–505
Matthias Corvinus: 223, 499, 502–503
Mayer am Pfarrplatz (Heiligenstadt): 1046
Mecsek Hills: 629
Medieval Art Museum (Prague): 66, 77
Međugorje: 974
Mehoffer, Józef: 266, 269, 284, 362; House (Kraków), 286
Melantrichova street (Prague): 74, 78
Memento Park (Budapest): 494, 540–546; map, 542
Memling, Hans: 412–413
Meštrović, Ivan: 739, 826, 827–828, 831–834, 920; Atelier (Zagreb), 926; Gallery (Split), 831, 833
Metelkova (Ljubljana): 674–675
Metković: 849, 974
Metric conversions: 1114–1115
Metro: Budapest, 487–490; Prague, 55, 60–62; Vienna, 987–988; Warsaw, 340–341
Michaelerplatz (Vienna): 1001
Michalská street (Bratislava): 205–206
Mickiewicz, Adam: 266, 276, 351
Milk bars, in Poland: 245, 272–273, 313, 376
Millennium Monument (Budapest): 535–536
Mimara Museum (Zagreb): 928
Minčeta Tower (Dubrovnik): 773, 779
Miniatures Museum (Prague): 110
Ministry of War (Budapest): 501
Minorite Church (Eger): 592
Mlinarica Gorge: 723
Młoda Polska: 262, 266, 269, 362
Mobile phones: 1091
Modern Hungarian Art Museum (Pécs): 627–628
Money: 14–21. *See also* Currency and exchange
Money-saving tips: *See* Discounts
Monte Cassino Heroes Street (Sopot): 424, 425
Montenegro: guided tours, 771
Monument Against War and Fascism (Vienna): 995–996
Monument of the Fallen Shipyard Workers (Gdańsk): 404–407
Moreška sword dances, in Korčula: 855
Mostar: 948–976; eating, 971–972; information, 954; layout of, 954; map, 953; nightlife, 968–969; planning tips, 952; sights/activities, 956–968; sleeping, 969–971; tours, 952, 954; transportation, 952, 954–955, 972–976
Mostar Old Bridge: 959–961
Motlawa River: 390–391, 419; cruises, 421–422
Motovun: 905–911
Mount Srd (Dubrovnik): 767, 791–793
Mount Straža: 700
Mount Triglav: 720
Movies, recommended: 1110
Mozart, Wolfgang Amadeus: 1017, 1020; concerts, 123–124, 1039–1040, 1042; House (Vienna), 999, 1021–1022, 1040; Museum (Prague), 123
Mozarthaus (Vienna): 999, 1021–1022, 1040
Mucha, Alfons: 41, 94, 116–117; Museum (Prague), 66, 94–95

Műcsarnok (Budapest): 537
Municipal House (Prague): 66, 95–96, 143
Museum of Applied Art (Vienna): 1031
Museum of Communism (Prague): 66, 96–97
Museum of Czech Cubism (Prague): 77–78
Museum of Ecclesiastical Art (Budapest): 505
Museum of Ethnography (Budapest): 512
Museum of Fine Arts (Budapest): 536–537
Museum of Herzegovina (Mostar): 965
Museum of Hungarian Agriculture (Budapest): 539
Museum of Medieval Art (Prague): 66, 77
Museum of Miniatures (Prague): 110
Museum of Modern Art (Ljubljana): 666
Museum of Modern Art (Vienna): 1026
Museum of the Old Bridge (Mostar): 961
MuseumsQuartier (Vienna): 1025–1027
Music: Budapest, 556–558; Dubrovnik, 794–795; Kraków, 300–301; Prague, 121–124; Rovinj, 882–883; Vienna, 1020, 1038–1043. *See also* Opera; *and specific composers*
Muslibegović House (Mostar): 967
Muslims of Mostar: 962–963
Muzeum Czartoryskich (Kraków): 259, 281–283
Muzeum Fryderyka Chopina (Warsaw): 342, 362–363
Muzeum Narodowe (Warsaw): 342, 360–362
Muzeum Powstania Warszawskiego (Warsaw): 343, 367, 369–370

N

Náci, Schöner: 207–209
Nagy, Imre: 462–463, 513, 514, 515, 535
Nakić House (Split): 828–829
Na Příkope (Prague): 93–96, 124–125
Národní Třída (Prague): 96–97, 125
Naschmarkt (Vienna): 991, 1030–1031
National and University Library (Ljubljana): 654, 670–671
National Dance Theater (Budapest): 501
National Gallery: Budapest, 494, 500; Ljubljana, 666
National Library: Prague, 66, 79; Vienna, 1019–1020
National Museum: Budapest, 495, 524–525; Gdańsk, 393, 412–413; Kraków, 281–286; Ljubljana, 665–666, 675; Prague, 88, 90; Warsaw, 342, 360–362
National Square (Pula): 903
National Theater: Bratislava, 210; Pécs, 617; Prague, 97, 99, 123
Na Valech Garden (Prague): 121
Neretva River: 954, 958–961
Neretva River Delta: 849, 974
Nerudova street (Prague): 102–103
Neuer Markt (Vienna): 997
Neum: 849, 974
Nevesinje: 976
New Bridge (Bratislava): 210–211, 214–215
New Cemetery (Kraków): 291–292
"New Europe" and the EU: 17
New Muslim Cemetery (Mostar): 964–965
New Palace Museums (Vienna): 990, 1002, 1015–1016
Newspapers: 14
New Town (Prague): 64, 66, 88–100; maps, 89, 132
New Town (Warsaw): 357–358
Nova Gorica: 725
Nové Mesto (Prague): *See* New Town
Nowa Huta (Kraków): 297–300
Nowý Most (Bratislava): 210–211, 214–215

Nowy Świat (Warsaw): 342–343, 346–347, 358–363; eating, 376–377
Nussdorf: 1045–1046

O
Óbuda (Budapest): 546
Oktogon (Budapest): 530–531
Old Bridge (Mostar): 959–961
Old Jewish Cemetery (Prague): 85–86
Old-New Synagogue (Prague): 86–87
Old Port (Dubrovnik): 760, 786–787
Old Royal Palace (Prague): 118–119
Old Synagogue (Kraków): 292
Old Town (Bratislava): 205–213
Old Town (Dubrovnik): 760, 773–786; eating, 806–808; map, 774–775; nightlife, 795–796; sleeping, 798–801, 803–804
Old Town (Gdańsk): 380–381
Old Town (Kraków): 252, 262–274; eating, 310–314; maps, 250–251, 304–305; nightlife, 301; sleeping, 302–309
Old Town (Prague): 64, 66, 69–88; eating, 137–144; maps, 70, 72, 127, 138; sleeping, 128–129
Old Town (Rovinj): 870, 873–874; eating, 888–889; sleeping, 884–886
Old Town (Split): 813, 819–824, 828–831; eating, 842–844; nightlife, 836; sleeping, 837–842
Old Town (Warsaw): 351–357; eating, 375–376; map, 337; sleeping, 371–375
Old Town Hall (Bratislava): 207, 212
Old Town Hall (Prague): 73–75
Old Town Market Square (Toruń): 444
Old Town Market Square (Warsaw): 342, 356, 376
Old Town Square (Prague): 66, 69, 71–76; map, 72; sleeping, 142–143
Oliwa Cathedral (Gdańsk): 393, 414
Opera: Budapest, 495, 556–557; Prague, 124; Vienna, 993–994, 1005–1006, 1041–1042
Orebić: 852, 854, 867
Organic architecture, of Hungary: 601
Oriental Art (Kraków): 281
Orlando's Column (Dubrovnik): 776
Ostrogski Castle (Warsaw): 362–363
Otočac: 945–946
Otok Island: 696–697

P
Packing checklist: 1117
Palace of Culture and Science (Warsaw): 343, 359
Palace on the Water (Warsaw): 365
Palach, Jan: 91, 96
Pálffy Gardens (Prague): 121
Palóc Folklore Museum (Eger): 594
Paprika: 465, 523, 560
Párisi Udvar Gallery (Budapest): 522
Parliament: Croatian (Zagreb), 921; Hungarian (Budapest), 494, 508–509; Slovenian (Ljubljana), 665
Passports: 9, 12
Path of Remembrance (Warsaw): 343, 366
Pavol the Master: 222, 223, 226
Pécs: 610–631; eating, 631; information, 611; map, 612–613; sights/activities, 614–629; sleeping, 629–630; transportation, 611, 614, 631
Pécs Cathedral: 624–625
Pécs City Walls: 628
Pécs Synagogue: 628–629
Pécs Town Hall: 616
People's Square (Split): 828–829
Pest (Budapest): 478, 494–495, 508–540; eating, 575–580; maps, 510–511, 564–565; sleeping, 562–570. *See also* Budapest
Pest Town Center (Budapest): 478, 508, 519–524; eating, 575–576; sleeping, 562–570
Peterskirche (Vienna): 1021

INDEX

Petřín Hill (Prague): 67, 106
Petřín Tower (Prague): 106
Petržalka (Bratislava): 215
Pharmacies: 13, 58
Pharmacy Under the Eagle (Kraków): 259, 294–295
Pieniny: 227–228
Pile: Dubrovnik, 761, 762, 772–773; eating, 808; sleeping, 801–802
Pile Gate (Dubrovnik): 760, 772–773
Piłsudski Square (Warsaw): 349
Pinkas Synagogue (Prague): 85
Planica: 720
Planty (Kraków): 258, 261
Plaszów Concentration Camp: 295
Plečnik, Jože: 650, 657–662, 667, 669–674; biographical sketch, 672–673; House (Ljubljana), 654, 671–674
Pletna boats: 697–698
Plitvice Lakes National Park: 934–946; eating, 944; information, 937; map, 936–937; science of, 938–939; sights/activities, 940–942; sleeping, 942–943; transportation, 935–936, 938–939, 945–946
Počitelj: 974–975, 976
Podgórze (Kraków): 294–296
Poland: 232–447; almanac, 234–235; currency, 15, 235; at a glance, 6; information, 1086; map, 233; overview, 232–247. *See also specific destinations*
Polish jokes: 242
Polish Plumber Syndrome: 28
Polish złoty: 15, 235
Polo, Marco: 739, 851, 855; House (Korčula), 858
Pomerania: 428–447
Poprad: 229–230
Population: Austria, 980; Bosnia-Herzegovina, 950; Croatia, 738; Czech Republic, 36; Hungary, 452; Poland, 234; Slovakia, 194; Slovenia, 636
Port Gruž: 761, 762
Postal Museum (Budapest): 495, 527, 529
Post offices: 1096; Bled, 692; Budapest, 486; Kraków, 255; Ljubljana, 653; Split, 817; Vienna, 987
Powder Tower (Prague): 96
Prague: 49–149; eating, 135–148; entertainment, 121–124; excursion areas, 150–170; festivals, 124; helpful hints, 58–60; information, 51; layout of, 64–65; planning tips, 50; rip-offs, 56–57, 136; shopping, 124–125; sights/activities, 69–121; sleeping, 125–135; tours, 63–65, 68–69; transportation, 51–58, 60–63, 148–149. *See also specific neighborhoods*
Prague Castle: 67, 114–120
Prague Castle Orchestra: 123
Prague Proms: 124, 1113
Prague Spring: 124, 1112
Prague Symphony Orchestra: 123
Prater (Vienna): 991, 1037
Prešeren, France: 639, 650, 656–657
Prešeren Square (Ljubljana): 656–659
Primate's Palace (Bratislava): 207, 212–213
Primate's Square (Bratislava): 207
Private rooms: overview, 25–26. *See also specific destinations*
Pršut: 642
Pula: 891–905; map, 895
Pula Amphitheater: 896–899
Pula Cathedral: 900
Pula Market Hall: 903, 904
Puppet Museum (Český Krumlov): 179

R

Ráday utca (Budapest): 558, 576–577
Radic Brothers Square (Split): 829–830
Radio Free Europe: 90, 110
Radobolja River Valley (Mostar): 957–958
Radovljica: 709–712
Radziwiłł Palace (Warsaw): 350–351

Rafting: Dunajec River, 227–228; Soča River, 694–695, 724–725; Vltava River, 183–184
Railpasses: 1099, 1107
Reader feedback: 30
Reading, recommended: 1109–1110
Rector's Palace (Dubrovnik): 767, 783–784
Red Hall (Gdańsk): 398–399
Rembrandt van Rijn: 114, 283, 928, 1016, 1025
Remu'h Synagogue (Kraków): 292
Restaurants: *See* Eating; *and specific destinations*
Ribčev Laz Village: 714
Riva (Split): 813, 834–835, 836
Riverside Market (Ljubljana): 654, 659–660
"Roads to Freedom" (Gdańsk): 392, 395, 409–410
Roma (Gypsies): 224–225, 322, 452, 925, 1109
Roman Amphitheater (Pula): 896–899
Roman Crypts (Pécs): 621–623
Roman Floor Mosaic (Pula): 901–902
Roman Forum (Pula): 900–901
Roman Theater (Pula): 904
Roosevelt tér (Budapest): 517
Round Tower (Český Krumlov): 180–181
Rovinj: 868–971; eating, 888–890; information, 871; map, 870–871; nightlife, 882–884; sights/activities, 873–882; sleeping, 884–888; transportation, 871–872, 891
Rovinj Aquarium: 881
Rovinj Bell Tower: 879–880
Rovinj Heritage Museum: 881
Rovinj Town Hall: 877
Royal Apartments (Vienna): 990, 1035–1036
Royal Castle (Warsaw): 342, 353–355
Royal Palace (Budapest): 499–500
Royal Private Apartments (Kraków): 281
Royal State Rooms (Kraków): 280
Royal Way (Gdańsk): 385–393
Royal Way (Kraków): 260–274
Royal Way (Prague): 65
Royal Way (Warsaw): 342–343, 346–351
Royal Wine House (Budapest): 501–502
Rubik, Erno: 451
Rupe Granary (Dubrovnik): 767, 790
Ruzyne Airport (Prague): 57–58

S

Sabor (Zagreb): 921
St. Adalbert Church (Kraków): 267
St. Agnes Convent (Prague): 66, 77
St. Anne's Church: Budapest, 557; Warsaw, 351
St. Barbara's Cathedral (Kutná Hora): 152–153
St. Blaise's Church (Dubrovnik): 778
St. Bridget's Church (Gdańsk): 394–395
St. Catherine's Church: Gdańsk, 394; Zagreb, 920
St. Charles' Church (Vienna): 991, 1027–1028
St. Dominus Cathedral (Split): 824–826
St. Euphemia Church (Rovinj): 878–879
St. Francis' Basilica (Kraków): 258, 269–271
St. George Basilica and Convent (Prague): 119–120
St. István's Basilica (Budapest): 495, 516–517
St. Jakob Beach (Dubrovnik): 793–794
St. James Church: Levoča, 222–223, 226; Prague, 76
St. John's Baptistery (Split): 826
St. John's Street (Warsaw): 355
St. John the Baptist Cathedral (Warsaw): 355–356
St. Joseph Church (Soca): 723–724
St. Lawrence Fort (Dubrovnik): 769, 772

St. Mark Church (Zagreb): 920
St. Mark's Cathedral (Korčula): 856–857
St. Mark's Square (Zagreb): 920
St. Martin in the Wall (Prague): 123
St. Martin's Cathedral (Bratislava): 211
St. Martin's Church (Warsaw): 352
St. Mary Formosa Basilica (Pula): 902
St. Mary's Church: Gdańsk, 391, 392, 400–402; Kraków, 258, 263–264
St. Mary the Victorious Church (Prague): 104–105
St. Michael's Gate (Bratislava): 205
St. Nicholas Church: Gdańsk, 394; Prague, 67, 72–73, 102
St. Peter's Church (Vienna): 1000, 1021
St. Savior Church (Dubrovnik): 773
Sts. Cyril and Methodius Serbian Orthodox Church (Ljubljana): 654, 666–667
Saints Peter and Paul Church (Kraków): 273
Sts. Peter and Paul Franciscan Church (Mostar): 956
St. Stephen's Cathedral (Vienna): 990, 1003–1005
St. Stephen's Church (Motovun): 907–908
St. Vitus Cathedral (Prague): 67, 115–118
St. Vitus Church (Český Krumlov): 177
Salt Hill Thermal Spa: 602–603, 609
Santa Casa (Prague): 111–112
Savica Waterfall: 715
Saxon Garden (Warsaw): 350
Schiele, Egon: 180, 1016, 1026; Art Center (Český Krumlov), 180
Schindler's Factory (Kraków): 259, 295
Schindler's List: 289, 290, 295–296, 328, 1110
Schönbrunn Palace (Vienna): 990, 1035–1037
Schwarzenberg Palace (Prague): 113
Seasons: 9
Secession, the (Vienna): 991, 1029, 1030
Sedlec Bone Church: 156–157
Serbian Herzegovina: 975–976
Serbian Orthodox Church: 789; Dubrovnik, 767, 788, 790; Ljubljana, 654, 666–667
Shopping: budgeting, 8–9; customs, 21; VAT refunds, 19–20. *See also* Markets; *and specific destinations*
Sightseeing: best three-week trip, 10–11; budgeting, 8; general tips, 21–23; priorities, 9. *See also specific sights and destinations*
Sirens' Valley: 604–605
Sisi, Elisabeth, Empress: 546, 1001–1002, 1008–1013, 1018; Museum (Vienna), 1009–1010
Skyscraper, the (Ljubljana): 653, 668
Slavonia: 640
Sleep code: 25
Sleeping: 23–29; budgeting, 8; reservations, 26–27, 29; reservations form, 1118; telephones, 1090–1091; types of accommodations, 24–26. *See also specific destinations*
Slovakia: 192–230, 640; almanac, 194; at a glance, 6; information, 1086; map, 193; overview, 192–199. *See also* Bratislava; Spiš Region
Slovak Paradise National Park: 227
Slovanský Ostrov (Prague): 99
Slovenia: 634–734; almanac, 636–637; currency, 15, 636, 639; at a glance, 7; information, 1086; map, 635; overview, 634–644. *See also* Julian Alps; Lake Bled region; Ljubljana
Slovenian Ethnographic Museum (Ljubljana): 655, 674–675
Slovenian Museum of Natural History (Ljubljana): 665–666

Slovenian National Gallery (Ljubljana): 666
Slovenian National Museum (Ljubljana): 665–666, 675
Slovenian Parliament (Ljubljana): 665
Slunj: 935
Smoking: 14
Soča Front: 639, 714–715, 722, 723–725, 729–733
Soča River: 722–725; rafting, 694–695, 724–725
Soča River Valley: 723–725
Soccer: 43, 234
Solidarity movement: 241–242, 392, 394–395, 404–412
Sopot: 423–426
Sopot Pier: 425–426
Sopron: 547
Spanish Riding School (Vienna): 991, 1018–1019
Spanish Synagogue (Prague): 88
Spas: *See* Baths
Special events: *See* Festivals
Spiš Castle: 226–227
Spiš Region: 220–230; map, 221
Spišská Nová Ves: 222, 227
Spittelberg (Vienna): 1065–1066
Split: 812–848; eating, 842–844; helpful hints, 816–818; information, 814; layout of, 813; maps, 815, 838–839; nightlife, 836; sights/activities, 819–836; sleeping, 837–842; tours, 818–819; transportation, 814–816, 818, 845–848
Split Archaeological Museum: 830–831
Split Bell Tower: 826
Split City Hall: 828
Split City Museum: 829
Split Gallery of Fine Arts: 830
Sponza Palace (Dubrovnik): 777
Sports, in the Czech Republic: 43
Square at the Bridge (Rovinj): 875–876
Square of the Republic (Ljubljana): 664–665
Srbsko: 169
Staatsoper (Vienna): 990, 993–994, 1005–1006, 1041–1042
Stadtpark (Vienna): 1037
Staré Mesto (Prague): *See* Old Town
Statue Park (Budapest): 494, 540–546; map, 542
Stephansdom (Vienna): 990, 1003–1005
Stephansplatz (Vienna): 998–999
Stephen, Saint: *See* István, Saint
Sternberg Palace (Prague): 114
Stolac: 976
Stoss, Veit: 263–264
Stradun (Dubrovnik): 760, 766, 773, 776
Strahov Monastery and Library (Prague): 67, 108–110
Straw Tower (Gdańsk): 387
Street of the Korčulan Statute of 1214: 856
Střelecký Ostrov (Prague): 99
Subway: *See* Metro
Šupljara Cave: 941–942
Swimming: *See* Beaches
Sword dances, in Korčula: 855
Synagogue Museum (Dubrovnik): 766, 787–788
Szabadság tér (Budapest): 495, 513
Széchenyi Baths (Budapest): 494, 539, 550–553, 558; map, 551
Széchenyi tér (Pécs): 616
Széchenyi utca (Eger): 596–599
Szentendre: 547
Szentháromság utca (Budapest): 506

T

Tadeusz Sendzimir Steelworks (Kraków): 299
Tatranská Lomnica: 230
Tatras Mountains: 229–230
Taxes: VAT refunds, 19–20
Taxis: tipping, 19. *See also specific destinations*
Telephone numbers, useful: 12–13, 1094–1095
Telephones: 1088–1093; Bosnia-Herzegovina, 951; Croatia, 744; Czech Republic, 38; Eger, 591; Hungary, 454–455; Poland, 237; Slovenia, 639
Tempel Synagogue (Kraków): 293

Tepa Market (Mostar): 965
Terezín Children's Art Exhibit (Prague): 85
Terezín Concentration Camp: 158–165; map, 162–163; tours, from Prague, 68
Terror Museum (Budapest): 495, 531–535
Tesla, Nikola: 739, 920
Teutonic Knights: 238, 434–435, 671
Theater an der Wien (Vienna): 1042
Thermal baths: *See* Baths
Third Man, The: 1048
Tiergarten (Vienna): 1036
Time zone: 13
Tipping: 18–19
Tito (Josip Broz): 687, 748, 832, 1073–1076; Vila Bled, 695–696
Tito Square (Rovinj): 876–877
Tivoli Park (Ljubljana): 667
Tkalčićeva (Zagreb): 922, 930–931
Tolmin: 725
Tomb of the Unknown Soldier (Warsaw): 349–350
Torture House (Gdańsk): 386
Torture Museum (Český Krumlov): 180
Toruń: 442–447
Toruń Ethnographic Park: 446
Tour guides: 12; tipping, 19. *See also specific destinations*
Tourist information: 1085–1086. *See also specific destinations*
Town under the Town (Eger): 598–599
Toy and Barbie Museum (Prague): 67, 120
Train travel: 1097, 1099; best three-week trip, 10–11; map, 1098; Auschwitz, 332; Bled, 689, 692, 708; Bratislava, 201, 204, 218; Budapest, 481–483, 486, 585–586; Český Krumlov, 173–174, 189; Dalmatian Coast, 745; Eger, 589, 609; Gdańsk, 381, 384, 421; Kraków, 253–254, 316; Kutná Hora, 152; Ljubljana, 651, 685; Malbork Castle, 429–430; Mostar, 954–955, 973–974; Pécs, 611, 631; Poland, 236; Prague, 52–56, 148; Pula, 895, 905; Split, 848; Toruń, 447; Vienna, 1066–1068; Warsaw, 338–340, 377–378; Zagreb, 915–916, 932–933
Transportation: 1096–1105; best three-week trip, 10–11; budgeting, 8; maps, 1098, 1101. *See also* Airports; Boat travel and cruises; Bus travel; Car travel; Train travel; *and specific destinations*
Travel smarts: 4–5
Trebinje: 976
Trenta: 723
Tri-City: 423–427. *See also* Gdańsk
Triglav National Park: 689, 717, 721–723
Trip costs: 5, 8–9
Triple Bridge (Ljubljana): 650, 657
Trogir: 819
Truffles: 641, 910
Tuđman, Franjo: 749–751, 855–856, 1077–1078, 1083–1084
Turanj: 935
Turul Bird (Budapest): 499
Twenty-Seven Crosses (Prague): 74
Týn Church (Prague): 73, 75–76

U

Ulica Chmielna (Warsaw): 346
Ulica Długa (Gdańsk): 388–389, 392
Üllői Út (Budapest): 539–540
Umschlagplatz (Warsaw): 343, 366
Ungelt Courtyard (Prague): 73, 76
Uphagen House (Gdańsk): 389, 393, 397–398
Upper Town (Zagreb): 913, 918–922, 926–928; eating, 932

V

Váci utca (Budapest): 520–521, 560; eating, 575–576
Vajdahunyad Castle (Budapest): 538–539
Varga, Imre: 526–527, 544, 546, 624
Vasarely, Viktor: 546; Museum (Pécs), 626–627

VAT refunds: 19–20
Velvet Divorce: 196–197
Velvet Revolution of 1989: 97, 98
Venice: transportation, 893
Venus of Willendorf: 1025
Via Musica (Prague): 73, 121
Vienna: 978–1068; cafés, 1043–1044; eating, 1058–1066; entertainment, 1038–1043; helpful hints, 986–987; information, 986; layout of, 983, 986; maps, 979, 984–985, 1050, 1054–1055, 1060–1061; nightlife, 1047–1048; planning tips, 982–983; shopping, 1038; sights/activities, 992–1038; sleeping, 1048–1057; tours, 989, 992; transportation, 987–989, 1066–1068; walking tour, 992–1003; wine gardens, 1044–1047
Vienna Boys' Choir: 1039
Vienna City Hall: 1047–1048, 1065
Vienna City Park: 1037
Vienna International Airport: 1068
Vienna Natural History Museum: 991, 1025
Vienna Secession: 1028–1029, 1030
Vienna State Opera: 990, 993–994, 1005–1006, 1041–1042
Viktor Vasarely Museum (Pécs): 626–627
Vila Bled: 695–696
Villa Bertramka (Prague): 123
Villa Richter (Prague): 137, 146
Vintgar Gorge: 712–713
Visegrád: 547
Vitus, Saint: 81, 117
Víziváros (Budapest): 478; eating, 580–581; sleeping, 570–573
Vltava River: 97, 99, 172, 176; canoeing and rafting, 183–184; cruises, 69
Vogel Mountain Cable Car: 714
VoIP (Voice over Internet Protocol): 1094
Vörösmarty tér (Budapest): 520, 584
Vrata Valley: 719
Vršič Pass: 719–722
Vysoké Tatry: 229–230

W

Wagenburg Coach Museum (Vienna): 1037
Wałesa, Lech: 237, 241–242, 387, 404, 406–412
Wallenberg, Raoul: 527
Wallenstein Palace Garden (Prague): 103
War Photo Limited (Dubrovnik): 767, 788
Warsaw: 334–378; eating, 375–377; information, 336, 338; maps, 337, 344–345; sights/activities, 342–370; sleeping, 370–375; tours, 341; transportation, 338–341, 377–378
Warsaw Castle Square: 342, 352–353
Warsaw Ghetto Uprising (1943): 336, 343, 364, 366
Warsaw Historical Museum: 343, 356–357
Warsaw Royal Castle: 342, 353–355
Warsaw University: 348
Warsaw Uprising (1944): 336, 366–370; Monument, 367; Museum, 343, 367, 369–370
Wawel Castle Grounds (Kraków): 258, 277–279
Wawel Castle Museums (Kraków): 280–281
Wawel Cathedral (Kraków): 258, 275–277
Wawel Hill (Kraków): 274
Weapons Historical Exhibition (Eger): 594
Weather: 9, 1115
Wenceslas, Saint: 41, 88, 90–91, 117
Wenceslas Square (Prague): 66, 88, 90–93
Westerplatte (Gdańsk): 414, 421–422
Wieliczka Salt Mine: 296–297
Wien: *See* Vienna
Wieners in Vienna: 1059
Wien Museum Karlsplatz (Vienna): 1028–1029

Wine: Croatia, 755, 911; Hungary, 467–469, 603–605
Wine gardens, in Vienna: 1044–1047
Wojtyła, Karol: *See* John Paul II, Pope
World War I: Hungary, 460–461; Slovenia, 639, 714–715, 721, 723–725, 729–733
World War II: 1072–1073; Austria, 979, 995–996; Croatia, 748; Czech Republic, 41–42, 82–83, 84, 158–165; Hungary, 461–462, 512–513, 531–533, 539–540; Poland, 239, 241, 290, 294–295, 317–331, 335, 364–370, 399, 414; Slovenia, 646. *See also* Concentration camps
Wyspiański, Stanisław: 237, 264, 266, 269–270, 272, 362; Museum (Kraków), 259, 283–284
Wyspiański Museum (Kraków): 259, 283–284
Wyszyński, Stefan: 348–349

Y

Yugoslavia: understanding, 1069–1084

Z

Zadružna Zveza (Ljubljana): 659
Zagreb: 912–933; eating, 930–932; information, 913–915; layout of, 913; map, 914–915; sights/activities, 918–928; sleeping, 928–930; tours, 917–918; transportation, 915–917, 932–933
Zagreb Arts and Crafts Museum: 928
Zagreb Botanical Garden: 928
Zagreb Cathedral: 926–928
Zagreb City Museum: 926
Zakopane: 229
Žehra: 227
Żelazowa Wola: 363
Žižkov Tower (Prague): 42, 110
Zlatá Koruna Abbey: 182–184
Zlote Tarasy Shopping Mall (Warsaw): 338, 359–360
Zoos: 538, 1036
Zsolnay Fountain (Pécs): 614–615
Zsolnay porcelain: 615, 626–627; Museum (Pécs), 628

MAP INDEX

COLOR MAPS
Eastern Europe Overview: iii–vii
Prague: viii
Budapest: x
The Dalmatian Coast: xii

INTRODUCTION
Top Destinations in Eastern Europe: xvi
Eastern Europe: Best Three-Week Trip by Public Transportation: 11

CZECH REPUBLIC
Czech Republic: 35

PRAGUE
Prague: 52
Prague Metro: 61
Prague Overview: 65
Prague's Old Town: 70
Old Town Square: 72
Prague's Jewish Quarter: 83
Prague's New Town: 89
Prague's Little Quarter: 101
Prague's Castle Quarter: 108
Hotels in Prague's Old Town: 127
Hotels & Restaurants in the Little Quarter: 130
Hotels & Restaurants in the New Town & Beyond: 132
Restaurants in the Old Town: 138

NEAR PRAGUE
Day Trips: 151
Kutná Hora: 154
Terezín: 162
Český Krumlov: 175

SLOVAKIA
Slovakia: 193

BRATISLAVA
Bratislava: 202
The Spiš Region: 221

POLAND
Poland: 233

KRAKÓW
Kraków's Old Town: 250
Kazimierz: 288
Kraków's Old Town Hotels and Restaurants: 304

AUSCHWITZ-BIRKENAU
Auschwitz I: 322
Auschwitz II–Birkenau: 329

WARSAW
Warsaw Overview: 337
Central Warsaw: 344

GDAŃSK AND THE TRI-CITY
Gdańsk: 382
Gdańsk Day Trips: 422

POMERANIA
Malbork Castle: 432

HUNGARY
Hungary: 451
Pre-Trianon Hungary: 460

BUDAPEST
Budapest Neighborhoods: 473
Budapest Overview: 476
Budapest Transit: 488
Buda Sights: 498
Pest Sights: 510
Andrássy Út: 528
City Park: 536
Memento Park: 542
Széchenyi Baths: 551
Pest Town Center Hotels & Restaurants: 565
Andrassy Út Hotels & Restaurants: 567
Buda Hotels & Restaurants: 571

EGER
Eger: 590

PÉCS
Pécs: 612

SLOVENIA
Slovenia: 635

LJUBLJANA
Ljubljana: 648

LAKE BLED
Bled Town: 690
Near Lake Bled: 710

THE JULIAN ALPS
The Julian Alps & Northwest Slovenia: 718

CROATIA
Croatia: 737

DUBROVNIK
Greater Dubrovnik: 762
Dubrovnik's Old Town: 774

SPLIT
Split Overview: 815
Diocletian's Palace: 822
Split Hotels & Restaurants: 838

KORČULA
Korčula: 853

ROVINJ AND ISTRIA
Rovinj: 870
Istria: 893
Pula: 895

ZAGREB
Zagreb: 914

PLITVICE LAKES NATIONAL PARK
Plitvice Lakes National Park: 936

MOSTAR (BOSNIA-HERZEGOVINA)
Mostar: 953

VIENNA (AUSTRIA)
Greater Vienna: 979
Vienna: 984
Vienna City Walk: 993
Vienna's Hofburg Palace: 1007
Kunsthistorisches Museum: 1023
Hotels in Central Vienna: 1050
Hotels and Restaurants Outside the Ring: 1054
Restaurants in Central Vienna: 1060

UNDERSTANDING YUGOSLAVIA
Yugoslav Succession: 1070

APPENDIX
Public Transportation in Eastern Europe: 1098
Driving: Distance & Time: 1101

Rick Steves®

EUROPEAN TOURS

ADRIATIC • ATHENS & THE HEART OF GREECE • BARCELONA & MADRID • BELGIUM & HOLLAND • BERLIN, VIENNA & PRAGUE
BEST OF EUROPE • BEST OF ITALY
BEST OF TURKEY • BULGARIA • EASTERN EUROPE • ENGLAND • FAMILY EUROPE
GERMANY, AUSTRIA & SWITZERLAND
HEART OF ITALY • IRELAND • ISTANBUL
LONDON • PARIS • PARIS & HEART OF FRANCE • PARIS & SOUTH OF FRANCE
PORTUGAL • PRAGUE & BUDAPEST • ROME
SAN SEBASTIAN & BASQUE COUNTRY
SCANDINAVIA • SCOTLAND • SICILY
SOUTH ITALY • SPAIN & MOROCCO
ST. PETERSBURG, TALLINN & HELSINKI
VENICE, FLORENCE & ROME • VILLAGE FRANCE • VILLAGE ITALY • VILLAGE TURKEY

VISIT **TOURS.RICKSTEVES.COM**

Great guides, small groups, no grumps

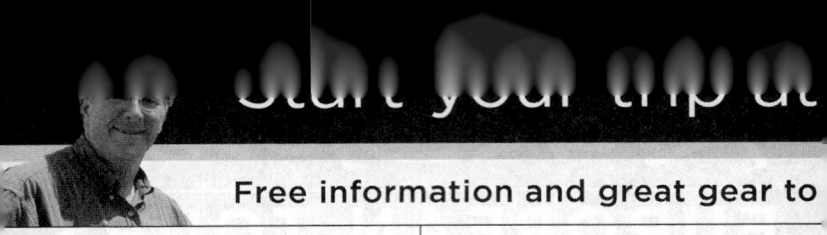

Free information and great gear to

▸ Plan Your Trip

Browse thousands of articles and a wealth of money-saving tips for planning your dream trip. You'll find up-to-date information on Europe's best destinations, packing smart, getting around, finding rooms, staying healthy, avoiding scams and more.

▸ Eurail Passes

Find out, step-by-step, if a rail pass makes sense for your trip—and how to avoid buying more than you need. Get a bunch of free extras!

▸ Graffiti Wall & Travelers' Helpline

Learn, ask, share—our online community of savvy travelers is a great resource for first-time travelers to Europe, as well as seasoned pros.

turn your travel dreams into affordable reality

Free Audio Tours & Travel Newsletter

Get your nose out of this guidebook and focus on what you'll be seeing with Rick's free audio tours of the greatest sights in Paris, Rome, Florence and Venice.

Subscribe to our free *Travel News* e-newsletter, and get monthly articles from Rick on what's happening in Europe.

Great Gear from Rick's Travel Store

Pack light and right—on a budget—with Rick's custom-designed carry-on bags, rollaboards, day packs, travel accessories, guidebooks, journals, maps and DVDs of his TV shows.

130 Fourth Avenue North, PO Box 2009 • Edmonds, WA 98020 USA
Phone: (425) 771-8303 • Fax: (425) 771-0833 • www.ricksteves.com

Rick Steves®

www.ricksteves.com

TRAVEL SKILLS
Europe Through the Back Door

EUROPE GUIDES
Best of Europe
Eastern Europe
Europe 101
European Christmas
Postcards from Europe

COUNTRY GUIDES
Croatia & Slovenia
England
France
Germany
Great Britain
Ireland
Italy
Portugal
Scandinavia
Spain
Switzerland

CITY & REGIONAL GUIDES
Amsterdam, Bruges & Brussels
Athens & The Peloponnese
Budapest
Florence & Tuscany
Istanbul
London
Paris
Prague & The Czech Republic
Provence & The French Riviera
Rome
Venice
Vienna, Salzburg & Tirol

PHRASE BOOKS & DICTIONARIES
French
French, Italian & German
German
Italian
Portuguese
Spanish

RICK STEVES' EUROPE DVDs
Austria & The Alps
Eastern Europe
England
Europe
France & Benelux
Germany & Scandinavia
Greece, Turkey, Israel & Egypt
Ireland & Scotland
Italy's Cities
Italy's Countryside
Rick Steves' European Christmas
Spain & Portugal
Travel Skills & "The Making Of"

PLANNING MAPS
Britain, Ireland & London
Europe
France & Paris
Germany, Austria & Switzerland
Ireland
Italy
Spain & Portugal

JOURNALS
Rick Steves' Pocket Travel Journal
Rick Steves' Travel Journal

RICK STEVES APPS FOR THE IPHONE OR IPOD TOUCH

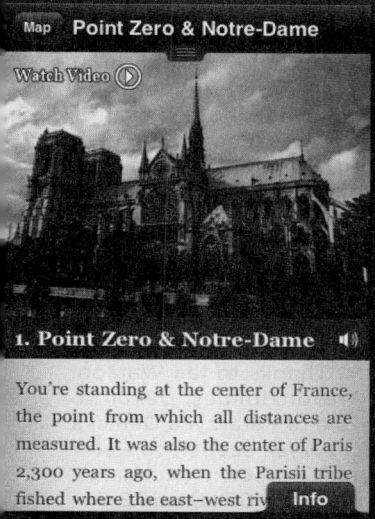

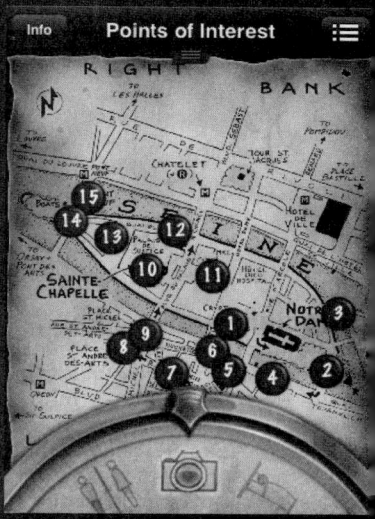

With these apps you can:

- Spin the compass icon to switch views between sights, hotels, and restaurant selections—and get details on cost, hours, address, and phone number.
- Tap any point on the screen to read Rick's detailed information, including history and suggested viewpoints.
- Get a deeper view into Rick's tours with audio and video segments.

Go to iTunes to download the following apps:

Rick Steves' Louvre Tour

Rick Steves' Historic Paris Walk

Rick Steves' Orsay Museum Tour

Rick Steves' Versailles

Rick Steves' Ancient Rome Tour

Rick Steves' St. Peter's Basilica Tour

Once downloaded, these apps are completely self-contained on your iPhone or iPod Touch, so you will not incur pricey roaming charges during use overseas.

Rick Steves books and DVDs are available at bookstores and through online booksellers.
Rick Steves guidebooks are published by Avalon Travel, a member of the Perseus Books Group.
Rick Steves apps are produced by Übermind, a boutique Seattle-based software consultancy firm.

Credits

Contributor

Gene Openshaw

Gene is the co-author of seven Rick Steves books. For this book, he wrote material on Europe's art, history, and contemporary culture (including this book's tour of the Kunsthistorisches Museum in Vienna). When not traveling, Gene enjoys composing music, recovering from his 1973 trip to Europe with Rick, and living everyday life with his daughter.

Special Thanks

The authors would like to acknowledge our friends and colleagues for their invaluable insights. Thanks to Ian Watson, Dave Hoerlein, Rick Garman, and Trevor Holmes; *Děkuji* to Honza Vihan (Czech Republic); *Dziękuję* to Katarzyna Derlicka and Agnieszka Syroka (Poland); *Köszönjük szépen* to Péter Pölczman, Andrea Makkay, and Elemér Boreczky (Hungary); *Hvala lepa* to Marijan Krišković, Tina Hiti, Sašo Golub, and Bojan Kočar (Slovenia and Croatia); and *D'akujeme* to Susana Minich (Slovakia).

Images

Location	Photographer
Title Page: Széchenyi Baths, Budapest, Hungary	Cameron Hewitt
Full-Page Color: Ulica Długa, Gdańsk, Poland	Cameron Hewitt
Introduction: Wawel Cathedral, Kraków, Poland	Cameron Hewitt
Czech Republic (full-page image): Charles Bridge, Prague	Cameron Hewitt
Prague: Vltava River, Charles Bridge, and Prague Castle	Cameron Hewitt
Near Prague: Konopiště Castle	Rick Steves
Český Krumlov: View of City	David C. Hoerlein
Slovakia (full-page image): St. Michael's Gate, Bratislava	Cameron Hewitt
Bratislava: Bratislava Castle	Cameron Hewitt
The Spiš Region: Spiš Castle	Cameron Hewitt
Poland (full-page image): Old Town Square, Warsaw	Cameron Hewitt
Kraków: Main Market Square	Cameron Hewitt
Auschwitz-Birkenau: Birkenau Guard Tower	Rick Steves
Warsaw: Castle Square and the Old Town	Cameron Hewitt
Gdańsk: Artus Court on Ulica Długa	Cameron Hewitt
Pomerania: Malbork Castle	Cameron Hewitt
Hungary (full-page image): Parliament, Budapest	Cameron Hewitt
Budapest: Chain Bridge Panorama	Cameron Hewitt
Eger: View from the Castle	Cameron Hewitt
Pécs: Main Square	Cameron Hewitt
Slovenia (full-page image): Julian Alps	Cameron Hewitt
Ljubljana: Ljubljana Castle overlooking Prešeren Square	Cameron Hewitt
Lake Bled: *Pletna* Boat on Lake Bled	Cameron Hewitt
The Julian Alps: Mountain Hut	Cameron Hewitt
Croatia (full-page image): Rovinj	Cameron Hewitt
Dubrovnik: View of Old Town	Cameron Hewitt
Split: Riva Promenade and Old Town	Cameron Hewitt
Korčula: Old Town	Cameron Hewitt
Rovinj and Istria: Rovinj Harbor	Cameron Hewitt
Zagreb: Zagreb Skyline	Cameron Hewitt
Plitvice Lakes National Park: Plitvice	Rick Steves
Bosnia-Herzegovina (full-page image): Old Bridge, Mostar	Cameron Hewitt
Mostar: Old Bridge	Cameron Hewitt
Austria (full-page image): St. Peter's Church, Vienna	Rick Steves
Vienna: Schönbrunn Palace	Cameron Hewitt

Rick Steves' Guidebook Series

Country Guides

Rick Steves' Best of Europe
Rick Steves' Croatia & Slovenia
Rick Steves' Eastern Europe
Rick Steves' England
Rick Steves' France
Rick Steves' Germany
Rick Steves' Great Britain
Rick Steves' Ireland
Rick Steves' Italy
Rick Steves' Portugal
Rick Steves' Scandinavia
Rick Steves' Spain
Rick Steves' Switzerland

City and Regional Guides

Rick Steves' Amsterdam, Bruges & Brussels
Rick Steves' Athens & the Peloponnese
Rick Steves' Budapest
Rick Steves' Florence & Tuscany
Rick Steves' Istanbul
Rick Steves' London
Rick Steves' Paris
Rick Steves' Prague & the Czech Republic
Rick Steves' Provence & the French Riviera
Rick Steves' Rome
Rick Steves' Venice
Rick Steves' Vienna, Salzburg & Tirol

Rick Steves' Phrase Books

French
French/Italian/German
German
Italian
Portuguese
Spanish

Other Books

Rick Steves' Europe 101: History and Art for the Traveler
Rick Steves' Europe Through the Back Door
Rick Steves' European Christmas
Rick Steves' Postcards from Europe
Rick Steves' Travel as a Political Act

Avalon Travel
a member of the Perseus Books Group
1700 Fourth Street
Berkeley, CA 94710, USA

Text © 2010 by Rick Steves
Cover © 2010 by Avalon Travel. All rights reserved.
Maps © 2010 by Europe Through the Back Door Printed in the USA by Worzalla. First printing March 2010.

Portions of this book were originally published in *Rick Steves' Germany & Austria* © 2009, 2008, 2007, 2006, 2005, by Rick Steves; in *Rick Steves' Germany, Austria & Switzerland* © 2004, 2003, 2002, 2001, 2000, 1999, by Rick Steves; in *Rick Steves' Prague & the Czech Republic* © 2009, 2008, 2007, 2006, 2005, by Rick Steves and Honza Vihan; in *Rick Steves' Budapest* © 2008, by Rick Steves and Cameron Hewitt; in *Rick Steves' Croatia & Slovenia* © 2009, 2008, 2007, by Rick Steves and Cameron Hewitt; and in *Rick Steves' Vienna, Salzburg & Tirol* © 2008, by Rick Steves.

For the latest on Rick Steves' lectures, guidebooks, tours, public radio show, and public television series, contact Europe Through the Back Door, Box 2009, Edmonds, WA 98020, tel. 425/771-8303, fax 425/771-0833, www.ricksteves.com, rick@ricksteves.com.

ISBN 978-1-59880-104-0
ISSN 1547-8505

Europe Through the Back Door Reviewing Editors: Jennifer Madison Davis, Cameron Hewitt
ETBD Editors: Gretchen Strauch, Tom Griffin, Cathy Lu, Cathy McDonald
ETBD Managing Editor: Risa Laib
Avalon Travel Senior Editor & Series Manager: Madhu Prasher
Avalon Travel Project Editor: Kelly Lydick
Copy Editor: Patrick Collins
Proofreader: Denise Silva
Indexer: Stephen Callahan
Production & Typesetting: McGuire Barber Design
Graphic Content Director: Laura VanDeventer
Maps & Graphics: David C. Hoerlein, Laura VanDeventer, Lauren Mills, Barb Geisler, Mike Morgenfeld, Chris Markiewicz, Brice Ticen, Albert Angulo
Photography: Cameron Hewitt, Rick Steves, David C. Hoerlein, Mike Potter, Honza Vihan, Rhonda Pelikan, Gene Openshaw, Dominic Bonuccelli, Gretchen Strauch, Debi Jo Michael
Front Matter Color Photos: page i: Széchenyi Baths, Budapest, Hungary © Cameron Hewitt; page ii: Gdańsk, Poland © Cameron Hewitt
Cover Photo: Lake Bled, Slovenia © Cameron Hewitt

Although the authors and publisher have made every effort to provide accurate, up-to-date information, they accept no responsibility for loss, injury, bad borscht, or inconvenience sustained by any person using this book.